AF706216

FEMINIST JUDGMENTS: REIMAGINING THE INTERNATIONAL CRIMINAL COURT

In the past decade, feminist scholars and women's rights activists have used the feminist judgment method to reimagine the relationship between law and gender justice, resulting in rewritten 'feminist' judgments from courts around the world. This groundbreaking book extends that approach and applies it to a wide range of decisions of the International Criminal Court (ICC), the Hague-based court with power to prosecute war crimes, crimes against humanity, genocide, and aggression in over 120 countries. With more than sixty contributors from the across the globe including countries where the ICC has been active, this book reflects an international and intersectional feminism. Diverse contributions reveal the gendered implications of crimes (both sexual and non-sexual), command responsibility, defences, complementarity, head-of-state immunity, sentencing, reparations, and more. This title is also available as Open Access on Cambridge Core.

Kcasey McLoughlin is Senior Lecturer in Law at Newcastle Law School. Her research examines the gendered assumptions that pervade legal and political institutions. Her first book, *Law, Women Judges and the Gender Order: Lessons from the High Court of Australia* (2022), was awarded the 2023 Carole Pateman Gender and Politics Book Prize Law and Society Association of Australia and New Zealand 2022 Book Prize.

Rosemary Grey is Senior Lecturer at Sydney Law School. Her research focuses on sexual, gender, and reproductive crimes in international law. Her scholarship and amicus curiae briefs have been cited by the International Criminal Court and Extraordinary Chambers in the Courts of Cambodia. Her past works include *Prosecuting Sexual and Gender-Based Crimes at the International Criminal Court* (2019).

Louise Chappell is Scientia Professor at the University of New South Wales, Sydney undertaking pioneering work on gender justice and institutions. Chappell publishes widely on gender in courts, parliaments, and bureaucracies. Her prize-winning books include *The Politics of Gender Justice at the International Criminal Court* (2015) and *Gendering Government* (2002).

Suzanne Varrall is Laureate Research Fellow at Melbourne Law School, University of Melbourne. She researches and teaches in international human rights law, international humanitarian law, and international criminal law. Varrall is a qualified lawyer with a background in foreign policy and national security.

Feminist Judgments Series

Editors

Bridget J. Crawford
Pace University, Elisabeth Haub School of Law

Kathryn M. Stanchi
University of Nevada, Las Vegas William S. Boyd School of Law

Linda L. Berger
University of Nevada, Las Vegas William S. Boyd School of Law

Advisory Panel for Feminist Judgments Series

Kathryn Abrams, *Herma Hill Kay Distinguished Professor of Law, University of California, Berkeley, School of Law*

Katharine T. Bartlett, *A. Kenneth Pye Professor Emerita of Law, Duke University School of Law*

Mary Anne Case, *Arnold I. Shure Professor of Law, The University of Chicago Law School*

April L. Cherry, *Professor of Law, Cleveland-Marshall College of Law*

Margaret E. Johnson, *Professor of Law, University of Baltimore School of Law*

Sonia Katyal, *Roger J. Traynor Distinguished Professor of Law, University of California, Berkeley, School of Law*

Nancy Leong, *Professor of Law and William M. Beaney Memorial Research Chair, University of Denver Sturm College of Law*

Rachel Moran, *Distinguished Professor of Emeritus of Law, University of California, Irvine School of Law*

Angela Onwuachi-Willig, *Dean and Ryan Roth Gallo & Ernest J. Gallo Professor of Law, Boston University School of Law*

Nancy D. Polikoff, *Professor of Law Emerita, American University Washington College of Law*

Daniel B. Rodriguez, *Harold Washington Professor, Northwestern University Pritzker School of Law*

Susan Deller Ross, *Professor of Law, Georgetown University Law Center*

Dean Spade, *Professor of Law, Seattle University School of Law*

Robin L. West, *Frederick J. Haas Professor of Law and Philosophy Emeritus, Georgetown University Law Center*

Verna L. Williams, *Chief Executive Officer, Equal Justice Works*

Feminist Judgments

REIMAGINING THE INTERNATIONAL CRIMINAL COURT

Edited by

KCASEY MCLOUGHLIN
University of Newcastle

ROSEMARY GREY
University of Sydney

LOUISE CHAPPELL
University of New South Wales, Sydney

SUZANNE VARRALL
University of Melbourne

CAMBRIDGE
UNIVERSITY PRESS

CAMBRIDGE
UNIVERSITY PRESS

Shaftesbury Road, Cambridge CB2 8EA, United Kingdom

One Liberty Plaza, 20th Floor, New York, NY 10006, USA

477 Williamstown Road, Port Melbourne, VIC 3207, Australia

314–321, 3rd Floor, Plot 3, Splendor Forum, Jasola District Centre, New Delhi – 110025, India

103 Penang Road, #05-06/07, Visioncrest Commercial, Singapore 238467

Cambridge University Press is part of Cambridge University Press & Assessment, a department of the University of Cambridge.

We share the University's mission to contribute to society through the pursuit of education, learning and research at the highest international levels of excellence.

www.cambridge.org
Information on this title: www.cambridge.org/9781009255288

DOI: 10.1017/9781009255271

© Cambridge University Press & Assessment 2025

This publication is in copyright. Subject to statutory exception and to the provisions of relevant collective licensing agreements, with the exception of the Creative Commons version the link for which is provided below, no reproduction of any part may take place without the written permission of Cambridge University Press & Assessment.

An online version of this work is published at doi.org/10.1017/9781009255271 under a Creative Commons Open Access license CC-BY-NC-ND 4.0 which permits re-use, distribution and reproduction in any medium for non-commercial purposes providing appropriate credit to the original work is given. You may not distribute derivative works without permission. To view a copy of this license, visit https://creativecommons.org/licenses/by-nc-nd/4.0

When citing this work, please include a reference to the DOI 10.1017/9781009255271

First published 2025

A catalogue record for this publication is available from the British Library.

A Cataloging-in-Publication data record for this book is available from the Library of Congress

ISBN 978-1-009-25528-8 Hardback

Cambridge University Press & Assessment has no responsibility for the persistence or accuracy of URLs for external or third-party internet websites referred to in this publication and does not guarantee that any content on such websites is, or will remain, accurate or appropriate.

For EU product safety concerns, contact us at Calle de José Abascal, 56, 1°, 28003 Madrid, Spain, or email eugpsr@cambridge.org.

Contents

Front Cover Image

Photographer and Rohingya refugee Omal Khair's striking image which graces the cover of our book was taken in one of the world's largest refugee camps, in Cox's Bazar, Bangladesh. The camp is home to more than 750,000 displaced people, mostly Rohingya, who fled alleged crimes against humanity and genocide in Rakhine State, Myanmar, with the largest influx arriving in 2017. Khair is a fellow with the Rohingya Media Fellows project, established in 2018 by the NGO Fortify Rights jointly with the media initiative Doha Debates.

We were drawn to this work by Omal Khair for several reasons. It was important to us that our cover image represented conflict outside the African continent, responding to critiques of the International Criminal Court's concentration on that region in its initial investigations, compared with its limited response to atrocity crimes committed elsewhere in the world. Capturing the aftermath of atrocities committed in Myanmar helps demonstrate the tragic reality of the extent of war and destruction across the globe.

This cover image beautifully captures an everyday moment of people uprooted by the Myanmar conflict, as the photographer herself has been. We are drawn in by the placement of the people in the image, all exercising agency, strength, and resilience, notwithstanding the (literal and figurative) precarity of their position. A woman balancing herself and a child on her hip, men and boys labouring to construct the overpass while another wades underneath. Each *appears* to be following gendered patterns, though the reality of these relationships is unknown to the viewer and requires deeper investigation. Incorrect assumptions about gender relations in conflict and post-conflict settings, as this volume shows, add to misrecognition and interfere with justice and accountability. One message emanating from this book is that judicial decision making will improve through contextualising experiences and discarding stereotyped views of people's lives across time and place.

Law limits its purview to specific instances of crimes, at specific moments, in specific places. By contrast, the photograph shows the cascade effect of conflict across borders and generations too often concealed by legal institutions. The bamboo scaffolding serves as a fitting metaphor for the legal scaffolding – the Rome Statute and other ICC rules – which both structure and constrain the reimagined judgments in this book.

The fragile structure of the bridge also represents for us the limits of international criminal law, as well as the reality of post-conflict life which requires survivors to balance precariously while constructing a new beginning. In this sense, the image shows the vulnerability of those forced to flee from conflict, but also provides some sense of hope for a better future.

In this book, we are privileged to be able to showcase more images from Omal Khair as well as two other Rohingya media fellows, Dil Kayas and Azimul Hasson, in the form of a photo essay in the Bangladesh/Myanmar section. Like our cover image, these photos speak to the limits of the law and the need to think creatively about how to express the costs of war and conflict, the burdens of survivorship, and the determination to rebuild shattered lives and seek justice and accountability, however it can be achieved.

Contributors

Mashal Aamir is a barrister and humanitarian. She is a graduate law student at the University of Oxford and graduate of the University of Cambridge and Glasgow University. Aamir is currently in South Korea assisting defectors from North Korea in upholding their human rights. She works as a researcher at the University of Dundee, Scotland. Previously she worked for the British government, the International Criminal Court, Legal Aid USA, and Pakistan's Supreme Court, among others. Aamir has written on transgender rights in prison, and feminist legal perspectives in Pakistan.

Salima Ahmadi is an international consultant and researcher. She worked for over a decade in Afghanistan, India, and Sri Lanka before having to migrate to Canada. She has worked with Amnesty International, Afghanistan Analysts Network, and New York University in Afghanistan. Her work focus has been on education, women's empowerment, and human rights and minority rights issues. Ahmadi holds an MBA from the University of Bedfordshire and a BA in International and Comparative Politics from the American University of Central Asia.

Afroza Anwary is Professor of Sociology at Minnesota State University, Mankato. She holds a PhD from the University of Minnesota, and her main research interests are social movements, contradictions of globalisation, human rights, gender-based violence, and genocide.

Sareta Ashraph is a barrister specialising in international criminal law. She serves as Senior Legal Adviser to the US Holocaust Memorial Museum's Center for the Prevention of Genocide and to the Center for Justice & Accountability. Ashraph served as Director of Investigations at the UN Investigative Team to promote accountability for the crimes committed by Da'esh/ISIL (2020–2022); Legal Analyst to the UN Commission of Inquiry on Syria (2012–2016) and the Commission of Inquiry on Libya (2012); Legal Adviser to the Defence Office of the International Criminal Court (2010–2011); and Defence Co-Counsel before the Special Court for Sierra Leone (2003–2009). She teaches 'Gender and International Crimes' at the Geneva Academy.

Kerstin Braun is Associate Professor and Associate Head (Research) at the School of Law and Justice at the University of Southern Queensland. Her interest is in criminal law and procedure, including international perspectives, comparative law, and human rights law. Prior to commencing work as an academic, Braun practised law as an associate at Baker & McKenzie at the Berlin office.

Louise Chappell is Scientia Professor of the Australian Human Rights Institute, the Faculty of Law and Justice at the University of New South Wales, Sydney, Australia. Chappell has published widely on gender and international law.

Maxine Beneba Clarke is an Australian of Afro-Caribbean descent, and the author of many books, including the bestselling memoir *The Hate Race* (2016), the Australian Book Industry Awards and Indie Award-winning short fiction collection *Foreign Soil* (2014), and the critically acclaimed poetry collections *Carrying the World* (2016), *How Decent Folk Behave* (2021), and *It's the Sound of the Thing:100 New Poems for Young People* (2023). She is the inaugural Peter Steele Poet in Residence at the University of Melbourne.

Lisa Davis is Professor of Law at City University of New York (CUNY) Law School, is Special Adviser on Gender Persecution to the International Criminal Court Prosecutor and is also Co-Director of the Human Rights & Gender Justice Clinic. Her work has focused on human rights and gender justice issues, including women's rights and LBGTQI+ rights in conflict and disaster settings. Davis has also testified before the US Congress, UK Parliament, the Inter-American Commission of Human Rights, and various other human rights bodies.

J. Jarpa Dawuni is Associate Professor of Political Science at Howard University. A lawyer by training, an educator by passion, and a social entrepreneur by calling, she is the founding director of the Howard University Centre of Women, Gender and Global Leadership, and founder of the non-profit organisation the Institute for African Women in Law. A multi-award winner, she is a leading scholar on women in law across Africa who has published pioneering work on women in the legal professions.

Alice Dieci is a human rights advocate and lawyer, having served for about a decade in the United Nations, civil society, and private law firms. Her work has included human rights monitoring and investigation in conflict, post-conflict, and crisis settings with the UN peacekeeping missions in the Democratic Republic of the Congo and the Central African Republic as well as with the UN High Commissioner for Human Rights in Colombia, Venezuela, and at its headquarters in Geneva, assisting the UN Special Rapporteur on trafficking in persons. Her areas of interest and expertise include sexual violence, gender issues and LGBTIQ+ rights, trafficking, peacebuilding, and transitional justice. She participated in research projects at the London School of Economics and the Geneva Academy and has been a teaching assistant at the Law Faculty of the University of Modena (Italy).

Sandrine de Herdt is Assistant Professor at the O. P. Jindal Global University, India, and a researcher at Athens Public International Law Centre, National and Kapodistian University of Athens. She obtained an LLM in Public International Law from the Catholic University of Louvain, Belgium.

Sarah Easy is an Australian lawyer who has a master's in Human Rights and Humanitarian Action from the Paris Institute of Political Sciences (Sciences Po). In parallel, she works as a research assistant at the Australian Human Rights Institute with a focus on gender issues. Easy has previously worked with human rights NGOs across Australia, Mexico, and Spain.

Souheir Edelbi is Lecturer in the School of Law at Western Sydney University. Her research is focused on race-making, coloniality, and international justice in the context of the complementarity principle and the International Criminal Court's interactions with African legal orders. Her research has an emphasis on the intersection of Third World approaches to international law, postcolonial studies, and critical race theory.

David Eichert is a PhD candidate at the London School of Economics. Eichert earned a JD from Cornell Law School and currently lectures about international law at the Paris Institute of Political Studies.

Kathryn Gooding is a public law and human rights solicitor with Irwin Mitchell LLP. She holds particular expertise in judicial review cases concerning the rights of asylum seekers and other migrant communities in the United Kingdom, as well as cases concerning sexual and gender-based violence against women and girls. Recently she has represented many Afghan asylum seekers with their judicial review challenges to policies and decisions of the UK government. Gooding has also interned with the Special Tribunal for Lebanon and worked as Research Associate for the Public International Law and Policy Group.

Priya Gopalan is a Malaysian international criminal lawyer and is currently Chair-Rapporteur of the UN Working Group on Arbitrary Detention. Her speciality is in gender and intersectionality. She has served as a prosecutor and appeals counsel at the ICTY, Legal Advisor for sexual and gender-based crimes at the International, Impartial and Independent Mechanism for Syria, Gender Advisor for the UN investigation on Sri Lanka, and Senior Advisor to the Truth, Reconciliation and Reparations Commission of the Gambia.

Laura Graham is Senior Lecturer at Northumbria Law School, Northumbria University. With a focus on gender and law, particularly sex work and human rights, reproductive autonomy, sexual offences, and feminist legal theory, she has examined whether the Human Rights Act 1998 could reform the law relating to sex work in England and Wales, and is currently using human rights as a strategic tool to fight for sex workers' rights and decriminalisation of sex work. In addition, Graham is Editor-in-Chief of the *International Journal of Gender, Sexuality and Law.*

Rosemary Grey is Senior Lecturer at the University of Sydney Law School. Her research focuses on gender and international criminal law, particularly in the International Criminal Court (ICC) and Extraordinary Chambers in the Courts of Cambodia (ECCC). Her previous book, *Prosecuting Sexual and Gender-Based Crimes in the International Criminal Court*, was published by Cambridge University Press in 2019. She has delivered professional training and presentations on gender issues for the ICC Assembly of States Parties, the ICC Office of the Prosecutor, and judges of the ICC, International Court of Justice, and ECCC.

Azimul Haas is a Rohingya photographer and poet from Myanmar. Since 2017, he has lived as a refugee in Bangladesh. For the past six years, he has photographed the daily lives of Rohingya people in the Cox's Bazar refugee camps, telling the world what he sees with his eyes. In 2022, he co-authored a photobook, *A Chance to Breathe*. Writing poetry is also his passion. It allows him to enter a world without injustice and discrimination. He has a strong ambition to receive a scholarship to help him become a professional journalist for his community one day.

Natalie Hodgson is Assistant Professor in the School of Law at the University of Nottingham. She is Head of the Forced Migration Unit in the Human Rights Law Centre and a member of the Criminal Justice Research Centre and the Nottingham International Law and Security Centre. Hodgson's research interests include criminology, criminal law, international criminal law, and refugee law.

Emma Irving is a consultant specialising in the intersection of international criminal justice, human rights, and technology. She also utilises her extensive experience in academia as a coach and mentor for PhD candidates and master's students.

Annika Jones is Associate Professor in Law at the University of Exeter. Her area of focus is in international criminal law and in particular international criminal procedure, judicial reasoning, and the relationship between international criminal courts and tribunals and other related institutions. Jones has worked in both the Trial and Appeals Chambers of the International Criminal Court, and on the development of the Implementing Legislation Database, one of the International Criminal Court's digital legal tools.

Olga Jurasz is Professor of Law at the Open University (United Kingdom). Her research focuses on legal responses to violence against women in national and international law, including prosecution of conflict-related gender-based crimes in international criminal law.

Dil Kayas is from Rakhine State, Myanmar. In 2017, she fled to Bangladesh from violent attacks by the Myanmar military, beginning her refugee life when she was twenty-four. She has dreamed of being a photographer since childhood. Three years ago, she received photography training, and her dream came true. Since 2018, she has been taking photographs with her mobile phone. In 2022, she co-authored *A Chance to Breathe*, a photobook published by FotoEvidence with support from Fortify Rights and Doha Debates. As a mother of three, her ambition is to educate her children so that they can have a better future.

Kirsten Keith is a lawyer with experience in international criminal law and human rights, having worked for the prosecution at various international, hybrid, and domestic courts. She acts as a consultant to human rights organisations and is a sessional academic at Southern Cross University, with a focus on international criminal justice and sexual and gender-based violence.

Omal Khair is from Rakhine State, Myanmar. Growing up, she dreamed of becoming a doctor to help women and children in her community. As she got older, she realised there was a greater need for journalists in her community, to shine a spotlight on the injustices Rohingya people face at the hands of the Burmese government. She fled to Bangladesh during the 2017 mass killings, where she now lives with her family. Despite their daily challenges, she continued to pursue her passion for photography, documenting the lives of her people and sharing their stories with the world.

Tonny Raymond Kirabira is a legal practitioner and academic in the field of international law and international relations, currently working as Lecturer at the University of Portsmouth. He holds a PhD in Law from the University of Portsmouth, an LLM in International Human Rights Law from the University of Notre Dame, and a Bachelor of Laws degree from Uganda Christian University. He was Visiting Fellow at the University of Copenhagen and has taught law courses at the University of Greenwich, University of Portsmouth, and Royal Holloway, University of London.

Sari Kouvo is Associate Professor of International Law in the University of Gothenburg's Department of Law, in addition to being an international consultant. Her work focuses on topics including Afghanistan, conflict, international law, human rights, transitional justice, and gender. She has served as Co-Director of the Afghanistan Analysts Network, Head of Program at the International Center for Transitional Justice, advisor to the European Union Special Representative for

Afghanistan, researcher at Amnesty International, and researcher and lecturer in the Department of Law at Gothenburg University.

Ramya Jawahar Kudekallu is currently the Telford Taylor Human Rights Visiting Instructor at the Benjamin N. Cardozo School of Law. Her research interest focuses on anti-discrimination frameworks within international human rights law, particularly labour, gender-based discrimination and access to justice, rights of minorities, and atrocity prevention through international intervention. She co-founded an international youth-led reproductive human rights organisation which advocates for youth access to sexual and reproductive health services as a human right and her previous work has included litigation at the Alternative Law Forum where her practice prioritised the rights of sex workers and LGBTIQ rights cases.

Marina Kumskova is Adjunct Professor at the John Jay College of Criminal Justice, as well as Senior UN Policy and Advocacy Advisor for the Global Partnership for the Prevention of Armed Conflict. She has worked extensively in the field of human rights including working to advance gender-sensitive conflict analysis and women's participation in peace work at the 2016 Women's International League for Peace and Freedom.

Naigaga Winifred Kyobiika is a magistrate with over ten years of experience in the domestic courts of Uganda. She currently heads the Chief Magistrates' Court of Ibanda in Western Uganda. She has written and published widely on legal issues such as gender, access to justice, and gender and judging. Kyobiika is also a change agent at the grassroots level with her involvement with the civil society organisations that target access to justice and development tools for vulnerable and marginalised women and girls in Ugandan society. She is a member of the board of the Federation for Women Lawyers, Uganda (FIDA-U) and a technical committee member of the International Association of Women Judges, Uganda Chapter (IAWJ-U). Kyobiika has consulted for the International Bar Association and is a certified trainer with the International Development Law Organisation, UN Women, and the International Association of Women Judges (IAWJ). She has trained several justice professionals, including: judicial actors, law enforcement, and other government officials.

Ameera Mahomed Ismail is an Australian lawyer specialising in criminal law. She has previously been a visiting professional at the International Criminal Court and has volunteered with organisations focusing on civil liberties, anti-discrimination, prisoner rights, and mental health.

Isabel Maravall-Buckwalter is Professor of Public International Law at CUNEF University, Madrid, Spain. She holds a PhD from the Universitat de València and the Università degli Studi di Palermo, as well as a master's in International Human Rights Law from the University of Oxford. Her research has focused on international human rights law, international and cross-border criminal law, and international health law.

Jill Marshall is a qualified lawyer and Professor of Law at Royal Holloway University of London. Her work focuses on gender justice, women's human rights, privacy, expression, and sexual violence in conflict. It includes analysis of international law, global justice, and human rights in their complexities of real-life situations. Marshall also works with an Afghan charity on diaspora work in London and Afghanistan, including workshops on sewing and human rights for the Being Human Arts Festival in London.

Melissa J. McKay is a Polish and Canadian barrister, born on the territory of the Anishinaab Nation (Treaty #3) and the traditional homelands of the Métis Nation. She has worked as a trial and appellate prosecutor in Canada, and has international criminal experience at the International Criminal Tribunal for the former Yugoslavia and Extraordinary Chambers in the Courts of Cambodia. She has also worked on strategic litigation relating to gender equality, and is interested in restorative justice.

Kcasey McLoughlin is Associate Professor in Law at Newcastle Law School. Her research examines the importance not only of greater diversity in our public institutions but also the need to critically interrogate the gendered assumptions that pervade legal and political institutions. Her first book *Law, Women Judges and the Gender Order: Lessons from the High Court of Australia* was awarded the Law and Society Association of Australia and New Zealand 2022 Book Prize.

Loyce Mrewa is an advanced PhD candidate at Western University's Faculty of Law. She has worked as a researcher for legal and multidisciplinary research institutes and is currently working with the Center for Research and Education on Violence against Women and Children. She has published in the areas of children's rights, gender justice in international criminal law, and transitional justice. Mrewa holds LLB and LLM degrees with a specialisation in international law and a master's in International Peace Studies.

Cassandra Mudgway is Senior Lecturer at the University of Canterbury Faculty of Law. She holds expertise in international human rights law, international criminal law, and gender, sexuality, and the law. Mudgway was involved in the Aoteroa New Zealand Feminist Judgment Project and is currently researching the use of 'patriarchy' in international human rights law with a particular interest in the role of the Convention on the Elimination of All Forms of Discrimination against Women in dismantling patriarchal structures globally.

Angela Mudukuti is Legal Advocacy Director of Waging Justice for Women Initiative at the Clooney Foundation for Justice. She is a Zimbabwean human rights lawyer, specialising in international criminal law. Mudukuti has worked for a number of organisations including the International Criminal Court, Open Society Foundations, Human Rights Watch, Wayamo Foundation, the Southern Africa Litigation Centre, and the International Institute for Criminal Justice and Human Rights. With a gender lens, she has focused on strategic litigation, advocacy, and capacity building. Her work experience includes training prosecutors and investigators to enhance domestic capacity to tackle international crimes; working on universal jurisdiction and precedent-setting cases before South African courts, including seeking the arrest of the former president of Sudan during his visit to South Africa. She has written and published on international criminal law issues in books, journals, and newspapers and has been featured in media such as the *Financial Times* and Al Jazeera. She sits on several editorial committees, including the *Oxford Journal for International Criminal Justice* and *Opinio Juris*.

Aparajitha Narayanan holds an LLM with a specialisation in international criminal law and previously worked in the defence team at the United Nations International Residual Mechamism for Criminal Tribunals in the Hague. She is currently a privacy advisor in the Netherlands, having settled there from India.

Melanie O'Brien is Associate Professor of International Law in the UWA Law School at the University of Western Australia. She is also the President of the International Association of Genocide Scholars. O'Brien has been cited by and been an amicus curia before the International Criminal Court. She has consulted for UN bodies and been cited by the global media for her expertise on international criminal law. She has conducted fieldwork and research across six continents while also being a member of the International Humanitarian Committee of the Australian Red Cross.

Claerwen O'Hara is Lecturer at La Trobe Law School, Co-Chair of the Australian and New Zealand Society of International Law Gender, Sexuality and International Law Interest Group and Managing Editor of the *Australian Feminist Law Journal*. Claerwen's research is on international human rights law and international economic law, with a particular focus on queer and feminist approaches to international law, alternative internationalisms, and law and political economy.

Phyu Phyu Oo is an independent scholar and practitioner, with over ten years of experience in development and humanitarian sectors, working with the United Nations and international NGOs across Asia and the Pacific. She was awarded a doctoral degree from Griffith University in 2023 and received a Master of Public Health from Johns Hopkins Bloomberg School of Public Health in 2015. Her research interests include the pressing issues of sexual and gender-based violence (SGBV) in conflict settings and interrogating state efforts in preventing and responding to the issues. She has contributed to multiple research projects focusing on SGBV in conflicts and consulted the United Nations on researching Myanmar following the military coup.

Valerie Oosterveld is Full Professor at Western University's Faculty of Law, Canada. She has published widely on the interpretation of sexual and gender-based crimes by international criminal tribunals and gender-sensitive investigation and prosecution. She was awarded the 2022 Royal Society of Canada Ursula Franklin Award in Gender Studies and is a member of the Canadian Partnership for International Justice. Oosterveld served on the Canadian delegation to various International Criminal Court-related negotiations, including the Assembly of States Parties, 2010 Review Conference and 1998 Diplomatic Conference.

Emma Palmer is Senior Lecturer at Griffith Law School, where she is a member of the Law Futures Centre and Griffith Asia Institute. Palmer has served as Director for Women's Legal Service NSW. Her research interests include international criminal law, international humanitarian law, human rights, transitional justice, infrastructure governance, gender issues, and norm adaptation in the Asia-Pacific region.

Navi Pillay is a distinguished expert on international criminal law and human rights. She served as the High Commissioner for Human Rights at the United Nations from 2008 to 2014. Prior to that, she was a judge at the International Criminal Court in The Hague from 2003 to 2008. She was the first and then only woman judge at the International Criminal Tribunal for Rwanda during 1995–2003, holding the Presidency for four years. Pillay has championed many human rights issues of which she herself had direct experience, having grown up under the Apartheid regime in South Africa. She plays an active role in numerous human rights organisations. Among other roles, she is the co-founder of Equality Now, an international women's rights organisation, and President of the Advisory Council of the International Nuremberg Principles Academy.

Akila Radhakrishnan is the Strategic Legal Advisor for Gender Justice for the Atlantic Council's Strategic Litigation Project, and former President of the Global Justice Center. Radhakrishnan is a globally recognised voice on issues of reproductive rights, gender-based violence, and justice and accountability. Her unique expertise as a feminist international lawyer is sought by policymakers, academics, media, and grassroots actors around the world. She has briefed the United Nations Security Council and the United Kingdom and European Parliaments, and regularly advises governments and multilateral institutions on issues of gender equality and human rights.

Catherine Renshaw is Professor in the School of Law at Western Sydney University. Her research focuses on Southeast Asia, particularly Myanmar, and she is a founding member of the Australian Myanmar Constitutional Democracy Project. Renshaw has authored many books, including *Human Rights and Participatory Politics in Southeast Asia* (2019) and *Experts, Networks and International Law* (2017, with Holly Cullen and Joanna Harrington).

Sophie Rigney is Senior Research Associate at the Indigenous Law Centres of the University of New South Wales. She is the author of *Fairness and Rights in International Criminal Procedure* (2022).

Adrienne Ringin is a qualified Australian lawyer, currently working as a Teaching Fellow while undertaking her PhD in law at La Trobe University, Australia. Being part of this project was a return to academic work for Adrienne after completing her Juris Doctor at the University of Melbourne. She has experience in government and the not-for-profit sectors in Australia, Geneva, and Tanzania.

Susana SáCouto directs the War Crimes Research Office of the Washington College of Law, where she is also Professorial Lecturer-in-Residence teaching courses on international criminal law and procedure. She has published widely on international criminal law topics and was awarded the Women's Law Center 22nd Annual Dorothy Beatty Memorial Award for significant contributions to women's rights.

Sara M. Saleh is a writer and human rights lawyer based in Sydney/Bidjigal land. Her poems, essays, and short stories have been published widely and she is co-editor of the ground-breaking 2019 anthology *Arab, Australian, Other: Stories on Race and Identity*. Her first novel is *Songs for the Dead and the Living* (2023). Her first poetry collection is *The Flirtation of Girls/Ghazal el-Banat* (2023) Saleh is the first and only poet to win both the 2021 Peter Porter Poetry Prize and the 2020 Judith Wright Poetry Prize. Saleh gained her Juris Doctor at UNSW. Her research interests include human rights and international humanitarian law, police accountability, the prison industrial complex, and the incarceration/detention of marginalised populations.

Patricia Viseur Sellers is an international criminal lawyer and is currently Special Advisor for Slavery Crimes to the Prosecutor of the International Criminal Court as well as part of the law faculty of the University of Oxford. She has served as the Legal Advisor for Gender, Acting Head of the Legal Advisory Section, and a prosecutor at the ICTY. She was also Legal Advisor for Gender at the ICTR. Her work includes litigation of the landmark cases of *Akayesu*, *Furundzija*, and *Kunarac*, which transformed the interpretation of sexual violence as war crimes, crimes against humanity, genocide, torture, and enslavement.

Anushka Sehmi is a Kenyan lawyer with over ten years of experience working in civil society in Kenya, the International Criminal Court, and the International Residual Mechanism for Criminal Tribunals (IRMCT). Sehmi holds degrees in law from the London School of Economics and the University of Oxford, having also recently completed a MSc in African Studies at the University of Oxford. She previously represented victims before the International Criminal Court in *Prosecutor v. Dominic Ongwen* and *Prosecutor v. Uhuru Muigai Kenyatta*. She has also worked at the International Criminal Court as Field Officer for the Victims' Participation and Reparations Section and as Associate Legal Officer with the ICC Registry.

Grant Shubin is a legal advisor at DIGNITY – the Danish Institute Against Torture – where his work focuses on ending impunity for torture and other ill-treatment, including when taking the form of sexual and gender-based violence and in mass atrocity contexts, by supporting the development of jurisprudence, institutional reform, and building capacity.

Immi Tallgren is Adjunct Professor of International Law at the University of Helsinki and Senior KONE Research Fellow. Her contribution was funded by the Kone Foundation. Tallgren has previously worked at the Finnish MFA, the Legal Affairs Unit of EUROPOL, the European Space Agency in Paris and Brussels, the Max Planck Institute, Luxembourg, and she has been a visiting fellow at various research centres at the London School of Economics. Her research interests are primarily in international criminal law, history of international law, feminist approaches to international law, and law and cinema.

Saumya Uma is Professor and Director for the Centre of Women's Rights at the Jindal Global Law School of O. P. Jindal Global University, India. She has twenty-nine years' combined experience as an academic, legal practitioner, researcher, writer, trainer, campaigner, and consultant, specialising in the intersections of gender, human rights, and the law. Uma worked as the National Coordinator of ICC India and has continued to engage with the jurisprudence of the ICC.

Suzanne Varrall is a Laureate Research Fellow at Melbourne Law School, University of Melbourne. She works, researches, and teaches in the areas of international humanitarian law, international criminal law, arms control, and human rights. Varrall has worked across the government, not-for-profit, and legal sectors. She was formerly the Associate Director of the Asia Pacific Centre for Military Law at the Australian Department of Defence, and has held various roles in the National Security and International Policy Division of the Department of the Prime Minister and Cabinet, including as Senior Adviser on non-proliferation and disarmament, and Adviser on Australia's civil–military engagement in Afghanistan.

Sarah Williams is Professor at the University of New South Wales, Faculty of Law & Justice, as well as Associate at the Australian Human Rights Institute and Centre for Crime, Law and Justice. She was the Dorset Fellow in Public International Law at the British Institute of International and Comparative Law, a senior legal researcher at the UK Foreign and Commonwealth Office, and Lecturer at Durham Law School, University of Durham. Her main research areas include international law, in particular international criminal law, international humanitarian law, international disaster law, and the law on the use of force.

Marie Wilmet holds a PhD from the European University Institute and is a research fellow at the Centre Thucydide (Université Paris-Panthéon-Assas). Adopting a socio-legal approach, Wilmet's research investigates the contributions of victims' procedural rights to gender justice in international criminal law through a case study of the Extraordinary Chambers in the Court of Cambodia.

Sarah Zarmsky is a PhD candidate and Assistant Lecturer in the Human Rights Centre at the University of Essex Law School. Her research focuses on intersections of international criminal law, human rights, and new and emerging technologies. In 2023, Zarmsky was Visiting Scholar in the Human Rights Center at UC Berkeley School of Law. She holds an LLM in Public International Law from Leiden University, and her experience includes working with multiple international courts and as an open-source investigator.

Foreword

This book is an exercise in gender-sensitive judging. The editors have invited a group of academics, advocates, and legal practitioners from various regions of the world to re-envision a range of judgments delivered by judges at the International Criminal Court (ICC), applying a feminist judgments methodology.

The outcomes are extremely enlightening, and hopefully will influence the future course of progressive jurisprudence. As a former judge myself, I became aware of the value of feminist perspectives, and believe that the book will be of great interest to judges, prosecutors, defence and victims' counsel, investigators, civil society organisations, and all of us who care about justice and accountability.

Although I myself disavowed the label 'feminist', judgments that I wrote, such as the *Akayesu* genocide judgment of the International Criminal Tribunal for Rwanda (ICTR), are often cited as examples of gender-sensitive decisions. Justice Claire L'Heureux Dube, formerly from the Canadian Supreme Court, also resisted the label of 'feminist' and instead embraced a commitment to protecting the rights of victims and human rights as the hallmark of her groundbreaking decisions on women's rights. I agree with Justice Brenda Hale of the United Kingdom that it is possible to be both a judge and a feminist once one understands that feminism underscores equality of women and men and that the experiences of women are as relevant as the experiences of men.

I champion the participation of women on the bench, based on the principles of equality and non-discrimination, and value the sensitivity and understanding they bring of the vulnerabilities of female victims within traditional gender structures, both in times of conflict and as victims of economic and social deprivations in society.

Having been born and practised as a lawyer in apartheid South Africa, I daily lived the experience of injustice of exclusion on the grounds of race, sex, and class. Many on the all-white male bench openly espoused racial and gender prejudices. Many of the judges were loyal to the official policy of superiority of the white race and the apprehensions about their safety from the Black danger (*swart gevaar*). They expressed prejudices, such as that Black women were sexually promiscuous and did not experience the shame or suffering that white women victims of rape would.

Prejudicial presumptions and ignorance of the context and living conditions of women, particularly poor women, is a common and pernicious barrier to justice, particularly for women victims and survivors of violence. Such stereotyping causes judges to reach a view about cases based on preconceived beliefs, rather than relevant facts and actual evidence. This is particularly relevant in sexual violence cases.

Prejudice also extends to suspicions that women judges have gender biases. It is no accident that the decisions of women judges at the International Criminal Tribunal for the former Yugoslavia (ICTY) and ICTR were challenged on appeal for their alleged gender biases towards women: in the *Akayesu* decision, I was singled out for allegedly being influenced by the women protestors on the streets of Kigali,[1] and at the ICTY, the impartiality of Judge Florence Mumba of Zambia was questioned on the basis that she should have recused herself because she had in the past represented her government before the UN Commission on the Status of Women (CSW).[2] Both these grounds of lack of impartiality were dismissed by the appeals chamber.

Gender is an issue not only in the elements of the crimes that the ICC deals with but also in the very composition of the court itself. The ICC is the first international court that has striven for a gender balance on the bench. The significance of the composition of the court is the subject of some reflection in the first part of this volume.

In *Akayesu*, we on the bench noted that in international law there was no commonly held definition of rape in conflict situations. The definition we created was born out of the experiences of women witnesses who testified at the trial. Witness 'JJ' was asked by the prosecutor whether the perpetrators had penetrated her. She replied that that was not the only thing they did. It was a combination of the violence, the acts they did on her, what they said, and the humiliation she felt as a mother, by the public nudity, and being raped in the presence of children and by young men. I listened to her with particular care to register how she had experienced the act of rape. I was convinced that the traditional 'body penetration' definition was not appropriate in the context of mass rapes in war and conflict situations and did not do justice to the way women perceived the violation. I tried to capture the essence of these voices of rape survivors in the line: 'Sexual violence was a step in the process of destruction of the Tutsi group – destruction of the spirit, of the will to live and of life itself.'[3]

1 See Appeal Judgment, *Akayesu* (ICTR-96-4-A), Appeals Chamber, 1 June 2001, §§ 197–200.

2 See Appeal Judgment, *Furundžija*, Appeals Chamber (IT-95-17/1-A), 21 July 2000 §§ 164–215.

3 See Judgment, *Akayesu*, Trial Chamber (ICTR-96-4-T), 2 September 1998, § 732.

The ICC's first conviction for acts of rape was delivered in the case concerning Jean-Pierre Bemba, on charges of rape, murder, and pillage committed in the Central African Republic by his troops. The judgment was reversed on appeal. Writers in this volume, Sarah Williams and Suzanne Varrall, have revisited the appeals decision by applying a feminist lens to liability under the principle of command responsibility, which is illuminating.

We have come a long way from defending women's rights to serve as judges to asserting exclusion and discrimination as violations of the right to equality and non-discrimination. We also still have some way to go. This volume makes an important contribution to these earlier efforts to achieve gender justice by once again bringing attention to the lived experiences of women in situations of war and conflict.

Navi Pillay

Acknowledgements

In Australia, we have a tradition of acknowledging the First Nations' lands that we live and work on. While this acknowledgement is a symbolic gesture, it helps to signify our understanding that this land was never ceded, and that the effects of colonialism and dispossession for Australia's indigenous peoples are ongoing, and that as editors from settler backgrounds, we have been privileged by colonialist structures. The editors of this project are grateful to have worked on the lands of the Aniwan, Awabakal and Worimi, Bedegal, Cammeraygal, Gadigal, Wurundjeri Woi-wurrung and Bunurong Boon Wurrung, Gamilaraay, and Dharug peoples. We are deeply grateful to be able to contribute to the long history of knowledge-sharing on these lands.

This extensive volume has been created over four years through a committed feminist process. The editorial team have sustained each other through illnesses, including cancer and COVID-19, and most importantly through our care responsibilities, which have included the birth of four precious children and the care of four precious others. Of course, there is also a village of invisible supporters who have stood beside and behind us, and who have enabled us to teach, write, edit, and manage our care commitments. We are each so grateful for those who have provided us the opportunity to have such full and rewarding (and sometimes exhausting!) lives.

As editors, we have been respectful of each other's views and critiques, finding a path through any differences. We have worked closely as a team, each taking up the editorial baton when passed to us, and feeling able to hand it back when the need arose. That said, we are indebted to Kcasey for a 'her'culean effort as the editorial mainstay, driving the book with such a careful and generous approach through its gestation. We are also grateful for Louise's mentoring, including showing us how to 'think outside the office', working hard while enjoying the wonders of nature – in this case the beautiful ocean pools on Bedegal and Awabakal and Worimi waters.

Essential to the completion and quality of this project have been two exemplary research assistants: Sarah Easy and Adrienne Ringin. It is true to say that this volume could not have been finished without their skills, expert knowledge, and timely and thoughtful responses, which have enabled us to gather a large collection including twenty-seven judgments, nine reflections, seven additional chapters, and poetic and photographic interventions. We know the authors too have been grateful for their support in identifying issues, tracking down footnotes, and guiding their contributions where necessary. We also appreciated Sarah and Adrienne making their own important contributions to the volume by donning fictional robes to write judgments on Cote d'Ivore, Afghanistan, and Uganda.

Developed over the course of a global pandemic, this book has been created during a unique and disruptive period for all our contributors, especially those with primary caring responsibilities, which includes almost everyone in this volume. Despite our disappointment at not being able to meet in person during the process of writing due to lockdowns, we are hugely grateful to every author who joined in online workshops and participated in group chats, and for ultimately producing outstanding chapters that collectively make a critically important contribution to the feminist judging methodology and international criminal law. We are thankful for their insights and imagination, and for them having the integrity to give us frank and constructive feedback when they saw the need.

There are many other individuals who have encouraged us in our endeavours in ways which have contributed significantly to this volume. Thanks to Bridget Crawford, Kathy Stanchi, and Linda Berger (Feminist Judgement Series at Cambridge University Press) for so enthusiastically encouraging our submission and supporting our proposal. We also acknowledge with gratitude Matt Galloway at Cambridge University Press, who has waited patiently for the manuscript and gently guided us through the production process.

We are grateful to Rosemary Hunter, Catherine O'Rouke, and Heather Douglas for helping us grapple with the conceptual and practical issues related to the use of the feminist judgments methodology, and for their encouragement of our ambition to bridge domestic-level analysis with international criminal law. Some of their guidance has been video-recorded and can be found here for those wishing to benefit from their wisdom.[1] We are also indebted to the Australian *Indigenous Legal Judgments* collection,[2] edited by Nicole Watson and Heather Douglas, for influencing our thinking and opening us up to more radical reimaginings of judicial writing.

[1] L. Chappell, R. Grey, K. McLoughlin, and S. Varrall, 'Reimagining Judging in International Criminal Courts: A Gendered Approach', Website (University of New South Wales and the Australian Human Rights Institute) available at www.humanrights.unsw.edu.au/research/current-research/reimagining-judging-international-criminal-courts-gendered-approach

[2] N. Watson and H. Douglas, *Indigenous Legal Judgments: Bringing Indigenous Voices into Judicial Decision Making* (Abingdon: Routledge, 2021).

We wish to thank Judges Navi Pillay and Hilary Charlesworth for being so supportive of the idea of this volume. We are indebted to Judge Pillay for sharing her wisdom in the Foreword, reinforcing the value of a diverse judiciary to the achievement of gender justice.

Inspired by other feminist judgment collections, we were keen to capture non-traditional expressions of the law. In this volume we have been privileged to work with two poets, Maxine Beneba Clarke and Sara Saleh, both of whom have a legal background. Through their rich and unique voices, Maxine and Sara capture more poignantly than any legal judgment ever could the struggle, tragedy, disappointment, and hope that the International Criminal Court provides to those who experience conflict. The editors also wish to acknowledge and thank Vanessa Chong and Fortify Rights for their assistance and support in connecting us with Azimul Haas, Omal Khair, and Dil Kayas – the Rohingya media fellows whose photographs feature on the cover of the book and in a dedicated photo essay.

We each offer our gratitude to our friends and colleagues from our academic homes at the University of Newcastle School of Law and Justice, Australian Human Rights Institute, Faculty of Law and Justice, University of New South Wales (UNSW), and Sydney University Law School. We're especially grateful to our co-workers, Pat Filmer-Sanky and Catherine Oddie from the College of Human and Social Futures, University of Newcastle, Steph Manefield, Oras Kalaf, and Susie Shaw at UNSW, and Professor Michele Ford, Professor Arlie Loughnan, and Research Manager Julia Robertson at the University of Sydney. We are indebted to everyone from our respective research offices who has assisted in establishing the financials and helped co-ordinate a complex, inter-university project. Thanks also to Paul Chappell and Geeta Arulampalam for their generous hospitality during our fruitful workshop in Newcastle.

The financial support of the Australian Research Council Discovery Program (DP210103628) has enabled us to pursue this ambitious project. We recognise how fortunate we are to have access to this publicly funded research scheme and for the assistance we have received.

Personal Acknowledgements

Kcasey: I am grateful to Dave, Arthur, and Imogen for their love and patience during this project. I am thankful to family and friends for their many acts of kindness, big and small. Thanks also to my wonderful colleagues at Newcastle School of Law and Justice, for their collegiality and support. Finally, I am grateful to the entire project team for cultivating such a positive and collaborative approach – it has been a genuine privilege to have learned from all of you. I acknowledge that my contribution is funded by the Australian Research Council DP210103628.

Louise: I would like to thank my precious gang, Robert, James, and Angus, who once again had my back while I worked on this book. I'd also like to acknowledge UNSW Law Dean Andrew Lynch and Head of School Theunis Roux, and my wonderful medical team, Doctors Kath Smartt, Rachel Dear, and Jeremey De Leon, who have enabled me to (mostly) keep on track. I acknowledge that my contribution is funded by the Australian Research Council DP210103628.

Rose: My lasting thanks to Sally, Annie, and Danny, and to my 'village' (including family and state-subsidised childcare) which, by taking care of the little ones, has enabled my involvement in this project. I acknowledge that my contribution to this project has been funded by the Australian Research Council DP210103628 and with the support of Sydney Law School. I have greatly enjoyed working with the co-editors, research assistants, and contributors on this collective endeavour. Few projects offer as many opportunities for community-building and ideas-sharing as this.

Suzanne: I would like to thank my family – Willem, Hazel, and Saskia – for their love and support. I am also exceptionally grateful to Louise, Kcasey, and Rose for so generously inviting me to be part of this amazing project, for sharing their invaluable experience and for their encouragement and support.

Contributor Acknowledgements

Mashal Aamir acknowledges her judgment concerns the situation in Afghanistan and wishes to highlight the victims and the continued impact left upon the lives of those affected.

Sareta Ashraph acknowledges and is grateful to those who gave their expertise and time to be interviewed for her contribution. She hopes the chapter reflects the challenges, many of them still unaddressed, under which the defence teams and offices at the hybrid tribunals continue to labour.

Alice Dieci acknowledges that her contribution was inspired by the courage and determination of all survivors of sexual violence she has had the opportunity to meet and listen to over the years. Her contribution is dedicated to them, with the hope that one day justice will be served. She also thanks her husband Thomas for always supporting her in the feminist struggle for gender equality. The views expressed in her contribution are solely her own and do not necessarily reflect those of the United Nations.

Souheir Edelbi acknowledges that she wrote her judgment on the unceded Barramattagal lands and waterways of the Darug Nation and pays her respects to the Barramattagal elders, both past and present.

Emma Irving would like to acknowledge the understanding and support of her co-author Sarah Zarmsky to complete the project as her son was born.

Naigaga Winifred Kyobiika acknowledges the support she got from her friend Brenda Nanyunja in putting together the judgment. She also acknowledges the enriching contribution of Sophie Rigney and Melanie O'Brien, without which this chapter would not be complete. Winfred thanks her family, Moses, Alexander, and Aristar, who support her every day in all ways.

Melissa J. McKay would like to thank Aicha Raeburn-Cherradi and Genevieve Westrope for their significant research support, without which her chapter would not be complete.

Loyce Mrewa would like to extend thanks to the Social Sciences and Humanities Research Council of Canada (SSHRC) and the Canadian Partnership for International Justice (CPIJ) for the funding that helped to support the research.

Valerie Oosterveld wishes to thank the Social Sciences and Humanities Research Council of Canada for its funding of the Canadian Partnership for International Justice (CPIJ). The CPIJ provided invaluable support for the completion of this project.

Emma Palmer wishes to thank all who cared for her two children during the process of writing in Arakwal-Bundjalung country, and to all those who supported surrounding communities during the flooding of 2022. Her contribution was funded by a Griffith University New Researcher Grant.

Adrienne Ringin acknowledges the support of her friends and family over the course of this project.

Immi Tallgren acknowledges that her contribution was funded by the Kone Foundation.

Saumya Uma acknowledges that all opinions expressed are her own and are not to be attributed to the institutions she is affiliated with.

Marie Wilmet acknowledges that her contribution is funded by the French Ministry of Higher Education and Research and the European University Institute. She is grateful to Andréa Feuillâtre, Carolin Lerch, and Sandrine de Sena for their helpful comments on earlier drafts.

Chronology

1872 – Gustav Moynier proposed a permanent court in response to the crimes committed during the Franco-Prussian War[1]
1919 – Calls for an ad hoc international court at the Treaty of Versailles
1945 – Establishment of the Nuremberg and Tokyo tribunals
1948 – Convention on the Prevention and Punishment of Genocide and the International Law Commission invited to 'study the desirability and possibility of establishing an international judicial organ for the trial of persons charged with genocide'
1989 – United Nations General Assembly invited the International Law Commission to resume work on a statute for an international criminal court
1990s – Establishment of the International Criminal Tribunal for Rwanda and International Criminal Tribunal for the former Yugoslavia
1994 – Draft statute for an international criminal court to the United Nations General Assembly
1995 – Establishment and meetings of the Ad Hoc Committee on the Establishment of an International Criminal Court
1996–1998 – Establishment and meetings of the Preparatory Committee on the Establishment of the ICC
17 July 1998 – 120 states adopted the Rome Statute[2]
1 July 2002 – Rome Statute entry into force after ratification by sixty countries[3]
June 2004 – Investigation in the Democratic Republic of the Congo authorised, ICC-01/04
July 2004 – Investigation in Uganda authorised, ICC-02/04

[1] Coalition of the ICC, 'ICC History – The Road to Rome' (Web page) available at www.coalitionfortheicc.org/icc-history,

[2] The ICC, 'The ICC at a Glance', available at www.icc-cpi.int/sites/default/files/ICCAtAGlanceEng.pdf

[3] *Ibid.*

June 2005 – Investigation in Darfur, Sudan authorised, ICC-02/05
May 2007 – Investigation in Central African Republic authorised, ICC-01/05
10 **June 2008** – Warrant of Arrest in the Case of the *Prosecutor v. Jean-Pierre Bemba Gombo*
4 **March 2009** – Public Redacted Version – Decision on the Prosecution's Application for a Warrant of Arrest against Omar Hassan Ahmad Al Bashir
15 **June 2009** – Decision Pursuant to Article 67(7)(a) and (b) of the Rome Statute on the Charges of the Prosecutor against Jean-Pierre Bemba Gombo
March 2010 – Investigation in Kenya authorised, ICC-01/09
18 **November 2010** – Preliminary Examination of Nigeria announced
March 2011 – Investigation in Libya authorised, ICC-01/11
3 **October 2011** – Investigation in Côte d'Ivoire authorised, ICC-02/11
2 **March 2012** – Decision on the Prosecutor's Application Pursuant to Article 58 for a Warrant of Arrest against Simone Gbagbo
14 **March 2012** – Thomas Lubanga Dylio convicted, ICC-01/04-01/06
January 2013 – Investigation in Mali authorised, ICC-01/12
7 **March 2014** – Germain Katanga convicted, ICC-01/04-01/07
September 2014 – Investigation in Central African Republic II authorised, ICC-01/14
11 **December 2014** – Decision on Côte d'Ivoire's Challenge to the Admissibility of the Case against Simone Gbagbo
3 **March 2015** – Judgment Decision in the case of the *Prosecutor v. Thomas Lubanga Dylio*
27 **January 2016** – Investigation in Georgia authorised, ICC-01/15
21 **March 2016** – Judgment Decision in the case of the *Prosecutor v. Jean-Pierre Bemba Gombo*. Bemba convicted, ICC-01/05-01/08
21 **June 2016** – Sentencing Decision in the case of the *Prosecutor v. Jean-Pierre Bemba Gombo*
27 **September 2016** – Judgment and Sentencing Decision in the case of the *Prosecutor v. Ahmad Al Faqi Al Mahdi*
4 **January 2017** – Second Decision to the Defence's Challenge to the Jurisdiction of the Court in Respect of Counts 6 and 9 in the case of the *Prosecutor v. Bosco Ntaganda*
17 **August 2017** – Reparations Order in the case of the *Prosecutor v. Ahmad Al Faqi Al Mahdi*
27 **September 2017** – Ahmad Al Faqi Al Mahdi convicted, ICC-01/12-01/15
25 **October 2017** – Investigation in Burundi authorised, ICC-01/17
22 **May 2018** – Decision on the Prosecutor's Application for the Issuance of a Warrant of Arrest for Al Hassan Ag Abdoul Aziz Ag Mohamed Ag Mahmoud
8 **June 2018** – Jean Pierre Bemba Gombo acquitted, ICC-01/05-01/08
12 **April 2019** – Decision Pursuant to Article 15 of the Rome Statute on the Authorisation of an Investigation into the Situation in the Islamic Republic of Afghanistan

6 May 2019 – In the Appeal of the Hashemite Kingdom of Jordan against the Decision of Pre-Trial Chamber II entitled 'Decision under Article 87(7) of the Rome Statute on the Non-Compliance by Jordan with the Request by the Court of Arrest and Surrender o[f] Omar Al-Bashir' of 11 December 2017

8 July 2019 – Judgment in the case of the *Prosecutor v. Bosco Ntaganda*. Ntaganda convicted, ICC-01/04-02/06

14 November 2019 – Investigation in Bangladesh and Myanmar authorised, ICC-01/19

14 November 2019 – Decision Pursuant to Article 15 of the Rome Statute on the Authorisation of an Investigation into the Situation in the People's Republic of Bangladesh/Republic of the Union of Myanmar

19 February 2020 – Preliminary Examination of Venezuela II announced

5 March 2020 – Investigation in Afghanistan authorised, ICC-02/17

1 June 2020 – Decision on the Prosecutor's Request to Amend the Charges against Alfred Yekatom

18 January 2021 – Decision Establishing the Principles of Victims' Representation during the Confirmation of Charges Hearing

4 February 2021 – Judgment in the case of the *Prosecutor v. Dominic Ongwen*. Ongwen convicted, ICC-02/04-01/15

3 March 2021 – Investigation in State of Palestine authorised, ICC-01/18

6 May 2021 – Sentencing Decision in the Case of the *Prosecutor v. Dominic Ongwen*

9 July 2021 – Decision on the Confirmation of Charges against Ali Muhammad Ali Abd-Al-Rahman ('Ali Kushayb')

15 September 2021 – Investigation in Republic of the Philippines authorised, ICC-01/21

3 November 2021 – Investigation in Venezuela I authorised, ICC-02/18

2 March 2022 – Investigation in Ukraine authorised, ICC-01/22

Cases

DOMESTIC COURTS

Australia

Court of Criminal Appeal, R v Pogson, R v Lapham, R v Martin [2012] NSWCCA 225

Supreme Court of New South Wales (Australia) R v MB 2017 NSWSC 619

Supreme Court of the Australian Capital Territory Samani v The Queen [2016] ACTCA 48

Supreme Court of the Northern Territory (Australia) R v Ebatarintja 2010 NTSC 6

Vartzokas v Zanker (1989) 51 SASR 277

Canada

British Colombia Court of Appeal (Canada) R v Reid 2002 B.C.J. No 845

Canada R v C.R.P. 2001 OJ No 1595

Canada R v L (R) 2004 CarswellOnt 5856 2004 O.J. No. 3502

Canada R v Stewart 1999 CarswellOnt 404 1999 S.J No 413 42 W.C.B. (2d) 546

Ontario Court of Appeal (Canada) R v Veenhof 2011 ONCA 195

Supreme Court of Canada R v Martineau [1990] 2 SCR 633 File No.:21122

R v Gladue [1999] 1 SCR 688

Supreme Court of Canada R v Ipeelee 2012 SCC 13

Supreme Court of Canada R v Middleton 2009 SCC 21

Supreme Court of Canada R v Proulx 2000 SCC 5

Yukon Francophone School Board, Education Area #23 v Yukon (Attorney General) 2015 SCC 25

India

Rajendar Mohan Rana & Ors v Prem Prakash Chaudhary & Ors 2011 8 AD (DELHI) 153, LPA 554/2-11
Supreme Court of India National Legal Services Authority v Union of India Writ Petition Civil No 604 of 2013
Supreme Court of India, State of Maharashtra v Chandrabhan Tale 1983 AIR 803, 1983 SCR (3) 327

New Zealand

Court of Appeal of New Zealand Mason v R 2021 NZCA 185
High Court of New Zealand Colvin v R 2021 NZHC 400
High Court of New Zealand R v Hodgson CRI 2009-044-10450 [2010] NZHC 1750

South Africa

Constitutional Court of South Africa S v M CCT 53/06 [2007] ZACC 18
High Court of South Africa (Gauteng) Mosikili v State (A339/2017) ZAGPPHC 813
South Africa S v Mambila (SH796/03) 2008 ZAGPHC 465
South Africa Supreme Court of Appeal S v Ingram 1995 (1) SACR 1 (A)
South Africa Supreme Court of Appeal S v Potgieter 1994 (1) SACR 61 (A)
Western Cape High Court (South Africa) S v Lakay (A 724/2010) 2012 ZAWCHC 14
S v Dikqacwi and Others (SS49/2012), High Court of South Africa [2013] ZAWCHC 6

Trinidad and Tobago

High Court of Justice Trinidad and Tobago, The State v Ramky Gayah for Manslaughter 2002 TTHC 12

United Kingdom

England and Wales Court of Appeal (Criminal Division) R v Wiles 2004 EWCA Crim 836
England and Wales High Court (Queen's Bench) Bird v Jones 1845 EWHC QB J64

United States of America

Heritage Farms, Inc v Markel Insurance Company 2012 WI 26

Zimbabwe

Bulawayo High Court S v Majaya Case no HC 168/2003 [2003] ZWBHC 15
Bulawayo High Court S v Sibanda (CRB G 440/10) and Another (CRB G 440-1/10 ZWBHC 79

INTERNATIONAL COURTS

European Court of Human Rights

Aydin v Turkey No. 23178/94, ECHR 1997-VI, 25 September 1997
Valašinas v Lithuania No. 44558/98, ECHR 2001-VIII, 24 July 2001

Inter-American Court of Human Rights

Advisory Opinion OC-24/17 on Gender Identity, and Equality and Non-Discrimination of Same-Sex Couples, 24 November, 2017
Caesar v Trinidad and Tobago IACHR Series C no 123 11, March 2005
Gelman v Uruguay Merits and Reparations IACHR. Series C No. 221, 24 February 2011
Miguel Castro-Castro Prison v Peru Merits, Reparations and Costs IACHR Ser. C No. 160 25 November 2006
Plan de Sánchez Massacre v Guatamala IACHR Series C no 116, 19 November 2004
Porfirio Rondin v Mexico IACHR Case 11.520, 18 February 1998
Raquel Marti de Mejia v Peru Case 10.970. Report No. 5/96, IACHR OEA/Ser.L/II.91 Doc. 7, 1 March 1996
Yakye Axa Indigenous Community v Paraguay IACHR Series C no 125, 17 June 2005

International Criminal Court

Prosecutor v Ahmad Al Faqi Al Mahdi ICC-01/12-01/15
Prosecutor v Al Hassan Ag Abdoul Aziz Ag Mohamed Ag Mahmoud ICC-01/12-02/18
Prosecutor v Alfred Yekatom and Patrice-Edouard Ngaïssona ICC-01/12-01/18
Prosecutor v Ali Muhammad Ali Abd-Al-Rahman ICC-02/05-01/20
Prosecutor v Bahr Idriss Abu Garda ICC-02/05-02/09
Prosecutor v Bosco Ntaganda ICC-01/04-02/06
Prosecutor v Callixte Mbarushimana ICC-01/04-01/10
Prosecutor v Dominic Ongwen ICC-02/04-01/15

Prosecutor v Francis Kirimi Muthaura et al ICC-01/09-02/11
Prosecutor v Germain Katanga ICC-01/04-01/07
Prosecutor v Germain Katanga and Mathieu Ngudjolo Chui ICC-01/04-01/07
Prosecutor v Jean-Pierre Bemba Gombo ICC-01/05-01/08
Prosecutor v Laurent Gbagbo ICC-02/11-01/11
Prosecutor v Mahmoud Busayf Al-Werfalli ICC-01/11-01/17
Prosecutor v Omar Hassan Ahmad Al Bashir ICC-02/05-01/09
Prosecutor v Saif al-Islam Gaddafi and Abdullah Al-Senussi ICC-01/11-01/11
Prosecutor v Simone Gbagbo ICC-02/11-01/12
Prosecutor v Thomas Lubanga Dyilo ICC-01/04-01/06
Prosecutor v Uhuru Muigai Kenyatta ICC-01/09-02/11
Prosecutor v William Samoei Ruto and Joshua Arap Sang ICC-01/09-01/11
Situation in the Democratic Republic of the Congo ICC-01/04
Situation in the Republic of Kenya ICC-01/09
Situation in the Republic of Côte d'Ivoire ICC-02/11
Situation in Georgia ICC-01/15
Situation in the Islamic Republic of Afghanistan ICC-02/17
Situation on the Registered Vessel of Comoros, Greece and Cambodia ICC-01/13
Situation in the People's Republic of Bangladesh/Republic of the Union of Myanmar ICC-01/19
Situation in the State of Palestine ICC-01/19-28

International Court of Justice

Case Concerning the Application of the Convention on the Prevention and Punishment of the Crime of Genocide (Bosnia and Herzegovina v Serbia and Montenegro) 2007 ICJ Rep 43
Case Concerning the Application of the Convention on the Prevention and Punishment of the Crime of Genocide (Croatia v Serbia) 2015 ICR Rep 3
Case Concerning the Application of the Convention on the Prevention and Punishment of the Crime of Genocide (Gambia v Myanmar) ICJ GL No. 178

International Military Tribunal

Major War Criminals International Military Tribunal, 1 October 1946
The Prosecutor v Krupp et al Case No. 214 United States Military Tribunal in Nuremberg
Trial of General Tomoyuki Yamashita United Stated Military Commission Maila 8 October–7 December 1945/Supreme Court of the United States, 4 February 1946

Trial of Major Karl Rauer and 6 Others British Military Court, Wuppertal, Germany, 18 February 1946

United States of America v Soemu Toyoda and Hiroshi Tamura Military Tribunal Appointed by the Supreme Commander of the Allies Powers, Tokyo, Japan, 1946–1949

United States v Josef Altstoetter, et al (Justice Case) United States Military Tribunal, Nuremberg 17 February–4 December 1947

United States v Wilhelm List (Hostages Trial) United States Military Tribunal, Nuremberg 8 July 1947–19 February 1948

United States v Wilhelm Von Leeh et al (High Command Trial) United States Military Tribunal, Nuremberg 27–28 October 1948

TRIBUNALS, COMMITTEES, TREATY BODIES

Committee against Torture

Abdelli v Tunisia CAT/C/31/D/188/2001

Thabati v Tunisia CAT/C/31/D/187/2001

ECCC

Case 002/01 002/19-9-09-2007/ECCC/TC-E313

Case 002 002-19-09-2007-ECCC/SC-F36

Co-Prosecutors v Duch Case 001-F28

Co-Prosecutors v Khieu Samphan and Nuon Chea 002/19-09-2007-ECCC/SC

Co-Prosecutors v Nuon Chea and Khieu Samphán Case 002/01-F23

Human Rights Committee

Clement Boodoo v Trinidad & Tobago CCPR/C/74/D/721

Darmon Sultanova v Uzbekistan CCPR/C/86/D/915/2000

George Osbourne v Jamaica CCPR/C/68/D/759/1997

Philip Afuson Njaru v Cameroon CCPR/C/89/D/1353/2005

ICTR

Prosecutor v Alfred Musema ICTR-96-13-T

Prosecutor v Théoneste Bagosora ICTR-98-41-A

Prosecutor v Casimir Bizimungu, Justin Mugenzi, Jérôme-Clément Bicamumpaka and Prosper Mugiraneza ICTR-99-50-T

Prosecutor v Clément Kayishema and Obed Ruzindana ICTR-95-1-T

Prosecutor v Elizaphan Ntakirutimana and Gérard Ntakirutimana ICTR-96-10-A and ICTR-96-17
Prosecutor v Sylvestre Gacumbitsi ICTR-2001-64-T
Prosecutor v Georges Anderson Nderubumwe Rutaganda ICTR-96-3-T
Prosecutor v Jean-Paul Akayesu ICTR-96-4-T
Prosecutor v Jean Kambanda ICTR-97-23-S
Prosecutor v Juvénal Kajelijeli ICTR-98-44A-T
Prosecutor v Édouard Karemera ICTR-98-44-T
Prosecutor v André Ntagerura ICTR-99-46-T
Prosecutor v Pauline Nyiramasuhuko et al ICTR-98-42-A
Prosecutor v Laurent Semanza ICTR-97-20-T
Prosecutor v Tharcisse Muvunyi ICTR-00-55A-AR73

ICTY

Prosecutor v Ante Gotovina et al IT-03-73-AR73.1
Prosecutor v Anto Furundžija IT-95-17/1-T
Prosecutor v Blagoje Simić et al IT-95-9-T
Prosecutor v Dario Kordić & Mario Čerkez IT-95-14/2-A
Prosecutor v Dragan Nikolić IT-94-2A
Prosecutor v Dragoljub Kunarac, Radomir Kovač and Zoran Vukovič IT-96-23 & 23/1
Prosecutor v Dragomir Milošević IT-98-29/1
Prosecutor v Duško Tadić IT-94-1
Prosecutor v Mile Mrksić et al IT-95-3-R61
Prosecutor v Milomir Stakić IT-97-24-T
Prosecutor v Milorad Krnojelac IT-97-25-T
Prosecutor v Miroslav Deronjić IT-02-61-S
Prosecutor v Miroslav Kvočka et al IT-98-30/1-T
Prosecutor v Mitar Vasiljević IT-98-32-T
Prosecutor v Mladen Naletilić et al IT-98-34-PT
Prosecutor v Radislav Krstić IT-98-33-T
Prosecutor v Radoslav Brdjanin IT-99-36-T
Prosecutor v Sefer Halilović IT-01-48-T
Prosecutor v Slobodan Milošević IT-02-54-T
Prosecutor v Vidoje Blagojević & Dragan Jokoć IT-02-60-T
Prosecutor v Vinko Pandurević & Trbić IT-05-86-AR73.1
Prosecutor v Vladimir Kovačević IT-97-24-AR73
Prosecutor v Vlastimir Dordević IT-05-87/1-A
Prosecutor v Vujadin Popović IT-05-88-T
Prosecutor v Zdravko Tolimir IT-05-88/2

Prosecutor v Zejnil Delalic, Zdravko Mucic also known as 'Pavo', Hazim Delic, and Esad Landzo also known as 'Zenga' IT-96-21-T
Prosecutor v Zejnil Delalić, Zdravko Mucić, Hazim Delić and Esad Landžo (Čelebići case) IT-96-21-A
Prosecutor v Zlatko Aleksovski IT-95-14/1-T
Prosecutor v Zoran Kupreškić et al IT-95-16

MICT

Prosecutor v Maxmilien Turinabo et al MICT-18-11-PT
Prosecutor v Petar Jojić and Vjerica Radeta MICT-17-111-R90

SCSL

Prosecutor v Alex Tamba Brima, Brima Bazzy Kamara and Santigie Borbor Kanu SCSL-04-16-T
Prosecutor v Charles Ghankay Taylor SCSL-03-01-T
Prosecutor v Issa Sesay, Kallon & Gbao SCSL-04-15-T
Prosecutor v Margaret Fomba Brima et al SCSL-2005-02
Prosecutor v Moinina Fofana and Allieu Kondewa SCSL-04-14-T

Special Panels for the Serious Crimes in East Timor

Prosecutor v Carlos Soares Carmona Case No 03 CG 2000 Special Panel for Serious Crimes

STL

Prosecutor v Akhbar Beirut S.A.L. Ibrahim Mohamed Al Amin STL-14-06/I/CJ
Prosecutor v Sarmento SP 18A/2001

Statutes, Legislation, and Treaties

DOMESTIC

Afghanistan Penal Code, 22 September 1976
Canada Criminal Code, R.S.C., 1985, c. C-46
Côte d'Ivoire Code pénal
Crimes (Sentencing Procedure) Act 1999 No 92 (NSW)
Criminal Code of Russia, 1996
Denmark Penal Code
Finland Criminal Code
Ireland Criminal Justice Act 2006
Ireland Prisons Act 1970, number 11 of 1970
Japan Penal Code
Penalties and Sentencing Act 1992 (Qld)
Sentencing Act, 2017 (SA)
United Kingdom Sentencing Act 2020
United States New York Consolidated Laws, Penal Law

REGIONAL

African Charter on Human and Peoples' Rights ('Banjul Charter'), 27 June 1981, CAB/LEG/67/3 rev. 5, 21 I.L.M. 58 (1982)
African Charter on the Rights and Welfare of the Child, 11 July 1990, CAB/LEG/24.9/49 (1990)
American Convention on Human Rights, 'Pact of San Jose', Costa Rica, 22 November 1969
European Prison Rules (Council of Europe June 2006)
Protocol to the African Charter on Human and People's Rights on the Rights of Women in Africa, 11 July 2003

INTERNATIONAL

Agreement between the United Nations and the Royal Government of Cambodia concerning the prosecution under Cambodian law of the crimes committed during the period of Democratic Kampuchea, 6 June 2003.

Agreement for Prosecution and Punishment of the Major War Criminal of the European Axis, and Charter of the International Military Tribunal, 8 August 1945

Beijing Declaration and Platform for Action, UN Doc. A/CONF. 177/20, 15 September 1995

Convention Against Torture and Other Cruel, Inhuman or Degrading Treatment or Punishment, United Nations, Treaty Series, vol. 1465, 10 December 1984

Convention Concerning the Protection of the World Cultural and Natural Heritage, 16 November 1972

Convention on the Elimination of All Forms of Discrimination Against Women, United Nations, Treaty Series, vol. 1249, p. 13, 18 December 1979

Convention for the Safeguarding of the Intangible Cultural Heritage, 17 October 2003

Convention of the Rights of the Child, United Nations 1989 Treaty Series, 1577, 3, 20 November 1989

Doha Declaration Global Program GA Res. 70/174, April 2015

Elements of Crimes, International Criminal Court, 2002

European Convention for the Protection of Human Rights and Fundamental Freedoms, as amended by Protocols Nos. 11 and 14, ETS 5, 4 November 1950

Geneva Convention for the Amelioration of the Condition of the Wounded and Sick in Armed Forces in the Field (First Geneva Convention), 75 UNTS 31, 12 August 1949

Geneva Convention Relative to the Protection of Civilian Persons in Time of War (Fourth Geneva Convention), 75 UNTS 287, 12 August 1949

Geneva Convention Relative to the Treatment of Prisoners of War (Third Geneva Convention), 75 UNTS 135, 12 August 1949

Hague Convention (IV) Respecting the Laws and Customs of War on Land and Its Annex: Regulations Concerning the Laws and Customs of War on Land, 18 October 1907

International Covenant on Civil and Political Rights, United Nations, Treaty Series, vol. 999, p. 171, 16 December 1966

International Covenant on Economic, Social, and Cultural Rights, Treaty Series, vol. 999, p. 171, 16 December 1966

International Convention on the Elimination of All Forms of Racial Discrimination, UN General Assembly Resolution 2106 (XX) 21 December 1965

International Convention on the Protection of the Rights of All Migrant Workers and Members of Their Families, A/RES/45/158, 18 December 1990

Landmark Resolution on Women Peace and Security, SC Res. 1235 2000

United Nations Security Council Resolution 2467, S/RES/2467(2019)

Protocol Additional to the Geneva Conventions of 12 August 1949, and relating to the Protection of Victims of International Armed Conflicts (Protocol I), 1125 UNTS 3, 8 June 1977

Protocol Additional to the Geneva Conventions of 12 August 1949, and relating to the Protection of Victims of Non-International Armed Conflicts (Protocol II), 1125 UNTS 609, 8 June 1977

Report of the Commission on the Responsibility of the Authors of the War and on Enforcement Penalties, 1920

Rules of Procedure and Evidence, International Criminal Court 2002

Rules of Procedure and Evidence, International Criminal Tribunal for Rwanda, 29 June 1995

Rules of Procedure and Evidence of the International Criminal Tribunal for the former Yugoslavia, 11 February 1994

Statute of the International Criminal Tribunal for the Former Yugoslavia, UNSCR 827 (1993), 25 May 1993

Statute of International Criminal Tribunal for the Prosecution of Persons Responsible for Genocide and Other Serious Violations of International Humanitarian Law Committed in the Territory of Rwanda and Rwandan Citizens Responsible for Genocide and Other Such Violations Committed in the Territory of Neighbouring States, between 1 January 1994 and 31 December 1994, UNSCR 955 (1994), 8 November 1994

Statute of the Special Court for Sierra Leone, 16 January 2002

Statute of the Special Tribunal for Lebanon, S/RES/1751(2007)

The Council of Europe Convention on Preventing and Combating Violence against Women and Domestic Violence (Istanbul Convention), November 2014

The Paris Principles and Guidelines on Children Associated with Armed Forces or Armed Groups (Paris Principles), February 2007

Rome Statute of the International Criminal Court (last amended 2010), 17 July 1998

Universal Declaration of Human Rights, UNGA Res 217A, 10 December 1948

United Nations Declaration of Basic Principles of Justice for Victims of Crime and Abuse of Power GA Res 40/34, 29 November 1985

United Nations Security Council Resolution 2456 (2019) on renewal of sanctions against Yemen imposed by Security Council resolution (2014) and extension of the mandate of the Panel of Experts until 28 March 2020, 26 February 2019

United Nations Standard Minimum Rules for Non-Custodial Measures (The Tokyo Rules) resolution adopted by the General Assembly, A/RES/45/110, 2 April 1991

Vienna Convention on the Law of Treaties United Nations Treaty Series, vol. 1155, p. 331, May 1969

1

The Hope of a Thousand Small Lights

Maxine Beneba Clarke

THE TASK

Joy, for many,

it is made up
of the simple wonders of this life.

Sometimes we do not know it,
and it's only at the end
we can recall
the feeling
of a tiny hand in ours:

cherubic face upturned,
wide-eyed with trust,

as we remind a young one
where to cross
  the road,
  their t's,
  a stitch they dropped,
  their plastic knitting needles,
  fingers, when they tell a fib,
and oh,
their tiny hearts

(which one day
we all know will break
over somebody
or some thing
that matters most).

The simple wonders of this life:

oh, innocence,
and, women
walking arm in arm
on quiet dusk-descended streets,
in safety:

laughter singing sisterhood,
Delightful in their whimsy.
Stunning in their calm ferocity.
At ease, and glorious
in casual and unthinking freedom.

Joy is the tiny wonders of this life,
bequeathed so readily to some:
    a meal with friends;
    shelter on icy nights;
    family together;
    dignity and hearth;
    a tender body,
    loving unconditionally when winter falls.

The space and strength to say:

    this life is mine,
    this right is mine,
    this body's mine,
    this choice is mine,
    this thought is mine,
and mine alone.

The simple wonders of this life,
and of these rights:
profound-unearned.
Intrinsic and inalienable.

Not to be sold,
or spent,
or spared.

Not to be spat at,
spurned or savaged.

That's the task.

That *is* the task:
to light up
the darkened corners
where these joys have been denied.

To strike the match
that lights the lamp.
And heavens, what an ask:
to flood with brightness,
and to search the shadows
where the worst of our humanity has gathered.

To square up against
the sure-unspeakable, and say:

Enough!
This can not be what we're made of.
This can not be what we sleep on.
This can not be what we let to breed,
and rot, and fester.

Oh, the horrors
found marauding in the margins
where the many do not tread.

That is the task:
to lay a hand on trauma's shoulder,
turn it round, and
look it in the eye.

To say:
this must be brought justice:
we are searching,
we are watching.
We will find you –
when we find you,
we will never look away.

To acknowledge
that there walk amongst us reapers:
scythes-at-ready,
riding on the horse of war and mayhem,

slaying all that we hold dear.
Sniffing the air
for scent

of those so vulnerable
they cannot – dare not –
raise:
  their fists to fight,
  their voices-loud,
  objection,
  international alarm.

Yes, this is what was realised
that Summer, there,
in the city of seven hills.

Oh, this is
what was born,
in Rome,

at the conception
of the International Criminal Court.

A vow, by hand of nations,
resolute-united,
saying:

> *we will chase the shadows*
> *to the round, unending edges*
> *of this aching earth.*
> *No matter famine, war or fire,*
> *fall-of-state or flood.*
>
> *No matter dissidence*
> *or disobedience,*
> *or tragedy, or ruin.*
>
> *Life itself*
> *is sacred.*
>
> *There are acts*
> *which chill the blood.*
>
> *And we will, together,*

will, we swear,

protect those folks
the greatest darkness

> *finds.*

THE MANDATE

Some say the law
ought not to bend.

That it should be a neutral,
certain thing.

But there are reasons
judgement and interpretation
are bequeathed
to human
– humane –
hearts, and heads.

Enter women, in coalition:

women, from the wings
of all the world,

who raised the plight
of territories

from the Balkans, to Rwanda.
From fields of conflict,
  and beyond.

These women urged the court
to recognise that category of crimes
which, by the horror of their calculation,
  target women

– target women, and their daughters
by the tent there, playing catch;

target women, and the sleeping children,
strapped to buckling backs;

target women, and their cheeky nephews,
dirt-drawing twig-in-hand;

target women, and the crawling babes, look,
right by their feet,

and the crimes which target
those whom gender,

(in the minds
of misogynistic men
and their supporters),

make
        as vulnerable
as these.

There are some crimes
which, by design,
so make of man
the enemy of all mankind.

So the sisterhood
walked the corridors of power:
lobbied, whispered, woke
and wrangled
in the halls of Rome.

The sisterhood
stole little sleep,

and guided by the hand
of some other-worldly strength,
– and bleary-eyed,
and sure of heart,

worked tirelessly

to see the statute recognise
the folk the greatest horrors

always find.

Whatever you do to the least of my sisters.
Every woman is a sister of mine.

And where war walks,
its bed-friend torture lounges,

to test the very limits
of what a broken body
                        can bear.

For those who gender makes a mark of
when the world forgets to watch,
for them,

the women guarding the statute of Rome,
they coalesced, they did their best

to weave through law
an equal hand.

To see that women always walk the halls,
and sit the benches:
see that there is always pause

to think of what it means
to be a woman in this world.

And to encourage those there judging
to bring to table, and to thinking,
all their living's taught them
(and perhaps the very things their living's
taught them are unimportant).

And oh, they were at pains to see
that academic theorisation

would not prove the enemy
of *just* interpretation.

And so it was the court,
there writ through treaty,

realised, and recognised
and ratified

a place,

the space,

for Feminist
consideration.

When, much later,
warm, just printed from the press,
the thing was set to paper,
they had achieved

not all their aims
(and many, true, lamented
that the hand of status quo

stripped back the goals
of progress).

But, still,

that they so tried,
and would not give in,
that they *believed,*

that was enough

to imbed
a gender mandate
in the ICC.

When all was said and done,
and when dawn broke in Rome,
there bled a sunset, peach and golden,
flecked with dappled rose,
that faded out
into the morning blue.

A glimmer of hope
that change would come.

Something had shifted,
                    everyone knew.

THE MEASURE

When the stench of terror
still hangs in the air,

and the slain
are yet to be given their rites;

when the shelling has stopped,
but the copters still whir
in near, not distant, memory.

When children crawl, shaking,
from out of their cupboards,

eyes terror-wide,
and darting.
When word finally spreads
that it's safe on the ground
and the task begins,
    of searching.

When mourning comes,
and the wailing continues;

with the damage surveyed,
and the losses inventoried.

When the shock sets in,
and the shaking starts,

and husbands crawl forward
to cradle their wives.

What, the measure of justice, then:
what, the measure of success.

What of the vow of '98:

the united hands
which would drive back hatred
and brutality; inhumanity, and fear.
What of a court built to raise survivors
– to raise their stories to the sky:
their brave whispers
        leading the justice cry.

Built to give pause
for interpreters to speak,
supports at the ready,
and *ready to hear*

the facts, unfettered,
and ferocious,
– *ferocious,* in their telling.

Built on the edge
of the northern sea,
deep in The Hague,
in the City of Peace:

Saltwater to truth.
An oceanic breeze.

Oh, let the light in

let the light in,
to dance through darkened halls.

To pirouette and tumble,
and to search out every shadow:

refracting,
and reflecting,
and unfiltered,
and a-glow.

Nominations of brilliant women,
were brought to the bench:
in numbers justice
and her sisters, favoured.
Women of all axes
persuasion, and thought:
there were some triumphs, after all.

But in creeped the corners
of status quo.

Unprecedent thrived,
and unwieldy process:

Expertise not decreed
a matter of course,
or consultancy diverse
   and broad.

Certain crimes
weren't recognised
as particular, in their horror:

   the plight of girl soldiers,
and their bodies as tools,
and their freedom denied,
and their labour subsumed,

and commanders well-shielded
   by the chain of command,

and bodies, forced-bared
   had their justice denied,

and they dismissed crimes designed
to de-masculinise,
and desexualise boys, and men.
And the experts were challenged,
and testimony decried,

and stigma stayed tongues,
and the states closed their eyes.

The corners of status quo crept in,
to restrict the justice there *could* have been
if what happened in Rome
hadn't stayed in Rome,
and the mandate
was followed through –

and the court stood proud,
and bared all teeth,

to do
what it was *born*
         to do.

THE MAP

What use the pen,
if not to protect.

What remedy ink,
if not a salve,

and what use reason,
if not to reason *well*.

What of a mandate for reform
without the *courage* to reform,

What becomes of a revolution
that doubts *itself*.

Well, now takes hold,
across the globe,
an epic reimagining:

a movement, whispering
across the wide-deep ocean.

A radical unpicking
of the neat, and patriarchal stitch

Imbedded in the fabric
of unwieldy man-made law.

For what wonder critique,
if condemnation withheld:
and judgements untouchable-revered.

And so, the many pens
of Feminist thought,

in deep and honest contemplation,

bleed ink for the judgements
that there might have been:

if bravery,
and courage
and equality
   and reform
had turned the corner of The Hague
and stared down, proper, face-to-face,

the casual-unthinking bias
of international criminal law.

Law made *by* men,
and made *for* men,
which makes *of* men
the perfect injured;
makes of men, defendants,
judges, sentencers, and all.

For some, the law's lean
cannot be unwritten

(through process, judge
or survivor's hearing),

for at its foundation there is rot,
and colonial conquer, and imposition.

But critique will cartograph the map:
myriad voices, in good faith and fact.

Let another scholar now spark their lamp,
and unwrite into the night.

And in the darkness, *there*, it flickers:
the hope of a thousand small lights.

As another,
and another,
and another,

unwrites,

and the harmony
of choral-collective
        takes flight.

And Feminist scholars
of all genders and creeds

light up the darkened corners
where world justice has been denied.

To strike the match
that glows the lamp.
And heavens, what an ask.
Oh, *change*.
Oh, women
– and their allies –
writing desk by desk
on quiet dusk-descending nights,
in starts, with distant gunfire,
tired, resolute, or charged,

their labour singing sisterhood,

at ease, and glorious,
in sure, and fierce, and thinking
                freedom.

PART I

Conceptual Approach

2

Introduction

Feminist Judgments and the International Criminal Court

Kcasey McLoughlin, Rosemary Grey, Louise Chappell, and Suzanne Varrall

INTRODUCTION

In the past decade, feminist scholars and women's rights activists have reimagined the relationship between law and gender justice using the feminist judgment method, resulting in rewritten 'feminist' judgments from courts in the United States, United Kingdom, Scotland, Ireland, Australia, New Zealand, Canada, and India.[1] Further extending the catalogue, we have seen publication of the international law project,[2] and domestic projects specialising in substantive areas of law.[3] Breaking new ground, this book is the first to apply the feminist judgment method to analyse decisions of the International Criminal Court (ICC), the Hague-based court with power to prosecute war crimes, crimes against humanity, genocide,

[1] 'Special Issue: Rewriting Equality' 18(1) *Canadian Journal of Women and the Law* (2006); R. Hunter, C. McGlynn, and E. Rackley (eds.), *Feminist Judgments: From Theory to Practice* (London: Hart, 2010); See e.g. H. Douglas et al., *Australian Feminist Judgments: Righting and Rewriting Law* (1st ed., London: Bloomsbury, 2014); K. Sanchi, L. Berger, and B. Crawford, *Feminist Judgments (Feminist Judgment Series: Rewritten Judicial Opinions)* (Cambridge: Cambridge University Press, 2016); M. Enright, J. McCandless, and A. O'Donoghue (eds.), *Northern/Irish Feminist Judgments: Judges' Troubles and the Gendered Politics of Identity* (London: Bloomsbury, 2017); E. McDonald et al. (eds.), *Feminist Judgments of Aotearoa New Zealand Te Rino, a Two-Stranded Rope* (Oxford: Hart, 2017); S. Cowan, C. Kennedy, and V. E. Munro (eds.), *Scottish Feminist Judgments: (Re)Creating Law from the Outside In* (Oxford: Hart, 2019); C. Aparna, J. Sen, and R. Chaudhary, 'Righting Together: An Introduction to the Indian Feminist Judgments Project' 56(1) *VRÜ Verfassung und Recht in Übersee* (2023) 5–16; V. Munro, 'Feminist Judgments Projects at the Intersection' (2021) 29 *Feminist Legal Studies* 251–261 (discussing the African Feminist Judgments Project (AFJP), which is still in its early conception phase).

[2] See L. Hodson and T. Lavers (eds.), *Feminist Judgements in International Law* (Oxford: Hart, 2019).

[3] In the United States, for example, scholars have extended the project to discrete subject matter disciplines such as corporation law, employment law, immigration law, reproductive justice, tax, torts, trusts, and estates (including those not covered by the original US Project, with its focus on SCOTUS decisions). See https://law.unlv.edu/us-feminist-judgments/series-projects.

and aggression in over 123 countries. Reflecting an international and intersectional feminism,[4] and drawing inspiration from collections that have enriched the feminist judgment method with indigenous, critical race, and queer perspectives,[5] the book's contributors include nearly fifty authors, of all genders, from almost twenty different countries including from African, Asian, and Middle Eastern countries where the ICC has been active. Bringing their diverse theoretical approaches, professional experience, and cultural backgrounds to the book, these contributors explore the connections between gender, race, nationality, ethnicity, faith, and sexual orientation in relation to the law and practice of the ICC.

Created in 1998 by the Rome Statute, the ICC is responsible for prosecuting those individuals most responsible for war crimes, crimes against humanity, aggression, and genocide.[6] The decisions of the ICC's judges, who are elected by state parties to the Rome Statute, have far-reaching consequences. Not only are these decisions influential within the ICC; they also function as persuasive precedents in other international, regional, and national criminal courts.

Although the terms 'gender-sensitive judging' or 'feminist judging' are not used in the Rome Statute, this treaty provides a firmer foothold for such an approach than the statute of any other international court. Its provisions enumerate a wide range of sexual and gender-based crimes, require that the law be interpreted and applied without adverse diction on gender grounds, and incentivise the election of both female judges *and* judges (of any sex or gender) with legal expertise on violence against women.[7] The Rome Statute is also the first to recognise the crime against humanity of persecution on 'gender' grounds – a crime which the Court has now applied in several situations including Mali and Afghanistan, where women and girls have been stripped of their rights and subjected to forced marriage and other sexual crimes; the Central African Republic and Darfur, in respect of mass killings of civilian men and boys by attacking forces; and Nigeria, where attacks on girls' schools, the use of female suicide bombers, and sex-selective attacks on men and boys have been described by the ICC Prosecutor's Office as gender-based persecution.

The book extends existing gender-oriented analyses of the ICC, which have tended to focus on how *investigation and prosecution* strategies have contributed

4 K. Crenshaw, 'Mapping the Margins: Intersectionality, Identity Politics, and Violence against Women of Color' (1991) 43 *Stanford Law Review* 1241–1299.

5 E.g. N. Watson and H. Douglas (eds.), *Indigenous Legal Judgments: Bringing Indigenous Voices into Judicial Decision Making* (London: Routledge, 2021); K. M. Mutcherson (ed.), *Feminist Judgments: Reproductive Justice Rewritten* (Cambridge: Cambridge University Press, 2020); N. Ferreira, M. Federica Moscati and S. Raj, 'Queer Judgments Project', available at www.queerjudgments.org/.

6 Rome Statute, Art. 5.

7 R. Grey, K. McLoughlin, and L. Chappell, 'Gender and Judging at the International Criminal Court: Lessons from Feminist Judgment Projects' 34(1) *Leiden Journal of International Law* (2021) 247–264.

to the ICC's initial failure to secure convictions for sexual and gender-based crimes, and its more recent advances in this regard.[8] Building on that work, our book focuses on a relatively under-examined dimension to ICC scholarship by examining the role that *judges* have played, and can play, in adjudicating those crimes. In this way, the book draws lessons from the extensive research on gender-sensitive judging in domestic courts,[9] bringing together insights from feminist scholarship in both national and international law.[10] By distilling the lessons learned from previous feminist judgment projects, this book illuminates new possibilities for feminist interventions in international criminal law.

In addition to being the first book to apply the feminist judgment method to a range of ICC cases,[11] it also advances and adapts the method for use in an *international* court that serves a global constituency and includes features of both common law and civil law systems. At times, taking a feminist perspective also compels our contributors to venture beyond the tasks ordinarily performed by ICC judges (interpreting and applying law, and making findings of fact), in order to discuss the shortcomings in international criminal law itself. Such critical reflections on law, while rare in real-life judicial analysis, are not unheard of,[12] and provide a

8 See, for illustrative examples: L. Chappell, 'Conflicting Institutions and the Search for Gender Justice at the International Criminal Court' 67(1) *Political Research Quarterly* (2014) 183–196; L. Chappell, *The Politics of Gender Justice at the International Criminal Court: Legacies and Legitimacy* (Oxford: Oxford University Press, 2016); N. Hayes, 'Sisyphus Wept: Prosecuting Sexual Violence at the International Criminal Court' in W. Schabas, Y. McDermott, and N. Hayes (eds.), *The Ashgate Research Companion to International Criminal Law* (Farnham: Ashgate, 2013) 7; R. Grey, 'ICC's First "Forced Pregnancy" Case in Historical Perspective' 15(4) *Journal of International Criminal Justice* (2017) 905–930; R. Grey, *Prosecuting Sexual and Gender-Based Crimes at the International Criminal Court* (Cambridge: Cambridge University Press, 2019); V. Oosterveld, 'The ICC Policy Paper on Sexual and Gender-Based Crimes: A Crucial Step for International Criminal Law' 24(3) *William & Mary Journal of Women and the Law* (2018) 1–15; K. O'Smith, 'Prosecutor v Lubanga: How the ICC Failed the Women and Girls of the Congo' 54(2) *Howard Law Journal* (2010–2011) 467–504; S. SáCouto and K. Cleary, 'The Importance of Effective Investigation of Sexual Violence and Gender-Based Crimes at the International Criminal Court' 17(2) *American University Journal of Gender, Social Policy and Law* (2009) 337–359.

9 R. Hunter, C. McGlynn, and E. Rackley (eds.), *Feminist Judgments: From Theory to Practice* (Oxford: Hart, 2010).

10 L. Hodson and T. Lavers (eds.), *Feminist Judgements in International Law* (Oxford: Hart, 2019).

11 Although no previous work has applied the feminist judgment to the ICC on the scale of this book, the method has been applied to certain discrete ICC judgments. See Y. Brunger, E. Irving, and D. Sankey, 'The Prosecutor v Thomas Lubanga Dyilo' in L. Hodson and T. Lavers (eds.), *Feminist Judgements in International Law* (Oxford: Hart, 2019) 409–444; see also K. Gooding, 'How Can the Methodology of Feminist Judgment Writing Improve Gender Sensitivity in International Criminal Law' 5 *LSE Law Review* (2020) 115–152 for a thoughtful feminist rewriting of *Ongwen*.

12 An example from our own jurisdiction is Justice Bell's dissent in the 2012 decision in *PGA v. The Queen*. She concluded that the historic common law immunity for marital rape was still in force at the time of the offending, but also expressed her view that this doctrine was 'demeaning to women'. *PGA v. The Queen*, 245 CLR 355 per Bell J § 246.

thought-provoking counterpoint to the more conventional feminist judgments in this collection.

STRUCTURE OF THE BOOK

The book commences with a foreword by Navi Pillay, former judge of the International Criminal Tribunal for Rwanda (ICTR) and ICC, which anchors this collection in real-world judicial experience. Among other things, Pillay reflects on being a judge in the first case to confirm that sexual violence can be an act of genocide (the ICTR's *Akayesu* case), and on accusations of bias that were levied against her and other judges who brought a conspicuous gender-sensitivity to their work. Following the foreword, Maxine Beneba Clarke's poem 'The Hope of a Thousand Small Lights' serves as the preface to this book. Beneba Clarke envisions the ICC as both the mechanism for, and barrier to, justice. This chapter sets out the book's contents and explains some of the editorial decisions we have taken, reflecting on questions of inclusion and exclusion.

Part I: *Conceptual Approach*

This introduction is followed by a series of chapters which set out the book's key concepts. These chapters frame the book's central provocation – how might the ICC's judgments have been different if a commitment to gender equality, and an awareness of gendered power relations, were at the forefront of the judges' minds? In the first of those framing chapters (Chapter 3), lead editor Kcasey McLoughlin asks, 'Do Feminists Believe in Fairytales?' as we seek to make the case for another feminist judgment project, interrogating the role of imagination in judgment and pondering the possibilities and dilemmas of judgment writing as feminist method. This chapter is followed by two 'in conversation' pieces. In the first, Patricia Sellers, the ICC Prosecutor's Special Advisor on Slavery Crimes, engages in a thought experiment with co-editor Rosemary Grey, reimagining what the ICC's jurisprudence on slavery crimes might have looked like had relevant cases in previous international criminal tribunals been decided differently (Chapter 4). By exploring those jurisprudential 'gaps', Sellers posits that recent decisions at the ICC, but also within previous international criminal tribunals, are hamstrung by the reticence and failures of past jurists to identify and label crimes accurately. The second 'in conversation' piece, between human rights lawyer Angela Mudukuti and co-editor Louise Chappell, highlights the lived experience of a practitioner navigating the implementation and tenuous shifting understandings of international criminal law (Chapter 5). Mudukuti emphasises the central importance of taking an intersectional approach to gender justice at the ICC, and the challenges that remain in achieving that aim.

The book turns to two reflections on the importance of intersectional gender analysis in the ICC, one by political scientist Jarpa Dawuni (Chapter 6) and another by international criminal lawyer Priya Gopalan (Chapter 7). As Gopalan argues in her piece, 'intersectionality can make visible other pertinent factors and structural inequalities, alongside gender, that are often disregarded or overlooked'. In Chapter 6, Dawuni explores the merits and demerits of intersectionality as a tool for feminist judgments. Questioning 'whose feminism', she argues that in engaging in feminist reimagination 'we must begin from a place of a feminist recasting of the challenges, social hierarchies, barriers, constraints, and opportunities that give rise to, maintain, and advance the multiple discriminations, exclusions, and erasures some groups of people face in societies across the world'.

Part II: *ICC Judgments Reimagined*

The second part of the book includes the rewritten ICC judgments. Each rewritten judgment begins with a brief outline, added by the editorial team, to orient readers. Some comments about the way that ICC cases are organised will assist readers to navigate this part of the book.

The ICC's proceedings are organised into 'situations' (a matter with jurisdictional boundaries both temporal and geographic, such as the situation concerning war crimes and crimes against humanity allegedly committed in Uganda since 2002) and 'cases' (proceedings against a particular person or persons, such as the case against former Lord's Resistance Army commander Dominic Ongwen). Rewriting judgments from every 'situation' that has come before the ICC was not feasible. However, in an effort to achieve broad coverage, the book's contributions address nine ICC situations: Afghanistan, Bangladesh/Myanmar, Central African Republic (I and II), Côte d'Ivoire, Democratic Republic of Congo, Mali, Sudan, and Uganda (Table 2.1).

These nine situations include crimes allegedly or proven to be perpetrated by nationals of African and Asian countries, as well as crimes allegedly committed by members of America's Central Intelligence Agency (CIA). This selection is intended to reflect the fact that in reality, although past and present ICC proceedings have focused primarily on perpetrators from the Global South, they have also implicated, to varying degrees, state officials and military personnel from the United States, United Kingdom, Israel, and Russia.

Within these nine situations, each of the cases is enormous, when compared with most criminal proceedings in domestic courts. Before a case is even opened, there may be need for a judicial decision to authorise an investigation by the Office of the

TABLE 2.1 *Rewritten judgments in this book, by situation and case*

Situation	Case (if applicable)	Rewritten decisions
Afghanistan	N/a	2019 decision on the Prosecutor's application to open an investigation
Bangladesh/ Myanmar	N/a	2019 Pre-Trial Chamber decision on the Prosecutor's application to open an investigation
Central African Republic I and II	*Bemba* case	2008 Pre-Trial Chamber arrest warrant decision 2009 Pre-Trial Chamber confirmation of charges decision 2016 Trial Chamber sentencing decision 2018 appeal judgment
	Yekatom case	2020 Pre-Trial Chamber decision on Prosecutor's application to amend the charges
Côte d'Ivoire	*(Simone) Gbagbo* case	2012 Pre-Trial Chamber arrest warrant decision 2014 Pre-Trial decision on admissibility of the case
Democratic Republic of Congo	*Lubanga* case	2015 Appeals Chamber decision on reparations
	Ntaganda case	2017 Trial Chamber decision on jurisdiction over Counts 6 and 9 (sexual crimes against child soldiers) 2019 trial judgment
Mali	*Al Mahdi* case	2016 Trial Chamber judgment and sentencing decision 2017 Trial Chamber reparations order
	Al Hassan case	2018 Pre-Trial Chamber arrest warrant decision
Sudan	*Al Bashir* case	2010 Pre-Trial Chamber arrest warrant decision (genocide) 2019 Appeals Chamber decision on head-of-state immunity
	Abd-al-Rahman case	2021 Pre-Trial Chamber confirmation of charges decision 2021 Pre-Trial decision on appointment of victims' legal representatives
Uganda	*Ongwen* case	2021 trial judgment 2021 Trial Chamber sentencing decision

Prosecutor.[13] This was necessary in relation to the Myanmar/Bangladesh and Afghanistan situations, for example. Once an investigation has been conducted and suspects have been identified, a typical ICC case will often run for over a

[13] If the situation was referred to the ICC Prosecutor by a state party or the UN Security Council, the Prosecutor can open an investigation provided that the statutory criteria of jurisdiction, admissibility, and interests of justice are satisfied. But if the Prosecutor has initiated proceedings *proprio motu* (on his/her own motion), authorisation from the Pre-Trial Chamber is needed before the investigation can proceed. See Rome Statute, Arts. 13, 15, and 53.

decade, and will include hundreds (if not thousands) of judicial decisions. For example, every case includes first-instance decisions (and often appeal decisions) on whether to issue an arrest warrant, whether to confirm the charges, and whether those charges have been proven beyond reasonable doubt. In the event of a conviction, there are further sentencing and reparations decisions. Most cases also include decisions about whether the case is already being adjudicated in a national court, whether fresh evidence is admissible, and whether the fair trial rights of the accused are being upheld.

Because ICC cases are so large, each of the rewritten decisions in this book focuses on just one issue of law, fact, or procedure that was addressed in the original judgment (some of which were identified by the contributors, and some suggested by the editors). This 'single-issue' approach is sensible because ICC judgments tend to be highly complex and lengthy (some exceeding 1,000 pages), with the result that rewriting the entire judgment would not be feasible.

We organised the rewritten judgments by situation and chronologically. Thus, we begin with the Democratic of Congo, which in 2004 became the first situation under investigation by the ICC, and we end with Afghanistan, which despite being under preliminary examination since 2007, did not progress to a formal investigation until 2020. Each situation is preceded by what we have termed as 'reflections' that introduce the relevant conflict, place the rewritten judgment within the context of the original judgment, and then critically reflect upon the reimagined work. Each reflection writer was also asked to consider how they might envision a different outcome, within or outside the bounds of the law, thus highlighting both opportunities for and constraints on transforming the ICC's practice.

The final intervention in Part II is not a rewritten ICC judgment, but a poem. Sara Saleh's compelling piece, 'The Checkpoint', evokes the daily realities of life in Palestine, drawing links with other colonised, indigenous, and subjugated peoples. By including Saleh's poem as the final contribution in the 'judgments' section, we hope to inspire readers to consider the future potential and work of the ICC, and to reflect on the lived experience of those affected by conflict but who are rarely seen or heard by international criminal law.

Part III: *Conclusion*

The book's conclusion reflects on the feminist judgment methodology and the ICC's legacy after two decades in operation. We observe that one of the major themes to emerge from this collection is the need for judges to make decisions from the perspective of the context and lived experiences of those suffering from international crimes. We argue that this book demonstrates the enormous transformative potential of judges, and the opportunity to enhance gender justice in the ICC, while also recognising the challenges confronting the Court given the destabilising realpolitik of the current historical period.

EDITORIAL DECISIONS: COLLABORATION, CONTEXT, AND OMISSIONS

It is important to contextualise and explain some of our editorial decisions regarding the selection of situations, judgments, and contributors.

Situations

Between July 2002, when the Rome Statute entered into force, and October 2023, when we completed this book, the ICC had instigated proceedings in twenty-eight situations concerning alleged crimes in twenty-six countries (twelve African states;[14] seven Asia and Pacific states;[15] two Eastern European states;[16] and four Latin American and Caribbean states[17]), and on flagships of Comoros, Greece, and Cambodia. Some of these situations have advanced so far as to include cases against specific individuals, some remain under investigation, and some have gone no further than the initial preliminary examination stage. Mostly, the alleged perpetrators have come from countries in the Global South. But, as shown in Table 2.2, they have included nationals from what the UN calls the 'Western European and Other' (WEOG) bloc.[18]

As feminist researchers, the question of which of these many situations and cases to include was a difficult one. Given our time and resource constraints, it was not feasible to include every possible option. But any decision to include a case necessarily meant a decision to exclude others. In making that choice, we very much wanted to avoid replicating patterns of inclusion and exclusion which, in the real world, mean that crimes committed in certain places, especially in relation to the ICC, in Africa, receive significantly greater condemnation, and significantly more effective responses, than others. This concern has, quite validly, been raised about the ICC's swift response to Russia's 2022 invasion of Ukraine compared with

[14] Burundi, Central African Republic, Côte d'Ivoire, Democratic Republic of Congo, Gabon, Guinea, Kenya, Libya, Mali, Nigeria, Sudan, and Uganda.

[15] Afghanistan, Bangladesh, Iraq, Myanmar, Palestine, the Philippines, and the Republic of Korea.

[16] Georgia and Ukraine.

[17] Bolivia, Columbia, Honduras, and Venezuela.

[18] Those from Israel as well as from Palestine in the Palestine situation, and the matter of Comoran-, Greek-, and Cambodian-registered ships; those from the United Kingdom in the Iraq/UK situation; and those from the United States of America in Afghanistan.

TABLE 2.2 *ICC situations and cases as of October 2023*

	Situation	Progress to date	States where alleged crimes occurred	States of which suspects/defendants are nationals
1	Afghanistan	Investigation	Asia and Pacific	WOEG; Asia and Pacific
2	Bangladesh/ Myanmar	Investigation	Asia and Pacific	Asia and Pacific
3	Bolivia	Preliminary examination	Latin American and Caribbean	Latin American and Caribbean
4	Burundi	Investigation	African	African
5	CAR I	Cases	African	African
6	CAR II	Cases	African	African
7	Columbia	Preliminary examination	Latin American and Caribbean	Latin American and Caribbean
8	Côte d'Ivoire	Cases	African	African
9	DRC I	Cases	African	African
10	DRC II	Preliminary examination	African	African
11	Comoros, Greece, and Cambodia	Preliminary examination	African; WEOG; Asia and Pacific	WEOG
12	Gabon	Preliminary examination	African	African
13	Georgia	Cases	Eastern European	Eastern European
14	Guinea	Preliminary examination	African	African
15	Honduras	Preliminary examination	Latin American and Caribbean	Latin American and Caribbean
16	Iraq/UK	Preliminary examination	Asia and Pacific	WEOG
17	Kenya	Cases	African	African
18	Libya	Cases	African	African
19	Mali	Cases	African	African
20	Nigeria	Preliminary examination	African	African
21	Palestine	Investigation	Asia and Pacific	WEOG; Asia and Pacific
22	Philippines	Investigation	Asia and Pacific	Asia and Pacific
23	Republic of Korea	Preliminary examination	Asia and Pacific	Asia and Pacific
24	Sudan	Cases	African	African
25	Uganda	Cases	African	African
26	Ukraine	Cases	Eastern European	Eastern European
27	Venezuela I	Investigation	Latin American and Caribbean	Latin American and Caribbean
28	Venezuela II	Preliminary examination	Latin American and Caribbean	Latin American and Caribbean

its slower response to humanitarian crises in Africa, Asia, and the Middle East,[19] but it is a perennial problem that preceded the Ukraine crisis. With this in mind, we were committed to selecting situations concerning crimes including in the part of the world where we are situated (the Asia-Pacific), with some alleged perpetrators from the WEOG region even though they remain under-represented in the ICC's caseload to date.

Alongside that consideration, we were also committed to selecting cases that would enable our judgment writers to grapple with a wide range of legal issues. 'Not only rape cases', we said, echoing other feminist scholars and lawyers who have called for a gender analysis in international criminal law that includes but goes *beyond* the issue of sexual crimes against female victims.[20] This is not to suggest that there is no more to say on that particular issue; to the contrary, there is great scope for ICC judgments to more sensitively and more fairly adjudicate crimes of sexual violence, as many of the rewritten decisions in this book show. But we also wanted to explore the possibilities for gender analysis on issues that remain on the fringes of feminist scholarship in international law. This motivated us to include judgments on the ICC's complementarity principle, on immunity from prosecution, on crimes with no obvious sexual content (such as deportation and pillage), and on what the Rome Statute calls 'grounds for excluding criminal responsibility' (that is, defences), for example.

[19] Y. Dutton and M Sterio, 'The War in Ukraine and the Legitimacy of the International Criminal Court', *Just Security*, 20 August 2022, available at www.justsecurity.org/82889/the-war-in-ukraine-and-the-legitimacy-of-the-international-criminal-court/; A. Mitrovica, 'An ICC Warrant against Putin Is Good – and Hypocritical', *Al Jazeera*, 20 March 2023, available at www.aljazeera.com/opinions/2023/3/20/an-icc-warrant-against-putin-is-good-its-also; N. Hedayat, 'The Response to Ukraine Is Laudable. But as a British Afghan, I'm a Little Jealous', *The Guardian*, 19 March 2022, available at www.theguardian.com/commentisfree/2022/mar/19/response-ukraine-laudable-british-afghan-jealous-kabul-crisis; N. Farrelly and A. Simpson, 'Why Has the West Given Billions in Military Aid to Ukraine, but Virtually Ignored Myanmar?', *The Conversation*, 30 January 2023, available at https://theconversation.com/why-has-the-west-given-billions-in-military-aid-to-ukraine-but-virtually-ignored-myanmar-198297; Z. Abuza, 'On Ukraine, the World Acts; on Myanmar, It Waits', Radio Free Asia, 3 March 2022, available at www.rfa.org/english/commentaries/myanmar-ukraine-03032022134344.html; M. O'Brien, 'Symposium on Myanmar and International Indifference: The Sloe Turning Wheels of Justice – Even for Genocide', *Opinio Juris*, 20 August 2022, available at https://opiniojuris.org/2022/08/30/symposium-on-myanmar-and-international-indifference-the-slow-turning-wheels-of-justice-even-for-genocide/.

[20] E.g. P. V. Sellers, 'Gender Strategy Is Not Luxury for International Courts' 17(2) *American University Journal of Gender, Social Policy & the Law* (2009) 327–335; I. Rosenthal, V. Oosterveld, and S. SáCouto, 'What Is "Gender" in International Criminal Law?' in *Gender and International Criminal Law* (Oxford: Oxford University Press, 2022) 11; J. Gardam, 'A New Frontline for Feminism and International Humanitarian Law' in M. Davies and V. Munro (eds.), *The Ashgate Research Companion to Feminist Legal Theory* (Farnham: Ashgate, 2013) 217; M. Jarvis, 'Overview: The Challenge of Accountability for Conflict-Related Sexual Violence Crimes' in S. Brammertz and M. Jarvis (eds.), *Prosecuting Conflict-Related Sexual Violence at the ICTY* (Oxford: Oxford University Press, 2016) 1, 10–14.

A factor that we chose to prioritise was seeking input from a diversity of authors – scholars, practitioners, or other experts, including those with lived experience of the conflicts that have come before the ICC. To this end, we circulated an open call for contributions on widely read international law blogs, asked colleagues to share the call with their networks, and offered support such as training in feminist judgment methods and access to research assistants and library resources, in order to diversify and enrich our pool of contributors. This process informed our selection of situations because where we had the option of including contributors from countries where the ICC has been active, we were especially motivated to include those countries so as to make full use of the contributors' expertise and experience.

The nine situations that we eventually settled upon reflect these various considerations and constraints. This enables our authors to consider crimes alleged to have been perpetrated in a range of African and Asian countries, including crimes allegedly committed by nationals of a Western country, and enables the book to explore a wide range of legal issues including (but not limited to) sexual violence against males, females, and third-sex people, and to engage with the three categories of crimes that have been adjudicated in the ICC so far, namely war crimes, crimes against humanity, and genocide.

Although our selection of situations and countries strikes a balance between all of the important considerations outlined above, we are the first to admit that it is imperfect and incomplete. To their credit, some of our contributors have, in principled and respectful ways, queried our selection decisions. We recognise the integrity and the value of these interventions, and have responded as best we could, given our constraints. Indeed, in selecting which situations and cases would be represented in this collection, we also found ourselves chafing against some of the drawbacks of the feminist judgment method. For example, we struggled with the fact that this method replicates existing gaps in the ICC's jurisprudence, because the task is to rewrite judgments that have actually been made by the Court (a point underscored in Patricia Sellers' contribution on the impact of 'absent jurisprudence' in Chapter 4). Thus, the method does not address the multitude of cases that could theoretically come before the ICC but are yet to do so, despite repeated calls for accountability by survivors and their supporters. We were also conscious that the craft of feminist judgment writing requires a high level of legal literacy, which limits the pool of contributors to those with legal training.

Acknowledging these limitations, we included several artistic contributions, in the form of two commissioned poetic reflections on the ICC (Chapters 1 and 18), as well as three photographic essays (Chapter 15). As already noted, in the first poem, Maxine Beneba Clarke weaves the potential embodied by the reimagined judgments through often untold stories about law and how its institutions touch our lives. The second poem, Sara Saleh's 'The Checkpoint', provides a personal perspective on a long-running conflict which continues to take a heavy toll on Palestinian and Israeli civilians. The inclusion of these poems is intended to transcend, symbolically at least, some of the constraints of the feminist judgment method. That is, we wanted to include voices not draped in the (imagined) trappings of judicial authority, in a further acknowledgement of the limits of the law. Responding to reflections by some of our contributors, the poems also extend the book's reach beyond the nine situations from which the judgments are sourced, in order to consider other sites of oppression, colonial domination, and violence.

In addition to the poetic interventions, the book contains three photographic essays featuring the works of Rohingya refugees Azimul Hassan, Omal Khair, and Dil Kayas, who fled persecution in Myanmar in 2017 for the relative security of life in the world's largest refugee camp in Cox's Bazar, Bangladesh. In 2018, Fortify Rights, an international human rights non-governmental organisation (NGO) that has been working in Myanmar for over a decade, along with Doha Debates, provided Hassan, Khair, and Kayas with smart phones and on-the-ground photography and media skills training in order to visually document and communicate their experiences of life in the camp. They have since established sizeable followings on Instagram, published a book of their photographs,[21] and won an award for their work.[22] The inclusion of Hassan, Khair, and Kayas' photographs at the conclusion of the Bangladesh/Myanmar section in Part II of the book contributes a powerful visual expression of the ongoing impacts of atrocities committed in Myanmar, by illustrating in full colour the people and lives at the centre of the foregoing rewritten decisions. The editors' decision to include photographs in the book in this way represents an attempt not only to go beyond the feminist judgment method and the limits of legal reasoning, but to break free of the constraints of the written word itself, transcending language and literacy barriers in the way that only an image can. These photographs are intended to complement the rewritten decisions on the Bangladesh/Myanmar situation, but also as a reminder that the individuals and lives that are rendered in black and white, through words on a page, in all of the rewritten ICC judgments in this book, exist beyond and outside of the confines of a judicial decision.

Our hope is that this book is the beginning of road for feminist judgment writing in international criminal law, but may pave the way for further projects which reach places, stories, and ideas beyond those covered in this book.

The agonising fact that after our selection was made the world continued to see the outbreak of new conflicts and escalation of others is one that also warrants

[21] O. Khair, D. Kayas, and A. Hassan, *A Chance to Breathe: A Photography Book by Rohingya Refugees* (Fortify Rights, 2022), available at www.fortifyrights.org/a-chance-to-breathe/.

[22] Shorty Social Goods Award, 2020 in the 'Best Work for Immigration and Refugees' category. Fortify Rights Annual Report 2021/22 (2022), available at www.fortifyrights.org/downloads/Fortify%20Rights%20Annual%20Report%202021.pdf.

discussion. For example, the book does not include a gender analysis of the crime of aggression because Russia's 2022 invasion of Ukraine occurred once our project was well underway. Nor could we have predicted the intensification of violence in Gaza and Israel following Hamas' actions in October 2023 and Israel's response, which is occurring in real time at a sickening pace as we go to print, claiming the lives of thousands of civilians, many of them children. That these and so many other conflicts erupted and morphed throughout our writing process meant that decisions we made when setting the scope of the book feel different several years later. This is a challenge for any scholarly enterprise that responds to events unfolding in real time, and invites reflection on how future feminist judgment collections might be designed so as to be more responsive to developments in the real world.

Contributors

Contributors to the book include academics, practitioners, poets, and photographers. In terms of the contributing judgment and reflections authors, the editors sought to ensure this cohort was reflective of an international and intersectional feminism,[23] and the book includes nearly fifty authors, of all genders, from almost twenty different countries. Bringing their diverse theoretical approaches, professional experience, and cultural backgrounds to the book, these contributors explore the connections between gender, race, nationality, ethnicity, faith, and sexual orientation in relation to the law and practice of the ICC. It was important to the editorial team that the book included perspectives from leading feminist scholars in international law as well as emerging voices in the field. This diversity among contributors was particularly important to us, in light of the relative homogeneity of our editorial team.

The selected authors include leading professors as well as emerging scholarly voices, international criminal law practitioners, and many current or former ICC/UN tribunal lawyers. This group includes people of all genders, several of whom hail from ICC situation countries, including Afghanistan, Kenya, Uganda, Myanmar, Palestine, and Bangladesh. All contributors share a commitment to feminist judgment writing, but bring diverse theoretical perspectives including Third World Approaches to International Law (TWAIL) and queer theory. Others bring experience from legal practice, including as prosecutors, defence counsel,

[23] K. Crenshaw, 'Demarginalizing the Intersection of Race and Sex: A Black Feminist Critique of Antidiscrimination Doctrine, Feminist Theory and Antiracist Politics' 1 *University of Chicago Law Forum* (1989) 139–167.

victims' counsel, and judicial officers. This diversity ensures a broad range of perspectives and, we hope, enables the book to speak to broad readerships and networks.

METHODOLOGY: FEMINIST JUDGMENT WRITING AND REFLECTION

Context

As feminist scholars it is important to reflect upon the personal and political circumstances in which this project was completed. Against the backdrop of a global pandemic, the lines of demarcation between the public and private blurred as many of us worked from home. The gendered dimensions of this blurring have not been fully appreciated, but early research[24] and the reflections of contributors to this project well demonstrate the gendered nature of care. In this important respect, this is a very much a book produced in the time of COVID. Just as many real-life courts moved online, so did our project. Most meetings moved online, and although this had some drawbacks in terms of facilitating the in-person connections which have been the hallmark of previous feminist judging projects, it also made the process far more accessible to those with funding limitations, work commitments, environmental concerns, and caring responsibilities that make travelling to in-person meetings difficult.

Aside from the global phenomenon of COVID, while in no way diminishing its impact, contributors to this project concurrently experienced the full gambit of life circumstances that often occur behind the scenes of large projects. Within the wider team we marked the birth of a number of children, as well as encountering grief and loss, health challenges, and other struggles including childcare and financial hardships. Others had to contend with climate disasters and emergencies. Global conflict was never far from the minds of those within the project, and we recognise that a number of contributors were living, if not with active conflict, then with the challenges of post-conflict settings. Contributors were also promoted, changed careers, and embarked on new adventures and achieved outstanding goals. The influences, and unique adventures and trials, have no doubt shaped the final thoughts and considerations of all involved in ways that would not have been contemplated at the beginning of this project.

[24] See e.g. B. R. Parry and E. Gordon, 'The Shadow Pandemic: Inequitable Gendered Impacts of COVID-19 in South Africa' 28(2) *Gender, Work & Organization* (2021) 795–806; S. Germain and A. Yong (eds.), *Beyond the Virus: Multidisciplinary and International Perspectives on Inequities Raised by COVID-19* (Bristol: Bristol University Press, 2023); M. Graham, V. Weale, K. Lambert, N. Kinsman, R. Stuckey, and J. Oakman, 'Working at Home' 63(11) *Journal of Occupational and Environmental Medicine* (2021) 938–943.

Process

In June 2021 we hosted two online workshops (offered at different times to accommodate different time zones) to introduce the methodology, set out a timeline, and build connections between collaborators. We facilitated participant roundtable discussions, inviting contributors to discuss what excited them about the project. Some contributors presented 'elevator pitches' about their ideas for writing their chosen judgment. In terms of introducing the feminist judgment methodology, we engaged our contributors in a discussion of a rewritten judgment from the Australian project to promote discussion about *what* made the piece feminist.

As part of these initial workshops, we also shared pre-recordings of interviews conducted by the editorial team with participants in previous feminist judgment projects: Heather Douglas (one of the editors of the Australian Feminist Judgment Project) and Catherine O'Rourke (one of the contributors to the Irish/Northern Irish Project).[25] These interviews provided a helpful grounding in the genre of judgment writing, with both providing insightful reflections and advice about the challenges which stem from donning the imagined judicial robes to produce a plausible legal judgment (in ways that they may not previously have attempted as academics) *and* ensure that the judgment is feminist. O'Rourke reflected on the framework of the original judgment as a 'useful guardrail' which she used as a vehicle to 'grow into' her judgment. Douglas encouraged contributors to 'throw out' the original judgment, starting with a blank page rather than tinkering with the original judgment, while also 'dropping the idea that you had to actually decide differently', meaning that the rewritten judgment might reach the same conclusion as the original judgment, but through different reasoning. These meditations on avenues to pursue provided options and scope for our own participants to work in a way that suited their own approach.

In response to submitted proposals, we were fortunate to be able to provide participants with an interview with Rosemary Hunter, one of the editors of the UK Feminist Judgment Project (and editor and valued advisor to many subsequent projects). Hunter's guidance built on her 2010 'checklist' for feminist judging, reminding participants that 'authority is not incompatible with feminism' and that the power of language will assist in allowing them to don the judicial robes, depart from the academic genre, and engage with the judicial voice. Memorably, this was condensed to the phrase 'just do it'. The generosity extended by these colleagues created a valuable bridge between this project and those within the global feminist judgment methodology community, and provided useful practical guidance for our contributors. We are grateful for their time and expertise in helping our participants craft their contributions.

25 These materials are available at our project website: www.humanrights.unsw.edu.au/research/current-research/reimagining-judging-international-criminal-courts-gendered-approach.

Rounding off our series of video resources to support contributors in finalising their judgments was an interview between the editors, Rosemary Grey and Kcasey McLoughlin. This interview focused on specific mechanisms, rules, and procedures which operate within the ICC, assisting the participants in bolstering the plausibility of their rewritten judgment. Grey encouraged participants to dive deeply into the source material, to find evidence or legal arguments which may have been overlooked or disregarded in the real judgment, especially in ensuring that victims' perspectives are heard, and to consider the Court's power to change the legal characterisation of facts where appropriate.[26]

Although practical reasons restricted face-to-face engagement, we were still determined to work in a collaborative way, utilising the skills and expertise of all involved to create a supportive, peer-driven experience for both judgment and reflection writers. To achieve this, we organised online 'discussion circles' to enable contributors to participate in a facilitated peer-review process and benefit from each other's creativity and expertise. This also permitted reflection writers to attend and gain an understanding of the individual approach of the judgment writers, strengthening the reflective chapters.

Beyond organising these meetings, we also encouraged contributors to reach out to each other for support and feedback in an attempt to further community building within the project itself. The editorial team additionally provided individual and general feedback on each judgment outline, and then later on the draft judgments. This was supplemented by material put together by the editorial team which sought to provide guidance on issues of evidence, facts and law at the ICC more specifically. As editors, it was important to us, following previous projects, not to be overly prescriptive about what counts as 'feminist'. For the most part, our feedback was not concerned with tone or style, but rather the plausibility of the judgment. That is, did the judgment read as legally tenable, even if the authors chose to depart from the style and conventions typically used in ICC judgments. While asked to stay within the bounds of the Rome Statute, our judges were encouraged to find their own authentic judicial voice, and we kept an open mind when contributors defended their decision to take their rewritten judgment in a direction that we had not anticipated.

The resulting judgments are as diverse as the contributors who wrote them. Some opted to adhere strictly to the traditional feminist judgment methodology, whereby their judgment reflects the formulations, rules, and structure of the original judgments while also focusing on concepts and evidence that were not afforded attention. Other contributors were perhaps more disruptive of the method – pushing the bounds of plausibility (at least insofar as the Court is currently constituted) and imagination. For example, Rigney's abolitionist approach, McKay's imposition of a

[26] An approach which, when utilised by then Judge Navanethem Pillay, saw the first convictions for rape in the case of the *Prosecutor v. Jean Paul Akayesu*, ICTR-96-4-T, 2 September 1998.

non-carceral sentence, and Zarsky and Irving's creation of an 'additional comment' have not been canvassed within the current judgments of the ICC, but they challenged us to consider what might be possible if the role of the judge was reimagined in more radical ways. The wealth of possibilities expose the rigidity of the current ICC system and missed opportunities to deliver gender justice, as well as highlighting potential ways forward for the Court.

The final submitted judgments were then passed to the reflection writers. Engaging in their own discussion circles, reflection writers were invited to read the reimagined judgments and compare them with the original, finding thematic lines for all the judgments within their situation. While the reflections are also as varied as those who authored them, all follow a similar structure. First, a brief contextual overview is offered, whereby key actors, events, judgments, and outcomes are identified to help situate the reader. Attention then moves to how the judgments differ from or align with the original judgment, interrogating what makes the reimagined judgment 'feminist'. Finally, the reflection offers a critical appraisal of the possibilities that ensue when gender is seriously considered within judicial deliberations. Where the reflection writer has considered it appropriate, they have also offered commentary on the approach undertaken by the judgment writer. Following the suggestion from reflection writer Immi Tallgren, this approach allowed the judgment and reflection writers the opportunity to 'think outside of the box',[27] not only to explore their own interpretation of the feminist judgment method but also to offer their own thoughts about what a more gender-sensitive international criminal law system might look like. Some respectfully disagree with the approach undertaken by the judgment writer while others prefer to draw attention to the context-specific realities that underpin the judgment in the first instance. Although judgment writers were not asked to respond to the reflection chapters in this book, contributors are free to continue to express and exchange ideas in other forums.

Focus

This project aligns with previous feminist and critical judgment projects whereby the intention is to suspend disbelief, thereby allowing the judgments to be read as legally plausible. The desire was to clearly demonstrate that each Chamber of the ICC had the ability to come to the judgment, within the parameters of the ICC's legal system, and based on the information that was available at the time, but that the current systems and processes of thinking utilised by the Court interfered with

[27] We acknowledge the important contribution of Immi Tallgren, who offered an 'outside-the-box' section in her first reflection draft, and the editorial team found it so engaging that we asked all reflection writers to follow Tallgren's lead in offering their own outside-the-box reflections.

that outcome. We therefore encouraged contributors to adhere to the information that was available to the Court at the time. We suggested scouring the testimony, documentary evidence, and expert evidence that had been submitted in the relevant case, even if it had not been cited in the real decision, to locate the reimagined decision within the ambit of the Court, reflecting the strict/classical feminist judgment method adhering to admissibility rules.

As we acknowledge, however, that part of the feminist judgment method is also disrupting the traditional paradigms of judicial processes; where contributors sourced material outside of these parameters, we decided not to be too restrictive. For example, Radhakrishnan and Shubin's judgment (about genocide in Darfur) cites some sources which post-date 4 March 2009, but have been retained for pedagogical purposes with an asterisk (*) notation because they are relevant and valuable sources that might assist with subsequent genocide decisions by the ICC and other courts. We also encouraged contributors to make full use of the ICC's legal framework, such as the provisions permitting the Court to request evidence[28] or to invite submissions from *amici curiae*.[29] Therefore, contributors were able to note the lack of evidence they wished to consider, such as social harms or gendered roles, and demonstrate the need for such evidence for a full determination to be made.

The second core focus was developing rewritten judgments that are 'feminist', focusing on and highlighting the lived experiences and evidence that is often dismissed or relegated at the ICC. Although we as editors wanted to leave space for our contributors to bring their own conceptions of feminism to the project, we were guided by Hunter's 'checklist'[30] for what constitutes feminist judging, such as asking the 'woman' question, including women and other marginalised actors, challenging gender bias on both legal doctrine and judicial reasoning, reasoning from context and with awareness of power relations, foregrounding the reality of women's lived experience, trying to redress 'injustices and improve the conditions of women's lives', promoting substantive equality, and drawing on ideas from feminist literature).

But going beyond that checklist, we also encouraged contributors to consider intersectional feminist analysis, and to amplify the voices of victims/survivors where possible. Contributors interpreted these cues in different ways. For example, Anushka Sehmi's reimagined judgment emphasises the importance of giving victims agency in the ICC, and Souheir Edelbi's judgment places victims at the centre of the 'interests of justice test'. Combining these 'feminist' techniques with other critical approaches, such as queer approaches and TWAIL approaches, were also

28 Rome Statute, Art. 69(3).

29 ICC Rules of Procedure and Evidence, Rule 103.

30 E.g. R. Hunter, 'An Account of Feminist Judging' in R. Hunter, C. McGlynn, and E. Rackley (eds.), *Feminist Judgments: From Theory to Practice* (Oxford: Hart, 2010).

welcome. The result of this process and focus is twenty-seven rewritten decisions that critically engage with international criminal law, demonstrating that within the current system, there is scope to render decisions that are feminist, victim-focused, and plausible.

IMAGINING NEW BOUNDARIES

The book unites two distinct fields of research. First, we hope that it will be relevant to a global audience of international criminal law scholars, students, and practitioners. Today, international criminal law is practised in multiple institutions, including: the Hague-based ICC, the UN stand-alone investigations into Syria, Central African Republic, Iraq, and Myanmar; the Extraordinary Chambers in the Courts of Cambodia; and the UN mechanism which is completing the work of the Rwanda and Yugoslavia tribunals. It will also be a valuable teaching tool for international law students in universities throughout the world, because it provides examples of clear, applied feminist critique of well-known (and some less well-known) ICC cases.

Second, we hope that the book will be a valued text for feminist scholars in international and national law. Both bodies of scholarship are extensive, but they are not in always in dialogue. In particular, there has been little engagement by international law scholars with the method of feminist judgment writing, while previous projects within this genre have focused on the domestic sphere. By extending this method to an international court, and by showcasing intersectional approaches to feminist judgment writing, we are offering something new to this target audience.

The book is also practical in its orientation, so will appeal to legal practitioners at all levels – lawyers, barristers, prosecutorial and judicial staff, and judges of international criminal courts – because it offers relevant and specific examples of how to apply their legal framework in a more gender-sensitive way. The book shows what feminist judging entails in real cases; it does not just describe the method in abstract terms. As editors, we have endeavoured to ensure that all authors use accessible language and explain theoretical concepts in straightforward terms.

The story of feminist engagement with law is the story of pushing and redrawing boundaries. A key aim is to demonstrate the consequences which stemmed from women's exclusion from the development of international law: to expose what Charlesworth and Chinkin describe as 'a narrow and inadequate jurisprudence that has legitimated the unequal position of women worldwide'.[31] In international criminal law, women's exclusion has likewise shaped the development of law and its institutions (notwithstanding the work of feminist scholars in seeking to shape the Rome Statute). In this book, we continue to push the boundaries of imagination and

[31] H. Charlesworth and C. Chinkin, *The Boundaries of International Law: A Feminist Analysis* (Manchester: Manchester University Press, 2000).

judgment, within the bounds of that statute. Importantly, the book demonstrates how *gender* has been framed in international criminal law – serving as an important reminder that gender is not a synonym for woman, and that a gender lens is crucial for accurately understanding the world. Indeed this neutrality is the fiction (or fairytale) which has for too long held sway in accounts of law, and adjudication. By setting out what might be possible if feminist and gender-sensitive voices echoed from the judiciary, this book imagines a new jurisprudence from the ICC.

3

Do Feminists Believe in Fairy Tales?

The Case for Bringing the Feminist Judgment Methodology to the International Criminal Court[*]

Kcasey McLoughlin

INTRODUCTION

A few years ago, following a presentation we (the editorial team) were delivering about applying the feminist judgment methodology to the International Criminal Court (ICC), an evidently exasperated audience member interjected and said something to the effect of 'But why do another feminist judgment project?' Although initially a little taken aback by the question, it nonetheless raises an important point – *why* indeed?

This is a question we have taken seriously in curating this project – it is perhaps a bigger question than it might appear at first glance. I do not know the thinking underpinning the questioner's tone and query at our presentation, although I might speculate. With time and popularity, perhaps some of the novelty or shine of this methodology has worn off. The framing of the question at the time felt as though it was suggesting, at best, a certain kind of naiveté on our part (a misplaced faith in law and its institutions) or, at worst, a complicity with law's violence, its subjugation of marginalised people. It thus might also be speculated that the question is at once an old *and* a new question about feminist method: to what extent should feminists engage with law? On what (or whose) terms, and to what ends? Is our faith in law misplaced? Are our attempts to mimic the judicial role just the stuff of wishful fairy tales?

In this chapter, I therefore want to address two, albeit interconnected, questions: *why* another feminist judgment project? and *why* the International Criminal Court? In so doing I aim to situate this book within the tradition of existing feminist projects

[*] This chapter draws on some of the arguments presented in an earlier article jointly authored by members of the editorial team for this book: R. Grey, K. McLoughlin, and L. Chappell, 'Gender and Judging at the International Criminal Court: Lessons from "Feminist Judgment Projects"' 34 (1) *Leiden Journal of International Law* (2021) 247–264. Any errors or omissions remain my own.

and to reflect on judgment writing as feminist method. Asking 'Do Feminists Believe in Fairy Tales?' unites these questions.

The fairy tale (or mythological) motif is, perhaps surprisingly, prominent in accounts of judging, from masculinist explanations of the nature of adjudication through Dworkin's superhuman Hercules[1] to the image of the (fairy-tale) woman judge cast so evocatively by Erika Rackley's analogy of the mermaid whose voice is dulled or diminished to fit in.[2] There is also the somewhat incongruous image of Lady Justice, as described by Clare McGlynn:[3] 'the mythical symbol of justice, the blind-folded figure holding the scales of justice, which appears above our courts, is female, yet women as judges, the dispensers of justice, are few and far between'.[4] Finally, the notion of fairy tales has also been invoked to rebut traditional, declaratory theories of judging, by suggesting that to believe that judges don't make law is akin to believing in fairy tales.[5] As Judge Lord Reid of the United Kingdom noted almost fifty years ago:

> There was a time when it was thought almost indecent to suggest that judges make law – they only declare it. Those with a taste for fairy tales seem to have thought that in some Aladdin's cave there is hidden the Common Law in all its splendour and that on a judge's appointment there descends on him knowledge of the magic words Open Sesame. Bad decisions are given when the judge has muddled the password and the wrong door opens. But we do not believe in fairy tales anymore.[6]

It might be countered that feminist legal theorists *never* believed in that particular cave and were always critical of law's supposed objectivity. The 'fairy tales' or fictions embedded in traditional theories came under heavy scrutiny in the second half of the twentieth century, when feminist theorists uncovered the deeply masculinist assumptions embedded in the law and called into question assumptions about law's

1 See R. Dworkin, *Taking Rights Seriously* (London: Duckworth, 1977).

2 I note that, in a recent piece, Rackley has somewhat disavowed the little mermaid framing (i.e. the idea that, like the little mermaid, the woman judge was an outsider and, to fit in, she too had to give up what made her distinctive). Indeed, at least part of Rackley's revision is the benefit of observing more real-life women judges (in her case, especially the feminist leadership of Brenda Hale in the United Kingdom). Although Rackley has moved on from this particular framing of the little mermaid, we think it is nonetheless useful to consider what it tells us about the evolving imagery of the woman judge – the apparent novelty of women's access means that evolving understandings should not surprise us. See E. Rackley, 'A Short History of Judicial Diversity' 76(1) *Current Legal Problems* (2023) 1–32.

3 Together with Rosemary Hunter, Clare McGlynn and Erika Rackley edited what we now describe as the 'English feminist judgment project'. Both have written extensively about gender and judging, and feminist approaches to legal adjudication in more domestic contexts. R. Hunter, C. McGlynn, and E. Rackley (eds.), *Feminist Judgments: From Theory to Practice* (London: Hart, 2010).

4 C. McGlynn, *The Woman Lawyer: Making the Difference* (London: Butterworths, 1998) 171.

5 See Lord Reid, 'The Judge as Law Maker' 12 *Journal of the Society of Public Teachers of Law* (1972) 22–29.

6 *Ibid.*

(assumed) impartiality. In fact, a major contribution of feminist thought (extending the earlier work of the realists)[7] has been in exposing the true nature of traditional jurisprudential theories as 'male theories about law',[8] in challenging the stories lawmakers have traditionally told about themselves. One of the most problematic of these stories is the way in which most prominent legal scholars, who have historically been men, have imagined the law (and their role in it) as an objective and apolitical enterprise.[9] Implicit in this story is the idea of 'the distinction between on the one hand regarding law as created by human beings, and on the other, as existing separately from deliberate human intervention'.[10] Feminist accounts of law have presented a rejoinder to 'the way in which a distinctly male view of the world has been masquerading as detached objectivity'.[11]

Of course, feminists have adopted a range of methods for demonstrating the law's partiality – the feminist judgment method is but one (relatively) recent innovation. Feminist judgment projects have emerged, at least in part, due to an exasperation with the legal system's failure to account for gender – they are one of many tools for demonstrating how a distinctly male view of the world has been masquerading as detached objectivity. Importantly, such projects have also taken place against the backdrop of significant shifts[12] in conceptualising the relationship between gender and judging. This conceptualisation has in many instances moved beyond earlier understandings of difference,[13] arguing that rather than expecting *women* judges to

7 I note that feminist legal theory was not the first to challenge the demarcation between the judge and the law – the key point of departure between feminist legal theory and other critical theories is that it aims to 'show that the supposed gender-blind approach to legal scholarship is problematic, since the claim of neutrality is often a cover-story for male orientated and discriminatory legal knowledge and policy'. See M. Davies (ed.), *Asking the Law Question* (3rd ed., Sydney: Lawbook Company, 2008) 213.

8 H. Barnett, *Sourcebook on Feminist Jurisprudence* (London: Cavendish, 1996) 301.

9 A. Scales, 'The Emergence of Feminist Jurisprudence: An Essay' 95(7) *Yale Law Journal* (1986) 1373–1403.

10 Davies, *supra* note 7, at 41.

11 C. A. MacKinnon, 'Feminism, Marxism, Method, and the State: Toward Feminist Jurisprudence' 8(4) *Signs* (1983) 635–658, at 636

12 See K. McLoughlin, *Law, Women Judges and the Gender Order: Lessons from the High Court of Australia* (Abingdon: Routledge, 2022), for a summary of some of the key shifts in conceptualising 'difference', particularly in canvassing how certain constructions of difference essentialised women, and how in many instances the search for women's purported different judicial voice was elusive.

13 The literature is vast, but I note some feminist theorists, responding at least in part to Carol Gilligan's 'ethic of care', hypothesised that women judges would be the panacea to the law's gender blindness. See e.g. C. Gilligan, *In a Different Voice: Psychological Theory and Women's Development* (Cambridge, MA: Harvard University Press, 1982); C. Menkel-Meadow, 'Portia in a Different Voice: Speculations on a Women's Lawyering Process' 1 *Berkeley Women's Law Journal* (1985) 39–63; S. Sherry, 'The Gender of Judges' 4 *Law and Inequality* (1986) 159–169. This is not to suggest that all feminists have subscribed to such a viewpoint, even contemporaneously. For example, for a critique of the essentialism embedded in feminist legal theory more broadly, see A. P. Harris, 'Race and Essentialism in Feminist Legal Theory' 42(3) *Stanford Law Review* (1990) 581–616.

make a difference, it is more plausible to expect that *feminists*[14] might make a difference insofar as their approach to legal reasoning is concerned. Although different feminist judgment projects have dealt differently with questions of temporality, place, history, and culture, they are united by the alluringly simple notion that legal judgments *could* have been decided differently. As a body of work, these projects powerfully make the case that it matters *who* judges are. More specifically, they demonstrate that there *were* always possibilities to bring a more gender-sensitive or feminist perspective to bear in the art and craft of judgment writing while staying within the guardrails of the law.

Although the notion of fairy tales serves as the central provocation for this chapter, I want to make clear that fairy tales operate on more than one level. First, I am interested in rebutting the notion that the feminist judgment methodology might simply be dismissed as mere 'fairy tale' or wishful thinking. Such an argument is premised on the notion that there is unmet promise and potential in adopting feminist or gender-sensitive approaches at the ICC. Second, while the notion of the judge as described by Lord Reid might have been roundly dismissed, it seems there is still a comfort, or at least resilience, in the fairy tale of 'the objective judge'. We see this in the extent to which real-life judges seek to eschew feminist identities. Of course, what Reid was saying was not especially controversial or radical for his time. Feminist jurisprudence extended the critique even further than the realists. As Scales observed, 'the realists did not press their critique deeply enough. They did not bring home its implications in the face of their failure. The system has clung even more desperately to objectivity and neutrality'.[15] On such a view, feminist judgments are not merely the stuff of fairy tales – in fact, they are part of the business of disrupting the orthodoxy. However, this is not to discount the *value* of fairy tales insofar as they might serve to imagine different ways of doing things. Indeed, historically the first fairy tales involved women critiquing the patriarchy.[16]

Thus, in posing the question 'Do Feminists Believe in Fairy Tales?', this chapter interrogates how the feminist judgment method contributes to this tradition of feminist legal theory in dispelling myths about the neutrality of law and challenging conceptions of the objective masculinised judge. I do so in considering the challenges and tensions which arise through feminist engagement with law and its institutions, especially when those very institutions have shown how resistant they are to feminist interventions. I further consider the tangible impact feminist

[14] See e.g. S. J. Kenney, *Gender and Justice: Why Women in the Judiciary Really Matter* (New York: Routledge, 2013); R. Hunter, 'Can Feminist Judges Make a Difference?' 15(1–2) *International Journal of the Legal Profession* (2008) 7–36.

[15] Scales, *supra* note 9.

[16] M. Ashley, 'The first fairytales were feminist critiques of patriarchy. We need to revive their legacy', *The Guardian*, 11 November 2019, available at www.theguardian.com/books/2019/nov/11/the-first-fairytales-were-feminist-critiques-of-patriarchy-we-need-to-revive-their-legacy; A. Neikirk, '. . .Happily Ever After (Or What Fairytales Teach Girls about Being Women)' 8 *Hohonu: A Journal of Academic Writing* (2009) 38–42.

judging[17] might have in the real world, dismissing the notion that such interventions are merely a fairy-tale exercise in reimagining. I make the case for another feminist judgment project, canvassing the ICC's record to date and the unmet promise of the Rome Statute, and arguing that judges have an important role to play in enhancing gender justice.[18] Throughout the discussion, I demonstrate that this notion of justice is about far more than questions of the sex composition of the bench.

WHY (ANOTHER) FEMINIST JUDGMENT PROJECT? OR DO WE STILL BELIEVE IN (FEMINIST) FAIRY TALES?

Who is the judge of our collective imagination? Thinking deeply about that question, Rackley pondered the extent to which we are still captivated by the particularly alluring fairy tale of neutrality as described by Lord Reid. Rather than taking it as a given, Rackley questioned whether we have indeed abandoned our commitment to the fairy-tale image of the judge as 'a person stripped of self and re-clothed with the magical attributes of "fairness", "impartiality", "disengagement" and "independence"'.[19] Cataloguing accounts of judging (albeit reflecting scholarship on the common law method in English-speaking countries), she argued:

> The judge who inhabits our legal imagination has no personality, no history and no voice. His identity is often hidden beneath a wig and gown, his humanity erased, his voice silenced, his actions directed and constrained. This suits us just fine. We expect the judge to have no identity. We like the idea of a judge who performs superhuman feats in human form, just like a superhero.[20]

By interrogating this fairy tale, Rackley presents a decidedly different kind of story – one which analyses the implications of women's exclusion and the way in which it continues to shape and constrain understandings of judges. Her argument is that, despite protestations to the contrary, for better or worse we remain trapped in a kind of fairy-tale conceptualisation of judging, even if it has been exposed as a myth. This framing is not only about how those external to the judicial role understand it but

[17] In this volume, we have taken an expansive view of what 'counts' as feminist judging. The editors were very much guided by Hunter's seven-point checklist; although accepting that feminism is not monolithic, we were also guided by our contributors in how they sought to frame their reimagined judgments as feminist (see R. Hunter, 'An Account of Feminist Judging' in R. Hunter, C. McGlynn, and E. Rackley (eds.), *Feminist Judgments: From Theory to Practice* (Oxford: Hart, 2010), 35; for a further discussion of the feminist judgment methodology see Chapter 2 in this book).

[18] For a definition of 'gender justice', see Nancy Fraser's 'trivalent model' in N. Fraser, *Scales of Justice: Reimaging Political Space in a Globalizing World* (New York: Colombia University Press, 2009), as discussed in L. Chappell, *The Politics of Gender Justice at the International Criminal Court* (Cambridge: Cambridge University Press, 2016).

[19] E. Rackley, 'Representations of the (Woman) Judge: Hercules, the Little Mermaid, and the Vain and Naked Emperor' 22(4) *Legal Studies* (2002) 602–624, at 613.

[20] *Ibid.*

also about the judges themselves. As Rackley argued, it is the insulation 'by his judicial or superhero identity from his own tainted sense of self' that enables the judge to 'execute the law's violence that might otherwise be too painful for him to perform'. Or, to put it another way, 'It is a belief in the possibility of his own superheroism that enables the judge to judge'.[21]

Such thinking suggests that the myth of Dworkin's Herculean judge, who has 'superhuman skill, learning, patience and acumen',[22] brings a level of comfort, trust, and reliance to those for whom the sphere of law has been determined to be a place of restricted entry. Perhaps this gives us some insight about why this image prevails, even if it has been exposed as a myth. What Rackley demonstrates so powerfully is the complex tension which has been born out of the feminist preoccupation with difference, including the important shift from expecting *women* judges to make a difference to the expectation that *feminist* judges will make a difference.[23]

> What does this have to do with the feminist judgment methodology? Certainly, it speaks to ways in which judicial voice might remain constrained by long held notions of exclusion and inclusion. It also brings into sharp relief questions of legitimacy. There is also a further, bigger question: extending the fairy tale motif, what kind of fairy tales underlie the feminist judgment methodology? Feminist judgments are themselves acts of (re)imagination – but are they fairy tales? Though they are fiction, feminist judgments are designed to exist in the realm of the possible. That is the precept at the very heart of the project: they aim to demonstrate what might be possible within the existing bounds of legal formalism.

In justifying another feminist judgment project, I necessarily seek to emphasise the success of the methodology. But what does success mean? Of course, in part this involves a re-examination of the goals of feminist judgment writing projects. These projects have variously been described as law reform projects, social projects, and educative projects. Certainly, such projects are a critique of the status quo – a practical demonstration of the contingency of legal judgment and a comment on law and the feminist method, and the judicial enterprise more broadly. These projects are also political – by demonstrating the contingency of legal reasoning, they are a clarion call to appoint judges with gender expertise. In both these ways, feminist judgment projects serve an educative purpose.

Does success therefore mean real-life judges taking up the feminist mantle? Is it something less ambitious? Is it as simple as the project leading some to question who has been (or still may be) the gatekeeper of knowledge in an area of society that governs and regulates their behaviour? Certainly, one might argue that the adoption of the methodology in various jurisdictions speaks to a certain measure

[21] *Ibid*, at 614.

[22] Dworkin, *supra* note 1, at 105.

[23] See e.g. Kenney, *supra* note 14; Hunter, *supra* note 14.

of success.[24] As the editors of the US Supreme Court project, Crawford, Berger, and Stanchi, have argued:

> The signature achievement of the feminist judgments projects has been to combat the myth of a purely logical judicial decision-making process and to demonstrate that judicial decision-making is rarely detached from personal background and experience. By re-imagining the reasoning of judicial opinions through the added insight of feminist theories and methods, while bound by the precedent and facts of the time, the feminist judgment authors are able to write and decide like actual judges, while still accounting for intersecting inequalities resulting from gender, race, class, disability, sexual orientation, gender identity, ethnicity, immigration status and national identity.[25]

Many of the arguments *for* feminist judgment writing as feminist method have been rehearsed elsewhere but they merit briefly revisiting here. For Rackley, one of the co-editors of the England and Wales Feminist Judgment Project, the academic value of judgment writing lies in the discipline of putting one's theoretical insights into judgment form, of 'really testing abstract theories and political commitments against the realities of actual cases'.[26] Indeed, feminist judgment projects are explicit about their own methodological limitations in terms of what can be done within the bounds of legal formalism and also in the tacit acknowledgement that feminists dressing up in judicial robes are not subject to the same institutional pressures as real judges. As Hunter and colleagues acknowledge, 'judgments are themselves a constrained and bound genre, and writing a judgment imposes certain expectations and constraints on the writer that inevitably affect – even infect – her theoretical purpose'.[27] Importantly, the value (which is in many instances framed as legal plausibility) of reimagined judgment also underscores potential limitations. Unlike ordinary academic critique, the genre of judgment writing makes demands of its

24 See e.g., H. Douglas et al., *Australian Feminist Judgments: Righting and Rewriting Law* (1st ed., London: Bloomsbury, 2014); K. Stanchi, L. Berger, and B. Crawford, *Feminist Judgments (Feminist Judgment Series: Rewritten Judicial Opinions)* (Cambridge: Cambridge University Press, 2016); M. Enright, J. McCandless, and A. O'Donoghue (eds.), *Northern/Irish Feminist Judgments: Judges' Troubles and the Gendered Politics of Identity* (London: Bloomsbury, 2017); E. McDonald et al. (eds.), *Feminist Judgments of Aotearoa New Zealand Te Rino, a Two-Stranded Rope* (Oxford: Hart, 2017); S. Cowan, C. Kennedy, and V. E. Munro (eds.), *Scottish Feminist Judgments: (Re)Creating Law from the Outside In* (Oxford: Hart, 2019); C. Aparna, J. Sen, and R. Chaudhary, 'Righting Together: An Introduction to the Indian Feminist Judgments Project' 56(1) *VRÜ Verfassung und Recht in Übersee* (2023) 5–16; V. Munro, 'Feminist Judgments Projects at the Intersection' 29 *Feminist Legal Studies* (2021) 251–261 (discussing the African Feminist Judgments Project (AFJP), which is still in its early conception phase).

25 L. Berger, K. Stanchi, and B. Crawford, 'Learning from Feminist Judgments: Lessons in Language and Advocacy' 98 *Texas Law Review Online* (2019) 40–70, at 44.

26 E. Rackley, 'Why Feminist Legal Scholars Should Write Judgments: Reflections on the Feminist Judgments Project in England and Wales' 24(2) *Canadian Journal of Women and Law* (2012) 389–413, at 397.

27 Hunter, *supra* note 17, at 5.

authors to suspend disbelief: a judicial voice must be adopted, a decision must be reached and academic judgment writers 'cannot reinvent or radically reshape the law (although they may push at its boundaries)'.[28]

It is therefore probably unsurprising that there has also been considerable reflection from feminist scholars about their engagement with this methodology. Certainly, some contributors to this project noted their own discomfort in engaging with the method – reflecting on the awkwardness of inhabiting the role of judge and the constraints inherent in upholding such a system. The performative aspect of judging (understood as a role inhabited by mere humans) is exposed in powerful ways by feminist judgment writing as a form of feminist critique. Responding to the method, Davies argues that 'drag is the judicial norm' rather than the exception, because all 'judges are performing a role'.[29] Because it is a performance contingent on plausibility, '[f]eminist judges are not at liberty to ignore legal conventions in favour of simply applying a feminist approach but rather must, like all drag artists, be faithful to pre-existing normative ideas'.[30]

But the fairy tale also provokes other questions: Methodologically, what does it mean to engage with law? Are we, as feminists, engaging in wishful (fairy-tale) thinking to engage with law? Should we, as feminist academics, work complicitly within a system that has excluded us. Returning to that provocative question: In pursuing another feminist judgment project (and reflecting on critiques of centring law), is the feminist judgment methodology itself a naïve belief in fairy tales? Is dressing up in judicial robes an example of the tale of the emperor's new clothes? Is it simply the stuff of fairy tales to imagine that law really can be done differently, and that real-life judges might be influenced by these feminist judgments.

Some insights are provided by real-life feminist judges who have engaged with the methodology in earlier projects – writing forewords, offering guidance about the art and craft of judgment writing, and the judicial role more broadly. For example, Sally Brown,[31] in the foreword to the Australian project, suggested: 'If more people who become judges are aware of the gendered nature of law and the overriding importance of equality, and more reflective about the fluidity of the judicial role and the effect of power on the operation of law, there will be judgments which grapple with the concerns of these authors.'[32] Similarly, Brenda Hale,[33] in the foreword to the UK project, pondered:

[28] *Ibid*, at 398 (footnotes omitted).

[29] M. Davies, 'The Law Becomes Us: Rediscovering Judgment, Review of Feminist Judgments: From Theory to Practice' 20(2) *Feminist Legal Studies* (2012) 167–181, at 173.

[30] *Ibid*.

[31] Sally Brown is an Australian judge. She was appointed Chief Magistrate of Victoria in 1990, and then a judge of the Family Court of Australia in 1993.

[32] S. Brown, 'Foreword' in H. Douglas et al. (eds.), *Australian Feminist Judgments: Righting and Rewriting Law* (Oxford: Hart, 2014).

[33] Brenda Hale served as president of the Supreme Court of the United Kingdom from 2017 until her retirement in 2020.

> So what difference would it make if there were more feminist judges? We take it as given that all judges have to work within their judicial oaths: to 'do right to all manner of people after the laws and usages of this realm without fear or favour affection or ill-will.' They cannot have an 'agenda' to shape the law to their own design. But they can certainly bring their own experience and understanding of life to the interpretation or development of the law or its application in individual cases.[34]

Hale went on to describe reading the UK feminist project as a 'chastening experience for any judge who believes himself or herself to be both true to their judicial oath and a neutral observer of the world'.[35] Or, put another way, what might judges make of the disruption of the 'myth of a purely logical judicial decision-making process and to demonstrate that judicial decision-making is rarely detached from personal background and experience'?[36] On one view, such an argument should not arouse *too* much controversy. And yet the notion that that feminism might be inimical to the judicial role has been hard to dislodge.

This is because this idea of the judge, as the 'objective' superhero continues to have enormous gravitational pull. Real-life judges have, in many instances, eschewed feminist identities. In those rare instances in which international criminal law (ICL) judges and actors have demonstrated a commitment to women's rights, it has come at a high personal cost, with accusations of 'bias and lack of impartiality' and 'judicial activism',[37] arguably making other judges reluctant to push at the gendered boundaries of ICL.[38] For instance, in the International Criminal Tribunal for the former Yugoslavia's (ICTY) *Furundžija* case, Judge Florence Mumba was accused by the defence of apprehended bias due to her former role on the UN Commission on the Status of Women (a claim that was ultimately dismissed by the Appeals Chamber).[39] This environment of suspicion or even outright hostility to gender sensitivity at the ICTY was captured by Patricia Viseur Sellers, former Legal Advisor for Gender in the ICTY Prosecutor's Office, who reflected that 'thoroughly normalizing the investigation and prosecution of sexual

34 B. Hale, 'Foreword' in R. Hunter, C. McGlynn, and E. Rackley (eds.), *Feminist Judgments: From Theory to Practice* (Oxford: Hart, 2010) v, vi.

35 *Ibid.*

36 *Ibid.*

37 L. Chappell, '"Newness", "Oldness", "Nestedness" and Gender Justice Outcomes' 10(4) *Politics & Gender* (2014) 572–594; L. Chappell and R. Grey, 'Gender Just Judging in International Criminal Courts: New Directions for Research' in S. Rimmer and K. Ogg (eds.), *Research Handbook on Feminist Engagement with International Law* (Cheltenham: Edward Elgar, 2019) 213–239.

38 H. Charlesworth and C. Chinkin, *The Boundaries of International Law: A Feminist Analysis* (Manchester: Manchester University Press, 2000); Chappell, *supra* note 18.

39 K. D. Askin, 'Prosecuting Wartime Rape and Other Gender Related Crimes: Extraordinary Advances, Enduring Obstacles' 21 *Berkeley Journal of International Law* (2003) 288–349, at 331–332.

violence created a perceptible backlash [at the ICTY]'.[40] Judge Elizabeth Odio Benito has also faced accusations of bias and politicisation following her gender-sensitive dissent in the *Lubanga* case.[41]

As such, we think that the bridging of theory and practice is important in opening dialogues between the academy and the profession. This is evident in former ICC Judge Navi Pillay's Foreword to this book in which she admits to having disavowed the label 'feminist' whilst at the same time acknowledging that 'it is possible to be both a judge and a feminist, once one understands that feminism underscores equality of women and men'. In a similar vein, at the launch of the Australian feminist judgment book, Justice Margaret McMurdo[42] stressed that being a feminist was entirely in keeping with the judicial role: 'How could the contextually appropriate advocating of women's rights on the ground of equality of the sexes result in a reasonable apprehension of bias? There is complete synergy between feminism and the judicial oath.'[43]

In this volume (as with other feminist judgment projects), we have the participation of real-life judges, such as the Honourable Naigaga Winifred Kyobiika from Uganda, in legitimising feminist approaches to judging. Through such projects, we demonstrate that 'judges can challenge the lingering suspicion that feminist judging comes at the cost of impartiality'.[44]

Since the central premise of the feminist judgment methodology is that the rewritten judgment must be possible within the time and space of the original decision, these reimaginations serve to reveal the masculine (and other) biases of law, as well as the potential to disrupt them. The insistence on operating within the bounds of the law in making decisions which would have been possible at the time (which is especially significant in some of the more historic rewrites) has enhanced the credibility of these projects. Evidently, credibility and being 'taken seriously' by legal practitioners is a trade-off for causing greater disruption to the legal processes which are often 'sites of oppression in themselves'.[45] Many authors in other volumes, as well as this one, have expressed difficulty in 'treading the line' wherein they may engage in the judgment-writing process, highlighting new opportunities for feminist interpretations, in a way that still permits a critique of the process itself.[46] Of course,

40 P. Viseur Sellers, 'Gender Strategy Is Not Luxury for International Courts' 17(2) *American University Journal of Gender, Social Policy & the Law* (2009) 301–326, at 312.

41 See R. Grey, K. McLoughlin, and L. Chappell, 'Gender and Judging at the International Criminal Court: Lessons from "Feminist Judgment Projects"' 34(1) *Leiden Journal of International Law* (2021) 247–264, at 253.

42 Margaret McMurdo is an Australian Judge who served as the President of Queensland Court of Appeal from 1998 until her retirement in 2017.

43 M. McMurdo, 'Address at the Launch of the Book *Australian Feminist Judgments: Writing and Re-writing Law*, Speech, 2 December 2014 (Banco Court, Brisbane: University of Queensland), available at https://law.uq.edu.au/files/19693/AFJP-booklaunch-address-mcmurdo021214.pdf.

44 See Grey et al., *supra* note 41, at 264.

45 Munro, *supra* note 24, at 255.

46 *Ibid.*

many of these tensions are even more apparent and complex against the backdrop of coloniality. As Dawuni notes in Chapter 6 in this volume, although colonisation may have ended, its effects are ongoing 'as an idea of subjugation continues to be a principal means of control over the political, economic, linguistic, and legal systems of former colonies'.

Some authors in our project have offered contributions which are more 'disruptive'; less willing to be bound by the genre of judgment writing.[47] While I agree that one of the most compelling features of feminist judgment writing has been its insistence on plausibility, it is also true that there are innumerable ways to engage with the law and legal system while maintaining scepticism about the law, its language and authority. One compelling example was the approach taken by the Indigenous authors in the Australian project whose contributions were not written as judgments because white man's law would not be adequate.[48] Taking these critiques further, the Indigenous Judgment Project was even more radical in its departure from the method – utilising poetry, narrative, and essay to challenge the hegemony of judgment.[49] These contributions provide an important counter to the notion that adopting feminist/critical judging techniques alone would be sufficient to effect widespread transformation in judicial reasoning and method.

Even through our project's engagement with the feminist judgment method I nonetheless acknowledge the dangers of engaging with law. As Otto argued in her review of the International Law Project, 'feminist encounters with law are therefore always fraught with danger for feminist ideas which are vulnerable to co-option into the service of imperial and masculinist agendas'.[50] She offers the following examples, all of which are salutary given our book's focus: 'when the US-led invasion of Afghanistan was defended as a measure to support women's rights, and the World Bank's promotion of women's equality and LGBTIQ inclusion because of their instrumental value in boosting free market economic productivity'.[51]

These examples underscore doubts some feminists have expressed about the capacity for women to transform legal practices and processes by working within

47 In this collection, for example, see Rigney's abolitionist approach, McKay's imposition of a non-carceral sentence, and Zarsky and Irving's inclusion of an 'additional comment'. These approaches all pushed the boundaries in terms of what is legally plausible under the Rome Statute.

48 See I. Watson, 'Response to *Kartinyeri v Commonwealth of Australia* (1998) 195 CLR H' in H. Douglas et al. (eds.), *Australian Feminist Judgments: Righting and Rewriting Law* (1st ed., London: Bloomsbury, 2014).

49 N. Watson and H. Douglas, *Indigenous Legal Judgments: Bringing Indigenous Voices into Judicial Decision Making* (1st ed., London: Routledge, 2022).

50 D. Otto, 'Feminist Judging in Action: Reflecting on the Feminist Judgments in International Law Project' 28(2) *Feminist Legal Studies* (2020) 445–446 (citations omitted).

51 *Ibid.*

the limits of the law.[52] Indeed, the disinclination of some feminist legal theorists to engage with the law stems from the view that legal processes are so inherently masculine that they are beyond transformation. While much is made of the arguments about decentring law, this was 'never meant to mean that feminists should ignore law nor indeed that they should never engage with its various guises'.[53] As Smart herself reflected, responding to the early formulation of feminist judgment projects:

> Indeed law (especially at the levels of both formulating legislation and case law) provides a vital site for the contestation of ideas and values. It provides an opportunity to voice feminist values and concerns, and even possible alternatives. ... The project, which is about revisiting actual reported cases and rewriting them from the basis of feminist values, seems to be entirely in keeping with the project of encouraging discursive struggle. What, I wonder, could be worse than remaining mute?[54]

Far from 'remaining mute' we have co-opted the fairy-tale motif, utilising its power of imagination, possibilities, and retelling to generate a new reality, one which is possible within the bounds that already exist. Using such techniques, it becomes more difficult for critics to dismiss the feminist project as creating something which is created as 'fake', 'forged', or 'false'. Rather, it is a demonstration of that which the judge *could* have decided but did not – either by explicit choice or by unconscious blindness. Feminist judgment projects are not (merely) wishful thinking, 'rather in showing how cases could have been decided differently within the constraints imposed on judicial decision making ... feminist judgments are a manifestation of political truth'.[55] The judgments provide a tangible and vivid demonstration 'not only of the importance of having a judiciary that reflects the communities it serves, but also the extent to which a diverse judiciary can bring different perspectives to bear'.[56]

In curating another feminist judgment project, we defend the feminist judgment methodology, acknowledging its limitations, and the limitations of law more broadly. To borrow Matsuda's powerful imagery, in this volume we have one foot in the courtroom and one foot outside – cognisant of law's power and possibilities, and its limitations.[57] Of course, *who* gets to stand inside the courtroom (imbued with any authority and voice) is itself contested, the product of all kinds of political machinations and hierarchies. This is the matter to which I now wish to turn:

[52] C. Smart, *Feminism and the Power of Law* (New York: Routledge, 1990); M. J. Mossman, 'Feminism and Legal Method: The Difference It Makes' 3 *Wisconsin Women's Law Journal* (1987) 147–168.

[53] C. Smart, 'Reflection' 20 *Feminist Legal Studies* (2012) 161–165, at 162.

[54] *Ibid*, at 162–163.

[55] Rackley, *supra* note 26, at 408.

[56] *Ibid*.

[57] M. Matsuda, 'When the First Quail Calls: Multiple Consciousness as Jurisprudential Method' 11(1) *Women's Rights Law Reporter* (1998) 7–10, at 8.

explaining why the ICC makes a compelling case study for extending the feminist judgment method to a new site.

WHY EXTEND FEMINIST JUDGMENT METHODOLOGY TO THE INTERNATIONAL CRIMINAL COURT?

What features of the ICC make it the suitable subject of another feminist judgment project? Here there are two matters which bear emphasis. The ICC's record means that it is rightly a site of feminist concern, one that has not lived up to its promise of gender justice – a promise that is significant (notwithstanding the many and valid critiques of the Rome Statute).[58] Although the ICC does not make any reference to feminist judging, the importance of gender sensitivity is 'baked into' the ICC's design, so to speak.[59] The feminist judgment methodology thus provides an important outlet to illustrate this promise, which can be more fully realised by thinking about the transformative role of judges.

The ICC's Poor Record in Attaining Gender Justice

Sexual and gender-based crimes (SGB) are endemic in periods of conflict,[60] and yet the ICC has secured just two convictions for such crimes, both towards the end of the second decade of its operation: *Ongwen* 2021[61] and *Ntaganda* 2019.[62] This low level of accountability creates a series of injustices: it leaves intact perpetrator impunity; it leaves victims without recognition or reparation; and it undermines the legitimacy of the ICC, given the commitment of its architects to advancing gender justice across all systems, jurisdictions, and societies.[63] But the ICC's weak contribution to gender justice runs much deeper than just failed convictions for SGB crimes; the ICC's failure to integrate a gender perspective has touched every stage of the trial. For example, the Court has not considered gendered barriers to justice when assessing whether its cases should be turned over to national courts,[64] and has excluded

58 See for example A. Facio, 'All Roads Lead to Rome, but Some Are Bumpier than Others' in S. Pickering and C. Lambert (eds.), *Global Issues, Women and Justice* (Sydney: Federation Press, 2004) 308–334; B. Schiff, *Building the International Criminal Court* (Cambridge: Cambridge University Press, 2008).

59 The editors of this volume developed this argument in Grey et al., *supra* note 41, at 250.

60 PRIO, 'Continued Failure to Address Wartime Sexual Violence', PRIO Policy Paper 07, 2018, available at https://cdn.cloud.prio.org/files/6602e342-5de5-4c2a-b4d8-a07c2d304ab1/Nordås%20Nagel%20Cohen%20-%20Continued%20Failure%20to%20End%20Wartime%20Sexual%20Violence%20PRIO%20Policy%20Brief%207-2018.pdf?inline = true.

61 Trial Judgment, *Ongwen* (ICC-02/04-01/15-1762-Red), Trial Chamber IX, 4 February 2021.

62 Trial Judgment, *Ntaganda* (ICC-01/04-02/06), Trial Chamber VI, 8 July 2019.

63 L. Chappell, 'The Gender Injustice Cascade: "Transformative" Reparations for Victims of Sexual and Gender-Based Crimes in the Lubanga Case at the International Criminal Court' 21 (9) *International Journal of Human Rights* (2017) 1223–1242.

64 L. Chappell, R. Grey, and E. Walker, 'The Gender Justice Shadow of Complementarity' 7(3) *International Journal of Transitional Justice* 455–475.

women's perspectives in cases relating to the destruction of cultural heritage.[65] Grey's work on prosecuting SGB crimes has shown how the proportion of SGB charges decreases significantly at each stage of trial in comparison to other crimes, illustrating an overarching issue with both prosecutorial and judging approaches.[66] To improve accountability for SGB crimes in the ICC, and to ensure that the Court develops a more gender-sensitive practice which places survivors at the centre, there is an urgent need to understand the reasons for this failure. This includes filling a research gap to interrogate the role of the judiciary in perpetuating the problem.

One such strategy for understanding the part the judiciary has played in the Court's poor gender justice record is adopting the feminist judgment methodology. The focus that the methodology brings to judging is currently lacking from the sophisticated critique of ICL which feminist scholars have been developing since the 1990s.[67] The focus of this work has primarily revolved around issues of how legal concepts and practices have historically been gendered in ways which lead to women's discrimination in the courtroom,[68] and how women survivors of SGB violence in conflict have been ignored, or their experiences rendered less grievous than other crimes.[69] However, missing from feminist ICL scholarship is the concept of 'feminist judging', a critical method which, as discussed above, has been used in domestic/national settings, and an understanding of how such an approach can be utilised in efforts to overcome gender biases embedded in ICL. To the extent that international legal studies have addressed gender and judging at all, the focus has (mostly) either been on increasing the number of women judges on relevant courts,[70] or on feminist judging in non-criminal international law venues.[71]

65 R. Grey, *Prosecuting Sexual and Gender-Based Crimes at the International Criminal Court* (Cambridge: Cambridge University Press, 2019).

66 'At each of these stages of proceedings, a decreasing proportion of gender-based crimes has been confirmed: just under 93 per cent at the arrest warrant/summons to appear stage; 74 per cent at the confirmation stage; and zero per cent at the end of the trial ... At every stage of proceedings, the OTP has been less successful in establishing charges of gender-based crimes than other crimes.' Grey, *supra* note 63, at 265.

67 See e.g. H. Charlesworth, C. Chinkin, and S. Wright, 'Feminist Approaches to International Law' 85 *American Journal of International Law* (1991) 613–645; Charlesworth and Chinkin, *supra* note 38; R. Copelon, 'Surfacing Gender: Re-engraving Crimes against Women in Humanitarian Law' 5 *Hastings Women' s Law Journal* (1994) 243–265; Chappell, *supra* note 18; R. Grey and L. Chappell, 'Prosecuting Sexual and Gender-Based Crimes in the International Criminal Court: Inching towards Gender Justice' in S. Mouthaan and O. Jurasz (eds.), *Gender and War: International and Transitional Justice Perspectives* (Cambridge: Intersentia, 2019) 209–234.

68 F. Ní Aoláin, D. F. Haynes, and N. Cahn, *On the Frontlines: Gender, War, and the Post-Conflict Process* (New York: Oxford University Press, 2011).

69 Charlesworth and Chinkin, *supra* note 38; Chappell, *supra* note 18.

70 N. Grossman, 'Sex on the Bench: Do Women Judges Matter to the Legitimacy of International Courts?' 12(2) *ChicagoUnbound* (2012) 647–684.

71 See L. Hodson and T. Lavers (eds.), *Feminist Judgments in International Law* (Oxford: Hart, 2019). Note that this important contribution includes just one ICC case. See also K. Gooding, 'How Can the Methodology of Feminist Judgment Writing Improve Gender Sensitivity in

Furthermore, as noted in Chapter 2, existing gender-oriented analyses of the ICC have tended to focus on how poor *investigation and prosecution* strategies have contributed to the ICC's initial failure to secure convictions for SGB crimes.[72] The ICC Prosecutor's Office recognises this fact and has consequently appointed gender advisors and published a comprehensive gender policy aimed at improving its track record across the board.[73] This focus has meant that there is comparatively little recognition or research (or at least the recognition has been slower) into the role that *judges* have played in adjudicating SGB crimes, and no collective action[74] by the ICC's judiciary to draw lessons from the extensive research on gender-sensitive judging in domestic courts.[75] As such, a feminist rewriting of ICC decisions examines the Court's poor conviction record from a new angle.

Gender Parity and Gender Expertise on the Bench

It is relevant to consider the ICC's own record in terms of gender parity and gender expertise on the bench and whether this makes the Court a suitable focus for another feminist judgment project. The importance of not conflating sex with gender expertise was at least to some extent addressed by the Rome Statute through its provisions for the election of judges. Notably, Article 36(8)(a) provides that states parties shall in the selection of judges 'take into account the need, within the membership of the Court, for: (i) The representation of the principal legal systems of the world; (ii) Equitable geographical representation; and (iii) A fair representation of female and male judges'. Importantly, it further specifies in Article 36(8)(b) that 'States Parties shall also take into account the need to include judges with legal

International Criminal Law' 5 *LSE Law Review* 115–152 for a thoughtful feminist rewriting of *Ongwen* prior to our ICC Feminist Judgment Project.

72 L. Chappell, 'Conflicting Institutions and the Search for Gender Justice at the International Criminal Court' 67(1) *Political Research Quarterly* (2014) 183–196; N. Hayes, 'Sisyphus Wept: Prosecuting Sexual Violence at the International Criminal Court' in W. Schabas, Y. McDermott, and N. Hayes (eds.), *The Ashgate Research Companion to International Criminal Law* (Farnham: Ashgate, 2013) 7; Grey and Chappell, *supra* note 67.

73 Office of the Prosecutor, 'Policy Paper on Sexual and Gender-Based Crimes', June 2014, available at https://www.icc-cpi.int/sites/default/files/iccdocs/otp/OTP-Policy-Paper-on-Sexual-and-Gender-Based-Crimes–June-2014.pdf; Office of the Prosecutor, 'Policy on Gender-Based Crimes', December 2023, https://www.icc-cpi.int/sites/default/files/2023-12/2023-policy-gender-en-web.pdf.

74 Although the judiciary itself may not have issued a practice manual or taken further collective action, I note the effective training programmes carried out by organisations such as African Legal Aid and Women's Initiatives for Gender Justice which have worked to incorporate gender expertise within the chambers. See e.g. African Legal Aid, 'Gender Mentoring Training Programme for Judges of International Criminal Courts', November 2022, available at www.africalegalaid.com/gender-mentoring-training-programme-for-judges-of-international-criminal-courts; WIGJ, 'Gender Training', 2004–2007, available at https://4genderjustice.org/home/gender-training.

75 Hunter, *supra* note 17; K. McLoughlin, 'A Particular Disappointment? Judging Women and the High Court of Australia' 23(3) *Feminist Legal Studies* (2015) 273–294.

expertise on specific issues, including, but not limited to, violence against women or children'.[76] Although these provisions do not conflate sex and expertise, they fall short of requiring equal gender representation and they do not put any particular weight on the matters to be taken account (for example, gender expertise).

The Rome Statute's provisions for judicial election provide some context to the Court's gender statistics, which have shown mixed success in embedding gender representation and expertise. From 2010 to 2014, women constituted the majority of justices on the ICC bench, reaching a peak of 61 per cent in 2011. However, underscoring the precarious nature of such gains, in 2015 female representation on the bench slipped to an all-time low of 33 per cent.[77] After the 2020 ASP Session, women held nine of eighteen judicial appointments.[78] At the 2023 ASP, two more women were elected to the bench, resulting in women again holding 61 per cent of all judicial positions.

As of March 2023, there were fourteen nominations to the positions, with six female to eight male nominations.[79] Notably, all three candidates from the Asia-Pacific states were male.[80] Accordingly, even specific provisions which account for a 'fair representation' have not necessarily been a safeguard for securing something akin (or close) to parity.

Perhaps more significantly for our purposes is the number of judges with specific gender expertise. In 2023, five out of the eighteen sitting justices self-identify as possessing gender expertise:[81]

(1) Judge Luz del Carmen Ibáñez Carranza, gender and children legal expertise.
(2) Judge Chang-ho Chung, gender legal expertise (ECCC).
(3) Judge Bertram Schmitt, gender legal expertise.
(4) Judge Althea Violet Alexis-Windsor, legal expertise in sexual violence.
(5) Judge Miatta Maria Samba, legal expertise in sexual violence.

Our point here is not to over-emphasise the significance of these numbers in any empirical sense. Understood in a wider historical context (which has denied women access to judicial roles) – parity or near parity on the bench must be set against that reality. But, as Kenney explains, numbers matter because they affect power in institutions, and we 'need to know if the institution is uniform, skewed, tilted, or

[76] The Rome Statute UN General Assembly, *Rome Statute of the International Criminal Court (last amended 2010)*, 17 July 1998, ISBN 92-9227-227-6, Art. 36(8)(b).

[77] The Coalition for the ICC Elections Team, 'Gender Representation on the ICC Bench' (2020), available at https://coalitionfortheicc.org/sites/default/files/cicc_documents/CICC%20Elections%20Team%20statement%20gender%20representation.pdf.

[78] ICC, 'Judges' (2022), available at www.icc-cpi.int/sites/default/files/Publications/JudgesENG.pdf.

[79] Assembly of States Parties, 'Nominations for Judges of the International Criminal Court', 23 March 2023, available at https://asp.icc-cpi.int/elections/judges/2023/Nominations.

[80] *Ibid.*

[81] ICC, 'Judges' (2023), available at www.icc-cpi.int/sites/default/files/Publications/JudgesENG.pdf.

balanced'[82] to understand how institutions are gendered.[83] Gender expertise is not the sole purview of women, and sex does not connote knowledge or authority. Two of the above five judges self-identifying as having expertise are male.[84] Moreover, I am not suggesting that this expertise is synonymous with a feminist approach to judging – although of course it stands to reason that this expertise might manifest itself this way (or at least increase the likelihood that a judge possessing such expertise might be more likely to show feminist or gender-sensitive approaches to judging). Rather, my point is about the relative importance that might be placed on ensuring that the ICC judiciary reflects the principles of fair representation, and the election of judges with gender expertise.[85] That is, despite these provisions, the Court has a mixed record, both in terms of gender parity and in the appointment of judges with specific gender expertise.

This record makes the ICC fertile ground for another feminist judgment project. The fact that the Court's provisions on gender representation and expertise have not been fully realised opens the door for asking: What if they had been? How might judgment differ if written by someone openly espousing feminist principles? Importantly, the fact that such expertise is explicitly recognised (to an extent) by the Statute itself renders its application more pertinent.

Highlighting the primary importance of gender expertise on the bench is even more important in light of the Court's continued preoccupation with numerical rather than substantive representation. Certainly, it feels as if this concern with parity remains significant – to the point that it might obscure other concerns – in accounts about judges and the role that they might play on the Court. For example, on International Women's Day (IWD) in 2023, the President of the Court, Judge Piotr Hofmański, made a point of emphasising the numerical picture:

> The ICC is proud to be at the forefront of the movement toward gender equality in the field of international justice. With nine female and nine male judges currently on our bench, we project to the world the critical importance of the equal participation of men and women in the field of law. Yet, much more remains to be done to achieve effective equality of opportunities in our workforce. As an International Gender Champion, I am strongly committed to treating this as a continuous priority that requires tangible efforts on a daily basis.[86]

[82] S. Kenney, 'New Research on Gendered Political Institutions' 49(2) *Political Research Quarterly* (1996) 445–466, at 456

[83] See McLoughlin, *supra* note 12, for an examination of the way in which the institutional features of a given court might be conceptualised as reflecting a particular 'gender regime' which in turn shapes the *institutional* and *individual* contributions of judges.

[84] ICC, *supra* note 83.

[85] Importantly, I note that regional representation is also significant in achieving gender justice due to the insights gained from regional diversity into intersectional power structures which exacerbate and underlie atrocity crimes.

[86] ICC, 'International Criminal Court Marks International Women's Day' (8 March 2023), available at www.icc-cpi.int/news/international-criminal-court-marks-international-womens-day-1.

In contrast, in his remarks on IWD, ICC Prosecutor Karim A. A. Khan KC also emphasised the ICC's working environment, but appeared to evidence a wider and more nuanced understanding of gender justice than focusing solely on equal representation. He said:

> On this International Women's Day, I reaffirm my commitment to the ICC's Gender Strategy and my conviction that gender equality, gender diversity, and empowerment of women within my Office are key prerequisites for high performance ... Our Office also protects women's rights in the crimes we investigate and prosecute. That includes the crime of gender persecution – the ultimate crime of discrimination towards women, including lesbian, bisexual, transgender, queer, and intersex women.

Now, of course these are isolated comments made in recognition of International Women's Day – they should not be taken as representing a complete picture regarding the institutional understanding of gender justice. But they nonetheless serve as another reminder that more work is needed in emphasising the role *judges* might play in improving gender justice.

Fulfilling the Promise of the Rome Statute

Finally, it is not merely the ICC's poor gender justice record or varying levels of gender expertise that make it a suitable forum for extending the feminist judgment methodology. Rather, the fact that the Rome Statute itself already contains substantial (and under-utilised) gender-sensitive provisions transforms the rewriting from an academic exercise into a real-world possibility. The editors of this volume have elsewhere canvassed the possibilities for ICC judges to engage in gender-sensitive or feminist judging, stressing the significant *promise* in the Rome Statute when it comes to delivering gender justice. As we argued, there are three main spheres of judicial activity which could be utilised by the bench to bring into effect the potential of the Statute: interpreting the law, making findings of fact, and making procedural decisions.[87]

During the Court's creation, the international feminist legal community successfully advocated for strong gender justice provisions in the Rome Statute.[88] These

87 As we argued: When interpreting decisions, there is scope for judges to think about the gendered consequences of a particular interpretation: will it have a discriminatory effect in practice, and if so, can this be avoided? Such questions give effect to Article 21(3) of the Rome Statute, which requires the Court to interpret and apply the law without adverse distinction on certain grounds, including gender. By thinking through how different interpretations of law might result in gender discrimination, judges can in substance engage in feminist judging, even if they choose not to describe their method in such terms. See Grey et al., *supra* note 41, at 268.

88 *Ibid*, at 250; B. Bedont and K. Hall-Martinez, 'Ending Impunity for Gender Crimes under the International Criminal Court' 6 *Brown Journal of World Affairs* (1999) 65–85; S. Mouthaan, 'The Prosecution of Gender-Based Crimes at the ICC: Challenges and Opportunities' 11(4) *International Criminal Law Review* (2011) 775–802.

provisions were supported by numerous states, as well as the Women's Caucus for Gender Justice, the key feminist organisation engaged in the negotiations.[89] Indeed, some of the proposed gender justice provisions had to be watered down in order to appease conservative states, particularly the provisions defining terms such as 'gender' and 'forced pregnancy'.[90] However, the Women's Caucus and like-minded states were successful in locking in many gender justice rules. For example, the Rome Statute recognises a wider range of sexual and gender-based crimes than any previous instrument of international law;[91] it refers to special measures to protect the dignity and well-being of victims of SGB violence;[92] and it requires that all sources of law applicable within the ICC are interpreted and applied without adverse distinction (discrimination) on gender grounds.[93] Of course, the Rome Statute's provisions aimed at securing gender expertise in the Chambers (that is, the judiciary),[94] Office of the Prosecutor,[95] and Registry[96] are all also important in embedding this expertise in the institution.

As such, embedded within the Rome Statute is an unrealised promise for gender justice. The Rome Statute provides a firm foothold for such an approach – and acknowledging, of course, that the method has been successfully deployed in reimagining historic and more contemporary decisions where arguably no such firm foothold exists. The feminist judgment methodology provides an important forum to explore the potential of this promise by changing *who* decides the law, testing the limits between legal plausibility and feminist principles.

It therefore presents something of a blueprint for what might be possible within existing institutions. Is it akin to belief in a fairy tale to imagine the appointment of real-life feminist judges? Here I think that at least part of the work of the feminist judgment methodology is to destigmatise the notion that bringing such a perspective to bear is antithetical to the judicial role. Indeed, even if ICC member states *want* to elect feminist judges, and even if serving judges *want* to become more gender sensitive, there is little guidance on the features of feminist judging in relation to this particular court, or in relation to ICL more generally. This is due to a lack of knowledge transfer from the extensive literature on and practice of feminist judging in domestic courts to the international arena.

89 Grey et al., *supra* note 41, at 252.

90 *Ibid*, at 250; M. Glasius, *The International Criminal Court: A Global Civil Society Achievement* (London: Routledge, 2006), 77–93; L. Chappell, 'Women's Rights and Religious Opposition: The Politics of Gender at the International Criminal Court' in Y. Abu-Laban (ed.), *Gendering the Nation-State: Canadian and Comparative Perspectives* (Vancouver: UBC Press, 2009) 139.

91 The Rome Statute UN General Assembly, *supra* note 76, Arts. 7(1)(g), 7(1)(h), 8(2)(b)(xxii), 8(2)(e)(vi).

92 *Ibid*, Arts. 54(1)(b), 68(1), 68(2).

93 *Ibid*, Art. 21(3)

94 *Ibid*, Art. 36(8)(b).

95 *Ibid*, Art. 42(9).

96 *Ibid*, Art. 43(6).

This book serves to bridge that gap. It demonstrates what might be possible on the international stage. It invites the legal community, and those beyond, to engage with the work already underway in many domestic spheres; to reimagine *who* the imagined international criminal law judge might be, and how they might approach their task. It reopens the possibilities that were in full force during the 1998 Rome Conference and earlier preparatory meetings. So, why another feminist judgment project? Because the promise and potential of the ICC for gender justice is not a fairy tale – and that is something we as feminists should believe in.

4

'The Richness of the Jurisprudence That Is Absent'

Imagining a Different Legal Past

Patricia Sellers in conversation with Rosemary Grey

INTRODUCTION

For over three decades, Professor Patricia Sellers has been a leading feminist voice in international criminal law. In 1994, she was hand-picked by the inaugural Prosecutor of the International Criminal Tribunal for the former Yugoslavia (ICTY) Richard Goldstone as his Special Advisor on Gender. She has since been Acting Head of the Legal Advisory Section and a prosecutor at the ICTY, and held three posts as Special Advisor to the ICC Prosecutor: first on prosecution strategies, then gender, and, since 2021, on slavery crimes. In 2024, she developed the ICC Prosecutor's inaugural Policy on Slavery Crimes. Sellers is on the law faculty and is a visiting fellow at Oxford University's Kellogg College, and has published widely on gender and enslavement in international criminal law. In 2000, she served as Chief Prosecutor of the Women's International War Crimes Tribunal on the Trial of Japan's Military Sexual Slavery, a people's tribunal that symbolically prosecuted and determined individual liability and state accountability for crimes committed against several hundred thousand 'comfort women' in Japanese military brothels before and during World War II.[1]

In this chapter, which is based on interviews with Rosemary Grey in 2022 and 2023, Sellers reflects on these experiences. The chapter extends this ICC feminist judgment collection in a unique way. In line with previous feminist judgment projects, most of this book's contributions take the form of a reimagined decision: the authors take an existing ICC judgment (or part of one) and rewrite it as if they had been on the Bench, equipped with the same submissions, evidence, and law as the real judges were, but rendering a judgment that seeks to be more gender-competent than the original.[2] This process can be described as a feminist rewriting of history: the

[1] T. Dolgopol, 'The Tokyo Women's Tribunal' in A. Byrnes and G. Simm (eds.), *Peoples' Tribunals and International Law* (Cambridge: Cambridge University Press, 2018) 84–106.

[2] Chapter 2, Introduction, in this book.

author goes back to their chosen moment in the ICC's past and produces an alternative decision, thereby revealing a road not taken in the Court's case law.

But here, Sellers takes us back even further in time, to cases adjudicated *before the creation of the ICC*. By imagining judgments that could have been made by previous international tribunals, she conjures up an alternative legal present and paves the way for an alternative legal future. Specifically, Sellers shows how contemporary jurisprudence on the crimes of 'enslavement' and 'slave-trading' might have been more gender-attuned had a deeper understanding of gender and intersectionality been embedded in international criminal tribunals in the past. Her thought-experiment reaches back to the beginning of contemporary international criminal law, with the trials of German and Japanese defendants in the International Military Tribunal (IMT or Nuremberg Tribunal) and International Military Tribunal for the Far East (IMTFE or Tokyo Tribunal) after World War II. It then moves on to the ICTY and International Criminal Tribunal for Rwanda (ICTR), and finally to current proceedings in the ICC.

By altering legal history in this way, the chapter resonates with the more experimental contributions to previous feminist judgment projects, such as Nicole Watson's entries in the Australian and Indigenous collections, which take the form of judgments that could hypothetically be rendered *if* Australia had made a treaty with its Indigenous people.[3] Such contributions veer off the guardrails of the 'feminist judgment method' proposed by Rosemary Hunter,[4] and in doing so reinterpret the method in thought-provoking ways.

In particular, Sellers' approach prompts us to consider the effect of legal precedent – of judicial analysis from past generations – on the development of international criminal law today. This issue of precedent is important in the ICC context. Legally speaking, the ICC is not bound by the principle of *stare decisis* (standing by past decisions) in the way that courts are in the common-law world. But in the practice of the ICC, legal precedents continue to loom large. In fact, ICC judgments regularly cite and follow decisions of the ICTY and ICTR, and sometimes also look to the Special Court of Sierra Leone (SCSL), Extraordinary Chambers in the Courts of Cambodia (ECCC), the Nuremberg and Tokyo Tribunals, and other courts that have adjudicated war crimes, crimes against humanity, and genocide. In addition, the career trajectories and educational pathways that lead lawyers and judges to the ICC provide an informal route by which ideas travel from past tribunals to this Court.

Therefore, to fully appreciate the limitations and possibilities of feminist judgment writing in the ICC, we need to contemplate the jurisprudence, absent jurisprudence, and forgotten jurisprudence of previous international criminal tribunals, as Sellers does here.

3 N. Watson, 'In the Matter of Djaparri (Re Tuckiar)' in H. Douglas, R. Hunter, T. Luker, and F. Bartlett (eds.), *Australian Feminist Judgments* (Oxford: Hart, 2014) 442–451; N. Watson and T. Broderick, 'Dempsey v Rigg [1914] St R Qd 245' in N. Watson and H. Douglas (eds.), *Indigenous Legal Judgments* (Abingdon: Routledge, 2021) 189–205.

4 See the discussion of Hunter's checklist in the Introduction to this book (Chapter 2).

THE CONVERSATION BEGINS

Sellers: I've been thinking a lot about the idea of absent jurisprudence. About the jurisprudence that we *don't* have, the jurisprudence that fails to inform us now. *I think we're living with the consequences of trying to imagine and legally characterise something that* could have been *given to us via precedent*, but was not. In international criminal law, we have certain 'holy books' of jurisprudence, but as feminist legal thinkers know, they are far from complete. I don't just mean the reductive call that 'there's no mention of the word rape in the Nuremberg judgment'. There's much more to it than that.

Grey: That is an intriguing way to begin, thank you. Where would you like to start?

On 'Comfort Women' and the Tokyo Tribunal

Sellers: I want to bring up the Tokyo judgment because it's so overlooked by most feminists. It speaks to something within us that we don't more closely examine the Tokyo jurisprudence for what is present in it. There's a lot of sexual violence present. But then, there is also a huge absence with the omission of the 'comfort women' crimes. Within the Tokyo Tribunal, there were no indictments that concerned the 'comfort women'. But we have an estimated 100,000 to 200,000 women wherein the crimes committed against them were not part of the evidentiary basis and certainly not part of the jurisprudence. Until today, we live in an absence of what that jurisprudence could have been like.

For example, that jurisprudence *might* have emphasised how women from a vast sphere of countries within Asia-Pacific were abducted, falsely recruited, and enslaved in a sexualised nature. And during their enslavement, continually transferred, reposted, etcetera, meaning continual slave-trading and enslavement. And because we don't have that as part of the IMTFE jurisprudence, we have an absence of understanding of that gendered aspect of enslavement and slave-trading over a long period of time in relationship to armed conflict. That lack of jurisprudence regarding 'comfort women' shows us very early on what could have been 'same-side sexual violence', an issue that we don't really understand until the ICC's *Ntaganda* case.[5]

Grey: When we discussed *Ntaganda* back in 2018, you described that appeal judgment as a 'high point' in the ICC's evolving jurisprudence, and

[5] The *Naganda* case is one of the ICC cases from the situation in the Democratic Republic of Congo. For background on the case, see discussion of the DRC in the Introduction to this book (Chapter 2).

observed that 'it hasn't really hit the international criminal law consciousness yet'.[6]

[*Editorial note:* In 2017 in the *Ntaganda* case, the ICC Appeals Chamber confirmed that the rape and sexual enslavement of female child soldiers by their commanders could constitute war crimes under Article 8(2)(e)(vi) of the Rome Statute, even though the putative victims and perpetrators were part of the same military force. This issue was contentious because the defence had argued that a war crime necessarily involves violations against persons or property affiliated with the 'other side', as opposed to crimes committed against members of one's own military force.[7]]

Would it have taken until 2017 to reach this 'high point' if the Tokyo Tribunal had addressed the question of 'same-side sexual violence' back in the 1940s?

SELLERS: I believe that if we'd had jurisprudence regarding the 'comfort women', particularly those from Korea, which was a Japanese colony at the time, we would already have dispelled the myth that you can't have war crimes over your 'own' people over seventy years earlier.

GREY: And now the *Ntaganda* ruling has been picked up in Colombia too, so the idea that sexual crimes *within* a military force can be a war crime is starting to travel across time and space.[8] But as you said, this could have happened decades ago, had the Tokyo Tribunal looked at this issue.

SELLERS: In addition, the Tokyo Tribunal could have provided a valuable intersectional analysis had it examined the slave-trading and enslavement of 'comfort women'. We can see the very racialised nature of enslavement within this context. Some of the women were indigenous, from Okinawa, Taiwan, Timor, and Burma. Those women's treatment were not only among the worst, but those were the women that enlisted men could have access to. Whereas some of the women who were the daughters of colonisers in Indonesia, who were white European women, were abused by the officer corps of the Japanese army. So, this racialisation of the different comfort

6 R. Grey, *Prosecuting Sexual and Gender-Based Crimes at the International Criminal Court* (Cambridge: Cambridge University Press, 2019) 142.

7 P. Viseur Sellers, 'Ntaganda: Re-alignment of a Paradigm' in F. Pocar (ed.), *The Additional Protocols 40 Years Later* (Sanremo: International Institute of Humanitarian Law, 2018) 116–136; Grey, *supra* note 6, at 274–278.

8 See C. Laverty and D. de Vos, '"Ntaganda" in Colombia: Intra-Party Reproductive Violence at the Colombian Constitutional Court', *Opinio Juris*, 25 February 2020, available at http://opiniojuris.org/2020/02/25/ntaganda-in-colombia-intra-party-reproductive-violence-at-the-colombian-constitutional-court/.

women was part of the ideology of the perpetrators. We shouldn't be surprised; in the Asia-Pacific arena at that time, there was a highly racialised war. Japan was blatantly claiming racial superiority over the other countries in Asia and South-East Asia and Asia-Pacific.

There were issues of class too. The women and girls recruited for work purposes were from working families that not only needed the money, but that could 'allow' their daughters to go to a foreign place with the hopes of bringing back money. But in the IMTFE, we really lacked this kind of intersectional gender analysis of the crimes committed against the 'comfort women'. I think that we have to be very cognisant of the richness of the jurisprudence that is absent by not having had that as part of the foundational Tokyo judgment jurisprudence.

GREY: The judgment from the Tokyo Women's Tribunal in 2000 showed us what that intersectional analysis of crimes against the 'comfort women' might have looked like.

[*Editorial note:* After an extensive intersectional analysis, the Tokyo Women's Tribunal concluded: 'The Japanese military targeted women and girls primarily of subjugated populations viewed as inferior by Japanese Imperial culture, for the provision of forced sexual services because they were female and thus seen as disposable . . . The creation of the "comfort women" system reflects the intersection of discrimination based on both gender and race/ethnicity.'[9]]

And so do the chapters by Pryia Gopalan, Angela Mudukuti and Jarpa Dawuni on intersectionality in this book.[10] It's incredible to imagine how advanced intersectional gender analysis might be in international criminal law today if that legal interpretive approach had begun with the Tokyo Tribunal in the 1940s.

On the Ravensbrück Camp and Nuremberg Trials

SELLERS: I also want to look at the other absent jurisprudence from the European theatre. We know that the Ravensbrück camp in Germany detained females (I assume they were female), let's say women, mostly above eighteen, but there might have been some younger. Why were they detained in this camp that wasn't necessarily a death camp for the Jewish population, but was certainly

[9] Judgment, *The Prosecutors and the Peoples of the Asia-Pacific Region v. Hirohito Emperor Showa et al.*, Women's International War Crimes Tribunal for the Trial of Japan's Military Sexual Slavery, 4 December 2001, § 929.

[10] Gopalan, Chapter 7 in this book.

a detention camp that the National Socialist [Nazi] regime set up for females? Well, in Nazi ideology these women were outcasts, enemies of society. They were 'prostitutes', today we would say commercial sex workers, or considered to be lesbian, and therefore were not adding to the Nazi birth project of increasing the procreation of the Aryan race. They were women who might have been criminals under national penal law. All of these 'unsociable' female elements were gathered together at the detention camp. They were basically detained for not performing the expected gender roles of women in society, which is not examined in jurisprudence after the war.

That jurisprudence has not been examined to the extent that it could have been, given that some trials did occur regarding the Ravensbrück camp.[11] These trials mainly concerned the female guards employed at the camp. We have to ask ourselves, who were these female perpetrators? Some had already been female guards at domestic women's prisons, and some might have been recruited specifically for Ravensbrück. Therefore, you see the use of women to be guards over women who are considered to be outcasts. Among some of these female guards, it appears from the readings I've done, but not in the court transcripts, that some were lesbian women. It's an interesting choice by the National Socialist regime to deploy lesbians on the one hand as a productive part of society, to guard other women who were considered 'a-sociable', some of them for that same reason.

We really haven't explored those Ravensbrück trials to the commensurate extent that we've explored other subsequent cases from that period: the medical trial, the judges' trial,[12] and others tried in Nuremberg under Control Council Law 10. Those Control Council cases have entered the common knowledge, at least of those who want to be a little more nerdy about the Nuremberg proceedings. But we haven't focused on trials against women defendants or about female camps. We have lost a richness in potential jurisprudence, even with its own prejudices of the day, that might have allowed us to better understand the gender ideology that related to imprisonment, to crimes against humanity against a

[11] See M. J. Bazyler and F. M. Tuerkheimer, *Forgotten Trials of the Holocaust* (New York: New York University Press: 2014) 129–157.

[12] Known officially as *United States of America v. Karl Brandt et al. and United States of America v. Josef Altstötter et al.*, both prosecuted between 1946 and 1947 by an American military tribunal in Nuremberg under Control Council Law 10.

female German population that was attacked, thus persecuted, by German society.

If we looked more closely at the Ravensbrück cases, it also would inform how we understand the detention of women during periods of armed conflict later on. For example, when we come to Yugoslavia, we find the Omarska camp and other gender-separated camps, where females and males are detained separately. We would see a slight continuum of past conflicts. *It is horrific and terrible, but we would have places in our legal historical memory in which to slot the detention of women and help us understand this type of crime.*

On Gendered Deportation and Enslavement

SELLERS: The last thing I will say, coming up from the Nuremberg and the Tokyo era, is that the relationship between deportation and slave labour was never analysed to the extent it might have been. Those tribunals certainly look at enslavement under crimes against humanity, more so with Nuremberg. In fact, there is part of the Nuremberg judgment that talks about 500,000 women being deported into Germany to work as domestic labourers.[13] This idea of deporting into enslavement is, I think, another way of saying they were slave-traded. We don't have that terminology within the jurisprudence, but certainly it could have been a more apt description of this very gendered example of slave-trading and enslavement.

And so, that consideration of gendered deportation, slave-trading, and enslavement is also absent from our jurisprudential background. There was no examination of the experience of this huge number of women being placed in German homes. As we know from historical experiences, they likely faced the kind of harsh treatment and sexual violence that maids and domestic workers confront when they're isolated in private houses, particularly by persons who are considered their enemy at this point in time. So, this is individualised domestic labour in relationship to armed conflict. It's not quite (imprisonment) detention, but it's a different type of framework. That type of framework might help us to understand more about the experience of enslaved Yazidi females, who have been placed in individualised homes today as 'domestic workers', and whose enslavement is also sexualised.

[13] See 'International Military Tribunal: Judgment and Sentence, October 1, 1946' 41(1) *American Journal of International Law* (1947) 172–333, at 330.

On Enslavement and the ICTY

Grey: I wrote down something you said before, 'the richness of the jurisprudence that is absent'. Building on that idea, what do you see as absent from the jurisprudence of the ICTY, the tribunal where you began to actively shape the international jurisprudence on sexual and gender-based crimes? Speaking about jurisprudence that we don't have, whose absence we're haunted by, we've previously talked about the ICTY's *Kunarac* case, in which you were on the prosecution trial team. Could you take us through your thoughts on that case?

[*Editorial note:* In 2001 in the *Kunarac* case, the ICTY rendered its first conviction of rape as a crime against humanity. The case also broke new legal ground by recognising that the detention by male Serb forces of Bosnian Muslim women and girls in homes in the Foča area of Bosnia and Herzegovina, where they were subjected to forced domestic and sexual servitude, amounted to the crime against humanity of enslavement. These historic convictions for rape and enslavement were upheld on appeal in 2002.[14]]

Sellers: Yes, I wanted to give this background, so I could finally elaborate upon the ICTY jurisprudence and the *Kunarac* case. Months ago, we were speaking about what's missing from the slavery jurisprudence. In doing that, I realised that the absences didn't start with *Kunarac*, and they probably won't end with *Kunarac*. I needed to recall the beginning, to the 1940s, to the foundations of international criminal law.

Within the ICTY jurisprudence, by the time the *Kunarac* case is delivered, we have already received the *Furundžija* and the *Čelebići* cases on sexual violence. There was an understanding from these cases that rape can be categorised as torture under the grave breaches of the Geneva Conventions, and also the customary-based war crime of outrages upon personal dignity. So, we're positioning ourselves within this 'rape as torture' compendium. Before that, there seemed to be a binary understanding of crimes against male and female. Males came under torture; women came under rape. False legal hierarchies were set up. We thought that if crimes against women could come under torture, that would show that we're as

[14] See K. D. Askin, 'Prosecuting Wartime Rape and Other Gender-Related Crimes under International Law: Extraordinary Advances, Enduring Obstacles' 21(2) *Berkeley Journal of International Law* (2003) 288–349, at 333–341.

important as men. So, there was this interest in linking rape and torture together.

At that time that we're investigating and drafting the indictment for *Kunarac*, we understand that *Čelebići* is coming out. There's a bit more comfort with understanding that rape, when done for certain purposes, can be torture. However, in *Kunarac*, we have evidence showing something *in addition* is happening to these females who were taken from the detention facility and into the soldier's homes, to be abused for weeks or months, which we eventually charged as their enslavement. I was legal advising on the case. It took some time to understand that there was something in addition to, if not more than, torture and rape. That in *Kunarac*, enslavement is happening, particularly when facts are being revealed of trading girls, and sales, and acts of that nature. *If we had had that World War II jurisprudence, that would have popped out at us without a blink.* We would have gone straight to charging enslavement, as opposed to having to go through the process of convincing colleagues, and making sure we could convince the judges.

At the time, this option [of charging forced sexual and domestic labour as enslavement] was completely off the radar of most of the feminists. We may make analogies by asking ourselves today: *what is off the radar, what can't we see because there hasn't been a precedent?*

On Slave-Trading

SELLERS: So, going forward with *Kunarac*, we started to better understand the choosing, gathering, and transferring of females for sexual violence, until they were reduced to a situation of enslavement. But we had missed legally categorising the transfers, the instances of trading and selling women, as slave-trading, which is a different crime to enslavement. Slave-trading is the precursory conduct that can lead to enslavement: the earlier steps of selecting, relocating, and sometimes transacting of people, so that they can be reduced to a situation of enslavement.

That understanding could have been reached via precedent if we'd better understood at Nuremberg what the deportation of 500,000 women into slave labour meant, or at Tokyo, what the transfer on Japanese wartime frigates or battleships meant for the 'comfort women'. We would have followed that legal logic when interpreting Article 3 of the Yugoslav Statute, which was not an exhaustive list of war crimes. Rather, it allowed the pursuit of a war crime as long as it was a serious violation of the laws and customs of war, and one could have individual criminal responsibility for it. It could be a war crime in treaty, or in customary international law. Therefore, both slavery and the slave trade could have been, or *should* have been, prosecuted under Article 3 of the ICTY Statute. This would have been following Rule 94 of the ICRC study of customary law.[15]

So those precedents also are missing from the ICTY. We don't have the customary law basis of slavery and [the] slave trade as war crimes inflicted upon the Foča women in the *Kunarac* case. The evidence was there, but neither the prosecution made submissions nor judges made observations of that nature in *obiter dicta*, which could have also clarified the issue. What they *did* say is that one does not need the sale of a person in order to prove enslavement. Now, we might go further and clarify that the sale of a person could indicate the war crime of slave-trading, but not necessarily enslavement. There were so many ways that this could have been clarified by submissions, or by adjudication. Instead, we have this absence in *Kunarac*. You also see that absence in the *Stanković* indictment.

[*Editorial note:* Like the *Kunarac* case, the *Stanković* case concerned the abuse of Bosnian Muslim women and girls by male Serb forces in the Foča area. Some of these girls were just twelve or fourteen years old. The prosecution alleged that defendant Radovan Stanković was in charge of an abandoned house owned by a man named Karaman. According to the indictment, Stanković 'not only stocked Karaman's House with Muslim girls and women so that Serb soldiers and other Serb men could sexually assault them, but also kept tight control on their movements'.[16] He was charged with the crimes against humanity of rape and enslavement, and the war crimes of rape and outrages on personal dignity, but there were no charges for the war crimes of enslavement or slave-trading. The case was referred from the ICTY to the Bosnia and Herzegovina State Court, where he was convicted of the crimes against humanity of enslavement, imprisonment, torture, and rape.[17]]

[15] This 2005 study by the ICRC is based on an extensive analysis of state practice in relation to the laws of war. Rule 94 recognises that under customary international law, slavery and the slave trade in all their forms are prohibited. See J.-M. Henckaerts and L. Doswald-Beck, *International Committee of the Red Cross: Customary International Humanitarian Law (Vol. I)* (Cambridge: Cambridge University Press, 2005) 327.

[16] Third Amended Indictment, *Radovan Stanković* (IT-96-23/2-I), ICTY, 8 December 2003, 'The Charges', § 3.

[17] K. Vigneswaran, 'Annex B: Charges and Outcomes in ICTY Cases Involving Sexual Violence' in S. Brammertz and M. Jarvis (eds.), *Prosecuting Conflict-Related Sexual Violence at the ICTY* (Oxford: Oxford University Press, 2016) 429–481, at 476.

I maintain that this missing jurisprudence has influenced, or, I like the word you used earlier, has 'haunted' our approach to the subsequent ICC cases of *Katanga*, *Ongwen*, and *Ntaganda*. It's clear in those cases that the abduction of boys and girls into militia groups was really the precursory conduct, the slave-trading conduct, in order to reduce them to enslavement.

On the Rome Statute's Silences around Enslavement and Slave-Trading

Grey: Listening to you just now, I had another thought about the ongoing impact of absences in past jurisprudence. As you've written about before, enslavement and the slave trade are not listed as war crimes under the Rome Statute. It doesn't appear that the drafters deliberately considered and excluded these crimes, it just seems to have slipped people's attention at Rome. I wonder, if there had been strong jurisprudence from Nuremberg, Tokyo, and the ICTY about enslavement and slave-trading as war crimes, maybe this wouldn't have been forgotten at Rome, and we'd now see those war crimes in Article 8 of the ICC Statute.

Sellers: Yes, I think they would have been in the Rome Statute because the jurisprudence from Tokyo, and particularly from Nuremberg, is just so pivotal. What also could have occurred to encourage the placement of these war crimes in the Rome Statute is if they were enumerated in the ICTR Statute. In 1977, in Article 4 of Additional Protocol II, there is a prohibition of slavery and the slave trade in all its forms.[18] Those prohibitions were not picked up in the ICTR Statute, although other parts of Protocol II were included. Maybe, there was a presumption that the Rwanda conflict was about genocide, rape, and so forth, but it wasn't about slavery and slave-trading, so there was no need for their inclusion. In any case, I think *that* absence in the ICTR Statute contributed to these war crimes not even being concertedly considered during the drafting of the Rome Statute.

Grey: In your previous answer, you mentioned the ICC's *Katanga*, *Ntaganda*, and *Ongwen* cases as examples where the transfer of people into enslavement could have been classified as slave-trading,

[18] Protocol Additional to the Geneva Conventions of 12 August 1949, and relating to the Protection of Victims of Non-International Armed Conflicts (Protocol II), 8 June 1977 (entered into force 7 December 1978), Art. 4(2)(f).

if that were a war crime in the Rome Statute. Could you elaborate on your reading of those cases?

Sellers: Right, I'm using *Katanga and Chui* as an illustration.[19] The Trial Chamber seems to have correctly adjudicated that sexual violence occurred; it was committed by the militia groups that Katanga and Chui were involved in, and female civilians were taken from one place to another. Here is where we get our preliminary jurisprudence on the 'sexual slavery' provision of the Rome Statute. But we can look at the facts prior to the sexual slavery, which is not attributed to the accused. Once again there is evidence of choosing, of transporting, of distributing women and girls. If we'd had the jurisprudence on slave-trading that I talked about before, we could have understood this evidence from *Katanga* as analogous to what happened to the 'comfort women', and what happened to the women in Foča. The judges might have characterised, in *obiter dicta*, those acts as slave-trading.

It's also a notable gap in *Ongwen*.[20] There, the Trial Chamber does a very thorough job of understanding the idea of abducting civilians to go into an enslaved workforce, and that within those civilians, the boys are later reduced to child soldiers, another form of enslavement. The girls are reduced to what is called '*ting tings*' [babysitters/domestic servants] if they are pre-menstrual, or to 'bush wives' if they are post-puberty and targeted to be sexually violated immediately. Now, looking back, we understand that the Trial Chamber is deliberating about their abduction and further distribution. These boys and girls were slave-traded until they were enslaved as child soldiers or as *tings tings* or as bush wives. When the fighter in charge of those enslaved children died, sometimes the children were slave-traded again. It perfectly fits into the 1926 and 1956 definition of slave-trading,[21] which can occur as a precursor to enslavement, but also subsequently, whenever enslaved persons are taken to new situations of enslavement. If we had the jurisprudential precedents that I spoke about earlier, and if that had led to the

[19] The *Katanga and Chui* case is one of the ICC cases from the situation in the Democratic Republic of Congo. For background on the case, see discussion of the DRC in the Introduction, in this book (Chapter 2).

[20] The *Ongwen* case is the ICC's only case on public record from the situation in Uganda. For background on the case, see discussion of Uganda in the Introduction in this book (Chapter 2).

[21] League of Nations, Convention to Suppress the Slave Trade and Slavery, 60 LNTS 253, 25 September 1926 (entered into force 9 March 1927), Art. 1(2); Supplementary Convention on the Abolition of Slavery, the Slave Trade, and Institutions and Practices Similar to Slavery, 266 UNS 3, 7 September 1956 (entered into force 30 April 1957), Art. 7(c).

inclusion of slave-trading as a war crime and as a crime against humanity in the Rome Statute, we could have understood this evidence in *Ongwen* as the slave-trading of children. *Ntaganda* gives us similar situations where children are abducted, kidnapped, transferred, and distributed.

GREY: And in your view, what are the stakes of the fact that slave-trading is not listed as a crime in the Rome Statute, that there isn't a legal lexicon to characterise that precursory conduct as 'slave-trading'. Could you explain, why does that matter?

SELLERS: That is a good question. One could say 'it really doesn't matter because there was enough other evidence that led to convictions', or 'it really doesn't matter because there are other important precedents set by those ICC cases', or 'why don't we just call that "other inhumane acts?"' But I would say those are insufficient answers for three reasons.

First, if we could return to the women placed in Nazi households as domestic workers, or to the 'comfort women' or to the women in Foča, and decidedly describe what happened to them, I think it was just as terrifyingly criminal to be chosen and relocated, prior to any of the enslavement occurring. Those very acts – placing me on your battleship and transferring me from Okinawa to the Philippines – those are criminal acts and that should have been characterised as slave-trading. I was in essence a victim/survivor of an international crime in that very moment; but it is a crime that international courts have chosen to ignore. So, from the victim/survivor point of view, to say that we'll examine enslavement but not slave-trading really is not to undertake responsibility as a judicial actor in relationship to the survivor. So, the first reason is that we're denying the survivor recognition of the panoply of crimes that were committed against them.

Second, international criminal law has evolved to become a combination of [Continental] civil law and Anglo-Saxon law. Within that civil law aspect, the judges are to be presented with as full a rendition of the criminal conduct as possible. For example, in the Yugoslav context, we didn't omit the detention crimes of someone. If they're killed in detention, we did not only focus on the murder. We'd look at the whole sequence: they were forcefully transferred, they were detained, and then the killing occurred. No one would say 'Let's just get the killings'. Likewise, one has to question why, when it comes to enslavement, particularly of women and children, do we jump over slave-trading? What is the impact of jumping over that crime, especially from a gender point of view?

The third rationale is that it is completely contrary to the idea of using the entire panoply of available legal tools, if we are really serious about atrocity crimes. Right now, there is a lot of discussion about use of the crime of aggression from customary international law, since it can't come before the ICC. It shows the importance of understanding the legal tools that are available, even the customary legal tools. So, skipping over or ignoring other legal tools, like the customary international crime of slave-trading, seems discordant with the project of access to justice, to judicial remedies, and, eventually, to reparations.

One could say that it's only because the slave-trade jurisprudence is absent, as you and I have discussed. Well, that's still not a reason for not utilising customary international law, or indeed for amending the Rome Statute to insert slave-trading under Article 7 as a crime against humanity and slavery and the slave trade under Article 8 as war crimes. These are among our earliest international crimes. They continue to haunt parts of society and are among the most egregious long-term crimes that states have perpetrated. They should not be overlooked.

On the Bifurcation of 'Enslavement' and 'Sexual Slavery'

GREY: I wanted to ask you now about two crimes that *are* in the Rome Statute: 'sexual slavery' and 'enslavement'. As you know, there's been a tendency in ICC cases to bring charges of 'sexual slavery' where sexual violence happens to a person who is enslaved. The option of charging that as 'sexual slavery' didn't exist before the ICC, because previous tribunals didn't have that crime in their statutes. Therefore, they used 'enslavement', as you did in *Kunarac*. A lot of feminist scholars see it as a win that the Rome Statute recognises both 'sexual slavery' and 'enslavement', and the Women's Caucus pushed for this at Rome. But as you've written about before, this isn't necessarily a step forward in all respects. It implies that sexual and reproductive violence are separate to 'enslavement', when in reality, losing control over one's sexuality and reproductive capacity have always been part of what it means to be enslaved.[22] Can you say a few words

[22] P. Viseur Sellers, 'Wartime Female Slavery: Enslavement?' 44 *Cornell International Law Journal* (2011) 115–142; P. Viseur Sellers and J. Getgen Kestenbaum, 'The International Crimes of Slavery and the Slave Trade: A Feminist Critique' in I. Rosenthal, V. Oosterveld, and S. SáCouto (eds.), *Gender and International Criminal Law* (Oxford: Oxford University Press, 2022) 157–186.

on this? What is *lost*, in your view, when sexualised enslavement is charged as 'sexual slavery' rather than 'enslavement'?

Sellers: Under the Rome Statute we have the crime of sexual slavery. In many ways, that was a feminist victory. That victory was very much influenced by the *Kunarac* case. We'd brought the first indictment (which included the enslavement charge) before the Rome Conference preparatory meetings concluded. The *Kunarac* appeals jurisprudence was rendered after. When you look at how enslavement is defined under customary international law, in that case, the judges opine about the psychological control over the person, the physical control, the control of the sexual access to the person, and so forth. Thus, the crime of enslavement has many indicia of how the powers attaching to the rights of ownership were exercised over the person. At that time period, there was very much of a fixation of the sexualised nature of the enslavement of the Foča women. *That sexualised component of the crime of enslavement became, in some manner, reduced into sexual slavery in the Rome Statute, as opposed to being enlarged into understanding that enslavement is sexualised.*

In the Rome Statute, the provision of sexual slavery highlights certain sexual acts and *actually swallows up the wider enslavement, including other sexualised acts of enslavement.* The elements of 'sexual slavery' are that someone is exercising powers of ownership over the person, *and* causing the person to engage in 'acts of a sexual nature'. In essence, sexual slavery has the proverbial tail wagging the dog. Historically, enslavement usually involved sexual harms. So, I advance that we need to recapture the conceptualisation of the sexualised nature of 'enslavement' and eliminate the provision on 'sexual slavery'.

Even as we examine sexualised enslavement today, being held out for an 'act of a sexual nature' is a reduction of what enslaved persons undergo. The current evidence of the enslavement of women and children, whether it's Yazidis, or in ICC cases, we can understand that sexualised enslavement can mean that a person has powers attaching to any or all of the rights of ownership even without being caused to engage in an 'act of a sexual nature'. For example, in the *Ongwen* case, the women who were subjected to forced pregnancy were all enslaved. But being pregnant is not seen as being caused to engage in an 'act of a sexual nature', so forced pregnancy was not charged as part of the sexual slavery. Likewise, the *ting ting* girls who were groomed as future wives, but were pre-menstrual, and who had not yet been raped, did not comprise part of the charges of sexual slavery either. Nevertheless, they endured sexualised enslavement because they *were* sexualised. Even while they were pre-menstrual, their enslavement was sexualised. They were guarded and watched to see what their physical sexual development would be, so that they could then be redistributed, that is slave-traded, as 'bush wives' when the time came. I think that boy soldiers are sexually enslaved also. They're told when they're allowed to rape, or be awarded a 'wife'.

Grey: I see your point. The crime of 'sexual slavery' as currently defined requires proof of an 'act of a sexual nature'. But there are ways that enslaved people are sexualised, even if they haven't been subjected to rape, or groping, etcetera, because their captivity is sexualised in other ways.

Sellers: Absolutely. And let me give you another historical example. When examining practices in what is referred to as the East African slave trade or Arab slave trade, very often boys under eighteen were slave-traded into the harems of the Ottoman empire. During a stage of the slave trade, these youthful males were castrated. The official word is gelded. Their enslavers wanted males whose physical reproductive system was neutered in order to interact with and guard the females of the harem, who also were sexually enslaved. So, in essence, both males and the females endured a sexualised enslavement. But one couldn't say these males would be victims under 'sexual slavery' in the ICC's definition, because they were not caused to engage in an 'act of a sexual nature' while enslaved as eunuchs.

On Feminist Judging

Grey: I have just loved what you've brought to this conversation, which is the idea of how a gap in the jurisprudence back in the 1940s can continue to limit our understanding of sexual and gender-based crimes. We've been talking mainly about the crimes most relevant to your current ICC advisory role, being slave-trading and enslavement. But your idea holds true for other crimes as well.

My final question is about what feminist or gender-sensitive judging means to you. In a way this whole interview answers that question, by thinking about how judges could have been more gender-sensitive decades ago, and how that missing jurisprudence makes it even harder for judges to fill in those gaps now. But is there anything else you would like to add to that?

Sellers: I think if we start with the premise that judgments are supposed to render justice, then a feminist lens has actually enlarged our understanding of what justice is. A feminist judgment really centres the human being in their complexity to make sure that that human receives justice. As with many social movements – the movement for ability or disability, or the movement for the environment – they allow other human beings, who might not be involved in those movements, a fuller expression of their ability to enjoy rights.

5

From Feminist Reimaginings to the Field

Reflections from an International Criminal Lawyer

Angela Mudukuti in conversation with Louise Chappell

INTRODUCTION

CHAPPELL: Angela, many thanks for agreeing to share your range of experiences as a practitioner in international criminal law [ICL] with us.

Can I start by you telling me about what inspired you to become an international criminal lawyer, and what positions have you held in this field?

MUDUKUTI: Thanks, Louise. I grew up in Zimbabwe and, at the time, it was still a racist and patriarchal society. And so, being a black woman, you find yourself at the bottom of the hierarchy. And, even as a young child, you see how people who look like you are treated. And so, from the very beginning, there was that desire, impetus, and that motivation to change things and to be a positive part of that change, and I felt like law was an empowering tool to do that. I felt very strongly about being a lawyer and being able to defend the rights of people who look like me and other people who are marginalised and not treated fairly in society. And that's where it all started. I decided to study law as an undergraduate degree, and then I did a masters in international criminal law and spent a brief time in private practice in Zimbabwe. After that I was lucky enough to get an internship at the International Criminal Court, back in the day when they still had paid internships. That was a truly formative experience because it opened my eyes to the world of international criminal law and reaffirmed all my choices, as far as wanting to be in human rights and international criminal law.

After my internship, I was retained by the Court. I worked within the Office of the Prosecutor and learnt a great deal about how international organisations work and the challenges that come with doing this kind of work. It was interesting and exciting to be at what I envisioned then as the pinnacle of international criminal law. But I also knew it would be very valuable to build more domestic experience and to work directly with affected communities as part of civil society. Working at the Southern Africa Litigation Centre, which is the Johannesburg-based human-rights organisation, provided such an opportunity. I ran the International Criminal Justice programme, and what we were doing there was strategic litigation using international criminal law domestically. Using domestic frameworks to bring international justice is very important because I feel international criminal law cannot just happen at the ICC or at the tribunals: it needs to happen at the domestic level as well, otherwise the principle of complementarity means nothing and the sustainability of the system remains in question. So, working at that level, I was able to work on universal jurisdiction cases, including for crimes against humanity committed in Zimbabwe, to be investigated and prosecuted in South Africa. Also, the attempts to arrest former Sudanese president Omar al-Bashir when he was in South Africa – that was one of my cases as well. And so, using international law at the domestic level, making it a reality, and making it palpable, tangible, and practical, was at the core of my work at the Southern Africa Litigation Centre. I also had the honour of working with the late Professor Cherif Bassiouni at his institute in Siracusa, Italy. And, at that point, we were writing a report on the human rights violations perpetrated by the Gaddafi forces and the rebels during the time of the conflict. My role was to assist with the IHL [international humanitarian law]/ICL analysis of those crimes in the context of this report. And it was, again, just a wonderful opportunity to put everything I'd learnt and experienced into practice, and to apply it to a new situation, and also to work in a situation where the violations were ongoing. Working with Professor Cherif Bassiouni who was, of course, just full of knowledge and insight and experience, was an incredible experience, one that I'm very grateful for. Since then, I've worked with many other civil society organisations, for example: Human Rights Watch, Open Society Foundation – and with both Human Rights Watch and Open Society Foundation the role was multifaceted, but one of the key things was institutional reform at the ICC. Because, of course, the ICC has had its struggles, it's not a perfect institution, and civil society is very proactively involved in trying to make sure we have the most efficient and effective court possible. That included looking at issues such as workplace harassment, bullying, the way in which officials are elected at the ICC, gender balance, geographical balance. Because, ultimately, we need institutions like the ICC to be in peak form internally, to better position themselves to fulfil their mandate. So, it was great to work in that context as well and, having been at the ICC, I knew how things worked on the inside. Working on the outside to improve the inside was a great experience. It was also an opportunity to remain constructively critical as a supporter of the Court, as a person who wants the best for the Court.

Over the course of my career, I have also been engaged in capacity-building: training investigators and prosecutors on how to best investigate and prosecute international crimes within their domestic contexts. I did this among other things at the Wayamo Foundation, where we were training prosecutors and investigators in several African countries – Nigeria, Kenya, Tanzania, Rwanda – and it was particularly interesting, again, because it was centred on this idea of making international justice sustainable, which means domestic prosecutors and investigators have to be equipped to do the job, otherwise it's very difficult to make progress. Working with different legal cultures, different legal traditions was particularly valuable because you have a much better appreciation of the constraints within each system. And so knowing that and how to best navigate these constraints depending on the situation was very helpful and also just a reality check as far as what happens at the international level and what happens at the domestic level, and how to marry those two, and how it is sometimes very difficult to do that. But finding ways was part of the role, and I enjoyed doing that work. I've been an independent consultant for the last couple of years and working with different organisations on different issues, including accountability for sexual and gender-based violence, and that's included amicus briefs at the ICC and before domestic courts. And also, speaking out and doing a lot of research and writing on decolonising international criminal justice and human rights, and reconsidering how we work within this framework that, unfortunately, does not acknowledge the inherent bias that's been built in over time. And so, in a nutshell – sorry, a very big nutshell – that's basically what I've been doing with my time.

ON INTERSECTIONALITY

CHAPPELL: That's incredible, Angela – such a diverse and rich range of experiences which very few people have. So many people in ICL get channelled into silos, either at the international or domestic level, but crossing over between them as you have done doesn't happen so often. You've really been able to see the key touchpoints across the entire ICL: the system, understanding where things link together and where they are falling short.

So, Angela, given your breadth of experience in the international criminal justice field, what's your view about the body of law that we have to work with: customary law, case law, jurisprudence of the different tribunals, and the Rome Statute, as it's been interpreted? Is it adequate for addressing the intersectional nature of atrocity and, if not, what would you suggest is needed to transform the ICL system to better recognise intersectionality?

MUDUKUTI: Intersectionality is key and it is built in, in some parts of the body of law you've mentioned. For example, the Rome Statute, Article 21 (3) talks about intersectionality – not that it names it explicitly – but that's the way the principle has been applied. And I think it makes a lot of sense. The current bodies of law that we have, they're obviously very useful and have been instrumental to bringing justice for core international crimes. But I do think that there is a lot more that can be done and, by that, I mean to be truly intersectional in our approach we need to understand that these laws, these institutions, were not built in a vacuum, they were built within a particular political and geopolitical dynamic which, unfortunately, has always been colonial in nature. And so, I think we need to understand that and understand how it's affected the jurisprudence, and how it's affected the laws we have today. The way in which we can understand that is to look at other disciplines. For example, third-world approaches to law or critical race theory, and all the different types of feminism. There's a very nice quote from Angela Davis. She says: 'Feminism involves so much more than gender equality. It involves so much more than gender.'[1] And this is exactly what we need to understand: within each of these disciplines, there are multiple lenses through which we can look at them. And I think international criminal law needs to be looked at through these

[1] A. Davis, *Freedom Is a Constant Struggle: Ferguson, Palestine, and the Foundations of a Movement* (Chicago: Haymarket Books, 2016) no page numbers.

different lenses. We need to understand that these disciplines bring value that will ultimately help us fully understand the intersectional nature of atrocity crimes. So I think we need to be more expansive in our thinking there.

I also think that we need to understand that the racial and the geographic makeup of these institutions – the ICC in particular, for example – leaves a lot to be desired. Right now at the International Criminal Court, out of the 473 professional staff at the ICC, 256 of them come from the Western Europe and Others group, otherwise known as the WEOG. It's essentially the Global North. That's more than half of the professional staff at the ICC who come from one of five regions. At the leadership level, nationals from WEOG also hold the most senior positions: currently a staggering 55.6 per cent of the most senior D1 positions; and high percentages across the second and third most senior roles, with 72 per cent of P5 positions and 56 per cent of P4 positions.

Given that we're talking about the coloniality of this field, having one group of people predominantly white, predominantly from the Global North, be responsible or in charge of these organisations, I think is detrimental. International institutions like the ICC have to be diverse. We have to have people from all regions. The system recognises five regions. We need to see that on staff. In reflecting on these worrying statistics, one has to think about how that came to be and one of the sources is an actual ASP [Assembly of States Parties] resolution, which states, in relation to staffing, 'the Court's selection of staff in the Professional category is guided by a system of desirable ranges based on that of the United Nations'.[2] The desirable ranges, or in other words percentages, are calculated by considering three factors: the total number of state parties, a state's financial contribution to the budget, and its population size. These factors are attributed weights that determine the final outcome.

At present, substantial weight is given to membership (40 per cent), which is equal for each state party, the greatest importance is given to the state's contribution (55 per cent), and the final 5 per cent is determined according to the population size of the country. Therefore, your state's financial contribution affects staffing positions at the ICC. I think this is hugely problematic

[2] ICC-ASP/1/Res. 10, 9 September 2002.

because it can result in the exclusion of those people who do not come from states that, for whatever reason, provide less money to the ICC. And that results in the skewed dynamic where most of the Court staff members come from Western Europe. I don't think that's a sustainable system. It needs to change.

The staff composition affects how cases are approached, how investigators engage with victims and survivors, how they interpret and collect evidence. This affects how the case is framed, presented, and brought before the judges and then, ultimately, on the bench itself, it has to be a diverse bench because how they render their judgments is influenced by their own legal and cultural background, and other factors such as race or their own intersecting identities, for example. We can't divorce these things. These things all influence the jurisprudence that comes out of the Court. So, my message is always one for diversity and not just racial diversity, not just geographical diversity, but also, of course, gender. At the ICC right now, unfortunately, we're still stuck in the two binaries. We only have statistics for men and women, there's nothing else, which is something that needs to be addressed but, even when we look at those statistics alone, at the ICC now, in terms of professional staff, it's roughly 48 per cent female and then the rest is male, which may not seem so bad but the problem is, when you dig deeper, you see that the leadership positions are predominantly held by men. And so what we have at the ICC is an organisation that is predominantly led by men from the Global North, who are usually white. Now, there are exceptions to this of course, but that's the general situation, and that has to change because we need a system that is fully representative and inclusive because all of this affects intersectionality. Intersectionality includes looking at who is doing the work and where they come from, and I think that's essential because it affects how they go about the work; and if we're actually going to deliver justice for core international crimes we have to be intersectional in our approach.

CHAPPELL: That's so important to bring that together, both the physical beings who are there as well as the way that anyone thinks about intersectionality . . .

MUDUKUTI: Louise, can I also just add: I think the primary thing we should all be focused on is understanding the lived experience of the victims and survivors. And, if everybody who is engaging with victims, witnesses, and survivors comes from one group, one region out of five regions, there's a lot that could be missed: cultural nuances, subtleties. And, if we fully want to understand the nature of atrocity, we have to fully understand the intersectional harm endured by victims and witnesses, and I just think we could all do more to improve this.

GEOGRAPHICAL AND GENDER REPRESENTATION INTEGRAL TO JUDICIAL INTEGRITY

Chappell: I agree with you Angela. I think you've really touched on a critical point there. I'd like to turn now to your publications and work on judicial integrity and independence and about the nomination and election of judges at the ICC. What reflections do you have about the composition of the bench in particular and the skills, qualifications, qualities, that are needed to be a judge at the ICC? And what are some of the ways to ensure that we get the most qualified judges possible?

Mudukuti: I think the first point is one that I made earlier, which is about the diversity of the bench; geographical representation on the bench. At this point, again, the bench is very heavy as far as WEOG representation is concerned. Currently, six out of eighteen judges are from WEOG. Before the 2020 election, the women were greatly outnumbered. There were six female judges and twelve men. Thankfully, that's changed now. We do have gender parity on the bench, which is wonderful, and it's taken long enough but I think these two metrics need to be considered as we look at the bench and the composition of the bench because, as I mentioned, it affects how international criminal jurisprudence develops. For example, we all know the influence Judge Navi Pillay has had on accountability for sexual violence when she sat on the ICTR [International Criminal Tribunal for Rwanda] bench.

I think we need to look at the responsibility state parties to the Rome Statute bear, because they nominate judicial candidates through their national nominations system and then they elect judges. They need to nominate women and men, not just men. They also need to conduct elections in a way that recognises the need for geographical representation. So I think the burden there is on state parties to rectify that system. As far as the qualities, qualifications, and skills are concerned, I think the Rome Statute does have some good criteria, including high moral character.

But I think there is a lack of specificity, for example, to be a P4 at the ICC, you need a certain number of years of experience before you're even considered for the job. For judges, there is no specified number of relevant years of legal experience. As a consequence, the levels of experience on the bench are inconsistent. So, I think we need more specificity and detail as far as the qualifications and skills requirement for judicial elections. But, again, this is something that state parties need to negotiate and agree on, and that hasn't always been easy. There's a lot of work to be done there.

Chappell: Do you think there's an appetite in the Assembly of States Parties to think about either adding more qualifications or even just paying more attention to the quality of the candidates? Have you noticed any moves in that direction at all?

Mudukuti: I think there are some states which recognise that this has been a problem and they're eager to change it. There's been a lot of discussion on improving national nomination processes because national nomination processes are how we get judges in the first place. States will put forward candidates, and in some states there is no process. You get nominated when you have friends in high places at the time regardless of your qualifications. Open Society Justice Initiative has done some great research in this area.
In some states, the national nomination procedure is not always merit-based and being part of the political elite has been the key to being nominated. There has been no process to vet you or to check your qualifications, or to check that you're the best person for the job. There are states which have shown leadership on this and have begun to change the national nomination processes, and are trying to encourage other states to do the same. But ultimately, I think there is a reluctance that, I wouldn't say is malicious, but I think, for some states, it's a case of prioritising. They don't see this as an urgent issue that needs to be resolved. Other states feel it's convenient that there is a quick and easy 'process' to nominate someone, so to be asked to go back to a national nomination process and to tell the public how you appointed someone, and what your process is, is seen as a nuisance and an inconvenience. But now the Advisory Committee on the Nomination of Judges plays a far more active role and they do request states to explain their national nomination process. Some states have done that, other states have not. There is potential and there is movement but it is going to

take some time until everybody feels like this is a priority and that the system should be standardised.

Chappell: That's so interesting. I do think that the committee's work is important but, as you say, there's a lot of reasons why states might make particular appointments and don't want the Assembly or the ICC getting involved in domestic affairs, necessarily. So, it's tough.

ON CIVIL SOCIETY AND ADVANCING GENDER AND RACIAL JUSTICE

Chappell: My next question for you is, given your experience working in civil society organisations in the international criminal justice field, what role do you think these organisations have in holding the ICC and other international tribunals to account, to advocate particularly for gender and racial justice, including on the bench? In your view, what could these organisations do better to advance these goals?

Mudukuti: I've worked as a member of civil society on exactly these issues and I can tell you that civil society organisations do a great deal in holding the ICC to account, including advocating for internal reform, for example, better workplace conditions and the eradication of discrimination and harassment, gender and geographical balance, as well as pushing the Court to more effectively execute its mandate. I think it's very important work. Civil society's been very active for many years in different ways, on institutional reform issues, but at the end of the day, it's about state parties changing the system. It's about state parties prioritising gender balance on the bench, gender balance at the ICC, and geographical balance. And it's the work of civil society to try and convince states to do that. But I think it's also on states to recognise the urgency and the need to change this because, as we've seen in the past, the ICC has been accused of targeting a certain group in its investigations and prosecutions. Whilst I think that accusation and resulting discussions lack nuance and have been oversimplified and abused by those seeking to escape accountability for grave crimes, the point is, it is a perception and having staff composed predominately of people from the WEOG region is not helping and ought to be addressed.

However, I should note that we have seen some important shifts: for example, the Office of the Prosecutor has diversified the geography of its docket – especially if you look at preliminary examinations. Five years ago they were mostly African situations and now that has shifted. So, there is a recognition of the need to geographically diversify the ICC's docket, as far as situations under investigation or prosecution.

But ultimately, state parties are responsible for championing issues of internal institutional reform because they have power as an Assembly to make important changes. So, it's not just up to civil society; I think we need to also acknowledge the role that state parties play in this, and the influence they have.

CHAPPELL: An important issue you're raising here is the importance for civil society not only to be operating at the international level in and around the Court but at the domestic level as well. It reinforces the point that we need to be working at multiple levels at once, to make sure that states are sensitive enough to issues of diversity and representation when they get to the floor of the ASP.

So, the next question: What do you think is required for judges at the ICC to acknowledge and act on the intersectional qualities of international crimes and their survivors?

MUDUKUTI: I think this ties up nicely with the first question. I would say that just an understanding that there are different disciplines that can inform how we approach international criminal justice, so looking at third-world approaches to international law, critical race theory, feminism, improves intersectional judging. I think it's very important for judges to be open to those disciplines as a lens. Obviously, at the end of the day they have to write a judgment that's founded on international criminal law and human rights law, having carefully weighed the evidence; but how you view the law, I think, can be positively influenced when you are aware of other schools of thought and the context in which the ICC and international criminal justice were born. So, I think knowledge of and an openness to understanding and appreciating what those different disciplines or schools of thought could bring is useful. I think judges also need to be open to continuous learning and approach it with humility. There is this perception – and I've seen this at the domestic level and international level, in all my capacity-building efforts – that you cannot have a workshop for judges and call it 'capacity-building' because some judges believe that is inappropriate given their level of seniority. So, you call it a 'retreat' instead, and that's fine, but the point is continuous learning for everybody is not a bad idea. The ICC does have annual retreats for judges, so I think there are valuable opportunities to augment the skills and experience judges already have.

I think the admission of amicus briefs is a practice that should continue. No one judge is an expert on absolutely every facet of the law: that's impossible. But, when you allow amicus briefs, you're giving other experts the opportunity to act as friend of the Court and provide insights that could positively contribute to the jurisprudence.

We saw it recently with the Ongwen Appeals Chamber process where they admitted roughly nineteen amicus briefs. This is a great practice because you're bringing different perspectives to the table. Acknowledging the realistic limits of any one person, any one judge, one bench, and allowing other experts to feed into the process is absolutely essential. What happened in the Ongwen Appeals Chamber process was progressive because different amicus briefs were accepted, many different perspectives were put before the Court, and the judges were able to draw from those in reaching their final conclusion. That should continue. Obviously, we need to be mindful of not extending judicial proceedings longer than they have to be, and that does happen when you have many amicus briefs, but I think there's a way in which to balance this, because we don't want trials that take decades of course, but we also want to make sure that we get the best judgment, especially at the appeals level, and amicus briefs can contribute a great deal.

ON THE VALUE OF AMICUS BRIEFS

CHAPPELL: Well, that brings us nicely to my last question. How important do you think it's been to have *amicus curiae* briefs presented in cases including sexual-violence crimes? Do you think these interventions have shifted the bench's view around sexual violence or intersectional issues in particular?

MUDUKUTI: I think, particularly looking at the Ongwen process where I submitted an amicus brief along with other incredible minds, including several authors in this book, was a good example of bringing different expertise to the process. For example, where certain issues were not covered by the main parties, *amici* were able to cover these issues. As with anything in life, you will have submissions that take us forward and some that do the opposite but accepting different views is very important from a due process standpoint. What I will say though is, when I look at all the amicus briefs that were accepted by the appeals chamber, unfortunately, again, it was mostly people from the Global North, and mostly there were a lot of briefs from men, for example, which is fine – it's valuable – but I think we need to make sure that voices or groups that are marginalised or usually excluded from these processes are included. I would have loved to see more submissions from African scholars, from Ugandan scholars, from women, regardless of whether they identify as feminist or not. That's a challenge that can be overcome. There are other challenges: for example, the deadlines were very tight. We had three weeks to submit leave to intervene and then the full brief was required a month later. Now, if you're a practitioner on the ground, working on several issues at the same time, it's very hard to turn over a draft in such a short space of time. Again, I am mindful of the need to have deadlines and not unnecessarily prolong proceedings, but balance is needed. And, also, how far and wide was this call for amicus briefs shared? I don't think it went very far. I have recently spoken to people who didn't even know it was an option. So, I think there are some things you can change including publishing calls for submissions as far as possible to reach a wider audience – and I think it's on all of us, not just the Court, not just civil society. I think anybody who cares about this field needs to be more proactive in bringing different voices to bear on international justice at the ICC.

CHAPPELL: Again, I think you're pointing to a resource issue here too, aren't you? If you have such a tight timeframe but you don't necessarily have the resources in your small NGO [non-governmental organisation], it's very hard to turn something around like that very quickly. Do you think there is anything in particular that explains why the Appeals Chamber allowed so many briefs in the *Ongwen* case? Is there something unique to *Ongwen*, or do you think the ICC is gradually becoming more open to amicus briefs in general?

MUDUKUTI: It's a very good question. I cannot say for certain but perhaps it was a combination of factors, such as a recognition that there are experts outside of the Court who can add value and should be allowed to participate in proceedings of this nature. I think that's also something that we've seen evolve over time. My hope is that other chambers will follow suit. But we have to balance that with the length of proceedings and just how long it takes to make all of this happen, and to make sure you're including everybody.

Chappell: It does stand out as a very good example, I think. And, as we've seen over the years, the expertise for writing these briefs is building over time, which is also important.

Angela, thank you again for providing such important insights into the operation of the ICC, intersectionality, and judging. It's been fascinating for me and I'm sure for the readers of our book too.

6

Intersectionality, Feminist Judgments, and the International Criminal Court

Whose Feminist Is It Anyway?

Jarpa Dawuni

INTRODUCTION

Chimamanda Ngozi Adichie's Ted Talk, 'We Should All Be Feminists',[1] has garnered over 5 million views on YouTube. The simple argument she makes is that despite the vastness of the term 'feminism', at the root of it is the need to respect, accept, and include the diversity in how feminism presents itself, how it is constructed, and, most importantly, how it affects different women differently. Despite the provocative examples drawn from her positionality as a Nigerian, an African, a woman of Igbo descent, a writer, and the list goes on, what is still not clear in her narrative is which feminism Adichie is referring to, or whose feminist/feminism she is talking about. How will she ascribe or describe feminism based on one single identity or the intersection of the multiple identities she embodies?

When I was invited to write a chapter for this edited volume, my first reaction was whether I could speak for and on behalf of the millions of women standing at the multiple intersections socially constructed by societies and the temporal spaces we occupy. Many of these intersections predate the historical development of this feminist judging project, and many other intersections keep developing each day. In line with feminist praxis and academic reflexivity,[2] I examined my positionality as woman, Black, African, Ghanaian, Basare, lawyer, academic, mother, and many other identities I inhabit. Did my positionality as a Black woman make me an expert on intersectionality? If not, who had the right or the qualifications to speak or write on this concept of intersectionality?

[1] See C. Adichie, 'We Should All Be Feminists', TEDTalk (TEDxEuston, December 2012) available at www.ted.com/talks/chimamanda_ngozi_adichie_we_should_all_be_feminists?language = en.

[2] On feminist reflexivity in research, see generally D. Macbeth, 'On "Reflexivity" in Qualitative Research: Two Readings, and a Third' 7(1) *Qualitative Inquiry* (2001) 35–68; K. England, 'Getting Personal: Reflexivity, Positionality, and Feminist Research' 46 *The Professional Geographer* (1994) 80–89.

Drawing on the works of an interdisciplinarity collection of Black feminist scholars, the concept of multiple and intersecting axes of oppression and exclusion has long informed the work of critical race scholars.[3] Taken up by Black feminist legal scholars,[4] the concept of intersectionality has travelled the colour and gender boundaries, as well as geographic boundaries, to gain global recognition and potency in explaining the lives, experiences, and complexities of minoritised people.[5]

In writing this chapter, I decided to adopt a critical approach in evaluating the feminist judgment projects (FJP) that exist to date. Having surveyed details about their beginnings, methodologies, and epistemological approaches, I understand that what binds all these projects together is applying a feminist lens to reimagine these judgments if they had considered gender as a socially constructed variable and ordering principle in societies. Most importantly, the goal of these projects, as I understand them, is to engage in a judicial and ideological rewinding and recasting of what a gender-inclusive law-making process would look like in order to expand access to justice for women. In applying a feminist lens and paying attention to gendered constructs, would future judgments from international courts, and the International Criminal Court (ICC) specifically, be fair and equitable? Would judges, prosecutors, and staffers question the gendered nature of the tools, paradigms, codes, and law-making processes they apply to arrive at the decisions they make?

In exploring the idea of a feminist reimagination, we must begin from a place of a feminist recasting of the challenges, social hierarchies, barriers, constraints, and opportunities that give birth to, maintain, and advance the multiple discriminations, exclusions, and erasures some groups of people face in societies across the world. The feminist reimagination must be anchored in helping us understand and bring

[3] R. Delgado and J. Stefancic, 'Introduction' in R. Delgado and J. Stefancic (eds.), *Critical Race Theory: The Cutting Edge* (2nd ed., Philadelphia: Temple University Press, 2000) xv–xix.

[4] A. Harris, 'Race and Essentialism in Feminist Legal Theory' 42 *Stanford Law Review* (1989) 581–616; K. Crenshaw, 'Demarginalizing the Intersection of Race and Sex: A Black Feminist Critique of Antidiscrimination Doctrine, Feminist Theory and Antiracist Politics' 1 *University of Chicago Law Forum* (1989) 139–167; P. Williams, *The Alchemy of Race and Rights: Diary of a Law Professor* (Cambridge, MA: Harvard University Press, 1991); A. Wing, 'International Human Rights and Black Women: Justice or Just Us?' in J. Levitt (ed.), *Black Women and International Law: Deliberate Interactions, Movements and Actions* (Cambridge: Cambridge University Press, 2015) 37–60; K. Crenshaw, 'Mapping the Margins: Intersectionality, Identity Politics, and Violence against Women of Color' 43 *Stanford Law Review* (1991) 1241–1299; J. Dawuni (ed.), *Intersectionality and Women's Access to Justice in Africa* (London: Rowman and Littlefield, 2022).

[5] Note that I use the term 'minoritised' and not minority because in some cases, the group suffering oppression are not minorities in the numeric or quantitative sense. For example, women make up at least 50 per cent of the world's population but they are often treated as minorities within power hierarchies. In South Africa, black people make up a majority of the national population, yet the lingering effects of apartheid cause them to be treated as minorities within the chambers of power.

into conversation the *normative* (what the 'feminine sensitive' law ought to be) versus the *empirical* (what the 'non-feminine-sensitive' law is). The chapters in this book attempt to peel back the historical layers of time, precedent, judicial reasoning, and legal principles that were cast in a male-centric gaze. Born out of a highly patriarchal system of international law[6] and a highly racist imperial system,[7] principles of international law and international justice have stood the test of time. These principles have endured because each time these cases made it to court as precedents (in common law jurisdictions), the masculine ethos upon which they were built re-emerge in one form or the other, thereby solidifying the magma of male-centred and male-biased judicial reasoning.

The current FJP is taking these pieces of gender-blind decisions and refashioning them as examples of feminist judicial decision-making. This time around, the magma is placed in the hands of individuals (academics, lawyers, activists, and so on) who are gender-aware, gender-conscious, and gender-sensitive. Their role as the new judicial goldsmiths is to turn this magma into something new – that is, a 'decision' that has all the contours, imagery, and marks of a feminist-informed and gender-inclusive work of art – a feminist-sensitive judgment.

Before I progress, I wish to position myself in relation to my reflection. I draw on liberatory academic praxis[8] in declaring that I speak from my positionality as a woman, a cisgender woman, a woman whose roots are in the continent of Africa, a highly educated woman (with a law degree and a doctorate). I also declare my positionality as a scholar whose works focus on Africa – a region too vast for me to claim to be an expert on all the forms and varieties of gender and feminist issues. I recognise that some claim to be 'African' experts, but I am opposed to this notion of a broad-brush representation of a continent of over a billion people and multiple cultures and lived experiences. With these declarations, I am making it clear that I do not stand as a voice that speaks on behalf of all women or gender issues explored

6 On gender in international law, see generally H. Charlesworth and C. Chinkin, *The Boundaries of International Law: A Feminist Analysis* (Manchester: Manchester University Press, 2000). For a discussion of gender at the international courts specifically, see L. Chappell, 'Women, Gender and International Institutions: Exploring New Opportunities at the International Criminal Court' 22(1) *Policy and Society* (2003) 3–25; R. Grey, K. McLoughlin, and L. Chappell, 'Gender and Judging at the International Criminal Court: Lessons from Feminist Judgments Projects' 34 *Leiden Journal of International Law* (2021) 247–264.

7 The pedagogical response to the imperial and racist nature of international law is captured in the genre of scholarship referred to as the Third World Approaches to International Law (TWAIL). See generally O. C. Okafor, 'Critical Third World Approaches to International Law (TWAIL): Theory, Methodology, or Both?' 10 *International Community Law Review* (2008) 371–378; M. Mutua, 'What Is TWAIL?' 94 *American Society of International Law Proceedings* (2000) 31–39; J. Gathii, 'Alternative and Critical: The Contribution of Research and Scholarship on Developing Countries to International Legal Theory' 41 *Harvard International Law Journal* (2000) 263–275; K. Mickelson, 'Rhetoric and Rage: Third World Voices in International Legal Discourse' 16 *Wisconsin International Law Journal* (1998) 353–419.

8 On feminist academic praxis and positionality, see *supra* note 2.

in this book and beyond. As a feminist scholar, I practise my liberatory feminism through the lens of African feminism, postcolonial feminism, and feminist legal theory. I have acquired the training and skills to critically analyse and evaluate other forms of feminism, bodies of knowledge, and theories. I am approaching this chapter with the goal of reflecting from my positionality as an African feminist academic to question how best the communities of scholars, activists, lawyers, and others engaged in gender equality might approach the issue of intersectionality in international criminal law. I recognise that the original discussions of intersectionality by Black feminist scholars sought to decentre race and gender as the two main axes of oppression.[9]

My understanding of the feminist judgment project is that it fixes its gaze on 'feminist methods, tools, and theories' as the defining feature of rewriting these judgments. Consequently, 'feminism' is used as a proxy to discuss how women and other marginalised groups are overlooked, erased, or treated unjustly through the judicial pens of some judges who made these earlier decisions. In the ensuing discussion, I explore the merits and demerits of applying an intersectional lens to the projects of feminist reimagination. In doing so, I briefly lay the cornerstones of the intersectionality framework as propounded by Black feminist scholars in the United States and popularised by the work of Black socio-legal scholar Kimberlѐ Crenshaw.[10]

The next section of the chapter raises a series of questions for scholars to think about as the feminist judgment project grows in number and breadth of coverage by geography and legal issue area. It grapples with, and attempts to answer, the following questions: What does intersectionality mean? What does/doesn't it bring to the law? The third section makes the connection between FJPs and intersectionality by posing and answering the question: How can the current project and other FJPs benefit from applying an intersectional lens to their judgment rewriting? It also weaves into the analyses of why the ICC needs to apply an intersectional lens in all its activities, from hiring staffers to delivering judgments. The fourth section provides recommendations and directions for three key constituents – the ICC Chambers/Assembly of State Parties, the Registry, and scholars/researchers writing these reimagined judgments. The last section concludes the chapter.

9 For a deeper exploration of the roots of intersectionality, see generally Crenshaw, 'Demarginalizing', *supra* note 4; P. H. Collins, 'Black Feminist Thought in the Matrix of Domination' in C. C. Lemert (ed.), *Social Theory: The Multicultural and Classic Readings* (Boulder, CO: Westview Press, 1993) 615–625; P. H. Collins, *Black Feminist Thought: Knowledge, Consciousness, and the Politics of Empowerment* (Abingdon: Routledge, 2000); P. H. Collins and S. Bilge, *Intersectionality: Key Concepts* (Cambridge: Polity, 2016); J. C. Nash, 'Re-thinking Intersectionality' 89 *Feminist Review* (2008) 1–15.

10 See the seminal critical race formulation of intersectionality theory, Crenshaw, 'Demarginalizing', *supra* note 4.

SOME MERITS AND DEMERITS OF INTERSECTIONALITY AS A TOOL FOR FEMINIST EQUITY AND JUDGMENT

As a theoretical framework for analysing different identities and how they intersect to create a multiplier effect on individuals facing discrimination, intersectionality has spread its theoretical tentacles around the world (geography) and subject matter (disciplines). Popularised by Kimberlè Crenshaw, the concept of intersectionality dominated the discussions of Black feminist scholars who examined how Black women are subjected to multiple axes of interconnected experiences of discrimination as a result of their race, gender, and other marginalised situatedness.[11]

Tracing the roots of the theory of intersectionality is itself an emancipatory act of feminism – one that requires the decentring of masculinities (gender) or, in this case, whiteness (race) as the loci of knowledge production and theoretical formulation. Crediting Black feminist scholars for developing this theory is itself a necessary act of recognising the need to centre the voice, agency, and capabilities of Black women as creators of knowledge.

But what do we know about intersectionality as a process to reach the desired end of achieving an equitable judicial decision? A decision that considers both the visible and invisible, the temporal and the non-temporal, the oppressors and the privileged? To what extent are all these oppositional forces, and many more not listed here, necessary when making a judicial decision?

Intersectionality as theory has helped expand our thinking of the possibilities of law – what the law can do when viewed through the lens of a feminist ideal of equity, fairness, and inclusion. The growing list of feminist rewritten judgments highlights how identities of race, gender, age, language, geography, sexuality, health status, marital status, and so on, may additively converge to create less optimal outcomes for those seeking justice. But are these projects truly inclusive? To what extent does each of these identities capture the centrality of different lived experiences? An analysis of the rewritten cases and commentaries in the current volume raises several questions that may be necessary for other feminist judgment projects.

The Merits

Intersectionality as a feminist framework has proven to possess the theoretical rigour to explain the lived experiences of diverse groups. The replicability and generalisability of intersectionality must however be weighed against the feminist principle of essentialism.[12] In applying an intersectional lens, judges, prosecutors, and judicial staff can understand how the racial, gender, class, and social categories affect and

[11] See generally notes 4, 9, and 10.

[12] See Harris, *supra* note 4; S. J. Kenney, 'Thinking about Gender and Judging' 15(1) *International Journal of the Legal Profession* (2008) 87–110.

determine who is a victim of a criminal offence. Through an intersectional lens, judges may also gain some insights into how language affects how defendants express themselves in court, thereby allowing judges to seek a deeper understanding of language, cultural, ethnic, and religious codes.[13] From a feminist perspective, intersectionality can help illuminate how women's lives are constructed as victims, why women victims may not express themselves with particular words, and how their age and social standing impact what they say in court. An example of the latter experience is captured in the words of Ugandan Judge Julia Sebutinde, the first African woman to serve on the bench of the International Court of Justice:

> Although I am a judge, I'm also a mother. I'm also a wife. I'm also somebody's daughter. Do I put my human emotions ... in these cases? Are we not the human face of justice? I think we are. For example, as I preside over the trial if I notice that a defense lawyer is harassing and badgering an old woman during cross-examination who is struggling to recount a horrific rape she endured, publicly, with a view maybe to intimidating or humiliating her, can you not forgive me for interjecting and saying: 'Counsel, you are out of order.' We understand the witness. Am I not allowed to read that women's body language? If she's not able to raise her eyes because of the feeling of shame? If all she can do is to mumble with her eyes downcast and narrate her story the best way she can, should we disbelieve her testimony? I recall a woman aged 70 years old who was gang-raped and had to testify before us about it. And this is a story I'm telling you that happened in Sierra Leone. She couldn't even look at the judges or anybody because her husband and grown children were sitting in the front row. These are gender sensitivities that our male colleagues may not even be aware of during the trial.[14]

The Demerits

There are several pitfalls that must be avoided in attempts to apply intersectionality in international criminal cases before the ICC or other criminal courts. First, it is critical to understand that not all individuals within a socially constructed group face the same oppression. For example, not all women victims of a criminal offence in a conflict will be heterosexual, of the same age, practise the same religion, or have the

[13] On the impact of language on proceedings at the ICC, see L. Swigart, 'The Impacts of English-Language Hegemony on the ICC' in F. Jeßberger, L. Steinl, and K. Mehta (eds.), *International Criminal Law – A Counter-Hegemonic Project?* (The Hague: T. M. C. Asser Press, 2022) 239–263; for a discussion of how religious and ethnic diversity can help with the adjudication of cases (but not necessarily as grounds for appointing judges), see the arguments by S. B. Balungi and G. L. Dossan, 'Ethnicity, Religion and Diversity at the International Criminal Court: Is More Too Much?' in F. Baetens (ed.), *Identity and Diversity on the International Bench* (Oxford: Oxford University Press, 2020) 446–461.

[14] Quoted in N. Grossman, 'Julia Sebutinde: An Unbreakable Cloth' in J. Dawuni and A. Kuenyehia (eds.), *International Courts and the African Woman Judge: Unveiled Narratives* (London: Routledge, 2018) 37–56, at 43.

same educational achievements. These categories show the need to adopt an intra-category approach to decipher the differences *within* groups.[15] Second, applying an intersectional lens may open a Pandora's box of claims that may not be apparent to the most well-versed scholars of intersectionality. For instance, how will judges react to new claims of categorical identities that claim special protections due to new identities developed out of artificial intelligence? Will an avatar or a robot be allowed to claim special prosecutorial or judicial protections? These are just two examples of what could emerge as judges grapple with new rights and freedoms.

REIMAGINING JUDGMENTS: IS FEMINISM ENOUGH?

Is the application of an intersectional lens enough to cover the universe of discriminatory treatments individuals face in society and by extension in the courtroom? In the same line of questioning, is feminism a concept that has near-universal application to the issues faced by women and other marginalised groups? In this section, I explore several questions and themes on whether 'feminism/feminist' is the right description for the rewritten judgments. I base my critique and evaluation on several assumptions inherent in the way these rewritten feminist judgments may have been constructed.

What Is Feminism and Whose Feminism?

If we proceed on the assumption that feminism is about seeking equality between men and women in society, several questions come to the fore. First, the question is, who is the woman we are referring to in this context? How can we assess the personal inclinations or lived experiences of the judgment writers to make an assessment of how well they understand the issues of Indigenous/Aboriginal/Native American/'Third World'/'Muslim', and other marginalised groups of women? Or the plight of immigrant, disabled, sex-trafficked women? To what extent are the lives of these 'other' women just an exercise in a dark alley of feminist knowing for the judgment writers if the writer has not lived in those conditions and experienced the daily and historical marginalisations of the very group they purport to 'save' through their rewriting exercise?

Who is the 'woman' for the purposes of these judgments? To what extent are these projects considering 'feminism' not from a biological deterministic binary of the female, but feminism more as a belief system (which, though it benefits from feminine ways of being) is not the exclusive preserve of women? Global feminist movements have helped to advance women's rights around the world. Yet these

[15] For a discussion of the distinctions between categorical, inter-categorical, and intra-categorical intersectionality, see L. McCall, 'The Complexity of Intersectionality' 30(3) *Signs* (2005) 1771–1800.

movements have not been without their tensions as feminist-ideological battles have been waged by and among women/feminists. Drawing on the works of postcolonial and decolonial feminists,[16] the bifurcation of the global feminist movement into the 'developed' and 'developing', 'first, second, and third' worlds has led to the 'othering' of a large swath of women in the world. Scholars have called for a true global sisterhood, informed by a collective and inclusive mobilisation around women's issues.[17] As the different FJPs attempt to reimagine a just world through a feminist lens, it is important to begin the exercise from a place of self-reflection to understand the extent to which the lives and experiences of 'othered' and 'third world women' may be centred vis-à-vis feminist legal principles that purport to produce just, equitable, and feminist-inclusive jurisprudence.

Which Intersections Matter or Which Are We (Re)marginalising?

At the heart of intersectionality is the need to recognise the multiplicity and simultaneity of oppressions. Women victims embody multiple identities; thus, it is when architects of justice choose one and not other identities that the gravest injustices can occur. The rewritten judgments in this volume run the risk of reproducing marginalisation. As the co-editors note in Chapter 2, due to the overwhelming number of issues in each of the ICC cases/situations under review, authors were tasked with picking and focusing on one issue only. Since this project is an exercise in showing the possibilities of future judgments, it is hoped that this message will be strongly shared with those who will be relying on these rewritten judgments as guideposts – there is more to be said and done. As suggested earlier, the task of judges, prosecutors, and judicial staff in peeling back their personal biases, stereotypes, and lack of knowledge about the lived realities of the litigants before them; and this requires training. Training programmes on (un)conscious bias and intercultural competence will be helpful in moving these actors to a place of awareness. Nonetheless, awareness is not enough to counteract the insidious impact of deep-seated biases. As the famous Black feminist scholar and poet Audre Lorde

[16] For a discussion on postcolonial and decolonial feminism, see generally C. T. Mohanty, 'Transnational Feminist Crossings: On Neoliberalism and Radical Critique' 38(4) *Signs* (2013) 967–991; C. T. Mohanty, A. Russo, and L. Torres (eds.), *Third World Women and the Politics of Feminism* (Bloomington: Indiana University Press, 1991); E. D. Velez, 'Decolonial Feminism at the Intersection: A Critical Reflection on the Relationship between Decolonial Feminism and Intersectionality' 33(3) *Journal of Speculative Philosophy* (2019) 390–406; A. Carastathis, 'Intersectionality and Decolonial Feminism' in *Intersectionality: Origins, Contestations, Horizons* (Lincoln: University of Nebraska Press, 2016) 199–232, available at https://doi.org/10.2307/j.ctt1fzhfz8.11.

[17] On the issue of how our global collective mobilisation can be effective in addressing women's issues, see J. Rami-Nogales, 'Revisiting the Category "Women"' in K. Ogg and S. H. Rimmer (eds.), *Feminist Approaches to International Law* (Cheltenham: Edward Elgar, 2019) 240–252.

noted, the 'master's tools will never destroy the master's house'.[18] The tools of patriarchy and racial, class, ethnic, and religious discrimination are 'houses' of oppression with deep foundations. To break down these 'houses' requires the adoption of holistic approaches to naming, centring, and hearing the voices of marginalised groups. How will judges and judicial staff determine which intersectional identities need to be protected? Will gender trump race? Will disability trump sexual orientation? Will social class trump geographical location (Global North versus Global South)? These are critical questions to be answered in order to avoid the vicissitudes of remarginalising groups that are already marginalised. When the latter happens, we are reconfirming the second part of Audre Lorde's famous quote, 'they may allow us temporarily to beat him at his own game, but they will never enable us to bring about genuine change'.[19]

Coloniality as a Vehicle for Patriarchy and Racism

Given the criticism against the ICC for its focus on the African continent, it is no surprise that the majority of the rewritten judgments in this volume deal with cases emanating from Africa.[20] The co-editors in Chapter 2, and some of the contributors, including Angela Mudukuti in Chapter 5, have reflected on the role of imperialism and colonisation as factors explaining the overwhelmingly African cases that have come before the ICC bench. Beyond the impact of colonisation on the spatial borders of these countries, it is essential to question the role of coloniality as a constant state of being, one that lies beyond physical occupation, as a continuity of imperial patriarchy and racism around the world. While physical colonisation may have ended, coloniality as an idea of subjugation continues to be a principal means of control over the political, economic, linguistic, and legal systems of former colonies.[21] The Rome Statute establishing the ICC attempted to create a diverse bench by considering geography and area of expertise. These modest gains at a diverse bench do not shield the court from failing to account for the nuances in the historical, socio-cultural, and myriad other contexts within which these cases

[18] Lorde's famous quote lies at the heart of her own frustrations in navigating the multiple identities and associated axes of oppression that come with her different positionalities; A. Lorde, 'The Master's Tools Will Never Dismantle the Master's House' in *Sister Outsider: Essays and Speeches* (Berkeley, CA: Crossing Press, 1984) 110–114.

[19] *Ibid.*

[20] Table 2.1 in Chapter 2 shows a breakdown of the 'situations', with African cases or situations leading, followed by Asia/Pacific, Latin America and the Caribbean, and Eastern Europe.

[21] For some discussion on the linkage between colonialisation and international law, see generally V. Nesiah 'The Ground Beneath Her Feet: "Third World" Feminisms' 4(3) *Journal of International Women's Studies* (2003) 30–38; A. Mudukuti, 'Gender Imbalance at the ICC: The Continued Hegemonic Entrenchment of Male Privilege in International Criminal Law' in F. Jeßberger, L. Steinl, and K. Mehta (eds.), *International Criminal Law – A Counter-Hegemonic Project* (The Hague: T. M. C. Asser Press, 2022) 265–280.

emerge. While the racial and gender diversity of the court has been touted, little has been said about the staffers and legal officers who handle the daily operations of these courts. These important issues are beginning to receive some scholarly attention and also form part of the conversation between Angela Mudukuti and Louise Chappell in this volume (Chapter 5).[22] To what extent are these staff positions diverse and inclusive? As these feminist judges emerge, how might authors (rewriting judgments) understand the continuity of coloniality and the extent to which it affects and determines the commission of some of these crimes? Who might charges be brought against, and who should be held accountable for the crimes? To what extent is coloniality a constant state of oppression that marginalises individuals along a wide spectrum of discriminatory acts and omissions?

The African Feminist Judgments: Is Africa a Continent or a Country?

The traction gained by the first feminist rewritten judgments is remarkable. One thing that has stood out about these projects is the focus on individual countries as the units of analysis.[23] Why is it that in the context of countries in Africa, the project has been lumped into the 'African Feminist Judgments Project'? Is this overgeneralisation and over-homogenisation of a continent of over a billion people not problematic and emblematic of how the issues that arise out of the first judgments stand to be repeated in other forms if the generalisation is not addressed? How can we realistically apply an intersectional lens to a continent that has probably one of the most diverse legal systems – combining transplanted civil law from the French colonial empire, common law from the British colonial empire, Islamic law from invasions from the Middle East, all of which operate side by side with indigenous customary legal systems? The historical, social, political, economic, linguistic, ethnic, and other identities and experiences are too numerous to cluster into one lived experience. What operates as patriarchy may operate as matriarchy in another culture within the same country.[24] How do we decipher and classify age as a social category and its impact in determining women's situational ranking in different national contexts?

[22] For a discussion on the staffers of international courts and tribunals, see a forthcoming chapter by N. Grossman, 'The "Invisible Court": Gender and Nationality in Registries and Secretariats' in N. Grossman, J. Ramji-Nogales, H. Ruiz-Fabris, and J. Dawuni (eds.), *Women and International Law* (Oxford: Oxford University Press, 2024).

[23] These examples include the projects on the United States, Canada, Scotland, Australia, India, England, and Brazil, to name a few.

[24] For some preliminary explanations on matriarchy, see generally J. Dawuni, 'Matri-legal Feminism: An African Feminist Response to International Law' in K. Ogg and S. H. Rimmer (eds.), *Feminist Approaches to International Law* (Cheltenham: Edward Elgar, 2019) 445–462.

Who are the Judges and the Registry Officials

Much of the early scholarship on international courts and tribunals focused on who international court judges were, and how they were selected.[25] While the issue of descriptive diversity on the bench is still instructive, other explorations of diversity beyond the usual issues of race, gender, and geography are gaining traction. Freya Baeten's edited volume *Identity and Diversity on the International Bench*[26] explores many themes, including language, ethnic, religious, and geographic diversity. While ethnic and religious diversity were debunked as not being critical factors in considering diversity on the bench, writing from personal experiences as an international judge, Judge Nosworthy maintained the importance of cultivating an inclusive climate on the bench that allows the minoritised judge from a 'tiny island' to be heard and seen as an equal voice.[27] Many other examples abound of minority (mostly women) judges who questioned how their intersecting identities would affect their presence on the bench.[28] These reflections by the judges who sit on these courts are instructive because they signal the continuity of social and judicial power hierarchies even on the benches of international courts.

Overwhelmingly, the staff who constitute the registry of these courts are also drawn from geographically dominant, Western countries. We must therefore question to what extent the feminist rewriters reproduce these inherent power hierarchies by failing to question the composition of those who provide essential administrative functions for the Court. What principles of soft law are at play when feminist judgment rewriters write from positions of relative privilege when compared to the lives of the people in the cases they are deliberating? To what extent are

25 For some works on the selection of international court judges, see generally D. Terris, C. P. R. Romano, and L. Swigart, *The International Judge: An Introduction to the Men and Women Who Decide the World's Cases* (Oxford: Oxford University Press, 2007); R. Mackenzie et al., *Selecting International Judges: Principle, Process and Politics* (Oxford: Oxford University Press, 2010); For discussions that focus on the election and appointment of women judges, see L. Hodson, 'Gender and the International Judge: Towards a Transformative Equality Approach' 35 *Leiden Journal of International Law* (2022) 913–930; N. Grossman, 'Achieving Sex-Representative International Court Benches' 110 *American Journal of International Law* (2016) 82–95; H. Vauchez, 'More Women – But Which Women? The Rule and Politics of Gender Balance at the European Court of Human Rights' 26(1) *European Journal of International Law* (2015) 195–221.

26 F. Baetens (ed.), *Identity and Diversity on the International Bench* (Oxford: Oxford University Press, 2020); K. Hessler, 'The Significance of Religious Diversity in International Human Rights Adjudication' in F. Baetens (ed.), *Identity and Diversity on the International Bench* (Oxford: Oxford University Press, 2020).

27 J. Nosworthy, 'Diversity, Inclusion, and Legitimacy in International Courts and Tribunals: Insights from Within, Perspectives from the Periphery – An Island Girl Speaks' in F. Baetens (ed.), *Identity and Diversity on the International Bench* (Oxford: Oxford University Press, 2020) 538–556.

28 Several international judges have raised this issue in various writings, these include Patricia Wald, Gabrielle Kirk McDonald, Navi Pillya, Florence Mumba, Julia Sebutinde, and Akua Kuenyehia. For the latter group, it was also the issue of their race they had to confront.

the original evidence and the facts of the case they are rewriting coded in language presenting barriers which they may not be able to decode? To what extent will the judgment rewriters have access to the non-verbal communications and cues that were present in the courtroom during the original cases, and how did such non-verbal communication influence the decisions of the judges? These are practical questions to explore as we engage in the liberatory exercise of (re)writing these feminist judgments through a feminist intersectional lens.

Women Judges and the Intersectional Burden

Most feminist analyses operate from the assumption that women will understand women's issues. This assumption leads to the expectation that women should be at the forefront of finding solutions to women's issues. These assumptions mostly hold true because women can relate to women's issues by 'stepping into' the imaginary shoes of other women. This ability to transpose into the reality of another woman was crucial in important international criminal cases such as the *Anto Furundzija* and *Kunarac et al.* cases, where Justice Florence Ndepele Mumba presided, and where for the first time the International Criminal Tribunal for the Former Yugoslavia (ICTY) pronounced sexual violence in the form of rape as crimes against humanity, war crimes, and torture. In the *Akayesu* case involving Judge Navi Pillay, the International Criminal Tribunal for Rwanda (ICTR) held rape as a war crime. Equally, in the Sierra Leone case Trial Chamber II, AFRC Judgment, Judge Sebutinde's concurring opinion in distinguishing between marriage in a time of peace and 'forced marriage' in a time of war helped established important principles of criminal conduct in conflict situations.[29]

Despite these examples of the contributions of women judges to developing jurisprudence on international criminal law, we must be cognisant of the fact that not all women are feminists, and not all women will understand the intersectional challenges of other women. In *Intersectionality and Women's Access to Justice in Africa*[30] I introduced the concept of layered intersectionality. This framework makes the argument that women judges face both oppression and privilege in their access to the courtroom as judges. The level of personal oppression they have faced can inform the extent to which they relate to other women facing similar or different challenges. The oppression need not be personal and can be communal, thus allowing them to relate to what others are facing as women.

[29] See the cases: *Prosecutor v, Dragoljub Kunarac, Radomir Kovac, and Zoran Vukovic* (IT-96-23-T); *Kunarac et al.* (IT-96-23 & 23/1); *Prosecutor v. Anto Furundzija* (IT-95-17/1); Trial Judgment, *Prosecutor v. Jean-Paul Akayesu* (ICTR-96-4-T)1 June 2001; Judgment on Appeal, *Armed Forces Revolutionary Council Trial*, Appeals Chamber (2008) Trial Chamber II, AFRC Judgment, Separate Concurring Opinion, 2007.

[30] See *supra* note 4.

Thus, while it may be easier for women to relate to these intersectional burdens, not all women can relate, while some make no effort to relate, limited by the judicial principles of 'impartiality'. An anti-essentialist reading of this burden women bear as frontline workers in understanding other women's experiences is important. Until the essence of anti-essentialism is achieved, the extent to which feminist judgment rewriters can explore the detailed socio-cultural understandings of the victims (or purported victims) must be at the forefront in grounding these judgments in an intersectional framework. Understanding women's situational identities should be the task of all judges – both men and women.

Feminist Judgments beyond Gender: Where Are the Men?

Is feminism intrinsically female? Can feminists confidently profess to represent the many marginalised voices that lie at the substrata of the intersectional barriers and challenges feminists claim to see from their academic towers or activist microphones? Beyond the pen of the academic and the advocacy of activists, can we really hear the voices of the marginalised and the newly emergent marginalised groups? In the current volume, most of the contributors are women. A review of the table of contents of other feminist judgment projects shows the same pattern, thus confirming that this challenge is not unique to the current volume. As an editor of several books, I know first-hand the difficulty of always hitting the diversity mark when selecting chapter contributors. My call to action is for feminist scholars to recruit male feminists. For these judgments to be sustainable and have the desired impact, they must extend beyond the confines of feminist circles and networks of feminist scholars. Including men who understand, respect, and can engage with intersectional and interdisciplinary feminisms is essential. Recruiting men who can rewrite a judgment from a feminist perspective will encourage male judges to descend from their judicial towers and engage with these rewritten judgments. It will also facilitate the efforts to use these feminist judgments as teaching materials in law schools.[31] If we do not make that extra effort to add men, we risk preaching to the choir. I do however recognise that some readers may ask why we need to 're'centre men in our writings and spaces as women.

RECOMMENDATIONS

The preceding analysis has offered some provocative thoughts and reflections on how architects of international criminal law may draw on intersectionality as a guiding framework in adjudicating international criminal law cases. In this section,

[31] See B. J. Crawford et al., 'Teaching with Feminist Judgments: A Global Conversation' 38(1) *Law and Inequality* (2020) 1–67, available at https://digitalcommons.pace.edu/cgi/viewcontent.cgi?article=2149&context=lawfaculty

I provide a few high-level recommendations for judges, the registry, and researchers engaged in other feminist judgment projects.

For Judges

Achieving a more intersectional and inclusive feminist judgment calls for several changes, two of which are presented here. First, judges must acknowledge their positionality relative to the socio-cultural context and temporality of the case and the victims who appear before them. Doing so will allow them to recognise the multiplicative and additive effects of intersectionality, thereby expanding the range of reliefs they order. But how might a judge understand the wide spectrum of intersectional identities? Is there a universe of identities from which a judge can draw when they apply an intersectional lens? Are judges required to consider extenuating circumstances in the two dominant legal traditions the ICC operates from, or do they have the knowledge and skills in understanding and interpreting pluralistic legal systems?

Second, judges must accept the need for continuous judicial education and attentiveness to the role of intersectionality in determining the circumstances that lead to the cases before them. As eloquently submitted by Mudukuti in Chapter 5 of this volume, while some judges may be averse to 'professional development', the adoption of creative techniques such as 'retreats' could be used. However, the caution here is to ensure that such training about intersectionality and (un)conscious biases should not be one-offs but rather a mainstreamed and continuous programme.

The Registry

As one of the four primary organs of the ICC, the registry plays important functional and administrative roles with consequences for the judicial outcomes of cases that come before the bench. These functions include administering court services, assisting external defence and counsel for victims, organising witness and victim protection, and facilitating victim participation and reparations.[32] These are important functions that bring the court closer to victims and legal counsel. Therefore, it is critical for the staffers working in the registry to have a deep and contextual understanding of how intersectionality and the multiple axes of oppressions and exclusions affect the people they deal with.

To what extent have these rewritten judgments considered the roles of these ancillary staff in the rewriting process? How might we engage the registries, clerks, and investigating authorities accountable for understanding and applying the concepts in these rewritten judgments? These questions are not a critique of the feminist judgment projects. They lead to two recommendations.

[32] See the functions of the registry at www.aba-icc.org/about-the-icc/structure-of-the-icc/.

First, there should be representational diversity in the rank and file of the registry. The data presented by Mudukuti supports several prior and ongoing advocacy efforts for the racial, geographic, and gender diversity needed in the ICC. A diverse organisation leads to optimal outcomes, and this is crucial for an organisation that deals with high-level crimes of impunity and the violation of human rights. The ICC registry must engage in conscious and intentional efforts to recruit an expert group of diverse staffers; this is not a call for some sort of affirmative action – it is simple: if they seek, they will find equally qualified racial minorities.

Second, it is essential for the ICC to reform its internal institutional/organisational norms and practices. It is not enough to recruit diverse candidates/staffers and dump them in an institutional environment that operates along toxic levels of overt and covert racism, gender discrimination, sexual harassment, and other forms of oppression. The UN and the ICC have attempted to address some of these issues, but more needs to be done.[33] In November 2022, the Institute for African Women in Law organised a public dialogue on intersectionality and decoloniality in collaboration with the ICC registry, the ICC Staff Union, the IRMCT[34] Focal Point for Diversity, Equity, and Inclusion, the ICC Gender Equality Focal Point, and the ICC Office of the Prosecutor (OTP) Focal Point for Gender to address issues of discrimination in their organisations. The seminar 'Decolonization of Workplaces: A Communal Dialogue' was hosted virtually with the goal of addressing hard issues such as the decolonisation of workplaces, different forms of workplace harassment, and the role of staffers in breaking the walls of oppression. While more such dialogues are needed, they should be backed by actionable plans by the leaders of these organisations to hear the voices of the oppressed and address their concerns. The intersectional oppressions that staffers in the registry face must be simultaneously addressed alongside the issues victims face. Justice cannot be served to victims if staffers are constantly navigating injustice and the multiple axes of oppression within the corridors of the organisation.

For Researchers

At the outset of this chapter, in line with feminist praxis and academic reflexivity, I presented my positionality (which is by no means universal or exhaustive) to contextualise how I intended to approach the issues to be discussed in the chapter. Throughout the analyses, I was conscious of how my privilege may influence my

33 Persisting allegations of abuse of authority, sexual harassment, and other forms of discrimination led to the study and report by the ICC in 2022. See The Registry, 'Addressing Discrimination, Harassment, including Sexual Harassment, and Abuse of Authority', available at www.icc-cpi.int/sites/default/files/2022-05/ICC-AI-2022-003%20%28ENG%29%20-%20ADDRESSING%20DISCRIMINATION%2C%20HARASSMENT%2C%20INCLUDING%20SEXUAL%20HARASSMENT%2C%20AND%20ABUSE%20OF%20AUTHORITY.pdf.

34 IRMCT refers to the International Residual Mechanisms for Criminal Tribunals.

writing, and this leads me to the following recommendations. First, exercising multiple consciousnesses[35] should be the guiding principle of all researchers and feminist scholars. Researchers must be in tune with their positionalities and how multiple layers of privilege and power may intersect and filter through the pen of their feminist judgment rewriting.[36]

Second, researchers should approach these judgments with an inclusive ethic of care that is focused on the additive and multiplicative impact of intersectional identities. If we privilege gender/women over other social identity categories (race, ethnicity, religion, ability, sexuality, age, and so on), we risk reproducing the same power hierarchies. In which case, we may just be moving the stakes one notch up or down, with little to no implication for the diverse lives affected by the decisions.

Third, beyond acknowledging positionality and privilege, scholars and researchers must constantly engage in self-reflection of the approaches, strategies, and tools being used to challenge the masculine legal norms and principles in the original judgments. Doing that will be essential to meeting the FJP goal of a feminist (re) imagining while eradicating the (re)marginalisation of the people we purport to liberate through the power of the feminist pen.

CONCLUSION

The editors of this volume have done a commendable job of compiling the first FJP focusing on international criminal law – and the ICC specifically. They have gone to great lengths to include a diversity of authors and interdisciplinary approaches to broaching the topic of women, gender, and feminism. While the Introduction lays out the parameters of the project and the gaps they self-identify, this book promises to open new avenues for judicial and legal practitioners, researchers, diplomats, and international law policymakers. By incorporating discussions on intersectionality in

[35] The concept of double consciousness was developed and popularised by African American scholar W. E. B. Dubois in his 1903 book the *Soul of Black Folks*. It raises the question of how one navigates between two dominant identities of being black and white and the challenges that come with both sides requiring a consciousness on both identities. The concept has since been developed by other scholars to include multiple identities, thereby leading to the phrase 'multiple consciousness'; see generally, D. D. Bruce, Jr., 'W. E. B. Du Bois and the Idea of Double Consciousness' 64(2) *A Journal of Literary History, Criticism, and Bibliography* (1992) 299–309; M. Matsuda, 'When the First Quail Calls: Multiple Consciousness as Jurisprudential Method' 7(9) *Women's Rights Law Report* (1989) 297–300; P. Giddings, *When and Where I Enter: The Impact of Black Women on Race and Sex in America* (New York: W. Morrow, 1984); N. Welang, 'Triple Consciousness: The Reimagination of Black Female Identities in Contemporary American Culture' 2 *Open Cultural Studies* (2018) 296–306.

[36] For a discussion of doing intersectional research, see J. Esposito and V. Evans-Winters, *Introduction to Intersectional Qualitative Research* (Thousand Oaks, CA: Sage Publications, 2021); A. Carastathis, 'The Invisibility of Privilege: A Critique of Intersectional Models of Identity' 3(2) *Les Ateliers de l'Ethique* (2008) 23–38; C. A. MacKinnon, 'Intersectionality as Method: A Note' 38(4) *Signs* (2013) 1019–1030.

this project, the book lends a voice to the countless marginalised people who are often the victims of horrific crimes yet remain largely unheard. The world cannot fully address impunity if the institutions (courts) do not represent the diversity in the world – gender, race, religion, sexuality, (dis)ability, and other identity categories. This book lays out several innovative approaches for the ICC as it continues to work towards achieving a more inclusive institution – one that respects not only the rights of minorities who work within it, but also recognises, respects, and protects the intersectional identities and lived experiences of the victims who appear before it.

7

Intersectional Approaches to Investigating and Prosecuting Sexual and Gender-Based Crimes

Speech Delivered at 'The International Criminal Court at Twenty: Reflections on the Past, Present and the Future' Conference Marking the Twentieth Anniversary of the Entry into Force of the Rome Statute of the International Criminal Court, The Hague, 1 July 2022

Priya Gopalan

Greetings to all. My remarks today will address 'Intersectional approaches to investigating and prosecuting sexual and gender-based crimes'. In doing so, I will focus on two areas: First: What is intersectionality? Second: Why does intersectionality matter when it comes to investigating and prosecuting sexual and gender-based crimes?

WHAT IS INTERSECTIONALITY?

The term intersectionality was coined in 1989 by African American legal scholar Kimberlé Crenshaw, to provide a multi-dimensional framework for discrimination law in the United States – a framework that recognises and accounts for the discrimination experienced by Black women on the basis of their race, sex, and class. In Crenshaw's words: 'Intersectionality is a lens through which you can see where power comes and collides, where it interlocks and intersects. It's not simply that there's a race problem here, a gender problem here, and a class or LBGTQ problem there.'[1]

Now, when it comes to international criminal law, intersectionality serves as an analytical framework that enables the surfacing of intersecting identities, systems of privilege and oppression (for example, patriarchy or colonialism) that drive and form the backdrop to international crimes.

HOW DO WE LINK INTERSECTIONALITY TO SEXUAL AND GENDER-BASED CRIMES?

The ICC Policy Paper on sexual and gender-based crimes recognises that 'multiple' factors of discrimination may underlie sexual and gender-based crimes – that these crimes 'may be motivated by underlying inequalities, as well as a "multiplicity" of

[1] Columbia Law School, 'Kimberlé W. Crenshaw, Isidor and Seville Sulzbacher Professor of Law', available at www.law.columbia.edu/faculty/kimberle-w-crenshaw.

other factors, *inter alia*, religious, political, ethnic, national, and economic reasons'.[2] The policy as such highlights underlying structural and systemic inequalities within a particular social context, which is the bedrock of an intersectional framework.

While still finding its feet in international criminal law, intersectional analysis is a well-established analytical tool in the human rights world. For example, decisions and general recommendations of the Convention on the Elimination of All Forms of Discrimination Against Women (CEDAW) Committee regularly address the intersectional aspects of women's human rights violations.

Recent reports of the Special Rapporteur on the right to health, Tlaleng Mofokeng, and the Independent Expert on protection against violence and discrimination based on sexual orientation and gender, Victor Madrigal-Borloz, have made explicit an intersectional approach in their work.

Pivoting back to international criminal law, an intersectional approach is embedded in Article 21(3) of the Rome Statute. This article requires that the application and interpretation of the law must be consistent with human rights law and 'without any adverse distinction founded on grounds such as gender [as defined in Article 7, paragraph 3], age, race, colour, language, religion or belief, political or other opinion, national, ethnic or social origin, wealth, birth or other status'.

Article 21(3) not only builds a bridge between international criminal law and international human rights law, in which intersectionality finds deeper roots. It also links an intersectional analysis to how the law is to be applied and interpreted.

Despite these snippets of intersectionality and some promising developments in the jurisprudence, the overriding approach in international criminal law has been to focus on one form of discrimination, such as gender-based discrimination.

Gender analysis has achieved much through surfacing the underlying unequal power structures embedded in patriarchal systems that drive violence against women.

That said, gender – while a significant aspect of a person's identity – is not the only defining aspect of an individual, and gender analysis alone is insufficient to surface the full breadth and depth of harms experienced by survivors. For this, we need to recognise and account for factors beyond gender.

Let's turn to some practical examples that demonstrate why intersectionality matters when it comes to investigating and prosecuting sexual and gender-based crimes.

A seminal case of conflict-related sexual violence was the sexual enslavement of women and girls by the Japanese military during World War II. Estimates indicate that up to 200,000 women and girls were captured, forced, or tricked into sexual slavery. These women and girls were drawn from various Japanese colonies at that time, including Korea. We know that sexual slavery is a sexual and gender-based crime; what can intersectionality add here?

[2] The Office of the Prosecutor, 'Policy Paper on Sexual and Gender-Based Crimes', Policy Paper, June 2014, § 19, available at www.icc-cpi.int/sites/default/files/iccdocs/otp/OTP-Policy-Paper-on-Sexual-and-Gender-Based-Crimes–June-2014.pdf.

Pyong Gap Min writes that in the case of the women and girls from Korea, Japan's colonisation of the country was a critical factor in their enslavement; a state-supported patriarchal system in Japan facilitated the establishment of military brothels, while patriarchal customs in Korea perpetuated further victimisation upon their return home. Being drawn largely from impoverished families, Korean victims were sexually enslaved due to their economic and social status.[3] This meant that when they were eventually freed from slavery, their future prospects were limited, forcing some to work as sex workers for economic survival.

Here we see how an intersectional approach allows us to broaden our vision to unpack the diverse drivers of the violations experienced. For these Korean women and girls, gender along with colonialism, ageism, patriarchy, and class coalesced to produce their unique violations that, for some, continued to permeate their lives well beyond the specific acts and temporal duration of their enslavement.

Let's take another example: The systematic killing of 8,000 Bosnian Muslim men and the removal of Bosnian women, children, and elderly people from the Srebrenica enclave in July 1995.

Expert testimony in the *Kristić* case at the ICTY identified the 'Srebrenica Syndrome' as a specific impediment to female survivors' recovery. One of the primary factors giving rise to the syndrome is that, with few exceptions, the majority of the men of Srebrenica were listed as missing, their fate unknown. For a Bosnian Muslim woman, having a clear marital status was paramount. A woman whose husband was missing lacked such status. On a psychological level, the women's recovery was impeded – without knowing with certainty the fate of their men, they were unable to bury and grieve for them.

An intersectional approach reveals that this syndrome was a specific response to the lived experiences of the women – the social and cultural context that permeated these violations – such as their religion as Bosnian Muslims and their stature in a patriarchal society, where marital status mattered immensely.

The individual harms experienced by each woman were also woven into the fabric of inter-community and inter-generational harms. In the words of one former Srebrenica resident, referring to her own family: 'With the fall of Srebrenica … from the face of the earth were wiped off three generations of men in the cruellest way possible.'[4] As the Trial Chamber stated, 'In little over one week, thousands of lives were extinguished, irreparably rent or simply wiped from the pages of history.'[5]

Analysing this context holistically demonstrates the full contours and complexities of harms experienced by the women as a result of the loss of their male family members.

[3] P. G. Min, 'Korean "Comfort Women": The Intersection of Colonial Power, Gender, and Class' 17(6) *Gender and Society* (2003) 938–957.

[4] Ms. Mirsada Malagić, T. 1983-84, *Prosecutor v. Radislav Krstić* (IT-98-33-T).

[5] Judgment, *Krstic* (IT-98-3-T), Trial Chamber, 2 August 2001, § 2.

A final example concerns conflict-related sexual violence in Sri Lanka experienced by ethnic Tamil men and boys, perpetrated by Singhalese state actors. Many survivors articulated feelings of shame and emasculation associated with sexual violence as a gendered crime. Many also felt degraded by the use of abusive language (ethnic slurs) by perpetrators that underscored their sense of superiority.[6] Here, gender intersected with nationalist narratives on the dominance of the Singhalese ruling class, the cultural and ethnic hierarchies that fed this dominance and fuelled sexual violence, juxtaposed against the minority status of being Tamil in Sri Lanka, and legacies of colonialism.

Let's wrap up: In the examples discussed, we see how factors such as gender, class, social and economic status, age, culture, ethnicity, religion, and colonial status intersected to compound and hone past violations and harms at an individual and community level, while straddling the present and the future.

This is why intersectionality matters – it seeks to uncover violations with an understanding of the past, as well as the present and future realities of survivors – as multi-dimensional complex human beings – that we all are.

Thus, intersectionality can make visible other pertinent factors and structural inequalities, alongside gender, that are often disregarded or overlooked. A single-axis analysis would not have done justice to survivors' experiences in this way.

An intersectional approach provides another tool in our armoury to deepen our contextual understandings of affected individuals, communities, and the systems of privileges and disadvantages that define them. It enables a more precise and comprehensive articulation of the nature of violations, harms, and their impacts.

This is what intersectionality can bring to the table when properly executed. Critically, it calls for intentionality in seeking to make visible what is excluded and unseen at first glance.

Intersectional analysis has the power to set us on a trajectory towards more survivor-responsive justice processes and outcomes – the very aim that has brought us all together today.

I will leave my remarks at that.

Finally, I would like to thank fellow participants in the Webinar series on 'Intersectionality and International Criminal Law' organised by the Emergent Justice Collective, for their insights that have informed my remarks today.

Thank you.

[6] A report by the International Truth and Justice Project Sri Lanka, an NGO that documents conflict-related sexual violence and torture in Sri Lanka, focuses on sexual violence against mostly Tamil men and boys. It contains a narrative analysis of the experiences of more than 100 male victims of sexual violence by the state security forces in Sri Lanka in 2014–2018. Most were detained and abused multiple times. See H. Touquet, *Unsilenced: Male Survivors Speak of Conflict-Related Sexual Violence in Sri Lanka* (International Truth and Justice Project, 2018), available at www.itjpsl.com/assets/ITJP_unsilenced_report-final.pdf.

PART II

ICC Judgments Reimagined

8

The Situation in the Democratic Republic of the Congo

8.1 REFLECTION: THE SITUATION IN THE DEMOCRATIC REPUBLIC OF THE CONGO

Aparajitha Narayanan and Sandrine de Herdt

INTRODUCTION

This chapter introduces the ICC decisions[1] concerning the *Lubanga* and *Ntaganda* cases delivered in the context of the situation in the DRC, and the reparations order of the *Lubanga* case.[2] It summarises the key facts and outcomes of each of these decisions and then considers how the authors of subsequent contributions have reimagined these ICC decisions from a feminist perspective. How the reimagined judgments depart from the original ICC decisions will be analysed and what makes them 'feminist' will be assessed. Finally, this contribution will conclude by critiquing the importance of the reimagined judgments in the context of 'gender-sensitive' ICC decision-making.

BACKGROUND TO THE CONFLICT

The *Lubanga* case in which Thomas Lubanga was charged with crimes related to child soldiers served as an ICC landmark for more reasons than one, chief among them being that it was the first case ever before the ICC. It was hoped by many

[1] *Prosecutor v. Thomas Dyilo Lubanga* (ICC-01/04-01/06-3129-AnxA), Appeals Chamber, 3 March 2015; Situation in the Democratic Republic of the Congo, *Prosecutor v. Bosco Ntaganda* (ICC-01/04-02/06-2359), Trial Chamber, 8 July 2019.

[2] Judgment on the appeals against the 'Decision establishing the principles and procedures to be applied to reparations' of 7 August 2012 with Amended order for reparations, *Prosecutor v. Thomas Dyilo Lubanga* (ICC-01/04-01/06-3129), Appeals Chamber (Annex A) and public annexes 1 and 2, 3 March 2015.

survivors of the DRC conflict and civil society advocates that the case would serve as a reminder that this 'new' system of international criminal justice would hold perpetrators of international crimes to account. The eventual guilty verdict and sentencing only managed to partially satisfy the wishes of the international community, especially those interested in gender justice.[3]

Prior to discussing the details of the cases before the ICC, it is important to set the factual scene against which the conflict associated with the ICC trials in the Democratic Republic of Congo (DRC), including that of Mr Ntaganda, took place. The multi-ethnic Ituri region of the DRC is known for its abundant natural resources, which include coltan, diamonds, gold, and petroleum.[4] However, from 1999 onwards, these resources became a root cause of inter-ethnic tensions in the region.[5] By 2002, Ituri was 'plunged into conflict over land distribution and the ownership of natural resources'.[6]

Prior to 2002, the dominant Hema ethnic group in Ituri coexisted peacefully with other ethnic groups, until DRC politicians whose primary aim was to (illegally) trade in Ituri's abundant natural resources became involved.[7] One of these politicians was Mr Thomas Lubanga Dyilo (hereinafter Mr Lubanga), who formed the Union des Patriotes Congolais (UPC). He also established and became head of a non-state armed group, the UPC's military wing, the Forces Patriotiques pour la Liberation du Congo (FPLC).[8] As the head of FLPC, between July 2002 and December 2003, Mr Lubanga, with other members, 'undertook the large-scale enlistment of children under the age of fifteen years who were trained in the FPLC training camps . . . and who subsequently participated actively in hostilities'.[9] Mr Bosco Ntaganda (hereinafter Mr Ntaganda), was also involved as the Deputy Chief of Staff and commander of the FPLC.[10]

It is important to the context of these cases to also note that the DRC has been recognised as a country with one of the highest rates of sexual violence in the world. There are reports stating that during the conflict, girl soldiers were regularly raped, and boy soldiers were forced to rape and were also raped themselves.[11]

3 L. Chappell, 'The Politics of Gender Justice at the ICC: Legacies and Legitimacy', EJIL:Talk!, Blog of the European Journal of International Law, 16 December 2016, available at www.ejiltalk.org/the-politics-of-gender-justice-at-the-icc-legacies-and-legitimacy/.

4 Closing Brief of the V02 Group of Victims, *Prosecutor v. Thomas Lubanga Dyilo* (ICC-01/04-01/06), Trial Chamber I, 1 June 2011, § 14.

5 *Ibid*, § 16.

6 *Ibid*, § 16.

7 *Ibid*, §§ 18–19.

8 *Ibid*, § 19.

9 *Ibid*, § 21.

10 For context, see generally: ICC, Case Information Sheet, available at www.icc-cpi.int/sites/default/files/CaseInformationSheets/NtagandaEng.pdf.

11 B. Inder, 'Reflection: Gender Issues and Child Soldiers – The Case of Prosecutor v Thomas Lubanga Dyilo', *International Justice Monitor*, 31 August 2011, available at www.ijmonitor.org/2011/08/reflection-gender-issues-and-child-soldiers-the-case-of-prosecutor-v-thomas-lubanga-dyilo-2/.

Sexual violence was used as a tool to demonstrate control over the child soldiers by the UPC and conscription of the children by the UPC was clearly not gender-neutral. In the *Lubanga* case, the UN Under-Secretary General for Children and Armed Conflict, Ms Radhika Coomaraswamy, provided testimony as an expert witness.[12] In her testimony, she specifically described the roles girl soldiers are forced to play in conflict situations, including that of cooks, porters, nurses, and translators, together with being sexually exploited.[13] However, while the ICC analysed the child soldiers issue in the *Lubanga* case, the Prosecutor's decision not to prosecute crimes of sexual violence and the failure to disclose exculpatory evidence to the defence stirred controversy among DRC survivors and civil society groups.[14] Further, when the Appeals Chamber reversed the Trial Chamber's decision to modify the legal characterisation of the facts to include the crimes of 'inhuman treatment' and 'sexual slavery', there was significant dissent. Many in the international criminal law community felt that the charges brought against Mr Lubanga were too narrow and did not accurately represent the full breadth of the crimes allegedly committed by him.

SITUATION IN THE DRC

In 2003, when the ICC commenced its work in earnest, it was announced by the then Prosecutor, Mr Luis Moreno Ocampo, that the DRC would be selected as the most urgent situation for investigation. In 2004, President of the DRC, Joseph Kabila, referred the situation to the ICC for all crimes occurring after 1 July 2002.

In June 2004, Prosecutor Luis Moreno Ocampo announced that he found reasonable basis to commence an investigation. Mr Lubanga was accused as a co-perpetrator of the war crime of enlisting and conscripting children under the age of fifteen and using them to participate actively in hostilities. An ICC arrest warrant was issued for Lubanga on 10 February 2006 and the charges were confirmed by Pre-Trial Chamber I on 29 January 2007. On 26 January 2009, the *Lubanga* trial opened before Trial Chamber I.

Mr Ntaganda was charged with thirteen counts of war crimes and five counts of crimes against humanity committed in 2002–2003 in the Ituri district of the DRC. The trial of Ntaganda opened on 2 September 2015 with closing statements from 28 to 30 August 2018. The ICC Prosecutor was Mr Karim A. A. Khan.

[12] Judgment, Situation in the Democratic Republic of the Congo, *Prosecutor v. Thomas Dyilo Lubanga* (ICC-01/04-01/06), Trial Chamber I, 14 March 2012, § 577.

[13] *Ibid.*

[14] K. J. Heller, 'A Problematic Take on the Lubanga Trial', *Opinio Juris*, 17 January 2018, available at http://opiniojuris.org/2018/01/17/a-revisionist-take-on-the-lubanga-trial/.

BACKGROUND TO THE RELEVANT ICC CASES

Lubanga

As stated above, Mr Lubanga was charged and later convicted by the ICC[15] along with his co-perpetrators for agreeing to, and participating in, a common plan to build an army, whose purpose was to establish and maintain control over the Ituri region. Owing to this common plan, children under the age of fifteen were conscripted into the UPC and FPLC between 1 September 2002 and 13 August 2003. The role Lubanga played in the UPC and FPLC, how aware he was of his specific role, his exercise of authority and implementation of UPC/FPLC plans, which included the recruitment of children under the age of fifteen and, most importantly, making them participate in hostilities, led to his charges and subsequent conviction by the ICC. Mr Lubanga was found guilty of the war crime of 'enlisting and conscription of children under the age of 15 years and using them to participate actively in hostilities' on 14 March 2012 and was sentenced on 10 July 2012 to fourteen years' imprisonment. This verdict and sentence was confirmed by the Appeals Chamber[16] of the ICC in December 2014.

In their judgment, the Chamber also found that the Office of the Prosecutor (OTP) should not have delegated its investigative responsibilities to intermediaries. This led to the submission of unreliable evidence and consequently contributed to a delay in the proceedings.[17] The Lubanga case spanned six years from arrest to conviction, largely due to two successive suspensions of proceedings. The length of ICC proceedings has been criticised due to its impact on the rights of the accused, as well as costs. The OTP did not make potentially exculpatory evidence available to the defence in the first instance.[18] Furthermore, in the second instance, the question of impossibility of a fair trial arose when it was found that the defence of the identity of an intermediary (whose veracity had been called into question) was not disclosed by the OTP, in spite of being ordered to do so by the Court.[19] The Appeals Chamber reversed both suspensions in October 2010, citing that sanctions should have been made instead.[20]

[15] Lubanga, Trial Chamber, *supra* note 1.

[16] Lubanga, Appeals Chamber, *supra* note 1.

[17] 'Thomas Lubanga Dyilo', Coalition for the ICC, available at www.coalitionfortheicc.org/cases/thomas-lubanga-dyilo.

[18] Decision on the Consequences of Non-Disclosure of Exculpatory Materials Covered by Article 54(3)(e) Agreements and the Application to Stay the Prosecution of the Accused, together with Certain other Issues Raised at the Status Conference on 10 June 2008, *Prosecutor v. Lubanga* (ICC-01/04-01-06/1401), 13 June 2008.

[19] Decision on the Prosecution's Urgent Request for Variation of the Time-Limit to Disclose the Identity of Intermediary 143 or Alternatively to Stay Proceedings Pending Further Consultations with the VWU, *Prosecutor v. Lubanga* (ICC-01/04-01/06-2517 Red), 8 July 2010.

[20] Lubanga, Order for Reparations, *supra* note 2.

Ntaganda

In the *Ntaganda* case, on 15 June 2017, the Appeals Chamber of the ICC handed down the verdict after the defence challenged the jurisdiction of the Court over the war crimes of sexual violence.[21] The scope of the appeal boiled down to whether the Rome Statute's jurisdictional reach extends to members of the same armed forces for the war crime of rape and sexual slavery listed in Article 8(2)(b) in a non-international armed conflict. In 2017, the Trial Chamber ruled that sexual violence crimes where the victims and perpetrators are members of the same fighting force (intra-party war crimes) can amount to war crimes under the ICC Statute.[22] That finding was subsequently upheld on appeal.[23] On 8 July 2019, Trial Chamber VI of the ICC found Ntaganda guilty of five counts of crimes against humanity and thirteen counts of war crimes.[24] On 7 November 2019, Mr Ntaganda was sentenced to a total of thirty years' imprisonment.[25]

On 30 March 2021, the ICC Appeals Chamber confirmed the conviction and the sentence in this case.[26] On 8 March 2021, Trial Chamber VI delivered its Order on Reparations to victims against Ntaganda.[27] On 12 September 2022, the Appeals Chamber issued its judgment outlining its reasoning in this case.[28]

CRITICAL REFLECTION OF THE REIMAGINED CASES

The following section introduces the relevant original ICC decisions in the *Lubanga* and *Ntaganda* cases, while critiquing the reimagined decisions written by Judges Marie Wilmet (Lubanga), Priya Gopalan and Olga Jurasz (Ntaganda); and Isabel Maravall-Buckwater (Ntaganda).

[21] Situation in the Democratic Republic of the Congo, *Prosecutor v. Ntaganda* (ICC-01/04-02/06-1962), Appeals Chamber, 15 June 2017.
[22] Situation in the Democratic Republic of the Congo, *Prosecutor v. Ntaganda* (ICC-01/04-02/06-1707), Trial Chamber VI, 4 January 2017.
[23] Situation in the Democratic Republic of the Congo, *Prosecutor v. Ntaganda* (ICC-01/04-02/06-1962), Appeals Chamber, 15 June 2017.
[24] Situation in the Democratic Republic of the Congo, *Prosecutor v. Ntaganda* (ICC-01/04-02/06-2359), Trial Chamber VI, 8 July 2019.
[25] Situation in the Democratic Republic of the Congo, *Prosecutor v. Ntaganda* (ICC-01/04-02/06-2442), Trial Chamber VI, 7 November 2019.
[26] Situation in the Democratic Republic of the Congo, *Prosecutor v. Ntaganda* (ICC-01/04-02/06-2666-Red), Appeals Chamber, 30 March 2021; *ibid*, (ICC-01/04-02/06-2667-Red), Appeals Chamber, 30 March 2021.
[27] Situation in the Democratic Republic of the Congo, *Prosecutor v. Ntaganda* (ICC-01/04-02/06-2659), Trial Chamber VI, 8 March 2021.
[28] Situation in the Democratic Republic of the Congo, *Prosecutor v. Ntaganda* (ICC-01/04-02/06-2782), Appeals Chamber, 12 September 2022.

Judge Marie Wilmet: Reimagining the 'Reparations for Child Soldiers'

In 2015, the Appeals Chamber issued its decision regarding the reparations order in the case against Mr Lubanga.[29] The Appeals Chamber ruled that Mr Lubanga was not liable for reparations for child soldiers who were alleged victims of sexual violence committed by members of the armed forces under his control. Referring to the sentencing decision, the Appeals Chamber noted that the failure of the Trial Chamber to include sexual violence as an aggravating factor meant that it did not 'establish harm from sexual and gender-based violence resulted from the crime for which Mr Lubanga was convicted'.[30]

At trial, the standard of proof is 'beyond reasonable doubt', and at the reparations stage it is a less exacting standard of a 'balance of probabilities'.[31] Judge Marie Wilmet, in her reimagined decision, reconsiders the trial evidence, applying what she determines is the correct standard of 'balance of probabilities' rather than the 'beyond reasonable doubt' standard originally applied, and determines that, but for the crimes Mr Lubanga was convicted of, the child soldiers would not have experienced the relevant sexual and gender-based harm. With this conclusion, Wilmet allows those victims to qualify for reparations.

Judge Wilmet reimagines the recruitment of child soldier crimes in the *Lubanga* judgment[32] by using Article 21(3) as an interpretative tool. She demonstrates that, while the evidence presented by witnesses was limited to gender-based violence committed against girl soldiers, it is erroneous that boy soldiers be automatically excluded from reparations, since they did suffer from sexual and gender-based violence as a result of their conscription, enlistment, and use in the armed conflict. Wilmet's view that 'anyone – male or female – demonstrating that they suffered from sexual and gender-based violence as a result of the crimes committed by Mr Lubanga is eligible to benefit from reparations' is, in our opinion, a strong case. We found this to be particularly respectful and inclusive, while not losing sight of the factual particularities of the case, and situating it against the backdrop of the DRC's socio-economic conditions. What Judge Wilmet does not do is go beyond this brief reference to boy soldiers' experiences of sexual violence, which she might have chosen to do to better highlight the extent of these experiences. However, girl soldiers, deservingly so in our view, given the extent of the crimes against them, get an in-depth analysis of the harms suffered at the hands of the perpetrators. By doing so, in reimagining the case Judge Wilmet has applied Article 21(3) in a manner that ensures that intersectional and gender-sensitive injuries are at the fore.

29 Lubanga, Appeals Chamber, *supra* note 1.

30 Lubanga, Order of Reparations, *supra* note 2.

31 Decision on Sentence pursuant to Article 76 of the Statute, Lubanga (ICC-01/04-01/06-2901), Trial Chamber I, 10 July 2012, § 67.

32 Lubanga, Order of Reparations, *supra* note 2.

As ICC Judge Odio Benito stated in her dissenting Trial Chamber opinion in *Lubanga*, the Chamber did in fact receive ample evidence of the conditions, including sexual violence, in which boys and girls were recruited, enlisted, and used in the hostilities and reminded us 'to keep in mind the differential gender effects and damages that these crimes have upon their victims, depending on whether they are boys or girls'.[33] Judge Wilmet shows the value in Odio Benito's feminist lens, and in her reimagining rigorously narrates how the original decision failed to consider women's unique circumstances and the existence of power relationships. In her rewritten decision, Judge Wilmet discusses how the seemingly gender-neutral war crime of conscription of children to actively participate in an armed conflict differently impact on girl and boy soldiers.

Critiques of the *Lubanga* case have focused on the constraints surrounding the 'recognition of harms experienced by girl child soldiers and whether gendered experiences and roles were sufficiently reflected'.[34] The route the Trial Chamber took in the original decision was viewed as suppressing the complexity of harms suffered by girls and established a hierarchy of harms; some were for substantive offences while others were categorised as being relevant for sentencing or reparations.[35] In a remarkably succinct paragraph, Judge Wilmet moves away from this approach and highlights the forms of 'physical or mental injury, emotional suffering, economic loss, or substantial impairment of his or her fundamental rights' applicable to this case. This exposition of how each of these forms of injury was suffered by the child soldier victims who were conscripted by the UPC also aids in understanding the gendered experiences of these child soldier victims, especially those to whom the original decision was blind.

Finally, Judge Wilmet, when holding that the child soldier victims qualify for reparations, clarifies that sexual and gender-based violence are also criminal acts which should be prosecuted as such. In doing so, Judge Wilmet's rewritten judgment strongly criticises the former Prosecutor Mr Ocampo's omission of sexual and gender-based crimes in the original charges.

33 Dissenting Opinion of Judge Odio Benito, Sentencing Decision, §§ 6, 7, 13.

34 S. Merope, 'Recharacterizing the Lubanga Case: Regulation 55 and the Consequences for Gender Justice at the ICC' 22 *Criminal Law Forum* (2011) 311–346; N. Hayes, 'Sisyphus Wept: Prosecuting Sexual Violence at the International Criminal Court' in W. Schabas, N. Hayes, and Y. Mcdermott (eds.), *Ashgate Research Companion to International Criminal Law: Critical Perspectives* (London: Routledge, 2013); Y. M. Brunger, E. Irving, and D. Sankey, 'The Prosecutor v. Thomas Lubanga Dyilo' in L. Hodson and T. Lavers (eds.), *Feminist Judgments in International Law* (Oxford: Hart, 2019), 409–444, at 413; see also L. Chappell, 'The Politics of Gender Justice at the ICC: Legacies and Legitimacy', EJIL:Talk!, Blog of the *European Journal of International Law*, 16 December 2016, available at www.ejiltalk.org/the-politics-of-gender-justice-at-the-icc-legacies-and-legitimacy/.

35 Brunger, Irving, and Sankey, *supra* note 34, at 415.

Judges Priya Gopalan and Olga Jurasz: Reimagining 'War Crimes within an Armed Group'

In 2017, Trial Chamber VI issued its decision regarding the challenge from the defence to the jurisdiction of the Court in respect to Counts 6 and 9 against Mr Ntaganda.[36] The Trial Chamber confirmed the charges of rape and sexual slavery of child soldiers as a war crime under Article 8(2)(e)(vi) of the Rome Statute, crimes allegedly committed as intra-party crimes. In this rewritten decision, Judges Priya Gopalan and Olga Jurasz confirm this decision. In doing so, they depart from the methods used by the original Chamber, instead, as explained below, situating their analysis in international humanitarian law (IHL) and treaty interpretation while simultaneously questioning the application of bodies of law created in historical contexts. Judges Gopalan and Jurasz also work to amplify the voices of victims, highlighting how nuances in gender relations influenced the commission of these crimes, particularly against female child soldiers.

More particularly, Gopalan and Jurasz's rewritten decision overlays a feminist lens onto the factual circumstances of the crimes. To begin with, they engage in feminist judging when 'asking the woman question',[37] pointing out how the apparently gender-neutral war crime of using children to participate actively in hostilities impacts differently on girl soldiers. Another important feature of feminist judging is the fact-telling process – that is, the contextualisation of women's experiences in the judgments' narrative. Judges Gopalan and Jurasz recognise the reality of girl soldiers' lives by pointing out a flaw in the Pre-Trial Chamber's legal grasp of sexual violence. In the rewritten decision, they bring the previously marginalised experience of girl soldiers to the fore and place the legal issues in a wider social context, taking into account the specificities of women's lives.[38] Finally, Judges Gopalan and Jurasz included specific and explicit references to 'girl soldiers' in their rewritten judgment, which gives a more realistic reading of the circumstances of the case. Yet, at the same time, one could highlight that these references make boy soldiers who suffered from rape invisible in the narrative of the judgment.

In concrete terms, they make a point of capturing the complexity of real-life experiences of girl soldiers, who are victims of the acts of sexual violence and threats thereof in armed conflicts. In doing so, they are drawing attention to the continuing nature of this crime. They concur with the Pre-Trial Chamber that girl soldiers were

[36] Situation in the Democratic Republic of the Congo, *Prosecutor v. Ntaganda* (ICC-01/04-02/06-1707), Trial Chamber VI, 4 January 2017. The Office of the Prosecutor charged Mr Ntaganda with, inter alia, '[r]ape of UPC/FPLC child soldiers, a war crime, punishable pursuant to article 8(2)(e)(vi)' (Count 6) and '[s]exual slavery of UPC/FPLC child soldiers, a war crime, punishable pursuant to article 8(2)(e)(vi)' (Count 9) (DCC, ICC-01/04-02/06-203-AnxA, pp. 57–58).

[37] K. T. Bartlett, 'Feminist Legal Methods' 103 *Harvard Law Review* (1990) 829–888, at 837.

[38] R. Hunter and E. Rackley, 'Feminist Judgments on the UK Supreme Court' 32 *Canadian Journal of Women and the Law* (2020) 85–113, at 96.

not contemporaneously taking part in hostilities during the time of the commission of the sexual violence and were therefore protected under IHL. They refute the Pre-Trial Chamber's basis for this conclusion, and in particular its focus on the specific and distinct time of the rape. In this context, they opine that the prevalence and frequency of acts of sexual violence experienced by girl soldiers as part of their daily lives and the long-standing impact of rape in both public and private spheres needed to be taken into account.[39]

While paying attention to the continuum of violence experienced by girl soldiers in and outside conflict settings, Judges Gopalan and Jurasz have shown concern for indirect victims such as the relatives of girl soldiers and the transgenerational transmission of trauma. It is telling that, in the Reparations Order in the same case, the ICC Chamber concluded that children who have been born out of rape and sexual slavery may qualify as direct victims, and are therefore entitled to reparations.[40] Judges Gopalan and Jurasz also argue that sexual violence is employed as a tactic of war to assert control over both the civilian population and the members of the same armed group, and that the sexual slavery and the participation in hostilities do not necessarily occur at distinct and different times. They highlight the perpetrators' powers of ownership that are continuously exercised across conflict and non-conflict settings. Furthermore, in their reimagining, these judges shed light on the socio-cultural tenets of the crime of sexual violence, identifying the need to take into account the patriarchal power structures in which sexual slavery is perpetrated in the DRC.

Judges Gopalan and Jurasz draw upon the Statute's reference to the 'established framework of international law' in order to permit recourse to IHL as a source of interpretation. In this context, they point to the evolutionary nature of the relevant treaties, including the Statute, the Geneva Conventions, and their Additional Protocols, in order to reflect the realities of child soldiering, and the protection of child soldiers, who shift regularly between different roles. Then, using Rome Statute Article 21(3) as an interpretive tool to reach their conclusion, they contextualise the gendered aspects of child soldiering and the use of girls for sexual purposes. They apply and interpret Article 21 in a manner that 'surfaces' gendered and intersectional harms. In their rewritten version, they include the experience of girl soldiers in the construction of legal rules and the rules of interpretation in particular.

In their rewritten judgment, Judges Gopalan and Jurasz make the gender issues visible within their feminist retelling of the facts; the complexity and continuity of

39 R. Grey, 'The Limits and Potential of International Criminal Law' 16(4) *International Feminist Journal of Politics* (2014) 601–621, at 613–614; A. Swaine, 'Beyond Strategic Rape and between the Public and Private: Violence against Women in Armed Conflict' 37(3) *Human Rights Quarterly* (2015) 755–786.

40 Public Redacted Version of the 'Submissions by the Common Legal Representative of the Victims of the Attacks on Reparations', *Prosecutor v. Bosco Ntaganda* (ICC-01/04-02/06-2477-Red), Trial Chamber VI, 28 February 2020, § 38.

the sexual violence in armed conflict is clearly underlined. One point that we felt was missing in their judgment was addressing the corrosive political and socio-economic effects of the sexual violence to cover the full spectrum of the temporal analysis of the crime.[41]

Judge Isabel Maravall-Buckwater: Reimagining 'Consent'

In 2019, Trial Chamber VI issued the judgment in the case against Bosco Ntaganda. Convicted of eighteen counts of war crimes and crimes against humanity, the volume of sexual violence, especially against women and girls, was a particular feature of this case.[42] In Judge Isabel Maravall-Buckwater's rewrite, the tension between age-related incapacity and consent is explored. She considers a global interpretation of consent while wanting to acknowledge the sexual agency of individuals, and in doing so uses the voices of victims to recount how the coercive environment within an armed conflict effectively eradicates consent. Through this approach, the reimagined judgment finds that multiple incidents of rape must be confirmed against Mr Ntaganda.

In international criminal law, it is unclear at what age, and in what circumstances, a child is legally capable of consenting to sexual acts. This issue has arisen in multiple cases concerning alleged sexual crimes against female children, including female child soldiers in the *Ntaganda* case. In her rewritten version of the 2019 *Ntaganda* trial judgment, Judge Maravall-Buckwater examines the law regarding age-related incapacity to consent. Age-related incapacity constitutes one of the circumstances which render consent immaterial to the crime of rape. As 'age-related incapacity' remains undefined in both the Statute and Articles 7(1)(g) and 8(2)(e)(vi) of the Elements of Crime, Maravall-Buckwater considers it appropriate to flesh out details on this point. She holds that, under Article 21(3), the absence of age of consent defined in the law is incompatible with international human rights standards. She has further used Article 21 to incorporate findings/reports of the Convention on the Rights of the Child and the Committee on the Elimination of Discrimination against Women to ascertain what should be considered as the minimum age for consent. Using these international standards, she reaches the conclusion that sixteen is an appropriate age of consent.

In her rewritten judgment, Judge Maravall-Buckwater includes distinctive feminist features. First, her feminist judging provides reasoning with reference to the

[41] Report of the Secretary General on Conflict-Related Sexual Violence, S/2022/272, 29 March 2022, available at https://documents-dds-ny.un.org/doc/UNDOC/GEN/N22/293/71/PDF/N2229371.pdf?OpenElement, § 13.

[42] Situation in the Democratic Republic of the Congo, *Prosecutor v. Ntaganda* (ICC-01/04-02/06-2359), Trial Chamber VI, 8 July 2019.

actual lived experience of individuals and gives social context to issues.[43] Maravall-Buckwater also provides contextual facts related to the age of the victims of sexual violence, thus enhancing the individual lived experiences of victims. Secondly, her reimagined decision is inclusive in nature. Even though girls are more affected, she does not focus solely on the implications for women; by considering the question of the age of consent, she incorporates the experiences of all victims of sexual violence. On another note, one point that we felt was missing in her reimagined exposition of facts was giving a name to the unnamed girl soldiers who suffer rape.[44] Giving a name is considered important to personify a victim, and to demonstrate empathy with the experience of litigants.

As Cronin has indicated in the New Zealand feminist judgments project, this methodology carves out spaces to 'see cases in ways that we have been blind to and may be continuing to be blind to. In that sense, the feminist project has larger implications, showing us how to engage with facts in a different way, by letting those facts inform the law, rather than disregarding or ignoring them'.[45]

8.2 CHILD SOLDIERS IN LUBANGA REPARATIONS ORDER

Wilmet

In 2015, the Appeals Chamber issued its decision regarding the reparations order in the case against Mr Thomas Lubanga Dyilo.[46] The Appeals Chamber ruled that Mr Lubanga was not liable for reparations for child soldiers who were alleged victims of sexual violence committed by members of the armed forces under the control of Mr Lubanga. Referring to the Sentencing Decision,[47] the Appeals Chamber noted that the failure of the Trial Chamber to include sexual violence as an aggravating factor meant that the Trial Chamber did not 'establish harm from sexual and gender-based violence resulted from the crime for which Mr Lubanga was convicted'.[48]

In this reimagining of the appeal decision, Marie Wilmet begins by highlighting the 'gender injustice cascade' characteristic of the *Lubanga* case at

[43] K. Gooding, 'How Can the Methodology of Feminist Judgment Writing Improve Gender-Sensitivity in International Criminal Law' 5 *London School of Economics Law Review* (2020) 115–151, at 124.

[44] See Hunter and Rackley, *supra* note 38, at 100.

[45] B. Toy Cronin, 'Feminist Judgments of Aotearoa, New Zealand and Te Rino: A Two-Stranded Rope' 1 *New Zealand Women's Law Journal* (2017) 192–199, at 198.

[46] Judgment on the appeals against the Decision establishing the principles and procedures to be applied to reparations of 7 August 2012, *Lubanga* (ICC-01/04-01/06-3129), Appeals Chamber, 3 March 2015.

[47] Sentence, *Lubanga* (ICC-01/04-01/06-2901), Trial Chamber I, 10 July 2012.

[48] Judgment on the appeals against the Decision establishing the principles and procedures to be applied to reparations of 7 August 2012, *Lubanga* (ICC-01/04-01/06-3129), Appeals Chamber, 3 March 2015, § 198.

the ICC.[49] Recalling the procedural background of the case, the author provides for judicial recognition from the ICC's highest Chamber of the Prosecutor's failure to include sexual and gender-based crimes within the charges and of Judge Odio Benito's gender-just interventions in dissenting opinions. Wilmet reconsiders the trial evidence, applying the correct standard of 'balance of probabilities' rather than the misused 'beyond reasonable doubt' standard originally applied, and determines that but for the crimes Mr Lubanga was convicted of, the child soldiers would not have experienced harms from sexual and gender-based violence. With this conclusion, Wilmet allows those victims to qualify for reparations.

No. ICC-01/04-01/06 A A 2 A 3
Date: 3 March 2015

Original: English

THE APPEALS CHAMBER(B)

Before: Judge Marie WILMET

SITUATION IN THE DEMOCRATIC REPUBLIC OF THE CONGO IN THE CASE OF THE *PROSECUTOR v. THOMAS LUBANGA DYILO*

Judgment

On the appeals against the Decision establishing the principles and procedures to be applied to reparations of 7 August 2012

Fourth Element: The Order for Reparations Must Define the Harm Caused to Direct and Indirect Victims as a Result of the Crimes for Which the Person Was Convicted, as well as Identify the Appropriate Modalities of Reparations Based on the Circumstances of the Case

Assessing the Harm Suffered by the Victims of Sexual and Gender-Based Violence

BACKGROUND AND RELEVANT PORTION OF THE IMPUGNED DECISION

192. In their victims' applications, 129 victims claim that they have suffered harm as a result of the enlistment or conscription of children under the age of fifteen, or their use to participate actively in the hostilities.[50] Of these victims, eighteen females and twelve males have referred to acts of sexual violence which they suffered or witnessed as part of the enlistment, conscription, or use of children under the age of

[49] L. Chappell, 'The Gender Injustice Cascade: 'Transformative' Reparations for Victims of Sexual and Gender-Based Crimes in the Lubanga Case at the International Criminal Court' 21(9) *International Journal of Human Rights* (2017) 1223–1242.

[50] Judgment pursuant to Article 74 of the Statute, *Lubanga* (ICC-01/04-01/06-2842), Trial Chamber I, 14 March 2012, § 16 (hereafter Article 74 Trial Judgment).

fifteen by the Union des Patriotes Congolais (UPC)/Forces Patriotiques pour la Liberation du Congo (FPLC).[51]

193. On 28 August 2006, the Prosecutor charged Thomas Lubanga Dyilo (Mr Lubanga) with enlisting and conscripting children under the age of fifteen into the FPLC and using them to participate actively in hostilities within the meaning of Articles 8(2)(b)(xxvi) and 25(iii)(a) of the Statute.[52] He did not charge Mr Lubanga with sexual and gender-based crimes.[53]

194. In the 29 January 2007 Decision on the confirmation of charges, Pre-Trial Chamber I found that there was sufficient evidence to establish substantial grounds to believe that Mr Lubanga was responsible for the charges of conscription, enlistment, and use of children under the age of fifteen into the UPC/FPLC.[54]

195. On 22 May 2009, the legal representatives of the victims filed a joint application pursuant to Regulation 55 of the Regulations of the Court.[55] They requested the Trial Chamber consider a legal re-characterisation of the facts in view of the large number of witnesses who referred to numerous cases of inhuman and cruel treatment as well as sexual violence before the Chamber.[56]

196. In its 14 July 2009 Decision, Trial Chamber I explained that it appeared 'to the majority of the Chamber that the legal characterisation of facts may be subject to change' in accordance with Regulation 55(2), Judge Fulford dissenting.[57] The majority of the Chamber stated that the defence, the prosecution, and the victims' legal representatives would be given an opportunity to make submissions on the requalification at a later stage of the proceedings.[58] On 8 December 2009, the Appeals Chamber reversed the decision on the grounds that the Trial Chamber erred in law 'when finding that Regulation 55 contained two separate procedures and that it was permissible under Regulation 55 (2) and (3) to include additional facts and circumstances that are not described in the charges'.[59]

[51] *Ibid.*

[52] Decision on the confirmation of charges, *Lubanga* (ICC-01/04-01/06-803-tEN), Pre-Trial Chamber I, 29 January 2007, § 9 (hereafter Confirmation of Charges Decision).

[53] Article 74 Trial Judgment, *supra* note 50, § 629.

[54] Confirmation of Charges Decision, *supra* note 52, at 156–157.

[55] Joint Application of the Legal Representatives of the Victims for the Implementation of the Procedure under Regulation 55 of the Regulations of the Court, *Lubanga* (ICC-01/04-01/06-1891-tENG), Trial Chamber I, 22 May 2009.

[56] *Ibid*, §§ 15 and 23.

[57] Decision giving notice to the parties and participants that the legal characterisation of the facts may be subject to change in accordance with Regulation 55(2) of the Regulations of the Court, *Lubanga* (ICC-01/04-01/06-2049), Trial Chamber I, 22 May 2009, § 35.

[58] *Ibid*, § 34.

[59] Judgment on the appeals of Mr Lubanga Dyilo and the Prosecutor against the Decision of Trial Chamber I of 14 July 2009 entitled 'Decision giving notice to the parties and participants that the legal characterisation of the facts may be subject to change in accordance with Regulation 55(2) of the Regulations of the Court', *Lubanga* (ICC-01/04-01/06-2205), Appeals Chamber, 8 December 2009, § 112.

197. On 14 March 2012, Trial Chamber I issued its Judgment pursuant to Article 74 of the Statute and convicted Mr Lubanga of the war crimes of enlisting, conscripting, and using children under the age of fifteen to participate in hostilities. The Chamber recognised it heard evidence from witnesses that girl soldiers were subjected to sexual violence and rape by UPC/FPLC commanders.[60] The majority, however, disagreed with the Prosecutor's argument that the recruitment of girls for sexual purposes and forced marriage was an integral part of the 'active participation in hostilities' of child soldiers,[61] and that sexual abuse was systematic in the training camps.[62] Considering 'the prosecution's failure to include allegations of sexual violence in the charges',[63] the Chamber did not make 'any findings of fact on the issue, particularly as to whether responsibility [was] to be attributed to the accused'.[64] As the relevant facts were not included in the Decision on the Confirmation of Charges, the majority found that 'it would be impermissible for the Chamber to base its Decision . . . on the evidence introduced during the trial'.[65] Judge Odio Benito dissented from the majority, stating that '[a]lthough the Majority of the Chamber recognises that sexual violence has been referred to in this case, it seems to confuse the factual allegations of this case with the legal concept of the crime, which are independent'.[66] The dissenting judge argued that sexual violence was an intrinsic part of using children to participate actively in the hostilities and could be subsumed under Article 8(2)(b)(xxvi) of the Statute.[67]

198. In its Decision on Sentence pursuant to Article 76 of the Statute of 10 July 2012, the Trial Chamber examined whether rape and other forms of sexual violence could be a relevant factor in the determination of the sentence under Rule 145(1)(c) of the Rules of Procedure and Evidence.[68] The majority found that it could not consider sexual violence as a relevant factor for sentencing, stating:

> On the basis of the totality of the evidence introduced during the trial on this issue, the Majority is unable to conclude that sexual violence against the children who were recruited was sufficiently widespread that it could be characterised as occurring in the ordinary course of the implementation of the common plan for which Mr Lubanga is responsible. Moreover, nothing suggests that Mr Lubanga ordered or encouraged sexual violence,

60 Article 74 Trial Judgment, *supra* note 50, §§ 890–896.

61 Prosecution's Closing Brief, *Lubanga* (ICC-01/04-01/06-2748-Red), Trial Chamber I, 1 June 2011, §§ 139–143.

62 *Ibid*, §§ 205, 229.

63 Article 74 Trial Judgment, *supra* note 50, §§ 629, 896.

64 *Ibid*, §§ 896, 913.

65 *Ibid*, § 630.

66 Separate and Dissenting Opinion of Judge Odio Benito, Trial Judgment, § 16.

67 *Ibid*, § 20.

68 Decision on Sentence pursuant to Article 76 of the Statute, *Lubanga* (ICC-01/04-01/06-2901), Trial Chamber I, 10 July 2012, § 67 (hereafter Sentencing Decision).

that he was aware of it or that it could otherwise be attributed to him in a way that reflects his culpability.[69]

199. Judge Odio Benito dissented from the majority considering that the Chamber received ample evidence during trial of the conditions, including sexual violence, in which boys and girls were recruited, enlisted, and used in the hostilities.[70] She insisted on the importance 'to keep in mind the differential gender effects and damages that these crimes have upon their victims, depending on whether they are boys or girls'.[71]

200. In the Decision establishing the principles and procedures to be applied to reparations of 7 August 2012 (Impugned Decision), the Trial Chamber identified victims of sexual and gender-based violence as beneficiaries of reparations.[72] It found that 'the Court should formulate and implement reparations awards that are appropriate for the victims of sexual and gender-based violence'.[73] The Trial Chamber stated that pursuant to Articles 21(3) and 68 of the Statute as well as Rule 86 of the Rules, reparations should be granted to victims without adverse distinction on the grounds of, inter alia, gender and take into account the needs of sexual and gender-based violence victims.[74]

SUBMISSIONS OF THE PARTIES AND PARTICIPANTS

201. Mr Lubanga submits that the Trial Chamber erred in law by finding that victims of sexual violence could benefit from reparations, contradicting the principle according to which the convicted person can only repair harms resulting from crimes he has been convicted of.[75] He argues that the Prosecutor limited the scope of the case to the crimes of recruiting, enlisting, and using children in hostilities, and that the Trial Chamber dismissed the contention that the commission of these crimes would necessarily lead to the perpetration of sexual violence, including at the sentencing stage.[76] Additionally, Mr Lubanga argues that Article 8 (2)(e)(vii) of the Statute, the corresponding elements of crimes, and international law do not link the commission of these crimes to sexual violence.[77]

69 *Ibid*, § 74.

70 Dissenting Opinion of Judge Odio Benito, Sentencing Decision, §§ 6, 7, 13.

71 *Ibid*, § 13.

72 Decision establishing the principles and procedures to be applied to reparations, *Lubanga* (ICC-01/04-01/06-2904), Trial Chamber I, 7 August 2012, § 207 (hereafter Impugned Decision).

73 *Ibid*, § 207.

74 *Ibid*, §§ 189, 191, 200 (the Trial Chamber recognises that priority may need to be given to certain victims, including victims of sexual and gender-based violence).

75 Mémoire de la Défense de M. Thomas Lubanga relatif à l'appel à l'encontre de la '*Decision establishing the principles and procedures to be applied to reparations*', rendue par la Chambre de première instance le 7 août 2012, *Lubanga* (ICC-01/04-01/06-2972), Appeals Chamber, 5 February 2013, §§ 122–137.

76 *Ibid*, §§ 129–132.

77 *Ibid*, § 135.

202. The Office of Public Counsel for Victims and the legal representatives of victims V02 submit that 'the recruitment of girls into armed forces is generally recognised as having as primarily aim [sic] their use as sex slaves', justifying the participation of victims of these crimes in the reparations proceedings.[78] They argue that the key consideration is not the nature of the crimes for which the person was convicted, but rather the harm produced as a result of such crimes which must be evaluated following the 'proximate cause' test.[79] In their view, harms of a sexual nature normally result from the crimes of which Mr Lubanga was convicted, thus warranting reparation before the Court.[80] The legal representatives of victims V01 argue that the key issue is the causal link between the crime committed and the harm suffered.[81] They contradict the defence's suggestion that a harm is necessarily an element of a crime and argue that the fact that sexual violence was not sufficiently widespread to be a relevant factor at sentencing does not prevent the harms being considered at the reparations stage.[82]

203. 'The Trust Fund notes that a distinction must be made between the legal qualification of the facts [– meaning the crimes for which Mr Lubanga was convicted] ... – [and] the harm ... that resulted from these crimes'.[83] It submits that '[t]he standard test is, whether during the course of those facts that are the basis of the charges ... acts of sexualised violence were committed that are directly linked to, and are a component of, the acts and facts underlying the charges'.[84] The Trust Fund subsequently argues that sexualised violence is inherently connected to the enlistment, conscription, and use of child soldiers,[85] and that therefore victims are entitled to reparations addressing this specific harm.[86]

Determination of the Chamber

204. As a preliminary matter, the Appeals Chamber notes that pursuant to Article 21(3) of the Statute, the application and interpretation of the Court's legal framework 'must be consistent with internationally recognized human rights, and be without any adverse distinction founded on grounds such as gender as defined in Article 7,

78 Joint Response to the '*Mémoire de la Défense de M. Thomas Lubanga relatif à l'appel à l'encontre de la "Decision establishing the principles and procedures to be applied to reparations", rendue par la Chambre de première instance le 7 août 2012*', *Lubanga* (ICC-01/04-01/06-3010), Appeals Chamber, 8 April 2013, § 85.

79 *Ibid*, §§ 86, 96.

80 *Ibid*, §§ 97, 101.

81 Réponse au Mémoire de la Défense relatif à l'appel contre la '*Decision establishing the principles and procedures to be applied to reparations*' du 7 août 2012, *Lubanga* (ICC-01/04-01/06-3007), Appeals Chamber, 7 April 2013, §§ 58, 63.

82 *Ibid*, §§ 61–62.

83 Observations of the Trust Fund for Victims on the appeals against Trial Chamber I 's 'Decision establishing the principles and procedures to be applied to reparations', *Lubanga* (ICC-01/04-01/06-3009), Appeals Chamber, 8 April 2013, § 151.

84 *Ibid*, § 153.

85 *Ibid*, §§ 153–166.

86 *Ibid*, §§ 158, 166.

paragraph 3'. Article 7(3) defines gender as 'the two sexes, male and female, within the context of society'. The Appeals Chamber also notes that pursuant to Rule 86 of the Rules of Evidence and Procedure, a Chamber 'in making any direction or order . . . shall take into account the need of all victims and witnesses in accordance with Article 68, in particular . . . victims of sexual or gender violence'.

205. The prosecution's failure to charge Mr Lubanga with rape and other forms of sexual and gender-based violence as separate crimes is not determinative of the question of whether the underlying acts are a relevant factor in the determination of the reparations for which the accused is responsible. The Chamber is entitled to consider sexual violence under the fourth principle, according to which 'the order for reparations must define the harm caused to direct and indirect victims as a result of the crimes for which the person was convicted', established pursuant to Article 75 of the Statute and Rule 85(a) of the Rules of Procedure and Evidence.

206. As indicated by the Trial Chamber, the Court's legal framework determines only in general terms the required causal link between the harm and the crime for which the person was convicted for the purpose of reparations.[87] The Appeals Chamber recalls its earlier finding that, pursuant to Rule 85(a) of the Rules of Procedure and Evidence, '[r]eparation is to be awarded based on the harm suffered as a result of the commission of any crime within the jurisdiction of the Court'[88] and the 'causal link between the crime and the harm for the purpose of reparations is to be determined in light of the specificities of a case'.[89] The Appeals Chamber must therefore decide whether harm from sexual and gender-based violence resulted from the crimes for which Mr Lubanga has been convicted. In the present case, the Appeals Chamber considers that it can.

207. The Appeals Chamber finds that the Trial Chamber has correctly applied the 'but/for' standard of causation to the relationship between the harm suffered and the crime for which the person was convicted for the purpose of reparations.[90] The crimes must be the 'proximate cause' of the harm for which the reparations are sought, meaning that the liability of the person is limited to the causes that are closely connected to the result of the act they were convicted of.[91] The Appeals Chamber emphasises that the causal nexus must be 'determined in light of the particular circumstances' of this case.[92]

208. In line with the previous jurisprudence, the Chamber adopts the standard of proof of a 'balance of probabilities' as appropriate for the reparations proceedings.[93]

[87] Impugned Decision, *supra* note 72, § 248.
[88] *Ibid*, § 79.
[89] *Ibid*, § 80.
[90] *Ibid*, § 82.
[91] *Ibid*, §§ 82, 129; *Black's Law Dictionary* (8th ed., St Paul, MN: Thomson/West, 2004), at 662.
[92] Impugned Decision, *supra* note 72, § 80.
[93] *Ibid*, §§ 83–84, 136.

The applicant must therefore show that it is more probable than not that the harm suffered is a consequence of the crimes of which Mr Lubanga was convicted.

209. The Appeals Chamber will now analyse the significance of Trial Chamber I's sentencing decision for the present determination. The Trial Chamber considered whether the evidence of sexual violence presented at trial could constitute a factor relevant to sentencing under Rule 145(1)(c) of the Rules as part of '(i) the harm suffered by the victims; (ii) the nature of the unlawful behaviour; and (iii) the circumstances of manner in which the crime was committed'.[94] On the basis of the evidence introduced during the trial, the majority found that because the link between Mr Lubanga and the sexual violence against the children who were recruited had not been established beyond reasonable doubt, this factor could not be taken into account for the purpose of sentencing.[95]

210. Concurring with Judge Odio Benito's Dissenting Opinion, the Appeals Chamber finds that the Trial Chamber disregarded the harm suffered by the victims and considered 'as relevant factors only: (a) the large-scale and widespread nature of the crimes committed; (b) the degree of participation and intent of the convicted person; and (c) the individual circumstances of the convicted person'.[96] As such, the Appeals Chamber does not consider that the Trial Chamber's considerations on sentence limit its assessment of the causal relationship between sexual violence and the crimes of which Mr Lubanga was convicted.

211. Additionally, the Appeals Chamber confirms the Trial Chamber's finding that reparation proceedings are fundamentally different from proceedings at trial.[97] While the standard of proof at trial is 'beyond reasonable doubt',[98] at the reparations stage the standard is a 'balance of probabilities'. In the sentencing decision, the Trial Chamber considered the evidence introduced at trial in light of the 'beyond reasonable doubt' standard.[99] As the standard is less exacting at the reparations stage, the Appeals Chamber is of the view that it must now reconsider the trial evidence. It will determine whether, on a balance of probabilities, but for the crimes of which Mr Lubanga was convicted, the child soldiers *in the particular circumstances of this case* would have suffered from sexual violence.

212. In their victims' applications, thirty victims have referred to acts of sexual violence which they have suffered or witnessed as part of their enlistment, conscription, or use by the UPC/FPLC.[100] Eight witnesses have provided evidence on the treatment of girl soldiers by commanders in training camps.[101] According to P-0046

[94] Sentencing Decision, *supra* note 68, § 67.
[95] *Ibid*, §§ 69, 74–75.
[96] *Ibid*, Dissenting Opinion of Judge Odio Benito, § 5.
[97] Impugned Decision, *supra* note 72, § 251.
[98] Sentencing Decision, *supra* note 68, § 33.
[99] *Ibid*, § 33.
[100] Article 74 Trial Judgment, *supra* note 50, § 16.
[101] Witnesses P-0007, P-0008, P-0213, and P-0298 were child soldiers who gave direct evidence during the trial stage. However, the Trial Chamber ruled that their testimonies were unreliable.

and P-0031, sexual violence against young girls was prevalent and systematic in the training camps.[102] P-0046 explained that 'all the young girls stated they had been sexually abused by their commanders most often, or by – by soldiers', including girls as young as twelve.[103] Several witnesses testified that this conduct took place once they were stationed with commanders as bodyguards.[104] P-0016 explained that girl soldiers were used as domestic servants by their commanders, forced to perform domestic chores, and to have sexual relations.[105] The sexual violence was committed during an extended period as the commanders took the girls as 'wives' or 'concubines'.[106] P-0089, for example, testified that commanders in the Mandro training centre would take girl soldiers 'as women [and] [t]hey would get them pregnant',[107] including girls who were under fifteen years old.[108]

213. The sexual violence had significant effects on the lives of girl soldiers. P-0031 and P-0046 testified that many girls suffered physical consequences from the sexual violence, including in the form of sexually transmitted diseases.[109] As a result of the sexual violence, several experienced early childbearing, and the obligation to raise children born of rape.[110] Others had to undergo abortions (voluntary or forced) to end the pregnancy.[111] Additionally, P-0046 referred to the mental difficulties experienced by the girl soldiers as a result of the sexual violence.[112] Expert witness Dr Elisabeth Schauer testified that the child soldier victims of rape had higher exposure to traumatic stressors, leading to a higher likeliness to develop post-traumatic stress disorder.[113] Additionally, Dr Schauer noted the increased risk to

Consequently, the Appeals Chamber could not use their testimonies for the purpose of assessing the harms resulting from the crimes of which Mr. Lubanga was convicted. See Article 74 Trial Judgment, *supra* note 50, §§ 246–247, 406, 441.

102 T-207, available at www.icc-cpi.int/sites/default/files/Transcripts/CR2012_04179.PDF, at 30–31, 35–39 (hereafter T-207); T-202, available at www.icc-cpi.int/sites/default/files/Transcripts/CR2012_04160.PDF, at 10 (hereafter T202).

103 T-207, *supra* note 102, at 30, 31, 35.

104 T-114, available at www.icc-cpi.int/sites/default/files/Transcripts/CR2012_05383.PDF, at 23–24, 39 (hereafter T-114); T-154, available at www.icc-cpi.int/sites/default/files/Transcripts/CR2012_06441.PDF, at 82–83; T-122, available at www.icc-cpi.int/sites/default/files/Transcripts/CR2012_05102.PDF, at 26 (hereafter T-122).

105 T-191, available at www.icc-cpi.int/sites/default/files/Transcripts/CR2012_03907.PDF, at 17. Although infrequently, T-178, available at www.icc-cpi.int/sites/default/files/Transcripts/CR2012_04490.PDF, at 78–79.

106 T-114, *supra* note 104, at 25–27; T-122, *supra* note 104, at 26; T-207, *supra* note 102, at 31.

107 T-196, available at www.icc-cpi.int/sites/default/files/Transcripts/CR2012_05152.PDF, at 8.

108 *Ibid*, at 7–8.

109 *Ibid*, at 31; T-202, *supra* note 102, at 10, 17.

110 T-202, *supra* note 102, at 10; T-207, *supra* note 102, at 36–37.

111 T-207, *supra* note 102, at 31, 36-38.

112 *Ibid*, at 31.

113 T-166, available at www.icc-cpi.int/sites/default/files/Transcripts/CR2010_00121.PDF, at 48–49; see also Expert Report of Dr Schauer, 'The Psychological Impact of Child Soldiering' (ICC-01/04-01/06-1729-Anx1), available at www.icc-cpi.int/sites/default/files/RelatedRecords/CR2009_01399.PDF, at 10, 12 (hereafter Schauer Report).

develop psychiatric disorder due to the proximity between the perpetrator of rape and the child solder.[114] The reintegration of the girls into their original communities was very difficult as they were stigmatised, especially in the event they had children.[115]

214. The Appeals Chamber recalls that following the Court's jurisprudence, harm denotes 'hurt, injury and damage',[116] in the form of 'physical or mental injury, emotional suffering, economic loss or substantial impairment of his or her fundamental rights'.[117] Child soldiers who were victims of sexual and gender-based crimes during their conscription, enlistment, and use in the hostilities suffered physical, mental, social, and *sui generis* harms. They have suffered physical harm from the act of rape, sexually transmitted diseases, forced pregnancy, and forced abortions. Moreover, they have suffered mental harm through the development of psychiatric disorders and, amongst other, post-traumatic stress disorder. By forcing them to perform domestic chores, the victims have suffered social harms by being reduced to their social identities as defined by the perpetrators.[118] Due to their difficult reintegration in their original communities and the need to care for children born as a result of the sexual violence, the child soldiers have also suffered *sui generis* harms. These harms include the loss of socio-economic opportunities, of standard of living, but also of their familial development that would have been possible under normal circumstances.

215. Finally, the Appeals Chamber finds that the child soldiers suffered a substantial impairment to their fundamental rights to physical and mental integrity as well as sexual and reproductive autonomy, in the case of forced pregnancy and forced abortion.[119]

216. Mr Lubanga was found guilty as a co-perpetrator of committing the war crimes of enlisting and conscripting children under the age of fifteen into the FPLC as well as using them to participate in hostilities.[120] The Trial Chamber held that, as

[114] T-166, *supra* note 113, at 58–49.

[115] T-207, *supra* note 102, at 39; T-202, *supra* note 102, at 10.

[116] Impugned Decision, *supra* note 72, § 228. See also Decision on victims' participation, Lubanga (ICC-01/04-01/06-1119), Trial Chamber I, 18 January 2008, § 35 (hereafter Decision on victims' participation); Judgment on the appeals of the Prosecutor and the Defence against Trial Chamber I's Decision on Victims' Participation of 18 January 2008, *Lubanga* (ICC-01/04-01/06-1432), Appeals Chamber, 11 July 2008, § 31; Schauer Report, *supra* note 113, at 28.

[117] Decision on victims' participation, *supra* note 116, §§ 35, 92.

[118] K. Campbell, 'The Gender of Transitional Justice: Law, Sexual Violence and the International Criminal Tribunal for the Former Yugoslavia' 1 *International Journal of Transitional Justice* (2007) 411–432, at 429; F. Ni Aolain, 'Exploring a Feminist Theory of Harm in the Context of Conflicted and Post-Conflict Societies' 35 *Queen's Law Journal* (2009) 219–244, at 234.

[119] Universal Declaration of Human Rights, Article 25; Charter of Fundamental Rights of the European Union, Article 3; Convention on the Elimination of All Forms of Discrimination against Women, Article 16; Convention of the Rights of the Child, Article 24; International Covenant on Civil and Political Rights, Article 17.

[120] Article 74 Trial Judgment, *supra* note 50, § 1358.

part of the enlistment and conscription, children were sent to training camps where they endured a harsh training regime and were subjected to a variety of severe punishments.[121] It considered that using children under the age of fifteen as bodyguards, a common practice among commanders of the UPC/FPLC – including Mr Lubanga himself – fell within the scope of Article 8(2)(e)(vii).[122] The Chamber also found that in addition to the other tasks they carried out as UPC/FPLC soldiers, such as acting as bodyguards, 'a significant number of girls under the age of fifteen were used for domestic work'.[123] According to the Trial Chamber, as President of the UPC/FPLC, Mr Lubanga was inter alia closely involved in making decisions on recruitment policy and 'personally used children below the age of fifteen amongst his bodyguards and he regularly saw guards of other UPC/FPLC members of staff who were below the age of fifteen'.[124]

217. The Chamber recalls the Trial Chamber's conclusion that due to their vulnerability, children need to be afforded particular protection, as recognised in various international treaties.[125] It concurs that '[t]his includes not only protection from violence and fatal or non-fatal injuries during fighting, but also the potentially serious trauma that can accompany recruitment, including . . . exposing them to an environment of violence and fear'.[126]

218. In light of the above, the Appeals Chamber finds that *in the particular circumstances of this case* from the evidence presented at trial, the presence of child soldiers at training camp exposed them to an environment of violence and fear which made them vulnerable to sexual violence. Their close contact with commanders during an extended period of time exposed child soldiers, and especially girl soldiers, to danger by becoming potential targets of sexual violence. Indeed, this prolonged exposure in the homes of the commanders, and their assignation to domestic chores, made them defenceless and susceptible of being taken as 'wives' by their superiors.

219. The Appeals Chamber considers it is clear from the evidence presented at trial that, had they not been enlisted, conscripted, or used by the UPC/FPLC, particularly as bodyguards to commanders, the girl soldiers would not have suffered the sexual violence harms described above.[127] As required by the 'proximate cause'

[121] *Ibid*, §§ 911–914.
[122] *Ibid*, §§ 915, 1247.
[123] *Ibid*, § 882.
[124] *Ibid*, § 1356.
[125] Sentencing Decision, *supra* note 68, § 37; Protocol Additional to the Geneva Conventions of 12 August 1949, and relating to the Protection of Victims of International Armed Conflicts (Protocol I), Article 77(2); Protocol Additional to the Geneva Conventions of 12 August 1949, and relating to the Protection of Victims of Non-International Armed Conflicts (Protocol II), Article 4(3)(c); Convention on the Rights of the Child, Article 38; African Charter on the Rights and Welfare of the Child, Article 22(2).
[126] Sentencing Decision, *supra* note 68, § 38.
[127] *Ibid*, § 19.

standard, the sexual and gender-based violence is closely connected to the crimes of conscription, enlistment, and use of children in hostilities.

220. The Appeals Chamber therefore finds that it is more probable than not that the sexual and gender-based violence suffered by child soldiers resulted from the crimes of which Mr Lubanga was convicted, satisfying the standard of proof of a balance of probabilities applicable to the reparations stage.

221. The evidence presented by witnesses at trial focused on the sexual and gender-based violence committed against girl soldiers. Nevertheless, the Appeals Chamber considers that this fact does not in any way exclude boy soldiers who suffered from sexual and gender-based violence as a result of their conscription, enlistment and use, from receiving reparations. The Chamber recalls that under Article 21(3) of the Statute the application and interpretation of the Statute must 'be without any adverse distinction founded on grounds such as gender'. As such, the Appeals Chamber finds that anyone – male or female – demonstrating that they suffered from sexual and gender-based violence as a result of the crimes committed by Mr Lubanga is eligible to benefit from reparations.

222. Consequently, the Appeals Chamber considers that harm from sexual and gender-based violence resulted from the crimes for which Mr Lubanga was convicted. Child soldier victims of sexual and gender-based violence can therefore benefit from reparations. The Appeals Chamber clarifies that this conclusion should not be interpreted to mean that sexual and gender-based violence do not constitute criminal acts which should be prosecuted as such. The Chamber concurs with the Trial Chamber and 'strongly deprecates the attitude of the former Prosecutor in relation to the issue of sexual violence' and his omission of sexual and gender-based crimes in the original charges.[128]

Judge Marie Wilmet

8.3 WAR CRIMES WITHIN AN ARMED GROUP IN NTAGANDA JURISDICTION ORDER

Priya Gopalan and Olga Jurasz

In 2017, Trial Chamber VI issued its decision regarding the challenge from the defence to the jurisdiction of the Court in respect to Counts 6 and 9 against Mr Bosco Ntaganda.[129] The Trial Chamber confirmed the charges of rape and sexual slavery of child soldiers as a war crime under Article 8(2)(e)(vi) of the Rome Statute, crimes allegedly committed as intra-party crimes.

128 Article 74 Trial Judgment, *supra* note 50, § 60.

129 Second decision on the defence's challenge to the jurisdiction of the Court in respect of Counts 6 and 9, *Ntaganda* (ICC-01/04-02/06-1707), Trial Chamber VI, 4 January 2017.

In this reimagining, Priya Gopalan and Olga Jurasz confirm this decision. In doing so, they depart from the methods used by the original Chamber, instead situating their analysis in international humanitarian law and treaty interpretation while simultaneously questioning the application of bodies of law created in historical contexts. Gopalan and Jurasz also work to amplify the voices of victims, highlighting the particular nuances of gender that influenced the committal of these crimes, particularly against female child soldiers.

No.: ICC-01/04-02/06
Date: 4 January 2017

Original: English

TRIAL CHAMBER VI(B)

Before: Judge Priya GOPALAN
Judge Olga JURASZ

SITUATION IN THE DEMOCRATIC REPUBLIC OF THE CONGO IN THE CASE OF THE *PROSECUTOR v. BOSCO NTAGANDA*

Public

Second decision on the defence's challenge to the jurisdiction of the Court in respect of Counts 6 and 9.

Trial Chamber VI (Chamber) of the International Criminal Court (Court), in the case of the *Prosecutor v. Bosco Ntaganda*, having regard to Articles 8 and 19 of the Rome Statute (Statute) and Rule 58 of the Rules of Procedure and Evidence (Rules), issues this Second decision on the defence's challenge to the jurisdiction of the Court in respect of Counts 6 and 9.

Counts 6 and 9 were based on evidence that:

> UPC/FPLC commanders and soldiers raped and sexually enslaved their soldiers without regard to age, including child soldiers under the age of 15 . . . UPC/FPLC [Union des Patriotes Congolais/Forces Patriotiques pour la Liberation du Congo] commanders and soldiers referred to child soldiers (and other girls and women in the UPC/FPLC above the age of 15) as *guduria*, a large cooking pot, to mean that they could be used for sex whenever the soldiers wanted them for that purpose.[130]

The crimes underlying Counts 6 and 9 are found in Article 8(2)(e)(vi) for non-international armed conflicts. The provision reads in relevant parts:

[130] Document Containing the Charges, *Ntaganda* (ICC-01/04-02/06), Pre-Trial Chamber 1, 10 January 2014, § 100.

APPLICABLE LAW

Article 8 War Crimes

1. For the purpose of this Statute, 'war crimes' means: ...
   e. Other serious violations of the laws and customs applicable in armed conflicts not of an international character, within the established framework of international law, namely, any of the following acts: ...
   (vi) Committing rape, sexual slavery, enforced prostitution, forced pregnancy, as defined in Article 7, paragraph 2 (f), enforced sterilisation, and any other form of sexual violence also constituting a serious violation of Article 3 common to the four Geneva Conventions.

ANALYSIS OF THE MERITS OF THE CHALLENGE

Submissions on the Merits of the Challenge to Jurisdiction over Counts 6 and 9

2. The defence submits that Counts 6 and 9 do not fall within the subject matter jurisdiction of the Court because:[131]

(i) Article 8(2)(e)(vi) of the Statute is subject to the established requirements of international law;[132]
(ii) according to Article 3 common to the Geneva Conventions of 1949 (Common Article 3), war crimes may not be committed by members of an armed force against fellow members of the same armed force;[133]
(iii) the prosecution has defined the victims of Counts 6 and 9 as being 'members' of the same armed force as the perpetrators;[134]
(iv) the notion of 'membership' of an armed force is not compatible with 'taking no active part in hostilities';[135] and
(v) international humanitarian law does not recognise any exception for child soldiers.[136]

[131] Consolidated submissions challenging jurisdiction of the Court in respect of Counts 6 and 9 of the Updated Document containing the charges, *Ntaganda* (ICC-01/04-02/06-1256), Trial Chamber VI, 7 April 2016, § 27.
[132] *Ibid*, § 15.
[133] *Ibid*, §§ 17–22.
[134] *Ibid*, §§ 23–24.
[135] *Ibid*, §§ 26–32.
[136] *Ibid*, §§ 33–39.

Chamber's Analysis of the Court's Subject Matter Jurisdiction in Respect to Counts 6 and 9

Applicable Law

STATUS REQUIREMENTS UNDER ARTICLE 8 OF THE STATUTE

3. Common Article 3 refers to 'persons taking no active part in the hostilities'. Additional Protocol II, which applies in non-international armed conflicts, states that children 'shall be provided with the care and aid they require'.[137]

4. The Pre-Trial Chamber held that individuals only lose their protection for such time as they are actively participating in hostilities, and that those who were raped and subjected to sexual violence were clearly not participating in hostilities at that time.[138] It found that children lose their protection when they take direct part in hostilities, for the duration of their participation in the hostilities.[139]

5. On this basis, the Pre-Trial Chamber determined that sexual violence committed against child soldiers constituted war crimes under Article 8(2)(e)(vi) of the Rome Statute because children were protected by international humanitarian law (IHL) during the commission of the sexual violence.[140] The Pre-Trial Chamber determined that whether the girl soldiers in question assumed the role of combatants in the same armed group as the perpetrator was irrelevant to this finding.[141]

6. This Chamber concurs with the conclusion of the Pre-Trial Chamber that child soldiers are protected under IHL but respectfully disagrees with the Pre-Trial Chamber's basis for this conclusion, namely that the girl soldiers in question could not logically have been taking a direct/active part in hostilities at the precise time sexual violence was being perpetrated against them.[142]

137 Article 4(3) specifies that 'in particular … children who have not attained the age of fifteen years shall neither be recruited in the armed forces or groups nor allowed to take part in hostilities' (Article 4(3)(c)) and 'the special protection provided by this Article to children who have not attained the age of fifteen years shall remain applicable to them if they take a direct part in hostilities despite the provisions of sub-paragraph (c) and are captured' (Article 4(3)(d).

138 Decision pursuant to Article 61(7)(a) and (b) of the Rome Statute on the Charges of the Prosecutor against Bosco Ntaganda, *Ntaganda* (ICC-01/04-02/06-309), Pre-Trial Chamber II, 9 June 2014, § 79 (hereafter Decision pursuant to Article 61(7)(a) and (b)).

139 *Ibid.*

140 *Ibid.*

141 *Ibid*, § 80.

142 *Ibid*, § 79. The Pre-Trial Chamber observed that the Special Court for Sierra Leone (SCSL) undertook a similar assessment, in the case of *Prosecutor v. Charles Ghankay Taylor*, For a similar assessment, see Judgment, *Taylor* (SCSL-03-01-T), Trial Chamber II, 18 May 2012, §§ 1179, 1206(vii), 1207, 1451. The Trial Chamber found that sexual violence against Akiatu Tholley (a girl soldier who was raped by a member of her own group) was the war crime of 'outrages on personal dignity', under Article3(e) of the SCSL Statute. In finding that Tholley was a victim of a war crime, the Trial Chamber did not specifically discuss her role in the same armed group as the perpetrator. The Trial Chamber explained that in relation to this charge, 'each of the victims was not taking an active part in the hostilities at the time of the sexual

7. The Chamber observes that this interpretation does not represent the full spectrum of the lived experiences of girl soldiers in conflict. The focus on the specific time of the rape to find that a victim could not have been taking a direct or active part in hostilities while being raped appears to presume that rape occurred infrequently and in limited circumstances. The Chamber finds this to be a rigid and unrealistic assessment of the nature, frequency, and consequences of sexual violence experienced by girl soldiers. It is also an approach that marginalises the lived experiences of girl soldiers. The trial record contains substantial evidence of the widespread and systematic perpetration of rape and other forms of sexual violence against child soldiers, particularly girls, by adult UPC/FPLC commanders.[143] Given the prevalence and frequency of sexual violence in this case, a temporal analysis that focuses on single acts does not reflect the multiplicity of acts of sexual violence experienced by girl soldiers as part of their daily lives as well as multiple and intertwined types of abuse perpetrated against them.

8. In addition, the Chamber notes that a narrow focus on the act or acts of rape precludes any considerations of the long-standing impact of rape – in particular, the psychological trauma resulting from rape, which is a defining feature of this crime and other forms of sexual violence: sexual and gender-based violence causes grave and long-lasting physical, psychological and social effects at multiple levels. Individuals, families and communities are affected whether before, during or after the conflict in the DRC, both in public and private spheres'.[144] Finally, this approach does not recognise the strategic function wielded by sexual violence.

9. Considering the strategic purpose of sexual violence, the Chamber notes the dual manner in which violence, sexual violence, and threats thereof can be used to obtain military advantage. Firstly, this is externally facing and directed at terrorising and instilling fear in the civilian population, as recognised by and captured in the

violence': Judgment, *Taylor* (SCSL-03-01-T), Trial Chamber II, 18 May 2012, § 1207. See also R. Grey, 'Sexual Violence against Child Soldiers: The Limits and Potential of International Criminal Law' 16(4) *International Feminist Journal of Politics* (2014) 601–621, at 612.

[143] Decision pursuant to Article 61(7)(a) and (b), *supra* note 138, § 82. The Chamber recalls evidence that 'Abelanga, a UPC/FPLC soldier, raped a girl under the age of 15 years who was his bodyguard from November 2002 until at least March–May 2003. Around mid-August–beginning of September 2002, young girls, including under the age of 15 years, were raped in Mandro camp. They were "domestic servants" and they "combined cooking and love services". Another girl, aged 13 years, was recruited by the UPC/FPLC and continuously raped by Kisembo, a UPC/FPLC soldier, until he was killed in Mongbwalu'.

[144] See e.g. Human Rights Watch, *Soldiers Who Rape, Commanders Who Condone: Sexual Violence and Military Reform in the Democratic Republic of Congo* (2009), available at www.hrw.org/report/2009/07/16/soldiers-who-rape-commanders-who-condone/sexual-violence-and-military-reform; United Nations Population Fund, 'Secretary General Calls Attention to Scourge of Sexual Violence in DRC' (1 March 2009), available at www.unfpa.org/news/secretary-general-calls-attention-scourge-sexual-violence-drc; Médecins Sans Frontières, *'I Have No Joy, No Peace of Mind': Medical Psychological and Socio-Economic Consequences of Sexual Violence in Eastern DRC* (2004), available at www.msf.org.za/sites/default/files/publications/sexual_violence_no_joy_no_peace_of_mind.pdf.

jurisprudence of the Special Court for Sierra Leone.[145] Secondly, it is internally directed against members of the same armed group in order to exercise power and control over members of that armed group. This is not uncommon practice, especially in the context of recruiting and using children to participate in hostilities – an international crime that has been examined at length and prosecuted by this Court.[146] The Chamber finds that rape and sexual slavery committed against members of the same armed force or group – specifically children who were recruited and used to participate in hostilities – in this case are examples of the latter. The deployment of sexual violence in this context is a tool of exercising power and control over the victims and, as noted by the ICC Office of the Prosecutor, 'in conflict situations, acts of sexual and gender-based crimes rarely occur in isolation from other crimes'.[147] The Chamber recalls terminology such as 'strategic rape' or 'rape as a weapon of war' which has been used to describe the strategic purpose for which sexual violence is deployed in conflict.[148]

10. Turning to the crime of sexual slavery, the Chamber observes that a defining feature of the crime of sexual slavery is that the perpetrator exercises rights of ownership over the victim or imposes on the victim a similar deprivation of liberty, and forces the victim to engage in sexual acts.[149] In the context of girl soldiers, a common-sense interpretation of this crime is that sexual slavery continues so long as the perpetrator exercises rights of ownership over the victim or similarly deprives the victim of her liberty, and on at least one occasion forces the victim to engage in a sexual act. Within this interpretation, the crime continues even while the victim is actively or directly participating in hostilities, cooking, engaging as a porter, laying mines, spying, and/or manning checkpoints. The presumption underlying

[145] Judgment, *Sesay, Kallon & Gbao* (SCSL-04-15-T), Trial Chamber I, 2 March 2009, §§ 1348–1351.

[146] Judgment, *Lubanga* (ICC-01/04-01/06), Trial Chamber I, 14 March 2012; A. Honwana, *Child Soldiers in Africa* (Pittsburg: University of Pennsylvania Press, 2006); N. Quénivet, 'Girl Soldiers and Participation in Hostilities' 16(2) *African Journal of International and Comparative Law* (2008) 219–235; M. A. Drumbl, *Reimagining Child Soldiers* (Oxford: Oxford University Press, 2012).

[147] ICC, Policy Paper on Sexual and Gender-Based Crimes (2014), available at www.icc-cpi.int/sites/default/files/iccdocs/otp/OTP-Policy-Paper-on-Sexual-and-Gender-Based-Crimes–June-2014.pdf, § 59.

[148] See e.g. Dr. Dennis Mukwege Foundation, 'Sexual Violence as a Weapon War' (undated), available at www.mukwegefoundation.org/the-problem/rape-as-a-weapon-of-war/; M. Eriksson Baaz and M. Stern, *Sexual Violence as a Weapon of War? Perceptions, Prescriptions, Problems in the Congo and Beyond* (London: Zed Books, 2013); A. Swaine, 'Beyond Strategic Rape and between the Public and Private: Violence against Women in Armed Conflict' 37(3) *Human Rights Quarterly* (2015) 755–786.

[149] Article 8(2)(b)(xxii)-2; Article 8(2)(e)(vi)-2, Elements of Crimes, available at www.icc-cpi.int/sites/default/files/iccdocs/otp/OTP-Policy-Paper-on-Sexual-and-Gender-Based-Crimes–June-2014.pdf.

the Pre-Trial Chamber's finding appears to be that that the sexual slavery and the participation in hostilities occur at distinct and different times.[150]

11. The Chamber finds additional support for the continuing nature of this crime in the socio-cultural tenets underpinned by the systemic gender inequalities of patriarchal power structures in the Democratic Republic of Congo (DRC). The Chamber observes that it was in this context that sexual slavery was perpetrated. Up to 52 per cent of women in DRC are survivors of domestic violence and 39 per cent report having been threatened or injured. Reports indicate that 27 per cent of women in DRC are victims of harmful traditional practices. In 2007 early marriages affected 39 per cent of women in their early twenties who were married or in a union before the age of eighteen.[151]

12. The Chamber recalls that according to the Paris Principles, '[g]ender inequalities, discrimination and violence are frequently exacerbated in times of armed conflict'.[152] Sexual and gender-based violence has been a hallmark of the conflict in the DRC, with Margot Wallström, the UN Secretary General's Special Representative on Sexual Violence in Conflict, declaring that the DRC was the 'rape capital of the world' in 2010.[153] Decades of armed conflict have led to the deaths of over 2 million civilians and estimates suggest over 1 million women have been raped.[154]

13. The Chamber observes that in this context, once a girl becomes associated with an armed group and is used sexually, she becomes identified socially as a 'military wife'.[155] If a girl has sexual contact with a man – whether voluntarily, by rape, or by assumption due to being taken by an armed group – outside of marriage and dowry, she is considered to 'no longer have any value' in society.[156] In certain communities in the DRC, a traditional justice approach to cases of rape or sexual relations outside of marriage is to force the perpetrator to pay a dowry/compensation to the family and marry the girl.[157]

14. As such, there is a strong socio-cultural conception that a girl has to remain with a sexual partner, whether that relationship originated with or without her consent, including where this may be rape, thus entrenching the continuous nature of this violation.[158] Many girls simply do not see leaving their 'military husband' or

[150] Grey, *supra* note 1422, at 611–612.

[151] UN Women, 'Democratic Republic of Congo' (undated), available at https://africa.unwomen.org/en/where-we-are/west-and-central-africa/democratic-republic-of-congo (hereafter UN Women).

[152] The Paris Principles and Guidelines on Children Associated with Armed Forces or Armed Groups, February 2007 (hereafter The Paris Principles), § 6.0.

[153] BBC News, 'UN official calls DR Congo rape capital of the world' (28 April 2010), available at http://news.bbc.co.uk/2/hi/africa/8650112.stm.

[154] UN Women, *supra* note 151.

[155] B. Verhey, *Reaching the Girls, Study on Girls Associated with Armed Forces and Groups Save the Children – UK and the NGO Group: CARE, IFESH and IRC* (November 2004), available at https://resource-centre-uploads.s3.amazonaws.com/uploads/2600.pdf, at 2.

[156] *Ibid.*

[157] *Ibid.*

[158] *Ibid.*

'enslaver' as a choice, which reinforces the continuing nature of the crime of sexual slavery.[159]

15. The Chamber will now analyse whether the 'established framework of international law' applicable in non-international armed conflicts protects members of the same armed force from crimes committed by other members of the same armed force, with the result that the acts of sexual violence constituted war crimes under Article 8(2)(e)(vi) of the Rome Statute.

The 'Established Framework of International Law' Applicable in International and Non-international Armed Conflicts

16. Article 8(2)(e) refers to 'other serious violations of the laws and customs applicable in non-international armed conflicts, *within the established framework of international law*'. Similarly, the 'Introduction' to the Elements of Crimes for Article 8 provides that the war crimes under paragraph 2 'shall be interpreted within the established framework of the international law of armed conflict' as expressed in IHL.

17. The question of whether acts of rape and sexual slavery committed against members of an armed force or group by members of the same armed force or group must be considered not only in the context of the principles of IHL and international criminal law (ICL) (specifically, the Statute), but also positioned within the broader principles of international law.

PRINCIPLES OF INTERNATIONAL LAW: TREATY INTERPRETATION

18. This issue goes to the heart of the object and purpose of treaties – here, the Statute, the Geneva Conventions, and their Additional Protocols – as well as a matter of treaty interpretation. The body of IHL was created in the late nineteenth and mid-twentieth century, with Additional Protocol II being adopted over forty years ago. Since then, the nature, typology, and duration of armed conflicts has changed dramatically and so has the international community's knowledge about the lived experiences of modern armed conflicts. This includes the growing ICL jurisprudence on sexual and gender-based crimes which has advanced (i) the knowledge of international courts on how sexual violence is used in conflict and (ii) practice in successful prosecutions of such crimes. Furthermore, whilst children's participation in armed conflicts is not a novel issue in the realm of IHL, the past two decades have been instrumental in conceptualising and advancing the understanding of child soldiering in contemporary armed conflicts.[160] Therefore,

[159] *Ibid.*

[160] Optional Protocol to the UN Convention on the Rights of the Child 1989 on the involvement of children in armed conflict (2000); Judgment, *Lubanga* (ICC-01/04-01/06), Trial Chamber I, 14 March 2012; *Sesay, Kallon & Gbao*, *supra* note 145.

the Chamber considers that an evolutionary approach to treaty interpretation[161] (which treats them as 'living instruments') is required in light of the above developments as well as the rapidly changing nature of violations of IHL and ICL, that better reflect the realities of child soldiering.

19. The Chamber observes that in the context of the changing nature of conflict around the world, including in African countries such as the DRC, and the increasingly asymmetrical nature of such conflicts, the bright-line rule that was drawn in traditional or formal armed forces between those on the front line and those playing supportive roles in rear bases is no longer clear or tenable. This opacity is evident when it comes to the protection of child soldiers who shift regularly between different roles, whether as active fighters, guards, porters, cooks, bush wives, or sex slaves.

20. The Chamber recalls that the object and purpose of Article 8 of the Statute is to punish criminal acts committed 'in the context of and associated with' an armed conflict of either international or non-international character.[162] This criterion ultimately differentiates war crimes from other crimes. The Chamber views acts referred to in Counts 6 and 9 as satisfying this criterion and notes that members of an armed force or group are not categorically excluded from protection against the war crimes of rape and sexual slavery under Article 8(2)(e)(vi) of the Statute when these acts are committed by members of the same armed force or group.

21. Furthermore, the Chamber notes that the non-exhaustive nature of the protections provided under IHL is recognised in the Preamble to the Additional Protocol II. Echoing the Martens clause,[163] the Preamble states that 'in cases not covered by the law in force, the human person remains under the protection of the principles of humanity and the dictates of the public conscience'.[164] Whilst Additional Protocol II, at the time of drafting, has not explicitly captured victimisation, exploitation, and violence directed by members of an armed force or group against members of the same armed force or group as a war crime, it has not explicitly excluded it either.

22. The Chamber notes that the scope of Article 8 of the Statute, whilst drawing upon the principles of IHL, is not a verbatim reproduction of the relevant IHL provisions. In fact, Article 8 differs in scope and phraseology from IHL provisions.

[161] See, for example, E. Bjorge, *The Evolutionary Interpretation of Treaties* (Oxford: Oxford University Press, 2014).

[162] Article 8, ICC Statute.

[163] Preamble to Hague Convention IV. The so-called Martens clause reads: 'Until a more complete code of the laws of war has been issued, the High Contracting Parties deem it expedient to declare that, in cases not included in the Regulations adopted by them, the inhabitants and the belligerents remain under the protection and the rule of the principles of the law of nations, as they result from the usages established among civilised peoples, from the laws of humanity, and the dictates of the public conscience'.

[164] Preamble to the Protocol Additional to the Geneva Conventions of 12 August 1949 and relating to the protection of victims of non-international armed conflicts (Protocol II), of 8 June 1977.

Considering the substance of the defence's challenge, specifically with regard to status requirements, the Chamber emphasises that crimes listed under paragraphs 2 (b)(xxii) and (e)(vi) do not identify a requirement for a particular victim status. This is in contrast with paragraphs 2(a) and (c) which stipulate specific victim status criteria.

23. The Chamber additionally observes that, whilst Additional Protocol II extends protection to those not taking or no longer taking part in hostilities, it remains silent on the issue of which side of the conflict these persons belong to. Additionally, the Chamber notes that ICL (including the jurisprudence of this Court[165]) and IHL both recognise the act of enlisting and conscripting children under the age of fifteen to participate in hostilities as a war crime.[166] This crime has not only been recognised as one of a continuous nature[167] for purposes of international criminal law but – in essence – constitutes a crime committed against members of the same armed group. Critically, these war crimes can only be perpetrated by members of a military force against victims who are from the same military force.

24. The Chamber observes that although in general IHL regulates conduct directed towards those external to a military force rather than to those internal to a military force, this general proposition does not constitute an irrebuttable presumption.

25. IHL accepts that the parties' objective to overcome the opposing side will result in certain suffering, damage, and harm, but specifically determines that such consequences ought only to follow from actions that are militarily necessary or that will result in a definite military advantage.[168] Yet sexual violence, including rape and sexual slavery, is increasingly being deployed by armed groups in an attempt to gain political and/or military advantage. In this regard, the Chamber notes the jurisprudence of the Special Court for Sierra Leone, which established that sexual violence can be, and was, deployed by armed groups with the specific intent to terrorise the civilian population and – therefore – commit acts of terror[169] contrary to Articles 4(2) (d) and 13(2) of Additional Protocol II.

26. This Chamber considers that acts of sexual violence, especially rape and enslavement, including sexual slavery, cannot under any circumstances be

[165] Judgment, *Lubanga* (ICC-01/04-01/06), Trial Chamber I, 14 March 2012.

[166] Article 8(2)(b)(xxvi) and Article 8(2)(e)(vii) ICC Statute; Article 77 of Additional Protocol I; Article 4 of Additional Protocol II.

[167] Judgment, *Brima et al.* (SCSL-04-16-T), Trial Chamber II, 20 June 2007, §§ 39–41; Judgment, *Taylor* (SCSL-03-01-T), Trial Chamber II, 18 May 2012, §§ 118–119; Decision on the confirmation of charges, *Lubanga* (ICC-01/04-01/06-803-tEN) (translation notified 14 May 2007), Pre-Trial Chamber I, 29 January 2007, § 248.

[168] ICRC, Customary International Law Database, Rule 14: Proportionality of Attack, available at https://ihl-databases.icrc.org/en/customary-ihl/v1/rule14; Article 51(5)(b) of the 1977 Additional Protocol I; Article 85(3)(b) of the 1977 Additional Protocol I.

[169] Judgment, *Taylor* (SCSL-03-01-T), Trial Chamber II, 18 May 2012, § 2035; Judgment, *Sesay, Kallon & Gbao* (SCSL-04-15-T), Trial Chamber I, 2 March 2009, §§ 1348–1351, upheld on appeal: Judgment, *Sesay, Kallon & Gbao* (SCSL-04-15-A), Appeals Chamber, 26 October 2009, § 990.

considered as legitimate acts in pursuance of military necessity or military advantage. Raping and sexually enslaving children under the age of fifteen,[170] or indeed any persons, would never bring any accepted military advantage, nor can there ever be a necessity to engage in such conduct. To do so would not only be in violation of the principle of legality but also in violation of customary international humanitarian law and the principle of *jus cogens*.

27. While most of the express prohibitions of rape and sexual slavery under IHL appear in contexts protecting civilians and persons *hors de combat* in the power of a party to the conflict, the Chamber does not consider those explicit protections to exhaustively define, or indeed limit, the scope of the protection against such conduct. The Chamber finds that rape and other forms of sexual violence have long been prohibited by IHL. The prohibition against rape and sexual slavery is a peremptory norm and such conduct is prohibited at all times, both in times of peace and during armed conflicts and against all persons irrespective of any legal status.[171]

Article 21(3) as an Interpretive Tool

28. In concluding sexual violence committed against child soldiers constituted war crimes under Article 8(2)(e)(vi) of the Rome Statute because the children were protected by IHL during the commission of the sexual violence, the Chamber also relies on Article 21(3) of the Statute, which compels it to interpret and apply the law in accordance with internationally recognised human rights,[172] without adverse distinction founded on grounds such as gender and age. In order to apply and interpret the law in this manner, this Chamber seeks to surface the gendered aspects of child soldiering as an intentional process of legal reasoning that is grounded in the realities of the conflict and lived experiences of child soldiers.

29. The Chamber recalls the UN Guidelines for the Demobilisation of Child Soldiers which emphasise that 'children, and girls in particular, perform numerous combat and non-combat functions that are essential to the functioning of the armed

[170] The Chamber recalls here that international humanitarian law contains specific rules aimed at protecting children from the effects of armed conflicts. See Article 50 of the Fourth Geneva Convention of 1949; Article 77 of Additional Protocol I; and Article 4(3) of Additional Protocol II.

[171] See, for example, the Martens Clause, Article 1(2) of Additional Protocol I and the Preamble of Additional Protocol II. See also International Court of Justice, Legality of the threat or use of nuclear weapons, Advisory Opinion, 8 July 1996, §§ 78 and 87; Judgment, *Furundžija* (IT-95-17/1), Trial Chamber, 10 December 1998, §137; Judgment, *Krupp et al.* (Case No. 214), United States Military Tribunal in Nuremberg, 31 July 1948; K. D. Askin, *War Crimes against Women: Prosecutions in International War Crimes Tribunals* (Leiden: Martinus Nijhoff, 1997) at 242; D. S. Mitchell, 'The Prohibition of Rape in International Humanitarian Law as a Norm of Jus Cogens: Clarifying the Doctrine' 15 *Duke Journal of Comparative Law & International Law* (2005) 219–257.

[172] Dissenting Opinion of Judge Odio Benito, Judgment, *Lubanga* (ICC-01/04–01/06), Trial Chamber I, 14 March 2012, § 6.

force or group'.[173] In her report, Dr Schauer highlights that girls' participation is central to sustaining a force because of their productive and reproductive labour.[174] The UN Special Representative of the Secretary-General on Children in Armed Conflict has stressed that 'during war, the use of children in particular includes sexual violence'.[175] The Chamber recalls that the Cape Town Principles include 'girls recruited for sexual purposes and forced marriage' in the definition of child soldiers[176] and that the Paris Principles reinforce this approach, acknowledging that 'girls are frequently used for sexual purposes'.[177]

30. The Chamber also recognises in this context the extensive scholarly critique[178] concerning the language of IHL, specifically where it concerns sexual violence, as well as the scope of protection afforded to women and girls. Although the use of girls for sexual purposes is well documented, the Chamber recalls that neither IHL nor ICL clearly regulate this conduct. As noted by Judge Odio-Benito in *Lubanga*, 'invisibility of sexual violence is the legal concept that leads to discrimination against victims of enlistment, conscription and use who systematically suffer this crime as an intrinsic part of the involvement with the armed group'.[179] Therefore, in light of the nature of the crimes in Counts 6 and 9, as well as the identities of the victims, a gender-competent and intersectional interpretation of the law is a positive obligation imposed on the Chamber under Article 21(3).

31. Article 21 calls for the law to be applied and interpreted in a manner that surfaces gendered and intersectional harms. Understanding the range of harms including sexual violence leads to a non-discriminatory analysis of sexual crimes, which in this context predominantly affected girl soldiers.[180] The Chamber observes the continuous nature of the violation of being recruited or enlisted as a child

[173] United Nations, 'Operational Guide to the Integrated Disarmament, Demobilization and Reintegration Standards' (1 August 2006) at 218, available at https://peacekeeping.un.org/sites/default/files/operational-guide-rev-2010-web.pdf; United Nations, *Report of the Secretary General 'Disarmament, Demobilisation and Reintegration'* (UN Doc A/60/705), 2 March 2006.

[174] Expert Report of Dr Schauer (EVD-CHM-0001), 'The Psychological Impact of Child Soldiering' (ICC-01/04-01/06-1729-Anx1), available at www.icc-cpi.int/sites/default/files/RelatedRecords/CR2009_01399.PDF, at 27–28.

[175] Written Submissions of the United Nations Special Representative of the Secretary-General on Children and Armed Conflict Submitted in application of Rule 103 of the Rules of Procedure and Evidence, March 2008.

[176] UNICEF, *Cape Town Principles and Best Practices on the Prevention of Recruitment of Children into Armed Forces and on Demobilization and Social Reintegration of Child Soldier in Africa* (April 1997) at 1.

[177] The Paris Principles, *supra* note 152, § 1.0. See also § 2.1.

[178] E.g. H. Durham and K. O'Byrne, 'The Dialogue of Difference: Gender Perspectives on International Humanitarian Law' 92(877) *International Review of the Red Cross* (2010) 31–52; J. Gardam, 'The Neglected Aspect of Women and Armed Conflict: Progressive Development of the Law' 52(2) *Netherlands International Law Review* (2005) 197–219.

[179] Dissenting Opinion of Judge Odio Benito, Judgment, *Lubanga* (ICC-01/04-01/06), Trial Chamber I, 14 March 2012, § 16.

[180] *Ibid*, § 6.

soldier, and the significance of contextualising these violations within societal norms, values, and attitudes to fully ventilate the harms arising from their multiple roles, including experiencing sexual violence committed by their own side. Accordingly, this Chamber makes plain the link between the *jus cogens* nature of the prohibition against rape and sexual slavery and its application to the girl soldiers.

32. Although the foregoing analysis centres on the experiences of girl soldiers, the Chamber notes that a gender-competent intersectional interpretative approach towards the law and offences pursuant to Article 21(3) is also the standard to be applied to the experiences of boy soldiers. Such an approach enables the recognition and unpacking of the experiences of child soldiering and permits a shift away from essentialist narratives that further the binary of the female victim and male perpetrator. Girl soldiers and boy soldiers experience conflict differently due to the gendered elements that underlie the perpetration of the crime of child soldiering. Article 21(3) permits the surfacing of these gendered and intersecting violations without adverse distinction.

The Special Protection Afforded to Children

33. The Chamber observes that the prohibition on conscripting or enlisting child soldiers or allowing children to directly participate in hostilities is an exception to the general proposition precisely in order to provide non-derogable protections for children as a particularly vulnerable group. The notion of vulnerability – traditionally determined through one's non-combatant status, be it civilian or *hors de combat* – underpins IHL provisions affording protection to selected persons/groups deemed specifically vulnerable.[181] Rape and sexual slavery committed against child soldiers by members of the same armed force or group heightens their vulnerability – first, resulting from recruitment and, second, as victims of sexual violence. This induced vulnerability is exploited by armed groups as an effective method of controlling child soldiers and is used to manipulate and subjugate the victims. The essence and motivations behind the acts underpinning crimes of rape and sexual slavery stand not only against the principles of customary international law, IHL, and ICL but also against key principles of humanity.

34. The Chamber recalls the legal basis for Counts 6 and 9, as explained in the document containing the charges, which stated that the rape and sexual enslavement of child soldiers by the UPC/FPLC commanders and soldiers constitute war crimes.[182] Child soldiers are afforded general protections against sexual violence under the fundamental guarantees afforded to persons affected by non-international armed conflicts under Article 4 of the Additional Protocol II and Common

[181] See, for example, the Fourth Geneva Convention of 1949.

[182] Document Containing the Charges, *Ntaganda* (ICC-01/04-02/06), Pre-Trial Chamber 1, 10 January 2014, § 100.

Article 3 of the 1949 Geneva Conventions.[183] They also have special protections because of their vulnerability as children under Article 4(3) of the Additional Protocol II.[184] The Chamber thus finds that the protection offered by these provisions supports the recognition of child soldiers as victims of sexual violence for the purposes of charges under Article 8(2)(e)(vi) of the Rome Statute.[185]

35. The Chamber thus concludes that sexual violence is used strategically in contemporary armed conflicts to exert power, influence, and control, irrespective of the status of its victims. [However, this is not accepted within the confines of the principles of military necessity and military advantage under IHL.] Having found that the protection against sexual violence under IHL is not limited to members of the opposing armed forces, who are *hors de combat*, or civilians not directly participating in hostilities, the Chamber does not need to address whether or not the persons alleged to have been 'child soldiers' in the facts and circumstances underlying Counts 6 and 9, or any persons alleged to have been held in sexual slavery by the UPC/FPLC, are to be considered as 'members' of this armed force at the relevant time.

Conclusion

36. Based on the foregoing analysis, the Chamber finds that members of the same armed force are not per se excluded as potential victims of the war crimes of rape and sexual slavery, as listed in Article 8(2)(e)(vi), based on the principles of treaty interpretation, the framework of international law including the *jus cogens* prohibition on sexual violence and the special protection afforded to children under IHL. Without prejudice to whether such acts have taken place, the Chamber therefore finds that it has jurisdiction over the conduct charged pursuant to Counts 6 and 9.

Judge Priya Gopalan and Judge Olga Jurasz

8.4 CONSENT AND SEXUAL CRIMES IN THE NTAGANDA JUDGMENT

Isabel Maravall-Buckwalter

In 2019, Trial Chamber VI issued the judgment in the case against Mr Bosco Ntaganda.[186] Convicted of eighteen counts of war crimes and crimes against humanity, the volume of sexual violence, especially against women and girls, was a particular feature of this case.

183 *Ibid*, § 107.
184 *Ibid*.
185 *Ibid*.
186 Judgment, *Ntaganda* (ICC-01/04-02/06-2359), Trial Chamber VI, 8 July 2019.

In Isabel Maravall-Buckwalter's rewrite,[187] age-related incapacity, as a circumstance defining the crime of rape, is explored. In *Ntaganda*, age was only considered as a circumstance sufficient to find rape in the case of a nine-year-old girl called Nadège. In the case of victims over the age of nine, additional circumstances were necessary for a finding of rape. Without diminishing the sexual agency of victims, the rewritten judgment argues against this standard and, by providing an interpretation in accordance with international human rights law and international humanitarian law, raises the age of consent to the acceptable standard in international law.

No.: ICC-01/04-01/06
Date: 8 July 2010

Original: English

TRIAL CHAMBER VI(B)

Before: Judge Isabel MARAVALL-BUCKWALTER

SITUATION IN THE DEMOCRATIC REPUBLIC OF THE CONGO IN THE CASE OF THE *PROSECUTOR v. BOSCO NTAGANDA*

Public

with public Annexes A, B, and C
Judgment

This case relates to events alleged to have occurred from on or about 6 August 2002 to on or about 31 December 2003, in Ituri, in the Democratic Republic of Congo (DRC). Mr Bosco Ntaganda is charged with thirteen counts of war crimes and five counts of crimes against humanity, of which specifically rape as a crime against humanity and as a war crime (Counts 4, 5, and 6) pursuant to Articles 7(1)(g) and 8(2)(e)(vi) of the Rome Statute (the Statute).

FACTUAL FINDINGS

Sexual Violence against Female Recruits and Soldiers

1. The Union des Patriotes Congolais (UPC)/Forces Patriotiques pour la Liberation du Congo (FPLC) extensively recruited individuals of all ages, from

[187] In accordance with the feminist judgment methodology, the reimagined judgment which follows draws on the materials that were available to, and cited in, the original judgment: Judgment, *Ntaganda* (ICC-01/04-02/06-2359), Trial Chamber VI, 8 July 2019. Wherever possible, the primary materials have been referenced in footnotes in the reimagined judgment. However, some of the primary materials that were referred to in the original judgment and relied on in the reimagined judgment are not publicly available (as referenced in footnotes 189–212).

June 2002.[188] Female members of the UPC/FPLC were regularly raped and subjected to sexual violence at the camps by male UPC/FPLC soldiers.[189] Sexual violence was committed against girls of all ages, including girls under the age of fifteen.[190] A number of these female members of the UPC/FPLC became pregnant during their time in the UPC/FPLC.[191] The Chamber has heard relevant evidence of sexual violence committed against girls over the age of fifteen, however it does not fall within the scope of the charges.[192]

2. P-0883 was under fifteen years old at the relevant time.[193] During her time at Bule camp she was raped by 'many soldiers'.[194] She was not able to state how often she was raped, and indicated that 'whether you were sitting down or sleeping, anyone who wanted to do so could rape you'.[195] Soldiers would come and take her and other girls 'whenever they wanted', whether they were inside or at the place of work of the soldier, sometimes saying that they would shoot them if they did not agree.[196] Later, after having been injured during a battle, P-0883 was sent to Camp Baudouin for treatment, where she found out that she was pregnant, without knowing 'who was responsible for that pregnancy'.[197]

3. A girl named Nadège, who was around nine years old at the time, and who was taken to training at Lingo camp, was raped; P-0758 explained that there was pus coming out of Nadège's vagina and that, as a result, she died.[198]

[188] The Chamber recalls its finding that both P-0883 and P-0898 were under fifteen when they joined the UPC/FPLC. In addition, the Chamber bases this finding on the presence of individuals under fifteen years of age in UPC/FPLC training camps, according to the evidence.

[189] P-0901: T-29, 57–58; P-0907: T-89, 61–64.

[190] In addition to the specific examples discussed here, the Chamber also heard other evidence about rape of PMFs under fifteen by UPC/FPLC soldiers or commanders: P-0031 reported that he was in contact with some young girls between thirteen and fourteen who reported having been raped within the UPC/FPLC; some of them had contracted sexually transmitted illnesses and others had a child (T-174, 27–29; DRC-OTP-2054-3760, 3778–3782; DRC-OTP-2054-3939, 3947–3948; and DRC-OTP-2054-4308, 4317–4318). P-0046 recalled having interviewed girls, including some under fifteen, who were sexually abused and taken as wives of the commanders and other soldiers (T-101, 68–69). P-0017 stated that he was told that Abelanga raped two bodyguards who were 12–13 years old (T-58, 51–52). The witness provided a reasonable explanation for his age assessment, referring to the girls' 'physiognomy', 'their sizes', and the fact that they played, and that 'they looked more like young boys because they didn't have any breasts'.

[191] P-0010: T-47, 34; P-0055: T-71, 94–96; P-0883: see below; and P-0901: T-29, 57. See also P-0031: DRC-OTP-2054-3760, at 3782; P-0046: T-101, 68.

[192] See testimony of P-0758 and P-0010.

[193] See credibility assessment of P-0883.

[194] P-0883: T-168, 31–32.

[195] P-0883: T-168, 32.

[196] P-0883: T-168, 32. See also P-0010: 36; and P-0907: T-89, 64.

[197] P-0883: T-168, 34, 36–37, and 42–44.

[198] P-0758: T-160, 89. In light of the details provided by P-0758 and having considered related findings on the conditions in the camps, the Chamber finds that the only reasonable conclusion to be drawn is that Nadège suffered a forceful vaginal penetration.

4. A girl by the name Mave, who was under fifteen years of age, was raped by many different soldiers on a regular basis. P-0887 testified that many soldiers 'slept with' Mave, 'treated her as a . . . soldier's woman', had sexual relations with her. The witness said she knew this because soldiers were talking about it amongst themselves, and she also spoke to Mave.[199] P-0907 testified as well that it was 'common knowledge' that Mave had been raped several times by soldiers and she began to suffer from fistula, and that he was present when Kisembo gave a speech to a gathering of soldiers in March 2003, where he told the soldiers that Mave had a fistula and prohibited the further rape of Mave.[200]

The Operations Involving the UPC/FPLC

5. During and in the immediate aftermath of the assault on Mongbwalu, UPC/FPLC soldiers forced women and girls to have sexual intercourse with them. P-0892, thirteen years old at the time, was taken to a house by UPC/FPLC soldiers.[201] Upon arrival, a UPC/FPLC commander named Saidi ordered the soldiers to undress the girl; the soldiers then violently ripped off her skirt and underwear and threw her onto the bed.[202] Saidi then penetrated the girl with his fingers, saying that she was a minor who had not 'known a man', after which he got on top of her and penetrated her vagina with his penis.[203] The girl started screaming, after which Saidi put a cloth over her mouth and continued.[204] After he finished, he said that she now was a 'woman', after which one of UPC/FPLC soldiers got on top of the girl and also penetrated her.[205]

6. P-0892 and P-0912 testified[206] that other women and girls were also taken away by UPC/FPLC soldiers and raped. One girl, who was approximately fourteen years old at the time, told her that she was forced to enter a bedroom, asked to lie down, and as she refused, the soldiers started hitting her. Subsequently, two people 'raped' her;[207] P-0912 testified that she overheard that the fourteen-year-old girl had been taken from the same house by soldiers who mentioned that they were taking girls to prepare food at the military camp. This girl later told P-0912 that she had been 'raped' and injured.[208] P-0887 testified that the UPC/FPLC soldiers committed 'rapes' and abductions of girls in Mongwalu and referred to one particular instance

[199] P-0887: T-93, 39–41, and 50.
[200] P-0887: T-93, 39–41, and 50; P-0907: T-89, 52, 55–57, and 63–64.
[201] P-0912: T-148, 32, and 60–62; and P-0892: T-85, 5–8.
[202] P-0912: T-148, 63–64; and T-149, 7–8; see also P-0892: T-85, 5 and 7.
[203] P-0912: T-148, 64–65. See also P-0892: T-85, 7.
[204] P-0912: T-148, 65.
[205] P-0912: T-148, 65–66. See also P-0892: T-85, 7.
[206] P-0912: T-148, 47.
[207] P-0892: T-85, 10–12.
[208] P-0912: T-148, 69–71.

in which he saw a girl from the neighbourhood being chased and pushed by a UPC/FPLC soldier with a gun, and who then spent a night with the soldier.[209] P-0888 also testified that he personally saw soldiers and commanders who raped 'little girls', although he could not provide their names.[210]

7. While in Kobu, UPC/FPLC soldiers detained several women and girls, in some instances for hours, in others over the course of several days; during these periods, UPC/FPLC soldiers raped them and otherwise subjected them to sexual violence on one or more occasion.[211] This included an eleven-year-old captured by Commander Simba during a mop-up operation in Kobu whom he brought with him to Bunia where she stayed until the Bunia operation and forced her to sleep with him; according to P-0017, she was forced to have 'sexual relationships' with Simba to save her life.[212]

APPLICABLE LAW

8. The crime against humanity of rape is laid down in Article 7(1)(g) of the Statute. The war crime of rape is laid down in Article 8(2)(e)(vi) of the Statute.[213]

9. The legal elements of the crime against humanity of rape as defined in Article 7 (1)(g)1 of the Elements of Crimes:

1. The perpetrator invaded the body of a person by conduct resulting in penetration, however slight, of any part of the body of the victim or of the perpetrator with a sexual organ, or of the anal or genital opening of the victim with any object or any other part of the body.
2. The invasion was committed by force, or by threat of force or coercion, such as that caused by fear of violence, duress, detention, psychological oppression or abuse of power, against such person or another person, or by taking advantage of a coercive environment, or the invasion was committed against a person incapable of giving genuine consent.
3. The conduct was committed as part of a widespread or systematic attack directed against a civilian population.
4. The perpetrator knew that the conduct was part of or intended the conduct to be part of a widespread or systematic attack directed against a civilian population.

[209] P-0887: T-93, 19, and 22–25.

[210] P-0888: T-105, 81.

[211] P-0790: T-54, 32.

[212] P-0017: T-60, 28–29.

[213] Parts of this section have been taken from I. Maravall-Buckwalter, 'The Inconsistencies of Age-Related Incapacity Thresholds in International Law: Child Rape Victims at a Disadvantage' 22 (2) *Human Rights Law Review* (2022) 18–20.

10. The legal elements of the war crime of rape are as defined in Article 8(2)(b)(xxii)1 of the Elements of Crimes:

1. The perpetrator invaded the body of a person by conduct resulting in penetration, however slight, of any part of the body of the victim or of the perpetrator with a sexual organ, or of the anal or genital opening of the victim with any object or any other part of the body.
2. The invasion was committed by force, or by threat of force or coercion, such as that caused by fear of violence, duress, detention, psychological oppression or abuse of power, against such person or another person, or by taking advantage of a coercive environment, or the invasion was committed against a person incapable of giving genuine consent.
3. The conduct took place in the context of and was associated with an armed conflict not of an international character.
4. The perpetrator was aware of factual circumstances that established the existence of an armed conflict.

11. As to the second element of the crime of rape as a crime against humanity and as a war crime, the fourth possible circumstance to be considered under the Statute is that an invasion of the body of the victim or the perpetrator may also constitute rape when committed 'against a person incapable of giving genuine consent'. The Elements of Crimes specifies that '[i]t is understood that a person may be incapable of giving genuine consent if affected by natural, induced, or age-related incapacity'.[214] Neither the Elements of Crimes nor the Statute establishes when a person is of age-related incapacity. Regarding this requirement, the Court's jurisprudence has stated that it is necessary that 'the Prosecution will only have to prove that the victim's capacity to give genuine consent was affected by natural, induced, or age-related incapacity'.[215] In 2014, in the *Prosecutor v. Germain Katanga* the ICC's Trial Chamber noted that, 'save the very specific situation of a person whose "incapacity" was "tak[en] advantage of", the Elements of Crimes do not refer to the victim's lack of consent, and therefore this need not be proven'.[216]

12. According to the Court's jurisprudence, 'at least one of the coercive circumstances or conditions set out in the second element is therefore sufficient alone for penetration to amount to rape'.[217]

13. Considering that age-related incapacity constitutes one of the circumstances which render consent immaterial to the crime of rape, the Chamber considers

[214] Article 7(1)(g)-1, Elements of Crimes; Article 8(2)(e)(vi)-1, Elements of Crimes.

[215] Judgment, *Prosecutor v. Jean-Pierre Bemba Gombo* (ICC-01/05-01/08), Trial Chamber III, 21 March 2016, § 107 (hereafter Bemba Trial Judgment).

[216] Judgment, *Prosecutor v. Germain Katanga* (ICC-01/04-01/07), Trial Chamber II, 7 March 2014, § 965.

[217] *Ibid*. See also Bemba Trial Judgment, *supra* note 215, §§ 105–106.

pertinent to give content to this circumstance, as it has been left undefined in the Statute and in the Elements of Crimes.

14. Article 21 of the Statute provides judges with the tools to interpret when the Court's primary sources, the Statute or the Elements of Crimes, fail to resolve an issue and there is a remaining lacuna in the law. First, according to Article 21.1(b), by resorting to the applicable treaties and the principles and rules of international law, including the established principles of the international law of armed conflict. Second, Article 21.1(c) establishes that if these also fail to resolve the issue, the Court may apply general principles of law derived from the national laws of the states that would normally exercise jurisdiction over the crime, provided they are consistent with international law. Article 21(2) allows the Court to apply principles and rules of law interpreted in its previous decisions and provides in Article 21(3) that the application and interpretation of law is consistent with international human rights law.

15. Judges must therefore ensure according to Article 21(3) of the Statute that the interpretation and application of the law is consistent with internationally recognised human rights. This obligation means that the law must not only be interpreted, but also applied in accordance with internationally recognised human rights law.[218] This requires that interpretation, resulting from Article 21(1) or Articles 31 and 32 of the Vienna Convention on the Law of Treaties will always have to produce a result which is compatible with international human rights law.[219]

16. Not having an age of consent defined in the law or adopting a threshold which is too low is not compatible with international human rights law standards. The Committee on the Rights of the Child (CRC) has noted, in General Comment No. 4 on the Right to Health of Adolescents, that 'States parties need to ensure that specific legal provisions are guaranteed under domestic law, including with regard to setting a minimum age for sexual consent',[220] and in General Comment No. 20 on the implementation of the rights of the child during adolescence that 'States parties should take into account the need to balance protection and evolving capacities, and define an acceptable minimum age when determining the legal age for sexual consent. States should avoid criminalizing adolescents of similar ages for factually consensual and non-exploitative sexual activity'.[221] The CRC has also

[218] *Prosecutor v. Thomas Lubanga Dyilo*, Appeals Chamber, Judgment on the Appeal of Mr. Thomas Lubanga Dyilo against Decision on the Defence Challenge to the Jurisdiction of the Court pursuant to Article 19 (2) (a) of the Statute of 3 October 2006 (ICC-01/04-01/06-772), 14 December 2006, § 37.

[219] G. Bitti, 'Part IV: The ICC and Its Applicable Law: Article 21 and the hierarchy or Sources of Law before the ICC' in C. Stahn (ed.), *The Law and Practice of the International Criminal Law* (Oxford: Oxford University Press, 2022) at 437.

[220] CRC, General Comment No. 4: *Adolescent Health and Development in the Context of the Convention on the Rights of the Child* (CRC/GC/2003/4), 1 July 2003, § 5.

[221] CRC, General Comment No. 20: *On the Implementation of the Rights of the Child during Adolescence* (CRC/C/GC/20), 6 December 2016, § 40.

disapproved states' lack of clarity in setting a legal minimum age of sexual consent or its absence from legislation in its concluding observations to state parties.[222]

17. Both the CRC and the Committee on the Elimination of all Forms of Discrimination Against women (CEDAW) have stressed in their concluding observations that when the age of sexual consent is undefined or set too low, it fails to protect the child from sexual exploitation and health-related risks. In order to protect children from such risks, both the CRC and the CEDAW have signalled the ages of twelve and thirteen as being too low.[223] The CRC has also shown concern 'at the rather low age for sexual consent (14 years), which may not provide adequate protection for children older than 14 years against sexual exploitation'[224] and has welcomed the adoption of legislative measures by states in raising the age of sexual consent to sixteen years.[225]

18. The recognition of sixteen as an acceptable age of consent is consistent with the CEDAW's and the CRC's Joint General Recommendation 31 which has highlighted in relation to child marriage that, 'as a matter of respecting the child's evolving capacities and autonomy in making decisions that affect her or his life, a marriage of a mature, capable child below 18 years of age may be allowed in exceptional circumstances, provided that the child is at least 16 years of age … without deference to culture or tradition'.[226]

19. These recommendations are in line with research showing that early sexual activity is correlated with negative psychosocial consequences for the child.[227] These range from unintended pregnancies, sexually transmitted infections, mental health risks, substance abuse, weaker attachments to conventional institutions, lower

[222] See for example Concluding Observations of the Committee on the Rights of the Child, Benin (CRC/C/BEN/CO/2), 2006, § 69; Concluding Observations of the Committee on the Rights of the Child, Madagascar (CRC/C/MDG/CO/3–4), 2012, § 45; Concluding Observations of the Committee on the Rights of the Child, Ukraine (CRC/C/UKR/3–4), 2011, § 26.

[223] Concluding Observations on the Combined Seventh And Eighth Periodic Reports of the Philippines (CEDAW/C/PHL/CO/7–8), 25 July 2016, § 26; Concluding Observations, Philippines (CRC/C/15/Add.259), 21 September 2005, § 85; Concluding Observations Indonesia (CRC/C/15/Add.223), § 81; Report of the Committee on the Elimination of Discrimination against Women, Thirty-second session (10–28 January 2005)/Thirty-third session (A/60/38) 5–22 July 2005, § 305; Concluding Observations on the Combined Seventh and Eighth Periodic Reports of Japan (CEDAW/C/JPN/CO/7–8), 7 March 2016, § 22.

[224] Concluding Observations of the Committee on the Rights of the Child, Iceland (CRC/C/15/Add.203), § 38.

[225] Concluding Observations of the Committee on the Rights of the Child, Lithuania (CRC/C/LTU/CO/3–4), 2013, § 3 c; Concluding Observations on the Combined Third to Fifth Periodic Reports of Malawi (CRC/C/MWI/CO/3–5), 6 March 2017, § 22.

[226] Joint General Recommendation No. 31 of the Committee on the Elimination of Discrimination against Women/General Comment No. 18 of the Committee on the Rights of the Child on Harmful Practices (CEDAW/C/GC/31-CRC/C/GC/18), 14 November 2014, § 20.

[227] A. S. Madkour et al., 'Early Adolescent Sexual Initiation as a Problem Behavior: A Comparative Study of Five Nations' 47(4) *Journal of Adolescent Health* (2010) 389–398, at 390 and 395–397.

academic achievement and aspirations, and poorer mental health.[228] Researchers have asserted that these negative psychosocial consequences 'tend to be concentrated among early initiators – those less than age 16 at sexual debut – or among girls'.[229] The maternal health consequences associated with early child marriage corroborate these findings in non-Western countries, where early sexual relations as a consequence of early child marriage entail a greater risk for maternal morbidity and mortality.[230]

20. This Chamber observes that the suggested age of sixteen is also compatible with the subsidiary sources embedded in Article 21(1)(b) and (c) of the Statute. Firstly, international humanitarian law prohibits in absolute terms the infliction of sexual violence against children. The special protection afforded children from any form of sexual violence can be found in Article 77(1) of Additional Protocol I,[231] which recognises the obligation of state parties to award children special respect and to protect them against any form of indecent assault,[232] and Article 4(2)(e) of Additional Protocol II,[233] which prohibits at any time and any place whatsoever outrages upon personal dignity, in particular humiliating and degrading treatment, rape, enforced prostitution, and any form of indecent assault.[234] This prohibition is recognised in customary international law.[235] This protection against *any* form of sexual violence[236] covers *all* children, even those children who have not attained the

[228] However, early sexual initiation is less convincingly associated with parental communication and inversely related to school attachment. *Ibid*, at 395–397.

[229] *Ibid*. See also A. L. Spriggs and C. T. Halpern, 'Sexual Debut Timing and Depressive Symptoms in Emerging Adulthood' 37(9) *Journal of Youth and Adolescence* (2008) 1085–1096, at 1085–1088 and 1091–1094; A. M. Meier, 'Adolescent First Sex and Subsequent Mental Health' 112(6) *American Journal of Sociology* (2007) 1811–1847, at 1814 ('Moreover, the risks of physical effects of sex (sexually transmitted diseases and pregnancy) disproportionately accrue to girls. This heightened threat may further induce psychological effects for girls who have sex early').

[230] A. Nove et al., 'Maternal Mortality in Adolescents Compared with Women of Other Ages: Evidence from 144 Countries' 2(3) *The Lancet Global Health* (2014) 155–164, at 163; N. M. Nour, 'Health Consequences of Child Marriage in Africa' 12(11) *Emerging Infectious Diseases* (2006) 1644–1649, at 1646–1647.

[231] International Committee of the Red Cross (ICRC), Protocol Additional to the Geneva Conventions of 12 August 1949, and relating to the Protection of Victims of International Armed Conflicts (Protocol I), 8 June 1977, 1125 UNTS 3.

[232] On a detailed analysis of the concept of 'indecent assault' see P. V. Sellers and I. Rosenthal, 'Chapter 17. Rape and Other Sexual Violence' in A. Clapham et al. (eds.), *The 1949 Geneva Conventions: A Commentary* (Oxford: Oxford University Press, 2015), at 355–357.

[233] International Committee of the Red Cross (ICRC), Protocol Additional to the Geneva Conventions of 12 August 1949, and relating to the Protection of Victims of Non-International Armed Conflicts (Protocol II), 8 June 1977, 1125 UNTS 609.

[234] On a detailed analysis of this legal framework see Sellers and Rosenthal, *supra* note 233.

[235] Rule 93: Rape and other forms of sexual violence are prohibited. J. M. Henckaerts and L. Doswald-Beck, *Customary International Humanitarian Law: Volume 1, Rules* (Cambridge: Cambridge University Press, 2005), at 323.

[236] 'According to customary law, the expressions "outrages upon personal dignity" and "any form of indecent assault" refer to any form of sexual violence', *ibid*, at 324.

age of fifteen years and take a direct part in hostilities or fall into the power of an adverse party.[237] This legal framework 'is continuous and not diminished by the fighter status or the civilian status of the child, even while in the hands of their own party'.[238] Articles 77(3) and 4(3)(d) do not set a higher age threshold for the provision of this privileged treatment; they only require that parties continue to protect children, including those under the age of fifteen, when they take up arms or are detained.[239]

21. Secondly, having satisfied Article 21(1)(b), it is not required that the Chamber apply 21(1)(c), which, in any case, were there to exist a recognised general principle on this subject matter, would still have to be consistent with the Statute and with international law and internationally recognised norms and standards, according to Article 21(1)(c). These, as mentioned earlier, agree on setting the age of consent at sixteen.

22. This Chamber therefore concludes that, considering the undefined age of capacity in the Statute and Articles 7(1)(g) and 8(2)(e)(vi) of the Elements of Crimes, an application of Article 21 of the Statute allows this Chamber to conclude that an interpretation which is compatible with the sources therein recognises the age of sixteen as the acceptable age of consent.

FINDINGS OF THE CHAMBER

23. Turning to the second legal element of the crime of rape, the Chamber notes that, in many instances, the perpetrators used force and threats of force and took advantage of a coercive environment to have sexual intercourse with girls or women.

24. The Chamber also considers that at the camps, UPC/FPLC soldiers repeatedly raped P-0883, a girl under fifteen years of age, at Camp Bule,[240] a girl named Nadège, approximately nine years old, at the Lingo training camp,[241] and a girl named Mave, who was under the age of fifteen.[242] Additionally, the Chamber notes

[237] Article 77(3) of API states: 'If, in exceptional cases, despite the provisions of paragraph 2, children who have not attained the age of fifteen years take a direct part in hostilities and fall into the power of an adverse Party, they *shall continue* to benefit from the special protection accorded by this Article, whether or not they are prisoners of war; Article 4.3 (d) of APII in very similar terms indicates that the special protection provided by this Article to children who have not attained the age of fifteen years *shall remain applicable* to them if they take a direct part in hostilities despite the provisions of sub-paragraph (c) and are captured.'

[238] P. Sellers, 'Ntaganda: Re-alignment of a Paradigm' in F. Pocar (ed.), *The Additional Protocols 40 Years Later: New Conflicts, New Actors, New Perspectives* (Milan: International Institute of Humanitarian Law and Franco Angeli, 2018), available at https://iihl.org/wp-content/uploads/2022/07/The-Additional-Protocols-40-Years-Later-New-Conflicts-New-Actors-New-Perspectives_2.pdf, at 130.

[239] Sellers and Rosenthal, *supra* note 232, at 356.

[240] See § 3.

[241] See § 4.

[242] See § 5.

that during the immediate aftermath of the assault on Mongbwalu, Witness P-0892 was thirteen years old at the time when she was raped[243] and witness P-0892 and P-0912 testified that another girl was fourteen years old.[244] In Kobu, UPC/FPLC soldiers detained several women and girls for hours, even days, and raped them during this time.[245] One of the girls was eleven years old.[246] The Chamber therefore is satisfied that perpetrators invaded the bodies of victims who were under the age of sixteen, and therefore under the acceptable age of consent.

25. Accordingly, the Chamber concludes that at least one, often more, of the coercive circumstances or conditions set out in the second legal element of the crime against humanity and of the war crime of rape is proven for all incidents listed.

Judge Isabel Maravall-Buckwalter

[243] See § 6.
[244] See § 7.
[245] See § 8.
[246] *Ibid.*

9

The Situation in Uganda

9.1 REFLECTION: THE SITUATION IN UGANDA

Melanie O'Brien

INTRODUCTION

This reflection addresses the feminist judgments concerning the International Criminal Court (ICC) in Uganda. It provides a background to the conflict in Uganda, before delivering an overview of the ICC in Uganda. A brief background of the *Prosecutor v. Dominic Ongwen* case (*Ongwen* case) is given, which is the only current ICC case in Uganda.[1]

A reflection is then provided of each of the three rewritings of the *Ongwen* case in this collection, explaining first the relevant findings from the original decision, before outlining how each of the rewritings differs from the original decision and reflecting on how the judges have incorporated a feminist perspective into their judgments. Finally, a reflection is given on how gender justice could be delivered beyond the existing rules and structure of the ICC.

Background to the Conflict

Uganda was a British colony, declaring independence in 1962. The postcolonial period has been dominated by violence and armed conflict, starting in 1964 with violent protests against the consolidation of power by the country's first prime minister, Milton Obote.[2] In 1971, General Idi Amin Dada carried out a coup. His

[1] The case against Joseph Kony is still at pre-trial stage, with arrest warrants issued. The ICC Prosecutor is seeking to move to Confirmation of Charges stage. Available at www.icc-cpi.int/uganda/kony.

[2] A. B. K. Kasozi, *Social Origins of Violence in Uganda, 1964–1985* (Montreal: McGill-Queen's University Press, 1994), at 74–80. Kasozi notes at 17–29 that the pre-colonial and colonial periods were also violent.

eight-year regime was characterised by violence, as he tortured and murdered anyone affiliated with the opposition, those perceived as supporting Obote, particularly Acholi and Langi peoples. 'It is estimated that between 300,000 and 500,000 Ugandans were killed during this period, which earned Amin the nickname "the butcher".'[3]

After the defeat of Amin's forces in 1979, Obote eventually returned to power in 1980 and retaliated against Amin's supporters, starting his own campaign of 'rape, torture, looting and destruction of property', during which another 300,000–500,000 people were killed.[4] Obote was once again ousted by the military in July 1985, although it too was then overthrown. In January 1986, Yoweri Museveni seized power and has been President of Uganda ever since, as he abolished all political parties except his own (National Resistance Movement), and continues to perpetuate violence against any opposition.

Uganda has fifty-six ethnic groups, and this has led to opposition, armed insurgencies, and resistance against the government, which continue today. After Museveni took power, conflict began in northern (and parts of eastern) Uganda and continued between government authorities and the Lord's Resistance Army (LRA), led by Joseph Kony. The LRA has abducted children to use as child soldiers, forced wives, and sexual slaves. It has also perpetrated atrocities against civilians, such as torture and murder.

To date, the only examples of accountability for LRA members are the conviction of Dominic Ongwen at the ICC and one ongoing Ugandan domestic trial against LRA commander Thomas Kwoyelo.[5] It has been reported that some LRA soldiers 'were integrated into the Ugandan military without investigation into crimes they may have committed in the LRA', although others remain 'in the bush', waging conflict.[6] A temporary ceasefire agreement was signed by LRA negotiators in 2008 (extending previous ceasefire agreements originally signed between November 2006 to 29 February 2008), and then a Demobilisation, Disarmament, and Reintegration (DDR) agreement and an implementation protocol on 29 February 2008. Kony himself did not participate in negotiations, and ultimately the negotiations for a full peace agreement fell apart due to his erratic behaviour.[7] Kony vowed never to sign a full peace agreement until ICC arrest warrants were withdrawn. Despite a high-profile campaign to find him in 2012, his whereabouts remain unknown.[8]

[3] J. R. Quinn, 'Getting to Peace? Negotiating with the LRA in Northern Uganda' 10(1) *Human Rights Review* (2009) 55–71, at 56.

[4] *Ibid.*

[5] Human Rights Watch, *World Report 2022, Uganda* (2022), available at www.hrw.org/world-report/2022/country-chapters/uganda.

[6] *Ibid.*

[7] See M. Schomerus, *The Lord's Resistance Army: Violence and Peacemaking in Africa* (Cambridge: Cambridge University Press, 2021), for details on the 2006–2008 peace negotiations.

[8] Al Jazeera, 'LRA and Uganda sign peace pact', 2 March 2008, available at www.aljazeera.com/news/2008/3/2/lra-and-uganda-sign-peace-pact.

The ICC in Uganda

In January 2004, the government of Uganda referred its own situation to the ICC, and investigations were opened in July 2004. The ICC's focus is on crimes committed in the armed conflict between the LRA and the government authorities. Alleged crimes are war crimes (including murder, cruel treatment of civilians, pillaging, rape, enlistment and use of child soldiers) and crimes against humanity (including murder, enslavement, sexual enslavement, rape, and other inhumane acts).

In 2005, the ICC issued an arrest warrant for LRA leaders Joseph Kony, Vincent Otti, Okot Odhiambo, Raska Lukwiya, and Dominic Ongwen. Kony and Otti remain at large; Lukwiya and Odhiambo are deceased (proceedings terminated). Ongwen surrendered himself to the ICC in January 2015, and, to this day, remains the only defendant to face trial at the ICC over crimes committed in Uganda. No crimes committed by Ugandan government authorities are being investigated by the ICC.

Background to the Ongwen *Case*

After surrendering himself to the ICC, Ongwen's trial began in December 2016, closing in March 2020. At the time of his surrender and arrest, Ongwen was the commander of the LRA's Sinia Brigade, with the rank of brigadier from 2004 onwards. Ongwen's history is complex. He was himself abducted by the LRA as a child, somewhere between the ages of eight and fourteen, although his exact age at abduction in the late 1980s is difficult to confirm. Ongwen was a particularly brutal leader, and was charged with over seventy counts of war crimes and crimes against humanity.[9] These included crimes of murder, attacking civilians, torture, enslavement, pillaging, other inhumane acts, persecution, destruction of property, rape, sexual slavery, forced pregnancy, outrages upon personal dignity, conscription of children into an armed group, and use of children in hostilities. These charges related to specific attacks on internally displaced persons (civilian) camps, and also to long-term and ongoing crimes (in particular, sexual and gender-based offences).

Ongwen was convicted by the ICC's Trial Chamber IX on 4 February 2021,[10] found guilty of sixty-one crimes (war crimes and crimes against humanity), and sentenced in May 2021 to twenty-five years in prison.[11] His conviction and sentencing were affirmed in the Appeal Judgment and Sentencing Appeal Judgment of 15 December 2022.[12]

[9] Decision on the Confirmation of Charges, *Ongwen* (ICC-02/04-01/15-422-Red), Pre-Trial Chamber II, 23 March 2016.

[10] Trial Judgment, *Ongwen* (ICC-02/04-01/15-1762-Red), Trial Chamber IX, 4 February 2021 (hereafter Ongwen Judgment).

[11] Sentence, *Ongwen* (ICC-02/04-01/15), Trial Chamber IX, 6 May 2021 (hereafter Ongwen Sentence).

[12] Appeal Judgment, *Ongwen* (ICC-02/04-01/15-2022-Red), Appeals Chamber, 15 December 2022.

Reflecting on the Feminist Judgments

All of the authors have reimagined aspects of the *Ongwen* Trial Judgment or Sentencing Decision, as the Appeal Judgment was released too late in this project (December 2022). Judges Kirabira, Ringin, and Grey rewrite the sentencing decision in relation to the crime of forced pregnancy; Judge Kyojiika writes a separate sentencing decision to incorporate the aggravating factor of the impact on children who were born as a result of Ongwen's sexual and gender-based crimes; and Judge Rigney looks at the defence of duress while applying the concept of abolitionism.

Sentencing for Crimes of Forced Pregnancy

Ongwen was convicted of forced pregnancy as a war crime and a crime against humanity, and sentenced to twenty years' imprisonment for each count. The forced pregnancy took place in the context of forced marriages, a systematic element of the LRA, in which girls and young women were abducted and 'given' to LRA soldiers as 'wives'. The 'wives' were regularly raped as part of their role as 'wife'. Ongwen had a number of 'wives', and the Trial Chamber found that he repeatedly raped his 'wives'. The Chamber found that two of his seven 'wives' became pregnant (P-0101 and P-0214); one birthed separately a girl and a boy, the other a girl. The Chamber found that the 'wives' were unable to escape, under threat of death, including the two pregnant 'wives', and that they were held in violent circumstances, including beatings and rape.

The Trial Chamber discussed the background to the Rome Statute definition of forced pregnancy. It then went on to detail the definition, namely when the perpetrator 'confine[s] one or more women forcibly made pregnant', with the two components of 'unlawful confinement' and 'forcibly made pregnant', and with the intent to 'affect the ethnic composition of any population or carry out other grave violations of international law'.[13] The trial judgment and sentencing judgment noted that the 'crime of forced pregnancy is grounded in the woman's right to personal and reproductive autonomy and the right to family', where forced pregnancy deprives a woman of reproductive autonomy. The sentencing judgment found the crime to be of a very high gravity, due to the forced pregnancy itself but also because the pregnancy resulted from rape. The defencelessness and multiplicity of victims was acknowledged as an aggravating factor, as was the discriminatory nature of the crime.

Judges Kirabira, Ringin, and Grey's sentencing judgment (Joint Judgment) differs from the original sentencing judgment in that it delves into the harm caused by forced pregnancy in significant detail, which the original sentencing judgment did not. The Joint Judgment explores four categories of harms. Firstly, the harms of

[13] Drawing from Articles 7(1)(g)-4 and 8(2)(e)(vi)-4 and the associated Elements of Crimes.

violation of personal and reproductive autonomy, which the judges note is a 'key aspect of human dignity'.

Next, they outline the physical harms stemming from rape, lack of medical assistance and perinatal care, birth complications, physically demanding domestic duties, and physical punishments. Here, the judges point out that insufficient evidence was collected of the physical harms experienced by the victims, which should be addressed in future cases.

Thirdly, the judges address psychological and emotional harm caused by fear and intimidation (threats of physical abuse). It was noted that the victims were still afraid of Dominic Ongwen, which diminished their willingness to fully cooperate with ICC investigators. Again, the judges noted a lack of evidence of the specific psychological harms to P-0101 and P-0214, although these could have included depression, anxiety, PTSD, shame, and more.

Finally, the Joint Judgment examines economic harms, including the 'significant economic burden' that can be placed on the victim from childcare responsibilities and the limited earning capacity due to parental responsibilities, while acknowledging that Ongwen's indigence left him unable to contribute to the welfare of the children he fathered. The judges also pointed out that the victims' education ceased once they were abducted, affecting their future earning capacity, and encouraged future Trial Chambers to pursue more detailed evidence of the socio-economic harms resulting from these crimes. A particularly feminist step in an international criminal court judgment taken here is to 'consider the provision of childcare in [the] reparations order in this case to address the financial burden'.

The judges include the same three aggravating factors that the original sentencing judgment included; however they also discuss social harms, namely the stigma attached to the victims in Uganda, which detrimentally affected their reintegration into society. As there was no evidence of this raised with regard to P-0101 and P-0214 specifically, the judges could not apply this aggravating circumstance but, again, urged this to be considered in future sentencing decisions. The judges do take cultural harms into consideration, such as the forced disconnection from cultural practices, including inheritance and land rights, as well as pregnancy rituals.

A strong feminist aspect of the Joint Judgment is to make obvious the lacunae in the evidence that results in the sentencing judges not being able to take some feminist-centred issues into account in their sentencing decision. This is an important commentary, making a critique of the trial process, which did not adequately explore how the women in this case were affected by the crimes they experienced.

A feminist approach to judging is to 'do no harm', and this is evident in the Joint Judgment. The judges are critical of the Trial Chamber for not seeking further testimony from P-0101 and P-0214 but decline to recall the witnesses so as to minimise the re-traumatisation caused by court appearances.

The judges ultimately conclude by pronouncing a sentence of life imprisonment each for the war crime and the crime against humanity of forced pregnancy, which they reduce to thirty years due to the mitigating circumstances of Ongwen's experiences as a child soldier. This is a longer sentence than that actually awarded to Ongwen (including on appeal), which ultimately better reflects the aggravating circumstances, thereby better taking the victims' experiences into account.

Considering Children Born of Sexual Offences

Rather than rewrite an existing part of either the trial or sentencing judgments, Judge Kyobiika has added to the sentencing judgment. Judge Kyobiika considers a wide range of the sexual and gender-based crimes against girls and women that Ongwen was convicted of (Counts 50–68): forced marriage as an 'other inhumane act'; torture; rape; sexual slavery; enslavement; forced pregnancy; and outrages upon personal dignity. Judge Kyobiika's focus, however, is on 'children born as a result of these sexual and gender-based crimes'. She treats the children as both a group of victims entitled to their own reparations and an aggravating factor in sentencing; this has not been considered by international courts. She discusses the context of the LRA's systematic abduction of girls and young women to take as forced 'wives', who were regularly raped by their 'husbands' and many of whom subsequently gave birth to children born from this rape.

Judge Kyobiika discusses the relevance of children's human rights, including to children's right to special care and assistance, and recognition that 'family is a fundamental group of society'. Children's growth, well-being, and development are all influenced by their experiences and environment. Obviously, being born of rape and growing up in an armed conflict environment, while not a definite predetermination of a child's ultimate life journey, is not in the best interests of a child. Such circumstances lead to significant obstacles to that child's enjoyment of human rights, such as the right to family and the right to education. Judge Kyobiika observes 'that some of the children born as a result of war have been treated with disdain and continue to face untold suffering, rejection, discrimination, and stigmatisation in the communities'; that patriarchal societal structures contribute to 'children's contested identities'; and that children born of war have a high risk of experiencing domestic and family violence. The forced 'wives' and the children born of rape in the LRA were also exposed to conflict, witnessing and experiencing horrific violence that may lead to serious mental health concerns from trauma, such as depression.

Ultimately, the radical nature of Judge Kyobiika's judgment is the inclusion of children born of sexual offences in the sentencing. By doing so, she is not merely acknowledging them as an aggravating factor, but actually considering these children and their needs as another category of victims. Judge Kyobiika finds that 'Ongwen denied some of his children the fundamental right of being born and raised in the security of a family', with resulting 'mental, economic, social, ethical, religious effects'. Thus, in addition to terms of imprisonment, Judge Kyobiika orders reparations for children who were members of Ongwen's homestead; children that were born as a result of forced pregnancy; children that witnessed some of the crimes; and children who were members of LRA soldiers' households.

Judge Kyobiika's judgment fills a significant gap in international criminal law jurisprudence. While 'women and children' is an oft-seen victim category, and in some cases rightly criticised for grouping these two types of people into one category, it is also the case that the plight of children is often directly connected to the plight of women, and thus it is appropriate to consider children in a sentencing decision. In particular, the children that Judge Kyobiika considers to have been very specifically impacted by the actions of Ongwen and the rest of the LRA, with their lives starting at a disadvantage. It is crucial that defendants are ordered to provide reparations to such victims, not just because they are in fact the children of Ongwen himself (which would lend itself to the traditional concept of child support) but because he brought these children into a world of violence and disadvantage, through an act of violence. The ICC has a reparations regime,[14] and it is surprising that this was not considered in the original Ongwen sentencing.

In relation to this reimagined judgment, I would like to see more detail about the reparations ordered. Certainly, financial reparations are appropriate, to assist with the rehabilitation of children, physical and mental health needs, education, living expenses, and more. What kind of reparations are appropriate for children born of war rape? Moffett discusses the need to shift 'the moral value system' of those responsible for atrocity crimes as part of reparations, which should be not just about money for victims (particularly if payments are merely symbolic) but also ensuring victims' rights.[15] Reparations for children, who have their lives ahead of them, are certainly challenging. Moffett notes that 'assessing the impact or measurable outcomes [of reparations] is complicated by the unpredictability of what will happen when societies move away from war. These issues reflect the disconnect between the idealism of rights and the reality of implementing remedies'.[16] Reparations must be feasible and secure 'adequate measures and processes to remedy victims' harm with responsible actors taking ownership to redress that harm, while at the same time not bankrupting a country, reinforcing inequalities, or humiliating responsible actors'.[17] It is a huge undertaking for a bench of judges to decide on appropriate remedies that achieve all of these, but it is necessary, as a general order for reparations may not address any of the harms suffered by children. Of course, a separate, more detailed reparations order may be made (see Articles 75 and 79 of the Rome Statute), and the

[14] L. Moffett, *Justice for Victims before the International Criminal Court* (London: Routledge, 2014).

[15] L. Moffett, *Reparations and War: Finding Balance in Repairing the Past* (Oxford: Oxford University Press, 2023), at 266, and chapter 2, 45–67. See also A. Sehmi, 'Emphasising Socio-economic Narratives of Truth, Justice and Reparations in the Prosecutor v. Dominic Ongwen' 26(6) *International Journal of Human Rights* (2022) 1083–1106.

[16] Moffett, *supra* note 15, at 287.

[17] *Ibid*, at 66.

lacunae in Article 75 'provide judges with the flexibility to determine the scope and extent of reparations'.[18] Ultimately, reparations for the children born of rape are necessary to remedy the victims' harm, and Judge Kyobiika's inclusion of these in her feminist judgment highlights a significant void in the original judgment.

Duress and Abolitionism

Part of Ongwen's defence was a claim for the defence of duress, and scholars have analysed the defence of duress in the *Ongwen* case.[19] The defence argued that Kony's control of LRA soldiers was 'allegedly maintained through a combination of strict disciplinary rules which severely punished non-compliance with orders, the tight supervision of commanders, and successful assertion of spiritual powers'.[20] The Trial Judgment considered multiple elements when analysing the duress defence: Ongwen's status in the LRA hierarchy and the applicability of the LRA disciplinary regime to him; executions of senior LRA commanders on Kony's orders; the possibility of escaping from or leaving the LRA; Kony's alleged spiritual powers; Ongwen's personal loyalty to Kony and his career advancement; and crimes committed in private.

It is outside the scope of this reflection to go through all of these elements; however, as an example, I will detail one of these elements: escape. The Trial Chamber noted that, if Ongwen engaged in the charged criminal conduct 'when escaping or leaving was possible is a strong indication that he acted on his own accord'.[21] The Chamber notes that evidence was given of other LRA soldiers, including of a high rank, who escaped, and that Ongwen was more afraid of being held accountable for the crimes he committed than of Kony. The Chamber held that Ongwen's 'high rank and position placed him in a relatively better position to escape, as compared to lower-ranking LRA members'.[22] Based on the evidence given, the Trial Chamber concluded 'that escaping from or otherwise leaving the LRA was a realistic option available to Dominic Ongwen ... as it was for many others who successfully escaped'.[23]

Ultimately, the Trial Chamber found 'no basis in the evidence to hold that Dominic Ongwen was subjected to a threat of imminent death or imminent or continuing serious bodily harm to himself or another person at the time of his conduct underlying the charged crimes'. The Trial Chamber determined that, quite the opposite, Ongwen 'frequently acted independently and even contested orders received from Kony'.

[18] Moffett, *supra* note 14, at 154.
[19] For example, W. Nortje and N. Quénivet, *Child Soldiers and the Defence of Duress under International Criminal Law* (Cham: Palgrave Macmillan, 2019).
[20] Ongwen Judgment, *supra* note 10, § 2568.
[21] *Ibid*, § 2619.
[22] *Ibid*, § 2634.
[23] *Ibid*, § 2635.

Judge Rigney concurs with the majority opinion in finding that the defence of duress is not open to Ongwen, but then goes on to discuss the limits of the defence of duress. Judge Rigney ponders the agency of the accused, why they made decisions, and what structural conditions influenced their actions. Drawing from this, she asks whether international criminal law can address 'the interconnectedness between personal and political violence', and, in doing so, questions whether there are alternatives to the international criminal justice system.

The feminist aspect of Judge Rigney's piece, which goes further than others in this collection, is that it questions the entire structure of international criminal law. As other feminist judgment projects have shown, some judgments are directed towards working within the system while others seek to disrupt the legal project entirely, and it is the latter that Rigney is seeking here. She questions the act of assigning individual criminal responsibility for collective wrongdoing when it is larger political, economic, or legal structures that have created the conditions for individual criminality. As Rigney points out, international criminal legal discourse largely does not engage with these structures and the conditions they create, resulting in the de-contextualisation of a defendant's actions from the conditions that led to them.

Judge Rigney then moves on to discuss the concept of abolition, a philosophy that 'ultimately aims to eliminate [the need for] imprisonment, policing and surveillance' (connecting this system to racism, capitalism, and slavery), introducing alternatives to punishment and imprisonment. Abolitionism has a strong feminist grounding, particularly in Black feminism, and looks at the root causes of harm and violence.

Judge Rigney's piece raised many questions for me. I would have liked to see in this judgment specific suggestions for future trials. Specifically, what does Judge Rigney think that judges (and/or lawyers) in future trials should implement to adopt an abolitionist perspective in their decisions? How does an abolitionist perspective fit with international criminal law generally? How does abolitionism in the context of a discussion about international criminal law (as opposed to domestic criminal law) differ from or overlap with atrocity prevention literature and strategies, which already focus on a societal structure that seeks to address risk factors, such as a human rights-focused society?[24] How can abolitionism engage with atrocity prevention theories and practice? How could international criminal law be adjusted to adapt transformative justice responses to address the social causes of violence and move away from incarceration? How could the court have addressed these concerns in this particular case, of Dominic Ongwen's experience as a child and adult soldier living in an

[24] See, for example, the work of Barbara Harff generally; H. Nyseth Brehm, 'Re-examining Risk Factors of Genocide' 19(1) *Journal of Genocide Research* (2017) 61–87; and the Framework of Analysis for Atrocity Crimes: A tool for prevention, developed by the UN Office on Genocide Prevention and the Responsibility to Protect (2014).

environment of long-term armed conflict? While these questions remain unanswered, Judge Rigney's reimagining opens new paths for thinking about the value of feminist engagement with international law and for looking to alternatives to achieve justice for all.

Imagining Gender Justice beyond the Existing Rules

One theme that emerges from the rewritten judgments of Judges Kirabira, Ringin, and Grey, and of Kyojiika is the need in sentencing to take into greater account any aggravating circumstances related to the impact of crimes on women and children. Ongwen's sentence of twenty-five years is something that I have struggled with. The details of the experiences and harms of the girls and women who were victims of the LRA are horrific and long-term: they did not cease when the women managed to escape. Crimes such as forced marriage and forced pregnancy have a lifelong impact. I had hoped that the sentence would be increased on appeal, and was disappointed it was not. I understand that the final sentence given to Ongwen was reduced because of the mitigating factor of his background as a child soldier. However, I found it difficult to balance the length of this sentence given the evidence which detailed the enthusiasm, violence, and cruelty with which Ongwen carried out his crimes. Ongwen may have been abducted as a child, but he was quick to engage with the LRA's way of life and to rise up through the ranks as he perpetrated atrocities in a way that other child soldiers did not. In addition, as the court noted in its rejection of the duress defence, Ongwen also had opportunities to leave the LRA, but did not do so.

This is perhaps why I find the idea of abolitionism advanced in the reimaged decision by Judge Rigney so challenging. As a scholar, I am open to the idea and can comprehend the arguments such as the need to address the root causes of violence: I agree prevention is better than punishment, if we can avoid the violence. However, when violence does take place, I cannot fathom not having a system of punishment. This is no doubt due to my ingrained education and subsequent work in criminal law. However, it is also due to my extensive empirical research with atrocity survivors. I have interviewed (often mostly women) survivors in Australia, Bangladesh, Bosnia, Cambodia, and Israel. I have delved in depth into survivor testimonies (oral and written) and memoirs, as well as accessing other sources of atrocity evidence such as photographs and film, and explored atrocity sites, memorials, and museums around the world. I have interviewed women who survived rape (including in rape camps) and forced marriage (some of which produced children). I have watched an elderly Holocaust survivor deliver her regular talk about her experience, and still struggle to talk about the loss of her mother over seventy years ago. The lifelong trauma that survivors carry is an incredibly heavy burden that never leaves them. The concept of punishment for crimes has always existed, although it is true that incarceration is historically a relatively new form of punishment, with its roots in racist and capitalist societies.[25] However, the idea that perpetrators of such horrific, deeply affecting atrocity crimes have the opportunity to 'rehabilitate' and live a free life is one I genuinely struggle with, particularly in the context of the crimes that women (and children) have experienced, and in the lifelong trauma and life disruption experienced by victims of genocide and other atrocities.[26] Thus, I want to see a stronger argument from abolitionists as to how abolitionism fits with atrocity crimes; how it would balance with the desire for justice that victims seek. To me, a gender-just outcome is one that honours the victims' wishes: what is the justice that they seek, and how can the international criminal justice system deliver that?

It would also be interesting to see how the judges in this collection would implement the *amicus curiae* contributions that were solicited by the ICC as part of the Ongwen appeal process, if these feminist judgments were at the appeal stage.[27] Some of the *amicus* briefs and oral presentations submitted to the court delivered perspectives on issues addressed here, including feminist-influenced arguments: duress, forced pregnancy, forced marriage, and, although not expressly using the word 'abolitionism', some relating to arguments about the context of violence in which Ongwen existed.[28] How would the judges in this collection have considered these *amicus* submissions? Would these submissions have contributed to or even strengthened the judges' findings? An interesting future project, perhaps.

The three *Ongwen* judgments in this book have two starkly competing feminist perspectives: one that works from inside the legal system and seeks to take the perspectives and experiences of children into account; and one that seeks to disrupt the legal system and urges it to take the context of atrocity violence into account to create new solutions. Yet all the judgments are grounded in a human rights perspective and language, always seeking to enhance and uphold the human rights of victims. Hence, this Uganda/Ongwen section of this book of feminist judgments is a microcosm of feminism, which comes in many forms and with many theories, although ultimately seeking equality, participation, non-violence, peace, and

[25] S. Bauer, *American Prison: A Reporter's Undercover Journey into the Business of Punishment* (New York: Penguin Books, 2019).

[26] M. O'Brien, *From Discrimination to Death: Genocide Process through a Human Rights Lens* (Abingdon: Routledge, 2023).

[27] Order inviting expressions of interest as *amicus curiae* in judicial proceedings (pursuant to rule 103 of the Rules of Procedure and Evidence), *Ongwen* (ICC-02/04-01/15-1884), Appeals Chamber, 25 October 2021.

[28] For example, Amicus Curiae Observations by Public International Law & Policy Group, ICC-02/04-01/15 A, 23 December 2021, available at https://engagedscholarship.csuohio.edu/fac_briefs/28/; and Submission of Amicus Curiae Observations in the Case of the *Prosecutor v. Dominic Ongwen*, ICC-02/04-01/15 A, 23 December 2021, available at https://scholarlycommons.law.wlu.edu/wlufac/692/. See also M. O'Brien, I. Rosenthal, and R. Grey, 'Historic Feminist Intervention at the International Criminal Court – the Appeals Hearing in *Prosecutor v. Dominic Ongwen*' 28(1) *Australian Journal of Human Rights* (2022) 176–182.

justice. Which, after all, is also what international criminal justice systems should deliver.

9.2 MENTAL INCAPACITATION AND DURESS IN THE ONGWEN JUDGMENT

Sophie Rigney

In 2021, Trial Chamber IX convicted Mr Dominic Ongwen of sixty-one counts of war crimes and crimes against humanity.[29] In this rewritten decision, Sophie Rigney interrogates the defence of duress to place Mr Ongwen firmly in the position of perpetrator and victim, eradicating the false dichotomy between the two. Rigney considers the constraints within which Mr Ongwen was operating and links these to broader questions of culpability. Rigney links these questions to carceral abolition movements.

Ultimately, Rigney confirms the finding of the original Trial Chamber and convicts Mr Ongwen of sixty-one counts of war crimes and crimes against humanity.

No.: ICC-02/04-01/15
Date: 4 February 2021

Original: English

TRIAL CHAMBER IX(B)

Before: Judge Sophie RIGNEY

SITUATION IN UGANDA
IN THE CASE OF THE *PROSECUTOR v. DOMINIC ONGWEN*

Public

Redacted Trial Judgment – Separate and Concurring Opinion of Judge Sophie Rigney

OVERVIEW

1. The man on trial was born Dominic Okumu Savio.[30] He was born into a Uganda that already knew significant political turmoil and conflict. When he was ten years old, or perhaps slightly younger, he was taken from the side of the road, abducted, and forced to become a soldier for the Lord's Resistance Army (LRA).

[29] Trial Judgment, *Ongwen* (ICC-02/04-01/15-1762-Red), Trial Chamber IX, 4 February 2021 (hereafter Ongwen Judgment).

[30] E. K. Baines, 'Complex Political Perpetrators: Reflections on Dominic Ongwen' 47(2) *Journal of Modern African Studies* (2009) 163–191, at 163 and 169.

This was a common occurrence, and there is evidence that his family had prepared him for such a possibility, including teaching him to provide a different name to his captors. This he did, telling them that his name was Dominic Ongwen.[31] Ongwen is now the name that he is known by, and is charged by in this trial. As he grew up within the LRA, Dominic also became adept at the various methods employed by the LRA, and was promoted through the ranks to eventually become a battalion and brigade commander. During this time, he turned eighteen, and thus became of age to be criminally responsible within the jurisdiction of the International Criminal Court for his actions. He is now charged with seventy counts of war crimes and crimes against humanity, and the majority judgment finds him guilty of sixty-one of those counts.[32]

2. Ongwen is the first person to come before this Court charged with crimes that we also know he was a victim of himself. Moreover, unlike many other cases in international criminal law, Ongwen was not a high-level commander or a president, issuing orders from behind a desk or hidden away behind palace doors. This is not to deny his position of power – as a commander, he held considerable authority in the LRA. But he was located within a hierarchy of power, rather than leading the hierarchical structure; and this relative position, as well as his victimhood, makes this case an unusual one.

3. There is a powerful narrative in popular discourse that portrays those charged with international crimes as monsters. However, the case of *Ongwen* has starkly shown the complexity of victimhood and perpetration, and how lines between these categories are 'porous',[33] with individuals often being both victim and perpetrator.

4. Perhaps more so than many other cases, this case sets out the devastation and depravity of war as experienced by its soldiers and commanders – and how this leads to conditions that allow, or even encourage, criminality. There are complex interactions that can be witnessed, between individual, local, and global conditions. These include questions of childhood and trauma, mental illness, and poverty; the role of international interventions in conflict and in criminal law; and the role of global capitalism which enables the market in arms and military spending. This case shows how these intersecting conditions can both structure individual decisions and agency, and simultaneously define what behaviour is criminalised and who is held accountable for it.

[31] *Ibid.*

[32] Ongwen Judgment, *supra* note 29.

[33] M. Drumbl, 'The Ongwen Trial at the ICC: Tough Questions on Child Soldiers', *Open Democracy*, 14 April 2015, available at www.opendemocracy.net/openglobalrights/mark-drumbl/ongwen-trial-at-icc-tough-questions-on-child-soldiers. See also M. Drumbl, 'Victims Who Victimise' 4(2) *London Review of International Law* (2016) 217–246, at 217; P. Clark, *Distant Justice: The Impact of the International Criminal Court on African Politics* (Cambridge: Cambridge University Press, 2018), at chapter 4; S. Rigney, *Fairness and Rights in International Criminal Procedure* (Edinburgh: Edinburgh University Press, 2022), at chapter 1.

5. Acknowledging these factors does not take away from the devastation and depravity experienced by other victims too, including crimes perpetrated by soldiers and commanders. The evidence in this case is overwhelming, particularly with regard to the use of sexual violence against young women and girls.[34] In the situation in Uganda, it was common that children were victims, and perpetrators, and victim-perpetrators.

6. All of this is particularly relevant to the defence of duress, which the defence has raised in this case. For reasons I will expand upon below, applying the law compels me to concur with the majority in this case, and find that the defence of duress is not open to Mr Ongwen. Nonetheless, I want to offer some comments on the defence of duress generally. It is my opinion that, even though it was not established on the evidence in this case, the defence of duress still permits us to examine the structure of international criminal law, alternative possibilities to this carceral system, and ultimately whether we can build an abolitionist movement for international criminal law. This separate and concurring opinion, then, shows the limits of the defence of duress as defined under the Rome Statute, but also shows what the defence of duress might allow us to understand about the structure and system of international criminal law.

OPINION

The Defence of Duress

7. Article 31 of the Rome Statute permits an accused a defence against their criminal responsibility for their conduct in situations where there was a 'threat of imminent death or of continuing or imminent serious bodily harm against that person or another person'.[35]

8. I agree with the majority's statements on the elements of the defence of duress. As they have set out, duress has three elements.[36] The first is the existence of a particular type of threat: there is a requirement that the conduct which is alleged to constitute the crime must have been caused by duress which resulted from a threat of imminent death or of continuing or imminent serious bodily harm, against the accused or another person.[37] The threat may be made by other persons, or may be constituted by other circumstances beyond the accused's control, but it is to be assessed at the time of the conduct in question which is alleged to constitute the crime. The requirement of imminence relates to the nature of the threatened harm

[34] See P. Bradfield, 'Preserving Vulnerable Evidence at the International Criminal Court – the Article 56 Milestone in Ongwen' 19(3) *International Criminal Law Review* (2019) 373–411.

[35] Article 31(1)(d) Rome Statute

[36] Ongwen Judgment, *supra* note 29, §§ 2581–2584.

[37] *Ibid*, § 2582.

(rather than the threat itself).[38] Hence, the threatened harm must be to be killed immediately, or to have serious bodily harm inflicted immediately or in an ongoing way.[39] Duress is not an available defence if this requirement of immediacy is not met; and an elevated probability of harm or an abstract danger will not be sufficient.[40]

9. The second element of the defence of duress is that the accused acted necessarily and reasonably to avoid the threat.[41] They are not required to take all conceivable action to avoid the threat. A determination of what 'necessarily and reasonably' would mean under the circumstances is a decision for the Trial Chamber, and should be assessed in relation to the totality of the circumstances in which the accused found themselves. The third element is that the person does not intend to cause a greater harm than the one sought to be avoided. This is a subjective element and relates to the intention of the individual, not whether or not they actually avoided the greater harm.[42]

10. The defence argues that Ongwen was 'under a continuing threat of imminent death and serious bodily harm from [Joseph] Kony and his controlling, military apparatus'.[43] They contend that Kony maintained control over the LRA through strict rules and severe punishment for non-compliance; supervision of commanders; and assertion of spiritual powers.[44] In total, the defence have led substantial evidence about the environment of the LRA and the horrors to which LRA members were subjected.[45]

11. The defence have also led significant evidence about Ongwen's mental state, and defence expert evidence suggested that 'the coercive and violent LRA, controlled by Kony (and the Spirits), with its "do or die" rules and regulations, disrupted [Ongwen's] development of any moral values and of the Acholi culture, leaving Mr Ongwen with no free will. Every activity that Mr Ongwen participated in while in the LRA was under duress'.[46] The defence argues that Mr Ongwen's mental state 'destroyed his capacity to "act reasonably and necessarily" in his situation to avoid the LRA's threats, and made it not possible for him to formulate any intent not to cause a greater harm'.[47]

12. The prosecution argues that the defence of duress is not applicable in this case. While the prosecution acknowledges that the LRA 'sometimes inflicted severe

38 *Ibid.*
39 *Ibid.*
40 *Ibid.*
41 *Ibid*, § 2583.
42 *Ibid*, § 2584.
43 Public Redacted Version of Corrected Version of Defence Closing Brief, filed on 24 February 2020, *Ongwen* (ICC-02/04-01/15-1722-Corr-Red), Trial Chamber IX, 13 March 2020, § 680.
44 Ongwen Judgment, *supra* note 29, § 2586.
45 Public Redacted Version of Corrected Version of Defence Closing Brief, *supra* note 43, §§ 681–691.
46 *Ibid*, § 538.
47 *Ibid*, § 602.

punishment on its members for breaking the armed group's rules, the Chamber has heard no evidence that Mr Ongwen's conduct was caused by a threat of imminent death or imminent or continuing serious bodily harm against him or another person'.[48]

13. In this case, the majority have concluded that the accused was not 'subjected to a threat of imminent death or imminent or continuing serious bodily harm to himself or another person at the time of his conduct underlying the charged crimes'.[49] In particular, they focus on evidence that during the period of the charges, Mr Ongwen did not face any prospective punishment by death or serious bodily harm when he disobeyed orders. Moreover, although Mr Ongwen had a realistic possibility of leaving the LRA, he chose not to do so and instead ascended through the ranks and attained greater power. Indeed, Mr Ongwen occasionally contested orders, and frequently acted independently.[50] This evidence is compelling, and I agree with the view of the majority that there has not been evidence brought to satisfy the particular elements of the defence of duress, particularly the requirement of immediate threat. In this case, then, the defence of duress has not been established and cannot excuse Mr Ongwen's conduct.

14. Nonetheless, due to the contestation of the defence of duress, significant evidence was brought which cast light on the conditions under which Mr Ongwen operated. Indeed, while duress has not been made out in this case, the defence itself – and the evidence that has been adduced by virtue of raising the defence – invites consideration of particular issues of morality, responsibility, power, and violence. Duress is fundamentally concerned with choice, and the structures that constrain or motivate that choice. What decision did the accused make about their actions, and why was that decision chosen? What drives the accused's agency? What structural conditions influenced their actions?

15. In raising such questions, the defence of duress allows us to consider the structure of international criminal law, its conditions of possibility, and whether it can address the interconnectedness between personal and political violence. In so doing, we are invited to consider whether there are other alternatives to this criminal justice system. These are the issues I want to address in my remaining comments.

International Criminal Law's Structural Features and Conditions

16. As a system of law, international criminal law has emerged relatively recently: the 1990s saw a huge momentum towards building institutions, substantive laws, and procedural laws. It is no coincidence that the growth of international criminal law

48 Public Redacted Version of Prosecution Closing Brief, *Ongwen* (ICC-02/04-01/15-1719-Red), Trial Chamber IX, 24 February 2020, § 475.

49 Ongwen Judgment, *supra* note 29, § 2668.

50 *Ibid.*

occurred at the same time as post-Cold War expansion of neoliberalism, with its attendant greater recourse to criminal law.[51] Neoliberalism 'often called for a strong punitive state', and 'criminal law played an important role in economic restructuring and rule of law projects throughout the world'.[52] Moreover, international criminal law's focus on individual responsibility mirrors the individualist ideologies of neoliberalism.[53]

17. Many argue that international criminal law is vulnerable: it is reliant on states for funding and logistics; it has no independent police force; and its jurisdiction is limited in many ways. Yet the suggestion that international criminal law is inherently vulnerable obscures the fact that it has some significant structural strengths. In particular, it is the powerful states and individuals that can either enforce or ignore international criminal law. Just as in domestic criminal systems, some are more criminalised than others. Far from being a flaw, the ways in which some powerful parties can flaunt international criminal law while others are captured by it is part of the design of the system.

18. There are various ways in which international criminal law structures criminality. Its relationships to global capitalism, race, and imperialism all determine who and what is criminalised.[54] International criminal law's focus on particular core crimes disregards other types of harm.[55] Its jurisdictional limitations mean that certain states and people are often concentrated on, and others escape examination. All of this means that race, nationality, class, and gender are powerful determinants

[51] K. Engle, 'Anti-Impunity and the Turn to Criminal Law in Human Rights Law and Advocacy' 100(5) *Cornell Law Review* (2015) 1069–1127, at 1070 and 1076.

[52] *Ibid.*

[53] For more on international criminal law's relationships with neoliberalism, see C. Schwöbel-Patel, *Marketing Global Justice: The Political Economy of International Criminal Law* (Cambridge: Cambridge University Press, 2021); K. Maxine Clarke, *Fictions of Justice: The International Criminal Court and the Challenge of Legal Pluralism in Sub-Saharan Africa* (Cambridge: Cambridge University Press, 2010); T. Krever, 'International Criminal Law: An Ideology Critique' 26(3) *Leiden Journal of International Law* (2013) 701–723; S. Kendall, 'Commodifying Global Justice: Economics of Accountability at the International Criminal Court' 13(1) *Journal of International Criminal Justice* (2015) 113–134.

[54] See, e.g., A. Anghie and B. S. Chimni, 'Third World Approaches to International Law and Individual Responsibility' 2(1) *Chinese Journal of International Law* (2003) 77–103; K. Maxine Clarke, 'Refiguring the Perpetrator: Culpability, History and International Criminal Law's Impunity Gap' 19(5) *International Journal of Human Rights* (2015) 592–614; R. C. DeFalco and F. Mégret, 'The Invisibility of Race at the ICC: Lessons from the US Criminal Justice System' 7(1) *London Review of International Law* (2019) 55–87; S. Rigney, 'Distant Justice: The Impact of the International Criminal Court on African Politics (Book Review)' 31(3) *European Journal of International Law* (2020) 1157–1161.

[55] C. Schwöbel-Patel, 'The Core Crimes of International Criminal Law' in K. Heller et al. (eds.), *The Oxford Handbook of International Criminal Law* (Oxford: Oxford University Press, 2020) 768–790; J. Reynolds and S. Xavier, '"The Dark Corners of the World": TWAIL and International Criminal Justice' 14(4) *Journal of International Criminal Justice* (2016) 959–983; M. Burgis-Kasthala, 'Scholarship as Dialogue? TWAIL and the Politics of Methodology' 14(4) *Journal of International Criminal Justice* (2016) 921–937.

of who will be brought before the Court – even more so than commission of a crime.[56]

19. International criminal law is galvanised by two powerful narratives, or aims of the system of law: 'ending impunity' and providing 'justice to victims'.[57] The first of these, 'ending impunity', is undertaken through criminal trials of individuals, and holding individuals criminally responsible for collective wrongdoing and for crimes perpetrated by others (through extended modes of liability and superior responsibility).[58] But in assigning *individual* criminal responsibility to particular people for acts that are often collective, international criminal trials 'exonerate[e] ... those larger (political, economic, even legal) structures within which the conditions for individual criminality have been created'.[59] Those structures, and the conditions they create – including 'poverty, discrimination, marginalization, and social exclusion' – are 'lost from sight' in international criminal legal discourse.[60] Thus, international criminal trials often decontextualise the actions of the accused, and refuse to examine these actions within the conditions that give rise to them.

20. A further structural feature of international criminal law is how this legal system addresses victimhood and perpetration. As mentioned, 'justice for victims' is a pre-eminent aim of international criminal law. Victims are seen as the ones in whose name criminal justice is dispensed. Yet they are also frequently 'feminized, infantilized and racialized'[61] in the process, and are made into a 'deity-like

56 I am inspired here by the phrasing in the domestic abolition literature, 'race, gender, class, and sexuality (are) more important determinants of who goes to prison than simply the commission of a crime' (A. Y. Davis, G. Dent, E. R. Meiners, and B. E. Richie, *Abolition. Feminism. Now* (Chicago: Haymarket, 2022) at 47–48).

57 See S. Rigney, 'Postcard from the ICTY: Examining International Criminal Law's Narratives' in D. Joyce and J. Hohmann (eds.), *International Law's Objects* (Oxford: Oxford University Press, 2018) 366.

58 Art. 7 ICTY Statute; Art. 25 and Art. 28 Rome Statute.

59 M. Koskenniemi, 'Between Impunity and Show Trials' 6(1) *Max Planck Yearbook of United Nations Law* (2002) 1–35, at 14; Krever, *supra* note 53, at 701; I. Tallgren, 'Sensibility and Sense of International Criminal Law' 13(3) *European Journal of International Law* (2002) 561–595, at 594; K. Maxine Clarke, 'We Ask for Justice, You Give Us Law: The Rule of Law, Economic Markets, and the Reconfiguration of Victimhood' in C. De Vos, S. Kendall, and C. Stahn (eds.), *Contested Justice: The Politics and Practice of International Criminal Court Interventions* (Cambridge: Cambridge University Press, 2015) 272–301; Burgis-Kasthala, *supra* note 55; Reynolds and Xavier, *supra* note 55.

Krever, *supra* note 53, at 719–720.

60 *Ibid.*

61 C. Schwöbel-Patel, 'The "Ideal" Victim of International Criminal Law' 29(3) *European Journal of International Law* (2018) 703–724, at 703. See also C. Schwöbel, 'The Market and Marketing Culture of International Criminal Law' in C. Schwöbel (ed.), *Critical Approaches to International Criminal Law* (London: Routledge, 2014) 279; L. Fletcher, 'Refracted Justice: The Imagined Victim and the International Criminal Court' in C. De Vos, S. Kendall, and C. Stahn (eds.), *Contested Justice: The Politics and Practice of International Criminal Court Interventions* (Cambridge: Cambridge University Press, 2015) 302–325.

abstraction' rather than a real person with their own needs and opinions.[62] Perpetrators (and alleged perpetrators) are similarly reduced. Ultimately, victimhood and perpetration are separated in international criminal law – presented as a dichotomy.[63]

21. Alongside this general dichotomy of victim and perpetrator, there is a more particular 'legal fiction' that paints child soldiers as 'faultless passive victim(s)'.[64] The reality is 'not so simple', with child soldiers often exercising agency and sometimes perpetrating crimes.[65] Indeed, Ongwen has become a personification of these issues: a small boy, vulnerable and victimised, who grew up to be a man accused of committing heinous crimes; accused himself of victimising others.

22. To summarise, we see that international criminal law, as a system of law, has particular structural features. These features are a consequence of its ideological underpinnings, which are linked to neoliberalism, as well as the relationships between international criminal law and race, global capital, and imperialism. The structural features include substantive and procedural laws that criminalise some and exonerate others. As a result, some wars (or 'situations'), and therefore some individuals, are brought into the realm of 'international criminal justice' while others are not. Even further, within these situations some are labelled as criminals and others are labelled as victims – and these binaries have an additional gloss when we consider the example of child soldiers, as in the current case. I now want to consider these structural features of international criminal law against the arguments of abolitionist movements.

Abolition

23. Abolition, as it refers to more modern understandings of the carceral system, is defined 'as a tradition, a philosophy, and a theory of change, [which] moves away from a myopic focus on the distinct institution of the prison toward a more expansive vision of the social, political, and economic processes that defined the context within which imprisonment came to be viewed as the legitimate hand of justice'.[66] Abolition ultimately aims to eliminate imprisonment, policing, and surveillance, and to create 'lasting alternatives to punishment and imprisonment'.[67]

[62] S. Nouwen, 'Justifying Justice' in J. Crawford and M. Koskenniemi (eds.), *The Cambridge Companion to International Law* (Cambridge: Cambridge University Press, 2012) 327–351, at 340.

[63] See Rigney, *supra* note 57. See also W. Nortje and N. Quénivet, *Child Soldiers and the Defence of Duress under International Criminal Law* (Cham: Palgrave Macmillan, 2020).

[64] M. Drumbl, *Reimagining Child Soldiers in International Law and Policy* (Oxford: Oxford University Press, 2012), at 19. See also Nortje and Quénivet, *supra* note 63.

[65] Drumbl, *supra* note 64.

[66] Davis et al., *supra* note 56, at 50.

[67] *Ibid.*

24. Abolitionist movements are guided by a philosophy which typically holds three central tenets:[68]

1. That the modern carceral punishment system has its origins in 'slavery and the racial capitalist regime it relied on and sustained';
2. That the carceral system 'functions to oppress black people and other politically marginalized groups in order to maintain a racial capitalist regime'; and
3. That 'we can imagine and build a more humane and democratic society that no longer relies on caging people to meet human needs and solve social problems'.[69]

25. Thus, abolitionist philosophy and movements aim to understand what is (in particular, the links between carceral systems and racial capitalism), and envisage what might be (imagining and building a better approach to complex social problems).

26. Abolition has been grounded in feminism, particularly the work of Black feminists and feminists that oppose racial capitalism. Indeed, it has been said that 'abolition is unimaginable without feminism ... feminism is unimaginable without abolition, and ... this dialogue is imperative'.[70]

27. In recent years, we have seen an uprising in domestic police and prison abolition movements in domestic jurisdictions. Increasingly, people are coming to better understand the causes of deviance and the links between capitalism, race, imperialism, and criminal 'justice'. While not seeking to detract from the experience of racialised carceral systems experienced in the United States of America, we can, I would argue, apply abolitionist theory and praxis to international criminal law. We can do so as follows.

28. First, we can understand the origins of international criminal law. As I have outlined above, these are linked to neoliberalism, capitalism, racism, and imperialism. Second, we can examine how these origins work to structure criminality. As I have also outlined above, international criminal law, by design, criminalises some – disproportionately those who are Black, and from the Global South – more than others. This, together with its steadfast refusal to engage with the causes of criminality, has meant that international criminal law has not shown itself to be capable of addressing the causes of mass violence.

29. This brings us to our final consideration: can we 'imagine and build a more humane (international) society that no longer relies on caging people to meet human needs and solve social problems'?[71] I believe we can, and I will return to

[68] D. E. Roberts, 'Abolition Constitutionalism' 133(1) *Harvard Law Review* (2019) 3–122, at 7–8.

[69] *Ibid.*

[70] Davis et al., *supra* note 56, at 10.

[71] Roberts, *supra* note 68, at 45.

this point in the conclusions. However, I first want to draw out why the defence of duress is particularly helpful for building an abolitionist movement.

The Defence of Duress and an Abolitionist Movement for International Criminal Law?

30. The defence of duress provides an important opportunity to understand several issues that are at the heart of abolitionist movements. These are (1) the factors that led to criminality; (2) the complexity of being both victim and perpetrator; and, relatedly, (3) the interconnectedness between personal and political violence, or between individual and state violence.

31. First, the defence of duress, as we have already seen, allows a conversation about *why* an individual acted in a particular way. What caused this person's criminality? In Mr Ongwen's case, the defence has emphasised the abduction of young Dominic and the crimes suffered by him, as well as the LRA's practices of harm and threat against its own soldiers. This may not be sufficient to excuse the criminal conduct alleged; the facts of the case may not satisfy the requirements of duress, particularly the need for 'imminence' of the threat.[72] Nonetheless, raising the defence of duress allows us to situate the accused and the reasons for his conduct. We can, and should, also look more broadly – to the political, legal, and economic causes of the situation of conflict (which includes considering who is benefiting financially from the war – arms manufacturers, particular individuals, and certain states and companies).

32. This broader examination is also at the heart of the abolitionist movement. Abolitionists 'address the root causes of harm by investing in people's basic needs and addressing the causes of interpersonal violence'.[73] In seeking to understand what causes criminality – those political, legal, and economic systems that lead to poverty, racism, and systems that criminalise some more than others – abolition also attempts to build solutions to those root causes. It is 'about presence, not absence. It's about building life-affirming initiatives'.[74]

33. Secondly, the defence of duress permits us a more nuanced and sophisticated understanding of victimhood and perpetration. The current case of Mr Ongwen has particularly highlighted the challenges for international criminal law accounting for 'victims who victimise',[75] or individuals who are both victim and perpetrator. As we have seen, international criminal law is structurally inept at understanding such

[72] See Article 31(1)(d) Rome Statute.
[73] Roberts, *supra* note 68, at 45.
[74] R. Wilson Gilmore, 'Making and Unmaking Mass Incarceration Conference', University of Mississippi, December 2019.
[75] Drumbl, 'Victims Who Victimise', *supra* note 33.

victim-perpetrators. But when an individual raises a defence of duress, we often hear evidence about their own victimhood. While they may even admit to the commission of the crime, they also explain how they were victims of the actions of another person and, perhaps, of particular systems and structures.[76] In Ongwen's case, and in other cases where duress is raised, perpetration and victimhood are entangled.

34. This interconnection between victimhood and perpetration might be difficult for international criminal law to accept, but in contrast, an abolitionist movement is concerned with contradictions 'which are often the spark for change'.[77] Contradictions – such as 'perpetrator' and 'victim' – are instead held onto as 'both/and'.[78] This allows the abolitionist movement to recognise 'the relationality of state and individual violence and thus frame our resistance accordingly: supporting survivors and holding perpetrators accountable ... sometimes messy and risky, these collective practices of creativity and reflection shape new visions of safety'.[79]

35. This brings us to the third area in which duress permits an understanding, which is also important to abolitionist movements – this interconnectivity between personal and political violences. An easy – yet false – critique of abolitionist movements would be that victims are forgotten; not provided with 'justice'. If we do not have a carceral system designed for retribution, what will happen to the victims?

36. It is worth recalling the crimes and victims in this particular case. Mr Ongwen is charged with committing acts of murder, attempted murder, torture, enslavement, outrages upon personal dignity, pillaging, destruction of property, persecution; the recruitment of child soldiers; and sexual and gender-based crimes including forced marriage, torture, rape, sexual slavery, enslavement, forced pregnancy, and outrages upon personal dignity. These acts and crimes all have victims.

37. It is not that abolitionists just want the end of the carceral system: they want the end of the need for the carceral system. Abolition feminists remember that 'to render prisons and policing obsolete we must also build movements demanding that society be reshaped with the goal of eliminating gender and sexual violence and their enabling of racist and heteropatriarchal structures'.[80] Moreover, abolition feminists point out that 'while it is critical to hold those who use violence accountable, advocating for greater involvement by the criminal legal system is counterproductive at best, and can actually further endanger some survivors'.[81]

76 See the guilty plea of Dražen Erdemović at the ICTY.
77 Davis et al., *supra* note 56, at 5.
78 *Ibid*, at 3.
79 *Ibid*.
80 *Ibid*, at 59.
81 *Ibid*, at 82.

38. Indeed, we see some of these problems in international criminal law. While it is a system that is galvanised by victims, there are significant issues with how victims are treated in international criminal law. At this Court, victim participation in trials has meant that some victims of crimes are granted participation status while other victims are not. This has the effect of creating a hierarchy of victimisation, and narrowing types of victimhood.[82] This system, then, can be challenging for victims.

39. In contrast, abolition practices ask, 'what does it mean ... to fight violence against women while simultaneously addressing the structural violence faced by the larger community?'[83] Or, put another way, 'how to acknowledge the structural character of gender violence alongside its intersections with violences generated by racism and capitalism'.[84] Thus, abolition of carceral justice attempts to prioritise victims by building a world where crimes do not occur in the first place.

Imagining a Different World

40. What would it have meant if Dominic Savio was born in a safe place? What if he was able to walk by the road without being kidnapped? What if he – and all other children in his community – had been able to go to school, had full bellies, safe beds, and high-quality universal healthcare? What if all children had been free from fear of violence, including sexual and gender-based violence?

41. It is my belief that we need to turn our attention from the 'ending impunity' rhetoric of international criminal law (which is already partial and skewed towards impunity for some and criminalisation of others), to instead focus on ending atrocities and the conditions that give rise to them.

42. Abolitionists work towards 'community-based transformative justice responses that address the social causes of violence and hold people accountable without exposing them to police violence and state incarceration'.[85] These practices might include community-building, properly funded education, robust healthcare, and rehabilitation. In a similar way, international criminal law needs to consider more

[82] See S. Kendall and S. Nouwen, 'Representational Practices at the International Criminal Court: The Gap between Juridified and Abstract Victimhood' 76 *Law and Contemporary Problems* (2013) 235–262. See also E. Haslam and R. Edmunds, 'Whose Number Is It Anyway? Common Legal Representation, Consultations, and the "Statistical Victim"' 15(5) *Journal of International Criminal Justice* (2017) 931–952; S. Vasiliev, 'Victim Participation Revisited – What the ICC Is Learning about Itself' in C. Stahn (ed.), *The Law and Practice of the International Criminal Court: A Critical Account of Challenges and Achievements* (Oxford: Oxford University Press, 2015) 1133; F. Mégret, 'The Strange Case of the Victim Who Did Not Want Justice' 12(3) *International Journal of Transitional Justice* (2018) 444–463, at 445; Maxine Clarke, *supra* note 53, at 276.

[83] Davis et al., *supra* note 56, at 109.

[84] *Ibid.*

[85] Roberts, *supra* note 68, at 46.

deeply what a world could look like without any need for international criminal law, and what strategies might be used to achieve this alternative world.

43. In this case, I concur with the majority, and find that the defence of duress is not satisfied. I feel some regret at this conclusion, because it is likely – subject to the separate sentencing judgment – that Dominic Ongwen will be imprisoned. However, we remain operating within the penal system of international criminal law, with its defences set out under the Rome Statute. In the case of duress, the defence is strictly defined, and limited to instances where the elements are satisfied. In this case, it has not been met.

44. But nevertheless, at a more abstract level, duress permits us to understand the limitations of international criminal law, its structural features, and what else might be possible. I hope we can work together to envisage this alternative reality where we have a safer, better, world for all – and then to form a movement to undertake the work to bring this world into being.

Judge Sophie Rigney

9.3 VIOLATION OF REPRODUCTIVE AUTONOMY IN THE ONGWEN SENTENCE

Tonny Raymond Kirabira, Adrienne Ringin, and Rosemary Grey

In 2021, an ICC Trial Chamber convicted Dominic Ongwen, one of the top commanders of the Lord's Resistance Army (LRA), of sixty-one counts of war crimes and crimes against humanity committed in northern Uganda.[86] This was the first ICC case to result in a conviction for the crime of 'forced pregnancy' as a war crime and crime against humanity under the Rome Statute.[87] The Trial Chamber sentenced Ongwen to terms of imprisonment ranging from eight to twenty years for each count, including twenty years for forced pregnancy as a war crime and twenty years for forced pregnancy as a crime against humanity, resulting in a total joint sentence of twenty-five years' imprisonment, taking into account mitigating circumstances concerning his abduction by the LRA as a child. In 2022, that sentence was confirmed on appeal.

The Trial Chamber's original sentencing decision provided only a fleeting analysis of the harms caused by forced pregnancy in this case. In their reimagining of that decision, Judges Kirabira, Ringin, and Grey revisit the available evidence to make detailed findings on these harms, including the violation of reproductive autonomy, and the physical, psychological, economic, and social harms suffered by the two survivors of forced pregnancy in this case.

[86] Trial Judgment, *Ongwen* (ICC-02/04-01/15-1762-Red), Trial Chamber IX, 4 February 2021.
[87] Sentence, *Ongwen* (ICC-02/04-01/15-1819-Red), Trial Chamber IX, 6 May 2021.

No.: ICC-02/04-01/15
Date: 6 May 2021

Original: English

TRIAL CHAMBER IX(B)

Before: Judge Tonny KIRABIRA, Presiding Judge (Uganda)

Judge Adrienne RINGIN (Australia)
Judge Rosemary GREY (Australia)[88]

SITUATION IN UGANDA
IN THE CASE OF THE *PROSECUTOR v. DOMINIC ONGWEN*

Public

Redacted Sentencing Decision

PROCEDURAL HISTORY

1. On 4 February 2021, Trial Chamber IX delivered its judgment in Mr Dominic Ongwen's case. It convicted him on sixty-one counts of war crimes and crimes against humanity committed in Uganda between 1 July 2002 and 31 December 2005, during an armed conflict between the Lord's Resistance Army and the Ugandan armed forces.

2. The conviction encompassed war crimes (intentionally attacking the civilian population; rape; sexual slavery; forced pregnancy; murder and attempted murder; torture; pillage; outrages on personal dignity; conscripting children under the age of fifteen into an armed group and using them to participate actively in hostilities; pillage; and destruction of property) and crimes against humanity (rape; sexual slavery; forced pregnancy; murder and attempted murder; torture; enslavement; persecution on political grounds; and inhumane acts including forced marriage).

3. Following conviction by Trial Chamber IX, the sentencing proceedings were assigned to this Chamber, Trial Chamber IX(B).

[88] The ideas in this brief were informed by the *amicius curiae* brief filed in the *Ongwen* case on behalf of the Global Justice Center, Women's Initiatives for Gender Justice, Amnesty International, and Rosemary Grey. We acknowledge, in particular, the intellectual contributions to that brief by Akila Radhakrishnan, Alix Vuillemin and Matthew Cannock. *Ongwen*, Amici Curiae Observations on the Rome Statute's definition of 'forced pregnancy' by Dr Rosemary Grey, Global Justice Center, Women's Initiatives for Gender Justice and Amnesty International (ICC-02/04-01/15-1938), Appeals Chamber, 23 February 2021; *Ongwen*, Transcript of Appeal Hearing (ICC-02/04-01/15-T-264-ENG), 15 February 2022, 68–73 and 94. The authors also acknowledge the input received from other editors and contributors to this book, including other authors in the 'Uganda' section.

SENTENCING RATIONALES

4. As in previous ICC sentencing decisions, the Chamber will offer observations on the rationales for sentencing. In this Chamber's view, the strongest rationale for imposing penal sanctions on individuals who have been convicted of one or more crimes under the Rome Statute (the Statute) is to express the international community's condemnation of these crimes. Rather than a means of exacting revenge, penal sanctions recognise the specific ways in which the perpetrator wronged the victims, their families, and their communities.[89] In this way, the sentence provides access to truth and justice as well as a unified international denunciation of such crimes.[90] The process of calculating the sentence must therefore include recognising the specific harms that resulted from each of the perpetrator's crimes.[91]

5. As recognised in the Statute's preamble, the prosecution and sentencing of individuals may also contribute to the prevention of crimes. At the specific level, the sentence may discourage the convicted person from recidivism. Access to rehabilitative services such as education and healthcare, particularly if such services have been inaccessible to the individual prior to ICC custody, may assist in decreasing the likelihood of recidivism. At the general level, sentencing aims to dissuade prospective perpetrators from committing similar crimes.[92]

6. The Chamber acknowledges that prosecuting and sentencing individual actors does not ameliorate the structural factors that contribute to the commission of crimes, including economic inequalities, postcolonial legacies, and entrenched beliefs about the inferiority of 'others' along ethnic, racialised and gendered lines. Sentencing is therefore not an effective deterrent in isolation; the structural causes of violence must also be addressed.

SENTENCING PRINCIPLES

7. In determining an appropriate penalty, the Chamber is directed by Articles 76–78 of the Statute and Rules 145–148 of the Rules of Procedure and Evidence (the Rules).[93] These provisions direct the Chamber to examine the gravity of a crime and

[89] For a similar view, see Decision on Sentence pursuant to Article 76 of the Statute, *Katanga* (ICC-01/04-01/07-3484-tENG-Corr), Trial Chamber II, 23 May 2014, § 38 (hereafter Katanga Sentencing Decision).

[90] Sentencing Judgment, *Ntaganda* (ICC-01/04-02/06-2442), Trial Chamber VI, 7 November 2019, §10(hereafter Ntaganda Sentencing Decision).

[91] For a similar view, see Katanga Sentencing Decision, *supra* note 89, § 38.

[92] Ntaganda Sentencing Decision, *supra* note 90, § 10.

[93] The Chamber notes that Art. 77(2) and Rules 146–148 of the Rules of Procedure and Evidence, which allow for fines and orders of forfeiture, do not apply in this case due to the indigence of Mr Ongwen.

the personal circumstances of the accused,[94] and then any mitigating and/or aggravating factors present.[95] The Chamber notes that factors used to determine the gravity of the crime will not be 'double counted' as aggravating factors.[96] Discretion is granted to the Chamber in determining the scope and weight of the relevant factors.[97]

8. The available penalties include imprisonment for a maximum of thirty years, or for life 'when justified by the extreme gravity of the crime and the individual circumstances of the convicted person'.[98] Capital or corporal punishment are impermissible under the Statute.

9. In the present decision, the Chamber will first summarise the parties' submissions, and then analyse *each specific crime* of which Mr Ongwen was convicted, before turning to those aggravating and mitigating circumstances that apply to the *totality* of his crimes.

THE PARTIES' SUBMISSIONS

10. Trial Chamber IX granted 4,095 victims standing to participate in Mr Ongwen's trial. Their legal representatives jointly argued that the crimes attributed to Mr Ongwen are 'extremely grave' and warrant a sentence of life imprisonment.[99] In relation to sexual and gender-based crimes, the victims' legal representatives submit that the 'particularly repugnant circumstances in which acts of rape; sexual slavery; torture, outrages upon personal dignity and enslavement considered under the ambit of sexual violence; forced marriage; and forced pregnancy . . . carry a specific high threshold of gravity'.[100]

11. In particular, some victims were 'satisfied and relieved' that forced pregnancy and forced marriage – neither of which had previously been prosecuted in the ICC – were recognised in this case.[101] In their view, forced pregnancy and forced marriage are 'very serious crimes worthy of life imprisonment in light of the

[94] Art. 78(1) ICCSt.

[95] *Ibid*; Rule 145(2) ICC RPE.

[96] Judgment and Sentence, *Al Mahdi* (ICC-01/12-01/15-171), Trial Chamber VIII, 27 September 2016, § 70; Katanga Sentencing Judgment, *supra* note 89, § 35; Ntaganda Sentencing Judgment, *supra* note 90, § 13.

[97] Rule 145(2)(b)(vi) ICC RPE allows the Chamber to consider as aggravating circumstances 'other circumstances which, although not enumerated [in the same Rule], by virtue of their nature are similar to those mentioned'. *See* also Judgment on the appeals of the Prosecutor and Mr Thomas Lubanga Dyilo against the 'Decision on Sentence pursuant to Article 76 of the Statute', *Lubanga* (ICC-01/04-01/06-3122), Appeals Chamber, 1 December 2014, § 43.

[98] Art. 77(1) ICCSt.

[99] Victims' Joint Submissions on sentencing, *Ongwen* (ICC-02/04-01/15-1808), Trial Chamber IX, 1 April 2021, §§ 40, 116 (hereafter Victims' Sentencing Brief).

[100] *Ibid*, § 43.

[101] *Ibid*, § 104.

tremendous harm suffered by the victims, especially the harm suffered through the children born out of rape'.[102] The victims emphasise the 'immensely challenging' situation of these children, as well as 'the difficult situation their mothers are confronted with, facing rejection from their families and communities', many of whom 'now live on the margins of the society with all the associated psychological, material and financial difficulties'.[103]

12. The prosecution submits that the crimes committed by Mr Ongwen would ordinarily warrant a sentence at the 'highest range available' under the Statute.[104] For sexual and gender-based crimes, the prosecution proposes a sentence of thirty years for each crime (to be served concurrently).[105] This proposal stems from the 'inherent gravity' and 'long-lasting' effect of the crimes perpetrated against Mr Ongwen's so-called wives as well as the indirect victims within his brigade.[106] However, considering the defendant's personal circumstances, particularly his status as both a victim and a perpetrator,[107] it recommends a one-third reduction in the total joint sentence, resulting in twenty years' imprisonment.[108]

13. The defence submits that Mr Ongwen's 'unique' circumstances warrant a sentence of no longer than ten years (if, indeed, their client is not acquitted on appeal).[109] These circumstances, according to the defence, include Mr Ongwen's mental defect, the harms suffered by him as an abducted child soldier, his willingness to undergo traditional justice mechanisms in Uganda, his family situation, and good deeds with the LRA.[110] The defence asks the Chamber to consider rehabilitation and reconciliation above retribution, arguing that deterrence should not be considered in this case.[111]

14. Informed by these submissions, the Chamber will now analyse the gravity and relevant circumstances of each specific crime.

SPECIFIC CRIMES

[Author note: Here, the judgment would consider each crime of which Mr Ongwen was convicted, but for the purposes of this reimagined judgment, only the analysis of the crime of forced pregnancy is shown.]

102 *Ibid*, § 104.
103 *Ibid*, § 44.
104 Prosecution's Sentencing Brief, *Ongwen* (ICC-02/04-01/15-1806), Trial Chamber IX, 1 April 2021, § 1.
105 *Ibid*, § 158.
106 *Ibid*, §§ 10–12, 21, 26.
107 *Ibid*, § 156.
108 *Ibid*.
109 Public Redacted Version of Corrected Version of Defence Brief on Sentencing, filed on 1 April 2021, *Ongwen* (ICC-02/04-01/15-1890-Corr-Red), Trial Chamber IX, 4 April 2021, §§ 18, 183.
110 *Ibid*, §§ 29, 52, 85, 112–128, 183.
111 *Ibid*, §§ 4–5, 14–21.

Forced Pregnancy

Evidentiary Considerations

15. Article 7(2)(f) of the Statute defines 'forced pregnancy' as the unlawful confinement of a victim who has been made forcibly pregnant with one of two specific intents: to affect the ethnic composition of any population, or to carry out other grave violations of international law. We note that this article refers to the victim of forced pregnancy as a 'woman'. However, the Statute's drafting history reveals no intention to exclude other victims who are capable of pregnancy, including girls of any age, or non-binary, intersex, or trans people. Moreover, Article 21(3) requires that the Statute must be applied and interpreted in accordance with 'internationally recognised human rights' and without any adverse distinction founded on grounds including age, gender identity, or intersex status. For these reasons, the Chamber will describe a person subjected to forced pregnancy using the gender-neutral term 'victim'.

16. The Chamber recalls that Mr Ongwen was convicted of forced pregnancy based on evidence that he impregnated and unlawfully confined two women who had been assigned to him as 'wives'. To protect their privacy, these two women are identified as P-0101 and P-0214 in the Court records.

17. Neither witness testified at trial, as would ordinarily happen for key witnesses in the ICC. Rather, Trial Chamber IX viewed a video-recording of the testimony that Mr Ongwen's forced 'wives' (including P-0101 and P-0214) had provided during the pre-trial proceedings. This measure was taken at the request of Prosecutor, in order to preserve the evidence and to limit the risk of re-traumatising the witnesses by reducing the number of times they had to testify.[112]

18. This is the first conviction of forced pregnancy by an international court. This Chamber recognises the value in a careful analysis of the many harms that can and did occur as a result of this crime. The copious evidence of harms proffered throughout the case records, including the testimony of P-0101 and P-0214, greatly enables this endeavour.

19. Notwithstanding this wealth of evidence, certain questions about P-0101 and P-0214's experiences of forced pregnancy remain unanswered. To fill that information gap, it would have been apt to seek further testimony from these two witnesses earlier in the proceedings.[113] However, mindful of our duty to protect the well-being

[112] Public Redacted Version of Second Prosecution application to the Pre-Trial Chamber to preserve evidence and take measures under Article 56 of the Rome Statute, *Ongwen* (ICC-02/04-01/15-310-Red), Trial Chamber IX, 27 May 2016; Decision on Request to Admit Evidence Preserved under Article 56 of the Statute, *Ongwen* (ICC-02/04-01/15-520), Trial Chamber IX, 10 August 2016.

[113] Article 69(3) of the Statute gives the Chamber the authority to request the submission of additional evidence that is considered necessary for the determination of the relevant facts.

of victims and witnesses,[114] and noting that calling P-0101 and P-0214 back to answer further questions about sexual violence might cause them distress,[115] this Chamber decided *not* to recall these witnesses to give further evidence at the sentencing phase. Instead, we will respond to the gaps in the evidence by raising questions that merit further consideration in subsequent cases where the crime of forced pregnancy is charged.

The Forced Pregnancies in This Case

20. Mr Ongwen was convicted of forced pregnancy as both a war crime and a crime against humanity on the basis that between July 2002 and December 2005 he confined P-0101 and P-0214, both whom he had impregnated, with the intent of continuing to subject them to grave violations of international law (forced marriage, torture, rape, and sexual slavery).[116] The charges of forced pregnancy were limited to three pregnancies within the temporal scope of the charges: P-0101's two pregnancies between 2002 and 2004, which resulted in the birth of a daughter and a son, and P-0214's pregnancy in 2002, which resulted in the birth of a daughter.[117]

21. Both women endured extreme violence in connection to their pregnancies. P-0101 was abducted in August 1996 by Mr Ongwen when she was aged fifteen.[118] He immediately claimed her as his 'wife' and raped her that night.[119] This initial rape is illustrative of the circumstances by which P-0101 later became forcibly pregnant. In her words, 'immediately the escorts held my hands and they forced me … He [Mr Ongwen] held me forcefully and he slept with me'[120] and 'He told me if I'm still resisting, can't I see the – what is there beside me, the gun?'[121]

22. P-0101 remained with Mr Ongwen for eight years.[122] Her duties as Mr Ongwen's 'wife' included cooking as well as enduring his repeated sexual assaults. P-0101 was under threat of death if she tried to escape. She explained: 'if you're caught when you're trying to escape, if you are not properly prepared for your

[114] Article 68(1) ICCSt.

[115] Public Redacted Version of Decision on the Second Prosecution application to the Pre-Trial Chamber to preserve evidence and take measures under Article 56 of the Rome Statute, *Ongwen* (ICC-02/04-01/15-316-Red), Pre-Trial Chamber II, 12 October 2015 (public redacted version dated 23 March 2016), § 12.

[116] Trial Judgment, *Ongwen* (ICC-02/04-01/15-1762-Red), Trial Chamber IX, 4 February 2021, § 3116 (hereafter Ongwen Judgment).

[117] *Ibid*, § 2069.

[118] T-13, www.icc-cpi.int/sites/default/files/Transcripts/CR2020_00648.PDF, at 16 (hereafter T-13).

[119] *Ibid*, at 16–18.

[120] *Ibid*, at 18.

[121] *Ibid*, at 50–51.

[122] *Ibid*, at 8–9. The Chamber notes that there is conjecture as to whether P-0101 was released or escaped but does not consider this debate to be important for the current discussion in this section.

escape, you would be killed without mercy, and for these reasons I was scared. People who tried to escape and were killed, I saw this'.[123]

23. During her eight years in Mr Ongwen's household, P-0101 conceived three children as a result of sexual assault by him: a daughter in 1999, another daughter between 2002 and 2004, and a son in 2004, shortly after her return from the bush when her second daughter was shot and taken during an assault from government armed forces.[124]

24. P-0214 was abducted by LRA forces in June 2000 when she was aged seventeen.[125] She was assigned as a 'wife' to Mr Ongwen by LRA leader Joseph Kony.[126] Thereafter, P-0214 endured repeated sexual assaults by Mr Ongwen under threat of physical force. In her words, this sexual activity 'wasn't my choice'.[127] Escape was virtually impossible. P-2014 explained: 'I could not escape as his [Mr Ongwen's] security guards guarded me well. They were all armed. And even if you escaped from the LRA, the Dinka and the Lutugu [other groups] in Sudan would kill you. I heard that they had killed people who fled the LRA.'[128] P-0214's chance at freedom eventually came in 2010, when she escaped with another of Mr Ongwen's 'wives'.[129]

25. During her ten years in Mr Ongwen's household, P-0214 conceived four times: in 2005 she delivered a child (sex unspecified); in 2007 she delivered a daughter, who died after a month; in 2007 her third pregnancy ended by miscarriage; and in 2009 she gave birth to a son.[130]

Harms Caused by the Crimes

26. The Chamber is cognisant that for some people, it is difficult to conceive of a pregnancy that results in a new life as a source of harm, even if that pregnancy was forced. Yet as the following analysis shows, forced pregnancy can result in serious and extensive harms. As well as being a grave violation of the victim's dignity and autonomy, this crime can cause serious physical, psychological, social, cultural, economic, and legal harms. The fact that it can *also* result in a new life – a life which is inherently valuable – does not erase those harms. Nor does it relieve this Court of its responsibility to punish the perpetrator. The fact that a victim of forced pregnancy may love the resultant child in no way dilutes the wrongdoing by the perpetrator.

[123] *Ibid*, at 44.
[124] *Ibid*, at 16; Ongwen Judgment, *supra* note 116, § 2088.
[125] Ongwen Judgment, *supra* note 116, § 2014.
[126] T-15, www.icc-cpi.int/sites/default/files/Transcripts/CR2016_25114.PDF, at 36 (hereafter T-15).
[127] *Ibid*, at 25.
[128] *Ibid*, at 26.
[129] Ongwen Judgment, *supra* note 116, at 211.
[130] T-15, *supra* note 126, at 29–30.

THE HARM OF VIOLATION OF PERSONAL AND REPRODUCTIVE AUTONOMY

27. Trial Chamber IX observed that the crime of forced pregnancy is grounded in the right to 'personal and reproductive autonomy'.[131] This statement is correct. The criminalisation of forced pregnancy protects the right of every individual to exercise agency over their body, their fertility, and their sexuality. The protection of reproductive autonomy was the rationale for the inclusion of the crime in the Statute. The recognition of this crime in the Statute and other international instruments,[132] and the ratification of the Statute by numerous states including Uganda, signals the importance placed on rights to reproductive autonomy by the international community.

28. Reproductive autonomy is a key aspect of human dignity. Rights pertaining to reproductive health and reproductive autonomy are protected in a range of international and regional human rights instruments,[133] and are the birthright of every individual regardless of their sex, gender, nationality, or culture. The distinctive violation of reproductive autonomy is reflected in the articulation of the crime of forced pregnancy as a crime in and of itself; it is not subsumed by rape or 'any other form of sexual violence'.[134] This violation has extensive and intergenerational implications. By subjecting P-0101 and P-0214 to forced pregnancy, Mr Ongwen violated their rights to personal and reproductive autonomy. As P-0101 explained, 'When I became pregnant with my three children to Ongwen, I did not think I had a choice as to whether I would become pregnant or not'.[135]

29. The state of pregnancy was used as a control mechanism by Mr Ongwen.[136] It was 'understood that pregnancy made it more difficult for women to escape'.[137] Whilst pregnant, P-0101 and P-0214 were physically confined and

[131] Ongwen Judgment, *supra* note 116, § 2717.

[132] See *Vienna Declaration and Programme of Action* 1993, UN Doc. A/CONF.157/23, 12 July 1993, § 38; *Draft Articles on Prevention and Punishment of Crimes against Humanity* 2019, International Law Commission A/74/10, 2019, Art. 2(g).

[133] General Comment No. 36 – Article 6: Right to Life, Human Rights Committee UN Doc. CCPR/C/GC/36, 3 September 2019, § 8; Proclamation of Teheran: Final Act of the International Conference on Human Rights, UN Doc. A/CONF.32/41, 13 May 1968, Art. 16; Convention on the Elimination of All Forms of Discrimination Against Women, UN Treaty Series, vol. 1249, 18 December 1979, Art. 10 and 16(1)(e); General Comment No. 22 (2016) on the Right to Sexual and Reproductive Health (Article 12 of the International Covenant on Economic, Social and Cultural Rights), Committee on Economic, Social and Cultural Rights UN Doc, E/C.12/GC/22, 2 May 2016, § 1; General Comment No. 20 on the Implementation of the Rights of the Child during Adolescence, UN Committee on the Rights of the Child UN Doc. CRC/C/GC/20, 6 December 2016, §§ 60, 63; General Recommendation No. 21:Equality in Marriage and Family Relations, CEDAW UN Doc. A/49/38(SUPP), 1994, § 22; 2003 Protocol to the African Charter on Human and Peoples' Rights on the Rights of Women in Africa, African Union, 11 July 2003, Art. 14.

[134] Ongwen Judgment, *supra* note 116, § 2722.

[135] T-13, *supra* note 118, at 21.

[136] Public Redacted Version of Prosecution Closing Brief, *Ongwen* (ICC-02/04-01/15-1719-Red), Trial Chamber IX, 24 February 2020, § 167 (hereafter Prosecution Closing Brief).

[137] *Ibid*, § 174.

monitored.[138] They were 'placed under heavy guard' and were unable to leave, and they were 'told or came to understand that if they tried to escaped they would be killed'.[139] There was no access to family planning or contraceptives and abortive attempts and successes were severely punished.[140]

PHYSICAL HARMS

30. P-0101 and P-0214 endured severe and prolonged physical harm as a result of forced pregnancy. The relevant pregnancies were achieved through sexual assault.[141] During and after these pregnancies, critical medical assistance and perinatal care was limited. P-0214 experienced pre-birth complications close to her due date and had to endure these in the bush with only the support of the other 'wives' and Mr Ongwen.[142] During the delivery, P-0214 stated that 'on that day that I had my baby there was no doctor, I was only with the girls in his household'.[143]

31. While pregnant, P-0101 and P-0214 were subjected to physically demanding domestic duties[144] as well as the constant threat and use of physical punishments for perceived failures.[145] P-0214 was beaten with a machete while pregnant for being 'too slow to bring' the bathing water.[146] While P-0214 was pregnant, Mr Ongwen continued to 'rape her, torture her, sexually enslave her, and enslave her for domestic purposes'.[147]

32. The available evidence does not divulge whether P-0101 or P-0214 experienced other pregnancy-related health issues disclosed by other victims, including birth-related complications, infertility, painful intercourse, and chronic pain,[148] although we are aware that P-0214 endured a miscarriage outside the charged period.[149] In future cases, we urge the parties and the Chamber to ask victims of forced pregnancy further questions about physical harms, so that these harms can be addressed in the sentencing decision.

[138] T-27, www.icc-cpi.int/sites/default/files/Transcripts/CR2016_25803.PDF, at 16 (hereafter T-27); Ongwen Judgment, *supra* note 116, §§ 3058–3059.

[139] Ongwen Judgment, *supra* note 116, § 3058.

[140] Prosecution Closing Brief, *supra* note 136, § 174.

[141] T-259, www.icc-cpi.int/sites/default/files/Transcripts/CR2021_01038.PDF, at 21–22; Public Redacted Version of Common Legal Representative of Victims' Closing Brief (ICC-02/04-01/15-1720-Conf), *Ongwen* (ICC-02/04-01/15-1720-Red), Trial Chamber IX, 28 February 2020, § 101 (hereafter Victims' Closing Brief).

[142] T-15, *supra* note 126, at 34–35.

[143] *Ibid*, at 29.

[144] Ongwen Judgment, *supra* note 116, § 208. Tasks included cooking, fetching laundry, chopping wood, and working in the garden.

[145] T-27, *supra* note 138, at 22; Ongwen Judgment, *supra* note 116, §§ 208, 3033.

[146] T-27, *supra* note 138, at 22.

[147] *Ibid*, at 22–23.

[148] Victims' Closing Brief, *supra* note 141, at 111, footnote 557.

[149] T-15, *supra* note 126, at 29–30.

PSYCHOLOGICAL AND EMOTIONAL HARM

33. Testimony provided by P-0101 and P-0214 reveals that they experienced serious psychological and emotional harm during their captivity, including during their pregnancies. Fear and intimidation were employed to keep them compliant.[150] P-0214 described being threatened when she refused to have sexual intercourse with Mr Ongwen: 'He told his security guards to get the sticks. The security guards scared me with the sticks so I went to Ongwen's place.'[151] This threatening environment was described by P-0101 as extending even when Mr Dominic Ongwen was physically injured: 'even if he was still weak physically, he could still use his mouth to give instructions or orders because if a superior gives instructions, you have to go and follow what he says'.[152]

34. The continuation of psychological trauma once the victim is released is evidenced by P-0101's concern about speaking with ICC investigators. She stated: 'During the last interview the reason that I did not want to answer questions about Ongwen is because I fear him and thought he might kill me if he came to learn what I was saying.'[153]

35. We note that the psychological burden on the victims of forced pregnancy can extend 'beyond the obvious physical effects of pregnancy and childbearing'.[154] The continual use of the word 'wife' to denote P-0101, P-0214, and the other women who were assigned to Mr Ongwen further perpetuates the continuing bond between the defendant and victims.[155] The situation can be even more complex in cases of forced pregnancy, when the perpetrator is the father of the resultant child and continues to be present in the victims' lives, as is the case with P-0101 and P-0214.[156] For example, the Chamber is aware that Mr Ongwen attempted to make financial payments to P-0214,[157] and the defence, prosecution, registry, and victims' legal representative have facilitated contact between Mr Ongwen and his children, with the consent of their mothers.[158] The victim may even express a degree of affection for the perpetrator, as P-0214 did at points in her testimony.[159]

[150] Ongwen Judgment, *supra* note 116, § 3029.
[151] T-15, *supra* note 126, at 22.
[152] Ongwen Judgment, *supra* note 116, § 1039.
[153] T-13, *supra* note 118, at 46.
[154] Ongwen Judgment, *supra* note 116, § 2748.
[155] Authors' note: This sentence is adapted from the real Ongwen sentencing decision, at § 292, although in the imaginative world in which this feminist judgment occurs, the real sentence does not yet exist.
[156] T-27, *supra* note 138, at 13.
[157] Public Redacted Version of Defence Response to the Prosecution Filing ICC-02/04-01/15-482-Conf, filed on 4 July 2016, *Ongwen* (ICC-02/04-01/15-490-Red), Trial Chamber IX, 7 July 2016, § 42 (hereafter Defence Response).
[158] T-261, www.icc-cpi.int/sites/default/files/Transcripts/CR2021_03573.PDF, at 39; CLRV's Response to Defence Request to Lift Communication Restrictions Placed Upon Mr Ongwen, *Ongwen* (ICC-02/04-01/15-1631-Red), Trial Chamber IX, 23 October 2019, § 23(iv).
[159] T-27, *supra* note 138, at 13. See also T-15, *supra* note 126, at 41; Ongwen Judgment, *supra* note 116, at 2519.

36. Expert testimony in the case further indicated that victims of sexual and gender-based crimes perpetrated by the LRA often experienced 'PTSD, depression, anxiety and dissociation, loss of perceived control, shame, increased sexual risk/ vulnerability'[160] and that 'When an individual does not perceive that she or he is safe, basic daily activities such as feeding, sleeping, and self-care are undermined and dysregulated … higher level pursuits such as taking care of others, gaining employment, and pursuing an education are also threated and rendered more challenging, if not impossible'.[161] The available evidence does not confirm whether P-0101 or P-0214 experienced these specific harms. In future cases, further evidence on the psychological impact of forced pregnancy on the victims would assist in sentencing.

37. There was also extensive evidence in this trial about the experience of *cen*, which in Acholi culture is a 'malevolent emanation that comes from those who have experienced or perpetrated violent acts'.[162] The Chamber did not receive evidence that P-0101 and P-0214 experienced this psychological harm. We suggest that in future cases there is a fuller examination of psychological harms resulting from forced pregnancy, including harms that are experienced in the victims' particular spiritual context.

ECONOMIC HARMS

38. Where forced pregnancy results in a child, and therefore caring responsibilities, a significant economic burden can be placed on the victim. Not only do parental responsibilities limit the victims' earning capacity, they also generate additional costs.

39. For example, according to the defence, almost all of Mr Dominic Ongwen's children are of school-going age or are quickly approaching this age.[163] Ugandan primary school costs are on average around Ugandan shillings (UGX) 100,000 per school quarter (€25.27) and this cost increases as the children advance through the school system.[164] UGX 100,00 in education costs is relatively expensive for the average household in the Acholi region of Uganda.

40. The Chamber is aware that in March 2016, while in ICC custody, Mr Ongwen attempted to contribute financially to some of his 'wives'.[165]

[160] Victims' Closing Brief, *supra* note 141, at § 109.

[161] *Ibid*, § 210.

[162] T-29, www.icc-cpi.int/sites/default/files/Transcripts/CR2017_00281.PDF, at 29–30.

[163] Public Redacted Version of Corrected Version of Defence Brief on Sentencing, filed on 1 April 2021, *Ongwen* (ICC-02/04-01/15-1809-Corr-Red), Trial Chamber XI, 4 April 2021, § 143 (hereafter Defence Sentencing Brief).

[164] *Ibid*, § 144.

[165] Defence Response, *supra* note 157, § 38; Decision on Prosecution Request for an order that Mr Ongwen cease and disclose payments to witnesses and that the Registry disclose certain calls made by Mr Ongwen, *Ongwen* (ICC-02/04-01/15-521), Trial Chamber XI, 10 August 2016, § 17, in which the single judge ordered the payments to stop in case they tainted witnesses.

However, any such future contribution will be limited. At the commencement of ICC proceedings he was indigent.[166] His current income in detention stands at €25 per week.[167] In this context, the Chamber is concerned that the financial burden of raising and educating the children that resulted from forced pregnancy may fall primarily on P-0101 and P-0214. The Chamber will further consider the provision of childcare in its reparations order in this case to address this financial burden and to assist in removing further barriers to employment in the immediate future.

41. When assessing the economic consequences of forced pregnancy, it is also relevant to consider how this crime affected the victims' education. In Uganda, educational attainment is associated with economic success, better health, and employment opportunities. P-0101 and P-0214 did not have these privileges. As this Chamber is aware, formal education commences for children in Uganda between the ages of six and eight, with seven years of primary school and six years of secondary school.[168] P-0101 was abducted when she was in primary 4,[169] and P-0214 in primary 7.[170]

42. The Chamber did not hear evidence as to how P-0101 and P-0214's lost educational opportunities affected their economic status, aside from the fact that P-0214 has been able to 'find work and survive, but not thrive'.[171] However, we were presented with evidence that, in general, time spent 'in the bush' placed victims in a worse economic position than their peers who were not abducted, and were therefore able to finish their education and gain employment without mental and physical trauma.[172] Regardless, the abduction and confinement of P-0101 and P-0214 immediately severed their educational opportunities. In future cases, we suggest that evidence is led on the impact of forced pregnancy on the victims' education, and subsequent earning capacity, noting that in some countries, education is legally and/or practically inaccessible during and after pregnancy.[173]

[166] Confidential ex parte Defence Only Defence Request for the Interim Release of Dominic Ongwen, *Ongwen* (ICC-02/04-01/15-332), Pre-Trial Chamber II, 29 October 2015, § 12.

[167] Defence Response, *supra* note 157, § 37.

[168] T-247, www.icc-cpi.int/sites/default/files/Transcripts/CR2019_06626.PDF, at 78 (hereafter T-247).

[169] T-13, *supra* note 118, at 16.

[170] T-15, *supra* note 121, at 5.

[171] Defence Response, *supra* note 157, § 42, noting that P-0214 was also designated D26-0010.

[172] See statement from P-0236, who was abducted for thirteen years, in Ongwen Judgment, *supra* note 116, at 2093.

[173] For example the Chamber is aware that in Tanzania, female students who become pregnant are legally unable to return to formal education after the child is born. Some other nations have similar bans for its female students. There are also barriers to return so that even if there is a technical right to return, in practice it is not possible. The Chamber notes that Uganda previously had such a law, but repealed it and in 2020 introduced new guidelines on pregnancy prevention and management in schools, see *Revised Guidelines for the Prevention and Management of Teenage Pregnancy in School Settings in Uganda*, 2020, available at www.ungei.org/sites/default/files/2021-02/Revised-Guidelines-Prevention-Management%20-Teenage-Pregnancy-School-Settings-Uganda-2020-eng.pdf.

43. As a final note in respect to the gravity of the crimes, the Chamber would like to make some recommendations regarding future forced pregnancy cases. There needs to be more detailed examination and specific evidence regarding physical, socio-economic, cultural, and psychological harms that are experienced by the victims of forced pregnancy.

Degree of Participation by Mr Ongwen

44. Mr Ongwen was convicted as the direct perpetrator of forced pregnancy. He personally confined the victims, with the intent of continuing to subject them to sexual and gender-based crimes. He was also the person responsible for forcibly impregnating the victims.[174]. As such, his direct involvement in the crime points in favour of a high sentence.

Aggravating Circumstances

45. The Chamber considers three aggravating factors in respect to Mr Ongwen's conviction of forced pregnancy, under Rule 145(2)(b).

COMMISSION OF A CRIME WHERE THE VICTIM IS PARTICULARLY DEFENCELESS

46. The Chamber heard evidence that within the LRA, young girls were targeted for rape and other sexual crimes because they were believed to be 'free from HIV/AIDS and sexually transmitted diseases'.[175] Mr Ongwen himself was frequently involved in the sexual assault of young girls.[176] These observations apply to P-0101 and P-0214, as detailed above. The victims' youth and gender, and the fact that they faced the threat of punishment or execution for escape, made them 'particularly defenceless'.[177]

COMMISSION OF A CRIME WITH PARTICULAR CRUELTY OR WITH MULTIPLE VICTIMS

47. Three pregnancies were imposed on two separate victims, utilising physical and psychological methods. The multiplicity of victims and the inherently cruel methods (use of force and threat of force, including death threats) used to perform the crime leads this to be a highly significant aggravating factor.[178]

48. We note that while Mr Ongwen's conviction of forced pregnancy is restricted to three incidents that occurred between 1 July 2002 and 31 December 2005, DNA

[174] This is not always the case with forced pregnancy. To establish this crime, it will suffice if the perpetrator confined the victim with the necessary intent and knowledge. The initial act of forcibly impregnating the victim can be done by a third party.

[175] T-247, *supra* note 168, at 62.

[176] *Ibid*; T-14, www.icc-cpi.int/sites/default/files/Transcripts/CR2016_25141.PDF, at 3.

[177] Rule 145(2)(b)(iii) ICC RPE.

[178] Rule 145(2)(b)(iv) ICC RPE.

evidence links Mr Ongwen to nine additional children delivered by his forced 'wives'.[179] These nine additional pregnancies were not charged, and therefore do not affect the sentence, but are recognised here as part of the Court's truth-telling role.

COMMISSION OF THE CRIME WITH DISCRIMINATORY MOTIVES

49. The systemic abduction of girls and women by Mr Ongwen, coupled with the forced pregnancy and other sexual crimes, illustrates a discriminatory motive, on the grounds of gender. This discriminatory motive constitutes another aggravating factor.

ADDITIONAL AGGRAVATING CIRCUMSTANCES

50. Cognisant of the non-exclusive list of aggravating factors under Rule 145(2)(b), the Chamber uses its discretion to consider additional aggravating circumstances,[180] in order to capture the full extent of damage caused by the crime of forced pregnancy.[181]

51. The first element worth considering relates to the social harms. Forced pregnancy results in a particular social stigma in Uganda.[182] Like others who returned from captivity with the LRA, victims of forced pregnancy were referred to as '*dwog cen paco*' (a derogatory term for 'somebody who has come back home').[183] Reintegration was detrimentally affected due to the violations inflicted upon them.

52. The Chamber does not have evidence that these social harms were experienced by P-0101 or P-0214. We urge these potential social consequences of forced pregnancy to be considered as additional aggravating circumstances in future sentencing decisions.

53. The second aspect worth considering relates to the resultant cultural harms to the victims. As many other victims of the LRA, P-0101 and P-0214 were unable to practise Acholi pregnancy rituals such as observing role changes and the preparation and consumption of specific food.[184] During labour, a traditional midwife called the *lacele* was not present to supervise and guide them through processes such as breastfeeding, nor was there a communal birthing ceremony.[185]

[179] These include the child delivered by P-0101 in 1999; the two children delivered by P-0214 in 2007 and 2009; the child delivered by P-0999 in 2002; the child delivered by P-0227 between 2005 and 2010; the three children delivered by P-0235 in 2007, 2010. and 2014; the child delivered by P-0236 in 2014.

[180] Under Rule 145(2)(b)(vi) of the Rules of Evidence and Procedure, the Chamber may consider as aggravating circumstances 'other circumstances which, although not enumerated [in the same Rule], by virtue of their nature are similar to those mentioned'.

[181] Rule 145(2)(b)(vi) ICC RPE.

[182] Victims' Closing Brief, *supra* note 141, § 105.

[183] T-247, *supra* note 168, at 36.

[184] Victims' Closing Brief, *supra* note 141, § 88.

[185] *Ibid.*

54. Expert evidence from Professor Musisi explained the consequences of the disconnection from cultural practices. Due to the Acholi culture being patrilineal, the mothers and children are unlikely to receive familial claims such as inheritance and fractal rights, which secure the land for Acholi women to work and provide for their family on.[186]

55. In its discretion, the Chamber considers the aggravating factor of cultural harms as relevant within the context of this case. This consideration does not amount to 'double counting' as social and cultural circumstances have not been considered for gravity purposes.

Sentencing Determination for Forced Pregnancy

56. As the above analysis shows, forced pregnancy is a crime of the most serious gravity. It violates a person's dignity, their body, and their reproductive autonomy. The impacts can reverberate through every facet of the victim's life.

57. In addition, the crime can result in a child, which even if welcomed, can place a heavy economic burden and caring responsibility on the victim. Forced pregnancy, therefore, resonates well after the pregnancy itself. It is a crime whose effects can endure for the duration of the victim's life, as well as there being intergenerational impacts felt by the child. [Editors' note: see below, Winfred Naigaga Kyobiika's reimagined judgment in this collection on the impact on children born of sexual violence (Chapter 9.4).]

58. Taking into account the damage caused by the crime, the direct role of Mr Ongwen, and the other aggravating factors noted above, and in keeping with previous sentences by this Court for analogous crimes,[187] it is appropriate to sentence Mr Ongwen to life imprisonment for the crime against humanity of forced pregnancy (Count 58) and the war crime of forced pregnancy (Count 59), to be served concurrently with his sentence for other crimes.

59. However, this sentence is to be reduced to thirty years taking into account the impact of Mr Ongwen's childhood experiences in the LRA on his moral and psychological development (see next section).

MITIGATING FACTORS

[Editors' note: save for the reference to mitigation in paragraph 59, the analysis of mitigating factors is omitted for the purpose of this reimaged judgment on forced pregnancy.]

[186] T-177, www.icc-cpi.int/sites/default/files/Transcripts/CR2018_02682.PDF, at 24.

[187] Ntaganda Sentencing Decision, *supra* note 90; Public with annexes I and II Decision on Sentence pursuant to Article 76 of the Statute, *Bemba* (ICC-01/05-01/08-3399), Trial Chamber III, 21 June 2016.

DISPOSITION

The Chamber pronounces the following sentences for each of the crimes committed by Dominic Ongwen:

For the crime against humanity of forced pregnancy (Count 58): life imprisonment;

For the war crime of forced pregnancy (Count 59): life imprisonment;

Mr Ongwen's total joint sentence would ordinarily be for life. However considering his mitigating circumstances, a reduced sentence of thirty years' imprisonment is justified in this case. Time spent in ICC custody will be deducted from this thirty-year sentence.

Judge Tonny Raymond Kirabira, Judge Adrienne Ringin, and Judge Rosemary Grey

9.4 CHILDREN BORN OF RAPE IN THE ONGWEN SENTENCE

W. Naigaga Kyobiika

In 2021, Trial Chamber IX convicted Mr Dominic Ongwen of sixty-one counts of war crimes and crimes against humanity.[188] In determining an appropriate sentence, the Chamber canvassed a number of aggravating and mitigating factors.[189]

In this rewritten sentencing decision, W. Naigaga Kyobiika inserts an additional aggravating circumstance, namely children born of war. In including this additional factor, Naigaga focuses in particular on the social and cultural experiences of these children, both during and after the war, noting the continuing nature of their harm due to the circumstances of their birth. Naigaga utilises the evidence provided at trial by experts to reframe the sentencing decision away from the perpetrator to the victims themselves, highlighting their voices and providing an avenue for closure denied in the original decision.

No.: ICC-02/04-01/15
Date: 6 May 2021

Original: English

TRIAL CHAMBER IX(B)

Before: Judge Winifred Naigaga KYOBIIKA

SITUATION IN UGANDA

IN THE CASE OF THE *PROSECUTOR v. DOMINIC ONGWEN*

Public

Redacted Sentencing Decision
Separate and Concurring Opinion of Judge Winifred Naigaga Kyobiika

[188] Trial Judgment, *Ongwen* (ICC-02/04-01/15-1762-Red), Trial Chamber IX, 4 February 2021.

[189] Sentence, *Ongwen* (ICC-02/04-01/15-1819-Red), Trial Chamber IX, 6 May 2021.

1. I agree with the final decision of the Trial Chamber as regards the individual criminal responsibility of Mr Dominic Ongwen. However, I respectfully wish to add to the conclusions of the majority of the Chamber as regards as an aggravating factor: the impact on children who were born as a result of the sexual and gender-based crimes for which Mr Ongwen has been convicted.

2. While sentencing Mr Ongwen for the crime of sexual and gender-based crimes directly and not directly perpetuated by Dominic Ongwen (Counts 50–68), the majority of the Trial Chamber states, and I agree, that there was a presence of aggravating circumstances of: a multiplicity of victims; victims being particularly defenceless; and a discriminatory motive as regards gender within the meaning of Rule 145(2)(b) of the Rules.

3. However, I wish to add another element: the concept of 'children born as a result of these sexual and gender-based crimes' as an aggravating factor. This element may be read into those circumstances covered by Rule 145(2)(b)(VI), which, although not enumerated in the Rules, is by its nature similar to the aggravating factors mentioned. Consequently, I consider it necessary to evaluate this factor.

4. It is important to note that the Rome Statute's provisions are applied and interpreted concerning specific charges brought against individuals. However, the Chamber must not disregard or shy away from discussing issues or interests that may arise while adjudicating a case. In the present case, it is an agreed fact that children were born as a result of sexual and gender-based crimes for which Mr Ongwen was convicted. It is therefore permissible for the Chamber to give a wide interpretation of the victims of crime to include those victims that arose as a result of far-reaching effects of charges with which Mr Ongwen was charged. Such an interpretation nurtures growth in the jurisprudence of the court and marks a step forward in the progressive development of international law in the area of a victim-centred approach.

5. I find that the majority of the Chamber addresses the purpose of the ICC trial proceedings: to decide on the guilt or innocence of an accused person. However, having regard to Article 75 of the Rome Statute, Rule 97 of the Rules of Procedure and Evidence of the Court, ICC trial proceedings through victim participation also attend to the effects embedded in the crimes of which one is charged that may become relevant during the determination of reparations. In our case, we have evidence of the existence of children born of war, some of whom may be indirect victims of the crime of which Dominic Ongwen is charged.

6. To analyse this additional aggravating factor, it is important to (a) discuss the legal framework that governs children in international law; and (b) expound on the complexity of children born as a result of the crimes Mr Ongwen has been convicted of.

7. The concept of 'children born as a result of war' is a relatively emerging area of law that has not previously been dealt with by this court or by any other international court in our present times. While hearing and deciding cases, the Chamber is compelled to use applicable treaties and the principles and rules of international

law; national laws of legal systems of the world; and principles and rules of law as interpreted in its previous decisions.[190]

8. International law on children, especially the 1989 UN Convention on the Rights of the Child, its Optional Protocols, and the African Charter on the Rights and Welfare of the Child, recognises that due to their physical and mental immaturity, children require special safeguards and care. The provisions for the special protection are guided by four general principles: non-discrimination; the best interests of the child; the right to life, survival, and development; and the right to express one's views and have them considered.[191] The protections include that a child has a right to: know and be cared for by his/her parents;[192] an identity including family relations;[193] be protected from all forms of physical or mental violence, injury or abuse, neglect or negligent treatment, maltreatment, or exploitation;[194] highest attainable standard of health and to facilities for the treatment of illness and rehabilitation of health[195] and education;[196] and protection against child abuse and torture;[197] among others. These safeguards seek to protect children from the multiple and different risks as they develop into adulthood, including in any context such as that of armed conflict

9. It is universally recognised that childhood is entitled to special care and assistance. The Chamber recognises that a family is a fundamental group in society and the natural environment for the growth and well-being of all its members particularly include children. It also notes that children have a right to be afforded the necessary protection and assistance in a family so that they can be prepared to fully assume their responsibilities within the community in adulthood. For the full and harmonious development of a child, that child should grow up in a family environment, in an atmosphere of happiness, love, and understanding. In the Inter-American Court's decision, in the case of *Gelman v. Uruguay*,[198] it was stated, in regard to enforced disappearance, that it is a violation of both the mental and psychological rights of a child if the mental state is a direct consequence of the enforced disappearance of the mother. The Court stated that this link was drawn because the enforced disappearance of one's mother meant a denial of identity and protection of a family, a right to a name and to a nationality. This further was a denial of the right to self-determination and a choice of one's preferred existence.

[190] Article 21(3) the Rome Statute.

[191] Articles 2, 3, 6, and 12 UN Convention on the Right of the Child; Articles 3, 4, and 5 African Charter on the Rights and Welfare of the Child.

[192] Article 7(1) UN Convention on the Right of the Child; Article 19 African Charter on the Rights and Welfare of the Child.

[193] Article 8(1) UN Convention on the Right of the Child; Article 6 African Charter on the Rights and Welfare of the Child.

[194] Article 19 UN Convention on the Right of the Child.

[195] Article 24 UN Convention on the Right of the Child.

[196] Article 28 UN Convention on the Right of the Child.

[197] Article 16 African Charter on the Rights and Welfare of the Child.

[198] *Gelman v. Uruguay*, Merits and Reparations, Inter-Am Ct. H.R., Series C No. 221 (24 February 2011).

The court emphasised that the denial of all these rights could be a result of the denial of protection to the mother.

10. I will now move to expound on the complexity surrounding children born of war. Mr Ongwen has been convicted of sexual and gender-based violence offences directly committed by him: forced marriage as another inhumane act and as a crime against humanity (Count 50); torture as a crime against humanity and as a war crime (Counts 51–52); rape as a crime against humanity and as a war crime (Counts 53–54); sexual slavery as a crime against humanity and as a war crime (Counts 55–56); enslavement as a crime against humanity (Count 57); forced pregnancy as a crime against humanity and as a war crime (Counts 58–59); and outrages upon personal dignity (Count 60).

11. Mr Ongwen has also been convicted of eight sexual and gender-based crimes not directly perpetrated by Dominic Ongwen which he committed – within the meaning of Article 25(3)(a) of the Statute – in the context of a coordinated and methodical effort in Sinia Brigade during the relevant period: forced marriage as an inhumane act and as a crime against humanity (Count 61); torture as a crime against humanity and as a war crime (Counts 62–63); rape as a crime against humanity and as a war crime (Counts 64–65); sexual slavery as a crime against humanity and as a war crime (Counts 66–67); and enslavement as a crime against humanity (Count 68).

12. This was a complex situation that went beyond the individual acts of Ongwen but, further, those perpetrated on his command. I take judicial notice of the proposals that the Lord's Resistance Army had a political agenda. Reports such as that of the Justice and Reconciliation project[199] have argued that there was a systematic plan to abduct young girls in part to develop a 'new moral order', a forceful purification of the old, and the birth of a 'new Acholi'. Forced marriage was a political project in which Acholi men and women, boys and girls were forced to 'marry' and bear children as 'families' in an effort to expand this new Acholi population.[200]

13. As a result of the forced marriages, some of the victims were mothers to children fathered by Mr Ongwen and his soldiers in the Sinia Brigade. To be precise, though Mr Ongwen had thirteen children at the time of the trial, ten of the thirteen children were fathered by him outside the period relevant to the charges. The three children who were fathered by Mr Ongwen during the period relevant to the charges were born to P-0101 and P-0214. Mr Ongwen also played a vital role in coordinating the Sinia Brigade to commit the offence of forced marriage which led to the fathering of many children. While precise findings as to the

[199] Justice and Reconciliation Project, 'We Are All the Same: Experiences of Children Born into LRA Captivity' (2015) 2, available at www.researchgate.net/publication/337158547_%27We_Are_All_the_Same%27_Experiences_of_Children_Born_into_LRA_Captivity.

[200] Article 5 of the UN Convention on the Rights of the Child.

number of children were not possible, the Chamber found in the Trial Judgment that at any time between 1 July 2002 and 31 December 2005 many children were conceived and born as a result of the rampant sexual abuse that took place during this time

14. Studies on children born of war, such as Brigitte Rohwerder's 2019 study,[201] generally observe that children born of wartime rape, and their mothers, are often stigmatised by their own communities due to their associations with political, ethnic, or religious enemies. She added that their identity and sense of belonging are contested, which creates dangers for their physical security and emotional well-being. She found that children born of wartime rape are at risk of violence, abuse, abandonment, discrimination, and marginalisation, at the hands of both families and communities. They often have less access to community resources, family protection, and education or livelihood activities, and are likely to grow up in poverty. They can face challenges in registering their birth and their right to citizenship. The experiences of children born of wartime rape can result in a lifetime of detrimental consequences, and the stigmatisation they experience continues long into the post-war period.

15. It is important to remind ourselves that being born as a result of war does not predetermine how a child will experience life's journey. Children's capacities and vulnerabilities do change according to time and contexts such as gender, perceived ethnicity, social and economic status, as well as structural gender discrimination, especially in patriarchal and patrilineal societies. Diane Amann[202] writes that 'children as persons with individual rights, as members of families and as constituents of multigenerational communities, may be impacted differently by crimes based on their sex, gender, or other status or identities'. She states that age and birth may give rise to multiple forms of discrimination and social inequalities, either alone or as they intersect with other factors, such as race, ability, or disability; religion or belief; political or another opinion; national, ethnic, or social origin; gender, sex, or other status or identity.

16. Indeed, the listing of child rights in the international human rights regime does not presume that all children always are vulnerable but instead requires attention to be paid to the evolving capacities of the child.

17. The discussion of experiences of children born as a result of rapes during war does not in any way suggest that I am lumping together the realities of children born as a result of war. I am aware that different children had different experiences. After the war, some relocated with their mothers from their ancestral villages to towns,

[201] B. Rohwerder, 'Reintegration of Children Born of Wartime Rape' (2019) 7–8, available at https://assets.publishing.service.gov.uk/media/5d431080ed915d09d7280ce4/628_Reintegration_of_Children_Born_of_Wartime_Rape.pdf.

[202] D. M. Amann, 'International Child Law and the Settlement of Ukraine-Russia and Other Conflicts' 99 *International Law Studies* (2022) 599–601, available at https://digital-commons.usnwc.edu/cgi/viewcontent.cgi?article=3022&context=ils.

where there was greater anonymity and people were less likely to know about their experiences in captivity, which contributed to reduced stigmatisation; others had a privileged social class and families that paid for their therapy and education in cities including Kampala; while others were welcomed back in their ancestral home and went on to have a loving family experience. However, I focus on those unfortunate children who were stripped of the protections of family life due to their status of being born because of rape.

18. It is a fact that forced marriages produce complex emotional and psychological effects on the victims and their children beyond the obvious physical effects of pregnancy and child-bearing. For example, I observe that some of the children born as a result of war have been treated with disdain and continue to face untold suffering, rejection, discrimination, and stigmatisation in the communities. On the maternal side, a majority of the children face discrimination because they were born outside the norms since their father never paid the dowry when he forcefully married their mothers. This fact in a way disrupted the social fabric – the belief in and sanctity of marriage. It should be noted that in northern Uganda having children out of wedlock is a practice that is generally frowned upon among the communities.[203] Secondly, some of these children and their mothers[204] have come to be identified as perpetrators or enablers of the conflict since the evidence in the Trial Chamber shows that they served as wives, cleaners, cooks, and actively took part in the conflict, among others.[205]

19. Joanne Neenan[206] and Mahlet Woldetsadik[207] report that the influence of patriarchy in Acholi communities contributes to children's contested identities, as paternal clan membership determines access to identity and belonging, social status, land and resources. They propose that contested clan membership reduces one's access to inherited family land and resources, leading to potential poverty, homelessness, and reduced prospects for marriage. They conclude that this is especially problematic for young men as, without a way to provide for spouses and families, they will experience greater social rejection than young women. It should be noted that some of these children face far more complex difficulties that are not comparable to those of other children born out of unsanctioned unions. For example, a situation where children are born as a result of elopement in peaceful times can be

[203] N. Mukasa, 'War-Child Mothers in Northern Uganda: The Civil War Forgotten Legacy' 27 *Development in Practice* (2017) 354–367, at 360.

[204] Mothers served as wives, cleaners, and cooks but at times were engaged in fighting.

[205] J. Neenan, 'Closing the Protection Gap for Children Born of War – Addressing Stigmatisation and the Intergenerational Impact of Sexual Violence in Conflict' LSE & FCO (2017), available at www.lse.ac.uk/women-peace-security/assets/documents/2018/LSE-WPS-Children-BornofWar.pdf.

[206] *Ibid.*

[207] M. A. Woldetsadik, 'Lessons from Northern Uganda: Post-Conflict Integration of "Children Born of War"', The RAND blog (2017), available at www.rand.org/blog/2017/04/lessons-from-northern-uganda-post-conflict-integration.html.

corrected with paying of dowry but the situation at hand cannot be corrected in the same way. Since the children of P-0099, P-0101, P-0214, and P-0227 fathered by Mr Ongwen were born out of an unsanctioned union, the chances that some of them may experience the rejections described above should not be disregarded.

20. Living outside the protection of family means that some of these children continue to be denied not only a sense of identity and belonging which correlates with inheritance and possession of land but also the provision of basic needs that are necessary to the full development of the child. It is important to note that the four witnesses mentioned above were aged between approximately nineteen and twenty-one at the time relevant to the crimes committed against them of which Dominic Ongwen has been found guilty. In a normal setting, these witnesses would have acquired skills at school during those formative years. The effect of the wasted years can be seen from the evidence of P-0236. When she was asked by the Trial Chamber to compare herself to her schoolmates now that she had returned home, she responded as follows:

> There is no comparison because right now they are much better off than I am. I'm back home. I've got – I have injuries. I'm weak. Maybe if I had not been abducted I would have not been shot at, I would have not been injured, I would have not had any – I would not be suffering. Most of the people that – my peers are okay. They are not injured. They're working. Some of them have finished their education. So they're in a much better off position than I am.[208]

21. Without skills, the victims are not a great fit for the labour market and unless supported may continue to be disadvantaged in giving their children the best chances in life.

22. If children born of war have been accepted with their mothers to live in their maternal home, in some extreme cases they stand a high chance of being victims of abuse in these maternal homes. Joanne Neenan[209] writes that such children are 'generally perceived as proxy members of the LRA, symbols of misfortune, and stereotyped as violent, unproductive, unequal members of society' and, as a result, they are discriminated against in everyday life. For example, some children shared that they were not allowed to share bedding with other children, and others were denied an opportunity to attend school and instead turned into casual labourers, among others. This is further exacerbated by the patrilineal culture where their mothers have no right to land, meaning the children have nothing to inherit apart from the segregation that their mothers suffer.[210]

[208] Judgment, *Ongwen* (ICC-01/04-01/15), Trial Chamber IX, 4 February 2021, § 2093.

[209] Neenan, *supra* note 205.

[210] V. Ladisch, 'From Rejection to Redress: Overcoming Legacies of Conflict-Related Sexual Violence in Northern Uganda', ICTJ (2015) 17–19, available at www.ictj.org/sites/default/files/ICTJ-Report-Uganda-Children-2015.pdf.

23. I now turn to discuss the effect of the offences of torture, rape, sexual slavery, enslavement, forced pregnancy, and outrages upon personal dignity on the children born of war.

24. Mr Ongwen's children and those of his soldiers in the Sinia Brigade were conceived, born, and raised in difficult circumstances. For example, P-0099 testified that in September 2002, while she was sick, she went to collect food with her three-month-old child. She successfully escaped and was taken to the government barracks where her baby started being fed on formula until she recovered. P-0101 testified that her group came under fire from two government gunships in July 2004. She stated that she was injured and her one-year-old daughter was shot and taken by government soldiers. P-0372 testified that abducted women and girls could occasionally be released after giving birth if they could not move with the group because of having to take care of the baby. The mothers and their children lacked proper medical attention, adequate food, accommodation, clothes, clean water, and education.

25. The evidence from the Trial Chamber also shows that as a result of the rape during the relevant period, P-0101 and P-0214 gave birth to children fathered by Dominic Ongwen, and other women who experienced sexual violence from the soldiers of the Sinia Brigade also gave birth. These children were born and conceived in violent circumstances and they grew up witnessing the rape of their mothers and other women by Mr Ongwen and his soldiers over a protracted period. It is important to note that other older children in Mr Ongwen's homestead and those who lived in the homestead of other members of the Sinia Brigade also witnessed this protracted violence perpetrated on their mothers.

26. Additionally, some of the children born of war witnessed and experienced violent events. The record of the Trial Chamber shows that Mr Ongwen and his soldiers often used violent acts such as beatings, rape, sexual slavery, and executions to discipline his army in his homestead. For example, P-0101 told the court about her first sexual encounter with Mr Ongwen. She stated that he threatened her with a gun before forcefully having sex with her while his escorts held her hands. She stated that she was fifteen years old at the time and in her own words she felt 'he violated my rights, I was young and there was absolutely nothing that I could say about it'. P-0099 testified that she and another woman refused to cook for Mr Ongwen or go to the garden. Mr Ongwen called his escorts and instructed them to beat them. P-0101 confirmed to the trial chamber that she was beaten by Mr Ongwen multiple times for refusing to have sex with him. P-0235 recalls an incident in Uganda when P-0214 was beaten when two months pregnant. Given that P-0214's evidence indicates that she was only in Uganda while pregnant for the first time, while all her other pregnancies occurred outside Uganda, the Trial Chamber concluded that the incident described by P-0235 took place during P-0214's first pregnancy in 2005, a time that falls within the period of the charges. P-0227 testified that at one time, when Mr Ongwen thought she was cunning and intended to escape, he ordered his

soldiers to beat her. She stated that the beating continued for a long time until her body was swollen and it was difficult for her to walk. P-0352 described being forced, on Dominic Ongwen's orders, to take part in the killing of another girl who had been accused of witchcraft, while P-0351 similarly stated that she was forced to kick to death a boy who had tried to escape but was caught.

27. From the above, I find that some of Mr Ongwen's children were conceived because of rape and were raised in a largely violent homestead. Professor Weierstall-Pust explained to the Court that when someone is exposed to traumatic events, it may lead to a trauma spectrum disorder. Professor Mezey's report gave the Trial Chamber a comprehensive description of the effect of a traumatic event on a person's mental health. It stated that victims of trauma may experience severe depressive illness, post-traumatic stress disorder (PTSD) and dissociative disorder (including depersonalisation and multiple identity disorder) as well as severe suicidal ideation and high risk of committing suicide, and from dissociative amnesia and symptoms of obsessive-compulsive disorder.

28. In his report, Professor Mezey described that a depressive disorder is characterised by a persistent severe lowering of mood, feelings of sadness, hopelessness, despair, often associated with an inability to see any future or to feel hopeless about the future. He added that this disorder is often associated with a high risk of suicidal tendencies. He stated that the more severe conditions will be associated with disruptions in the individual's physical health and functioning and will include symptoms such as a reduction of appetite, loss of weight, disruption to sleep, particularly inability to get to sleep, and waking early in the morning. Professor Mezey stated that the condition can result in an individual becoming socially withdrawn and disruption of the individual's cognitions so that they are unable to concentrate well. He stated that people who have undergone traumatic experiences may become retarded, so that the person's speech and their movements are slowed down; they may lack spontaneity in terms of expressing themselves, but also in terms of their facial expressions or ability to verbalise or vocalise. He also stated that they often express unreasonable feelings of worthlessness, low self-esteem, and guilt, sometimes to an extreme extent, so that they feel guilty about the war and things they cannot possibly be held responsible for.

29. Professor Mezey also noted in his report that PTSD is significant clinical distress associated with symptoms that are so severe and so intrusive that they stop the individual from being able to carry on with their normal day-to-day functioning. For example, children may fail to study, help with household chores, or interact with friends.

30. Concerning dissociative identity disorder, Professor Mezey explained that dissociation is a disruption to the person's identity, their sense of self, and their sense of agency. He stated that this disorder is characterised by two or more distinct personalities operating, essentially, side by side and neither personality knows of the other person's existence. He added that this is an enduring condition that does not remit or relapse in the way that other illnesses might do.

31. The Chamber also called Ms Elisabeth Schauer as an expert witness on the topic of children with trauma, particularly post-traumatic stress disorder. During her testimony, Ms Schauer stated that the trauma suffered by child soldiers has intellectual and cognitive consequences for the children. Children who have suffered trauma have problems with their memory and may have learning difficulties, particularly as regards reading and writing comprehension. She also affirmed that this trauma never goes away. The expert further stated that although persons with PTSD may recall events that occurred in the past, their ability to answer and remember these events will depend on the way questions are asked, and if they are asked chronologically. She stated, 'you probably have a hard time just wanting to know – jumping and wanting to know little details here and there'.

32. I find the evidence of these medical experts entirely convincing and do believe that some of Mr Ongwen's children and some of the other children born to his soldiers in the Sinia Brigade stand a high risk of suffering from the mental disorders discussed by the medical experts.

33. I find that Mr Ongwen denied some of his children the fundamental right of being born and raised in the security of a family. The central element and underlying act for children born of war is the imposition of this status on the victim. Such a status, as seen above, has mental economic, social, ethical, and religious effects, among others.

34. I recall that Dominic Ongwen himself had in the past been a victim of war, having been abducted as a child and integrated as a fighter into the LRA ranks. He described the great suffering of the children abducted by the LRA when providing an account of his own experience. It cannot go unnoticed that Dominic Ongwen, despite being well aware of such suffering, which he had been subjected to several years earlier and fully appreciating its wrongfulness, did nothing to spare similar experiences to other children after him, but, on the contrary, wilfully sustained and contributed to perpetuating the systemic, methodical, and widespread fathering of children for the LRA.

35. From the foregoing, I thus sentence as follows:

- For the crime against humanity of forced marriage as another inhumane act of P-0099, P-0101, P-0214, P-0226, and P-0227 (Count 50) a term of twenty years of imprisonment; and in addition I order reparations for any of the children that were members of Mr Ongwen's homestead during the period relevant to this offence.
- For the crime against humanity of torture of P-0101, P-0214, P-0226, and P0227 (Count 51) a term of twenty years of imprisonment; and in addition I order reparations for any of the children that were members of Mr Ongwen's homestead during the period relevant to this offence.
- For the war crime of torture of P-0101, P-0214, P-0226, and P-0227 (Count 52) a term of twenty years of imprisonment; and in addition I order

reparations for any of the children that were members of Mr Ongwen's homestead during the period relevant to this offence.

- For the crime against humanity of rape of P-0101, P-0214, P-0226, and P-0227 (Count 53) a term of twenty years of imprisonment; and in addition, I order reparations for any of the children that were members of Mr Ongwen's homestead during the period relevant to this offence.
- For the war crime of rape of P-0101, P-0214, P-0226, and P-0227 (Count 54) a term of twenty years of imprisonment; and in addition, I order reparations for any of the children that were members of Mr Ongwen's homestead during the period relevant to this offence.
- For the crime against humanity of sexual slavery of P-0101, P-0214, P-0226, and P-0227 (Count 55) a term of twenty years of imprisonment; and in addition, I order reparations for any of the children that were members of Mr Ongwen's homestead during the period relevant to this offence.
- For the war crime of sexual slavery of P-0101, P-0214, P-0226, and P-0227 (Count 56) a term of twenty years of imprisonment; and in addition I order reparations for any of the children that were members of Mr Ongwen's homestead during the period relevant to this offence.
- For the crime against humanity of enslavement of P-0099, P-0235, and P-0236 (Count 57) a term of twenty years of imprisonment; and in addition, I order reparations for any of the children that were members of Mr Ongwen's homestead during the period relevant to this offence.
- For the crime against humanity of forced pregnancy of P-0101 and P-0214 (Count 58) a term of twenty years of imprisonment; and in addition, I order reparations for the children that were born as a result of this offence.
- For the war crime of forced pregnancy of P-0101 and P-0214 (Count 59) a term of twenty years of imprisonment; and in addition, I order reparations for any of the children that were members of Mr Ongwen's homestead during the period relevant to this offence.
- For the war crime of outrages upon personal dignity of P-0226 and P-0235 (Count 60) a term of fourteen years of imprisonment; and in addition, I order reparations for any of the children that witnessed this crime while it was happening.
- For the crime against humanity of forced marriage as another inhumane act, from at least 1 July 2002 until 31 December 2005 (Count 61), a term of twenty years of imprisonment; and in addition, I order reparations for any of the children that were members of the Sania Brigade soldiers' homesteads during the period relevant to this offence.
- For the crime against humanity of torture, from at least 1 July 2002 until 31 December 2005 (Count 62), a term of twenty years of imprisonment; and in addition, I order reparations for any of the children that were

members of the soldiers' homesteads during the period relevant to this offence.

- For the war crime of torture, from at least 1 July 2002 until 31 December 2005 (Count 63), a term of twenty years of imprisonment; and in addition, I order reparations for any of the children that were members of the soldiers' homesteads during the period relevant to this offence.
- For the crime against humanity of rape, from at least 1 July 2002 until 31 December 2005 (Count 64), a term of twenty years of imprisonment; and in addition, I order reparations for any of the children that were members of the soldiers' homesteads during the period relevant to this offence.
- For the war crime of rape, from at least 1 July 2002 until 31 December 2005 (Count 65), a term of twenty years of imprisonment; and in addition, I order reparations for any of the children that were members of the soldiers' homesteads during the period relevant to this offence.
- For the crime against humanity of sexual slavery, from at least 1 July 2002 until 31 December 2005 (Count 66), a term of twenty years of imprisonment; and in addition, I order reparations for any of the children that were members of the soldiers' homesteads during the period relevant to this offence.
- For the war crime of sexual slavery, from at least 1 July 2002 until 31 December 2005 (Count 67), a term of twenty years of imprisonment; and in addition, I order reparations for any of the children that were members of the soldiers' homesteads during the period relevant to this offence.
- For the crime against humanity of enslavement, from at least 1 July 2002 until 31 December 2005 (Count 68), a term of twenty years of imprisonment; and in addition, I order reparations for any of the children that were members of the soldiers' homesteads during the period relevant to this offence.

Judge W. Naigaga Kyobiika

10

The Situation in Sudan

10.1 REFLECTION: THE SITUATION IN SUDAN

Sareta Ashraph

CONTEXT

In February 2003, violence erupted in Sudan's western Darfur region and quickly evolved into a civil war between the Government of Sudan and several organised armed groups, in particular the Sudanese Liberation Movement/Army (SLM/A) and the Justice and Equality Movement (JEM).[1] Following the 25 April 2003 SLM/A attack on an airport in northern Darfur, the Government of Sudan, led by then-President Omar Al Bashir, issued a general call for the mobilisation of the Janjaweed militia in response.[2] Sudanese government forces – including the Sudanese armed forces and their allied Janjaweed militia – launched a counter-insurgency campaign in Darfur, a core component of which were unlawful attacks on the civilian population, largely belonging to the Fur, Masalit, and Zaghawa communities, who were perceived to be aligned with one or more of the various armed groups.[3]

Within a year of the campaign's start, the United Nations estimated that more than 750,000 people were displaced in Darfur and upwards of 110,000 had fled across the border into Chad.[4] The refugees and internally displaced came bearing accounts of horrific violence against the civilian population.[5] By December 2003,

[1] J. Flint and A. de Waal, *Darfur: A New History of a Long War* (London: Zed Books, 2008).

[2] *Prosecutor v. Al Bashir*, Warrant for the Arrest of Omar Hassan Ahmad Al Bashir (ICC-02/05-01/09), 4 March 2009 (hereafter Al Bashir Warrant – First Decision).

[3] *Ibid.*

[4] UN News, 'Sudan: Humanitarian crisis in Darfur deteriorating, U.N. agencies say', 30 March 2004.

[5] Including accounts of killings, sexual violence, abductions, destruction of food and water sources, burning of villages, looting of private property, and forced displacement. Human

UN Secretary-General Kofi Annan voiced alarm at the 'reports of widespread abuses against civilians, including killings, rape and the burning and looting of entire villages'.[6]

On 18 September 2004, the UN Security Council adopted Resolution 1564 requesting that the Secretary-General 'rapidly establish an international commission of inquiry in order immediately to investigate reports of violations of international humanitarian law and human rights law in Darfur by all parties, to determine also whether or not acts of genocide have occurred, and to identify the perpetrators of such violations with a view to ensuring that those responsible are held accountable'.[7] The International Commission of Inquiry on Darfur, chaired by Antonio Cassese, began its work in late October 2004. It submitted a full report on its findings to the Secretary-General on 25 January 2005, and found that,

> Government forces and militias conducted indiscriminate attacks, including killing of civilians, torture, enforced disappearances, destruction of villages, rape, and other forms of sexual violence, pillaging and forced displacement, throughout Darfur. These acts were conducted on a widespread and systematic basis, and therefore may amount to crimes against humanity. The extensive destruction and displacement have resulted in a loss of livelihood and means of survival for countless women, men, and children. In addition to the large-scale attacks, many people have been arrested and detained, and many have been held incommunicado for prolonged periods and tortured. The vast majority of the victims of all of these violations have been from the Fur, Zaghawa, Massalit, Jebel, Aranga and other so-called 'African' tribes.[8]

The Report's findings that the Sudanese government forces and militias had committed acts that may have amounted to multiple crimes against humanity and war crimes were overshadowed in media reports by the fact that the Commission did not make a finding of genocide due to insufficient information on the specific intent required for the crime.[9]

Rights Watch, *Darfur in Flames: Atrocities in Western Sudan* 16(5) (A), April 2004, 13–35; Amnesty International, 'Darfur: "Too many people killed for no reason"', 3 February 2004 (HRW, *Darfur in Flames*) 9–25.

6 UN News, 'Annan alarmed at reports of widespread abuses of civilians in Darfur, Sudan', 9 December 2003.

7 UN Security Council, S/RES/1564 (2004), 18 September 2004, § 12.

8 Report of the International Commission of Inquiry on Darfur to the Secretary-General, Pursuant to Security Council Resolution 1564 (2004) of 18 September 2004, UN Doc. S/2005/60, 1 February 2005, 3 (hereafter Commission's Final Report).

9 Commission's Final Report, *supra* note 8, at 4; W. Hoge, 'UN finds crimes, not genocide in Darfur', *New York Times*, 1 February 2005; C. Lynch, 'UN panel finds no genocide in Darfur but urges tribunals', *Washington Post*, 1 February 2005; E. MacAskill, 'Sudan's Darfur crimes not genocide, says UN Report', *Guardian* (UK), 1 February 2005. For a critical analysis of the Commission's finding, see D. Luban, 'Calling Genocide by Its Rightful Name: Lemkin's Word, Darfur, and the UN Report' 7(1) *Chicago Journal of International Law* (2006), Article 14, 303–320.

THE DARFUR CASES

On 31 March 2005, the Security Council, through its Resolution 1593 and acting under its Chapter VII powers, referred the situation in Darfur to the ICC and required Sudan to give its full cooperation.[10] This marked the first time that the Security Council had successfully referred a situation to the ICC. It would also be the first ICC investigation on the territory of a non-state party to the Rome Statute.

The Office of the Prosecutor, then under Luis Ocampo, opened its investigation on 1 June 2005,[11] focusing on allegations of genocide, war crimes, and crimes against humanity committed in Darfur, Sudan, since 1 July 2002. Since April 2007, the ICC has issued summons to appear and/or warrants for arrest for seven men alleged to bear responsibility for various crimes committed in Darfur: Omar Hassan Ahmad Al Bashir; Ali Muhammad Ali Abd-Al-Rahman; Ahmad Harun;[12] Abdel Raheem Muhammad Hussein;[13] Bahr Idriss Abu Garda;[14] Abdallah Banda Abakaer Nourain;[15] and Saleh Mohammed Jerbo Janus.[16]

[10] UN Security Resolution 1593, S/Res/1593 (2005), 31 March 2005; UN News, 'Security Council refers situation in Darfur, Sudan, to Prosecutor of International Criminal Court', 31 March 2005.

[11] International Criminal Court, 'The Prosecutor of the ICC opens investigation in Darfur', 6 June 2005.

[12] In April 2007, the Pre-Trial Chamber found reasonable grounds to believe that Mr Harun, in his role as Minister of State for the Interior, was criminally responsible for commission of crimes against humanity and war crimes between August 2003 and March 2004 in predominantly Fur localities in West Darfur. Following the April 2019 coup, Mr Harun was arrested by local authorities in Sudan, where he is believed to remain in custody. As he has not been transferred to the seat of the Court, his case remains at the pre-trial stage. *Prosecutor v. Harun and Abd-Al-Rahman*, Warrant for the Arrest of Ahmad Hurun (ICC-02/05-01/07), 27 April 2007.

[13] On 1 March 2023, the Pre-Trial Chamber held there were reasonable grounds to believe that Mr Hussein, while Minister of the Interior and the Sudanese President's Special Representative in Darfur, was responsible for crimes against humanity and war crimes relating to attacks on civilians in predominantly Fur localities in West Darfur during 2003 and 2004. Arrested after the April 2019 coup d'état, Mr Hussein is believed to be in custody in Sudan. Mr Hussein's case remains at the pre-trial stage. *Prosecutor v. Hussein*, Warrant of Arrest for Abdel Raheem Muhammad Hussein (ICC-02/05-01/12), 1 March 2012.

[14] The Chamber did not confirm charges – comprising three counts of war crimes arising from a JEM attack on an African Union Mission base, Military Group Site (MGS) Haskanita, in North Darfur on 29 September 2007 – and later rejected the Prosecutor's application to appeal the decision. The case is considered closed, barring presentation of new evidence by the prosecution. *Prosecutor v. Abu Garda*, Decision on the 'Prosecution's Application for Leave to Appeal the "Decision on the Confirmation of Charges"' (ICC-02/05-02/09-267), 23 April 2010.

[15] On 7 March 2011, Pre-Trial Chamber I confirmed war crimes charges against Mr Banda relating to the 2007 attack on Military Group Site (MGS) Haskanita and committed Mr Banda to trial. On 11 September 2014, the Chamber issued an arrest warrant to ensure his presence at trial. Mr Banda remains at large, with his trial postponed until his arrest and transfer to the Court. *Prosecutor v. Banda*, Warrant of Arrest for Abdallah Banda Abakaer Nourain (ICC-02/05-03/09-606), 11 September 2014.

[16] While war crimes charges against Mr Jerbo – related to the 2007 attack on MGS Haskanita – were confirmed, the Chamber terminated the trial proceedings in October 2013, based on

Prosecutor v. Omar Hassan Ahmad Al Bashir

In its 2009 Decision on the Prosecution's Application for a Warrant of Arrest (First Decision), Pre-Trial Chamber I determined there were reasonable grounds to believe that around April 2003, along with other top political and military leaders of the Sudanese government, Mr Al Bashir – then President of the Republic of Sudan and the commander-in-chief of the Sudanese armed forces – established a common plan to carry out a counter-insurgency campaign against armed groups opposing the government, and that a core component of the campaign was the unlawful attack on that part of the civilian population of Darfur belonging largely to the Fur, Masalit, and Zaghawa groups; and he used the 'apparatus' of the Sudanese state to direct hundreds of attacks against the Fur, Masalit, and Zaghawa civilian population taking no direct part in hostilities.[17] In issuing the warrant, the Chamber held that there were reasonable grounds to believe that Mr Al Bashir was criminally responsible for the war crimes of attacking civilians and pillage, arising from various attacks taking place between August 2003 and May 2008 on specified localities,[18] and the crimes against humanity of murder, extermination, forcible transfer, and rape arising from attacks on named localities in West and South Darfur in various periods between August/September 2003 and May 2008.

In its second decision regarding the warrant of arrest (Second Decision), issued on 12 July 2010, the Pre-Trial Chamber held that there were reasonable grounds to believe that Mr Al Bashir was criminally responsible for the commission of the three counts of genocide against the Fur, Masalit, and Zaghawa ethnic groups.[19] Following his overthrow in the 2019 coup d'état, Al Bashir was arrested by local authorities and is currently in Sudanese custody. As he has not been transferred to the seat of the Court, his case remains at the pre-trial stage.

Ali Muhammad Ali Abd-Al-Rahman (Ali Kushayb)

Mr Abd-Al-Rahman is alleged to be a senior leader in the Janjaweed militia in Wadi Salih area of West Darfur, a member of the Popular Defence Forces, and commander of thousands of militia/Janjaweed from August 2003 to March 2004.[20]

evidence that pointed to Mr Jerbo's death on 19 April 2013. *Prosecutor v. Banda*, Public redacted Decision terminating the proceedings against Mr Jerbo (ICC-02/05-03/09-512-Red), 4 October 2013.

17 Al Bashir Warrant – First Decision, *supra* note 2.

18 Namely, Kodoom village; Bindisi town; Mukjar town; Arawala town; Shattaya town and its surrounding villages; Kailek; towns and villages in Buram locality; Muhajerlya; Saraf Jidad; Silea; Sirba; Abu Suruj; civilian centres in Jebel Moon; and Shegeg Karo.

19 *Prosecutor v. Al Bashir*, Second Warrant for the Arrest of Omar Hassan Ahmad Al Bashir (ICC-02/05-01/09), 12 July 2010 (hereafter Al Bashir – Warrant Second Decision).

20 *Prosecutor v. Abd-Al-Rahman*, Prosecutor's Application under Article 58 (7), 27 February 2007 (ICC-02/05-55-US-Exp) (public redacted version notified on the same day, ICC-02/05-56).

On 27 April 2007, Pre-Trial Chamber I granted the Prosecutor's application under Article 58(7) of the Statute[21] and decided[22] to issue a warrant of arrest against Mr Abd-Al-Rahman for crimes against humanity and war crimes allegedly committed in the localities of Kodoom, Bindisi, Mukjar, Arawala, and their surrounding areas in Darfur, Sudan, between August 2003 and March 2004.[23] On 16 January 2018, Pre-Trial Chamber II granted the Prosecutor's application to amend the first warrant,[24] issuing a second warrant of arrest for crimes against humanity and war crimes allegedly committed in the locality of Deleig and surrounding areas in Darfur, Sudan, on or about 5–7 March 2004.[25]

Mr Abd-Al-Rahman is charged with thirty-one counts of war crimes and crimes against humanity – including murder, rape, forcible transfer, torture, persecution, pillage, cruel treatment, intentionally directing attacks against the civilian population, destruction of property, and outrages upon personal dignity – committed in 2003 and 2004 in four villages in West Darfur. He is charged with directing attacks, and also mobilising, recruiting, arming, and providing supplies to Janjaweed militia under his command.

On 9 June 2020, Mr Abd-Al-Rahman voluntarily surrendered himself in the Central African Republic and was transferred into ICC custody. In June 2020, as ordered by the Chamber,[26] Mr Abd-Al-Rahman made his first appearance before the single judge,[27] during which his case was severed from his co-defendant Mr Harun's case. Pre-Trial Chamber II confirmed all thirty-one charges on 9 July 2021. Mr Abd-Al-Rahman's trial commenced on 5 April 2022 and is ongoing at the time of writing.

FEMINIST REIMAGININGS OF SELECT JUDGMENTS AND DECISIONS

Our authors have engaged in the feminist reimagining of four judgments: two from the *Al Bashir* case and two from the *Abd-Al-Rahman* case.

21 *Ibid.*

22 *Prosecutor v. Abd-Al-Rahman*, Decision on the Prosecution Application under Article 58(7) of the Statute (ICC-02/05-01/07-1-Corr).

23 *Prosecutor v. Abd-Al-Rahman*, Warrant of Arrest for Ali Kushayb (ICC-02/05-01/07-3-Corr), 27 April 2007 (hereafter Abd-Al-Rahman – First Warrant).

24 *Prosecutor v. Abd-Al-Rahman*, Prosecution's application pursuant to Article 58(6) of the Rome Statute to amend the warrant of arrest for Ali Muhammad Ali Abd-Al-Rahman (Ali Kushayb) by adding new crimes (ICC-02/05-01/07-73-Secret-Exp), 3 November 2017 (confidential redacted and public redacted versions notified on 26 June 2020, ICC-02/05-01/20-6-Conf-Red and ICC-02/05-01/20-6-Red2).

25 *Prosecutor v. Abd-Al-Rahman*, Second warrant of arrest for Ali Muhammad Ali Abd-Al-Rahman (Ali Kushayb) (ICC-02/05– 01/07-74-Secret-Exp) (public redacted version notified on 11 June 2020, ICC-02/05-01/07-74-Red) (hereafter Abd-Al-Rahman – Second Warrant).

26 *Prosecutor v. Abd-Al-Rahman*, Decision on the convening of a hearing for the initial appearance of Mr Ali Kushayb (ICC-02/05-01/07-82), 11 June 2020.

27 *Prosecutor v. Abd-Al-Rahman*, Transcript of hearing of Initial Appearance (ICC-02/05-01/20-T-001-ENG), June 2020 (hereafter Initial Appearance).

Prosecutor v. Al Bashir, *Second Decision on the Prosecutor's Application for a Warrant of Arrest*

Judge Akila Radhakrishnan and Judge Grant Shubin deliver their reimagining of the ICC Pre-Trial Chamber's Second Decision on the Prosecutor's Application for a Warrant of Arrest, issued in 2010 against Sudan's then president in respect of his responsibility for the alleged genocide in Darfur against the Fur, Masalit, and Zaghawa peoples.

While the Pre-Trial Chamber's Second Decision explored the evidence adduced by the prosecution in support of the material elements of each of the alleged counts of genocide being met, their examination's approach to the victims was gender-blind and ageless, often referring to victims as 'people' or 'civilians'[28] – apart from sexual violence, where only women were highlighted as victims.[29] The original Second Decision, in the absence of an intersectional approach, did not grapple with how the gendered and age-disaggregated commission of genocide, by design, was more likely to specifically target and/or impact on victims who are routinely less visible in documentation and jurisprudence, such as children and women, as well as deepening the annihilative impact of the crime.

Judges Radhakrishnan and Shubin's reimagined decision takes as its starting point the Pre-Trial Chamber's exploration of the specific material elements of each of the three counts of genocide. It illuminates how gendered understandings are woven into the Sudanese government's planning and commission of coordinated acts that make up the continuum of genocidal violence, and how through these gendered annihilative acts the perpetrators maximised the crime's destructive impact on the Fur, Masalit, and Zaghawa ethnic groups.

Alighting first on the count of genocide by killing, the judges delve into the gendered manner of the killings, emphasising that civilians were targeted in specific ways by reason not only of their ethnicity but also of their perceived gender. The Chamber makes the significant choice – given the paucity of information as to the gender and age of the victims within the evidence presented by the prosecution – to include testimony from the UN Darfur Commission report, which charts the targeted killing of men and boys from the three ethnic groups, including the seeking out and killing of young boys being hidden by their families.[30] Radhakrishnan and Shubin also highlight how the crime of murder was committed in different ways

[28] For example, and with regard to the count of genocide by killing, the Pre-Trial Chamber reviewed the evidence of the murder of 'thousands of civilians belonging primarily to the Fur, Masalit and Zaghawa groups' between April 2003 and 14 July 2008. Al Bashir – Warrant Second Decision, *supra* note 19, § 22.

[29] Ibid, § 29.

[30] Radhakrishnan and Shubin, Reimagined Decision, para. 10.

against victims of different genders, a facet that is obscured in the original decision's use of the gender-blind term 'civilians'. In one example, the judges, in their reimagining, direct focus to the gendered nature of killing, juxtapositioning the killings of men and boys through gunshot at the onset of an attack, and an attack where the women suffered far slower deaths, having been abducted, transferred to a military garrison, paraded naked, and raped continuously for several days, in the course of which three were killed.[31]

In the second count of genocide by causing serious bodily and mental harm, Judges Radhakrishnan and Shubin explore the legacy of the International Criminal Tribunal for Rwanda (ICTR) *Akayesu* case, in discussing rape and sexual violence as constitutive acts of genocide. While both the prosecution and Chamber refer to the rape of 'thousands of women', the reimagined decision renders visible the experience of girls, highlighting sections of the prosecution's application stating that 'girls as young as five ... were raped'.[32] Also discussed are the particular gender-specific impact on women and girls in society, with the gendered impact layered atop the harm done as a result of pre-existing structural inequalities and practices. In Darfur, that includes not only the physical and psychological damage, but particularly physical damage – including increased risk of fistula – in those who had previously been subjected to female genital mutilation.

As well as exploring the gendering of the third count of genocide, Judges Radhakrishnan and Shubin centre the gendered dimensions of evidencing genocidal intent, unexplored in the original decision. They note that judicial and non-judicial determinations of genocide have largely focused on intent to physically destroy as evidenced through mass killing. They posit that, considering the gendered underpinnings of the acts in question, equally relevant is the intent to biologically destroy, which aims at the target group's regenerative capacity and its ability to ensure long-term survival – and which has specific consequences for women and girls, who are perceived to be the main reproductive agents of the group, in the gendered role of bearers of life.[33]

While limited by the gender-blindness of the underpinning evidence, Judges Radhakrishnan and Shubin's reimagined decision underscores that female and male members of targeted groups, by the perpetrators' own design, experience genocide in distinct ways by reason of their gender. In particular, they successfully illuminate how genocidal violence directed at women and girls is fed by existing misogynistic attitudes in society, and the traumatic impacts are magnified by the financial, social, and cultural inequalities to which women and girls are subjected.

[31] *Ibid*, §§ 11, 13.
[32] *Ibid*, §§ 20, 22.
[33] *Ibid*, § 24.

Prosecutor v. Al Bashir, *Judgment in the Jordan Referral of the Al Bashir Appeal*

Judges Saumya Uma and Ramya Jawahar Kudekallu have handed down their reimagining of the Appeals Chamber's May 2019 judgment in the Jordan referral of the Al Bashir appeal.[34]

The original judgment addressed the question about the extent to which states are legally obligated to cooperate with the Court, in which the Appeals Chamber decided that Jordan, as a state party to the Rome Statute, had an obligation to arrest and surrender Mr Al Bashir, despite Sudan not being a state party to the Statute and despite Mr Al Bashir then holding the post of President of Sudan. The reimagined judgment focuses on the question of whether Jordan had failed to comply with its Rome Statute obligations, examining the issue of state cooperation and accountability from a feminist analytical perspective.

The original and the reimagined judgments share commonalities. Both confirm the Pre-Trial Chamber's decision, finding that Jordan had failed to comply with its obligations under the Statute by not executing the Court's request for the arrest of Mr Al Bashir and his surrender to the Court while he was on Jordanian territory on 29 March 2017.[35] In the underlying reasoning, both judgments concur that there is no customary law recognising head-of-state immunity before an international court, and such immunity cannot be claimed under Article 27(2) of the Rome Statute.[36]

Further, both judgments agree that parties to the Rome Statute are under an obligation to cooperate fully with the Court in accordance with the Statute, and that this obligation must be 'understood in the context of the Statute as a whole and bearing in mind *its object and purpose*'.[37] In this, the original judgment notes that the ICC was established to exercise jurisdiction 'over persons for the most serious crimes of international concern' and its state parties express their determination to 'put an end to impunity for the perpetrators of these crimes'.[38] The original judgment states: 'The obligation to cooperate with the Court reinforces the obligation *erga omnes* to prevent, investigate and punish crimes that shock the conscience of humanity, including in particular those under the jurisdiction of the Court and it is this *erga omnes* character that makes the obligation of States Parties to cooperate with the Court so fundamental.'[39]

Nevertheless, Judges Uma and Kudekallu's reimagined judgment explores, with greater sensitivity and nuance, both how state cooperation impacts on victim

34 *Prosecutor v. Al Bashir*, Judgment in the Jordan Referral of the Al Bashir Appeal (ICC-02/05-01/09 OA2), 6 May 2019 (hereafter Appeals Judgment – Jordan Appeal).

35 *Ibid*, § 215.

36 *Ibid*, §§ 102, 113.

37 *Ibid*, § 121.

38 *Ibid*.

39 *Ibid*, § 123.

communities, and specifically victims from marginalised communities including women, girls, and those belonging to sexual orientation and gender identity (SOGI) minorities. With great clarity, they emphasise how Jordan's breach of its obligation to cooperate with the Court in failing to arrest and surrender Mr Al Bashir also fails the victims of the alleged crimes, which include multiple war crimes and crimes against humanity as well as the crime of genocide – 'an undesirable outcome that is diametrically opposed to the objectives for which this Court was established'.[40]

In further contrast to the original judgment, Judges Uma and Kudekallu's reimagining explores the intrinsic interconnections between state cooperation with the ICC in arresting and surrendering a suspect to the Court, and ending impunity for ICC crimes, especially crimes of sexual and gender-based violence. As they note, a failure of states to cooperate opens up 'chasms in access to justice for victims', while assisting the accused to take refuge in other jurisdictions. The reimagined judgment further observes that Jordan has also fallen foul of its duty to discharge its state obligations under other conventions that it has ratified, including (but not limited to) the Genocide Convention and/or Torture Convention.

In contrast with the original judgment, Judges Uma and Kudekallu's feminist reimagining confronts the international legal community with the reality that a failure of a state party, here Jordan, to live up to its obligations to arrest and surrender Mr Al Bashir has profound implications for victims' access to justice.

Prosecutor v. Abd-Al-Rahman, *Decision on the Confirmation of Charges*

In this rewritten decision, Judges Lisa Davis and Marina Kumskova consider whether the Chamber had the evidence before it to request, under Article 61(7) of the Rome Statute, the Prosecutor to present evidence on the crime of gender persecution.

In the original Rahman Confirmation of Charges Decision, the Chamber found that the contextual elements of war crimes and crimes against humanity had been proven to the requisite standard.[41] Following an examination of the evidence put forward by the prosecution, and taking into account the submissions by the defence, Office for the Public Counsel for Victims, and legal representatives of victims, the Chamber confirmed the multiple counts of war crimes and crimes against humanity, including persecution as a crime against humanity.[42]

The charge of persecution concerned targeted attacks on persons in Kodoom, Bindi, and surrounding areas, the population of which were predominantly Fur and who were perceived as belonging to, or being associated with, or supporting the

40 Uma and Kudekallu, Reimagined Judgment, § X

41 Decision on the confirmation of charges against Ali Muhammad Ali Abd-Al-Rahman (Ali Kushayb) (ICC-02/05-01/20-433), 9 July 2021, available at www.icc-cpi.int/sites/default/files/CourtRecords/CR2021_10734.PDF, §§ 67–68.

42 *Ibid*, §§ 54–57.

rebel armed groups. The prosecution asserted that Mr Abd-Al-Rahman targeted these persons on political and ethnic grounds, severely depriving them of fundamental rights, including the rights to life, bodily integrity, private property, freedom of movement and residence, and not to be subjected to rape, torture, or cruel, inhumane, or degrading treatment.

In their reimagined decision on confirmation of charges in the Abd-Al-Rahman case, Judges Davis and Kumskova engage with the question of whether to confirm the charge of persecution on the ground of gender, under Article 7(1)(h) of the Statute. More specifically, they look at the question of whether, drawing from the facts as presented in the prosecution's submissions, the prosecution established substantial grounds to believe that Mr Abd-Al-Rahman committed the crime of gender persecution in Kodoom, Bindisi, and surrounding areas between 15 and 16 August 2003; in Mukjar and surrounding areas between the end of February 2004 and the beginning of March 2004; and in Deleig and surrounding areas between 5 and 7 March 2004.

Judges Davis and Kumskova's judgment explores the gendered dimensions of the attacks on persons from the Fur population, illuminating how the attacks were planned and committed against women and men, girls and boys in specific ways because of the gender roles they were perceived to inhabit. For example, the reimagined decision explores the targeted killing and torture of Fur men and older boys in the attacks on Mukjar and Deleig and highlights that the perpetrators were driven by the view of men as fighters and boys as revenge-seekers, based on entrenched perceptions of the biological and sociological roles of men and boys in that society. Analysing the evidence contained in the prosecution submissions with regard to the rape of Fur women and girls, the reimagined judgment explores the intersection of the perceived marginalised identities of the victims as black women, highlighting the perpetrator's use of forced nudity and often public rapes, as well as the import of the derogatory epithets by which the perpetrators referred to the women, notably as slaves.

The reimagined judgment delves deeper into the gendered design and impact of the crimes. The judges' analysis illuminates how the attacks on Fur men and boys draws from the understanding of males as protectors of the group, while attacks on women and girls pay heed to their role of holders of community honour – often defined in terms of socially enforced control over their sexuality. The attacks on Fur women, girls, men, and boys therefore not only serve to imprint the dominance of the perpetrator group, but also to break the will and destroy the social bonds within the Fur community.

The facts in the case render visible that targeting of the Fur lay at the intersection of race, gender, and political grounds. Indeed, that the underlying facts are present in the prosecution's submission – which is to say, they required no reimagining – underscores the urgent need for the feminist approach that Judges Davis and Kumskova model in their reimagining.

Prosecutor v. Abd-Al-Rahman, *Decision Establishing the Principles on Victims' Representation during the Confirmation of Charges Hearing*

Judge Anushka Sehmi's feminist reimagining of the 2021 Decision establishing the principles on victims' representation during the Confirmation of Charges Hearing in the Abd-Al-Rahman case makes up the fourth and final reimagining of the Darfur cases. The original decision centred on the way that victims from Sudan would participate, and be legally represented, in the Abd-Al-Rahman case.

Judge Sehmi rewrites this decision from a feminist perspective, looking at the importance of consulting with victims on their choice of legal representation. The reimagined decision focuses on what is meant by the need for victims' participation in proceedings to be 'meaningful' – long recognised in ICC jurisprudence – as opposed to 'purely symbolic'.[43] The single judge noted that such meaningful participation requires the implementation of strategies that aim at ensuring two-way communication between the affected communities and the Court, most appropriately via the mandates of the Public Information and Outreach Section (PIOS) and the Victims Participation and Reparations Section (VPRS).

The reimagined decision emphasises that the success of victim participation is profoundly dependent on proper outreach and public information activities directed towards victims,[44] and moves to explore the gendered implications of designing and conducting such outreach through an intersectional lens. This includes, necessarily Judge Sehmi asserts, proactive engagement with women, girls, and non-binary individuals who may qualify as victims in the Abd-Al-Rahman case. The reimagined decision reminds the international legal community that the violations committed in Darfur, and as alleged by the prosecution, were heavily gendered and exacerbated structural gender inequalities, rendering women and girls even more vulnerable to being the victims of sexual and gender-based crimes. In turn, women and girls suffered particularly physical, psychological, financial, and social traumatic impacts as a result of being the victims of alleged crimes, which magnified the entrenched pre-existing structural inequalities.

While the original decision treats victims as a monolithic group (though not always in agreement, at least as regards legal representation), Judge Sehmi takes care to embed an intersectional feminist approach, underscoring that while greater outreach is needed to ensure the meaningful participation of women and girls, strategies aimed at achieving this 'must allow for the full diversity of women, including those of different ethnicities, minority religious or ethnic groups, as well as those from rural or urban backgrounds'.[45] She further underscores the need for a

[43] Sehmi, Reimagined Decision, § 13.
[44] *Ibid*, § 19.
[45] *Ibid*, § 34.

specific strategy for outreach of child victims, who are so often overlooked in trials which evince an adult-centric understanding of violence and harm.[46]

Judge Sehmi illuminates how structural inequalities may limit the participation of marginalised groups, including women and girls, in the ICC proceedings – whether as a result of having more limited access to education and corresponding higher likelihood of illiteracy; being tasked with childcare; the stigma of sexual violence, with speaking out exacting high social costs; and living in a patriarchal context where men are assumed to be the ones interacting with authority, such as may be the perception of the ICC. The reimagined decision sets out clear practical steps that PIOS and VPRS should take to ensure meaningful gender-sensitive and inclusive participation in the Abd-Al-Rahman proceedings.

On victim representation, the reimagined decision tackles the widely recognised – but rarely officially discussed – matter of the Registry neither having an inclusive approach to obtaining the views of victims, expressly including those from marginalised communities, on their preferred legal representation nor tackling the lack of diversity within the pool of representation offered. Sehmi's single judge asserts the need for a more inclusive approach to recruiting victims' counsel and the importance, given the scale of sexual and gender-based crimes committed against women and girls in Darfur, of counsel having expertise in working with survivors of such crimes.[47]

This reimagined judgment in the Darfur cases underscores that a feminist approach needs not only to inform our understanding of the planning, commission, and impact of alleged crimes, but must flow through the operations of the Court if it is to carve a path to justice that leaves no victims in the shadows.

CONCLUSION: INCLUDING THOSE SO OFTEN OBSCURED IN THE PURSUIT OF JUSTICE

Early documentation of the violations committed in Darfur showed the urgent need for a feminist intersectional approach to the investigation, analysis, and prosecution of the alleged crimes and to understanding the context in which they were committed.

A troubling intersection of gender, race, and age was laid bare as early as the 2004 Human Rights Watch report, which included the testimony of an eighteen-year-old woman who recounted being assaulted by Janjaweed who inserted a knife in her vagina, saying, 'You get this because you are black'.[48] In its 2009 Request for Warrant in the Al Bashir case the prosecution asserted, 'Perpetrators often verbally

[46] *Ibid*, § 44.
[47] *Ibid*, § 57.
[48] HRW, *Darfur in Flames*, *supra* note 5, 29.

berated the women and girls, calling them slaves, telling them that they would now bear a "free" child, and asserting that they (the perpetrators) are wiping out the non-Arabs'.[49]

The interplay of violence committed against those with intersecting marginalised identities was most visible in the documentation and ensuing discussion of sexual violence committed against Darfurian women and girls. While this arguably shows the progress made on the documentation of sexual violence, it raised questions about the depth of the intersectional approach to investigating other crimes, and whether a feminist intersectional approach would also guide the Court's own operations, including its outreach to the affected communities.

One of the clear challenges for some authors, as judges, was that they – like the judges delivering the original judgments and decisions – were constrained by the evidence adduced and arguments made by the parties before them. In Judges Radhakrishnan and Shubin's analysis of genocide, for example, the blindness of the prosecution materials as to the multiple and potentially overlapping identities of the marginalised identities of those described as victims led to moving beyond the materials in front of the Chamber into documentation from non-governmental organisations. However, as Judges Davis and Kumskova show in their exploration of gender persecution, the foundations of a charge of gender persecution existed in the materials, obscured perhaps by the lesser seriousness with which the prosecution and the Chamber seem to approach gender-based targeting, notably, but not solely, of women and girls.

Judge Sehmi's reimagined decision, focusing on how to achieve meaningful victims' participation in the proceedings, shows a path very much open to, but not taken, in the original decision. Similarly, Judges Uma and Kudekallu's reimagined judgment underscores that relatively little effort could have been expended by the original Trial Chamber to open a richer discussion of how state cooperation impacts on victim communities.

A feminist intersectional approach can, indeed, be more radical – calling into question whether the International Criminal Court, and its founding Statute and Rules for Procedure and Evidence, are suitable instruments for achieving a more equal world, with full dignity for marginalised communities, including women and girls who constitute an opposed global majority. This is particularly when questions of criminal accountability, especially in common law systems, writ large focus very narrowly on the question of criminal liability of one of more accused and are without incentive to delve into the underlying multifaceted and often historical roots of why and how individuals cross the line into becoming perpetrators of mass atrocities, and the opacity through which the international justice experiment sees

[49] Al Bashir Warrant – First Decision, *supra* note 2, § 130.

(and does not see) the victims. Whether genuine progress towards a feminist permanent world court requires a more radical questioning and approach remains a core political and philosophical question with which international justice actors would do well to engage.

All four reimagined judgments and decisions, however, give weight to an arguably far more tantalising viewpoint: that much can be achieved within the current workings of the Court. Each underscores that a feminist intersectional approach could be implemented relatively easily to signal and effect the inclusion of marginalised – and often multiply marginalised – individuals and communities into the Court's work and processes, if there was greater understanding of and commitment to such an approach by those who people the Court, now and in the future.

To be sure, the calls for revolution sit on firm conceptual ground. The reimagined judgments in the Darfur cases, however, make a firm and optimistic case for how a feminist reality can root itself in the processes and outcomes of an evolving International Criminal Court.

10.2 GENOCIDE IN THE AL BASHIR WARRANT

Akila Radhakrishnan and Grant Shubin

In 2009, Pre-Trial Chamber I issued a Warrant of Arrest for Mr Omar Al Bashir, then President of Sudan, for two counts of war crimes and five counts of crimes against humanity.[50] The Chamber did not authorise charges for the crime of genocide; however, that aspect was later overturned by the Appeals Chamber citing an error of law.[51]

In their rewritten decision on the Warrant of Arrest, Akila Radhakrishnan and Grant Shubin apply the correct interpretation of genocide to the decision but engage more thoroughly with how gender was exploited in the alleged committal of the crime. They highlight the gender differentiation used by Government of Sudan forces by exploring the different methods applied to genders, from execution-style killing to rape and sexual slavery, cultural and social humiliation to confinement in unsafe and unhealthy conditions in the displacement camps. In giving voice to the victims, Radhakrishnan and Shubin give an expansive tour of the evidence which was available to the original Chamber and include the crime of genocide in the Warrant of Arrest against Omar Al Bashir.

[50] Warrant of Arrest, *Al Bashir* (ICC-02/05-01/09-3), Pre-Trial Chamber I, 4 March 2009.

[51] Judgment on the appeal of the Prosecutor against the 'Decision on the Prosecution's Application for a Warrant of Arrest against Omar Hassan Al Bashir', *Al Bashir* (ICC-02/05-01/09-73), Appeals Chamber, 3 February 2010.

No.: ICC-02/05-01/09
Date: 4 March 2009[52]

Original: English

PRE-TRIAL CHAMBER I(B)

Before: Judge Akila Radhakrishnan, Presiding Judge
Judge Grant Shubin

SITUATION IN DARFUR, SUDAN
IN THE CASE OF THE *PROSECUTOR v. OMAR HASSAN AHMAD AL BASHIR* (*'OMAR AL BASHIR'*)

Public Redacted Version

Decision on the Prosecution's Application for a Warrant of Arrest against Omar Hassan Ahmad Al Bashir

BACKGROUND

1. On 14 July 2004 the Prosecutor filed an application under Article 58 of the Rome Statute (the Statute) seeking a warrant for the arrest of Mr Omar Al Bashir (Bashir) for his alleged criminal responsibility in the commission of genocide, crimes against humanity, and war crimes against members of the Fur, Masalit, and Zaghawa groups in Darfur from 2003 to 14 July 2008.

WHETHER THE COMMON REQUIREMENTS UNDER ARTICLE 58(1) OF THE STATUTE FOR THE ISSUANCE OF A WARRANT OF ARREST HAVE BEEN MET

Whether There Are Reasonable Grounds to Believe That at least One of the Crimes within the Jurisdiction of the Court Referred to in the Prosecution Application Has Been Committed

2. The Court observes that under Article 58(1) of the Statute, it shall issue an arrest warrant if the existence of genocidal intent is only one of several reasonable conclusions available on the materials provided by the prosecution.

[52] Editors' note: Some of the sources cited in this judgment post-date 4 March 2009, but have been retained for pedagogical purposes with an asterisk (*) notation because they are relevant and valuable sources that might assist with subsequent genocide decisions by the ICC and other courts.

Genocide

3. The crime of genocide is defined in Article 6 of the Statute as follows:

> For the purpose of this Statute, 'genocide' means any of the following acts committed with intent to destroy, in whole or in part, a national, ethnical, racial or religious group, as such:
> (i) Killing members of the group;
> (ii) Causing serious bodily or mental harm to members of the group;
> (iii) Deliberately inflicting on the group conditions of life calculated to bring about its physical destruction in whole or in part;
> (iv) Imposing measures intended to prevent births within the group;
> (v) Forcibly transferring children of the group to another group.

4. The prosecution submits that there are reasonable grounds to believe that Omar Al Bashir bears criminal responsibility under Article 25(3)(a) of the Statute for the crime of genocide as a result of:

(i) the killing of members of the Fur, Masalit, and Zaghawa ethnic groups [Article 6(a) – Count 1];
(ii) causing serious bodily or mental harm to members of the Fur, Masalit, and Zaghawa ethnic groups [Article 6(b) – Count 2]; and
(iii) deliberately inflicting on the Fur, Masalit, and Zaghawa ethnic groups conditions of life calculated to bring about the groups' physical destruction [Article 6 (c) – Count 3].

5. Having gone through other elements of genocide elsewhere, the Court here wants to pay specific attention to the gendered manner of the commission of crimes alleged by the Prosecutor.

KILLING MEMBERS OF THE FUR, MASALIT, AND ZAGHAWA ETHNIC GROUPS (ARTICLE 6(A) – COUNT 1)

6. For the purposes of the *actus reus* of genocide by killing, the Court must be convinced that the prosecution has shown to the applicable standard that members of each target group were killed with the intention of destroying the group as such.[53]

7. Killing is often the privileged genocidal act, and consequently examinations of the commission of genocide largely revolve around the numbers killed. However, genocidal killing is in fact a highly gendered activity, with men and boys targeted for different reasons and killed in different ways than women and girls.

8. Males, particularly men and adolescent boys, are targeted for killing because they occupy gendered roles that genocide's perpetrators find particularly threatening: those of heads of households, community leaders, political figures,

[53] Article 6(a), Elements of Crimes; see Judgment, *Kajelijeli* (ICTR-98-44A-T), Trial Chamber II, 1 December 2003, § 813 (hereafter Kajelijeli Trial Judgment); Judgment, *Semanza* (ICTR-97-20-T), Trial Chamber III, 15 May 2003, § 319 (hereafter Semanza Trial Judgment).

religious authorities, guardians of the group's identity (particularly so in patrilineal cultures), fighters, and patriarchs. Where women and girls are targeted for genocidal killings, those killings – like the killing of men and boys – tend to reflect the gendered view of the role and uses of females in that society. Assaults on women and girls pay heed to their roles as mothers, wives, daughters, bearers of future life, keepers of the communities' and families' honour, and sources of labour within the home.

9. In genocides, men and boys are also more likely to die 'fast' (but not necessarily less horrific) deaths. They tend to be killed first and, usually, very shortly after being located or captured. These killings are usually presaged by the separation of men and older boys from the rest of the protected group.

10. The attacks against the Fur, Masalit, and Zaghawa groups bear this out, where attacks were characterised by indiscriminate killings, as well as specific targeting of Fur, Masalit, and Zaghawa men of military age. According to the United Nation's Commission of Inquiry on Darfur, witness testimonies reflected in the reports describe attackers with Kalashnikovs and other automatic weapons shooting either indiscriminately or targeting specific people, usually men of military age.[54] The massacre in Surra is a revealing example of the gendered manner in which Bashir's forces conducted their killings. There, at least 250 people were killed when Bashir's forces attacked in the early hours of the morning.[55] Initially, they fired mortars at unarmed civilians, shooting indiscriminately with rifles and machine guns.[56]

> They entered the homes and killed the men. They gathered the women in the mosque. There were around 10 men hidden with the women. They found those men and killed them inside the mosque. They forced women to take off their *maxi* (large piece of clothing covering the entire body) and if they found that they were holding their young sons under them, they would kill the boys.[57]

11. A similar gendered targeting is seen in the killings in Deleig, where Bashir's forces went from house to house looking for specific individuals, and arrested many men who were subsequently taken to the local police station.[58] The men were then separated into different groups and certain groups were placed on a truck and transported to the Garsila area.[59] The truck would come back empty and leave

[54] *Report of the International Commission of Inquiry on Darfur to the Secretary-General, Pursuant to Security Council Resolution 1564 (2004) of 18 September 2004*, UN Doc. S/2005/60, 1 February 2005, § 269 (hereafter UN COI Final Report).

[55] *Ibid*, § 272.

[56] *Ibid.*

[57] *Ibid*, § 272.

[58] *Ibid*, § 275.

[59] *Ibid.*

again with a new group of men.[60] Most of those taken away were executed.[61] In the end, more than 120 men were killed.[62]

12. The gendered undercurrent to the killings continued after the initial attacks into the context in which members of the Fur, Masalit, and Zaghawa were confined in squalid internally displaced persons (IDP) camps. According to one witness, 'Young girls can't leave the camp. We are scared to send them out. They rape them. We can't send the young men out because they will kill the men'.[63]

13. This gendered underpinning can also be seen in methods by which killings were carried out against male and female members of the target groups. As described above, in many cases Fur, Masalit, and Zaghawa men were killed by gunshot at the onset of, or during, an attack; women and girls on the other hand were often killed by sexual violence and rape.[64] For example, take the paradigmatic case in Arawala, where Bashir's forces captured and detained a group of women at the local military garrison.[65] Upon arrival at the garrison, the women were stripped naked and 'inspected' by a military commander.[66] 'The soldiers then raped the women continuously over several days. Three of the women died while they were in captivity.'[67]

14. In a particularly gruesome example of the convergence of gender killing, a Fur baby had also been killed and was lying on his back with his penis cut off and stuffed in his mouth.[68]

15. In sum, the alleged methods of killing tend to display not only the specific targeting of the Fur, Masalit, and Zaghawa groups on the part of Bashir's forces, but also a deeply engrained misogyny soaked with deeply gendered conceptions of dominance, power, and masculinity. Accordingly, the Court finds that there is a reasonable basis to believe that genocidal acts of killing were committed by Bashir's forces.

CAUSING SERIOUS BODILY OR MENTAL HARM TO MEMBERS OF THE FUR, MASALIT, AND ZAGHAWA ETHNIC GROUPS (ARTICLE 6(B) – COUNT 2)

16. For the purposes of the *actus reus* of genocide by causing serious bodily and/or mental harm to members of each target group, the Court must be convinced that the Prosecution has shown to the applicable standard that serious bodily or mental harm was inflicted on members of the target groups with the intention of destroying

60 *Ibid.*
61 *Ibid.*
62 *Ibid.*
63 Prosecutor's Application under Article 58 (ICC-02/05-157-AnxA), § 204, 14 July 2008 (hereafter Prosecutor's Request for Warrant).
64 Notably, in many attacks, women and girls were also victims of killings by gunshot and indiscriminate motor fire and bombings.
65 Prosecutor's Request for Warrant, *supra* note 63, § 219.
66 *Ibid*, § 219.
67 Ibid, § 219.
68 Ibid, § 113.

the groups as such.[69] Serious bodily or mental harm 'must involve harm that goes beyond temporary unhappiness, embarrassment or humiliation. It must be harm that results in a grave and long-term disadvantage to a person's ability to lead a normal and constructive life'.[70]

17. This second prohibited act, when committed with the requisite intent, can encompass a wide range of non-fatal genocidal acts. The International Criminal Tribunal for Rwanda (ICTR) and International Criminal Tribunal for former Yugoslavia (ICTY) have held that rape and sexual violence; torture and other cruel, inhuman, or degrading treatment or punishment; and deportation and forcible transfer are among the acts that may cause serious bodily or mental harm.[71] This understanding has been confirmed by the International Court of Justice (ICJ).[72]

Sexual Violence in Darfur

18. Sexual violence, when employed as a genocidal strategy, aims to destroy the victim as an incremental step to annihilating the group, as famously confirmed in the ICTR's *Akayesu* case.[73] It is simultaneously an assault on the victim and on the existence, identity, and cohesiveness of the group.

19. Most genocidal campaigns have explicitly and implicitly sanctioned sexual violence against women and girls of the target group. This includes, for example, the sexual enslavement of Armenian women and girls by the Ottoman Turks[74] – echoes

[69] Article 6(b), Elements of Crimes. See Semanza Trial Judgment, *supra* note 53, § 323; see also Judgment, *Musema* (ICTR-96-13-T), Trial Chamber, 27 January 2000, § 165 (hereafter Musema Trial Judgment); Judgment, *Rutaganda* (ICTR-96-3), Trial Chamber, 6 December 1999, § 60 (hereafter Rutaganda Trial Judgment); Judgment, *Akayesu* (ICTR-96-4-T), Trial Chamber, 2 September 1998, § 521 (hereafter Akayesu Trial Judgment).

[70] Judgment, *Krstić* (IT-98-33), Trial Chamber, 20 December 2004, § 513 (hereafter Krstić Trial Judgment).

[71] Semanza Trial Judgment, *supra* note 53, § 320; Judgment, *Ntagerura* (ICTR-99-46-T), Trial Chamber, 24 February 2004, § 664 (hereafter Ntagerura Trial Judgment); Akayesu Trial Judgment, *supra* note 69, §§ 731–732; Judgment, *Stakic* (IT-97-24-T), Trial Chamber, 31 July 2003, § 516 (hereafter Stakic Trial Judgment).

[72] *Case Concerning the Application of the Convention on the Prevention and Punishment of the Crime of Genocide (Bosnia and Herzegovina v. Serbia and Montenegro)*, judgment of 26 February 2007, at 300 (hereafter Bosnia and Herzegovina v. Serbia and Montenegro Judgment).

[73] Akayesu Trial Judgment, *supra* note 69, § 731: 'Rapes resulted in physical and psychological destruction of Tutsi women, their families and their communities. Sexual violence was an integral part of the process of destruction, specifically targeting Tutsi women and specifically contributing to their destruction and to the destruction of the Tutsi group as a whole'; § 732: 'Sexual violence was a step in the process of destruction of the Tutsi group – the destruction of the spirit, of the will to live, and of life itself'; see also Judgment, **Karemera* (ICTR-98-44-T), Trial Chamber, 2 February 2012, §§ 1665–1668 (hereafter Karemera Trial Judgment).

[74] *A. Holslag, 'Exposed Bodies: A Conceptual Approach to Sexual Violence during the Armenian Genocide' in E. Randall (ed.), *Genocide and Gender in the Twentieth Century: A Comparative Survey* (London: Bloomsbury Academic, 2015) 97–106, at 97–99.

of which reverberate in Rwanda where an estimated 100,000–250,000 women and girls were raped in three months.[75]

20. Violence in Darfur fits these patterns. Bashir's forces conducted a campaign of systematic rape of women and girls, with the frequent sexual mutilation of victims. Countless reports and testimonies indicate thousands of women and girls belonging to the target groups were raped systematically and continuously for five years.[76] Girls as young as five and women as old as seventy were raped.[77] Gang rape was a distinctive and pronounced feature of the attacks by Bashir's forces.[78]

21. From the numerous cases of rape and sexual violence allegedly committed by Bashir's forces against Fur, Masalit, and Zaghawa women and girls submitted to and reviewed by the court, a distinctive pattern emerged. First, during attacks on villages there were deliberate aggressions and violence against women and girls, including gang rapes.[79] Second, women and girls were abducted, held in confinement for several days, and repeatedly raped.[80] Third, rape and other forms of sexual violence continued during flight and subsequent displacement, including when women left towns and displaced persons' sites to collect wood or water or perform other essential activities.[81] As to this last stage – rape and sexual violence in the context of displacement – one witness testified:

> When we see them [Bashir's forces], we run. Some of us succeed in getting away, and some are caught and taken to be raped – gang-raped. Maybe around 20 men rape one woman [...] These things are normal for us here in Darfur. These things happen all the time. I have seen rapes too. It does not matter who sees them raping the women – they don't care. They rape women in front of their mothers and fathers.[82]

22. As just one example, following the joint attacks by Bashir's forces in the surrounding area, up to 30,000 people were confined in Kailek, southern Darfur, for about fifty days.[83] Women and children were separated from the men, physically confined, and eventually transported to a new location.[84] Here, the women and girls, including some as young as ten years old, were gang raped for protracted periods of time.[85]

[75] See 'Outreach Programme on the 1994 Genocide against the Tutsi in Rwanda and the United Nations', available at www.un.org/en/preventgenocide/rwanda/supporting-survivors.shtml.

[76] Prosecutor's Request for Warrant, *supra* note 63, § 121.

[77] *Ibid*, § 121.

[78] *Ibid*, § 121.

[79] UN COI Final Report, *supra* note 54, § 334.

[80] *Ibid*, § 334.

[81] *Ibid*, § 334.

[82] Prosecutor's Request for Warrant, *supra* note 63, § 24.

[83] UN COI Final Report, *supra* note 54, § 343.

[84] *Ibid*, § 343.

[85] *Ibid*, § 343.

23. Cases of rape and sexual violence are often underreported and, as previous prosecutions have demonstrated, it is difficult to assess a total number of victims.[86] Notably, however, 2.5 years after Bashir's forces began their campaign against the Fur, Masalit, and Zaghawa groups, sources in Darfur were documenting 'new cases of rape on a weekly basis, perpetrated by armed men alleged to be members of the Government armed forces, law enforcement agencies and Janjaweed'.[87]

24. While rape per se meets the severity threshold of, indeed beyond, 'serious bodily or mental harm',[88] the Court will nevertheless take note of the particular bodily and psychological damage suffered by Fur, Masalit, and Zaghawa women and girls. The prevalence of female genital mutilation (FGM) in Darfur exacerbated the physical damage inflicted during rape, in particular increased incidence of fistula.[89] According to one witness interviewed by the prosecution, for 'virgins who had FGM and were sexually assaulted, the impact was particularly painful and debilitating'.[90] A health specialist treating victims in Darfur testified that most of the 'victims exhibited symptoms of post-traumatic stress disorder, including extreme shame, grief, hopelessness, anger and rage, flashbacks, nightmares, and inability to interpret their environment'.[91] These symptoms have been aggravated by the inability to resort to state authorities for help. One victim testified, 'those who rape you wear fatigues and those who protect you wear fatigues. We don't know any more who to run from and who to run to'.[92]

Torture and Other Cruel, Inhuman, or Degrading Treatment in Darfur

25. Torture and other cruel, inhuman, or degrading treatment can amount to genocidal acts. Torture occurs when someone deliberately causes very serious and cruel physical or mental suffering to another person. This encompasses a wider range of conduct including, for example, beatings, blinding, and mutilations. It also includes acts of sexual violence.[93] The findings cited above and describing gang

[86] Prosecutor's Request for Warrant, *supra* note 63, § 126.

[87] *Ibid*, § 124.

[88] Judgment, *Kunarac, Kovac and Vukovic* (IT-96-23/1-A), Appeals Chamber, 12 June 2001, §§ 150–151 (hereafter Kunarac, Kovac and Vukovic Appeal Judgment); see also Judgment, *Delalić et al.* (IT-96-21-T), Trial Chamber, 16 November 1998, § 480 (hereafter Delalić et al. Trial Judgment); Judgment, *Furundžija* (IT-97-17/1-A), Appeals Chamber, 21 July 2000, § 114 (hereafter Furundžija Appeal Judgment).

[89] Prosecutor's Request for Warrant, *supra* note 63, § 129.

[90] *Ibid*, § 129.

[91] *Ibid*, § 25.

[92] *Ibid*, § 27.

[93] Kunarac, Kovac and Vukovic Appeal Judgment, *supra* note 88, § 150; Judgment, *Mucić* (IT-96-21-T), Trial Chamber, 16 November 1998, §§ 493, 495 (hereafter Mucić Trial Judgment); Akayesu Trial Judgment, *supra* note 69, § 731; see also **Report of the Independent International Commission of Inquiry on the Syrian Arab Republic, Pursuant to Human Rights Council Resolutions 43/28 and 45/21 of 19 June 2020*, UN Doc. A/HRC/46/54, 21 January 2021, § 103 'sexual and physical violence, together with the severe mental trauma, which Yazidi women

rapes, rapes, and sexual slavery support a finding that these acts also constitute acts of torture and cruel, inhuman, or degrading treatment against the Fur, Masalit, and Zaghawa groups.

26. Additionally, being forced to witness loved ones or others being killed or ill-treated can in and of itself constitute cruel, inhuman, or degrading treatment.[94] In Darfur, such forced witnessing took particularly gendered hues when Bashir's forces made mothers witness the murder of their children. According to the UN Commission of Inquiry for Darfur, 'extreme mental torture was inflicted on many mothers who saw their children burn alive after they were snatched from their arms by the Janjaweed and thrown into the fire'.[95] In one gruesome instance, a mother was repeatedly raped in the vicinity of her baby who cried for three straight days. On the third day a member of Bashir's forces 'grabbed the baby, cut his throat and smashed his head on the floor'.[96]

27. Finally, concerning degrading treatment, international tribunals have qualified forced public nudity as constituting such treatment.[97] In Darfur, stripping women of their clothes and the use of derogatory language as a means of humiliation and degradation were nearly ubiquitous characteristic in Bashir's forces' abductions and subsequent rape.[98]

28. Accordingly, and in light of all of the foregoing, the Court finds adequate reason to believe that in perpetrating widespread and brutal sexual violence and torture and other cruel, inhuman, and degrading treatment against the Fur, Masalit, and Zaghawa groups, the *actus reus* of the second act of genocide is satisfied.

DELIBERATELY INFLICTING ON THE FUR, MASALIT, AND ZAGHAWA ETHNIC GROUPS CONDITIONS OF LIFE CALCULATED TO BRING ABOUT THE GROUPS' PHYSICAL DESTRUCTION (ARTICLE 6(C) – COUNT 3)

29. For the purposes of the *actus reus* of genocide by deliberately inflicting conditions of life calculated to bring about the group's physical destruction, the Court must be convinced that the prosecution has shown to the applicable standard that Bashir's forces inflicted on the Fur, Masalit, and Zaghawa groups methods of destruction by which the perpetrator does not immediately kill the members of the

and girls over the age of nine experience at the hands of ISIS rises to the level of torture, causing them serious physical and psychological harm'.

94 See Inter-American Commission on Human Rights, *Case 11.520 (Mexico)*, Report, 1998, § 76; Inter-American Court of Human Rights, *Caesar v. Trinidad and Tobago*, Judgment, 2005, § 78; ICRC, Commentary on the First Geneva Convention: Convention (I) for the Amelioration of the Condition of the Wounded and Sick in Armed Forces in the Field, 2nd ed., 2016, § 622.

95 UN COI Final Report, *supra* note 54, § 365.

96 Prosecutor's Request for Warrant, *supra* note 63, § 139.

97 Kunarac, Kovac and Vukovic Trial Judgment, *supra* note 88, §§ 766–774.

98 UN COI Final Report, *supra* note 54, § 366.

group, but which, ultimately, seek their physical destruction.[99] Such methods include, inter alia, 'subjecting the group to a subsistence diet; failing to provide adequate medical care; systematically expelling members of the group from their homes; and generally creating circumstances that would lead to a slow death such as the lack of proper food, water, shelter, clothing, sanitation, or subjecting members of the group to excessive work or physical exertion'.[100]

30. The ICTR Trial Chamber in the *Kayishema* case found that rape could be a method of imposing conditions of life that do not 'lead immediately to the death of members of the group'.[101] Moreover, in the ICJ's 2015 judgment in *Croatia v. Serbia*, the Court indicated that rape could fall within Article II(c) of the Genocide Convention but noted that in that particular case, 'it has not been shown that these occurrences [of rape] were on such a scale to have amounted also to inflicting conditions of life on the group that were capable of bringing about its physical destruction in whole or in part'.[102]

31. With the backdrop of other measures imposed by Bashir's forces to physically destroy the Fur, Masalit, and Zaghawa groups (addressed elsewhere in this decision) – including destroying food, wells, and water-pumping machines, shelter, crops and livestock, physical structures capable of sustaining life or commerce, and denying access to humanitarian relief – the characteristics of Bashir's forces' rape in the context of displacement can be viewed as conditions of life calculated to physically destroy the Fur, Masalit, and Zaghawa groups.

32. As a preliminary matter, the displacement of a very large part of the population of Darfur is a fact beyond dispute. Data from refugee camps in Chad and internally displaced persons' camps within Darfur confirm that virtually the entire population of the target groups has been forcibly displaced.[103]

33. Within the camps, the Fur, Masalit, and Zaghawa continued to be subjected to attacks. There was a complete absence of meaningful government aid, and Bashir's forces hindered other efforts to bring humanitarian aid to the target groups. Sudan's Ministry of Humanitarian Affairs works in close association with the

99 Akayesu Trial Judgment, *supra* note 69, §§ 505–506.

100 Judgment, **Tolimir* (IT-05-88/2-A), Trial Chamber, 8 April 2015, §§ 225–226; See also Akayesu Trial Judgment, *supra* note 69, § 506. This definition has been affirmed in the Rutaganda Trial Judgment, *supra* note 69, § 52; Musema Trial Judgment, *supra* note 69, § 157; Stakić Trial Judgment, *supra* note 71, § 517. The ICC Elements of Crimes defines 'conditions of life' as including, but not necessarily restricted to, 'deliberate deprivation of resources indispensable for survival, such as food or medical services, or systematic expulsion from homes', Article 6, Elements of Crimes.

101 Judgment, *Kayishema* (ICTR-95-1-T), Trial Chamber, 21 May 1999, § 116, where ICTR Trial Chamber determined that the infliction of rape was also a method of destruction that does not 'lead immediately to the death of members of the group'.

102 **Case Concerning the Application of the Convention on the Prevention and Punishment of the Crime of Genocide (Croatia v. Serbia)*, judgment of 3 February 2015, at 362–364 (hereafter Croatia v. Serbia Judgment).

103 Prosecutor's Request for Warrant, *supra* note 63, §§ 19–22.

government's intelligence and security apparatus and blocked the publication of nutrition surveys, delayed the delivery of aid, expelled relief staff, denied visas and travel permits, and imposed unnecessary bureaucratic requirements on aid workers.[104]

34. Importantly, basic amenities like food, water, and firewood were located far from where IDPs were confined. This meant that girls and women had to leave the borders of their camps to collect these essential-for-life resources (because they were less likely to be killed than men or boys), and in the process traverse areas patrolled by Bashir's forces and local militias that Bashir allegedly recruited, armed, and purposefully failed to disarm, which are stationed in the vicinity of the camp.

35. As noted above, rape and other forms of sexual violence were widely reported during these junctures. That is, for more than five years Fur, Masalit, and Zaghawa women and girls were raped continuously and systematically when they ventured from the relative, if still limited, security of IDP camps to collect essentials for life (which the Court notes is a highly gendered responsibility).[105]

36. A Masalit woman from Habila, West Darfur testified:

> Sometimes we go to collect grass, to sell in the market to buy things we need for our children. They [the Janjaweed] send two people, and the rest of them set up an ambush. They stop their car in a khor or a hill. Some of them act as guards. The two people then approach us and, when we see them, we run. Some of us succeed in getting away, and some are caught and taken to be raped – gang-raped. Maybe around twenty men rape one woman.[106]

37. Rapes of women and girls venturing outside displaced person locations for food, water, firewood, or the market to sell goods for their families have reportedly occurred in the Abu Shouk and Kassab camps in northern Darfur, the Ardamata, Azeoni, Garsila, Krinding, Magarsa, Masteri, Mornei, Mukjar, Riyadh, and Sisi camps in western Darfur, and the Al Jeer, Derej, Kalma, Kass, and Otash camps in southern Darfur, among others.[107] Abductions and subsequent sexual slavery were also reported to occur on the borders of the IDP camps.[108]

38. A health specialist treating IDPs in Darfur testified that many of the girls who had been raped when they went to get firewood outside IDP camps were repeatedly retraumatised because they had no choice but to revisit the places where they had been raped.[109] According to this witness, the absence of any mental health or

[104] *Ibid*, § 34.
[105] *Ibid*, § 24.
[106] *Ibid*, § 145.
[107] UN COI Final Report, *supra* note 54, § 346.
[108] *Ibid*, § 342.
[109] Prosecutor's Request for Warrant, *supra* note 63, § 25.

psychosocial support services in the camp was an exacerbating factor that was liable to prolong or worsen the suffering of the victims.[110]

39. Cases of rape by Bashir's forces surrounding IDP camps instilled fear among women and girls of the target groups, and led to their virtual confinement inside those sites.[111] In some cases, women and girl IDPs belonging to the target groups were unable to move even a few metres from their camp for fear of being raped.[112]

40. According to one witness, residents of the camps are afraid to send men out of the camps for fear of death, and afraid to send women and girls out of the camps for fear of rape.[113] Another witness shared similar experiences: 'We were afraid to use the toilet at night because we were surrounded by the attackers, and they were on the look-out for women to rape.'[114] The impact of this sexual violence was amplified by the fact that women and their families depended on the collection of firewood for their livelihood and survival.[115]

41. It is here where Bashir's forces' rape and sexual violence can be viewed as a condition of life calculated to physically destroy the Fur, Masalit, and Zaghawa groups. The Court is satisfied that by forcing the groups from their homes, confining them to squalid IDP camps, limiting the ingress of essential humanitarian supplies, and then raping the women and girls who are then forced to leave the camps to gather essentials for survival, thereby inflicting massive trauma that in many cases rendered victims unable to leave the camps, the natural and foreseeable outcome of which would be the slow physical destruction of all of the camp's residents, Bashir's forces can reasonably be seen to have committed the third prohibited genocidal act.

INTENT TO DESTROY

42. In order to support the issuance of a warrant, the Court must be satisfied that there are reasonable grounds to believe that the above-alleged genocidal acts occurred with the intent to destroy the Fur, Masalit, or Zaghawa groups, in whole or in part, as such. This means that in order to constitute genocide, 'acts must have been committed against one or more persons because such person or persons were members of a specific group, and specifically, because of their membership in this group'.[116] Thus, the victim is targeted not because of their individual identity, but because of their being a member of a national, ethnic, racial, or religious group.

43. Because direct evidence of the special intent to destroy is highly uncommon, courts have inferred the intent to destroy from defendants' conduct, including their statements, as well as 'deeds and utterances considered together, as well as from the

110 *Ibid*, § 132.
111 UN COI Final Report, *supra* note 54, § 347.
112 *Ibid*, § 396.
113 Prosecutor's Request for Warrant, *supra* note 63, § 204.
114 UN COI Final Report, *supra* note 54, § 344.
115 *Ibid*, § 346.
116 Rutaganda Trial Judgment, *supra* note 69, § 60.

general context of the perpetration of other culpable acts systematically directed against the same group'.[117] Relevant conduct includes the physical targeting of the group and/or their property, the use of derogatory language towards members of the targeted group, and methodological planning.[118] The scale of atrocities committed, their general nature, and the fact of deliberately and systematically targeting victims on account of their membership in a particular group, while excluding members of other groups, are other factors from which one can infer genocidal intent.[119]

44. The concept of 'destruction' refers to both physical and biological destruction.[120] To date, judicial and non-judicial determinations of genocide have largely focused on physical destruction through mass killing. However, it should be noted, considering the gendered underpinnings of the acts in question, that equally relevant is the intent to biologically destroy, which aims at the target group's regenerative capacity and its ability to ensure long-term survival.[121] The Genocide Convention itself, as well as the decisions of the ICTY have consistently confirmed that acts intending to bring about biological destruction do fall under its ambit.[122]

45. The intent must be to physically or biologically destroy a protected group in whole or in part. Concerning what constitutes 'a part' of the protected group, the ICTY and ICTR have made clear that the intended destruction must refer at least to a 'substantial part' of the group.[123] While there is no specific threshold or formula for understanding substantiality, courts have frequently looked to three sets of factors: numbers, function, and geography.[124] Notably, the ICTY's *Krstic* appeals chamber found that '[t]hese considerations, of course, are neither exhaustive nor dispositive. They are only useful guidelines. The applicability of these factors, as well as their relative weight, will vary depending on the circumstances of a particular case'.[125]

[117] Judgment, *Gacumbitsi* (ICTR-2001-64-T), Trial Chamber, 17 June 2004, § 252.

[118] Kayishema Trial Judgment, *supra* note 102, § 93.

[119] Akayesu Trial Judgment, *supra* note 69, § 523; Kajelijeli Trial Judgment, *supra* note 53, §§ 804–805.

[120] See for example Krstić Trial Judgment, *supra* note 70, § 580 (affirmed in Krstić Appeals Judgment (IT-98-33-A), Appeals Chamber, 19 April 2004, § 25); Croatia v. Serbia Judgment, *supra* note 102, at 136.

[121] Croatia v. Serbia Judgment, *supra* note 102, at 136: 'It was accordingly decided to limit the scope of the Convention to the physical or biological destruction of the group . . . [re: act e] this can also entail the intent to destroy the group physically, in whole or in part, since it can have consequences for the group's capacity to renew itself, and hence to ensure its long-term survival.' See also S. Ashraph, 'Beyond Killing: Gender, Genocide, & Obligations under International Law', Global Justice Center (2018), available at www.globaljusticecenter.net/files/Gender-and-Genocide-Whitepaper-FINAL.pdf, at 32–33.

[122] See for example Krstić Trial Judgment, *supra* note 70, § 580 (affirmed in Krstić Appeals Judgment, § 25); Croatia v. Serbia Judgment, *supra* note 102, at 136.

[123] See for example Krstić Appeals Judgment, *supra* note 121, § 12; Bagilishema Trial Judgment (ICTR-95-1A-T), Trial Chamber I, 7 June 2001, § 64; Popović Trial Judgment (IT-05-88-T), Trial Chamber II, 10 June 2010, § 831. See also Bosnia and Herzegovina v. Serbia and Montenegro Judgment, *supra* note 72, at 198.

[124] Krstic Appeals Judgment, *supra* note 121, §§ 12–13.

[125] *Ibid*, § 14.

This view has also been endorsed by the ICJ in the *Bosnia* case: 'Much will depend on the Court's assessment of those and all other relevant factors in any particular case.'[126] Building on this analysis and giving priority to the numeric requirement, the ICJ in the *Croatia* case further noted that 'in evaluating whether the allegedly targeted part of a protected group is substantial in relation to the overall group, the Court will take into account the quantitative element as well as evidence regarding the geographic location and prominence of the allegedly targeted part of the group'.[127]

46. While the numerical understanding of substantiality has often been the focus,[128] geography and function can be highly illustrative of substantiality.[129] For example, in determining substantiality on the basis of prominence of the targeted part of the group, the *Krstic* court looked at whether the targeted members of the group were essential to the group's survival or emblematic of the overall group.[130]

47. Indeed, in the case of the Fur, Masalit, and Zaghawa groups, an analysis looking at the intersections of these three factors, in particular through the lens of the widespread perpetration of sexual violence and an intent to destroy, leads to a reasonable basis to believe Bashir and his forces were operating with genocidal intent.

48. An analysis of these three factors weighing the presence of whether a substantial part of the group was targeted for biological destruction would be incomplete without special consideration of the manner and means by which Bashir's forces sought to destroy different members of the Fur, Masalit, and Zaghawa groups. This necessarily includes taking into consideration the gendered reasons the forces chose certain types of violence for certain members of these groups. Under this light, the forces' intent to biologically destroy the Fur, Masalit, and Zaghawa groups can be seen through the (1) geographical confinement to IDP camps and subsequent (2) large number of brutal rapes against (3) women and girls – members of the groups charged with ensuring the groups' regeneration, through obtaining essentials for life as well as through reproduction.

126 Bosnia and Herzegovina v. Serbia and Montenegro Judgment, *supra* note 72, at 201.

127 Croatia v. Serbia Judgment, *supra* note 102, at 142.

128 See for example: **Case Concerning the Application of the Convention on the Prevention and Punishment of the Crime of Genocide (Gambia v. Myanmar)*, verbatim record of 11 December 2019, at 47, where Counsel for Myanmar asserted with respect to arguments on the intent to destroy that 'does the application specify the number of deaths, the total number of deaths, and compare this with the size of the population that was allegedly attacked'.

129 Bosnia and Herzegovina v. Serbia and Montenegro Judgment, *supra* note 72, at 198; Croatia v. Serbia Judgment, *supra* note 102, at 142; Krstic Appeals Judgment, § 12; Jelisić Trial Judgment (IT-95-10-T), Trial Chamber, 14 December 1999, § 82: '[Genocidal intent] may also consist of the desired destruction of a more limited number of persons selected for the impact that their disappearance would have upon the survival of the group as such. This would then constitute an intention to destroy the group "selectively".'

130 Krstic Appeals Judgment, *supra* note 121, § 12.

49. Taking these factors one by one to then look at them in conjunction, the context of confinement is a highly probative geographical factor. The scale and intensity of attacks on Fur, Masalit, and Zaghawa villages can be viewed as a push factor forcing surviving members of the group into enclosed and squalid conditions within IDP camps devoid of essentials for survival – in effect creating a siege environment where commerce stalled, resupply was forbidden, and resources dwindled.

50. These dire conditions had the highly predictable effect of forcing women and girls to venture outside the confines of the camps to acquire essentials. As noted above, it was the women who left the camps because of their higher likelihood of survival, and the gendered roles ascribed to them. But while women and girls might survive (not be killed) by Bashir's forces outside the camps, they were often raped – which implicates the second factor: the numerical assessment.

51. Rape and other forms of sexual violence in atrocity situations are significantly underreported, owing to the stigma often imposed on survivors. This is no less true in Darfur than anywhere else with evidence of sexual violence of this scale. Additional factors leading to the impossibility of definitively stating a specific quantitative amount relate to the Government of Sudan's refusal to allow humanitarian actors to access the IDP camps, as well as the general denial of the rape and sexual violence occurring in Darfur.[131] However, despite the inability to authoritatively state a specific number, evidence supports the conclusion that many, many thousands of women and girls were raped by Bashir's forces in the context of their confinement. This conclusion is all the more evident when it is recalled that it has been widely reported that systematic rape in the context of confinement occurred in Darfur for more than five years, that Bashir's forces allegedly only raped women and girls belonging to African tribes in Darfur (that is, they did not rape Arab women in Darfur),[132] and that there were roughly 2.5 million people living in IDP camps at the relevant time, including significant portions of the protected groups.[133]

52. But a genocidal intent analysis should not be so two-dimensional as to only look at *what numbers* of people were targeted for destruction and *where*. The Court is also compelled to look at what *function* these targeted persons served in the targeted group. In the case of the Fur, Masalit, and Zaghawa women and girls, these members of the groups were serving two essential functions for the groups' continued biological survival.

53. Firstly, and as noted above in the section on the imposition of measures calculated to physically destroy the group, Fur, Masalit, and Zaghawa women and girls were responsible for leaving the relative safety of the IDP camps in efforts to

[131] See Prosecutor's Request for Warrant, *supra* note 63, § 396: 'On 19 March 2007, speaking on the issue of rapes, he said that "It is not in the Sudanese culture or people of Darfur to rape. It doesn't exist. We don't have it".' Al Bashir also insisted that 99 per cent of alleged cases of rape are fabricated in order to place blame on the government.

[132] UN COI Final Report, *supra* note 54, § 221.

[133] Prosecutor's Request for Warrant, *supra* note 63, §§ 23, 24, 34.

obtain essentials for their families. It was on these excursions that they were raped and abducted. Report after report makes clear that Fur, Masalit, and Zaghawa women and girls were raped and abducted when they went to fetch water, when they went to gather firewood for cooking, when they went into towns to attempt to sell items to buy medicine for their families. By raping and abducting into sexual slavery the members of the groups performing these absolutely essential functions, Bashir's forces were creating massive disincentives for these women and girls to continue performing these tasks, to continue exposing themselves to the risks of repeated and brutal rape and sexual violence.

54. In so doing, Bashir's forces created an environment where the Fur, Masalit, and Zaghawa groups were deprived of essentials, which would foreseeably lead to their eventual death and physical destruction. Thus, there is a reasonable basis to believe that in confining large portions of the Fur, Masalit, and Zaghawa groups to IDP camps, then subjecting those responsible for day-to-day survival to brutal sexual violence and sexual slavery, essentially guaranteeing these women and girls would stop leaving the camps and therefore stop obtaining essentials for the groups, that Bashir's forces were acting with the intent to physically destroy the groups.

55. But these day-to-day tasks were not the only functions the Fur, Masalit, and Zaghawa women and girls performed. The sexual violence against them must also be seen against the backdrop of the broader social context in which they lived. That is, as a means of destroying the victim group, sexual violence has been particularly effective when employed in more strongly patriarchal cultures where the protection of female members of the group is believed to be the ultimate responsibility of their male relatives.

56. In this way, sexual violence against a group's female members is also often perpetrated and understood as a means of deliberate attack on the group's men, or more specifically on the gender roles that men are expected to play. Where men are expected to act as protectors of their female relatives and the female members of their particular group more generally, they may interpret the rape of 'their' women as evidence of their own powerlessness, and thus as a cogent assault on their identity as men.[134]

57. This is particularly apparent when perpetrators commit rapes of women and girls publicly, as occurred in Darfur. Rapes were often committed in front of others, including husbands, fathers, mothers, and children of the victims, who were forced to watch and prevented from intervening, amplifying the humiliation wrought on all parties.[135] These rapes are reported as having been inflicted upon a wide age range, from girls under ten to women of seventy or older.[136]

134 S. Ashraph, 'Acts of Annihilation: Understanding the Role of Gender in the Crime of Genocide', *The Cairo Review of Global Affairs* (2004), available at www.thecairoreview.com/essays/gender-and-genocide/, at 65.

135 T. Gingerich and J. Leaning, 'The Use of Rape as a Weapon of War in the Conflict in Darfur, Sudan' (US Agency for International Development/OTI, 2004) 1–56, at 15, 18.

136 *Ibid*, at 15.

58. Moreover, rapes and episodes of sexual violence were extremely brutal. According to a report prepared by Harvard University's School of Public Health, Bashir's forces 'engaged in vaginal and anal penetration, including penetration with objects. In the course of raping women, the assailants also inflicted beatings, cutting them with knives on the legs in a method similar to that used for branding slaves, and mutilate them sexually'.[137] Additionally, perpetrators often verbally berated the women and girls, 'calling them slaves, telling them that they would now bear a "free" child, and asserting that they (the perpetrators) are wiping out the non-Arabs'.[138]

59. This system and method of rape left an enduring mark on the groups' social fabric. Individuals, families, and the wider Fur, Masalit, and Zaghawa communities were highly traumatised by the systematic and brutal sexual violence they suffered and witnessed. This trauma carries with it gendered implications.

60. In contexts where women and girls are held up as repositories of the family's honour, such as in the Fur, Masalit, and Zaghawa communities, female survivors of sexual violence are more likely to be cast out by their own community, left unable to marry, abandoned by their husbands. For example, one Zaghawa witness interviewed by the prosecution stated: '[I]n my community sexual violence is emotionally shattering. … The impact of rape and sexual violence on the victims is such that those who are not married would have difficulty finding a husband, and the people look at [a rape victim] as though she has a terminal disability.'[139] Another witness testified, 'in this society if you rape one woman, you have raped the entire tribe'.[140]

61. These consequences break down the bonds between members of the targeted communities, reducing social cohesion and diminishing the ability of the protected group to replenish itself through sexual reproduction.[141]

62. In other words, the rape and sexual violence perpetrated against Fur, Masalit, and Zaghawa women and girls can be seen as an effort to leverage the conservative, cultural norms of those community which equated honour and marriageability with the sexual 'purity' of its female members. In this way, perpetrators used gender norms to maximise the destructive impact of their geographical confinement and numerically massive rape campaign by further facilitating the traumatisation, stigmatisation, and ostracisation of victims, adversely impacting their ability to become or to remain married or contemplate procreative relationships.[142]

63. In sum, the Court finds that there is a reasonable basis to believe that Bashir's forces harboured genocidal intent to biological destroy a substantial part of the Fur, Masalit, and Zaghawa groups in view of the confinement of the target groups, the

[137] *Ibid.*
[138] *Ibid.*
[139] Prosecutor's Request for Warrant, *supra* note 63, § 130.
[140] *Ibid*, § 130.
[141] J. Gottschall, 'Explaining Wartime Rape' 41 *Journal of Sex Research* (2004) 129–136, at 131.
[142] Ashraph, *supra* note 134, at 35.

subsequent and massive campaign of rape against those in the groups responsible for their daily survival and longer-term biological regeneration.

64. The Court is reminded that while the crime of genocide is a crime of intention, it does not require that the intended destruction succeed – much less when the question put before the Court in this instance is whether there is a reasonable basis to believe that the requisite intent exists. On the basis of the facts elaborated above, the Court finds that such a reasonable basis does in fact exist.

65. Thus, it is the Court's conclusion that there exists a reasonable basis to believe that the genocidal acts of killing, causing serious mental or physical suffering, and inflicting conditions calculated to physically destroy were committed with the required special intent to destroy the Fur, Masalit, and Zaghawa groups.

Judge Akila Radhakrishnan and Judge Grant Shubin

10.3 STATE COOPERATION AND ACCOUNTABILITY IN THE AL BASHIR JORDAN APPEAL

Saumya Uma and Ramya Jawahar Kudekallu

Then President of Sudan, Mr Omar Al Bashir, visited the Hashemite Kingdom of Jordan in March 2017. The ICC had issued a Warrant of Arrest for Mr Al Bashir on 4 March 2009[143] and 12 July 2010[144] respectively, and requested Jordan to arrest and surrender Mr Al Bashir during his visit.[145] Jordan refused, stating that head-of-state immunity protected Mr Al Bashir from arrest and that, further, as Sudan was not a state party to the Rome Statute, there was no obligation to arrest.[146]

In 2019, the Appeals Chamber decided that Jordan was under an obligation to arrest and surrender Mr Al Bashir because as a state party to the Rome Statute, Jordan had accepted that head-of-state immunity cannot act as a bar to the jurisdiction of the ICC.[147]

In this rewritten appeal decision, Saumya Uma and Ramya Jawahar Kudekallu confirm Jordan's obligation to arrest and surrender Mr Al Bashir, but situate this obligation through an examination of how the tolerance and acceptance of immunities, such as head-of-state immunity, increases the likelihood that sexual and gender-based crimes are treated with impunity. They bolster the obligation with a

[143] Warrant of Arrest, *Al Bashir* (ICC-02/05-01/09-3), Pre-Trial Chamber 1, 4 March 2009.

[144] Second Decision on the Prosecution's Application for a Warrant of Arrest, *Al Bashir* (ICC-02/05-01/09-94), Pre-Trial Chamber I, 12 July 2010.

[145] Public redacted version of Annex 1 to the Report of the Registry on information received regarding Omar Al Bashir's potential travel to the Hashemite Kingdome of Jordan, *Al Bashir* (ICC-02/05-01/09-291-Anx1-Red), Registry, 24 March 2017.

[146] Decision under Article 87(7) of the Rome Statute on the non-compliance by Jordan with the request by the Court for the arrest and surrender of Omar Al Bashir, *Al Bashir* (ICC-02/05-01/09-309), Pre-Trial Chamber II, 11 December 2017, §§ 7–8, 14–19.

[147] *Ibid*, § 32–34, 39.

close reading of the Statute, the submissions of amici and also consider how accession to international conventions, such as the conventions on torture and genocide, operate to require both state party and non-state party members to assist the ICC, further dismantling the notion that being a non-state party further authorises the lack of obligation.

No. ICC-02/05-01/09 OA2
Date: 6 May 2019

Original: English

THE APPEALS CHAMBER(B)

Before: Judge Saumya UMA
Judge Ramya Jawahar KUDEKALLU

SITUATION IN DARFUR, SUDAN
IN THE CASE OF THE *PROSECUTOR v. OMAR HASSAN AHMAD AL BASHIR*

Public Document

Judgment in the Jordan Referral re Al Bashir Appeal

The Appeals Chamber of the International Criminal Court

In the appeal of the Hashemite Kingdom of Jordan against the decision of Pre-Trial Chamber II entitled 'Decision under Article 87(7) of the Rome Statute on the non-compliance by Jordan with the request by the Court for the arrest and surrender o[f] Omar Al Bashir' of 11 December 2017 (ICC-02/05-01/09-309) (Jordan Referral re Al Bashir Appeal).

After deliberation, based on a unanimous decision, the judges deliver the following judgment.

JUDGMENT

1. Pre-Trial Chamber II found that the Hashemite Kingdom of Jordan (Jordan) had failed to comply with its obligations under the Rome Statute (Statute) by not executing the Court's request for the arrest of Mr Omar Hassan Ahmad Al Bashir (Mr Al Bashir) and his surrender to the Court when Mr Al Bashir was on Jordanian territory on 29 March 2017. This decision was appealed by Jordan. While the judgment of Pre-Trial Chamber II addressed multiple issues, this decision is confined to addressing and determining one core issue, namely whether Jordan complied with its duty to cooperate with the Court.

2. The Appeals Chamber unanimously concludes that Jordan breached its international obligations under the Statute by failing to comply with the request of the Court to execute the arrest warrant issued by it, when Mr Al Bashir was on Jordanian territory on 29 March 2017. Jordan's act of recognising head-of-state immunity, and

its non-compliance with the request of this Court to arrest the suspect, affected the effective functioning of the Court in ending impunity for the most serious crimes of international concern. Thus, the Pre-Trial Chamber's decision on this issue is confirmed, for the reasons given below.

(i) This Court finds that immunity for heads of state as a customary practice does not eclipse or override the jurisdiction of this Court, nor should it interfere or disrupt a consistency required of the Court, which is state cooperation and ending impunity for heinous crimes. Mr Al Bashir is being charged with ten counts on the basis of his individual criminal responsibility under Article 25(3)(a) of the Rome Statute as an indirect (co)perpetrator.

(ii) These crimes include five counts of crimes against humanity, specifically murder under Article 7(1)(a), extermination under Article 7(1)(b), forcible transfer under Article 7(1)(d), torture under Article 7(1)(f), and rape under Article 7(1)(g) of the Statue.

(iii) Mr Al Bashir has also been charged with two counts of war crimes, in particular intentionally directing attacks against a civilian population and against individual civilians not taking part in hostilities under Article 8(2)(e)(i)), and pillaging under Article 8(2)(e)(v)

(iv) In addition to the above, three counts of the crime of genocide, with Mr Al Bashir allegedly committing genocide by killing under Article 6-a, genocide by causing serious bodily or mental harm under Article 6-b, and genocide by deliberately inflicting on each target group conditions of life calculated to bring about the group's physical destruction under Article 6-c.

(v) Pre-Chamber I considered that there are reasonable grounds to believe that Mr Al Bashir targeted thousands of civilian women belonging primarily to Fur, Masalit, and Zaghawa groups, subjecting them to acts of rape, forcible transfer, and torture.[148]

REASONS

Key Findings

3. Customary international law has limits to immunity for heads of state. There is no suggestion in any instruments that immunity of heads of state can prevent or exonerate persons from being prosecuted before an international court for international crimes. The drafters of the Statute would have surely been aware of the immunity accorded to heads of state under customary international law, in the context of ICC crimes within the jurisdiction of the Court through Article 27(2).

[148] *Prosecutor v. Omar Hassan Ahmad Al Bashir* (ICC-02/05-01/09), at § 105

Applicable Law

4. A close reading of Article 21 of the Statute lends credence to this reasoning. Article 21 reads as follows:

> Article 21 Applicable law
> 1. The Court shall apply:
>   a. In the first place, this Statute, Elements of Crimes, and its Rules of Procedure and Evidence;
>   b. In the second place, where appropriate, applicable treaties and the principles and rules of international law, including the established principles of the international law of armed conflict;
>   c. Failing that, general principles of law derived by the Court from national laws of legal systems of the world including, as appropriate, the national laws of states that would normally exercise jurisdiction over the crime, provided that those principles are not inconsistent with this Statute and with international law and internationally recognised norms and standards.

5. Article 21 allows recourse to customary or treaty law *only* if a matter is not addressed by the sources of law enumerated in Article 21(1)(a).[149] Article 21 ranks the applicable sources by prioritising the ICC-specific sources of law. In the present case, it is clear that the Statute has addressed the issue of immunities and rejected them in Article 27. *We believe and hold that customary international law cannot override an explicit statutory provision that has dismantled immunity for heads of state for ICC crimes. This was done in the Statute to facilitate accountability for the perpetration of such crimes by the highest echelons of power.*

State Obligation to Execute an Arrest Warrant Issued by the Court

6. Article 58(1) of the Statute provides for the issuance of a warrant of arrest by the Pre-Trial Chamber, in situations where it concludes that there are reasonable grounds to believe that the suspect has committed an ICC crime and their arrest appears necessary. The issuance of the warrant of arrest is accompanied by the issuance of a summons to appear, in order to compel the attendance of the suspect before the Court.[150] Given that a trial cannot proceed in the absence of the suspect

[149] Request by Professor Nicholas Tsagourias and Dr Michail Vagias for Leave to Submit Observations on the Merits of the Legal Questions Presented in the Hashemite Kingdom of Jordan's Appeal against the Decision under Article 87(7) of the Rome Statute on the Non-Compliance by Jordan with the Request by the Court for the Arrest and Surrender of Omar Al Bashir of 12 March 2018, *Al Bashir* (ICC-02/05-01/09), Appeals Chamber, 29 April 2018, at 4.

[150] UN General Assembly, *Rome Statute of the International Criminal Court* (last amended 2010), 17 July 1998. Article 58(1) of the Rome Statute of the ICC states: 'At any time after the initiation of an investigation, the Pre-Trial Chamber shall, on the application of the Prosecutor, issue a warrant of arrest of a person if, having examined the application and the evidence or other information submitted by the Prosecutor, it is satisfied that: (a) There are reasonable grounds to believe that the person has committed a crime within the jurisdiction of the Court; and (b) The

before the Court, as per Article 63 of the Statute, the execution of the arrest warrant is of utmost importance so as to ensure that the trial is not rendered infructuous and the effort to ensure accountability of the suspect is not aborted. Jordan had a legal and moral obligation to execute the arrest warrant. This is more so as by acceding to the Statute, Jordan accepted Article 27(2) which paved way for the ICC to exercise its jurisdiction even against heads of states. As submitted by the Prosecutor, this Court agrees that Jordan understood the regime created when ratifying the Statute, including 'the issue and execution of requests of arrest and surrender of officials of States ... bound by the ... Statute'.[151] Jordan's act of refusal is not merely an unlawful act due to its breach of state parties' obligations to cooperate with the Court as clearly mandated by the Statute, but also one that undermines rule of law and fails the victims of the alleged ICC crimes.

Irrelevance of Immunity for Heads of State

7. We acknowledge and foreground, with deep concern and trepidation, the ramifications of a sitting head of state's access to power to potentially continue committing atrocities (including ICC crimes), to threaten victims and potential witnesses and scuttle processes for justice and accountability particularly against vulnerable communities – women, girls, and sexual orientation and gender identity (SOGI) minorities. We conclude that allowing immunity for heads of state could also lead to impunity for crimes against such communities – an undesirable outcome that is diametrically opposite to the objectives for which this Court was established.

8. Article 27 of the Statute is of immense relevance to the present case.

9. Article 27 explicitly states the irrelevance of official capacity as a head of state or government for serious crimes of international concern enumerated in the Statute. This standard has to be concurrent with the cooperation of states broadly while simultaneously pursuing an individual who, very obviously, wields the power, political clout, and has the means to cross state boundaries. State parties ratify the Statute, and are therefore cognisant of the jurisdiction of this Court with respect to the aforesaid crimes. Jordan, as a state party to the Statute, carries the obligation of executing the ICC's warrant of arrest.

arrest of the person appears necessary: (i) To ensure the person's appearance at trial; (ii) To ensure that the person does not obstruct or endanger the investigation or the court proceedings; or (iii) Where applicable, to prevent the person from continuing with the commission of that crime or a related crime which is within the jurisdiction of the Court and which arises out of the same circumstances.'

151 Prosecution Response to the Hashemite Kingdom of Jordan's Appeal against the 'Decision under Article 87(7) of the Rome Statute on the non-compliance by Jordan with the request by the Court for arrest and surrender [of] Omar Al Bashir', *Al Bashir* (ICC-02/05-01/09), Appeals Chamber, 3 April 2018, §§ 7, 15.

Importance of State Cooperation with the Court

10. From the drafting stages of the Statute, state cooperation in the Court's investigative, prosecutorial, and judicial functions was a key principle built into the Statute. Part 9 of the Statute contains aspects of international cooperation and judicial assistance. The focus on state cooperation – an edifice of the Statute – arises from the need to delicately balance states' concerns about infringement of their sovereignty with efforts at ending impunity for ICC crimes globally. As a result, the ICC is a judicial institution with no independent police force, enforcement agency, or prison facilities (only facilities to hold in custody those persons detained under the authority of the ICC). For this reason, the Court relies on the cooperation of its state parties to the Statute and willing states which are not parties to the Statute, and institutions. The obligation of states that are parties to the Statute to cooperate entails not only complying with requests of the ICC for arrest and surrender of the accused; it extends beyond the same and includes persuading other nations that are not state parties to the ICC (such as Sudan, in this instance) to cooperate with the ICC. This is in order to reduce or eliminate safe havens for evading prosecution and escaping accountability.[152] Jordan failed in its duty to fulfil and discharge both these state obligations.

11. Deficiency of cooperation, where war crimes, crimes against humanity and genocide are concerned, opens up chasms in access to justice for victims while assisting accused persons to take refuge in other jurisdictions. This court takes cognisance of the evidence submitted whereby witnesses interviewed by the prosecution, the UN Commission of Inquiry into Darfur (UNCOI), other UN bodies, and numerous NGOs have reported that, since March 2003, thousands of women and girls belonging to the target groups were raped in all three states of Darfur by members of the armed forces and militia/Janjaweed. Girls as young as five and women as old as seventy have been raped.[153] The importance of the voice and participation of victims has been an evolving key priority for the court.[154] Yet the execution of justice would ring hollow if the Court did not determine with clarity that states too, through the principles of *jus cogens* and *erga omnes*, owe equity to victims and must ensure that their participation is not reduced to being tokenistic.

12. State parties have a legal obligation to cooperate with the ICC at all stages of the trial and its outcome. These include implementation of arrest warrants and surrender of suspects to the ICC for trial. Non-cooperation by state parties is

[152] See also 'The International Criminal Court offers new hope for a permanent reduction in the phenomenon of impunity' and the establishment of the ICC is '[u]ndoubtedly the most significant recent development in the international community's long struggle to advance the cause of justice and the Rule of Law', Report of the Secretary-General, 23 August 2004, S/2004/616, § 49.

[153] *Prosecutor v. Omar Hassan Ahmad Al Bashir* (ICC-02/05-01/09) at § 105.

[154] M. Pena and G. Carayon, 'Is the ICC Making the Most of Victim Participation?' 7(3) *International Journal of Transitional Justice* (2013) 518–535.

addressed in Article 87(7) while non-cooperation with the Court by states not party to the Statute is dealt with in Article 87(5). The issue is not merely about what was agreed upon by the state parties at the Rome Conference, but how to make the provisions on state cooperation with the Court effective and workable in practice. The Court, being a judicial institution, has the discretion to make a judicial finding to the effect of non-cooperation by a state party to the Rome Statute. However, not every situation of non-compliance leads to a finding of non-cooperation; for instance, following Mr Omar Al Bashir's visit to the Federal Republic of Nigeria (Nigeria) in July 2013, Pre-Trial Chamber II requested Nigeria to arrest and surrender him to the Court, without making a finding on the issue of non-cooperation.[155]

13. The specific procedural moments of this Court's process are an important factor. The Court has issued multiple warrants of arrest with obligations to multiple states, including those few that have ratified the Statute.[156] It has been over eight years of consistent follow-up by the prosecution to secure the defendant. Since March 2009, the defendant made more than eighty-five trips to more than twenty nation states without deterrence or limits to movements.[157] By failing to meet obligations of arrest and surrender for widespread crimes, particularly gendered in nature, involving sexual violence against populations, the non-cooperation of states retains a dangerous culture of tolerance and encouragement to the most heinous crimes under international law.[158]

14. Mr Al Bashir has been freely travelling across the world, making numerous international trips with no fear of being arrested, founded in his confidence of non-cooperation by state parties to the Statute in executing this Court's warrant.[159] It is pertinent to note that the ICC has been addressing the issue of non-cooperation for the past few years, in instances such as *Kenyatta*[160] and *Gaddafi*.[161] Further, Jordan is

[155] Decision Regarding Omar Al Bashir's Visit to the Federal Republic of Nigeria, *Al Bashir* (ICC-02/05-01/09), Pre-Trial Chamber II, 15 July 2013.

[156] 'Request to all States Parties to the Rome Statute for the Arrest and Surrender of Omar Al Bashir' (ICC-02/05-01/09-7), 6 March 2009, and 'Supplementary Request to all States Parties to the Rome Statute for the Arrest and Surrender of Omar Al Bashir' (ICC-02/05-01/09-96), 21 July 2010.

[157] *8132nd Meeting Reports of the Secretary-General on the Sudan and South Sudan*, UN Doc. S/PV.8132, 12 December 2017, at 8.

[158] The Office of the Prosecutor, *Policy Paper on Sexual and Gender-Based Crimes*, June 2014, § 75, available at www.icc-cpi.int/sites/default/files/iccdocs/otp/OTP-Policy-Paper-on-Sexual-and-Gender-Based-Crimes–June-2014.pdf.

[159] Nuba Reports, 'Wanted frequent flyer: Sudan's president has made 74 trips across the world in the seven years he's been wanted for war crimes', QUARTZ Africa, 4 March 2016, available at https://qz.com/africa/630571/sudans-president-has-made-74-trips-across-the-world-in-the-seven-years-hes-been-wanted-for-war-crimes/.

[160] Second decision on prosecution's application for a finding of non-compliance under Article 87 (7) of the Statute, Kenyatta (ICC-01/09-02/11), Trial Chamber V9B), 19 September 2016.

[161] Decision on the non-compliance by Libya with requests for cooperation by the Court and referring the matter to the United Nations Security Council, *Saif Al-Islam Gaddafi* (ICC-01/11-01/11), Pre-Trial Chamber I, 10 December 2014.

not the first country to refuse to cooperate with the Court with respect to the arrest and surrender of Mr Al Bashir. Other such states include Malawi,[162] Democratic Republic of Congo,[163] Djibouti,[164] Uganda,[165] Kenya,[166] and Chad.[167] This is a clear indication of the fact that Mr Al Bashir enjoys an unparalleled, de facto impunity for alleged commission of most serious crimes of international concern – that which this court resolves to end.

Relationship between State Cooperation and Ending Impunity for Sexual and Gender-Based Violence

15. There exist intrinsic interlinkages between state cooperation with the ICC in arresting and surrendering a suspect to the court, and ending impunity for ICC crimes, especially crimes of sexual and gender-based violence. Feminist scholars of international law have, time and again, drawn attention to the gendered impact of armed conflict on women.[168] At the Beijing conference on women in 1995, the global community affirmed this by acknowledging that 'while entire communities suffer the consequences of armed conflict and terrorism, women and girls are particularly affected because of their status in society and their sex'.[169] In General Recommendation 30, the Convention on Elimination of Discrimination Against

[162] *Prosecutor v. Omar Hassan Ahmad Al Bashir*, Corrigendum to the Decision pursuant to Article 87(7) of the Rome Statute on the Failure by the Republic of Malawi to Comply with the Cooperation Requests Issued by the Court with Respect to the Arrest and Surrender of Omar Hassan Ahmad Al Bashir (ICC-02/05-01/09), Pre-Trial Chamber I, 13 December 2011.

[163] *Prosecutor v. Omar Hassan Ahmad Al Bashir*, Decision on the Cooperation of the Democratic Republic of the Congo Regarding Omar Al Bashir's Arrest and Surrender to the Court (ICC-02/05-01/0)9, Pre-Trial Chamber II, 9 April 2014.

[164] *Prosecutor v. Omar Hassan Ahmad Al Bashir*, Decision on the non-compliance by the Republic of Djibouti with the request to arrest and surrender Omar Al Bashir to the Court and referring the matter to the United Nations Security Council and the Assembly of the State Parties to the Rome Statute (ICC-02/05-01/09), Pre-Trial Chamber II, 11 July 2016.

[165] *Prosecutor v. Omar Hassan Ahmad Al Bashir*, Decision on the non-compliance by the Republic of Uganda with the request to arrest and surrender Omar Al Bashir to the Court and referring the matter to the United Nations Security Council and the Assembly of State Parties to the Rome Statute (ICC-02/05-01/19), Pre-Trial Chamber II, 11 July 2016.

[166] ICC, *Prosecutor v. Omar Hassan Ahmad Al Bashir*, Decision informing the United Nations Security Council and the Assembly of the States Parties to the Rome Statute about Omar Al Bashir's presence in the territory of the Republic of Kenya (ICC-02/05-01/09), Pre-Trial Chamber I, 27 August 2010.

[167] ICC, *Prosecutor v. Omar Hassan Ahmad Al Bashir*, Decision informing the United Nations Security Council and the Assembly of the States Parties to the Rome Statute about Omar Al Bashir's recent visit to the Republic of Chad (ICC-02/05-01/09), Pre-Trial Chamber I, 27 August 2010.

[168] J. Gardam, 'Women and the Law of Armed Conflict – Why the Silence? 46(1) *International and Comparative Law Quarterly* (1997) 55–80, at 55, 58; C. Chinkin and H. Charlesworth, *The Boundaries of International Law: A Feminist Analysis* (Manchester: Manchester University Press, 2000) at 250–257; S. Brownmiller, *Against Our Will: Men, Women and Rape* (Harmondsworth: Penguin Books, 1986).

[169] UN Doc. A/CONF. 177/20, 17 October 1995, § 135.

Women (CEDAW) committee too expressed concern about the gendered impact of conflicts.[170] There is emerging research on the sharp rise in violence based on SOGI in countries that are adversely impacted by conflict.[171] Suffice it to note, at this juncture, the pervasive nature of ICC crimes against such vulnerable communities in the context of war and conflict, and their adverse and disproportionate impact on women and girls, as well as SOGI minorities. Thus, state parties' non-cooperation in the arrest and surrender of suspects of alleged ICC crimes would result in impunity for ICC crimes, which would have negative ramifications on access to justice for women, girls, and SOGI minorities. Seen in this light, Jordan's non-compliance with the Pre-Trial Chamber's request to arrest and surrender Mr Al Bashir has consequences that are adverse and far-reaching. Jordan's avoidance with respect to the arrest and surrender of the defendant is inconsistent with its obligations under international law, specifically human rights.

Rape as Torture

16. Rape and other forms of sexual violence have been recognised as torture under international law by various courts and tribunals. For instance, in *Aydin v. Turkey*, decided in 1997 by the European Court of Human Rights, the Court found that rape could also constitute a violation of the prohibition of torture, enshrined in Article 3 of the European Convention.[172] In this case, a Turkish police officer had been charged with the rape of a seventeen-year-old Kurdish girl who had been illegally detained. Similarly in *Martí de Mejía v. Perú*, the Inter-American Commission on Human Rights held that rape violated the prohibition against torture, stated in Article 5.[173] In the International Tribunal for the Prosecution of Persons Responsible for Serious Violations of International Humanitarian Law committed in the Territory of the Former Yugoslavia since 1991 (ICTY), four members of the Bosnian armed forces were prosecuted for rape and sexual violence against Bosnian Serb civilians detained in a prison camp in Čelebići. The trial chamber, in its judgment of 1998, observed that the rape of any person was a 'despicable act which strikes at the very core of human dignity and physical integrity'.[174] It held that acts of

[170] CEDAW/C/GC/30, 1 November 2013, § 2.

[171] World Bank, *Sexual Orientation and Gender Identity in Contexts Affected by Fragility, Conflict, and Violence* (Washington, DC: World Bank, 2020), available at https://openknowledge.worldbank.org/handle/10986/33722 License: CC BY 3.0 IGO; A. Margalit, 'Still a Blind Spot: The Protection of LGBT Persons during Armed Conflict and other Situations of Violence' 100(1–3) *International Review of the Red Cross* (2018) 237–265.

[172] *Aydin v. Turkey* (1998) 25 EHRR 251.

[173] Case 10.970, Inter-American Commission on Human Rights, Report No. 5/96, OEA/Ser.L/V/II.91 Doc. 7, 1996, at 157.

[174] *Prosecutor v. Zdravko Mucic aka 'Pavo', Hazim Delic, Esad Landzo aka 'Zenga', Zejnil Delalic*, Trial Judgment, IT-96-21-T, International Criminal Tribunal for the former Yugoslavia (ICTY), 16 November 1998.

rape may constitute torture under customary international law.[175] In 2001, the appeals chamber of the ICTY upheld the judgment.[176] This was significant as it was the first judgment of the ICTY holding that rape satisfied the prerequisites of torture. Further, the ICTY stated that it is not required that each act be widespread or systematic, provided that the act forms part of a widespread or systematic attack against a civilian population.[177] A 2014 report that examined the torture of thirty-four women by state security forces in the Democratic Republic of Congo found that rape and sexual violence ought not to be seen in isolation; it must be seen in the broader pattern of widespread torture.[178]

17. The resolve to end impunity for sexual and gender-based violence is of utmost importance, particularly due to the historic wrongs committed during Nuremberg and Tokyo tribunals, where a deliberate failure to prosecute persons for crimes committed against women in a systematic manner during World War II was evident.[179] There is an urgent need to 'right' the wrongs by ending impunity for ICC crimes. On this ground, too, non-cooperation with the Court for arrest and surrender of suspects, including heads of state, can be neither tolerated nor condoned.

18. Even if some countries are not state parties of the Statute, they have a duty to discharge their state obligations under other conventions that they have ratified, including (but not limited to) the Genocide Convention and/or Torture Convention. For instance, although Sudan is not a state party to the Statute, it acceded to the Genocide Convention on 13 October 2003 and is bound to discharge its state obligations under the same. For those countries that are state parties to the Statute as well as other relevant conventions, they have additional state obligations under multiple conventions, which need to be addressed holistically. For instance, in addition to being a state party to the Statute, Jordan acceded to the Genocide Convention on 3 April 1950, and it acceded to the Torture Convention on

[175] *Ibid.*

[176] *Prosecutor v. Zdravko Mucic aka 'Pavo', Hazim Delic, Esad Landzo aka 'Zenga', Zejnil Delalic*, Appeal Judgment, IT-96-21-A, 20 February 2001.

[177] *Prosecutor v. Tadić*, Appeal Judgment, IT-94-1-A, 15 July 1999, n. 311 to § 248, citing *The Prosecutor v. Mile Mrkšić et al.*, Trial Chamber I, 'Review of Indictment Pursuant to Rule 61 of the Rules of Procedure and Evidence', IT-95-13-R61, 3 April 1996, § 30: '*As long as there is a link with the widespread or systematic attack against a civilian population, a single act could qualify as a crime against humanity. As such, an individual committing a crime against a single victim or a limited number of victims might be recognised as guilty of a crime against humanity if his acts were part of the specific context identified above.'

[178] Freedom from Torture, 'Rape as Torture in the DRC: Sexual Violence beyond the Conflict Zone', 2 June 2014, available at https://reliefweb.int/report/democratic-republic-congo/rape-torture-drc-sexual-violence-beyond-conflict-zone.

[179] C. J. (Kay) S. Picart, 'Attempting to Go Beyond Forgetting: the Legacy of the Tokyo IMT and Crimes of Violence against Women' 7 *University of Pennsylvania East Asia Law Review* (2011) 1–49; N. Buchowska, 'Violated or Protected. Women's Rights in Armed Conflicts after the Second World War' 2(2) *International Comparative Jurisprudence* (2016) 72–80.

13 November 1991. We note that rape and other forms of sexual and gender-based violence constitute torture and, in specific situations, are characterised as genocide, war crimes, and crimes against humanity.[180] Thus, we conclude that Jordan's abject failure to discharge its state obligations are not only under the Statute but also under allied conventions that it is a party to.

19. The Court will engage in the nature of power in relation to immunity enjoyed by the defendant, noting that he had access to ample resources to travel safely, and to stay in several jurisdictions. The Prosecutor has submitted that the Court could consider an agent in executing the Court's arrest warrant, and consequently the enforcement jurisdiction would be that of the Court and not that of the requested state, Jordan.

Victims' Right to Reparative Justice

20. This Court remains committed to a reparative justice approach that centres victim participation in legal proceedings and adjudication with reparations.[181] Essentially, such an approach would encompass 'restitution, compensation, rehabilitation, satisfaction (disclosure of the truth) and guarantee of non-repetition'.[182] Beyond individual accountability for international crimes, as well as conviction and punishment of the defendant for the same, the Court is committed to engaging with member states in support of such practices that would reinforce a deliberate intent towards prevention of future crimes.[183] Additionally, a priority of this Court is to protect and uphold the interests of the victims and affected communities. This would contribute to securing long-term stability in post-conflict societies – an imperative of state parties to the Statute.[184] This approach should be realised so that victims are perceived and treated as 'active agents' rather than 'passive objects' in international criminal justice processes.[185] Such an approach is

[180] *Prosecutor v. Anto Furundzija*. Trial Judgment, IT-95-17/1-T, International Criminal Tribunal for the former Yugoslavia (ICTY), 10 December 1998; also *Prosecutor v. Dragoljub Kunarac, Radomir Kovac and Zoran Vukovic*, Trial Judgment, IT-96-23-T & IT-96-23/1-T, International Criminal Tribunal for the former Yugoslavia (ICTY), 22 February 2001.

[181] 'Victims before the ICC: A Guide for the Participation of Victims in the Proceedings of the Court', ICC Booklet, 2016, available at www.icc-cpi.int/NR/rdonlyres/8FF91A2C-5274-4DCB-9CCE-37273C5E9AB4/282477/160910VPRSBookletEnglish.pdf.

[182] C. Evans, *The Right to Reparations in International Law for Victims of Armed Conflict* (Cambridge: Cambridge University Press, 2012) 13–14.

[183] *Prosecutor v. Jean-Pierre Bemba Gombo*, Judgment on the appeal of Mr Jean Pierre Bemba Gombo against Trial Chamber III's Judgment pursuant to Article 74 of the Statute (ICC-01/05-01/08), 8 June 2018.

[184] International Criminal Court, 'Justice is Key to Durable Peace', Statement of the President of the ICC, Judge Silvia Fernandez de Gurmendo, ICC Press Release, 21 September 2015 (ICC-CPI-20150921-PR1152), available at www.icc-cpi.int/Pages/item.aspx?name=pr1152.

[185] C. Garbett, 'From Passive Objects to Active Agents: Changing Conceptions of Victim Identities at the ICTY and ICC' 15(1) *Journal of Human Rights* (2016) 40–59.

also supported by the Office of the Prosecutor, which, in its policy paper on sexual and gender-based crimes, emphasises a gender-inclusive approach to reparations, taking into account the gender-specific impact on, as well as the harm caused to, and suffering of, the victims affected by the crimes for which an individual has been convicted.[186] Additionally, General Recommendation 30 of the CEDAW committee, on women in conflict prevention, conflict, and post-conflict situations, provides a framework of state obligations, including due diligence obligations, prior to, during, and after a conflict.[187] It is pertinent to note that General Recommendation 30 applies to international and internal armed conflict. Jordan is a state party to the CEDAW.

Towards Universal Jurisdiction and a Borderless World

21. This Court further opines that reducing or eliminating safe havens for suspects of ICC crimes is of prime importance, given the heinous nature of such crimes. While the Statute presently does not provide for universal jurisdiction, this Court observes, with satisfaction, the positive movement towards universal jurisdiction for ICC crimes, where an increasing number of national courts are willing to prosecute suspects for serious crimes under international law. In the years 1994–2009, a number of countries, including Australia, Austria, Belgium, Canada, Denmark, France, Finland, Germany, Norway, The Netherlands, Spain, Senegal, Sweden, Switzerland, the United Kingdom, and the United States started to apply the principle of universal jurisdiction in relation to crimes against humanity, torture, or genocide.[188] The principle is premised on the notion that perpetrators of such crimes are *hostes humani generis* (enemies of all mankind), so any country should have the jurisdiction and legal authority to hold the perpetrators accountable, regardless of the country where the crime was allegedly committed or the nationality of the perpetrator or the victims.[189] In 2009, an African Union–European Union Expert Report on the Principle of Universal Jurisdiction emphasised as follows: '[T]emporal, geographical, personal and subject-matter limitations on the jurisdiction of international criminal courts and tribunals mean that universal jurisdiction remains a vital element in the fight against impunity.'[190] A 2012 report of Amnesty International notes that a total of 147 states have exercised universal jurisdiction for

[186] The Office of the Prosecutor of the ICC, 'Policy Paper on Sexual and Gender-Based Crimes' 3 (2014), § 102.

[187] CEDAW/C/GC/30, 18 October 2013.

[188] Human Rights Watch, 'Basic Facts on Universal Jurisdiction', 19 October 2009, available at www.hrw.org/news/2009/10/19/basic-facts-universal-jurisdiction.

[189] J. Greene, 'Hostis Humani Generis' 34(4) *Critical Inquiry* (2008) 683–705, available at https://doi.org/10.1086/592540.

[190] Council of the European Union, *The AU-EU Expert Report on the Principle of Universal Jurisdiction*, 8672/1/09 REV 1, 16 April 2009, § 28.

one or more crimes in international law.[191] We believe that universal jurisdiction for the most serious crimes under international law does not weaken or diminish the ICC's jurisdiction over heinous crimes in any manner whatsoever; to the contrary, it complements and strengthens the philosophy behind the establishment of the ICC, which is to end impunity for ICC crimes.

22. Further, the legal concept and practice of universal jurisdiction reinforces and strengthens the futuristic vision of a borderless world, grounded in principles of freedom and equality, where people can move freely as global citizens, where migrants and refugees face no violations, and where natural resources belong to all human beings across the world.[192] Given that most wars are fought over territories or for control over natural resources, often in the name of state sovereignty and territorial integrity, with sexual and gender-based violence as a logical corollary of such wars, a borderless world would go a long way in preventing wars and their aftermath. A borderless world would also ensure justice and accountability for perpetrators of ICC crimes, as they would have no safe havens through which they could potentially thwart arrest and production before the Court. Drawing inspiration from Gayatri Spivak, the only borders to be respected should be the 'seemingly permeable female body'.[193] Though this may sound like a feminist utopian dream, we believe that it is the spark of a dream today that lights the path towards its achievement in future.

23. In conclusion, a warrant of arrest, alongside a summons to appear, issued by Pre-Trial Chamber I of this Court against Mr Al Bashir, is intended to ensure accountability of the defendant for the alleged commission of ICC crimes, secure justice for the victims, and thereby end impunity for heinous crimes that may have been perpetrated. Jordan bears the legal and moral obligation to execute the arrest warrant and cooperate with this Court. Such an obligation is not obliterated by head-of-state immunity recognised under customary international law. Since Jordan is a state party to the Rome Statute and is presumed to be fully aware of the provisions of the Rome Statute that it accepted, including Article 27 (irrelevance of official capacity), we conclude that by refusing to execute the arrest warrant, Jordan has deliberately and intentionally failed to discharge its obligations under international criminal law to cooperate with this Court.

Judge Saumya Uma and Judge Ramya Jawahar Kudekallu

[191] Amnesty International, 'Universal Jurisdiction: A Preliminary Survey of Legislation around the World – 2012 Update' (2012), available at www.amnesty.org/en/documents/ior53/019/2012/en/.

[192] C. T. Mohanty, *Feminism without Borders: Decolonizing Theory, Practicing Solidarity* (Durham, NC: Duke University Press, 2003) at 1–13. See also M. A. Miyoshi, 'Borderless World? From Colonialism to Transnationalism and the Decline of the Nation-State' 19(4) *Critical Inquiry* (1993) 726–751, available at www.jstor.org/stable/1343904.

[193] G. C. Spivak. 'A Borderless World?' in R. Braidotti and P. Gilroy (eds.), *Conflicting Humanities* (London: Bloomsbury, 2016) 47–60, at 51.

10.4 VICTIM PARTICIPATION IN THE ABD-AL-RAHMAN CONFIRMATION OF CHARGES

Anushka Sehmi

In 2021, single judge of Pre-Trial Chamber II, Judge Rosario Salvatore Aitala, appointed the Office of Public Counsel for Victims as the common legal representative for all participating victims in the case against Mr Ali Muhammad Ali Abd-al-Rahman (Ali Kushayb).[194] This decision was made without prior consultation with any of the victims, with the single judge citing time constraints and practical limitations.[195]

In her rewrite, Anushka Sehmi focuses on the agency of victims, which must be supported to provide meaningful participation. Sehmi uses the governing statutes of the ICC as well as its previous decisions to firmly assert that victims must be consulted with regard to their choice of representative. In using this agency of choice, Sehmi highlights how victims of sexual and gender-based violence may feel more empowered as victims to nominate, knowing that their experiences are to be represented by a person chosen by themselves, thereby ensuring a greater capture of evidence and testimonies. Further, in choosing their own representative, the ICC may avail itself to counsel with specific and necessary subject and socio-cultural expertise which again may ensure greater access to justice for those involved.

No.: ICC-02/05-01/20-259
Date: 18 January 2021

Original: English

PRE-TRIAL CHAMBER II(B)

Before: Judge Anushka SEHMI

SITUATION IN DARFUR, SUDAN
IN THE CASE OF THE *PROSECUTOR v. ALI MUHAMMAD ALI ABD-AL-RAHMAN ('ALI KUSHAYB')*

Public

Decision Establishing the Principles on Victims' Representations during the Confirmation of Charges Hearing

Judge Anushka Sehmi, acting on behalf of Pre-Trial Chamber II of the International Criminal Court (the Court), taking into consideration Articles 57(3)

[194] Decision establishing the principles applicable to victims and representation during the Confirmation Hearing, *Abd-Al-Rahman* (ICC-02/05-01/20-259), Pre-Trial Chamber II, 18 January 2021.

[195] *Ibid*, § 35.

(c), 67(1)(c) and (2) and 68(1) and (3) of the Rome Statute (the Statute), Rules 16 and 85–93 of the Rules of Procedure and Evidence (RPE) and Regulations 79, 80, and 86 of the Regulations of the Court (the Regulations), I hereby issue this Decision establishing the principles applicable to victims' participation and representation during the Confirmation of Charges Hearing.

PROCEDURAL HISTORY

1. On 9 June 2020, Mr Ali Muhammad Ali Abd-Al-Rahman (Mr Abd-Al-Rahman) surrendered himself and was transferred to the Detention Centre of the Court. On 15 June 2020, as ordered by the Chamber,[196] Mr Abd-Al-Rahman made his first appearance before the single judge.[197]

2. On 9 October 2020, the Registry, through the Victims Participation and Reparations Section (VPRS), submitted a request to modify the standard application form for victim participation in the present case (VPRS Request)[198] and on 4 November 2020, the Chamber granted the VPRS Request.[199]

3. On 17 November 2020, the VPRS submitted observations and recommendations on aspects related to the admission process for victims seeking to participate in the proceedings (Registry Observations).[200]

4. On 11 January 2021, the legal representative of potential victims requested the Chamber to clarify the temporal and geographical scope of the charges and to be provided with guidance in terms of the modalities for legal representation, including access to documents in the case file (Request for Guidance).[201] On 13 January 2021, the defence responded to the request for clarification from the legal representative.[202]

[196] Decision on the convening of a hearing for the initial appearance of Mr Ali Kushayb, *Ali Kushayb*, (ICC-02/05-01/07-82), Pre-Trial Chamber II, 11 June 2020.

[197] T-001, available at www.icc-cpi.int/sites/default/files/Transcripts/CR2020_02436.PDF (hereafter Initial Appearance).

[198] Public Redacted version of Registry Request for Authorization to Use a Modified Standard Application Form to Facilitate Victim Participation in the Case, *Ali Kushayb* (ICC-02/05-01/20-178-Conf), 8 October 2020 (A public redacted version was filed on 2 November 2020, ICC-02/05-01/20-178-Red).

[199] Decision on the Registry's Request for Authorisation to Use a Modified Standard Application Form for Victim Participation, *Ali Kushayb* (ICC-02/05-01/20-198), Pre-Trial Chamber II, 4 November 2020, at 8.

[200] Registry Observations on Aspects Related to the Admission of Victims for Participation in the Proceedings, *Ali Kushayb* (ICC-02/05-01/20-203), 17 November 2020.

[201] Request for Guidance on Modalities for Submissions relating to Applications for Victim Participation, *Ali Kushayb* (ICC-02/05-01/20-251), 11 January 2021 (hereafter Request for Guidance).

[202] Observations en Réponse à la Requête, *Ali Kushayb* (ICC-02/05-01/20-255), 13 January 2021.

ANALYSIS

Preliminary Matter

5. The single judge notes that the Request for Guidance was filed by the legal representative on behalf of a number of individuals who have filed applications to participate in the proceedings as victims of crimes that fall within the scope of this case. In this respect, a valid power of attorney has been submitted to the Registry. Consequently, the present decision sets out the applicable principles and modalities of victim participation with respect to the upcoming confirmation of charges hearings.

MEANINGFUL VICTIM PARTICIPATION AS THE CORE PRINCIPLE GUIDING MODALITIES OF VICTIM PARTICIPATION

6. In the opinion of the single judge, a discussion of the modalities of victim participation is of little value without elaborating on the concept of *meaningful* victim participation and what it entails in the context of these pre-trial proceedings.

7. Article 68(3) of the Rome Statute provides that:

> Where the personal interests of the victims are affected, the Court shall permit their views and concerns to be presented and considered at stages of the proceedings determined to be appropriate by the Court and in a manner which is not prejudicial to or inconsistent with the rights of the accused and a fair and impartial trial. Such views and concerns may be presented by the legal representatives of the victims where the Court considers it appropriate, in accordance with the Rules of Procedure and Evidence.

8. The jurisprudence before this Court emphasises that the participation of victims in proceedings must be 'meaningful' as opposed to 'purely symbolic'.[203] It is the opinion of the single judge that practice before this Court has demonstrated that there are at least three main overarching principles that must be adhered to in

[203] Decision on Victims' Participation, *Lubanga* (ICC-01/04-01/06-1119), Appeals Chamber, 22 January 2008, § 85; Judgment on the appeals of the Prosecutor and the Defence against Trial Chamber I's Decision on Victims' Participation of 18 January 2008, *Lubanga* (ICC-01/04-01/06-1432), Appeals Chamber, 11 July 2008, § 97; Order on the Organisation of Common Legal Representation of Victims, *Katanga and Ngudjolo* (ICC-01/04-01/07-1328), Trial Chamber II, 22 July 2009, § 10(a); Decision on the Modalities of Victim Participation at Trial, *Katanga and Ngudjolo* (ICC-01/04-01/07-1788-tENG), Trial Chamber II, 22 January 2010, § 57; Decision on Common Legal Representation of Victims for the Purpose of Trial, *Bemba* (ICC-01/05-01/08-1005), Trial Chamber III, 10 November 2010, § 9(a).

order to ensure that victim participation is meaningful. The first is a gender-sensitive and inclusive approach to victim participation which considers the gendered dynamics of conflict; secondly, effective communication and consultation between victims of conflict and the Court; and lastly, ensuring victim agency in their choice of legal representation.

A Gender-Sensitive and Inclusive Approach to Victim Participation

9. According to the single judge, *meaningful* victim participation must be gender-sensitive and inclusive. The Rome Statute is the first international instrument that expressly includes sexual and gender-based crimes, including rape, sexual slavery, enforced prostitution, forced pregnancy, enforced sterilisation, and other forms of sexual violence as underlying offences of both war crimes and crimes against humanity. The Statute also prohibits persecution based on gender as a crime against humanity. Sexual and gender-based crimes may also fall under the Court's jurisdiction if they constitute acts of genocide or other acts of crimes against humanity or war crimes. Furthermore, in 2014, the Office of the Prosecutor launched its Policy Paper on Sexual and Gender-Based Crimes, which seeks to help ensure the effective investigation and prosecution of these crimes and enhance access to justice for victims.[204]

10. Article 21 of the Statute outlines the sources of law that are applicable by the Court, which include treaties and 'principles of international law'. As stated by the Appeals Chamber in relation to Article 21(3), 'the law applicable under the Statute must be interpreted as well as applied in accordance with internationally recognised human rights. Human rights underpin the Statute; every aspect of it, including the exercise of the jurisdiction of the Court'.[205] According to the single judge, applying best practices from the normative international human rights law framework is particularly important in ensuring gender-sensitive and inclusive victim participation.

11. The right of women to participate in transitional justice processes is guaranteed under a number of human rights instruments and conventions, including the Universal Declaration of Human Rights (UDHR),[206] the International Covenant on Civil and Political Rights (ICCPR),[207] and the Convention on the Elimination

[204] Office of the Prosecutor, 'Policy Paper on Sexual and Gender-Based Crimes' (June 2014), available at www.icc-cpi.int/sites/default/files/iccdocs/otp/OTP-Policy-Paper-on-Sexual-and-Gender-Based-Crimes–June-2014.pdf, at 5–6.

[205] Judgment on the Appeal of Mr. Thomas Lubanga Dyilo against the Decision on the Defence Challenge to the Jurisdiction of the Court pursuant to article 19 (2) (a) of the Statute of 3 October 2006, *Lubanga* (ICC-01/04-01/06-772), Appeals Chamber, 14 December 2006, § 37.

[206] Arts. 2, 6, 7 and 8, Universal Declaration of Human Rights (UDHR) 1948, (UNGA Resolution 217 A), adopted 10 December 1948.

[207] Arts. 3 and 25, International Convention on Civil and Political Rights, opened for signature 16 December 1966, 999 UNTS 171 (entered into force 23 March 1976).

of All Forms of Discrimination Against Women (CEDAW).[208] This right is premised on the inherent dignity and the equal and inalienable right of all people to participate in political and public life, including people of all genders.

12. In its landmark Resolution 1325 (2000) on Women, Peace and Security, the United Nations Security Council (UNSC) recognised the importance of the equal participation and full involvement of women in maintaining and promoting peace and security.[209] In Resolution 2467 (2019), the UNSC specifically called for women's meaningful participation in transitional justice processes.[210]

13. A gender-inclusive and sensitive approach to victim participation must guide the entire process of facilitating the participation of victims in ICC proceedings and their participation through their legal representative/s. Indeed, a gender-inclusive approach to victim participation is especially important as conflict often exacerbates societal gender inequalities, leaving women and girls even more vulnerable to gross human rights violations and sexual and gender-based crimes (SGBC).[211] Thus, the process of victim participation should borrow from human rights law best practices and encourage a gender and women's rights perspective which allows women to exert their agency.

[208] Art. 7, Convention on the Elimination of All Forms of Discrimination Against Women, opened for signature 1 March 1980, 1249 UNTS 13 (entered into force 3 September 1981). See also General Recommendation No. 30 on Women in Conflict Prevention, Conflict and Post-conflict Situations, CEDAW/C/GC/30, 1 November 2013, §§ 46(b) and 81(e); § 46(b) articulates the importance of ensuring 'women's equal representation at all decision making levels in national institutions and mechanisms', including inter alia 'transitional justice mechanisms (judicial and non-judicial)'; § 81(e) emphasises the importance of ensuring that 'women are involved in the design, operation and monitoring of transitional mechanisms at all levels so as to guarantee that their experience of conflict is included, their particular needs and priorities are met and all violations suffered are addressed; and ensure their participation in the design of all reparations programmes'. Sudan has not signed or ratified CEDAW; however it has ratified the ICCPR.

[209] SC Res. 1325 (2000). See the Preamble, which confirms the 'important role of women in the prevention and resolution of conflicts and in peace-building' and stresses 'the importance of their equal participation and full involvement in all efforts for the maintenance and promotion of peace and security, and the need to increase their role in decision-making with regard to conflict prevention and resolution'.

[210] SC Res. 2467 (2019).

[211] See Guidance note of the Secretary-General: United Nations approach to transitional justice, ST/SG(09)/A652, March 2020, at 5, which highlights that 'transitional justice approaches should pay special attention to abuses committed against groups most affected by conflict, particularly women. Gender inequality is one of the most pervasive forms of societal inequality and is often exacerbated by conflict and situations of gross human rights violations. Entrenched forms of gender-based violence also make women and girls particularly vulnerable to conflict-related human rights abuses, including systematic sexual violence which often continues unabated even after conflict ends. The social stigma and trauma associated with reporting such crimes and women's exclusion from public decision-making processes make it particularly challenging for women to engage with transitional justice mechanisms'. Furthermore, during her 2014 Statement to the UNSC, the former Prosecutor Fatou Bensouda emphasised ongoing atrocities in Darfur and their disproportionate impact on women and girls.

14. Furthermore, victim participation in ICC proceedings should aim to address underlying structural causes of gender inequality. For example, UNSC Resolution (2019) states as follows:

> Transitional justice processes should seek to address the underlying gender inequality in societies. Redressing such inequality entails addressing the needs and priorities of all women and girls, lesbian, gay, bisexual, transgender, queer and intersex individuals, and survivors of sexual and gender-based violence, including men and boys, as well as guaranteeing their safe and meaningful participation in those processes.[212]

15. Consequently, addressing the structural causes of gender inequality requires that the Court adopt a 'transformative' approach to victim participation. Rees and Chinkin argue that 'transformative justice' must have 'gender relations at its center'.[213] In the opinion of the single judge, 'transformative' victim participation in the context of ICC proceedings requires a contextual, bottom-up, and locally grounded approach geared towards addressing structural inequalities, including those related to gender, which arguably are some of the root causes of conflict.[214]

16. Furthermore, the idea of transformative justice has been articulated in several UN documents on reparations. For example, the Guidance Note of the Secretary General on Reparations for Conflict-Related Sexual Violence (CRSV) instructs that '[R]eparations should strive to be transformative, including in design, implementation and impact'.[215] In the opinion of the single judge, transformative justice is not only limited to the reparations phase of the proceedings, but also to victim participation.

17. White has articulated an ascending scale of four general forms of participation: nominal; instrumental; representative, and transformative.[216] In the opinion of the

[212] United Nations Security Council, *Women, Peace and Security: Report of the Secretary General*, S/2019/800 (9 October 2019), at 20, § 65, available at https://documents.un.org/doc/undoc/gen/n19/308/37/pdf/n1930837.pdf.

[213] M. Rees and C. Chinkin, 'Exposing the Gendered Myth of Post Conflict Transition: The Transformative Power of Economic and Social Rights' 48(4) *New York University Journal of International Law and Politics* (2016) 1211–1226, at 1213.

[214] S. Robins, 'Failing Victims? The Limits of Transitional Justice in Addressing the Needs of Victims of Violations' 11(1) *Human Rights and International Legal Discourse* (2017) 41–58, at 41; P. Gready and S. Robins, 'From Transitional to Transformative Justice: A New Agenda for Practice' 8 *International Journal of Transitional Justice* (IJTJ) (2014) 339–343; E. Schmid, *Taking Economic Social and Cultural Rights Seriously in International Criminal Law* (Cambridge: Cambridge University Press, 2015), at 33.

[215] United Nations, *Guidance Note of the Secretary-General: Reparations for Conflict-Related Sexual Violence*, ST/SG(02)/R425 (2014), at 1, available at https://digitallibrary.un.org/record/814902?v=pdf. Other UN documents that refer to a 'transformational' approach to justice include CEDAW General Recommendation No. 30, *supra* note 208, §§ 34, 79.

[216] S. C. White, 'Depoliticising Development: The Uses and Abuses of Participation', in J. Pearce (ed.), *Development, NGOs, and Civil Society: Selected Essays from Development in Practice* (Oxford: Oxfam GB, 2000) at 142–155.

single judge, these principles of participation are wholly applicable to victim participation at the ICC and consequently victim participation should aim to be transformative, empowering victims as opposed to those acting on their behalf, and allow them to engage with the Court on their own terms.[217]

18. There exist varied gendered experiences and consequences of conflict, and therefore women's inclusion must be proactively sought throughout the process of facilitating victim participation in order to ensure that it is meaningful. However, meaningful and 'transformative' victim participation should not be tokenistic and performative through the mere numerical inclusion of women; rather, it should aim to ensure that they can communicate their views and concerns and have their input incorporated into any relevant processes. In addition, given that victim communities do not exist in a vacuum and often form part of larger patriarchal social and political structures dominated by men, it is necessary for the Registry to expect some resistance to gender-inclusive victim participation and design strategies that will counter such resistance.

19. Furthermore, it is important to recognise that women are not a monolithic group, and victim participation processes must allow for the full diversity of women, including those of different minority religious or ethnic groups, as well as those from rural or urban backgrounds, to participate in ICC proceedings. In particular, the Registry and their interlocutors must proactively seek to engage with women, girls, and non-binary individuals who may be eligible to participate in ICC proceedings.

20. Steps should be taken at every stage of the victim participation process in order to ensure the participation of marginalised groups or persons depending on the victim's sex or gender identity. It is crucial for the Registry to ensure the inclusion of women and girls who may have a disadvantaged socio-economic status. In line with international human rights standards, the single judge submits that the facilitation of victim participation by VPRS and its intermediaries must be fulfilled without discrimination based on sex, gender identity, ethnicity, race, age, political affiliation, class, marital status, sexual orientation, nationality, religion, and disability, or any other status.

21. In addition to the victim's sex or gender identity, any other intersecting factors, such as a victim's social or political identity, must also be considered in order to prevent any discrimination against them during the facilitation of victim participation. Indeed, discrimination against women can affect them in intersectional ways (including race, ethnicity, age, sexual orientation, and gender identity, amongst others).[218] Thus, it is necessary for the Registry to remain mindful of intersectional forms of discrimination when facilitating victim participation.

[217] *Ibid*, at 144–147.

[218] See UN Committee on the Elimination of Racial Discrimination (CERD), General Comment 32, Seventy-Fifth Session, August 2009, § 7 on intersectionality.

22. Furthermore, women and girls also face significant structural and cultural inequalities in many contexts within which this Court operates and generally worldwide.[219] For example, women and girls may face greater obstacles than their male counterparts in having their voices heard in processes that impact their interests.[220] Some of these obstacles may be practical, such as childcare responsibilities or those relating to work, especially in the home.[221] In addition, in certain cultures women's voices may generally be marginalised due to traditional, religious, and cultural practices that operate within many contexts, including in Sudan.[222]

23. In addition, women and girl survivors of SGBC may face even greater obstacles to having their voices heard given their trauma or the silencing of their experiences.[223] Furthermore, in certain communities women may be discouraged from attending school or may be married at a younger age, limiting their educational opportunities.[224] This may have a direct and disproportional impact on their levels of literacy, and consequently their ability to complete victim application forms or adequately convey their views with regard to their choice of legal representation.[225]

[219] Rees and Chinkin, *supra* note 213, at 1216: 'Put simply, an analysis of the structures of power – ownership of and access to land, property and resources, access to tools, education, paid employment, positions of authority in the economy, governance and state institutions, and the media – who has it, who uses it, and how, shows that men dominate power structures. Across all such structures, it is clear that there is an overwhelming dominance of men.'

[220] *Ibid.*

[221] For example, 'by law, men are the sole financial providers within the family, and women are the sole caregivers within the family' in Sudan. See L. Tønnessen, 'Women at Work in Sudan: Marital Privilege or Constitutional Right?' 26 *Social Politics* (2019) 223–244, at 223; see also World Bank, 'Sudan', World Bank's Women, Business and the Law Index, 2021, available at https://wbl.worldbank.org/content/dam/documents/wbl/2021/snapshots/Sudan.pdf.

[222] See for example, UN Women, Sudan, Country Fact Sheet, available at https://data.unwomen.org/country/sudan.

[223] Rees and Chinkin, *supra* note 213, at 122: 'many women are in a position of vulnerability post conflict caused through the commission of war crimes and crimes against humanity against them, displacement, the continued operation of the predatory political economy, and the constructions of femininity that render them "passive and victims"'. See also CEDAW General Recommendation 30, *supra* note 208; Committee on the Elimination of Discrimination Against Women, Concluding Comments of the Committee on the Elimination of Discrimination against Women: Bosnia and Herzegovina, 37, UN Doc. CEDAW/C/BIH/CO/3 (2 June 2006).

[224] S. S. O. Mohamed, 'Assessment of the Gender Gap in Sudan', UNU-MERIT Working Paper No. 2011-004, 1 January 2011, available at http://dx.doi.org/10.2139/ssrn.1856543.

[225] Rees and Chinkin, *supra* note 213, at 1219: '[F]or instance . . . without access to their economic and social entitlements, survivors of and witnesses to wartime atrocities are less likely to be able to participate in court proceedings, or truth commissions, thereby denying access to justice and sustaining perpetrator impunity. The same is true for participation in peace processes and the political, institutional, and social structures for reconstruction. Such participation would be a luxury for those lacking, for instance, adequate food, shelter, and employment. This in turn lessens the likelihood of achieving the sought-after stability and human security post conflict (including food, health, gender, and physical security).'

24. Therefore, it is critical for the Registry to assess whether such obstacles exist and implement strategies in order to ensure the equal participation of women in the victim participation process. This could be through the organisation of 'women only' spaces which would allow women to speak more freely, or through separate meetings for survivors of SGBC.

25. Furthermore, women's meaningful participation in roles of leadership can also actively confront patriarchal power structures and entrench women's status as equal rights bearers within a community.[226] In relation to VPRS's intermediaries, the single judge notes that it can be the case that men and male voices are amplified over others, such that men may be more likely to volunteer as intermediaries for VPRS. As such, the single judge submits that VPRS must take steps to ensure that women are given the opportunity to participate in this type of 'leadership' role as per the ICC Guidelines on Intermediaries.[227]

26. The reason for this is twofold: firstly, it will engender a gender-sensitive and inclusive approach to victim participation if women are afforded such positions of leadership, effectively allowing them to exercise their agency throughout the victim participation process. Secondly, the presence of female intermediaries will possibly make it easier for other female victims or victims of SGBC to give a fuller account of the harm they have suffered. Given that it is often the case that VPRS intermediaries, rather than staff of VPRS, assist victims in the completion of victim application forms, ensuring that victims are comfortable enough to express the totality of the harm they have suffered must be a key consideration in the choice of intermediary. Furthermore, it may be easier for female intermediaries to access networks of victims who may be hesitant to speak to men. In this way, women's inclusion in leadership positions, such as that of a VPRS intermediary, or the spokesperson for a group of victims, rather than solely as 'victims, for example of SGBC', can help cement the role of women in transitional justice processes.

27. The suspect in this case, Mr Al-Rahman, has been charged by the Prosecutor in Counts 8–9 of perpetrating rape as a crime against humanity and a war crime.[228] In Bindisi and the surrounding areas, militia/Janjaweed and Government of Sudan

[226] F. Stewart, 'The Fourth Domain for Gender Equality: Decision-Making and Power' in *Achieving Gender Equality, Women's Empowerment and Strengthening Development Cooperation*, Report by Department of Economic and Social Affairs, Office for ECOSOC Support and Coordination, UN (New York: United Nations, 2010), at 31, available at www.un.org/en/ecosoc/docs/pdfs/10-50143_(e)_(desa)dialogues_ecosoc_achieving_gender_equality_women_empowerment.pdf.

[227] ICC, Guidelines Governing the Relations between the Court and Intermediaries: for the Organs and Units of the Court and Counsel working with intermediaries (March 2014), at 7–9, available at www.icc-cpi.int/sites/default/files/GRCI-Eng.pdf.

[228] Public redacted version of Second Corrected Version of Document Containing the Charges, 29 March 2021 (ICC-02/05-01/20-325-Conf-Anx1), 22 April 2021 (ICC-02/05-01/20-325-Conf-Anx1-Corr2), *Ali Kushayb* (ICC-02/05-01/20-325-Anx1-Corr-2-Red), 23 April 2021 (hereafter Document Containing the Charges).

forces allegedly raped at least seventeen women.[229] However, as is often the case in times of conflict, the number of sexual violence survivors may be greater than those stated in official figures.[230] Therefore, it is highly likely that VPRS and their intermediaries will encounter a larger number of victims of SGBC.

28. Although it may be harder to ensure that victims of SGBC come forward and participate in ICC proceedings due to the possibility of stigma and ostracism, the single judge believes that a well-thought-out strategy for victim participation will ensure that victims of any gender will feel comfortable enough to participate in ICC proceedings. At the same time, it is important to remain mindful that although women are disproportionately impacted by SGBC, the Registry should avoid equating 'woman or girl victims' with 'victims of sexual violence', as this could further victimise women and sideline male and gender-non-binary victims of SGBC.

29. Lastly, special attention must be paid to the participation of child victims in ICC proceedings, including their age, maturity, and the harm that they have suffered, in order to prevent further harm or trauma. Child victims should feel comfortable enough to express their views and concerns freely and the VPRS should implement measures in order to ensure the protection of their rights, especially those girls who may be affected by SGBC. However, at the same time, VPRS and their intermediaries must remain aware of potential violations against men and boys, which tend to result in stigma and silence.[231] To this end, the single judge encourages a statistical evaluation of the number of victim application forms received in order to ensure sufficient gender representation. However, it must be borne in mind that gender inclusiveness cannot be solely represented by numbers, but, rather, 'meaningful' participation requires that women, girls, and non-binary individuals are able to exert their agency and influence through justice processes, such as victim participation in ICC proceedings. Thus, the single judge stresses that the representation of women and girls should not be limited to the cosmetic and numerical 'inclusion of women' but should also ensure that women are heard, and able to exercise their agency.

[229] *Ibid*, §§ 51–53.

[230] UNSG, Conflict-Related Sexual Violence, Report of the Secretary General, S/2022/272, 29 March 2022.

[231] S. Sivakumaran, 'Sexual Violence against Men in Armed Conflict' 18(2) *European Journal of International Law* (2007) 253–276, at 267; S. Mouthaan, 'Sexual Violence against Men and International Law – Criminalising the Unmentionable' 13(3) *International Law Review* (2013) 665–695, at 691; and see 677 for an in-depth discussion on how international law has a tendency to leave out men as victims, but readily views them as perpetrators; D. Lewis, 'Unrecognized Victims: Sexual Violence against Men in Conflict Settings under International Law', 27(1) *Wisconsin International Law Journal* (2009) at 7, citing A. N. Groth, *Men Who Rape: The Psychology of the Offender* 2 (New York: Plenum, 1979).

Effective Communication

30. It has been argued that an essential element of meaningful victim participation is 'frequent communication and consultation between victims and the Court'.[232] Meaningful participation necessarily requires that victims are not treated as an 'abstract or symbolic entity, but as individual rights-bearers with opinions' that are relayed to the Court.[233]

31. The single judge concurs that one of the foundational elements of meaningful victim participation is the implementation of strategies aimed at ensuring consistent two-way communication between affected communities and the Court. Indeed, as highlighted in the previous section, consultation is also an essential element of transitional justice.[234] This function appropriately falls within the mandate of the Public Information and Outreach Section (PIOS) and VPRS.

32. The role of the VPRS in assisting victims in completing victim application forms, as well as collecting application forms is underscored by Regulation 86(9) of the Regulations of the Court (RoC) and Rule 16(1) of the RPE. Regulations 5*bis* and 6 of the Regulations of the Registry outline the Registry's role in ensuring public dissemination of appropriate, neutral, and timely information concerning the activities of the Court through public information and outreach programmes. Further to this, public information programmes must be aimed at 'fostering public understanding and support for the work of the Court'.[235]

33. Pre-Trial Chamber I in the situation in Palestine[236] called on the Registrar to create an information and communication system between the Court and victims, stating that 'outreach and public information activities in situation countries are quintessential to foster support, public understanding and confidence in the work of the Court. At the same time, they enable the Court to better understand the concerns and expectations of victims, so that it can respond more effectively and clarify, where necessary, any misconceptions'.[237] Similarly, Pre-Trial Chamber III has stated that, 'in order to be able to properly exercise their rights, victims should be

[232] A. Sehmi, 'Now That We Have No Voice, What Will Happen to Us?': Experiences of Victim Participation in the *Kenyatta* Case' 16(3) *Journal of International Criminal Justice* (2018) 571–591, at 580.

[233] *Ibid*.

[234] See generally, Report of the Special Rapporteur on the promotion of truth, justice, reparation and guarantees of non-recurrence, UN GA, A/71/567 (2016); and the Report of the Special Rapporteur on the promotion of truth, justice, reparation and guarantees of non-recurrence on Participation of victims in transitional justice measures, UN GA A/HRC/34/62 (2016), § 79.

[235] Regulation 5*bis*(2), Regulations of the Registry, available at www.icc-cpi.int/sites/default/files/RegulationsRegistryEng.pdf.

[236] Decision on Information and Outreach for the Victims of the Situation, Situation in the State of Palestine (ICC-01/18-2), Pre-Trial Chamber I, 13 July 2018.

[237] *Ibid*, § 7.

provided with sufficient and accurate information about the Court's role and activities'.[238]

34. The Assembly of States Parties (ASP) has also underscored the importance of providing victims and affected communities with information regarding the activities of the Court, 'in order to put into effect, the unique mandate given to the International Criminal Court towards victims'.[239]

35. Furthermore, the ICC's Integrated Strategy for External Relations, Public Information and Outreach has defined outreach as a 'process of establishing sustainable two-way communication between the Court and communities affected by the situations that are subject to investigations. It aims to provide information, promote understanding and support for the Court's work and to provide access to judicial proceedings'.[240]

36. Consequently, for the Court to properly fulfil its mandate, it is essential that its role and activities are clearly understood by affected communities. Outreach and public information activities are critical not only to engender support for the Court but, more importantly, to establish a two-way form of communication between the Court and affected communities.

37. In the opinion of the single judge, outreach plays an integral role in informing victims of their participatory rights under the Statute. The success of victim participation in ICC proceedings is highly dependent on proper outreach and public information activities directed towards victims by both PIOS and the VPRS. Outreach regarding victim participation ensures that victims are aware of their participatory rights under Article 68(3) of the Statute. Furthermore, it lays the groundwork for the dissemination and collection of victim application forms within affected communities by the VPRS.

38. Therefore, it is crucial for the VPRS and PIOS to work together in order to inform victim communities of their right to participate in ICC proceedings under the Statute; the practicalities of the victim participation process, including the temporal, material, and territorial scope of the case; and respond to relevant questions from victim communities. To this end, the Registry must employ a bottom-up and focused strategy, and enable harmony between victims' needs and institutional

[238] *Ibid*, § 11; Order on Information and Outreach for the Victims of the Situation, Situation in the People's Republic of Bangladesh/Republic of the Union of Myanmar, Order on Information and Outreach, 2020 (ICC-01/19-28), Pre-Trial Chamber III, 20 January 20202, § 7.

[239] See, for example, Resolution adopted at the Review Conference in Kampala, RC/Res.2, 8 June 2010, The Impact of the Rome Statute System on Victims and Affected Communities; most recently see ICC-ASP/13/Res.4, 17 December 2014, Resolution on Victims and Affected Communities, Reparations and the Trust Fund for Victims; ICCASP/16/Res. 6, Strengthening the International Criminal Court and the Assembly of States Parties, 14 December 2017, §§ 93–94.

[240] ICC, 'Integrated Strategy for External Relations, Public Information and Outreach', available at www.icc-cpi.int/sites/default/files/NR/rdonlyres/425E80BA-1EBC-4423-85C6-D4F2B93C7506/185049/ICCPIDSWBOR0307070402_IS_En.pdf.

responses. Victim participation should be viewed as an ongoing process, entailing dialogue and constant adaptation, in order to ensure that it is meaningful.

39. At the same time, the single judge is cognisant of several obstacles that have prevented PIOS and VPRS from conducting outreach with affected communities and informing eligible victims of their right to participate in these proceedings.

40. Firstly, the Registry has been unable to establish a field presence in Darfur as a result of budgetary constraints and the attendant need to allocate the Court's limited resources across multiple situations and cases.[241] Consequently, this means that at present there is potentially a huge information vacuum in Darfur regarding the Court's activities and mandate that must be addressed.

41. Secondly, ongoing security concerns in Darfur and the surrounding areas over the past few years has meant that the establishment of a Field Office has faced significant hurdles, apart from those related to budgetary concerns.[242] The single judge is aware that the security situation has meant that many victims have left the region and are living either in other parts of Sudan or have left the country entirely and now form part of the Darfurian diaspora.[243]

42. Thirdly, the COVID-19 worldwide pandemic has greatly affected the mobility and ability of staff members of the Court to conduct field missions, in Darfur or where members of the Darfurian diaspora may reside, in order to carry out general outreach,[244] inform victims of their right to participate, and solicit their views on the choice of their legal representation in proceedings, should they be eligible to participate.[245]

43. However, the single judge contends that despite these obstacles the Court still has a binding duty to fulfil its mandate to the best of its ability, bearing in mind that

[241] On 12 December 2014, the former Prosecutor Fatou Bensouda informed the UNSC of the decision to hibernate investigative activities in Darfur due to limited resources of the Court, lack of oversight of the Security Council, and difficulties in bringing the accused individuals to justice. Statement to the United Nations Security Council on the Situation in Darfur, pursuant to UNSCR 1593 (2005), 12 December 2014, § 4. Louise Arbour, former UN High Commissioner for Human Rights, also called for 'an increased visible presence of the ICC in Sudan', insisting that it 'is possible to conduct serious investigations of human rights during an armed conflict in general, and Darfur in particular, without putting victims at unreasonable risk', Observations of the United Nations High Commissioner for Human Rights Invited in Application of Rule 103 of the Rules of Procedure and Evidence, Situation in Darfur (ICC-02/05-19), Pre-Trial Chamber I, 10 October 2006, § 64.

[242] Registry Observations on Aspects Related to the Admission of Victims for Participation in the Proceedings, *Ali Kushayb* (ICC-02/05-01/20-203), 17 November 2020, § 9.

[243] Registry Report on Proof of Identity Documents Available to Victims of the Case, *Ali Kushayb* (ICC-02/05-01/20-211), 24 November 2020.

[244] Public Redacted version of Registry Request for Authorization to use a Modified Standard Application Form to Facilitate Victim Participation in the Case, 8 October 2002, ICC-01/05-01/20-178-Conf, *Ali Kushayb* (ICC-02/05-01/20-178-Red), 2 November 2020, § 5.

[245] *Ibid*; see also Public redacted version of Registry Observations on the Defence's Réponse à la Requête ICC-02/05-01/20-178 (ICC-02/05-01/20-182-Conf), 26 October 2020, ICC-02/05-01/20-194-Conf, *Ali Kushayb* (ICC-02/05-01/20-194-Red), 29 October 2020, § 39.

in some instances this may necessitate adapting to a new set of circumstances, especially considering the COVID-19 pandemic. Indeed, the Court simply cannot fulfil its mission without ensuring that the affected communities are able to understand the Court's mandate, the judicial proceedings, and their right to participate in proceedings and claim reparations.

44. Consequently, PIOS and VPRS, in consultation with the relevant Registry sections, must consider the feasibility of conducting field missions in Chad, Darfur, or other locations where potential victims reside, in order to commence the process of consulting with victims, providing them with information regarding the application process, disseminating victim application forms either directly or through VPRS intermediaries, and collecting completed victim application forms either manually or electronically.

45. Given the pervasive and unpredictable impact of the COVID-19 pandemic on the operations of the Court, the single judge supports creative solutions that would enable communication between the Court and victim communities. For example, where logistical and security considerations make it difficult to consult with victims directly, VPRS should consider the possibility of consulting victims though secure online platforms, in collaboration with VPRS intermediaries, and in consultation with the relevant security sections within the Court. In addition, given the easing of travel restrictions, PIOS and VPRS should consider the feasibility to travelling to countries where a significant number of the affected Darfurian diaspora reside.

Legal Representation of Victims

46. Lastly, meaningful victim participation is not possible without quality legal representation. It has been argued that the entire system of victim participation at the ICC 'feminizes and infantilizes' victims and they are consistently treated as 'weaker' participants who do not need to be consulted on major decisions that impact on their interests.[246] One of these major decisions is victims' choice of legal representation. However, ensuring a meaningful and gender-inclusive system of victim participation will entrench a system of victim participation that seeks to empower victims, and not marginalise them.

47. Consultations with victims must not only be limited to their participation in legal proceedings but should include their views on their choice of legal representative. The system of victim participation at this Court must seek to empower victims, rather than marginalise them; it must ensure that victims are not 'infantilised' and disempowered in these processes; and consequently, victims must be consulted on decisions that impact on their interests. In the opinion of the single judge,

[246] C. Schwobel-Patel, 'The "Ideal" Victim of International Criminal Law' 29(3) *European Journal of International Law* (2018) 703–724, at 724.

one of the most important decisions that victims can make is their choice of legal representative/s.

48. As noted by the Pre-Trial Chamber in the Situation in the Republic of Kenya:

> [W]hen deciding on the selection of the Common Legal Representative, the Chamber must balance a number of requirements. These requirements include in particular (a) the need to ensure that the participation of victims, through their legal representative, is as meaningful as possible, as opposed to purely symbolic; (b) the purpose of common legal representation, which is not only to represent the views and concerns of the victims, but also to allow victims to follow and understand the development of the trial.[247]

49. To this, the single judge would add that the process of in-person consultation and engagement with victim communities is arguably the core function of the legal representative and potentially may also have a restorative justice function.[248]

50. Rule 90(1) of the RPE provides that 'A victim shall be free to choose a legal representative'. However, given the often large number of victims who are eligible to participate in proceedings, Rule 90(2) provides that 'the Chamber may, for the purposes of ensuring the effectiveness of the proceedings, request the victims or particular groups of victims, if necessary, with the assistance of the Registry, to choose a common legal representative or representatives'.

51. The single judge notes that the legal representative of potential victims in their Request for Guidance represents 102 individuals who are seeking permission to participate in the confirmation of charges hearings.[249] The legal representative in question notes that she 'has been instructed to represent a number of victim advocacy groups',[250] and through her work with these organisations, she has identified 102 potential survivors who have suffered harm that potentially falls within the scope of the charges in this case.[251]

52. The single judge notes that the process of an appointment of legal representation for victims should be driven by consultation with victims and through an open and transparent recruitment process of counsel, whether the outcome is the Office of Public Counsel for Victims (OPCV) or external counsel. In this respect, the single judge notes with concern two issues in relation to the ongoing practice for appointment of counsel for victims at the Court. Firstly, there has been a tendency to appoint the OPCV as the common legal representative for victims without due

[247] Decision on victims' representation and participation, *Muthaura & Kenyatta* (ICC-01/09/02/11-498), Trial Chamber V, 6 October 2012, § 58.

[248] Sehmi, *supra* note 232, at 590–591.

[249] Request for Guidance, *supra* note 201.

[250] *Ibid*, § 5.

[251] *Ibid*.

consideration to victims' views or existing representation.[252] Secondly, it has been the case that external counsel who have been able to establish 'first contact', so to speak, with victim communities have the expectation that they will automatically be appointed as common legal representative in their respective cases.[253]

53. Both practices are problematic in their own way. The blanket representation of victims by the OPCV in all situations before this Court clearly raises issues of a lack of diversity in representation and perhaps prevents victims from choosing lawyers from their own country, or those with a different set of expertise. This lack of diversity also has an impact on the complementary nature of the Court and the importance of creating/harnessing expertise on victim representation and international criminal law more broadly beyond The Hague through external legal representatives and their support staff.

54. For example, it could be the case that victims would like to be represented by lawyers who are able to speak to them in their own language or be able to establish a permanent field presence in the relevant country. At the same time, there may be groups of victims who would prefer to be represented by the OPCV given their institutional positioning and familiarity with the Court's practices and jurisprudence.

55. With regard to counsel who are 'first on the scene', so to speak, either as a result of them being from the same country or for other reasons, and are able to obtain powers of attorney from victim communities first, the single judge notes that this practice must not be systematised within court procedures such that these lawyers are automatically appointed as common legal representative by virtue of them being the first to have obtained powers of attorney from victims.

56. Victim communities are often traumatised and vulnerable in the aftermath of conflict, and therefore may appoint the lawyer that happens to approach them first. It may be the case that these lawyers are not well versed in international criminal law, or not well suited to represent victims for other reasons – for example, there may exist conflicts of interest or potentially better suited candidates with specific expertise, on SGBC, for example. Thus, it is the opinion of the single judge that all lawyers who are interested in representing victims, including the OPCV, must go through a competitive recruitment process in order to ensure they have the necessary expertise to represent victims in a particular situation country. Furthermore, and more importantly, victims must be consulted on their opinion of the candidates, including those who may already be representing them, in order to ensure that victims are given proper agency in the appointment of a legal representative.

[252] Human Rights Watch, 'Who Will Stand for Us?' (2017), at 14, available at www.hrw.org/sites/default/files/report_pdf/ijongweno817_web.pdf.

[253] Legal framework and experience to date on common legal representation, *Ruto & Sang* (ICC-01/09-01/11-243-Anx1), 1 August 2011, at § 8. This remark is not directed at Ms Clooney et al., who have obtained powers of attorney for a number of victims who may or may not fall within the scope of the present case.

57. Thus, taking into consideration the above, the single judge notes that in order to ensure that the system of victim participation at this Court empowers victims, victims must be able to have a choice in the appointment of their counsel, and a fair and transparent recruitment process of victims' counsel must take place in order to ensure that the counsel selected have the necessary expertise in representing victims in international criminal proceedings, such as those before the ICC. Such expertise may include specific language skills; familiarity with the local context; previous expertise in representing victims; expertise in international criminal law; an established practice of working with victims of SGBC; proximity to the local communities; amongst others.

58. Again, the single judge would like to emphasise the importance of ensuring that consultations with victims on their choice of legal representation include the views of women and girls, whether victims of SGBC or not, male victims of SGBC, and other non-binary individuals. Consultations with victims must not be dominated by male voices and there must be room for women and girls, as well as other marginalised and intersecting groups, to have the opportunity to air their views and opinions.

59. Lastly, given the prevalence of SGBC in conflict, whether charged or not, it is the opinion of the single judge that counsel appointed to represent victims will have the necessary expertise with working with victims of SGBC or will endeavour to appoint team members with the necessary expertise.

FOR THESE REASONS, THE SINGLE JUDGE HEREBY

ORDERS the Registry, to establish, as soon as practicable, a system of public information and outreach activities relating to victim participation for the benefit of the victims and affected communities in Darfur and report back to the single judge in compliance with the principles established in the present decision.

ORDERS the Registry, in consultation with ICC Security Section, to undertake the feasibility of a mission to South Sudan/Chad to consult with victims, or alternatively arrange meetings with victims in neighbouring states, as well as consider meeting victims who may be in the diaspora.

ORDERS the Registry to facilitate the participation of victims through outreach, liaising with intermediaries, and the dissemination and collection of victim application forms in line with the principles laid out in this Decision.

ORDERS the Registry to consult victims on their choice of legal representation and report back to the Chamber regarding the outcome these consultations, with the view to conducting an open recruitment process in relation to the organisation of common legal representation.

Judge Anushka Sehmi

10.5 GENDER-BASED PERSECUTION IN THE ABD-AL-RAHMAN CONFIRMATION OF CHARGES

Lisa Davis and Marina Kumskova

In 2021, Pre-Trial Chamber II confirmed charges of war crimes and crimes against humanity against Mr Ali Muhammad Ali Abd-Al-Rahman (Ali Kushayb).[254] In this rewritten decision, Lisa Davis and Marina Kumskova consider whether the original Chamber had sufficient evidence before it to establish substantial grounds to believe that Mr Abd-Al-Rahman committed the crime against humanity of gender persecution under Article 7(1)(h) of the Rome Statute at the sites of Kodoom, Bindisi, Mukjar, and Deleig, as well as the surrounding areas, and request the Prosecutor, under Article 61(7)(c) of the Rome Statute, to amend its Document Containing Charges.[255]

Davis and Kumskova dissect the requirements of gender persecution, namely that there was a deprivation of liberty, that there was targeting of a collectivity, that this targeting was on gender grounds and was in connection with any act referred to in Article 7(1) of the Rome Statute, and then use these requirements and available evidence to analyse the evidence presented regarding all incidents in Sudan.

Davis and Kumskova find that the evidence satisfies the threshold that both Fur males and females were the victims of gender persecution, albeit in connection with differing Article 7(1) crimes, ultimately request the prosecution to include the charge of gender persecution in all incidents, and adjourn the confirmation of charges hearing for such a request to be made. Moreover, the rewritten decision suggests that any act of rape, torture, murder, other inhumane acts, or outrages upon personal dignity, if used to target a civilian group by reason of their gender, and if proven by the Court, are enough to find charges of gender persecution.

No.: ICC-02/05-01/20-433
Date: 9 July 2021

Original: English

PRE-TRIAL CHAMBER II (B)

Before: Judge Lisa Davis, Presiding Judge
Judge Marina Kumskova

SITUATION IN DARFUR, SUDAN
IN THE CASE OF

[254] Decision on the Confirmation of Charges against Ali Muhammad Ali Abd-Al-Rahman (Ali Kushayb), *Abd-Al-Rahman* (ICC-02/05-01/20-433), Pre-Trial Chamber II, 9 July 2021.

[255] Public Redacted Version of Second Corrected Version of Document Containing the Charges, 29 March 2021, ICC-02/05-01/20-325-Conf-Anx1, *Abd-Al-Rahman* (ICC 02/05-01/20-325-Conf-Anx1-Corr2), Pre-Trial Chamber II, 22 April 2021.

THE *PROSECUTOR V. ALI MUHAMMAD ALI ABD-AL-RAHMAN ('ALI KUSHAYB')*

Public

Decision on the Confirmation of Charges against Ali Muhammad Ali Abd-Al-Rahman (Ali Kushayb)

CHARGES

1. This decision on the confirmation of charges in the case against Mr Ali Muhammad Ali Abd-Al-Rahman (Mr Abd-Al-Rahman), also known as Ali Kushayb, a national of the Republic of the Sudan (Sudan), addresses the legal question of whether there is sufficient evidence to establish substantial grounds to believe that Mr Abd-Al-Rahman committed the crime against humanity of gender persecution under Article 7(1)(h) of the Rome Statute (Statute) in Kodoom, Bindisi, and surrounding areas between 15 and 16 August 2003, in Mukjar and surrounding areas between the end of February 2004 and the beginning of March 2004, and in Deleig and surrounding areas between 5 and 7 March 2004.

2. The Chamber adjourns the confirmation of charges hearing and requests the Prosecutor to amend its Document Containing the Charges,[256] pursuant to Article 61 (7)(c)(ii) of the Statute. First, the Chamber requests the Prosecutor to consider whether all war crimes and crimes against humanity that Mr Abd-Al-Rahman allegedly committed in Kodoom, Bindisi, and surrounding areas between 15 and 16 August 2003 (Counts 1–10), in Mukjar and surrounding areas between the end of February 2004 and the beginning of March 2004 (Counts 12–20), and in Deleig and surrounding areas between 5 and 7 March 2004 (Counts 22–30) can be separately and cumulatively charged as gender persecution. Second, the Chamber requests the Prosecutor to conduct further investigation with respect to gender persecution in Kodoom, Bindisi, and surrounding areas between 15 and 16 August 2003 (in addition to political and ethnic persecution under Count 11).

3. The Chamber concludes that, in circumstances where a civilian group is targeted on gender grounds by the acts of rape, torture, murder, other inhumane acts, and outrages upon personal dignity, such crimes either separately or cumulatively rise to the level of the crime against humanity of gender persecution under Article 7(1)(h) of the Statute and should be charged as such. In other words, each one of the war crimes or crimes against humanity, if used to target a civilian group by reason of their

[256] Public Redacted Version of Second Corrected Version of Document Containing the Charges, 29 March 2021, ICC-02/05-01/20-325-Conf-Anx1, *Abd-Al-Rahman* (ICC02/05-01/20-325-Conf-Anx1-Corr2), Pre-Trial Chamber II, 22 April 2021 (hereafter Second Corrected Version of Document Containing the Charges).

gender, and if proven by the Court, are enough to establish the crime against humanity of gender persecution.

BACKGROUND AND PROCEDURAL HISTORY

4. On 31 March 2005, pursuant to Article 13(b) of the Statute,[257] the United Nations Security Council referred to the Prosecutor the situation in Darfur, Sudan, as of 1 July 2002.[258]

5. In the present decision, the Chamber renders its determination under Article 61 (7)(c) of the Statute as to whether there is sufficient evidence to establish substantial grounds to believe that Mr Abd-Al-Rahman committed the crime against humanity of persecution on the grounds of gender in Darfur, Sudan. The purpose of the confirmation of charges procedure is to ensure that the charges that are supported by 'sufficient evidence to establish substantial grounds to believe that the person committed each of the crimes charged'.[259] While having carefully considered all of the arguments advanced by the parties and participants as part of its determination, the Chamber will only refer in this decision to those elements which it considers necessary to show the line of reasoning underpinning its conclusions.

CRIME AGAINST HUMANITY OF PERSECUTION

6. For the purposes of the Statute, 'crimes against humanity' means any acts enumerated under Article 7(1) of the Statute, including murder, torture, and rape, when committed as part of a widespread or systematic attack against a civilian population, with the perpetrator's knowledge of the attack. The chapeau elements for crimes against humanity were found to be sufficiently met for all charges in the case against Mr Abd-Al-Rahman and thus are not discussed here.

7. The crime against humanity of gender persecution requires, under the Statute, that (1) the perpetrator severely deprived, contrary to international law, one or more persons of fundamental rights; (2) the perpetrator targeted such person or persons by reason of the identity of a group or collectivity or targeted the group or collectivity as such; (3) such targeting was based on gender as defined in Article 7(3) of the Statute; and (4) the conduct was committed in connection with any act referred to in Article 7(1) of the Statute or any crime within the jurisdiction of the Court.[260] These elements are discussed below. Elements (5) and (6) pertaining to the chapeau elements for crimes against humanity are omitted.

[257] Art. 13(b), ICCSt.

[258] ICC Statement, 'Security Council Refers Situation in Darfur to ICC Prosecutor' (ICC-OTP-20050401-96), 1 April 2005, available at www.icc-cpi.int/news/icc-security-council-refers-situation-darfur-icc-prosecutor (hereafter ICC Statement).

[259] Art. 61(5), ICCSt.

[260] Art. 7(1)(h), ICCSt.

The Perpetrator Severely Deprived One or More Persons of Fundamental Rights

8. Article 7(2)(g) of the Statute defines 'persecution' as 'the intentional and severe deprivation of fundamental rights contrary to international law by reason of the identity of the group or collectivity'.

9. The Statute also requires, under the fourth element of persecution, a connection between gender persecution and an act under its Article 7(1) or any crime within the jurisdiction of the Court. Since all crimes under the Statute are violations of fundamental rights and all persecutory conduct violates the fundamental right to be free from discrimination, the violation of the right to be free from discrimination in connection with any relevant crime prohibited by the Statute always constitutes a severe deprivation of fundamental rights.[261]

10. The Court also recognises that it is in the interest of justice to consider all human rights violations that cumulatively constitute a severe deprivation of fundamental rights in connection to an act or acts of gender persecution.[262] For this reason, the Court considers a broad range of human rights violations.[263]

11. The Chamber notes that the Statute should be interpreted and applied in accordance with internationally recognised human rights pursuant to Article 21(3) and may consult 'applicable treaties' where 'appropriate' under Article 21(1)(b).[264] Such rights are enshrined in, for example, the Universal Declaration of Human Rights (UDHR), the International Covenant on Civil and Political Rights (ICCPR), and the International Covenant on Economic, Social and Cultural Rights (ICESCR) (taken together these are known as the 'international bill of human rights'); the Convention Against Torture and Other Cruel, Inhuman or Degrading Treatment or Punishment; the Convention on the Elimination of All Forms of Discrimination Against Women; the Convention on the Rights of the Child; the International Convention for the Elimination of Racial Discrimination; the Convention on the Rights of Persons with Disabilities; the African Charter on Human and Peoples' Rights; the American Convention on Human Rights; the

261 Office of the Prosecutor, 'Policy on the Crime of Gender Persecution', December 2022, available at www.icc-cpi.int/sites/default/files/2022-12/2022-12-07-Policy-on-the-Crime-of-Gender-Persecution.pdf, at § 39.

262 *Ibid.*

263 Judgment, *Kupreškić* (IT-95-16-T), Trial Chamber, 14 January 2000, § 618; Judgment, *Krnojelac* (IT-97-25-T), Trial Chamber II, 15 March 2002, § 433.

264 E.g., in *Al Hassan*, the Pre-Trial Chamber identified the following acts as constituting the severe deprivation of fundamental rights: flogging, restrictions on the freedom of movement, detention in inhuman conditions, as well as the control of educational freedoms may constitute severe deprivations of fundamental rights. See Decision on Confirmation of Charges, *Al Hassan* (ICC-01/12-01/18-461-Corr-Red), Pre-Trial Chamber I, 13 November 2019, §§ 665, 683, 684, 690.

European Convention on Human Rights; and other international or regional instruments on international human rights.[265]

12. The Chamber therefore calls on the Prosecutor to consult applicable treaties and other relevant international or regional human rights law in its analysis of the severe deprivation of fundamental rights in connection to any acts of persecution in its charges against Mr Abd-Al-Rahman.

The Perpetrator Targeted Persons by Reason of the Identity of a Group or Collectivity or Targeted the Group or Collectivity as Such

13. The Statute requires that the perpetrator targets a person or persons either based on 'the identity of a group or collectivity' or 'targeted the group or collectivity'.[266]

14. The 'targeted group' may be, and frequently is, larger than persons who are perceived to exhibit the criteria of the group and must be interpreted broadly.[267] In accordance with tribunal jurisprudence, the 'targeted group' is *defined by the perpetrator* and may include such victims who, due to their affiliations or sympathies for members of the identity protected under the prohibited grounds for persecution, may become part of the targeted group.[268] The targeted group may also be defined as non-members of a specific group, meaning persons targeted for being perceived as non-members of an *accepted* group.[269]

15. For gender persecution, this means the targeted group may simply be *anyone* who does not exhibit the acceptable gender criteria such as the roles, behaviours, activities, or attributes assigned to groups relevant for discriminatory targeting.[270] As the policy on the crime of gender persecution notes, '[g]roups targeted for gender persecution include, for example, women, girls, men, boys and LGBTQI+ persons, and subsets of these groups'.[271]

The Perpetrator's Targeting Was Based on Gender Grounds

16. Under Article 7(3) of the Statute, the term 'gender' refers to 'the two sexes, male and female, within the context of society'.[272] The policy explains that 'gender' refers to sex characteristics and social constructs and criteria used to define maleness and

[265] Office of the Prosecutor, *supra* note 262, at § 37.
[266] ICC Statement, *supra* note 258, Art. 7(1)(h)(2).
[267] Judgment, *Naletilić & Martinović* (IT-98-34-T), Trial Chamber, 31 March 2003, § 636 (citing Judgment, *Kvočka* (IT-98-30/1-T), Trial Chamber, 2 November 2001, § 195 (footnote omitted)).
[268] Judgment, *Ntaganda* (ICC-01/04-02/06), Trial Chamber VI, 8 July 2019, § 1011.
[269] Judgment, *Ongwen* (ICC-02/04-01/15-1762-Red), Trial Chamber IX, 4 February 2021, § 2735 (hereafter Ongwen Judgment).
[270] Office of the Prosecutor, *supra* note 262, at §§ 42, 45.
[271] *Ibid*, at § 5.
[272] ICC Statement, *supra* note 258, Art. 7(3).

femaleness, including roles, behaviours, activities and attributes'.[273] The policy further clarifies that 'gender persecution is committed against persons because of sex characteristics and/or because of the social constructs and criteria used to define gender'.[274] The Chamber accepts the policy's interpretation of Article 7(3) of the Statute because this interpretation is in accordance with decades of internationally recognised human rights, which is relevant in this Court by virtue of Article 21(3) of the Statute. Accordingly, the inextricable link between 'gender' and 'sex' should not be conflated.

The Conduct Was Committed in Connection with Any Act Referred to in Article 7, Paragraph 1 of the Statute

17. As noted above, the persecutory conduct must be committed *in connection with* any act referred to in Article 7(1) of the Statute (underlying act) and results in the severe deprivation of a victim's fundamental rights.[275] The policy notes that,

> The threshold for element one of gender persecution is always met when the crime[s] under the Statute are committed with discriminatory intent. This is because all crimes under the Statute are violations of fundamental rights and all persecutory conduct violates the fundamental right to be free from discrimination. Taken together, the violation of the right to be free from discrimination in connection with any relevant crime prohibited by the Statute always constitutes a severe deprivation of fundamental rights.[276]

18. In addition to satisfying its own elements pursuant to Article 7(1) of the Statute, an underlying act may also trigger other multiple and severe fundamental rights deprivations. As the policy notes, 'fundamental rights deprivations based on discriminatory grounds, should always be considered cumulatively'.[277] Identifying these additional deprivations helps to establish sufficient evidence to support the charge of gender persecution, providing a holistic and accurate historical record of atrocities and a clearer pathway to the non-repetition of crimes and sustainable peace.

AMENDED COUNT 11: GENDER PERSECUTION AS A CRIME AGAINST HUMANITY COMMITTED AGAINST THE FUR MEN AND WOMEN IN KODOOM, BINDISI, AND SURROUNDING AREAS

19. On 22 April 2021, the prosecution submitted its second corrected version of the Document Containing the Charges,[278] charging persecution as a crime against

[273] Office of the Prosecutor, *supra* note 262, at 3.
[274] *Ibid.*
[275] Ongwen Judgment, *supra* note 269, at §§ 2733, 2738.
[276] Office of the Prosecutor, *supra* note 262 at § 39 (footnote omitted).
[277] *Ibid.*
[278] Public Redacted Version of Second Corrected Version of Document Containing the Charges, *supra* note 256.

humanity on political and ethnic grounds committed in Kodoom, Bindisi, and surrounding areas between 15 and 16 August 2003 for targeting persons perceived as belonging to, or being associated with, or supporting the rebel armed groups (Count 11).[279] The Prosecutor did not charge gender as a ground of persecution for Count 11 (Bindisi and surrounds). Nor did the prosecution recognise women and girls as victims of gender persecution for Count 11. Therefore, the Court requests amendments for Count 11 under Article 61(7)(c) to include charges for gender persecution as a crime against humanity by way of the criminal acts listed under Counts 1–10.

20. In Kodoom, Bindisi, and surrounding areas (Counts 1–11), perpetrators tortured and killed Fur men, women, boys, and girls because of their ethnicity, political views and gender. While the militia/Janjaweed and Government of Sudan forces killed fleeing 'young boys, men, women and children',[280] victims were targeted on the basis of gender. The militia members were specifically instructed to keep men at the checkpoints.[281] The Fur women were asked about their husbands and often raped[282] but not targeted for killing in the same manner as men. In particular, the perpetrators captured fleeing men and women and separated them by their gender.[283] The men in particular were forced to keep their backs turned to their female counterparts and were threatened with death if they failed to obey the order.[284]

21. Most women were stripped of their clothing and raped, with their clothing stuffed in their mouths.[285] Women were often referred to as *khadim* (servants).[286] This is according to the perpetrators' belief that because of Fur women's gender and their ethnicity this is their prescribed gender role. Often egregious crimes are carried out as punishments for when victims are perceived to deviate from their prescribed gender role.[287] Stripping women of their clothes and the use of derogatory language were used as a means of humiliation, and mental torture was also common to many incidents.[288] Some of the women were raped in full view and/or hearing of other

[279] *Ibid*, at § 57.
[280] *Ibid*, at § 39.
[281] Public Redacted Version of Prosecution's Pre-Confirmation Brief, 16 April 2021, ICC-02/05-01/20-346-Conf-AnxA, *Abd-Al-Rahman* (ICC-02/05-01/20), Pre-Trial Chamber II, 21 May 2021, § 137 (hereafter Public Redacted Version of Prosecution's Pre-Confirmation Brief).
[282] *Ibid*, § 181.
[283] Public Redacted Version of Second Corrected Version of Document Containing the Charges, *supra* note 256, at § 45.
[284] *Ibid*.
[285] *Ibid*, at §§ 48, 51.
[286] Public Redacted Version of Prosecution's Pre-Confirmation Brief, *supra* note 281, at § 181.
[287] L. Davis, 'Reimagining Justice for Gender-Based Crimes at the Margins: New Legal Strategies for Prosecuting ISIS Crimes against Women and LGBTIQ Persons' 3 *William & Mary Journal of Race, Gender, and Social Justice* (March 2018) 513–558, at 546.
[288] *Report to the United Nations Secretary-General*, International Commission on Inquiry on Darfur, 25 January 2005, § 366, available at www.un.org/ruleoflaw/blog/document/report-of-the-international-commission-of-inquiry-on-darfur-to-the-united-nations-secretary-general/ (hereafter *Report to the United Nations Secretary-General*, International Commission on Inquiry on Darfur).

detained persons.[289] Fur women were also killed, including when they resisted rape.[290] In this context, women were targeted on gender grounds as a punishment for not complying with their presumed roles, behaviours, activities, and attributes assigned to women and not fulfilling their destiny to sexually serve perpetrators who are men. Gender persecution inevitably includes efforts to aggressively reinforce binary gender roles and advance punishment for any transgression.

22. Sexual and gender-based violence also reinforced masculinities and manhood among Government of Sudan forces and militia/Janjaweed. After finding a virgin, some perpetrators fired guns in the air and shouted, 'I have found a virgin woman'.[291] Mr Abd-Al-Rahman and militia/Janjaweed demonstrated an intent to commit persecution as indicated in his language, such as 'we have taken Tora Bora's wives, praise be to god', while raping women in villages.[292] In addition to reinforcing their roles as enslaved persons, women's bodies were being used to reduce their value as the future, attack their own honour and the honour of their husbands, terrorise the population, and ensure control over the population.[293]

23. The evidence also shows the gendered nature of crimes in the statements by Government of Sudan forces and militia/Janjaweed about the fact that they will take the 'beautiful' women as wives and the 'ugly' ones will be servants.[294] This capitalises on the social pressures faced by women as a result of men's attempt to control their roles and responsibilities in public and domestic settings.

24. Other torturous or inhumane acts committed against men or boys may also rise to the level of gender persecution in Kodoom, Bindisi, and surrounding areas. In detention, men were mistreated and kept in inhumane conditions.[295] Specifically, evidence shows that victims were treated so as to show that they are in the power of the perpetrators.[296] The militia/Janjaweed and Government of Sudan forces also humiliated, degraded, or otherwise violated the dignity of their victims, amounting to an outrage upon personal dignity.[297] Finally, Government of Sudan forces and militia/Janjaweed used pejorative and derogatory language against the Fur men and boys during the course of the attack, uttering epithets such as 'slave' and 'servant', and made derogatory references linked to detainees' skin colour,

[289] Public Redacted Version of Second Corrected Version of Document Containing the Charges, *supra* note 256, at §§ 49, 53.

[290] *Ibid*, at § 38.

[291] Public Redacted Version of Prosecution's Pre-Confirmation Brief, *supra* note 281, at § 190.

[292] *Ibid*, §§ 136, 190.

[293] *Report to the United Nations Secretary-General*, International Commission on Inquiry on Darfur, *supra* note 288, at § 353.

[294] Public Redacted Version of Prosecution's Pre-Confirmation Brief, *supra* note 281, at § 181.

[295] Public Redacted Version of Second Corrected Version of Document Containing the Charges, *supra* note 256, at §§ 38, 40.

[296] *Ibid*, § 40.

[297] *Ibid*, at § 50.

while also stating that the Government of Sudan sent them to kill every Black person.[298]

25. These multiple intersecting persecutory grounds capture aspects of the targeting that go beyond killing and include other crimes or inhumane acts. Fur men and boys were targeted because of their ethnicity, political beliefs, and gender. Abuses committed against such men and boys, as well as women and girls, for said reasons constitute the grounds of gender persecution. Absent the gendered perception that all Fur men are fighters and supporters of the rebel movements (specifically supporting these movements by joining them in their fighting role), these men would not be subjected to murder, torture, and other criminal acts. Similarly, women would not be raped if not in an attempt to humiliate and destroy communities. Therefore, Fur men, women, boys, and girls were not only targeted with killing because of their ethnicity and political beliefs but also because of their gender.

26. Pursuant to Article 61(7) of the Statute, the Chamber requests the Prosecutor to amend its Document Containing the Charges, so as to charge the acts of rape, torture, other inhumane acts, cruel treatment, outrages upon personal dignity, in addition to murder and attempted murder committed against the Fur men, women, boys, and girls in Kodoom, Bindisi, and surrounding areas between 15 and 16 August 2003 as the crime against humanity of persecution on the grounds of gender.

ADDITIONAL COUNTS 21 AND 31: GENDER PERSECUTION AS A CRIME AGAINST HUMANITY COMMITTED AGAINST THE FUR MEN AND WOMEN IN MUKJAR, DELEIG, AND SURROUNDING AREAS

27. On 22 April 2021, the prosecution submitted its second corrected version of the Document Containing the Charges,[299] charging persecution as a crime against humanity on political, ethnic, and gender grounds committed against the Fur men and boys in Mukjar and surrounding areas between the end of February 2004 and the beginning of March 2004 and in Deleig and surrounding areas between 5 and 7 March 2004 (Counts 21 and 31).[300] Pursuant to Article 61(7)(c) of the Statute, the Chamber further requests the Prosecutor to amend its Document Containing the Charges to include an additional charge of gender persecution for rape, murder, other inhumane acts, and outrages on personal dignity committed against women in Mukjar and surrounding areas between the end of February 2004 and the beginning of March 2004, and in Deleig and surrounding areas between 5 and 7 March 2004. The Chamber recognises both the differential and

[298] *Ibid*, at § 47.
[299] *Ibid*.
[300] *Ibid*, at §§ 93, 136.

common impact of such persecutory conduct as rape against men, boys, women, and girls of the Fur tribe.

28. In Mukjar and surrounding areas, rapes have been committed and should be interpreted as an underlying crime of gender persecution.[301] Similar to the Kodoom and Bindisi incidents, these acts of rape served to subject women and girls to severe deprivation of their fundamental rights, including through mass rape and sexual violence.[302] Upon further investigation, the prosecution could establish that the impact could have included humiliation, degrading treatment, or inflicting serious injury to the victim's body or to their mental or physical health. Rape may be committed to enforce a role or because it is the prescribed role, which is a central characteristic of sexual slavery/enslavement.

29. In Mukjar and surrounding areas, the evidence shows that the perpetrators also demonstrated an intent to commit persecution as indicated in their language, such as 'I am going to f*** you today' and subjecting men to beatings.[303] Such language is used to undermine men's status by making them appear feeble, like 'women',[304] and can evidence intent to discriminate against both men and women. The policy elaborates on this, explaining that perpetrators may target men and/or women through rape based on gender discrimination:

> Perpetrators may target women and girls because they view them as 'chattel' or 'war booty' (based on their belief that women are lesser than men and should be treated like property). At the same time, perpetrators may target men and boys through rape as a strategy to 'feminize' them and/or to invoke the 'indignity' of being treated as a woman or a 'homosexual' (based on their belief that men enjoy a higher standing than women or LGBTQI+ persons).[305]

30. In Mukjar, Deleig, and surrounding areas, Mr Abd-Al-Rahman also mistreated the detainees, particularly by striking them with an axe or an axe-like object, as well as by whipping them across the back.[306] Such physical abuse is an indication of dominance over the Fur men and boys. Perpetrators inflicted the pain and suffering on Fur men and boys to obtain information or a confession. The crimes of torture, other inhumane acts, cruel treatment, and outrages upon personal dignity served to terrorise and intimidate the detained Fur men and boys and constituted the crime of

[301] Public Redacted Version of Prosecution's Pre-Confirmation Brief, *supra* note 281, at § 50; *Report to the United Nations Secretary-General*, International Commission on Inquiry on Darfur, *supra* note 288, at § 341.

[302] *Ibid*.

[303] Public Redacted Version of Prosecution's Pre-Confirmation Brief, *supra* note 281, at §§ 138, 139, 238, 271.

[304] Davis, *supra* note 287, at 20.

[305] Office of the Prosecutor, *supra* note 262, at § 51.

[306] Public Redacted Version of Second Corrected Version of Document Containing the Charges, *supra* note 256, at §§ 79, 80, 85, 123, 129, 147.

persecution on the basis of intersecting political, ethnic, and gender grounds. Such treatment destroys the capacity of men and boys to lead and protect their families and communities by showing dominance, thus violating their manhood and inflicting psychological trauma.

31. In connection with these crimes, Government of Sudan forces and militia/ Janjaweed targeted women based on political, ethnic, and gender grounds. Women and girls comprise the majority – if not totality – of rape victims during the selected attacks.[307]

32. Therefore, the Chamber finds that available evidence appears to establish gender persecution within the jurisdiction of the Court based on the acts of rape, murder, other inhumane acts, and outrages on personal dignity committed against Fur men and women in Mukjar and surrounding areas between the end of February 2004 and the beginning of March 2004, and in Deleig and surrounding areas between 5 and 7 March 2004.

CONCLUSION

33. Not charging rape, torture, murder, other inhumane acts, and outrages upon personal dignity conducted as the crimes against humanity of gender persecution would be a travesty. The Chamber therefore adjourns the confirmation of charges proceeding and requests the Prosecutor to amend the Document Containing the Charges, pursuant to Article 61(7)(c)(ii) of the Statute, to (1) amend Count 11 to specify that the acts of torture, rape, other inhumane acts, cruel treatment, outrages upon personal dignity, murder, and attempted murder committed against men, women, boys, and girls in Kodoom, Bindisi, and surrounding areas between 15 and 16 August 2003 (Counts 1–11) constitute the crime against humanity of gender persecution (as well as intersecting with political and ethnic persecution); (2) amend Counts 21 and 31 to specify that the acts of torture, rape, murder, and other inhumane acts against men, women, boys, and girls in Mukjar and surrounding areas between the end of February 2004 and the beginning of March 2004 (Counts 12–20), as well as in Deleig and surrounding areas between 5 and 7 March 2004 (Counts 22–30), constitute the underlying conduct of the crime against humanity of gender persecution, in addition to political and ethnic persecution.

Judge Lisa Davis and Judge Marina Kumskova

[307] *Report to the United Nations Secretary-General*, International Commission on Inquiry on Darfur, *supra* note 288, at §§ 354–488.

11

The Situations in the Central African Republic

11.1 REFLECTION: THE SITUATIONS IN THE CENTRAL AFRICAN REPUBLIC

Alice Dieci and Cassandra Mudgway

INTRODUCTION

This sub-chapter provides a critical reflection on the feminist reimagining of five selected decisions from the two ICC situations in the Central African Republic (CAR), known as 'CAR I' and 'CAR II'. It begins by providing background to the relevant conflicts, as well as the procedural history of the cases prosecuted at the ICC. It goes on to summarise the key facts and outcomes of the ICC proceedings, before discussing how the authors of the reimagined decisions have departed from the original in adopting a feminist perspective. The sub-chapter considers what makes each decision 'feminist' and reflects upon how gender justice might be effected if we were to act beyond the 'existing rules' of international criminal law.

Background to the Conflict

Since gaining independence in 1960, CAR has experienced political instability, military coup attempts and army mutinies, and almost a constant state of rebellion which erupted into armed conflict a number of times. In 2001, (then) President Ange Félix Patassé faced two attempted coups, and in 2002 he faced another rebellion led by General François Bozizé. Unable to rely on his weakened army to fend off Bozizé's rebellion, Patassé obtained the support of Democratic Republic of Congo (DRC) politician Jean-Pierre Bemba Gombo's military group, the Mouvement de libération du Congo (MLC), which operated mostly in the southern CAR regions bordering the DRC. But Patassé was unsuccessful: the MLC was unable to defeat the rebels, and in 2003 Bozizé seized the presidency. Since that

2003 coup by Bozizé, the majority of the territory, and especially the northern areas, have been controlled by rebels.

In 2004, the CAR armed forces waged war against the Union of Democratic Forces for Unity (UFDR) but, despite efforts to achieve peace and disarmament, attacks against civilians persisted. In 2013, a coalition of various rebel groups known as Séléka (a predominantly Muslim group) accused the government of failing to abide by the peace agreements and seized the capital Bangui. Bozizé fled the country and Séléka leader Michel Djotodia declared himself president. Renewed fighting began between Séléka and militias opposed to them, called Anti-Balaka (a predominantly Christian coalition). In September 2013, President Djotodia disbanded the Sélékan, which had lost its unity after taking power, and resigned in 2014. He was replaced by Catherine Samba-Panza, but the conflict continued. Faustin-Archange Touadéra, who was elected president in 2016, ran and won the 2020 election. That triggered the main rebel factions to form an alliance opposed to the election, called the Coalition of Patriots for Change, which was coordinated by former President Bozizé. This non-international armed conflict in CAR is ongoing and has resulted in targeted violence against civilians suspected of being supporters of either group or on the basis of their religious or ethnic affiliation.

Situation in the Central African Republic I

After receiving a referral from the government of the CAR led by President Bozizé in 2004, the (then) ICC Prosecutor, Luis Moreno-Ocampo, opened a preliminary examination and investigation into alleged crimes against humanity and war crimes committed on the territory of CAR from 1 July 2002 to March 2003.[1] Notably, there would be no ICC trials against Bozizé's forces; the ICC only prosecuted crimes committed by the opposing MLC.

The main case to be prosecuted was against Mr Jean-Pierre Bemba Gombo (Mr Bemba), commander of MLC forces, for war crimes and crimes against humanity committed by those forces, including the murder and rape of civilians and the pillaging of their homes and workplaces.[2] Proceedings were also initiated against Bemba and four other individuals for offences against the administration of justice, in connection with the *Bemba* case: Aimé Kilolo Musamba, Fidèle Babala Wandu, Jean-Jacques Mangenda Kabongo, and Narcisse Arido.

Bemba, as MLC president and commander-in-chief, deployed those troops to the CAR at the request of former CAR President Patassé. Between October 2002 and March 2003, MLC troops directed a widespread attack against the civilian population of the CAR, committing brutal murders, rapes, and pillaging. In 2016, he was

[1] Decision Assigning the Situation in the Central African Republic to Pre-Trial Chamber III (ICC-01/05), Pre-Trial Chamber III, 19 January 2005.

[2] Judgment on Appeal, *Bemba* (ICC-01/05-01/08-3636-Red), Appeals Chamber, 8 June 2018.

convicted of crimes against humanity and war crimes by the ICC Trial Chamber on the basis that he was responsible for the crimes committed by MLC troops in the CAR under the principle of command responsibility. However, he was acquitted of all charges on appeal in 2018, when the majority of the Appeals Chamber overturned the Trial Chamber's findings on command responsibility.[3]

The following rewritten judgments reimagine four decisions in the *Bemba* case, including the Warrant of Arrest, Confirmation of Charges, Sentencing, and Appeal.

Feminist Reimagining of Select Judgments and Decisions

Judge David Eichert's Reimagining of the Crime of 'Forced Nudity'

THE PRE-TRIAL CHAMBER'S ORIGINAL JUDGMENT In the original judgment, the Pre-Trial Chamber declined to include forced nudity in the Warrant of Arrest against Mr Bemba.[4] The Chamber decided that the alleged acts of members of the MLC in ordering civilians (including cisgender[5] men) to remove their clothes in public could not be considered 'other forms of sexual violence' as charged by the Prosecutor.[6] In the Chamber's view, forced nudity was not conduct of 'a gravity comparable to the other offences' in Article 7(1)(g) of the Statute, such as rape, sexual slavery, enforced prostitution, forced pregnancy, or enforced sterilisation, or, regarding Article 8(2)(e)(vi), of comparable gravity to a serious violation of Common Article 3 of the Geneva Conventions.[7] The Chamber did not give any further reasoning for the exclusion.

THE REIMAGINED DECISION AND CRITICAL REFLECTION The essential legal issue for the rewritten judgment was whether there were reasonable grounds to believe the specific acts of forced nudity by MLC members were of comparable gravity to other sexual offences found in Article 7(1)(g) or Article 8(2)(e)(vi).[8] Judge David Eichert concludes that, in this case, there were such reasonable grounds.

Although international tribunals have established that forced nudity can be considered a sexual crime, this is not always the case. As noted by the rewritten judgment, whether or not forced nudity is a sexual crime depends on the context of

[3] ICC Prosecutor Press Release, 'Prosecutor opens investigation in the Central African Republic', 22 May 2007, available at https://reliefweb.int/report/central-african-republic/prosecutor-opens-investigation-central-african-republic.

[4] Warrant of Arrest, *Bemba* (ICC-01/05-01/08-14-tENG), Pre-Trial Chamber III, 10 June 2008.

[5] 'Cisgender' uses the prefix 'cis' to indicate someone who is not trans. Cisgender people generally identify their gender with the sex assigned to them at birth.

[6] Bemba Warrant of Arrest, *supra* note 4, § 63.

[7] Article 7(1)(g)-6, Elements of Crimes; Article 8(2)(e)(vi)-6, Elements of Crimes.

[8] Judge David Eichert, Rewritten Decision on the Prosecutor's Application for a Warrant of Arrest against Jean-Pierre Bemba Gombo (Forced Nudity), § 7.

the acts themselves.[9] However, it is the particular context where international tribunals and the ICC have declined to acknowledge forced nudity and other acts similarly not specified in Articles 7(1)(g) and 8(2)(e)(vi) as 'sexual crimes' that has been considered problematic by scholars, including feminist scholars,[10] and specifically in cases where victims have been cisgender men.

Historically, conflict-related sexual violence against anyone was largely ignored by national and international regimes alike. Through decades of feminist scholarship and advocacy there are now well-established international instruments and norms that recognise the victimisation of cisgender women and girls by conflict-related sexual violence, including the Rome Statute itself. However, it was not until relatively recently that cisgender men and boys were recognised as a unique category of victims of such violence. The international criminal tribunals for Rwanda and for the former Yugoslavia tried a number of cases that defined rape and sexual violence in a way that included violence against cisgender men and boys.[11] The Rome Statute also incorporates gender-neutral definitions of sexual violence. Nevertheless, as Sandesh Sivakumaran has argued, despite the recent recognition, problems remain in the implementation of the law.[12] For example, where victimisation of cisgender men and boys was not prosecuted as 'sexual violence' but as torture instead,[13] or where individual acts of violence against men were acknowledged but not prosecuted at all (as in this case).[14] Such approaches reinforce the idea that the violence that happens to men during conflict is not 'sexual' or that it is separate from, and in some cases perceived as 'less serious' than, the violence perpetrated against women.[15] Failing to recognise or prosecute such violence also ignores and invalidates the unique harm that victims suffer.

9 *Ibid*, § 10.

10 V. Oosterveld, 'Sexual Violence Directed at Men and Boys in Armed Conflict or Mass Atrocity' 10 *International Law & International Relations* (2014) 107–128; S. Sivakumaran, 'Sexual Violence against Men in Armed Conflict' 18 *European Journal of International Law* (2007) 253–276; E. A. P. Gorris, 'Invisible Victims? Where Are Male Victims of Conflict-Related Sexual Violence in International Law and Policy?' 22 *European Journal of Women's Studies* (2015) 412–427.

11 See for example, Judgment, *Češić* (IT-95-10/1-S), Trial Chamber, 11 March 2003; Judgment, *Stakić* (IT-97-24-A), Appeals Chamber, 22 March 2006; Judgment, *Todorović* (IT-95-9/1), Trial Chamber, 31 July 2001.

12 S. Sivakumaran, 'Lost in Translation: UN Responses to Sexual Violence against Men and Boys in Situations of Armed Conflict' 92 *International Review of the Red Cross* (2010) 259–277, at 273–274.

13 See for example, Judgment, *Simić et al.* (IT-95-9-T), Trial Chamber, 17 October 2003; Decision on Prosecutor's Application for Summonses to Appear, *Kenyatta et al.* (01/09-02/11), Pre-Trial Chamber II, 8 March 2011 § 27.

14 See for example, Judgment, *Bagosora et al.* (ICTR-98-41-T), Trial Chamber, 18 December 2008 § 1908; Decision on the Confirmation of Charges, *Kenyatta et al.* (01/09-02/11) Pre-Trial Chamber II, 23 January 2012 § 257–266.

15 Oosterveld, *supra* note 10, at 123.

The catch-all words in Articles 7(1)(g) and 8(2)(e)(vi), 'any other form of sexual violence', potentially capture a range of violent acts perpetrated against cisgender men and boys; however, as illustrated by Valerie Oosterveld's research, the ICC Prosecutor is rarely successful in arguing for the inclusion of such acts.[16] Judge Eichert's rewritten judgment seizes an opportunity for the Chamber to fill the legal gap and recognise that forced nudity may, in some circumstances, be used to weaponise cultural ideas and beliefs about 'gender, sexuality, religion, chastity, respect, social position, or dignity'.[17] Starting from an understanding of the crime of forced nudity that captures its potential to weaponise norms of gender, Judge Eichert creates space for the recognition of cisgender men, and, as further explored below, gender-diverse people, including trans people, as victims of a 'sexual' crime.

Judge Eichert outlines the unique 'sexual' harm of forced nudity that is tied to cultural and social context. All societies have socially constructed ideas about gender and sexuality, and a perpetrator can use forced nudity to weaponise these ideas against any gender. He describes such harm as mental anguish, being traumatising and humiliating.[18] By taking into consideration the social context, Judge Eichert acknowledges the potential psychological harm that can be inflicted on victims of forced nudity. His judgment also makes clear that perpetrators of any gender can weaponise such norms against a person of any other gender.[19] Forced nudity is therefore committed within the context of the perpetrators and the victim's gender in light of the socially constructed norms of gender and sexuality. Thus, in certain circumstances the act of forced nudity can be just as dehumanising and harmful as the physical manifestations of sexual violence specified in Articles 7(1)(g) and 8(2)(e)(vi).

Unlike in the Pre-Trial Chamber's original judgment, where the voices of victims were absent, in assessing the gravity of the particular alleged acts presented by the ICC Prosecutor, the reimagined judgment centres the victims' experience. Judge Eichert stresses the importance of listening to victims when considering the social and cultural context that informs the gender norms being weaponised as 'sexual' harm. In doing so, he decides that there are reasonable grounds to believe the acts of forced nudity are of sufficient gravity to be included in the arrest warrant as 'other forms of sexual violence'.

[16] See *ibid.*

[17] Judge Eichert, *supra* note 8, §§ 13 and 17.

[18] *Ibid*, § 15.

[19] *Ibid*, § 16; Judge Eichert purposefully uses 'weaponise' throughout his judgment to focus on the motives of the perpetrator and not of the victim, see also D. Eichert, '"Homosexualization" Revisited: An Audience-Focused Theorization of Wartime Male Sexual Violence' 21 *International Feminist Journal of Politics* (2019) 409–433, at 416.

Utilising queer theory, the rewritten judgment also challenges gender duality by recognising the existence of transgender, intersex, and gender minorities and acknowledging the unique harms that forced nudity inflicts on such groups.[20] Traditionally, international law has reproduced a gender binary and, with that, unequal relations of power based on (cis)gender, thereby rendering gender-diverse people invisible and at risk of violence, including sexual violence, perpetrated to enforce rigid ideas about gender – that is, to maintain the heterosexual, binary order.[21] As a result, gender-diverse people are all but absent from international law and in international criminal trials. In the rewritten judgment, Judge Eichert makes these invisible victims visible.[22] Further, the kind of harm experienced by gender-diverse people as victims of forced nudity is different to cisgender people. For example, Judge Eichert explains how gender-diverse people's bodies may not conform to socially policed ideas about gender and so being forced to be naked may lead to social exclusion; that their gender-diverse status may be exposed, leading to increased risk of violence; they may suffer gender dysphoria and again suffer mental anguish, humiliation, and further dehumanisation.[23]

Judicial decisions can serve as a source of knowledge and is one way in which societies construct or reconstruct reality. Feminists have criticised what is considered accepted 'knowledge' as representing a male perspective of 'reality', thereby excluding women's experiences.[24] That perspective is also predominantly a Western one. Similarly, the absence of gender minorities from international criminal trials reproduces the gender binary and excludes the particular experiences of those groups. If the ICC were to listen and publish the voices of such groups, especially those from non-Western societies, it would disrupt the power of the gender binary and redistribute some of that power to gender-diverse people.

However, such inclusion of gender-diverse people must be made in connection to gender-diverse communities themselves. Although Judge Eichert impresses the importance of listening to victims, if victims themselves are reluctant to expose their gender-diverse status then the responsibility will fall to the ICC Prosecutor to bring such existence and harms to the attention of the Chamber. Accordingly, the rewritten judgment also raises important questions about the sensitivities towards gender identity and sexuality of those who conduct investigations into atrocity crimes and the Office of the Prosecutor.

20 See generally D. Otto (ed.), *Queering International Law: Possibilities, Alliances, Complicities, Risks* (London: Routledge, 2018).

21 D. Eichert, 'Decolonizing the Corpus: A Queer Decolonial Re-Examination of Gender in International Law's Origins' 43 *Michigan Journal of International Law* (2022) 557–594, at 572.

22 Judge Eichert also considers other specific harm to other groups who may not comply with cultural beliefs about gender and sexuality, including sex workers; see *supra* note 8, § 21.

23 *Ibid*, § 19.

24 A. P. Harris, 'Race and Essentialism in Feminist Legal Theory' 42 *Stanford Law Review* (1990) 581–616.

Judge Loyce Mrewa's Reimagining of Confirmation of Charges for the Crime of Rape

THE PRE-TRIAL CHAMBER'S ORIGINAL JUDGMENT In 2009, Pre-Trial Chamber II confirmed the charges against Mr Bemba on five counts: the war crimes of rape, murder, and pillage, and the crimes against humanity of rape and murder.[25]

However, the Prosecutor's submission and the Document Containing the Charges also included the charges of torture as a war crime and as a crime against humanity, as well as outrages upon personal dignity as a war crime.[26] These three charges utilised the same factual content that the Prosecutor presented to the Chamber regarding the charges of rape also imposed against Mr Bemba.

In the original confirmation of charges, the Pre-Trial Chamber refused to apply the doctrine of cumulative charging,[27] stating that both torture and outrages upon personal dignity were entirely subsumed by the crime of rape, and therefore declined to confirm those charges.[28]

THE REIMAGINED DECISION AND CRITICAL REFLECTION In her reimagined confirmation of charges, Judge Loyce Mrewa confirms the ability of the Pre-Trial Chamber to apply the doctrine of cumulative charging by using a feminist approach and reflecting on the importance of a judicial understanding of the gender implications of cumulative charging for sexual and gender-based crimes. This approach arguably prevents flawed and gender-insensitive legal reasoning and reflects the extent of victimisation on the ground.[29]

Judge Mrewa first focuses on demonstrating, through the jurisprudence of international tribunals,[30] that cumulative charging is permitted under international criminal law as a component of the fair labelling of crimes, considered a general principle of law, although not explicitly spelled out in the Rome Statute.[31] Basing her reasoning on prior authoritative jurisprudence, she argues that the accused can be charged and convicted with different offences in relation to the same set of facts

[25] Confirmation of Charges, *Bemba* (ICC-01/05-01/08-424), Pre-Trial Chamber II, 15 June 2009 (hereafter Confirmation of Charges).

[26] Annex 3 of the Amended Document containing the charges filed on 30 March 2009, *Bemba* (ICC-01/05-01/08-395-Anx3), Pre-Trial Chamber II, 20 March 2009.

[27] Cumulative charging is the process by which an accused can be charged with different offences in relation to the same set of underlying facts, where each offence has a distinctive element.

[28] Confirmation of Charges, *supra* note 25, § 501(e).

[29] In this regard, see also L. Green, 'First-Class Crimes, Second-Class Justice: Cumulative Charges for Gender-Based Crimes at the International Criminal Court' 11 *International Criminal Law Review* (2011) 529–541.

[30] See for instance Judgment, *Prosecutor v. Delalic et al.* (IT-96-21-A), Appeals Chamber Judgment, 20 February 2001, § 412 and Judgment, *Prosecutor v. Akayesu* (ICTR-964-S), Trial Chamber I, 2 September 1998, § 468.

[31] Judge Joyce Mrewa, Rewritten Decision on Confirmation of Charges, *Bemba* (ICC-01/05-01/08-424), Pre-Trial Chamber II, 15 June 2009, at § 27.

under international criminal law if the relevant statutory provisions are designed to protect different social interests, each offence has a distinctive element, and the charges reflect the total culpability of the accused.[32]

In the case under examination, Judge Mrewa recalls that the Prosecutor submitted cumulative charges for torture and outrages upon personal dignity which are based on the same factual conduct and are mainly related to acts of rape. She argues that rape is often used to achieve different ends, which should be carefully considered and distinguished from each other. For instance, the crimes of torture and rape protect different human rights, namely physical and mental integrity and physical autonomy and protection from non-consensual violations of bodily autonomy, respectively.[33] The threshold of suffering is also different, as torture requires 'severe suffering' whereas for rape non-consensual bodily invasion or penetration is sufficient.[34] Similarly, outrages upon dignity committed through acts of rape expand on the psychological harm caused by rape, reflecting on its far-reaching consequences such as humiliation, degradation, and attack on personal dignity.[35]

Therefore, subsuming these crimes would fail not only to respect the principle of fair labelling, but also to reflect the full culpability of the accused and the extent of the harm suffered by victims.[36] Charging and convicting the accused for torture and outrages upon personal dignity allegedly committed through acts of rape shows the severity of rape, the intent to perpetrate 'severe suffering' as well as to humiliate, undermine personal dignity, and disempower the victim through sexual violence.

By reimagining the confirmation of charges through a feminist lens, Judge Mrewa successfully underlines the shortcomings of judicial decisions that oversimplify the breadth of lived experiences of survivors of conflict-related sexual violence and the complexity and interrelated nature of sexual crimes with other serious human rights violations and abuses.

Like Judge Eichert, Judge Mrewa places the voices of the victims at the centre of the discussion, noting that to ignore the reality of rape as a method of torture or an outrage upon personal dignity excludes the lived experiences of survivors.

While Judge Mrewa's legal reasoning effectively encompasses a feminist lens in her analysis of cumulative charging through fair labelling of different crimes, she could have further expanded on the practical gender implications of the lack of cumulative charging for torture or outrages upon personal dignity by referring to factual elements of the case, as included in the Prosecutor's Amended Document containing the charges. For instance, the Prosecutor indicated that:

[32] *Ibid*, at §§ 1 and 35.
[33] *Ibid*, at § 24.
[34] *Ibid*, at § 40.
[35] *Ibid*, at § 46.
[36] *Ibid*, at § 50.

> Civilian properties were systematically looted, and civilians were forced to cook and clean for the MLC troops against their will and with no payment. Men, women and children were raped by multiple MLC perpetrators in their homes, raped in front of family members, forced to watch rapes of family members, and raped in public locations including streets, fields and farms. Many of the women victims of rapes and gang-rapes contracted HIV, and became pregnant as a result of these rapes. Civilians that were killed included those who tried to prevent or resist rapes, attacks or lootings.[37]

More specifically, in the case of civilians raped in front of family members or in public locations, charging the accused solely with rape without considering the element of public humiliation through the crime of outrages upon personal dignity and related long-term psychological trauma of both survivors of sexual violence and family members forced to watch their loved ones being abused, fails to reflect the extent of victimisation on the ground and minimises the complexity of sexual violence in conflicts and its societal impact beyond the direct victims of crime.

Judge Mrewa could have also reflected on the wide range of survivors of sexual violence and the specific impact that the lack of cumulative charging could have on men or gender-diverse victims. As discussed above, historically there has been a certain reluctance to include men and boys as victims of sexual violence and whenever the abuse was recognised it was hardly seen as sexual violence 'for the issue was often buried under the rubric of abuse or torture'.[38]

Concepts of masculinity, virility, and procreative capacity also play out in relation to the frequency of violence and torture aimed at male reproductive organs during conflicts, as 'survivors of sexual torture often relate anxiety about the possibility of having children to injury of sexual organs or fear of no longer being considered fully a man or to function as a man'.[39] Therefore, failure to recognise the interconnected nature of torture and conflict-related sexual violence, including through cumulative charging, gives the false idea that international crimes are gender-blind, whereas acts of rape may constitute torture and torture may be intrinsically gendered and perpetrated with the intention of causing a gender-based crime.

Judge Kirsten Keith's Reimagining of Sentencing for 'Pillaging'

THE TRIAL CHAMBER'S ORIGINAL JUDGMENT In 2016, Trial Chamber III handed down the sentencing decision for Mr Bemba.[40] Bemba had been convicted for the war crimes of murder, rape, and pillaging, and the crimes against humanity of

[37] Annex 3 of the Amended Document containing the charges filed on 30 March 2009, *Bemba* (ICC-01/05-01/08-395-Anx3), Pre-Trial Chamber II, 20 March 2009, § 39.

[38] Sivakumaran, *supra* note 10, at 256.

[39] *Ibid*, at 273.

[40] Decision on Sentence, *Bemba* (ICC-01/05-01/08-3399), Trial Chamber III, 21 June 2016 (hereafter Sentence Decision).

murder and rape committed by soldiers of the MLC who were proven to be under Bemba's effective authority and control, in CAR between 26 October 2002 and 15 March 2003.[41] For the war crime of pillaging, Bemba was sentenced to sixteen years' imprisonment.[42] The ICC judgment is the first to include a conviction for rape as a war crime and a crime against humanity, marking an important turning point in terms of accountability for sexual violence as an international crime.

In determining the gravity of the crime as the principal consideration to impose the sentence,[43] the Trial Chamber noted the special nature of the crimes of rape and pillaging.[44] In particular, it considered the aggravating circumstances for both crimes, such as the location of the crime (victims' homes, churches, hospitals), the victims' ages (as young as ten years old for sexual violence), the duration and repeated nature of the acts (against the same victim, in the presence of the victim's family members, and committed by multiple MLC soldiers), the perpetrator's motives, and the violent and humiliating nature of the acts, finding beyond reasonable doubt that Bemba knew the factors relevant to prove the alleged aggravating circumstances for both rape and pillaging.[45]

In determining the aggravating circumstances, the Chamber found that 'many of the same factors considered in relation to the circumstances aggravating the crimes of rape are equally applicable in assessing the aggravating circumstances alleged for pillaging'.[46] For instance, after having displayed great sensitivity to the psychological, medical, and societal impact of rape on victims in CAR,[47] while determining the particular cruelty of the crime of rape as an aggravating circumstance, it highlighted that 'all acts of rape were committed together with, or during the course of, acts of murder and pillaging'.[48]

Likewise, when assessing the gravity of the crime of pillage, the Chamber found that 'MLC soldiers pillaged property from CAR civilians on a large scale and with grave consequences for the victims, impacting various aspects of their personal and professional lives, often leaving victims with nothing',[49] including the necessities. The Chamber also found that acts of pillage were often accompanied by acts of murder and rape and always by physical and verbal abuse, threats of violence, death, and/or rape.[50] The *modus operandi* for pillage and rape proved to be similar: during acts of pillaging, MLC soldiers often targeted the unarmed victims in their homes, places of civilian sanctuary such as churches and hospitals, or in the bush while

[41] *Ibid*, § 21.
[42] *Ibid*, § 94.
[43] *Ibid*, § 15.
[44] *Ibid*, § 24.
[45] *Ibid*, §§ 25–26.
[46] *Ibid*, § 52.
[47] *Ibid*, §§ 36–38.
[48] *Ibid*, § 44.
[49] *Ibid*, § 50.
[50] *Ibid*, § 54.

seeking refuge. They committed the crime repeatedly against the same victims and families, without regard to the victims' age, gender, social status, livelihood, or well-being, 'such as the ability to seek treatment, arrange burial or funeral services, or even feed their families'.[51] Common to both rape and pillage was also the MLC soldiers' underlying motive of self-compensation,[52] for not receiving sufficient financial gain from their military operations, confirming the traditional use of rape victims as war booty.

In sentencing Bemba for the crime of rape as a war crime and crime against humanity, the original Trial Chamber's verdict has the merit of reiterating many of the Rome Statute's important gender-sensitive legal standards, to provide for a detailed account of some of the most appalling rape cases against men, women, and children and even to return to expert opinions to offer a comprehensive analysis of the magnitude of negative and permanent psychiatric, medical, and social consequences faced by rape victims in CAR. However, when it comes to pillage, while the Court clearly stated that it occurred simultaneously with rape and recognised its long-term negative impact on victims' lives and well-being,[53] it failed to further expand on the broader socio-economic context and financial consequences for victims as well as to explore its gender dimension.

THE REIMAGINED JUDGMENT AND CRITICAL REFLECTION Judge Keith fills this gap by considering the broader socio-economic context within which the crime of pillaging occurred. In her judgment, this approach helps to 'frame the Chamber's understanding of the gravity of the crime and the physical, social, and economic distress it creates for its victims, rather than viewing the impacts of the crime in isolation'.[54] Keith does so by recalling that CAR is one of the poorest countries in the world, ranking 169 out of 175 countries in 2003 on a world poverty index, and by identifying the personal experiences recalled by victims and witnesses during trial.[55] The gravity of the crime of pillage in CAR's socio-economic context is particularly evident in the factual circumstances of the case reported in testimonies: many victims were killed in an attempt to protect their property from destruction or confiscation,[56] showing the centrality of certain daily items that, despite not having an objective considerable financial value, were deemed necessary to preserve victims' human dignity and survival. In doing so, Judge Keith highlights the difficulty of international criminal law in considering individual experiences in the face of mass atrocities, as well as its selectivity and inability to redress harm experienced by all conflict-related victims. She also notes the need to refrain from considering

51 *Ibid*, § 53.
52 *Ibid*, § 47.
53 *Ibid*, § 53.
54 Judge K. M. F. Keith, Rewritten Sentencing Decision in the Bemba Case, § 10.
55 *Ibid*, §§ 12–13.
56 Sentence Decision, *supra* note 40, §§ 28, 54.

victims of international crimes as homogenous groups while also stressing the inevitable need to consider victims' common socio-economic background. In integrating victims' voice into the narrative, Keith demonstrates that robbing civilians of everyday items such as clothing, food, cooking utensils, foam mattresses, money, and vehicles in a context characterised by extreme poverty deprived them of their basic necessities, whose impact is still visible today.[57] She demonstrates the grave harm caused by destruction and confiscation of property during conflict, a violation that, like many economic, social, and cultural rights violations, is often overlooked in international human rights law and, even more so, in international criminal law.[58] Importantly, she also explores the financial loss caused by pillage, with lack of access to medical treatment and education.[59]

Judge Keith partially develops the notion of the gendered impact of poverty, which affects women differently as they often bear the sole financial responsibility for their children in times of conflict.[60] This is particularly true when women have been victims of rape and have to raise children born out of rape, either because their husbands left them due to cultural stigma or because they have been killed. So, even when women's financial situation is not the direct consequence of pillaging, the 'crime of pillaging can leave women in a position of financial precariousness'.[61] While the original judgment solely focuses on the psychological impact of rape on victims, Keith comprehensively addresses the multidimensional nature of pillaging, which also includes a psychological component as it is often perpetrated in conjunction with other heinous crimes such as rape and murder. Similar to the original judgment, Keith concludes by confirming the serious gravity of the crime of pillage, highlighting its enduring impacts on victims and their families' lives, which 'exacerbate their vulnerabilities'.[62]

Judge Keith's reimagined judgment reveals the limitations of international criminal law in investigating both the socio-economic dimension of conflict-related sexual violence and the gendered nature of economic and social rights violations that may amount to international crimes, such as pillage. However, her feminist approach, which considers the wider contextual lives of women in legal reasoning, could have been broadened.

While Judge Keith sheds light on some of the gendered aspects of pillage, such as the lack of financial means for girls to access education or medical treatment as a

57 Judge Keith, *supra* note 54, § 15.

58 For a comprehensive analysis on the definition of economic, social, and cultural rights (ESCR) violations entailing individual criminal responsibility and on the overlapping between ESCR violations and international criminal law, see E. Schmid, *Taking Economic, Social and Cultural Rights Seriously in International Criminal Law* (Cambridge: Cambridge University Press, 2015).

59 Judge Keith, *supra* note 54, §§ 29–33.

60 *Ibid*, § 34.

61 *Ibid*.

62 *Ibid*, § 37.

result of pillaging, she mainly focuses on the socio-economic dimension of the crime of pillage. An important element indicated in the original judgment which Keith could have built on is that 'all acts of rape were committed together with, or during the course of, acts of murder and pillaging'.[63] This means that all rape victims have also been victims of pillage (other than having witnessed the murder of one or more family members) in their household.

Applying feminist contextual reasoning implies considering how pillage affects men and women differently because of gender discrimination, especially when perpetrated in connection with rape and against the same victims. Given that rape disproportionately affected women and girls who were also victims of pillage within their households, while the negative consequences of pillage impacted all family members, depriving them of their basic necessities, it is self-evident that women and girls had to bear the worst physical, psychological, and financial consequences resulting from both crimes. In a context already characterised by widespread poverty and gender discrimination, pillage exacerbated women's and girls' vulnerabilities, for instance by depriving them of the financial resources necessary to access medical treatment to prevent sexually transmitted diseases and unwanted pregnancies that may have resulted from the rape suffered or by forcing them to resort to coping strategies, such as forced marriage or trafficking in persons for sexual exploitation (for example, 'survival sex') to feed the family and their children after having lost everything.[64] As indicated also in the testimonies of some of the victims,[65] pillage further deteriorated the already dire living conditions of many families in CAR. Extreme poverty forced many children, especially girls, to drop out of school to take up employment in the informal sector, exposing them to further risks of gender-based violence, depriving them of the opportunity to continue their education and thus access better employment opportunities with the hope to improve their lives and break the cycle of poverty and violence.

In conclusion, international justice must take seriously the intergenerational trauma for women and girls stemming from the links between conflict-related sexual violence and intergenerational poverty which is exacerbated by the crime of pillage. In a 2021 UN report by the Special Representative of the Secretary General on Sexual Violence in Conflict (SRSG-SVC), reflecting voices of survivors worldwide, sexual violence survivors from CAR noted that one of their most frequent and unmet demands over the course of the past twenty years has been the necessary financial assistance to gain economic independence, which is essential for accessing other rights (including food, healthcare, education, access to justice) for themselves and their dependants.[66] The follow-up of the SRSG-SVC in 2022 noted that survivors of

[63] Sentence Decision, *supra* note 40, § 44.
[64] See for instance, A/73/171 (2018) and A/71/303 (2016).
[65] Judge Keith, *supra* note 54, § 25.
[66] Office of the Special Representative of the Secretary General for Sexual Violence in Conflict, *In Their Own Words: Voices of Survivors of Conflict-Related Sexual Violence and Service*

conflict-related sexual violence in CAR 'continued to come from socioeconomically marginalized communities, including in remote and rural areas'.[67] Providing a gender lens to economic, social, and cultural rights violations may help international justice to better reflect the extent and heterogeneity of victims' grievances and experiences and move a step forward towards recognition and redress of the multifaceted nature of the harm suffered.

Judges Suzanne Varrall and Sarah Williams' Reimagining of Command Responsibility

THE APPEAL CHAMBER'S ORIGINAL JUDGMENT Having been convicted for war crimes and crimes against humanity in 2016, Mr Bemba successfully appealed his conviction in 2018. The Appeal Chamber's acquittal of Bemba on all charges, including those relating to rape and sexual violence, was a bitter disappointment for victims and a setback for feminist advocates and scholars, who criticised the decision as allowing immunity for sexual and gender-based crimes.[68]

The original decision was in part based on the third ground of Bemba's appeal – that the Trial Chamber used the wrong legal standard of command responsibility according to Article 28(a). Of particular interest is the Appeals Chamber's interpretation of Article 28(a)(ii): 'that military commander or person failed to take *all necessary and reasonable* measures within his or her power to prevent or repress their commission or to submit the matter to the competent authorities for investigation and prosecution'.[69] In the original judgment, the majority of the Appeals Chamber accepted Bemba's argument that commanders were allowed to undertake 'cost/benefit analysis when deciding which measures to take, bearing in mind their overall responsibility to prevent and repress crimes committed by their subordinates', thereby de-emphasising the word 'all' and instead emphasising the words 'necessary' and 'reasonable'.[70] Additionally, the Chamber introduced the concept of a 'remote commander' as Bemba was located in the DRC.[71] According to the Appeals Chamber, this impacted on what 'necessary and reasonable' measures were 'feasible'.[72]

THE REWRITTEN JUDGMENT AND CRITICAL REFLECTION Judges Suzanne Varrall and Sarah Williams focus on Article 28(a)(ii) and the failure of a commander

Providers (2021) §§ 23–41, available at www.un.org/sexualviolenceinconflict/in-their-own-words-voices-of-survivors-of-conflict-related-sexual-violence-and-service-providers.

67 S/2022/272, § 13.

68 S. SáCouto and P. V. Sellers, 'The Bemba Appeals Chamber Judgment: Impunity for Sexual and Gender-Based Crimes' 27 *William & Mary Bill of Rights Journal* (2019) 599–622.

69 Emphasis added.

70 Judgment on Appeal, *Bemba* (ICC-01/05-01/08-3636-RED), Appeals Chamber, 8 June 2018, (Appeal Judgment) § 170.

71 *Ibid*, §§ 191–192.

72 *Ibid*, § 188.

to take 'all necessary and reasonable measures'. They begin by centralising the concept of protection under international humanitarian law (IHL) and argue that this rationale informs and underlies command responsibility itself.[73] Furthermore, the rewritten judgment utilises a textual interpretation of 'necessary' and 'reasonable' in Article 28(a)(ii) to articulate the 'correct' legal standard, finding that there are minimum actions that must be taken by commanders.[74] Unlike the original judgment, Varrall and Williams do not limit those minimum necessary actions according to the geographical remoteness of the commander. Applying what they argue is the 'correct' legal standard, the rewritten judgment dismisses Bemba's appeal as he failed to take the minimum necessary actions informed by the protective concept of IHL which included, inter alia, ensuring troops are properly trained in IHL.

Judges Varrall and Williams place a feminist lens at the heart of their rewritten judgment by first centralising the protective concept of IHL. One of the key principles of IHL is the protection of people who do not take part in the fighting. Importantly, this includes the protection of civilians against all forms of violence and degrading treatment.[75] Additionally, certain groups considered especially vulnerable, including women and girls, are specified as needing special protection from certain kinds of violence.[76] Article 27 of Additional Protocol I to the Geneva Conventions dictates that women are to be especially protected against rape and sexual violence. Varrall and Williams state that this concept of protection also underlies the notion of command responsibility. Under IHL, commanders are expected to exert control over their forces and train them in IHL, including the obligation to protect civilians.[77] Article 28(a) holds commanders responsible for the crimes committed by their own subordinates, including violence against civilians. Consequently, Varrall and Williams argue that the rationale for command responsibility must be informed by the protective principle of IHL. Therefore, the protection of everyone from rape and sexual violence, as a central part of the concept of protection, informs the rewritten judgment's approach to the legal standard of 'all necessary and reasonable' measures.

Another key principle under IHL is that of 'proportionality'. According to this principle, some degree of harm to civilians is permitted, provided it is not disproportionate to the anticipated military advantage.[78] However, Varrall and Williams state that there is no possible military advantage to be gained by the targeting of civilians for sexual violence.[79] By taking this argument off the table, the principle of

[73] Judges S. Varrall and S. Williams, Reimagining of Command Responsibility in the Bemba Appeals Judgment, § 6.
[74] *Ibid*, §§ 14–26.
[75] Additional Protocols I and II to the Geneva Convention 1977.
[76] Article 76, Additional Protocol I to the Geneva Convention; Article 4, Additional Protocol II to the Geneva Convention.
[77] Judges Varrall and Williams, *supra* note 73, §§ 24–25.
[78] Articles 51(5)(b) and 57 of Additional Protocol I of the Geneva Conventions.
[79] Judges Varrall and Williams, *supra* note 73, § 25.

protection in the context of crimes of rape and sexual violence will always be a paramount consideration. This is a powerful feminist statement. Due to the prevalence of sexual and gender-based violence during armed conflict, particularly against women and girls, this approach recognises both the gravity of the harm such violence causes and elevates the protection of vulnerable groups of civilians above that of military advantage. Moreover, the rewritten judgment links this to command responsibility, arguing that all commanders should be considered to be effectively on notice of the risk of sexual and gender-based violence and of their duty to take all necessary and reasonable measures to minimise it.[80] Overall, although absent from the original judgment, Varrall and Williams consider their legal reasoning having regard to the particular nature of the crimes committed by MLC forces, specifically rape and sexual violence.

When discussing the 'correct' legal standard of Article 28(a)(ii), the rewritten judgment uses a textual interpretation of 'all necessary and reasonable measures' according to the Vienna Convention on the Law of Treaties.[81] Because the protective concept of IHL underlies command responsibility, Varrall and Williams begin by asserting that there must be a high standard expected of commanders to exercise control over their troops.[82] In contrast to the original judgment, Varrall and Williams emphasise the word 'all' so that what is determined as 'necessary and reasonable' cannot be watered down.[83] Accordingly, assessment of measures must start with that which is 'necessary' to prevent or repress the commission of crimes by subordinates. Importantly, what is necessary should be informed by the obligation to protect civilians from known risks associated with armed conflict: sexual and gender-based violence.

Judges Varrall and Williams then break down the three distinct obligations created by Article 28(a)(ii): 'first to prevent crimes; second to repress crimes; and third to submit criminal matters to competent authorities for investigation and prosecution'.[84] They link the protective rationale of IHL to each of these obligations. Applying this reasoning to the facts, Varrall and Williams determine that part of the basic requirements of responsible command includes ensuring that subordinates are properly trained in the rules of IHL.[85] As already set out, essential to these rules is the principle of protection of civilians from risks that armed conflict creates.[86] A further basic requirement of responsible command is ensuring adequate supervision of troops, especially where there are known risks to civilians due to the armed conflict,

80 *Ibid*, § 29.
81 Article 31, Vienna Convention on the Law of Treaties 1969.
82 Judges Varrall and Williams, *supra* note 73, § 26.
83 *Ibid*, § 23.
84 *Ibid*, § 27
85 *Ibid*, §§ 39–40.
86 *Ibid*, § 39.

especially of rape and sexual violence.[87] Leaving open the possibility that there may be circumstances where such measures would not be reasonable, the rewritten judgment makes it clear that this was not the case with Bemba. The rewritten judgment finds that Bemba had extensive material ability to prevent or repress crimes and failed to take necessary and reasonable measures arising from the basic requirements of responsible command.[88] Significantly, this included a failure to ensure that MLC troops were trained in the rules of IHL and adequate supervision of troops.

The rewritten judgment's approach to Article 28(a)(ii) frames sexual and gender-based violence during armed conflict as a central concern for commanders where their failure to train and supervise their troops contributes to an environment of rape and sexual violence. The judgment also elevates the so-called special protected status according to IHL of women and girls above that of military necessity or advantage in a way that challenges the traditional patriarchal view that sexual violence against civilians is inevitable or, in some cases, purposefully weaponised against them. Judges Varrall and Williams are careful not to limit the protection of victims to only women and girls. Such an articulation of 'women and girls' as an especially vulnerable and protected group under IHL, while a feminist position in and of itself (for reasons outlined above), is equally contested within feminist scholarship. The merging of 'womenandchildren' as one category under international law has been critiqued as both erasing the agency and individual experiences of children and infantilising women as passive victims of violence in need of masculine protection.[89] Therefore, the rewritten judgment avoids similar criticism of being a continuation of (a Western patriarchal) law essentialising the experience of women and the assumption that women lack agency and individual personhood separate to that of children. However, although Varrall and Williams specifically mention men as a class of victims, they do not acknowledge gender-diverse people, which may be criticised as silencing the experiences of such victims of sexual and gender-based violence.

Judges Varrall and Williams' approach also has implications for the responsibility of commanders that go beyond Mr Bemba. Although the rewritten judgment highlights the importance of assessing 'reasonable' measures contextually and that such measures do not need to be successful, the assertion that commanders should be considered put 'on notice' regarding sexual and gender-based crimes raises the issue of strict liability. As noted in the rewritten judgment itself, there is a significant link between increased sexual violence and armed conflict. It is difficult to imagine

87 *Ibid*, § 40.

88 *Ibid*, §§ 50–51.

89 C. Enloe, *The Morning After: Sexual Politics at the End of the Cold War* (Berkeley: University of California Press, 1993) at 166; E. Burman, 'Beyond "Women vs Children" or "Womenandchildren": Engendering Childhood and Reforming Motherhood' 16 *Journal of Children's Rights* 177–194.

a situation where such crimes are being committed by subordinates, and a commander, although they may make some efforts to repress those crimes, would not be found to have responsibility to them given the emphasis in the rewritten judgment on Mr Bemba's overall lack of 'adequate' supervision of MLC forces. During the drafting stages of Article 28(a), drafters were careful not to create such situations of strict liability. However, this risk of strict liability should be considered against the risk of ongoing impunity for sexual and gender-based crimes. It can be argued that the duty on commanders should be a heavy burden.

Situation in the Central African Republic II

The ICC Prosecutor, Fatou Bensouda, opened a preliminary investigation in 2014 and determined there was a reasonable basis to believe war crimes and crimes against humanity had been committed in CAR since 2012.[90] Alleged war crimes and crimes against humanity committed by both Séléka and Anti-Balaka include inter alia murder, torture, persecution and other inhumane acts, use of child soldiers, rape, and sexual violence.

The subject of the final rewritten judgment is the first case arising from the ICC's second investigation into the CAR, against Alfred Yekatom, alleged former Anti-Balaka commander, and Patrice-Edouard Ngaïssona, alleged former senior leader in the Anti-Balaka movement, who both had warrants of arrest issued against them in 2018.[91]

Judge Valerie Oosterveld's Reimagining of Amending Charges Using Evidence of Sexual Violence

THE PRE-TRIAL CHAMBER ORIGINAL JUDGMENT In 2019, Pre-Trial Chamber II partially confirmed charges of war crimes and crimes against humanity against Mr Alfred Yekatom concerning events in CAR between 5 December 2013 and August 2014.[92] In March 2020, pursuant to Article 61(9) of the Rome Statute, the prosecution requested the Pre-Trial Chamber to amend the charge of rape confirmed against Ngaïssona to include and confirm a second instance of rape under Counts 40 and 41 of the Document Containing the Charges (DCC) and notified its intention to seek to add additional charges against Yekatom to include the war

[90] Decision Assigning the Situation in the Central African Republic II to Pre-Trial Chamber I (ICC-01/14-1) Trial Chamber I, 18 June 2018; The Office of the Prosecutor, *Article 53(1) Report, Situation in the Central African Republic II*, 24 September 2014, § 20.

[91] Decision, *Warrant of Arrest for Alfred Yekatom* (ICC-01/14-01/18-1-Red), Trial Chamber II, 11 November 2018; Decision, *Warrant of Arrest for Patrice-Edouard Ngaïssona* (ICC-01/14-01/18-89-Red), Trial Chamber II, 13 December 2018.

[92] Decision on the Confirmation of Charges against Alfred Yekatom and Patrice-Edouard Ngaïssona, *Yekatom and Ngaïssona* (ICC-01/14-01/18-403-Red), Pre-Trial Chamber II, 11 December 2019.

crimes of rape and sexual violence.[93] However, Pre-Trial Chamber II declined to include those charges, adopting a 'precautionary and restrictive approach', noting that such an approach was required in order to avoid 'unjustified recourse to this prerogative by the Prosecutor turn[ing] into abuse'.[94] The Chamber cautioned the prosecution for continuing to investigate following the confirmation of charges and noted that Article 61(9), while sanctioned, cannot be used to address 'gaps' in the case of the prosecution.[95] Throughout its reasoning, the Chamber put at the centre the fundamental rights of the accused, including the right to be tried expeditiously, affirming that such was the rationale of Article 61(9) during the preparatory works of the Statute, which also guides international human rights treaties and the jurisprudence of international criminal tribunals in relation to implementation of Article 61 (9) of the Statute. Importantly, the Chamber's reasoning almost exclusively focused on the request to amend charges for the accused Ngaïssona, on which also heavily relied the decision on the Prosecutor's request to add additional charges against Yekatom, with no separate analysis. Consequently, although the Prosecutor submitted witness statements from victims detailing alleged sexual violence, there were no charges of rape against Ngaïssona or Yekatom.

THE REWRITTEN JUDGMENT AND CRITICAL REVIEW Judge Valerie Oosterveld expertly re-examines Article 61(9) of the Rome Statute, granting the Prosecutor's request to introduce additional charges against Yekatom, while she rejects the request to amend charges against Ngaïssona by including and confirming a second instance of rape. Contrary to the original decision, Judge Oosterveld's arguments largely focus on Yekatom, rather than Ngaïssona, distinguishing the Prosecutor's request to amend charges for Ngaïssona from the request to add additional charges for Yekatom on the basis that the latter 'considers entirely new charges with new evidence justified by different reasons' while the former was aimed at 'reintroducing non-confirmed charges for which evidence was lacking'.[96] As a result, regarding Ngaïssona, Oosterveld rejects the request for amendment as it 'would not satisfy the accused's fair trial rights'.[97]

Judge Oosterveld begins by partially challenging the procedural history of the case[98] and briefly examines the arguments of both the defence and the prosecution.[99] Importantly, she further substantiates what in the original Prosecutor's

[93] Prosecution Motion to Amend the Charges against Alfred Yekatom, *Yekatom and Ngaïssona* (ICC-01/14-01/18-518-Red), Pre-Trial Chamber II, 22 May 2020.

[94] Decision on the Prosecutor's Request to Amend the Charges against Alfred Yekatom, *Yekatom and Ngaïssona* (ICC-01/14-01/18-538), Pre-Trial Chamber II, 1 June 2020, §§ 12, 14.

[95] *Ibid*, § 19.

[96] Judge Valerie Oosterveld, Reimagining of Amending Charges Using Evidence of Sexual Violence, § 38.

[97] *Ibid*.

[98] *Ibid*, §§ 1–8.

[99] *Ibid*, §§ 9–13.

submission was vaguely anticipated as mere notice of intention, by clarifying that the additional charges of rape and sexual slavery as war crimes against Yekatom are 'fully substantiated and more fully reflect his alleged culpability' and that, in light of the 'seriousness and importance of these charges, the proposed amendment is in the interest of justice'.[100] Judge Oosterveld also anticipates the Chamber's main objection on the need to ensure the right to defence by introducing an important factual element, namely that no trial date has been set and highlighting the Court's duty to establish the truth.[101] Importantly, she integrates the view of the common legal representatives of the former child soldiers and of the victims of other crimes (CLRV), stating that it is in the interest of the victims that the proposed charges are added, considering also that concerns about the lack of charges related to gender-based crimes has already been expressed by the CLRV in their 9 July 2019 submissions.[102] Such an approach acknowledges that individual victims of sexual and gender-based crimes do not often report those crimes immediately, due to trauma and cultural or social barriers that are not always apparent to an international tribunal located outside of that context. Access to justice is better served when these localised and victim-centred contexts are recognised and mainstreamed throughout the entire trial process.

Judge Oosterveld's core argument revolves around the three Article 61(9) factors, namely: (1) the importance of the additional charges to ensure a complete understanding and full consideration of the relevant issues; (2) the reasonable diligence of the Prosecutor in bringing additional charges, including the reasonableness of continuing investigations after the Pre-Trial Chamber's confirmation of charges; and (3) whether the adjudication of additional charges would cause undue prejudice to the rights of the accused.[103] Regarding the first factor, Judge Oosterveld cites the Court's jurisprudence as well as that of other international criminal tribunals such as the International Criminal Tribunal for the Former Yugoslavia (ICTY), which recognised that 'the duty to establish the truth is not limited to the time before the confirmation hearing' so the Prosecutor must be allowed to continue the investigation beyond the confirmation hearing.[104] Consequently, she found that, since the war crimes of rape and sexual slavery are the only proposed charges of conflict-related sexual violence against the accused, 'the victims, in particular, have an interest in the full consideration of the responsibility of the accused and the extent of victimisation'.[105]

The rewritten judgment's feminist approach is most obvious regarding discussion of the second factor. Judge Oosterveld clarifies that the underlying rationale of

[100] *Ibid*, § 11.
[101] *Ibid*, § 12.
[102] *Ibid*, § 14.
[103] *Ibid*, § 20.
[104] *Ibid*, § 23.
[105] *Ibid*, § 25.

Article 61(9) is that the continued investigation should only be related to essential pieces of evidence that were not known or could not have been collected by the Prosecutor prior to the confirmation hearing and the reasons for such an investigation must be properly justified.[106] Judge Oosterveld comprehensively expands on the Prosecutor's original submission by meticulously detailing the factual circumstances hampering the Prosecutor in providing such evidence prior to the confirmation hearing. In particular, Oosterveld demonstrates the material lack of time for the Prosecutor to carry out field missions to CAR, including during the COVID-19 pandemic and related travel restrictions, as well as to assess risks related to witness and victim protection and related procedural matters, such as translation into French. Importantly, Oosterveld incorporates a feminist approach by highlighting the inherent challenges related to collecting credible evidence on conflict-related sexual violence, such as survivors' reluctance in revealing the crime suffered due to security threats, as well as societal and cultural stigma. Oosterveld also recalls how trauma, lack of meaningful protection mechanisms, and health reasons should not be underestimated when dealing with survivors of conflict-related sexual violence.[107]

Regarding the third factor, in assessing the right to a fair trial of the accused, Judge Oosterveld considers the duration of pre-trial custody, the extent of the delay in case of adjudication of additional charges, and whether it would amount to undue delay.[108] She skilfully relies on the same ICC jurisprudence – namely *Al Hassan* and *Ruto and Sang*[109] – already cited in the original judgment, proving that it could equally serve to substantiate her arguments and showing how the Court already previously balanced the search for the truth with the fairness and expeditiousness of the proceedings, prioritising the former over the latter.[110] Judge Oosterveld concludes by affirming that the proposed charges are limited both in scope and time and connected to existing charges. Hence, only the defence would have to carry out an additional investigation, which would be narrow in focus, in consideration also of the fact that the trial is unlikely to happen in the near future.[111] Finally, Oosterveld also offers mitigating steps to ensure the rights of the accused, such as prompt disclosure of witness statements to the defence and subtracting time in custody in case of conviction, showing that the Chamber could have opted for a less restrictive approach, better balancing two competing and equally relevant interests.[112]

Judge Oosterveld's reimagined judgment clearly highlights how a restrictive and excessively procedural approach to the amendment of charges following the Pre-Trial Chamber's confirmation of charges poorly serves the interest of justice, failing

[106] *Ibid*, § 27.
[107] *Ibid*, § 32.
[108] *Ibid*, § 35.
[109] *Prosecutor v. William Samoei Ruto and Joshua Arap Sang*, ICC-01/09-01/11.
[110] Judge Oosterveld, *supra* note 96, §§ 36–37.
[111] *Ibid*, § 39.
[112] *Ibid*, § 43.

to recognise the extent and complexity of survivors' experiences and needs, especially with regard to conflict-related sexual violence. The Chamber's blank dismissal of the charges of rape and sexual slavery, justified almost exclusively on the need to safeguard the accused's right to defence, without even minimally factoring in the gravity of the crimes allegedly committed or the severity of the consequences on victims' rights and lives, is concerning for international justice. Such a decision confirms, inter alia, how the gender analysis referred to in ICC policy papers is still largely lacking in practice and needs to be updated and mainstreamed throughout all phases of the proceedings.[113]

By following the procedural and legal steps of the original judgment, Judge Oosterveld fills this gap, attributing gender-based crimes the centrality they deserve in an international criminal tribunal. While carefully considering the procedural and restrictive approach of the Chamber, Oosterveld strikes a balance between the need to preserve the accused's right to a fair trial – including by offering mitigating measures to ensure an expeditious trial – and the duty to establish the truth in the interest of justice, adopting a victim-centred, trauma-informed, and gender-sensitive approach. Her feminist approach is particularly evident in the examination of the second factor, namely the reasonableness of continuing investigation after the confirmation of charges. In this context, she offers factual details on the two incidents affecting the additional victims which were missing in the original Prosecutor's request and also delves into the specific challenges related to the collection of evidence of conflict-related sexual violence. While some of these challenges are inherent to most survivors of human rights violations, such as security risks, lack of protection measures, and investigators' difficulties to find confidential spaces to conduct interviews during ongoing conflicts, specific cultural and societal barriers leading to further stigmatisation for survivors of conflict-related sexual violence were also highlighted. This paragraph is central to the purpose of rewriting ICC decisions through a gendered lens and could have probably been further expanded, for instance by providing a more detailed analysis on the crime of sexual slavery and additional challenges of individuals subjected to extreme forms of exploitation and completely deprived of their freedom and agency to timely and meaningfully testify on the multiple violations suffered without the risk of re-victimisation. In addition, this feminist approach could have been integrated throughout the other two factors examined in the rewritten judgment, namely that of the importance of the additional allegations to a complete understanding of the Prosecutor's case and that of whether the additional charges would cause undue

[113] See, for instance, The Office of the Prosecutor, *Policy Paper on Sexual and Gender-Based Crimes* (International Criminal Court, June 2014): See also R. Grey, *Prosecuting Sexual and Gender-Based Crimes at the International Criminal Court* (Cambridge: Cambridge University Press, 2019); and I. Rosenthal, 'ICC Preliminary Examinations: Where Is the Gender Analysis', *Opinio Juris*, 11 January 2022, available at http://opiniojuris.org/2022/01/11/icc-preliminary-examinations-where-is-the-gender-analysis/.

prejudice to the rights of the accused. While this was partially done, it could be further strengthened, for instance highlighting the gravity of the crimes by referring to victims' testimonies, as well as to CLRV's previous submissions.

Overall, Judge Oosterveld illustrates, using a feminist approach, that it is possible to respect the rationale of Article 61(9) of the Rome Statute exercising caution on the risk of abuse by the Prosecutor, while fully recognising the extent of victims' lives and experiences, in the interest of justice and truth. Judge Oosterveld's rewritten judgment also highlights the importance of mainstreaming a gender-sensitive and trauma-informed analysis throughout all phases of judicial proceedings and not just during the investigation phase. While survivors of gross human rights and humanitarian law violations share similar challenges in accessing international justice, survivors of conflict-related sexual violence face additional cultural and social barriers, such as family and community stigma and lack of social and economic support which may deter them from testifying before an international accountability body. The risk of re-victimisation is also higher for survivors of conflict-related sexual violence, especially when they face social exclusion, have to raise children born out of rape, or are rejected by their families. Victims of sexual slavery in particular, due to the severe and protracted multifaceted exploitation, are often compromised in their capacity to take decisions for themselves, and the time required to recover from the long-term effects of such trauma may at times be incompatible with the legalistic requirements of tribunals. However, Judge Oosterveld proves that a balance between respect for the rights of the accused and recognition of the extent of victimisation on the ground is possible even when dealing with amendment of charges following a confirmation decision and that a feminist approach is key to avoiding sexual violence charges being left out of international courtrooms, failing to provide survivors with justice and redress, which is the ultimate goal for which international tribunals were created.

Imagining Gender Justice beyond the Rules

The preceding reflections of rewritten judgments highlight both the opportunities but also the limitations of using a feminist approach within the confines of international criminal law and the Rome Statute. Engaging in truly feminist legal reasoning requires reasoning from context rather than reasoning from the abstract. Thus, consideration must be given to the lived experiences of victims of international crimes, such as gender-based crimes, and how those crimes may be experienced differently depending on gender (norms). Therefore, judges should be free to incorporate information that contextualises the crimes further, and should include the contextualisation of gender norms as it relates to gender-diverse people.

As an example, in Judge Keith's rewritten judgment, she could have further expanded on the socio-economic consequences of rape, including victims' financial lack of capacity to be able to access a series of basic rights, such as healthcare, education, and employment opportunities as essential components of their reintegration into society. An analysis of structural gender-based discrimination predating the conflict and further exacerbated by it could also have enriched the contextual background. For instance, in its concluding observations on the Central African Republic in 2000, the UN Committee on the Rights of the Child expressed its concern about 'extensive discrimination against girls with regard, in particular, to access to education and inheritance rights'.[114] Similarly, in 2006, the UN Human Rights Committee noted with concern a persistent pattern of discrimination against women, both in the exercise of their political rights and in the area of education. It was also concerned about discrimination against women in the marriage relationship, in particular with regard to the exercise of parental authority and the choice of residence.[115] In addition, the Committee expressed its concern with regard to the practices of female genital mutilation and polygamy that adversely impact women's rights.[116] Structural gender inequalities and stereotyping, including discriminatory access to education, employment opportunities, and therefore financial resources, significantly hamper women's and girls' rehabilitation, empowerment, and social inclusion, which are also key for prevention and non-recurrence of sexual violence.[117]

Another example relates to Judge Eichert's reimagining of 'forced nudity'. The gendered harm of the crime could have been better contextualised in a non-Western setting where sexual orientation and gender identity are not really publicly discussed. In this regard, going beyond the rules may include making an extra effort to search for cultural, customary, or other traditional practices that could support integration of gender-diverse people and recognition of forced nudity as a form of gender-based violence grounded in agreed cultural norms in that society which may not necessarily coincide with codified international criminal law.

We conclude by observing that there is no one universal feminist frame used throughout all rewritten judgments. This is both purposeful and necessary. When (re)writing judgments concerning diverse peoples with diverse conceptions of pain and loss, it is useful and necessary to approach complex legal issues with fully contextualised understanding of those issues, including contexts of gender, sexuality, race, and culture.

11.2 FORCED NUDITY IN THE BEMBA WARRANT

David Eichert

In 2008, ICC Pre-Trial Chamber III issued a warrant of arrest against Mr Jean-Pierre Bemba Gombo for crimes which allegedly occurred between 25 October 2002 and

[114] CRC/C/15/Add.138, § 28.
[115] CCPR/C/CAF/CO/2, § 9.
[116] *Ibid*, §§ 10–11.
[117] See for instance CEDAW/C/GC/35 (2017).

14 March 2003 in CAR while Mr Bemba led the Mouvement de Libération du Congo (MLC).[118] The prosecution's application for arrest included forced nudity as both a crime against humanity under Article 7(1)(g) and as a war crime under Article 8(2)(e)(vi) of the Rome Statute.[119]

The warrant issued by the Chamber authorised three counts of crimes against humanity and five of war crimes but declined to include the crime of forced nudity, stating that it did not meet the 'comparable gravity threshold' as either a war crime or crime against humanity; that is, the Chamber found forced nudity not to be as grave as sexual crimes such as rape or sexual slavery.[120]

In his rewritten warrant of arrest, David Eichert confirms the crime of forced nudity and explores the idea of comparable gravity, focusing on the way forced nudity weaponises cultural ideas and norms of gender, utilising the approaches of international conventions and courts. Drawing attention to the social impact of such a crime, Eichert notes that any person can experience harm through this crime, but that cisgender men and gender-diverse individuals experience a unique harm which has often been disregarded at the ICC, and he directs his focus to the voices of such victims.

No.: ICC-01/05-01/08
Date: 10 June 2008

Original: English

PRE-TRIAL CHAMBER III(B)

Before: Judge David EICHERT

SITUATION IN THE CENTRAL AFRICAN REPUBLIC
IN THE CASE OF THE *PROSECUTOR v. JEAN-PIERRE BEMBA GOMBO*

Public Document

Decision on the Prosecutor's Application for a Warrant of Arrest against Jean-Pierre Bemba Gombo

PROCEDURAL HISTORY

1. On 9 May 2008 the Chamber was seized of the Prosecutor's application, in which the Prosecutor sought the issuance of a warrant of arrest against Jean-Pierre Bemba Gombo (Mr Bemba) for four counts of crimes against humanity and six

[118] Warrant of Arrest, *Bemba* (ICC-01/05-01/08-14-tENG), Pre-Trial Chamber III, 10 June 2008.
[119] Prosecutor's Submission on Further Information and Materials, *Bemba* (ICC-01/05-01/08-29-Red), Pre-Trial Chamber III, 27 May 2008.
[120] Bemba Warrant of Arrest, *supra* note 118, §§ 40, 63.

counts of war crimes.[121] On 23 May 2008 the Prosecutor filed an Application for Request for Provisional Arrest under Article 92 and later that same day an arrest warrant pursuant to Article 58 of the Rome Statute was issued.[122] On 27 May 2008 the Prosecutor submitted additional information and supporting material (Prosecutor's Submission on Further Information and Materials).[123]

2. Included among these allegations was the claim that members of the MLC, under the command of Mr Bemba, committed the crime of sexual violence in violation of Articles 7(1)(g) and 8(2)(e)(vi) of the Rome Statute during the time period being investigated. Specifically, the Prosecutor alleged that members of the MLC forced civilians to undress in public in order to humiliate them, and that these acts amounted to crimes against humanity and war crimes.[124] The Prosecutor alleged that Bemba, as commander in chief of the MLC forces, is criminally responsible under Article 25(3)(a) of the Statute, jointly with another person or through other persons, for such acts.[125]

3. The Prosecutor's allegations focus on three separate instances of forced nudity, although they included additional redacted acts of sexual violence which are not discussed here.[126]

4. The first allegation of forced nudity comes from a twenty-two-year-old man who was attacked by a group of ten MLC combatants. After being beaten and robbed, the man was taken aside and forced to undress by a female combatant. Once naked, he was forced to have sex with the woman, who threatened to tell her male colleagues to beat him again if he did not comply.[127]

5. Another allegation involved a male government minister who was told to strip naked by female MLC combatants. Amnesty International notes that this was done in a context of active armed conflict in which the wives of other ministers and government officials were being raped by combatants. Allegedly the perpetrators who forced the man to undress 'wanted to see a naked government minister because they had not seen one before', in a manner meant to humiliate the victim.[128]

[121] Prosecutor's Application for Warrant of Arrest under Article 58, *Bemba* (ICC-01/05-01/08-26-Red 15-12-2009 1/62 EO PT), Pre-Trial Chamber III, 9 May 2008, at 8–11 (hereafter Prosecutor's Application).

[122] Prosecutor's Application for Request for Provisional Arrest under Article 92, *Bemba* (ICC-01/05-01/08-28 24-06-2008 1/6 SZ PT), Pre-Trial Chamber III, 23 May 2008; Warrant of Arrest for Jean-Pierre Bemba Gombo, *Bemba* (ICC-01/05-01/08-1-tENG 09-06-2008 1/8 VW PT), Pre-Trial Chamber III, 23 May 2008.

[123] Prosecutor's Submission on Further Information and Materials, *Bemba* (ICC-01/05-01/-8-29-Red 15-12-2009 1/1- EO PT), Pre-Trial Chamber III, 27 May 2008 (hereafter Prosecutor's Submission).

[124] *Ibid*, § 6(c)(v).

[125] Prosecutor's Application, *supra* note 121, at 9–10.

[126] *Ibid*, at 9–10; Prosecutor's Submission, *supra* note 123, § 6(c)(v).

[127] Prosecutor's Submission, *supra* note 123, at 8 (citing Amnesty International, *Central African Republic: Five Months of War against Women* (2004) at 5–6).

[128] Prosecutor's Submission, *supra* note 123, at 8 (citing Amnesty International, at 9).

6. The final allegation of forced nudity involved a woman who was forced to undress by a group of MLC men who wanted to rape her. However, they saw that she was suffering from scabies and did not rape her.[129]

7. The question before this Chamber is whether, pursuant to Article 58(1)(a), there are reasonable grounds to believe that such acts are of sufficient gravity as to justify further action by the Court. This gravity requirement is outlined in the Elements of Crimes: Article 7(1)(g)-6(2) requires that an act of sexual violence be 'of a gravity comparable' to the other sexual offences outlined in Article 7(1)(g), while Article 8(2)(e)(vi)-6(2) requires that acts alleged to be war crimes must constitute 'a serious violation of Article 3 common to the four Geneva Conventions'.[130]

DETERMINATION BY THE CHAMBER

8. This Chamber affirms that forced nudity can meet these requirements and, where appropriate, should be considered a crime of sexual violence in violation of the Rome Statute. Allegations of forced nudity and other acts of sexual violence should be assessed on a case-by-case basis to determine the gravity of such claims, taking into consideration the culturally situated messages about gender conveyed by such acts.

Previous Treatment of Forced Nudity in International Legal Sources

9. Forced nudity has been recognised in multiple international contexts as a serious violation that is comparable to other sexual crimes and forms of inhuman treatment. Notably, the Istanbul Protocol, an authoritative United Nations document about torture, states that '[s]exual torture begins with forced nudity … An individual is never as vulnerable as when naked and helpless. Nudity enhances the psychological terror of every aspect of torture, as there is always the background of potential abuse [or] rape'.[131]

10. Forced nudity has been addressed in cases before other international tribunals. Notably, in *Akayesu* the International Criminal Tribunal for Rwanda (ICTR) ruled that the accused was criminally responsible for various crimes of sexual violence, including one episode where a young girl was forced to undress and do gymnastics

[129] *Ibid.*

[130] A similar gravity requirement for the war crime of sexual violence during international armed conflicts is included in Article 8(2)(b)(xxii)-6(2) of the Elements of Crimes.

[131] *The Istanbul Protocol: Manual on Effective Investigation and Documentation of Torture and Other Cruel, Inhuman or Degrading Treatment or Punishment* (Geneva: United Nations, 2004), at 41.

for a group of soldiers.[132] The International Criminal Tribunal for the former Yugoslavia (ICTY) similarly found that sexual violence had occurred in the judgment for *Kunarac et al.*, where three women were forced to dance on a table nude,[133] and in *Brđanin*, where a woman was forced to undress in front of a crowd of cheering male soldiers.[134]

11. Moreover, pursuant to Article 21(3) of the Statute which requires that the interpretation of law be consistent with internationally recognised human rights, it is notable that human rights courts and treaty bodies have ruled on the issue of forced nudity. Both the Inter-American Court of Human Rights and the European Court of Human Rights have found forced nudity to be a serious human rights violation, especially where the victim is forced to be nude in unhealthy or cold conditions,[135] in the presence of unmuzzled dogs,[136] or before an officer of a different gender.[137] The UN Human Rights Committee and the Committee against Torture have similarly ruled that forced nudity can amount to a serious human rights violation, such as in cases where the victim was whipped while naked,[138] forced to comply with humiliating strip searches,[139] forced into painful poses while naked,[140] or forcibly undressed before family members.[141] Furthermore, the Human Rights Committee has even ruled that being threatened with public nudity without actually being forced to undress can amount to a human rights violation, as in the case of one man who experienced threats that the police would 'parade him naked in front of women and female children'.[142]

12. The potential seriousness of forced nudity was also reaffirmed by the Appeals Chamber for the Special Court of Sierra Leone, which asserted that the prohibition on 'inhumane acts' could include different forms of sexual violence, including the 'forced undressing of women and marching them in public, forcing women to perform exercises naked, … torture, sexual violence, humiliation, harassment, psychological abuse, and confinement in inhumane conditions'.[143]

[132] Judgment, *Akayesu* (ICTR-96-4-T), Trial Chamber, 2 September 1998, §§ 429, 452.

[133] Judgment, *Kunarac, Kovac & Vukovic* (IT-96-23-T & IT-96-23/1-T), Trial Chamber, 22 February 2001, §§ 766–774.

[134] Judgment, *Brđanin* (IT-99-36-T), Trial Chamber, 1 September 2004, § 1013.

[135] Judgment (Merits, Reparations and Costs), *Miguel Castro-Castro Prison v Peru* (Ser. C No. 160), 25 November 2006, § 308.

[136] See *ibid*, § 260.

[137] Judgment, *Valašinas v. Lithuania* (no. 44558/98, ECHR 2001-VIII), 24 October 2001, §§ 114–118.

[138] Communication, *George Osbourne v. Jamaica* (CCPR/C/68/D/759/1997), 15 March 2000, § 3.4.

[139] Communication, *Clement Boodoo v. Trinidad & Tobago* (CCPR/C/74/D/721/1996), 2 April 2002, § 2.7.

[140] E.g., Communication, *Abdelli v. Tunisia* (CAT/C/31/D/188/2001), 14 November 2002, § 2.3; Communication, *Thabati v. Tunisia* (CAT/C/31/D/187/2001), 14 November 2003, § 2.4.

[141] Communication, *Darmon Sultanova v. Uzbekistan* (CCPR/C/86/D/915/2000), 30 March 2006, § 2.3.

[142] Communication, *Philip Afuson Njaru v. Cameroon* (CCPR/C/89/D/1353/2005), 19 March 2007, § 2.7.

[143] Judgment, *Brima, Kamara & Kanu (the AFRC Accused)* (SCSL-04-16-T), Appeals Chamber, 22 February 2008, § 184.

Discussion

Understanding Sexual Violence in Context

13. Forced nudity may be a sufficiently serious crime when such acts weaponise closely held beliefs about gender, sexuality, religion, chastity, respect, social position, or dignity. In many parts of the world public nudity is believed to be a shameful act, and many religions and legal systems restrict nudity to a small number of acceptable situations. Many societies also place special significance on being nude in the presence of individuals from a different gender, which may further intensify the harm of being forced to undress in public. Alternatively, in some social contexts public nudity in the presence of individuals of the same gender may be interpreted as perverted or homosexual, which can be similarly harmful to victims.

14. The Prosecutor has not included specific information about the cultural meaning of public nudity in the Central African Republic (CAR), but from limited UN material it appears that public nudity is often interpreted as being deeply shameful.[144]

15. While being forced to undress can be a serious violation by itself, forced nudity can also be accompanied by situational considerations which aggravate the harm even more. For example, if a victim becomes involuntarily aroused during the experience, that can be personally confusing to the individual or inspire further violence. Perpetrators may take photographs and videos of the crime or threaten to tell other members of the victim's community about the nudity. Such threats contribute to the harm and dehumanisation that can be experienced by victims, leading to mental anguish.

16. For victims of any gender, forced nudity may result in traumatic feelings associated with vulnerability, shame, and humiliation. Victims of forced nudity may have traumatic fears about the possibility of further sexual assault or rape once they are naked. This is especially true in situations like the one currently before the Court, where armed forces are alleged to have committed widespread sexual assault on civilians. Furthermore, one of the three victims included in the Prosecutor's submission was allegedly raped after being forced to undress, while another was allegedly forced to undress so that soldiers could carry out their intention of raping her. It is therefore reasonable to conclude, given the potential for serious physical abuse and mental harm due to forced nudity, that the crimes alleged by the Prosecutor could be sufficiently serious to merit further attention from this Court.

17. Forced nudity also preys upon norms about gender and can cause long-term harm in a person's life. For cisgender women, being forced to undress may result in

[144] M. J. Mathey et al., 'The Role Played by Women of the Central African Republic in the Prevention and Resolution of Conflicts' in *Women and Peace in Africa: Case Studies on Traditional Conflict Resolution Practices* (Paris: UNESCO, 2003) 35–46, at 41–42.

social isolation or rejection for the perceived violation of norms about modesty and chastity. Cisgender women may also lose their standing in their community or be perceived negatively by community members.

18. Similarly, cisgender men who are forced to publicly undress may experience negative social repercussions for the perceived violation of community norms. Some men may lose their social position due to a perceived inability to protect themselves from sexual humiliation or be shunned for violating religious rules around nudity. In instances where a female perpetrator forces a man to undress publicly, such an act may be interpreted as humiliating or sexually exploitative due to culturally specific ideas about sexual autonomy and control. Notably, for the government minister who was forced to undress by female soldiers, it would be reasonable to assume that the alleged crime could have been influenced by social norms about nudity and social status, and therefore potentially traumatic for the victim.

19. Forced nudity may similarly be harmful to transgender, intersex, and gender-minority individuals whose bodies do not conform to widespread beliefs about gender. In such situations, forced nudity may expose individuals to further social exclusion or result in greater feelings of insecurity. This is especially true for individuals who are not public about their gender-minority status or who live in situations where knowledge about a person's gender-minority status would put them at greater risk of physical violence. Moreover, for individuals with gender dysphoria, being forced to publicly undress may result in significant anguish and humiliation connected to their mental state.

20. These examples are not exhaustive, and ideas about modesty, chastity, social position, or strength can be weaponised to harm individuals of any gender.

21. Additionally, individuals who do not comply with cultural norms about nudity and sexuality can also be victims of forced nudity. For example, sex workers may experience tremendous harm and humiliation from being forced to undress publicly, even if they have consented to public nudity in the past. Similarly, individuals who have non-normative beliefs about nudity, who engage in non-normative sexual relationships, or who otherwise fall outside conventional beliefs about public morality may all nevertheless experience harm from forced nudity in a situation of armed conflict.

Using Victim Testimony to Understand the Gravity of Forced Nudity

22. While expert opinion may be useful for understanding the significance and gravity of forced nudity in a specific cultural context, ultimately the most reliable source is the victim or survivor who experienced the crime. Victims are the most qualified individuals for articulating how a crime made them feel, the long-term ramifications of the crime, and how ideas about gender or sexuality were weaponised by the crime. Presenting victims' perspectives is therefore essential for understanding the gravity of a particular situation, especially for a crime like sexual violence whose use is informed by nuanced and culturally specific ideas about gender and sexuality.

23. Situating victims' claims in the wider context of an armed conflict can clarify the significance and gravity of forced nudity. This is because the crime of forced nudity rarely happens in a vacuum; rather, forced nudity often occurs at the same time as other sexual crimes and outrages upon personal dignity. Victims' beliefs about the gravity of their experiences can thus be confirmed by situating those claims in the wider context of sexual and non-sexual violence at the time. For example, a victim who is forced to undress in a situation where sexual assault is a well-known occurrence, such as in this case, may report much higher rates of traumatisation than a person who undresses in a more peaceful situation.

24. This deference to victims' claims is particularly important when considering sexual crimes against men, which have featured in relatively fewer cases before international tribunals. Notably, in some instances allegations of sexual violence against men have been classified as 'cruel treatment' or another non-sexual label,[145] while in other cases no charges have been brought despite evidence of sexual violence against men being available.[146] While much of the international case law regarding sexual violence involves situations where cisgender women have been harmed by cisgender men, it is important to note that men sometimes also experience sexual violence which can have a serious effect on their well-being. As shown in two of the allegations submitted by the Prosecutor, cisgender women are capable of committing acts of sexual violence against cisgender men, often in conjunction with other male or female combatants, and these crimes should not be interpreted as less serious just by virtue of the victims' gender.

25. Similarly, crimes against transgender, intersex, or gender-minority individuals have been absent from international criminal trials about sexual violence, even though they too can be victims of forced nudity and other sexual crimes. These harms demonstrate the importance of trusting victims of all genders to correctly express and articulate the gravity of their experiences, since this articulation is essential to a proper understanding of the scope of violence in a specific context.

The Categorisation of Non-Penetrative Sexual Violence

26. Finally, identifying forced nudity as a 'sexual' crime, rather than as an outrage upon personal dignity or cruel treatment, can be important for understanding the

[145] For example, in *Tadić* the Prosecutor introduced evidence of the accused forcing male prisoners to engage in oral sex but charged him with exclusively non-sexual crimes: committing torture or inhuman treatment, wilfully causing great suffering or serious injury to body and health, cruel treatment in violation of the laws or customs of war, and the crime against humanity of inhumane acts. Second Amended Indictment, *Tadić* (IT-94-1), 14 December 1995, at 5–6.

[146] For example, in *Brima, Kamara, & Kanu*, the Trial Chamber only considered evidence regarding sexual violence against women, despite evidence of sexual violence against men being also presented. Judgment, *Brima, Kamara & Kanu (the AFRC Accused)* (SCSL-04-16-T), Appeals Chamber, 22 February 2008, §§ 966–1188.

scope and meanings of a certain act. The crimes listed in Articles 7(1)(g) and 8(2)(e)(vi) weaponise ideas about gender and sexuality in specific ways not reflected by other categorisations, and this weaponisation allows perpetrators to target both an individual's bodily autonomy and wider community cohesion through gendered shame and humiliation. Identifying a crime as 'sexual' can therefore be useful for reflecting the gravity and meaning of certain crimes in a specific instance of armed conflict. This is not to say that forced nudity cannot also be categorised as an outrage upon personal dignity or cruel treatment, but rather that the categorisation of 'sexual' is useful for expressing some of the unique harms associated with such crimes.

27. Moreover, the delegates who drafted the Rome Statute felt it necessary to include the crime of sexual violence as outlined in Articles 7(1)(g) and 8(2)(e)(vi) as a distinct category separate from other sexual crimes. The crime of sexual violence is thus distinct from rape in that there is no penetrative element, but despite this absence, the categorisation is still considered serious enough to be included as both a crime against humanity and a war crime. As noted in a previous case, '[t]he crimes listed in Articles 5 to 8 of the Statute have been carefully selected'[147] and thus the inclusion of a non-penetrative form of sexual violence is not accidental.

28. While the crime of sexual violence must be of comparable gravity to the other enumerated sexual crimes, there is no hierarchy among these crimes. If a victim reasonably alleges that a non-penetrative form of sexual violence such as forced nudity has occurred, and that such an act led to serious harm for the victim, the allegation should be sufficient for believing that such an act is serious enough to merit further consideration by this Court.

Request for Further Information

29. In all three allegations submitted by the Prosecutor, it would be reasonable to assume that the victims experienced significant harm from the weaponisation of gendered ideas and the humiliation of public nudity. Moreover, the threat of rape after being forced to undress could have left victims with a deep feeling of insecurity and unease, especially given the larger context of alleged rape by MLC combatants. These elements suggest that the charges listed by the Prosecutor are of sufficient gravity to merit further consideration by this Court.

30. Pursuant to Article 69(3) of the Rome Statute, the Court has 'the authority to request the submission of all evidence that it considers necessary for the determination of the truth'. Because the Prosecutor provided little background about the

[147] Judgment on the Prosecutor's Appeal against the Decision of Pre-Trial Chamber I Entitled 'Decision on the Prosecutor's Application for Warrants of Arrest, Article 58', *Situation in the Democratic Republic of Congo* (ICC-01/04-169 23-09-2008 1/49 CB PT OA), Appeals Chamber, 13 July 2006, § 71.

meaning of forced nudity in the CAR, this Chamber deems it necessary to request that all parties provide specific information about gendered norms which are relevant to understanding public perceptions of nudity in the local context. Ideally much of this information should come from the victims themselves, who are the most capable of articulating the feelings evoked by their experiences. Such testimony can be complemented by expert testimony about gender in the CAR and evidence about other crimes committed during the conflict to situate victims' allegations of harm.

FOR THESE REASONS, THE CHAMBER HEREBY

DECIDES that forced nudity can qualify as sexual violence as described in Articles 7(1)(g) and 8(2)(e)(vi) of the Rome Statute;

DECIDES to issue a warrant of arrest against Jean-Pierre BEMBA GOMBO, as a separate document in the place of the warrant issued on 23 May 2008, for his alleged criminal responsibility within the meaning of Article 25(3)(a) of the Statute in the commission of crimes against humanity and war crimes under the following counts:

- rape as a crime against humanity under Article 7(1)(g);
- other forms of sexual violence as a crime against humanity under Article 7(1)(g);
- rape as a war crime under Article 8(2)(e)(vi);
- other forms of sexual violence as a war crime under Article 8(2)(e)(vi);
- torture as a crime against humanity under Article 7(1)(f);
- torture as a war crime under Article 8(2)(c)(i);
- outrages upon personal dignity, in particular humiliating and degrading treatment, as a war crime under Article 8(2)(c)(ii);
- murder as a crime against humanity under Article 7(1)(a);
- murder as a war crime under Article 8(2)(c)(i);
- pillaging a town or place as a war crime under Article 8(2)(e)(v); and

REQUESTS all parties to provide additional context about the culturally specific meaning of sexual violence and forced nudity in the Central African Republic, to aid in understanding how the alleged acts may be seen in the local context.

Judge David Eichert

11.3 CHARGING SEXUAL CRIMES IN THE BEMBA CONFIRMATION OF CHARGES

Loyce Mrewa

Pre-Trial Chamber II confirmed the charges against Mr Jean-Pierre Bemba Gombo in 2009.[148] The Prosecutor's submission, the Document Containing the Charges, contained the charges of torture as a war crime and as a crime against humanity, as well as

[148] Confirmation of Charges, *Bemba* (ICC-01/05-01/08-424), Pre-Trial Chamber II, 15 June 2009.

outrages upon personal dignity as a war crime.[149] These three charges utilised the same factual conduct that the Prosecutor presented to the Chamber regarding the charges of rape also levied against Mr Bemba. In the original confirmation of charges, the Pre-Trial Chamber declined to confirm the crime of torture as a war crime because the Prosecutor failed to prove the specific intent requirement related to this crime.[150] The Pre-Trial Chamber also refused to apply the doctrine of cumulative charging, stating that both torture as a crime against humanity and outrages upon personal dignity as a war crime were entirely subsumed by the crime of rape, and therefore declined to confirm those charges.

In this reimagined confirmation of charges decision, Loyce Mrewa focuses on the charges of torture as a crime against humanity and outrages upon personal dignity as a war crime, which the Pre-Trial Chamber declined to confirm as cumulative charges. Mrewa confirms the ability of the Pre-Trial Chamber to apply the doctrine of cumulative charging to the charges of torture as a crime against humanity and outrages upon personal dignity as a war crime. In considering the application of the doctrine from other international tribunals, Mrewa places the voices of the victims at the centre of the discussion, noting that to ignore the reality of rape as a method of torture or an outrage upon personal dignity is a failure not just to apply the requirement of fair labelling but is akin to denying the lived experiences of the victims and relegating their harm without comment.

Mrewa applies a close reading of the Elements of Crime to conclude that the charges under consideration meet the threshold of being materially different while protecting different interests and that cumulative charging is necessary to record the full culpability and blameworthiness of the accused and to accurately characterise the experiences of victims of sexual and gender-based crimes. Mrewa concludes that cumulative charging using the same factual conduct for multiple counts is authorised, and these counts would likely be confirmed if additional evidence was publicly accessible because the accused, Mr Bemba, was convicted of the crime of rape at trial.[151]

No.: ICC-01/05-01/08-424 B
Date: 15 June 2009

Original: English

PRE-TRIAL CHAMBER II(B)

Before: Judge Loyce MREWA

SITUATION IN THE CENTRAL AFRICAN REPUBLIC
IN THE CASE OF THE *PROSECUTOR v. JEAN-PIERRE BEMBA GOMBO*

[149] Annex 3 of the Amended Document containing the charges filed on 30 March 2009, *Bemba* (ICC-01/05-01/08-395-Anx3), Pre-Trial Chamber II, 20 March 2009.

[150] Bemba Confirmation of Charges, *supra* note 148, §§ 289–300.

[151] Public with Annexes I, II, and A–F: Judgment pursuant to Article 74 of the Statute, *Bemba* (ICC-01/05-01/08-3343), Trial Chamber III, 21 March 2016, § 752(c)(d).

Public

Decision pursuant to Article 61(7)(a) and (b) of the Rome Statute on Charges of the Prosecutor against Jean-Pierre Bemba Gombo

PRE-TRIAL CHAMBER II (the Chamber) of the International Criminal Court (the Court) issues this decision pursuant to Article 61(7)(a) and (b) of the Rome Statute (the Statute), on the charges brought by the Prosecutor in the case of the *Prosecutor v. Jean-Pierre Bemba Gombo* (the Case).

THE PERSON CHARGED

1. The Prosecutor of the Court submits the charges against Mr Jean-Pierre Bemba Gombo (Mr Bemba) a national of the Democratic Republic of the Congo (DRC).[152] In 1998, Mr Bemba established a military movement known as the Mouvement de Libération du Congo (MLC), in Kisangani, DRC.[153] He was the president and commander-in-chief of the MLC until 13 July 2002, when he obtained the rank of a general.[154]

PROCEDURAL BACKGROUND

2. The Central African Republic referred to the Prosecutor of the Court the situation in the CAR in a letter dated 18 December 2004.[155] The letter referred to the situation in which crimes against humanity and war crimes within the jurisdiction of the Court had allegedly been committed on the territory of the CAR since 1 July 2002.[156]

3. The Presidency of the Court assigned the situation in the CAR to Pre-Trial Chamber III pursuant to Regulation 46(2) of the Regulations of the Court on 19 January 2005.[157]

4. On 9 May 2008, the Prosecutor submitted an application for the issuance of a warrant of arrest against Mr Bemba on four counts of crimes against humanity and six counts of war crimes.[158]

[152] Annex 3 Public Redacted Version of the Amended Document containing the Charges Filed on 30 March 2009, *Bemba* (ICC-01/05-01/08-395-Anx3), Pre-Trial Chamber II, 30 March 2009, § 1 (hereafter Bemba Annex 3 Amended Charges Document).

[153] *Ibid*, at § 4.

[154] *Ibid*, at § 5.

[155] Decision on the Prosecutor's Application for a Warrant of Arrest against Jean-Pierre Bemba Gombo, *Bemba* (ICC-01/05-01/08-14-tENG), Pre-Trial Chamber III, 10 June 2008, § 1 (hereafter Bemba Prosecutor's Application for an Arrest Warrant).

[156] *Ibid*, at § 1.

[157] *Ibid*, at § 2.

[158] *Ibid*, at § 4.

5. On 21 May 2008, the Chamber issued the Decision Requesting Additional Information in Respect of the Prosecutor's Application for Warrant of Arrest under Article 58 of the Statute, in which, inter alia, it requested the Prosecutor to provide additional information and supporting material on various aspects of the application, in particular on the counts of other forms of sexual violence and murder, both offences being characterised under crimes against humanity and war crimes.[159]

6. On 23 May 2008, the Prosecutor filed an Application for Request for Provisional Arrest under Article 92 of the Statute, in which, inter alia, he requested the Chamber to consider the prosecution's application for a warrant of arrest of Mr Bemba, filed on 9 May 2008, on an expedited basis in light of the circumstances where the possibility of apprehending Mr Bemba could disappear, while apprehension in the Kingdom of Belgium appeared feasible.[160]

7. The accused, Mr Bemba, was arrested on 24 May 2008 by the authorities of the Kingdom of Belgium, after an arrest warrant was issued against him on 23 May 2003 on two counts of crimes against humanity and four counts of war crimes.[161] On 27 May 2008, the Prosecutor submitted additional information and supporting material in response to the Chamber's decision of 21 May 2008 (Prosecutor's Submission on Further Information and Materials).

8. On 10 June 2008, in light of the Prosecutor's Submission on Further Information and Materials, the Chamber deemed it necessary to issue a new warrant of arrest replacing the original warrant of arrest issued on 23 May 2008.[162] The new warrant of arrest referred to the same events allegedly committed in the CAR between 25 October 2002 and 15 March 2003 and added two counts of murder as both crimes against humanity and war crimes to the original two counts of crimes against humanity and four counts of war crimes.[163]

9. On 12 January 2009, the Confirmation of Charges Hearing commenced but was adjourned by the Chamber and the Prosecutor was requested to submit amended charges establishing the mode of liability under Article 28 of the Statute, and within the context and meaning of Article 61(7)(c)(ii) of the Statute.[164]

10. On 19 March 2009, the Presidency assigned the CAR situation to Pre-Trial Chamber II and dissolved Pre-Trial Chamber III.[165]

[159] *Ibid*, at § 5.

[160] Prosecutor's Application for Request for Provisional Arrest under Article 92, *Bemba* (ICC-01/05-01/08-28), Pre-Trial Chamber III, 23 May 2008, §§ 5–14 (hereafter Bemba Prosecutor's Request for Provincial Arrest).

[161] Bemba Prosecutor's Application for an Arrest Warrant, *supra* note 155, at §§ 6–8.

[162] *Ibid*, at § 10.

[163] *Ibid*, at §§ 7 and 10.

[164] Decision Adjourning the Hearing pursuant to Article 61(7)(c)(ii) of the Rome Statute, *Bemba* (ICC-01/05-01/08-388), Pre-Trial Chamber III, 3 March 2009, at §§ 6 and 49 (hereafter Bemba Article 61(7)(c)(ii) Decision).

[165] Decision on the Constitution of Pre-Trial Chambers and on the Assignment of the Central African Republic Situation (ICC-Pres-01-09), The Presidency, 19 March 2009, at 3.

11. On 30 March 2009, the Prosecutor submitted an amended document containing the charges (DCC) against the accused, together with the Prosecutor's Amended List of Evidence and Amended In-Depth Analytical Chart of Incriminatory Evidence.[166] The prosecution charged Mr Bemba pursuant to Article 25(3)(a) of the Statute with eight counts of the crimes against humanity and war crimes referred to in Articles 7 and 8 of the Statute. Alternatively, the prosecution charged Mr Bemba pursuant to Article 28(a) or Article 28(b) of the Statute for the crimes against humanity and war crimes in Counts 1–8 by virtue of his superior–subordinate relationship with the MLC troops.[167]

12. In the amended DCC, the Prosecutor, pursuant to his authority under Article 61(3)(a) of the Statute, charged Mr Bemba with war crimes and crimes against humanity, as set forth below:

(i) **Count 1** (Rape constituting a crime against humanity in violation of Articles 7(1)(g) and 25(3)(a) or 28(a) or 28(b) of the Statute);
(ii) **Count 2** (Rape constituting a war crime in violation of Articles 8(2)(e)(vi) and 25(3)(a) or 28(a) or 28(b) of the Statute);
(iii) **Count 3** (Torture constituting a crime against humanity in violation of Articles 7(1)(f) and 25(3)(a) or 28(a) or 28(b) of the Statute);
(iv) **Count 4** (Torture constituting a war crime in violation of Articles 8(2)(c)(i) and 25(3)(a) or 28(a) or 28(b) of the Statute);
(v) **Count 5** (Outrages upon personal dignity constituting a war crime in violation of Articles 8(2)(c)(ii) and 25(3)(a) or 28(a) or 28(b) of the Statute);
(vi) **Count 6** (Murder constituting a war crime in violation of 8(2)(c)(i) and 25(3)(a) or 28(a) or 28(b) of the Statute);
(vii) **Count 7** (Murder constituting a crime against humanity in violation of Articles 7(1)(a) and 25(3)(a) or 28(a) or 28(b) of the Statute);
(viii) **Count 8** (Pillaging constituting a war crime in violation of Articles 8(2)(e)(v) and 25(3)(a) or 28(a) or 28(b) of the Statute).[168]

13. The Chamber observes that the Prosecutor presented the same factual conduct, related mainly to acts of rape, for Count 3, torture as a crime against humanity under Article 7(1)(f) of the Statute,[169] Count 4, torture as a war crime under Article 8(2)(c)(i) of the Statute,[170] and Count 5, outrages upon personal dignity as a war

[166] Public Document Prosecution's Submission of Amended Document Containing the Charges, Amended List of Evidence and Amended In-Depth Analysis Chart of Incriminatory Evidence, *Bemba* (ICC-01/05-01/08-395), Pre-Trial Chamber II, 30 March 2009 (hereafter Bemba Public Prosecution's Submission of Amended Document Containing the Charges).
[167] *Ibid*, at § 11.
[168] Bemba Annex 3 Amended Charges Document, *supra* note 152, at 33.
[169] *Ibid*, at 35.
[170] *Ibid*.

crime under Article 8(2)(c)(ii) of the Statute.[171] The Chamber further notes that the Prosecutor submitted cumulative charges for Count 3,[172] Count 4,[173] and Count 5.[174]

14. In view of the available evidence, the Chamber will begin by assessing the permissibility of cumulative charging for Count 3 on torture as a crime against humanity and Count 5 on outrages upon personal dignity based on the same factual conduct to determine whether the Prosecutor's submissions are in accordance with the applicable law.

THE APPLICABLE LAW

Legality of Cumulative Charging in International Criminal Law

15. Concerning the question of the legality of cumulative charging, the Chamber will consider the developments in international criminal law. The Chamber notes that cases from ad hoc criminal tribunals have mapped the developments and legality of cumulative charging, including the conditions in which this practice is permissible in the field of international criminal law. Due regard will be given to relevant case law within the field.

16. At the International Criminal Tribunal for the former Yugoslavia (ICTY), the Appeals Chamber in the *Delalic* case found 'that multiple criminal convictions entered under different statutory provisions but based on the same conduct are permissible only if each statutory provision involved has a materially distinct element not contained in the other'.[175] The *Delalic* judgment indicates that cumulative charging is permitted when the charges relate to crimes containing materially distinct elements from the other crimes.

17. Trial Chamber I of the International Criminal Tribunal of Rwanda (ICTR) reached a similar conclusion in the *Akayesu* case by finding that:

> On the basis of national and international law and jurisprudence, the Chamber concludes that it is acceptable to convict the accused of two offences in relation to the same set of facts in the following circumstances: (1) where the offences have different elements; or (2) where provisions creating the offences protect different interests; or (3) where it is necessary to record a conviction for both offences in order fully to describe what the accused did.[176]

[171] Ibid, at 36; T-10, www.icc-cpi.int/sites/default/files/Transcripts/CR2009_00218.PDF, at 9 and 10 (hereafter T-10).
[172] Bemba Annex 3 Amended Charges Document, *supra* note 152, at 35.
[173] Ibid, at 35.
[174] *Ibid*, at 36; T-10, *supra* note 171, at 9 and 10.
[175] Judgment, *Delalic et al.* (IT-96-21-A), Appeals Chamber Judgment, 20 February 2001, § 412.
[176] Judgment, *Akayesu* (ICTR-964-S), Chamber I, 2 September 1998, § 468.

18. Multiple cases from the ICTR, ICTY, and the Special Court for Sierra Leone confirm that multiple criminal charges can be based on the same factual conduct.[177] In the *Kupreskic* case, the ICTY Trial Chamber endorsed cumulative charging if the statutory provisions relied on are designed to protect different social values and if each offence has a distinctive element.[178] This is demonstrated by the Trial Chamber's finding that 'the Prosecutor may be justified in bringing cumulative charges when the Articles of the Statute referred to are designed to protect different values and when each Article requires proof of a legal element not required by the others'.[179]

19. Trial Chamber II of the ICTR also used a similar test for the concurrence of crimes and reached a similar conclusion in the *Kayishema & Ruzindana* case by finding that 'it is only acceptable to convict an accused of two or more offences in relation to the same set of facts in the following circumstances: (1) where offences have differing elements or (2) where the laws in question protect differing social interests'.[180]

20. Judge Tafazzal H. Khan, the dissenting judge in the *Kayishema & Ruzindana* case,[181] stressed the need for charges and convictions to reflect the total culpability of the accused rather than the distinct elements of cumulative crimes by finding that:

> What must be punished is culpable conduct; this principle applies to situations where the conduct offends two or more crimes, whether or not the factual situation also satisfies the distinct elements of the two or more crimes, as proven[182] . . . where the culpable conduct was part of a widespread and systematic attack specifically against civilians, to

[177] Delalic Judgment, *supra* note 175, at § 400; Trial Judgment and Sentence, *Musema* (ICTR–96–13–T), Trial Chamber I, 27 January 2000, §§ 289–299; Trial Judgment and Sentence, *Rutaganda* (ICTR-96-3-T), Trial Chamber I, 6 December 1999, §§ 108–119; Trial Judgment, *Kayishema & Ruzindana* (ICTR-95-1-T), Trial Chamber II, 21 May 1999, §§ 625–636, 639–650; Akayesu Judgment, *supra* note 176, at § 468; Judgment, *Brima et al.* (SCSL-2004-16-A), Appeals Chamber, 22 February 2008, §§ 202 and 215; Judgment, *Fofana and Kondewa* (SCSL-04-14-A), Appeals Chamber, 28 May 2008, §§ 220 and 225.

[178] Decision on the Defence Challenges to Form of Indictment, *Kupreskic et al.* (IT-95-16-T), Trial Chamber, 15 May 1998.

[179] *Ibid.*

[180] Kayishema & Ruzindanda Judgment, *supra* note 177, at § 627.

[181] The majority came to a different conclusion by finding that the charges brought under Articles 3(a) and (b) of the ICTRSt, namely murder as a crime against humanity and extermination as a crime against humanity, respectively, were fully subsumed within the counts brought under Article 2 of the ICTRSt on genocide. The majority, therefore, found Clement Kayishema not guilty on counts 2, 3, 9, 14, 15, 20, and 21 and Obed Ruzindana not guilty on counts 20 and 21, see Kayishema & Ruzindanda Judgment, *supra* note 177, at VIII: The Verdict, § 1.

[182] Separate and Dissenting Opinion of Judge Tafazaal Hossain Khan Regarding the Verdicts under the Charges of Crimes against Humanity/Murder and Crimes against Humanity/ Extermination, *Kayishema & Ruzindana* (ICTR-95-1-T), Trial Chamber II, 21 May 1999, § 13 in Musema Judgment, *supra* note 177, at § 294 (hereafter Separate and Dissenting Opinion of Judge Khan).

record a conviction for genocide alone does not reflect the totality of the accused's culpable conduct.[183]

21. In assessing the tenability of cumulative charging and convictions, the ICTR Trial Chamber in *Musema* adopted Judge Khan's reasoning regarding cumulative charging.[184] Thus, Judge Khan's reasoning was used to assess the legality and scope of the application of cumulative charges and convictions in *Musema*, and cannot be regarded as *obiter dicta*: his opinion has been transformed into *ratio decidendi*, which has guided subsequent cases within the ICTR.

22. The ICTY and ICTR case law demonstrates the development of the criteria for cumulative charging but does not set a legally binding precedent for this Chamber. These cases, however, clarify the legality of cumulative charging in international criminal law and provide authoritative and persuasive reasoning for accepting cumulative charges. Moreover, the Rome Statute does not provide any contrary direction; thus the interpretations of the ICTY and ICTR will be considered in this Chamber's evaluation of the cumulative charges submitted by the Prosecutor in accordance with Article 21 of the Statute.

23. The drafters of the ICC Elements of Crimes (EoC) also foresaw the likelihood of cumulative charging based on the same factual conduct.[185] The general introduction of the EoC stipulates that 'a particular conduct may constitute one or more crimes'.[186] However, the general introduction of the EoC is a background and preamble, which is persuasive but not legally binding. The *travaux préparatoires* and preambular wording are used to aid the interpretation of the rights and duties arising from treaties.[187] In this particular case, the preambular wording will guide the Chamber in interpreting the Prosecutor's submission of cumulative charges for torture (Count 3) and outrages upon personal dignity (Count 5).

24. The Chamber notes that each individual offence enshrined within the Statute has distinct elements and protects different interests. Article 7(1)(f) of the Statute recognises and prohibits 'torture', while Article 7(1)(g) of the Statute prohibits 'rape, sexual slavery, enforced prostitution, forced pregnancy, enforced sterilisation, or any other form of sexual violence of comparable gravity' committed, as crimes against humanity. The Chamber, therefore, further observes that the Statute allows for the prosecution of distinct forms of sexual and gender-based crimes within its provisions.

[183] Separate and Dissenting Opinion of Judge Khan, *supra* note 182, at § 33 in Musema Judgment, *supra* note 177, at § 295.

[184] Musema Judgment, *supra* note 177, at §§ 294–299.

[185] *Report of the Preparatory Commission for the International Criminal Court, Addendum Part II: Finalized Draft Text of the Elements of Crimes*, UN Doc. PCNICC/2000/1/Add.2, 2 November 2000, General Introduction, § 9.

[186] General Introduction § 9, Elements of Crimes. The ICC Elements of Crimes are legally binding under Art. 21(1)(a) ICCSt. and assist the Court in interpreting and applying Articles 6, 7, and 8 in a manner consistent with the Statute, see Art. 9(1) ICCSt.

[187] Art. 31(2) Vienna Convention on the Law on Treaties.

The Chamber holds that the distinct recognition of offences under the Statute demonstrates how these are separate offences that are prohibited to protect different human rights interests.

25. The Chamber gives due regard to the interests that disparate statutory provisions of the Statute are meant to protect. In this case, the prohibition of torture as a crime against humanity aims to protect physical and mental well-being whilst rape as a crime against humanity focuses on physical autonomy and protection from non-consensual violations of bodily autonomy.[188]

26. In light of the foregoing, notably the guidance provided by the case law from *Kayishema & Ruzindana*, *Musema*, and *Kupreskic*, the preambular wording of the Elements of Crimes, and the Statute itself, the Chamber concludes that it is justified to permit cumulative charging based on the same factual conduct under certain circumstances. The Chamber observes that a criminal act that meets the elements of multiple offences may constitute one or more crimes. The Chamber, therefore, holds that cumulative charging and convictions are acceptable in international criminal law if the relevant statutory provisions are designed to protect different social interests, each offence has a distinctive element, and the charges reflect the total culpability of the accused.[189] As a result, it is generally understood that the Prosecutor is permitted to cumulatively charge offences based on the same criminal conduct.

27. Turning to the case at hand, a full assessment of the culpability of the accused includes recognition of the varied uses of rape to achieve torture (Count 3) and outrages upon dignity (Count 5). The perpetration of torture and outrages upon personal dignity, through the instrument of rape,[190] highlights the breadth of uses of sexual and gender-based violence during conflict. The evidence in the case at hand shows that rape can be used to torture (Count 3), humiliate as outrages upon personal dignity (Count 5), and disempower when the power dynamics of rape itself are considered. The Chamber notes that the charges submitted by the Prosecutor categorise the different uses of rape to achieve different ends.

The Principle of Fair Labelling

28. The Chamber notes that the Statute does not directly mention fair labelling[191] but stipulates the importance of facilitating fair and expeditious

[188] Art. 7(l)(f) § 1, Elements of Crimes; Art. 7(1)(g)-1, § 1, Elements of Crimes.

[189] Separate and Dissenting Opinion of Judge Khan, *supra* note 182, at §§ 13 and 33 in Musema Judgment, *supra* note 177, at §§ 294–295; Kayishema & Ruzindanda Judgment, *supra* note 177, at § 627; Delalic Judgment, *supra* note 175, at § 412; Musema Judgment, *supra* note 177, at §§ 296–299; Kupreskic Decision, *supra* note 178.

[190] Bemba Annex 3 Amended Charges Document, *supra* note 152, at 35–36; T-10, *supra* note 171, at 9 and 10.

[191] Although I rely on secondary literature written after June 2009 to discuss the principle of fair labelling, the insights and debates shared were already relevant at the time of the 2009 decision but were simply codified when these articles were published.

trials.[192] In the determination of charges, the accused is entitled to a fair hearing with minimum guarantees, including 'to be informed promptly and in detail of the nature, cause and content of the charge'.[193] The requirement to inform an accused of the charges in specific terms is also confirmed by scholars and cases from national and international courts such as the ICTR.[194] The Canadian Supreme Court also directly mentions the importance of labelling and punishing a person as a way to 'stigmatise' and attach 'blameworthiness' to the accused in a manner proportionate to the conduct of the accused.[195] Fair labelling of crimes accurately describes and distinguishes criminal conduct in proportion to blameworthiness.[196] Fair labelling is, therefore, important for describing, categorising, and communicating crimes to the accused clearly and fairly in accordance with Article 67(1)(a) of the Statute.

29. The Chamber further notes that Article 21(1)(c) of the Statute provides that general principles from domestic legal systems may be applied by the Court. Fair labelling is a general principle of law in most domestic legal systems because the description, distinguishing, and codification of crimes in domestic criminal codes and laws is an affirmation of fair labelling.[197] Scholars such as Zawati confirm the importance of fair labelling of crimes and argue that the objectives of domestic and international criminal law systems are similar and compatible, including fundamental principles such as fair labelling.[198] The application of fair labelling within the Chamber's assessment of the charges brought by the Prosecutor is justified based on principles of fairness in the ICC Statute and the compatibility of general principles between domestic and international criminal law systems.

192 Art. 64(2) and 3(a) ICCSt.

193 Art. 67(1)(a) ICCSt.

194 Supreme Court of Canada, *R v. Martineau*, [1990] 2 SCR 633, File No. 21122, at 634, 645, and 647; Decision on Prosecution Interlocutory Appeal against Trial Chamber II Decision of 23 February 2005, *Muvunyi* (ICTR-00-55A-AR73), Appeals Chamber, 12 May 2005, §§ 18–19; Judgment, *Ntakirutimana* (ICTR-96-10-A and ICTR-96-17), Appeals Chamber, 13 December 2004, §§ 469–470; Judgment, *Rutaganda* (ICTR-96-3-A), Appeals Chamber, 26 May 2003, § 301; A. Ashworth, 'Principles and Policies' in A. Ashworth (ed.), *Principles of Criminal Law* (6th ed., New York: Oxford University Press, 2009) 44–83, at 78–80; J. Chalmers and F. Leverick, 'Fair Labelling in Criminal Law' 71(2) *Modern Law Review* (2008) 217–246, at 218–222.

195 *R v. Martineau, supra* note 194, at 634 and 647.

196 Chalmers and Leverick, *supra* note 194, at 224–225; T. De Souza Dias, 'Recharacterisation of Crimes and the Principle of Fair Labelling in International Criminal Law' 18(5) *International Criminal Law Review* (2018) 788–821, at 799.

197 Fair labelling began in English criminal law scholarship and has evolved over time and influenced other criminal justice systems, see Ashworth, *supra* note 194, at 88; De Souza Dias, *supra* note 196, at 792–796. De Souza Dias argues, for instance, that fair labelling, although originating in the English criminal system, is a general principle that is reflected in the characterisation and labelling of crimes in most legal systems, including criminal codes and laws.

198 H. Zawati, 'Fair Labelling as a Common Legal Principle in Criminal Law' in H. Zawati (ed.), *Fair Labelling and the Dilemma of Prosecuting Gender-Based Crimes at the International Criminal Tribunals* (New York: Oxford University Press, 2014) 25–39, at 33–35.

30. The Chamber notes that cumulative charging is consistent with the legal norm relating to the fair labelling of crimes in international criminal law. This principle of fair labelling requires that 'distinctions between [the] kinds of offences and degrees of wrongdoing are respected and signalled by the law, and that offences are subdivided and labelled so as to represent fairly the nature and magnitude of the law-breaking'.[199] The Chamber further notes that the principle of fair labelling also extends to sentencing and stresses the need for the labelling of a crime to correspond to blameworthiness and proportionality between sentencing and guilt.[200] Consequently, accurate labelling of crimes and accurate descriptions of the degree of wrongfulness promotes justice for victims and the accused by ensuring the full recognition of harms endured by victims, proportionate punishment to the degree of wrongfulness, and consistency in sentencing and convictions.[201]

31. In light of the above, the principle of fair labelling is important because it acknowledges the types and severity of wrongdoing and guarantees the legal recognition of various types of harm. This principle ensures an accurate description of the scope of wrongfulness, communicates reprehensible behaviour to society, recognises various types of harm, and ensures proportionate conviction and sentencing to the degree of wrongfulness.[202]

32. Fair labelling of crimes also helps to fulfil the Article 21(3) requirement of the application and interpretation of the Statute in light of norms of non-discrimination on grounds such as gender.[203] The Chamber notes that fair labelling helps to bring visibility to sexual and gender-based crimes, which have failed to be adjudicated at all, or properly adjudicated, in the past, a situation which the ICC Statute aimed to remedy.[204] Such recognition also contributes to society's understanding of the complexity of gendered violence, including its various forms, effects, and severity,

[199] Ashworth, *supra* note 194, at 78.

[200] H. Zawati, 'Introduction: Structure and Scope' in H. Zawati (ed.), *Fair Labelling and the Dilemma of Prosecuting Gender-Based Crimes at the International Criminal Tribunals* (New York: Oxford University Press, 2014) 10–20, at 19–20.

[201] Zawati, *supra* note 198, at 27–33; Chalmers and Leverick, *supra* note 194, at 224–237.

[202] Zawati, *supra* note 198, at 27–33.

[203] Art. 21(3) ICCSt.

[204] R. Copelon, 'Gender Crimes as War Crimes: Integrating Crimes against Women into International Criminal Law' 46(1) *McGill Law Journal* (2000) 217–240, at 220–233; Human Rights Watch, *Shattered Lives: Sexual Violence during the Rwandan Genocide and Its Aftermath*, 24 September 1996, available at www.hrw.org/report/1996/09/24/shattered-lives/sexual-violence-during-rwandan-genocide-and-its-aftermath, at Introduction; Problems Documenting Gender-Based Crimes; C. J. Fountain, 'Sexual Violence, the Ad Hoc Tribunals and the International Criminal Court: Reconciling Akayesu and Kunarac' 19(2) *ILSA Journal of International and Comparative Law* (2013) 251–262; K. Askin, 'Gender Crimes Jurisprudence in the ICTR: Positive Developments' 3(4) *Journal of International Criminal Justice* (2005) 1007–1018; S. SáCouto and K. Cleary, 'The Importance of Effective Investigation of Sexual Violence and Gender-Based Crimes at the International Criminal Court' 17(2) *American University Journal of Gender, Social Policy & the Law* (2009) 337–360.

which is instrumental in dispelling myths and assumptions about the nature of this violence.

33. The Chamber holds that the principle of fair labelling also demands an accurate and full representation of sexual and gender-based crimes within criminal charges. This approach avoids minimising and/or mischaracterising the experiences of victims of sexual and gender-based crimes and, therefore, contributes to the recognition of cumulative charging and convictions of these crimes.

34. The Chamber further notes that the Court attends to the crimes within its jurisdiction to protect the rights of all persons but also recognises its social function of clarifying the law and reinforcing norms. Addressing sexual and gender-based crimes acknowledges the complexity of these crimes, through the identification of acts that target and exploit gender identities, roles, and expectations, and develops progressive gender norms that could trickle down to domestic criminal justice systems.[205] The Chamber holds that fair labelling recognises and accurately describes sexual and gender-based violence, including how this violence can be used to achieve various objectives, which could guide domestic criminal justice systems in similar cases.

35. In conclusion, the Chamber holds that recognising torture and outrages upon personal dignity committed through rape as separate crimes fairly labels the types of harm done to victims and gives legal recognition to their lived realities. Therefore, fair labelling also leads to non-discriminatory and gender-sensitive recognition of torture and outrages upon personal dignity. Based on the foregoing, the Chamber deems it necessary to assess the nature and extent of the cumulative charges brought by the Prosecutor in the context of the principle of fair labelling and in accordance with Article 21(3) of the Statute.

Legal Findings of Cumulative Charging of Crimes

36. The Chamber recalls that cumulative charging and convictions are acceptable in international criminal law if the relevant statutory provisions are designed to protect different social interests, each offence has distinct elements, and the charges reflect the total culpability of the accused.[206] According to Judge Khan in *Kayishema & Ruzindana*, and as accepted by the majority in *Musema*, an assessment of charges should be proportionate to the blameworthiness of the accused.[207]

[205] This trickle-down effect is possible because the ICC is meant to complement domestic justice systems in accordance with Art. 17 ICCSt. and relies on cooperation with both state and non-state actors to function effectively according to Arts. 86–90 ICCSt.

[206] Separate and Dissenting Opinion of Judge Khan, *supra* note 182, at §§ 13 and 33 in Musema Judgment, *supra* note 177, at §§ 294–295, 296–299; Kayishema & Ruzindanda Judgment, *supra* note 177, at § 627; Delalic Judgment, *supra* note 175, at § 412; Musema Judgment, *supra* note 177, at §§ 296–299; Kupreskic Decision, *supra* note 178.

[207] Separate and Dissenting Opinion of Judge Khan, *supra* note 182, at §§ 13 and 33 in Musema Judgment, *supra* note 177, at §§ 294–295; Musema Judgment, *supra* note 177, at §§ 294–295.

A full assessment of criminal charges must reflect the total culpability of the accused.[208] The Chamber concurs with these conditions of cumulative charging in international criminal law.

37. The Prosecutor submitted cumulative charges for torture (Count 3) and outrages upon personal dignity (Count 5).[209] These charges are based on the same factual conduct and are mainly related to acts of rape.[210] The Chamber further notes that the Prosecutor's request to cumulatively charge acts of torture and outrages upon personal dignity allegedly perpetrated through acts of rape[211] is vital for adhering to the principle of fair labelling.

38. The Chamber recalls that the legal requirement to fairly and accurately label crimes is satisfied if criminal charges are proportionate to the blameworthiness of the accused and the severity of the criminal conduct.[212] Criminal charges must reflect the facts and the severity of criminal conduct. Acts of rape that meet the elements of torture and outrages upon personal dignity constitute forms of torture and outrages upon personal dignity that ought to be represented as such in the criminal charges against the accused.

39. Based on the foregoing, the Chamber holds that cumulative charging of torture (Count 3) and outrages upon personal dignity (Count 5), allows for the recognition of the full culpability of the accused and protects separate interests enshrined in distinct provisions of the Statute, including crimes not directly categorised as sexual and gender-based crimes. Therefore, the Chamber must consider whether the conditions for cumulative charging are met in the case at hand.

40. Despite being allegedly carried out through acts of rape, the charges brought by the Prosecutor are different crimes from rape as they have elements distinct from the crime of rape.[213] The conditions for cumulative charging require that the charges brought by the Prosecutor based on the same factual conduct, in this case of rape, contain distinct elements.[214] The Chamber will assess whether Counts 3 and

[208] Separate and Dissenting Opinion of Judge Khan, *supra* note 182, at § 33 in Musema Judgment, *supra* note 177, at § 295; Musema Judgment, *supra* note 177, at § 295.

[209] Bemba Annex 3 Amended Charges Document, *supra* note 152, at 35–36; T-10, *supra* note 171, at 9 and 10.

[210] Bemba Annex 3 Amended Charges Document, *supra* note 152, at 35–36; T-10, *supra* note 171, at 9 and 10.

[211] Bemba Annex 3 Amended Charges Document, *supra* note 152, at 35–36.

[212] Zawati, *supra* note 198, at 27–33.

[213] Torture, outrages upon personal dignity, and rape are protected within separate statutory provisions and have distinct elements in the Elements of Crimes document. In this case, torture as a crime against humanity is regulated within Art. 7(1)(f) ICCSt, outrages upon personal dignity as a war crime is prohibited within Art. 8(2)(c)(ii) ICCSt, rape as a crime against humanity or war crime is regulated within Arts. 7(1)(g) and 8(2)(c)(i) ICCSt respectively, and the elements of these crimes are codified according to the structure of the corresponding provisions within the ICC Statute.

[214] Separate and Dissenting Opinion of Judge Khan, *supra* note 182, at §§ 13 and 33 in Musema Judgment, *supra* note 177, at §§ 294–295; Kayishema & Ruzindanda Judgment, *supra* 177, at

5 should be confirmed as torture and outrages upon personal dignity respectively. This assessment will analyse whether these crimes have materially different elements, are conceptually different, and protect different social values.

Count 3: Torture as a Crime against Humanity

41. The Chamber observes that the material elements of rape as a crime against humanity are different from the material elements of torture as a crime against humanity.[215] Torture requires the infliction of severe physical or mental suffering by the perpetrator whilst rape requires an act of bodily invasion by the perpetrator resulting in the penetration of any part of a victim's body.[216]

42. For the crime of rape, 'psychological oppression' is an element of the crime that can be used as a means to exert control.[217] Although 'psychological oppression' is an element of the crime of rape, the inherent material element of rape is bodily invasion,[218] unlike the infliction of severe physical or mental pain or suffering, in the custody or control by the perpetrator, necessitated for fulfilling the material elements of torture.[219]

43. Additionally, torture requires 'severe physical or mental pain or suffering' while for the crime of rape, bodily invasion or penetration, 'however slight', committed by 'force, or by threat of force or coercion . . . or against a person incapable of giving genuine consent' is sufficient.[220] The wording in the Elements of Crimes shows that for the crime of rape, any violation of bodily integrity by non-consensual invasion or penetration is considered severe.[221] In other words, any invasion of bodily integrity in a sexual manner is a severe offence that can amount to a crime against humanity. This distinction suggests differences in the nature of conduct necessary to fulfil the elements of the crime of rape and torture.

44. The crimes of rape and torture are also conceptually different and protect distinct human rights (different social interests). The prohibition of torture aims to protect physical and mental well-being and related interests whilst rape focuses on physical autonomy and protection from non-consensual violations of bodily

§ 627; Delalic Judgment, *supra* note 175, at § 412; Musema Judgment, *supra* note 177, at §§ 296–299; Kupreskic Decision, *supra* note 178.

[215] Art. 7(l)(f) § 1, Elements of Crimes; Art. 7(1)(g)-1 § 1, Elements of Crimes.

[216] Art. 7(l)(f) § 1, Elements of Crimes; Art. 7(1)(g)-1 § 1, Elements of Crimes.

[217] Art. 7(1)(g)-1 § 2, Elements of Crimes.

[218] The inherent material element of rape is bodily invasion, which can be committed or facilitated 'by the threat of force or coercion such that caused by fear of . . . psychological oppression or abuse of power, against such person or another person, or by taking advantage of a coercive environment, or the invasion was committed against a person incapable of giving genuine consent', see Art. 7(1)(g)-1 § 2, Elements of Crimes.

[219] Art. 7(l)(f) §§ 1–2, Elements of Crimes.

[220] Art. 7(l)(f) § 1, Elements of Crimes; Art. 7(1)(g)-1 §§ 1–2, Elements of Crimes.

[221] Art. 7(1)(g)-1 § 1, Elements of Crimes.

autonomy.[222] Charging torture allegedly committed through acts of rape shows the severity of rape, including the severe violation of both the physical and mental well-being of the victims.

45. The Chamber holds that the differences between the material elements of rape and torture demonstrate that Count 3 on torture meets the conditions for cumulative charging: the fair reflection of the harm caused as well as the total culpability of the accused, distinct criminal element, and the protection of different human rights.[223] Additionally, the Chamber finds that Count 3 should not be subsumed in other crimes such as rape because it violates the principle of fair labelling, does not reflect the full blameworthiness of the accused, and fails to recognise the complexity of sexual and gender-based violence.

46. In conclusion, this Chamber finds that the three conditions for cumulative charging have been fulfilled for Count 3 on torture as a crime against humanity within the meaning of Article 7(1)(f) of the Statute.[224]

Count 5: Outrages upon Personal Dignity as a War Crime

47. The Chamber recalls that the elements of outrages upon personal dignity and rape as a war crime are different.[225] The elements of outrages upon personal dignity as a war crime are focused on whether 'the perpetrator humiliated, degraded or otherwise violated the dignity of one or more persons'.[226] Therefore, this crime requires criminal conduct that is intended to inflict grave psychological and mental harm aimed at humiliating, degrading, and violating the dignity of victims.[227] The subjective psychological effect of criminal conduct that results in humiliation, degradation, and the violation of dignity is the distinct element and interest protected by this provision.

48. The material elements of the crime of rape are focused on bodily invasion 'resulting in penetration, however slight' and 'committed by force, or by threat of force or coercion ... or against a person incapable of giving genuine consent'.[228] This wording demonstrates how the Court ought to recognise any invasion of a person's body in a sexual manner as a serious offence that has a severe impact on the victim.

49. The crime of rape and outrages upon personal dignity committed as war crimes are also conceptually different. The essence of each crime captures a

[222] Art. 7(l)(f) § 1, Elements of Crimes; Art. 7(1)(g)-1 § 1, Elements of Crimes.

[223] Separate and Dissenting Opinion of Judge Khan, *supra* note 182, at §§ 13 and 33 in Musema Judgment, *supra* note 177, §§ 294–295; Kayishema & Ruzindanda Judgment, *supra* note 177, at § 627; Delalic Judgment, *supra* note 175, at § 412; Musema Judgment, *supra* note 177, at §§ 296–299; Kupreskic Decision, *supra* note 178.

[224] The test used to assess the permissibility of cumulative charging is discussed above in § 25.

[225] Art. 8(2)(c)(ii) §§ 1, 2, and 4, Elements of Crimes; Art. 8 (2)(e)(vi)-1 §§ 1–2, Elements of Crimes.

[226] Art. 8(2)(c)(ii) § 1, Elements of Crimes.

[227] Art. 8(2)(c)(ii) §§ 1, 2, and 4, Elements of Crimes.

[228] Art. 8 (2)(e)(vi)-1 §§ 1–2, Elements of Crimes.

different social value. The crime of rape deals with the violation of bodily integrity and autonomy and the crime of outrages upon personal dignity deals with violations of one's dignity.[229] In other words, the crime of rape captures the invasion of bodily integrity, while the crime of outrages upon personal dignity captures the violation of a person's sense of worth or being as a person.[230] The *Aleksovski* and *Kunarac* cases, of the ICTY, confirm that the crime of outrages upon personal dignity prohibits inhumane acts that cause humiliation and degradation,[231] and protects 'respect for the human personality'.[232]

50. The elements of the crimes of rape and outrages upon personal dignity also protect different social interests. The prohibition of outrages upon personal dignity aims to protect human dignity, a fundamental guarantee protected in instruments such as the Universal Declaration of Human Rights.[233] The prohibition of rape protects physical autonomy and protection from non-consensual violations of bodily autonomy.[234] Given these distinct elements, these crimes should be fairly labelled as separate offences falling within the Statute and considered as separate criminal charges. Charging outrages upon personal dignity allegedly committed through acts of rape shows the psychological effects of a violation of bodily autonomy, which can have far-reaching consequences such as humiliation, degradation, and/or violation of one's dignity.

51. This Chamber, therefore, holds that an act of physical bodily invasion in a sexual manner can satisfy the legal definition of both rape and outrages upon personal dignity. The Chamber further holds that the differences in the material elements and protected interests of these crimes demonstrate that Count 5 on outrages upon personal dignity meets the conditions for cumulative charging: the fair reflection of the harm caused as well as the total culpability of the accused, distinct criminal element, and the protection of different human

[229] Art. 8(2)(c)(ii) § 1, Elements of Crimes; Art. 8 (2)(e)(vi)-1 § 1, Elements of Crimes.

[230] This is demonstrated by the definition of rape, which protects bodily autonomy and the definition of outrages upon personal dignity in the Elements of Crimes where the deliberate humiliation of persons takes into account the cultural background of a victim and is broad enough to include deceased persons, see Art. 8(2)(c)(ii) § 1, Elements of Crimes; Art. 8(2)(e)(vi)-1 §§ 1–2, Elements of Crimes.

[231] Judgment, *Kunarac et al.* (IT-96-23 & 23/1-T), Trial Chamber, 22 February 2001, §§ 500–502; Judgment, *Aleksovski* (IT-95-14/1-T), Trial Chamber, 25 June 1999, §§ 54–55. This definition of outrages upon personal dignity is based on the four Geneva Conventions but is relevant and authoritative because the war crimes codified in the Statute are also based on grave breaches of the Geneva Conventions of 12 August 1949, see Art. 8(2)(a) ICCSt.

[232] Aleksovski Judgment, *supra* note 231, at § 54.

[233] Art. 1 of the UDHR. Most of the rights and freedoms codified in the Universal Declaration of Human Rights have been incorporated into binding treaties and conventions and have become part of customary international law, see *Observance of Human Rights by States Which Are Not Parties to United Nations Human Rights Conventions*, UN Doc. E/CN.4/Sub.2/2000/2, 7 June 2000, § 5, at 3; United Nations, *Universal Declaration of Human Rights*, available at www.un.org/en/about-us/universal-declaration-of-human-rights.

[234] Art. 8(2)(e)(vi)-1 §§ 1–2, Elements of Crimes.

rights.[235] Cumulative charging for Count 5 on outrages upon personal dignity highlights the full blameworthiness of the accused, recognises the effects of sexual acts, and complies with Article 21(3) ICC Statute in respect of fair labelling and non-discriminatory application of the law based on gender or another status.

52. In conclusion, this Chamber finds that the three conditions for cumulative charging have been fulfilled for Count 5 on outrages upon personal dignity within the meaning of Article 8(2)(c)(ii) of the Statute.[236]

53. In light of the foregoing, the Chamber shall determine whether the evidentiary standard for confirming Count 3 on torture as a crime against humanity and Count 5 on outrages upon personal dignity and the other criminal charges submitted by the Prosecutor have been met. Having thoroughly assessed the evidence, the Chamber adjourns the Confirmation of Charges hearing and requests additional evidence from the Prosecutor, in accordance with Article 61(7)(c) of the Statute.[237]

For These Reasons, the Chamber

(a) **DECIDES** to adjourn the hearing;

(b) **REQUESTS** the Prosecutor to consider submitting to the Chamber no later than 31 September 2009 an amended document containing additional evidence, including witness statements, and an in-depth analysis chart on the basis of any new evidence and evidence already submitted to the Chamber;

(c) **INVITES** the Defence to respond to the amended document, with a written submission not exceeding thirty pages, no later than 31 October 2009;

(d) **INVITES** the legal representatives for victims to submit written observations not exceeding thirty pages, no later than 30 October 2009;

(e) **DECIDES** that the sixty-day period required for the issuance of the decision on the confirmation of charges will commence anew as of the date of receipt of the last written submission.

[235] Separate and Dissenting Opinion of Judge Khan, *supra* note 182, at §§ 13 and 33 in Musema Judgment, *supra* note 177, §§ 294–295; Kayishema & Ruzindanda Judgment, *supra* note 177, at § 627; Delalic Judgment, *supra* note 175, at § 412; Musema Judgment, *supra* note 177, at §§ 296–299; Kupreskic Decision, *supra* note 178.

[236] The test used to assess the permissibility of cumulative charging is discussed *supra* in § 25.

[237] The evidence submitted by the Prosecutor is not publicly available and the few facts mentioned are not sufficient for analysing whether Counts 3 and 5 can be confirmed. The Chamber has, therefore, decided to adjourn the hearing and request additional information from the Prosecutor. However, given Bemba's conviction at trial for rape, one might assume that enough evidence is present to also support or provide proof, at this stage, for acts of rape that amount to torture and outrages upon personal dignity, see Public with Annexes I, II, and A–F: Judgment pursuant to Article 74 of the Statute, *Bemba* (ICC-01/05-01/08-3343), Trial Chamber III, 21 March 2016, § 752(c)(d).

Done in both English and French, the English version being authoritative.
Judge Loyce Mrewa

11.4 PILLAGE IN THE BEMBA SENTENCING

Kirsten M. F. Keith

In 2016, Trial Chamber III handed down the sentencing decision for Mr Jean-Pierre Bemba Gombo.[238] For the war crime of pillaging, Mr Bemba was sentenced to sixteen years' imprisonment.[239] In this rewritten sentence by Kirsten M. F. Keith, the gendered aspects of pillaging are brought to the fore. Utilising evidence available to the original Chamber, Keith provides a greater analysis of the socio-economic context of Central African Republic (CAR) and how the impacts of pillaging resonate in a particular way for this society.

In considering a variety of harms, both the direct and indirect impacts are unpacked, with a particular focus on the financial and psychological aftermath. In delving into the harm experienced, Keith situates gender, highlighting realities not explored in the original sentence, noting the differentiated harms, as well as the similarities.

No.: ICC-01/05-01/08
Date: 21 June 2016

Original: English

TRIAL CHAMBER III(B)

Before: Judge Kirsten M. F. KEITH

SITUATION IN UGANDA

IN THE CASE OF THE *PROSECUTOR v. JEAN-PIERRE BEMBA GOMBO*

Public with Annexes I and II

Decision on Sentence pursuant to Article 76 of the Statute

INTRODUCTION/SUMMARY OF CONVICTION

1. On 21 March 2016, the Trial Chamber convicted Mr Jean-Pierre Bemba Gombo (Mr Bemba) of murder as a war crime and crime against humanity under Articles 7(1)(a) and 8(2)(c)(i) of the Rome Statue (Statute), rape as a war crime and crime against humanity under Articles 7(1)(g) and 8(2)(e)(vi) of the Statute, and pillaging as war crime under Article 8(2)(e)(vi) of the Statute. Mr Bemba was

[238] Decision on Sentence, *Bemba* (ICC-01/05-01/08-3399), Trial Chamber III, 21 June 2016.
[239] *Ibid*, § 94.

convicted for the crimes committed by Mouvement de libération du Congo (MLC) forces based on his responsibility as a person effectively acting as a military commander of those forces, pursuant to Article 28(a) of the Statute.

APPLICABLE LAW REGARDING THE DETERMINATION OF SENTENCE

2. Article 78(1) of the Statute and Rule 145 of the Rules of Procedure and Evidence (Rules) provide the framework for the determination of sentence. While Article 78(1) requires the Court 'to take into account such factors as the gravity of the crime and the individual circumstances of the convicted person', Rule 145(1)(c) provides a non-exhaustive list of additional factors that may be considered in the determination of sentence. These include 'the extent of the damage caused, in particular the harm caused to the victims and their families, the nature of the unlawful behaviour and the means employed to execute the crime'. Additionally, Rule 145(2) requires the Court to 'take into account, as appropriate', any mitigating and aggravating circumstances.

3. In accordance with Rule 145(1)(b), the Chamber is to 'balance all relevant factors, including any mitigating and aggravating factors and consider the circumstances both of the convicted person and of the crime', based on 'its intimate knowledge of the case'.[240]

4. The framework for the determination of sentence, therefore, requires the Chamber to (a) identify and assess factors relevant to sentencing and (b) weigh and balance them and pronounce a sentence for each crime pursuant to Rule 145(1)(b).[241] However, the Statute and Rules are silent as to any requirements for such a process. Consequently, it falls to the Chamber, in the exercise of its discretion, to balance and weigh those factors it deems relevant to sentencing. The importance of this broad discretion was highlighted by the Appeals Chamber when it held that 'the weight given to an individual factor and the balancing of all relevant factors in arriving at the sentence is at the core of a Trial Chamber's exercise of discretion'.[242]

Gravity

5. One of the principal considerations in the determination of a sentence, as specified in Article 78(1), is the gravity of the crime.[243] Consistent with jurisprudence from the International Criminal Tribunal for the former Yugoslavia (ICTY), when

[240] Judgment on the Appeals of the Prosecutor and Mr Thomas Lubanga Dyilo against the Decision on Sentence pursuant to Article 76 of the Statute, *Lubanga* (ICC-01/04-01/06-3122 01-12-2014 1/50 NM A4 A6), 1 December 2014, § 34.

[241] *Ibid*, at § 33.

[242] *Ibid*, § 43.

[243] *Ibid*, § 36.

assessing the gravity of a crime within the context of persons convicted on the basis of command responsibility, two factors must be considered:

1. the gravity of the underlying crime committed by the subordinates; and
2. the gravity of the convicted person's own conduct in failing to prevent or repress the underlying crimes.[244]

6. Gravity is generally assessed *in abstracto*, by analysing the legal elements of the crime and the mode of liability in general terms, and *in concreto*, by assessing the particular circumstances of the case, the gravity of crimes committed by subordinates and the convicted person's culpability.[245] Factors that are considered in relation to the gravity of a crime cannot be 'double-counted' and taken into account as aggravating circumstances for the same crime, and vice versa.[246]

ANALYSIS OF THE CRIMES

7. The Chamber will now address the crime of pillaging, with regard to the gravity of the offence and, if applicable, any aggravating and/or mitigating circumstances. Mr Bemba's culpability, individually and as a military commander, and his convictions for rape and murder are addressed in subsequent sections of this Decision, where the Chamber pronounces a sentence for each crime in accordance with Article 78(3).

Pillaging

8. The Chamber convicted Mr Bemba of the war crime of pillaging on the basis that pillaging was committed by MLC forces against civilians in the CAR with grave consequences for the victims.[247]

[244] See Judgment, *Čelebići* (IT-96-21-A), Appeals Chamber, 20 February 2001, §§ 732 and 741, where the Appeals Chamber stressed that the gravity of a subordinate's crime remains an 'essential consideration' in assessing the gravity of the superior's own conduct in sentencing.

[245] See Judgment on the Appeals of the Prosecutor and Mr Thomas Lubanga Dyilo against the Decision on Sentence pursuant to Article 76 of the Statute', *supra* note 240, §§ 62–65, where the Appeals Chamber considered both approaches to assessing the gravity of the crime. It ultimately concluded that it was not necessary to consider which was the correct approach to take but rather to ensure that the Trial Chamber considered 'all relevant factors and made no error in the weighing and balancing exercise of these factors in arriving at the sentence'. See also Judgment, *Vasiljević* (IT-98-32-A), Appeals Chamber, 25 February 2004, § 156, where the Appeals Chamber quoted from a prior ruling that: 'the determination of the gravity of the crime requires a consideration of the particular circumstances of the case, as well as the form and degree of the participation of the accused in the crime'.

[246] Decision on Sentence, *Lubanga* (ICC-01/04-01/06-2901 10-07-2012 1/52 RH T), 10 July 2012, § 35. See also Judgment, *Krajišnik* (IT-00-39-A), Appeals Chamber, 17 March 2009, § 787: 'What is important is to avoid double-counting (i.e. . . . no factor should be taken into account twice in sentencing)'. The same Appeals Chamber also noted, however, that 'while a Trial Chamber should strive to distinguish between the gravity of the criminal conduct and aggravating circumstances, it might be difficult or artificial to separate the two in some cases'.

[247] Judgment pursuant to Article 74 of the Statute, *Bemba* (ICC-01/05-01/08-3343 21-03-2016 1/364 NM T), 21 March 2016, §§ 563, 646, and 648.

Factors Relevant to the Determination of Sentencing the Crime of Pillaging

GRAVITY

9. In assessing the gravity of the crime, the Chamber considers Mr Bemba's ongoing failure, as someone acting as a military commander, to fulfil his duty to prevent or repress the crime of pillaging. Such failure to act may have the implicit effect of encouraging subordinates to believe they can commit further crimes with impunity. Although this issue has not been previously considered by this Court, such reasoning accords with jurisprudence from the ICTY. In the *Halilović* case, the Trial Chamber considered '[t]he argument that a failure to punish a crime (committed by subordinates) is tacit acceptance of its commission is not without merit'.[248] Drawing on the words of the International Committee of the Red Cross (ICRC) Commentary to the Additional Protocol, the ICTY Trial Chamber held that a commander who fails to act has 'tolerated breaches of the law of armed conflict'.[249] In view of such judicial reasoning, this Chamber finds that Mr Bemba's ongoing failure to act is of serious gravity.

10. In its assessment of the gravity of the crime, the Chamber also considers the following factors listed in Rule 145(1)(c): the circumstances of manner, time, and location, and the extent of damage caused, in particular the harm caused to the victims and their families. Before doing so, and in the exercise of its discretion in identifying and assessing relevant factors, the Chamber will first consider the broader socio-economic context within which the crime of pillaging occurred. This contextual approach helps frame the Chamber's understanding of the gravity of the crime and the physical, social, and economic distress it creates for its victims, rather than viewing the impacts of the crime in isolation.

11. The Chamber is cognisant that in assessing the gravity of the crime of pillaging, it is also important to consider the harm caused from multiple dimensions. This requires the Chamber to consider the compounding effects of the harm, particularly when viewed within the socio-economic context of the CAR, and to assess the harm against victims not as a homogenous group but as persons with their own unique lived experiences resulting from the crime of pillaging.

Socio-economic Context

12. With more than 66.6 per cent of the population living on less than US$1 per day, the CAR is one of the poorest countries in the world, with the rate of poverty increasing to 75 per cent in 2003.[250] According to the Human Development Index,

[248] Judgment, *Halilović* (IT-01-48-T), Trial Chamber, 16 November 2005, § 95.

[249] *Ibid.*

[250] EVD-P-0014, CAR-OTP-0004-0409, FIDH, *Central African Republic: Forgotten, Stigmatised: The Double Suffering of Victims of International Crimes*, No. 457/2, October 2006, p. 46. See also the testimony of P-6, who gave evidence regarding the unstable economic and social situation in the CAR. T-95, www.icc-cpi.int/court-record/icc-01/05-01/08-t-95-red-eng, at 60–61; and T-96, www.icc-cpi.int/court-record/icc-01/05-01/08-t-96-red2-eng, at 50, lines 22–25.

in 2003 it ranked 169 out of 175 countries, with a schooling rate of 31 per cent, literacy at 48.6 per cent, and a life expectancy of forty-two years.[251] As explained by the International Federation for Human Rights (FIDH), the 'total collapse of the economy over the last ten years' is 'due mainly to bad government and to repeated cycles of political and military violence'.[252] Against this backdrop, the cost of provision of care and social security is prohibitive, leaving the 'system on its last legs'.[253]

13. The lived experiences heard before this Chamber reflect the above data. Witnesses recounted that, prior to the conflict, they led subsistence lives, running small businesses trading goods, such as coffee and food, or working as small-scale farmers.[254] For many, their earnings were sufficient to provide their families with shelter and basic necessities; victims worked hard for many years to accrue their possessions and any savings. Those fortunate enough to complete more advanced education were able to enter professions and provide a greater degree of comfort for their families and their homes.[255]

14. Framed within this socio-economic context, it is evident that the crime of pillaging has severe, long-term consequences for victims. As considered further below, the loss of their most essential belongings, many of which are necessary for the basic provision of food and shelter, has a multifaceted and enduring impact on victims. For some, the pillaging directly and significantly impacted on their livelihoods, as they lost the means to generate an income. For others, the pillaging also resulted in the loss of a person's own agency and independence as, faced with nothing, they are compelled to return to live with family. The pillaging of items essential for their survival therefore impacts on the victims' most basic of human rights.

The Circumstances of Manner, Time, and Location

15. The Chamber found that large-scale acts of pillaging occurred throughout the 2002–2003 CAR military operation, across a broad geographical area where MLC soldiers were present.[256] The Chamber found that a wide range of property was taken from civilians without their consent, covering everyday items such as clothing, food, cooking utensils, foam mattresses, radios, televisions, fridges, generators, suitcases, money, vehicles, and items of personal value.[257] The Chamber found that the

[251] EVD-P-0014, CAR-OTP-0004-0409, FIDH, Central African Republic, *supra* note 250, p. 6.

[252] *Ibid*, p. 45.

[253] *Ibid*, p. 57.

[254] See for instance the transcript of V-480, whose father was a goat and sheep farmer and was also part of a collective buying and reselling goods. V-480, T-369, www.icc-cpi.int/court-record/icc-01/05-01/08-t-369-red-eng, 66, line 3.

[255] See for instance the testimonies of P-6, P-9, and P-108.

[256] Judgment pursuant to Article 74 of the Statute, *Bemba* (ICC-01/05-01/08-3343 21-03-2016 1/364 NM T), §§ 646, 648, and 563, referring to the locations covering a large geographical area that were subject to pillaging.

[257] *Ibid*, § 646.

MLC soldiers pillaged personal items for pecuniary gain[258] and with no regard for the victim's livelihood or well-being, which included being able to feed their families, seek treatment, or arrange burial services.[259]

16. The pillaging was systematic, forming part of the MLC's *modus operandi*. When they took control of an area, they conducted house-to-house searches for remaining rebels and during these searches they pillaged goods.[260] Witness P-38 testified that the MLC also erected checkpoints to control the entire area and they would stop persons and ask them for money. If they had no money, they were stripped of their clothing and if the person had jewellery or a mobile phone, they would also take that.[261] Other witnesses explained that when houses were pillaged, they took everything except for the items they destroyed.[262] Many houses were occupied by the MLC during the CAR operation. Witnesses testified about the behaviour of the soldiers, who occupied these civilian houses with blatant disrespect for their belongings and homes, destroying whatever was left in the houses.[263] For instance, the Chamber recalls the testimony of P-73, who explained that the MLC looted the houses and left them empty and damaged, with the doors used as firewood. P-73 testified that if people fled their homes, the soldiers would then occupy their homes and do whatever they wanted to them 'and you would be forced to struggle in order to buy everything all over again'.[264] Similarly, P-108 testified that he was 'in a state of total desolation' when he returned to his house as he could not recognise it. 'It was beyond recognition. They practically took away everything, except those items that were destroyed . . . The house was very, very dirty.'[265]

17. Items were also pillaged directly from victims while they were fleeing to safety. For instance, P-68 testified that she and her sister decided to flee from their house as the shooting and shelling in their neighbourhood made them very frightened.[266] While fleeing from their house to seek refuge in PK5, they were attacked by a group

[258] *Ibid*, §§ 565–567, and 644.

[259] P-42, T-64, www.icc-cpi.int/court-record/icc-01/05-01/08-t-64-red2-eng, at 44, lines 13–14; and at 48, line 14–49, line 6; and V-1, T-220, www.icc-cpi.int/court-record/icc-01/05-01/08-t-220-eng, at 45, lines 21–46, line 5. *See also* a/0394/08: T-228, www.icc-cpi.int/court-record/icc-01/05-01/08-t-228-red-eng, at 7, lines 10–24; a/0511/08: T-228, at 22, lines 3–9.

[260] Judgment pursuant to Article 74 of the Statute, *Bemba* (ICC-01/05-01/08-3343 21-03-2016 1/364 NM T), §§ 565–567, and 644.

[261] Witness P-38, T-34, www.icc-cpi.int/court-record/icc-01/05-01/08-t-34-red2-eng, at 42, lines 2–8.

[262] Witness P-108, T-132, www.icc-cpi.int/court-record/icc-01/05-01/08-t-132-red2-eng, at 37, describing how saddened he was to return to his house to see it 'was beyond recognition. They practically took everything, except those items they destroyed [. . .] The house was very dirty'.

[263] P-73, T-70, www.icc-cpi.int/court-record/icc-01/05-01/08-t-70-red2-eng, at 23–24.

[264] *Ibid*, at 24, lines 10–11.

[265] Witness P-108, T-132, www.icc-cpi.int/court-record/icc-01/05-01/08-t-132-red2-eng, at 37, lines 15–18.

[266] Witness P-68, T-48, www.icc-cpi.int/court-record/icc-01/05-01/08-t-48-red2-eng, at 11, lines 1–5.

of soldiers. These soldiers took the few possessions P-68 had managed to take with her while fleeing and then subjected her to multiple violent rapes.[267]

The Extent of Damage Caused, in Particular the Harm to Victims and Their Families

18. The Chamber found that the consequences of pillaging were far-reaching, impacting various aspects of victims' personal and professional lives. Victims were often left with nothing, not even basic necessities,[268] with the impacts of the crime still evident today. As P-42 testified, 'they looted everything I had and they left me with nothing at all, so until today I continue to sleep on a mat'.[269]

19. The sense of loss and destitution was a recurring theme in many testimonies.[270] P-23, for instance, stated that upon completion of his testimony in the Hague, he would return home to 'live in the poverty that [he] was plunged into'.[271] The knock-on effect of this is that many victims have been unable to rebuild their lives and homes; as P-73 described, 'it's difficult for us to be able to get our lives back. Everything that we had [. . .] we'd made a huge effort to accumulate what we had'.[272]

20. While recognising that the harm caused to victims and their families by the pillaging is unique to each individual, for the purposes of assessing the extent of the harm, the Chamber finds it useful to consider the financial and psychological impact of the crime on victims' lives.

FINANCIAL IMPACTS

21. The Chamber heard evidence of the severe financial impacts that the acts of pillaging had on victims. Among these, direct financial losses were incurred, including money that was taken directly from victims or their homes, much of it representing their hard-earned savings. P-87, for instance, spoke of the theft of 67,000 francs that she had earned from selling coffee and 600,000 francs that belonged to her parents.[273] It also includes the costs of trying to replace or rebuild what was pillaged. P-108, for instance, explained that the estimated loss they incurred from the pillaging is between 20–30 million francs.[274] He further explained that even today, he has not been able to return the house to its former state because

[267] *Ibid*, at 11, lines 24–12, and 18, lines 10–19.

[268] Judgment pursuant to Article 74 of the Statute, *Bemba* (ICC-01/05-01/08-3343 21-03-2016 1/364 NM T), § 646.

[269] P-42, T-64, www.icc-cpi.int/court-record/icc-01/05-01/08-t-64-red2-eng, at 44, lines 13–14.

[270] See for instance, P-69, who referred to the general conditions in the area, saying 'the inhabitants of Bangui are living in desolate conditions'. P-69, T-193, www.icc-cpi.int/court-record/icc-01/05-01/08-t-193-red2-eng, at 37, line 24.

[271] P-23, T-52, www.icc-cpi.int/court-record/icc-01/05-01/08-t-52-red2-eng, at 6, lines 2–3.

[272] P-73, T-70, www.icc-cpi.int/court-record/icc-01/05-01/08-t-70-red2-eng, at 40, lines 1–4. See also, P-69, T-193, www.icc-cpi.int/court-record/icc-01/05-01/08-t-193-red2-eng, at 37, lines 22–24, and at 38, lines 1–8.

[273] T-44, www.icc-cpi.int/court-record/icc-01/05-01/08-t-44-red3-eng, at 43, lines 13–14.

[274] P-108, T-132, www.icc-cpi.int/court-record/icc-01/05-01/08-t-132-red2-eng, at 35, lines 17–19.

as a civil servant his salary was owed in arrears and he had existing bank loans, so it was not easy to repair the house.[275] Other witnesses also spoke of being unable to rebuild their lives and their homes owing to the financial constraints they face as a result of the pillaging.[276]

22. The acts of pillaging also directly impacted victims' businesses. Many lost items that were crucial to their business operations; without such items, their businesses ceased to operate. The Chamber, for instance, found that V-20's tailoring business never recovered after his sewing machines were pillaged.[277] V-20 described how the loss of the machines and his clients' clothing still makes him very sad.[278] Likewise, Witness P-23 testified about the many items pillaged from his house, including the vehicle he used to earn a living.[279] He later found the ruins of his car after all its parts had been taken; this was the only item of his that was found.[280] Other witnesses spoke of their livestock or food supplies being pillaged – items that were essential to their business that provided a means of subsistence.[281]

23. The financial impact on businesses and the loss of potential earnings is hard to quantify and was not fully explored during witnesses' testimony. However, it is evident that losing a business, which generates an income, has a severe and enduring impact on victims, particularly given the socio-economic context in the CAR.

24. The Chamber recognises that while the monetary value of items pillaged from the victims varies depending on their personal and professional circumstances, these items were essential to their lives. Consequently, regardless of the actual monetary value of the items pillaged, they were of great value to the victims and their loss resulted in severe consequences for the victims; many are living in prolonged poverty unable to rebuild their lives and their homes.

25. The financial harm caused by the pillaging continues to impact other aspects of victims' lives, including their education. Some witnesses testified that as a result of the pillaging, they no longer have access to education as they cannot afford it. As Witness A/555/08 recalled, she was a child attending school when soldiers came to her area. She was then raped and abducted by the soldiers and eventually managed to flee and return to her family home four years later. On return she found her family 'had been totally stripped of their belongings. They were living in

[275] *Ibid*, at 38, lines 16–25.

[276] Witness P-69, T-193, www.icc-cpi.int/court-record/icc-01/05-01/08-t-193-red2-eng, at 38, lines 1–8, who testified that 'the inhabitants of Bengui are living in desolate conditions' with many victims still sleeping on straw mats, while the houses are empty and none of their property has been restored, though the 'civilians are making great effort to replace their property, to get it back'.

[277] V-20, T-223, www.icc-cpi.int/court-record/icc-01/05-01/08-t-132-red2-eng, at 53, lines 19–24, at 54, line 3.

[278] *Ibid*, at 53, lines 19–24.

[279] P-23, T-51, www.icc-cpi.int/court-record/icc-01/05-01/08-t-51-red2-eng, at 49.

[280] P-23, T-52, www.icc-cpi.int/court-record/icc-01/05-01/08-t-52-red2-eng, at 7, lines 20–24.

[281] Judgment pursuant to Article 74 of the Statute, *Bemba* (ICC-01/05-01/08-3343 21-03-2016 1/364 NM T), §§ 566 and 643.

poverty. They were farming and involved in a little bit of trading in order to be able to afford something to eat, even clothing themselves was difficult'.[282] As a result of the pillaging, her father can no longer afford to send her to school and she is deeply hurt by this.[283] She talked about seeing some of her peers who managed to complete their schooling and who have managed to secure employment with salaries.[284] She is severely depressed and has suicidal thoughts as a result of what happened to her and when she sees the huge difference between her life and others who work and have a salary.[285]

26. A/555/08's experience also highlights the intergenerational impact of pillaging vis-à-vis access to education, with her children also unable to attend school. She explained that she survives by the small-scale trading of vegetables, enabling her to just manage to feed and take care of her children, but she lacks the financial resources to send them to school.[286]

27. The intergenerational impact of pillaging on access to education is also evident in A/480/08's testimony. She explained that due to the events that occurred, including the pillaging, her children have been unable to return to school as there is no money to pay for it.[287]

28. The Chamber notes the overarching importance of an education, with education being one of the UN Sustainable Development Goals that form part of a blueprint for global peace and prosperity.[288] An education provides people with knowledge and skills to help them gain employment, which links to better health and greater financial resources. It is, therefore, a critical tool that is essential to helping lift victims and their families out of poverty. For women and girls, in particular, education provides them with opportunities that may enable them to have greater autonomy over their lives. It represents hope and aspirations for a future that includes secure employment, enabling them to determine their own lives, rather than being dependent on family.

29. The harm resulting from pillaging therefore extends beyond the immediate loss of quantifiable possessions, to that which is intangible: the loss of an individual's access to education and the resulting loss of opportunities associated with an education. Given the socio-economic context in the CAR, this Chamber considers that the intergenerational loss of access to education is significant and contributes to the enduring impact of pillaging on victims.

30. In addition to impacting individuals' access to education, the crime of pillaging has also resulted in many victims lacking the financial resources to access

[282] A/555/08, T-369, www.icc-cpi.int/court-record/icc-01/05-01/08-t-369-red-eng, at 51, lines 15–17.
[283] *Ibid*, at 51, lines 15–19 and 52, lines 6–10.
[284] *Ibid*, at 54, lines 17–22.
[285] *Ibid*, at 54, lines 17–22.
[286] *Ibid*, at 54, lines 8–14.
[287] A/480/08, T-369, www.icc-cpi.int/court-record/icc-01/05-01/08-t-369-red-eng, at 68, lines 16–18.
[288] For further information, see www.un.org/sustainabledevelopment/development-agenda/.

medical treatment. The Chamber, for instance, found that P-73 lacked money to pay for medical treatment following the pillaging.[289]

31. The loss of financial resources to pay for healthcare has added significance when viewing this factor contextually. As considered below, the Chamber found that the pillaging was accompanied by other crimes, including rape and other sexual violence against men, women, and children. As a result of these crimes, many victims have medical issues, including HIV, which require ongoing medical treatment.[290] However, the Chamber heard evidence that many of these victims were left destitute following the pillaging and are unable to afford the treatment.[291] For instance, P-81 testified that as a consequence of the rape, she has stomach problems but she cannot afford to get 'treatment from an appropriate doctor'. As she has no one to help her pay for a doctor, she gets traditional treatment but 'the results have not been good'.[292] Other victims, including Witness P-68, have to rely on family for financial help for their treatment.[293] The lack of access to treatment for ongoing medical conditions caused by rape highlights the intersectionality of the crimes and the continuing vulnerabilities of victims.

32. The Chamber heard evidence regarding the shame and humiliation facing victims of rape and other sexual violence, which has devastated their lives and communities.[294] Cognisant of this, the Chamber further considers that the reliance on family members to assist with payment for medical treatment adds considerable stress to the burdens they are already carrying.

33. The impact of pillaging and the consequent lack of financial means to access medical treatment is viewed within the context of the situation in the CAR. The International Federation of Human Rights found that despite the trauma victims suffering due to the crimes committed, there is no national support programme to

[289] P-73, T-70, www.icc-cpi.int/court-record/icc-01/05-01/08-t-70-red2-eng, at 40, lines 1–9.

[290] For instance, P-68 testified that as a result of the rape she suffers depression, a fear of armed soldiers, vaginal and stomach ailments, and HIV. T-48, www.icc-cpi.int/court-record/icc-01/05-01/08-t-48-red2-eng, 41, line 4.

[291] P-69, T-193, www.icc-cpi.int/court-record/icc-01/05-01/08-t-193-red2-eng, at 29, lines 15–18, and at 29–30, lines 2–7. See also P-221, Dr Akinsulure-Smith, whose report findings were read onto the transcript: 'The survivors of these acts of sexual violence continue to experience the devastating negative physical, psychological and social outcomes of these experiences. Many reported an inability to seek medical attention due to limited financial resources. This population not only carries the burden of their distressing histories and stressful life circumstances, but the shame and humiliation of sexual experiences that have devastated their lives, their families and their communities.' T-39, www.icc-cpi.int/court-record/icc-01/05-01/08-t-39-eng, at 8, lines 16–21.

[292] P-81, T-55, www.icc-cpi.int/court-record/icc-01/05-01/08-t-55-red2-eng, at 32, lines 1–6.

[293] P-68, T-48, www.icc-cpi.int/court-record/icc-01/05-01/08-t-48-red2-eng, at 41, lines 3–4.

[294] For instance, A/555/08 explained how she was stigmatised and the population turned its back on her when she returned to her home town with a child that was born as a result of rape by her captor. T-369, www.icc-cpi.int/court-record/icc-01/05-01/08-t-369-red-eng, at 49–51. See also P-80, T-61, www.icc-cpi.int/court-record/icc-01/05-01/08-t-61-red2-eng, at 26, lines 1–12; and P-81, T-55, www.icc-cpi.int/court-record/icc-01/05-01/08-t-55-red2-eng, at 32, lines 7–22.

provide them with medical and psychological assistance. Yet such support is essential given the prohibitive cost of care and the fact that social security is collapsing.[295]

34. The Chamber also recognises a gendered dimension to the impact of pillaging in relation to the poverty in the CAR. Although many live in poverty, the situation facing women with sole financial responsibility for their children is particularly acute. There are numerous reasons why they bear such responsibility. For instance, some husbands left their rape-victim wives due to the associated cultural stigma rape brings to the family, particularly where there are children born of rape.[296] In other cases, husbands were killed, either outright or as a result of injuries sustained by violent physical attacks. Faced with severe financial hardship, some women received support from organisations such as Medicines sans Frontiers or Caritas,[297] although that support was intermittent and is no longer available. With sole financial responsibility for their children, the Chamber notes that the crime of pillaging has left some women in a position of desperate financial precariousness and vulnerability. The Chamber finds, therefore, that the crime of pillaging has an additional and significant impact on women and children.

PSYCHOLOGICAL IMPACT

35. The crime of pillaging also has a direct psychological impact on the victims. As Witness P-108 explained, prior to the conflict he had a good life, working as a magistrate, and he did everything he could to make his family comfortable. Then, 'in one day's time, we had to leave, we had to sleep on rugs on the floor. Before we were able to sleep in proper beds and, therefore, the children felt the impact of that; and still today they're suffering from that, because in one day they had lost everything. So there is really truly psychological impact'.[298] P-108 estimated that if the moral and psychological damage to his family were included in the cost of harm, 'it would bring the amount up to 60 million francs CFA'.[299]

36. The Chamber notes that the full psychological impact on victims of the crime of pillaging is hard to gauge given many victims were subjected to other crimes. Further, most of the evidence adduced regarding the psychological impacts of crime focused on the impact of rape on victims and their families rather than the other crimes. Given this, the Chamber is unable to make a finding on the psychological impact of the crime of pillaging alone. However, in assessing the gravity of the

[295] EVD-P-00014, CAR-OTP-0004-0409, FIDH, Central African Republic, *supra* note 250, at 57.

[296] A/555/08 recalled how she was stigmatised because of the child she had that was born of rape, although her family welcomed her. Her first husband died and the second one left her because of the children. As a result, she had to return and live with her family as she had no financial means to cover living costs. T-369, www.icc-cpi.int/court-record/icc-01/05-01/08-t-369-red-eng, at 53, lines 1–18.

[297] See for instance, P-68, T-48, www.icc-cpi.int/court-record/icc-01/05-01/08-t-48-red2-eng, at 39–40, lines 1–15.

[298] P-108, T-132, www.icc-cpi.int/court-record/icc-01/05-01/08-t-132-red2-eng, at 41–42, lines 21–24.

[299] *Ibid*, at 35, lines 17–19.

crime, and drawing on the testimony of Dr Reicherter, the Chamber recognises the compounding effects of traumatic events, including pillaging, where one traumatic event has a clear mental health impact that is then exacerbated by other risk factors, including other acts of violence or the death of family.[300]

37. The Chamber finds, therefore, that the harm caused by the acts of pillaging is multidimensional. It has an enduring impact on victims and their families' lives that exacerbate their vulnerabilities. In particular, the Chamber has considered the intergenerational and gendered impact of the crime of pillaging, which has a significant impact on women, children, and other victims of rape and sexual violence. Such impact goes beyond the quantifiable harm caused by pillaging, namely the financial loss associated with pillaged belongings, to the intangible, non-financial harm. As mentioned, this includes the loss of agency and opportunities associated with an education that victims can no longer afford to access.

38. In view of the above circumstances, in particular the harm caused to victims and their families, the Chamber finds that the crime of pillaging is of serious gravity.

Aggravating Circumstances

39. The Chamber will now consider factors that support aggravating circumstances in the determination of sentence: where the victim is particularly defenceless and the commission of the crime with particular cruelty. It notes that these aggravating factors also apply to the other crimes Mr Bemba was convicted of. However, as the Chamber is bound to apply a sentence for each crime individually,[301] it holds that the same aggravating circumstance factors can be applied for each different crime.

VICTIM IS PARTICULARLY DEFENCELESS

40. The Chamber found that civilians, including children, were subject to pillaging without distinction as to age, gender, profession, or social status.[302] Armed MLC soldiers targeted these unarmed civilians in or around their homes or their businesses, places of sanctuary including churches and hospitals, on MLC bases, in isolated locations including the bush, and/or while seeking refuge.[303]

41. Witnesses spoke of the general sense of insecurity and chaos that prevailed during this period, with the arrival of armed soldiers causing many to flee the

[300] P-0925 Dr Reicherter, T-368, www.icc-cpi.int/court-record/icc-01/05-01/08-t-368-eng, at 87, lines 1–2, and at 96, lines 13–22; T-369, www.icc-cpi.int/court-record/icc-01/05-01/08-t-369-red-eng, at 3, lines 7–16, 10, lines 17–22, and 14, lines 17–25.

[301] Rome Statute, Article 78(3).

[302] Judgment pursuant to Article 74 of the Statute, *Bemba* (ICC-01/05-01/08-3343 21-03-2016 1/364 NM T), § 563.

[303] *Ibid*, sections V(C)(3), V(C)(4), V(C)(5), V(C)(9), and V(C)(11), and §§ 462, 467, 471, 485, 487, 496, 502, 510, 522, 531, 543, 563–564, 625–626, 634, 641–642, 664, 673, 676, 680, and 695.

area.[304] Confronted with armed soldiers pillaging their personal belongings, victims were rendered defenceless. As P-87 stated in response to a question whether the items were taken with her consent:

> Well, they come into your house, they have weapons and they say, 'Give us the money, give us the money and we won't fire', but if we don't give them our belongings, if we put up a resistance, they will kill us. So when they came into our houses, we would just let them do what they wanted and take away our belongings. It was to save our own lives.[305]

42. In view of the above, the Chamber finds that the crime of pillaging was committed where the victims were particularly defenceless, as an aggravating circumstance provided in Rule 145(2)(b)(iii).

COMMISSION OF THE CRIME WITH PARTICULAR CRUELTY

43. The Chamber found that acts of pillaging were often accompanied by other crimes, including rape, murder, and other forms or threats of physical violence or verbal abuse.[306] As P-6 recalled: 'The looting was concomitant with the acts of rape. It was at the time the MLC troops were being deployed in the neighbourhoods when they went from house-to-house, searching these houses. At one and at the same time as the rapes were being committed, property of interest was being stolen.'[307]

44. The Chamber heard from multiple survivors, both male and female, who were raped during the pillaging events. P-68 recalled how she was fleeing to safety when she and her sister-in-law were attacked by soldiers, who took their possessions. She was then threatened with a weapon and raped by two soldiers; her sister-in-law was raped by three soldiers.[308] Others who attempted to resist the pillaging were beaten or killed. P-69 testified that MLC soldiers entered his compound and demanded money from his sister. When she refused, they threw her on the ground, taking the money off her.[309] She was then shot 'a bullet right into the head . . . it was as if an animal's skull had been hit'.[310]

45. The Chamber also found that many victims and their family members were subject to multiple acts of pillaging and other forms of violence.[311] For instance, P-87

[304] P-87, T-44, www.icc-cpi.int/court-record/icc-01/05-01/08-t-44-red3-eng, at 19, lines 5–10.

[305] *Ibid*, at 35, lines 3–8.

[306] Judgment pursuant to Article 74 of the Statute, *Bemba* (ICC-01/05-01/08-3343 21-03-2016 1/364 NM T), §§ 674, 676.

[307] P-6, T-96, www.icc-cpi.int/court-record/icc-01/05-01/08-t-96-red2-eng, at 7, lines 7–10.

[308] Judgment pursuant to Article 74 of the Statute, *Bemba* (ICC-01/05-01/08-3343 21-03-2016 1/364 NM T), §§ 462–466.

[309] *Ibid*, § 496.

[310] P-29, T-192, www.icc-cpi.int/court-record/icc-01/05-01/08-t-192-red2-eng, at 16, lines 10–14.

[311] Judgment pursuant to Article 74 of the Statute, *Bemba* (ICC-01/05-01/08-3343 21-03-2016 1/364 NM T), §§ 497–501.

testified that groups of armed soldiers came to her house twice on the same day just hours apart. The first time they took the TV, radio, furniture, and mattresses.[312] The second time they came, she was raped by multiple soldiers while other soldiers were pillaging the savings she had earned from selling coffee.[313]

46. Based on the factors considered above, the Chamber finds that the war crime of pillaging was committed with particular cruelty, as an aggravating circumstance under Rule 145(2)(b)(iv).

Concluding Remarks on the Crime of Pillaging

47. The Chamber has identified and assessed the factors it considers relevant for determining a sentence for the crime of pillaging. In doing so, it has explored the far-reaching consequences this crime has on victims and their families, many of whom have been unable to rebuild their lives as a direct result. In particular, the Chamber has considered the harm pillaging causes, from a financial and psychological perspective, and the intergenerational and gendered effect of pillaging.

48. The Chamber finds that women and children are disproportionately impacted by the crime of pillaging. It impedes their access to education, which is critical given the socio-economic context and poverty rates in the CAR, and consequently impacts their potential for independence, agency, and earnings. Further, many women and girls, but also some men, are also victims of rape. This has a compounding impact on the trauma they endure, being victims of multiple crimes. Given the cultural stigma and sensitivity associated with rape, the Chamber is particularly aware of the indirect harm pillaging has on women and girls, particularly where they have to rely on family to pay for the ongoing medical treatment that is required as a result of the rapes. In the Chamber's view, it is important to employ such a gendered lens when assessing the harm caused by pillaging in order to more readily reflect the lived experiences of the victims.

49. The Chamber finds these were acts deliberately targeted against vulnerable, defenceless civilians, including children, women, and the elderly. Their vulnerability was further compounded by the circumstances in which the crimes occurred. The pillaging of personal items and civilian property occurred in the context of a military operation, which forced many civilians to flee their home and seek safety elsewhere. It was committed by armed MLC soldiers, and accompanied by other serious crimes, including rape and murder.

50. The Chamber found that as a result of the systematic pillaging of civilians, and their homes and businesses, the victims were stripped of their belongings and resources. Their houses were also often destroyed following the pillage.

[312] P-87, T-44, www.icc-cpi.int/court-record/icc-01/05-01/08-t-44-red3-eng, at 14–15, 27, lines 20–25.
[313] *Ibid*, at 14–15, 28.

Consequently, many victims were forced to live in poverty, which continues today. The Chamber finds that, while each victim has their own lived experience, the commonality between them is the overwhelming losses they suffered due to the pillaging. This has had multidimensional and enduring consequences on their lives and those of their families. Viewed within the context of the CAR, with its socio-economic challenges, it is evident that the crime of pillaging has a significant impact on vulnerable civilians, with many living an existence of prolonged poverty.

51. In view of the above, the Chamber finds the war crime of pillaging is a crime of serious gravity. The Chamber also finds that two aggravating circumstances apply to the crime of pillaging; it was committed:

(i) against particularly defenceless victims and
(ii) with particular cruelty.

52. On the basis of the above, coupled with Mr Bemba's ongoing failure to prevent or repress the crimes committed by his subordinates, the Chamber sentences Mr Bemba to sixteen years of imprisonment for the crime of pillaging as a war crime.

Judge Kirsten M. F. Keith

11.5 COMMAND RESPONSIBILITY IN THE BEMBA APPEAL

Suzanne Varrall and Sarah Williams

In 2016, Mr Jean Pierre Bemba Gombo was found guilty of the war crimes and crimes against humanity of murder, rape, and pillage.[314] He was subsequently sentenced to eighteen years' imprisonment.[315] In 2018, the Appeals Chamber acquitted Mr Bemba on all charges.[316] In this rewritten appeal decision, Suzanne Varrall and Sarah Williams reflect on the significance of the case as the first before the ICC to see convictions for sexual violence charges and for command responsibility as a mode of liability. Varrall and Williams critically engage with the doctrine of command responsibility and apply a feminist lens to the interpretation of the phrase 'all necessary and reasonable measures' in determining Mr Bemba's third ground of appeal.

Varrall and Williams' decision interprets and applies the correct legal standard for 'all necessary and reasonable measures', reflecting the protective function of international humanitarian law (IHL) and its special regard for women and children at risk of sexual violence. While they agree with the original Appeal Chamber's finding that commanders cannot do the impossible, and that a case-by-case assessment of

[314] Judgment Pursuant to Article 74 of the Statute, *Bemba* (ICC-01/05-01/08-3343), Trial Chamber III, 21 March 2016.

[315] Decision on Sentence, *Bemba* (ICC-01/05-01/08-3399), Trial Chamber III, 21 June 2016.

[316] Judgment on Appeal, *Bemba* (ICC-01/05-01/08-3636-Red), Appeals Chamber, 8 June 2018.

the facts must be applied, they categorically dismiss the use of criteria of 'feasibility' or 'proportionality' in interpreting the standard. Instead, Varrall and Williams note that the rules and principles of IHL that underpin responsible command establish a protective rationale for the doctrine and assign a special status to women and children and to sexual violence. Drawing on this framework, Varrall and Williams highlight the basic requirements of responsible command and situate these within the distinct obligations to prevent and repress crimes, and to submit them for investigation and prosecution. Comparing these requirements to the measures taken by Mr Bemba, Varrall and Williams find the basic requirements of responsible command have not been met and dismiss this third ground of appeal.

No.: ICC-01/05-01/08 A
Date: 1 June 2018

Original: English

THE APPEALS CHAMBER (B)

Before: Judge Suzanne VARRALL
Judge Sarah WILLIAMS

SITUATION IN THE CENTRAL AFRICAN REPUBLIC
IN THE CASE OF THE *PROSECUTOR v. JEAN-PIERRE BEMBA GOMBO*

Public Document

Judgment on the Appeal of Mr Jean-Pierre Bemba Gombo against Trial Chamber III's Judgment pursuant to Article 74 of the Statute

The Appeals Chamber of the International Criminal Court, in the appeal of Mr Jean-Pierre Bemba Gombo (Mr Bemba) against the decision of Trial Chamber III entitled 'Judgment pursuant to Article 74 of the Statute' of 21 March 2016 (ICC-01/05-01/08-3343), by majority, delivers the following Judgment.

BACKGROUND

1. Mr Bemba's case represents a landmark for this Court on at least two fronts. It is the first case before the Court in which a charge and conviction has been recorded on the basis of command responsibility. Mr Bemba's case is also the first case to include charges and a conviction for crimes of sexual violence. The Appeals Chamber notes that incidents of sexual violence outnumber the other crimes in this case: Mr Bemba was convicted of murder, rape, and pillaging on the basis of three murders, approximately twenty-two cases of pillage, and the rape of twenty-eight people (comprising twenty-six women and

two men).[317] The sexual violence charges in this case were found to be of 'utmost, serious gravity',[318] committed against particularly defenceless victims, including children, and with particular cruelty.[319]

THIRD GROUND OF APPEAL

Overview

2. The third ground of appeal concerns Mr Bemba's submission that the Trial Chamber erred when it found that he was responsible as a commander, pursuant to Article 28(a) of the Rome Statute, for crimes committed by troops under his control during the 2002–2003 operations in the Central African Republic (CAR Operation) – those being the crimes against humanity of murder and rape, and the war crimes of murder, rape, and pillaging. Mr Bemba was, at all relevant times, the president of the Mouvement de libération du Congo (MLC), a political party founded by him, and the commander-in-chief of its military branch.

3. As outlined in Article 28(a), command responsibility for crimes committed by subordinates comprises three elements: first, the commander had effective command and control, or authority and control, over those subordinates;[320] second, the commander knew, or should have known, that those forces were committing or about to commit crimes within the jurisdiction of this Court;[321] and third, the commander failed to take all necessary and reasonable measures within his or her power to prevent or repress their commission or to submit the matter to the competent authorities for investigation and prosecution.[322]

4. The Appeals Chamber accepts the reasoning and conclusions of the Trial Chamber with respect to the first and second of these elements. It will therefore limit its assessment to arguments concerning the third element and Mr Bemba's submissions in relation to the Trial Chamber's finding that he failed to take all necessary and reasonable measures within his power.[323]

5. The Appeals Chamber considers that the first of Mr Bemba's five submissions, being that the Trial Chamber failed to apply the correct legal standard, is the decisive issue and will limit its considerations to this point. Because the underlying

[317] Judgment Pursuant to Article 74 of the Statute, *Prosecutor v. Jean-Pierre Bemba Gombo* (ICC-01/05-01/08), Trial Chamber III, 21 March 2016, (hereafter Conviction Decision).

[318] Decision on Sentence Pursuant to Article 76 of the Statute, *Prosecutor v. Jean-Pierre Bemba Gombo* (ICC-01/05-01/08), Trial Chamber III, 21 June 2016, § 40 (hereafter Sentencing Decision).

[319] *Ibid*, §§ 41–47.

[320] Art. 28(a) ICCSt.

[321] Art. 28(a)(i) ICCSt.

[322] Art. 28(a)(ii) ICCSt.

[323] Public Redacted Version of Appellant's document in support of the appeal, *Prosecutor v. Jean-Pierre Bemba Gombo* (ICC-01/05-01/08), Appeals Chamber, 28 September 2016, §§ 129–413 (hereafter Appeal Brief).

rationale for the mode of liability contained in Article 28(a) of the Rome Statute is critical to a correct interpretation of the relevant legal standard and its application, the following reasoning will commence with an exposition of how the concept of protection under IHL informs the doctrine of command responsibility. The Appeals Chamber will then outline the correct legal standard and apply this to the facts in Mr Bemba's case.

The Protection Rationale Underlying Command Responsibility

The Relevance of International Humanitarian Law

6. As one of the oldest branches of international law, IHL forms the *lex specialis* governing conduct in warfare with the aim of mitigating the human suffering borne both by combatants and non-combatants. A primary focus of IHL is, therefore, the protection of the civilian population from the effects of hostilities.[324] Crucially, under IHL, women and children are entitled to special respect and protection from sexual violence.[325] This principle recognises the heightened risk of sexual and gender-based violence that armed conflict entails and the impact of this type of violence on women and girls. The Appeals Chamber notes that the Rome Statute and Rules also accord a special status to sexual crimes, crimes against children, and the victims thereof,[326] in recognition of their especially grave nature and consequences.

7. The Appeals Chamber considers the rules and principles of IHL to be central to applying and interpreting Article 28(a) of the Rome Statute concerning command responsibility for the following reasons. First, Mr Bemba has been convicted of serious violations of the laws of armed conflict, collectively described as war crimes under Article 8 of the Rome Statute, the nature of which are directly informed by IHL.[327] Second, the Rome Statute specifically provides that the Court shall apply the rules of IHL in its application and interpretation of the Statute, Elements of Crimes, and Rules.[328] Finally, the mode of liability of command responsibility codified in Article 28(a) of the Rome Statute is derived from IHL, as will be outlined further below.

Command Responsibility under IHL

8. It is from the rules and principles of IHL that the concept of responsible command derives. The notion that armed forces should always be 'commanded by a

[324] Art. 51(1), Protocol Additional to the Geneva Conventions of 12 August 1949, and relating to the Protection of Victims of International Armed Conflicts, 8 June 1977 (hereafter Additional Protocol I).

[325] *Ibid*, Arts. 76 and 77.

[326] See Arts. 36(8)(b), 42(9), 43(6), 54(1)(b), and 68(1) to (2) ICCSt; and Rules 16(1)(d), 17(2)(a)(iv), 17(2)(b)(iii), 17(3), 19(f), 63(4), 70, 72(1), 86, 88(1), 88(5), and 112(4) of the ICC Rules.

[327] Art. 8. ICCSt.

[328] Art. 21(b) ICCSt.

person responsible for his subordinates' was contained in Article 1(1) of the Regulations Respecting the Laws and Customs of War on Land annexed to the 1907 Fourth Hague Convention.[329] The principle of responsible command also featured in post–World War I international conventions (the precursors to the 1949 Geneva Conventions).[330]

9. A positive legal duty for commanders was codified in the 1977 Additional Protocol I to the 1949 Geneva Conventions.[331] Article 86(2) provides that commanders are not absolved of responsibility for breaches by their subordinates 'if they knew, or had information enabling them to conclude' that the breaches were being committed or were about to be committed, and they did not take reasonable measures to prevent them.[332] Article 87 requires commanders to 'prevent and, where necessary, to suppress and report' breaches of the Geneva Conventions and Additional Protocol I, 'ensure that members of the armed forces under their command are aware of their obligations', and 'initiate disciplinary or penal action against violators'.[333]

10. The imposition of individual *criminal* responsibility on commanders for the breach of this duty was established in the statutes of various international criminal tribunals[334] and in jurisprudence in the aftermath of World War II.[335] The responsibility of commanders for crimes committed by their subordinates is based on the commanders' failure to take measures to prevent, repress, or report the commission of such crimes. In the post–World War II trial of Japanese General Tomoyuki Yamashita, a US Military Commission in the Philippines explained the liability thus:

[329] Art. 1(1), Hague Convention (IV) Respecting the Laws and Customs of War on Land and Annexed Regulations, 1907.

[330] See Art. 26, Geneva Convention for the Amelioration of the Condition of the Wounded and Sick in Armies in the Field, 1929; and Art. 18, Geneva Convention Relative to the Treatment of Prisoners of War, 1929.

[331] Additional Protocol I, *supra* note 324.

[332] *Ibid*, Art. 86(2).

[333] *Ibid*, Art. 87.

[334] See Art. 7(3) ICTYSt; Art. 6(3) ICTRSt; Art. 6(3) Statute of the Special Court for Sierra Leone; Article 3(2) Statute of the Special Tribunal for Lebanon.

[335] In several of the post–World War II trials commanders were found guilty of war crimes committed by their subordinates; for example: *Trial of Major Karl Rauer and 6 others*, British Military Court, Wuppertal, Germany, 18 February 1946; *United States v. Wilhelm Von Leeb, et al. (High Command Trial)*, United States Military Tribunal, Nuremberg, 27–28 October 1948; *United States v. Wilhelm List (Hostages Trial)*, United States Military Tribunal, Nuremberg, 8 July 1947–19 February 1948; *Trial of General Tomoyuki Yamashita*, United States Military Commission, Manila, 8 October–7 December 1945, and the Supreme Court of the United States, 4 February 1946 (hereafter *Yamashita* case); *Major War Criminals*, International Military Tribunal, 1 October 1946; and *United States of America v. Soemu Toyoda and Hiroshi Tamura*, Military Tribunal Appointed by the Supreme Commander of the Allied Powers, Tokyo, Japan, 1946–1949.

> [The] assignment to command military troops is accompanied by broad authority and heavy responsibility. This has been true in all armies throughout recorded history . . . where murder and rape and vicious, revengeful actions are widespread offences, and there is no effective attempt by a commander to discover and control the criminal acts, such a commander may be held responsible, even criminally liable, for the lawless acts of his troops, depending upon their nature and the circumstances surrounding them.[336]

11. The Rome Statute codifies commanders' criminal liability for the crimes of subordinates under Article 28. The responsibility of commanders and other superiors in this provision specifically adds to 'other grounds of criminal responsibility' found elsewhere in the Rome Statute. The provision distinguishes between the responsibility of military commanders and persons effectively acting as military commanders on the one hand, and other superiors (often referred to as 'non-military' or 'civilian superiors') on the other.

12. The responsibility of the former is addressed in Article 28(a), which applies to both international and non-international armed conflicts.[337] Responsibility will arise where three criteria are satisfied. First, the commander must have effective control over the troops. Second, the commander must have actual or constructive knowledge of the commission or potential commission of crimes. Third, the commander must have failed to take all necessary and reasonable measures within his or her power to prevent or repress the crimes or submit them to the competent authorities.

13. The Appeals Chamber considers that the application and interpretation of Article 28(a) concerning the command responsibility mode of liability must be consistent with the protective function of IHL and the special status it accords to women and children in relation to sexual violence. In particular, this approach must be applied in determining and applying the correct legal standard under Article 28 (a)(ii) for whether a commander has taken all necessary and reasonable measures within his or her power to prevent, repress, or submit subordinates' crimes to competent authorities.

The Correct Legal Standard: Article 28(a)(ii)

14. Mr Bemba argues that the Trial Chamber failed to assess his conduct in relation to the obligation to take all necessary and reasonable measures against the correct legal standard. The Trial Chamber found that whether or not a commander

336 *Yamashita* case, *supra* note 335.

337 The Rome Statute explicitly provides for this rule in the context of non-international armed conflicts, and its inclusion did not occasion any controversy during the negotiation of the Statute. See Report of the Preparatory Committee on the Establishment of an International Criminal Court, 25 March–12 April 1996, A/AC-249/1 (hereafter Report of the Preparatory Committee).

failed to take all necessary and reasonable measures should be established on a 'case-by-case basis', focusing on the 'material power' of the commander.[338] Mr Bemba submits that a commander need only take such measures that are 'within his material possibility'[339] and that his conduct should be judged by a standard of what measures were 'feasible and practicable at that time'.[340]

15. In determining the correct legal standard to be applied, the Appeals Chamber notes that Article 21 of the Rome Statute stipulates the sources of law that the Court shall apply. The first of these is the Statute itself, as well as the Elements of Crimes and Rules of Procedure and Evidence.[341] In the second place, where appropriate, the Court shall apply relevant treaties, rules, and principles of international law including the established principles of IHL. The significance of this body of law has been discussed above and will be referred to throughout the following section of the judgment as relevant. Furthermore, Article 21(3) establishes a positive obligation on the Court to apply a gender-sensitive and intersectional interpretation of the law consistent with internationally recognised human rights.

16. As per the general rules of treaty interpretation, construing the provisions of Article 28(a)(ii) must commence with a textual interpretation, in accordance with the ordinary meaning of the words in their context and in light of the object and purpose of the Rome Statute.[342] The drafting history of the relevant provision may thereafter be considered in order to confirm the meaning resulting from the textual interpretation if required.[343]

17. The text of Article 28(a)(ii) outlines the third criterion that must be satisfied before a military commander with effective control of his or her troops can be criminally responsible for crimes committed by those troops (the first criterion requires effective control and the second criterion requires actual or constructive knowledge). The text of the third criterion takes the following form: 'That military commander or person failed to take all necessary and reasonable measures within his or her power to prevent or repress their commission or to submit the matter to the competent authorities for investigation and prosecution.' The following inquiry shall consider firstly the phrase 'all necessary and reasonable measures within his or her power', and subsequently the three distinct obligations to 'prevent', 'repress', or 'submit'.

All Necessary and Reasonable Measures within a Commander's Power

18. The relevant categories of measures stipulated in Article 28(a)(ii) are described as those that are necessary and reasonable – not feasible, practicable, proportional,

[338] Conviction Decision, *supra* note 317, §§ 197–198.
[339] Appeal Brief, *supra* note 323, at § 338.
[340] *Ibid*, para. 341.
[341] Art. 21(a) ICCSt.
[342] Art. 31, Vienna Convention on the Law of Treaties, 1969.
[343] *Ibid*, Art. 32.

plausible, or any other formulation. The Appeals Chamber therefore cannot accept Mr Bemba's submission that his conduct should be judged by a standard of what measures were 'feasible and practicable at that time'.[344] A commander cannot be expected to do the impossible, certainly. But while it is appropriate to adopt a case-by-case approach to what is necessary and reasonable in the circumstances, an alternative and lesser standard of 'feasible and practicable' is neither warranted nor permissible. Although the word 'feasible' is used in Article 86(2) of Additional Protocol I, it was not included in Article 28(a)(ii), and we must assume this to be a deliberate choice by the drafters. Nor is 'feasible' used in the relevant provisions of the statutes of other international criminal tribunals, which use the 'necessary and reasonable' formulation.

19. An examination of the Rome Statute *travaux préparatoires* confirms this understanding and provides no reason to infer any intention that the provision should be construed beyond the ordinary meaning of the words 'necessary and reasonable'. The choice of these words was not a contentious issue during the drafting process. The formulation was adopted in all drafts with no objections or amendments, and ultimately incorporated by the drafting committee.[345] It is the ordinary meaning of the words 'necessary and reasonable' that must guide an interpretation of the relevant provision.

20. The word 'necessary' means 'needed', 'indispensable', 'vital', or 'essential'.[346] For example, water is necessary to sustain life. The word 'reasonable' means 'within the limits of what it would be rational or sensible to expect', 'not extravagant or excessive', 'moderate'.[347] What is reasonable is inherently informed by context. Of course, what is necessary and reasonable to prevent or repress the commission of a crime by subordinates, or to submit those crimes for investigation and prosecution, is far from straightforward. Nevertheless, it is the task given to this Court under the Rome Statute to make such a determination, consistent with the rules and principle of IHL and internationally recognised human rights.

21. Attention must also be given to the use of the term 'all' preceding the categories of necessary and reasonable in Article 28(a)(ii). The use of this word in this context, given its ordinary meaning, stipulates that no exceptions or exclusions can be accepted in relation to the extent of measures to be taken within the relevant categories. If any necessary and reasonable measure has not been taken, then the standard has not been met.

22. However, Article 28(a)(ii) qualifies that the measures a commander must take are limited to those that are 'within his or her power'. The Trial Chamber correctly stated that the word 'power' in this context is not to be understood as limited to a

[344] Appeal Brief, *supra* note 323, at § 138.

[345] Report of the Preparatory Committee, *supra* note 337, at 15, 16, 85.

[346] *OED Online*, Oxford University Press, June 2022, www.oed.com/view/Entry/125629.

[347] *Ibid*.

commander's 'explicit legal capacity' but that it relates to the de jure and/or de facto power of the commander.[348] The scope of an individual commander's power will therefore inform what measures are necessary and reasonable in the circumstances.

23. The Appeals Chamber notes, however, that command responsibility applies to *all* commanders, irrespective of their seniority, and whether they are physically in the field commanding troops or issuing orders from a distance. Both circumstances are relevant in Mr Bemba's case. Thus, while Article 28(a)(ii) recognises the relevance of the *scope* of a commander's power, it does not make any differentiation as to the *standard* applied to the actions (or omissions) of a commander based on either their seniority or their physical proximity to troops. Such a distinction is not only factually illogical, it would also be inconsistent with this Court's duty to apply the Rome Statute equally to all persons without any distinction based on official capacity.[349]

24. The phrase 'within his or her power' allows for consideration of the circumstances that may constrain a commander's ability. A commander cannot do the impossible. However, this does not justify the failure to take measures on the basis that they may prove difficult, inconvenient, or even disadvantageous. It is true that, at a broad level, IHL allows for the balancing of military necessity against the protection of civilians. The principle of military necessity, first codified in the Lieber Code of 1863, requires that parties to a conflict adopt only 'those measures which are indispensable for securing the ends of the war, and which are lawful according to the modern law and usages of war'.[350] So while military necessity recognises that the obligation to protect is never an absolute one, given the realities of war, it also maintains that unlawful means and methods of warfare are never permissible.

25. The Appeals Chamber agrees with the prosecution's submission that conduct contrary to IHL, and *a fortiori* criminal conduct, is never a permitted means or method of warfare.[351] The Appeals Chamber considers that sexual and gender-based violence cannot under any circumstances be considered as legitimate acts in pursuance of military necessity or military advantage. The rape of women, men, and children would never bring any lawful military advantage, nor can there ever be a necessity to engage in such conduct. Such acts are always contrary to IHL.

26. In sum, the Appeals Chamber considers that the ordinary meaning of the words 'all necessary and reasonable measures within his or her power' establishes a high standard for commanders, but one which allows for consideration of factual limitations and does not require a commander to perform impossible feats.

348 Conviction Decision, *supra* note 317, at § 199.

349 Art. 27, ICCSt.

350 Art. 14, Instruction for the Government of Armies of the United States in the Field (Lieber Code), 24 April 1863.

351 Prosecution's Final Submissions following the Appeal Hearing, *Prosecutor v. Jean-Pierre Bemba Gombo* (ICC-01/05-01/08), Appeals Chamber, 19 January 2018, § 9.

Nevertheless, this is a standard that cannot be incrementally lowered in response to what may or not be militarily advantageous, convenient, or economical at a particular point in time.

Prevent or Repress Crimes, or Submit to Competent Authorities

27. Article 28(a)(ii) specifies that all necessary and reasonable measures within a commander's powers are to be taken to 'prevent or repress' the commission of crimes within the Court's jurisdiction, 'or to submit the matter to the competent authorities for investigation and prosecution'. This approach follows that found in Article 87 of Additional Protocol I, which requires commanders to 'prevent and, where necessary, to suppress and report' breaches.[352] The provision thus creates three distinct obligations on commanders, who must take all necessary and reasonable measures within their power first to *prevent* crimes; second to *repress* crimes; and third to *submit* criminal matters to competent authorities for investigation and prosecution. Each of these obligations captures a distinct temporal relationship to the commission of crimes. While IHL does not provide a list of the measures that are necessary and reasonable for a commander to take to fulfil these obligations and the standard must be considered on a case-by-case basis, basic requirements can be determined nevertheless on the grounds of the temporal dimensions of each obligation as well as the fundamental obligations of IHL and responsible command.

OBLIGATION TO PREVENT

28. To 'prevent' means 'to stop something from happening or someone from doing something'.[353] An obligation to prevent therefore exists in relation to a future event, and in the context of Article 28(a)(ii), a future crime. What measures are necessary and reasonable for a commander to take to prevent the commission of crimes by subordinates will be heavily context-dependent and should be determined on a case-by-case basis. However, the following observations are relevant universally on the basis that preventive measures are those measures that must be undertaken *prior to* the commission of a crime.

29. First, the obligation to take measures to prevent crimes compels commanders to make an assessment of the known and likely risks of military operations. The protective rationale of IHL underpinning command responsibility further requires commanders to have particular regard to the increased risk of sexual violence that accompanies armed conflicts, and the disproportionate impact of this on women and children. Armed conflict brings with it a range of characteristic and notorious risks, including but not limited to an increased likelihood of sexual and gender-based violence. According to the 2007 Paris Principles, '[g]ender inequalities,

[352] Art. 87, Additional Protocol I, *supra* note 324.
[353] *OED Online*, *supra* note 346.

discrimination and violence are frequently exacerbated in times of armed conflict'.[354] It is a deeply distressing but well-known fact that there is a long-standing tendency of troops engaged in armed conflict, especially male combatants, to commit such crimes, particularly but not only against women and girls, and that this is amplified by failures of command to exercise proper control. It is the view of the Appeals Chamber that the commonly understood risk to women and girls that accompanies any and all armed conflicts must therefore inform the legal standards of both the knowledge element of command responsibility, and the requirement to take all necessary and reasonable measures.

30. Second, the obligation to take preventive measures encompasses the broadest temporal scope of the three obligations. This obligation does not only arise in the days or hours before a crime may be committed; nor does it only take effect when troops are deployed, or operations commence. Furthermore, preventive measures will not only be required in the days of operational planning or training. The obligation to take preventive measures will exist from the moment an individual takes command of troops, and it will continue to exist for the duration that the individual maintains a position of command.

31. Given commanders must consider the risks of certain crimes being committed by troops, particularly sexual violence crimes against women and children, and given the obligation to take preventive measures is ongoing from the time an individual takes command, certain basic requirements must be satisfied in order to fulfil the obligation to take all necessary and reasonable preventive measures. As noted above, some obligations under IHL are fundamental, such as the responsibility of commanders to ensure their troops are aware of their obligations under IHL.[355] Thus training troops in IHL, and particularly making them aware of prohibitions on sexual violence, at the earliest opportunity possible would constitute one such basic requirement of preventive measures. As would issuing lawful orders in accordance with the rules and principles of IHL. In addition, taking steps to ensure adequate supervision of troops and to establish clear communication and investigative and disciplinary procedures would also form basic requirements from the time of assuming command.

OBLIGATION TO REPRESS

32. To 'repress' means 'to not allow something ... to be expressed'; 'to control what people do, especially by using force'.[356] Repression relates to something that is occurring in the present, and in the context of Article 28(a)(ii), the contemporaneous commission of a crime. The temporal context is critical to assessing what

[354] The Paris Principles and Guidelines on Children Associated with Armed Forces or Armed Groups, February 2007 (Paris Principles), § 6.0.

[355] Art. 87(2), Additional Protocol I, *supra* note 324.

[356] *OED Online*, *supra* note 346.

measures are necessary and reasonable for a commander to take to repress the commission of crimes by his or her subordinates. Unlike preventive measures, measures to repress crimes must be taken in response to unlawful conduct that has occurred and is continuing, or may continue, to occur. A commander must take all necessary and reasonable measures to repress the criminal conduct at the earliest possible opportunity, and must continue to do so for so long as the unlawful conduct or its probability persists.

33. The circumstances will determine what form such measures must take, and which lie within a commander's power. Once again, however, the basic requirements of responsible command are instructive in such an assessment. Measures to repress criminal conduct must be responsive and timely and should at a minimum involve adequate supervision of troops and the issuance of lawful orders. Furthermore, investigative and disciplinary action must be undertaken to the fullest extent possible. Depending on the temporal span of the criminal activity, additional measures may become necessary and reasonable over time, including resolving the shortcomings or absence of investigative and disciplinary procedures. As with preventive measures, a commander's obligation cannot be considered to be fulfilled on the basis of a one-off response.

OBLIGATION TO SUBMIT MATTER TO COMPETENT AUTHORITIES FOR INVESTIGATION AND PROSECUTION

34. To 'submit' means 'to give or offer something for a decision to be made by others'.[357] In the context of Article 28(a)(ii), what is to be submitted to the competent authorities for investigation and prosecution is the details of crimes that have already been committed. To do so will require a commander to facilitate the collection and communication of such details. There are no specifications under Article 28(a)(ii) as to what form this submission must take. It can be assumed, however, that a basic requirement of fulfilling this obligation necessitates, to the extent it is within a commander's power, that he or she must ensure all the known details of criminal conduct are collected, documented, and provided in a fulsome, unprejudiced, and timely manner.

35. This obligation also entails another complexity, through the use of the adjective 'competent' to describe the nature of the relevant authority. A competent authority is not defined in Article 28(a)(ii); however, elsewhere the Rome Statute does provide guidance on the competence of national judicial systems.[358] The inability to carry out investigations and prosecutions is understood here as 'a total or substantial collapse or unavailability' of the judicial system in question. It is unlikely that a military commander is in a position to undertake a sophisticated assessment of the competence of relevant authorities; thus, for the purposes of

[357] *Ibid.*
[358] Art. 17(3) ICCSt.

Article 28(a)(ii), the Appeals Chamber considers a competent authority will be that which has the jurisdiction to conduct investigation and prosecution of the criminal matter in question and which is not affected by the 'total or substantial collapse or unavailability' of the judicial system.

RELEVANCE OF OUTCOME AND MOTIVE

36. It should be noted that the nature of the obligations encapsulated in Article 28(a)(ii) is one of action, not outcome. There is nothing in this provision that requires the crimes in question to be successfully prevented or repressed – indeed, the issue of a commander's liability may not arise if such an outcome had been achieved. Nor is there an obligation on the commander as to the outcome of any investigation or prosecution relating to crimes, although the referral must be made in good faith that the investigation and/or prosecution will be genuine and not a sham. The commander must do all that is necessary and reasonable to submit a matter to the competent authorities, not ensure any particular result.

37. The Trial Chamber effectively recognised this approach in stating that a commander that has taken all necessary and reasonable measures cannot be held liable 'even if the crimes nonetheless ultimately occur or the perpetrators go unpunished'.[359] The Appeals Chamber considers any implication to the contrary in the Trial Chamber's decision to be erroneous and irrelevant, as is any direct reference to the inadequacy of the results of measures taken by Mr Bemba.[360] However, it is the Appeals Chamber's view that such implications and references do not reach the threshold of having a material impact on the outcome of the decision.

38. Furthermore, there is no mention made in Article 28(a) as to the motivations behind a commander's actions, and the Appeals Chamber does not accept that this should be a relevant consideration in making an assessment as to whether or not a commander failed to meet the requirements of Article 28(a). Beyond the fact that determining motives is an extremely subjective endeavour, it is possible, and in fact highly likely, that a commander will have multiple motivations in following any particular course of action. It is sufficient to note for present purposes that while the Appeals Chamber does not agree with the Trial Chamber's treatment of motivation as an 'aggravating' factor in the Appellant's case,[361] this approach has not materially affected the outcome and has no impact on the Appeals Chamber's decision in the present appeal.

Basic Requirements of Responsible Command

39. As demonstrated above, it is possible to identify a number of basic requirements of responsible command that should inform the assessment of whether all

[359] Conviction Decision, *supra* note 317, at § 200.
[360] *Ibid*, at § 720.
[361] *Ibid*, at § 727.

necessary and reasonable measures have been taken to prevent and repress the commission of crimes and to submit criminal matters to competent authorities for investigation and prosecution. These basic requirements are reflective of what is required by international law in recognition of the inherent risks of armed conflict and the importance of properly trained, supervised, and disciplined troops. This standard is informed by the rules and principles of IHL, including the obligation to protect civilians and the special protection of women and children from sexual violence.

40. The Prosecutor's submission identifies several such basic requirements of commanders,[362] including ensuring troops are properly trained in IHL; ensuring adequate supervision of troops; issuing proper and lawful orders; facilitating investigations, prosecutions, and punishments in light of potentially unlawful conduct; and replacing, dismissing, and removing subordinates as necessary. The Appeals Chamber concurs with this assessment and considers that it provides a non-exhaustive list of those basic requirements that must be considered in determining whether the criteria of Article 28(a)(ii) are satisfied. However, the Appeals Chamber would add that given the risk of sexual violence inherent in armed conflict, a responsible commander should adopt measures specifically aimed at the prevention, repression, and investigation/prosecution of sexual violence.

Conclusion

41. The Appeals Chamber considers that the correct legal standard in relation to the criteria contained in Article 28(a)(ii) requires a case-by-case approach to both: determining what measures were necessary and reasonable for a commander to take to prevent or repress crimes, or submit criminal matters to competent authorities, which at a minimum should include (but not be limited to) the basic requirements of responsible command; and assessing the commander's de jure or de facto power and whether any necessary and reasonable measures were beyond this scope. Where a commander has failed to implement any necessary and reasonable measures within his or her power (and the other fault elements of effective control and knowledge have also been satisfied), then he or she will incur criminal liability.

Assessment of Measures Taken by Mr Bemba

Trial Chamber's Findings

42. The Trial Chamber found Mr Bemba took 'a few measures' over the course of the 2002–2003 CAR Operation,[363] specifically that he:

[362] Public Redacted Version of Corrected Version of Prosecution's Response to Appellant's Document in Support of Appeal, *Prosecutor v. Jean-Pierre Bemba Gombo* (ICC-01/05-01/08), Appeals Chamber, 19 January 2017 (hereafter Prosecution Response to Appeal Brief).

[363] Conviction Decision, *supra* note 317, at § 719.

(a) Established the Mondonga Inquiry which investigated alleged crimes committed by MLC troops in Bangui and produced a brief of evidence in relation to allegations of pillaging, but did not question suspects about the crime of murder or pursue reports of rape;[364]
(b) Met with the UN representative in the CAR, General Cissé, and CAR President Patassé in November 2002, and reportedly committed to a progressive and organised withdrawal of troops and the punishment of soldiers who committed crimes, noting some had already been identified and disciplined;[365]
(c) Addressed MLC troops in November 2002, referring to allegations of crimes against civilians and warning against further misconduct;[366]
(d) Facilitated the trial of seven soldiers for pillaging at the Gbadolite Court-Martial, including by appointing the presiding judge and prosecutor (all seven accused were convicted);[367]
(e) Sent an investigative commission to Zongo to investigate allegations of pillaging in December 2002, but which was unable to establish that MLC soldiers had committed the crime of pillaging;[368]
(f) Wrote to General Cissé on 4 January 2003 stating that the MLC would not ignore serious violations of human rights, advising he had ordered the arrest of soldiers whose behaviour was contrary to instructions given before their departure to CAR, and requesting assistance with an investigation involving the CAR population;[369]
(g) Wrote to the president of the International Federation for Human Rights (FIDH) on 20 February 2003 responding to a report on its investigative mission in Bangui;[370] and
(h) Dispatched a delegation of soldiers and officials to Sibut in response to reports of abuses in the towns of Sibut and Bozoum.[371]

43. The Trial Chamber concluded that the measures taken by Mr Bemba were 'limited in mandate, execution, and/or results'.[372] The Trial Chamber further found that '[i]n addition to or instead of the insufficient measures' Mr Bemba took, and in light of his extensive material ability to prevent or repress the crimes, he could have inter alia taken a number of other measures. These included:

[364] *Ibid*, at §§ 582–589.
[365] *Ibid*, at §§ 590–593.
[366] *Ibid*, at §§ 594–596.
[367] *Ibid*, at §§ 597–600.
[368] *Ibid*, at §§ 601–603.
[369] *Ibid*, at §§ 604–606.
[370] *Ibid*, at §§ 607–611.
[371] *Ibid*, at §§ 612–620.
[372] *Ibid*, at § 720.

(a) Ensuring MLC troops in CAR were properly trained in IHL and properly supervised for the duration of the CAR operation;
(b) Initiating genuine and full investigations into the commission of crimes and properly tried and punished any soldiers alleged to have committed crimes;
(c) Issuing further and clear orders to commanders of the troops in CAR to prevent the commission of crimes;
(d) Altering the deployment of troops, including to minimise contact with civilian populations;
(e) Removing, replacing, or dismissing officers or soldiers that committed or condoned crimes;
(f) Sharing relevant information with CAR authorities and others and supporting them in investigations.[373]

Notice of Measures

44. Mr Bemba submits that he was not given notice of the measures which the Trial Chamber found he could have taken because of their 'hypothetical' nature, and therefore it would be unfair to convict him without giving him the opportunity to defend himself. Mr Bemba asserts that the Trial Chamber erroneously compared his conduct to 'a list of hypothetical measures' compiled with the 'benefit of hindsight from its *post hoc* position of superior information'.[374] He claims it was not the Trial Chamber's role to speculate as to what measures might have 'stemmed or mitigated the commission of the crimes' and then evaluate Mr Bemba's conduct against this hypothetical list.

45. The Appeals Chamber unequivocally rejects these arguments. It is not in dispute that an accused is entitled to notice of the factual allegations made against him or her in order that they may prepare an informed defence.[375] However, given the assessment to be made under Article 28(a)(ii) relates to the *failure* of a commander to take all necessary and reasonable measures, the inquiry is naturally concerned with *omissions*. This requires a judicial assessment as to what was not done but should have been. One may label this as hypothesising with the benefit of hindsight, but it is the nature of the task given to this Court by the Rome Statute. The Trial Chamber made no error in identifying a list of hypothetical necessary and reasonable measures that Mr Bemba could have taken but did not, as this was precisely what was required of it.

46. The Appeals Chamber notes that notice of necessary and reasonable measures not taken may be specific or general in form. With regard to the former, notice of

[373] *Ibid*, at § 729.
[374] Appeal Brief, *supra* note 323, at § 340.
[375] Art. 67, ICCSt.

specific measures should be provided through the indictment and confirmation of charges procedure. In relation to the latter, all commanders should be considered at all times to be on notice of measures which are in effect the inherent duties of command and would apply in every case, as discussed above.

47. In the present case, the Appeals Chamber agrees with the Prosecutor that Mr Bemba was given 'sufficient notice'[376] of the scope and nature of measures he was found to have failed to take. First, all of the measures the Trial Chamber found Mr Bemba had failed to take fell within the scope of the notice provided to Mr Bemba through the Confirmation Decision and the Corrected Revised Second Amended Document Containing the Charges. Second, the Prosecutor submits and the Appeals Chamber accepts that at least four of the measures the Trial Chamber found Mr Bemba did not take can be considered to be basic requirements of responsible command, including ensuring proper IHL training and adequate supervision of troops.

Appeals Chamber's Findings

48. The Appeals Chamber does not dispute the findings of the Trial Chamber as to what measures Mr Bemba took, or its view that these were limited and ultimately insufficient. However, the reasoning by which we have reached this conclusion differs, and is based upon the correct legal standard, as outlined above, to be applied to establish that the provisions of Article 28(a)(ii) have been met.

49. As noted above, the legal standard required by Article 28(a)(ii) sets a high threshold for the conduct of commanders in fulfilling their responsibility to exercise effective control over their troops, reflecting the protective function of IHL and its special regard for women and children at risk of sexual violence. The test to be applied is whether all necessary and reasonable measures within the commander's power have been taken to prevent or repress crimes, or submit criminal matters to competent authorities. Although this assessment takes into account the scope of the commander's de jure and/or de facto power, the provision contains no other criteria involving feasibility, seniority, outcome, or motive, and these do not form part of the relevant legal test for liability. While a case-by-case approach cognisant of contextual considerations is warranted, the basic requirements must be satisfied for a commander to fulfil the obligations placed upon them under international law and required under Article 28(a)(ii).

50. The Appeals Chamber notes that among the list of additional or alternate actions the Trial Chamber identified as necessary and reasonable measures that Mr Bemba failed to take are several basic requirements of responsible command, including his failure to ensure MLC troops were properly trained in IHL and adequately supervised for the duration of the CAR Operation. Mr Bemba's

[376] Prosecution Response to Appeal Brief, *supra* note 362, at § 202.

submissions on appeal fail to address these findings, or offer a justification for why such measures were not within his power.

51. Ensuring troops are properly trained in IHL and made aware of the prohibitions on sexual violence against women and children is a basic requirement of responsible command and constitutes a necessary and reasonable measure for a commander to take to prevent violations of IHL by troops. Ensuring adequate supervision of troops, including issuing clear orders concerning the prohibition of sexual violence, is similarly an essential preventive measure and critical to repressing prohibited conduct. Failure to take these measures alone, without regard to the adequacy of his actions in submitting criminal matters for investigation and prosecution, mean that Mr Bemba has not fulfilled the obligations required of him. The Appeals Chamber therefore finds that Mr Bemba's conduct did not satisfy the legal test for taking all necessary and reasonable measures as per Article 28(a)(ii) and that he is subject to criminal liability under the doctrine of command responsibility.

Conclusion

52. For the reasons outlined above, the Appeals Chamber finds that the Trial Chamber erred in referring to irrelevant considerations of outcome and motive in its reasoning. However, the weight given to these considerations in determining whether Mr Bemba failed to take all necessary and reasonable measures was limited and does not materially affect the findings or decision of the Trial Chamber.

53. In conclusion, the Appeals Chamber concurs with the Trial Chamber – but distinguishes its reasoning – in finding that Mr Bemba failed to take all necessary and reasonable measures within his power to prevent or repress the commission of crimes by his subordinates during the 2002–2003 CAR Operation, or to submit the matter to the competent authorities. The third ground of appeal is therefore dismissed.

Judge Suzanne Varrall and Judge Sarah Williams

11.6 CHARGING SEXUAL CRIMES IN THE YEKATOM CHARGE AMENDMENT

Valerie Oosterveld

In 2019, Pre-Trial Chamber II partially confirmed charges of war crimes and crimes against humanity against Mr Alfred Yekatom concerning events in Central African Republic (CAR) between 5 December 2013 and August 2014.[377] In May 2020, the Prosecutor filed a request under Article 61(9) of the Rome Statute to add charges of

[377] Decision on the Confirmation of Charges against Alfred Yekatom and Patrice-Edouard Ngaïssona, *Yekatom and Ngaïssona* (ICC-01/14-01/18-403-Red), Pre-Trial Chamber II, 11 December 2019.

rape and sexual slavery as war crimes.[378] In June 2020, Pre-Trial Chamber II declined to include those charges, adopting a 'precautionary and restrictive approach', noting that such an approach was required in order to avoid 'unjustified recourse to this prerogative by the Prosecutor turn[ing] into abuse'.[379] The Chamber cautioned the prosecution for continuing to investigate post the confirmation of charges and noted that Article 61(9), while sanctioned, cannot be used to address 'gaps' in the case of the prosecution.[380]

In this rewritten decision concerning the Prosecutor's request to amend the charges, Valerie Oosterveld reconsiders the three Article 61(9) factors permitting the introduction of additional charges, focusing on the inescapable realities of collecting evidence regarding sexual violence faced by investigating teams. In doing so, she criticises the restrictive approach undertaken by the Chamber, turning to the experience of other international tribunals to demonstrate how, particularly in the situation of sexual crimes, there is a need for a full appreciation of the experience of victims and ultimately confirms the inclusion of such charges against Mr Yekatom.

No.: ICC-01/14-01/18
Date: 1 June 2020

Original: English

PRE-TRIAL CHAMBER II(B)

Before: Judge Valerie OOSTERVELD

SITUATION IN THE CENTRAL AFRICAN REPUBLIC II

IN THE CASE OF THE *PROSECUTOR v. ALFRED YEKATOM AND PATRICE-EDOUARD NGAÏSSONA*

Public

Decision of the Prosecutor's Request to Amend the Charges against Alfred Yekatom

PRE-TRIAL CHAMBER II of the International Criminal Court issues this Decision on the Prosecutor's Request to Amend the Charges against Alfred Yekatom.

PROCEDURAL HISTORY

1. On 11 December 2019, the Chamber issued the Decision on the confirmationof charges against Alfred Yekatom and Patrice-Edouard Ngaïssona (Confirmation

378 Prosecution Motion to Amend the Charges against Alfred Yekatom, *Yekatom and Ngaïssona* (ICC-01/14-01/18-518-Red), Pre-Trial Chamber II, 22 May 2020.

379 Decision on the Prosecutor's Request to Amend the Charges against Alfred Yekatom, *Yekatom and Ngaïssona* (ICC-01/14-01/18-538), Pre-Trial Chamber II, 1 June 2020, at §§ 12, 14.

380 *Ibid*, at § 19.

Decision, Yekatom, and Ngaïssona, respectively), in which, inter alia, it confirmed the charges presented against Yekatom and Ngaïssona to the extent specified in the decision and committed them to trial on the charges as confirmed.[381]

2. On 2 March 2019, the Prosecutor filed a request for reconsideration or leave to appeal this decision.[382] On 11 March 2019, the Chamber rejected this request.[383]

3. On 13 March 2020, the Registry transmitted the record of the proceedings to the Presidency,[384] which constituted Trial Chamber V and referred the case against Yekatom and Ngaïssona to it on 16 March 2020.[385]

4. On 31 March 2020, the Prosecutor's Request to Amend Charges pursuant to Article 61(9) and for Correction of the Decision on the Confirmation of Charges, and Notice of Intention to Add Additional Charges (Ngaïssona Article 61(9) Request) was filed:[386] the Prosecutor requested the Chamber, inter alia, to 'amend the charges of rape confirmed against' Ngaïssona by 'includ[ing] and confirm[ing] a second instance of rape'.

5. On 14 May 2020, the Chamber issued the Decision on the Prosecutor's Request to Amend Charges pursuant to Article 61(9) and for Correction of the Decision on the Confirmation of Charges, and Notice of Intention to Add Additional Charges (14 May 2020 Decision), rejecting the Ngaïssona Article 61(9) Request.[387]

6. Also on 14 May 2020, the Prosecution Motion to Amend the Charges against Alfred YEKATOM (Request) was filed:[388] the Prosecutor seeks that the Chamber (i) 'grant permission to amend the charges' confirmed against Yekatom 'under Article 61(9) to add charges of rape and sexual slavery as war crimes' and (ii) 'issue a

[381] Yekatom and Ngaïssona Decision on the Confirmation of Charges, *supra* note 378.

[382] Prosecution's Request for Reconsideration of, or alternatively Leave to Appeal, the Decision on the Confirmation of Charges against Alfred Yekatom and Patrice-Edouard Ngaïssona, *Yekatom and Ngaïssona* (ICC-01/14-01/18-437), Prosecutor, 2 March 2020.

[383] Decision on the Prosecutor's Request for Reconsideration or, in the Alternative, Leave to Appeal the Decision on the Confirmation of Charges against Alfred Yekatom and Patrice-Edouard Ngaïssona, *Yekatom and Ngaïssona* (ICC-01/14-01/18-447), Pre-Trial Chamber II, 11 March 2020.

[384] Transmission to the Presidency of the Record of the Proceedings, including the Decision on the Confirmation of Charges against Alfred Yekatom and Patrice-Edouard Ngaïssona, *Yekatom and Ngaïssona* (ICC-01/14-01/18-449), Registry, 13 March 2020.

[385] Decision Constituting Trial Chamber V and Referring to it the case of *Prosecutor v. Alfred Yekatom and Patrice-Edouard Ngaïssona*, *Yekatom and Ngaïssona* (ICC-01/14-01/18-451), Presidency, 16 March 2020.

[386] Prosecution's Request to Amend Charges Pursuant to Article 61(9) and for Correction of the Decision on the Confirmation of Charges, and Notice of Intention to Add Additional Charges, *Yekatom and Ngaïssona* (ICC-01/14-01/18-468-Red), Prosecutor, 31 March 2020.

[387] Decision on the Prosecution's Request to Amend Charges pursuant to Article 61(9) and for Correction of the Decision on the Confirmation of Charges, and Notice of Intention to Add Additional Charges, *Yekatom and Ngaïssona* (ICC-01/14-01/18-517), Pre-Trial Chamber II, 14 May 2020 (hereafter Ngaïssona Art. 61(9) Decision).

[388] Prosecution Motion to Amend the Charges against Alfred YEKATOM, *Yekatom and Ngaïssona* (ICC-01/14-01/18-518-Red), Prosecutor, 14 May 2020 (hereafter Prosecution Art. 61 (9) Yekatom Request).

scheduling order for the confirmation hearing [on those charges] for as soon as practicable'.

7. On 26 May 2020, the Yekatom Defence Response to Motion to Amend the Charges (Yekatom Response), opposing the Request, was filed before Trial Chamber V.[389]

8. On 26 May 2020, the common legal representatives of the former child soldiers and of the victims of other crimes (CLRV) filed their joint response, seeking that the Chamber grant the Request in its entirety.[390]

SUBMISSIONS OF THE PARTIES AND PARTICIPANTS

Defence for Yekatom

9. As a preliminary matter, the Chamber notes that the corrected version of the Yekatom Response, addressed to Pre-Trial Chamber II, was received by the Registry on 27 May 2020, at 15:51 hours, after the time limit for responses to the Request had expired. The defence for Yekatom did not request an extension of time prior to the expiration of the deadline. Accordingly, the Chamber will not consider the Yekatom Response.

Prosecutor

10. The Prosecutor submits that 'credible evidence of rape and sexual slavery allegedly committed by Anti-Balaka elements subordinate to' Yekatom, in the form of witness statements, was uncovered '[d]uring the course of finalising [the] investigation into the conscription, enlistment, and use of children under the age of 15 years'. Accordingly, charges of rape and sexual slavery as war crimes should be added by amending the charges confirmed against Yekatom, pursuant to Article 61(9) of the Statute.

11. In the view of the Prosecutor, these additional charges are 'fully substantiated and more fully reflect [Yekatom's] alleged culpability'; in light of the 'seriousness and importance' of these charges, the 'proposed amendment is in the interests of justice'.

12. The Prosecutor submits that 'the requested amendment is timely, justified, and entails no unfair prejudice to' Yekatom because: (i) 'no trial date has as yet been set

[389] On 27 May 2020, the Defence for Yekatom filed a corrected version of the filing, in which it replaced the cover page in order to reflect Pre-Trial Chamber II and its composition: Corrected version of Yekatom Defence Response to Motion to Amend the Charges, *Yekatom and Ngaïssona* (ICC-01/14-01/18-532-Red-Corr, with corrected public redacted Annex, ICC-01/14-01/18-532-Red-Corr-Anx), Defence for Yekatom, 27 May 2020.

[390] Common Legal Representatives' Joint Response to the Prosecution Motion to Amend the Charges against Alfred YEKATOM (ICC-01/14-01/18-531-Red), CLRV, 26 May 2020 (hereafter CLRV Art. 61(9) Response).

and … an actual trial is unlikely to commence soon'; (ii) the additional charges, being 'predicated on sufficient evidence', are 'adequately substantiated' and feature 'among the Rome Statute's most serious', which renders them 'important to the Court's duty to establish the truth and to ensure the Trial Chamber's "full consideration of the relevant issues"'; (iii) the Prosecutor 'acted with reasonable diligence in pursuing the investigation and the [a]dditional [c]harges', including with regard to the gathering of the relevant evidence; and (iv) the 'amendment of charges … would not unfairly prejudice' Yekatom, nor would the Prosecutor 'gain any tactical advantage', since the defence would 'have ample opportunity to prepare' and there would be 'no clear impact on the expeditious conduct of a prospective trial'.

13. Should the Request be granted, the Prosecutor also 'requests that the Chamber schedule a date for the confirmation hearing on the [a]dditional [c]harges for as soon as practicable'. Further particulars of the Prosecutor's argument are indicated below.

Common Legal Representatives of the Former Child Soldiers and Common Legal Representatives of the Victims of Other Crimes (CLRV)

14. In the view of the CLRV, the Request should be granted in its entirety, based inter alia on the following submissions: (i) it is in the interest of the victims that the proposed charges are added in order for them to have effective 'access to justice, recognition of their victimisation and eventually the possibility to claim reparations'; (ii) the prosecution only received credible information on conflict-related sexual violence in mid-July 2019, which did not provide sufficient time for it to gather and integrate the evidence into the Document Containing the Charges (DCC); (iii) this timing required investigation 'necessary to establish the truth … of grave crimes' beyond the submission of the DCC and the issuance of the Decision on the Confirmation of Charges; (iv) this investigation faced 'practical and logistical constraints' which explained the timing of the current request; (v) adding new charges of limited scope at this juncture 'would not negatively impact the fairness and expeditiousness of the proceedings', given that 'the date of the commencement of the trial is yet to be set'; (vi) concerns about the lack of charges related to gender-based crimes had already been expressed by the CLRV in their 9 July 2019 submissions; (vii) the Chamber must assess and balance the rights of victims, which include consideration of the full extent of their victimisation, as well as those of the accused; and (viii) it is not satisfactory to have a speedy trial 'if said trial fails to uncover the truth about the responsibility of those involved'.

DETERMINATION OF THE CHAMBER

15. The Trial Chamber must consider the criminal responsibility of the accused based on the facts confirmed in the Pre-Trial Chamber's Decision on the

Confirmation of Charges.[391] The Decision on the Confirmation of Charges therefore sets the factual boundaries for each trial and the accused cannot be convicted for acts that fall outside of those particularised in that decision.

16. Article 61(9) of the Statute provides for the possibility of amending the charges after the issuance of the Decision on the Confirmation of Charges and before the start of trial. It states, in part: 'After the charges are confirmed and before the trial has begun, the Prosecutor may, with the permission of the Pre-Trial Chamber and after notice to the accused, amend the charges. If the Prosecutor seeks to add additional charges or to substitute more serious charges, a hearing under this article to confirm those charges must be held.' The phrase 'before the trial has begun' refers to 'the true opening of the trial when the opening statements, if any, are made prior to the calling of witnesses'.[392]

17. The drafters of the Statute, in adding Article 61(9), reflected the procedures to amend an indictment in the International Criminal Tribunals for the Former Yugoslavia and Rwanda (ICTY and ICTR, respectively), crafted to fit the differing procedure of the ICC.[393]

18. This Court has previously determined that the Prosecutor may request permission to amend the charges up until the actual commencement of the trial, provided that a request to this effect is properly 'supported and justified'.[394] This is not an unfettered right, as the Court must also consider whether granting such a request would 'negatively affect other competing interests, such as the fairness and expeditiousness of the proceedings, which would result in causing prejudice to the rights of the accused'.[395]

19. The prosecution's request to add entirely new and separate charges not already reflected in the Decision on the Confirmation of Charges raises issues of first instance. This Court has considered requests under Article 61(9) to amend and

[391] ICC St, Art 74(2); Judgment on the Appeals of Mr Lubanga Dyilo and the Prosecutor against the Decision of Trial Chamber I of 14 July 2009 entitled 'Decision Giving Notice to the Parties and Participants that the Legal Characterisation of the Facts may be Subject to Change in Accordance with Regulation 55(2) of the Regulations of the Court', *Lubanga* (ICC-01/04-01/06-2205), Appeals Chamber, 8 December 2009.

[392] Decision on the Status before the Trial Chamber of the Evidence Heard by the Pre-Trial Chamber and the Decisions of the Pre-Trial Chamber in Trial Proceedings, and the Manner in Which Evidence Shall Be Submitted, *Lubanga* (ICC-01/04-01/06), Trial Chamber I, 13 December 2007, § 39 (reference omitted).

[393] Draft Statute for the International Criminal Court and Draft Final Act, UN Doc. A/CONF.183/2/Add.1, 14 April 1998, at 97–98 ('Further options for Articles 58 to 61'); Rule 50 ICTY RPE; Rule 50 ICTR RPE; Rule 50 IRMCT RPE.

[394] Decision on the Prosecution's Request to Amend the Final Updated Document Containing the Charges Pursuant to Article 61(9) of the Statute, *Kenyatta* (ICC-01/09-02/ll-700-Corr), Pre-Trial Chamber II, 21 March 2013, § 21 (hereafter Kenyatta Art. 61(9) Decision).

[395] Decision on the Prosecution's Request to Amend the Updated Document Containing the Charges Pursuant to Article 61(9) of the Statute, *Ruto and Sang* (ICC-01/09-01/11-859), Pre-Trial Chamber II, 16 August 2013, § 31 (hereafter Ruto and Sang Art. 61(9) Decision).

extend existing charges,[396] and this prior jurisprudence provides guidance. Additionally, other international criminal tribunals have considered requests for the addition of new charges under rules that bear some similarity to Article 61 (9);[397] even though the procedures of those tribunals differ from the Confirmation of Charges procedures of the ICC, their jurisprudence may also be instructive.

20. These sources lead to the conclusion that the relevant factors are, when considering an Article 61(9) request for the addition of new charges:

1. The importance of the additional allegations to a complete understanding of the prosecution's case and a full consideration of the relevant issues;[398]
2. The reasonable diligence of the prosecution in bringing the additional charges, including the reasonableness of continuing investigations after the Decision on the Confirmation of Charges and whether the request is supported and justified;[399] and
3. Whether the adjudication of the additional charges would cause undue prejudice to the rights of the accused.[400]

21. These factors will be considered in turn.

Importance of the Additional Allegations to a Complete Understanding of the Prosecution's Case and a Full Consideration of the Relevant Issues

22. The Prosecutor submits that permitting the requested amendment to add charges against Yekatom of rape and sexual slavery as war crimes would lead to a

[396] The Ngaïssona Article 61(9) Decision (*supra* note 387) addressed the prosecution's request to amend an existing charge of rape to include a second instance of rape. This differs from the Prosecution Art. 61(9) Yekatom Request (*supra* note 388), which seeks to add two new additional charges. See also Kenyatta Art. 61(9) Decision, *supra* note 394; Ruto and Sang Art. 61(9) Decision, *supra* note 395; Decision on the Applicable Procedure following the Prosecutor's Filing of her Request for Corrections and Amendments for the Decision to Confirm the Charges, *Al Hassan* (ICC-01/12-01/18-608-Red), Pre-Trial Chamber I, 21 February 2020 (hereafter Al-Hassan Art. 61(9) Decision); and Version publique expurgée du Rectificatif de la Décision portant modification des charges confirmées le 30 septembre 2019 à l'encontre d'Al Hassan Ag Abdoul Aziz Ag Mohamed Ag Mahmoud, *Al-Hassan* (ICC-01/12-01/18-767-Conf), Pre-Trial Chamber I, 8 May 2020 (hereafter Al-Hassan Decision on Amendment of Charges).

[397] See e.g. Written Reasons for Decision on Prosecution Motion to Amend the Second Amended Indictment, *Tolimir* (IT-05-88/2-PT), Trial Chamber II, 16 December 2009; Decision on Vinko Martinović's Objection to the Amended Indictment and Mladen Naletilić's Preliminary Motion to the Amended Indictment, *Naletilić et al.* (IT-98-34-PT), Trial Chamber, 14 February 2001; Order Granting Leave to Amend the Croatia Indictment, *Milošević* (IT-02-54-T), Trial Chamber, 4 November 2002; Decision on the Prosecution Motion to Amend the Indictment, *Turinabo et al.* (MICT-18-116-PT), Single Judge, 17 October 2019 (hereafter Turinabo Amendment Decision).

[398] Kenyatta Art. 61(9) Decision, *supra* note 394, at §§ 35–36.

[399] Ruto and Sang Art. 61(9) Decision, *supra* note 395, at § 34, Kenyatta Art. 61(9) Decision, *supra* note 394, at §§ 21, 37.

[400] Kenyatta Art. 61(9) Decision, *supra* note 394, at §§ 22, 32, 42.

more complete understanding of the case against the accused: 'The Additional Charges are important to the Court's duty to establish the truth and to ensure the Trial Chamber's "full consideration of the relevant issues".'[401]

23. The Appeals Chamber has recognised that '[t]he duty to establish the truth is not limited to the time before the confirmation hearing. Therefore, the Prosecutor must be allowed to continue his investigation beyond the confirmation hearing, if this is necessary in order to establish the truth'.[402] The Appeals Chamber identified when such situations may be necessary: when a failure to do so would 'deprive the Court of significant and relevant evidence ... particularly in situations where the ongoing nature of the conflict results in more compelling evidence becoming available for the first time after the confirmation hearing'.[403]

24. This Court has also recognised that the ICC's 'Statute and the Rules accord a special status to sexual violence crimes, crimes against children, and the victims thereof' and that '[d]uring the drafting process of the Rome Statute, the especially grave nature and consequences of sexual violence crimes ... were recognised'.[404] In the *Ntaganda* case, Trial Chamber VI observed, citing the ICTY trial chamber in *Kunarac et al.*, that 'rape is one of the worst sufferings a human being can inflict upon another'.[405] Citing *Mucić et al.*, Trial Chamber VI also considered '[t]he rape of any person to be a despicable act which strikes at the very core of human dignity and physical integrity'.[406] Trial Chamber VI concluded that rape and sexual slavery as crimes against humanity and war crimes are grave crimes, ultimately sentencing Ntaganda to seventeen and fourteen years' imprisonment respectively.[407] Other international criminal tribunals have come to the same conclusion, with Trial Chamber II of the Special Court for Sierra Leone categorising these acts as 'of the utmost gravity'.[408]

25. The Prosecutor is requesting the addition of charges for the war crimes of rape and sexual slavery. These are the only proposed charges of conflict-related sexual

[401] Prosecution Art. 61(9) Yekatom Request, *supra* note 388, at § 15, citing Turinabo Amendment Decision, *supra* note 397, at § 10.

[402] Judgment on the Prosecutor's Appeal against the Decision of Pre-Trial Chamber I entitled 'Decision Establishing General Principles Governing Applications to Restrict Disclosure pursuant to Rule 81 (2) and (4) of the Rules of Procedure and Evidence', *Lubanga* (ICC-01/04-01/06-568), Appeals Chamber, 12 October 2006, § 52 (hereafter Lubanga General Principles).

[403] *Ibid*, at § 54.

[404] Sentencing Judgment, *Ntaganda* (ICC-01/04-02/06), Trial Chamber VI, 7 November 2019, § 95 (hereafter Ntaganda Sentencing Judgment), citing Decision on Sentence pursuant to Article 76 of the Statute, *Bemba* (ICC-01/05-01/08-3399), Trial Chamber III, 21 June 2016, § 35.

[405] Ntaganda Sentencing Judgment, *supra* note 404, at § 96, citing Judgment, *Kunarac et al.* (IT-96-23-T& IT-96-23/1-T), Trial Chamber, 22 February 200, § 655.

[406] Ntaganda Sentencing Judgment, *supra* note 404, at § 96, citing Judgment, *Mucić et al.* (IT-96-21-T), Trial Chamber, 16 November 1998, § 495.

[407] Ntaganda Sentencing Judgment, *supra* note 404, at §§ 96–120, 246.

[408] Sentencing Judgment, *Taylor* (SCSL-03-01-T), Trial Chamber II, 30 May 2012, § 70.

violence against the accused. The victims, in particular, have an interest in the full consideration of the responsibility of the accused and the extent of victimisation.

26. Given the gravity of the proposed additional charges, they may provide 'significant and relevant evidence' as well as context for the previously confirmed charges. Therefore the requirement to demonstrate the importance of the additional allegations to a complete understanding of the prosecution's case and a full consideration of the relevant issues has been met.

Reasonable Diligence of the Prosecution in Bringing the Additional Charges, including the Reasonableness of Continuing Investigations after the Confirmation of Charges and whether the Request Is Supported and Justified

27. The 'underlying rationale [of Article 61(9)] is that continued investigation should be related only to such essential pieces of evidence which were not known or available to the Office of the Prosecutor prior to the confirmation hearing or could not have been collected for any other reason, except at the later stage'.[409] The reasons for such an investigation must be properly justified.[410]

28. In June 2019, the prosecution indicated that it was 'continu[ing] to investigate the commission of sexual and gender based crimes … and may seek the confirmation of such charges, should the evidence obtained satisfy the requisite threshold'.[411] It received relevant information relating to sexual violence in mid-July 2019.[412] The DCC was due on 19 August 2019. In order to incorporate this information into the DCC, the prosecution would have needed to organise and undertake missions (involving travel arrangements for all participants, including the witnesses), assess any risks to the witnesses based on the evidence provided and their personal circumstances before disclosure could take place, and translate the statements into French for the purposes of the Rules of Procedure and Evidence and Rules of the Court in order to rely on them as evidence at the confirmation hearing – all within one month.[413] There was therefore not sufficient time.[414] Additionally, the prosecution had earlier sought and obtained a delay in the Confirmation of Charges hearing[415] and it was not feasible to request a further delay.

409 Kenyatta Art. 61(9) Decision, *supra* note 394, at § 37.

410 *Ibid*, §§ 21, 37; Ruto and Sang Art. 61(9) Decision, *supra* note 395, at § 31; Al-Hassan Art. 61(9) Decision, *supra* note 396, at § 53; Ngaïssona Art. 61(9) Decision, *supra* note 387, at § 22.

411 Prosecution's Additional Observations on the Registry's'First Assessment Report on Applications for Victims' Participation in Pre-Trial Proceedings (ICC-01/14-01/18-198', *Yekatom and Ngaïssona* (ICC-01/14-01/18-224-Conf), Prosecutor, 14 June 2019, § 9.

412 Prosecution Art. 61(9) Yekatom Request, *supra* note 388, at § 23.

413 *Ibid*, at § 23.

414 *Ibid*.

415 Decision on the 'Prosecution's Request to Postpone the Confirmation Hearing and all Related Disclosure Deadlines, *Yekatom and Ngaïssona* (ICC-01/14-01/18), Pre-Trial Chamber II.

29. The prosecution sought to interview two victims. The prosecution alleges that the first individual, a victim of rape and sexual slavery, was deprived of her liberty while with the Anti-Balaka, told that she 'had to do anything they ordered [her] to do', and was raped under threat of death by an intermittently armed direct perpetrator.[416] The prosecution alleges that a second individual, another victim of rape and sexual slavery, was threatened by the direct perpetrator and deprived of her liberty.[417]

30. The prosecution indicates that the first individual was screened in late August 2019, and interviewed within three weeks, in September 2019, once the presence of a psychosocial expert was ensured.[418] The prosecution indicates that it faced considerable difficulties initially in contacting the second individual.[419] The date for her first interview was rescheduled to late November 2019 due to the unavailability of a psychosocial expert.[420] The prosecution conducted a second interview in January 2020 to obtain 'additional details and clarifications in order to determine whether to seek the amendment of charges'.[421] The prosecution submits that witness-related work was hampered by the considerable budget restraints in place at the Court during the last quarter of 2019, which permitted only a single investigative team to conduct field work in the Central African Republic.[422] The prosecution viewed the evidence of the first and second individuals as interconnected,[423] which is why it secured evidence from both before proceeding to an internal evidence review, which concluded on 27 March 2020, and the filing of its motion to add additional charges on 31 March 2020.[424]

31. The time period between the prosecution's initial receipt of relevant information on sexual violence and issuance of the request to amend the charges was 8.5 months. Within this time period, the prosecution only had the evidence for both charges in hand as of January 2020.[425]

32. This delayed surfacing of the evidence on conflict-related sexual violence, and the difficulties in securing such evidence and putting into place protective measures for victims, are not unusual. There are inherent challenges to collecting credible evidence of conflict-related sexual violence which have an impact upon the speed at which such evidence can be uncovered, considered, and integrated into prosecution

[416] Prosecution Art. 61(9) Yekatom Request, *supra* note 388, at § 18.
[417] Ibid, at § 19.
[418] *Ibid*, at § 24.
[419] *Ibid*, at § 26.
[420] *Ibid*.
[421] *Ibid*, at § 27.
[422] *Ibid*, at § 28.
[423] *Ibid*, at §§ 15 and 18; one of the victims is a female captured by the Anti-Balaka, perhaps as a child soldier, and thus the prosecution may argue that the rape and sexual slavery charges are connected to the child soldiering charges.
[424] Prosecution Art. 61(9) Yekatom Request, *supra* note 388, at §§ 29–30.
[425] This can be contrasted with Ruto and Sang Art. 61(9) Decision, *supra* note 395, at § 37, where the prosecution had the evidence in hand.

cases.[426] Survivors may be reluctant to reveal their victimisation to investigators because they face threats to their security and well-being or societal, cultural, and other barriers such as stigmatisation and ostracism.[427] Survivors may be in a precarious position, affiliated with or living in a community with those who perpetrated the sexual violence against them. Survivors may be dealing with trauma, fatigue, health conditions, insufficient support mechanisms within their families and communities for survivors of sexual violence, and lack of access to meaningful victim protection.[428] They may therefore need to be interviewed more than once in order to build trust and secure further details.[429] Investigators may not have access to survivors or to secure private locations in which to interview survivors.[430] All of these difficulties can lead to the delayed reporting of sexual violence, as well as delays once evidence of sexual violence initially comes to light. Investigators and prosecutors have responsibilities for carrying out investigation of conflict-related sexual violence in a measured, careful manner to avoid harming victims, which takes time.[431]

33. Indeed, in *Al-Hassan* the Pre-Trial Chamber indicated that the prosecution cannot be reproached for decisions that belong solely to the witnesses, such as their hesitance to cooperate and to give evidence.[432]

34. Given the prosecution's explanation of the reasons for the timing of the investigation of the alleged incidents of sexual violence, and considering the inherent difficulties in investigating conflict-related sexual violence, the Chamber finds that it was reasonable for the prosecution to continue investigating after the Decision on the Confirmation of Charges, and that the timeline indicates that the prosecution was reasonably diligent in bringing its motion to amend the charges.

Whether the Adjudication of the Additional Charges Would Cause Undue Prejudice to the Rights of the Accused

35. In considering whether the adjudication of the additional proposed charges would cause undue prejudice to the rights of the accused, this Chamber must consider: the ability of the accused to prepare a timely defence to the additional charges, and any delay the additional charges may cause to the proceedings,

426 M. Jarvis and K. Vigneswaran, 'Challenges to Successful Outcomes in Sexual Violence Cases' in S. Brammertz and M. Jarvis (eds.), *Prosecuting Conflict-Related Sexual Violence at the ICTY* (Oxford: Oxford University Press, 2016) 33–72, at 33.
427 *Ibid*, at 42.
428 *Ibid*, at 42–43.
429 *Ibid*, at 43.
430 *Ibid*, at 44.
431 *Ibid*, at 45.
432 Al-Hassan Decision on Amendment of Charges, *supra* note 396, at § 27.

including to the duration of pre-trial custody.[433] These two considerations are interrelated: the granting of a request under Article 61(9) will naturally cause some disruption and delay as the defence would need to: review the information disclosed by the prosecution, conduct its own investigation, potentially adjust its strategy; and respond to the charges in an additional Confirmation of Charges hearing. It is therefore important to consider the potential extent of such a delay and whether it would amount to undue delay.

36. In *Al Hassan*, the Pre-Trial Chamber agreed to modify the existing charges of sexual slavery, rape, persecution, outrages on personal dignity, and other inhumane acts (forced marriage) in order to include additional facts on ten charges involving twelve victims.[434] The Chamber indicated that these additions were not so significant that they would delay the start of the trial and, although they would impact on the way the defence prepared for trial, this relatively small impact was outweighed by the necessary search for the truth by the prosecution.[435] The current case involves two new charges involving two victims, and is thus comparable.

37. In *Ruto and Sang*, the Pre-Trial Chamber stated that an amendment done well in advance of the scheduled trial respected 'the fairness of the proceedings, their expeditiousness and respect for the rights of the accused to receive a proper trial'.[436] The current case is also comparable, as the trial date has not been scheduled and is likely to be affected by the ongoing COVID-19 restrictions. Thus, a grant of the requested amendment sufficiently in advance of the trial can preserve the accused's rights.

38. In *Ngaïssona*, this Chamber found that granting the requested amendment would not satisfy the accused's fair trial rights. That decision can be distinguished from the current case because, in *Ngaïssona*, this Chamber found that the prosecution's request to amend the charges to include a charge of rape was aimed at 'reintroduc[ing] non-confirmed charges for which evidence was lacking pursuant to a supplemental investigation'.[437] In contrast, the current case considers entirely new charges with new evidence justified by different reasons.

39. In the view of this Chamber, the extent of any delay is likely to be minimal for two reasons. First, the proposed charges are limited both in scope and time, and are connected to existing charges. The prosecution has already completed its investigation and therefore only the defence would be required to undertake an additional investigation. This additional investigation would be narrow in focus. Second, the proceedings in this case are at an early stage. No trial date has been set and the trial is unlikely to happen in the near future due to COVID-19-related

[433] Ngaïssona Art. 61(9) Decision, *supra* note 387, at §§ 26–27.
[434] Al-Hassan Decision on Amendment of Charges, *supra* note 388, at § 24.
[435] *Ibid*, at § 24.
[436] Ruto and Sang Art. 61(9) Decision, *supra* note 395, at § 36.
[437] Ngaïssona Art. 61(9) Decision, *supra* note 387, at § 23.

restrictions.[438] Indeed, in this situation, the prosecution would be exercising its recourse to Article 61(9) 'under circumstances and conditions which would not impact the … trial'.[439]

40. Even if the trial date is likely to be set in the near future, a short delay would not be undue. For example, in the ICTY, a delay of seven months was not considered undue and was deemed to still afford the accused a fair trial, even though the trial date had already been set.[440]

41. Additionally, the effects of any delay could be substantially mitigated through the disclosure of witness statements to the defence as 'attorneys-eyes-only', to allow the defence immediate access to the evidence while still protecting the security of the witnesses.[441] Additionally or alternatively, witness statements could be disclosed to the accused and the CLRV in the form of extracts or excerpts, to the extent the security situation allows. In addition, any delays caused by such an amendment could also be mitigated by subtracting time in custody from the sentence in the event of a conviction, in accordance with Article 78(2) of the Statute.

42. In sum, any potential delay would not be undue and could be mitigated.

43. In light of the above, and after careful consideration of the rights of the accused, the Chamber finds that any potential disruption and delay caused to the defence by the granting of the prosecution's Article 61(9) request may be counterbalanced by these mitigating steps: (1) disclosure of relevant prosecution witness statements to the defence as 'attorneys-eyes-only' within five days of the release of this decision; (2) disclosure of witness statements to the accused and the CLRV in the form of key extracts or excerpts, to the extent the security situation allows, within ten days; and (3) subtracting time in custody from the sentence in the event of a conviction, in accordance with Article 78(2).

44. In conclusion, this Chamber finds that the three factors identified in paragraph 20 above have been fulfilled.

FOR THESE REASONS, THE CHAMBER HEREBY

GRANTS the Request.

Done in both English and French, the English version being authoritative.

Judge Valerie Oosterveld

[438] ICC, 'Guidelines for the Judiciary Concerning the Holding of Court Hearings during the COVID-19 Pandemic', Chambers, 23 June 2020, available at www.icc-cpi.int/news/guidelines-judiciary-concerning-holding-court-hearings-during-covid-19-pandemic.

[439] Ngaïssona Art. 61(9) Decision, *supra* note 387, at § 36.

[440] Decision Stating Reasons for Appeals Chamber's Order of 29 May 1998, *Kovačević* (IT-97-24-AR73), Appeals Chamber, 2 July 1998, § 31.

[441] Under ICCSt Art. 68, '[t]he Court shall take appropriate measures to protect the safety, physical and psychological well-being, dignity and privacy of victims and witnesses. In so doing, the Court shall have regard to all relevant factors, including age, gender … and the nature of the crime, in particular, but not limited to, where the crime involves sexual or gender violence or violence against children'.

12

The Situation in Côte d'Ivoire

12.1 REFLECTION: THE SITUATION IN CÔTE D'IVOIRE

Immi Tallgren

INTRODUCTION

My observations on the contexts relevant here do not start with the alleged crimes in Côte d'Ivoire but the temporalities of feminist rewriting as a critical practice. The first feminist rewritings in international law that marked the audiences concerned old judgments, such as the judgment in the *Lotus* case by the Permanent Court of Justice, decided in 1927.[1] Another important one was the International Court of Justice's decision on the Reservations to the Convention on the Prevention and Punishment of the Crime of Genocide, of 1955.[2] At the time when the original decisions were made, not only the international judges, counsel, and legal experts active on the cases, but almost all scholars, experts, negotiators, and professors – the most visible part of the intellectual and professional community of international lawyers – were men.

What difference does the (historical) context make? Early feminist rewriting could move freely in a realm of possibilities, in a liberty of constraints, a space of reimagination that resembles the often controversial 'what if?' histories, referred to as counterfactual or alternative histories in historiographical research. With the ongoing sex and gender transformation in international law that started in the 1990s, that moment of 'what if there were a woman' or even several women on

[1] C. Chinkin et al., '*Bozkurt Case*, aka the *Lotus Case (France v Turkey)*: Ships that Go Bump in the Night' in L. Hodson and T. Lavers (eds.), *Feminist Judgments in International Law* (Oxford: Hart, 2019) 27–52.

[2] K. McCall-Smith, R. Smith, and E. Yahyaoui Krivenko, 'Reservations to the Convention on the Prevention and Punishment of the Crime of Genocide' in L. Hodson and T. Lavers (eds.), *Feminist Judgments in International Law* (Oxford: Hart, 2019) 55–82.

the bench – or as counsel – has passed, in some sub-disciplines of international law at least. Amongst these disciplines, international criminal law (ICL) is generally considered the leading example of progress towards more equal sex and gender representation in authoritative and visible roles.

In the first decision concerning the alleged crimes in Côte d'Ivoire addressed here, Pre-Trial Chamber III consisted of three members, two of whom were women, Judge Silvia Fernández de Gurmendi presiding. The second decision was adopted by an all-female panel in Pre-Trial Chamber I. This change in the context of rewriting is brought about by very positive developments which remain aleatory and primarily restricted to ICL.[3] At the same time, the new context accentuates the challenges of rewriting as a creative critical exercise, by underlining the question of the difference between a decision by an all-female panel and a feminist decision. What is feminism(s) today, and who decides on the matter? I will return to this question in the concluding remarks.

I will proceed by giving a brief account of the conflict in Côte d'Ivoire which gave rise to the ICC's intervention before outlining each of the cases concerning Côte d'Ivoire. I will then analyse each rewritten decision separately, concluding with general reflections. I start with Judge Natalie Hodgson's rewritten Decision on the Prosecutor's Application Pursuant to Article 58 for a Warrant of Arrest against Simone Gbagbo and continue with Judge Sarah Easy's rewriting of the Decision on Côte d'Ivoire's challenge to the admissibility of the case against Simone Gbagbo.

BACKGROUND TO THE CONFLICT

Côte d'Ivoire experienced post-election violence after the results of the 2010–2011 presidential election were disputed. Mr Laurent Gbagbo claimed victory although the electoral commission stated that his opponent, Mr Alassane Ouattara, had won. It was reported that unrest ensued, with systematic and widespread attacks occurring against the civilian population. Witnesses described instances of raids with excessive force used, while others detailed incidences of rape, murder, disappearances, and mass graves. It was estimated that during the conflict, approximately 1 million people were displaced. The investigation focused on both pro-Gbagbo and pro-Ouattara forces, but so far only pro-Gbagbo personnel have been charged.

BACKGROUND TO THE CASES

Côte d'Ivoire accepted the jurisdiction of the ICC in April 2003 and ratified the Rome Statute on 15 February 2013. On 3 October 2011, the Office of the Prosecutor

[3] H. Charlesworth, 'The Institut de Droit international in Today's World' in M. Kohen and I. van der Heijden (eds.), *150 ans de contributions au développement du droit international: livre du sesquicentenaire de l'Institut de droit international (1873–2023)/150 Years of Contributing to the Development of International Law: Sesquicentenary Book of the Institute of International Law (1873–2023)* (Paris: A. Pedone, 2023) 147–168.

(OTP) was granted permission to open a *proprio motu* investigation in relation to alleged crimes committed since November 2010. On 22 February 2012, this was expanded to include alleged crimes committed since 10 September 2002. On 23 November 2011, a warrant of arrest was issued for Mr Laurent Gbagbo while on 21 December 2011 a warrant was issued for Mr Charles Blé Goudé, a military leader within Mr Gbagbo's party. On 29 February 2012, Ms Simone Gbagbo had a warrant of arrest issued against her for the crimes against humanity of murder, rape and other sexual violence, persecution, and other inhuman acts. While the charges against Mr Laurent Gbagbo and Mr Charles Blé Goudé proceeded to trial (where they were eventually acquitted), the warrant against Ms Simone Gbagbo was vacated on 19 July 2021.

FEMINIST REIMAGININGS

Prosecutor v. Simone Gbagbo, *Decision of the Prosecutor's Application Pursuant to Article 58 for a Warrant of Arrest against Simone Gbagbo*

Judge Natalie Hodgson's rewriting appears to have two primary objectives, the first less explicit than the second. First, her revisions to the original try to bring order and logic to an ICC decision. She uses titles that structure the corpus text of the decision and organises the questions the court must resolve. Her drafting closely follows the language and order of appearance of the Rome Statute's diverse criteria about what the Court must be convinced of at this stage of the proceedings. Her initiative suggests that feminist rewriting also comprises the general objective of communication and clarity. I welcome the suggestion for clarity, considering how gender, social class, and other structural circumstances and factors have for long restrained access to international law, to its education, its professions, and its intellectual and professional communities. Those less familiar with international law, the general public, civil society activists, students, and others should be provided with more pedagogical and approachable legal instruments, as Hodgson seems to suggest. Substantially, Judge Hodgson's decision reproduces the findings of the Pre-Trial Chamber on jurisdiction and admissibility.

The second objective of this feminist rewriting relates to the qualification of Simone Gbagbo's role in the examination of the 'reasonable grounds' test. The rewritten decision introduces supplementary information on Simone Gbagbo, thereby altering the way in which her personality, political importance, and agency are presented. In contrast to the original decision in which Simone Gbagbo is predominantly and repeatedly represented as the wife of Laurent Gbagbo, as if an auxiliary to 'her husband',[4] the rewritten judgment mentions the circumstance that Simone Gbagbo is married to Laurent Gbagbo only once. At a later part of the

[4] This language is used (three) times as a synonym of Laurent Gbagbo in § 10 of the decision.

decision, Judge Hodgson refers to Simone Gbagbo's 'relationship with Laurent Gbagbo', without specifying it. The fact that Laurent Gbagbo was, at the time of the alleged crimes, the president or the ex-president of Côte d'Ivoire, is noted only once.

In contrast to framing Simone Gbagbo in the Pre-Trial Chamber (para. 10) as the wife who was ideologically and professionally very close to her husband, the rewritten decision presents an inner circle 'comprising individuals occupying formal and informal positions in Mr Gbagbo's government' (para. 24), of which Simone Gbagbo is a member. Under the heading 'Whether There Are Reasonable Grounds to Believe That Ms Gbagbo Is Criminally Responsible for the Crimes Alleged by the Prosecutor', Judge Hodgson's decision introduces specific reasons why Simone Gbagbo should be considered an indirect co-perpetrator under Article 25(3)(a) of the Statute. The image that appears is not that of a wife following the president-husband, who even (mischievously?) 'acted as an alter ego for her husband' (PTC para. 10) but a power-couple of two independent, notable, long-term politicians at the centre of the inner circle of the Côte d'Ivoire government.

The rewritten decision details, for example, that 'Ms Gbagbo had her own cabinet within the presidency with its own staff. In a country where women are significantly underrepresented in political positions, Ms Gbagbo was an active decision maker and possessed significant political power' (para. 34). That power has a history in 'her long political career', including the fact that she was a 'founding member' of the *Front populaire ivorien* (para. 35). Thereafter, Judge Hodgson refers to elements concerning meetings, military equipment, and orders given to militias. These matters were also addressed in the original decision but Judge Hodgson emphasises them differently to suggest that Simone Gbagbo was able to 'exercise joint control over the crimes' (para. 38), 'made a co-ordinated and essential contribution to the crime' (para. 39), and 'acted with the necessary degree of intent and knowledge in performing her role within the common plan' (para. 40).

Judge Hodgson provides a more substantiated analysis of Simone Gbagbo's role than in the original judgment by demonstrating that the legal requirements for issuing a warrant of arrest are independent (of 'the husband'). She explains how Simone Gbagbo's arrest warrant depends, in accordance with Article 58(1) and in addition to the reasonable grounds test addressed above, on whether the arrest is necessary to: (i) ensure her appearance before the Court; (ii) ensure that she does not use her connections and resources to obstruct or endanger the investigation; and (iii) prevent the further commission of crimes within the jurisdiction of the Court. The rewritten decision proceeds to analyse these aspects individually, relying on ICC case law, commenting in paragraph 44 on how:

> A person's past and present political position, international contacts, financial and professional background, their access to necessary networks and financial resources, and the likely length of any potential sentence are factors that might increase the

> risk that an individual will abscond or avoid arrest.[5] Additionally, a person's access to networks and financial status is a relevant factor in determining whether they have the means to interfere with the investigation or safety of witnesses.[6]

The decision then replies to these requirements, stating how Simone Gbagbo has a 'long political history and strong political connections throughout Côte d'Ivoire' and that 'her supporters have called for her release and oppose her transfer to the ICC' (para. 45). On international connections, the decision details that Simone Gbagbo 'has studied abroad in Senegal and France, as well as having completed multiple international training courses' (para. 46). The decision suggests that these connections 'could assist her to abscond' (para. 46). Furthermore, Judge Hodgson's decision notes that 'the Prosecutor has provided evidence that Ms Gbagbo has access to significant financial resources' (para. 46), and that her 'connection to high-profile members of the former government and her relationship with Mr Gbagbo might also assist her to access relevant contacts and resources in order to abscond' (para. 46).

To strengthen the arrest warrant further, Judge Hodgson's decision introduces additional information on the situation in Côte d'Ivoire at the moment of the consideration of the arrest warrant. It refers to allegations about previous concealing of 'crimes committed by members of the inner circle' (para. 55), and provides information on how 'supporters of Ms Gbagbo are currently discussing strategies for regaining political power in Côte d'Ivoire. The pro-Gbagbo forces that remain loyal to Ms Gbagbo and the other members of the inner circle continue to have access to significant material resources, including weapons' (para. 49).

The rewriting culminates in a section entitled 'Concluding Comments' that starts with the following statement: 'Ms Gbagbo is the first woman to be the subject of an application for an arrest warrant before this Court' (para. 51). As such a section is not habitual in ICC or other international criminal court decisions, it somewhat diminishes the impression of reading a 'real' decision of the ICC Pre-Trial Chamber. But it certainly allows Judge Hodgson to be more explicit about her message. After explaining – in a scholarly manner – how women's general under-representation in politics and the military has meant the rarity of their qualification as suspects or accused in international criminal trials, the rewriting returns to a more judge-like voice: 'The issue before this Court is not whether Ms Gbagbo's conduct

5 Decision on the Prosecutor's Application for a Warrant of Arrest against Jean-Pierre Bemba Gombo, *Prosecutor v. John-Pierre Bemba Gombo* (ICC-01/05-01/08-14-tENG), Pre-Trial Chamber III, 10 June 2008, § 87; Judgment on the Appeal of the Prosecutor against Pre-Trial Chamber II's Decision on the Interim Release of Jean-Pierre Bemba Gombo and Convening Hearings with the Kingdom of Belgium, the Republic of Portugal, the Republic of France, the Federal Republic of Germany, the Italian Republic, and the Republic of South Africa, *Prosecutor v. John-Pierre Bemba Gombo* (ICC-01/05-01/08-631-Red), Appeals Chamber, 2 December 2009, § 70.

6 Judgment on the Appeal of the Prosecutor against Pre-Trial Chamber II's Decision, *supra* note 5, §§ 44, 74.

adhered to the traditional gender roles that woman are expected to perform, or whether Ms Gbagbo should be punished for her relationship with her husband, but rather the extent to which Ms Gbagbo herself is or is not guilty of perpetrating international crimes' (para. 53, footnote omitted).

The Female Perpetrator of International Crimes as a Hard Case for Feminism(s)

An astute academic article authored by Natalie Hodgson that precedes the rewriting project by several years helpfully adds background and nuances to her reimagined judgment.[7] In her article, stereotypes regarding gender, femininity, violence, and conflict that shape legal discourses are analysed and deconstructed in the cases of six defendants in international criminal courts. Hodgson identifies three narratives used in international criminal courts to frame women defendants: mother, monster, and wife,[8] and localises them via discourse analysis in the case materials. Regarding the ICC case of Simone Gbagbo, one of the six analysed in the article, Hodgson suggests that motherly characteristics of Gbagbo are referred to by the defence. The article quotes Côte d'Ivoire's challenge to the admissibility of Simone Gbagbo's case: 'She has devoted most of her adult life, striving to advance the education of the people of Côte d'Ivoire in so far as they came under her sphere of influence in general and the women and children of Abidjan in particular.'[9]

For Hodgson, 'the use of motherly attributes' in the case of Simone Gbagbo 'suggests that the themes of domesticity and motherhood pervade all stages of a female defendant's case, and that females are analysed with respect to these themes even when the defendant's character or conduct is not the main issue before the court'.[10] Pertinently, she gives primary importance in Simone Gbagbo's case to the wife narrative by the ICC prosecution and the Pre-Trial Chamber. The language used, such as the recurrent choice of the word 'husband', 'emphasises the personal

7 N. Hodgson, 'Gender Justice or Gendered Justice? Female Defendants in International Criminal Tribunals' 25 *Feminist Legal Studies* (2017) 337–357.

8 See also L. Sjoberg and C. Gentry, *Mothers, Monsters, Whores: Women's Violence in Global Politics* (London: Zed Books, 2007); C. Gentry and L. Sjoberg, *Beyond Mothers, Monsters, Whores: Thinking about Women's Violence in Global Politics* (London: Zed Books, 2015); C. Sperling, 'Mother of Atrocities: Pauline Nyiramasuhuko's Role in the Rwandan Genocide' 33(2) *Fordham Urban Law Journal* (2006) 637–127, at 653–656; D. Brown, *The Beautiful Beast: The Life and Crimes of SS-Aufseherin Irma Grese* (Ventura, CA: Golden West Historical Publications, 1996); U. Weckel and E. Wolfrum, *'Bestien' und 'Befehlsempfänger': Frauen und Männer in NS-Prozessen nach 1945* (Göttingen: Vandenhoeck & Ruprecht, 2003); N. Hogg, 'Women's Participation in the Rwandan Genocide: Mothers or Monsters?' 92 *International Review of the Red Cross* (2010) 69–102.

9 Hodgson, *supra* note 7, at 346, referring to *Prosecutor v. Ghagbo* Response on behalf of Simone Gbagbo to the 'Requête de la République de Côte d'Ivoire sur la recevabilité de l'affaire, le Procureur c. Simone Gbagbo et demande de sursis à exécution en vertu des articles 17, 19 et 95 du Statut de Rome' (ICC-02/11-01/12-39), Pre-Trial Chamber II, 8 April 2014.

10 Hodgson *supra* note 7, at 346.

and familial connection between the two'.[11] The patriarchal stereotyping appears most striking in how the Pre-Trial Chamber presupposes that the motivation for Simone Gbagbo's alleged crimes was not to retain her own political power or her political party's power, as is granted to be the case for the inner circle of President Gbagbo, but rather 'her husband's power'.[12]

How does other academic scholarship in criminology, sociology, history, and criminal law see perpetrator women? There is a broad concordance about the starting point that women's participation in violent crime is significantly minor in quantity compared to that of men, and that women's participation differs in quality.[13] I entitled this section 'The Female Perpetrator of *International Crimes* as a Hard Case for Feminism(s)' to mark a focus in a discussion that risks exceeding the limited space available. Why call the female perpetrator of international crimes a hard case? I try to explain by a short excursion into the narratives of women in international law and their incompatibility with the real-life eventuality of women's transgression to perpetration of international crimes.

Women have a history of perpetrating international crimes, including sexual violence against women and men, at all levels of responsibility.[14] National trials after World War II and the armed conflicts and episodes of large-scale violence in the Democratic Republic of Congo (DRC), Rwanda, and former Yugoslavia, to name only a few, have dealt with the criminal responsibility of women, including women who committed direct violence. Women prosecuted in international criminal trials have so far been accused as indirect perpetrators, indirect co-perpetrators, and involved in joint criminal enterprise. Despite these examples, the paradigmatic image of women in international criminal justice remains that of victims of sexual and gendered violence. That is likely to relate the arguably essentialised, ahistorical notions and narrative strategies of women's general propensity to preserve life,

[11] *Ibid*, at 349–350.

[12] *Ibid*, at 350, referring to the Pre-Trial Chamber decision.

[13] N. Rafter and E. A. Stanko, *Judge, Lawyer, Victim, Thief: Women, Gender Roles, and Criminal Justice* (Boston, MA: Northeastern University Press, 1982); C. Cardi and G. Pruvost, 'Thinking Women's Violence' 5 *History of the Present* (2015) 200–216.

[14] For examples of literature, see K. Allar, 'Setting the Picture Straight: The Ordinary Women of Nazi Germany and Rwanda Who Participated in Genocide' in K. Auerbach (ed.), *Aftermath – Genocide, Memory and History* (Melbourne: Monash University Press, 2015); S. Linton, 'Women Accused of International Crimes: A Trans-Disciplinary Inquiry and Methodology' 27(2) *Criminal Law Forum* (2016) 159–226; S. Brown, 'Female Perpetrators of the Rwandan Genocide' 16 *International Feminist Journal of Politics* (2014) 448–469; L. Sharlach, 'Gender and Genocide in Rwanda: Women as Agents and Objects of Genocide' 1(3) *Journal of Genocide Research* (1999) 387–399; S. Tabak, 'False Dichotomies of Transitional Justice: Gender, Conflict and Combatants in Colombia' 44 *NYU Journal of International Law and Policy* (2011) 103–161; A. Jones, 'Gender and Genocide in Rwanda' 4 *Journal of Genocide Research* (2002) 65–94; A. Smeulers, 'Female Perpetrators: Ordinary or Extra-ordinary Women?' 15(2) *International Criminal Law Review* (2015) 207–253.

aversion to violence, or otherwise higher values, hardly leaving space for deviance, violence, and crimes by women.[15]

Women's history in international law, as its explicit objects, subjects, agents, and actors, is typically considered short and modest, but perhaps it is more adequately qualified as obscured and ignored.[16] The red line can be sketched in a few main roles and routes in diverse temporalities, grossly simplified. Women are seen to have entered international law as pacifists acting in the law against war; as empathetic and solidary carers for others in international humanitarian law and abolition of slavery;[17] as equal citizens in the advocacy for suffrage and women's rights more broadly, and as victims of sexual and gendered violence; experts of it and combatants against it in international criminal law.[18] These roles remain to a large extent, despite the diverse contexts, marked by gendered assumptions of women's character and moral disposition, and not least by women themselves.

Should that situation be 'redressed' and if yes, how? Sociological and physical limits to women's role as direct perpetrators are diminishing, as women more broadly access positions of leadership in various contexts and modern weapons technologies provide an array of 'smart' solutions for conducting warfare.[19] For legal

[15] See M. A. Drumbl, '"She Makes Me Ashamed to Be a Woman": The Genocide Conviction of Pauline Nyiramasuhuko, 2011' 34 *Michigan Journal of International Law* (2013) 559–603; H. Charlesworth, 'Are Women Peaceful? Reflections on the Role of Women in Peace-Building' 16(3) *Feminist Legal Studies* (2008) 347–361; J. York, 'The Truth about Women and Peace' in L. A. Lorentzen and J. Turpin (eds.), *The Women and War Reader* (New York: New York University Press, 1998) 19–25; K. Engle, 'Judging Sex in War' 106 *Michigan Law Review* (2008) 941–961; C. Coutler, 'Female Fighters in the Sierra Leone War: Challenging the Assumptions?' 88 *Feminist Review* (2008) 54–73.

[16] See generally I. Tallgren (ed.), *Portraits of Women in International Law: New Names and Forgotten Faces?* (Oxford: Oxford University Press, 2023).

[17] J. G. Gardam, 'The Law of Armed Conflict: A Gendered Regime?' in D. G. Dallmeyer (ed.), *Reconceiving Reality: Women and International Law*, Studies in Transnational Legal Policy No. 25 (Washington, DC: ASIL, 1993) 174–175.

[18] K. Askin, 'Gender Crimes Jurisprudence in the ICTR: Positive Developments' 3 *Journal of International Criminal Justice* (2005) 1007–1018; K. L. King and M. Greening, 'Gender Justice or Just Gender? The Role of Gender in Sexual Assault Decisions at the International Criminal Tribunal for Former Yugoslavia' 88 *Social Science Quarterly* (2007) 1049–1071; C. MacKinnon, 'The ICTR's Legacy on Sexual Violence' 14 *New England Journal of International and Comparative Law* (2008) 211–221. For critical views, see J. Halley, 'Rape in Berlin: Reconsidering the Criminalisation of Rape in the International Law of Armed Conflict' 9(1) *Melbourne Journal of International Law* (2008) 78–124; J. Halley, 'Rape in Rome: Feminist Interventions in the Criminalization of Sex-Related Violence in Positive International Criminal Law' 30(1) *Michigan Journal of International Law* (2008) 1–123; K. Engle, *The Grip of Sexual Violence in Conflict: Feminist Interventions in International Law* (Redwood City, CA: Stanford University Press, 2020).

[19] See S. A. Labenski, 'The Importance of Women as Villains and Violators: Scenes from the ICTY, the ICTR, and Abu Ghraib', Master's thesis, June 2013, American University of Cairo. On women's agency in armed conflict and political violence, see C. Moser and F. Clark (eds.), *Victims, Perpetrators or Actors? Gender, Armed Conflict and Political Violence* (London: Zed Books, 2001). On the 'prototypical constructions' of women as non-combatants, 'the Beautiful

academic Doris Buss, asking 'where are the women?' directs us to roles and places often obscured in dominant narratives and 'opens up a range of questions about what war and armed conflict are, how they are understood, practiced, and represented, and how women and men, femininities and masculinities, are involved in and produced through war'.[20] Diversity of women's and men's real experiences in conflict, including violence and criminality, should be 'recognized as valid, rather than being excluded from the discourse or reduced to stereotype'.[21]

Many commentaries suggest that international criminal trials have a role in 'writing history'.[22] From that perspective, the transformation of gender balance of the benches in international criminal trials may also alter the authorship of histories about violence and international crime. The unease that persists regarding women's perpetuation of international crimes is, however, also current, perhaps in particular amongst women, and feminists. The infamous photos of Karen England's and other US personnel's cruel violence on detainees in Abu Ghraib prison in Iraq shocked because, as one commentator put it, 'this is not how women are expected to behave. Feminism taught me 30 years ago that not only had women gotten a raw deal from men, we were morally superior to them. When it came to distinguishing right from wrong, the needle of our compass always pointed to true north'.[23]

On the IntLawGrls, a website on women and international law, a blog series titled 'Women in Nuremberg' celebrated women amongst the prosecutorial staff and defence counsels, as well as staffers, interpreters, and journalists. In contrast, the very few women accused of international crimes were barely mentioned, with the suggestion they are 'Not Our Sisters'.[24] As the editors noted, '[t]he crimes of which these women were convicted ought to be unimaginable, and will remain, here at least, unprintable'.[25] The desire to identify only with the positive accomplishments of women remains. It has, however, been met with scholarship striving to dissipate the obscurity surrounding women perpetrators in crimes of totalitarian regimes. A branch of German and international academic discussion on Nazi criminality has since the 1980s sought an end to 'the rituals of innocence in the women's

Soul', and men as fighters, 'the Just Warrior', see J. B. Elshtain, *Women and War* (New York: Basic Books, 1987).

20 D. Buss, 'Seeing Sexual Violence in Conflict and Post-Conflict Societies: The Limits of Visibility' in D. Buss et al. (eds.), *Sexual Violence in Conflict and Post-Conflict Societies: International Agendas and African Contexts* (New York: Routledge, 2014) 3, at 5.

21 H. Durham and K. O'Byrne, 'The Dialogue of Difference: Gender Perspectives on International Humanitarian Law' 92(877) *International Review of the Red Cross* (2010) 31–52, at 51.

22 E.g. L. Douglas, *The Memory of Judgment: Making Law and History in the Trials of the Holocaust* (New Haven, CT: Yale University Press, 2001).

23 M. J. Melone, 'We've come a long, and wrong, way', *St. Petersburg Times*, 7 May 2004.

24 B. Van Schaack, 'Not Our Sisters', INTLAWGRRLS, 31 July 2007, on file with author.

25 *Ibid.*

movement and in women's history'.[26] In international (criminal) law, this turn is in the making, and the rewritten decision of Simone Gbagbo's arrest warrant makes an important contribution to it.

Complementarity Test in Simone Gbagbo's Admissibility Decision, Prosecutor v. Simone Gbagbo, *Decision on Côte d'Ivoire's Challenge to the Admissibility of the Case against Simone Gbagbo*

In the five years from the first International Law Commission (ILC) draft in 1993 for a statute of an international criminal court to the adoption of the Rome Statute in the 1998 diplomatic conference attended by the delegations representing 161 states, the issue of delimitation of the international and national criminal jurisdiction was among the most difficult to negotiate.[27] The solutions found, substantially in Article 17 entitled 'Issues of Admissibility', packaged together with Article 20 on '*Ne bis in idem*', became parts of a multifarious compromise package that made the adoption possible. As the lengthy Articles 18–19 spell out, the concrete application of the delimitation was likely to become cumbersome. Articles 17–20 are typically read in connection with the preamble of the Statute's tenth paragraph, 'Emphasizing that the International Criminal Court established under this Statute shall be complementary to national criminal jurisdictions'. This paragraph provides the origin of the discourse on 'the complementarity principle'.[28]

This legal and doctrinal landscape on complementarity is at the centre of Judge Sarah Easy's 'Separate and dissenting opinion' to Pre-Trial Chamber I decision on Côte d'Ivoire's challenge to the admissibility of the case against Simone Gbagbo. Judge Easy explains the motivation of her dissent as follows: 'In governing the relationship between the (ICC) and domestic criminal courts, Article 17(1)(a) is of great consequence for women and minority groups for whom such institutions have historically been unavailable or ineffective in securing justice.'[29] The dissent relates

[26] See C. Koonz, *Mothers in the Fatherland* (New York: St. Martin's Press, 1987); L. Gravenshort and C. Tatschmurat (eds.), *Töchter-Fragen, NS-Frauen-Geschichte* (Freiburg im Breisgau: Kore, 1990); G. Bock, 'Equality and Difference in National Socialist Racism' in J. Scott (ed.), *Feminism and History* (Oxford: Oxford University Press, 1996) 267–290; J. Stephenson, *Women in Nazi Germany* (London: Routledge, 2001); Weckel and Wolfrum *supra* note 8; K. Kompisch, *Täterinnen: Frauen im Nationalsozialismus* (Köln: Böhlau, 2008).

[27] W. A. Schabas and M. M. El Zeidy, 'Article 17: Issues of Admissibility' in O. Triffterer and K. Ambos (eds.), *The Rome Statute of the International Criminal Court: A Commentary* (3rd ed., London: Bloomsbury, 2016) 781–831; D. N. Ntanda Nsereko, 'Article 18: Preliminary Rulings Regarding Admissibility' in O. Triffterer and K. Ambos (eds.), *The Rome Statute of the International Criminal Court: A Commentary* (3rd ed., London: Bloomsbury 2016) 832–848; I. Tallgren and A. Reisinger Coracini, 'Article 20: Ne bis in idem' in O. Triffterer and K. Ambos (eds.), *The Rome Statute of the International Criminal Court: A Commentary* (3rd ed., London: Bloomsbury, 2016) 899–931.

[28] 1998 Rome Statute of the International Criminal Court, 2187 UNTS 3, preamble.

[29] Separate and Dissenting Opinion of Judge Sarah Easy, § 5 (footnote omitted).

to how the Pre-Trial Chamber arrived at its conclusion to dismiss the inadmissibility challenge by Côte d'Ivoire. In doing so, Judge Easy dismisses the Pre-Trial Chamber's decision.

Judge Easy's feminist reimagining rejects the Pre-Trial Chamber I use of the 'same person/same conduct' test as being too narrow and vague.[30] In doing so, she refers to the language used in the Appeals Chamber decision on Libya's appeal against the Pre-Trial Decision in the case against Saif Al-Islam Gaddafi.[31] In this case, the Appeals Chamber dismissed the admissibility challenge by Libya. In her judgment, Judge Easy regrets that the Pre-Trial Chamber 'has not seized the opportunity to further clarify the content of this [same person/same conduct] test and address the gender justice concerns arising out of its application'.[32] At this point, it is necessary to return to the observations about the context of the feminist redrafting exercise that I started with. Who were the judges deciding the case that is now 'reimagined'? Silvia Fernández de Gurmendi (presiding), Ekaterina Tredafilova, and Christine Van den Wyngaert. A bench of three women resorted to an interpretation that is, to quote Easy, 'likely [to] operate in a discriminatory manner against women who are statistically significantly more likely to be victims of sexual and gender-based violence, by precluding them from seeking redress at both the national and international level'.[33]

The main critique of Judge Easy's dissent is, however, not directed at the Pre-Trial Chamber's decision, but the state of Côte d'Ivoire, its legal system, judiciary, and 'court and law enforcement personnel'.[34] The sharp rewriting fails to pay attention to the history of Côte d'Ivoire's relationship with the ICC as a movement towards a closer relation – the acceptance of its jurisdiction as a non-state party in 2003, the *proprio motu* investigation in 2011, state party to the Rome Statute in 2013. In contrast, Judge Easy underlines that the court must exercise 'the expressive function of denouncing state conduct which fosters impunity',[35] having inquired about the quality and the conduct of the national law enforcement authorities and judiciary. This position mirrors a contentious aspect in the Statute negotiations that the Court has tried not to dwell on extensively in its case law.

Judge Easy explains how 'evidence before me indicates that entrenched discriminatory attitudes towards women and girls in Côte d'Ivoire present a significant barrier to the genuine investigation of incidents of sexual and gender-based violence'.[36] She quotes at length a report by an NGO describing shocking events of

30 *Ibid*, § 4.

31 Judgment on the Appeal of Libya against the Decision of Pre-Trial Chamber I of 31 May 2013 entitled 'Decision on the Admissibility of the Case against Saif Al-Islam Gaddafi', *Gaddafi and Al-Senussi* (ICC-01/11-01/11), Appeals Chamber, 21 May 2014.

32 Separate Opinion of Judge Easy, § 5.

33 *Ibid*, § 9.

34 *Ibid*, § 32.

35 *Ibid*, § 24.

36 *Ibid*, § 27.

sexual and gendered violence in detail.[37] She further finds that there is evidence suggesting 'that the pervasive trivialisation of these crimes is so significant that even if the justice system had not been disrupted by political turmoil and conflict, lacunae in the prosecution of sexual and gender-based crimes would prevail'.[38] Judge Easy further argues that 'gender-based discrimination is not only practised by the general population but evinced by the very institutions charged with effecting justice. Of great concern is the systematic encouragement by the Ivorian police for the victims to seek an amicable solution with their rapist'.[39]

I am, firstly, surprised by how this feminist rewriting outright refuses to consider whether any co-operation with or support to the Côte d'Ivoire authorities would be meaningful.[40] While Judge Easy mentions the efforts of the UN operation in Côte d'Ivoire (UNOCI) to train the national and local police in sexual and gender-based violence, they are considered as 'unlikely to have a transformative effect ... due to the nature of structural discrimination which is omnipresent across economic and socio-political spheres'.[41] Judge Easy appears to choose a straightforward polarisation of the national and the international jurisdiction – an outcome the Rome Statute negotiators struggled to avoid.[42] Her decision flags the prioritisation of international law and the 'international community', trusting both with inherently superior qualities, at least regarding the interests of women and girls. The ICC is presented as being able and potentially willing to completely take over the administration of criminal justice in Côte d'Ivoire. The domestic judiciary and administration of the post-colonial state are painted in indelible dark colours, as a despicable nest of violence, brutality, and injustice. Consideration is given exclusively to the interests of victimised women, in particular those who relate to the ICC favourably, potentially having received attention and promises of international reparations to be granted subsequently

A second issue with Judge Easy's feminist reimagining is the exclusive focus on criminal trials, and on punishment in particular. A prison sentence as lengthy as possible is considered the only ever acceptable consequence for perpetrators of any sexual violence.[43] No empirical evidence is deemed necessary by Judge Easy to demonstrate the explicit and extraordinary value of international criminal trials from

[37] *Ibid*, § 31.

[38] *Ibid*, § 32

[39] *Ibid*, § 32 (footnote omitted).

[40] For a remarkable recent volume on the possibilities and challenges of accountability in several African countries, see E. C. Lubaale and N. Dyani-Mhango, *National Accountability for International Crimes in Africa* (London: Palgrave Macmillan, 2022). For a study on the earlier practice, S. Nouwen, *Complementarity in the Line of Fire: The Catalysing Effect of the International Criminal Court in Uganda and Sudan* (Cambridge: Cambridge University Press, 2013).

[41] Separate Opinion of Judge Easy, § 32.

[42] Schabas and El Zeidy, *supra* note 27; Ntanda Nsereko, *supra* note 27; Tallgren and Reisinger Coracini, *supra* note 27.

[43] See Separate Opinion of Judge Easy, § 33.

the point of view of victims, for example, or the societal effects of international punishments, in general.[44] This certainty of the superiority of international criminal justice departs from scholarship searching also for alternative, not criminal prosecution-based models of resolution of conflicts in transitional justice or more broadly in post-conflict societies.[45] It contrasts with the experience that 'in terms of the relative significance of the local fit and international frame in retributive justice outcomes for women, international norms must always work their influence through the filter of domestic structures and domestic norms'.[46] Judge Easy's separate and dissenting opinion is not so inclined; instead it sees as a particular risk 'the prevalence of customary law, particularly in northern rural regions' (of Côte d'Ivoire) which 'further enshrines structural discrimination and inadequate protections for victims of sexual violence'.[47]

Further, Judge Easy's dissent does not introduce any attempt to balance the goal of retribution with other interests, such as granting a fair trial to the accused. This might be because of gendered assumptions about the identity of the parties in a criminal trial at the ICC: the male perpetrators and the female victims, notwithstanding the current case. Judge Easy admits that the Court has established that 'the assessment of the conduct forming the subject of domestic proceedings in the context of an admissibility challenge must focus on the underlying incidents and not their legal characterisation'.[48] That the reasons for that position can be seen as diverse, including the acknowledgement of the heterogeneity of legal cultures, criminal law, and justice systems in the world, is not addressed.

There is a connection, as Judge Easy also notes, to the *ne bis in idem* principle in Article 20, 'which protects the accused from double penalisation of the same acts under different labels of criminality'.[49] Easy 'regret[s]', however, 'that this interpretation is likely to adversely impact victims ... by confining the ambit of recognition and reparations available to those prescribed for ordinary crimes'.[50] She further undertakes an astute, if somewhat complex, examination of the procedural and doctrinal minutiae of Articles 17 and 20 in light of the growing ICC case law to ground her conclusions. Because of the various 'significant barriers to justice for women and girls in Côte d'Ivoire, it cannot be said that the ongoing investigation into Ms Simone Gbagbo's criminality' by the justice system of Côte d'Ivoire

44 F. Jessberger and J. Geneuss (eds.), *Why Punish Perpetrators of Mass Atrocities? Purposes of Punishment in International Criminal Law* (Cambridge: Cambridge University Press, 2020).

45 For discussion, see e.g. L. Yarwood (ed.), *Women and Transitional Justice* (Abingdon: Routledge, 2013); C. O'Rourke, *Gender Politics in Transitional Justice* (Abingdon: Routledge, 2013).

46 O'Rourke, *supra* note 45, at 96.

47 Separate Opinion of Judge Easy, § 32.

48 *Ibid*, § 12.

49 *Ibid*.

50 *Ibid*.

'constitutes a genuine investigation',[51] Judge Easy believes. She therefore concurs 'with the Majority in finding that the present case is admissible before the Court'.[52]

Judge Sarah Easy's feminist rewriting has the merit of strong internal consistency: it makes the legal and procedural interests of female victims of sexual and gender-based violence in an international criminal trial the superior, if not the only, objective of the ICC. A concern I have with the approach used by Judge Easy is that should one wish to extend the reflection to potential real-life consequences of this rewriting for Ivorians in the narrated context, several challenges appear. Who (that is, what constituency of power) guarantees the sustainability of such an exclusively punitive policy? In the tensions of the fragile 'international community', with its wavering and often racialised policies of international criminal justice, the ICC has so far been struggling annually to gather the financial resources for its functioning. Its longevity is a real concern: in the reimagined situation of Côte d'Ivoire, what happens to the victims when the odds are reversed in the ICC and the international crews pack their bags to focus on another situation?

The decision therefore gives reason to inquire about the nature of 'justice' in a feminism where everything should be sacrificed for the ambition of 'saving' a number of 'women and girls' from the hands of their own malicious post-colonial state, its authorities, customary law, the legal profession as a whole, denounced for 'conduct which fosters impunity',[53] 'weak effort',[54] 'pervasive trivialisation of these crimes'[55] – to such a fatal and lasting extent that even any future proceedings 'of such crimes would likely not be considered genuine'.[56] I am not ignorant of or insensitive to the suffering and injustices encountered by individuals and communities facing or having faced sexual violence. Rather, I wish to take issue with the feminist anti-impunity position upon which Judge Easy's reasoning is based, and I would like to respectfully encourage open discussions on the civilisational assumptions of feminist approaches that emphasise international criminal prosecutions at the expense of the (post-colonial, African) national state and its own efforts towards post-conflict justice.

The issue could be approached in terms of universalism of international criminal law and 'women's rights', opposing them to particularism(s), local culture, as early post-colonial feminist theory did.[57] Yet, to my understanding, the main questions are no longer there. After the 'Me Too' movement and the global backlash on feminism (s), including the deplorable spectacle of annihilation of the Women, Peace and

[51] *Ibid*, § 34.
[52] *Ibid*, § 35.
[53] *Ibid*, § 24.
[54] *Ibid*, § 31.
[55] *Ibid*, § 33.
[56] *Ibid*.
[57] See e.g. R. Lewis and S. Mills (eds.), *Feminist Postcolonial Theory: A Reader* (Edinburgh: Edinburgh University Press, 2003).

Security agenda in Afghanistan since 2021, is it plausible to argue for some imagined perfection, a superiority of legal protection of women's rights or universal 'international law' safeguarding women's interests at the *centre* that could be as clearly juxtaposed with its 'lack' in the *periphery*?[58] Women's lives and their rights, their bare existence, to start with their physical inviolability, sexuality, and their political and economic survival as members of society are globally under threat or already attacked, be it in Finland, Australia, the United States, or Côte d'Ivoire. Why should feminist reimagining so resolutely turn its back on the possibilities of exchanges and collaboration between the local, national, and international judiciary and law enforcement – experts, judicial personnel, representatives of victims? Finally, whose interests are served by excluding any chance of a transformative reform in Côte d'Ivoire as a whole: what does such a hopeless image, as one of 'The Dark Corners of the World',[59] convey to Ivorians of the future of their own democratic state?

THE REMAINS OF THE REWRITING

I have raised many questions in the preceding pages, such as the following: Is feminist reimagining constrained by the international law in force and its established structures, its sediments of institutional practice, formed when (almost) all women, their ideas and interests were absent? How should feminism(s) relate to that long absence, so full of consequences for current law and jurisprudence? Should a feminist remain always combative or rather try to show resilience – to whom? I started my reflections by calling for attention to the contexts in which feminist rewriting takes place. In the instructions for this fascinating project, the rewriters were invited to imagine themselves in the same position of knowledge as the ICC judges were at the time of rendering their decisions. Inside the frames formed by that rule, the authors have creatively searched for ways to change, to transform, to remedy, by rewriting decisions of the ICC.

The two rewritten decisions discussed above reflect diverse and to some extent contradictory desires. Natalie Hodgson's rewriting aims, primarily, at discrediting certain stereotypical categorisations of the roles and behaviour of women and men, deconstructing the discursive choices of the original decision and offering a new rationality for approaching perpetration of international crimes. In that sense, and in my subjective understanding, it is primarily based on the rationale of emancipation of women aiming at a formal equality of sexes and genders. The second rewriting by Sarah Easy is feminist in a different manner, more frontal and ambitious in how it

[58] R. Kapur, '"The First Feminist War in All History": Epistemic Shifts and Relinquishing the Mission to Rescue the "Other Woman"' 116 *AJIL Unbound* (2022) 270–274; K. Bennoune, 'Multi-Directionality and Universality: Global Feminisms and International Law in the Twenty-First Century' 116 *AJIL Unbound* (2022) 275–280.

[59] J. Reynolds and S. Xavier, '"The Dark Corners of the World": TWAIL and international Criminal Justice' 14(4) *Journal of International Criminal Justice* 959–983.

aims at rewriting the political architecture of the Rome Statute: its (in)famous oscillation between the acknowledgement of national sovereignty, the past status quo of impunity and the complementary international criminal jurisdiction. The impression of a categorical, civilisational dismissal of the ailing post-colonial state is a risk that I have touched on.

Beyond the temporal contexts, feminist reimagining can be approached in terms of the places of rewriting, the situations of the exercise in geographical, political, cultural spaces, languages, and discourses: the locations of, firstly, committing the alleged international crimes, secondly, taking the original decision, and thirdly, the feminist rewriting each flavour the exercise. How do feminism(s) relate to populations, languages, everyday lived experiences 'on the ground' of the interventions of international criminal courts and tribunals in 'the situation of Côte d'Ivoire'?

The violence addressed as (alleged) international crimes by the prosecutor of the ICC in The Hague took place in Côte d'Ivoire, a state that became independent from its colonisation by France in 1960.[60] The international crimes were allegedly committed both by and against nationals or residents of Côte d'Ivoire, a population of 29 million. Seventy-eight languages are spoken in Côte d'Ivoire.[61] The official language, imposed during the colonial period, is French, currently understood by an estimated 80 per cent of the population.[62] It is the language used in the media, election campaigns, and the administration of justice. The literacy rate at the time of the alleged violence (2012) was 40.98 per cent.[63] The latest estimation (2019) is 89.89 per cent.[64]

The feminist rewriting took place in Australia and the United Kingdom, by native speakers of English. The draft decisions discussed in November 2022 contained no or few references to local academic or media sources or other locally produced knowledge about Côte d'Ivoire. In that sense, the feminist justice rendered may appear, from the point of view of the local population, its academic scholars, media, and civil society, to remain as distanced from the contexts of everyday life and of the violence, the victims, and the perpetrators as the regular ICC practice has been critically claimed to be.[65] A difference of importance exists, however, in how the ICC judges have access to a dedicated staff researching, collecting, translating, interpreting, analysing, and synthesising materials, and writing drafts of the decisions. Part of that work became available for the feminist rewriters via documents of

60 See e.g. www.agi-ivoiriens.com/cote_ivoire/cote_ivoire_histoire.html; J. N. Loucou, *Côte d'Ivoire: les résistances à la conquête coloniale* (Abidjan: Éditions CERAP, 2007).

61 Ethnologue, 'Côte d'Ivoire', available at www.ethnologue.com/country/CI/.

62 *La langue française dans le monde: Édition 2019* (Paris: Gallimard and OIF, 2019).

63 www.indexmundi.com/facts/c%C3%B4te-d%27ivoire/indicator/SE.ADT.LITR.ZS.

64 *Ibid.*

65 For a recent contribution, see O. Ba, K.-J. Bluen, and O. Owiso, 'The Geopolitics of Race, Empire, and Expertise at the ICC', *International Studies* (Oxford: Oxford Research Encyclopedia of International Studies, 2023).

the Court. The pro bono feminist judgment authors we are reading in this volume had no or very limited means at their disposal to engage translators, for example.

Distance can be seen in a positive light, as an element of impartiality, an intrinsic value in criminal justice. Even more so, one could argue, in a situation of violence that could be qualified as 'political violence' since it occurs, in the narrative of the ICC at least, between adherents to conflicting political parties in a national state. Distance may, however, also cause ignorance, so that the knowledge and experiences of the distant other – 'the Other' of what is close/known – are neglected or marginalised. Lack of local sources of information in making decisions in a central question of a particular society can signal indifference, or at worst a standing as hierarchically superior masters who believe they should have the last word. Here I would make a distinction between the legal questions of jurisdiction and competence and the intellectual, value-based positionings, bearing in mind how 'feminist justice' is at times associated with aspirations towards the experience of a palpable, human, material justice by the persons concerned, eventually engaged in dialogues, and less concerned for the formal procedures.

In that sense, the astute rewritings discussed here do not exhaust the possibilities of a feminist reimagining of Côte d'Ivoire. As we have been invited in this project to think 'outside the box', I shall shortly try to explain that remark. One example of an 'outside-the-box' reflection would be to openly question the choice of international criminal justice as the central instrument for a feminist reimagining of 'the situation of Côte d'Ivoire'. It would mean countering another kind of inability or unwillingness, namely that of the 'international community' and international lawyers to critically evaluate the limits of their institutional practices. In such an evaluation, the Côte d'Ivoire situation might figure as a poignant example of structural violence where the focus on individual criminal responsibility is inapt, so that any international resources and attention should at best be directed differently.

To arrive at that reflection requires admitting that the *actus reus* of Simone Gbagbo's and the other accused's crimes, casually characterised as 'election violence', exceed the conceptual frame of criminal responsibility in which the ICC tried to make it fit. The 'election violence' or a threat of it was and remains recurrent and omnipresent, not restricted to the temporal jurisdiction of the ICC in 'the situation in the Republic of Côte d'Ivoire', or to the acts or omissions of the accused that featured in the ICC case materials. Therefore, instead of the frame set by the ICC, a feminist rethinking might rather try to address the general, structural, constitutional, and legal difficulties of peaceful democratic governance in a young state scarred by colonialism and the slave trade, surrounded by neighbouring states confronting comparable problems, aggravated by the fact that they are situated in Africa, a continent and populations exploited, discriminated, othered, and ostracised like no other.

The thinking 'outside the box' would therefore question whether an efficient cure to a tense and dysfunctional political system in a confrontational social environment that is turning every upcoming election into a potential starting point for a new outbreak of violence can be found in the elegant courthouse in The Hague, or in the international prison-house in Scheveningen. A feminist rethinking might even ask to what extent the ICC and the overwhelming, passionate commitment, activism, and academic investment in international criminal punishment forms part of a global political economy that adds to the already manifold challenges faced by post-colonial states.

Another line of 'outside-the-box' thinking might dig even deeper, analysing the ideological, cultural, and civilisational underpinnings of the arguably 'Western' and gendered conceptions of the hierarchies of violence. Why is rape, in particular, as if intuitively, considered a 'fate worse than death'?[66] Since when, where, and why should one think so? Do feminism(s) have to integrate the ideologies or cultural mythologies of the magical 'purity' of virgins of Christianity and other religions, thus confirming the male control of female sexuality and the patriarchal demands on the familial and national lineage of children?[67] Similarly, it comes across that diverse types of sexual conduct or victims are valued in civilisational, culture-based ways, too. Is anal sex more serious or less serious violence than vaginal penetration, for example, and what civilisational assumptions or fears might figure behind such hierarchies? Finally, why is 'violent gang rape of … grandmothers'[68] more serious or shocking a crime than the same conduct regarding persons not having biological descendants?

These are complex and sensitive issues to study and discuss. Leaving the security of the like-minded 'box' may become a risky excursion into unknown or even hostile territory, thus prone to misunderstandings and manifold confusion. Yet the word 'feminist' would seem to call for a courageously critical reconsideration of the gendered and European-originated 'international' humanitarian law, the basis of the current international criminal law on sexual and gendered violence: what and who have been the protected interests behind the criminalisation of this violence, and where and among whom did these norms first take form?[69] Why should the victims of sexual violence be burdened, in addition to physical and mental pain and eventual bodily injury, with the tragic, ominous stigma, as if 'damaged goods for life'? A feminist rewriting at its best would make sure that the shame and stigma change sides, not 'soiling' the victims, and this without regard to their sex, gender, sexual orientation, age, ability, motherhood or not, or civil status.

Some of the 'outside-the-box' feminist rewritings of the ICC decisions would abstain from applying every rule of the current order of international law. Instead,

66 See C. McGlynn, 'Rape as "Torture"? Catherine MacKinnon and Questions of Feminist Strategy' 16(1) *Feminist Legal Studies* (2008) 71–85.

67 See e.g. Y. Knibiehler, *La virginité féminine: Mythes, fantasmes, émancipation* (Paris: Odile Jacob, 2012).

68 Separate Opinion of Judge Easy, § 31.

69 See e.g. H. Matthews, 'Redeeming Rape: Berlin 1945 and the Making of Modern International Criminal Law' in I. Tallgren and T. Skouteris (eds.), *The New Histories of International Criminal Law – Retrials* (Oxford: Oxford University Press, 2019) 90–109; Engle, *supra* note 18.

they would question and reflect. They might also choose not to use the money from donors to queue for an audience with the staff of the ICC Prosecutor's Office at the margins of the meeting of the Assembly of States Parties to the Rome Statute. They would, instead, launch a broad public reflection on the sense of trying to enforce individual criminal responsibility for long-term structural societal and political problems in a post-colonial African state by an international court in Europe. Thereby they would also question the use of resources available for and in Côte d'Ivoire, such as the short and at times erratic attention span of the Western/Global North's governments, media, and public on a small selection of *jus in bello* violence, instead of focusing on peace and thus the prohibition of violence in general (*jus ad bellum*).[70] This would require facing the challenge of imagining together with the civil society, academia, judiciary, and law enforcement personnel of Côte d'Ivoire different, hopefully better adapted, ways to channel the general desire for justice and progress, and profit from the benevolent intellectual energies of international lawyers – perhaps feminists at the forefront.

12.2 FEMALE DEFENDANTS IN THE SIMONE GBAGBO WARRANT

Natalie Hodgson

In 2012, the Pre-Trial Chamber III issued a warrant under Article 58 of the Statute for the arrest of Ms Simone Gbagbo,[71] the first female defendant in the history of the Court. The Chamber found there were reasonable grounds for believing that Ms Gbagbo had committed the crimes against humanity of murder, rape, other forms of sexual violence, persecution, and other inhumane acts.[72] The Chamber determined that Ms Gbagbo's criminal responsibility could reasonably be established as an indirect co-perpetrator under Article 25(3)(a), based upon her involvement in the 'inner circle' of her husband, Mr Laurent Gbagbo.[73] Furthermore, the Chamber held that, despite Ms Gbagbo's detention in custody, the issuance of the warrant was necessary in light of her political contacts, economic resources, and propensity to commit further crimes within the jurisdiction of the Court.[74]

In this reimagined judgment, Natalie Hodgson endorses the Chamber's decision to issue the warrant of arrest for Ms Gbagbo whilst refuting the gendered stereotypes encoded in the original presentation of the facts. Employing gender-neutral language that avoids overemphasis of Ms Gbagbo's status as a 'wife and mother', Hodgson challenges traditional narratives of the passive, disenfranchised female

[70] Matthews, *supra* note 69, develops this argument in general with regard to 'the feminist anti-impunity project'.

[71] Decision on the Prosecutor's Application pursuant to Article 58 for a Warrant of Arrest against Simone Gbagbo, *Simone Gbagbo* (ICC-02/11-01/12-2), Pre-Trial Chamber III, 2 March 2012.

[72] *Ibid*, § 19.

[73] *Ibid*, §§ 29–30.

[74] *Ibid*, §§ 41–45.

defendant, as well as broader ideas about femininity and conflict. Hodgson concludes by offering some thoughts on the relevance and irrelevance of a defendant's gender in criminal prosecutions.

No.: ICC-02/11-01/12
Date: 2 March 2012

Original: English

PRE-TRIAL CHAMBER III(B)

Before: Judge Natalie HODGSON

SITUATION IN THE REPUBLIC OF CÔTE D'IVOIRE
IN THE CASE OF THE *PROSECUTOR v. SIMONE GBAGBO*

Public redacted version

Decision on the Prosecutor's Application pursuant to Article 58 for a Warrant of Arrest against Simone Gbagbo

Pre-Trial Chamber III (Chamber) of the International Criminal Court (ICC or Court) issues the following decision on the Prosecutor's Application Pursuant to Article 58 as to Simone GBAGBO (Prosecutor's Application).

PROCEDURAL HISTORY

1. On 3 October 2011, the Pre-Trial Chamber authorised an investigation into the situation in the Republic of Côte d'Ivoire.[75]

2. On 30 November 2011, the Pre-Trial Chamber issued a warrant of arrest against Laurent Gbagbo (Mr Gbagbo).[76]

3. On 7 February 2012, the Prosecutor filed an application for a warrant of arrest against Simone Gbagbo (Ms Gbagbo). The Prosecutor argues that Ms Gbagbo is responsible, as an indirect co-perpetrator under Article 25(3)(a) of the Rome Statute (Statute), for the crimes against humanity of murder,[77] rape and other sexual violence,[78] other inhumane acts,[79] and persecution.[80]

4. Under Article 58(l) of the Statute, to issue an arrest warrant, the Chamber shall determine whether there are reasonable grounds to believe that the person

[75] Corrigendum to Decision pursuant to Article 15 of the Rome Statute on the Authorisation of an Investigation into the Situation in the Republic of Côte d'Ivoire, *Situation in the Republic of Côte d'Ivoire* (ICC-02/11-14-Corr), Pre-Trial Chamber III, 15 November 2011.

[76] Decision on the Prosecutor's Application pursuant to Article 58 for a Warrant of Arrest against Laurent Koudou Gbagbo, *Prosecutor v. Laurent Gbagbo* (ICC-02/11-01/11-9-Red), Pre-Trial Chamber III, 30 November 2011.

[77] Art. 7(1)(a) ICCSt.

[78] Art. 7(1)(g) ICCSt.

[79] Art. 7(1)(k) ICCSt.

[80] Art. 7(1)(h) ICCSt.

concerned has committed a crime within the jurisdiction of the Court, and that the arrest of the person appears necessary.

THE JURISDICTION OF THE COURT AND THE ADMISSIBILITY OF THE CASE AGAINST MS GBAGBO

Jurisdiction

5. For conduct to fall within the Court's jurisdiction, three criteria must be satisfied:

(i) The conduct amounts to a crime listed in Article 5 of the Statute;
(ii) The crime occurred within the relevant timeframe specified in Article 11 of the Statute; and
(iii) The crime satisfies the territorial or nationality criteria in Article 12 of the Statute.

6. Given the similarities between this application and the application against Mr Gbagbo, the Chamber adopts its earlier reasoning from the Decision on the Prosecutor's Application for a Warrant of Arrest against Mr Gbagbo and concludes that the case against Ms Gbagbo falls within the temporal, territorial, and nationality jurisdiction of the Court.[81]

7. For the reasons listed below, the Chamber also concludes that the case against Ms Gbagbo falls within the Court's subject-matter jurisdiction.

Admissibility

8. The Prosecutor submits that the current case is admissible. Although there are domestic proceedings against Ms Gbagbo, the Prosecutor submits that these concern 'economic' crimes which are not substantially the same conduct as the present case.

9. The Prosecutor further submits that the case is of sufficient gravity, based on the scale, nature, and manner of the commission of the crimes and the impact of these crimes on the victim.

10. Article 19(1) of the Statute grants the Chamber the discretionary power to determine the admissibility of a case on its own motion. The Appeals Chamber has held that, at the arrest warrant stage where the Prosecutor's application is made on a confidential and *ex parte* basis, the Chamber should only exercise its discretion in exceptional circumstances, so as to preserve the interests of the relevant person.[82]

[81] Decision on the Prosecutor's Application pursuant to Article 58 for a Warrant of Arrest against Laurent Koudou Gbagbo, *Prosecutor v. Laurent Gbagbo* (ICC-02/11-01/11-9-Red), Pre-Trial Chamber III, 30 November 2011.

[82] Judgment on the Prosecutor's Appeal against the Decision of Pre-Trial Chamber I entitled 'Decision on the Prosecutor's Application for Warrants of Arrest, Article 58', *Situation in the Democratic Republic of the Congo* (ICC-01/04-169-US), Appeals Chamber, 13 July 2006, §§ 52, 53.

11. The Chamber notes its reasoning from the Decision Authorising the Investigation in the Republic of Côte d'Ivoire, where the Chamber was satisfied that potential cases arising in the situation would be admissible and of the requisite gravity. It is inappropriate at this stage for the Chamber to examine the admissibility of the case against Ms Gbagbo more fully.

WHETHER THERE ARE REASONABLE GROUNDS TO BELIEVE THAT ONE OR MORE CRIMES FALLING WITHIN THE JURISDICTION OF THE COURT HAVE BEEN COMMITTED

12. The Prosecutor submits that Ms Gbagbo is criminally responsible for the crimes against humanity of (1) murder, (2) rape and other forms of sexual violence, (3) other inhumane acts, and (4) persecution.

13. When the 2010 presidential election in Côte d'Ivoire was held, the Front populaire ivoirien (FPI), the political party of which Ms Gbagbo was a member, was in power. The incumbent president of Côte d'Ivoire was Mr Gbagbo, Ms Gbagbo's husband. On 2 December 2010, the Independent Electoral Commission announced that Alassane Ouattara (Mr Ouattara) had won the election with 54 per cent of the vote. Mr Ouattara was a member of the Rassemblement des Républicains (RDR) political party. On 3 December 2010, the Constitutional Council announced that the election results were invalid and Mr Gbagbo was the winner.[83]

14. The Prosecutor submits that in subsequent months, Ms Gbagbo along with Mr Gbagbo and other members of his inner circle orchestrated significant violence against individuals perceived to be supporters of Mr Ouattara, as part of an alleged plan to retain their political power by all means necessary.

Contextual Elements of the Crimes against Humanity

15. Under Article 7(1) of the Statute, a crime against humanity involves any of the specified acts (underlying acts) when committed as part of a widespread or systematic attack directed against any civilian population with knowledge of the attack. An 'attack directed against any civilian population' is a course of conduct involving the multiple commission of the acts referred to in Article 7(1), pursuant to or in furtherance of a state or organisational policy to commit such an attack.[84]

Widespread or Systematic Attack against a Civilian Population

16. The Chamber finds that there are reasonable grounds to believe that between 28 November 2010 and 8 May 2011, multiple attacks were committed against civilians who were or were perceived to be supporters of Mr Ouattara.

[83] Twenty-Seventh Progress Report of the Secretary-General on the United Nations Operation in Côte d'Ivoire, UN Doc No S/2011/211, 30 March 2011, ICC-02/11-24-US-Exp-Anx5.36, §§ 14–15.

[84] Art. 7(2)(a) ICCSt.

17. The materials provided by the Prosecutor indicate that victims were attacked because they lived in areas believed to support Mr Ouattara.[85] Victims were also identified on ethnic, religious, or national grounds as perceived supporters of Mr Ouattara.[86] The attacks were carried out by the Ivorian Defence and Security Forces (FDS), youth militia, and mercenaries (collectively, the pro-Gbagbo forces).[87]

18. Members of the inner circle, including Ms Gbagbo, distributed weapons to the pro-Gbagbo forces. The pro-Gbagbo forces were also given direct and indirect instructions and training on how to target supporters of Mr Ouattara.[88]

19. The materials indicate that attacks continued over a period of five months and resulted in between 706 and 1,059 murders, 35 rapes, the arbitrary arrest of at least 520 individuals, and the infliction of serious bodily injury and suffering on at least 90 people.[89] The attacks involved multiple incidents and occurred in the city of Abidjan, in the west of Côte d'Ivoire (including Bedi-Goazon, Bloléquin, Duékoué, and Gagnoa), and in the coastal areas of Côte d'Ivoire (including Sassandra).[90]

20. The materials indicate that violence followed a consistent pattern. The pro-Gbagbo forces erected road blocks in order to identify individuals who, based on their ethnicity or religious background, may have supported Mr Ouattara. Attacks on civilians were carried out concurrently in multiple locations, demonstrating coordination among the pro-Gbagbo forces.

21. The Chamber therefore concludes that there are reasonable grounds to believe that in the aftermath of the Côte d'Ivoire presidential elections, pro-Gbagbo forces attacked the civilian population, targeting people who they believed were supporters of Mr Ouattara.

22. The Chamber further concludes that there are reasonable grounds to believe that these attacks were both widespread and systematic.

Pursuant to or in Furtherance of a State or Organisational Policy to Commit such an Attack

23. The Prosecutor submits that Mr Gbagbo and his inner circle constituted an 'organisation'.

[85] J. T. Balima, 'Afrique de l 'Ouest: Crise Ivorienne – L'ABSF fait un décompte macabre', *All Africa*, 10 July 2011, ICC-02/11-24-US-Exp-Anx6.35.

[86] *Ibid.*

[87] Twenty-Seventh Progress Report of the Secretary-General on the United Nations Operation in Côte d'Ivoire, UN Doc. No. S/2011/211, 30 March 2011, ICC-02/11-24-US-Exp-Anx5.36, 10–12.

[88] Video material ICC-02/11-24-US-Exp-Anx7.1. See Decision on the Prosecutor's Application pursuant to Article 58 for a Warrant of Arrest against Laurent Koudou Gbagbo, *Prosecutor v. Laurent Gbagbo* (ICC-02/11-01/11-9-Red), Pre-Trial Chamber III, 30 November 2011, n. 80.

[89] See Decision on the Prosecutor's Application pursuant to Article 58 for a Warrant of Arrest against Laurent Koudou Gbagbo, *Prosecutor v Laurent Gbagbo* (ICC-02/11-01/11-9-Red), Pre-Trial Chamber III, 30 November 2011, n. 34.

[90] See *ibid*, § 35.

24. The Chamber is satisfied that there are reasonable grounds to believe that an inner circle existed, comprising individuals occupying formal and informal positions in Mr Gbagbo's government. Ms Gbagbo was a member of this inner circle.[91]

25. The materials provided by the Prosecutor indicate that the inner circle adopted a policy to attack Mr Ouattara, members of the RDR political party, and civilians who were believed to support Mr Ouattara, in order to retain their political power by all means necessary.

26. The existence of this policy can be inferred by: the consistent and widespread attacks by pro-Gbagbo forces against civilians believed to support Mr Ouattara; the provision of finance and weapons to pro-Gbagbo forces by members of the inner circle; and instructions provided by members of the inner circle to pro-Gbagbo forces.

27. The Chamber therefore concludes that there are reasonable grounds to believe that the attacks occurred pursuant to, or in furtherance of, an organisational policy to commit such an attack.

Underlying Acts

28. The Prosecutor submits that Ms Gbagbo, as an indirect co-perpetrator, committed the crimes against humanity of murder (Count 1),[92] rape and other forms of sexual violence (Count 2),[93] other inhumane acts (Count 3),[94] and persecution (Count 4).[95]

29. The Prosecutor refers to the following four incidents in support of the charges:

(i) The attacks relating to the Radiodiffusion Télévision Ivoirienne (RTI) demonstrations between 16 and 19 December 2010.

(ii) The attack on the women's march in Abobo on 3 March 2011.

(iii) The Abobo market shelling on 17 March 2011.

(iv) The Yopougon massacre on 12 April 2011.

30. The Chamber notes that, in the Decision on the Prosecutor's Application for a Warrant of Arrest against Mr Gbagbo, the Chamber found that there were reasonable grounds to believe that the acts of murder, rape, and other forms of sexual violence, persecution, and other inhumane acts had been committed by pro-Gbagbo forces during these incidents.[96]

[91] See V. Hugeux, 'Simone Gbagbo femme fatale', *L'Express*, 20 February 2003, available at https://web.archive.org/web/20040619003526/http://www.lexpress.fr/info/monde/dossier/cotedivoire/dossier.asp?ida = 376354.

[92] Art. 7(1)(a) ICCSt.

[93] Art. 7(1)(g) ICCSt.

[94] Art. 7(1)(k) ICCSt.

[95] Art. 7(1)(h) ICCSt.

[96] Decision on the Prosecutor's Application pursuant to Article 58 for a Warrant of Arrest against Laurent Koudou Gbagbo, *Prosecutor v. Laurent Gbagbo* (ICC-02/11-01/11-9-Red), Pre-Trial Chamber III, 30 November 2011.

31. As such, the Chamber adopts its earlier reasoning and concludes that there are reasonable grounds to believe that the charged crimes were committed in Côte d'Ivoire during the period between 16 December 2010 and 12 April 2011.

WHETHER THERE ARE REASONABLE GROUNDS TO BELIEVE THAT MS GBAGBO IS CRIMINALLY RESPONSIBLE FOR THE CRIMES ALLEGED BY THE PROSECUTOR

32. The Prosecutor submits that Ms Gbagbo is responsible for the alleged crimes as an indirect co-perpetrator.[97]

33. The Chamber is satisfied that there are reasonable grounds to believe that Ms Gbagbo fulfils the elements of co-perpetration.

34. Immediately prior to the 2010 election, Ms Gbagbo had her own cabinet within the Presidency with its own staff. In a country where women are significantly underrepresented in political positions, Ms Gbagbo was an active decision maker and possessed significant political power.[98] Many perceived her as the alter ego of the president.

35. Ms Gbagbo's significant political power reflects her long political career. She was a founding member of the FPI. In addition, she has served as a member of the Parliament for Abobo and secretary of the Congrès national pour la résistance et la démocratie (CNRD) political group.[99]

36. This Chamber has already found that there is a reasonable basis to believe that members occupying formal and informal positions in the government comprised an 'inner circle' who operated pursuant to a policy to retain their political power by all means necessary. Ms Gbagbo was a member of this inner circle.

37. During the relevant period, the materials provided by the Prosecutor indicate that Ms Gbagbo participated in meetings of the inner circle to plan and coordinate attacks against Ouattara supporters, in order to retain her political position and her own political power. Ms Gbagbo instructed the pro-Gbagbo forces to commit crimes against individuals who were perceived to support the political opponents of the FPI. Ms Gbagbo held meetings with officials in the FDS and supplied them with military equipment. The FDS perpetrated violence on her orders. Ms Gbagbo also provided instructions to members of the youth militia to commit crimes against Ouattara supporters.

38. The Chamber finds that there are reasonable grounds to believe that a common plan existed among the inner circle and that Ms Gbagbo and the other members of the inner circle were aware that implementing this plan would lead to the commission of the offences discussed above in the ordinary course of events.

[97] Art. 25(3)(a) ICCSt.

[98] See Hugeux, *supra* note 91.

[99] *Ibid.*

Given her position in the inner circle, Ms Gbagbo was aware of the relevant circumstances that enabled her and other members of Mr Gbagbo's inner circle to exercise joint control over the alleged crimes.

39. Further, by virtue of the various roles they occupied and actions they performed, Ms Gbagbo and the other members of the inner circle made a co-ordinated and essential contribution to the alleged crimes. The pro-Gbagbo forces complied with the orders they received from the inner circle with almost automatic compliance.

40. There are reasonable grounds to believe that Ms Gbagbo acted with the necessary degree of intent and knowledge in performing her role within the common plan.

41. Therefore, the Chamber concludes that there are reasonable grounds to believe that Ms Gbagbo is responsible for the crimes as an indirect co-perpetrator.

WHETHER THE REQUIREMENTS FOR THE ARREST OF MS GBAGBO UNDER ARTICLE 58(1)(B) OF THE STATUTE HAVE BEEN MET

42. Pursuant to Article 58(1) of the Statute, when there are reasonable grounds to believe that a person has committed crimes within the jurisdiction of the Court, the Chamber shall issue a warrant of arrest if the arrest of the person appears necessary.

43. The grounds on which an arrest may appear necessary are: (i) ensuring the person's appearance at trial; (ii) ensuring that the person does not obstruct or endanger the investigation or court proceedings; and (iii) to prevent the person from continuing with the commission of the crime or a related crime within the jurisdiction of the Court which arises from the same circumstances.[100]

44. A person's past and present political position, international contacts, financial and professional background, their access to necessary networks and financial resources, and the likely length of any potential sentence are factors that might increase the risk that an individual will abscond or avoid arrest.[101] Additionally, a person's access to networks and financial status is a relevant factor in determining whether they have the means to interfere with the investigation or safety of witnesses.[102]

45. Ms Gbagbo has a long political history and strong political connections throughout Côte d'Ivoire. Ms Gbagbo no longer holds a position of power and is

[100] Art. 58(1)(b) ICCSt.

[101] Decision on the Prosecutor's Application for a Warrant of Arrest against Jean-Pierre Bemba Gombo, *Prosecutor v. John-Pierre Bemba Gombo* (ICC-01/05-01/08-14-tENG), Pre-Trial Chamber III, 10 June 2008, § 87; Judgment on the Appeal of the Prosecutor against Pre-Trial Chamber II's Decision on the Interim Release of Jean-Pierre Bemba Gombo and Convening Hearings with the Kingdom of Belgium, the Republic of Portugal, the Republic of France, the Federal Republic of Germany, the Italian Republic, and the Republic of South Africa, *Prosecutor v John-Pierre Bemba Gombo* (ICC-01/05-01/08-631-Red), Appeals Chamber, 2 December 2009, § 70.

[102] Judgment on the Appeal of the Prosecutor against Pre-Trial Chamber II's Decision, *supra* note 101, at § 74.

currently being detained in Côte d'Ivoire. However, evidence indicates that she still enjoys a significant degree of political support. Her supporters have called for her release and oppose her transfer to the ICC.[103]

46. Ms Gbagbo has studied abroad in Senegal and France, as well as having completed multiple international training courses. This suggests that Ms Gbagbo has international connections that could assist her to abscond. The Prosecutor has provided evidence that Ms Gbagbo has access to significant financial resources. Further, Ms Gbagbo's connection to high-profile members of the former government and her relationship with Mr Gbagbo might also assist her to access relevant contacts and resources in order to abscond.

47. As discussed above, there are reasonable grounds to believe that Ms Gbagbo is responsible for serious crimes within the jurisdiction of the Court that could attract a significant penal sanction if proven.

48. Forces loyal to the FPI are alleged to have been previously involved in concealing crimes committed by members of the inner circle. The United Nations has reported that pro-Gbagbo forces allegedly involved in murder and other human rights violations in Côte d'Ivoire have denied the UN access to alleged mass graves, preventing any investigation of their conduct.[104]

49. Supporters of Ms Gbagbo are currently discussing strategies for regaining political power in Côte d'Ivoire. The pro-Gbagbo forces that remain loyal to Ms Gbagbo and the other members of the inner circle continue to have access to significant material resources, including weapons.[105]

50. The Chamber is therefore satisfied that Ms Gbagbo's arrest is necessary: (i) to ensure her appearance before the Court; (ii) to ensure that she does not use her connections and resources to obstruct or endanger the investigation; and (iii) to prevent the further commission of crimes within the jurisdiction of the Court.

CONCLUDING COMMENTS

51. Ms Gbagbo is the first woman to be the subject of an application for an arrest warrant before this Court. As it is likely that this case will attract interest due to the gender of the accused, it is worth making some final remarks.

52. Historically, women have been involved in conflict in a range of ways, including as perpetrators, enablers, and bystanders to violence.[106] However, the

[103] 'La Grande Marche de la Liberté le 18 Février 2012 à la Haye', 9 January 2012, ICC-02/11-35-US-ExpAnx1.17; 'La Grande Marche européenne en faveur de la libération du président Gbagbo: la diaspora ivoirienne et africaines dans les rues de Paris le 12 novembre', *FPI-Allemagne*, 10 November 2011, ICC-02/11-35-US-Exp-Anx1.18.

[104] Report of the High Commissioner for Human Rights on the Situation of Human Rights in Côte d'Ivoire, UN Doc. A/HRC/17/49, 15 February 2011, ICC-02/1 l-24-US-Exp-Anx5.38, 39.

[105] *Ibid*, 35.

[106] See e.g. M. Alison, *Women and Political Violence: Female Combatants in Ethno-National Conflict* (Abingdon: Routledge, 2009); N. Hogg, 'Women's Participation in the Rwandan Genocide: Mothers or Monsters?' 92(877) *International Review of the Red Cross* (2010) 69–102.

underrepresentation of women in politics and the military, particularly in leadership positions, means that women have been less likely to be identified as those who are potentially 'most responsible' for alleged international crimes. Thus, women have rarely been selected for prosecution before international criminal tribunals.

53. All accused persons before this Court have the right to a fair hearing conducted impartially.[107] This Court's application and interpretation of the law must be without any adverse distinction as to gender.[108] The issue before this Court is not whether Ms Gbagbo's conduct adhered to the traditional gender roles that woman are expected to perform,[109] or whether Ms Gbagbo should be punished for her relationship with her husband, but rather the extent to which Ms Gbagbo herself is or is not guilty of perpetrating international crimes.

54. There may be times when an accused's gender becomes legally relevant. Similarly to how international criminal tribunals have previously drawn on expert cultural evidence,[110] expert gender evidence may provide assistance in understanding an accused's actions and how these may have been influenced by a patriarchal social context. Hypothetically, one can imagine a situation where such evidence might assist the court in understanding, for example, the extent of an accused's political influence.[111] Such evidence is most likely to provide an explanation for a defendant's actions, but not legally excuse the defendant's conduct.[112]

FOR THESE REASONS, THE CHAMBER

DECIDES that the conditions established by Article 58(1) of the Statute in order to issue a warrant of arrest against Simone Gbagbo are met in relation to her alleged criminal responsibility within the meaning of Article 25(3)(a) of the Statute for the crimes against humanity of (1) murder under Article 7(l)(a); (2) rape and other forms of sexual violence under Article 7(1)(g); (3) other inhumane acts under Article 7(l)(k); and (4) persecution under Article 7(l)(h) of the Statute committed in the territory of Côte d'Ivoire during the period between 16 December 2010 and 12 April 2011.

Judge Natalie Hodgson

[107] Art. 67(1) ICCSt.

[108] Art. 21(3) ICCSt.

[109] See A. Worrall, *Offending Women: Female Lawbreakers and the Criminal Justice System* (London: Routledge, 1990).

[110] See e.g. Decision on Casimir Bizimungu's Urgent Motion for the Exclusion of the Report and Testimony of Déo Sebahire Mbonyinkebe (Rule 89(c)), *Prosecutor v. Casimir Bizimungu, Justin Mugenzi, Jérôme-Clément Bicamumpaka and Prosper Mugiraneza* (ICTR-99-50-T-22241), Trial Chamber II, 2 September 2005.

[111] For example, Biljana Plavšić has claimed that she was excluded from high-level meetings because of her gender: B. Plavšić, *Svedocim* (Banjaluka: Trioprint, 2005) 113.

[112] On cultural evidence in mitigation, see e.g. Judgment, *Prosecutor v. Carlos Soares Carmona* (Case No. 03 C G 2000) Special Panel for Serious Crimes, Trial Chamber, 8 March–5 April 2001, 9.

12.3 COMPLEMENTARITY TEST IN THE SIMONE GBAGBO ADMISSIBILITY DECISION

Sarah Easy

In 2014, Pre-Trial Chamber I rejected a challenge to the admissibility of the case against Ms Simone Gbagbo brought by Côte D'Ivoire in accordance with Article 19(2)(b) of the Statute, and on the ground of inadmissibility under Article 17(1)(a).[113] The Chamber held that Côte D'Ivoire had failed to establish that an investigation into the same case was being conducted at the national level on the basis that the investigative steps taken by the national authorities in order to ascertain Simone Gbagbo's criminality were not 'tangible, concrete and progressive' but rather 'sparse and disparate'.[114] Furthermore, the Chamber found that the contours of the national investigation were so unclear that it was not in a position to discern, with sufficient clarity, that the subject matter of the national investigation covered the same conduct as described in the Article 58 decision.[115]

In this rewritten decision, Sarah Easy injects gendered considerations into the so-called same person/same conduct test which has failed to expressly recognise the absence of the prosecution of sexual and gender-based crimes as a factor supporting the admissibility of a case. Easy offers a novel interpretation of the term 'genuinely' under Article 17(1)(a) which would restrict the class of proceedings to which the ICC has to defer to a genuine prosecution that is capable of bringing perpetrators of sexual and gender-based crimes to justice. Ultimately, Easy concurs with the Chamber in determining that Côte D'Ivoire has provided insufficient information to establish it is investigating the same conduct but goes further in identifying the gendered barriers obstructing the existence of a national genuine investigation.

No.: ICC-02/11-01/12
Date: 6 May 2021

Original: English

TRIAL CHAMBER IX(B)

Before: Judge Sarah EASY

SITUATION IN THE REPUBLIC OF CÔTE D'IVOIRE

IN THE CASE OF THE *PROSECUTOR v. SIMONE GBAGBO*

Public Redacted Version

Decision of Côte d'Ivoire's Challenge to the Admissibility of the Case against Simone Gbagbo

[113] Decision on Côte d'Ivoire's Challenge to the Admissibility of the Case against Simone Gbagbo, *Simone Gbagbo* (ICC-02/11-01/12-47), Pre-Trial Chamber I, 11 December 2014, § 78.
[114] *Ibid*, § 65.
[115] *Ibid.*, § 76.

SEPARATE AND DISSENTING OPINION OF JUDGE SARAH EASY

1. I agree with the Majority of the Chamber that the challenge to the admissibility of the case against Ms Simone Gbagbo brought by Côte d'Ivoire (the Admissibility Challenge) must be rejected. Notwithstanding my agreement, I append the following separate and dissenting opinion to present my views on certain aspects of the judgment. I clarify that I only address the issues arising in this matter which I consider require my attention.

APPLICABLE LAW

2. As recalled by the Majority of the Chamber, the Admissibility Challenge is brought by Côte d'Ivoire as a state having jurisdiction over the case against Ms Gbagbo, in accordance with Article 19(2)(b) of the Rome Statute (the Statute), and on the ground of inadmissibility under Article 17(1)(a) of the Statute. Article 17 (1)(a) provides that 'the Court shall determine that a case is inadmissible where ... [t]he case is being investigated or prosecuted by a State which has jurisdiction over it, unless the State is unwilling or unable genuinely to carry out the investigation or prosecution'.

3. The majority judgment confirmed that the second tier of the assessment of admissibility under Article 17(1)(a), concerning the question of unwillingness or inability, should only be considered when the state, having jurisdiction, is inactive in investigating or prosecuting the case before the Court.[116] As such, the Chamber must first determine whether the state has discharged its burden of demonstrating the existence of an ongoing investigation or prosecution of the case by its domestic authorities.[117]

Same Person/Same Conduct Test

4. In assessing the parameters of the case before the Court, the Majority of the Chamber applied the definition of a 'case' as previously set out by the Appeals Chamber, being: (i) the suspect against whom the proceedings before the Court are being conducted; and (ii) the conduct giving rise to criminal liability under the Statute that is alleged in the proceedings.[118] In adopting this definition, the Majority of the Chamber implicitly accepted the narrow and vague 'same person/same conduct' test for determining whether the first tier of the assessment of admissibility under Article 17(1)(a) had been satisfied, being that the state is investigating or prosecuting the same case before the Court.

116 Majority Judgment, *Gbagbo* (ICC-02/11-01/12), Pre-Trial Chamber 1, 11 December 2014, § 27 (hereafter Gbagbo Majority Decision).

117 *Ibid*.

118 *Ibid*, § 33.

5. It should be noted that the so-called same person/same conduct test is not prescribed by Article 17(1)(a), having evolved through interpretations of the chambers of this Court.[119] In governing the relationship between the International Criminal Court and domestic criminal courts, Article 17(1)(a) is of great consequence for women and minority groups for whom such institutions have historically been unavailable or ineffective in securing justice.[120] As such, it is regrettable that the majority judgment has not seized the opportunity to further clarify the content of this test and address the gender justice concerns arising from its application.

6. In my view, and contrary to the opinion of the Majority of the Chamber, the same person/same conduct test, if confirmed in its current form, would likely give rise to adverse distinctions upon gender grounds, contrary to Article 21(3) of the Statute. This is of particular significance to the case at hand, given that Ms Simone Gbagbo is charged with individual criminal responsibility for crimes against humanity, including the gender-based crimes of rape and other forms of sexual violence under Article 7(1)(g), and other inhumane acts under Article 7(1)(k).[121] Some of these crimes allegedly took place in the context of the 2011 women's march in Abobo, where thousands of women protested against the Gbagbo government.[122]

7. Firstly, there remains considerable ambiguity as to what degree of similarity the conduct being investigated or prosecuted by the domestic authorities must bear in relation to the conduct charged by the Prosecutor for the case to be deemed inadmissible. This ambiguity has been exacerbated by the relaxation of the admissibility test to require only 'substantially the same conduct'.[123] The Appeals Chamber opined that the incidents being investigated or prosecuted domestically may constitute substantially the same conduct where they 'form the crux of the Prosecutor's case and/or represent the most serious aspects of the case'.[124] I consider that defining

[119] See e.g. Judgment on the Appeal of Mr. Germain Katanga against the Oral Decision of Trial Chamber II of 12 June 2009 on the Admissibility of the Case, *Katanga* (ICC-01/04-01/07-1497), Appeals Chamber, 25 September 2009, §§ 1, 75–79; Judgment on the Appeal of the Republic of Kenya against the Decision of Pre-Trial Chamber II of 30 May 2011 entitled 'Decision on the Application by the Government of Kenya Challenging the Admissibility of the Case Pursuant to Article 19(2)(b) of the Statute', *Situation in Kenya* (ICC-01/09-02/11-274), Appeals Chamber, 30 August 2011, §§ 2 and 61.

[120] See for example L. Chappell, 'The Role of the ICC in Transitional Gender Justice: Capacity and Limitations' in S. Buckley-Zistal and R. Stanley (eds.), *Gender and Transitional Justice* (Basingstoke: Palgrave Macmillan, 2011) at 43.

[121] Warrant of Arrest, *Simone Gbagbo* (ICC-02/11-01/12), Pre-Trial Chamber II, 29 February 2012, § 8.

[122] *Ibid*.

[123] Judgment on the Appeal of the Republic of Kenya against the Decision of Pre-Trial Chamber II of 30 May 2011 entitled 'Decision on the Application by the Government of Kenya Challenging the Admissibility of the Case Pursuant to Article 19(2)(b) of the Statute', *Muthaura, Kenyatta, and Ali* (ICC-01/09-02/11 OA), Appeals Chamber, 30 August 2011, § 39.

[124] Judgment on the Appeal of Libya against the Decision of Pre-Trial Chamber I of 31 May 2013 entitled 'Decision on the Admissibility of the Case against Saif Al-Islam Gaddafi', *Gaddafi and Al-Senussi* (ICC-01/11-01/11), Appeals Chamber, 21 May 2014, § 72.

admissibility criteria in relation to the 'crux' or 'seriousness' of the case is not only unworkable in its vagueness but poses a grave risk to the effective prosecution of sexual and gender-based crimes. This is due to the traditional treatment of sexual and gender-based crimes as lesser crimes or simply the inevitable byproduct of conflict.[125]

8. Furthermore, the Chamber has clarified that the fact that incidents which are described in the Article 58 Decision as 'particularly violent' or which appear to be significantly representative of the conduct attributed to the suspect are not covered by the national proceedings, may be taken into account in the Chamber's ultimate determination of whether those proceedings cover the same conduct with which the respondent is charged.[126] To date, the Court is yet to recognise that *gendered* incidents, described in the Article 58 Decision as sexual or persecutory in nature, which are not covered by the national proceedings, may equally constitute a factor supporting the admissibility of a case.

9. Accordingly, under the existing interpretation of 'substantially the same conduct', one could argue that a domestic case investigating virtually all of the conduct charged by the Prosecutor but omitting an incident or incidents constituting sexual and gender-based crimes would be inadmissible before the International Criminal Court. Such an interpretation would likely operate in a discriminatory manner against women, who are statistically significantly more likely to be victims of sexual and gender-based violence, by precluding them from seeking redress at both the national and international level.

10. In my opinion, the definition of a 'case' under Article 17(1)(a) by reference to the 'same conduct' has textual support through the parallel definition of the closely linked *ne bis idem* principle under Article 20(1).[127] There is nothing, however, in the Statute or the reasoning of the Appeals Chamber which provides a sound legal basis for the easing of this test of 'substantially the same conduct'. For this reason, and taking into account the potential gendered consequences of the existing interpretation, I consider that for a case to be deemed inadmissible under Article 17(1)(a), the conduct being investigated or prosecuted by the state must cover *all of the same* conduct charged in the Article 58 Decision. The degree of permissible dissimilarity between the conduct being investigated and the conduct charged should be confined to minor discrepancies in the description of the underlying facts, so that the conduct is the same in time, location, and subject matter.

[125] See e.g. R. Copelon, 'Gender Crimes as War Crimes: Integrating Crimes against Women into International Criminal Law' 46(1) *McGill Law Journal* (2000) 217–240.

[126] Decision on the Admissibility of the Case against Abdullah Al-Senussi, *Al-Senussi* (ICC-01/11-01/11), Pre-Trial Chamber I, 11 October 2013, § 79.

[127] Article 20(1) of the Rome Statute states: 'Except as provided in this Statute, no person shall be tried before the Court with respect to conduct which formed the basis of crimes for which the person has been convicted or acquitted by the Court.'

11. For the avoidance of doubt, a domestic case which *goes beyond* the crimes charged in the warrant of arrest, by investigating or prosecuting additional conduct, will not be deemed inadmissible, provided it covers the 'same conduct' at a minimum.

Defining Conduct

12. It is well settled by the Chambers of this Court that the assessment of the conduct forming the subject of domestic proceedings in the context of an admissibility challenge must focus on the underlying incidents and not their legal characterisation.[128] This finding upholds the closely linked *ne bis idem* principle under Article 20(1), which protects the accused from double penalisation of the same acts under different labels of criminality.[129] I regret that this interpretation is likely to adversely impact victims in states which have not incorporated international crimes into their domestic law, by confining the ambit of recognition and reparations available to those prescribed for ordinary crimes. However, there is no provision in the Statute capable of supporting an alternative interpretation by mandating the manner in which states must incorporate the substantive crimes listed under Article 5 into their domestic legal system.

13. Although there may be discrepancies between the way a particular act is criminalised under the Statute and under domestic law, Article 17(1)(a) is clear that the state must nevertheless 'have jurisdiction' over the case, and thus criminalise the same conduct. Consequently, to use the example of the crime against humanity of rape, the Prosecutor must be careful in ensuring that all relevant incidents of penetration criminalised at the international level are punishable under domestic law. Thus, a state which restricts the definition of rape to penile–vaginal penetration only may not be said to have jurisdiction over a case involving anal, oral, or other forms of penetration. As such, I consider that an inquiry into the manner in which the conduct is criminalised by the domestic legal system is necessary and permissible to the extent of establishing that the same conduct is in fact within the jurisdiction of the state.

Genuine Proceedings

14. Article 17(a) renders a case admissible if the state is unwilling or unable *genuinely* to carry out the investigation or prosecution, yet the Chambers have directed little to no attention to the interpretation of 'genuinely' as a standalone

[128] Decision on the Admissibility of the Case against Abdullah Al-Senussi, *supra* note 126, § 66; Decision on the Admissibility Challenge by Dr Saif Al-Islam Gadafi, *Gadafi* (ICC-01/11-01/11-344), Pre-Trial Chamber, 5 April 2019, §§ 85 and 88.

[129] This finding is further reinforced by the contrasting use of the terms 'conduct' as opposed to 'crime' under Article 20(1).

term. There appears to be tacit understanding that this term operates so as to require a genuine unwillingness and/or genuine inability on the part of the state to render a case inadmissible. For instance, the second tier of the admissibility test has been formulated as 'the genuineness of Libya's willingness and ability to investigate'.[130] This formulation has sometimes led to the introduction of extraneous criteria into Article 17(1)(a): 'the allocation of the burden to the State is also consistent with the raison d'être of the principle of complementarity: to prove a case inadmissible, the State must establish that it is undertaking a *meaningful* investigation that genuinely seeks to ascertain the criminal responsibility of the suspect'.[131] Reference to the investigation as 'meaningful', a term not present in the text of the Statute, reflects the prosecution's struggle to establish some standard of adequacy concerning the national proceedings that would render a case inadmissible before the Court. Such a standard is in fact provided for by a proper reading of the term 'genuinely'.

15. A closer examination of the context in which the term 'genuinely' is employed reveals that it in fact modifies the objective quality of the investigation or prosecution to which the Court must defer under Article 17(1)(a), requiring a genuine investigation or prosecution. This is evident under Article 17(1)(b) wherein the adverb 'genuinely' is repeated and positioned more closely to the verb 'prosecute', reading: 'unless the decision resulted from the unwillingness or inability of the State genuinely to prosecute'. Furthermore, Articles 17(2) and 17(3), which set out the criteria for determining unwillingness and inability respectively, make no mention of the term genuinely. This interpretation of 'genuinely' has been endorsed by the Court to the extent that it has confirmed that proceedings may be deemed 'inconsistent with an intent to bring the person to justice', where the violations of the rights of the suspect are so egregious that the proceedings can no longer be regarded as capable of providing any *genuine* form of justice.[132] In this way, the Court has acknowledged that it is the genuineness of the proceedings, as opposed to the genuineness of the state's unwillingness or inability, which is relevant to admissibility.

16. As such, the term 'genuinely' restricts the class of national proceedings that requires deference from the Court. Without the inclusion of the word 'genuinely', any national proceedings where there was an intent to bring the accused to justice, and the system was not unavailable, would preclude action by the Court, even if the proceedings were so inadequate as to be incapable of bringing the accused to justice.

[130] Prosecution's Response to Libyan Government's Further Submissions on Issues Related to the Admissibility of the Case against Saif Al-Islam Gaddafi, *Gaddafi* (ICC-01/11-01/11-276 Gaddafi), Pre-Trial Chamber, 13 February 2013, § 23.

[131] Judgment on Kenya's Appeal on the Admissibility of the Case, *Muthaura, Kenyatta & Ali* (ICC-01/09-02/11-274OA), Appeals Chamber, 30 August 2011, § 61, emphasis added.

[132] Appeal on behalf of Abdullah Al-Senussi, *Al-Senussi* (ICC-01/11-01/11-565), Appeals Chamber, 17 October 2013, § 3.

17. The drafting history of the Statute confirms that it was the states' intention to modify the class of proceedings precluded from the purview of the Court, with the term evolving from 'effectively prosecute' to 'duly prosecute' before arriving at 'genuinely prosecute'.[133] Whilst it is clear that the term was not intended to set aside national proceedings simply because the Office of the Prosecutor could develop a more effective prosecutorial strategy, the term cannot be interpreted in a way that is permissive to impunity and thus contrary to the object and purpose of the Statute.

18. The term 'genuine' is defined by the *Oxford Dictionary* as 'having the supposed character, not sham or feigned'.[134] Genuineness is thus a distinct concept from unwillingness or inability. Rather, the genuineness of an existing prosecution informs the Court as to whether the state is truly willing or able to carry out the prosecution. Whilst a state may intend to bring someone to justice by appropriately investigating their criminality (demonstrating willingness) and enjoy a functioning national justice system, in the sense that it is not unavailable as a result of conflict or natural disaster (demonstrating ability), it may still, by the disingenuous design or inadequate workings of its system, be incapable of bringing the accused to justice.

19. This interpretation of genuineness is more closely aligned with the overall object and purpose of the Statute. Whilst the principle of complementarity has often been described as striking a balance between state sovereignty and an effective and credible ICC,[135] it must be emphasised that state sovereignty and effective prosecution by the Court are not competing *objects* of the Rome Statute. Rather, the Preamble establishes that the overall, singular object and purpose of the Statute is to ensure that 'the most serious crimes of concern to the international community must not go unpunished' and to 'put an end to impunity'. This object is pursued primarily by states through domestic proceedings and complementarily by the Court when the state is found unwilling or unable. If the prosecution of a case is so inadequate as to be incapable of ever bringing the accused to justice, it cannot be said to be a genuine prosecution for the purpose of Article 17(1)(a).

20. The requirement for a genuine investigation or prosecution in the assessment of admissibility is aligned with the 'Policy Paper on Sexual and Gender Based Crimes 2014', adopted by the Prosecutor, which separates the evaluation of 'the existence of genuine proceedings' under paragraph 40 from the assessment of 'whether such proceedings are vitiated by an unwillingness or inability' under paragraph 42.[136]

[133] *United Nations Diplomatic Conference of Plenipotentiaries on the Establishment of the International Criminal Court, Rome*, 15 June–17 July 1998, Vol. II, 90–96.

[134] *Oxford English Dictionary Online* (Oxford: Oxford University Press, 2022).

[135] See e.g. W. Schabas, C. Stahn, and M. El Zeidy, 'The International Criminal Court and Complementarity: Five Years On' 19 *Criminal Law Forum* (2008) 1–3.

[136] ICC Office of the Prosecutor, Policy Paper on Sexual and Gender-Based Crimes (June 2014), at 41. The Policy Paper lists potential barriers to genuine proceedings, including: 'discriminatory attitudes and gender stereotypes in substantive law, and/or procedural rules that limit access to justice for victims of such crimes, such as inadequate domestic law criminalising conduct proscribed under the Statute; the existence of amnesties or immunity laws and statutes

21. As such, I find that the state challenging the admissibility of a case before the Court must demonstrate the existence of an ongoing investigation or prosecution which covers all of the same conduct against the same person being investigated or prosecuted by the Court. If the state discharges this burden, it must further establish its willingness and ability to genuinely carry out the ongoing investigation or prosecution.

ANALYSIS

Existence of an Ongoing Investigation

22. As stated above, I agree with the determination made by the Majority of the Chamber that Côte d'Ivoire's challenge to the admissibility of the case against Ms Gbagbo before the Court must be rejected.[137] However, for reasons set out below, I respectfully disagree with the reasoning employed by the majority in reaching its decision.

23. The Majority of the Chamber found that Côte d'Ivoire failed to establish that an investigation into the same case was being conducted at the national level on the basis that the investigative steps taken by the national authorities to ascertain Ms Gbagbo's criminality were not 'tangible, concrete and progressive' but rather 'sparse and disparate'.[138] However, a plain reading of Article 17(1)(a) reveals that the first tier of the admissibility assessment requires only that 'the case is being investigated'. Introducing extraneous criteria as to the efficiency of the investigation obfuscates the distinction between 'inaction' and 'unwillingness or inability' under the two-step admissibility test that the majority itself confirmed in its judgment.[139] Indeed, the majority's consideration of the temporal aspects of the investigation are directly provided for by the second tier of the test under Article 17(2)(b), which states that 'unjustified delay' may be a determinative factor of unwillingness.

24. I find concerning the continued efforts to construct a hurdle to the first tier of the admissibility assessment, in what may be perceived to be an attempt by this Court to avoid the evaluation of a state's criminal legal system.[140] The finding of

of limitation, and the absence of protective measures for victims of sexual violence. Other indicators of an absence of genuine proceedings may be the lack of political will, including official attitudes of trivialisation and minimisation or denial of these crimes; manifestly insufficient steps in the investigation and prosecution of sexual and gender-based crimes, and the deliberate focus of proceedings on low-level perpetrators, despite evidence against those who may bear greater responsibility'.

[137] Gbagbo Majority Decision, *supra* note 116, at § 78.

[138] *Ibid*, at § 65.

[139] *Ibid*, at § 27.

[140] See e.g. Decision on the Confirmation of Charges, *Samoei Ruto, Kiprono Kosgey, Arap Sang* (ICC-01/09-01/11-373), Pre-Trial Chamber, 4 February 2012; Application on behalf of the Government of the Republic of Kenya pursuant to Article 19 of the ICC Statute, *Kirimi Muthaura, Kenyatta and Hussein Ali* (ICC-01/09-02/11-26), Pre-Trial Chamber II, 31 March 2011.

unwillingness or inability by the Court serves the expressive function of denouncing state conduct which fosters impunity for the most serious crimes of international concern. It is an important judicial responsibility mandated by Article 17(2), from which we must not shy away.

25. Upon review of the uncontested evidence provided by Côte d'Ivoire, I find that the relevant domestic authorities have:

(a) formally initiated an investigation to ascertain the criminality of Ms Gbagbo;[141]
(b) detained Ms Gbagbo as a result of said investigation;[142]
(c) interrogated Ms Gbagbo in furtherance of this investigation;[143]
(d) questioned a civil party concerning the conduct of Ms Gbagbo;[144] and
(e) attempted to collect evidence relevant to her crimes.[145]

In light of these investigative steps undertaken by the domestic authorities, I find that there is an ongoing investigation into the criminal conduct of Ms Gbagbo on the part of the state. To determine otherwise, as the majority have done, would be farcical.

Same Conduct/Same Person Test Applied

26. I now turn to whether the case against Ms Gbagbo currently being investigated by Côte d'Ivoire is the same case, in that it is investigating all of the same conduct against the same person. In order for the admissibility challenge at hand to succeed, Côte d'Ivoire must establish that it is currently investigating conduct constituting the basis of *all of the conduct* forming the basis of the charges against Ms Gbagbo, including the crimes against humanity of (1) murder under Article 7(l)(a), (2) rape and other forms of sexual violence under Article 7(1)(g), (3) other inhumane acts under Article 7(l)(k), and (4) persecution under Article 7(l)(h) of the Statute committed in the territory of Côte d'Ivoire:

(i) in the context of the march on the Radiodiffusion Télévision Ivoirienne (RTI) building on 16 December 2010;
(ii) in the context of the women's march in Abobo on 3 March 2011;
(iii) in the context of the Abobo market shelling on 17 March 2011; and
(iv) in relation to the Yopougon massacre on 12 April 2011.

27. I share the view of the Majority of the Chamber that the economic crimes alleged in the first set of proceedings against Ms Gbagbo, referred to as RI-09/2012, RI-33/2012, and RI-04/2012, are evidently of a different nature to the conduct alleged

[141] Gbagbo Majority Decision, *supra* note 116, § 65.
[142] *Ibid.*
[143] *Ibid*, § 73.
[144] *Ibid*, § 60.
[145] *Ibid*, § 72.

in the case before this Court.[146] Similarly, the crimes against the state alleged in the second set of proceedings, referred to as RI-01/2011, fail to cover the same conduct as the case before this Court, namely killings, rapes, or acts causing great suffering or serious injury to individuals.[147] Finally, I concur that the contours of the national investigation are so unclear that I am not in a position to discern, with sufficient clarity, that the subject matter of the third set of proceedings covers all of the same conduct as described in the Article 58 decision.[148]

28. Despite the failure of Côte D'Ivoire to satisfy the first tier of the admissibility test under Article 17(1)(a), for the sake of completeness and in order to clarify the content of this test, I will proceed to assess the unwillingness or inability of the state to carry out a genuine prosecution, as detailed in Article 17(2) and (3) of the Statute.

Unwillingness or Inability

29. As described above, the Majority of the Chamber's finding that the investigative steps taken by the national authorities in order to ascertain Ms Gbagbo's criminality were not 'tangible, concrete and progressive' but rather 'sparse and disparate'[149] should be characterised more appropriately as an 'unjustified delay' constituting unwillingness on the part of the state to prosecute Ms Gbagbo under Article 17(2)(b), as opposed to the non-existence of an investigation.

30. In the alternative, the fact that the state's ongoing investigation cannot be said to be genuine, in that it is incapable of bringing Ms Gbagbo to justice, may also evince unwillingness on the part of Côte D'Ivoire. Whilst the definition of 'unwillingness' under Article 17(2) appears to be exhaustive, in that it enumerates the factors to be taken into account by the Court in its interpretation of this term, the state must nevertheless establish under Article 17(1)(a) willingness to carry out a genuine investigation, as opposed to any investigation which the authorities deem fit.

31. The evidence before me indicates that entrenched discriminatory attitudes towards women and girls in Côte D'Ivoire present a significant barrier to the genuine investigation of incidents of sexual and gender-based violence with which Ms Simone Gbagbo is charged. While the Criminal Code of Côte D'Ivoire (the Criminal Code) provides a prison term of between five and twenty years for the crime of rape,[150] the evidence submitted by the victims indicates that neither the

[146] *Ibid*, § 47.
[147] *Ibid*, § 49.
[148] *Ibid*, § 76.
[149] *Ibid*, § 65.
[150] *Côte d'Ivoire: Code pénal*, art. 354, 1981-640; 1995-522, 31 July 1981. A term of life sentence can be imposed in the cases of gang rape if the perpetrator is related to the victim or holds authority over them. The Code fails to criminalise spousal rape.

Gbagbo nor the Ouattara governments enforce this law in practice.[151] Indeed, officials from both governments as well as rebel leaders have been accused of authorising the use of sexual violence against women as a tool for political control.[152] The investigative steps taken by the Ivorian authorities to date constitute a weak effort to address even the most serious incidents of sexual violence. Such incidents, which remain unpunished, allegedly include the violent gang rape of women, including grandmothers, children as young as six, and pregnant women whose family members were sometimes forced to watch or participate.[153] Other women were abducted and endured sexual slavery for extended periods of time, sometimes forced to give birth to children conceived through rape. Many died because of the egregious sexual violence inflicted upon them. Human Rights Watch describes an environment of increasingly entrenched lawlessness in which impunity for such sexual and gender-based crimes persists.[154]

32. The evidence suggests that the pervasive trivialisation of these crimes is so significant that even if the justice system had not been disrupted by political turmoil and conflict, lacunae in the prosecution of sexual and gender-based crimes would prevail. Importantly, gender-based discrimination is not only practised by the general population but evinced by the very institutions charged with effecting justice. Of great concern is the systematic encouragement by the Ivorian police for victims to seek an amicable solution with their rapist.[155] In other instances, women's claims of sexual and gender-based violence are simply ignored. Both court and law enforcement personnel are described as suffering from an inadequate understanding of sexual violence, typically allowing perpetrators to escape prosecution.[156] Disturbingly, women have even reported the solicitation of sexual favours from magistrates in exchange for a favourable judicial decision.[157] Whilst there have been recent efforts by the United Nations Operation in Côte d'Ivoire (UNOCI) to train the national and local police in sexual and gender-based violence,[158] these are

[151] Human Rights Watch, 'Turning Rhetoric into Reality, Accountability for Serious International Crimes in Côte D'Ivoire', April 2013, available at www.hrw.org/sites/default/files/reports/CDI0413_ForUpload.pdf, in Observations des victimes, *Gbagbo* (ICC-02/11-01/12-40-Red), Pre-Trial Chamber I, 9 April 2014, § 71.

[152] FIDH, MIDH, and LIDHO, 'Côte d'Ivoire: La lutte contre l'impunité à la croisée des chemins', October 2013, available at www.fidh.org in Observations des victimes, *Gbagbo* (ICC-02/11-01/12-40-Red), Pre-Trial Chamber I, 9 April 2014, § 71. *Ibid.*

[153] *Ibid.*

[154] Human Rights Watch, *supra* note 151, at § 71.

[155] *Ibid.*, § 71.

[156] FIDH, MIDH, and LIDHO, *supra* note 152, at § 71.

[157] Unité de l'Etat de Droit de l'Unoci, Étude d'évaluation du système judiciaire ivoirien – L'organisation et le fonctionnement du système judiciaire en Côte d'Ivoire, juin 2007, cited in Observations des victimes, *Gbagbo* (ICC-02/11-01/12-40-Red), Pre-Trial Chamber I, 9 April 2014, § 71 (on file with author).

[158] Voir Conseil de Sécurité des Nations Unies, Trente et unième rapport périodique du Secrétaire général sur l'Opération des Nations Unies en Côte d'Ivoire, U.N. Doc. S/2012/964, 31 December 2012, at 22 and 23, available at www.refworld.org/reference/countryrep/unsc/

unlikely to have a transformative effect in the short term, especially if conducted in isolation. This is due to the nature of structural discrimination which is omnipresent across economic and socio-political spheres, as well as being rooted in historically unequal power relationships.[159] Furthermore, the prevalence of customary law, particularly in northern rural regions, further enshrines structural discrimination and inadequate protections for victims of sexual violence.[160] Reports suggest that victims are further discouraged from pursuing legal recourse by members of their family who view sexual violence as a 'family problem' and thus may advocate for reconciliation with the perpetrator.[161]

33. Furthermore, significant inadequacies in the procedural rules governing the prosecution of sexual and gender-based crimes in Côte D'Ivoire mean that future proceedings of such crimes would likely not be considered genuine. Although the *cour d'assises* has jurisdiction over cases of rape, the evidence reveals a systematic practice of mischaracterising the crime as indecent assault.[162] This is coordinated so that the crime will be tried before a lesser court in order to relieve some of the pressure on the *cour d'assises*, which suffers from a lengthy backlog of cases.[163] Whilst trying rape as a lesser crime may not impair the efficiency, impartiality, or independence of the proceedings, and thus still evince an intention to secure a conviction against the accused under Article 17(2), I consider the penalties available for indecent assault under the Criminal Code to be manifestly inadequate, standing at just two months' to two years' imprisonment.[164] The real possibility that the incidents of rape with which Ms Simone Gbagbo is charged would be tried as lesser crimes casts serious doubt as to the genuineness of the investigation being conducted by the Ivorian authorities.

34. The absence of a legislative framework establishing protective measures for victims of sexual violence in Côte D'Ivoire represents a further barrier to genuine proceedings as it is likely to significantly diminish the number of witnesses willing to testify. Indeed, in relation to the situation in Côte D'Ivoire, the Security Council determined that '[i]t is likely that a significant number of rapes went unreported because the victims were afraid of retaliation or did not trust the judicial system'.[165] The concern most often voiced by the victims themselves is the lack of guarantees

2, cited in Observations des victimes, *Gbagbo* (ICC-02/11-01/12-40-Red), Pre-Trial Chamber I, 9 April 2014, at § 64.

[159] E. Henn, *International Human Rights Law and Structural Discrimination: The Example of Violence against Women* (1st ed., Berlin: Springer, 2019).

[160] FIDH, MIDH, and LIDHO, *supra* note 152, at § 71.

[161] Human Rights Watch, *supra* note 151, at § 71.

[162] *Ibid.*

[163] *Ibid.*

[164] *Côte d'Ivoire: Code penal*, Art. 360, 1981-640; 1995-522, 31 July 1981.

[165] Conseil de Securite des Nations Unies, Trentième rapport périodique du Secrétaire général sur l'Opération des Nations Unies en Côte d'Ivoire, U.N. Doc. S/2012/506, 29 June 2012, available at www.refworld.org/reference/countryrep/unsc/2012/en/90296, at 26, cited in Observations des victimes, *Gbagbo* (ICC-02/11-01/12-40-Red), Pre-Trial Chamber I, 9 April 2014, § 64.

that their rights will be respected by the Ivorian justice system, should the case against Ms Simone Gbagbo be pursued before the national courts.[166] The absence of protective measures for victims of sexual violence may also impede their ability to testify by causing additional psychological strain.[167] Although the views of victims are not mandated as part of the legal criteria for assessing admissibility, the Chamber values this opportunity to hear their perspective which is grounded in their lived experience. It should be highlighted that the vast majority of victims have expressed their desire for Ms Simone Gbagbo to be tried before this Court.[168] In light of these significant barriers to justice for women and girls in Côte D'Ivoire, it cannot be said that the ongoing investigation into Ms Simone Gbagbo's criminality constitutes a genuine investigation.

CONCLUSION

35. I conclude that Côte d'Ivoire has not demonstrated that the same case against Ms Simone Gbagbo alleged in the proceedings before the Court is currently subject to genuine domestic proceedings within the meaning of Article 17(1)(a) of the Statute. Accordingly, I concur with the majority in finding that the present case is admissible before the Court.

Judge Sarah Easy

[166] Observations des victimes, *Gbagbo* (ICC-02/11-01/12-40-Red), Pre-Trial Chamber I, 9 April 2014, § 98.

[167] D. Jjuko, 'Double Victimization? Using a Human Security Framework to Assess the Effectiveness of the Witness Protection Regime in Kenya' 15(3) *African Security* (2022) 189–212, at 196.

[168] Observations des victimes, *supra* note 166, § 97.

13

The Situation in Mali

13.1 REFLECTION: THE SITUATION IN MALI

Kerstin Braun

INTRODUCTION

This chapter reflects on the Mali situation and the cases before the ICC, including the reimagined judgments. It first offers background to the conflict in Mali, before outlining the ICC proceedings relating to the situation in the Republic of Mali at the ICC. It then briefly introduces the original ICC cases in this situation, the *Al Hassan* and *Al Mahdi* cases. The focus is on the *Al Mahdi* judgment, sentencing decision[1], and reparations order[2], and the *Al Hassan* arrest warrant decision.[3]

The chapter then considers the feminist reimagining of select judgments and decisions. It first outlines the key facts and conclusions of each real decision, then considers how those decisions have been re-imagined from a feminist perspective in this book by authors Ameera Mahomed Ismail, Melissa McKay, Laura Graham, Annika Jones, Sarah Zarmsky and Emma Irving. This is followed by critical reflection on each rewritten decision.

The discussion closes by reflecting on what is needed to achieve more gender-just outcomes at the ICC and ponders whether this can only be achieved by going beyond existing rules.

[1] Judgment and Sentence, *Al Faqi Al Mahdi* (ICC-01/12-01/15-171), Trial Chamber VIII, 27 September 2016 (hereafter Al Mahdi Judgment and Sentence).

[2] Public Reparations Order, *Al Faqi Al Mahdi* (ICC-01/12-01/15-236), Trial Chamber VIII, 17 August 2017 (hereafter Al Mahdi Public Reparations Order).

[3] Decision on the Prosecutor's Application for the Issuance of a Warrant of Arrest for Al Hassan Ag Abdoul Aziz Ag Mohamed Ag Mahmoud, *Situation in the Republic of Mali*, Public Redacted Version (ICC-01/12-01/18-35-Red2-tENG), Pre-Trial Chamber I, 22 May 2018 (hereafter Al Hassan Arrest Warrant Decision).

BACKGROUND TO THE CONFLICT

In January 2012, a non-international armed conflict arose in the West African Republic of Mali when the armed rebel group *Mouvement national de libération de l'Azawad* (National Movement for the Liberation of Azawad, MNLA) attacked the Malian armed forces military base in Menaka, a town in the north of Mali.[4] In April 2012, the Malian armed forces withdrew from Mali's north and armed groups subsequently took control of the area. From this point on, the conflict mostly concerned confrontations between different alliances trying to gain territorial control of the north including government forces, including government forces, the MNLA, al-Quaeda in the Islamic Maghreb (AQIM), Ansar Dine, *Le Mouvement pour l'unicité et le jihad en Afrique de l'Ouest* (Movement for Oneness and Jihad in West Africa, MUJAO), and 'Arab militias'.[5] As of the time of writing in June 2023, the conflict is ongoing.

After a military coup d'état in March 2012, the groups Ansar Dine and AQIM took control of the city of Timbuktu from early April 2012 until January 2013, imposing their religious and political stance on the local population. During the occupation, crimes against humanity and war crimes, including the destruction of historical and religious sites in Timbuktu, have been reported.

THE SITUATION IN THE REPUBLIC OF MALI BEFORE THE ICC

The Malian government referred the situation to the International Criminal Court (ICC) in July 2012. In 2013, the ICC Office of the Prosecutor (OTP) commenced an investigation into the alleged crimes carried out in Mali since January 2012, and concluded that there was a reasonable basis to believe that war crimes had been committed, including murder, the passing of sentences and the carrying out of executions without due process, cruel treatment and torture, intentionally directing attacks against protected objects, pillaging, and rape.[6] The situation in Mali was subsequently assigned to Pre-Trial Chamber I in 2013.

Thus far two cases exist within the situation in Mali. The first is the *Ahmad Al Faqi Al Mahdi* case (*Al Mahdi* case), concerned with war crimes relating to the destruction of protected objects. The case was heard by Trial Chamber VIII and resulted in the 2016 conviction of the defendant, who had pleaded guilty, and was sentenced to a nine-year term of imprisonment. In 2017, Trial Chamber VIII issued a reparations order for victims in this case. At the time of writing in June 2023, the second case, the *Al Hassan Ag Abdoul Aziz Ag Mohamed Ag Mahmoud* case (*Al Hassan* case), concerned with war

4 ICC (OTP), 'Situation in Mali, Article 53(1) Report' (16 January 2013) 4, available at https://www.icc-cpi.int/sites/default/files/itemsDocuments/SASMaliArticle53_1PublicReportENG16Jan2013.pdf.

5 *Ibid.*

6 *Ibid.*

crimes and crimes against humanity, was being heard by Trial Chamber X *[Editors' note: in 2024 Al Hassan was convicted of certain crimes, but notably, not gender-based persecution. The judgment will not be appealed. That same year, the Court unsealed documents showing that the (then) Prosecutor had in 2017 initiated a third Mali case against the leader of Ansar Dine, with gender persecution among the charges].*

BACKGROUND TO THE ICC CASES CONCERNING THE SITUATION IN MALI

The below briefly introduces and provides background to the original ICC decisions within the situation in Mali, the *Al Mahdi* and *Al Hassan* cases, selected aspects of which have been reimagined in the coming chapters.

Prosecutor v. Ahmad Al Faqi Al Mahdi *Judgment and Sentence*

The 2016 ICC *Al Mahdi* judgment and sentence[7] concerned Al Mahdi's 2012 involvement in the war crime of intentionally directing attacks against buildings of a religious and historical character in Timbuktu, Mali, by armed forces between June and July 2012, pursuant to Article 8(2)(e)(iv) of the Rome Statute.[8] The buildings comprised nine mausoleums as well as one mosque. Most of the buildings were protected as UNESCO World Heritage sites. In 2015, Pre-Trial Chamber I issued a warrant for Al Mahdi's arrest for the aforementioned crime. After the confirmation of charges by Pre-Trial Chamber I in March 2016, Trial Chamber VIII was allocated the case, which was ultimately tried in August 2016. Al Mahdi admitted guilt in relation to the charged war crime and signed a plea agreement with the prosecution ahead of the confirmation of charges.

In September 2016, Al Mahdi was found guilty of attacking the respective protected sites as a war crime according to Article 8(2)(e)(iv), in the capacity of a principal within the meaning of Article 25(3)(a), and was sentenced to nine years' imprisonment. In the context of sentencing considerations, the Court pointed out that the charge was unique, in that Al Mahdi had been charged with crimes against property only and not with crimes against persons.[9] It should be noted that this case marks the first ICC judgment concerned with war crimes in the form of destruction of monuments and buildings. On 25 November 2021, Al Mahdi's sentence was reduced by two years.[10]

7 Al Mahdi Judgment and Sentence, *supra* note 1.

8 ICC Case Information Sheet, *Situation in the Republic of Mali, Prosecutor v. Ahmad Al Faqi Al Mahadi*, ICC-01/12-01/15 last updated January 2022, available at www.icc-cpi.int/sites/default/files/CaseInformationSheets/Al-MahdiEng.pdf (hereafter Case Information Sheet). All articles without further reference to legislation are those of the Rome Statute.

9 Al Mahdi Judgment and Sentence, *supra* note 1, at § 77.

10 Case Information Sheet, *supra* note 8.

Prosecutor v. Ahmad Al Faqi Al Mahdi *Reparations Order*

After the 2016 judgment and sentence in the *Al Mahdi* case, in August 2017, Trial Chamber VIII handed down a Public Reparations Order (Reparations Order) holding Al Mahdi liable for €2.7 million in individual and collective reparations associated with the above crime.[11] The Reparations Order became final in March 2018.[12]

Decision on the Prosecutor's Application for the Issuance of a Warrant of Arrest for Al Hassan Ag Abdoul Aziz Ag Mohamed Ag Mahmoud

In 2018, ICC Pre-Trial Chamber I was tasked with deciding on the issuance of a warrant for Al Hassan's arrest, which marks the commencement of the second Malian case before the ICC.

On 20 March 2018, an application for the arrest of Al Hassan was filed by the Prosecutor.[13] The Prosecutor submitted that reasonable grounds existed to believe that Al Hassan was criminally liable for crimes against humanity, including torture, rape, sexual slavery, persecution on religious and gender grounds, and other inhumane acts carried out in Timbuktu between April 2012 and January 2013. In addition, there were reasonable grounds to believe that Al Hassan was criminally responsible for war crimes, including violence to persons, rape and sexual slavery, as well as intentionally directing attacks against buildings dedicated to religion and historic monuments.[14] On 27 March 2018, Pre-Trial Chamber I issued a warrant for the arrest of Al Hassan. Al Hassan was surrendered to the ICC by the Malian authorities and arrived at the Court's detention centre in the Netherlands on 31 March 2018.[15]

After the decision by Pre-Trial Chamber I on the Prosecutor's application for the issuance of a warrant in the *Al Hassan* case (re-imagined by Zarmsky and Irving in this volume), on 30 September 2019, Pre-Trial Chamber I committed Al Hassan to trial, making him the first person to sent to trial for gender-based persecution in the ICC. Charges against him were subsequently partially modified on 23 April 2020 and the trial commenced before Trial Chamber X on 14–15 July 2020. Trial Chamber X declared the closure of the submission of evidence on 8 February

[11] Al Mahdi Public Reparations Order, *supra* note 2, at § 134.

[12] ICC Press Release, 'Al Mahdi Case: Reparations Order Becomes Final' (8 March 2018), available at www.icc-cpi.int/news/al-mahdi-case-reparations-order-becomes-final.

[13] Requête urgente du Bureau du Procureur aux fins de délivrance d'un mandat d'arrêt et de demande d'arrestation provisoire à l'encontre de M. Al Hassan Ag Abdoul Aziz Ag Mohamed Ag Mahmoud, *Situation in the Republic of Mali* (ICC-01/12-01/18-1-Secret-Exp), 20 March 2018.

[14] Al Hassan Arrest Warrant Decision, *supra* note 3, at § 2.

[15] ICC Case Information Sheet, *Situation in the Republic of Mali, Prosecutor v. Al Hassan Ag Abdoul Aziz Ag Mohamed Ag Mahmoud* (ICC-01/12-01/18), last update February 2022, available at www.icc-cpi.int/sites/default/files/CaseInformationSheets/al-hassanEng.pdf.

2023 and heard closing statements in May 2023.[16] At the time of writing in June 2023, the Chamber's judgment has not yet been pronounced [*Editors' note:* in 2024 Al Hassan was convicted of certain crimes, but notably, not gender-based persecution].

FEMINIST REIMAGINING OF SELECT JUDGMENTS AND DECISIONS

This section considers the feminist reimagining of select judgments and decisions from the Mali situation.

Judge Ameera Mahomed Ismail: 'Cultural Heritage in Mali'

Original Decision

As per the established facts of the 2016 *Al Mahdi* judgment and sentence,[17] Al Mahdi had been a member of Ansar Dine since April 2012. During their occupation of northern Mali, Ansar Dine and AQIM established a local government, which included an Islamic tribunal and a morality brigade called Hesbah, tasked with preventing and supressing all things considered vices by the government. Al Mahdi headed up the morality brigade between April 2012 and September 2012 and was also involved in consulting for the Islamic tribunal, due to being recognised as a religious expert.[18]

The mausoleums and mosques held great religious importance for the people of Timbuktu. Especially the mausoleums, which were frequently visited to perform prayers, with some people considering them places of pilgrimage.

In his role as a religious expert and head of Hesbah, Al Mahdi, together with other Islamic jurists, unanimously opined that constructions over tombs were prohibited.[19] On this basis, at the end of June 2012, the leader of Ansar Dine instructed him as head of Hesbah to destroy the mausoleums. Even though Al Mahdi harboured initial reservations about this order, based on not wanting to upset relations between the occupiers and the local population, he, together with other individuals, executed the attacks between 30 June 2012 and 11 July 2012. Overall, he was involved in the destruction of ten of the most important sites in Timbuktu dedicated to religion and historic monuments, nine of which were considered UNESCO World Heritage sites. In his role, he organised the attacks and sourced the required equipment, which he distributed to brigade members during the relevant attacks.[20] He was personally present during the destruction of each site and supervised and directed perpetrators. He was actively involved in the destruction of a minimum of five sites.[21]

[16] See Situation in the Republic of Mali, Al Hassan Case – Summary, available at www.icc-cpi .int/mali/al-hassan.
[17] Al Mahdi Judgment and Sentence, *supra* note 1.
[18] *Ibid*, at § 33.
[19] *Ibid*, at § 36.
[20] *Ibid*, at §§ 37–40.
[21] *Ibid*, at § 53.

Reimagined Decision

In her reimagined decision, Judge Mahomed Ismail points out that the original 2016 judgment and sentence in the *Al Mahdi* case is largely free of reference to the relationship between women and the destroyed cultural property. She therefore reimagines the decision by analysing the significance of the mausoleums in Timbuktu to women, and how women have been impacted by their destruction.

Firstly, the rewritten decision differs significantly from the original as it provides in-depth contextualisation of the importance of the impacted mausoleums and mosques, by highlighting how they form an integral part of the religious lives of the local community.

Secondly, Judge Mahomed Ismail identifies a mismatch between the seemingly gender-neutral war crime of intentionally directing attacks against buildings,[22] which is traditionally interpreted to relate only to tangible objects, and the 'realities of cultural heritage and its destruction, which is that when tangible cultural heritage is destroyed, there is often a corresponding destruction of intangible cultural heritage'.[23] The judge defines intangible cultural heritage in line with the Report of the Special Rapporteur in the field of cultural rights as 'traditions, customs and practices, aesthetic and spiritual beliefs, vernacular or other languages, artistic expressions and folklore'.[24] The reimagined decision highlights that 'women, in particular, are central to the maintenance and vitality of cultural heritage worldwide and that this is often through women's roles in relation to intangible heritage'.[25] Consequently, Judge Mahomed Ismail points out that they would have liked to consider whether the intangible cultural heritage of Mali 'is so intertwined with the mausoleums and mosques that it should be considered as falling within the definition' of a war crime.[26] Judge Mahomed Ismail concludes, however, that they are currently prevented from broadening said definition due to the provision's clear wording. Subsequently, the judge calls upon state parties 'to consider the need to expand the current understanding of cultural heritage to better ensure that decisions, sentences, and reparations are commensurate with the entirety of cultural loss, not merely that which is "tangible"'.[27]

In the rewritten sentencing considerations, the question of the gravity of the crime is addressed. The decision highlights the particular importance of mausoleums for women, noting that a woman 'might seek solace or pray at a mausoleum if she cannot have children'.[28] Further, in the context of the gravity of the crime, Judge

[22] Article 8(2)(e)(iv) Rome Statute.
[23] Ameera Mahomed Ismail, Reimagined Decision, at § 24.
[24] *Ibid*, at § 20.
[25] *Ibid*, at § 25.
[26] *Ibid*, at § 26.
[27] *Ibid*, at § 27.
[28] *Ibid*, at § 93.

Mahomed Ismail highlights that an example of intangible heritage in this context is the plastering of the mosque, also referred to as *crépissage*, which must occur annually to preserve the buildings. Especially women and elderly persons are tasked with preparing the clay balls on the ground level which are then passed up to males to attach to the sides of the mosque.

Critical Reflection

Judge Mahomed Ismail's reimagined decision takes the opportunity to highlight how traditional judicial interpretations of seemingly gender-neutral war crimes can exclude the lived experiences of women from ICC decisions. By shining a light on the relationship between women and the destroyed cultural property, especially in relation to intangible property, she convincingly demonstrates that women's lived experiences are not always appropriately reflected in traditional interpretations of war crimes. Continuing to rely on a narrow interpretation and application of the law, which in this case focuses on tangible objects only, may mean missing opportunities for gender-sensitive judging at the ICC.

Her statement that she would have liked to interpret cultural heritage in a more gender-sensitive way than is currently permitted by law emphasises the shortfalls of the current definition of cultural heritage in relation to the special circumstances of women. What would be required to overcome this issue and allow for more holistic assessments would be the broadening of the current conventional narrow definition of cultural property.

Despite being unable to move beyond this restriction rooted in current law, the judge calls upon state parties to create change regarding this situation, thus providing a clear example of what makes this judgment feminist.

Judge Melissa McKay: 'Al-Mahdi, Sentencing'

The subsequent rewriting, also concerned with the *Al Mahdi* case, turns its focus exclusively to the sentencing decision.

Original Decision

In the original sentencing decision, the Court found that retribution and deterrence are the primary objectives of punishment at the ICC.[29] To determine the relevant sentence, the Chamber subsequently considered the gravity of the crime, Al Mahdi's culpable conduct, and his individual circumstances.[30] The Chamber noted that while 'crimes against property are generally of lesser gravity than crimes against persons',[31] the damage Al Mahdi caused made the crime significant in this case

[29] Al Mahdi Judgment and Sentence, *supra* note 1, at § 66.
[30] *Ibid*, at § 75.
[31] *Ibid*, at § 77.

based on the following: ten sites (nine of which were UNESCO heritage sites) were completely destroyed, the attacks were carefully planned, and their impact on the population was intensified due to media reporting.[32] The Court did not find aggravating circumstances and saw mitigating circumstances in the fact that Al Mahdi was initially reluctant to destroy the respective sites and did not recommend using a bulldozer for their destruction.[33] Furthermore, he admitted his guilt,[34] cooperated with the prosecution,[35] expressed remorse and empathy for the victims,[36] and displayed good behaviour in detention.[37] On this basis, the Court sentenced Al Mahdi to nine years' imprisonment.

Reimagined Decision

In the rewritten sentencing decision, Judge McKay identifies a third purpose of sentencing, being the rehabilitation of the convicted person and their reintegration into society. This stands in contrast to the original decision, which considers retribution and deterrence as the primary objectives of punishment at the ICC. This third purpose is informed by restorative and transformative justice concepts, which focus on the offender taking responsibility for their actions as well as the provision of restitution to victims.

In the rewritten decision, Judge McKay, through treaty interpretation, clarifies that Article 77 provides the Court with discretion as to what type of penalty it can apply, and that penalties are not limited to custodial sentences. This marks a departure from traditional interpretations of Article 77, which seem to suggest that the ICC penalties regime does not allow for non-custodial sentences.[38] In support of this wider interpretation, however, Judge McKay draws on the Tokyo Rules, an international instrument designed to 'promote greater community involvement in the management of criminal justice',[39] in support of non-custodial sentences at the ICC. After providing an overview of domestic legal traditions and the imposition of 'alternative' sentences, the rewritten sentencing decision concludes that imposing alternative sentences is in accordance with the Rome Statute and that the Chamber has the authority to consider whether an alternative sentence is appropriate in this case.

Judge McKay outlines the respective mitigating circumstances, namely: (1) admission of guilt; (2) cooperation with prosecution; (3) remorse and empathy expressed to

32 *Ibid*, at § 78.
33 *Ibid*, at § 93.
34 *Ibid*, at §§ 98–100.
35 *Ibid*, at §§ 101–102.
36 *Ibid*, at §§ 103–104.
37 *Ibid*, at § 97.
38 See Dejana Radisavljevic, 'ICC Commentary (Article 77)', Case Matrix Network (last updated 20 August 2020), available at https://cilrap-lexsitus.org/clicc/clicc/77/77; W. Schabas, *The International Criminal Court: A Commentary on the Rome Statute* (2nd ed., Oxford: Oxford University Press, 2016) 1159.
39 Melissa McKay, Reimagined Judgment, at § 71.

the victims; (4) initial reluctance to commit the crimes; and (5) good behaviour in detention, then departs from the original decision by also focusing on Al Mahdi's rehabilitative potential and capacity for him to give back to the harmed community.

Consequently, the sentence imposed in the rewritten judgment does not exclusively rely on incarceration, as the original decision does, but sentences Al Mahdi to seven years of custodial imprisonment along with 3,765 hours of community service in the Trust Fund for Victims (TFV), UNESCO, or, pending Court and community approval, another similar organisation focused on culturally relevant and appropriate activities. Judge McKay points out that while the focus of this community service must be 'on rebuilding what Mr Al Mahdi helped destroy', the work undertaken in the context of the community service may also focus more broadly 'on building respect for religious diversity'.

Critical Reflection

Judge McKay finds a gap in the interpretation of sentencing objectives at the ICC which traditionally do not focus on rehabilitation. The conventional narrow interpretation of the purpose of sentencing excludes the possibility for offenders to make amends with victims and communities in the context of international criminal law. The rewritten decision seeks to close this gap by making the case for imposing non-carceral sentences at the ICC, thus calling into existence a new sentencing pathway. Such a novel approach requires not only an offender who is willing to undertake community service but also a harmed community which is willing to accept the service provided by the offender. While the formal structure of sentencing decisions limits the reimagined decision in commenting on this tension in depth, the decision does touch on balancing potentially competing interests by ordering the community service to be undertaken at the same time as the imprisonment. Consequently, the offender will not perform community service directly in the impacted community but serve it in the TFV or similar. Imposing non-carceral sentences at the ICC, although not without opposition, has the potential to positively impact both victims and offenders in future and marks a departure from the traditional focus on punishment in sentencing.

Through the rewrite of the *Al Mahdi* sentencing decision, Judge McKay builds on ideas from the feminist abolitionist movement. The rewritten decision emphasises the need to move away from the traditional, punitive interpretation of sentencing objectives and towards integrating rehabilitative approaches within sentencing at the ICC, if making amends with harmed communities and individual victims is to be taken seriously. That traditional punishment and mass incarceration does not necessarily have the potential to prevent crime against women[40] has long been

[40] See C. Maxwel and J. Garner, 'The Crime Control Effects of Criminal Sanctions for Intimate Partner Violence' 3(4) *Partner Abuse* (2012) 469–500.

noted in the national context by the anti-carceral feminist movement.[41] This movement challenges traditional punitive criminal responses to gendered violence, instead pointing to alternatives such as transformative and restorative justice.[42] Through the reimagined decision, Judge McKay ultimately advances these national reflections to the sentencing level at the ICC. Yet, and while acknowledging its structural constraints, the reimagined decision could have taken this further by emphasising the link to a greater extent, thereby strengthening the decision's feminist approach.

Laura Graham and Annika Jones: 'Reparations for Destruction of Cultural Property in Mali'

Judges Graham and Jones focus on rewriting the 2017 reparations order handed down in the Al Mahdi case.

Original Decision

In its 2017 Public Reparations Order decision in the *Al Mahdi* case, Trial Chamber VIII highlighted the importance of international cultural heritage,[43] noting that the attacks on protected buildings in this case had 'not only destroyed and damaged the physical structures',[44] but heavily impacted the identity of the local population. The decision identified that the reparations in the case at hand were designed 'to relieve the suffering caused by the serious crime committed, address the consequences of the wrongful act committed by Mr Al Mahdi, enable victims to recover their dignity and deter future violations'. The Chamber concluded that reparations could also assist in 'promoting reconciliation between the victims of the crime, the affected communities and the convicted persons'.[45] The order defined cultural heritage in line with its importance to the local community, here the people of Timbuktu, as well as its importance to humanity in general.[46]

The Chamber ordered reparations for three kinds of harm. Firstly, it noted that for the damage caused to the protected buildings, the reparations should be 'aimed at rehabilitating the Protected Sites with effective measures to guarantee

[41] See discussion in C. Taylor, 'Anti-Carceral Feminism and Sexual Assault – A Defense: A Critique of the Critique of the Critique of Carceral Feminism' 34 *Social Philosophy Today* (2018) 29–49.

[42] See, for example, discussion in M. Kim, 'Transformative Justice and Restorative Justice: Gender-Based Violence and Alternative Visions of Justice in the United States' 27(2) *International Review of Victimology* (2021) 162–172; C. McGlynn, 'Challenging Anti-Carceral Feminism: Criminalisation, Justice and Continuum Thinking' 93 *Women's Studies International Forum* (2022) 1–8, at 1.

[43] Al Mahdi Public Reparations Order, *supra* note 2, at § 13.

[44] *Ibid*, at § 19.

[45] *Ibid*, at § 28.

[46] *Ibid*, at § 51.

non-repetition of the attacks directed against them'.[47] The liability was set at €97,000.[48] Secondly, for consequential economic loss from the attacks, it ordered individual reparations, in the form of compensation, to address the losses suffered by those 'whose livelihoods *exclusively* depended upon the Protected Buildings'. This included, for example, businesses selling holy sand from the respective sites.[49] Moreover, as consequential economic losses also existed for the community of Timbuktu as a whole, the Chamber ordered collective reparations in the form of rehabilitation to address the economic harm to the community. The liability was set at €2.12 million.[50] Thirdly, the Chamber ordered individual reparations to compensate for the moral harm suffered by those whose ancestors' grave sites had been damaged by the attacks. In addition, it ordered collective reparations for the disruption of the culture of the Timbuktu community and the causing of mental pain and anguish, in the form of 'collective rehabilitation to address the emotional distress suffered as a result of the attack on the Protected Building'.[51] The liability was set at €438,000.[52]

Reimagined Decision

In their rewritten reparations order, Judges Graham and Jones argue that the original Trial Chamber's findings as to which victims could receive individual damages for economic loss discriminated against women. On this basis, the judges reimagine the decision by incorporating a feminist perspective.

In contrast to the original reparations order, the rewritten order refers to traditional gender roles when contemplating the impact of economic harm. It highlights that women's economic links to mausoleums are more likely indirect as they are only allowed inside once they reach a certain age. In the rewritten order, Judges Graham and Jones caution that in order to avoid entrenchment of discrimination, there should not be a distinction between direct and indirect economic losses in relation to the destruction of the protected buildings. Rather, the focus should be on the extent to which victims were impacted by their destruction.

In the original reparations order, the Chamber did not consider Al Mahdi's crime as the proximate cause of property loss incurred when victims fled Timbuktu in the aftermath of the attacks.[53] In stark contrast, however, the rewritten decision does recognise economic losses suffered in this context. It highlights that this loss should be included in the reparations to ensure that particularly women and children are

47 *Ibid*, at § 67. The buildings had already been restored at the time the Order was made.
48 *Ibid*, at § 118.
49 *Ibid*, at § 81.
50 *Ibid*, at § 128.
51 *Ibid*, at §§ 90, 104.
52 *Ibid*, at § 133.
53 *Ibid*, at § 102.

not negatively affected by an otherwise exclusive focus on the economic losses of business owners.

Comparable to the original decision, in the rewritten reparations order the judges award collective reparations for the community of Timbuktu as a whole. However, departing from the original, the rewritten order suggests, inter alia, that collective reparations could include programmes or actions designed to assist women, youth, and others towards generating income, as well as initiatives which promote the training of women and 'fostering discussions of the issue of non-discrimination in access to cultural heritage sites as a means of guaranteeing non-repetition of the abuses in this case'.[54]

The original decision simply ordered that Al Mahdi make necessary individual reparations for the mental pain and anguish of those whose ancestors were buried in the mausoleums damaged in the attacks.[55] Applying a feminist perspective to this aspect, Judges Graham and Jones in the rewritten order identify that male victims are more readily able to establish this connection due to the patrilineal method of family record keeping. As a consequence, the judges emphasise the importance of recognising 'female-based lines of ancestry', in the context of identifying groups which have a 'strong emotional connection to the destroyed sites', and orders individual reparations for 'those with a stronger emotional connection to the destroyed sites than the rest of the Timbuktu population'.[56]

Based on the above, the rewritten decision expands the award of individual reparations for consequential economic losses from only those 'whose livelihoods exclusively depended upon the Protected Buildings',[57] to also include those 'whose livelihoods were significantly affected by their destruction' and 'those who otherwise suffered significant personal economic loss as a consequence of their destruction, such as the loss of their homes as a result of displacement'. The Chamber concludes that this is warranted as 'their loss relative to the rest of the community is more acute and exceptional'.

The reimagined order also goes beyond the original in the context of implementation, noting that 'women's views are ordinarily only heard in certain conditions, such as "when they are old and considered wise"', thus cautioning that care must be taken to ensure that women are included in the process of developing a reparation scheme and as victims wishing to access the scheme. The Chamber remarks that this is particularly the case as the wife is subordinate in the 'Malian traditional family structure' and that women may therefore struggle to access the reparation schemes. The Chamber thus calls upon the TFV to introduce a process designed to allow women to increase their recognition and involvement in the development of a reparations scheme.

[54] Laura Graham and Annika Jones, Reimagined Decision, at § 89.

[55] Al Mahdi Public Reparations Order, *supra* note 2, at § 90, as well as collective reparations for the disruption of culture of the Timbuktu community as a whole.

[56] Graham and Jones, *supra* note 54, at § 97.

[57] Al Mahdi Public Reparations Order, *supra* note 2, at § 104.

Critical Reflection

Judges Graham and Jones identify parts of the original decision in which the Chamber failed to consider traditional gender roles. The original decision interprets economic harm extremely narrowly. The economic losses of business owners, who are more likely to be male than female, with women having more indirect economic links to the mausoleums, are considered economic harm. Yet the original Chamber refused to recognise the loss of personal property, including, for example, household items of persons fleeing Timbuktu, as consequential economic loss. The narrowness of the interpretation has the potential to negatively impact women and children as the loss of household items, livestock, and store wares will primarily impact females, who, in the traditional Malian family setting, are largely responsible for domestic tasks. By applying a feminist lens, Judges Graham and Jones demonstrate how the original decision discriminates against women by failing to consider their unique circumstances and the existence of power relationships.

In addition, the narrow definition of eligible victims qualifying for reparations for moral harm as only those persons whose ancestors had been buried in the destroyed mausoleums largely excludes women unable to prove this connection due to traditional record keeping. The judges clearly demonstrate that reliance on narrow interpretations, which fail to consider notions of privilege, discrimination, and gender roles, more likely exclude women from reparations schemes and hinder them from recuperating their losses. Judges Graham and Jones plausibly outline how the law could have been applied to avoid disadvantaging women and sketch convincing avenues of how women can be included to a greater extent in the process of developing and carrying out reparation schemes.

The rewritten order highlights the importance for ICC judicial decisions to be more mindful of traditional gender roles and how these roles may impact a particular situation.

Sarah Zarmsky and Emma Irving: 'Digital Evidence'

While the previous rewritten decisions all focused on the *Al Mahdi* case, Judges Zarmsky and Irving deal with aspects of the *Al Hassan* case.

Original Decision

Pre-Trial Chamber I decided on the Prosecutor's Application for the Issuance of a Warrant of Arrest for Al Hassan on 27 March 2018. It provided the analysis of the evidence and other information submitted by the Prosecutor separately on 22 May 2018.[58] The Pre-Trial Chamber's decision to issue a warrant for the arrest of Al Hassan is based on the following considerations.

58 Al Hassan Arrest Warrant Decision, *supra* note 3.

Firstly, Al Hassan was a member of Ansar Dine and de facto chief of the Islamic police, playing a significant role and providing essential contributions between May 2012 and January 2013 in northern Mali. He was also involved in the work of the Islamic tribunal in Timbuktu and participated in executing its decisions. As part of his role, he participated in the destruction of mausoleums through the Islamic police.[59]

In its decision, the Pre-Trial Chamber found that there were reasonable grounds to believe that Al Hassan, as a co-perpetrator, had committed crimes against humanity against civilians as per Article 7 and war crimes according to Article 8.[60] The Chamber noted that evidence submitted by the Prosecutor inter alia included videos showing public whippings ordered by the Islamic tribunal, some of which were carried out by Islamic police and Hesbah.[61] The evidence particularly showed that women 'were insulted, beaten and whipped relentlessly, sometimes until they bled, at the market and in their homes, for reasons such as that they were not sufficiently covered'.[62]

Reimagined Decision

In their reimagined decision, Judges Zarmsky and Irving depart from the original decision concerning the issuance of a warrant of arrest for Al Hassan by providing additional remarks on the use of video evidence and its evidentiary value before the Court. The first part of the additional remarks is concerned with the importance of the use of video evidence in the context of offences pertaining to violence against women, while the second part focuses on what impact crime recordings posted on internet platforms can have on victims.

After pointing out that the application by the Prosecutor in this case contains more than seventy mentions of the term 'video' in relation to various submissions, Judges Zarmsky and Irving note the increasing significance of video evidence in front of the ICC. This includes the *Al Mahdi* case, where video evidence was introduced at trial showing the accused destroying, and participating in the destruction of, protected buildings. The judges identify that video evidence appears to be traditionally used for crimes occurring in public spaces, such as the destruction of protected buildings in the *Al Mahdi* case, as opposed to crimes frequently occurring in private settings, including sexual and gender-based violence. The judges therefore note 'with satisfaction' that the use of video evidence in the Al Hassan case departs from this traditional approach as it is also used to support arguments relating to violence against women and girls. The judges call for an end to considering video evidence unsuitable in these cases and suggest that its value in establishing sexual and gender-based violence crimes should not be overlooked.

59 *Ibid*, at §§ 172–178.
60 *Ibid*, at § 14.
61 *Ibid*, at § 73
62 *Ibid*, at § 72.

Judges Zarmsky and Irving then turn to the posting of recorded crimes on the internet by perpetrators and others and contemplate the question of additional harm arising from this conduct. They conclude that the posting should be considered as an aggravating circumstance in the context of assessing the gravity of the crime in relation to the threshold that a case must meet to be admissible before the ICC. In the case at hand, Ansar Dine publicly posted videos of crimes on the internet, including executions and whippings. The judges argue that this conduct increases the gravity of the crime as victims are likely to experience additional harm through posts about their ordeal on internet platforms, which greatly widens the audience of their suffering. The harm may also be more severe in this case as unsuspecting relatives may come across the videos on the internet, thus leading to additional suffering. The sharing of videos via the internet, which is difficult to end, and which may continue for decades, may particularly impact female victims. The Chamber points out that stigma continues to be associated with certain offences which women frequently experience. Therefore, women may be haunted by these videos shared on the internet for the rest of their lives. With reference to domestic trials in which the posting of war crime videos on the internet was found to be a war crime itself, the Chamber leaves open the possibility for similar findings in future at the ICC under Article 8.

Critical Reflection

Judges Zarmsky and Irving offer unique insights into the importance of not overlooking the value of video evidence for establishing sexual and gender-based violence crimes as appears to have been standard practice at the ICC in the past. In addition, they apply a feminist lens when contemplating the consequences for victims of posted video recordings of crimes. It may not be legally plausible that judges at the ICC provide 'additional remarks' on issues they consider particularly important. Nevertheless, Judges Zarmsky and Irving's rewritten decision generally highlights the scope for gender-sensitive analysis when using digital evidence at the ICC.

The rewritten decision begins where the original decision ends. It reflects on the importance of video technology and what it means, especially for women, to have war crimes against them broadcast on the internet. The narrow and traditional use of video evidence in practice means that it is frequently considered unsuitable in cases concerning sexual and gender-based violence and is not relied upon. In addition, the rewritten decision calls attention to the fact that the posting of videos can have particularly severe and long-lasting consequences for female victims as stigma remains for certain offences frequently committed against women and girls. Yet the ICC has not given due consideration to this aspect in past decisions – in the context of the gravity threshold a case must meet to be admissible before the ICC or in considering the posting of respective videos as a war crime itself. Changing the above approaches may increase the use of video evidence in proceedings concerned with domestic and sexual violence offences, possibly increasing conviction rates. It may also lead to a more appropriate reflection in ICC judgments of the suffering and stigma women can experience when crimes against them are broadcast on the internet.

After considering the original and reimagined decisions and pondering what makes them feminist, the below reflects on what would be needed to achieve more gender-just outcomes in ICC cases.

IMAGINING GENDER JUSTICE BEYOND EXISTING RULES?

Some may argue that law reform and going beyond existing rules is required to enhance gender-justice principles at the ICC. However, to effect change and improve a particular situation it is important to firstly identify any underlying issues. The feminist judgments relating to the situation in Mali have done precisely that. The four rewritten decisions focus on different aspects of ICC proceedings. Each shines a feminist light on gaps and spaces in the original decisions, where the situation and experiences of girls and women could and should have been considered, but where the Court failed to do so or did not do so holistically. As such, all rewritten decisions begin where the original decisions stop short. In addition, all rewritten decisions apply the law in a more gender-sensitive way than the original, thus showing what would have been possible in this context or how the law could be applied in future cases.

Without the feminist judgments relating to the situation in Mali, the gaps and blank spaces each rewritten decision identifies may have gone undetected. Illuminating these omissions and rewriting how they could have been addressed in a more meaningful gender-sensitive way offers exciting new perspectives on how gender can be taken more seriously in the context of ICC judicial decisions.

The point of feminist judgment writing is to demonstrate how the law can be applied in a gender-sensitive way within the existing legal system as opposed to focusing on how the law could be changed to achieve more gender justice. The novel perspectives offered in the rewritten judgments have the potential to influence and inspire ICC judges to strengthen their commitment to gender-sensitive judging. As such, the judgments are not only an important aspect of identifying shortfalls but also vital examples of how a gender-sensitive approach to judging at the ICC could look in future.

While law reform, including, for example, reform of the Rome Statute, may be one approach to achieve gender justice, this does not mean that change cannot be accomplished without such law reform. The feminist judgment project has the potential to inspire an attitudinal and behavioural change regarding gender justice at the ICC which may offer greater benefits than law reform could in this context. It remains to be seen whether more judges at the ICC will adopt a gender-sensitive perspective and, relatedly, whether gender justice will become an integral part of ICC processes.

13.2 CULTURAL HERITAGE IN THE AL MAHDI JUDGMENT AND SENTENCE

Ameera Mahomed Ismail

In 2016, Trial Chamber VIII handed down the judgment and sentence in the case of Mr Ahmad Al Faqi Al Mahdi.[63] Mr Al Mahdi pleaded guilty to the Article 8(2)(e)(iv) war crime of intentionally directing attacks against buildings dedicated to religion, committed during the occupation of Timbuktu by Ansar Dine in 2012. As part of a common plan, Mr Al Mahdi help to destroy ten of the most well-known and important mosques and mausoleums in Timbuktu. Trial Chamber VIII sentenced Mr Al Mahdi to nine years' imprisonment and the reparations order[64] required him to pay €2.7 million in individual and collective reparations.

Ameera Mahomed Ismail confirms the judgment and sentencing decision of the Trial Chamber, but considers the shortcomings of Article 8(2)(e)(iv), which permits a sole focus on tangible cultural heritage, and how Article 65 can result in the Court not hearing from marginalised victims. In doing so, Mahomed Ismail comments that 'hidden' labour, often undertaken by women, can only then be considered at the sentencing and reparations stage rather than forming part of the judgment itself. Mahomed Ismail's work discusses the current international norms and understanding of culture and asks that the ICC's jurisprudence be broadened when addressing this specific crime and plea agreements.

No.: ICC-01/12-01/15
Date: 27 September 2016

Original: English

TRIAL CHAMBER VIII(B)

Before: Judge Ameera MAHOMED ISMAIL

SITUATION IN THE REPUBLIC OF MALI

IN THE CASE OF THE *PROSECUTOR v. AHMAD AL FAQI AL MAHDI*

Public

Judgment and Sentence

TRIAL CHAMBER VIII(B) (Chamber) of the International Criminal Court (Court or ICC) issues the following judgment and sentence, in the case of the *Prosecutor v. Ahmad Al Faqi Al Mahdi*, having regard to Articles 8(2)(e)(iv), 23, 25(3)

[63] Judgment and Sentence, *Al Mahdi* (ICC-01/12-01/15-171), Trial Chamber VIII, 27 September 2016.
[64] Reparations, *Al Mahdi* (ICC-01/12-01/15-236), Trial Chamber VIII, 17 August 2017.

(a), 65 and 76 to 78 of the Rome Statute (Statute) and Rules 139 and 145 of the Rules of Procedure and Evidence (Rules).

INTRODUCTION ...

The Accused and the Charge

9. Mr Ahmad Al Faqi Al Mahdi (Mr Al Mahdi), also known as Mr Abu Turab, was born in Agoune in the region of Timbuktu, Mali,[65] to a family recognised in his community for having a particularly high knowledge of Islam.[66] He is a Touareg from the Ansar Touareg tribe and the son of a marabout (a Muslim religious leader and teacher)[67] who has a thorough knowledge of the Quran.[68] He is between thirty and forty years old.[69] In April 2012, Mr Al Mahdi joined Ansar Dine.[70]

10. Mr Al Mahdi is charged with intentionally directing attacks against ten buildings of a religious and historical character in Timbuktu, Mali, between around 30 June 2012 and 11 July 2012: (i) the Sidi Mahamoud Ben Omar Mohamed Aquit Mausoleum; (ii) the Sheikh Mohamed Mahmoud Al Arawani Mausoleum; (iii) the Sheikh Sidi El Mokhtar Ben Sidi Mouhammed Al Kabir Al Kounti Mausoleum; (iv) the Alpha Moya Mausoleum; (v) the Sheikh Mouhamed El Mikki Mausoleum; (vi) the Sheikh Abdoul Kassim Attouaty Mausoleum; (vii) the Sheikh Sidi Ahmed Ben Amar Arragadi Mausoleum; (viii) the Sidi Yahia Mosque door; and the two mausoleums adjoining the Djingareyber Mosque, being (ix) the Ahmed Fulane Mausoleum and (x) the Bahaber Babadié Mausoleum.

JUDGMENT

Applicable Law

Crime Charged

11. The war crime of attacking protected objects under Article 8(2)(e)(iv) of the Statute punishes the following act: 'Intentionally directing attacks against buildings dedicated to religion, education, art, science or charitable purposes, historic monuments, hospitals and places where the sick and wounded are collected, provided they are not military objectives.'

12. This is the charge to which the defendant has admitted guilt.

13. In order to prove the crime charged, the prosecution must show that:

[65] Public redacted version of ICC-01/12-01/15-78-Conf-Exp-Anx1-tENG, *Al Mahdi* (ICC-01/12-01/15), Prosecution, 9 September 2016, § 39 (hereafter Agreement).

[66] T-6, www.icc-cpi.int/sites/default/files/Transcripts/CR2016_05729.PDF, at 39–40.

[67] T-4, www.icc-cpi.int/sites/default/files/Transcripts/CR2016_05767.PDF, at 31.

[68] T-6, *supra* note 66, at 40.

[69] T-2, www.icc-cpi.int/sites/default/files/Transcripts/CR2016_01929.PDF, at 4.

[70] T-6, *supra* note 66, at 13.

1. The perpetrator directed an attack.
2. The object of the attack was one or more buildings dedicated to religion, education, art, science, or charitable purposes, historic monuments, hospitals, or places where the sick and wounded are collected, which were not military objectives.
3. The perpetrator intended such building or buildings dedicated to religion, education, art, science, or charitable purposes, historic monuments, hospitals, or places where the sick and wounded are collected, which were not military objectives, to be the object of the attack.
4. The conduct took place in the context of and was associated with an armed conflict not of an international character.
5. The perpetrator was aware of factual circumstances that established the existence of an armed conflict.[71] …

19. The conventional understanding of cultural heritage is that it is made up of both tangible and intangible aspects. Nonetheless Article 8(2)(e)(iv) reflects the twentieth-century understanding of culture as solely constituting tangible objects. For example, Article 1 of the 1954 Convention for the Protection of Cultural Property in the Event of Armed Conflict defines 'cultural property' as 'a) movable or immovable property of great importance to the cultural heritage of every people … b) buildings whose main and effective purpose is to preserve the movable or cultural property … c) centers containing a large amount of cultural property'. This 'tangible objects' approach continued in the 1972 Convention Concerning the Protection of World Cultural and Natural Heritage, where 'cultural heritage' was defined in Article 1 as being confined to 'monuments', 'groups of buildings', and 'sites'.

20. On the other hand, intangible cultural heritage is made up of 'traditions, customs and practices, aesthetic and spiritual beliefs, vernacular or other languages, artistic expressions and folklore'.[72]

21. Intangible cultural heritage is defined in Article 2 of the 2003 Convention for the Safeguarding of the Intangible Cultural Heritage as 'the practices, representations, expressions, knowledge, skills … that communities, groups and, in some cases, individuals recognize as part of their cultural heritage'. Article 2 notes that intangible cultural heritage 'is constantly recreated by communities and groups in response to their environment, their interaction with nature and their history, and provides them with a sense of identity and continuity'.

22. Further, the Preamble to that Convention considers 'the importance of the intangible cultural heritage as a mainspring of cultural diversity' and 'the *deep-seated interdependence between the intangible cultural heritage and the tangible cultural*

[71] War crime of attacking protected objects, Article 8(2)(e)(iv), Elements of Crimes.

[72] *Report of the Special Rapporteur in the Field of Cultural Rights*, A/HRC/31/59, 3 February 2016, § 49.

and natural heritage' (emphasis added). It also recognises 'that communities . . . play an important role in the production, safeguarding, maintenance and re-creation of the intangible cultural heritage, thus helping to enrich cultural diversity and human creativity'.

23. Earlier this year, the Special Rapporteur in the field of cultural rights reported that both tangible and intangible cultural heritage 'should be understood in broad and holistic terms'.[73] The Special Rapporteur's report pointed out that there is a significant overlap between tangible and intangible heritage, and that attacks on each are interconnected.[74]

24. Article 8(2)(e)(iv) of the Statute is therefore in conflict with the realities of cultural heritage and its destruction, which is that when tangible cultural heritage is destroyed, there is often a corresponding destruction of intangible cultural heritage. In fact, some say that tangible and intangible cultural heritage are two sides of the same coin.[75]

25. The Chamber also recognises that women, in particular, are central to the maintenance and vitality of cultural heritage worldwide and that this is often through women's roles in relation to intangible heritage.[76]

26. Here, the Chamber would have liked to consider whether the intangible cultural heritage of Mali is so intertwined with the mausoleums and mosques that it should be considered as falling within the definition of Article 8(2)(e)(iv). However, the Chamber is currently unable to do so due to the clear wording of Article 8(2)(e)(iv).

27. The Chamber therefore urges state parties to the Statute to consider the need to expand the current understanding of cultural heritage to better ensure that decisions, sentences, and reparations are commensurable to the entirety of cultural loss, not merely that which is 'tangible'. This would allow the Court to consider the destruction of cultural property from a holistic perspective. . . .

Article 65 of the Statute . . .

30. As this is the first time Article 65 has been applied at this Court, the Chamber will briefly address some relevant matters relating to this provision. . . .

37. Pursuant to Articles 64(8)(a) and 65 of the Statute, an accused may make an admission of guilt at the commencement of the trial. However, Article 65 requires the Chamber to conclude that the admission is 'supported by the facts of the case',

[73] *Ibid*, § 49.

[74] *Ibid*, § 77.

[75] M. Bouchenaki, 'Editorial', 56 *Museum International* (2004) 10.

[76] UNESCO, *Synthesis Report. Activities in the Domain of Women and Intangible Heritage: International Editorial Meeting and Future Activities in the Domain*, June 2001, available at https://ich.unesco.org/doc/src/00160-EN.pdf, at 2.

such that the admission of guilt must be considered 'together with any additional evidence presented'.[77]

38. The Chamber acknowledges the Separate Opinion of Judge Péter Kovács,[78] in particular Judge Kovács' concern that Pre-Trial Chamber I's majority opinion 'gives the impression that it rests on mere assumptions due to the lack of support from the evidence presented to the Chamber'. It is unlikely that Judge Kovács' concerns would have been valid if Mr Al Mahdi had pleaded not guilty.

39. While this Chamber does not arrive at the same conclusion as Judge Kovács, it concedes that plea negotiations might necessarily confine the issues and truncate the court process. However, the process by which the prosecution and defence make oral submissions by way of evidence, from the bar table, may not foster an environment such that the Chamber can deliver a decision that presents a 'full account of the relevant facts and law in order to reveal the transparency of the judicial process and guarantee a considerable degree of persuasiveness'.[79] This is notwithstanding the fact that the Chamber can access freely all evidence relevant to the case without the requirement that evidence must be tendered through a witness.[80]

40. Furthermore, the Chamber acknowledges that victim participation can be lost when the prosecution and defence enter into plea negotiations rather than the case proceeding to a contested trial. This means that the Chamber cannot be certain that it has heard from a diverse range of witnesses, in particular marginalised categories of victims.

41. Lastly, the Chamber acknowledges the view that international criminal courts establish 'an accurate and publicly accessible historical record'.[81] The convenience of an admission of guilt must weigh against this, and other factors.

Established Facts of the Case

42. The Chamber now turns to the established facts of the case.

43. The Chamber notes that Mr Al Mahdi's decision to plead guilty has the unfortunate effect of limiting the types of evidence that the Chamber was presented with, namely the views of victims and a consideration of the types of harm that the crime engages with. . . .

[77] Article 65(1)(c) and (2) of the Statute.

[78] Separate Opinion of Judge Péter Kovács, *Al Mahdi* (ICC-01/12-01/15), Pre-Trial Chamber I, 9 May 2016.

[79] Separate Opinion of Judge Péter Kovács, *Situation in Georgia* (ICC-01/15), Pre-Trial Chamber I, 27 January 2016, § 12.

[80] Article 65 of the Statute.

[81] R. E. Rauxloh, 'Negotiated History: The Historical Record in International Criminal Law and Plea Bargaining' 10 *International Criminal Law Review* (2010) 739–770, at 739.

Context

45. Mali has a diverse cultural heritage,[82] and Timbuktu is at the centre of this. The residents of Timbuktu are diverse,[83] and Islam is the common denominator that brings together the city's residents.[84]

46. Timbuktu played an important role in the early dissemination of Islam, and became a centre of training and education in the West African region due to the existence of scholars, universities, and the city's status as a centre of trade.[85] Most of these scholars became saints.[86] Timbuktu is also known as 'the City of 333 Saints'.[87]

CONTEXTUALISING THE MAUSOLEUMS AND MOSQUES

47. The mausoleums of these saints and the mosques were an integral part of the religious lives of the city's residents, who frequently visited them as places of worship and pilgrimage.[88] They reflected the people's commitment to Islam and provided psychological safety nets, to the extent that they were viewed as protection.[89]

48. The Sheikh Sidi El Mokhtar Ben Sidi Mouhammed Al Kabir Al Kounti Mausoleum was visited by the people of Timbuktu to pray if they were faced with a dilemma or important decision.[90] Locals attended the Alpha Moya Mausoleum to make offerings, and to pray on Tabaski and in Ramadan.[91] Many worshippers prayed at the tomb of Sheikh Sidi Ahmed Ben Amar Arragadi, including pilgrims of Kunti origin from Morocco, Algeria, Niger, Libya, Mali, and Tunisia.[92] Worshippers would go to the Sheikh Mouhamed El Mikki Mausoleum for spiritual retreats.[93] The Sidi Yahia Mosque door had not been opened for 500 years, and, according to legend, opening it would lead to the Last Judgment.[94] The Ahmed Fulane and Bahaber Babadié Mausoleums adjoined the western wall of the Djingareyber Mosque, located at the heart of Timbuktu; many people visited them on Mondays and Fridays, as well as during major religious festivals.[95]

82 T-5, www.icc-cpi.int/sites/default/files/Transcripts/CR2016_05772.PDF, at 77.
83 Agreement, *supra* note 65, at § 26.
84 *Ibid*, at § 26.
85 T-5, *supra* note 82, at 78.
86 *Ibid*, at 78.
87 Agreement, *supra* note 65, at § 105.
88 Ibid, at § 26.
89 T-5, *supra* note 82, at 80.
90 Agreement, *supra* note 65, at § 67.
91 *Ibid*, § 73.
92 *Ibid*, § 82.
93 *Ibid*, § 85.
94 *Ibid*, § 89.
95 *Ibid*, § 96.

THE ROLE OF THE COMMUNITY

49. The Chamber can gather from the material before it that the mausoleums and mosques were 'cherished by the community'.[96] The population of Timbuktu itself was involved in the upkeep of the monuments through the process of *crépissage*, or the plastering of the mosque.[97] At the neighbourhood level, materials are collected and meetings are held.[98] The event brings together the community as a whole.[99]

50. The Chamber considers this further in its analysis of the gravity of the crime.

Decision to Attack the Mausoleums and Mosques …

The Attack and Mr Al Mahdi's Responsibility

54. The attack was carried out between 30 June 2012 and 11 July 2012.[100] Mr Al Mahdi and other individuals adhering to the same common plan destroyed ten of the most well-known and important sites in Timbuktu.

55. These sites were all dedicated to religion and historic monuments, and none were military objectives. Except for the Sheikh Mohamed Mahmoud Al Arwani Mausoleum, all of the buildings were protected UNESCO World Heritage Sites.[101] …

Findings

72. In view of these findings, the Chamber considers that all of the elements for the war crime of attacking protected objects are established. …

Conclusion

74. The Chamber is satisfied beyond reasonable doubt that all of the essential facts of the crime charged are proven, having regard to the admission of guilty, the hearings held, and the evidence brought forward.

SENTENCE

75. Having concluded that Mr Al Mahdi is responsible for intentionally attacking the above-mentioned objects as a co-perpetrator, the Chamber will now turn to the determination of the appropriate sentence. The submissions made by the parties and participants are addressed in the course of the analysis. …

96 T-2, *supra* note 69, at 6, 19, 21.

97 *Ibid*, at 25.

98 T-4, *supra* note 67, at 18.

99 *Ibid*, at 18.

100 Agreement, *supra* note 65, at § 30.

101 *Ibid*, § 33; T-5, *supra* note 82, at 53.

Applicable Law

Analysis

84. In order to determine the appropriate sentence, the Chamber will consider: (i) the gravity of the crime; (ii) Mr Al Mahdi's culpable conduct; and (iii) his individual circumstances. Rule 145(1)(c) factors and aggravating and mitigating circumstances are discussed in the course of the analysis when relevant. ...

Gravity of the Crime

88. Mr Al Mahdi has been charged with crimes against property. Although this may be considered of lesser gravity than crimes against persons,[102] this crime has 'hit and harmed the people in question at all levels, intellectually, spiritually, and at the very core of their being'.[103]

89. The legal representative for victims, Mr Mayombo Kassongo, provided valuable assistance to the Chamber in determining the gravity of the crime. He submitted that 'heritage is not something frivolous or a luxury item, heritage is part of whom we are, it is an extension of ourselves ... if heritage is destroyed we are like a traveller without any belongings, like beings without a soul, history or memory'.[104]

90. The Chamber also accepts the Prosecutor's assertion that 'culture is who we are. Our ancestors created paintings, sculptures, mosques, temples and other forms of cultural possessions all around us. They put their hearts and souls into the creation of such cultural heritage so that it represents the cultural identity of their times and is passed on for the benefit of future generations'.[105]

91. The impact of the destruction had a calamitous effect on the citizens of Timbuktu. During the destruction of the mausoleums, an inhabitant of Timbuktu cried out in desperation that 'Timbuktu is about to lose its soul ... Timbuktu has on its throat the sharp knife of coldblooded assassins'.[106] Another inhabitant said, '[t]hey have destroyed everything we have'.[107] The Minister of Culture of Mali called the destruction 'an attack on the lifeblood of our souls, on the very quintessence of our

[102] Decision on Sentence Pursuant to Article 76 of the Statute, *Katanga* (ICC-01/04-01/07), Trial Chamber II, 23 May 2014, §§ 42–43; Observations de la Défense sur les principes devant gouverner la peine et les circonstances aggravantes et/ou atténuantes en la cause, en conformité avec l'ordonnance ICC-01/12-01/15-99 de la Chambre (ICC-01/12-01/15-141-Conf), *Al Mahdi* (ICC-01/12-01/15), Defence, 20 September 2016, §§ 121–123, 127–128; T-6, *supra* note 66, at 52–58.

[103] T-6, *supra* note 66, at 8.

[104] *Ibid*, at 6.

[105] T-4, *supra* note 67, at 19.

[106] T-2, *supra* note 69, at 12.

[107] *Ibid*, at 12.

cultural values. Their purpose was to destroy our past . . . our identity and, indeed, our dignity'.[108]

92. It is clear that the mausoleums and mosques are important to the people of Mali and the international community. They are not merely walls and stones.[109] At a national level, the mausoleums and mosques have important religious, cultural, and social significance.[110] At the international level, they stand as symbols of Timbuktu's intellectual and spiritual past.[111] In fact, the Chamber heard evidence that Timbuktu is considered to match the role that the city of Florence played in Renaissance Europe as a centre of intellectual and religious life and teaching.[112] In that way, the mausoleums and mosques were the embodiment of Malian history in tangible form.[113]

93. In some Muslim countries such as Mali, mausoleums are used by the community when they find themselves in a position of weakness and an inability to find solutions to the problems themselves.[114] The community then looks to the saints, who are perceived to be close to God, and pleads with them.[115] For example, a woman might seek solace or pray at a mausoleum if she cannot have children.[116]

94. According to UNESCO Witness P-151, the population is extremely attached to both their tangible heritage, being the mosques and mausoleums, and intangible heritage.[117] One example of intangible heritage is *crépissage*, or the plastering of the mosque. Due to climatic events that erode the plastering, *crépissage* must be done annually to preserve the structures.[118] Witness P-151 testified that *crépissage* is a collective effort done by the population.[119] Women and the elderly prepare balls of clay at the bottom, which are passed up to the males hanging on the sides of the mosque.[120]

95. The practice of *crépissage* is not merely technical. Rather, it corresponds with a ritual found in many African societies which aims to ward off bad luck and to ensure good rains.[121] This link is important; the belief that blessings will be received (good rains) makes the task of *crépissage* more attractive.[122]

108 *Ibid*, at 15–16.
109 *Ibid*, at 13.
110 Agreement, *supra* note 65, § 27.
111 *Ibid*, § 27.
112 T-5, *supra* note 82, at 44.
113 T-4, *supra* note 67, at 17.
114 T-6, *supra* note 66, at 41.
115 *Ibid*, at 41.
116 *Ibid*, at 41.
117 T-5, *supra* note 82, at 39.
118 *Ibid*, at 39.
119 *Ibid*, at 39.
120 *Ibid*, at 39–40.
121 MLI-OTP-0028-0598, *Rapport d'expertise sur l'état inteérieur et extérieur des mausolées, mosques et autres monuments situés à Tombouctou et sa region*, 27 February 2015, available at www.icc-cpi.int/sites/default/files/Evidence/MLI-OTP-0028-0586_redacted.pdf, at 12–13.
122 *Ibid*, at 12–13.

DEFENCE SUBMISSIONS ON GRAVITY

96. The defence, in their oral submissions, outlined how different schools of thought within Islam were created.[123] They submitted that Ansar Dine considered that it followed the Wahhabi school, which totally forbade people from building tombs.[124]

97. Mr Kassongo confirmed that the notion of seeking assistance from saints has become a debated issue within Islam. He submitted that the Maliki sect, prominent in North Africa and some sub-Saharan regions, has allowed for Sufism to find a place for seeking this assistance.[125] This is in contrast to the Wahhabi sect, which prohibits and condemns these practices.[126]

98. While the Chamber considers this to be a relevant factor, it does not consider it to be a mitigating or aggravating factor.

FURTHER EVIDENCE THE CHAMBER MAY HAVE CONSIDERED

99. The Chamber appreciates that it has received evidence regarding the views of the community. However, the Chamber reiterates its view that given the circumstances of this matter, it has not had the benefit of being presented the views of further victims and a consideration of the types of harm that results from such a crime, specifically with respect to women and other minority groups.

100. As this is the first time this Chamber has considered the application of Article 8(2)(e)(iv) of the Statute, it may have benefited from submissions regarding the destruction of cultural heritage at a national level.

101. In a similar fashion, commencing in October 2011, several Sufi shrines, tombs, and libraries were desecrated or destroyed in Libya.[127]

102. Earlier this year in Tasmania, Australia, ochre stencils on a cave wall were destroyed. Indigenous Australian traditional owners said the hand stencils were made during large clan gatherings between 800 and 8,000 years ago. The chairman of the Tasmanian Land Council, Clyde Mansell, reported that 'what makes it sacred is the way in which it was used, and the process that went into making those hand stencils … It's not just a hand stencil, it's the story that goes with the hand stencils that turns it into a sacred site. If we can't protect that hand stencil, then we can't keep it in our interpretation for generations to come'.[128]

[123] T-6, *supra* note 66, at 41–42.

[124] *Ibid*, at 41.

[125] *Ibid*, at 41–42.

[126] *Ibid*, at 42.

[127] UN, 'UN Independent Experts Condemn Destruction of Sufi Religious Sites in Libya', UN News, 10 September 2012, available at https://news.un.org/en/story/2012/09/419122#:~:text = In%20August%2C%20several%20sites%20were,and%20libraries%20were%20also%20targeted.

[128] C. Wahlquist, 'Aboriginal sacred site up to 8,000 years old destroyed by "cultural vandals"', *The Guardian*, 3 June 2016, available at www.theguardian.com/australia-news/2016/jun/03/aboriginal-sacred-site-up-to-8000-years-old-destroyed-by-cultural-vandals.

103. An understanding of how the destruction of cultural heritage affects communities at large would have benefited the Chamber in its determination of the sentence. …

Determination of the Sentence

110. The Chamber finds that the crime for which Mr Al Mahdi is being convicted is of significant gravity. The Chamber has considered the aggravating and mitigating factors. Taking into account all of these factors, the Chamber sentences Mr Al Mahdi to nine years of imprisonment.

111. The Chamber notes that none of the parties or participants requests the imposition of a fine or order of forfeiture under Article 77(2) of the Statute and Rules 146 and 147 of the Rules. As such, the Chamber finds that imprisonment is a sufficient penalty.

112. Pursuant to Article 78(2) of the Statute, Mr Al Mahdi is entitled to have the time he has spent in detention deducted from his sentence, in accordance with an order of this Court.

FOR THE FOREGOING REASONS, THE CHAMBER HEREBY

CONVICTS Mr Al Mahdi of the war crime of attacking protected objects as a co-perpetrator under Articles 8(2)(e)(iv) and 25(3)(a) of the Statute;

SENTENCES Mr Al Mahdi to nine years of imprisonment;

ORDERS the deduction of the time Mr Al Mahdi has spent in detention, pursuant to an order of this Court, from his sentence; and

INFORMS the parties and participants that reparations to victims pursuant to Article 75 of the Statute shall be addressed in due course.

Done in both English and French, the English version being authoritative.

Judge Ameera Mahomed Ismail, Presiding Judge
Dated 27 September 2016
At the Hague, The Netherlands

13.3 SENTENCING AL MAHDI

Melissa McKay

In 2016, Trial Chamber VIII sentenced Mr Ahmad Al Faqi Al Mahdi to nine years' imprisonment after he pleaded guilty to the Article 8(2)(e)(iv) offence of intentionally directing attacks against buildings dedicated to culture and religion in Mali, Timbuktu, in 2012.[129]

[129] Judgment and Sentence, *Al Mahdi* (ICC-01/12-01/15-171), Trial Chamber VIII, 27 September 2016.

In this rewritten sentence, Melissa McKay disrupts the notion that Articles 77 and 78 of the Rome Statute restrict the ICC to imposing sentences of imprisonment. Using principles of restorative justice and placing a strong focus on the objective of rehabilitation, McKay explores how non-carceral sentences are available at the ICC due to the use of the permissive language of 'may' rather than the directive language of 'shall'. She notes that such a sentence should only be considered where the situation of the crime and the affected community permit such a sentence to be delivered. McKay places the convicted offender as part of the global community that the preamble of the Rome Statute professes to advocate for, noting that while each person will have a different rehabilitative potential, the gains from such an approach are evident through domestic jurisprudence.

In applying this approach, McKay sentences Mr Al Mahdi, with the support of the community of Timbuktu and Mr Al Mahdi himself, to seven years of custodial imprisonment with 3,765 hours of community service to be served concurrently. In doing so, McKay provides a framework for future judicial officers to examine the possibilities available to them in sentencing applications and appeals.

No.: ICC-01/12-01/15
Date: 27 September 2016

Original: English

TRIAL CHAMBER VIII(B)

Before: Judge Melissa MCKAY

SITUATION IN THE REPUBLIC OF MALI
IN THE CASE OF THE *PROSECUTOR v. AHMAD AL FAQI AL MAHDI*

Public

Judgment and Sentence

SENTENCE

1. Having concluded that Mr Al Mahdi is responsible for intentionally attacking the above-mentioned protected objects as a co-perpetrator, the Chamber will now turn to the determination of the appropriate sentence. The submissions made by the parties and participants are addressed in this analysis.[130]

Applicable Law

2. For the purposes of determining the sentence, the Chamber has considered, inter alia, Articles 21, 23, 76, 77, and 78 of the Statute and Rules 143–148 of the Rules.

[130] The Chamber would like to thank Aicha Raeburn-Cherradi and Genevieve Westrope for their invaluable research support, without which this judgment would not be complete.

Purposes of Sentencing

3. Articles 77 and 78 of the Statute do not specify the purpose of sentences at the Court.

4. Deterrence is one objective of sentencing, as is denunciation, or the 'expression of society's condemnation of the criminal act and of the person who committed it'.[131] A third objective is the rehabilitation of the convicted person and the promotion of their reintegration into society.[132] Rehabilitation of the perpetrator is crucial where criminal sentences seek to incorporate concepts of restorative and transformative justice, which have, in the past few decades, become increasingly common elements of domestic criminal law while also gaining international prominence.[133]

5. The Chamber understands restorative justice to focus on the provision of restitution to the victims, the perpetrator taking responsibility for their actions, and the role of a sentence in contributing to reconciliation.[134] In essence, it focuses on repairing the broader harm caused by criminal behaviour, ideally through an inclusive and cooperative process.[135] In placing a greater emphasis on restorative justice, a sentence may assist in repairing harms suffered by individual victims and the community as a whole, as well as developing a more meaningful opportunity for the convicted person to take responsibility for their actions. A correct application of restorative justice approaches will consider the needs of the victim, the community, and the perpetrator, which necessitates an analysis of their rehabilitative potential.[136]

6. The Chamber notes the unique circumstances of the present case, where Mr Al Mahdi has pleaded guilty to the crime with which he has been charged, and considers that a 'guilty plea is accepted as a first step to rehabilitation of the perpetrator and a positive factor towards reconciliation of the offended community'.[137]

7. The Chamber views this as an opportune moment to provide further guidance on the sentencing objective of rehabilitation.

131 Decision on Sentence, *Katanga* (ICC-01/04-01/07), Trial Chamber, 23 May 2014, § 38 (hereafter Katanga Sentence).

132 See, for example, *ibid*, at § 38. Referred to by this Chamber as simply 'rehabilitation'.

133 In 2005, it was estimated that 80–100 countries were using some form of restorative justice in addressing crime, see D. Van Ness, *An Overview of Restorative Justice around the World*, Eleventh United Nations Congress on Crime Prevention and Criminal Justice: Workshop 2: Enhancing Criminal Justice Reform, Including Restorative Justice, April 2005, 1, 5–15. In the international context, see for example, *Handbook on Restorative Justice Programmes* (1st ed., New York: UNODC, 2006).

134 Supreme Court of Canada, *R v. Gladue*, [1999] 1 SCR 688, judgment of 23 April 1999 (hereinafter *Gladue*), at § 43; ECOSOC Res. 2000/12, 13 August 2002, section I, §§ 2–4.

135 Van Ness, *supra* note 133, p. 3.

136 GA Res. 45/110, 14 December 1990 (hereafter Tokyo Rules), Rules 1.4 and 1.5.

137 Sentencing Judgment – Separate Opinion of Judge Mumba, *Deronjić* (IT-02-61-S), Trial Chamber, 30 March 2004, § 2 (hereafter Deronjić Separate Opinion of Judge Mumba).

8. Regrettably, the rehabilitative objective has not been judicially examined in earnest by this Court, as the *Katanga* sentencing decision simply stated that rehabilitation was to be accorded limited weight.[138] There, without reference to jurisprudence or any other sources, the *Katanga* Chamber held that the objective of easing the convicted person's reintegration into society 'cannot be considered to be primordial as the sentence on its own cannot ensure the social reintegration of the convicted person'.[139] The *Katanga* Chamber provided no further analysis on this point.

9. With respect to the *Katanga* Chamber's suggestion that, for an objective of sentencing to be primordial the sentence must, on its own, ensure the objective is achieved, this Chamber disagrees. Were the *Katanga* Chamber's statement true with respect to rehabilitation then, likewise, neither deterrence nor denunciation could be primordial objectives of sentencing. A sentence cannot *ensure on its own* that an individual, or the general public for that matter, is deterred from committing a crime.[140] Nor can a sentence be said to satisfy every party to the process, or global observer for that matter, in terms of denunciation – it is trite to say that the appropriateness of a sentence, for either being too harsh or too lenient, is an oft-debated topic, in both domestic and international criminal law.

10. Sentencing, at its core, is about judging another human being – a member of our global community, with whom we share common bonds. It is a delicate science, guided by the law of this Court as well as general criminal legal principles, where judges are tasked with imposing sentences that best reflect each objective in light of all the circumstances of the individual and the crime in question. Though it is the intention of any criminal court to impose a sentence that achieves its objectives, the law is subject to the practical limitations of reality: 'Justice is the aspirational application of law to life.'[141] A court, on its own, cannot ensure any single objective;

[138] Katanga Sentence, *supra* note 131, at § 38.

[139] *Ibid*, at § 38.

[140] It is long-acknowledged that individual sanctions may not result in a sufficient deterrent ('I am too well aware of the weaknesses of juridical action alone to contend that in itself your decision under this Charter can prevent future wars. Judicial action always comes after the event. Wars are started only on the theory and in the confidence that they can be won. Personal punishment, to be suffered only in the event the war is lost, will probably not be a sufficient deterrent to prevent a war where the warmakers feel the chances of defeat to be negligible.' 'Second Day, Wednesday, 11/21/1945, Part 04', in Trial of the Major War Criminals before the International Military Tribunal. Volume II. Proceedings: 11/14/1945–11/30/1945. [Official text in the English language.] Nuremberg: IMT, 1947, 98–102). Further, the Chamber takes note of academic literature that has consistently demonstrated that neither general nor specific deterrence is so straightforward that recidivism is reduced through the application of a criminal sanction, see M. Drumbl, *Atrocity, Punishment, and International Law* (Cambridge: Cambridge University Press, 2007); M. Mennecke, 'Punishing Genocidaires: A Deterrent Effect or Not?' in S. Totten (ed.), *The Prevention and Intervention of Genocide* (New York: Routledge, 2008) 319–339.

[141] Supreme Court of Canada, *Yukon Francophone School Board, Education Area #23 v. Yukon (Attorney General)*, 2015 SCC 25, judgment of 14 May 2015 (hereinafter *Yukon Francophone School Board*), at § 34.

a court can only impose a just and appropriate sentence that is mindful of each of its objectives, and enforceable pursuant to its law.

11. Acknowledging life outside the legal corridors through which we tread, including the reality that sentences pronounced in a courtroom are subject to limitations in terms of their practical impact, is not to say that the sentencing process and its underlying objectives are moot. Rather, it is to acknowledge the complexities of the overarching context, and that the criminal trial process is but one avenue through which justice, accountability, and healing are pursued.

12. In the international criminal context, certain perpetrators may be prosecuted as the relevant conflict rages on, while others may appear before a court decades after the fact. Each of these scenarios, and those existing between the two ends of that spectrum, present challenges in crafting appropriate sentences.

13. The existence of such challenges, combined with the apparent tension between the objective of rehabilitation and a traditionally punitive approach to sentencing, have regrettably served to sideline the rehabilitative component of sentencing in the international criminal context.

14. Turning to the consideration of rehabilitation at the ad hoc and hybrid tribunals, the Chamber considers the *Čelibići* Trial Chamber's general reference to the objective of rehabilitation, where it noted the following:

> The factor of rehabilitation considers the circumstances of reintegrating the guilty accused into society. This is usually the case when younger, or less educated, members of society are found guilty of offences. It therefore becomes necessary to reintegrate them into society so that they can become useful members of it and enable them to lead normal and productive lives upon their release from imprisonment. The age of the accused, [their] circumstances, [their] ability to be rehabilitated and availability of facilities in the confinement facility can, and should, be relevant considerations in this regard.[142]

15. In a separate opinion, Judge Mumba expanded on rehabilitation: international justice 'is not about unfair retribution; if that were the case, humanity should forget about reconciliation'.[143] Judge Mumba further cautioned against an overemphasis on vengeance, which could manifest through harsh sentences following guilty pleas, and opined that 'rehabilitation, after turmoil, may serve to reduce the incidence of political instability and conflict'.[144]

[142] Judgment, *Mucić et al.* (IT-96-21), Trial Chamber, 16 November 1998 (hereafter Čelebići TJ), § 1233.

[143] Deronjić Separate Opinion of Judge Mumba, *supra* note 137, § 3.

[144] *Ibid.*

16. Generally, ad hoc tribunals have supported access to rehabilitative programming,[145] but, as in *Katanga*, have held the objective itself subject to an 'undue weight' caveat.[146] For example, the *Čelibići* Appeals Chamber considered that:

> Although both national jurisdictions and certain international and regional human rights instruments provide that rehabilitation should be one of the primary concerns for a court in sentencing, this cannot play a *predominant* role in the decision-making process . . . Accordingly, although rehabilitation (in accordance with international human rights standards) should be considered as a relevant factor, it is not one which should be given undue weight.[147]

17. The jurisprudence from the ad hoc tribunals has not, however, provided guidance on the threshold for undue weight in balancing any sentencing objective.[148] Though rehabilitation has typically been accorded lesser weight, judges have equally held that deterrence 'must not be accorded undue prominence in the overall assessment of the sentences to be imposed'.[149] In fact, the *Čelibići* Appeals Chamber further held that it was erroneous for a trial chamber to state that deterrence was the most important factor to consider.[150]

18. Meanwhile, domestic sources of law suggest that, for certain crimes, though the objectives of deterrence and denunciation may be more prominent, this does not negate the rehabilitative component of the sentence.[151] Domestic law

[145] Judgment, *Furundžija* (IT-95-17/1-T), Trial Chamber, 10 December 1998, (hereafter Furundžija TJ), § 291.

[146] See, for example, Judgment, *Mucić et al.* (IT-96-21-A), Appeals Chamber, 20 February 2001 (hereafter Čelebići AJ), § 806; Sentencing Judgment, *Brima et al.* (SCSL-04-16-T), Trial Chamber, 19 July 2007 (hereinafter *Brima* SJ), §§ 14–17; Judgment, *Kordić & Čerkez* (IT-95-14/2-A), Appeals Chamber, 17 December 2004 (hereafter Kordić & Čerkez AJ), §§ 1073–1083.

[147] Čelebići AJ, *supra* note 146, at § 806.

[148] In several cases where an appellant has alleged 'undue weight' has been placed in one of the sentencing objectives, Chambers have dismissed the appeal ground for the appellant's failure to adequately articulate the error. See, for example, Čelebići AJ, *supra* note 146, at § 803; Judgment in Sentencing Appeals, *Tadić* (IT-94-1-A & IT-94-1-A *bis*), Appeals Chamber, 26 January 2000 (hereafter Tadić Sentencing AJ), § 48.

[149] Tadić Sentencing AJ, *supra* note 148, at § 48. See also Čelebići AJ, *supra* note 146, at §§ 801–803; Judgment, IT-95-14/1-A), Appeals Chamber, 24 March 2000 (hereinafter Aleksovski AJ), § 185.

[150] Čelebići AJ, *supra* note 146, at §§ 801, 803. See also Kordić & Čerkez AJ, *supra* note 146, at § 1078; Judgment on Sentencing Appeal, *Dragan Nikolić* (IT-94-2A), Appeals Chamber, 4 February 2005 (hereafter Dragan Nikolić SAJ), § 46; Aleksovski AJ, *supra* note 149, at § 185; Tadić Sentencing AJ, *supra* note 148, at § 48.

[151] These are generally violent crimes against vulnerable populations, in line with the fundamental principle of proportionality and the degree of responsibility of the perpetrator. See, for example, Finland, Criminal Code Chapter 2(c), ss. 11 and 12 (for certain crimes and where the sentence exceeds three years, the court may, on request of the prosecutor, order the convicted person to serve the entire sentence in prison; however, after being ordered to serve the entire sentence in prison, that person will be released after serving five-sixths of their sentence or once they have been deemed no longer dangerous); Canada, Criminal Code, ss. 718.01–718.04

additionally suggests that rehabilitation is to be considered for all perpetrators, not simply those who are subject to personal or social disadvantages.[152]

19. Given the gravity of the crimes before the Court, the Chamber is of the view that victims, including both the specifically harmed community and the global community, are owed sentences that have a strong emphasis on denunciation and deterrence.

20. The Chamber, however, also views the first line of the Preamble to the Statute as a significant directive, and considers that all parties are likewise owed sentences that attempt to contribute to the healing of the 'common bonds' and 'shared heritage' through which *all* people, including the convicted person, are united.[153]

21. The Preamble's acknowledgement that international crimes may shatter the 'delicate mosaic' of humanity is reminiscent of the way in which certain indigenous communities view crimes as a tear in the 'community fabric', which may be repaired through restorative justice mechanisms.[154] In this regard, the Chamber considers that a more a deliberate emphasis on rehabilitation is required in its sentencing practices.

22. In considering how the Court can more effectively incorporate the rehabilitative objective, it is important to examine how the sentencing objectives intersect.

23. The Chamber first notes the long-standing principle in criminal law that it is the certainty rather than severity of punishment that more effectively deters criminality.[155] Perpetrators serving longer prison sentences may, in fact, be *more likely* to reoffend, due to the negative impact of being removed from factors that promote rehabilitative potential.[156] The Chamber thus views the imposition of lengthy sentences as fulfilling, primarily, the denunciatory objective.

24. With respect to deterrence, it appears as though sentences focusing on an individual's rehabilitative potential through initiatives such as job and education

(crimes against children, participants of the justice system, certain animals, and vulnerable people), 718(d), 718.2(d), and 718.2(e) (nevertheless they articulate rehabilitation and alternative sentences as ongoing considerations); Australia (New South Wales), Crimes (Sentencing Procedure) Act 1999 No. 92, s. 5(1) (articulates imprisonment as a last resort).

[152] Supreme Court of South Australia, *Vartzokas v. Zanker* (1989) 51 SASR 277, judgment of 5 July 1989, at 3–4.

[153] Preamble, ICCSt.

[154] A. W. Blue and M. A. Blue, 'The Case for Aboriginal Justice and Healing: The Self Perceived through a Broken Mirror' in M. L. Hadley (ed.), *The Spiritual Roots of Restorative Justice* (New York: SUNY Press, 2001) 57–79.

[155] C. Beccaria, 'Dei delitti e delle pene (Crimes and Punishment)', 1766 ed., § XXVII, Venturi (ed.), 1965, p. 59. For a modern approach, see, for example, S. Durlauf and D. Nagin, 'Imprisonment and Crime: Can Both Be Reduced?' 10(1) *Criminology & Public Policy* (2011) 13–54; V. Wright, *Deterrence in Criminal Justice: Evaluating Certainty vs. Severity of Punishment*, The Sentencing Project, November 2010, available at www.antoniocasella.eu/nume/Wright_2010.pdf.

[156] Wright, *supra* note 155, at 6–8.

training, therapeutic treatment, and social connections are more likely to reduce recidivism.[157]

25. Additionally, these sentences benefit the perpetrator through various outcomes, including the acquisition of knowledge and skills, strengthened self-perception, and greater self-understanding.[158] It is suggested that rehabilitative programming may allow an individual to transform their perspectives to become more inclusive, open, and reflective, thereby gaining greater control over their lives as socially responsible, clear-thinking decision-makers.[159]

26. The Chamber thus notes the potential for a positive impact on the convicted person themselves through a sentence emphasising rehabilitation. Not only does such a sentence aim to protect the community by reducing recidivism; it also has the additional benefit of allowing the perpetrator the opportunity to take meaningful accountability for their crimes, and to possibly return to the community at some point in the future as a contributing member who is better equipped to make decisions with the entire community in mind.

27. The Chamber further views that the rehabilitation of the perpetrator is an inextricable component of deterrence and, indeed, opines that without considering *how* the convicted person can be rehabilitated, specific deterrence is entirely unmet. The objectives of deterrence and rehabilitation are distinct, yet indivisible, as meaningful deterrence requires rehabilitation, and the aim of that rehabilitation is to allow the perpetrator the opportunity to make better, non-destructive choices in the future, thereby deterring future criminal activity.

28. Finally, the Chamber considers the way in which sentences that incorporate aspects of restorative justice, such as rehabilitation, may contribute to a community's sense of peace and justice. Overall, restorative justice programming in domestic

[157] C. J. Smith et al., *Correctional Industries Preparing Prisoners for Re-entry: Recidivism & Post-Release Employment*, US Dept. of Justice Report No. 214608 (2006), available at www.ojp.gov/pdffiles1/nij/grants/214608.pdf; C. Uggen, 'Work as a Turning Point in the Life Course of Criminals: A Duration Model of Age, Employment, and Recidivism' 65(4) *American Sociological Review* (2000) 529–546; E. Gunnison et al., 'Correctional Practitioners on Reentry: A Missed Perspective' 2(1) *Journal of Prison Education and Reentry* (2015) 32–54; J. Petersilia, *When Prisoners Come Home: Parole and Prisoner Reentry* (New York: Oxford University Press, 2003); L. M. Davis et al., *Evaluating the Effectiveness of Correctional Education: A Meta-Analysis of Programs That Provide Education to Incarcerated Adults* (Santa Monica, CA: RAND Corporation, 2013).

[158] Uggen, *supra* note 157; Davis et al., *supra* note 157; N. Ronel and E. Elisha, 'A Different Perspective: Introducing Positive Criminology' 55(2) *International Journal of Offender Therapy and Comparative Criminology* (2011) 305–325; B. B. Roth et al., 'The Relationship between Prisoners' Academic Self-Efficacy and Participation in Education, Previous Convictions, Sentence Length, and Portion of Sentence Served' 3(2) *Journal of Prison Education and Reentry* (2016) 106–121.

[159] C. Calleja, 'Jack Mezirow's Conceptualisation of Adult Transformative Learning: A Review' 20 (1) *Journal of Adult and Continuing Education* (2014) 117–136; D. Patton, 'The Need for New Emotionally Intelligent Criminal Justice & Criminological Approaches to Help End the "War on Terror"' (September 2016), available at https://ssrn.com/abstract=2860881.

settings, which includes a focus on rehabilitation in sentencing, appears to result in increased victim and perpetrator satisfaction with the overall process, greater fear reduction for victims, and the development of increased empathy in the convicted person.[160] The Chamber notes that, depending on the status of the conflict at issue, outcomes in the international criminal context may differ significantly. Nevertheless, the Chamber considers that at least some of these outcomes may result.

29. Based on the above, the Chamber is of the mind that there is no implicit hierarchy between denunciation, deterrence, and rehabilitation. In other words, no one objective of sentencing is determinative, but rather each objective is relevant to the balancing test that sentencing judges must perform. These objectives are fulfilled through the imposition of a just and appropriate sentence, which 'reflects the degree of culpability while contributing to the restoration of peace and reconciliation in the communities concerned'.[161]

30. Each perpetrator will have a different rehabilitative potential. A trial chamber has broad discretion in determining an appropriate sentence considering all the unique circumstances of the individual and case,[162] and equally holds such discretion in assessing how the sentence properly fulfils each objective.

31. The sentence should make its objectives plain. To do so, the sentence must simply speak to each objective in the context of the case. This is distinct from articulating a particular objective as primordial or assigning a hierarchy amongst the objectives. It is sufficient that the sentence reflects each of the objectives logically and accessibly. This is a fact-specific analysis, and, as such, there may be some cases where a certain objective is more relevant than another. It is the context of the specific case before it that will determine the weight a chamber attributes to each objective in delineating the sentence.

32. Based on the inclusion of rehabilitation as an equal objective of sentencing, the Chamber, in undertaking to pronounce a just, appropriate, and individualised sentence within the context of this case, turns to consider the types of sentences that may be imposed upon convicted persons at this Court.

[160] Van Ness, *supra* note 133, at 5–6, 13; M. Umbreit et al., 'The Impact of Restorative Justice Conferencing: A Multinational Perspective' 1(2) *British Journal of Community Justice* (2002) 21–48, at 22–28 (satisfaction with process), 32–37 (recidivism), 44–45.

[161] Katanga Sentence, *supra* note 131, at § 38, referring to Rule 145(1)(a).

[162] Judgment on the appeals of the Prosecutor and Mr Thomas Lubanga Dyilo against the Decision on Sentence pursuant to Article 76 of the Statute, *Lubanga* (ICC-01/04-01/06-3122), Appeals Chamber, 1 December 2014 (hereafter Lubanga Sentence Appeal), §§ 36–46 and all the citations therein; Judgment, *Duch* (Case 001-F28), Supreme Court Chamber, 3 February 2012 (hereafter *Duch* AJ), § 354; Judgment, *Nuon Chea and Khieu Samphân* (Case 002/01-F36), Supreme Court Chamber, 23 November 2016 (hereafter Case 002/01 AJ), § 1107. See further Judgment and Sentence, *Kambanda* (ICTR 97-23-S), Trial Chamber, 04 September 1998 (hereafter Kambanda Sentence), § 30; Judgment (IT-98-29/1) *Milošević (Dragomir)* (IT-98-29/1), Appeals Chamber, 12 November 2009 (hereafter Milošević (Dragomir) AJ), § 297; Čelebići AJ, *supra* note 146, at §§ 725, 780, 787 and the citations therein.

Applicable Penalties

33. At the outset, the Chamber notes the principle of *nulla poena sine lege*,[163] which prevents the arbitrary imposition of criminal sanctions and ensures legal certainty.

34. The Chamber considers the text of Article 77 of the Statute, which states that the Court *may* impose one of the following penalties: imprisonment for a specified number of years[164] or life imprisonment.[165] In addition to imprisonment, the Court *may* order a fine and/or a forfeiture of proceeds, property, and assets derived from the crime.[166]

35. This Chamber first notes that the text of the Statute employs the permissive language of '*may* impose' but does not state that the Court '*shall* impose' those penalties. Both Articles 77(1) (setting out terms of imprisonment) and 77(2) (setting out pecuniary penalties) employ this permissive language. This is distinct from Article 78, which prescribes factors the Court '*shall* ... take into account'[167] in determining a sentence, and further states that the Court '*shall* deduct'[168] previous time spent in detention.[169]

36. International jurisprudence has interpreted that the statutory inclusion of 'shall' prescribes a mandatory directive,[170] while 'may' has been interpreted to confer a discretionary power.[171] This interpretation likewise appears in domestic jurisprudence.[172]

[163] Art. 23, ICCSt.

[164] Art. 77(1)(a), ICCSt.

[165] Art. 77(1)(b), ICCSt.

[166] Art. 77(2), ICCSt.

[167] Art. 78(1), ICCSt (emphasis added).

[168] Art. 78(2), ICCSt (emphasis added).

[169] This language is also reflected in the French version of the Statute, where Article 77 states 'la Cour *peut* prononcer' (emphasis added) while similar permissive language is absent from Article 78 (for example, 'la Cour tient compte'; 'la Cour en déduit le temps'; 'la Cour prononce').

[170] See, for example, Decision on *Amicus Curiae*'s Appeal against the Order Referring a Case to the Republic of Serbia, *Petar Jojić and Vjerica Radeta* (MICT-17-111-R90), Appeals Chamber, 12 December 2018, § 11.

[171] Judgment, *Nyiramasuhuko et al.* (ICTR-98-42-A), Appeals Chamber, 14 December 2015, §§ 69–71; Appeal Decision on Joinder, *Gotovina et al.* (IT-03-73-AR73.1), Appeals Chamber, 25 October 2006, §§ 16–17; Decision on Vinko Pandurević's Interlocutory Appeal against the Decision on Joinder, *Pandurević & Trbić* (IT-05-86-AR73.1), Appeals Chamber, 24 January 2006, § 7, with each case considering Rule 48 of the ICTY Rules on Joinder, which state that 'persons ... *may* be jointly charged and tried' (emphasis added). See further Judgment, *Bagosora* (ICTR-98-41-A), Appeals Chamber, 14 December 2011, § 533 ('there is nothing in Rule 54 of the Rules that makes it mandatory for the Trial Chamber to issue a subpoena', where the text of Rule 54 reads 'a Trial Chamber *may* issue' (emphasis added)).

[172] See, for example, Judgment, *Rajendar Mohan Rana & Ors vs Prem Prakash Chaudhary & Ors* (2011 8 AD (DELHI) 153, LPA 554/2011), Delhi High Court (Appeals Chamber), 1 September 2011, §§ 7–10; Review of a Decision of the Court of Appeal, *Heritage Farms, Inc. v. Markel Insurance Company* (2012 WI 26), Supreme Court of Wisconsin, 16 March 2012, § 32.

37. To be clear, the Chamber is not of the view that the drafters of the Statute intended to create a situation wherein *no* penalty would be imposed – this would produce an unreasonable result and run contrary to the Preamble's determination to end impunity – but rather that flexibility in what the judges *may* impose in terms of 'imprisonment' was contemplated.[173]

38. The *travaux préparatoires* further illuminate the level of judicial discretion in sentencing. For example, mandatory minimum periods of imprisonment were contemplated,[174] but ultimately not included in the Statute. The drafters considered mandating the imposition of the highest penalty provided for by the law of the state of which the convicted person was a national, the state where the crime was committed, or the state which had jurisdiction over the accused;[175] such requirement, likewise, was not included.

39. Conditionally suspended sentences were also contemplated,[176] as was probation in limited circumstances.[177] Though these were not explicitly included in the Statute, certain documents from the *travaux préparatoires* suggest that judges could have recourse to sentencing practices and provisions from certain states.[178] This aligns with the final text of the Statute, which includes general principles of domestic legal systems as a source of law.[179]

40. Finally, it is noteworthy that the drafters of the Statute considered it to be a living document, that could be revisited and reassessed as the number and types of cases grew,[180] and of further relevance that the application and interpretation of the law at the Court must be consistent with internationally recognised

[173] This is supported, for example, by International Commission of Jurists, *The International Criminal Court: Third ICJ Position Paper*, August 1995 (hereafter Third ICJ Position Paper), 61, 62 ('The ICJ recognises that it is important for the Court to have discretion in sentencing in order to tailor specific sentences to specific cases').

[174] See, for example, Draft Statute for an International Criminal Court, Prepared by a Committee of Experts, July 1995 (hereafter 1995 Siracusa Draft), 72–74 (suggesting the language of the Statute include 'imprisonment for a time not less than one year' because 'the minimum sentence should be no less than one year'); Working Group on Penalties, *Penalties*, UN Doc. A/AC.249/1997/CRP.1, 13 August 1997 (hereafter August 1997 Penalties Draft), 3; Working Group on Penalties, *ILC Draft Articles 46(2) and 47 – Applicable Penalties*, UN Doc. A/AC.249/1997/WG.6/CRP.1, 2 December 1997, 2; *Identification of the Main Issues Pertaining to Methods of Proceedings* (Informal paper prepared by an open ended Working Group under the chairmanship of Mr Gerard Hafner), UN Doc. UD/A/AC.244/1995/IP.4, 4 April 1995 (hereafter April 1995 Informal Paper), 12; *Summary of the Proceedings of the Ad Hoc Committee during 3–13 April 1995*, Ad Hoc Committee on the Establishment of an International Criminal Court, UN Doc. A/AC-244/2, § 113, Annex II, 2(vi).

[175] August 1997 Penalties Draft, *supra* note 174, at 5.

[176] 1995 Siracusa Draft, *supra* note 174, at 57; April 1995 Informal Paper, *supra* note 174, at 12, § 59.

[177] 1995 Siracusa Draft, *supra* note 174, at 73 (Draft Article 47 a (3)).

[178] 1995 Siracusa Draft, *supra* note 174, at 74.

[179] Article 21(1)(c), which allows the Court, in certain circumstances, to apply national principles of law if they are not in conflict with the Rome Statute or international law.

[180] 1995 Siracusa Draft, *supra* note 174, at 13.

human rights[181] – a field of law that continues to evolve through the inclusion of more diverse voices and legal approaches.

41. Sentencing judges thus have significant discretion regarding all aspects of the penalty imposed upon a perpetrator, including the *type* of penalty. This corresponds with the need for an individualised sentence, and the fundamental principles underlying the discretion of a sentencing judge.[182] Sentencing discretion is nevertheless limited by the requirement that the punishment be appropriate to the crime while maintaining consistency with internationally recognised human rights,[183] and that the punishment respect the Statute and the Rules of the Court.

42. As for the types of penalty that judges may impose, the Chamber notes that 'imprisonment' is not defined in the Statute or the Rules and has not been judicially interpreted at this Court. It further does not appear as though the meaning of 'imprisonment' has been judicially examined in the hybrid or ad hoc tribunals, though there has been flexibility in the types of sentences imposed.

43. In contempt proceedings, for example, international chambers have imposed sentences that are variations on those specifically articulated in the relevant Statute and/or Rules.[184] Further, the Special Court for Sierra Leone (SCSL) held that, when the relevant texts provide that certain punishments may be imposed by setting out a maximum sentence without reference to a minimum sentence, sentencing judges have 'an inherent power to impose a sentence other than a fine or imprisonment ... [including] a conditional discharge ... subject to the particular circumstances of the case'.[185]

44. This Chamber has difficulty imagining a scenario outside a contempt proceeding where a conditional discharge would be appropriate in this jurisdiction; however, the Chamber views this jurisprudence as reinforcing the significant discretionary power of sentencing judges in terms of the *type* of sentence imposed. The Chamber also considers that the omission of a mandatory period of imprisonment is indicative of the high discretionary authority to craft an appropriate sentence without necessarily resorting to a custodial sentence.[186]

[181] Art. 21(3), ICCSt.

[182] There is broad discretion in determining a sentence, and there exists a high threshold to appeal these decisions. See Lubanga Sentence Appeal, *supra* note 162, at §§ 36–46 and the citations therein; Duch AJ, *supra* note 162, at § 354; Case 002/01 AJ, *supra* note 162, at § 1107; Milošević (Dragomir) AJ, *supra* note 162, at § 297.

[183] Art. 21(3), ICCSt.

[184] Decision in Proceedings for Contempt with Orders in lieu of an Indictment, *Akhbar Beirut S.A.L. Ibrahim Mohamed Al Amin* (STL-14-06/I/CJ), Contempt Judge, 31 January 2014, §§ 9–13; Judgment on Allegations of Contempt against Prior Counsel, Milan Vujin, *Dusko Tadić* (IT-94-1-A-R77), Appeals Chamber, 31 January 2000, §§ 165–172.

[185] Sentencing Judgment in Contempt Proceedings, *Margaret Fomba Brima et al.* (SCSL-2005-02), 21 September 2005, § 35. See further § 19.

[186] This is consistent with domestic jurisprudence, which suggests that where there is no mandatory minimum sentencing regime, non-custodial sentences are a valid option; see, for example,

45. There are several international instruments that support the use of non-custodial measures, perhaps most notably the Tokyo Rules, which predate this Court, having been adopted by the United Nations General Assembly in 1990. The Tokyo Rules serve as 'a set of basic principles to promote the use of non-custodial measures' and are 'intended to promote greater community involvement in the management of criminal justice, specifically in the treatment of perpetrators, as well as to promote among perpetrators a sense of responsibility towards society'.[187]

46. Rule 2.1 requires the rules to be applied to *all persons* subject to prosecution, at all stages of the administration of justice, and Rules 1.5 and 2.4 encourage the development of new non-custodial measures. Possible non-custodial measures are enumerated in Rule 8.2, including, inter alia: conditional discharge; economic sanctions; restitution orders; suspended sentences; judicial supervision; community service orders; and house arrest.

47. The more recently pronounced Doha Declaration additionally calls upon States to 'adopt comprehensive and inclusive ... criminal justice policies and programmes that fully take into account ... the root causes of crime, as well as the conditions conducive to its occurrence', to 'implement and enhance policies for prison inmates that focus on education, work, medical care, rehabilitation, social reintegration and the prevention of recidivism', and to 'create[e] opportunities for community service and support ... the social reintegration and rehabilitation of perpetrators'.[188]

48. Domestically, there exist multiple flexible sentencing regimes that can be tailored to individual circumstances and to the gravity of the crime. Such sentences include conditional or community-based sentences, where an individual serves their sentence in the community subject to strict rules;[189] intermittent sentences, where an individual serves the custodial portion of their sentence intermittently while being subject to conditions when not in custody;[190] or suspended sentences, where an individual's sentence is deferred, subject to their following the conditions of release and not reoffending.[191]

Sentence Judgment, *S v. Dikqacwi and Others* (SS49/2012), High Court of South Africa [2013] ZAWCHC 67, 15 April 2013 (hereafter Sentence Judgment, *S v. Dikqacwi*), § 28.

[187] Tokyo Rules, *supra* note 136, at Rules 1.1 and 1.2.

[188] GA Res. 70/174 (Doha Declaration), 8 January 2016, Arts. 5(a), (j), (k), 10(d), (k). See further ECOSOC Res. 2017/19, §§ 1–2.

[189] South Australia, Sentencing Act (hereafter South Australia Sentencing Act), s. 25(4); Canada, Criminal Code, s. 742.1; Finland, Criminal Code (780/2005), Chapter 2(c), s. 5; Ireland, Criminal Justice Act, 2006, s. 101; Queensland, Penalties and Sentences Act, 1992, s. 32; United Kingdom, Sentencing Act 2020, ss. 200–202.

[190] Canada Criminal Code, s. 732; United States, New York Consolidated Laws, Penal Law, Part II, § 85.00.

[191] South Australia Sentencing Act, *supra* note 189, at s. 25(4); Canada, Criminal Code, s. 731(1)(a); Ireland, Criminal Justice Act, 2006, ss. 99–100; Japan, Penal Code (Act No. 45 of 1907), 2017, s. 25; Russian Criminal Code, Article 73; United Kingdom, Sentencing Act 2020, s. 277; Denmark, Penal Code, Articles 56–60.

49. Domestic legislation has further included more substantive definitions of 'imprisonment', and jurisprudence addressing these regimes has considered its meaning extensively. For example, the Irish Criminal Justice Act defines imprisonment to include detention in 'places other than prisons',[192] and the South Australian Sentencing Act includes community-based custodial sentences and suspended sentences under the 'sentence of imprisonment' umbrella.[193] The Canadian Criminal Code expressly names community-based sentences as 'conditional sentences of imprisonment'.[194]

50. The Supreme Court of Canada has also articulated that a conditional sentence is a term of imprisonment.[195] South African courts have used the term 'direct imprisonment' to distinguish sentences that involve time spent in prison, while taking care to note that these are not necessarily more lenient sentences,[196] and Australian courts have imposed sentences of imprisonment to be served in the community[197] while explicitly stating that these are sentences of imprisonment.[198] Zimbabwean jurisprudence has articulated community service as a form of imprisonment,[199] while the Supreme Court of India has held that 'sentenced to imprisonment' does not equate to 'condemned to prison upon conviction'.[200] Courts in the United Kingdom, meanwhile, have defined a term of imprisonment as 'an order of restriction of freedom on the perpetrator',[201] and held that 'every confinement of the person is an imprisonment, whether it be in a common prison, or in a private house'.[202]

[192] Ireland, Criminal Justice Act, s. 98, referring to the Prisons Act, 1970, s. 2.

[193] South Australia Sentencing Act, s. 25(3)(a)(i). Further, the Queensland (Australia) Penalties and Sentences Act, 1992, ss. 111–113 sets out 'intensive correction orders:, whereby an individual convicted of a crime 'serve[s] the sentence of imprisonment by way of intensive correction in the community'.

[194] Canada, Criminal Code, s. 742.1.

[195] Supreme Court of Canada, *R v. Proulx*, 2000 SCC 5, judgment of 31 January 2000, at § 29.

[196] Constitutional Court of South Africa, *S v. M* (CCT 53/06) [2007] ZACC 18, judgment of 26 September 2007, at §§ 58–63; Sentence Judgment, *S v. Dikqacwi*, *supra* note 186, at §§ 25–28.

[197] Supreme Court of the Australian Capital Territory (Court of Appeal), *Samani v. The Queen* [2016] ACTCA 48, judgment of 12 September 2016, at §§ 32–38, 42–47; Court of Criminal Appeal, *R v. Pogson*, *R v. Lapham*, *R v. Martin* [2012] NSWCCA 225, decision of 22 October 2012, at §§ 96–98, 105–111.

[198] Court of Criminal Appeal, *supra* note 197, at, at § 109 ('An ICO deprives a perpetrator of his or her liberty in a real and not merely fictional sense').

[199] Bulawayo High Court, *S v. Sibanda* (CRB G 440/10) and Another (CRB G 440-1/10), [2011] ZWBHC 79, review judgment of 21 April 2011 ('both accused persons have already served 4 *months imprisonment in the form of community service*' (emphasis added)). See also Denmark, Criminal Code (Order No. 909, 2005), Arts. 62–64 (where a custodial sentence may be suspended on the condition that a convicted person undertakes community service); South Australia Sentencing Act, *supra* note 189, at Art. 25(3)(b)(iii).

[200] Supreme Court of India, *State of Maharashtra v. Chandrabhan Tale* (1983 AIR 803, 1983 SCR (3) 327), judgment of 7 July 1983, at 348–350.

[201] England and Wales Court of Appeal (Criminal Division), *R v. Wiles* [2004] EWCA Crim 836, judgment of 4 March 2004, at §§ 14–15.

[202] England and Wales High Court (Queen's Bench), *Bird v. Jones* [1845] EWHC QB J64, judgment of 11 January 1845.

51. Generally, the appropriateness of these 'alternative' sentences is guided by legislation, which may restrict their use based on the severity of the crime, the vulnerability of the victims, or the length of a maximum sentence. Domestic courts, however, and in some cases domestic legislation itself, have further articulated that carceral imprisonment is a last resort, and should only be used in the absence of suitable non-custodial sentences,[203] particularly when a convicted person is themself a victim of systemic inequality.[204]

52. Domestically, alternative forms of imprisonment have been imposed upon individuals convicted of violent offences, including killings and attempted killings;[205] sexual assaults, including where the victim is a minor;[206] other physical assaults, including spousal violence, instances where the victim was strangled, and where there was intent to injure;[207] death threats;[208] and kidnapping,[209] among others.[210]

[203] Bulawayo High Court, *S v. Majaya* (Case No. HC 168/2003) [2003] ZWBHC 15, review judgment of 29 January 2003, at §§ 3–4; *Gladue*, *supra* note 134, at §§ 36, 40; Supreme Court of Canada, *R v. Ipeelee*, 2012 SCC 13, judgment of 23 March 2012, at §§ 47–48, 50–51, 68. Criminal Code of Canada, s. 718.2(e); Crimes (Sentencing Procedure) Act 1999 (New South Wales), s. 5(1). This is also reflected in the Tokyo Rules, *supra* note 136, at Rule 1.5, which requires member states to provide options other than incarceration, taking into account the rehabilitative needs of the perpetrator, and is further reflected in the European Prison Rules (Council of Europe, June 2006), Chapter 1 ('no one shall be deprived of liberty save as a measure of last resort').

[204] Criminal Code of Canada, s. 718.2(e); *Gladue*, *supra* note 135, at §§ 37, 61, 65, 68; *Ipeelee*, *supra* note 203, at §§ 64–79.

[205] High Court of South Africa (Gauteng), *Mosikili v. State* (A339/2017) [2018] ZAGPPHC 813, Appeals Chamber, judgment of 3 May 2018, §§ 5–16; Western Cape High Court (South Africa), *S v. Lakay* (A 724/2010) [2012] ZAWCHC 14, Appeals Chamber, judgment of 2 March 2012, §§ 21–31; South Africa Supreme Court of Appeal, *S v. Potgieter* 1994 (1) SACR 61 (A), judgment of 29 November 1993, pp. 83–90; South Africa Supreme Court of Appeal, *S v. Ingram* 1995 (1) SACR 1 (A); High Court of New Zealand, *R v. Hodgson* (CRI 2009-044-10450 [2010] NZHC 1750), judgment of 28 September 2010, §§ 20–22; High Court of Justice (Trinidad & Tobago), *State v. Ramkay Gayah for Manslaughter*, [2002] TTHC 12, judgment of 4 June 2002; Supreme Court of New South Wales (Australia), *R v. MB* [2017] NSWSC 619, §§ 73–79. Japan: The Kyoto District Court sentenced a woman who strangled her son to death to a suspended sentence, see 'Woman gets suspended sentence for killing mentally disabled son', *Japan Today*, 15 December 2021, available at https://japantoday.com/category/crime/woman-gets-suspended-sentence-for-killing-mentally-disabled-son.

[206] Canada: *R v. Stewart* 1999 CarswellSask 404, [1999] S.J. No. 413, 42 W.C.B. (2d) 546; *R v. C.R. P.* (2001) O.J. No. 1595; *R v. L. (R.)* 2004 CarswellOnt 5856 [2004] O.J. No. 3502; South Africa: *S v. Mambila* (SH796/03) [2008] ZAGPHC 465 (22 September 2008).

[207] British Columbia Court of Appeal (Canada), *R v. Reid* (2002) B.C.J. No. 845, judgment of 24 April 2002; Ontario Court of Appeal (Canada), *R v. Veenhof* 2011 ONCA 195, judgment of 7 March 2011; Court of Appeal of New Zealand, *Mason v. R* [2021] NZCA 185, judgment of 14 May 2021; High Court of New Zealand, *Colvin v. R* [2021] NZHC 400, judgment of 5 March 2021; Supreme Court of the Northern Territory (Australia), *R v. Ebatarintja* [2010] NTSC 6, judgment of 11 March 2010.

[208] Supreme Court of Canada, *R v. Middleton* 2009 SCC 21, judgment of 22 May 2009.

[209] Sentence Judgment, *S v. Dikqacwi*, *supra* note 186.

[210] For example, one particular restorative justice youth diversion programme in the United States prioritises serious offences, with 62 per cent of their restorative case conferences involving felonies,

53. In imposing non-custodial sentences, the involvement of the community is essential, to rehabilitate the perpetrator as well as to ensure that meaningful reconciliation is considered.[211]

54. The Chamber recalls that it may, in certain circumstances, apply national principles of law if they are not in conflict with the Rome Statute or international law.[212] The Chamber finds that the imposition of 'alternative' sentences, a widespread practice in domestic legal traditions, is in line with international law, as evidenced by the Tokyo Rules and the European Prison Rules. The Chamber further finds that imposing alternative sentences does not conflict with the Rome Statute.

55. Finally, the Chamber notes that each case must be carefully considered in light of all the relevant circumstances before finding an alternative sentence is appropriate, with attention to each of the sentencing objectives, the gravity of the crime, the circumstances of the accused, and the input of the victims.

56. The Chamber holds that it has the legal authority to consider whether an alternative sentence is appropriate in this case.

Factors to Be Considered pursuant to the Statute and Rule 145

57. To determine the appropriate sentence, the Chamber will consider: (i) the gravity of the crime; (ii) Mr Al Mahdi's culpable conduct; and (iii) his individual circumstances. Rule 145(1)(c) factors and aggravating and mitigating circumstances are discussed when relevant.

[The author relies on paragraphs 76–105 of the original judgment.]

Determination of the Sentence

58. The prosecution submits that Mr Al Mahdi's sentence should be between nine and eleven years.[213] The defence made extensive submissions on the adequate assessment of the gravity of the crime charged, the absence of aggravating circumstances and the importance of the mitigating circumstances in this case.[214] The

such as robberies, battery causing great bodily injury, assaults with a deadly weapon, sexual battery, arson, and crimes involving the exhibition of a deadly weapon besides a firearm, see S. Baliga, S. Henry, and G. Valentine, *Restorative Community Conferencing: A Study of Community Works West's Restorative Justice Youth Diversion Program in Alameda County*, Impact Justice, available at https://impactjustice.org/wp-content/uploads/CWW_RJreport.pdf, at 7–8.

211 Tokyo Rules, *supra* note 136, at Rule 1.2. See also GA Res. 40/34, 29 November 1985 (UN Declaration of Basic Principles of Justice for Victims of Crime and Abuse of Power), Art. 6(b).

212 Art. 21(1)(c), ICCSt.

213 Public redacted version of Prosecution's submissions on sentencing, 22 July 2016, ICC-01/12-01/15-139-Conf, § 3.

214 Observations de la Défense sur les principes devant gouverner la peine et les circonstances aggravantes et/ou atténuantes en la cause, en conformité avec l'ordonnance ICC-01/12-01/15-99 de la Chambre ICC-01/12-01/15-141-Conf, 20 September 2016, ICC-01/12-01/15-141-Corr-Red 20-09-2016 1/28 RH T, §§ 131–201.

victims' legal representative (LRV) requests that the sentence handed down to Mr Al Mahdi be severe and exemplary, without specifying a sentencing range.[215]

59. The Chamber stresses that sentencing an individual for crimes that they committed is a unique exercise for which comparison with different cases can be of only very limited relevance, if any.

60. As set out above, the Chamber must balance all the relevant factors, including any mitigating and aggravating circumstances, and consider the circumstances of both the convicted person and the crime. To sufficiently and adequately reflect the moral and economic harm suffered by the victims of the present case and fulfil the objectives of sentencing, the Chamber must impose a sentence that is proportionate to the gravity of the crime and the individual circumstances and culpability of Mr Al Mahdi.

61. The Chamber finds that the crime for which Mr Al Mahdi is being convicted is of significant gravity. That said, the Chamber has found no aggravating circumstances and five mitigating circumstances, namely: (i) Mr Al Mahdi's admission of guilt; (ii) his cooperation with the prosecution; (iii) the remorse and the empathy he expressed for the victims; (iv) his initial reluctance to commit the crime and the steps he took to limit the damage caused; and (v), even if of limited importance, his good behaviour in detention despite his family situation.

62. The Chamber additionally notes the defence submissions regarding Mr Al Mahdi's profession and 'good character'.[216] Though not mitigating, the Chamber views these as positive factors in assessing Mr Al Mahdi's rehabilitative potential, as well as determining *how* Mr Al Mahdi's sentence could incorporate his education and skills to allow him to give back to the harmed community, while also allowing him the opportunity to rebuild his positive life skills.

63. The Chamber further considers that the defence submissions regarding Mr Al Mahdi's background, in terms of the social context in which he was raised,[217] are pertinent to the sentence.

64. As noted above,[218] there is life outside these processes, as well as a broader context to consider when judging a fellow human. Though the criminal process serves a strict purpose in determining guilt or innocence and the penalty for convicted persons, such determinations should not occur in a void: 'Judges should be encouraged to experience, learn and understand "life" – their own and those whose lives reflect different realities.'[219]

65. Mr Al Mahdi grew up as an ethnic minority, a Tuareg, in northern Mali, a region that has suffered from political and economic exclusion, ethnic conflicts, and

[215] Observations des victimes tendant à la fixation d'une peine exemplaire pour crimes de guerre, 22 July 2016, ICC-01/12-01/15-135 28-09-2016 1/13 EK T, §§ 46–50.

[216] Observations de la Défense sur les principes devant gouverner la peine et les circonstances aggravantes et/ou atténuantes en la cause, en conformité avec l'ordonnance ICC-01/12-01/15-99 de la Chambre, *Al Mahdi* (ICC-01/12-01/15-141-Corr-Red 20-09-2016 1/28), Trial Chamber, 20 September 2016 (hereafter Al Mahdi Defence Submissions), §§ 131–136.

[217] Al Mahdi Defence Submissions, §§ 137–149.

[218] *Supra* § 11.

[219] *Yukon Francophone School Board, supra* note 141, at § 34.

violence, as well as environmental hardships.[220] Mr Al Mahdi was further educated with a strict interpretation of Sharia,[221] and does not appear to have previously had the opportunity to effectively challenge that interpretation. Given his background, it is perhaps not all that surprising that Mr Al Mahdi engaged in destructive behaviour and extremist methods.

66. To be clear, Mr Al Mahdi's background is not an excuse for his actions, which were manifestly criminal. The Chamber further rejects the defence submissions that Mr Al Mahdi's motive is mitigating.[222] So-called good intentions are no excuse for the crimes under this Court's jurisdiction, and a stated motivation or goal that is not inherently criminal, if it nevertheless involves the commission of crimes to achieve it, cannot mitigate a convicted person's actions. As articulated by the LRV, 'to attack the culture and heritage of a people is to attack its soul and its roots', which is precisely what Mr Al Mahdi did.[223]

67. Nevertheless, the Chamber considers his background and overarching social context as relevant in considering Mr Al Mahdi's rehabilitative potential, as it provides greater understanding of how and why Mr Al Mahdi made the choices that led him to this Court.

68. Finally, in considering Mr Al Mahdi's rehabilitative potential, the Chamber again notes his genuine remorse for his actions.

69. Considering all these factors, the Chamber departs from the Court's traditional reliance on incarceration as the sole form of punishment, and sentences Mr Al Mahdi to seven years of custodial imprisonment, along with an additional 3,765 hours of community service.[224]

70. The hours of community service will be served in the Trust Fund for Victims, UNESCO, or, with approval of the Court and in consultation with relevant stakeholders from the harmed community, another similar organisation focused on culturally relevant and appropriate activities. The work undertaken as part of his community service must focus on rebuilding what Mr Al Mahdi helped destroy, but can be contemplated in broader terms that the work could, for example, focus on building respect for religious diversity. A panel of relevant stakeholders from the harmed community as well as the above-named organisations will be assigned to

[220] T-4-Red-ENG, Trial Chamber, www.icc-cpi.int/sites/default/files/Transcripts/CR2016_05767.PDF, at 31; 'Minorities and Indigenous Peoples in Mali – Tuareg', Minority Rights Group International, available at https://minorityrights.org/minorities/tuareg/.

[221] T-4-Red-ENG, *supra* note 220, at, at 31–34, 43–44, 59–60, 102–108.

[222] Al Mahdi Defence Submissions, *supra* note 216, at §§ 147–148 (wherein the defence submits that the motive was to test a new political and religious experiment with the goal of improving the economic and social situation in northern Mali).

[223] Observations des victimes tendant à la fixation d'une peine exemplaire pour crimes de guerre (ICC-01/12-01/15-135 28-09-2016 1/13), *Al Mahdi*, Trial Chamber, 22 July 2016, §§ 23–24, 27–31.

[224] The number of hours was calculated based on a commitment of engaging in community service activities for a seven-and-a-half-hour working day, with a five-day work week, over a period of two years (7.5 hours x 251 days x 2 years = 3,765 hours total).

monitor Mr Al Mahdi's work to ensure it is relevant, assess his contributions, and provide updates to the Court.

71. While performing his community service hours, Mr Al Mahdi will not have any access to the internet or a cell phone. Any tasks that require access to a computer or phone will be supervised to ensure that he does not send any communications.

72. The hours of community service are to be completed concurrently, while Mr Al Mahdi is serving his custodial sentence.

73. The Chamber notes that it did not hear submissions from any party with respect to a prospective imposition of community service, and given the impact that this sentence will have on Mr Al Mahdi's time in custody, considers it appropriate to allow Mr Al Mahdi to respond. Mr Al Mahdi is to file a written response to this decision within thirty days, indicating whether he wishes to participate in the community service sanction. If Mr Al Mahdi is unwilling to engage in community service as part of his sentence, for whatever reason, the community service portion of the sentence, equivalent to two years, will be applied as an additional two-year period of incarceration, bringing his sentence to nine years of incarceration.

74. If Mr Al Mahdi fails to complete the hours of community service by the end of the seven-year custodial sentence, the outstanding balance will be converted into a custodial period.

75. For clarity, notwithstanding this directive, all parties, including Mr Al Mahdi, retain the right to appeal this decision through the regular channels and procedures.

76. Lastly, noting that none of the parties or participants requests the imposition of a fine or order of forfeiture under Article 77(2) of the Statute and Rules 146 and 147 of the Rules, the Chamber finds that this term of imprisonment and community service is a sufficient penalty.

77. Pursuant to Article 78(2) of the Statute, Mr Al Mahdi is entitled to have deducted from his sentence the time he has spent in detention in accordance with an order of this Court, namely since his arrest pursuant to the warrant of arrest issued on 18 September 2015.

Judge Melissa McKay

13.4 DESTRUCTION OF CULTURAL PROPERTY ON THE AL MAHDI REPARATIONS ORDER

Laura Graham and Annika Jones

In 2017 Trial Chamber VIII issued the reparations order for Mr Ahmad Al Faqi Al Mahdi,[225] a decision that was confirmed on appeal in 2018.[226] The order required

[225] Reparations, *Al Mahdi* (ICC-01/12-01/15-236), Trial Chamber VIII, 17 August 2017.

[226] Judgment on the Appeal of the Victims against the Reparations Order, *Al Mahdi* (ICC-01/12-01/15-259-Red2), Appeals Chamber, 8 March 2018.

Mr Al Mahdi to pay €2.7 million in individual and collective reparations to the victims of the destruction of cultural heritage in Mali, Timbuktu, in 2012. This order found that those who could demonstrate direct economic loss from the destruction would be eligible for consequential economic loss reparations, without considering the informal economy operating from the sites, mainly managed by women and girls. The order also focused on the patrilineal succession lines marking ancestral connection to the sites, again overlooking the moral connections of women and girls.

In this rewritten reparations order, Laura Graham and Annika Jones emphasise the cultural underpinnings that may result in women's harm being indirect rather than direct and how that aspect needs to be considered in the distribution of reparations. They also critique traditional implementation and application methods used to identify victims, noting that cultural and social norms may impact women and girls applying. As a practical way to counter these issues, Graham and Jones support matrilineal as well as patrilineal ancestral mapping, and recognition of the impact on the informal economy, in the allocation of individual reparations; include initiatives focusing on marginalised communities as part of collective reparations; and emphasise the importance of including women in the implementation of the order.

No.: ICC-01/12-01/15
Date: 17 August 2017

Original: English

TRIAL CHAMBER VIII(B)

Before: Judge Laura GRAHAM

Judge Annika JONES

SITUATION IN THE REPUBLIC OF MALI

IN THE CASE OF THE *PROSECUTOR* v. *AHMAD AL FAQI AL MAHDI*

Public

Reparations Order

PRINCIPLES ON REPARATIONS AND APPLICABLE LAW ...

Harm Suffered, Types of Reparations and Modalities

Harm

42. To be eligible for reparations, a victim must have suffered harm as a result of the commission of the crime of which Mr Al Mahdi was convicted. ...

45. As the 'First Expert Report' rightly notes, this is the first engagement of the 'ICC' with the situation in Mali and it is, therefore, essential that the Chamber

understands the harms that flow from this crime in the context of the wide range of abuses that were carried out during the occupation and the ideology that informed the attacks.[227]

46. The Chamber has noted that the destruction of the protected buildings was ordered because the attackers considered them to be sites of vice.[228] Mr Al Mahdi, as head of the *Hesbah* morality brigade, was entrusted with regulating the morality of the people of Timbuktu, and of preventing, suppressing, and repressing anything perceived by the occupiers to constitute a visible vice.[229] These visible vices included freedom of dress and freedom of movement, especially for women.[230] Mr Al Mahdi has personally referenced 'not wearing the veil, revealing one's physical appearance [and] gender mix[ing]' as examples of vice suppressed by *Hisbah*.[231] The *Hesbah* organised patrols to make sure that women complied with the dress codes imposed by the armed groups.[232] In addition, women were subjected to a range of abuses, including rape and sexual assaults, which escalated as the attackers were mobilised.[233]

47. It is within this context that the war crime of attacking the Protected Buildings occurred. Therefore, while the reparations order must focus on compensation for the effects of Mr Al Mahdi's crimes, the Chamber notes the importance of taking a gender-sensitive approach to reparations in this case,[234] ensuring that the losses and harms experienced by women are not further marginalised by this reparations order, or through its implementation. . . .

Consequential Economic Loss

72. When pronouncing Mr Al Mahdi's sentence, the Chamber concluded that Mr Al Mahdi caused economic harm.[235]

73. The victims have requested compensation for the effect that the attacks on the protected buildings had on their livelihood. The tourist economy was decimated as a result of the attacks.[236] Prior to the destruction of the protected buildings, people

[227] Brief by Ms. Karima Bennoune, UN Special Rapporteur in the Field of Cultural Rights, *Al Mahdi* (ICC-01/12-01/15-214-AnxI-Red3), Trial Chamber VIII, 27 April 2017, at 25 and 33 (hereafter First Expert Report).

[228] Judgment and Sentence, *Al Mahdi* (ICC-01/12-01/15-171), Trial Chamber VIII, 27 September 2016, §81 (hereafter Al Mahdi Judgment).

[229] *Ibid*, § 33.

[230] Transcript of Confirmation of Charges Hearing, *Al Mahdi* (ICC-01/12-01/15-T-2-Red2-ENG), Pre-Trial Chamber I, 1 March 2016, at 39.

[231] *Ibid*, at 46.

[232] *Ibid*.

[233] First Expert Report, *supra* note 227, at 24–25.

[234] As suggested in *ibid*, at 35.

[235] Al Mahdi Judgment, *supra* note 228, § 108.

[236] Submissions of the Legal Representative of Victims on the principles and forms of the right to reparation, *Al Mahdi* (ICC-01/12-01/15-190-Red-tENG), Trial Chamber VIII, 3 January 2017, § 66 (hereafter First LRV Submissions).

came from all over the world to see the mausoleums and to pray to the saints.[237] On given days, people would visit the mausoleums to offer monetary donations or sacrifice animals (mostly in the case of women, who could not enter the mausoleums).[238] The destruction of the protected buildings was understood by the community as destroying the souls and spirits of the saints.[239] Without the belief that the saints might listen to the prayers and grant their wishes, visitors have become rare.[240] According to one victim, 'the damage sustained by the Timbuktu area is incommensurable. It will take generations for the situation to return to how it was before 2012'.[241]

74. The Chamber notes three overlapping categories of economic losses. There is no hierarchy between these categories. Instead, the losses incurred by the victims should be understood on their own merits. This is important given that women, children, and the elderly are unlikely to be included in the first category and should not be disadvantaged in the implementation of the reparations order.

75. The first category comprises those victims whose livelihoods exclusively depended upon the protected buildings. These include the guardians of the mausoleums, the *maçons* tasked with prominent responsibilities in maintaining them,[242] and people whose businesses could not exist without the protected buildings. The victims' legal representative (LRV) has drawn attention to the particular harm suffered by this category of victims.[243]

76. The second category includes victims whose livelihoods have been indirectly harmed, including as a result of the losses of tourism and economic activity in the years following the attack.[244] Consequential economic loss falling into this category has been detailed in the 'Second Expert Report'.[245]

77. The Chamber notes that traditional gender roles may have an impact on the way the economic harm is felt. Individuals who are restricted from entering into the mausoleums, including women under a certain age,[246] are more likely to suffer

[237] *Ibid*, § 67.

[238] Public redacted version of Corrigendum with one explanatory annex: Final submissions of the Legal Representative on the implementation of a right to reparations for 139 victims under Article 75 of the Rome Statute, *Al Mahdi* (ICC-01/12-01/15-224-Corr-Red-tENG), Trial Chamber VIII, 14 July 2017, § 31 (hereafter Final Submissions of the LRV).

[239] *Ibid*.

[240] *Ibid*.

[241] First LRV Submissions, *supra* note 236, at § 66.

[242] The LRV defines a '*maçon*' (mason) as 'a pivotal figure in the historical and religious shrine. He alone is the embodiment of expertise in the building of the shrine and its bequeathal to the next generation. He is greatly skilled in the substantial aspects of the mausoleum and oversees building and burials. He is selected in a unique and fitting process by the prominent family of the descendants of the mausoleum' see First LRV Submissions, *supra* note 236, at § 25(f).

[243] *Ibid*, § 67.

[244] *Ibid*, §§ 65–71.

[245] Expert Report – Reparations Phase: Dr Marina Lostal, *Al Mahdi* (ICC-01/12-01/12-214-AnxII-Red2), Trial Chamber VIII, 3 May 2017, §§ 80–84 (hereafter Second Expert Report).

[246] *Ibid*, at § 86.

indirect harm as a result of their destruction. Attacks on the informal economy are also likely to have a particularly strong impact on some sectors of the population, including women and girls. These economic losses are more difficult to quantify because of the absence of accounting records. Nonetheless, as the LRV has observed, the effect of the destruction has been no less real for the victims.[247] It is important that distinctions are not drawn between direct and indirect economic loss when assessing the impact of the destruction of the protected buildings on victims for the purpose of allocating reparations. This is to ensure that reparations do not contribute to the entrenchment of discrimination and, to the extent that it is possible, play a role in disrupting pre-existing inequalities and patterns of structural discrimination.[248]

78. The third category of economic losses comprises those resulting from the abandonment of property as a result of fleeing Timbuktu in the wake of the destruction out of fear that 'Mr Al Mahdi and his co-perpetrators would turn their attention to people after striking stone and mortar'.[249] In fleeing, victims 'were forced to abandon not only their property, livestock and money, but their occupations and businesses as well'.[250] This economic loss should be included in reparations to ensure that affected victims, including women, children, and the elderly, are not excluded by a narrow focus on loss of business owners alone.

79. The Chamber is satisfied that Mr Al Mahdi's crime is both the actual and proximate cause of these three categories of economic harm. It was reasonably foreseeable that attacking cultural property integral to the community in Timbuktu would have a lingering economic impact. Indeed, the protected buildings were targeted in large part because of their prominent community role.[251]

80. As noted in the Second Expert Report,[252] the general consequential economic loss caused by the attack reverberated across the entire community in Timbuktu. The Chamber considers that the harm caused by Mr Al Mahdi's actions is primarily collective in character. It is much larger and of a different nature than the harm suffered by the 139 applicants grouped together. Aggregating their losses and prioritising their compensation would risk dramatically understating and misrepresenting the economic loss actually suffered.

81. Nevertheless, the LRV argues that compensation should be given to all reparations applicants who suffered financial losses, and that a further €250 be granted to each victim applicant to address their collective harm.[253]

247 Final Submissions of the LRV, *supra* note 238, at § 38.
248 First Expert Report, *supra* note 227, at § 46.
249 First LRV Submissions, *supra* note 236, at § 69.
250 Final Submissions of the LRV, *supra* note 238, at § 37.
251 Al Mahdi Judgment, *supra* note 228, at §§ 34–37.
252 Second Expert Report, *supra* note 245, §§ 80–84.
253 Final Submissions of the LRV, *supra* note 238, at 37.

82. When focusing on the extent of compensation, the Chamber considers it more equitable to use individual reparations to compensate victims on the basis of the extent of the harm suffered or sacrifice made, whether as part of the formal or informal economy, directly or indirectly, rather than solely on whether a victim had applied for reparations. To do otherwise would exacerbate gender-based discrimination faced by women who may, in this cultural context, be less likely to make individual applications.

83. The Chamber notes that reparations applicants in the present case already obtain several procedural advantages which are not necessarily available to other members of the Timbuktu community who suffered similar harm. By virtue of having already prepared applications and supporting materials, the applicants can take part in the screening procedure, specified later in the present order, without significant additional effort. The applicants provided information considered by the Chamber in tailoring the reparations award, giving them more influence over the parameters set in the present order. The applicants also continue to avail themselves of the assistance of the LRV, a Court-appointed lawyer who receives legal assistance to represent their interests and advocate for them. Furthermore, inclusion and participation in the reparations process has been understood to provide reparation in itself, insofar as it restores agency to victims.[254]

84. Compensating the applicants – to the exclusion of similarly harmed people – beyond these procedural advantages puts undue emphasis on the filing of applications rather than on the extent of the harm suffered or the sacrifice made by the victims. Doing so may exacerbate gender-specific disadvantages where women's voices have not been heard as part of these applications. There is no reason to believe that the reparations applicants, simply by virtue of applying, suffered to a different degree compared with the rest of the Timbuktu community. It is important to ensure that a broader range of victims, including women, children, and the elderly, benefit from the reparations process to promote their agency and challenge their previous exclusion. As noted by the LRV, there is a high risk of frustration in awarding reparations only to those who have reparations applications pending before the Chamber.[255] The Second Expert Report also recommends that reparations in the present case should be 'awarded on a collective basis as far as possible'.[256]

85. Accordingly, the Chamber awards individual reparations for consequential economic loss only to those (i) whose livelihoods exclusively depended upon the protected buildings, including those whose livelihood was to maintain and protect those buildings; (ii) whose livelihoods were significantly affected by their destruction; or (iii) those who otherwise suffered significant personal economic loss as a consequence of their destruction, such as the loss of their homes as a result of

[254] First LRV Submissions, *supra* note 236, at § 111.
[255] Final Submissions of the LRV, *supra* note 238, at §§ 87–91.
[256] Second Expert Report, *supra* note 248, at § 125.

displacement. An individualised response is more appropriate for them, as their loss relative to the rest of the community is more acute and exceptional.

86. The Chamber considers that the number of victims and the scope of the consequential economic loss make a collective award more appropriate for those beyond these identified groups. This is not to say that other individual businesses and families beyond these three categories could not receive financial support in the implementation of these collective reparations, but rather that the Chamber considers a collective response is more appropriate to adequately address the harm suffered. As indicated by the Appeals Chamber, 'the decision not to award reparations on an individual basis does not prejudice the individuals who filed individual reparations requests with respect to their eligibility to participate in any collective reparations programme'.[257]

87. The Chamber therefore considers that the economic harm caused by Mr Al Mahdi necessitates: (i) individual reparations for those whose livelihoods exclusively depended upon the protected buildings, who were significantly affected by their destruction, or who otherwise suffered significant personal economic loss as a consequence of their destruction; and (ii) collective reparations for the community of Timbuktu as a whole.

88. As for the modalities, the Chamber considers that individual reparations are to be implemented through compensation to address the financial losses suffered. The modalities for collective reparations should be aimed at rehabilitating the community of Timbuktu to address the economic harm caused. Collective measures in this regard may include: community-based educational and awareness-raising programmes to promote Timbuktu's important and unique cultural heritage; return/resettlement programmes; the development of actions or programmes aimed at assisting women, youth, and others towards generating income; a 'microcredit system' that would assist the population to generate income; a school/university; a project that would generate jobs not only for the women, but for youth and others; or other cash assistance programmes to restore some of Timbuktu's lost economic activity.[258]

89. Moreover, a fully gender-sensitive approach to the protection of cultural heritage and to combating its destruction is essential.[259] As recommended in the First Expert Report, such reparations could include initiatives such as promoting training for women and fostering discussions of the issue of non-discrimination in

[257] Judgment on the appeals against the Decision establishing the principles and procedures to be applied to reparations of 7 August 2012 with AMENDED order for reparations (Annex A) and public annexes 1 and 2, *Lubanga* (ICC-01/04-01/06-3129), Appeals Chamber, 3 March 2015, § 155 (hereafter Lubanga Reparations Appeals Judgment).

[258] *See* First Expert Report, *supra* note 245, at 46; PUBLIC Redacted Annex I to Registry's observations pursuant to Trial Chamber VIII's Decision ICC-01/12-01/15-172 of 29 September 2016, *Al Mahdi* (ICC-01/12-01/15-193-AnxI-Red), 5 December 2016, § 44 (hereafter Registry's Observations).

[259] First Expert Report, *supra* note 245, at 46.

access to cultural heritage sites as a means of guaranteeing non-repetition of the abuses in this case.[260] As the First Expert Report notes, 'if there was no specific provision made for reparations for women, women will be unlikely to be beneficiaries of the reparations. The reparations process can afford an opportunity to strengthen their recognition and involvement in the protection, care and transmission of cultural heritage'.[261]

Moral Harm

90. When pronouncing Mr Al Mahdi's sentence, the Chamber concluded that Mr Al Mahdi had caused moral harm.[262]

91. Every victim applicant before the Chamber alleges some sort of moral harm as a result of the attack on the protected buildings. The Chamber considers that the victims established the following forms of moral harm to the requisite standard: (i) mental pain and anguish, including losses of childhood, opportunities, and relationships among those who fled Timbuktu because the protected buildings were attacked and (ii) disruption of culture.[263]

92. The Chamber has also received other information describing the emotional distress and harm suffered across the Timbuktu community. In particular, the protected buildings were widely perceived in Timbuktu as being the protectors of the community from outside harm. The attack on the protected buildings not only destroyed cherished monuments, but also shattered the community's collective faith that they were protected.[264] Collective events at the mausoleums also brought members of the community together; the *crépissage*, or plastering of the mosques, is done collectively, with women and the elderly at the base and young men at the top.[265]

93. In relation to moral harm stemming from the disruption of culture, the Chamber has acknowledged in its sentencing judgment the particular loss of intangible cultural heritage that women have faced in their ritual of cleaning the

[260] *Ibid.*

[261] *Ibid.*

[262] Al Mahdi Judgment, *supra* note 228, at § 108.

[263] Forms of moral harm related to disruption of culture have been recognised in international human rights jurisprudence. Judgment (Reparations), *Plan de Sánchez Massacre v. Guatemala* (IACHR Series C No. 116), Inter-American Court of Human Rights (IACtHR), 19 November 2004, §§ 77, 85–88; Judgment (Merits, Reparations and Costs), *Yakye Axa Indigenous Community v. Paraguay* (IACHR Series. C. no 125), IACtHR, 17 June 2005, §§ 154, 203.

[264] RAPPORT Rédigé par un college d'Experts, *Al Mahdi* (ICC-01/12/01-15-214-AnxIII-Red2), Trial Chamber VIII, 4 August 2017, at 146–149 (hereafter Third Expert Report); Second Expert Report, *supra* note 245, § 65; First Expert Report, *supra* note 227, at 29.

[265] Transcript of Trial Hearing, *Al Mahdi* (ICC-01/12-01/15-T-5-Red-ENG), Trial Chamber VIII, 23 August 2016, at 39–40.

shrines.[266] Women were the most frequent visitors to the mausoleums, even though they were unable to enter the protected buildings.[267] They often prayed at these buildings, making wishes to have children, or wishing for the success of their children.[268] Having acknowledged the particular links that women have with the mausoleums, the First Expert Report stresses the significance of including a 'gender specific component of the reparations that recognizes women's connections to the cultural heritage that was targeted, their suffering during the jihadist occupation and the [REDACTED] in countering the fundamentalist ideology that inspired the destructions'.[269]

94. The Chamber is satisfied that Mr Al Mahdi's crime is both the actual and proximate cause of this moral harm. It was reasonably foreseeable that attacking cultural property integral to the community in Timbuktu would cause these kinds of distress.

95. The LRV argues at length that the moral harm suffered is best addressed by giving compensation to the applicants as individual and collective reparations.[270] For the same reasons provided when discussing consequential economic loss, the Chamber considers such a compensation-centric approach for the benefit of the reparations applicants to be problematic. The Chamber again emphasises that it considers that such a course understates the variety of other information proving that Timbuktu's community at large – and not only the victim applicants – suffered moral harm.

96. The Registry has noted that documentary evidence of harm, proving a victim was 'faithful' or was harmed by the destruction of the buildings, and quantifying moral harm would prove difficult for most victims.[271] The defence argues in its submissions that psychological harm in the present case can be proven *only* by asking for a direct kinship between the people claiming the harm and the deceased whose mausoleums were attacked.[272] The Chamber agrees with the defence – and LRV,[273] for that matter – that those whose ancestors' burial sites were damaged in the attack (such as the 'descendants of the saints') have a different kind of emotional connection to the destroyed sites than the rest of the Timbuktu population. However, it considers that the community-wide impact of moral harm is minimised by sole reliance on direct kinship as a means of proving moral harm. Furthermore, given that male victims are more likely to be able to prove a connection with the 'descendants of the saints', due to the patrilineal way that familial records are kept,

266 M. McKay, Reimagined Mali Sentencing Decision, Chapter 13.3 above.

267 First Expert Report, *supra* note 227, at 22.

268 *Ibid*, at 21.

269 *Ibid*, at 46.

270 Final Submissions of the LRV, *supra* note 238, §§ 44–59.

271 Registry's Observations, *supra* note 258, at 13.

272 General Defence Observations on Reparations, *Al Mahdi* (ICC-01/12-01/15-191-tENG), at 23 (hereafter First Defence Submissions).

273 First LRV Submissions, *supra* note 236, § 77.

narrowly interpreting this moral harm could reinforce structural and material exclusion of women.

97. With this in mind, the Chamber stresses the importance of recognising female-based lines of ancestry alongside 'descendants of the saints' when identifying groups that have a particularly strong emotional connection to the destroyed sites. The Chamber considers that individual reparations through compensation are necessary to address the mental pain and anguish that these victims suffered. But the remainder of the reparations awarded to the entire community of Timbuktu must be collective in character and should prioritise collective opportunities for sections of the population who may be marginalised in the distribution of individual reparations.

98. The Chamber therefore orders that the moral harm caused by Mr Al Mahdi necessitates: (i) individual reparations for the mental pain and anguish of those with a stronger emotional connection to the destroyed sites than the rest of the Timbuktu population, including those whose ancestors' burial sites were damaged in the attack and (ii) collective reparations for the mental pain/anguish and disruption of culture of the Timbuktu community as a whole.

99. As for the modalities, the Chamber considers that individual reparations are to be implemented through compensation and collective reparations through rehabilitation to address the emotional distress suffered as a result of the attack on the protected buildings. These collective reparations can also include symbolic measures – such as a memorial, commemoration, or forgiveness ceremony – to give public recognition of the moral harm suffered by the Timbuktu community and those within it. As noted by the LRV, the implementation of reparations must not result in any discrimination – including gender-based discrimination – among victims.[274] It is important, therefore, that all victims, including women, children, and the elderly, be included in decisions around collective reparations. . . .

IMPLEMENTATION

135. The Chamber has concluded that Mr Al Mahdi is liable for €2.7 million in expenses for individual and collective reparations. The Chamber has also ordered some symbolic measures. . . .

137. The LRV has suggested that the reparation scheme should involve local traditional and religious leaders to ensure communication with and inclusion of communities in decision making.[275] It is recognised that some methods of reparation 'could unintentionally strengthen the dominant group, and leave the marginalised members of the community worse off'.[276] The Chamber notes, in particular,

[274] Final Submissions of the LRV, *supra* note 238, § 97.

[275] First LRV Submissions, *supra* note 236, § 22.

[276] Second Expert Report, *supra* note 245, § 124.

evidence in the Second Expert Report that women's views are ordinarily only heard in certain conditions, such as when 'they are old and considered wise … [where they] do not expose themselves in public … [or where they play a] role of counsellor … [to] their husbands'.[277] The report also notes that women are at a disadvantage in relation to property rights given that male descendants receive twice as much as female descendants and widows are only entitled to one-eighth of the property of their deceased husband.[278] With this in mind, the Trust Fund for Victims (TFV) must ensure that the involvement of community leaders does not further the exclusion of women, but rather that women's inclusion both in the process of developing the scheme and as victims using the scheme is facilitated.

138. It is not the Chamber's responsibility at this time to give detailed information about the implementation component of the reparations phase. However, the Chamber will advance the following preliminary considerations to guide the implementation of its order. …

140. Second, the Chamber notes that the modalities of reparations it has ordered mutually reinforce each other. In other words, addressing the discrete moral harm may have residual effects that ameliorate the discrete forms of economic harm and vice versa. Care must be taken, however, to avoid any assumption that addressing economic harms to a family unit, which is traditionally headed by a man, does not supersede reparations for moral harms to other members of the family, including women and children, who occupy a vulnerable and submissive position in society.[279] The TFV is not limited to the Chamber's intermediate liability calculations when designing an implementation plan; the TFV is limited only by the Chamber's final determination on the defendant's liability.

141. Third, specific provisions must be made in the implementation phase to ensure equitable distribution of reparations to women.[280] Women may find it difficult to make individual claims for reparations because of the Malian traditional family structure and subordination of the wife. The TFV should consider a process that affords an opportunity for women to strengthen their involvement in developing an appropriate reparations scheme, which ensures adequate financial reparation and inclusive participation.

142. Fourth, the Chamber notes that it has received only 139 applications during the reparations phase, despite determining that collective harm was suffered across Timbuktu (a city of approximately 70,000 people around the time of the attack).

[277] *Ibid*, § 115.

[278] *Ibid*, § 114.

[279] Second Expert Report, *supra* note 245, § 114.

[280] The LRV have emphasised the importance of equal treatment of victims regardless of gender and the need to need to ensure that '[f]emale victims … [are] able to receive directly, and under the same conditions as male victims, any reparations awarded to them' in order to avoid gender-based discrimination in the implementation of reparations. See Final Submissions of the LRV, *supra* note 238, § 97.

The LRV acknowledges that 'the victims whom he met on his assignment in Mali represent just a fraction of the victims in the case'.[281] The Chamber notes the potential for these applications to be gendered because of the effect of conservative social values that curtail women's ability to negotiate or advocate for themselves in legal processes.[282] The Chamber also notes the information received that the security situation in Timbuktu makes travelling there or contacting victims difficult,[283] a situation exacerbated for women. For these reasons, the Chamber considers that the names of all the victims meeting its parameters for individual reparations are simply not known and considers that it would be impracticable for the Chamber to attempt to identify and assess them all itself.

143. As recognised by the Appeals Chamber,[284] the regulations of the TFV explicitly contemplate individual reparations for unidentified beneficiaries.[285] This is in juxtaposition to the TFV regulations governing individual reparations in cases where the Court identifies each beneficiary.[286] When the Court does not identify the beneficiaries, it falls to the TFV to establish a verification procedure to determine that any persons who identify themselves to the TFV are in fact members of the beneficiary group.[287] The Chamber considers that proceeding in this manner is an alternative to an application-based process, whereby the Chamber assesses the reparation requests of identifiable beneficiaries filed pursuant to Rule 94 of the ICC Rules of Procedure and Evidence.

144. For the reasons above, the Chamber considers that the impracticability of identifying all those meeting its individual reparations parameters justifies an eligibility screening during the implementation phase. The Chamber therefore considers it best that individual reparations be awarded on the basis of an administrative screening by the TFV.[288] However, the TFV should recognise that because of the patrilineal nature of familial records, the particular role of women in the informal economy, and the submissive position of women in society, these verification procedures must be such that they do not reinforce exclusion.

145. The Chamber notes that given the particular role of the descendants of the saints in guarding and maintaining the protected buildings, it is likely that many of those identified as suffering economic loss and moral harm will be the same individuals. Bearing this in mind, the Chamber considers that one screening for

[281] First LRV Submissions, *supra* note 236, § 54.
[282] Second Expert Report, *supra* note 245, § 114.
[283] See First LRV Submissions, *supra* note 236, § 129; Final Submissions of the LRV, *supra* note 238, §§ 14–15.
[284] First LRV Submissions, *supra* note 236, §§ 142, 167.
[285] Regulations 60–65 of the Regulations of the TFV.
[286] Regulation 59 of the Regulations of the TFV.
[287] Regulations 62–65 of the Regulations of the TFV.
[288] The TFV has made submissions confirming its capacity to conduct administrative screenings. See First TFV Submissions, *Al Mahdi* (ICC-01/12-01/15-187), Trial Chamber VIII, 2 December 2016, §§ 56–63.

both categories is sufficient for these applicants. It is also emphasised at the outset that anyone not participating in the screening can still participate in collective reparations programmes – the screening process concerns only individual reparations.

146. This screening process itself must respect the rights of both the victims and the convicted person.[289] The Chamber considers that the full details of this screening are to be determined by the TFV, but it can already set out the following general parameters:

(i) Reasonable efforts must be made to identify individuals who may be eligible under the screening process, within a timeframe to be proposed by the TFV. These efforts must ensure the inclusion of eligible women, and identify and ameliorate difficulties for women in meeting eligibility criteria.

(ii) Individuals who wish to be considered for the screening process are to provide a reparations application and any supporting documents. It is noted in this regard that this step has already been taken by the reparations applicants in the present case, and these persons should be considered first by the TFV if they apply to be screened. However, it must also be recognised that in the provision of reparations this must not prioritise those who have already made applications, as that would have an indirect effect of reinforcing exclusion of marginalised groups.

(iii) Both the applicant, on their own or through a legal representative, and the defence must be given an opportunity to make representations before the TFV assesses any applicant's eligibility. In assessing eligibility, the TFV may base itself only on information made available and to which the defence has had an opportunity to access and respond. Recognition must be made that the informal economy and patriarchal family registration means that women in particular may be reliant on informal documentation or accounts to support their eligibility. For instance, to demonstrate that they are descendants of the saints, women may be more likely to rely upon oral testimony and statements rather than registration documents.

. . .

147. Fifth, the Chamber has received conflicting information about the extent to which traditional justice mechanisms should be used in implementing the Chamber's order. Some note the paramount role these play in Timbuktu's culture and how the validity of any reparations order depends on using them.[290] Others

[289] Rule 97(3) of the ICC Rules of Procedure and Evidence.

[290] See Second Expert Report, *supra* note 245, at §§ 89, 103, 112–113, 119, 121–123. See also Third Expert Report, *supra* note 264, at 136–142; First LRV Submissions, *supra* note 236, § 133; Final Submissions of the LRV, *supra* note 238, §§ 74, 98.

emphasise that certain traditional justice mechanisms in Timbuktu have a history of discrimination, especially against neglected groups such as women, children, and slaves, and that care should be taken in relying upon them.[291] Given this conflicting information, and the Chamber's commitment to equitable distribution of reparations, the Chamber will not require that traditional justice mechanisms be part of the implementation of its award.

148. Lastly, the Chamber emphasises that implementation of the present order must be responsive to local conditions while being consistent with the Court's reparations principles, including the principle of non-discrimination. The TFV is expected to devise a draft implementation plan bearing this dichotomy in mind, consulting all relevant stakeholders – including the parties – and recommending any implementation measures it considers appropriate.[292] The parties will also be given an opportunity to file written submissions on the draft implementation plan proposed. As emphasised above, the TFV's discretion in drafting the implementation plan will be subject to approval by way of a second decision of the Chamber.

Judge Laura Graham and Judge Annika Jones

13.5 DIGITAL EVIDENCE IN THE AL HASSAN WARRANT

Sarah Zarmsky and Emma Irving

In 2018, Pre-Trial Chamber I issued a Warrant of Arrest for Mr Al Hassan Ag Abdoul Aziz Ag Mohamed Ag Mahmoud.[293] In this rewritten decision, Sarah Zarmsky and Emma Irving provide additional remarks on the aspect of digital evidence that is intended to come before the Chamber at trial.

Zarmsky and Irving explore how the benefit of digital evidence is also the disadvantage, namely that the violence can be shared globally and never completely eradicated. Zarmsky and Irving note that the digital aspect of the evidence compounds the harm experienced by victims while also providing a clear portrayal of the violence and thereby greatly assisting the Court. They highlight the safeguards that should be enacted to protect victims but note that as digital evidence becomes more frequently used, the lack of such evidence, notably in regard to sexual and gender-based crimes, should not act as a barrier to conviction and should still enjoy proper and thorough investigatory practices.

[291] Second Expert Report, *supra* note 245, at §§ 89, 114–118, 124; First Expert Report, *supra* note 227, at 48–49.

[292] *As requested in* Final Submissions of the LRV, *supra* note 238, §§ 101, 110.

[293] Warrant of Arrest, *Al Hassan* (ICC-01/12-01/18-35-Red2-tENG), Pre-Trial Chamber I, 22 May 2018.

No.: ICC-01/12-01/18
Date: 22 May 2018

Original: French

PRE-TRIAL CHAMBER I

Before: Judge Sarah ZARMSKY
Judge Emma IRVING

SITUATION IN THE REPUBLIC OF MALI

IN THE CASE OF THE *PROSECUTOR v. AL HASSAN AG ABDOUL AZIZ AG MOHAMED AG MAHMOUD*

Public Redacted Version

Decision on the Prosecutor's Application for the Issuance of a Warrant of Arrest for Al Hassan Ag Abdoul Aziz Ag Mohamed Ag Mahmoud

ADDITIONAL REMARKS

1. Having found reasonable grounds to believe:

(a) That crimes against humanity and war crimes were committed in Timbuktu, Mali, between April 2012 and January 2013;

(b) That Mr Al Hassan has incurred individual criminal responsibility under Articles 25(3)(a) and (b) of the Rome Statute for these crimes; and

(c) That the conditions under Article 58(1)(b) of the Rome Statute for arresting Mr Al Hassan Ag Abdoul Aziz Ag Mohamed Ag Mahmoud are satisfied,

the Chamber sees fit to issue some additional remarks on two subjects that it considers pertinent to the present case and to future cases in which similar conditions arise.

2. The first subject is that of video evidence and its evidentiary value before this Court. The second subject concerns the additional gravity considerations which arise due to the fact that the crimes committed were filmed and posted online.

The Use of Video Evidence

3. The Chamber notes the Prosecutor's inclusion of a number of videos in the evidence supporting her application for the present arrest warrant. In said application, the term 'video' is mentioned seventy-four times in support of a range of submissions.[294] This conspicuous use of video material reflects the growing

[294] Version publique expurgée de la 'Requête urgente du Bureau du Procureur aux fins de délivrance d'un mandat d'arrêt et de demande d'arrestation provisoire à l'encontre de M. Al Hassan Ag ABDOUL AZIZ Ag Mohamed Ag Mahmoud', 20 March 2018, ICC-01/12-54-Secret-

importance that video evidence – as well as digital evidence more generally – is coming to play in international criminal accountability. For this reason, the Chamber considers it opportune to issue some remarks on the subject of video evidence.

4. Videos have played a role in International Criminal Court (ICC) proceedings since its first case, when videos depicting child soldiers were shown in the courtroom during the trial the *Prosecutor v. Thomas Lubanga Dyilo*.[295] Since that time, two cases have come before this Court in which video evidence was a significant part of the case.

5. The first such case was the *Prosecutor v. Ahmad Al Faqi Al Mahdi*. On 27 September 2016, Mr Al Mahdi was found guilty as a co-perpetrator of the war crime of intentionally directing attacks against religious and historic buildings in Timbuktu, Mali, in 2012. The evidence presented to Trial Chamber VIII included a large number of videos that, among other things, depicted the accused taking part in the destruction of protected buildings and giving instructions and moral support to others to do the same.[296]

6. The second such case was the *Prosecutor v. Mahmoud Mustafa Busayf Al-Werfalli*. In 2017 and 2018 respectively, two warrants of arrest were issued for Mr Al-Werfalli for both directly committing and ordering the commission of murder as a war crime.[297] The alleged murders took place in the context of eight incidents, seven of which were captured on video and uploaded to social media sites. The total number of alleged murder victims is forty-three, corresponding to the number of individuals whose death is purportedly depicted in the videos. At the time the present arrest warrant was issued, Mr Al-Werfalli was still at large, and reported by some sources as deceased.

7. In both above cases, the Prosecutor limited her charges to one war crime: in *Al Mahdi* the intentional directing of attacks against religious and historic buildings, and in *Al-Werfalli* murder. This narrow focus fed into and reinforced (and was possibly a consequence of, though that is not for this Chamber to say) a commonly held belief that video evidence is predominantly of use for a certain category of crimes only. These are crimes that take place in public or semi-public spaces, such as the very public destruction of buildings in Mali or executions on the street in Libya. This stands in contrast to crimes more often perpetrated in private and

Exp, *Al Hassan Ag Abdoul Aziz Ag Mohamed Ag Mohmoud* (ICC-01/12-01/18), Pre Trial Chamber I, 20 March 2018 (hereafter Prosecutor's Arrest Warrant Application).

[295] For an overview of the use of video in the Lubanga case, see Witness, 'From the DRC to the ICC: The Prosecutor v Lubanga: The Role of Video in the Criminal Justice Process', available at https://vae.witness.org/portfolio_page/role-of-video-in-the-criminal-justice-process/.

[296] See Judgment and Sentence, *Ahmad Al Faqi Al Mahdi* (ICC-01/12-01/15), Trial Chamber VIII, 27 September 2016, § 40 (hereafter Al Mahdi Judgment and Sentence).

[297] Warrant of Arrest, *Mahmoud Mustafa Busayf Al-Werfalli* (ICC-01/11-01/17), Pre-Trial Chamber, 15 August 2017; Second Warrant of Arrest, *Mahmoud Mustafa Busayf Al-Werfalli* (ICC-01/11-01/17), Pre-Trial Chamber, 4 July 2018.

frequently stigmatised, in particular sexual and gender-based violence crimes (SGBV).

8. In addition to noting the extensive use of video evidence in the Prosecutor's application for the present arrest warrant, the Chamber notes with satisfaction that video is used to support a range of submissions, including arguments relating to violence against women and girls.[298] This marks a move away from the approach seen in *Al Mahdi* and *Al-Werfalli* and gives force to the idea that video evidence can play a larger evidentiary role than hitherto thought.

9. On the basis of the evidence presented by the Prosecutor in her application, including videos, the Chamber has made a number of findings in this arrest warrant. While these are addressed in detail elsewhere in this decision, the Chamber will draw attention to a few points that pertain to the use of video evidence in submissions related to SGBV.

10. First, in establishing – as a contextual element of crimes against humanity – that Ansar Dine and al-Qaeda in the Islamic Maghreb (AQIM) had a policy of attacking the civilian population, the Chamber takes note of videos showing how the armed groups wished to impose their authority and new religious order on the civilian population. Under this policy, those who failed to demonstrate the necessary religiosity, in particular women and girls, were to be punished.[299]

11. Second, video evidence played a part in establishing reasonable grounds to believe that torture and persecution as crimes against humanity took place in Timbuktu, Mali, and that women and girls were particular targets. With respect to the crime of torture, the Prosecutor submitted video evidence of women being subjected to whipping at the market and in their homes.[300] The reasons given for this conduct included not being sufficiently covered or wearing colourful clothes.[301] With respect to the crime of persecution, the Prosecutor referenced videos showing that under the pretext of enforcing Ansar Dine and AQIM's religious vision, women were harassed in the street, in hospitals, in schools, and in their own homes;[302] they were subjected to daily abuse, searches, and detention.[303] In one video referenced by the Prosecutor, Ansar Dine/AQIM preacher Abou Al Baraa declares that women 'must not speak seductively and softly; and they must not make tingling sounds when they walk; and they must not embellish themselves'.[304]

12. These findings illustrate that some categories of SGBV crimes can take place in public spaces and that video recordings capturing elements of these crimes do

[298] See sections 72 and 73 of the present arrest warrant.
[299] Section IV(A)(1) of the present arrest warrant.
[300] See sections 72 and 73 of the present arrest warrant.
[301] Video, *Al Jazeera*, 'Frances calls for Mali peace talks' (31 January 2013), cited in Prosecutor's Arrest Warrant Application, *supra* note 294, n. 316.
[302] *Ibid*, § 121.
[303] *Ibid*, n. 330.
[304] Prosecutor's Arrest Warrant Application, *supra* note 294, at § 110.

exist and can have evidentiary value. It is time, therefore, for a shift in mindset away from viewing video evidence as limited in utility, and in particular away from viewing video evidence as unhelpful in proving crimes against women and other victims of SGBV crimes.

13. The Chamber does not deny that some SGBV crimes are more difficult than others to establish using video evidence. Notably, the Chamber finds reasonable grounds to believe that the crimes against humanity of rape, sexual slavery, and forced marriage as an inhumane act, and the war crime of rape, were committed in Timbuktu, Mali; however, the Chamber does not cite video evidence as supporting evidentiary material for these findings.

14. Recent research shows, however, that while direct video evidence of sexual violence being perpetrated is rare,[305] video evidence has a valuable role to play in corroborating and supporting other forms of evidence. Alexa Koenig and Ulic Egan found through interviews with practitioners that digital open-source information (including video evidence) can be useful in establishing contextual elements of international crimes, for example by documenting television statements made in the lead-up to an attack, or recording troop and vehicle movements.[306] Furthermore, digital evidence can capture more 'visible' conflict-related phenomena that correlate with sexual violence. That way, the 'visible phenomena can act as a signal that evidence of sexual violence may be nearby'.[307] Events such as village burnings, forcible transfers, the use of detention centres, slave labour, and the presence of large groups of armed men are often indicators that sexual violence could have taken place.[308] Koenig and Egan recommend that investigators work creatively when looking for SGBV-related evidentiary material and that they take into account the fact that evidence of this category of crimes may not be labelled as such[309] and may be reported in different ways than other crimes.[310] When carrying out investigations online, they found that SGBV-related material was often hidden on the dark web, and therefore more challenging to find.[311]

15. The Chamber has been keen to express its support for widening the understanding of the role that video evidence can play in proceedings before this Court and in other accountability fora. In an age when videos are so easily made on

305 But not unheard of. As described by Sellers and Kestenbaum, ISIS is said to have carefully documented the sale of Yazidi women and girls, registering their names, ages, marital statuses, along with photos and purchase prices. P. V. Sellers and J. G. Kestenbaum, 'Missing in Action: The International Crime of the Slave Trade' 18 *Journal of International Criminal Justice* (2020) 517–542, at 524–525.

306 A. Koenig and U. Egan, 'Power and Privilege: Investigating Sexual Violence with Digital Open Source Information' 19 *Journal of International Criminal Justice* (2021) 55–84.

307 *Ibid*, 73.

308 *Ibid*, 73.

309 *Ibid*, 75.

310 *Ibid*, 64.

311 *Ibid*, 65.

smartphones and other digital devices, and so easily shared through social media and communication apps, to overlook the value of this source of evidence for establishing SGBV crimes risks rendering such crimes more invisible than they already are. The digital age provides a wealth of tools for investigators and lawyers that should be put to work to address marginalisation and silence. That being said, there are two cautionary notes that these additional remarks on video evidence will conclude with.

16. First, where there is video evidence of SGBV crimes, especially direct evidence of the perpetration of such crimes, a strong and robust ethical framework is needed to ensure victims' rights and the safety of the individuals who captured the video.

17. Second, in cases where video evidence simply does not exist, caution should be exercised to ensure that SGBV crimes are still given the proper investigatory attention. There are a range of reasons why video evidence may be scarce, including that the internet was cut off during the conflict, a lack of digital infrastructure in the conflict-affected area, unequal access to technology between men and women/young and old/rural and city dwellers, unequal (digital) literacy, the existence of domestic legislation that makes reporting SGBV crimes difficult, a lack of services, and so on. Crimes where the perpetrator is captured on video directly perpetrating or ordering the crime are attractive from an investigative and prosecutorial standpoint, but the relative ease of prosecuting these crimes should not mean that other crimes, and in particular the often difficult to prosecute SGBV crimes, should escape investigation and accountability.

Gravity Considerations

18. In addition, with the development of smartphones and the accessibility of the internet around the globe, it is now common for individuals to post footage of atrocities to social media. This phenomenon occurs for multiple reasons; sometimes bystanders may begin recording as an instinctual mechanism to deal with the shock of seeing a crime, or witnesses may post footage to try and raise awareness about a particular event or conflict. However, sharing videos of crimes may not always be done with the purest of intentions, as terrorist organisations and other perpetrators now frequently use social media to distribute footage for purposes of spreading propaganda, instilling fear, and further humiliating the victims and their families.[312]

19. When footage of crimes is shared on social media, this element of publication can aggravate the gravity of the crimes. As the Pre-Trial Chamber stated in the case

[312] See for instance A. Barr and A. Herfroy-Mischler, 'ISIL's Execution Videos: Audience Segmentation and Terrorist Communication in the Digital Age' 41 *Studies in Conflict & Terrorism* (2018) 946–967; S. Sandberg and T. Ugelvik, 'Why Do Offenders Tape Their Crimes? Crime and Punishment in the Age of the Selfie' 57 *British Journal of Criminology* (2017) 1023–1040.

against Mr Al-Werfalli, 'the posting on social media of the videos depicting executions' and 'the manner in which the crime was committed and publicized was cruel, dehumanizing, and degrading'.[313] This Chamber considers that the publication element should have been further discussed in the case against Mr Al-Werfalli when assessing gravity. Focus should have been placed on the additional harm suffered by the victims from having their suffering posted to public online platforms, which extended the audience of this suffering far beyond the group of onlookers on the street that day.

20. Returning to the present case, the Prosecutor submits in her application that one of the reasons the attacks against the population of Timbuktu can be considered widespread and systematic is 'the mode of executions, in public and in the presence of the population summoned for this purpose'.[314] The Prosecutor argues that the executions were 'brutal and public' in order to 'instil fear in the population'.[315] Further, the Prosecutor emphasises that the public nature of the executions rendered them particularly humiliating for the victims.[316] These elements of the application add to this Chamber's view that the way in which offences were committed publicly and posted online aggravate the seriousness of the crimes.

21. Further, in her application the Prosecutor makes frequent reference to videos of the executions, some of which were posted to social media platforms such as YouTube by Ansar Dine.[317] The Prosecutor submits that these videos 'show the victims bent over in pain. The repetition of the blows contributes to accentuate their suffering, perceptible through their cries and their groans. Some have bloodstains, others have their private parts exposed for all to see, contributing to a sense of public humiliation'.[318]

22. The Chamber considers that the posting of videos of executions to social media platforms such as YouTube by Ansar Dine itself demonstrates a desire to further degrade the victims before a widespread audience. It is the Chamber's view that this factor aggravates the offence and should be noted in considering the gravity of the crimes committed. When footage of crimes is posted to the internet, those depicted are victimised even further through the humiliation of their suffering being shared globally and the fear of not knowing how far the footage will be circulated. Once a video is posted online, it is extremely difficult to remove it completely and stop it from being continuously shared, which can leave victims feeling helpless and humiliated for much longer than if the crime was not filmed and shared. It is also

[313] Warrant of Arrest, *Mahmoud Mustafa Busayf Al-Werfalli* (ICC-01/11-01/17), Pre-Trial Chamber, 15 August 2017, § 29; Second Warrant of Arrest, *Mahmoud Mustafa Busayf Al-Werfalli* (ICC-01/11-01/17), Pre-Trial Chamber, 4 July 2018, § 31.

[314] Prosecutor's Arrest Warrant Application, § 130 (translated from French).

[315] *Ibid*, § 80 (translated from French).

[316] *Ibid*, § 136 (translated from French).

[317] *Ibid*, § 228, n. 626 (translated from French).

[318] *Ibid*, § 304 (translated from French).

important to note that in instances where footage of crimes is posted to social media, women and girls may likely be affected disproportionately to men. This is due to the fact that the stigma surrounding being victims of certain crimes may be worse for women and girls, and can continue to haunt them throughout their lives.

23. The Chamber also considers that the public nature of the executions and the fact that they were circulated online adds to the harm experienced by those close to the victims, such as friends and family members, who may come across the footage and be unable to escape the reality of what has happened to their loved ones. The mental toll of seeing crimes perpetrated on relatives of victims was considered by the Chamber in the cases of the *Prosecutor v. Moinina Fofana and Allieu Kondewa* at the Special Court for Sierra Leone and the *Prosecutor v. Miroslav Kvočka et al.* at the International Criminal Tribunal for the Former Yugoslavia. For example, in *Fofana and Kondewa*, the Trial Chamber stated that 'a third party could suffer serious mental harm by witnessing acts committed against others, particularly against family or friends ... the Accused may be held liable for causing serious mental harm to a third party who witnesses acts committed against others'.[319] Further, in *Kvočka*, the Trial Chamber found that 'the mental suffering caused to an individual who is forced to watch severe mistreatment inflicted on a relative would rise to the level of gravity required under the crime of torture'.[320]

24. Thus, in both the aforementioned cases, the Court decided that the harm caused by viewing a crime committed against others could constitute the level of gravity needed to constitute its own crime. In the present case, the additional element of posting of crimes to social media could have potentially increased the number of family members or friends of the victims who bore witness to the heinous acts committed against them. Therefore, the Chamber considers this elevated risk of vicarious victimisation as well in its assessment of the gravity of the acts charged.

25. In addition, the publication of footage of international crimes can also harm not just the victims and those close to them, but the community and broader population as well. This was noted by the Trial Chamber in the case against Mr Al Mahdi, in which it was found that 'the impact of the attack on the population was heightened by the fact that it was relayed in the media'.[321] When making this finding, the Trial Chamber referred to the Office of the Prosecutor's (OTP's) submissions on sentencing, in which the OTP argued that publicity was used 'as a tool in the attack', and that this 'intentionally "high-profile" nature of the attack heightened the suffering of the people of Timbuktu and allowed the armed groups to reach, and thus to victimise, a broader audience'.[322] The Chamber considers that

[319] Judgment, *Moinina Fofana and Allieu Kondewa* (SCSL-04-14-T), Trial Chamber I, 2 August 2007, § 153.

[320] Judgment, *Miroslav Kvočka et al.* (IT-98-30/1-T), 2 November 2001, § 149.

[321] Al Mahdi Judgment and Sentence, *supra* note 296, at § 78.

[322] Public redacted version of Prosecution's submissions on sentencing, *Ahmad Al Faqi Al Mahdi*, (ICC-01/12-01/15) Trial Chamber VIII, 21 August 2016, § 35.

this argumentation may be applied to the present case, in which social media was used to publicise the executions.

26. Further, it is commonly known that terrorist and armed groups such as Ansar Dine and AQIM utilise social media to spread fear and political messages to a global audience.[323] The Chamber is thus of the view that in posting execution videos online, members of Ansar Dine intended not only to degrade the victims depicted in the footage, but to harm other internet users who may have stumbled across the content. Notably, in its sentencing judgment for the *Prosecutor v. Bosco Ntaganda* case, Trial Chamber VI considered that crimes 'irreversibly impacted not only the direct victims but also those who witnessed them'.[324] The Chamber therefore submits that this should also be factored into the assessment of gravity, as by sharing videos to platforms like YouTube, Ansar Dine expanded its range of victims outside of those executed and in the direct vicinity of the crimes to include virtually any internet user as well.

27. The Chamber notes that the posting of executions online has been acknowledged as a separate crime and charged as an outrage on the dignity of the deceased in domestic trials. For example, in The Netherlands, a man was convicted for the war crime of assault on personal dignity for posting a photo to Facebook of himself posing next to a man who was executed and tied to a cross.[325] Months later, another man was convicted for the same crime for posting to YouTube footage of him kicking and spitting on dead bodies.[326] In both instances, the Hague Court ruled that the footage posted to social media constituted the level of humiliating and degrading treatment necessary to be considered a war crime.[327] Similar cases have occurred in Finland, Germany, and Sweden, in which individuals were sentenced to imprisonment for war crimes for sharing videos of dead bodies and crimes being

[323] See for instance E. Vermeersch, J. Coleman, M. Demuynck, and E. Dal Salto, *The Role of Social Media in Mali and Its Relation to Violent Extremism: A Youth Perspective*, International Centre for Counter-Terrorism The Hague and United Nations Interregional Crime and Justice Research Institute, March 2020, available at www.icct.nl/sites/default/files/import/publication/Social-Media-in-Mali-and-Its-Relation-to-Violent-Extremism-A-Youth-Perspective.pdf.

[324] Sentencing Judgment, *Bosco Ntaganda* (ICC-01/04-02/06), Trial Chamber VI, 7 November 2019, § 52.

[325] ECLI:NL:GHDHA:2021:103, available at https://uitspraken.rechtspraak.nl/inziendocument?id=ECLI:NL:GHDHA:2021:103, at 2.

[326] ECLI:NL:RBDHA:2021:3998, available at https://uitspraken.rechtspraak.nl/inziendocument?id=ECLI:NL:RBDHA:2021:3998. See para. 5.4.2.3 of the judgment, translated from Dutch to English: 'All of this behavior was subsequently filmed and this film was distributed through a public YouTube channel, continuing the humiliation and dishonor by allowing a large audience to learn about it. In the opinion of the court, these humiliating and degrading behaviours – certainly viewed in conjunction with each other – are of such a nature that one can speak of an assault on personal dignity.'

[327] ECLI:NL:GHDHA:2021:103, *supra* note 325, at 26; ECLI:NL:RBDHA:2021:3998, *supra* note 326, at 41.

committed to the internet.[328] The Chamber leaves open the possibility of applying the same analysis at the ICC, which has jurisdiction over the war crimes listed under Article 8 of the Rome Statute.[329]

28. Further, regarding the consideration of other victims outside those directly affected by the executions, such as online users, the Chamber notes that other crimes under the jurisdiction of the Court take into account victimisation outside of those in the immediate vicinity of the crimes. For instance, in its Policy on Cultural Heritage, the OTP notes that '[t]he victims of crimes against or affecting cultural heritage may include persons affected both directly and indirectly ... The impact of an attack on cultural heritage may transcend the socio-geographical space it occupies, resulting in a global impact'.[330]

29. Including this element in the gravity consideration renders visible harms perpetrated through digital means important in all cases where violence is published online. This will be particularly significant in cases involving sexual and gender-based violence, where the additional stigma involved in the violence being made public requires recognition as part of what renders the crimes particularly grave.

Conclusion

30. The digital age is changing how international crimes are committed and how accountability for crimes is pursued before criminal courts, both international and domestic. These additional remarks have drawn attention to two issues that will be important going forward and to which attention must be paid by actors in the accountability space, from lawyers to investigators. First, video evidence will continue to grow in importance and its potential should be viewed more broadly than has been the case until now. Second, there is an additional harm that takes place when a recording of a crime is posted to social media, and this harm should be acknowledged and factored into an assessment of the gravity of the crime.

Judge Sarah Zarmsky and Judge Emma Irving

[328] For example, in Finland, two men were convicted for posting on Facebook images of themselves holding decapitated heads – one was convicted for desecrating the corpse of the dead fighter, and the other was convicted for an outrage upon the personal dignity of the deceased. In Germany, one man was prosecuted for posing with severed heads of enemy combatants impaled on metal rods and uploading the photos to Facebook 'with limited privacy settings', and another was convicted on similar grounds for recording himself mutilating the bodies of dead soldiers. In Sweden, a man was convicted for posing next to multiple severed heads and posting the photos on Facebook. See Eurojust, 'Prosecuting war crimes of outrage upon personal dignity based on evidence from open sources – Legal framework and recent developments in the Member States of the European Union' (The Hague, February 2018) 7–10.

[329] Article 8(2)(b)(xxi) includes the war crime of 'outrages upon personal dignity; in particular humiliating or degrading treatment'.

[330] The Office of the Prosecutor, Policy on Cultural Heritage, June 2021, § 27.

14

The Situation in Bangladesh/Myanmar

14.1 REFLECTION: THE SITUATION IN BANGLADESH/ MYANMAR

Catherine Renshaw and Afroza Anwary

INTRODUCTION

This sub-chapter provides a critical reflection on the feminist reimagining of two selected decisions from the situation in Bangladesh/Myanmar at the ICC. It begins by providing background to the 2016 'clearance operation' carried out by the government of Myanmar, as well as the procedural history of the situation at the ICC. It goes on to summarise the key facts and outcome of the ICC proceedings, before discussing how the authors of the reimagined decisions have departed from the original in adopting a feminist perspective. The sub-chapter considers what makes each decision 'feminist' and reflects upon how gender justice might be effected if we were to act beyond the existing rules of international criminal law.

BACKGROUND TO THE CONFLICT

From 9 October 2016 until 9 February 2017, the government of Myanmar carried out what it labelled 'clearance operation' in northern Rakhine State, in response to an attack by insurgents on three border guard posts.[1] During this period, according to a report by the United Nations Office of the High Commissioner for Human

[1] The Republic of the Union of Myanmar – President's Office, 'Tatmadaw ends area clearance operations in northern Rakhine', available at www.president-office.gov.mm/en/?q = print/7288; W. Lone, K. S. Oo, S. Lewis, and A. Slodkowski, 'Myanmar forces and Buddhist villagers torched Rohingya homes, then killed', Reuters, 8 February 2018, available at www.reuters.com/article/us-myanmar-rakhine-events-precis/myanmar-forces-and-buddhist-villagers-torched-rohingya-homes-then-killed-idUSKBN1FS3BL.

Rights, government forces carried out a series of atrocities against local populations.[2] The military, known as the Tatmadaw, used helicopters to fire bullets and drop grenades on villagers as they worked on their farms, shopped in markets, or fished. On the ground, soldiers burned and looted villages, raped and tortured the inhabitants, and summarily executed imams, religious scholars, and community leaders. Tens of thousands of people fled over the border into Bangladesh.[3]

The targets of the 2016 operation were known as the Rohingya, an ethnic and religious minority within the majority Buddhist, predominantly ethnic Bamar population.[4] The Rohingya follow Islamic faith practices, speak Chittagonian dialect, and are not recognised as one of the ethnic groups entitled to citizenship under Myanmar law.[5] They have been marginalised, discriminated against, and oppressed by successive governments. In the 1970s and 1990s, pogroms displaced hundreds of thousands of Rohingya. In 2012, following sectarian violence, government forces participated in the burning of Rohingya villages and the murder of hundreds of Rohingya men, women, and children. Many Rohingya people were displaced and herded into ghettos, where they were denied the ability to work or to access adequate food, water, medical care, education, or humanitarian assistance.[6]

Against this backdrop, the brutality and scale of the 2016 attacks led United Nations officials and some of Myanmar's Southeast Asian neighbours to accuse the Tatmadaw of carrying out a campaign of ethnic cleansing against the Rohingya.[7] In April 2017, the United Nations Human Rights Council resolved to establish an Independent International Fact Finding Mission (IIFFM) to investigate allegations of arbitrary detention, torture and inhuman treatment, rape and other forms of sexual violence, extrajudicial, summary, or arbitrary killings, enforced disappearances, forced displacement, and unlawful destruction of property.[8]

In August 2017, as the IIFFM prepared to begin its work, the Tatmadaw carried out a second and more extensive campaign against the Rohingya. In response to

2 Office of the High Commissioner for Human Rights, 'Report of OHCHR Mission to Bangladesh: Interviews with Rohingyas Fleeing from Myanmar since 9 October 2016: Flash Report' (1 February 2017).

3 *Ibid*, 42.

4 See M. Gravers, *Exploring Ethnic Diversity in Burma* (Copenhagen: Nordic Institute of Asian Studies, 2007) 191–283.

5 M. Chowdhury, 'The Advent of Islam in Arakan and the Rohingyas', ARNO, 22 October 2006, available at www.rohingya.org/the-advent-of-islam-in-arakanand-the-rohingyas/; A. Chan, 'The Development of a Muslim Enclave in Arakan (Rakhine) State of Burma (Myanmar)' 3 *SOAS Bulletin of Burma Research* (2005), 396–420, at 396.

6 Kofi Annan Foundation, Advisory Commission on Rakhine State (2017) available at www.kofiannanfoundation.org/publication/rakhine-final-report/.

7 UN News, 'UN human rights chief points to "textbook example of ethnic cleansing" in Myanmar', 11 September 2017, available at https://news.un.org/en/story/2017/09/564622-un-human-rights-chief-points-textbook-example-ethnic-cleansing-myanmar; Al Jazeera, 'Malaysia: Myanmar pursues ethnic cleansing of Rohingya', 3 December 2016, available at www.aljazeera.com/news/2016/12/3/malaysia-myanmar-pursues-ethnic-cleansing-of-rohingya.

8 Human Rights Council; HRC Res. 34/22, 24 March 2017.

another coordinated attack by Rohingya insurgents, the Tatmadaw mobilised forces across a broad geographic area of Rakhine, encompassing hundreds of predominantly Rohingya villages. Soldiers carried out similar procedures in each village. They approached at dawn, while families slept, and opened fire indiscriminately. Some people were killed while fleeing their homes. The elderly, people with disabilities, and young children, who were unable to escape, were forced back into burning houses, or locked in buildings which were then set on fire.[9] In at least ten village tracts, soldiers perpetrated large-scale gang-rapes, often in public spaces and in front of families and the community.[10] Following the rapes, many women and girls were killed.[11] Pregnant women were among those specifically targeted, and rapes were accompanied by language such as: 'We are going to kill you this way, by raping you.'[12] Men and boys were also subjected to rape, genital mutilation, and sexualised torture.[13]

In October 2017, the military declared that the clearance operation was complete.[14] By that time, 10,000 people had been killed, 392 villages had been totally or partially destroyed, and 750,000 Rohingya had fled across the border to Bangladesh,[15] many of whom remain there at the time of writing in June 2023.

The IIFFM published its final report into the violence in September 2018. It concluded that there was sufficient information to warrant the investigation and prosecution of senior Tatmadaw officials for the international crimes of genocide, war crimes, and crimes against humanity. In relation to genocide, the IIFFM stated that the Rohingya had been subjected to four of the five prohibited genocidal acts (killing; causing serious bodily or mental harm; inflicting conditions of life calculated to bring about the physical destruction of the group in whole or in part; imposing measures intending to prevent births).[16] The IIFFM considered that the critical element of 'genocidal intent' was likely to be present, given the manner in which the crimes were perpetrated, their similarity, and their gravity and scope.[17] The IIFFM considered the possible argument that the Tatmadaw's intention may not have been to commit genocide – the ultimate destruction of the Rohingya, in whole or in part – but merely to drive the Rohingya out of Rakhine State.[18] The IIFFM rejected this argument because of the scale and scope of the violence, the

9 Report of the Independent International Fact-Finding Mission on Myanmar, UN Doc. HRC/39/64, 12 September 2018, § 633, at 92.

10 *Ibid*, § 1372.

11 *Ibid*.

12 *Ibid*, § 1378.

13 *Ibid*, § 675; 'Sexual and Gender-Based Violence in Myanmar and the Gendered Impact of Its Ethnic Conflicts', UN Doc. HRC/42/CRP, 22 August 2019.

14 Republic of the Union of Myanmar, *supra* note 1.

15 IIFFM, *supra* note 9, § 959.

16 *Ibid*, §§ 1393–1410.

17 *Ibid*, §§ 84–85.

18 *Ibid*, §§ 1434–1438.

intensity and brutality of the attacks, and the mass demolition of Rohingya villages and homes.[19] The only possible conclusion that could be drawn from the facts, in the view of the IIFFM, was that the Tatmadaw intended to obliterate the Rohingya, at least in part.

In 2019 the IIFFM published a second report, titled 'Sexual and Gender-Based Violence in Myanmar and the Gendered Impact of Its Ethnic Conflicts'.[20] The report described a situation of sexual and gender-based violence perpetrated by the Tatmadaw against Rohingya (and other ethnic minority) women and girls, men and boys, and people from the transgender community. The IIFFM amassed 'a vast amount of information about incidents of mass gang rapes, rapes, sexually humiliating acts, sexual slavery and sexual mutilations'.[21] The gravity and brutality of the violence was striking. The Mission concluded that the sexual violence perpetrated against women and girls was a factor that indicated the Tatmadaw's genocidal intent to destroy the Rohingya people, including by means of killing female members of the Rohingya community, causing Rohingya women and girls serious bodily or mental harm, deliberately inflicting on the Rohingya women and girls conditions of life calculated to bring about the destruction of the Rohingya in whole or in part, and imposing measures that prevented births within the group. The killing of women and girls was widespread and systematic, women and girls of reproductive age were targeted for rape, pregnant women and babies were attacked, the reproductive organs of girls and women were mutilated and injured, there was physical branding of bodies by bite marks on their cheeks, neck, breasts, and thighs, and victims were so severely injured that they may be unable to have sexual intercourse with their husbands or to conceive or carry children.[22]

Myanmar is not a party to the Rome Statute and therefore not directly subject to the jurisdiction of the International Criminal Court (ICC). The IIFFM recommended that the Security Council refer Myanmar to the ICC or that the Security Council create an ad hoc international tribunal to investigate and prosecute international crimes carried out in Myanmar. Practically and politically, however, Security Council action was unlikely. Two of the Council's permanent members, China and Russia, routinely blocked action against Myanmar.[23] The following section explains how the jurisdictional issue was addressed and the Prosecutor was granted authorisation to proceed with an investigation.

[19] *Ibid*, § 1438.

[20] 'Sexual and Gender-Based Violence in Myanmar and the Gendered Impact of Its Ethnic Conflicts', *supra* note 13. *See* V. Hospodaryk, 'Male and Gender-Diverse Victims of Sexual Violence in the Rohingya Genocide: The Selective Narrative of International Courts' 17(2) *International Journal of Transitional Justice* (2023) 252–267.

[21] 'Sexual and Gender-Based Violence in Myanmar and the Gendered Impact of Its Ethnic Conflicts', *supra* note 13, § 73.

[22] *Ibid*, § 96.

[23] Reuters, 'China, Russia block U.N. council concern about Myanmar violence', 26 October 2016, available at www.reuters.com/article/us-myanmar-rohingya-un-idUSKBN16O2J6.

SITUATION IN BANGLADESH/MYANMAR

The Rome Statute of the International Criminal Court confers jurisdiction in cases where the conduct that gives rise to the crime occurs on the territory of a state on the territory of a state party, inter alia.[24] In April 2018, the ICC Office of the Prosecutor (OTP) requested a ruling on whether the ICC could exercise jurisdiction over the displacement of the Rohingya across the border separating Myanmar and Bangladesh.[25] The Prosecutor argued that the crime against humanity of deportation may have occurred.[26] The crime of deportation, argued the Prosecutor, involves conduct that takes place on the territory of two states: the state from which the victim population is displaced and the state into which the victim population is moved. In the case of the Rohingya, this may mean that part of the crime of deportation took place on the territory of Bangladesh. Bangladesh signed the Rome Statute in 2010. Thus, argued the Prosecutor, the Court has jurisdiction to investigate the crime against humanity of deportation in relation to the Tatmadaw's treatment of the Rohingya.

On 6 September 2018, Pre-Trial Chamber I delivered its opinion. The Chamber agreed with the Prosecutor that the crime of deportation involves the victims' displacement across an international border.[27] For this reason, the 'conduct' of the crime necessarily takes place in two different states. In cases where coercive acts that instigate deportation are initiated in a state that is not party to the Statute and are completed in a state that is a party to the Statute, then the Court has jurisdiction. It was the drafters' intention, the Chamber held, to allow for the exercise of the Court's jurisdiction where one element of the crime is committed on the territory of a state party.[28] Therefore, in relation to the alleged deportation of Rohingya civilians across the Myanmar–Bangladesh border, the Court had jurisdiction to investigate.

The Chamber emphasised that the Rome Statute definition of deportation specifies that displacement takes place by means of 'expulsion or other coercive acts'.[29] Deportation is therefore an 'open-conduct crime', meaning that 'several different conducts can amount to expulsion or other coercive acts'.[30] The relevant conduct can include deprivation of fundamental rights, killing, sexual violence, torture, enforced disappearance, destruction, and looting. The Chamber held that

[24] Article 12(1)–(2) ICCSt.

[25] Prosecution's Request for a Ruling on Jurisdiction under Article 19(3) ICCSt, ICC-RoC46(3)-01/18, 8 April 2018.

[26] Article 7(1)(d) ICCSt. The Statute defines 'deportation or forcible transfer of population' as the 'forced displacement of the persons concerned by expulsion or other coercive acts from the area in which they are lawfully present, without grounds permitted under international law'.

[27] Decision on the Prosecution's Request for a Ruling on Jurisdiction under Article 19(3) of the Statute, ICC-RoC46(3)-01/18, 6 September 2018.

[28] *Ibid*, § 71.

[29] Article 7(2)(d) ICCSt.

[30] Reuters, *supra* note 23, § 61.

examination of evidence relating to all these acts, which may have occurred solely on the territory of Myanmar, was within the Court's jurisdiction.

The Chamber also emphasised that the cross-border rationale which provided jurisdiction for the crime of deportation might apply to other international crimes as well. The Chamber provided two examples. One was the crime against humanity of persecution.[31] The Rome Statute defines 'persecution' as 'the intentional and severe deprivation of fundamental rights contrary to international law'. The Chamber noted that under international human rights law, no one may be arbitrarily deprived of the fundamental right to enter their own country. The Rohingya, forced to endure appalling conditions in the refugee camps of Bangladesh while the authorities of Myanmar impeded their return home, may have been deprived of their fundamental right to enter their own country, contrary to international law. Part of this conduct, which could amount to the crime against humanity of persecution, may also have taken place on the territory of Bangladesh. The other example provided by the Chamber was the catch-all crime against humanity provision of '[o]ther inhumane acts of a similar character intentionally causing great suffering, or serious injury to body or to mental or physical health'.[32] Such acts, the Chamber noted, were also potentially inflicted on the Rohingya when they were uprooted from their homes and forced to leave their country and seek refuge in Bangladesh. The overall conclusion was that in circumstances where victims are made to flee to the territory of a state party, or victims languish on the territory of a state party and are prevented from returning to their homes, then the jurisdiction of the Court may be invoked.

The Pre-Trial Chamber decision on jurisdiction caused significant controversy. Some critics feared that in providing a 'backdoor to the Hague'[33] the Chamber had overreached, and that the Court's legitimacy, already precarious, may be undermined.[34] Others were concerned with the practical question of how the ICC would prosecute cases for crimes committed by Myanmar officials on Myanmar territory without the support of the Myanmar government. The Court's track record in states not party to the Statute, for example, in Sudan in relation to the arrest warrants issued against former President Omar al-Bashir and in Libya in relation to the arrest warrant against Saif al-Islam Gaddafi – provided little ground for optimism.[35] There were also concerns about the legal foundations of the decision, because the Chamber seemed to blur the line between 'conduct' and 'consequence' in relation

31 *Ibid*, § 75.

32 *Ibid*, § 77.

33 P. Akhavan, 'The Radically Routine Rohingya Case: Territorial Jurisdiction and the Crime of Deportation under the ICC Statute' 17 *Journal of International Criminal Justice* (2019) 325–345, at 325.

34 D. Guilfoyle, 'The ICC Pre-Trial Chamber Decision on Jurisdiction over the Situation in Myanmar' 73(1) *Australian Journal of International Affairs* (2019) 2–8.

35 Omar Al Bashir, President of Sudan since 1993, was the subject of ICC arrest warrants issued on 4 March 2009 and 12 July 2010. He remains at large.

to a particular action.[36] Other commentators noted that the Chamber's decision did not address (although nor did it rule out) the possibility of jurisdiction extending to the crime of genocide.[37] It seemed arguable that certain forms of genocide, such as genocide 'by deliberately inflicting conditions of life calculated to bring about physical destruction',[38] could – similar to the crime of deportation – be thought of as involving several elements, some of which might occur on the territory of a country that was not a party to the Rome Statute, while other elements occurred on the territory of a state that was. In the Rohingya case, the difficulty would be in establishing that the *dolus specialis* of genocide – an intention to *destroy* – was not incompatible with the *mens rea* of deportation – an intention to displace.[39]

The Prosecutor faced unpalatable choices. Investigating crimes *other* than genocide, even serious crimes against humanity such as deportation, might be viewed as only partial or inferior justice for the victims. Those who defended the Chamber's decision answered that surely partial justice was better than no justice at all.[40] But an outcome of 'no justice at all' was also a possibility, and even a likelihood, given that Myanmar was not a party to the Rome Statute, was not cooperating in the case, and the Prosecutor was unlikely to be able to execute any arrest warrants.

In July 2019, following the decision on jurisdiction, the Prosecutor requested authorisation to investigate crimes in which at least one element took place on the territory of Bangladesh, and which occurred within the context of the 2016 and 2017 waves of violence in Rakhine State. The Prosecutor submitted that there was reasonable basis to believe that since 9 October 2016, members of the Tatmadaw, with the border guard police and the Myanmar police force, committed the crime against humanity of deportation; other inhumane acts; and persecution on the grounds of ethnicity and/or religion. Other crimes, submitted the Prosecutor, might also come to light once an investigation commenced. Pre-Trial Chamber III authorised that investigation on 14 November 2019, and parts of that decision have been re-written from a 'feminist' perspective in this volume [*Editors' note: in 2024, the Prosecutor applied for an arrest warrant for Myanmar's acting President, General Min Aung Hlaing, in connection to alleged crimes against humanity of deportation and persecution against Rohingya people committed in part in Myanmar, and in part in Bangladesh*].

36 C. Wheeler, 'Human Rights Enforcement at the Borders: International Criminal Court Jurisdiction over the Rohingya Situation' 17 *Journal of International Criminal Justice* (2019) 609–631.

37 Y. Nagakoshi, 'The Scope and Implications of the International Criminal Court's Jurisdictional Decision over the Rohingya Crisis' 43(2) *Human Rights Quarterly* (2021) 259–289.

38 Article 6(c) ICCSt.

39 This is the difficulty that Croatia encountered in the International Court of Justice in *Croatia v. Serbia*, when it failed to convince the Court that the extreme violence that underpinned mass displacement was indicative of the special intent to destroy. M. Steinfeld, 'When Ethnic Cleansing Is not Genocide: A Critical Appraisal of the ICJ's Ruling in *Croatia v. Serbia* in Relation to Deportation and Population Transfer' 28(4) *Leiden Journal of International Law* (2015) 937–944.

40 Akhavan, *supra* note 33.

FEMINIST REIMAGINING OF SELECT JUDGMENTS AND DECISIONS

Judges Emma Palmer and Phyu Phyu Oo

The rewritten judgment by Judges Palmer and Oo examines the 'coercive acts' which forced the Rohingya to leave Bangladesh. The judges employ devices that allow the reader to appreciate the historical and contextual background to the violence perpetrated on the Rohingya, and the impact of intersecting grounds of persecution. The opening of the judgment, for example, is striking. The authors use direct quotations from Rohingya refugees to signal to the reader that it is the concrete person before the Chamber, rather than the abstract legal person. Palmer and Oo also describe in detail the long-term oppression and dispossession suffered by the Rohingya, and the climate of impunity in which the specific violence of 2016 and 2017 took place. For many decades, the Rohingya were denied citizenship, limits were set on the number of children they could have, and they were prohibited from marrying, working, and receiving education or medical care.[41] When the immediate violence commenced, the Rohingya knew from the experience of generations of persecution that if they wished to save their lives, then they must flee. Those who fled, Judges Palmer and Oo note, were not an abstract mass, but hundreds of thousands of individuals.[42] Palmer and Oo also draw attention to the wretched conditions that awaited those who fled to the refugee camps of Bangladesh, and they also note the absences – those who did *not* arrive in the refugee camps of Bangladesh but who lost their lives in Rakhine or along the way. They ask future Trial Chambers or other Chambers to inquire specifically into what happened to people of different genders, including Hijra people (see below), to children, and to disabled persons, who suffered violence and coercion in Rakhine, and whose experiences of terror and pain will be distinct.

In their reasoning, the approach adopted by Judges Palmer and Oo pursues a feminist method in that it assists a deeper and more nuanced understanding of the complex history of Rohingya suffering. The authors make clear that the setting in which interactions take place must be considered in depth and detail, including the background of 'racial, patriarchal, repressive, environmental, discriminatory, economic, or other structures upon individuals and communities'.[43] The authors set out the wretched history of the Rohingya in Rakhine State and the long-term misery of their existence in a country where they were not recognised as citizens. The authors might have added that Myanmar society – which existed under British colonial rule for more than 100 years and then under military rule for almost half a century – was profoundly militaristic and heteronormative in nature. In its Report on Sexual and

[41] M. Zarni and A. Cowley, 'The Slow-Burning Genocide of Myanmar's Rohingya' 23(3) *Pacific Rim Law & Policy Journal* (2014) 681–752; C. Renshaw, 'Myamar's Genocide and the Legacy of Forgetting' 48 *Georgia Journal of International and Comparative Law* (2019) 425–472.

[42] Palmer and Oo, Reimagined Judgment, § 58.

[43] *Ibid*, § 21.

Gender-Based Violence, the IIFFM notes the larger problem of extreme gender inequality in Myanmar and that Myanmar ranks 148 of 189 countries in the United Nations' Gender Inequality Index.

Rakhine was under a state of emergency from 2013 to 2016. There are long-term societal effects to existence under conditions of colonial and military oppression, and to subjection to continual arbitrary exercises of power and denigration. For more than a century, 'race', 'sex', 'ethnicity', and 'religious association' were viewed as calcified categories by those who held power in Rakhine State. By 2016, the potential for choice or self-determination over any aspect of the lives of Rohingya women was close to non-existent. How they married, raised families, gathered food and fuel, provided shelter, and survived was severely circumscribed.

One important contribution of Palmer and Oo's judgment is that it clarifies, where the original decision does not, that the jurisdictional question addressed in relation to the crime against humanity of deportation may also apply to the crime of genocide. This, again, is a 'feminist' contribution in the sense that the conclusion gives voice to what victims themselves experienced as happening. Rohingya people believe that the military was trying to wipe them out.[44] In Palmer and Oo's discussion of the crime of genocide, they appropriately leave it for a later court to clarify whether the 'special intent' to destroy, necessary for the crime of genocide, has a sufficient nexus with the acts and consequences that took place.

An alternative feminist judgment might have delved more deeply into issues around the nature of harm. Linear and dichotomising conceptions of time (acts/consequences) used in the reimagined judgment preclude more multi-layered, complex, interactive, and cyclical notions of time that encompass longer-term and intergenerational pain. Judges Palmer and Oo might at least have called for the need for further evidence of harm at later stages of the case. In their discussion about the consequences of violence and deportation, they do note some longer-term, complex consequences of sexual violence.[45] But at times the language used is clinical and objective: for example, 'negative coping strategies' is used as a term to describe consequences of sexual violence such as forced labour and forced prostitution.[46] Judges Palmer and Oo might have drawn attention, as did the IIFFM, to self-harm and suicide as a result of sexual violence.[47] The isolation and disconnection bound up in the crime of deportation, and the psychological trauma that accompanies the rupture to routine daily life, also warrants attention. There is an established body of

[44] Rohingya poets such as Mayyu Ali provide the subjective experience of intended destruction: 'That year [2012] was a turning point . . . The Rohingya had always been discriminated against, but now the authorities' aim was to make us disappear.' C. Cabot, '"When I write, I exist and so does my community", says Rohingya poet Mayyu Ali', *France 24*, 4 September 2022, available at www.france24.com/en/asia-pacific/20220904-when-i-write-i-exist-and-so-does-my-community-says-rohingya-poet-mayyu-ali.

[45] Palmer and Oo, Rewritten Judgment, § 54.

[46] *Ibid.*

[47] IIFFM, supra note 9, § 1398.

literature on social and geographical embeddedness,[48] on the psychological and social effects of displacement,[49] and on the ways in which the effects of deracination are not gender-neutral.[50] Deportation punctuates the concrete practices of daily existence (in Rohingya villages, these include collecting firewood, attending the mosque, fetching water, shopping at the market, readying children for school) in ways that disproportionately impact women. The need for emotional and caring labour, also provided by women, is acute. Dislocation manifests in a myriad of quotidian traumas, which feminist jurisprudence must speak to.

Judge Claerwen O'Hara

The central problem Judge O'Hara wrestles with in their decision is whether it is possible, given the Rome Statute's definition of 'gender', for the crime of persecution to apply to Hijra persons. Hijra people are third-gender persons from the region of South Asia. Some Hijra people follow Hindu faith practices, and may choose to undergo a castration ceremony as part of Hindu ritual; others follow the Muslim faith. The common characteristic most Hijra people share is communal life with other Hijra people, removed from wider society. Following the attacks on the Rohingya in Myanmar, some Rohingya Hijra reported to the IIFFM that they believed they had been targeted for sexual violence due to a combination of their non-conformity with gender norms and their Rohingya ethnicity.[51]

Persecution on the basis of gender is a crime against humanity under Article 7(1)(h) of the Rome Statute. The difficulty with applying this provision to the persecution of Hijra people is that the Rome Statute defines gender restrictively. Article 7(3) of the Statute states: 'For the purposes of this Statute, it is understood that the term "gender" refers to the two sexes, male and female, within the context of society. The term "gender" does not indicate any meaning different from the above.' On one reading of the text, the definition of gender in the Rome Statute includes only the two sexes – male and female – as recognised targets for persecution.

Judge O'Hara overcomes the restrictions of the Article 7(3) definition using a process of reasoning that emphasises the significance of the phrase 'in the context of society'. O'Hara reasons that the inclusion of this phrase means that 'male and female' cannot be understood solely to refer to the narrow biological categories denoted.[52] 'Male and female' must, O'Hara argues, encompass the social context,

[48] E. Casey (ed.), *Getting Back into Place: Towards a Renewed Understanding of the Place-World* (Bloomington: Indiana University Press, 2009).

[49] L. Eckenwiler, 'Displacement and Solidarity: An Ethic of Place-Making' 32 *Bioethics* (2018) 562–568.

[50] D. Indra (ed.), *Engendering Forced Migration: Theory and Practice* (New York: Berghahn Books, 2001); C. Nolin (ed.), *Transnational Ruptures: Gender and Forced Migration (Gender in a Global/Local World)* (London: Routledge, 2001).

[51] O'Hara, Reimagined Judgment, § 36.

[52] *Ibid*, §§ 20–23.

dynamics, and interactions that give those dyadic categories meaning. O'Hara draws support for this interpretation from debates about the definition of gender at the time of the Statute's drafting. States rejected a non-social definition of gender, insisting on the inclusion of the phrase 'in the context of society' as part of the definition.[53] Judge O'Hara also notes developments in the jurisprudence of UN human rights treaty bodies and human rights instruments that support a broad contextual and social interpretation of gender, such as the definition of gender in the Council of Europe Convention on Preventing and Combating Violence against Women and Domestic Violence.[54] O'Hara notes that the Rome Statute must be interpreted in a manner consistent with international human rights law.[55]

Applying the broader understanding of gender to Hijra people in Rakhine State, Judge O'Hara finds (i) that some Hijra people may have been targeted on the basis of their non-conformity with norms and expectations that have formed around sex-based categories of male and female, which may constitute gender-based persecution for the purposes of Article 7(1)(h) of the Statute; (ii) that some Hijra people who are intersex may have been subjected to persecution because they do not conform with expected bodily appearances of males and females;[56] and (iii) that other Hijra people may have been targeted for rape and sexual violence because they do not conform with expected bodily appearances of males and females.[57] O'Hara concludes that 'to the extent that the Hijra people who were allegedly targeted for rape and sexual violence were also Rohingya, the persecution may have been based on the intersecting grounds of gender, ethnicity, and religion'.[58]

Judge O'Hara succeeds in reinterpreting the definition of gender in a way that encompasses gender as a social construction – which in Western law and society generally is the more common way in which 'gender' is now understood. The Office of the Prosecutor confirmed this interpretation in its 2022 policy paper on the crime of gender persecution:

> As for all forms of persecution, persons may be targeted for gender persecution because of sex characteristics and/or because of the social constructs and criteria used to define gender roles, behaviours, activities and attributes. For example, persons may be targeted for gender persecution when they are perceived to have or carry (gender) criteria prohibited by the perpetrator; or are perceived to not have or carry (gender) criteria required by the perpetrator.[59]

[53] *Ibid*, § 25.
[54] Art. 210 CETS; O'Hara, Reimagined Judgment, § 26.
[55] O'Hara, Reimagined Judgment, § 26.
[56] *Ibid*, § 33.
[57] *Ibid*, §§ 32–34.
[58] *Ibid*, § 35.
[59] The Office of the Prosecutor, Policy on the Crime of Gender Persecution, 7 December 2022, § 42, available at www.icc-cpi.int/sites/default/files/2022-12/2022-12-07-Policy-on-the-Crime-of-Gender-Persecution.pdf.

On Judge O'Hara's argument, not only is persecution on the grounds of male or female sex criminalised, but also discrimination that takes place because perpetrators have gendered ideas about males and females, including towards intersex, non-binary, inter-gender, and transgender people, and Hijra persons. Judge O'Hara thus brings the discrimination and harm suffered by Hijra people in Myanmar within the scope of the Rome Statute. Following O'Hara's redefinition of gender, the relevant issue is whether one of the reasons the Tatmadaw inflicted pain and suffering on Hijra people is because the victims were *not* a 'man or woman' as traditionally, biologically understood. O'Hara's judgment has the salutary effect of advancing the jurisprudence on recognition of impermissible persecution. O'Hara follows a line of scholarship that lays the foundation for this interpretation, which includes the work of Grey,[60] Suhr,[61] Leddy,[62] and Oosterveld.[63]

One question Judge O'Hara might have asked a future Trial Chamber to consider is whether all or most Hijra people believed they were persecuted because they are something *other* than male or female. It might be, for example, that some Hijra people feel that atrocities were committed against them for a different reason – not because of what they are *not*, but perhaps because of what they *are* – which is an altogether different thing to just an 'absence' of male or female biological attributes.[64] The distinction in this regard is not trivial. One of the points of a feminist interpretation is to reflect, speak to, and recognise harm as it is experienced by the victim. Reliance on the negative ('Hijra people were persecuted on the basis that they did not conform to the male/female binary') runs the danger of drawing us into to the very tendency that a feminist approach might wish to avoid: the constitution of the subject through negation of the gender categories male and female. In O'Hara's decision, Hijra and others are constructed to mirror the male/female binary. This approach replicates traditional (colonialist) gender hierarchies and accepts difference as relational, rather than upholding the fluid potential that inheres in the intersubjective constitution of gender.

Judge O'Hara's negation of the binary as a basis for advancing an interpretation of how Article 7(3) might apply to Hijra persons matters because the language of the Rome Statute has a constructive aspect. Our concern with O'Hara's judgment is that

60 R. Grey et al., 'Gender-Based Persecution as a Crime against Humanity' 17(5) *Journal of International Criminal Justice* (2019) 957–979.

61 V. Suhr (ed.), *Rainbow Jurisdiction at the International Criminal Court – Protection of Sexual and Gender Minorities under the Rome Statute* (The Hague: T. M. C. Asser Press, 2021).

62 N. Leddy, 'Investigative and Charging Considerations for International Crimes Targeting Individuals on the Basis of Sexual Orientation and Gender Identity' 20(4) *Journal of International Criminal Justice* (2022) 911–942.

63 V. Oosterveld, 'The Definition of "Gender" in the Rome Statute of the International Criminal Court: A Step Forward or Back for International Criminal Justice?' 64 *Harvard Human Rights Journal* (2005) 55–84.

64 D. Cornell and A. Thurschwell, 'Feminism, Negativity, Intersubjectivity' in S. Benhabib and D. Cornell (eds.), *Feminism as Critique* (Minneapolis: University of Minnesota Press, 1987) 143–162.

in using an interpretive technique that bends the law into a more favourable shape to do justice in the immediate case,[65] a seemingly progressive decision may disqualify, repress, and absorb counter-discourses that may have more affinity with the truth as it is experienced by those who are persecuted. In Judge O'Hara's decision, value is attributed to the socially constructed roles of man and woman at the expense of the unmentioned 'Other'. A more expansive feminist method, in contrast, would attempt to favour that which most severely disrupts identity-bound thought. The Yogyakarta Principles on the Application of International Human Rights Law in Relation to Sexual Orientation and Gender Identity affirm that 'each person's self-defined sexual orientation and gender identity is integral to their personality and is one of the most basic aspects of self-determination, dignity and freedom'.[66]

The OTP's Policy on Gender Persecution confirms that 'all persons can be subjected to gender persecution because all persons have gender identities just as all persons have racial and ethnic identities'.[67] Women, girls, men, boys, and LGBTQI+ persons may be discriminated against on the basis of their roles, behaviours, activities, and attributes. O'Hara's judgment makes a salutary contribution to jurisprudence by demonstrating what is possible within the law as it stands – but from our perspective, this should not be the end of the story. Reform of the Statute is required, to recognise 'gender' without any constraining definition. The preservation of the word 'gender' within the text of the Rome Statute, without any caveats as suggested by the feminist lawyers involved in its drafting, would signal acceptance of the mutability, fluidity, and ambiguity of 'gender'. Such reform would do more to honour the particularised harm experienced by victims than adopting the perpetrator's view that harm was inflicted because the victim was not what they ought to be. 'Gender' standing alone would affirm the discursive openness of the term, including its gaps and the possibility of multiple meanings and ways of being.

CONCLUSION

Hospodaryk observes that the pre-trial ICC proceedings in the Rohingya case represent an incomplete attempt to elevate the voices of victims (the point made by Judges Palmer and Oo), and that the proceedings fail to capture the full range of sexual crimes, particularly against gender-diverse people (the point made by Judge O'Hara).[68] Hospodaryk suggests that one reason why the Court fails to present a more inclusive picture of what happened to Rohingya people is because of structural limitations to the capabilities of the Victims Participation and Reparations Section (VPRS) of the OTP. In this reflection we have suggested that feminist reimaginings

[65] C. Smart, *Law, Crime and Sexuality* (London: Sage, 1995), at 198.

[66] Art. 3, Yogyakarta Principles on the Application of International Human Rights Law in relation to Sexual Orientation and Gender Identity (2006).

[67] Office of the Prosecutor, *supra* note 59, § 45.

[68] Hospodaryk, *supra* note 20.

such as those provided by Judges Palmer and Oo and by Judge O'Hara function as a reminder of law's potential to expand the possibilities for justice, even within the confines of the existing statutory framework and limited evidentiary resources.

14.2 DEPORTATION AS A GENDERED CRIME IN THE BANGLADESH/MYANMAR INVESTIGATION

Emma Palmer and Phyu Phyu Oo

In 2019, Pre-Trial Chamber III authorised the Prosecutor to commence an investigation into the situation in Bangladesh/Myanmar in accordance with Article 15(4) of the Rome Statute.[69] The Chamber held that the Prosecutor could reasonably believe that coercive acts towards the Rohingya forced them to leave Bangladesh, which may amount to the crimes against humanity of deportation[70] and persecution on the ground of religion and/or ethnicity.[71] In establishing jurisdiction, the Chamber was satisfied that the alleged crimes had been committed at least partially on the territory of Bangladesh, which ratified the Statute on 23 March 2010.[72] The Chamber held that the scope of the investigation extended to acts committed on at least part of the territory of other states which would accept the jurisdiction of the Court, insofar as they were sufficiently linked to the situation.[73] Furthermore, the Chamber expanded the scope of the investigation beyond the crimes alleged by the Prosecutor in the request to *any crimes* sufficiently linked to the situation, stressing that limiting the incidents to be investigated at the preliminary stage would be contrary to the obligation under Article 54(1)(a) to 'cover all facts and evidence … [i]n order to establish the truth'.[74]

In this reimagined decision, Emma Palmer and Phyu Phyu Oo explore the underlying crime of deportation from a gendered perspective by expanding the definition of 'coercive acts' in a way that considers the lived experience of women and girls. Palmer and Oo employ a historical perspective that investigates the structural nature of violence and lasting legacies of colonialism in Myanmar. Their decision considers whether there is scope to elevate the findings on deportation to constitute the crime of genocide. In doing so, they ultimately reach the same conclusion as the Court in authorising the investigation.

[69] Decision Pursuant to Article 15 of the Rome Statute on the Authorisation of an Investigation into the Situation in the People's Republic of Bangladesh/Republic of the Union of Myanmar, *Situation in the People's Republic of Bangladesh/Republic of the Union of Myanmar*, Pre-Trial Chamber III, ICC-01/19–27, 14 November 2019, § 126.

[70] *Ibid*, § 108.

[71] *Ibid*, § 109.

[72] *Ibid*, §§ 113–114.

[73] *Ibid*, § 124.

[74] *Ibid*, §§ 126–128.

No.: ICC-01/19
Date: 14 November 2019

Original: English

PRE-TRIAL CHAMBER III(B)

Before: Judge Emma PALMER
Judge Phyu Phyu OO

SITUATION IN THE PEOPLE'S REPUBLIC OF BANGLADESH/ REPUBLIC OF THE UNION OF MYANMAR

Public

Decision pursuant to Article 15 of the Rome Statute on the Authorisation of an Investigation into the Situation in the People's Republic of Bangladesh/Republic of the Union of Myanmar

JUDGMENT

Deportation

1. The Chamber recalls again that one victims' representation noted: 'We lost our family members. We survive with [gunshot] wounds. We lost our property, our houses, our lands and cattle and everything. Kicked out from our motherland and made us refugee. Destroyed our everything.' Another representation, submitted on behalf of women, also states that the 'atrocities of August 2017 were the turning point of the Rohingya crisis, after this date none of the women represented could return to their motherland Myanmar'. A representation submitted on behalf of alleged victims living in the same refugee camp in Bangladesh similarly states that victims 'decided to escape and save our lives from the extra-judicial killings [. . .] the people had just one way to save their lives. [It] was to come to Bangladesh'.[75]

Applicable Law

2. The Chamber now turns to the question of whether, based on the facts, a reasonable prosecutor could believe that coercive acts towards the Rohingya forced them to flee to Bangladesh, which may amount to the crime against humanity of deportation.

[75] *Ibid*, § 28, referring consecutively to: Victims' representation r/00001/19, First Registry Transmission, ICC-01/19-14-Conf-Exp-Anx1, p. 3; see also video annex to victims' representation r/00242/19, available only to the Chamber in Third Registry Transmission, ICC-01/19-24; Victims' representation r/00017/19, First Registry Transmission, ICC-01/19-14-Conf-Exp-Anx17, p. 4; Victims' representation r/00025/19, First Registry Transmission, ICC-01/19-14-Conf-Exp-Anx25, p. 2.

3. The Chamber notes that, under international law, deportation of a state's nationals as well as the arbitrary or collective expulsion of aliens is generally prohibited.[76] There is a long history of instruments that have aimed to prevent or ensure accountability for forcible displacement.[77]

4. Article 21 of the Rome Statute sets out a hierarchical list of sources of interpretation: firstly, the Statute, its Elements of Crimes, and its Rules; secondly, applicable treaties and principles of international law; and thirdly, principles of law derived from national and other international criminal courts and tribunals.

5. Article 21(3) provides that the 'application and interpretation of law ... must be consistent with internationally recognized human rights'. In that context, we note that crimes that may appear apparently 'gender neutral' can have differently gendered effects,[78] intersecting with other cultural, social, and economic issues.

6. Article 7 of the Rome Statute addresses crimes against humanity: 'any of the following acts when committed as part of a widespread or systematic attack directed against any civilian population, with knowledge of the attack: ... (d) Deportation or forcible transfer of population'.

7. 'Deportation or forcible transfer of population' is defined as 'forced *displacement* of the persons concerned by *expulsion or other coercive acts* from the area in which they are *lawfully present, without grounds permitted* under international law'.[79]

[76] Decision, *supra* note 69, § 98: Art. 12(3) and 13, *International Covenant on Civil and Political Rights*, 19 December 1966, 999 UNTS 17955, 18 December 1966 (ICCPR); Art. 22, *American Convention on Human Rights*, 1144 UNTS 17955, 22 November 1969 (IACHR); Art. 12, Organization of African Unity, *African Charter on Human and Peoples' Rights*, 10 June 1998 (ACHPR); Arts. 2–4 of Protocol 4 ECHR; Art. 22, *International Convention on the Protection of the Rights of All Migrant Workers and Members of Their Families*, UN Doc. A/RES/45/158, 18 December 1990; V. Chetail, 'Is There Any Blood on My Hands? Deportation as a Crime of International Law' 29 *Leiden Journal of International Law* (2016) 926–928 (international law generally prohibits collective expulsion of aliens, arbitrary deportation of aliens without due process, or expulsions which severely infringe basic rights).

[77] Such as the Lieber Code of 1863, and there may be ancient precursors, at least addressing the government of occupied territories – see for instance Chapter VII, §§ 251–253, of the 'Laws of Manu', 'Indian History Sourcebook: The Laws of Manu, c. 1500 BCE, translated by G. Buhler', 1998, available at https://sourcebooks.fordham.edu/india/manu-full.asp. See also Arts. 42–56, 1907 *Hague Regulations*; 1920 *Report of the Commission on the Responsibility of the Authors of the War and on Enforcement of Penalities*; Art. 6(b) and (c) 'Nuremberg Charter' of the International Military Tribunal; Control Council Law No. 10, 'Punishment of Persons Guilty of War Crimes, Crimes Against Peace and Against Humanity' 3 *Official Gazette Control Council for Germany* (1946) 50–55; Art. 49, Geneva Convention IV; Art. 85(4)(a) of Additional Protocol I in 1977; Art. 17, Additional Protocol II of 1977; Arts. 5 and 6, Law on the Establishment of the Extraordinary Chambers in the Courts of Cambodia, with inclusion of amendments, 27 October 2004; Art. 2, ICTY Statute; Arts. 5(d) and 3(d) of the ICTR Statute.

[78] R. Grey, 'Interpreting International Crimes from a Female Perspective: Opportunities and Challenges for the International Criminal Court' 17(2) *International Criminal Law Review* (2016) 325–350.

[79] Art 7(2)(d) ICCSt.

8. The terms 'expulsion', 'coercive acts', 'lawfully present', 'grounds permitted under international law', and 'territory' have been elucidated in the jurisprudence of international courts and tribunals, including the International Criminal Tribunal for Rwanda (ICTR),[80] the Extraordinary Chambers in the Courts of Cambodia (ECCC) (forced transfers were charged as a crime against humanity of 'other inhumane acts'),[81] and the International Criminal Tribunal for Former Yugoslavia (ICTY).[82]

DEPORTATIONS OR FORCIBLE TRANSFERS

9. While the Rome Statute defines deportation or forcible transfer as forced displacement, after some contradiction and, arguably, confusion,[83] ICTY jurisprudence indicates that forcible transfers do not necessarily have a trans/cross-boundary nature,[84] although deportations might encompass forcible transfers.

10. The Prosecutor chose to argue that the crime of deportation requires or 'inherently'[85] involves the crossing of a boundary,[86] given the need to establish this Court's jurisdiction, based in this situation upon territoriality.

11. However, we see no need to minimise potential intersections between deportation and forcible transfers, including, for example, for women[87] and others who may flee to a range of places as part of their deportation/displacement.

'EXPULSION OR OTHER COERCIVE ACTS'

12. Forced displacement must be perpetrated 'by expulsion or other coercive acts'.[88] The Elements of Crimes do not define these terms, but international courts

[80] E.g. Judgment, *Prosecutor v. Jean-Paul Akayesu* (ICTR-96-4-T), Trial Chamber I, 2 September 1998 (hereafter *Akayesu*), § 688; Alongside other international institutions – for instance at the Eritrea–Ethiopia Claims Commission, which arguably applied narrower understanding of the 'forced' nature of displacements than some ICTY cases: A. M. Abebe, 'Displacement of Civilians during Armed Conflict in the Light of the Case Law of the Eritrea–Ethiopia Claims Commission' 22 *Leiden Journal of International Law* 823–851.

[81] Judgment, Case 002/01 (002/19-09-2007/ECCC/TC-E313), Trial Chamber, 7 August 2014; Appeals Judgment, Case 002 (002-19-09-2007-ECCC/SC-F36), 23 November 2016.

[82] E.g. Judgment, *Prosecutor v. Vujadin Popović et al.* (IT-05-88-T), Trial Chamber, 10 June 2010 (hereafter *Popović et al.*); Judgment, *Prosecutor v. Zdravko Tolimir* (IT-05-88/2-T), Trial Chamber, 12 December 2012 (hereafter *Tolimir*).

[83] See Judgment, *Prosecutor v. Krnojelac* (IT-97-25-T), Trial Chamber, 15 March 2002, § 474; Judgment, *Prosecutor v. Krstić* (IT-98-33-T), Trial Chamber, 2 August 2001 (hereinafter *Krstić*), § 521.

[84] *Tolimir*, *supra* note 82, § 793.

[85] Office of the Prosecutor, Prosecution's Request for a Ruling on Jurisdiction under Article 19(3) of the Statute (ICC-RoC46(3)-01/18-1), 8 April 2018, § 49 (hereafter Prosecutor's Request).

[86] *Ibid.*, 26.

[87] For the avoidance of doubt, 'women' is used inclusively to include trans women, *apwint*, and others identifying as women/womxn, and our analysis also considers non-binary individuals, although distinct forms of discrimination may be experienced by different women; see L. J. Chua and D. Gilbert, 'State Violence, Human-Rights Violations and the Case of Apwint in Myanmar' in A. Barrow and J. L. Chia (eds.), *Gender, Violence and the State of Asia* (Abingdon: Routledge, 2016) 169–185.

[88] *Popović et al.*, *supra* note 82, § 896.

and tribunals have considered the meaning of 'forced' alongside the concepts of coercion and expulsion.[89]

13. The Elements of Crimes at Article 7(2)(d) notes that the term 'forcibly' is 'not restricted to physical force, but may include threat of force or coercion, such as that caused by fear of violence, duress, detention, psychological oppression or abuse of power against such person or persons or another person, or by taking advantage of a *coercive environment*'.

14. This definition is supported by other international criminal tribunals' jurisprudence[90] and is the same wording adopted in the Elements of Crimes for the commission of the crime against humanity of rape, for example.[91]

15. The ICTR Trial Chamber observed, in the context of sexual violence, that '[c]oercive circumstances need not be evidenced by a show of physical force' but can 'be inherent in circumstances like armed conflict or military presence of threatening forces on an ethnic basis'.[92] International crimes can (and should) be understood within their dynamic contexts, including or especially when analysing the coercive environments underlying allegations.

16. Coercive acts can include shelling, burning property, and other acts designed to terrify the population into leaving,[93] such as sexual and gender-based violence.

17. However, those specific acts are not necessarily required, as confirmed in the *Ruto* case at the ICC.[94] The attacks should also not 'be viewed in isolation, but must be seen in the context of the pattern of excessive use of force', which may also provide evidence of criminal responsibility, intention (to change the ethnic composition of an area, for example),[95] and other elements of the crime (such as the '*chapeau*' elements of crime against humanity).

[89] See also Decision on the Confirmation of Charges Pursuant to Article 61(7)(a) and (b) of the Rome Statute, *Prosecutor v. William Samoei Ruto et al.* (ICC-01/09-01/11-373), 23 January 2012 (hereinafter *Ruto et al.*), § 244.

[90] *Tolimir, supra* note 84, § 795. See *Popović et al., supra* note 82: 'Threats of force or coercion have been found to include those caused by fear of violence, duress, detention, psychological oppression or abuse of power, or by taking advantage of a coercive environment'; Judgments, *Prosecutor v. Milomir Stakić* (IT-97-24-T), Appeals Chamber, 22 March 2006, § 281 (hereafter *Stakić*). The ECCC TC referred to 'coercion, fraud, exploitation of a panic and the pressure of terror', which the Supreme Court Chamber considered 'conforms with the approach taken by the ICTY' in Appeals Judgment, *Prosecutor v. Khieu Samphan and Nuon Chea* (002/19-09-2007-ECCC/SC), 23 November 2016, § 595.

[91] Art. 7(1)(g) ICCSt; Elements of Crimes, 8, with the additional wording 'or the invasion was committed against a person incapable of giving genuine consent'; and for 'enforced prostitution', 9.

[92] *Akayesu, supra* note 80, § 688.

[93] *Popović et al., supra* note 82, § 896, quoting Judgment, *Prosecutor v. Simić et al.* (IT-95-9-T), Trial Chamber, 17 October 2003 (hereafter *Simić et al.*), § 126, referring to *Krstić, supra* note 83, § 147.

[94] *Ruto et al.* (ICC-01/09-01/11-373), 23 January 2012, § 688.

[95] Judgment, *Prosecutor v. Đorđević* (IT-05-87/1-A), Appeals Chamber, 27 January 2014 (hereafter *Đorđević*), § 704.

'BY'/CAUSATION

18. To show that displacement was really 'forced' and not voluntary, and occurred *by* expulsion or other coercive acts or 'as a result of the force', some courts have required a 'link' between the 'threat of force or coercion' and the displacement.[96]

19. To do so, in the *Simic* case ICTY Trial Chamber II suggested that it 'should look beyond formalities to all the circumstances surrounding the person's displacement' to determine whether the person was 'faced with a real choice'.[97] The Chamber analysed the 'intention' of the person, despite noting that this is difficult given the potential 'lack of genuine choice' in 'circumstances of discrimination or persecution'. The Chamber proposed that: 'whether a person would have wished to leave the area absent circumstances of discrimination or persecution may also be considered as indicative of a person's wish.'[98]

20. However, determining what anyone's intention might have been 'absent' the circumstances is incredibly difficult within situations of long-term structural and intersecting discrimination, violence, and other human rights violations. The need for any examination of the 'leaving' person's subjective intent is undermined by the reality also recognised at the ICTY that, '[w]hile those displaced may consent to, or even request to be removed, that consent must be given voluntarily and as a result of the individual's free will, assessed in the light of the surrounding circumstances'.[99] We consider that the 'trier of fact must consequently consider the *prevailing situation and atmosphere*, as well as all relevant *circumstances*, including in particular the victims' *vulnerability*, when assessing whether the displaced victims had a genuine choice to remain or leave and thus whether the resultant displacement was unlawful'.[100]

21. It is hard to see what assistance would be gained from requiring evidence of the actual, subjective intention of the person(s) fleeing – or what that intention might have been in different circumstances. This is particularly important for marginalised (rather than necessarily 'vulnerable') communities, including women, who may have had multiple changing reasons to consider, or even dream of, leaving a particular social setting, even before the immediate circumstances that led to their displacement. These reasons may result from the impacts of (for instance) racial, patriarchal, repressive, environmental, discriminatory, economic, or other structures upon individuals and communities.

'LAWFULLY PRESENT'

22. The wording about individuals transferred being from 'the area in which they were *lawfully present*' should be given its 'common meaning and should not be equated to the legal concept of lawful residence'.[101]

96 *Popović et al., supra* note 82, § 893.
97 *Simić et al., supra* note 93, § 126.
98 *Ibid*, § 126.
99 *Popović et al., supra* note 82, § 896.
100 Judgment, *Prosecutor v. Blagojević & Jokić* (IT-02-60-T), Trial Judgment, 17 January 2005 (hereafter *Blagojević & Jokić*), § 596.
101 *Popović et al., supra* note 82, § 900.

23. As the ICTY Trial Chamber opined in 2010:

> The clear intention of the prohibition against forcible transfer and deportation is to prevent civilians from being uprooted from their homes and to guard against the wholesale destruction of communities. In that respect, whether an individual has lived in a location for a sufficient period of time to meet the requirements for residency or whether he or she has been accorded such status under immigration laws is irrelevant. Rather, what is important is that the protection is provided to those who have, for whatever reason, come to 'live' in the community – whether long term or temporarily.[102]

24. This broad understanding of 'lawful presence' is consistent with the Elements of Crimes *mens rea* requirement that the 'perpetrator was aware of the factual circumstances that established the lawfulness of such presence'. This wording indicates that it is only awareness of the 'factual circumstances' of individuals or communities living or having their home in a particular place that must be established – even 'temporary homes after being uprooted from their original community'.[103]

25. We agree with Pre-Trial Chamber I's observation that the 'legal interest commonly protected by the crimes of deportation and forcible transfer is the right of individuals to live in their area of residence. However, the legal interest protected by the crime of deportation further extends to the right of individuals to live in the State in which they are lawfully present'.[104] While (as noted) there is overlap between the crimes of deportation and forcible transfers, deportation outside of one's state may have particular impacts (for different people, including, for example, for displaced children and children born of rape) denied the right to live in their home state. Those deported across borders may lack documentation, become stateless, be at risk of further displacement (including trafficking and other intersecting harms), and be adversely affected by their engagement with various 'regimes of care', including access to health and education, all affected by the fragility of their residence within other states.

'WITHOUT GROUNDS PERMITTED'

26. There are situations where evacuations might be permitted, but this should be 'an exceptional measure'.[105] Examples of grounds that might permit forced displacements under international humanitarian law include where the transfer is of prisoners of war out of combat zones and into internment facilities the text inside the round brackets should be Article 19 of Geneva Convention III or where conducted for the security of those involved 'or for imperative military reasons' the text inside the round brackets should be Article 49 of Geneva Convention IV and Article 17(1) of Additional Protocol

[102] *Ibid*, § 900.
[103] *Ibid*, § 900; *Tolimir*, *supra* note 82, § 797.
[104] Decision on the Prosecution's Request for a Ruling on Jurisdiction under Article 19(3) of the Statute (ICC-RoC46(3)-01/18), Pre-Trial Chamber I, 6 September 2018, § 58.
[105] *Popović et al.*, *supra* note 82, § 901.

IIthe text inside the round brackets should be Article 49 of Geneva Convention IV and Article 17(1) of Additional Protocol IIthe text inside the round brackets should be Article 49 of Geneva Convention IV and Article 17(1) of Additional Protocol IIthe text inside the round brackets should be Article 49 of Geneva Convention IV and Article 17(1) of Additional Protocol II [106] – including intensive bombing.[107]

27. If evacuations do take place, those affected must be properly provided for in terms of accommodation, hygiene, health, safety, and nutrition.[108] This would include responding to the particular needs of women and other genders, including, for the avoidance of doubt, Hijra and trans/intersex persons, children, and for intersecting cultural needs.

28. It follows from these exceptions that the evacuation should last only while the circumstances warranting evacuation persist, after which the transferred population should (be able to) return home.[109] The Chamber considers that it would therefore be relevant to consider the medium- and longer-term ongoing effects of any displacement when assessing this element.

29. However, the ICTY consistently held that it 'is not necessary for the Accused to intend to displace the victims on a permanent basis'.[110]

30. For the purposes of this section, we note that although it is for the Prosecutor to establish that the exceptions were not met,[111] it is sufficient to observe that the ordinary meaning of the wording concerning 'exceptional measure[s]' and 'imperative' reasons suggests that these exceptions are limited.

31. Further, these exceptions do not apply where the humanitarian crisis that caused the displacement resulted from the perpetrators' unlawful activity.[112]

Deportations and Other Crimes

32. The Chamber notes that there is scope to consider forcible displacements as part of other international crimes beyond crimes against humanity (including persecution and other inhumane acts as discussed elsewhere in this Decision). These include war crimes most explicitly in the Rome Statute (see Articles 8(2)(a)(vii), (b)(viii)), but also, in particular circumstances, genocide.

33. During the drafting of the Genocide Convention in 1948, Syria presented a proposal to include 'imposing measures intended to oblige members of a group to

[106] *Tolimir*, *supra* note 82, § 901.
[107] *Blagojević & Jokić*, *supra* note 100, 598.
[108] See *Popović et al.*, *supra* note 82, § 902; Judgment, *Prosecutor v. Sarmento* (SP, 18A/2001), 12 August 2003 (hereafter *Sarmento*), § 99: 'Therefore the standard is the same for international or internal conflicts: if civilians have to be moved for either of those two reasons – safety or military imperatives – their evacuations are to be under protected, hygienic, and humane conditions, and as short-lived as possible.'
[109] *Sarmento*, *supra* note 108, § 99.
[110] *Tolimir*, *supra* note 82, § 801; *Stakić*, *supra* note 90, § 317; *Popović et al.*, *supra* note 82, § 905.
[111] *Đorđević*, *supra* note 95, § 705.
[112] *Stakić*, *supra* note 90, § 287.

abandon their homes' as a form of genocide.[113] This was not taken up, resisted by the Allies apparently 'out of fear that it might imply the ethnic cleansing perpetrated against German minorities in Europe following the war',[114] which had involved sexual violence,[115] could be captured by that crime.

34. Nevertheless, deportation could be charged under Article II(a), (b), or (e) of the Genocide Convention if other requirements, including the presence of genocidal intent, are met,[116] as recognised by later ICTY and ICTR cases finding that practices of forced displacement might cause 'serious bodily or mental harm',[117] or 'conditions of life … calculated to bring about' a group's destruction.[118]

35. The Chamber considers that the underlying practice of forcible displacements could therefore in principle – subject of course to other admissibility, jurisdiction, and *chapeau* requirements, and the requirement for the special intent to destroy the group in whole or in part – in some circumstances also fall within at least Article 6 (b) of the Rome Statute as causing 'serious bodily or mental harm', (c) deliberately inflicting conditions of life calculated to bring about the relevant group's physical destruction in whole or in part, or (e) forcibly transferring children. At least it remains open to this Court to determine that the intent behind these crimes is not mutually exclusive, since (for instance, as noted) both displacement and genocide could potentially involve an intent to impose intolerable conditions that destroy a group, and it seems plausible that attempts to perpetrate genocide could be associated with displacements, given our discussion about 'coercive acts'. The Chamber recalls the victims' representation that victims 'decided to escape and save our lives from the extra-judicial killings […] the people had just one way to save their lives. [It] was to come to Bangladesh'.[119]

36. In addition, where displacement appears gendered, in the sense that more women and children are recorded as being deported, there may be a suggestion that

[113] J. Nilsson, 'The Vucković Trial in Kosovo – Deportation and Forcible Transfer under the Definition of Genocide' 71 *Nordic Journal of International Law* (2002) 545–555, at 549.

[114] W. A. Schabas, 'Problems of International Codification – Were the Atrocities in Cambodia and Kosovo Genocide?' 35(1) *New England Law Review* (2001) 287–302, at 296; see A. de Zayas, 'The Illegality of Population Transfers and the Application of Emerging International Norms in the Palestinian Context' 6 *Palestine Yearbook of International Law* (1990) 17–55, at 26.

[115] See M. Gebhardt (trans. by N. Somers), *Crimes Unspoken: The Rape of German Women at the End of the Second World War* (Cambridge: Polity, 2016).

[116] See E. Haslam, 'Unlawful Population Transfer and the Limits of International Criminal Law' 61(1) *Cambridge Law Journal* (2002) 66–75.

[117] Chetail, *supra* note 76, at 939; *Krstić*, *supra* note 83, § 513; Second Decision on the Prosecution's Application for a Warrant of Arrest, *Al Bashir* (ICC-02/05–01/09), P.T.Ch. I, 12 July 2010, § 30.

[118] Art. II The Genocide Convention. See also Elements of the Crimes, 7; *Application of the Convention on the Prevention and Punishment of the Crime of Genocide (Bosnia and Herzegovina v. Serbia and Montenegro)*, Judgment of 26 February 2007, [2007] ICJ Rep. 43, § 190; Chetail, *supra* note 76, at 939; Nilsson, *supra* note 113, at 550.

[119] Decision, *supra* note 69, at § 28, referring to: Victims' representation r/00025/19, First Registry Transmission, ICC-01/19-14-Conf-Exp-Anx25, at 2.

men were possibly targeted for other crimes, including killings. Especially when considered alongside intersectional cultural considerations (including in patriarchal or patrilineal societies), in such circumstances displacements would also seem consistent with an attempt to destroy a group in whole or in part.[120]

37. Therefore, this Chamber considers that there is no *in principle* legal barrier to investigations of certain practices associated with deportation being considered as part of an investigation of other crimes, such as genocide (persecution is addressed elsewhere in this Decision).

Alleged Facts

Deportation

38. The Chamber now turns to the specific situation involving Myanmar and Bangladesh. The Chamber has noted the breadth of relevant conduct and importance of appreciating dynamic contexts and 'vulnerability' when assessing both 'expulsion' or 'coercive acts' in relation to deportation, and whether 'victims had a genuine choice'. It follows that the so-called waves of 'clearance operations' in 2016 and 2017 cannot be disaggregated as separate events and assessed in semi-isolation, but rather form part of a pattern of violence and a 'coercive environment' that in this case has a long and difficult history.[121]

39. The emergence of Rohingya movements within and since the post-colonial independence era in Myanmar demands recognising the 'Rohingya' as an ethic national identity, and the cultural formation of Muslims as an important part of the fabric of the country.[122] Instead, Rohingya people have endured, and continue to endure, multiple forms of oppression from the military regime in Myanmar and discrimination from many Buddhist communities in Rakhine State, who have promoted Buddhist nationalism in Rakhine since the early 1950s. The adoption of the 1974 Emergency Immigration Act and subsequent implementation of 'Operation Nagamin' in 1977 involved an effort to filter out those labelled or perceived as foreigners prior to a national census and reportedly forced over 200,000 Rohingya to flee to Bangladesh.[123] These events were reportedly

[120] Though noting *Case Concerning the Application of the Convention on the Prevention and Punishment of the Crime of Genocide (Croatia v. Serbia)*, Judgment of 3 February 2015, [2015] ICR Rep. 3, § 514; M. Steinfeld, 'When Ethnic Cleansing Is Not Genocide: A Critical Appraisal of the ICJ's Ruling in Croatia v. Serbia in relation to Deportation and Population Transfer' 28 *Leiden Journal of International Law* (2015) 937–944.

[121] OHCHR, 'Report of the OHCHR mission to Bangladesh: Interviews with Rohingyas fleeing from Myanmar since 9 October 2016: Flash Report', 3 February 2017, at 42.

[122] J. P. Leider, 'Competing Identities and the Hybridized History of the Rohingyas' in R. Egreteau and F. Robinne (eds.), *Metamorphosis: Studies in Social and Political Change in Myanmar* (Singapore: NUS Press, 2015) 151–178.

[123] Human Rights Watch, 'Historical Background' (2000), available at www.hrw.org/reports/2000/burma/burm005-01.htm.

accompanied by human rights violations perpetrated against Rohingya by the Burmese army.[124] In addition, the 1982 Citizenship Law and accompanying registration process clearly denied the citizenship rights of Rohingya. Individuals already holding citizenship cards (pink or green) as assigned by the former regime were no longer eligible to receive those cards, but instead were issued 'white cards'.[125] White cards as defined under the 1951 Union Residents Registration Rules are understood as an interim form of documentation, and a substitute for permanent identification documents, and nearly a million Rohingya people in Myanmar held white cards.[126]

40. Following the transition towards democracy and civilian government in 2011, the government created different pathways for Rohingya to claim their identity without success. For instance, in 2011, the government cancelled the white cards and offered a pathway to register and verify their national identity for those who had lost 'white cards', although it was soon suspended due to public opposition.[127]

41. Beyond these successive processes that have complicated Rohingya's entitlement to secure formal citizenship, the government has also imposed several measures restricting Rohingya people's activities, including restricting their movement between villages and townships. Such measures applied to men and women, but affected all aspects of the lives of women and girls, and non-binary persons, differently,[128] including by limiting their access to medical care, food, adequate housing, and involving forced labour and restrictions on marriages and pregnancies.[129] For instance, women seeking emergency obstetric care have been required to secure approval and pay fees to the local authority before they can access the appropriate medical care, increasing the risk of maternal death. In addition, Rohingya women do not have equal access to registering births.

42. The Chamber observes that systematic state-based discrimination intersects with other experiences to exacerbate coercive circumstances. For instance, gendered social norms and stereotypes within the Rohingya communities compounded the effects of discriminatory laws and institutions. In Rohingya society, we understand that women and girls and non-binary persons are often expected to remain in the domestic realm and take up traditional gender roles, such as housework and

[124] *Ibid.*

[125] N. Cheesman, 'How in Myanmar "National Races" Came to Surpass Citizenship and Exclude Rohingya' 47(3) *Journal of Contemporary Asia* (2017) 461–483.

[126] C. Win and T. Kean, 'Communal Conflict in Myanmar: The Legislature's Response, 2012–2015' 47(3) *Journal of Contemporary Asia* (2017) 413–439.

[127] *Ibid.*

[128] Amnesty International, 'Myanmar: Briefing to the UN Committee on the Elimination of Discrimination against Women, 64th Session', July 2016, available at www.amnesty.org/en/documents/asa16/4240/2016/en/.

[129] United Nations, Committee on the Elimination of Discrimination against Women, 'Concluding Observations of the Committee on the Elimination of Discrimination against Women: Myanmar', UN Doc. CEDAW/C/MMR/CO/3, 7 November 2008.

childcare.[130] Women mainly interact with women in their own household, family members, and their closest neighbours and rely on the women in their households for religious knowledge and information about women's health and reproductive issues,[131] access to which was then further restricted by state-based discrimination. Women generally do not work outside the home, and thus marriage is the only form of financial security for them. Consequently, early and forced marriage is a common practice among the Rohingya population, not only as an element of culture but also as an adaptation for economic security.[132] The Chamber observes that the United Nations High Commissioner for Refugees (UNHCR) reports that over 40 per cent of Rohingya girls who have fled Myanmar since 2012 were married before the age of eighteen,[133] without legal protection.[134]

43. The Myanmar government appears aware of the impact of its discriminatory policies within this cultural context and indeed particular decisions seem designed to exacerbate these effects. In the late 1990s, a local order was issued in North Arakan requiring Rohingya communities to seek permission from the local authority before couples can get married (unlike other groups in Myanmar) and to sign a document agreeing to limit the number of children, violating the reproductive rights of women.[135] Marriage authorisations are granted on the payment of fees and bribes and the process can be prolonged.[136] Those requirements of seeking approval for marriage and the lengthy process increase the risk of exposing women and girls to multiple harms. For instance, women who become pregnant without official marriage authorisation often undergo unsafe abortions, an illegal practice in Myanmar, contributing to the number of maternal deaths. Some women register their newborn child with another legally married couple, or with their own parents, while many

[130] S. Ripoll et al., 'Social and Cultural Factors Shaping Health and Nutrition, Wellbeing and Rohingya within a Humanitarian Context', October 2017, available at https://opendocs.ids.ac.uk/opendocs/bitstream/handle/20.500.12413/13328/Ripoll_2017_Social_and_cultural_factors_wellbeing_and_protection_of_the_Rohingya.pdf?sequence = 1&isAllowed = y.

[131] *Ibid.*

[132] *Ibid.*

[133] UNHCR, 'Mixed-Movements in South East Asia' (2016), available at http://reporting.unhcr.org/sites/default/files/UNHCR%20-%20Mixed%20Movements%20in%20South-East%20Asia%20-%202016%20–%20April%202017_0.pdf.

[134] Gender Equality Network, 'Myanmar Laws and CEDAW: The Case for Anti-Violence against Women Laws' (2013), available at www.burmalibrary.org/en/myanmar-laws-and-cedaw-the-case-for-anti-violence-against-women-laws-english?__cf_chl_tk = 2t.h30ffHH10N7Gq0.PJNbYOnClASozq1NxsOLuk6fo-1653878430-0-gaNycGzNBqU.

[135] Amnesty International, *supra* note 128; ISCG, 'Gender Profile No. 1 For Rohingya Refugee Crisis Response', December 2017, available at https://reliefweb.int/sites/reliefweb.int/files/resources/iscg_gender_profile_rohingya_refugee_crisis_response_final_3_december_2017_.pdf.

[136] C. Lewa, 'North Arakan: An Open Prison for the Rohingya in Burma. Statelessness' 32 *Forced Migration Online* (2009) 11–13.

children born are reportedly unregistered. In some cases, young couples, unable to obtain permission to marry, flee to Bangladesh to live together.[137]

44. Furthermore, the adoption of Race and Religion Protection Laws in 2015 presented a clear threat to Rohingya women, compounded with these other violations. The Religious Law discriminates against women by restricting their ability to marry men of other religions. The Population Control Law also restricts the reproductive rights of women. For example, and in the context of publicised fears about Rohingya population growth,[138] the Population Law provides the regional governments an authority 'to request a presidential order limiting reproductive rates if it is determined that population growth, accelerating birth rates, or rising infant or maternal mortality rates are negatively impacting regional development', or that there exists an 'imbalance between population and resources, low socio-economic indicators and regional food insufficiency because of internal migration'.[139]

45. The combined effect of these discriminatory policies was to restrict Rohingya's population growth and ability to move and engage in social life, generating a pattern of excessively discriminatory policies openly aimed at changing the ethnic composition of the area.

46. In addition to these state-directed oppressive policies over many decades, communal tensions between largely Buddhist communities and the Rohingya persisted and were encouraged in the Rakhine State region. The creation of the '969' campaign in early 2012 led by Buddhist extremists fuelled these communal tensions between Muslims and Buddhists across different parts of the country. The campaign specifically aimed to increase hatred against Muslims in Myanmar by calling upon followers to boycott Muslim-owned businesses, displaying 969 logos in businesses owned by Buddhists to show their solidarity with the campaign, and leading to multiple forms of violence against Muslims, while encouraging anti-Muslim feelings across the nation.[140] In the same year (2012) two violent outbreaks between Rakhine and Muslim groups, in June and October, were triggered by the reported rape and killing of a Buddhist woman by Rohingya men, followed by the killing of Muslim Rohingya by Buddhist mobs, driving 125,000 Rohingya and other Muslims to internally displaced camps.[141] Instead of protecting the population, the

[137] *Ibid.*

[138] '2-child limit in Rohingya towns', *The Hindu*, 26 May 2013, available at www.thehindu.com/todays-paper/2child-limit-in-rohingya-towns/article4752431.ece.

[139] N. Zaw, 'Union Parliament Passes Population Control Bill', Blog: The Irrawaddy, April 2015, available at www.irrawaddy.com/news/burma/union-parliament-passes-population-control-bill.html.

[140] N. G. Thompson, 'The 969 Movement and Burmese Anti-Muslim Nationalism in Context', Blog: Buddhist Peace Fellowship, July 2013, available at www.bpf.org/blog/the-969-movement-and-burmese-anti-muslim-nationalism-in-context.

[141] Human Rights Watch, '"All You Can Do is Pray": Crimes against Humanity and Ethnic Cleansing of Rohingya Muslims in Burma's Arakan State' (2013), available at www.hrw.org/sites/default/files/reports/burma0413webwcover_0.pdf.

government further repressed Muslims by preventing their access to markets, livelihoods, and humanitarian assistance. Furthermore, responses from the national and local government promoted anti-Rohingya hatred and encouraged the departure of Rohingya from the area.[142] For example, the then president, Thein Sein, called for 'illegal' Rohingya to be sent to 'third countries', stressing their lack of legal status in the country and implying that the majority of Rohingya did not belong in Myanmar.[143]

47. Rohingya communities have for many years witnessed crimes committed against their family members and suffered from sexual and gender-based violence (including perpetrated by military officers without commensurate accountability),[144] a lack of adequate food, shelter, education for their children, and medical care. These have wider consequences for families, for instance women are direct victims of human rights violations, but also suffer indirectly as family members of those who were killed and disappeared[145] and may be forced to become the breadwinners in addition to, or affecting, their culturally promoted family and home-focused roles.[146] These factors illustrate the violence, and its gendered effects, in the period *prior* to the so-called waves of violence, which already presented multiple intersecting factors that had in the past led to mass forcible displacement of Rohingya refugees into Bangladesh on several occasions.

48. We note that these factors of historic violence against the Rohingya are so serious that they are alleged to amount to genocide at the International Court of Justice. To be clear, *we do not think that such a high threshold of contextual violence as is found in this situation is required to establish that there may be 'coercive acts' in relation to deportation*. We observe again that acts such as shelling, burning property, and others including sexual violence, are sufficient to amount to 'expulsion or other coercive acts' leading to forcible displacement. These acts also occurred, among them the killing of babies and young children and sexual violence, as detailed elsewhere in this Decision, including in paragraph 86 noting that 'Hijra' individuals, non-binary, transgender, and intersex persons were reportedly targeted for sexual violence.[147]

49. While enmeshed within earlier contexts and structures of violence and dispossession, events in 2016 resulted in a further intensification of oppressive measures against the Rohingya inside Myanmar, forcing 87,000 Rohingya people, some of whom would have been carrying or leaving family members as well as

[142] *Ibid.*

[143] 'UN rejects Thein Sein's potential Rohingya plan', *Democratic Voice of Burma*, July 2012, available at https://reliefweb.int/report/myanmar/un-rejects-thein-sein%E2%80%99s-potential-rohingya-plan.

[144] Human Rights Watch, *supra* note 141.

[145] *Ibid.*

[146] *Ibid.*

[147] ICC, *Article 15 Decision*, PTC III, § 86.

homes, cultural lives, and livelihoods, to flee to Bangladesh – although we note there is a lack of available gender-disaggregated data. In addition to existing restricted movements, security forces, camps, and checkpoints were increased, with even more extreme restrictions on movement.[148] During these security searches, women are disproportionately affected, including the intruders strip searching their bodies for valuables and possible weapons.[149]

50. The scale, brutality, and systematic nature of sexual and gender-based violence indicate that rape and sexual violence formed part of a deliberate strategy to intimidate, terrorise, or punish a civilian population, and were used as a tactic to generate a violent environment.[150] In many cases, sexual violence was accompanied by degrading behaviour, including insults and spitting, as recounted in numerous victims' representations.[151] However, the national government defended the acts of the military and denied the allegations of the crimes, responding to the misconduct in official press statements as 'fake rape' claims.[152] This degree of normalisation and dismissal of sexual violence reflects the climate of long-standing impunity, including for military perpetrators of violence – across Myanmar as well as, or especially, in Rakhine State.[153]

51. Many internally displaced Rohingya from the 2016 and earlier events remained in precarious situations and even temporary accommodation in 2017. The events of

148 UNHRC, 'Report of the Independent International Fact-Finding Mission on Myanmar', September 2018, available at www.ohchr.org/Documents/HRBodies/HRCouncil/FFM-Myanmar/A_HRC_39_64.pdf.

149 United States Department of State, 'Documentation of Atrocities in Northern Rakhine State', January 2019, available at www.state.gov/wp-content/uploads/2019/01/Documentation-of-Atrocities-in-Northern-Rakhine-State.pdf.

150 UNHRC, *supra* note 148.

151 Victims' representation, r/00033/19, r/00032/19, r/00039/19, r/00040/19, r/00034/19, r/00041/19, r/00042/19, r/00053/19, r/00054/19, r/00058/19, r/00060/19, r/00075/19, r/00089/19, r/00090/19, r/00098/19, r/00096/19, r/00112/19, r/00114/19, r/00111/19, r/00115/19, r/00116/19, r/00120/19, r/00119/19, r/00121/19, r/00125/19, r/00122/19, r/00132/19, r/00131/19, r/00130/19, r/00147/19, r/00152/19, r/00149/19, r/00151/19, r/00154/19, r/00166/19, r/00169/19, r/00171/19, r/00189/19, r/00191/19, r/00192/19, r/00208/19, r/00207/19, r/00211/19, r/00210/19, r/00209/19, r/00217/19, r/00226/19, r/00222/19, r/00220/19, r/00219/19, r/00234/19, r/00230/19, r/00228/19, r/00227/19, r/00239/19, r/00238/19, r/00237/19, r/00236/19, r/00235/19, r/00243/19, r/00244/19, r/00242/19, r/00302/19, r/00303/19, r/00268/19, r/00036/19, r/00035/19, r/00038/19, r/00092/19, r/00037/19, r/00163/19, r/00168/19, r/00176/19, r/00179/19, r/00180/19, r/00186/19, r/00190/19, r/00185/19. Representations are available in the corresponding confidential ex parte annexes in the First Registry Transmission, ICC-01/19-14-Conf-Exp-Anx; Second Registry Transmission, ICC-01/19-21; Third Registry Transmission, ICC-01/19-24. See also video annex to victims' representation r/00190/19, at 10:40, video annex to victims' representation r/00200/19, video annex to victims' representation r/00242/19, available only to the Chamber in Third Registry Transmission, ICC-01/19-24.

152 'Myanmar: Report adds to mounting rights abuse claims in Arakan', *Democratic Voice of Burma*, May 2017, available at https://reliefweb.int/report/myanmar/myanmar-report-adds-mounting-rights-abuse-claims-arakan.

153 This has long been reported in Myanmar, see e.g. B. Apple, 'School for Rape: The Burmese Military and Sexual Violence', *EarthRights International*, 1998, available at https://earthrights.org/wp-content/uploads/publications/school-for-rape.pdf.

2016 alone had internally displaced more than 23,000 individuals, over half of them women and girls.[154] The protracted displacement with limited access to international humanitarian aid, restrictions of movement, and overcrowded shelters with no privacy led to increased pressure on families, increasing the various forms of gender-based violence towards women and children. Adolescents have had limited access to youth services and other opportunities, further increasing the incidence of child marriage, child labour, and risky migration.[155]

52. Those remaining in Myanmar 'lived' there, and were in that sense '*lawfully present*'.

53. The further violence in 2017 represented a continuation, albeit of greater scale (see elsewhere in this Decision), of the violent and allegedly genocidal context and appears to be a culmination of long-term efforts to change the ethnic composition of Rakhine State by removing, through multiple discriminatory policies and violent acts, the Rohingya population.

54. While both men and women are affected by this violence, women were (and are) disproportionately traumatised by the gendered forms and severity of crimes, including the incidents of sexual and gender-based violence. The United Nations and other organisations noted an increase in the number of pregnant women and girls in the refugee camps in Bangladesh between May and June 2018.[156] Recognition of children born out of rape is challenging for women due to the stigma associated with rape and often the resentment of the husband. A survivor of rape described her child born out of rape as 'not our child – a lost child'.[157] Further, losing the male household members forced women to become breadwinners, yet many have limited skills and literacy. The circumstances have led them to engage in negative coping strategies[158] to overcome economic hardship. After 2017 this continued to include early marriage and selling child brides, as was noted above after 2016.[159]

[154] UNOCHA, 'Myanmar' 4 *Humanitarian Bulletin* (2016), available at https://reliefweb.int/report/myanmar/myanmar-humanitarian-bulletin-issue-4-october-2016-january-2017-enmy.

[155] UNOCHA, 'Humanitarian Response Plan' (2016), available at https://reliefweb.int/report/myanmar/2016-humanitarian-response-plan-monitoring-report-january-december-2016.

[156] United Nations International Children's Emergency Fund, 'More than 60 Rohingya Babies Born in Bangladesh Refugee Camps Every Day', 17 May 2018, available at www.unicef.org/press-releases/more-60-rohingya-babies-born-bangladesh-refugee-camps-every-day-unicef#:~:text= .

[157] UNHRC, 'Sexual and Gender-Based Violence in Myanmar and the Gendered Impact of Its Ethnic Conflicts', August 2019, available at www.ohchr.org/sites/default/files/Documents/HRBodies/HRCouncil/FFM-Myanmar/sexualviolence/A_HRC_CRP_4.pdf.

[158] J. Ferrie, 'Rohingya refugee girls were sold into forced labor, UN says', Blog: Global Citizen, October 2018, available at www.globalcitizen.org/en/content/refugee-girls-sold-into-forced-labour-bangladesh; N. Iqbal, 'Rohingya women in Bangladesh face "forced prostitution"', Blog: BBC, November 2017, available at www.bbc.com/news/world-asia-41928555.

[159] A. Taylor, 'Child marriage in the Rohingya camps in Bangladesh', Blog: The Atlantic, December 2017, available at www.theatlantic.com/photo/2017/12/child-marriage-in-the-rohingya-camps-in-bangladesh/548408/.

55. For the purposes of this Decision, it is sufficient to observe that these reported experiences alone illustrate a coercive environment in which, among so many orchestrated oppressive factors, it is arguably pointless to isolate particular subjective motivations for leaving. Indeed, it is correspondingly easy to identify how ongoing forms of displacement and enduring harms were caused by multiple and deliberately intersecting coercive circumstances.

Exceptions and Limitations

56. The Chamber observes that there is no suggestion that any of the limited exceptions potentially applicable to the crime of deportation were present, and that no humanitarian assistance of any kind, let alone of a gender-sensitive nature, was provided by the government to those displaced. Further, the Chamber observes that the Rohingya population largely remains displaced as there has been no meaningful guarantee of their safety upon any return to Myanmar.[160]

57. The displacement was also not temporary.

58. At this point, the Chamber stresses that this 'Rohingya population' that fled Myanmar is not an amorphous mass or abstract concept, but many hundreds of thousands of individuals, 80 per cent of whom are women and children,[161] as well as non-binary people, and all of them have experienced systematic discrimination and direct or indirect forms of violence and displacement.

59. Reports also clarify that this includes 'single mothers (11%), persons with serious medical condition (4%), older persons at risk (4%), persons with disabilities (4%), child-headed households (3%), older persons with children (2%), separated children (2%), unaccompanied children (1%), single fathers (1%). Increasing gendered isolation and restricted mobility of women and girls limits their access to life-saving assistance, services and information'.[162] These are individuals who continue to experience the crime of deportation in their daily lives, whether they now live in refugee camps or elsewhere. Victims' representations also suggest that many still fear further deportation or forced displacement, including back to Myanmar or to other destinations within Bangladesh, such as Bhasan Char.[163]

60. Those who did *not* arrive include family members – men, children, elderly parents, and others with restricted mobility – many of whom were killed. The fact that 80 per cent of those displaced have been recorded as being women and girls suggests that gender was a factor, and even that numerous men may have been killed. The Prosecutor might further investigate the extent to which gender and

[160] C. Gluck, 'Rohingya say rights guarantees key to Myanmar return', Blog: UNHCR, January 2018, available at www.unhcr.org/en-au/news/latest/2018/1/5a6a00b29/rohingya-say-rights-guarantees-key-myanmar-return.html.

[161] ISCG, *supra* note 135.

[162] *Ibid.*

[163] Representations of victims from Tula Toli (ICC-01/19-19), 23 October 2019.

intersectional considerations (including 'hate speech' concerning population control discussed elsewhere in this Decision) contributed to the non-temporary nature of the displacement, as well as the intent of those behind it.

61. The report issued by an international independent fact-finding mission in 2018 showed a clear pattern of racial discrimination and prohibition of cultural and religious rights, formally and informally, *within* refugee camps.[164] This includes unsafe living conditions, high levels of sexual and gender-based violence, risks of trafficking for women and children, income insecurity, challenges in securing culturally appropriate health or education services, children born of rape (and cultural stigma), lack of shelter, and other intersectional issues.[165]

62. Again, the Chamber observes that, although women's civil society organisations are emerging among refugees, some materials suggest that forcible displacement has exacerbated existing, partly cultural or religious, challenges for Rohingya women. A growing number of domestic violence incidents and child marriages have been reported within the Rohingya community in protracted and overcrowded displaced camps, compounded by the lack of livelihoods (including because of the absence of primary earners and lack of culturally appropriate work opportunities) and increases in poverty.[166]

63. The Chamber considers this context to be relevant to the crime of deportation, even though these circumstances occur outside of Myanmar, since, as noted above, even if met, the exceptions allowing for displacement require the preservation of such rights to the extent appropriate. There is no information suggesting any intention on the part of Myanmar authorities or Tatmadaw to maintain the safety of those displaced, while the long history and ongoing nature of the challenges and risks in refugee camps in Bangladesh was very likely known to them.

64. In light of the above, a reasonable prosecutor could believe that coercive acts towards the Rohingya forced them to flee to Bangladesh, which may amount to the crime against humanity of deportation.

Cultural and Gender Considerations

65. The Chamber takes this opportunity to note that the information provided suggests that the alleged facts occurred in a very complex context involving nuanced and layered forms of harm. We expect that the parties will find it useful to present evidence, including expert evidence, to assist any future Trial Chamber or other Chambers to better understand specific and intersecting gendered, cultural, and

164 UNHRC, *supra* note 148.

165 *Ibid.*

166 *Ibid*; documented since at least 2015: F. Islam et al., 'Situation of Sexual and Gender Based Violence among the Rohingya Migrants Residing in Bangladesh' 22(2) *Injury Prevention* (2016) 260.

religious influences among Rohingya women, those of non-binary genders (including Hijra), children, and other groups such as the disabled.

66. While the crime of deportation may appear gender 'neutral' in the sense that it does not directly refer to gendered issues, the Chamber also observes that the ICC Prosecutor's Policy Paper on Sexual and Gender-Based Crimes has recognised that deportation and forcible transfer of population 'may also have a sexual and/or gender element',[167] although such recognition has not led to convictions on that basis.[168] The Chamber considers that investigators, prosecutors, and judges also do not operate in 'gender-neutral' institutions, and there remain opportunities for the ICC to interpret 'seemingly gender-neutral crimes in order to reflect the distinct experiences of women and girls'.[169] At the very least, the Chamber reminds the parties that careful and culturally sensitive approaches to investigation are warranted in international crimes trials.[170]

67. We also reiterate our support for the Registry and other parties to ensure that culturally and gender-appropriate witness protection initiatives, including trauma-informed and psychosocial supports, are in place.

68. Finally, the Chamber invites *amicus curiae* briefs providing culturally informed analyses of the intersecting effects of the alleged crimes, including upon women and children.

Judge Emma Palmer and Judge Phyu Phyu Oo

14.3 PERSECUTION OF NON-BINARY PEOPLE IN THE BANGLADESH/MYANMAR INVESTIGATION

Claerwen O'Hara

In 2019, the Pre-Trial Chamber III authorised the Prosecutor to commence an investigation into the situation in Bangladesh/Myanmar in accordance with Article 15(4) of the Statute.[171] The Chamber held that the Prosecutor could reasonably believe that coercive acts towards the Rohingya forced them to leave Bangladesh, which may amount to the crimes against humanity of deportation,[172]

[167] ICC Office of the Prosecutor, 'Policy Paper on Sexual and Gender Based Crimes', June 2014, available at www.icc-cpi.int/sites/default/files/iccdocs/otp/OTP-Policy-Paper-on-Sexual-and-Gender-Based-Crimes–June-2014.pdf, at 34.

[168] Grey, *supra* note 78, at 327.

[169] Consistent with the requirements of Article 21(3) of the Rome Statute, see *ibid.* at 326; L. Chappell, *The Politics of Gender Justice at the International Criminal Court* (Cambridge: Cambridge University Press, 2016).

[170] ISCG, *supra* note 135; Advisory Commission on Rakhine State, 'Final Report of the Advisory Commission on Rakhine State', 24 August 2017, available at www.kofiannanfoundation.org/wp-content/uploads/2017/08/FinalReport_Eng.pdf.

[171] Decision Pursuant to Article 15 of the Rome Statute on the Authorisation of an Investigation into the Situation in the People's Republic of Bangladesh/Republic of the Union of Myanmar, *Situation in the People's Republic of Bangladesh/Republic of the Union of Myanmar*, Pre-Trial Chamber III, ICC-01/19–27, 14 November 2019, § 126.

[172] *Ibid*, § 108.

and persecution on the ground of religion and/or ethnicity.[173] In establishing jurisdiction, the Chamber was satisfied that the alleged crimes had been committed at least partially on the territory of Bangladesh, which ratified the Statute on 23 March 2010.[174] The Chamber held that the scope of the investigation extended to acts committed on at least part of the territory of other states which would accept the jurisdiction of the Court, insofar as they were sufficiently linked to the situation.[175] Furthermore, the Chamber expanded the scope of the investigation beyond the crimes alleged by the Prosecutor in the request to *any crimes* sufficiently linked to the situation, stressing that limiting the incidents to be investigated at the preliminary stage would be contrary to the obligation under Article 54(1)(a) to 'cover all facts and evidence … [i]n order to establish the truth'.[176]

In this rewritten judgment, Claerwen O'Hara authorises the investigation into the situation in Bangladesh/Myanmar in a manner which brings the experience of Hijra, transgender, and intersex peoples to the forefront of the decision. Whilst the Chamber's original decision only briefly references sexual violence against Hijra individuals,[177] O'Hara discusses in depth the persecution of gender-diverse Rohingya people on the intersecting grounds of gender, ethnicity, and religion. In doing so, O'Hara offers an interpretation of gender under Article 7(3) of the Statute which encompasses gender-diverse people and the socially constructed nature of gender.

No.: ICC-01/19
Date: 14 November 2019

Original: English

PRE-TRIAL CHAMBER III(B)

Before: Judge Claerwen O'HARA

SITUATION IN THE PEOPLE'S REPUBLIC OF BANGLADESH/ REPUBLIC OF THE UNION OF MYANMAR

Public

Decision pursuant to Article 15 of the Rome Statute on the Authorisation of an Investigation into the Situation in the People's Republic of Bangladesh/Republic of the Union of Myanmar

[Extract from the judgment]

173 *Ibid*, § 109.
174 *Ibid*, §§ 113–114.
175 *Ibid*, § 124.
176 *Ibid*, §§ 126–128.
177 *Ibid*, § 86.

THE FACTS

1. In 2016 and 2017, the armed forces of Myanmar, the Tatmadaw, are alleged to have launched 'clearance operations' against the Rohingya civilian population in Myanmar, resulting in waves of violence which forced over 700,000 Rohingya to seek refuge in Bangladesh.[178]

2. Representations submitted on behalf of alleged victims recount frequent occurrence of incidents of rape and other forms of sexual violence during the 2016 and 2017 waves of violence.[179] Most alleged rapes were reportedly carried out by the Tatmadaw, although members of the border guard police, the Myanmar government, Myanmar police force, and local civilians are also alleged to have committed such acts.[180]

[178] Fortify Rights, 'They Gave Them Long Swords/Preparations for Genocide and Crimes against Humanity against Rohingya Muslims in Rakhine State', Myanmar, July 2018, available at www.fortifyrights.org/downloads/Fortify_Rights_Long_Swords_July_2018.pdf, at 13 (700,000); Inter Sector Coordination Group, 'Situation Report Rohingya Refugee Crisis', November 2018, available at https://reliefweb.int/sites/reliefweb.int/files/resources/iscg_situation_report_29_nov.pdf, at 2 (700,000); Kaladan Press Network, 'Rape by Command: Sexual Violence as a Weapon against the Rohingya', February 2018, at 11 (680,000); Independent International Fact-Finding Mission on Myanmar, 'Report of the Detailed Findings of the Independent International Fact-Finding Mission on Myanmar', United Nations Human Rights Council, UN Doc. A/HRC/39/CRP.2, 17 September 2018 (hereafter UNFFM Report), § 751, at 180 (725,000); Physicians for Human Rights, '"Please Tell the World What They Have Done to Us" – The Chut Pyin Massacre: Forensic Evidence of Violence against the Rohingya in Myanmar', July 2018, available at https://phr.org/wp-content/uploads/2020/03/BurmaReport_ChutPyin_ExecutiveSummary_FINAL.pdf, at 3 (720,000). The supporting material further suggests that others have fled to Malaysia, Pakistan, Saudi Arabia, India, the United Arab Emirates, Thailand, and Indonesia: Public International Law & Policy Group, 'Documenting Atrocity Crimes Committed against the Rohingya in Myanmar's Rakhine State: Factual Findings & Legal Analysis', available at https://static1.squarespace.com/static/5900b58e1b631bffa367167e/t/5c058268c2241b5f71a0535e/1543864941782/PILPG+-+ROHINGYA+REPORT+-+Factual+Findings+and+Legal+Analysis+-+3+Dec+2018+%281%29.pdf, at 7.

[179] Victims' representation, r/00033/19, r/00032/19, r/00039/19, r/00040/19, r/00034/19, r/00041/19, r/00042/19, r/00053/19, r/00054/19, r/00058/19, r/00060/19, r/00075/19, r/00089/19, r/00090/19, r/00098/19, r/00096/19, r/00112/19, r/00114/19, r/00111/19, r/00115/19, r/00116/19, r/00120/19, r/00119/19, r/00121/19, r/00125/19, r/00122/19, r/00132/19, r/00131/19, r/00130/19, r/00147/19, r/00152/19, r/00149/19, r/00151/19, r/00154/19, r/00166/19, r/00169/19, r/00171/19, r/00189/19, r/00191/19, r/00192/19, r/00208/19, r/00207/19, r/00211/19, r/00210/19, r/00209/19, r/00217/19,r/00226/19, r/00222/19, r/00220/19, r/00219/19, r/00234/19, r/00230/19, r/00228/19, r/00227/19, r/00239/19, r/00238/19, r/00237/19, r/00236/19, r/00235/19, r/00243/19, r/00244/19, r/00242/19, r/00302/19, r/00303/19, r/00268/19, r/00036/19, r/00035/19, r/00038/19, r/00092/19, r/00037/19, r/00163/19, r/00168/19, r/00176/19, r/00179/19, r/00180/19, r/00186/19, r/00190/19, r/00185/19. Representations are available in the corresponding confidential *ex parte* annexes in the First Registry Transmission, ICC-01/19-14-Conf-Exp-Anx; Second Registry Transmission, ICC-01/19-21; Third Registry Transmission, ICC-01/19-24. See also video annex to victims' representation r/00190/19, at 10:40, video annex to victims' representation r/00200/19, video annex to victims' representation r/00242/19, available only to the Chamber in Third Registry Transmission, ICC-01/19-24.

[180] UNFFM Report, *supra* note 178, § 920, at 215.

3. The available information suggests that in some instances Hijra individuals, who are third-gender persons, transgender women, and intersex persons in South Asia who were assigned a masculine gender at birth,[181] were targeted for rape and sexual violence.[182] In its report on sexual and gender-based violence in Myanmar, the Independent International Fact-Finding Mission on Myanmar found that the gender-diverse people who were allegedly subjected to rape and sexual violence during the 'clearance operations' were also largely of Rohingya ethnicity.[183]

APPLICABLE LAW

4. Having established that that there exists a reasonable basis to believe that the contextual elements of crimes against humanity may be fulfilled in relation to the 2016 and 2017 waves of violence, the Chamber will now consider whether there is a reasonable basis to believe that the alleged rape and sexual violence perpetrated against Hijra and other gender-diverse people in Myanmar may constitute persecution within the meaning of the Statute.

Persecution

5. Persecution, within the meaning of Article 7(1)(h) and (2)(g)[184] of the Statute, is committed, either through a single act or a series of acts,[185] when:

1. The perpetrator severely deprived, contrary to international law,[186] one or more persons of fundamental rights.

[181] The Women's Refugee Commission, 'It's Happening to Our Men as Well: Sexual Violence against Rohingya Men and Boys', 8 November 2018, available at www.womensrefugeecommission.org/wp-content/uploads/2020/04/Rohingya-Report-Final.pdf (hereafter WRC Report), at 5.

[182] Victims' representation r/00003/19, ICC-01/19-14-Conf-Exp-Anx3; WRC Report, *supra* note 4, at 35; Independent International Fact-Finding Mission on Myanmar, 'Sexual and Gender-Based Violence in Myanmar and the Gendered Impact of Its Ethnic Conflicts', UN Human Rights Council, UN Doc. A/HRC/42/CRP.4, 22 August 2019 (hereafter 2019 UNFFM Report), §§ 180–187, at 43–44.

[183] 2019 UNFFM Report, *supra* note 182, § 180, at 43. Note that the UNFFM refers to these alleged victims in its report as transgender Rohingya.

[184] Article 7(2)(g) of the ICCSt. stipulates: '"Persecution" means the intentional and severe deprivation of fundamental rights contrary to international law by reason of the identity of the group or collectivity'.

[185] Decision pursuant to Article 15 of the Rome Statute on the Authorization of an Investigation into the Situation in the Republic of Burundi (ICC-01/17-9-Red), Pre-Trial Chamber III, 9 November 2017, § 130.

[186] Footnote 21 of the Elements of Crimes stipulates: 'This requirement is without prejudice to paragraph 6 of the General Introduction to the Elements of Crimes'. Paragraph 6 of the General Introduction reads: 'The requirement of "unlawfulness" found in the Statute or in other parts of international law, in particular international humanitarian law, is generally not specified in the elements of crimes.'

2. The perpetrator targeted such person or persons by reason of the identity of a group or collectivity or targeted the group or collectivity as such.
3. Such targeting was based on political, racial, national, ethnic, cultural, religion, or gender, as defined in Article 7, paragraph 3 of the Statute, or other grounds that are universally recognised as impermissible under international law.
4. The conduct was committed in connection with any act referred to in Article 7, paragraph 1 of the Statute or any crime within the jurisdiction of the Court.[187]

Serious Deprivation of Fundamental Rights

6. Not every infringement of human rights amounts to persecution, but only a 'severe deprivation' of a person's '*fundamental* rights contrary to international law'.[188] The commission of an act considered to be a crime against humanity will, in principle, result in a sufficiently severe deprivation of fundamental rights to meet the threshold for persecution.[189]

7. As stated above, there is evidence before the Chamber that Hijra and other gender-diverse people were targeted for rape and sexual violence by Tatmadaw soldiers, police, and members of ethnic Rakhine communities during the waves of violence in Myanmar in 2016 and 2017.

8. Alleged victims recount being tied up, beaten, and subjected to anal and oral rape, sometimes by large groups of men.[190] Some victims have described the sexual violence they experienced as a form of torture. In recounting her experience during the 2016 and 2017 waves of violence, one transgender woman told the Independent International Fact-Finding Mission on Myanmar: 'They always tortured transgender women like myself. They threatened us and did bad things to us; they forced me to do bad things. They remove our clothes and did bad things if we refused. We were threatened and risked being killed.'[191]

9. The Mission also concluded that these instances of sexual violence amounted to torture or other forms of cruel, inhuman, or degrading treatment or punishment for the purposes of both international human rights law and international criminal law.[192]

[187] Article 7(1)(h), Elements of Crimes. Footnote 22 of the Elements of Crimes stipulates: 'It is understood that no additional mental element is necessary for this element other than that inherent in element 6.'

[188] Article 7(1)(h), Elements of Crimes (emphasis added).

[189] Judgment, *Ntaganda* (ICC-01/04-02/06), Trial Chamber VI, 8 July 2019, § 994.

[190] 2019 UNFFM Report, *supra* note 182, §§ 183–187, at 43–44.

[191] *Ibid*, § 182, at 43.

[192] *Ibid*, § 188, at 44.

10. Further, this sexual violence is alleged to have occurred against a backdrop of general coercion, in which gender-diverse Rohingya people were routinely subject to harassment and arrest by the authorities. According to local activists, Article 377 of the Penal Code, which forbids 'carnal intercourse against the order of nature', has long provided legal cover for ill-treatment of gender and sexually diverse people in Myanmar.[193] One transgender victim described the effects of this ill-treatment on her as follows: 'I can't be myself because of fear ... Sometimes we are insulted and called names, motherfuckers, all sorts of abusive language.'[194]

11. Rape and other forms of sexual violence of comparable gravity are recognised by Article 7(1)(g) of the Statute as acts that may constitute crimes against humanity. Torture is also designated as such an act by Article 7(f) of the Statute and it is well established that rape can constitute a form of torture in both international criminal law[195] and international human rights law.[196] In addition, deportation by coercive acts is recognised as a crime against humanity by Article 7(1)(d) of the Statute, as are other inhumane acts of a similar character intentionally causing great suffering, or serious injury to the body or to mental or physical health by Article 7(k).

12. As the rape and sexual violence allegedly committed against Hijra and other gender-diverse people in Myanmar in 2016 and 2017, causing many of them to flee to Bangladesh, may amount to such acts, the Chamber finds that there is a reasonable basis to believe that there may have been a sufficiently severe deprivation of fundamental rights to qualify as persecution under the Statute.

Identifiable Group or Collectivity

13. The second element of the crime against humanity of persecution is that the perpetrator must have targeted the person or persons by reason of the identity of a group or collectivity, or targeted the group or collectivity as such.[197] This requires there to be an identifiable group or collectivity.

[193] *Ibid*, §153, at 36.

[194] *Ibid*, § 181, at 43.

[195] Judgment, *Mucić et al.* (IT-96-21), Trial Chamber, 16 November 1998, §§ 480–496; Judgment, *Furundžija* (IT-95-17/1-T), Trial Chamber, 10 December 1998, §§ 163 and 171; Judgment, *Kunarac et al.* (IT-96-23 & IT-966-23/1-A), Appeals Chamber, 12 June 2002, §§ 149–151; Judgment, *Akayesu* (ICTR-96-4-T), Trial Chamber, 2 September 1998, § 597.

[196] Committee Against Torture, 'General Comment No. 2: Implementation of Article 2 by States Parties', UN Doc. CAT/C/GC/2, 24 January 2008 (hereafter CAT General Comment No. 2), § 22, at 6; Committee Against Torture, 'Decision Adopted by the Committee under Article 22 of the Convention, concerning Communication No. 854/2017', UN Doc. CAT/C/67/D/854/2017, 22 August 2019; J. E. Méndez, 'Report of the Special Rapporteur on Torture and Other Cruel, Inhuman or Degrading Treatment or Punishment', UN Doc. A/HRC/31/57, 5 January 2016, §§ 51–53, at 14–15.

[197] Article 7(1)(h), Elements of Crimes.

14. The separation of elements two and three of the crime against humanity of persecution in the Elements of Crimes[198] indicates that the identity of the group or collectivity need not be defined according to the political, racial, national, ethnic, cultural, religious, gender, or other impermissible grounds mentioned in Article 7(2)(g) of the Statute. Those grounds constitute the prohibited reasons for targeting an identifiable group or collectivity, rather than the characteristics of the group in question.

15. Pre-Trial Chamber II's decision confirming the charges against Dominic Ongwen illustrates the separate operation of elements two and three of the crime against humanity of persecution. The identifiable group alleged to have been targeted in that case were civilian residents of certain internally displaced person camps. Mr Ongwen's alleged targeting of the group was said to have been based on political grounds, as he perceived them to be affiliated with and/or supporting the Ugandan government.[199]

16. In assessing whether a group is identifiable, a mixed approach may be adopted,[200] considering both objective and subjective criteria.

17. The academic literature indicates that Hijra people have been culturally recognised as a distinct gender or sex-based group in South Asia for millennia.[201] Encompassing non-binary, transgender, and intersex persons, Hijra people often live together in communal households[202] and have their own myths, rituals, and spiritual practices.[203]

18. In the twenty-first century, several South Asian states have legally recognised Hijra people as having a third gender or sex. In 2014, for example, the Indian Supreme Court ruled that 'Hijras, Eunuchs, apart from binary gender, be treated as "third gender" for the purpose of safeguarding their rights under Part III of our Constitution'.[204] That same year, the Government of Bangladesh published in its *Gazette* that it had 'recognized the Hijra community of Bangladesh as a Hijra sex'.[205]

[198] *Ibid.*

[199] Decision on the confirmation of charges against Dominic Ongwen (ICC-02/04-01/15-422-Red), Pre-Trial Chamber II, 23 March 2016, § 52.

[200] Judgment, *Ntaganda* (ICC-01/04-02/06), Trial Chamber VI, 8 July 2019, §§ 1010–1011. See also Judgment, *Kayishema et al.* (ICTR-95-1-T), Trial Chamber, 21 May 1999 § 98; Judgment, *Brđanin* (IT-99–36-T), Trial Chamber, 1 September 2004, §§ 682–684.

[201] G. Reddy, *With Respect to Sex: Negotiating Hijra Identity in South Asia* (Chicago: Chicago University Press, 2005), at 9; G. Kalra, '*Hijras*: The Unique Transgender Culture of India' 5(2) *International Journal of Culture and Mental Health* (2012) 121–126, at 121; B. Ghosh, 'A Diachronic Perspective of Hijra Identity in India' in S. Manna, S. Patra, and S. Roy (eds.), *Sociology of Motherhood and Beyond* (Kolkata: Levant Books, 2018) 107–119, at 107.

[202] Reddy, *supra* note 201, at 9–11.

[203] A. Hossain, 'Beyond Emasculation: Being Muslim and Becoming *Hijra* in South Asia' 36(4) *Asian Studies Review* (2012) 495–513.

[204] *National Legal Services Authority v. Union of India*, Writ Petition (civil) No. 604 of 2013, Supreme Court of India, 15 April 2014, § 129.

[205] Quoted in Human Rights Watch, '"I Want to Live With My Head Held High": Abuses in Bangladesh's Legal Recognition of Hijras', 23 December 2016, available at www.hrw.org/sites/default/files/report_pdf/bangladesh1216_web.pdf, at 1.

Despite this recognition, Hijra and other gender-diverse people in India and Bangladesh continue to face marginalisation and social exclusion.[206]

19. Hijra people have also been specifically named as having a distinct cultural and gender identity by international human rights courts and bodies, including the Office of the United Nations High Commissioner for Human Rights,[207] the UN Independent Expert on Sexual Orientation and Gender Identity,[208] and the Inter-American Court of Human Rights.[209]

20. Although Hijra people are not legally recognised as having a third sex or gender in Myanmar, the academic literature suggests that they view themselves as a distinct group or collectivity. For example, as in other parts of South Asia, Hijra people in Myanmar tend to live together in communities, with their own distribution of labour and communal living practices.[210] Tight kinship networks are also common amongst transgender and non-binary people living in Myanmar who do not necessarily identify as 'Hijra'.[211]

21. Further, Hijra and gender-diverse people in Myanmar appear to be viewed as a distinct group or collectivity by others. In early 2016, for example, there were widespread reports of transgender people being targeted by police for arrest, bribes, and sexual violence in Myanmar on account of their gendered appearance.[212] Further, research reports on the marginalisation and social exclusion of Hijra Rohingya in refugee camps in Bangladesh suggest that gender-diverse people from Myanmar continue to be viewed differently by others, including the wider Rohingya community.[213]

[206] A. Hossain, 'The Paradox of Recognition: *Hijra*, Third Gender and Sexual Rights in Bangladesh' 19(12) *Culture, Health & Sexuality* (2017) 1418–1431; S. Mal, 'The Hijras of India: A Marginal Community with Paradox Sexual Identity' 34(1) *Indian Journal of Social Psychiatry* (2018) 79–85.

[207] The United Nations Office of the High Commissioner for Human Rights, 'Born Free and Equal: Sexual Orientation and Gender Identity in International Human Rights Law' (2012) 9, fn 2.

[208] UN Independent Expert on Sexual Orientation and Gender Identity, 'Report of the Independent Expert on Protection against Violence and Discrimination Based on Sexual Orientation and Gender Identity', UN Doc. A/74/181, 17 July 2019, § 3.

[209] Inter-American Court of Human Rights, Advisory Opinion OC-24/17 on Gender Identity, and Equality and Non-Discrimination of Same-Sex Couples, 24 November 2017, §§ 32, 17, and 20.

[210] D. Gilbert and N. H. M. Thar, 'Moving from the Shadows: Law and SOGIE Rights in Myanmar's Democratic Transition' 20(1) *Australian Journal of Asian Law* (2019) 187–195, at 193.

[211] D. F. Gilbert, *Everyday Transgender Belonging in Transitioning Yangon* (PhD Thesis, ANU, March 2016), 73: 'For trans Burmese and hijra, operating outside of a kinship network is virtually unthinkable.'

[212] C. England, 'Myanmar's transgender people not just chasing rainbows in fight for equality', *The Guardian*, 2 February 2016, available at www.theguardian.com/global-development/2016/feb/02/myanmar-transgender-people-lgbt-colors-rainbow-equality; J. Nickerson, 'Myanmar's abused, intimidated LGBT people long for acceptance in new era', Reuters, 16 November 2016, available at https://jp.reuters.com/article/uk-myanmar-gay-idUKKBN13B0oR.

[213] WRC Report, *supra* note 181, at 34–35.

22. In light of the above, the Chamber is satisfied that Hijra and other gender-diverse people in Myanmar may constitute an identifiable group or collectivity and that Hijra and other gender-diverse individuals were targeted for rape and sexual violence during the 2016 and 2017 'clearance operations' by reason of the identity of that group or collectivity. As there is no requirement for the identity of the group to be based on the characteristics mentioned in Article 7(2)(g) of the Statute, it is unnecessary for the Chamber to consider whether, as a group, Hijra and gender-diverse people in Myanmar come within the definition of 'gender' in Article 7(g) of the Statute.

The Targeting Was Based on Prohibited Grounds

23. The targeting of the group or collectivity must have been based on political, racial, national, ethnic, cultural, religious, gender – as defined in Article 7, paragraph 3 of the Statute – or other grounds that are universally recognised as impermissible under international law.[214]

24. Article 7(3) of the Statute provides: 'For the purpose of this Statute, it is understood that the term "gender" refers to the two sexes, male and female, within the context of society. The term "gender" does not indicate any meaning different from the above.'

25. According to Article 31 of the Vienna Convention on the Law of Treaties,[215] treaty provisions are to be interpreted in good faith according to their ordinary meaning in their context and in the light of the object and purpose of the treaty. The ordinary meaning of the term 'sexes' is 'the two main categories (male and female) into which humans and many other living things are divided on the basis of their reproductive functions'.[216] The ordinary meaning of 'context' is 'the situation within which something exists or happens, and that can help explain it'.[217] The ordinary meaning of 'society' is 'a large group of people who live together in an organised way, making decisions about how to do things and sharing the work that

[214] Article 7(1)(h), Elements of Crimes.

[215] 1155 UNTS 331, 23 May 1969 (entered into force 27 January 1980) (hereafter VCLT). Article 21 (b) of the ICCSt. stipulates that the Court shall apply '[i]n the second place, where appropriate, applicable treaties and the principles and rules of international law'.

[216] 'Sex' in *Oxford English Dictionary* (3rd ed., Oxford: Oxford University Press, 2008; most recently modified version published online March 2022, available at https://dictionary.cambridge.org/dictionary/english). See also 'Sex' in *Merriam Webster*, Online Dictionary (Springfield, MA: Encyclopædia Britannica), available at www.merriam-webster.com/dictionary: 'either of the two major forms of individuals that occur in many species and that are distinguished respectively as female or male especially on the basis of their reproductive organs and structures'.

[217] 'Context' in *Cambridge Dictionary*, *supra* note 216. See also 'Context' in *Merriam Webster*, Online Dictionary, *supra* note 216: 'the interrelated conditions in which something exists or occurs'.

needs to be done'[218] or 'an enduring and cooperating social group whose members have developed organised patterns of relationships through interaction with one another'.[219] A good-faith interpretation of Article 7(3) of the Statute requires reading these words together.

26. When read together, the ordinary meaning of the words 'sexes', 'in the context of', and 'society' suggests that 'gender', as defined in Article 7(3) of the Statute, refers to the division of people into two reproductive categories (male and female), as exists within, and which may be explained by, the interactions of groups of people living together in an organised way. There are two implications that can be drawn from this understanding of gender. The first is that the Statute appears to recognise that the division of people into two biological categories based around their reproductive functions is itself socially constructed. This does not mean that biology is irrelevant to the designation of people as 'male' or 'female'. Rather, the combination of the words 'sexes' and 'in the context of society' in Article 7(3) acknowledges that it is through large-scale group interactions that any bodily differences associated with the sex-based categories 'male' and 'female' are given meaning.

27. The second implication that can be drawn from reading the words 'sexes' and 'in the context of society' together is that, for the purposes of the Statute, the term 'gender' encompasses not only the division of people into sex-based categories, but also the 'organised patterns of relationships' that have formed around, and which help to produce and sustain, those categories. These organised patterns of relationships may include expectations about how people who are assigned 'male' or 'female' are to interact with one another, as well as norms, behaviours, and social and economic roles associated with each category.

28. This reading is consistent with the Office of the Prosecutor's understanding of Article 7(3): 'This definition acknowledges the social construction of gender, and the accompanying roles, behaviours, activities, and attributes assigned to women and men, and to girls and boys.'[220] An interpretation of the term 'gender' that emphasises social dynamics also coheres with the Preamble to the Statute, which begins by recognising all peoples as living in a 'delicate mosaic' made up of 'cultures', 'shared heritage', and 'common bonds'.

29. The ordinary meaning of the second sentence in Article 7(3), which reads '[t]he term "gender" does not indicate any meaning different from the above', is that the first sentence in Article 7(3) exhaustively defines the term 'gender' for the purposes of the Statute.

30. To confirm the meaning resulting from the application of Article 31 of the Vienna Convention on the Law of Treaties, Article 32 of that treaty provides that

[218] 'Society' in *Cambridge Dictionary*, *supra* note 216.

[219] 'Society' in *Merriam Webster*, Online Dictionary, *supra* note 216.

[220] Office of the Prosecutor, ICC, 'Policy Paper on Sexual and Gender-Based Crimes', June 2014, available at www.icc-cpi.int/sites/default/files/iccdocs/otp/OTP-Policy-Paper-on-Sexual-and-Gender-Based-Crimes–June-2014.pdf, at 3.

recourse may be had to supplementary means of interpretation, including the preparatory work of the treaty and the circumstances of its conclusion.[221] The *travaux préparatoires* to the Statute reveal little about the meaning of 'gender' in Article 7(3), other than that some states wished to emphasise the binary categories of 'male' and 'female' around which the notion of gender is organised.[222] Some states also queried whether the use of the term 'gender' in connection with the crime against humanity of persecution may be broad enough to bring the criminalisation of homosexual acts within the jurisdiction of the Court, but the matter was not resolved.[223]

31. Literature on the circumstances of the treaty's conclusion indicates that there was some debate about the inclusion of a reference to the social dimension of gender, with several states preferring a biological definition.[224] However, a majority of states disagreed with that position and the words 'in the context of society' were ultimately included in Article 7(3) by consensus.[225] The fact that a non-social definition of gender was considered and rejected by the states parties supports the conclusion that the words 'in the context of society' must be given work to do.

32. Article 21(3) of the Statute provides that the Court's interpretation of the applicable law, including the Statute itself, must be consistent with internationally recognised human rights. The term 'gender' only appears in one international human rights treaty: the Council of Europe Convention on Preventing and Combating Violence against Women and Domestic Violence.[226] In that treaty, 'gender' is defined as 'the socially constructed roles, behaviours, activities and

[221] VCLT, *supra* note 215.

[222] A footnote in one of the negotiating documents provided that 'gender' 'refers to male or female': 'Recommendations of the Coordinator regarding article 5', UN Doc. A/CONF.183/C.1/L.44, 7 July 1998 in United Nations Diplomatic Conference of Plenipotentiaries on the Establishment of an International Criminal Court, 15 June–17 July 1998, Official Records, Vol. III, Reports and other documents, at 221, n 15 (hereafter UN Diplomatic Conference). At the 28th meeting of the Committee of the Whole, the delegate for Kuwait observed that a later negotiating document 'did not take into account the reference in document A/CONF.183/C.1/L.44 and Corr.l indicating that the word "gender" referred to both male and female' and stated, '[t]hat aspect should be highlighted', see *ibid*, § 13, at 289. See also the statement by the delegate of Bahrain, quoted in *ibid*, § 22, at 284.

[223] The delegate for Azerbaijan stated that 'his delegation was concerned about the use of the word "gender" in paragraph 1 (h) under "Crimes against humanity"'. He asked for clarification as to whether that provision implied 'that a conviction by a national court for homosexual acts might be regarded as persecution and thus fall within the jurisdiction of the Court as a crime against humanity', see United Nations Diplomatic Conference, *supra* note 222, § 61, at 272.

[224] V. Oosterveld, 'The Definition of "Gender" in the Rome Statute of the International Criminal Court: A Step Forward or Back for International Criminal Justice?' 18 *Harvard Human Rights Journal* (2005) 55–84, at 60–65; C. Steains, 'Gender Issues' in R. S. Lee (ed.), *The International Criminal Court: The Making of the Rome Statute* (Alphen aan den Rijn: Kluwer Law International, 1999) 357–390, at 372–375.

[225] Oosterveld, *supra* note 224, at 65.

[226] CETS 210, 11 May 2011 (entered into force 1 August 2014).

attributes that a given society considers appropriate for women and men'.[227] This definition is consistent with an interpretation of the term 'gender', as defined in Article 7(3) of the Statute, that encompasses the social patterns of relationships that produce and regulate the division of people into two reproductive categories.

33. Although the term 'gender' does not appear in other international human rights treaties, some UN human rights treaty bodies have read the notion into their respective treaties. In its General Recommendation 28, the UN Committee on the Elimination of Discrimination against Women (CEDAW Committee) stated that although the Convention on the Elimination of All Forms of Discrimination against Women[228] only explicitly mentions sex-based discrimination, references to 'customs and practices'[229] and 'social and cultural patterns of conduct'[230] in the Convention indicate that it covers gender-based discrimination as well.[231] The CEDAW Committee went on to distinguish between the notions of 'sex' and 'gender'. In the Committee's view, whereas 'sex' refers to 'biological differences between men and women', the term 'gender' encompasses 'socially constructed identities, attributes and roles for women and men and society's social and cultural meaning for these biological differences resulting in hierarchical relationships between women and men and in the distribution of power and rights favouring men and disadvantaging women'.[232]

34. While the Statute does not draw such a clear distinction between the notions of 'sex' and 'gender', the CEDAW Committee's comments lend weight to a reading of the term 'gender' in the Statute that includes socially constructed norms, behaviours, and roles. Its comments also support the idea that the concept of 'sex' must be understood in light of these social patterns because they are, in the words of the CEDAW Committee, what give 'social and cultural meaning' to any bodily differences associated with the two dominant sex-based categories.

[227] *Ibid*, Art. 3(c).

[228] 1249 UNTS 13, 18 December 1979 (entered into force 3 September 1981).

[229] *Ibid*, Art. 2(f).

[230] *Ibid*, Art. 5(a).

[231] Committee on Economic, Social and Cultural Rights, General Recommendation 28 on the Core Obligations of States Parties under Article 2 of the Convention on the Elimination of All Forms of Discrimination against Women, UN Doc. CEDAW/C/GC/28, 16 December 2010 (hereafter CEDAW General Recommendation 28), § 5, at 2. The Committee was also influenced by Article 1 of the Convention, which states: 'For the purposes of the present Convention, the term "discrimination against women" shall mean any distinction, exclusion or restriction made on the basis of sex which has the effect or purpose of impairing or nullifying the recognition, enjoyment or exercise by women, irrespective of their marital status, on a basis of equality of men and women, of human rights and fundamental freedoms in the political, economic, social, cultural, civil or any other field.' In the view of the Committee, this provision meant 'that identical or neutral treatment of women and men might constitute discrimination against women if such treatment resulted in or had the effect of women being denied the exercise of a right because there was no recognition of the pre-existing gender-based disadvantage and inequality that women face': *Ibid*.

[232] *Ibid*.

35. The UN Committee on Economic, Social and Cultural Rights (CESCR) has taken a different approach to the CEDAW Committee. Rather than drawing a clear distinction between the concepts of 'sex' and 'gender', in its General Comment No. 20, the CESCR provided an expansive reading of the term 'sex' in the International Covenant on Economic, Social and Cultural Rights,[233] which included social elements. It said: 'Since the adoption of the Covenant, the notion of the prohibited ground "sex" has evolved considerably to cover not only physiological characteristics but also the social construction of gender stereotypes, prejudices and expected roles, which have created obstacles to the equal fulfilment of economic, social and cultural rights.'[234] These comments confirm that, in contemporary international human rights law, sex and gender should not be construed in ways that overlook social dynamics.

36. Having determined the meaning of 'gender', as defined in Article 7(3) of the Statute, the Chamber must now turn to whether the targeting of Hijra and gender-diverse people was based on gender grounds.

37. The UN Committee against Torture has recognised that actual or perceived non-conformity with social gender roles can put people at risk of torture and ill-treatment.[235] The UN High Commissioner for Refugees has also recognised people whose bodies do not fit with binary perceptions of sex can be exposed to harm.[236] Given the Statute's recognition of the centrality of both social dynamics and binary thinking to the notion of 'gender', both of these forms of targeting could constitute persecution on gender grounds.

38. As noted above, the term 'Hijra' applies to third-gender persons, transgender women, and intersex persons in South Asia who were assigned male at birth.[237] Some members of this group may have been targeted for rape and sexual violence during the 'clearance operations' in 2016 and 2017 due to their non-conformity with gendered behaviours and social roles. For example, the Independent International Fact-Finding Mission on Myanmar reports that transgender women, who are

[233] 993 UNTS 3, 16 December 1966 (entered into force 3 January 1976).

[234] Committee on Economic, Social and Cultural Rights, 'General Comment No. 20: Non-discrimination in Economic, Social and Cultural Rights (Art. 2, para. 2, of the International Covenant on Economic, Social and Cultural Rights)', UN Doc. E/C.12/GC/20, 2 July 2009, § 20, at 6.

[235] CAT General Comment No. 2, *supra* note 196, § 22, at 6: 'Both men and women and boys and girls may be subject to violations of the Convention on the basis of their actual or perceived non-conformity with socially determined gender roles.'

[236] UN High Commissioner for Refugees, 'Guidelines on International Protection No. 9: Claims to Refugee Status Based on Sexual Orientation and/or Gender Identity within the Context of Article 1A(2) of the 1951 Convention and/or Its 1967 Protocol Relating to the Status of Refugees', UN Doc. HCR/GIP/12/09, 23 October 2012 (hereafter UNHCR Guidelines), at 4: 'Not fitting within accepted binary perceptions of being male and female, [transgender people] may be perceived as threatening social norms and values. This non-conformity exposes them to risk of harm.'

[237] WRC Report, *supra* note 181, at 5.

women who were assigned male at birth, face high levels of discrimination in Myanmar because their feminine mannerisms, clothing, and behaviour do not align with social expectations regarding the gender expression of people who are assigned male at birth.[238] This may also be the case for Hijra and gender-diverse people who identify as non-binary or third gender, rather than as women or men.

39. As the notion of gender, as defined in Article 7(3) of the Statute, appears to encompass the social norms and expectations that have formed around, and which help to produce and sustain, the sex-based categories of 'male' and 'female', the targeting of Hijra people on the basis of their non-conformity with such norms and expectations may constitute persecution on the grounds of gender for the purposes of Article 7(1)(h) of the Statute.

40. Other Hijra people may have been targeted for rape and sexual violence during the 'clearance operations' due to their non-conformity with the very sex binary around which the notion of gender is organised, such as Hijra people who are intersex. The UN Office of the High Commissioner on Human Rights defines intersex people as people who 'are born with physical sex characteristics that do not fit the normative definitions for male or female bodies'.[239] These sex characteristics may include sexual anatomy and/or chromosome patterns that do not fall neatly into either of the dominant sex-based categories.[240]

41. According to the UN High Commissioner for Refugees, intersex people can be subjected to persecution because they do not conform with expected bodily appearances of 'males' and 'females'.[241] To the extent that intersex Hijra people in Myanmar were targeted on a similar basis, this may also constitute persecution on the grounds of gender, as defined in Article 7(3). This is because the social belief that humanity can be divided into two binary sexes would be the motivating force behind the targeting.

42. Earlier in this decision, the Chamber established that there exists a reasonable basis to believe that members of the Tatmadaw, jointly with other security forces and with some participation of local civilians, may have committed acts that qualify as the crime against humanity of persecution on grounds of ethnicity and/or religion against the Rohingya population. To the extent that the Hijra and other gender-diverse people who were allegedly targeted for rape and sexual violence were also Rohingya, the persecution may have been based on the intersecting grounds of gender, ethnicity, and religion.

43. UN human rights bodies have recognised that discrimination based on sex and gender is often inextricably linked with other factors, including race, ethnicity,

[238] 2019 UNFFM Report, *supra* note 182, §§ 151–152, at 36.

[239] UN Office of the High Commissioner for Human Rights, 'Born Free and Equal: Sexual Orientation, Gender Identity and Sex Characteristics in International Human Rights Law', 2nd ed., UN Doc. HR/PUB/12/06/Rev.1 (2019), at 5.

[240] UNHCR Guidelines, *supra* note 236, at 5.

[241] *Ibid.*

religion or belief, health, status, age, class, caste, and sexual orientation and gender identity.[242] In the case of gender-diverse Rohingya people, the Independent International Fact-Finding Mission on Myanmar received reports from transgender women who believed that they had been targeted for sexual violence during the 'clearance operations' in 2016 and 2017 due to a combination of their non-conformity with gender norms and their Rohingya ethnicity.[243] This led the Mission to conclude that, 'transgender people of Rohingya ethnicity are victimised twice: as Rohingya and as transgender people'.[244] The actual or perceived identity of Hijra Rohingya people as Muslim may have also contributed to their alleged targeting.

44. In light of the above, the Chamber is satisfied that there is a reasonable basis to believe that the targeting of Hijra and other gender-diverse people may have been based on gender grounds, as well as ethnic and religious grounds in the case of Hijra and gender-diverse Rohingya.

The Conduct Was Connected with a Crime within the Jurisdiction of the Court

45. The final non-contextual element of the crime against humanity of persecution is that the conduct was committed in connection with any act referred to in Article 7, paragraph 1 of the Statute or any crime within the jurisdiction of the Court.[245]

46. Earlier in this decision, the Chamber determined that a reasonable Prosecutor could believe that coercive acts perpetrated against the Rohingya civilian population in Myanmar in 2016 and 2017 forced them to flee to Bangladesh. If established, this may amount to the crime against humanity of deportation under Article 7(1)(d) of the Statute. The Chamber further determined that the Court may assert jurisdiction *ratione loci* over this alleged crime as Bangladesh is a state party to the Statute and it is possible to conclude that the *actus reus* of the crime of deportation was completed in the territory of Bangladesh.

47. The rape and sexual violence perpetrated against Hijra and other gender-diverse people in Myanmar during the 2016 and 2017 'clearance operations', causing many of them to seek refuge in Bangladesh, may also amount to the crime against humanity of deportation by coercive acts.

[242] CEDAW General Recommendation 28, *supra* note 231, § 18, at 4. See also CAT General Comment No. 2, *supra* note 196, § 22, at 6: 'Being female intersects with other identifying characteristics or status of the person such as race, nationality, religion, sexual orientation, age, immigrant status etc. to determine the ways that women and girls are subject to or at risk of torture or ill-treatment and the consequences thereof.'

[243] 2019 UNFFM Report, *supra* note 182, § 180, at 43.

[244] *Ibid.*

[245] Article 7(1)(h), Elements of Crimes.

48. As the conduct that allegedly deprived Hijra people in Myanmar of their fundamental rights would be the same conduct that allegedly forced them to flee to Bangladesh, the Chamber is satisfied that there is a sufficient connection between the conduct underlying the persecution and the crime against humanity of deportation under Article 7(1)(d) of the Statute.

Conclusion

49. Upon review of the available information, the Chamber accepts that there exists a reasonable basis to believe that since at least 9 October 2016, members of the Tatmadaw, jointly with other security forces and with some participation of local civilians, may have committed rape and sexual violence that could amount to the crime against humanity of persecution against Hijra and gender-diverse people in Myanmar under Article 7(1)(h) of the Statute on the grounds of gender and, in the case of Hijra and gender-diverse Rohingya, gender, ethnicity, and/or religion.

Judge Claerwen O'Hara

15

Photo Essays: Myanmar/Bangladesh

Azimul Hassan, Omal Khair, and Dil Kayas

At the time of writing in 2023, it was four years since the Office of the Prosecutor commenced an investigation into the situation in Bangladesh/Myanmar in accordance with Article 15(4) of the Rome Statute.[1] It was also six years since the mass displacement of Rohingyas from Rakhine state in Myanmar, which Pre-Trial Chamber III held may amount to the crimes against humanity of deportation[2] and persecution on the ground of religion and/or ethnicity.[3] According to the United Nations, around 10,000 people were killed in an alleged genocidal operation, and more than 700,000 people fled to Bangladesh.[4] Most of these people have found themselves in the Kutupalong-Balukhali expansion site in Cox's Bazar – the largest and most densely populated refugee camp in the world.[5] Living conditions in the camp are challenging. Shelters are built from bamboo and tarpaulin and are closely packed together. Access to clean water, sanitation, healthcare, and education is limited. Residents must contend with overcrowding, outbreaks of disease, fires, monsoons, and cyclones. The COVID-19 pandemic added another layer of complexity to the crisis. The future for refugees in the camp remains uncertain, with limited prospects for safe and voluntary return to Myanmar, local integration in Bangladesh, or resettlement to a third country.

In this photo essay, Azimul Hassan, Omal Khair, and Dil Kayas – Media Fellows with Fortify Rights – have captured the hardships of camp life, but also the resilience and adaptability of the refugees living there, as well as their moments of joy and

[1] Decision Pursuant to Article 15 of the Rome Statute on the Authorisation of an Investigation into the Situation in the People's Republic of Bangladesh/Republic of the Union of Myanmar, *Situation in the People's Republic of Bangladesh/Republic of the Union of Myanmar* (ICC-01/19-27), Pre-Trial Chamber III, 14 November 2019, § 126.

[2] *Ibid*, § 108.

[3] *Ibid*, § 109.

[4] UNCHR. Rohingya Refugee Crisis Explained, 24 August 2024, available at www.unrefugees.org/news/rohingya-refugee-crisis-explained/.

[5] *Ibid*.

hope. These images and the photographers' accompanying text are evidence of the ongoing impacts of the atrocities committed in Myanmar, yet at the same time they are testament to the tenacity of the human spirit and the great power of art and creative expression to transcend the physical and non-physical borders we construct between us.

15.1 THE DAILY LIFE, SUFFERING AND CULTURE OF ROHINGYA REFUGEES

by Azimul Hassan

These images tell the world about the situation of the Rohingya people in the refugee camps. They not only illustrate the daily lives and suffering of Rohingya people in the camps but also Rohingya culture.

PHOTO 15.1 Boy on roof at sunset by Azimul Hassan

PHOTO 15.2 Boys playing football behind barbed wire by Azimul Hassan

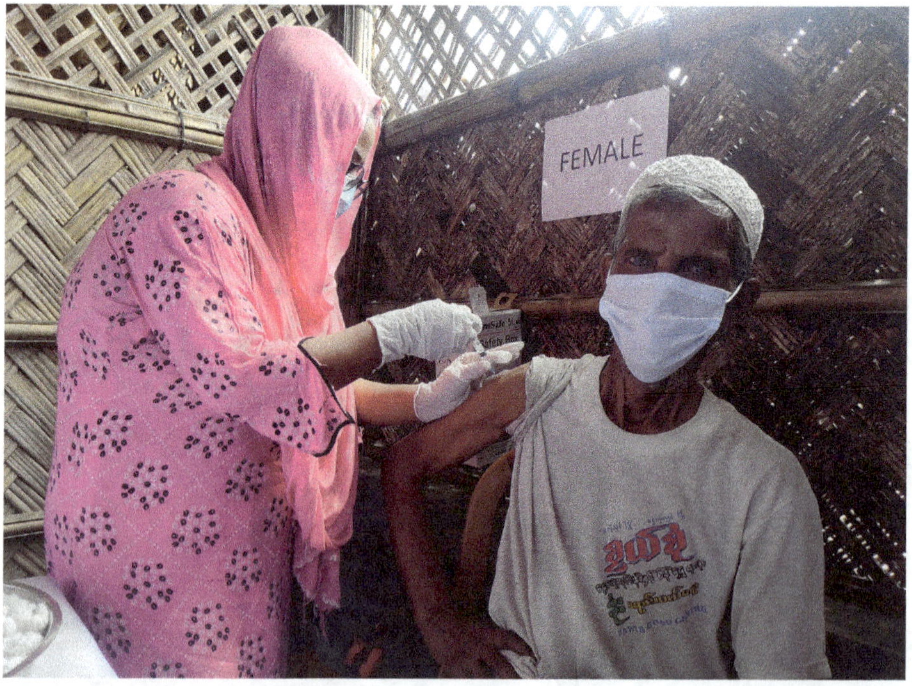

PHOTO 15.3 Man receiving vaccination by Azimul Hassan

PHOTO 15.4 Woman drying fish on a net in the sun by Azimul Hassan

15.2 A WINDOW INTO THE LIFE OF ROHINGYA REFUGEES

by Omal Khair

These photos offer a window into Rohingya refugees' lives. For example, one of the photos shows the makeshift infrastructure refugees create to navigate the challenging living conditions. One captures the everyday reality of how Rohingya refugees manage essential tasks like bathing in a constrained environment and another shows

PHOTO 15.5 Girls collecting water by Azimul Hassan

PHOTO 15.6 Children at school by Azimul Hassan

PHOTO 15.7 Man showering with pot by Azimul Hassan

PHOTO 15.8 Boys looking out over refugee camp by Azimul Hassan

how refugees collect water from a hand pump well. I've also highlighted the limited play spaces available for children in the overcrowded camps, but the photo shows the incredible resilience of the kids, finding moments of joy in this challenging situation. Another photo shows how the children of Rohingya refugees are studying at a learning centre. This is against the breathtaking scenery surrounding the camp, providing viewers with a unique perspective on the refugees' daily lives.

15.3 TELL THE WORLD

by Dil Kayas

The images taken between 2018 and 2022 show on-the-ground reality in the Rohingya refugee camps in Cox's Bazar, Bangladesh. From daily life to the hardships endured, the photos tell the world about the lived experience of the Rohingya refugees.

PHOTO 15.9 Two men wading through flood water by Dil Kayas

PHOTO 15.10 Girls by a barbed wire fence by Dil Kayas

PHOTO 15.11 Refugees after the fire by Dil Kayas

16

The Situation in Afghanistan

16.1 REFLECTION: THE SITUATION IN AFGHANISTAN

Salima Ahmadi and Sari Kouvo

INTRODUCTION

In August 2021, the Taliban marched into Kabul and once again became the de facto government of Afghanistan, overthrowing the government of the Islamic Republic of Afghanistan which held power from 2004 to 2021. The Taliban takeover came just a little less than two decades after the 9/11 attacks on the Twin Towers in New York that started the US-led 'War on Terror' in Afghanistan and beyond. For some, the Taliban takeover marks an end to the conflict: both the US forces and the elected Afghan president departed the country, leaving a security and governance void that the Taliban filled. For others, the relative stability of the first years of Taliban rule is simply a lull in the conflict. Since 1978, Afghans have experienced many phases of conflict, each with its own dynamic of human rights violations and war crimes.[1]

At the time of writing in 2023, there has been next to no accountability for any past crimes in Afghanistan, and few attempts to deal with conflict-related grievances and trauma. In the sporadic peace and power-sharing deals of the past four decades, de jure and de facto amnesty for war crimes and crimes against humanity has been the general rule *[Editors' Note: In January 2025, the Prosecutor applied for arrest warrants for Taliban leaders on the charge of gender-based persecution, including against women, their allies, and LGBTIQ+ persons.]*.

[1] There are few comprehensive analyses about violations during the different phases of the conflict, the most complete officially published account remains the reports of the Afghanistan Justice Project covering the period 1978–2001. The civilian casualties reporting by the UN Assistance Mission for Afghanistan (UNAMA) provides some insights into violations of the past decades of conflict.

The aim of this sub-chapter is to contextualise the rewritten decisions of the International Criminal Court (ICC) on the situation in Afghanistan, from a feminist perspective. For the time being, the ICC is the only justice mechanism focusing on Afghanistan. Its engagement is a reminder that there *should* be no amnesty for war crimes. When embarking on a feminist reflection of the role of the ICC in Afghanistan, it is important to note that while accountability for atrocity crimes has been scarce in Afghanistan, accountability for these crimes have even more seldom included a gender dimension, although this dimension is ever present. Throughout the Afghanistan conflict, women and girls, their appearance and role in society and the family, have been one of the key ideological battlegrounds. The conflict has accentuated and brutalised already existing discriminatory practices, and lessened opportunities to challenge existing gender norms. With men away fighting the war or abroad trying to earn a living, women have been left to head large multi-generational households in complicated and insecure circumstances. The conflict has also changed the lives of men and boys while strengthening and privileging opportunistic and violent forms of masculinity.

Background to the Conflict in Afghanistan

The conflict in Afghanistan started in 1978 with a communist coup that set the stage for the Soviet occupation a year later. By the time Soviet forces withdrew in 1989, the occupation had cost at least a million civilian lives.[2] The Mujahideen government that was formed after the withdrawal quickly imploded and a new phase of the civil war started. During the civil war over 6 million Afghans sought refuge in neighbouring Iran and Pakistan.[3] The Mujahideen's failure to form a centralised state contributed to the birth of the Taliban movement. The Taliban came to power in 1996 and under their regime, women and ethnic and religious minorities were the main targets of serious human rights violations. The Taliban also provided a haven for the Al Qaeda network, and it is believed that the 9/11 attacks against the United States were planned from Afghanistan. Consequently, Afghanistan become the first theatre in the US 'War on Terror', with the government of the Islamic Republic of Afghanistan, the United States, North Atlantic Treaty Organization (NATO) forces and a 'coalition of the willing' fighting the Taliban and non-state actors.

The 'War on Terror' continued until a peace agreement was signed in February 2020 between the Taliban and the US government under the Trump administration. In April 2021, President Biden announced a full US withdrawal from Afghanistan by August of that year, leaving the government of the Islamic Republic of Afghanistan to fend for itself. The Taliban had already, for several years,

[2] S. R. Samady, *Education and Afghan Society in the Twentieth Century* (Paris: UNESCO, 2001) 18, available at https://reliefweb.int/report/afghanistan/education-and-afghan-society-twentieth-century.

[3] *Ibid*, 69.

been the de facto powerholders in much of rural Afghanistan; after the US withdrawal they quickly took provincial capitals and finally the national capital, Kabul. While overrunning cities and districts, the Taliban committed revenge killings of people supportive of the former government, targeted killings and torture of civilians and human rights defenders, and looted civilian properties.[4]

The Afghanistan conflict came at a heavy price. After two decades of war, official reports record the deaths of 47,245 Afghan civilians, 66,000 Afghan forces, 51,191 Taliban and other fighters, 444 aid workers, 72 journalists, and 3,846 US and other fighters from the 'coalition of the willing'.[5] These deaths represent but a fraction of the human rights violations and war crimes committed in Afghanistan.

Throughout Afghanistan's history and the conflict, Afghan women have been used as political tools. The women's issue has shaped rulers' political agenda – some seeking to limit women's rights, some 'liberating' them through socialism or liberal democracy. Gender – the role of men and women in society and family – runs across cleavages within Afghan society. However, the politicisation of gender issues has further deepened existing cleavages between the elites and the poor, the educated and the illiterate, the secular and the religious, the Western-oriented liberals and the conservatives.

Besides the political and ideological football that the different factions have played with women's rights, they have also used women and their bodies as weapons of war.[6] To protect themselves from attacks, women had to at times unveil and at other times veil.[7] During the civil war, insecurity and poverty reached record levels; families were forced to sell their daughters into marriages and sexual violence was rampant.[8] The Taliban's treatment of women was even harsher. During their 1990s reign, they outlawed women's public appearance 'for the sake of their protection'.[9] They deprived women of a wide range of civil-political, socio-economic, and judicial rights, including freedom of thought and expression, freedom of religion, freedom to travel, and the right to education and work. The group was accused of women's rights violations, which included stoning, public beatings, execution, arrest, and penalties for inappropriate dress.[10]

4 A. Coren and S. Sidhu, 'Taliban fighters execute 22 Afghan commandos as they try to surrender', CNN, 13 July 2021, available at https://edition.cnn.com/2021/07/13/asia/afghanistan-taliban-commandos-killed-intl-hnk/index.html. See also www.amnesty.org/en/latest/press-release/2021/10/afghanistan-13-hazara-killed-by-taliban-fighters-in-daykundi-province-new-investigation/.

5 A. Knickmeyer, 'Cost of the Afghanistan War, in lives and dollars', AP, 17 August 2021, available at https://apnews.com/article/middle-east-business-afghanistan-43d8f53b35e80ec18c130cd683e1a38f. See also BBC, 'Afghanistan: What has the conflict cost the US and its allies?', 1 September 2021, available at www.bbc.com/news/world-47391821.

6 S. Samar, 'Feminism, Peace and Afghanistan' 72 *Journal of International Affairs* (2019) 145–148.

7 M. Zulfacar, 'The Pendulum of Gender Politics in Afghanistan' 25(1–2) *Central Asian Survey* (2006) 27–59.

8 *Ibid*, 26.

9 *Ibid*, 1.

10 A. Bukhari, 'Taliban's return has Afghan women living in fear', *The Diplomat*, 17 August 2021, available at https://thediplomat.com/2021/08/talibans-return-has-afghan-women-living-in-fear/.

Progress was made to improve women's rights after the 2001 US military intervention and the UN-supported state-building exercise: laws, policies, and institutional practices changed in order to open up opportunities for women. By the time of the collapse of the government of President Ashraf Ghani, a quarter of civil servants across the country were women, women accounted for 36 per cent of media workers, 28 per cent of parliamentarians, and the governors or deputy governors in more than half of Afghanistan's thirty-four provinces.[11] Progress was uneven though, and sexual harassment and violence was rampant.[12] As girls and women are considered to carry the family honour, reporting harassment or violence remained challenging as girls and women often choose not to report so as not to bring shame on the family.

Each phase of the conflict has had its own dynamic of atrocities, while only a handful of perpetrators have been held to account.[13] To date, all Afghan power-sharing or peace agreements have included direct references to amnesty or have left the issue of legacies of war crimes unaddressed. Although Afghanistan acceded to the Rome Statute of the ICC in 2003, efforts to promote transitional justice have largely failed.[14]

In the post-2001 era, there have been a few exceptions to the culture of silence and impunity for war crimes that has reigned in Afghanistan. A few low-level commanders or commanders who no longer could rely on friends in high places have been prosecuted in Afghanistan.[15] In the United Kingdom and the Netherlands, there have also been some prosecutions making use of universal jurisdiction.[16] There is no indication that the Taliban will change the trend of impunity. The possibility of an ICC investigation into war crimes in Afghanistan remains the only accountability mechanism open to victims of the conflict.

Background to the ICC Cases Concerning the Situation in Afghanistan

The Afghan government was an early adopter of the Rome Statute, acceding to it in 2003. At that point there was a lull in the conflict, and the ICC did not have jurisdiction over crimes committed during previous phases of the Afghanistan conflict. That is, adopting the Rome Statute did not seem to have any practical

[11] Afghanistan, Performance Report. Independent Administrative Reform and Civil Services Commission, 2018, no longer available online at https://iarcsc.gov.af/fa/wp-content/uploads/sites/2/2019/05/IARCSC-Annual-Report-1397.pdf.

[12] VoA, 'More than 1,500 cases of violence against women registered', *Voice of America*, 2021, www.darivoa.com/a/violence-1500-registered-against-woman-in-afghanistan/5933616.html.

[13] For an overview of accountability in Afghanistan, see S. Kouvo and P. Gossman, 'Tell Us How This Ends?', AAN Report, 30 June 2013, available at www.afghanistan-analysts.org/en/special-reports/tell-us-how-this-ends-transitional-justice-and-prospects-for-peace-in-afghanistan/

[14] S. Kouvo, 'Transitional Justice in the Context of Ongoing Conflict: The Case of Afghanistan', International Centre for Transitional Justice, September 2009, available at www.ictj.org/sites/default/files/ICTJ-Afghanistan-Conflict-Briefing-2009-English.pdf.

[15] Kouvo and Gossman, *supra* note 13.

[16] *Ibid.*

significance for Afghanistan, as the warring decades of the 1980s and 1990s were outside the Court's remit. The lull in the conflict did not last.

In 2007, the first ICC Prosecutor, Luis Moreno Ocampo, initiated a preliminary analysis into the situation in Afghanistan. It took a decade for the Office of the Prosecutor (OTP) to conclude that crimes meeting the ICC's gravity threshold had been committed in Afghanistan since the Rome Statute's entry into force in respect of Afghanistan in 2003.[17] In its 2016 Preliminary Examinations report, the OTP concluded that there was reasonable basis to believe crimes reaching the ICC threshold had been committed in Afghanistan.[18] The alleged crimes identified all parties to the conflict, including crimes against humanity and war crimes by the Taliban and the Haqqani Network, war crimes by the Afghan government, in particular the Afghan intelligence agency, and war crimes by the US military forces deployed in Afghanistan. The OTP report provided a detailed account of the crimes, including extensive targeting of civilians, extrajudicial killings, torture, rape, and illegal detention.

The Afghanistan case was not referred to the ICC, rather it was initiated by Prosecutor Ocampo under the *proprio motu* powers of the Rome Statute. In such cases, a decision by the Pre-Trial Chamber is needed to decide whether to open an actual investigation. Before starting its deliberations, the Pre-Trial Chamber invited victims to share their views on whether an investigation would 'serve the interests of justice'. The responses showed resounding support for an investigation.[19] However, the Pre-Trial Chamber decided to go against the OTP and the victims' recommendations. In 2019, the Pre-Trial Chamber declined to authorise the investigation, holding that although the jurisdiction and admissibility tests were satisfied, an investigation at this stage 'would not serve the interests of justice' because the likelihood of successful prosecutions was too limited.[20]

The ICC's second Prosecutor, Fatou Bensouda, and victims' groups successfully appealed the Pre-Trial Chamber's decision. On 5 March 2020, the Appeals Chamber decided to allow the Prosecutor to pursue an investigation, but few concrete steps were taken in the year before the Taliban takeover.[21] Shortly after the takeover, the third ICC Prosecutor, Karim Khan, stated that, since the Taliban's recapture of power, the Prosecutor had decided to continue the investigation but, referring to the limited resources available, he proposed only to investigate crimes committed by the Taliban and Islamic State in Afghanistan.[22] This new prosecution

[17] E. Qaane, 'Investigating Post-2003 War Crimes: Afghan Government Wants "One More Year" from the ICC', Afghanistan Analysts Network, 27 June 2017, available at www.afghanistan-analysts.org/en/reports/rights-freedom/investigating-post-2003-war-crimes-afghan-government-wants-one-more-year-from-the-icc/.

[18] OTP Report on Preliminary Examination Activities (2016), International Criminal Court, 43, available at www.icc-cpi.int/iccdocs/otp/161114-otp-rep-PE_ENG.pdf.

[19] www.icc-cpi.int/CourtRecords/CR2019_02068.PDF.

[20] *Ibid*, § 96.

[21] www.icc-cpi.int/CourtRecords/CR2020_00828.PDF.

[22] https://www.icc-cpi.int/news/statement-prosecutor-international-criminal-court-karim-khan-qc-following-application.

strategy excluded both the crimes committed by the Afghan intelligence service of the former Islamic Republic of Afghanistan government, as well as by US and other international forces present in Afghanistan during the 'War on Terror'.

Feminist Reimagining of Select Judgments and Decisions

In this chapter, six authors – Mashal Aamir and Adrienne Ringin, Jill Marshall, Kathryn Gooding, Souheir Edelbi, and Susana SáCouto – have each undertaken a feminist reinterpretation of different aspects of the ICC's Afghanistan proceedings.[23] The five legal issues were: (1) the notion of gender-based persecution by the Taliban in the Pre-Trial Chamber's decision to open an investigation into Afghanistan; (2) the jurisdiction test; (3) the gravity test; (4) the complementarity test; and (5) the interests of justice test. In line with the feminist methodology used for this volume, the authors were asked to write their contributions *as if* they were ICC judges.

The five legal issues chosen are all central to the ICC's engagement on Afghanistan from 2007 to 2020. Importantly, however, all the issues pre-date the August 2021 Taliban takeover of Afghanistan. Consequently, the authors are reimagining ICC decisions adopted when the Islamic Republic of Afghanistan, backed by US and other international forces, was fighting the Taliban and other non-state armed groups, not at the time when the Republic has fallen, US forces have left the country, and the Taliban has become the de facto government.

Judge Susana SáCouto: Gender-Based Persecution in Afghanistan

In 2019, the ICC Pre-Trial Chamber accepted the Prosecutor's submission that there was a reasonable basis to believe that Taliban forces had committed gender-based persecution in Afghanistan.[24] However, in its decision the Chamber offered no commentary on what that crime involved, and what 'gender' means in the ICC Statute. The Chamber's decision focused on if, based on the Prosecutor's submission, the Court has jurisdiction and if the cases met the threshold of the Court. The Prosecutor's submission encompassed alleged crimes committed by all parties to the conflict, including the Taliban and other non-state armed groups, the Afghan government, and the US and other international forces.

In her reimagined decision, Judge Susana SáCouto examines gender-based persecution in the decision through a feminist lens. Judge SáCouto takes as her starting point the Rome Statute's definition of gender under Article 7(3), which defines gender as referring to 'the two sexes, male and female, within the context of society'. The definition can be read as an attempt by the drafters of the statute to equate gender with biological sex. Judge SáCouto takes a different view. She makes use of the rules of interpretation, focusing on the ordinary meaning of the terms and

[23] The court files relevant to the ICC proceedings on Afghanistan can be accessed at www.icc-cpi .int/afghanistan.

[24] ICC 02/17 (12 April 2019).

their drafting history. In her reinterpretation, she argues that the meaning of gender has evolved since the adoption of the Rome Statute so that its ordinary meaning, when situated in the 'context of society', is socially and culturally construed and changeable. That is, what Judge SáCouto does is attempt to show that the ordinary meaning of equating gender with 'male and female in the context of society' has changed between when the Rome Statute was adopted and now: in the early 2000s we may have understood the reference as meaning gender equals sex, today we understand gender as a social construction and changeable.

Using this interpretation, Judge SáCouto proceeds to analyse what an understanding of gender as evolving, and as socially and culturally construed, means for the crime of gender-based persecution, and for the ICC's investigation into crimes committed in Afghanistan. She notes that 'gender-based persecution includes persecutory acts that are motivated by beliefs, attitudes, and perceptions regarding appropriate social behaviour for males and females', and concludes that,

> having examined not only direct harms to the women and girls targeted by the Taliban, but also the long-lasting adverse impacts of these acts on the ability of victims and their families to subsist and on women's and girls' access to critical services and support, this Chamber finds that women and girls in Afghanistan were severely deprived of their fundamental rights.

Judge SáCouto's analysis differs from the original decision in that she focuses on the definition of gender-based persecution. She seeks to update the ICC's definition of gender by arguing – successfully so, in our view – that since the adoption of the Rome Statute our common understanding of gender has changed. Her analysis also differs from the original decision regarding the amount of attention given to the gender-based crimes committed by the Taliban. Judge SáCouto places these crimes at the centre. We welcome the shift made by Judge SáCouto's reinterpretation: it is unusual and refreshing to read such extensive focus on crimes committed towards women in an international criminal law decision.

Judges Mashal Aamir and Adrienne Ringin: The 'Jurisdiction' Test in Afghanistan

To open an investigation, the ICC Prosecutor must first establish under Article 53(1) that there are reasonable grounds to believe that crimes within the ICC's subject-matter jurisdiction were committed. In 2019, the ICC Pre-Trial Chamber ruled that this jurisdiction test was satisfied in relation to the situation in Afghanistan.

Rewriting this decision from a feminist perspective, Judges Aamir and Ringin do not change the decision. As in the real ICC decision, they decide that the jurisdiction test is satisfied, as there is reasonable basis to believe that war crimes and crimes against humanity have been committed. However, the rewritten judgment increases the focus on crimes with a gender-based and sexual nature. Judges Aamir and Ringin have used public sources to include more and different violations to the list of crimes within the scope of the investigation. Their account provides an overview of gender-based and sexual violence committed *by all parties to the conflict*, including rape of men and women, torture and threats of torture focused on genitalia, forced nudity, and other forms of degrading treatment. What the increased attention to gender-based and sexual crimes starkly shows is the deeply gendered and sexualised nature of the conflict, and the brutality of all parties to the conflict.

The fact that Judges Aamir and Ringin focus not only on violence by the Taliban, but also on how members of the Taliban have been treated when detained by the security forces of the Islamic Republic and international forces, is relevant also for the current situation wherein the Taliban are the de facto government of Afghanistan. The recorded brutality of the Taliban in and out of government clearly includes extreme violations of international criminal law. However, as this judgment makes clear, they are not the only ones to have committed atrocities; indeed over the past decades attention to the crimes committed against Taliban members by international forces have been cursory at best. Judges Aamir and Ringin's feminist analysis therefore contributes to a levelling of the playing field: violations by all parties to the Afghanistan conflict get the attention they deserve.

Judge Jill Marshall: The 'Gravity' Test in Afghanistan

After the 'jurisdiction' test, the ICC Prosecutor must establish that the alleged crimes meet the 'gravity threshold' to be authorised to open an investigation. In its 2019 decision, the Pre-Trial Chamber ruled that war crimes and crimes against humanity allegedly committed by the Afghan army and the Taliban within Afghanistan, and by American forces against Afghan detainees, were sufficiently serious to pass this 'gravity threshold'.[25] In her decision, Judge Marshall reimagines the 'gravity threshold' through a gender lens.

Specifically, Judge Marshall guides the reader through the ICC's assessment of the gravity of the crimes by all parties to the conflict. The assessment focuses on the scale, nature, manner, and impact of the violations. In contrast to the original decision, Judge Marshall's decision includes a gender analysis to assess both how the violations have been committed, and what they mean in the context of the Afghan conflict and the discrimination, deprivation, and trauma that they have caused in this situation. This analysis is further strengthened by Judge Marshall in the impact section, underlining the importance of recognising the consequences of living with the experiences of the violations in the broader context of the conflict.

In explicating her decision, Marshall also reflects on the challenge of using feminist analysis while remaining within the limits of what the ICC and legal rules prescribe. Feminism in law, Judge Marshall notes, 'makes use of the power that law

[25] *Ibid.*

holds, whilst resisting that same power'. Navigating this paradox is not an easy task; it demands making the most of law, without falling into the trap of reproducing patriarchal structures that view Afghan women mainly as victims. Judge Marshall manages this but her judgment points to the balancing act underlying the exercise of feminist reimagination in itself.

Judge Kathryn Gooding: The 'Complementarity' Test in Afghanistan

The 'complementarity' test must also be satisfied for the ICC Prosecutor to open an investigation. Under this test, the ICC can only investigate and prosecute crimes in the absence of genuine proceedings at the national level. In its 2019 decision, the Pre-Trial Chamber ruled that the crimes of interest to the ICC were not already the subject of genuine proceedings in Afghanistan or the United states, making them admissible to the ICC. Judge Kathryn Gooding's rewritten decision approaches the complementarity test from a feminist angle.[26]

Judge Gooding argues it is unlikely that either the Afghan or the US judicial system would be able and willing to prosecute the alleged gender-based crimes genuinely. She notes in her decision that, given the record of the current Afghanistan government, it is likely that the proceedings would focus on crimes against the state, and not the many gender-based crimes committed during the conflict. Similarly, Judge Gooding is of the view that, given its record, the US government would most likely not give enough attention to the gender-based and sexual offences committed by US forces in particular. She notes that Afghan law does not adequately recognise sexual and gender-based crimes, and that the United States has demonstrated a lack of political will to prosecute its own soldiers for such atrocities. Therefore, in the view of Judge Gooding, the ICC can jurisdiction. Gooding's focus is potentially the most radical of the rewritten Afghanistan decisions because it puts gender-based and sexual crimes at the centre of the complementarity test. Given the history of the ICC, this focus still seems like an improbability. By taking this stance, Judge Gooding's decision is revelatory, demonstrating how marginalised gender-based and sexual crimes remain in the sphere of ICC crimes.

Judge Souheir Edelbi: The 'Interests of Justice' Test in Afghanistan

Judge Souheir Edelbi's feminist redrafting relates to the Appeal Chamber's 2020 decision on Afghanistan, which focuses on whether the Pre-Trial Chamber erred in its interpretation of Article 15(4) of the Statute when it found itself bound to assess the factors under Article 53(1) (interests of justice test) of the Statute.[27] The Pre-Trial Chamber's decision received considerable attention from both the international

[26] *Ibid.*
[27] *Ibid.*

legal community and Afghan human rights activists.[28] The Pre-Trial Chamber originally took a very far-reaching interpretation of the interests of justice, allowing it to decide that largely because of the ICC's financial situation, there was little chance of successful prosecutions in Afghanistan. The Pre-Trial Chamber's determination that the investigation was not in the interests of justice centred on the 'availability of evidence dating back so long in time' (para. 93), 'the prospects of securing meaningful cooperation from the relevant authorities' (para. 94), and the 'significant amount of resources' required to conduct the investigation (para. 95). As such, pursuing prosecution in Afghanistan was not in the interests of justice. The Pre-Trial Chamber's decision was overturned by the Appeals Chamber in March 2020.[29]

Judge Edelbi's rewritten version of that 2020 decision agrees with the Appeals Chamber's verdict, but takes the decision further. She underscores that the interests of justice test in the Rome Statute is a negative test, and that the Afghanistan investigation is in the interests of justice unless it is clear that potential victims consider that an investigation would harm them. However, Edelbi extends the reasoning, noting that the ICC's task is a complex one: to provide justice for victims in situations where national avenues for justice are limited or unavailable, but to do this within its own legal system of the Rome Statute that is itself limited and cannot provide real redress for the many victims and many crimes of, in this case, the Afghanistan situation. Judge Edelbi also adds a dimension of meta reflection to her decision, noting that the abstract reasoning of the ICC creates a false sense of detachment and objectivity. While some consider abstraction necessary for judicial decision making, it can be counterproductive to the interests of justice for victims who seek accountability from the Court.

Critical Reflection

Reading the rewritten decisions was an interesting experience for us. First, because they focused much more on gender-based and sexual crimes than the original decisions did. Second, because some of the rewritten decisions broadened the scope from the immediate violations to showing the cost of conflict in terms of lost socio-economic opportunities and the crippling effects of conflict-related trauma. And, finally, because these reimagined judgments focus on violations by all parties to the conflict, not just one side of the conflict. The decision by the ICC Prosecutor to mainly focus on the violations committed by the Taliban over the past two decades

[28] One of the authors of this chapter has written about it together with colleagues at the Afghanistan Analysts Network, see www.afghanistan-analysts.org/en/reports/rights-freedom/legal-arguments-and-war-crimes-the-icc-appeals-hearing-on-afghanistan-in-five-questions/. Under the heading the 'ICC abandons the field', Human Rights Watch also questioned the Court's decision, see at www.hrw.org/news/2019/04/23/afghanistan-icc-abandons-field.

[29] ICC 02/17-138 (5 March 2020).

gives the impression that a generation of violations have been swept under the carpet. The rewritten statements counterbalance this, emphasising that the past two decades, violations have been committed by the Taliban and other non-state armed groups, but also by the Islamic Republic and its international allies.

Since the late 1970s, Afghans have lived with conflict and/or repressive governments. Women's rights have been an ideological football throughout the conflict, and the conflict itself has cemented discriminatory attitudes and harmful customary practices. As lamented by a female judge whom one of the authors interviewed several years back, Afghanistan is the only country where the next generation is always more conservative and less educated than the previous one.[30]

For many proponents of transitional justice in Afghanistan, an ICC prosecution is the only remaining hope for some form of accountability. While it is important that the ICC pursues its investigation into Afghanistan, it will take time for the Prosecutor to build cases against specific individuals, and even the most ambitious prosecution strategy would only capture a fraction of the possible cases. While the original preliminary analysis by the Prosecutor focused on alleged crimes committed by all parties to the Afghan conflict, his final decision means that there will be no accountability for crimes committed by the Islamic Republic and its international allies. The decision will also not help the often-voiced criticism that the ICC is a European or Western court, as opposed to a truly *international* criminal court.

The challenge for any efforts to reimagine ICC decisions on the Afghanistan situation is that they all focus on the time prior to the withdrawal of US forces from Afghanistan, before the fall of the Islamic Republic and the Taliban takeover, and the current period of the Taliban as the de facto government of Afghanistan. The Taliban is of course also an exceptionally misogynistic and brutal regime. A refreshing feature of the rewritten decisions is that all the judges expand the view to focus on alleged crimes committed by all parties to the conflict. Consequently, the rewritten decisions do not fall into the all-too-common trap of (Western) feminist analysis of viewing Afghan women as oppressed victims to be saved by the United States and its allies.

All the rewritten decisions for the Afghanistan situation not only take a more complex approach to the violations suffered by Afghan women, but they also expand the focus of the ICC's decisions in a few important ways. First, the rewritten decisions focus extensively on sexual and gender-based violations committed by all parties to the conflict, including how sexual humiliation was allegedly part of both the US and the Islamic Republic's repertoire in detention. The focus on these crimes shows the gendered nature of conflict itself and the extent to which power is sexualised in conflict and that this needs to be recognised and addressed by the ICC and other post-conflict justice mechanisms. Second, the rewritten statements also

[30] Interview with female judge in Kabul 2013. The interview was part of a series of interviews conducted for a research project on change from a gendered perspective. The research was published as S. Kouvo and C. Levine, 'Law as a Placeholder for Change? Women's Rights and Realities in Afghanistan' in K. Rubenstein and K. G. Young (eds.), *The Public Law of Gender: From the Local to the Global* (Cambridge: Cambridge University Press, 2016).

focus on the broader effects of conflict, making the socio-economic consequences relevant for the contextual understanding of the ICC's decision. That is, while the ICC may focus only on specific crimes, it is important to understand these crimes in the wider context of conflict. This last point is particularly significant in the case of ICC proceedings on Afghanistan. The ICC is currently the only existing accountability mechanism focusing on Afghanistan, and even in the best-case scenario it will only focus on a fraction of the violations committed over the past two decades. Afghans have faced uncountable violations in a conflict that has been going on for over four decades.

It is interesting to try to do a feminist reinterpretation *within* law, as these reimagined judgments have done. However, if we think beyond the limitations of the Rome Statute, and provide a meta reflection, the complexities of the Afghanistan case become much more apparent, and it reminds us that law can only ever provide a partial solution. For the sake of the many victims of gross violations, it is also important to recognise that the language of law does not capture the experiences of all those who have suffered. Accountability for gross violations is important, but it very seldom equals justice. It is important that feminist judicial reimaginings are clear about these limitations, while also recognising the need to also look elsewhere to achieve accountability and change.

16.2 THE JURISDICTION TEST IN THE AFGHANISTAN INVESTIGATION

Mashal Aamir and Adrienne Ringin

In 2017, the Prosecutor requested authorisation from the ICC Pre-Trial Chamber to initiate an investigation into alleged war crimes and crimes against humanity committed on the territory of the Islamic Republic of Afghanistan since 1 May 2003.[31] In 2019, Pre-Trial Chamber II denied that request, stating that such an investigation would not be in the interests of justice.[32] This decision was subsequently overturned unanimously by the Appeals Chamber in 2020.[33]

In their rewritten version of that 2019 Pre-Trial Chamber decision, Mashal Aamir and Adrienne Ringin reconsider the evidence used to determine the jurisdiction test. As in the real decision, Aamir and Ringin find that there is satisfactory evidence that crimes within the Court's jurisdiction were committed, but they use the information

[31] Public redacted version of Request for Authorisation of an Investigation pursuant to Article 15, 20 November 2017, ICC-02/17-7-Conf-Exp, *Situation in Afghanistan* (ICC-02/17-7-Red), Pre-Trial Chamber III, 20 November 2017.

[32] Decision pursuant to Article 15 of the Rome Statute on the Authorisation of an Investigation into the Situation in the Islamic Republic of Afghanistan, *Situation in Afghanistan* (ICC-02/17-33), Pre-Trial Chamber II, 12 April 2019.

[33] Judgment on the appeal against the Decision on the Authorisation of an Investigation into the Situation in the Islamic Republic of Afghanistan, *Situation in Afghanistan* (ICC-02/17-138), Appeals Chamber, 5 March 2020.

presented to the original Chamber to further emphasise the satisfaction of the jurisdiction test and thereby centre the lived experiences of victims throughout the decision.

No.: ICC-02/17
Date: 12 April 2019

Original: English

PRE-TRIAL CHAMBER II(B)

Before: Judge Mashal AAMIR, Presiding Judge
Judge Adrienne RINGIN
SITUATION IN THE ISLAMIC REPUBLIC OF AFGHANISTAN

Public

Decision pursuant to Article 15 of the Rome Statute on the Authorisation of an Investigation into the Situation in the Islamic Republic of Afghanistan

PRE-TRIAL CHAMBER II(B) (the Chamber) of the International Criminal Court (the Court) issues this Decision pursuant to Article 15 of the Rome Statute (the Statute) on the authorisation of an investigation into the situation in the Islamic Republic of Afghanistan (Afghanistan).

This request originates from a *proprio motu* examination conducted on the initiative of the Office of the Prosecutor in accordance with Article 15(1) of the Statute.

HISTORY

1. The situation in Afghanistan has been in a state of flux, particularly since the events of 11 September 2001 and the resultant global 'War on Terror'.[34] There have been numerous incidents of both brief and protracted conflict within the territory, initiated by various actors. This turbulence has led to continued suffering by the people of Afghanistan. In 2016 alone there was a 66 per cent increase in the number of people fleeing their homes due to conflict, 56 per cent of whom were children.[35] Indeed, even at this early stage of examination, the Court has received 699 representations on behalf of victims including 668 representations on behalf of 6,220 individuals, 17 representations on behalf of 1,690 families, 13 representations on behalf of several millions of victims including 26 villages, and 1 representation on behalf of an institution.[36]

[34] Public redacted version of Request for Authorisation of an Investigation pursuant to Article 15, 20 November 2017, ICC-02/17-7-Conf-Exp, Situation in Afghanistan (ICC-02/17-7-Red), Pre-Trial Chamber III, 20 November 2017, §§ 2, 15–18 (hereafter OTP Request).

[35] United Nations Assistance Mission in Afghanistan, *Afghanistan: Protection of Civilians in Armed Conflict – Annual Report 2016*, February 2017, available at https://unama.unmissions.org/sites/default/files/protection_of_civilians_in_armed_conflict_annual_report_2016_final280317.pdf, at 36–37 (hereafter UNAMA 2016 Annual Report).

[36] Annex 1-Red to the Final Consolidated Registry Report on Victims' Representations pursuant to the Pre-Trial Chamber's Order ICC-02/17-6 of 9 November 2017, *Situation in Afghanistan* (ICC-02/17-29-Anx1-Red), Pre-Trial Chamber III, 20 February 2018, §§ 23, 28–29.

2. Afghanistan acceded to the Statute on 10 February 2003, therefore accepting the jurisdiction of the Court over Article 5 crimes, genocide, war crimes, crimes against humanity, and aggression committed on its territory after 1 May 2003.[37]

3. The Office of the Prosecutor (OTP) began conducting a preliminary examination of the situation in Afghanistan in 2006.[38] This led to an official request on 20 November 2017 through the submission of the Request for authorisation of an investigation pursuant to Article 15 (the Request). Through the Request, the OTP petitions the Pre-Trial Chamber

> to authorise the commencement of an investigation into the Situation in the Islamic Republic of Afghanistan in relation to alleged crimes committed on the territory of Afghanistan in the period since 1 May 2003, as well as other alleged crimes that have a nexus to the armed conflict in Afghanistan and are sufficiently linked to the situation and were committed on the territory of other States Parties in the period since I July 2002.[39]

4. The OTP has deliberately excluded from the Request acts that occurred on the territory of Cuba, namely at Guantanamo Bay. The Chamber will therefore not make a comment on that topic in this decision.

5. The Request specifies the following actors as those responsible for the crimes committed: (1) The Taliban and other armed groups; (2) Afghan forces; and (3) Forces of the United States of America (US forces) and the Central Intelligence Agency (CIA).[40]

6. The Chamber wishes to emphasise that at this stage of the proceedings, all persons, organisations, and acts mentioned in this decision are alleged and that decisions of other Chambers at later dates will deliberate on the veracity of such allegations.

7. The Chamber draws attention to the implicit assertion made by the OTP that, despite the length of time Afghanistan has endured conflict, there has been a distinct lack of prosecution for the crimes at domestic, regional, and international levels. While it is not the place of this Chamber to make a determination at this stage, and leaving open the possibility for dispute from concerned parties, the Chamber wishes to note that should this allegation be true, then there has been a distinct failure of the international global community in allowing ongoing impunity for such crimes.[41]

[37] OTP Request, *supra* note 34, §§ 2, 50.

[38] *Ibid*, § 22.

[39] *Ibid*, § 376.

[40] *Ibid*, §§ 53–71.

[41] See Decision pursuant to Article 15 of the Rome Statute on the Authorisation of an Investigation into the Situation in the Republic of Kenya, *Situation in the Republic of Kenya* (ICC-01/09-19-Corr), Pre-Trial Chamber II, 31 March 2010, §§ 17–63; Corrigendum to Decision pursuant to Article 15 of the Rome Statute on the Authorisation of an Investigation into the Situation in the Republic of Côte d'Ivoire, *Situation in the Republic of Côte d'Ivoire* (ICC-02/11-14-Corr), Pre-Trial Chamber III, 15 November 2011, §§ 16–18.

ELEMENTS OF JURISDICTION

8. The test for jurisdiction is satisfied through the fulfilment of three separate checks: *ratione loci* or *personae*, *ratione materiae*, and *ratione temporis*.

9. To satisfy the jurisdiction test, the OTP has relied on evidence from organisations and bodies such as the following: the United National Assistance Mission in Afghanistan (UNAMA), the Afghanistan Independent Human Rights Commission (AIHRC), Amnesty International (AI), Human Rights Watch (HRW), Physicians for Human Rights (PHR), the CIA, the United States Senate Select Committee on Intelligence, the United States Senate Armed Services Committee, and the United States Department of Defence.

10. While at this stage of the analysis the Chamber is limited to the evidence placed before it, the Chamber notes that it considers the information relied upon to be from reputable sources and therefore, at this stage of the proceedings, there is no reason to doubt the information presented before this Chamber.

11. The Chamber will turn to an analysis of each of these elements in the present application.

Ratione Loci *or* Ratione Personae

12. Article 12(2) is satisfied should either *ratione loci* or *ratione personae* be met, that is, whether the alleged crimes were committed on the territory of a state party by a national of any state, or by a national of a state party on any territory.

13. As Afghanistan is a party to the Rome Statute, *ratione loci* is satisfied concerning the crimes committed on the territory of Afghanistan by the Taliban and other forces, Afghan forces, US forces, and the CIA.

14. Turning to the crimes committed on the territory of the states parties, the Republic of Poland, Romania, and the Republic of Lithuania, the Chamber notes that the temporal period articulated in the Request is specific to when a non-international armed conflict was occurring. In this way, the Chamber is required to analyse whether there is a sufficient nexus between the crimes and the armed conflict.

15. The Chamber wishes to reinforce that an analysis of each situation will reveal whether sufficient nexus has been achieved. The test is not as simplistic as to whether or not a criminal act occurred on a specific territory of interest. Rather, it is whether the criminal act occurred in the context of and associated with the armed conflict on the specific territory of interest.

16. This interpretation accords with the originating article, Article 3 of the four Geneva Conventions, and subsequently reflected in Article 8 of the Elements of Crime, whereby the nexus requirement is stated as 'the conduct took place in the context of and was associated with an international armed conflict [or alternatively not of an international character]'. Note the lack of reference to territory.

17. The Chamber therefore agrees with the OTP that 'the transfer of a detainee outside of a theatre of armed conflict does not render the protections to which he/she is entitled under international humanitarian law inapplicable' and that the detention and treatment of detainees on the territories of Lithuania, Poland, and Romania after their detention and treatment in Afghanistan does constitute a sufficient nexus.[42]

18. To avoid confusion, this finding does not provide legitimacy, tacit or otherwise, to whether the crimes were committed by any of the parties so far nominated. The Chamber is instead concerned with the correct interpretation of the relevant law. A decision regarding the committal of any offence on any territory will be made by an appropriate Chamber at an appropriate date. Parties concerned may then avail themselves of the Article 19(2) procedure to challenge the question of jurisdiction.

Ratione Materiae

19. For jurisdiction to be satisfied, the subject matter must be categorised as one of the crimes in Article 5: genocide, crimes against humanity, war crimes, or the crime of aggression.

20. The OTP states that, based on the information acquired so far, there is a reasonable basis to believe that incidents amounting to crimes against humanity and/or war crimes have occurred.

21. The Chamber will now examine the information provided.

Contextual Elements of Crimes against Humanity and War Crimes …

22. [. . .] Therefore, the Chamber agrees that that contextual elements of crimes against humanity and war crimes have been satisfied.

Taliban and Other Armed Groups

23. The OTP has limited its application to the conduct of the Taliban and its affiliate, the Haqqani Network.[43]

24. The Request categorises the following crimes against humanity under Article 7 against the Taliban and Haqqani Network: murder (Article 7(1)(a)), imprisonment or other severe deprivation of physical liberty (Article 7(1)(e)), and political and gender persecution (Article 7(1)(h)).

25. The Request further categorises the following war crimes under Article 8 against the Taliban and Haqqani Network: murder (Article 8(2)(c)(i)), intentionally directing attacks against the civilian population (Article 8(2)(e)(i)), intentionally directing attacks against humanitarian personnel (Article 8(2)(e)(iii)), intentionally

[42] OTP Request, *supra* note 34, § 251.

[43] *Ibid*, § 53.

directing attacks against protected objects (Article 8(2)(e)(iv)), conscripting or enlisting children under the age of fifteen or using them to participate actively in hostilities (Article 8(2)(e)(vii)), and killing or wounding treacherously a combatant adversary (Article 8(2)(e)(ix)).

26. The Chamber recognises, but does not validate, the existence of the *Layha*, a document utilised by the Taliban and referred to as a type of Code of Conduct.[44] The Chamber gives no weight to the assertion that such a document negates the formal, institutionalised, and universally approved laws of war.

27. The following acts are illustrative of conduct that the OTP claims the Taliban or the Haqqani Network have declared responsibility for or have been implicated in:

MURDER – ARTICLE 7(1)(A) AND ARTICLE 8(2)(C)(I)

(a) in september 2006, director of women's affairs safiye amajan was executed in kandahar province. taliban commander mullah hayat khan stated 'she worked for the government ... "we have told people again and again that anyone working for the government, and that includes women, will be killed"'.[45]
(b) In 2010, UNAMA and AIHRC documented 381 assassinations and executions.[46]
(c) In 2016, the Taliban claimed responsibility for 149 civilian causalities from targeted and deliberate killings.[47]

IMPRISONMENT OR OTHER SEVERE DEPRIVATION OF PHYSICAL LIBERTY – ARTICLE 7(1)(E)

(a) In 2007, a man was detained by the Taliban for three months, allegedly due to his brother working as a Prosecutor.[48]
(b) In January 2008, a man was abducted by the Taliban and only released after accepting the demand for his wife to cease her teaching job and after the provision of a financial payment.[49]

44 See Amnesty International, 'Afghanistan: All who are not friends, are enemies: Taleban abuses against civilians', 19 April 2007, available at www.amnesty.org/en/documents/asa11/001/2007/en/ , at 45 for an example of the *Layha* (hereafter Amnesty International All Who Are Not Friends Report).

45 *Ibid*, at 23.

46 United Nations Assistance Mission in Afghanistan, *Afghanistan: Protection of Civilians in Armed Conflict – Annual Report 2010*, March 2011, available at https://unama.unmissions.org/sites/default/files/engi_version_of_poc_annual_report_2011.pdf; https://unama.unmissions.org/sites/default/files/protection_of_civilians_in_armed_conflict_annual_report_2016_final280317.pdf, at 11 (hereafter UNAMA 2010 Annual Report).

47 UNAMA 2016 Annual Report, *supra* note 35, at 64.

48 Afghanistan Independent Human Rights Commission, 'Insurgent Abuses against Afghan Civilians', December 2008, available at www.legal-tools.org/doc/b961fc/pdf/, at 19 (hereafter AIHRC Insurgent Abuses 2008).

49 *Ibid*, at 18.

POLITICAL AND GENDER-BASED PERSECUTION – ARTICLE 7(1)(H)

(a) The 2009 provincial and parliamentary elections were deemed insecure enough that women candidates from Kandahar campaigned from outside the province,[50] while 196 of the 200 students reportedly poisoned were female.[51]

(b) On 3 June 2011, the head of the Bamyan provincial council was abducted and his body was found on 7 June 2011.[52]

INTENTIONALLY DIRECTING ATTACKS AGAINST THE CIVILIAN POPULATION – ARTICLE 8(2)(E)(I)

(a) In December 2005, Taliban insurgents demanded that farmers pay tax. Those who could not afford to pay financially were reportedly told to pay in kind, including being beaten, shot, or having their sons abducted.[53]

(b) On 25 October 2006, Taliban spokesperson Qari Yousef Ahmadi stated: 'There is no difference between the armed people who are fighting against us and civilians who are co-operating with foreigners.'[54]

(c) In May 2011, the Haqqani network claimed responsibility for the deaths of thirty-six construction workers and the wounding of thirteen others when a road construction company was attacked in Paktika province.[55]

(d) In 2016 the Taliban claimed responsibility for 358 civilian deaths, 1,106 civilian causalities, and 260 civilian abductions through 225 incidents.[56]

INTENTIONALLY DIRECTING ATTACKS AGAINST HUMANITARIAN PERSONNEL – ARTICLE 8(2)(E)(III)

(a) In June 2011, the Taliban claimed responsibility for a twenty-year-old female suicide bomber attack on an international military convoy in Marawara district, Kunar province.[57]

(b) The Aid Worker Security Database recorded twenty-seven attacks against humanitarian personnel during 2015.[58] Three of those attacks

[50] Human Rights Watch, '"We Have the Promises of the World" – Women's Rights in Afghanistan', 6 December 2009, available at www.hrw.org/report/2009/12/06/we-have-promises-world/womens-rights-afghanistan (hereafter HRW Promises of the World).

[51] Ibid.

[52] United Nations Assistance Mission in Afghanistan, *Afghanistan: Protection of Civilians in Armed Conflict – Mid-Year Report 2011*, 14 June 2011, available at https://reliefweb.int/report/afghanistan/mid-year-report-2011-protection-civilians-armed-conflict, at 19 (hereafter UNAMA 2011 Mid-Year Report).

[53] Amnesty International All Who Are Not Friends Report, *supra* note 44, at 30.

[54] *Ibid*, at 11.

[55] UNAMA 2011 Mid-Year Report, *supra* note 52, at 13.

[56] UNAMA 2016 Annual Report, *supra* note 35, at 75.

[57] UNAMA 2011 Mid-Year Report, *supra* note 52, at 5.

[58] Aid Worker Security Database, 'Afghanistan 2015', available at https://aidworkersecurity.org/incidents/search?start=2015&end=2015&detail=1&country=AF.

were attributed to the Taliban while the rest were largely identified as 'unknown' or 'not applicable'.[59]

INTENTIONALLY DIRECTING ATTACKS AGAINST PROTECTED OBJECTS – ARTICLE 8(2)(E)(IV)

(a) From April to August 2009, 102 schools were attacked leading to the deaths of 105 students and teachers.[60]
(b) In May 2011, the Taliban claimed responsibility for an attack on a military hospital in Kabul which killed six students and wounded twenty-three others.[61]
(c) The UNAMA 2012 mid-year report found seventy-four incidents against schools and education. These incidents included burning of schools, threats to teaching staff, improvised explosive devices (IEDs) near schools and fourteen incidents of occupation of schools.[62]
(d) In 2013, attacks against mullahs and places of worships tripled.[63]

CONSCRIPTING OR ENLISTING CHILDREN UNDER THE AGE OF FIFTEEN OR USING THEM TO PARTICIPATE IN HOSTILITIES – ARTICLE 8(2)(E)(VII)

(a) On 12 February 2007, local Afghani children were used as human shields during fighting in Kajaki district, Helmand province.[64]
(b) A 2017 Human Rights Watch report detailed thirteen boys who were recruited to various Taliban units, some when under the age of fifteen, and who were subsequently active in hostilities.[65] Two of these boys, Qasem, fifteen, and Ahmad, fourteen, were killed after being deployed during a ground incident with Afghan forces.[66]

59 *Ibid.*

60 HRW Promises of the World, *supra* note 50.

61 UNAMA 2011 Mid-Year Report, *supra* note 52, at 4.

62 United Nations Assistance Mission in Afghanistan, *Afghanistan: Protection of Civilians in Armed Conflict – Annual Report 2012*, February 2013, available at https://unama.unmissions.org/sites/default/files/2012_annual_report_eng_0.pdf, at 12 (hereafter UNAMA 2012 Annual Report).

63 United Nations Assistance Mission in Afghanistan, *Afghanistan: Protection of Civilians in Armed Conflict – Annual Report 2013*, February 2014, available at https://unama.unmissions.org/sites/default/files/feb_8_2014_poc-report_2013-full-report-eng.pdf, at 29 (hereafter UNAMA 2013 Annual Report).

64 Amnesty International All Who Are Not Friends Report, *supra* note 44, at 12.

65 Human Rights Watch, 'Afghanistan: Taliban Child Soldier Recruitment Surges', 17 February 2016, available at www.hrw.org/news/2016/02/18/afghanistan-taliban-child-soldier-recruitment-surges (hereafter HRW Child Soldier Recruitment).

66 *Ibid.*

KILLING OR WOUNDING TREACHEROUSLY A COMBATANT ADVERSARY – ARTICLE 8(2)(E)(IX)

(a) In April 2011, the Taliban used an ambulance to conduct a suicide attack on a police training centre in Kandahar.[67]

(b) On 6 December 2012, a male suicide bomber falsely presented himself as a peace envoy before detonating himself in an attempt to kill the National Directorate for Security (NDS) chief, Asadullah Khalid.[68]

28. Victims have spoken about the impact of experiencing such events:

(i) A man in Zabul province stated: 'After receiving this warning [about his daughters attending school] I disconnected my phone. Since that time, I have stopped my two daughters from attending school.'[69]

(ii) A victim of a remote-controlled improvised explosive device stated: 'Since that day, my life has changed for the worse. My leg is injured and is often painful. I can no longer walk easily to attend lessons at university. Sometimes, I hear children crying as I remember that terrible day.'[70]

(iii) Kathreen Wida, the editor of *Cheragh Daily* explained: 'Women journalists have been murdered, like Zakia Zaki and Shakiba Sanga Amaaj, so of course I worry that the same thing will happen to me . . . I worry for my children.'[71]

(iv) The difficulty faced by health officials are evidenced by the following: 'We were . . . transferring a pregnant woman in an ambulance. Suddenly, Anti-Government Elements opened fire on the ambulance and wounded the patient in her neck . . . After two hours, and negotiations by community elders with the Anti-Government Elements, it was clear to them that the ambulance was transporting a pregnant woman and not any Afghan Local Police members. They finally allowed us to transfer the patient to Mehterlam public hospital for treatment.'[72]

(v) The relative of a fifteen-year-old boy, Mati, who was recruited by the Taliban, stated: 'They cheated him. Mati's uncle went to bring him back, but the Taliban would not let him go . . . Then fighting [with Afghan government forces] erupted [in July 2015], and . . . Mati was killed in an airstrike.'[73]

67 UNAMA 2011 Mid-Year Report, *supra* note 52, at 14.

68 Agence France Presse, 'Afghan spy chief wounded by underpants bomber', NDTV, 7 December 2012, available at www.ndtv.com/world-news/afghan-spy-chief-wounded-by-underpants-bomber-506851.

69 AIHRC Insurgent Abuses 2008, *supra* note 48, at 17.

70 UNAMA 2016 Annual Report, *supra* note 35, at 52.

71 HRW Promises of the World, *supra* note 50.

72 UNAMA 2016 Annual Report, *supra* note 35, at 27.

73 HRW Child Soldier Recruitment, *supra* note 65.

(vi) Nasima Niazi explained her decision not to contest an election in 2010 due to the security risks: 'Every day when I leave home to go to parliament, I fear that they might blow me up, so I say goodbye to my daughters, and give them advice, and leave them some money just in case I don't come back.'[74]

(vii) A community elder described: 'The local population cannot say anything against the Taliban, or to the benefit of the government since they are always scared of being executed by the Taliban in accusation of spying for the government.'[75]

(viii) A female police officer stated after her close encounter with a suicide attack: 'My daughter is nine years old and every day before I leave for work she cries and says "Mama don't go to work. I don't need to eat".'[76]

Afghan Forces

29. The Afghan National Defence and Security Forces (ANSF) consists of several organs such as: the Afghan National Army (ANA), the Afghan Air Force (AAF), the NDS, the Afghan National Police (ANP), the Afghan Local Police (ALP), and the Afghan National Border Police (ANBP).

30. The Request alleges the following war crimes under Article 8: torture and cruel treatment (Article 8(2)(c)(i)), outrages upon personal dignity (Article 8(2)(c)(ii)), and sexual violence (Article 8(2)(e)(vi)). These alleged incidents have taken place at various ANSF facilities throughout the territory of Afghanistan.[77]

31. The Chamber notes the inability to provide a 'bright line' test to differentiate between the crimes of torture, cruel and degrading treatment, and outrage upon personal dignity. In this way, the Chamber agrees with the reality that 'experience demonstrates that the conditions that give rise to ill-treatment frequently facilitate torture and therefore the measures required to prevent torture must be applied to prevent ill-treatment'.[78]

[74] HRW Promises of the World, *supra* note 50.

[75] United Nations Assistance Mission in Afghanistan, *Afghanistan: Protection of Civilians in Armed Conflict – Mid-Year Report 2012*, July 2012, available at https://unama.unmissions.org/sites/default/files/2012_mid-year_report.pdf, at 27 (hereafter UNAMA 2012 Mid-Year Report).

[76] United Nations Assistance Mission in Afghanistan, *Afghanistan: Protection of Civilians in Armed Conflict – Annual Report 2011*, February 2012, available at https://unama.unmissions.org/sites/default/files/unama_poc_report_final_feb_2012.pdf, at 16 (hereafter UNAMA 2011 Annual Report).

[77] OTP Request, *supra* note 34, § 165.

[78] United Nations Assistance Mission in Afghanistan, *Treatment of Conflict Related Detainees: Implementation of Afghanistan's National Plan on the Elimination of Torture*, April 2017, available at https://unama.unmissions.org/sites/default/files/treatment_of_conflict-related_detainees_24_april_2017.pdf, at 6 (hereafter UNAMA 2017 National Plan on the Elimination of Torture).

32. The Chamber notes that UNAMA has been systematically reporting on the treatment of conflict-related detainees since 2011 and has revealed a continued disregard for the protection and proper treatment of such persons.[79]

33. The use of torture to elicit confessions during interrogations had implicit approval, as was articulated by a provincial chief of the ANP Criminal Investigation Department: 'All suspects have the right to remain silent. That presents an obstacle to our police work. What can we do if they don't speak? We have to find out what happened; we need to use certain methods to find out what really happened.'[80]

34. Information gathered has revealed the following acts as being illustrative of those which allegedly occurred:

TORTURE AND CRUEL TREATMENT – ARTICLE 8(2)(C)(I)

(a) UNAMA and AIHRC reports detail the following: beatings on the soles of the feet, legs, shoulders, back, and chest with instruments such as cables, pipes, hoses, and/or wooden sticks; punching, hitting, kicking, and/or jumping on a detainee's body; suspension by the wrists for a period of time; electric shocks; forced prolonged standing; stress positions – such as standing and sitting down repeatedly and standing outside in cold weather conditions for long periods; use of cigarette lighters to burn the soles of detainees' feet; removal of fingernails and/or toe nails; and the stuffing of cloth or plastic bags in the mouths of detainees in order to cause asphyxiation.[81]

OUTRAGES UPON PERSONAL DIGNITY – ARTICLE 8(2)(C)(II)

(a) UNAMA and AIHRC reports detail the following: forced drinking of excessive amounts of water; denial of food, water, and prayer time; threats of execution and/or sexual assault.[82]

79 United Nations Assistance Mission in Afghanistan, *Treatment of Conflict Related Detainees in Afghan Custody 2011*, October 2011, available at https://unama.unmissions.org/sites/default/files/october10_2011_unama_detention_full-report_eng.pdf (hereafter UNAMA 2011 Treatment of Conflict-Related Detainees); United Nations Assistance Mission in Afghanistan, *Treatment of Conflict Related Detainees in Afghan Custody 2013*, January 2013, available at https://unama.unmissions.org/sites/default/files/master_unama_detention_report_20_jan_2013_final.pdf (hereafter UNAMA 2013 Treatment of Conflict-Related Detainees); United Nations Assistance Mission in Afghanistan, *Update on the Treatment of Conflict Related Detainees in Afghan Custody 2015: Accountability and Implementation of Presidential Decree 129*, February 2015, available at https://unama.unmissions.org/sites/default/files/unama_detention_report_2015_revised.pdf (hereafter UNAMA 2015 Treatment of Conflict-Related Detainees); UNAMA 2017 National Plan on the Elimination of Torture, *supra* note 78.

80 UNAMA 2015 Treatment of Conflict-Related Detainees, *supra* note 79, at 53.

81 OTP Request, *supra* note 34, § 166.

82 UNAMA 2011 Treatment of Conflict-Related Detainees, *supra* note 79, at 19, 29, 30; UNAMA 2013 Treatment of Conflict-Related Detainees, *supra* note 79, at 4, 50; UNAMA 2015 Treatment of Conflict-Related Detainees, *supra* note 79, at 19, 71, 123; UNAMA 2017 National Plan on the Elimination of Torture, *supra* note 78, at 7, 37; Afghanistan

(b) In October 2016, ANA Special Forces reportedly stripped a seventeen-year-old boy naked and photographed him at a school in Paktya province.[83]

SEXUAL VIOLENCE – ARTICLE 8(2)(E)(VI)

(a) UNAMA and AIHRC reports detail the following: deliberate injuries to the genitalia of victims by twisting, squeezing, beating, or burning their penises and/or testicles including with pliers or wrench-like devices; administering electric shocks to the testicles; hanging weights from the testicles; and whipping their penises and testicles with cables.[84]

(b) In 2012, ALP members were found to be involved in the process of *baad*, where a female member of a perpetrator's family was 'given' to a victim's family as compensation for a crime.[85]

(c) Also in 2012, a commander in the Chahardara district was found to have carried out or ordered torture, sexual assault, and ill treatment, including the sexual assault of a sixteen-year-old boy,[86] while in Baghlan province, an ALP commander detained five boys for five years who were reportedly sexually abused while performing the roles of bodyguards and 'dancing boys'.[87]

(d) In 2016, two incidents of sexual violence, including rape and sexual exploitation, against boys by the ALP were reported.[88]

35. Victims have recounted the following in relation to alleged experiences:

(i) 'He showed me a cable and said, "I will shock you with electricity." And then he shocked me [displays visible injury]. After that, I did not know where I was or who I was. When I was okay again, I saw that I was back in my cell. But both of my thumbs had ink on them. I did not know it, but they had taken my thumbprints [as proof of a confession].'[89]

(ii) '[O]ne of them held my penis in his hand and twisted it severely until I passed out. After I woke up, I had to confess because I could not stand the pain, and I did not want that to happen to me again and suffer the same severe and unbearable pain.'[90]

Independent Human Rights Commissions and Open Society Foundations, *Torture, Transfers and Denial of Due Process: The Treatment of Conflict-Related Detainees in Afghanistan*, 17 March 2012, at 43.

83 UNAMA 2016 Annual Report, *supra* note 35, at 21.

84 OTP Request, *supra* note 34, § 183.

85 UNAMA 2012 Mid-Year Report, *supra* note 75, at 43.

86 *Ibid*, at 46.

87 *Ibid*, at 56.

88 UNAMA 2016 Annual Report, *supra* note 35, at 21.

89 UNAMA 2011 Treatment of Conflict-Related Detainees, *supra* note 79, at 16.

90 *Ibid*, at 18–19.

(iii) 'I was beaten with a cable for half an hour and they accused me of being a Talib and being involved in a murder case. They beat my body cruelly and told me to confess. During the interrogation they also had two electric wires which they used on my body until I became unconscious. I forcibly confessed that I was involved in the person's killing. Then I was transferred to the NDS provincial facility, they again slapped me and one of them choked me four times. They wanted me to confess my membership of the Taliban but I denied this. They threatened me to death if I did not confess and so I did.'[91]

(iv) 'On the third day, NDS officials threatened me that they would insert a wooden stick pasted with chilli powder in my anal canal.'[92]

(v) 'They tied me on the door of the interrogation office and I was hanged from it for few hours and I was not feeling anything in my hands. The process continued for almost a week.'[93]

US Forces and the CIA

36. The Request states that in pursuit of answers to the 11 September 2001 attack, US forces and the CIA aggressively pursued a detention and interrogation plan of persons suspected of being connected to the planning and execution of the attack.[94] The existence and approval of this plan is demonstrated through official US reports, documentation, and authorisations as well as independent UN reports.[95]

37. During the course of this detention and interrogation plan, the Request alleges the following war crimes under Article 8 were committed: torture and cruel treatment (Article 8(2)(c)(i)), outrages upon personal dignity (Article 8(2)(c)(ii)), and rape and other forms of sexual violence (Article 8(2)(e)(vi)).

[91] UNAMA 2015 Treatment of Conflict-Related Detainees, *supra* note 79, at 44.

[92] UNAMA 2011 Treatment of Conflict-Related Detainees, *supra* note 79, at 22–23.

[93] UNAMA 2017 Treatment of Conflict-Related Detainees, *supra* note 79, at 26.

[94] OTP Request, *supra* note 34, §§ 230, 241.

[95] See Physicians for Human Rights, *Break Them Down: Systematic Use of Psychological Torture by US Forces*, 2005, available at https://phr.org/wp-content/uploads/2005/05/break-them-down.pdf, at 40, 'The psychologically abusive techniques formalized in 2003 for Afghanistan remained in effect until the Abu Ghraib scandal became public in May 2004'; and at 45, 'The UN Independent Expert on the Situation of Human Rights in Afghanistan, M. Cherif Bassiouni, visited the country in August 2004 and conducted research and consultations. He found that Coalition forces at that time were employing forced nudity, public embarrassment, sleep deprivation, prolonged standing, hooding, and sensory deprivation. A follow up report in March 2005 repeated the allegations of these abuses; at 15, 'In April 2005, a draft of the Administration's new detainee operations policy was leaked. Although the document says that there is no military exception to the requirement that detainees be treated humanely, it contradicts that statement only seven pages later by formalizing the category of "enemy combatant" and declaring that their humane treatment is subject to military necessity' (hereafter PHR Break Them Down).

38. The Request states that these crimes occurred in CIA-run detention facilities on the territory of Afghanistan and on the territory of third-party states such as Poland, Romania, and Lithuania predominantly during 2003–2004.[96]

39. The following information is illustrative of the acts alleged to have been conducted by the US forces and the CIA:

TORTURE AND CRUEL TREATMENT – ARTICLE 8(2)(C)(I)

(a) Documents reveal the use of: solitary confinement for various amounts of time; sensory deprivation including the use of black-out goggles and sound-blocking earphones; sensory over-stimulation including the use of loud music and flashing lights; stress positions; suspension including from the ceiling; sleep deprivation and/or manipulation; physical assault including grasping, slapping, hitting, or kicking, 'rough take downs',[97] and 'wallings';[98] confinement in small spaces such as boxes; 'water boarding',[99] water dousing or deluging, and/or placing detainees in ice baths.[100]

OUTRAGES UPON PERSONAL DIGNITY – ARTICLE 8(2)(C)(II)

(a) Documents reveal the use of: items of religious importance in an offensive way; sexual humiliation in the form of being exposed to a member of the opposite sex while naked; being photographed naked; diapering; phobias such as dogs to intimidate and threaten detainees; insulting language; food manipulation and/or deprivation; forced

96. OTP Request, *supra* note 34, § 189.

97 See *ibid*, at § 197: 'CIA detainees at the "Cobalt" detention facility in Afghanistan, for example, were "walked around naked or were shackled with their hands above their heads for extended periods of time", and "were subjected to what was described as a 'rough take down', in which approximately five CIA officers would scream at a detainee, drag him outside of his cell, cut his clothes off, and secure him with Mylar tape. The detainee would then be hooded and dragged up and down a long corridor while being slapped and punched".'

98 Wallings involve the detainee being forcibly thrown or slammed into an artificial wall by the interrogation team. For further information on this act, see Central Intelligence Agency, 'Background Paper on CIA's Combined Use of Interrogation Techniques', 30 December 2004, available at www.thetorturedatabase.org/document/fax-cia-olc-providing-generic-description-cias-combined-use-various-interrogation-technique, at 7 (hereafter CIA Background Paper); Senate Select Committee on Intelligence, 'Committee Study of the Central Intelligence Agency's Detention and Interrogation Program, Declassification Revisions', 3 December 2014, available at https://irp.fas.org/congress/2014_rpt/ssci-rdi.pdf, at 3–4 (hereafter Senate Select CIA Study); OTP Request, *supra* note 34, § 193(x).

99 See OTP Request, *supra* note 34, § 193(xiii), which explains water boarding as 'suffocation by water . . . which simulated drowning (and, potentially, imminent death) by pouring water over a cloth covering the mouth and nose of a restrained person'; see also the Senate Select CIA Study, *supra* note 98, at 3–4, which described water boarding as 'physically harmful, inducing convulsions and vomiting'.

100 OTP Request, *supra* note 34, at §§ 193–194. See also Senate Select CIA Study, *supra* note 98; CIA Background Paper, *supra* note 98; PHR Break Them Down, *supra* note 95.

nudity including in front of other detainees; being shown pornography; forced grooming; manipulation of the environment including the use of extreme cold or heat; and mock executions.[101]

RAPE AND OTHER FORMS OF SEXUAL VIOLENCE – ARTICLE 8(2)(E)(VI)

(a) Documents reveal the use of: physical sexual molestation; sexual assault by a female soldier; beatings focused on the testicles of a detainee; penetration of the anus; rectal feeding;[102] forced masturbation; and the posing of detainees in sexually degrading positions.[103]

40. The experience and the immediate as well as ongoing impact of such acts were articulated by victims either themselves or through the medium of a care institution:

(i) PHR notes: 'Short and long-term effects can include memory impairment, reduced capacity to concentrate, somatic complaints such as headache and back pain, hyperarousal, avoidance, irritability, severe depression with vegetative symptoms, nightmares, feelings of shame and humiliation, and posttraumatic stress disorder.'[104]

(ii) Some detainees reported 'depression, thoughts of suicide and nightmares, memory loss, emotional problems, and are quick to anger and have difficulties maintaining relationships and employment'.[105]

(iii) The Berlin Center for the Treatment of Torture Victims (CVT) found that 'Muslim victims of sexual torture forever carry a stigma and will often be ostracised by the community'[106] and that 'merely being stripped naked implies the breaking of a strict taboo, which leaves victims feeling extremely exposed and humiliated'.[107]

(iv) Said Nabi Siddiqi, an Afghan citizen allegedly detained at several facilities in Afghanistan between July and August 2003, reported that he 'has had depression, thoughts of suicide and nightmares, is quick to anger, and has suffered from memory loss'.[108]

[101] OTP Request, *supra* note 34, at §§ 193–194; PHR Break Them Down, *supra* note 95, at 7, 26. This documentary evidence include photographs concerning the mock executions of bound and hooded detainees at Fire Base Tycze, Dah Rah Wood in Afghanistan.

[102] OTP Request, *supra* note 34, at § 212. Public health experts have also disputed the existence of any medical justification for rectal feeding, which they describe as 'a technique of sexual assault' of which goal is 'dominance and punishment'.

[103] OTP Request, *supra* note 34, at § 216; Physicians for Human Rights, *Broken Laws, Broken Lives: Medical Evidence of Torture by US Personnel and Its Impact*, June 2008, available at https://phr.org/wp-content/uploads/2008/06/BrokenLaws_ExecSummary14.pdf, at 7 (hereafter PHR Broken Laws, Broken Lives).

[104] PHR Break Them Down, *supra* note 95, at 9.

[105] *Ibid.*

[106] *Ibid*, at 11–12, 57–58.

[107] *Ibid.*

[108] *Ibid*, at 53.

(v) Haji Abdul Rahman, allegedly detained at several facilities between December 2003 and May 2004, reported that he 'suffers vision problems and memory lapses, has emotional problems and is quick to anger, "which has caused difficulties with his family and work"'.[109]

(vi) Tarek Dergoul, allegedly detained at facilities in Afghanistan as well as Guantánamo Bay, reported: 'I get migraines, I'm depressed and I suffer from memory loss. There's stuff that happened, embedded in my head, that I can't remember.'[110]

Ratione Temporis

41. Article 11 restricts jurisdiction to crimes committed after the Statute came into force, which occurred on 1 July 2002. Where a state becomes a party after that date, then jurisdiction is held over crimes committed following the accession date. Afghanistan acceded to the Statute on 10 February 2003,[111] while Poland, Romania, and Lithuania ratified the Statute on 12 November 2001, 11 April 2002, and 12 May 2003 respectively.[112]

42. Therefore, *ratione temporis* is satisfied ...

THE IMPACT ON THE LIVES OF THE PEOPLE OF AFGHANISTAN

44. Decades of conflict in Afghanistan have left its citizens facing layered and multifaceted impacts. Mass migration to flee the instability has resulted in millions leaving their homes and seeking refuge in neighbouring states, such as the Islamic Republics of Pakistan and Iran.[113] Those who remain continue to suffer from a deteriorating security situation in many parts of the country and face routine attacks. The governor from a district of the Kandahar province explained:

> 45. The life of civilians in this district is extremely difficult. On the one hand, when the Taliban plants IEDs, civilians cannot defuse them for fear of Taliban reactions. If they defuse them, the Taliban will kill them. On the other hand, the government pressures people to tell them where and why the Taliban plants IEDs in their villages ... Civilians are stuck in between, and are always in trouble. There is no third source to listen to the people and solve these problems.[114]

46. The conflict has left local infrastructure, systems, and politics in a state of dilapidation. One area where the ramifications will continue to be seen is in the area

[109] *Ibid*.
[110] *Ibid*, at 54.
[111] OTP Request, *supra* note 34, §§ 2, 50.
[112] *Ibid*, § 51.
[113] *Ibid*, § 13.
[114] UNAMA 2012 Annual Report, *supra* note 62, at 62.

of education, where generational and cyclical poverty is endemic due to low literacy rates translating into limited employment options. Women in particular face insurmountable challenges in pursuit of education, first from a safety perspective and then from official decrees from the Taliban and Haqqani Network.[115] Refugee children face similar barriers to educational opportunities, particularly when they are forced to flee to states with little to no welfare support.

47. That children are constantly affected is a concern for this Chamber. This state of despair was articulated by a man who lost one of his nieces to an improvised explosive device in 2011, while another niece and his daughter were also injured: 'These children were not part of the conflict, they had very hopeful aspirations for their future, but this useless war took their future dreams and lives.'[116]

48. Health and medical services have suffered similarly. Afghanistan is one of only two countries in the world where polio is still endemic. The 'failure to deliver poliomyelitis vaccinations has serious consequences for children's health and a direct effect on the efforts to eradicate poliomyelitis in Afghanistan. Cases of polio in Afghanistan tripled in 2011, creating concern of a reversal of several years of decline'.[117]

49. The Chamber wishes to note that civilian deaths and injuries have also resulted from tactics used by pro-government forces.[118] While not addressed in the list of crimes thus far alleged, these should by no means be less regretted, or be overlooked or forgotten. Furthermore, evidence of rape and sexual assault is presented in the information provided but not brought forward at this stage. Therefore the Chamber calls upon the OTP to investigate such instances for inclusion if evidence dictates.

CONCLUSION ON JURISDICTION

50. In light of the above, the Chamber is satisfied that there is a reasonable basis to believe that the contextual elements of both crimes against humanity and war crimes are satisfied in respect of the alleged events, in particular in light of their scale and magnitude. Suffice to say, at this stage, that according to UNAMA, civilian

[115] OTP Request, *supra* note 34, §§ 116–118, 121; Amnesty International All Who Are Not Friends Report, *supra* note 44, at 2.

[116] UNAMA 2011 Mid-Year Report, *supra* note 52, at 1.

[117] UNAMA 2012 Mid-Year Report, *supra* note 75, at 30.

[118] See UNAMA 2010 Annual Report, *supra* note 46; UNAMA 2011 Annual Report, *supra* note 76; UNAMA 2012 Annual Report, *supra* note 62; UNAMA 2013 Annual Report, *supra* note 63; United Nations Assistance Mission in Afghanistan, *Afghanistan: Protection of Civilians in Armed Conflict – Annual Report 2014*, February 2015, available at https://unama.unmissions.org/sites/default/files/2014-annual-report-on-protection-of-civilians-final.pdf; United Nations Assistance Mission in Afghanistan, *Afghanistan: Protection of Civilians in Armed Conflict – Annual Report 2015*, February 2016, available at https://unama.unmissions.org/sites/default/files/poc_annual_report_2015_final_14_feb_2016.pdf; UNAMA 2016 Annual Report, *supra* note 35.

casualties in the period 2009–2016, as witnessed throughout the Afghan territory, exceed 50,000, of which 17,700 are deaths and over 33,000 injuries.[119]

Judge Mashal Aamir and Judge Adrienne Ringin

16.3 THE GRAVITY TEST IN THE AFGHANISTAN INVESTIGATION

Jill Marshall

In 2019, Pre-Trial Chamber II decided whether to authorise an investigation into crimes allegedly committed on the territory of the Islamic Republic of Afghanistan since 1 March 2003.[120] While the Chamber ultimately decided that an investigation would not be in the interests of justice, the Chamber did conclude that the crimes allegedly committed by the Afghani army, the Taliban, and American Central Intelligence Agency (CIA) forces against Afghani detainees were severe enough to merit passing the ICC's gravity test.

In this rewritten decision, Judge Marshall concurs with the original Chamber's finding through a critical engagement with the role of gender, and in particular sexual violence, prevalent in the crimes allegedly committed. In doing so, Marshall expands the section on gravity, allowing for an exploration of the intersectionality of race, ethnicity, and other social factors, placing the survivors at the centre of the discussion and analysing the actions of all protagonists in the conflict.

No.: ICC-02/17
Date: 12 April 2019

Original: English

PRE-TRIAL CHAMBER II(B)

Before: Judge Jill MARSHALL
SITUATION IN THE ISLAMIC REPUBLIC OF AFGHANISTAN

Public

Decision pursuant to Article 15 of the Rome Statute on the Authorisation of an Investigation into the Situation in the Islamic Republic of Afghanistan

119 The authors wish to note this paragraph comes from the original decision, Decision pursuant to Article 15 of the Rome Statute on the Authorisation of an Investigation into the Situation in the Islamic Republic of Afghanistan, *Situation in Afghanistan* (ICC-02/17-33), Pre-Trial Chamber II, 12 April 2019, § 66.

120 Decision pursuant to Article 15 of the Rome Statute on the Authorisation of an Investigation into the Situation in the Islamic Republic of Afghanistan, *Situation in Afghanistan* (ICC-02/17-33), Pre-Trial Chamber II, 12 April 2019.

INTRODUCTION

1. This Chamber notes the importance of victims' representations complementing and supplementing the information provided by the Prosecutor on the facts alleged in support of the Request. A high number of victims of the situation have come forward to present their views on whether the Chamber should authorise the commencement of this Prosecutor's investigation. The Court has received a large number of representations in various languages: 668 representations on behalf of 6,220 individuals; 17 representations on behalf of 1,690 families; 13 representations on behalf of several millions of victims, including 26 villages; and 1 representation on behalf of an institution. It is fundamental to hear the voices of women and girls, as well as other alleged victims and survivors of the acts falling under investigation. A survivor-centred approach is in keeping with norms and resolutions of other parts of international law, and international criminal law will be enriched by considering these issues holistically within the wide international legal framework.[121]

2. In terms of court procedure, Article 15 of the Rome Statute states that the Prosecutor may initiate an investigation on their own motion. Such investigation must be authorised by a pre-trial chamber with the assessment being provisional in nature because it is conducted in abstract pending commencement of investigations. To reinterpret and transform laws for a better, more just future as a court, we need to use those tools currently at our disposal as a starting point.[122]

ADMISSIBILITY ...

Gravity

19. The next decision relates to gravity. Any crime falling within the jurisdiction of this Court is serious. However, Article 17(l)(d) states that a case may be inadmissible if it 'is not of sufficient gravity to justify further action by the Court'. The prosecution makes detailed submissions arguing that all the crimes alleged in the Request meet the threshold of sufficient gravity. Assessing gravity is crucial, requiring information regarding those most responsible for the most serious crimes within the situation. Any assessment must be carried out consistently, irrespective of the states or parties involved, or the person(s) or group(s) concerned.[123]

20. The Rome Statute does not define gravity. It generally refers to the seriousness of the crimes but lacks a clear definition. The Appeals Chamber has dismissed the

[121] For example, United Nations Security Council Resolution 2467 (2019) which states that a survivor-centred approach is necessary to provide justice at a global level to survivors of gender-based violence.

[122] See R. Dworkin, *Taking Rights Seriously* (London: Duckworth, 1977); A. Lorde, *Sister Outsider* (Harmondsworth: Penguin Modern Classics, 2019, originally 1984).

[123] See the Office of the Prosecutor Policy Paper on Preliminary Examinations, November 2013, available at www.icc-cpi.int (hereafter OTP Policy Paper 2013).

setting of an overly restrictive legal bar to the interpretation of gravity that would hamper the deterrent role of the Court. It has also observed that the role of persons or groups may vary considerably depending on the circumstances of the case and therefore should not be exclusively assessed or predetermined on excessively formulistic grounds.[124]

21. The Court has read the detailed submissions from the prosecution and refers to selected relevant information within its assessment below.

Assessment

22. The assessment of gravity must be done from both a quantitative and a qualitative viewpoint. The factors that guide the prosecution's assessment include the scale, nature, manner of commission of the crimes, and their impact.[125] These factors are helpful in reaching this decision and will be used together with the Request's classification of three groups allegedly responsible for the crimes, namely: the Taliban and affiliated forces; the Afghan National Security Forces and others (ANSF); and US forces and the CIA. The persons or groups of persons identified in accordance with Regulation 49(2)(c) include persons with levels of responsibility in directing, ordering, facilitating, or otherwise contributing to the commission of alleged crimes. The persons or groups of persons so identified include those who devised, authorised, or bore oversight responsibility for the implementation of the incidents, including persons with levels of responsibility for interrogating detainees within a given facility or region, and developing, authorising, directing, supervising, and implementing the commission of alleged crimes.

WHAT IS THE SCALE, NATURE, AND MANNER OF COMMISSION OF THE CRIMES AND THEIR IMPACT?

scale

23. What is 'scale' and how is it assessed? In line with past practice of this Court, factors to consider include:

(i) the number of direct and indirect victims;
(ii) the extent of the damage caused by the crimes, in particular the bodily or psychological harm caused to the victims and their families;

[124] See *Situation in the Democratic Republic of the Congo*, Judgment on the Prosecutor's Appeal against the Decision of Pre-Trial Chamber I entitled 'Decision on the Prosecutor's Application for Warrants of Arrest, Article 58' (ICC-01/04-169), under seal 13 July 2006; reclassified public 23 September 2008, §§ 69–79.

[125] As stipulated in Regulation 29(2) of the Regulations of the Office of the Prosecutor (OTP), *Situation in the Republic of Kenya*, Decision pursuant to Article 15 of the Rome Statute on the Authorisation of an Investigation into the Situation in the Republic of Kenya, 31 March 2010, §§ 50, 58, 60–62, and 188; *Situation in the Republic of Côte d'Ivoire*, Decision pursuant to Article 15 of the Rome Statute on the Authorisation of an Investigation into the Situation in the Republic of Côte d'Ivoire, 15 November 2011, §§ 202–205; *Situation in Georgia*, Decision pursuant to Article 15 of the Rome Statute on the Authorisation of an Investigation, 27 January 2016, § 51. For all, see the OTP Policy Paper 2013, *supra* note 123.

(iii) or their geographical or temporal spread (high intensity of the crimes over a brief period or low intensity of crimes over an extended period).[126]

24. The prosecution provides extensive information regarding the background to the series of armed conflicts and instability within Afghanistan for decades. It recalls that since 1 May 2003 – when the Rome Statute entered into force for Afghanistan – conflict intensified, as an armed insurgency waged a widespread guerrilla-style war against the government, as well as international forces supporting it. The prosecution submits that, according to statistical data collected since 2009, many thousands of civilians, including many women, have been victims of continuous acts of serious violence, potentially constituting crimes within the jurisdiction of the Court.[127]

Nature

25. The nature of the crimes refers to the specific elements of each offence such as:

(i) killings;
(ii) rapes and other crimes involving sexual or gender violence;
(iii) crimes committed against children;
(iv) persecution, or the imposition of conditions of life on a group calculated to bring about its destruction.[128]

Manner

26. The manner of commission of the crimes may be assessed by considering:

(i) the means employed to execute the crime;
(ii) the degree of participation and intent of the perpetrator (if discernible at this stage);
(iii) the extent to which the crimes were systematic or result from a plan or organised policy or otherwise resulted from the abuse of power or official capacity;
(iv) elements of particular cruelty, including the vulnerability of the victims;

[126] Regulation 29(2), *supra* note 125; *Situation in the Republic of Côte d'Ivoire*, Decision, *supra* note 125; *Situation in Georgia*, Decision, *supra* note 125, § 51. For all, see OTP Policy Paper 2013, *supra* note 123.

[127] See relevant prosecution documents.

[128] Regulation 29(4), Regulations of the OTP; *Prosecutor v. Germain Katanga and Mathieu Ngudjolo Chui*, Judgment on the Appeal of Mr Germain Katanga against the Oral Decision of Trial Chamber II of 12 June 2009 on the Admissibility of the Case, 25 September 2009, § 56. *Situation in the Democratic Republic of the Congo*, Judgment on the Prosecutor's appeal against the decision of Pre-Trial Chamber I entitled 'Decision on the Prosecutor's Application for Warrants of Arrest, Article 58', See in concurrence *Prosecutor v. Abu Garda*, Decision on the Confirmation of Charges.

(v) any motives involving discrimination, or the use of rape and sexual violence as a means of destroying groups.

Impact

27. The impact of crimes may be assessed through looking at:
(i) the suffering endured by the victims and their increased vulnerability;
(ii) the terror subsequently instilled;
(iii) or the social, economic, and environmental damage inflicted on the affected communities.

ALLEGATIONS AGAINST THE TALIBAN AND AFFILIATED GROUPS

Scale

28. Since mid-2003, remnants of the Taliban, formerly in power, and other armed anti-government groups, clashed with Afghan forces and those international forces supporting it. The civilian population suffered greatly as the anti-government groups attacked civilians including those perceived or believed to be associated with the Afghan government or related to the international community.

29. Annex 2A to the Request provides a non-exhaustive list and detailed description of several of the most serious incidents, which are said to have taken place in as many as twenty-five provinces of Afghanistan. An extensive catalogue of crimes, including statistics, were alleged to have been committed by them as part of a widespread and systematic attack; these include many and varied incidents on an extensive scale, as further described below in relation to the nature of the acts.

30. Over the period 2009–2016, the prosecution states that 50,802 civilian casualties (17,770 deaths and 33,032 injuries) were attributed to anti-government armed groups, mostly from their use of improvised explosive devices (IEDs) as well as suicide and complex attacks. The information available suggests that much of the alleged conduct was committed with particular cruelty or in order to instil terror and fear among the local civilian population.[129] The prosecution mainly relies on the findings of the United Nations Assistance Mission in Afghanistan (UNAMA) and the Afghan Independent Human Rights Commission (AIHRC). For example, UNAMA documented 11,002 civilian casualties (3,545 deaths and 7,457 injured) in 2015 alone, exceeding the previous record levels of civilian casualties that occurred in 2014. These figures show an overall increase of 4 per cent during 2015 in total civilian casualties from the previous year. UNAMA began its systematic documentation of civilian casualties in 2009. Ground engagements between parties to the conflict caused the highest number of total civilian casualties (fatalities and injuries), followed by IEDs and suicide and complex attacks. Ground engagements caused the most fatalities amongst civilians, followed by targeted and deliberate killings.

31. The prosecution alleges that the Taliban and other anti-government groups can be held responsible for these incidents. While making some submissions on the

[129] See relevant prosecution documents.

structure of the Taliban and other anti-government armed groups in Afghanistan, the prosecution underlines that information available at this stage does not lead to any conclusive determination as to which specific groups, or association of groups, may have carried out the alleged crimes.

Nature

32. The Request's list of Taliban acts consists of a variety of incidents including, without limitation, the following: attacks by gunmen, bombers, and suicide bombers resulting in numerous murders and injuries of civilians gathered in public and private places – among them mosques, hospitals, and schools – as well as foreigners regarded as supportive of the Afghan government; executions of alleged collaborators and spies of the government and foreign entities, sometimes followed by the gruesome display of mutilated bodies to which written messages threatening the population were attached; abductions of civilians; attacks against civil servants, police officers, judges and other officials of judicial authorities, governors, members of parliament and of district and provincial councils, religious, tribal, and other local community leaders, teachers, healthcare providers, journalists, farmers, and workers on de-mining or road construction sites; schoolgirls and female officials. Other incidents involving the multiple commission of prohibited acts and furthering an organisational policy leading to a high number of direct and indirect victims, including widespread attacks on humanitarian aid workers.

33. The prosecution alleges that the Taliban and other anti-government groups can be held responsible for attacks on United Nations, NGO, and humanitarian workers; suicide attacks resulting in the killing or wounding of members of Afghan forces and of soldiers of the International Security Assistance Force (ISAF) established by the UN Security Council; and the use of child soldiers, in some cases in connection with suicide bombings.[130]

Manner

34. This orchestrated, systematic, cultural structure of violence based on ideologies of hate, inequality, and terror appeared to permeate the country, contributing to intentional cruelty, including rape and sexual violence, potentially as a means to destroy certain groups.

35. This structural order could instil a notion of recurring harms simply expected in women's lives, with access to resources virtually impossible and violence against women and girls a reflection of wider unequal power relationships between men and women in society.[131] Thought-provoking research on suffering indicates there is

[130] See relevant prosecution documents.

[131] Adapted from A. Swaine writing in a different context: A. Swaine, *Conflict-Related Violence against Women: Transforming Transition* (Cambridge: Cambridge University Press, 2018), at 110–114.

a body of work that gives voice to the physical and emotional pain of people battling with chronic poverty, social marginalisation, and routinised violence. It focuses on disruption and regulation: how ordinary social life 'hurts' and how this hurt becomes part of the social experience.[132] In this regard, there is much evidence of Taliban attacks or threats towards the education sector undermining the rights of girls and women to education without discrimination under international law. Attacks occurred not only in schools, but in places of worship and against civilians, all contrary to international law. These alleged crimes were committed in a manner inflicting maximum harm and injury on the largest number of victims, through suicide bombings in crowded public gatherings, including against humanitarian workers. The information available suggests that much of the alleged conduct was committed with particular cruelty, or intended to instil terror and fear among the local civilian population. Victims were deliberately targeted on a discriminatory basis based on their actual or perceived political allegiance or on gender grounds, with attacks particularly directed to civic and community leaders. For example, in 2015, UNAMA documented a 37 per cent increase in female casualties and a 14 per cent increase in child casualties.

36. UNAMA indicates that women continue to suffer greatly from the armed conflict. In 2018, women comprised 10 per cent of conflict-related civilian casualties, and 12 per cent in 2017. UNAMA documented 1,152 women casualties from the armed conflict (350 deaths and 802 injured), a 6 per cent decrease from 2017. Together with the direct impact on women, they are also disproportionately affected by the broader effects of the armed conflict. This exacerbates their vulnerability to marginalisation, poverty, discrimination, and violence. Further, internally displaced women and children face particular risks of abuse of their basic rights, in particular access to adequate shelter, food, and health services. Women suffer harm from the loss of male family members, critical to the socio-economic survival and security of the nuclear and extended family unit. Women's access to health services is severely impeded in locations of active hostilities as service providers either flee the fighting or cannot provide services due to ongoing insecurity. UNAMA noted that incidents of armed attacks, ground fighting, and IED detonations contributed to a heightened sense of fear amongst women for their physical safety and that of their family. Women thus remained within their homes and villages with their families, restricting their freedoms on a day-to-day basis, eliminating women's visibility from public life and their right to make contributions without fear of repercussions on them directly or on their families. The National Action Plan on UN Security Council Resolution 1325 on Women, Peace and Security to protect women and girls from violence – in law, policy, and practice – needs to be taken into account in this regard to ensure underlying structural discrimination policies are eliminated at source, in the design of governmental policies, and provide full redress for failures to do so.

[132] J. Davis, 'The Anthropology of Suffering' 5 *Journal of Refugee Studies* (1992) 149–161.

37. The public nature of 'executions', and displaying mutilated bodies, has been noted in the context of genocide as destroying communities and having cultural significance.[133] This example is from Rwanda and awareness of cultural understandings of suffering and death are often specific. In the context of Rwanda, and in certain religious understandings, 'suffering a bad death',[134] including the separation of the head from the rest of the body, can have further spiritual resonance. It is clear this constitutes significant cruelty, including towards vulnerable victims.

38. The Request submits that such conduct qualifies as crimes against humanity under Article 7 of the Statute and, specifically, as the crimes of murder, imprisonment, or other severe deprivation of physical liberty and persecution on political and gender grounds, committed since 1 May 2003 as part of a widespread and systematic attack against civilians. The Request further submits that these acts qualify as war crimes in the context of an armed conflict not of an international character under Article 8 of the Statute and, specifically, as the crimes of murder; intentionally directing attacks against the civilian population, humanitarian personnel, and protected objects; conscripting or enlisting children under the age of fifteen or using them to participate actively in hostilities; and killing or wounding treacherously a combatant adversary.

Impact

39. The Chamber specifically highlights the devastating and unfinished systemic consequences on the lives of innocent people of the brutal violence inflicted over a prolonged period; the gruesome public display of violence aimed at instilling fear and inspiring subjugation in the population as well as the recurrent targeting of women, including very young and vulnerable civilians. The widespread use of such tactics placed the civilian population at increased risk of attack from governmental and international forces, contributing to increased civilian casualties.[135]

40. The daily endurance and duration of these crimes has had a severe social and psychological impact on the population. The campaign of targeted killings of politicians, government workers, tribal and community leaders, teachers, and religious scholars has deprived local communities of functioning institutions. In many

[133] See analysis in the Rwandan context by R. Korman, 'The Tutsi Body in the 1994 Genocide: Ideology, Physical Destruction, and Memory' in E. Anstett and J.-M. Dreyfus (eds.), *Destruction and Human Remains: Disposal and Concealment in Genocide and Mass Violence* (Manchester: Manchester University Press, 2014) 226–242. Korman includes evidence that victims were deliberately openly stripped in broad daylight for the public to laugh and join in to inflict further cruelty of cultural resonance.

[134] *Ibid.*

[135] United Nations Assistance Mission in Afghanistan, *Afghanistan: Protection of Civilians in Armed Conflict – Annual Report 2016*, February 2017, available at https://unama.unmissions.org/sites/default/files/protection_of_civilians_in_armed_conflict_annual_report_2016_final280317.pdf, and all related prosecution documents.

parts of the country, the population has been denied access to humanitarian assistance and basic government services, including healthcare, because of the insurgent strategy of targeting government and aid workers, including medical staff and de-miners. Areas have become effectively out of bounds to humanitarian assistance workers, while continued attacks against foreigners have forced many international aid organisations to cease their operations, making the effective delivery of essential aid or development programmes more difficult.

41. The alleged crimes have had a particularly broad and severe impact on women and girls. Not only have they suffered conflict-related sexual violence; girls' education has come under sustained attack, thereby depriving thousands of girls of their fundamental human right to education.[136] UNAMA evidence shows that the armed conflict took a heavy toll on education in 2018. Between 1 January and 31 December, UNAMA recorded 191 incidents affecting education, including attacks targeting or incidentally damaging schools; the killing, injury, and abduction of educational personnel; and threats against education facilities and personnel. Women who were left as sole income-providers for their households after the death or injury of their husbands have experienced long-lasting social and economic consequences, with poverty forcing many women to give their daughters in marriage in exchange for debts or to take their children out of school, often to work, with potentially long-lasting negative impact on the lives of women and girls and wider society.[137]

42. Such allegations are of an extremely grave nature. If proven, they demonstrate the structural nature of violence against a population, particularly discriminatory, abusive, and violent towards women and girls, and indicate that an investigation into gender-based crimes is required.

ALLEGATIONS AGAINST THE ANSF AND OTHER FORCES

Scale

43. Alleged crimes are said to have been committed institutionally in certain facilities on a large scale with high percentages of detainees reportedly subjected to torture or cruel treatment. For example, UNAMA evidence that in 2016 alone, ANSF caused 1,663 civilian casualties (457 deaths and 1,206 injured) during ground engagements, a 41 per cent increase compared to 2015. This figure does not include

[136] See Article 26 of the Universal Declaration of Human Rights, Article 13 of the International Covenant on Economic, Social and Cultural Rights 1966, General Comment No. 13 of the Committee of the Economic, Social and Cultural Rights Committee 1999, available at www.ohchr.org/en/resources/educators/human-rights-education-training/d-general-comment-no-13-right-education-article-13-1999.

[137] See related prosecution documents. See also J. True, 'The Political Economy of Gender in UN Peacekeeping' in G. Heathcote and D. Otto (eds.), *Rethinking Peacekeeping, Gender Equality and Collective Security* (New York: Palgrave Macmillan, 2014), at 245. True examines the socio-economic inequality affecting silenced men and women, leaving them vulnerable to poverty and violence after armed conflicts.

103 civilian casualties (18 deaths and 85 injured) attributed to pro-government armed groups or 7 civilian deaths attributed to international military forces. In 2015, UNAMA attributed 1,177 civilian casualties (321 deaths and 856 injured) from ground engagements to ANSF (not including 81 civilian casualties – 19 deaths and 62 injured attributed to pro-government armed groups).

Nature

44. With regard to the ANSF and other forces, and the US forces and CIA, the alleged crimes include killings, torture, and crimes of a sexual nature, as detailed below.

Manner

45. The prosecution submits that, since 1 May 2003, members of the ANSF and others committed crimes against persons removed from combat by detention, or civilians who were not taking active part in the hostilities and were detained for security reasons related to the ongoing armed conflict. Evidence was produced that torture was widely practised to force confessions, obtain information, or punish. The Request details cases of infliction of severe physical and mental pain or suffering to detainees, some of which are particularly brutal, cruel, and hurtful and some resulting in the victim's death; cases of humiliating and degrading treatment, or other inhumane treatment violating victims' dignity, including by depriving them of fundamental material and spiritual needs, such as sleep, food, and water, and praying; as well as cases of acts of sexual violence, at times resulting in the permanent impairment of the victims' sexual integrity. In 2016, UNAMA verified eleven cases of conflict-related sexual violence against women, girls, and boys committed by parties to the conflict including the Afghan National Border Police and the Afghan Local Police (as well as the Taliban). Of these cases, just two perpetrators (members of the Afghan National Border Police) were convicted and sentenced to imprisonment. The eleven incidents include four documented cases of '*bachah bazi*', involving the sexual abuse and enslavement of boys by men in positions of power, many of whom are linked to the Afghan National Defence and Security Forces. Efforts led by the AIHRC to criminalise this practice resulted in draft legislation in March 2016.[138] A report by an independent government watchdog listed 5,753 cases of what it describes as gross human rights abuses by Afghan forces. Many of those abuses involve routine enslavement and sexual abuse of underage boys by Afghan commanders.[139] The limited presence of women in the Afghan National Police (1.8 per cent) contributes to the continuing underreporting

[138] See UN Report of the Secretary-General, *Conflict-Related Sexual Violence*, 15 April 2017/S/2017/249, at 10.

[139] See www.npr.org/2018/01/24/580433652/how-the-u-s-military-ignored-child-sexual-abuse-in-afghanistan-for-years, accusing the US military of ignoring this practice.

of sexual violence. The prosecution submits that there are reasonable grounds to believe that, since 1 May 2003, the war crimes of torture and cruel treatment, outrages upon personal dignity, and sexual violence have been committed in the context of a non-international armed conflict against persons so detained.

46. The 'special gravity' of torture is noted. Senior officials have admitted that detainees were subjected to cruel treatment in the relevant facilities under their authority.[140] Torture's prohibition represents a peremptory norm of international law (*jus cogens*).[141] It 'is absolute and non-derogable in any circumstances', 'applies at all times', 'no exceptional circumstances whatsoever may be invoked by a State Party to justify acts of torture in any territory under its jurisdiction', with no exceptions including 'a state of war or threat thereof, internal political instability or any other public emergency', or 'any threat of terrorist acts or violent crime as well as armed conflict, international or non-international'. This prohibition is 'grounded in a widespread international practice and on the *opinio juris* of States … appears in numerous international instruments of universal application … has been introduced into the domestic law of almost all States'.[142] It is therefore clear that where torture is allegedly involved, the matter of gravity is made out.

Impact

47. Detainees were forced to give false confessions, with threat of further punishment, resulting in potentially innocent detainees incarcerated for longer periods with further deprivation of their, and their families', rights.[143]

48. The alleged crimes had severe short-term and long-term impacts on detainees' physical and mental health, including permanent physical injuries. Often the pain during interrogation caused lost consciousness. Some detainees are described as 'broken husks' after abuse, suffering insomnia, chronic pain, and forgetfulness.[144]

49. Families of victims were often left in a state of uncertainty about the fate of loved ones; their communities came under suspicion of harbouring loyalties to the Taliban, or Al Qaeda, or were tainted by such accusations. The information available suggests that victims were deeply traumatised by their treatment in custody.

[140] See relevant prosecution documents. See also Human Rights Watch, 'On the Precipice: Insecurity in Northern Afghanistan', *A Human Rights Watch Briefing Paper*, June 2002.

[141] Questions Relating to the Obligation to Prosecute or Extradite (*Belgium v. Senegal*), Judgment of 20 July 2012, ICJ Reports 2012, § 99; *Furundžija Trial Judgment*, §§ 153–154; *Prosecutor v. Delalic*, IT-96-21-T, ICTY Trial Judgment of 16 November 1998, § 454.

[142] See relevant prosecution documents referring to numerous international human rights and humanitarian laws, including ICC-02/17-26 with three public annexes.

[143] *Ibid.*

[144] See related prosecution documents and UN Committee against Torture, General Comment No. 2, CAT/C/GC/2, 24 January 2008, § 26.

ALLEGATIONS AGAINST US FORCES AND THE CIA

Scale

50. The alleged crimes appear to have been inflicted on a small percentage of all persons detained by US armed forces over a limited time period, after which the use of such techniques by US armed forces worldwide was formally rescinded and the US Army Field Manual restored the Geneva Conventions in its detainee treatment and interrogation. The acts allegedly committed were serious both in their number and in their effect and, although implemented pursuant to authorised interrogation policies adopted locally rather than at headquarters level, they implicated personal responsibility within the command structure.

Nature

51. With regard to US armed forces and the CIA, the alleged crimes include killings, torture, and crimes of a sexual nature.

Manner

52. The prosecution argue that the treatment of CIA detainees appears to have been particularly grave on a qualitative assessment. The alleged crimes appear to have been committed with particular cruelty, involving the infliction of serious physical and psychological injury, over prolonged periods, and including acts committed in a manner calculated to offend cultural and religious values, and leaving victims deeply traumatised. Detainees who were subjected to 'enhanced interrogation techniques' and extended isolation exhibited psychological and behavioural issues, including hallucinations, paranoia, insomnia, and attempts at self-harm and self-mutilation. A specific section of the Request is devoted to the alleged policies of US armed forces and the CIA for interrogating detainees. The specific incidents included inflicting severe physical and mental pain or suffering to hors de combat detainees or to other persons not taking active part in the hostilities in the non-international armed conflict, some of which are extremely cruel, brutal, and gruesome; cases of humiliating, degrading, or inhumane treatment violating the victims' dignity, among which the deprivation of fundamental material and spiritual needs (including sleep, food and water, and praying); acts implying offence, distress, and shame, including acts of a sexual nature, invading intimate, private dignity, bodily, and psychological integrity, all fully protected under international law. Socio-cultural norms and religious factors particular to Afghan society, known for its social conservativism especially regarding sexual matters,[145] may have caused incidents of detainee abuse to be under-reported, especially in cases of sexual violence such as forced nudity and sexual humiliation. These victims may

[145] H. Bamik, 'Talking about Sexual Attitudes and Behaviors: A Cultural and Social Taboo in Afghanistan' (July 2018), available at www.researchgate.net/publication/326446311_Talking_about_Sexual_Attitudes_and_Behaviors_a_cultural_and_Social_Taboo_in_Afghanistan.

experience shame, guilt, and fear of being stigmatised by their communities. The prosecution received information that victims are afraid to report the abuse because of threats to harm their families or fear of retaliation and reprisals. Some who did speak publicly were threatened, harassed, or attacked after doing so. There has been no reporting mechanism in place attempting to collect accounts from witnesses and survivors located in remote and insecure areas of Afghanistan or that has been available to victims who have been willing to come forward with their testimonies.[146]

53. According to the prosecution, there is a reasonable basis to believe that, since May 2003, members of the US armed forces and the CIA have committed the war crimes of torture and cruel treatment, outrages upon personal dignity, and rape and other forms of sexual violence pursuant to a policy approved by the US authorities.[147]

54. The prosecution further indicates there may be other crimes committed by members of the other international forces deployed in Afghanistan.[148] A determination on these has not yet been reached due to currently insufficient information or analysis. Several victims' representations refer to incidents in which individuals not participating in hostilities as well as non-military buildings, including of a protected nature, were indiscriminately or deliberately attacked by air strikes and drones by US and other international forces, despite lacking a military target, and that such attacks resulted in civilian deaths. Although the prosecution is not requesting authorisation to investigate these yet, it notes that these allegations 'can be subjected to proper investigation and analysis if an investigation of the Situation is authorised'. Further, it states 'should an investigation be opened, these and other alleged crimes that may occur after the commencement of the investigation ... could be assessed within the scope of the authorised situation'.[149]

55. These alleged crimes appear to have been committed with particular cruelty, involving the infliction of serious physical and psychological injury, over prolonged periods, including acts committed in a manner calculated to offend cultural and religious taboos, leaving victims deeply traumatised. Detainees so subjected exhibited psychological and behavioural issues, including hallucinations, paranoia, insomnia, and attempts at self-harm and self-mutilation.[150]

56. The treatment of CIA detainees appears to have been particularly grave on a qualitative assessment, with interrogations being 'brutal and far worse than the CIA represented to policymakers and others'. The CIA applied its 'enhanced interrogation' techniques 'with significant repetition for days or weeks at a time', with

[146] All as described in relevant prosecution documents.

[147] The prosecution mainly relies on the findings of the US Senate Select Committee on Intelligence, the US Senate Armed Services Committee, and the US Department of Defense.

[148] This includes complicity in the torture of detainees and civilian casualties.

[149] See relevant prosecution documents.

[150] G. Smith, 'From Canadian custody into cruel hands', *Globe and Mail*, 23 April 2007, and further information in prosecution documents.

techniques 'used in combination, frequently concurrent with sleep deprivation'.[151] Further details can be found in the US Senate Report regarding the horrors of 'waterboarding' and the particularly harsh conditions of confinement for CIA detainees allegedly forming an integral part of the interrogation process. Information available is, however, limited by the clandestine nature of the detention and interrogation programme; efforts to conceal the number and identity of victims; denying access to national and international reporting mechanisms mandated to monitor and report these detentions, together with the destruction of CIA videotapes of this behaviour.[152]

Impact

57. The prosecution point out the psychological impact on CIA detainees who were told they would not leave custody alive.[153] Threats to harm children or sexually abuse mothers of detainees are detailed. Psychological and behavioural issues were identified, including hallucinations, paranoia, insomnia, and attempts at self-harm and self-mutilation. It is noted that '[m]ultiple psychologists identified the lack of human contact experienced by detainees as a cause of psychiatric problems'.[154] Being carried out by a democratic country seen by many to be the 'land of the free' and 'leaders of the free world' with developed standards of integrity, accountability, and transparency, such behaviour is especially hypocritical. This has corresponding effects on any understanding of trust in liberal democracies. Further, women are involved as alleged perpetrators of torture and other crimes. All these issues can undermine support for substantive gender equality, instead being used to substantiate arguments supporting the negative influence of westernising feminism on Afghan society, in general, and Afghan women, in particular.

58. Previous international criminal case law has secured convictions for sexual violence and raised the profile of the global phenomenon of conflict-related sexual violence and the cultural, religious, and societal consequences of such crimes that must be considered in any assessment of gravity. As noted by Brammertz and Jarvis, former lead prosecutors at the International Criminal Tribunal for the former Yugoslavia (ICTY), 'we must engage in an honest dialogue about why conflict-related sexual violence presents such an accountability challenge and how we can improve the situation. We cannot simply rest on the successes we managed to secure in the past – we must continue to insist on more effective strategies for the future'.[155]

[151] All from Senate Select Committee on Intelligence, Committee Study of the Central Intelligence Agency's Detention and Interrogation Program, Declassification Revisions, 3 December 2014, AFG-OTP0003-5696 (Report of the Senate Select Committee on Intelligence, Melville House, 2015).

[152] *Ibid.*

[153] The CIA allegedly suggested to one detainee that he would only leave in a coffin-shaped box.

[154] See related prosecution documents.

[155] S. Brammertz and M. Jarvis (eds.), *Prosecuting Conflict-Related Sexual Violence at the ICTY* (Oxford: Oxford University Press, 2016). Witnesses and scholars have extensively expressed, and/

As part of that, this Court needs to acknowledge the structural gender disadvantages suffered by women in Afghan society during the time in question in this decision.

Conclusions on Gravity

59. All these allegations meet the gravity threshold set out in Article 17(1)(d) in respect of all the 'categories' of crimes for which the prosecution requests authorisation to investigate committed by the Taliban, members of the ANSF and others, US armed forces and members of the CIA. There appear to be multiple failures from all sides.

60. In relation to the crimes allegedly committed by the ANSF, US forces and the CIA, the Chamber notes the gravity per se of the crime of torture, which is banned by international law, and that the conduct was allegedly committed by public officials in their functions, the high number of victims, the nature of the crimes, the manner of the conduct and its impact on the victims.

61. As my decision draws to a close, I would like to refer to the risks and tensions of feminist perspectives in legal decisions and judgments such as this. Feminism in law depends on paradoxes – to acknowledge the power of discourses, such as international criminal law, that reinforce the existing status quo yet require the transforming potential for resistance. In this regard, we need to challenge the notion of violent acts that can be prosecuted and addressed whilst also accounting for their enabling structures and ideologies, to expand and pluralise our vocabularies of justice and redress, but to do this without reinscribing narratives that reinforce patriarchal norms.[156] This is 'not so much a space of resistance but an entirely different geometry through which we can think power, knowledge, space and identity in critical and, hopefully, liberatory ways'.[157] It is hoped that this short

or analysed, how rape affects different women, and women in different cultures. Whilst a subjective intimate experience with many reactions and impacts, H. M. Zawati, for example, has said that raping a Muslim woman 'simply means sentencing her to death, physically, psychologically, and socially. Assaulted women might be killed, abandoned, or "at best" socially rejected. Moreover, women could be killed by their own families or commit suicide as a preventive measure against being raped'. See H. M. Zawati, 'Sexual Violence as a Weapon of War in the Ongoing Syrian Conflict: Testimony before the Subcommittee on International Human Rights of the Standing Committee on Foreign Affairs and International Development of the House of Commons', Parliament of Canada, 1 May 2014.

156 This paraphrases and changes the emphasis provided by V. Nesiah, 'Missionary Zeal for a Secular Mission: Bringing Gender to Transitional Justice and Redemption to Feminism' in S. Kouvo and Z. Pearson (eds.), *Feminist Perspectives on Contemporary International Law: Between Resistance and Compliance* (London: Hart, 2014) 137–157, at 153. Nesiah cites Joan Scott and Chandra Mohanty as analysed by S. Stone-Mediatore, 'Chandra Mohanty and the Revaluing of "Experience"' 13 *Hypatia* (1998) 116–133.

157 G. Rose, *Feminism and Geography: The Limits of Geographical Knowledge* (Minneapolis: University of Minnesota Press, 1993), at 151–155, 159, cited and discussed by Z. Pearson, 'Feminist Project(s): The Spaces of International Law' in S. Kouvo and Z. Pearson (eds.), *Feminist Perspectives on Contemporary International Law: Between Resistance and Compliance* (London: Hart, 2014) 47–68, at 55. See also J. Marshall, 'Law, Everyday Spaces and Objects,

decision contributes fruitfully to such a future of transformative international criminal justice.

Judge Jill Marshall

16.4 THE COMPLEMENTARITY TEST IN THE AFGHANISTAN INVESTIGATION

Kathryn Gooding

In 2019, Pre-Trial Chamber II concluded that the complementarity test had not been met by belligerent parties in prosecuting alleged crimes committed in the Islamic Republic of Afghanistan from 1 March 2003. Therefore, the potential cases arising from the Afghanistan situation appeared admissible to the ICC.[158]

In this rewritten decision, Kathryn Gooding confirms this finding. In doing so, Gooding applies a feminist lens to several aspects of complementarity including the 'substantially the same conduct' test as well as the framing of 'unwilling', 'unable', and 'genuine', noting how domestic cases against the Taliban forces, Afghan National Security Forces, US armed forces, and the Central Intelligence Agency (CIA) failed to be conducted in a gender-sensitive manner. This is demonstrated through the absence of language around sexual violence in Afghan law, and the discriminatory requirements for proof in the matter of rape. Gooding also engages with the prosecution for Afghan National Security Forces, US armed forces, and the CIA in the treatment of male sexual assault survivors and how social and cultural understanding of male sexual assault acts as a barrier to effective prosecution.

No.: ICC-02/17
Date: 12 April 2019

Original: English

PRE-TRIAL CHAMBER II(B)

Before: Judge Kathryn GOODING
SITUATION IN THE ISLAMIC REPUBLIC OF AFGHANISTAN

Public

Decision pursuant to Article 15 of the Rome Statute on the Authorisation of an Investigation into the Situation in the Islamic Republic of Afghanistan

and Being Human' in C. Stychin (ed.), *Law, Humanities and the COVID Crisis* (London: University of London Press, 2023, on file with the Court).

[158] Decision pursuant to Article 15 of the Rome Statute on the Authorisation of an Investigation into the Situation in the Islamic Republic of Afghanistan, *Situation in Afghanistan* (ICC-02/17-33), Pre-Trial Chamber II, 12 April 2019.

DETERMINATION BY THE CHAMBER ON THE ISSUES ON ADMISSIBILITY

[...]

Introduction

70. As per Article 53(1)(b), the Chamber is required at this stage to assess whether prospective cases, which could arise out of an investigation by the Prosecutor, would be admissible before the Court pursuant to Article 17 of the Statute. This assessment is conducted by reference to the conduct identified by the Prosecutor in her Request,[159] which could constitute crimes within the jurisdiction of the Court. This is, however, without prejudice to further cases that may subsequently be identified by the Prosecutor. The admissibility assessment contained within Article 17 is three-fold; Article 17(1)(a)–(d) sets out the two-stage complementarity assessment[160] and gravity assessment that the Chamber must carry out. Firstly, the Chamber must consider whether there are, or have been, any domestic investigations or prosecutions of cases that could arise from any authorised investigation into the situation in Afghanistan. And if this is answered in the affirmative, whether these cases relate to the same case that may be the subject of proceedings before the Court, and whether a decision has been made not to prosecute the individuals concerned.

71. Secondly, the Chamber must assess whether the state with jurisdiction is genuinely willing and able to carry out the relevant investigations or prosecutions identified at stage 1 and whether a decision not to prosecute any individual concerned arose out of any unwillingness or inability of the state to genuinely prosecute.

72. The Chamber must finally consider whether the relevant cases identified are of sufficient gravity to justify investigation by the Court.

Complementarity

73. The Pre-Trial Chamber has provided guidance as to the requirements contained within Article 17(1)(a). The Court is required to conduct a judicial assessment of whether the case that the state is investigating sufficiently mirrors the one that the Prosecutor is investigating.[161] The focus must be on the nature of the conduct, not its legal characterisation in the national legal system.[162] The Pre-Trial Chamber has

[159] Request for Authorisation of an Investigation pursuant to Article 15, *Situation in the Islamic Republic of Afghanistan* (ICC-02/17/-7-Red), Pre-Trial Chamber, 20 November 2017.

[160] Judgment on the Appeal of Mr Germain Katanga against the Oral Decision of the Trial Chamber II of 12 June 2009 on the Admissibility of the Case, *Katanga* (ICC-01/04-01/07-1297), Appeals Chamber, 25 September 2009, § 78 (hereafter Katanga Appeal Judgment).

[161] Judgment on the Appeal of Libya against the Decision of the Pre-Trial Chamber I of 31 May 2013 entitled 'Decision on the Admissibility of the Case against Saif Al-Islam Gaddafi', *Gaddafi and Al-Senussi* (ICC-01/11-01/11-547-Red), Appeals Chamber, 21 May 2014, § 73.

[162] Decision on the Admissibility of the Case against Saif Al-Islam Gaddafi, *Gaddafi and Al-Senussi* (ICC-01/11-01/11-344-Red), Pre-Trial Chamber I, 31 May 2013, § 85.

found that the unwillingness and inability tests are disjunctive;[163] therefore, if either one is satisfied, the case is admissible before the Court. Article 17(2) and (3) sets out a number of factors which may indicate unwillingness or inability on the part of the investigating and/or prosecuting state, including national proceedings not being conducted independently or impartially. Inability must be assessed in the context of the relevant national system and procedures[164] to determine whether the national authorities are capable of investigating or prosecuting the accused.

74. The Trial Chamber has found that the statutory definition of 'unwillingness' contained within Article 17(2) is not exhaustive.[165] The Chamber therefore considers that the definition can be extended to encompass gender-sensitive considerations to assess the extent to which Afghanistan and the United States can be considered willing or able to investigate or prosecute the cases contained within the Prosecutor's Request.

75. In relation to national proceedings carried out in Afghanistan against members of the Taliban and affiliated armed groups, the Prosecutor submits that members of such groups have been accused predominantly of committing crimes against the state.[166] Articles 173–253 of Afghanistan's 1976 Penal Code set out crimes against the external and internal security of the state. These offences encompass efforts to change the constitution or form of the state by force, or to impair the independence or territorial integrity of Afghanistan. The Chamber considers that these offences do not cover substantially the same conduct as the conduct alleged by the Prosecutor to constitute the crime of persecution on political and gender grounds contrary to Article 7(1)(h). The Chamber notes that the national proceedings, focusing on conduct considered to weaken the state, emanate from the ideologically competing, yet similarly patriarchal, visions of statehood of the Western-backed government and the Taliban.

76. In contrast, the crime of persecution on gender grounds, as identified by the ICC Prosecutor, reflects in this case the individual harms suffered by women and girls, targeted simply for being women. The national proceedings in no way capture the extent of the harm, or the discriminatory rationale, nature, and effect of the offences committed against Afghan women and girls. The Chamber is therefore satisfied that potential cases against members of the Taliban and affiliated armed groups would be admissible under Article 17 because the first limb of the test is not satisfied (that is, the Afghan authorities are not investigating or prosecuting the same conduct that is of interest to the ICC).

77. In addition, even if there was a greater degree of overlap between the national and ICC proceedings, these cases would still be admissible to the ICC under the

[163] Katanga Appeal Judgment, *supra* note 160, § 78.

[164] Decision on the Admissibility of the Case against Abdullah Al-Senussi, *Gaddafi and Al Senussi* (ICC-01/11-01/11-466-Red), Pre Trial Chamber I, 11 October 2013, § 203.

[165] Reasons for the Oral Decision on the Motion Challenging the Admissibility of the Case (Article 19 of the Statute), *Katanga* (ICC-01/04-01/07-1213-tENG), Trial Chamber II, 18 June 2009, § 77.

[166] Request for Authorisation, *supra* note 159, at 270.

second limb of the test. That is, the Chamber considers that Afghanistan is unwilling to investigate or prosecute the potential cases arising from the Request, as a result of the inadequacies of the Afghan legal system in its treatment of sexual and gender-based violence. Although equality between men and women is enshrined in Article 22 of the Afghan Constitution, it is the observation of the Chamber that this is not the case in practice. The Afghan legal system is defined by legal pluralism, with Islamic *Hanafi* jurisprudence dictating the punishments for *hudud* (crimes committed against the public interest) and *qisas* (crimes against the bodily integrity of a person).[167] The *hudud* offence of *zina*, contrary to Article 429 of the 1976 Penal Code, prohibits adultery, fornication, and rape, although rape is neither mentioned nor defined. This ambiguity has reinforced the blurring between consensual and non-consensual sexual relations and has led to the widespread incarceration of female rape victims on charges of adultery.[168] Furthermore, discriminatory procedural requirements obstruct investigations into and convictions for rape. In support of her complaint, a female complainant must obtain the testimony of four trustworthy male Muslims, each of whom were present at the time of the offence, and each of whom saw the actual act of penetration.[169]

78. The Chamber notes that of relevance is paragraph 41 of the Prosecutor's Policy Paper on Sexual and Gender-Based Crimes, which states that the absence of genuine national proceedings being undertaken can be demonstrated by discriminatory attitudes and gender stereotypes evident in the substantive law of the country under investigation, and procedural rules that limit access to justice for victims of sexual and gender-based crimes.[170] The Chamber is therefore satisfied at this stage that potential cases arising from crimes committed by members of the Taliban would be admissible under the second limb of the test, as a result of the unwillingness of the Afghan authorities to genuinely investigate or prosecute conduct constituting the crime of prosecution on political and gender grounds contrary to Article 7 (1)(h) of the Statute.

79. With regard to the alleged crimes committed by Afghan National Security Forces, US armed forces, and the CIA, the Prosecutor's Request details a number of acts constituting sexual violence contrary to Article 8(2)(e)(vi), carried out against predominantly male conflict-related detainees. The acts alleged in the Request include deliberate injuries and electric shocks to the genitals, penetration of the anal openings of detainees in circumstances of sexual humiliation, forced nudity, and sexual molestation. The Chamber notes that the Prosecutor's Request refers to a

[167] Art. 1 1976 Penal Code of Afghanistan, AFG-1976-L-105007, 7 October 1976.

[168] *Report of the Special Rapporteur on Violence against Women, Its Causes and Consequences, Yakin Ertürk*, UN Doc. E/CN.4/2006/61/Add.5, 15 February 2006, § 41.

[169] E. Sugarman et al., *An Introduction to the Criminal Law of Afghanistan* (2nd ed., Stanford, CA: Stanford Law School, 2009), at 90.

[170] ICC Office of the Prosecutor, 'Policy Paper on Sexual and Gender-Based Crimes', June 2014, § 41.

number of investigations conducted by Afghan authorities for torture and cruel treatment, and by US authorities for assault and murder. This characterisation of the acts detailed in the Request by the relevant authorities fails to reflect the sexual and gender dimensions of the crimes – specifically that the crimes were likely carried out for the purposes of punishment, humiliation, and degradation of the detainee against the backdrop of cultural and religious taboos against homosexuality prevalent in Afghanistan.[171]

80. It is the opinion of the Chamber that the sexual and gender dimensions of these alleged acts go to the very nature of the conduct, such that the investigations by Afghan and US authorities into acts of torture, cruel treatment, assault, and murder do not sufficiently mirror the cases detailed by the Prosecutor in her Request. The Chamber further notes the importance of correctly characterising sexual and gender-based violence, to undermine the dichotomy of female/victim and male/perpetrator, and the idea that a male survivor is emasculated and weak, due to sexual violence casting aspersions of homosexuality. The Chamber concludes that the Afghan and US authorities are not investigating or prosecuting cases constituting the same conduct as that contained within the Prosecutor's Request, and therefore such cases are admissible under Article 17.

81. The Chamber observes that the first limb of the test for complementarity has been met in relation to investigations and prosecutions conducted by Afghan and US authorities; however, these cases would nevertheless be admissible under the second limb. The Chamber notes with concern the significant lack of protections for male survivors of sexual violence in Afghanistan. Sodomy and sexual acts between men that do not result in penetration, *tafkhez*, are offences contrary to Articles 646, 647, and 649 of the 2017 Penal Code.[172] It has been reported that men and boys who report rape and other sexual violence to the relevant authorities are branded as homosexual and are incarcerated for these offences.[173] It is the conclusion of the Chamber that the structural discrimination evident in the Afghan legal system precludes any impartial proceedings and demonstrates Afghanistan's unwillingness to conduct genuine proceedings that reflect the sexual and gender dimensions of the crimes contained within the Request.

82. Furthermore, the Chamber also notes its concern regarding the approach of the US authorities in conducting predominantly non-judicial and administrative proceedings[174] in relation to offences perpetrated by members of the US armed

[171] All Survivors Project and Youth Health and Development Organization, 'Enhancing Survivor-Centred Healthcare Response for Male Victims/Survivors of Sexual Violence in Afghanistan', March 2021, available at https://allsurvivorsproject.org/enhancing-survivor-centred-healthcare-response-for-male-victims-survivors-of-sexual-violence-in-afghanistan/, at 48.

[172] 2017 Penal Code of Afghanistan, AFG-2017-L-105003, 15 May 2017.

[173] Afghanistan: Implementing Alternatives to Imprisonment, in Line with International Standards and National Legislation Assessment Report, UN Doc. AFG/R87, May 2008, at 37.

[174] Request for Authorisation, *supra* note 159, § 306.

forces and the CIA, which demonstrates the unwillingness of the US authorities to genuinely carry out prosecutions of individuals for cases contained within the Prosecutor's Request. The Chamber notes with interest paragraph 41 of the Prosecutor's Policy Paper on Sexual and Gender-Based Crimes, which states that the absence of genuine national proceedings can be indicated by the lack of political will, including official attitudes of trivialisation and minimisation or denial of the crimes contained within the Prosecutor's Request, and manifestly insufficient steps in the investigation and prosecution of sexual and gender-based crimes.[175]

83. The Church Report found that as of September 2004, twenty-seven investigations had been initiated following allegations of detainee abuse by US personnel in Afghanistan, involving sixty-five service members and between twenty-five and fifty detainees. The twenty-seven investigations concluded that the allegations were either unsubstantiated or led to administrative action including a letter of reprimand or suspension from operations involving detainees.[176] The Chamber concludes that the non-judicial and administrative proceedings conducted by US authorities serve to perpetuate impunity for sexual and gender-based violence against male conflict-related detainees, and appear to reflect the attitude of US authorities to investigating and prosecuting such crimes, which appears to be one of trivialisation and minimisation. For the foregoing reasons, the Chamber deems the potential cases arising from crimes committed by members of US armed forces, the CIA, and the Afghan National Security Forces admissible under both limbs of the test in Article 17.

Conclusion

84. The Chamber concludes that the national proceedings conducted by Afghan and US authorities do not cover the same conduct that is subject to proceedings before the Court, as the national cases do not adequately capture the gendered basis of the crimes contained within the Prosecutor's Request. The Chamber notes that even if there is a degree of overlap between some of the domestic cases and the cases detailed in the Prosecutor's Request, there are gendered deficiencies in national law, particularly in Afghan law, and lack of political will on the part of the US and Afghan authorities to prosecute sexual and gender-based crimes, which mean that both states are unwilling or unable to genuinely conduct these proceedings. Although not made explicit by the text of Article 17 of the Statute, the Chamber observes that gender analysis is relevant to both limbs of the complementarity test.

85. The Chamber is therefore satisfied at this stage that potential cases arising from crimes committed by members of the Taliban, Afghan National Security

[175] ICC Office of the Prosecutor, *Policy Paper on Sexual and Gender-Based Crimes*, June 2014, § 41.

[176] Church Report, AFG-OTP-0003-4294, at 4529–4530.

Forces, US armed forces, and the CIA would be admissible under Article 17 of the Statute.

Judge Kathryn Gooding

16.5 THE INTERESTS OF JUSTICE TEST IN THE AFGHANISTAN INVESTIGATION

Souheir Edelbi

In 2017, after a decade-long preliminary examination into the conflict in Afghanistan, Prosecutor Bensouda concluded that the criteria for opening an investigation were satisfied, there being a reasonable basis to believe that Rome Statute crimes had been committed by the Taliban and Afghan National Security Forces within Afghanistan.

Implicating a Western power for the first time in the ICC's history, she also found there was a reasonable basis to believe that Rome Statute crimes had been committed by members of the US armed forces and US Central Intelligence Agency (CIA) in Afghanistan and in secret facilities in Eastern Europe where suspected Taliban and Al Qaeda members were detained.[177]

In 2019, the Pre-Trial Chamber dismissed the Prosecutor's request to open this investigation, on the basis that the investigation would not serve the 'interests of justice'.[178] In 2020, the Appeals Chamber reversed that decision, finding that the Pre-Trial Chamber was not empowered to adjudicate the 'interests of justice' question.[179] In her reimagined version of that 2020 appeal decision, Souheir Edelbi comes to that same conclusion but, in doing so, provides an original, victim-centred analysis of the 'interests of justice'. She further finds that the Pre-Trial Chamber abused its discretion by failing to consider the views expressed by the victims who had participated in the proceedings.

No.: ICC-02/17
Date: 5 March 2020

Original: English

Appeals Chamber

Before: Judge Souheir EDELBI
SITUATION IN THE ISLAMIC REPUBLIC OF AFGHANISTAN

177 Public Redacted Version of Request for Authorisation of an Investigation pursuant to Article 15, *Situation in Afghanistan* (ICC-02/17-7-Red), Pre-Trial Chamber III, 20 November 2017.

178 Decision pursuant to Article 15 of the Rome Statute on the Authorisation of an Investigation into the Situation in the Islamic Republic of Afghanistan, *Situation in Afghanistan* (ICC-02/17-33), Pre-Trial Chamber II, 12 April 2019.

179 Judgment on the Appeal against the Decision on the Authorisation of an Investigation into the Situation in the Islamic Republic of Afghanistan, *Situation in Afghanistan* (ICC-02/17-138), Appeals Chamber, 5 March 2020.

Public

Judgment on the appeal against the decision on the authorisation of an investigation into the situation in the Islamic Republic of Afghanistan

1. The present appeal by the Prosecutor concerns the situation in the Islamic Republic of Afghanistan and the outcome of the Prosecutor's request for authorisation of an investigation by Pre-Trial Chamber II. On 12 April 2019, the Pre-Trial Chamber unanimously held, pursuant to Article 53(1)(c), that a criminal investigation into allegations of war crimes and crimes against humanity would not serve the interests of justice and on this basis declined to authorise the Prosecutor's request for an investigation into the situation in Afghanistan (Impugned Decision). It did so having found that there *is* a reasonable basis to believe the incidents underlying the Prosecutor's request occurred and may have constituted crimes within the jurisdiction of the Court, and that the relevant requirements for admissibility had been met.[180]

2. The Prosecutor appeals the Impugned Decision on the grounds that the Pre-Trial Chamber abused its discretion when assessing the scope of the 'interests of justice' (first ground of appeal) and erred in law by assessing the Prosecutor's determination of the interests of justice (second ground of appeal). These issues bring into question the concept and scope of the interests of justice as formulated in Article 53(1)(c) of the Rome Statute. Therefore, the present appeal will focus on these issues as relevant to the Pre-Trial Chamber's decision to decline to authorise the investigation into the situation in Afghanistan.

FIRST GROUND OF APPEAL: DID THE PRE-TRIAL CHAMBER ABUSE ITS DISCRETION WHEN ASSESSING THE SCOPE OF THE 'INTERESTS OF JUSTICE'?

The Concept of 'Interests of Justice'

3. The Prosecutor argues that the Pre-Trial Chamber abused its discretion when determining that the initiation of an investigation into the situation in Afghanistan was not in the interests of justice. The Prosecutor argues that the Pre-Trial Chamber misapprehended factors that it took into account, that it took into consideration factors that it should not have taken into account, and that it failed to take sufficient account of relevant factors.

[180] Decision pursuant to Article 15 of the Rome Statute on the Authorisation of an Investigation into the Situation in the Islamic Republic of Afghanistan (ICC-02/17), Pre-Trial Chamber II, 12 April 2019, §§ 60 and 79.

4. The 'interests of justice' is of great significance to the Rome Statute's legal framework for initiating an investigation. This is because Article 53(1)(c) of the Statute is an 'access to justice' provision and, consequently, triggers questions of importance for victims who are unable to secure a measure of accountability in domestic criminal jurisdictions.[181] It is an issue that the Prosecutor is obliged to consider when assessing whether to initiate an investigation. For this reason, the Appeals Chamber outlines some observations regarding the Pre-Trial Chamber's approach to the concept.

5. First, the Appeals Chamber underlines that one of the strengths of the Court lies in creating a source of legal redress for victims where domestic avenues of justice are either limited or unavailable. This particular strength, however, is tempered by the fact that the Rome Statute is limited by design to a narrow sense of 'justice' in the form of criminal trials, which is intended to provide only a certain measure of individualised accountability for crimes that fall under the Statute. As one academic acknowledges, criminal trials 'are not appropriate fora to deal with the greater context or root causes of a conflict or repressive regime', nor are the procedural and evidential modalities of criminal law necessarily victim-friendly.[182]

6. In this regard, tensions may arise between the interests of victims and the criminal law nature of the Court's inherent functions. Judges are called upon to observe the limits of the text, purpose, and context of the Rome Statute and to apply caution to judicial reasoning to avoid stretching judicial interpretation beyond the actual text of the Statute. The Appeals Chamber acknowledges these limits in order to avoid unnecessarily inflating the expectations of victims. Victims are not served well by a discourse of 'justice' that ignores the inherent limits in which the Court and the Rome Statute operate. To be clear, Article 53(1)(c) is not directly concerned with substantive outcomes or broader forms of justice such as truth and reconciliation, peace agreements, or redistributive justice, which very often form part of victims' submissions before this Court. In this regard, it is simply not designed to cater to more substantial visions of justice.

7. Instead, Article 53(1)(c) of the Statute is more narrowly concerned with the procedure for initiating an investigation. Questions of procedure, however, need not be reduced to an abstract and mechanical method of interpretation, removed from the interests of victims and their specific context and lived experiences. Such abstract reasoning would lead to unnecessary judicial detachment from those whom the law should most serve and create a false impression of objectivity that is hardly suited to the task of assessing the interests of justice under Article 53(1)(c). This is because this particular provision tilts heavily towards the interests of victims and the

[181] Victims' Joint Appeal Brief against the Decision pursuant to Article 15 of the Rome Statute on the Authorisation of an Investigation into the Situation in the Islamic Republic of Afghanistan (ICC-02/17), Appeals Chamber, 30 September 2019, § 1.

[182] D. Robinson, 'Serving the Interests of Justice: Amnesties, Truth Commissions and the International Criminal Court' 14 *European Journal of International Law* (2003) 481–505, at 484.

presumption that securing these interests requires the opening of an investigation. In this regard, the plain wording of Article 53(1)(c) supports the need for the Prosecutor to conduct a contextual assessment of the interests of justice by considering the gravity of the crimes and the interests of victims within the context of the particular situation.

8. In assessing the interests of justice, the Pre-Trial Chamber placed emphasis on the feasibility of an effective investigation in light of difficulties highlighted by the Prosecutor in securing cooperation from relevant authorities during the preliminary examination. It argued that '[a]n investigation can hardly be said to be in the interests of justice if the relevant circumstances are such as to make such investigation not feasible and inevitably doomed to failure'.[183] The Pre-Trial Chamber drew a distinction between the preliminary examination stage of proceedings and the investigation stage in the context of 'timing, type of activities or resources'.[184] Having done so, it pointed to the limited resources available to carry out a complex investigation and also questioned the availability of evidence for historical crimes.[185] Of considerable note was the Pre-Trial Chamber's finding that the protracted nature of the preliminary examination and the likely difficulties in obtaining cooperation from state authorities at the investigation stage.[186] According to the Pre-Trial Chamber, the changing 'political landscape' in Afghanistan and 'key states (both parties and non-parties to the Statute)' – the latter presumably referring to the United States – was likely to hamper a successful investigation.[187] As a result of these challenges, it found that an investigation was likely to be contrary to the interests of victims and was also likely to undermine the Court's legitimacy.[188]

9. The Pre-Trial Chamber's reasoning reflects the inherent tension between the broader interests of justice and the interests of victims. There may be situations where there are significant gravity issues or substantial reasons to believe that a criminal investigation would not serve the interests of justice in a particular situation. The interests of justice analysis must be conducted on a case-by-case basis, noting that where the alleged crime is grave and serious, the Prosecutor is not required under Article 53(1)(c) to balance the interests of victims against any other criterion or factors. As such, the broad wording of Article 53(1)(c) tilts the provision towards the interests of victims. This is made clearer when Article 53(1)(c) is read in conjunction with the Statute's criminal justice imperative located in Article 17 of the Statute establishing the principle of complementarity. Complementarity is not only a

[183] Decision ICC-02/17, *supra* note 180, § 90.

[184] *Ibid*, § 92.

[185] *Ibid*, §§ 92–93.

[186] *Ibid*, § 91.

[187] *Ibid*, § 96 (according to the Pre-Trial Chamber, 'the current circumstances of the situation in Afghanistan are such as to make the prospects for a successful investigation and prosecution extremely limited').

[188] *Ibid*.

core structuring principle that governs the Court's operations, but it also embeds a criminal justice imperative in the Rome Statute which guides the application and scope of the interests of justice. The wording of the interests of justice in Article 53(1)(c) together with the complementarity principle dictates that the Prosecutor must presume that an investigation *is* in the interests of justice unless there are substantial reasons to suggest otherwise.

10. However, it should not be presumed that the constraining factors identified by the Pre-Trial Chamber (such as difficulty securing cooperation, complex nature of an investigation, limited resources) necessarily always undermine or contradict the interests of victims. Indeed, they may reflect the diverse and divergent interests of victims. For example, some victims may demand a more substantial form of accountability than what carceral justice can offer. Some victims may wish to avoid criminal justice altogether due to fears of retaliation. As noted by the Registry, a group of victims within the victims' representations expressed the view that they did not wish the Pre-Trial Chamber to authorise an investigation because of 'security concerns' and 'doubts as to the likelihood that the Prosecutor's investigation would result in the perpetrators being brought to justice'.[189]

11. Although Article 53(1)(c) operates to frame criminal justice as inherently positive for victims, caution must be exercised in relation to this assumption. This may not bear out for all victims within a situation. Victims may articulate competing and complex views or express their interests, contrary to the broad assumption that international criminal justice is an inherent good. Indeed, victims may regard the highly structured rules and procedures of criminal justice as antithetical to their own conceptions of justice and lived realities as victims. Therefore, where criminal justice remains an inherently limited form of accountability for dealing with complex injustices, substantive or transformative change, where available, in societies impacted by conflict and atrocity should be encouraged at an early stage of proceedings.[190] In these circumstances, the Prosecutor may choose to exercise discretion by refraining from opening an investigation in the context of a referral or by declining to seek authorisation to open an investigation *proprio motu*, thereby indirectly lending support to the substantive interests of victims who seek to pursue structural change.

[189] As noted by the Registry, 680 victim representations indicated that the victims wanted the Prosecutor to investigate the situation. However, fifteen representations stated that the victims did not want the Prosecutor to be authorised to open an investigation. See Public Redacted Version of Annex I-Red to the Final Consolidated Registry Report on Victims' Representations Pursuant to the Pre-Trial Chamber's Order of 9 November 2017, ICC-02/17-29-Anxl-Red, Registry, 20 February 2018, § 40.

[190] F. Mégret, 'What Sort of Global Justice Is "International Criminal Justice"?' 13 *Journal of International Criminal Justice* (2015) 77–96, at 79.

Victims' Representations

12. In the present situation before the Appeals Chamber, however, the express views of the victims were almost uniform in calling for a criminal investigation.[191] Of the 699 victim applications received by the Pre-Trial Chamber, 680 welcomed an investigation.[192] In addition, a separate group of victims 'LVR 1', 'LVR 2', and 'LVR 3', representing eighty-two victims, six victims, and an individual victim respectively, filed notices of appeal against the Impugned Decision in favour of authorising a criminal investigation.[193] There is no indication that the Pre-Trial Chamber took the views of the victims as expressed in the victims' representations into account when assessing the Prosecutor's request, nor did the Pre-Trial Chamber invite the victims to address whether an investigation would be in the interests of justice.[194]

13. The Appeals Chamber notes that prior to reaching its decision, the Pre-Trial Chamber ordered the Prosecutor to provide additional information in relation to 'allegations attributed to special forces of a number of international forces operating in Afghanistan' and 'the structure, organisation and conduct of the Afghan Forces, the structure, organisation of the Islamic State operating in Afghanistan, and the structure and interrogation policies of the United States of America for specific time periods'. In response, the Prosecutor provided 806 items of supporting material, amounting to 20,157 pages.[195] However, the Pre-Trial Chamber assessed the materials in relation to the effectiveness of an investigation rather than the interests of justice. It drew negative inferences regarding the prospects of a successful investigation including the availability of resources to carry out a complex investigation contrary to the interests of the victims. For example, as stated in the Impugned Decision, '[i]f the judicial authorisation is granted, the Prosecutor is required to investigate thoroughly and expeditiously; this may prove critically difficult in a

[191] *Ibid*, at 87.

[192] *Ibid*.

[193] By majority of the Appeals Chamber, with Judge Ibáñez Carranza dissenting, the notices of appeal were found to be inadmissible under Article 82(1)(a) of the Statute on the basis that while victims could participate in the proceedings by the Prosecutor seeking authorisation of an investigation *proprio motu*, they did not have the right to trigger an appeal within the procedural context of Article 15 as this 'right is reserved for the Prosecutor'. See Reasons for the Appeals Chamber's Oral Decision Dismissing as Inadmissible the Victims' Appeals against the Decision Rejecting the Authorisation of an Investigation into the Situation in Afghanistan (ICC-02/17 OA OA2 OA3 OA 4), Appeals Chamber, 4 March 2020, § 20.

[194] Corrigendum of Victims' Joint Appeal Brief against the Decision Pursuant to Article 15 of the Rome Statute on the Authorisation of an Investigation into the Situation in the Islamic Republic of Afghanistan of 30 September 2019 (ICC-02/17-75, ICC-02/17), Appeals Chamber, 1 October 2019, § 4.

[195] Decision ICC-02/17, *supra* note 180, § 11.

complex situation like the one under scrutiny'.[196] The Pre-Trial Chamber further stated that:

> [I]n light of the nature of the crimes and the context where they are alleged to have occurred, pursuing an investigation would inevitably require a significant amount of resources ... this will go to the detriment of other scenarios (be it preliminary examinations, investigations or cases) which appear to have more realistic prospects to lead to trials and thus effectively foster the interests of justice, possibly compromising their chances for success.[197]

14. Despite the possible complexities in an investigation of this kind involving many years of examination and several states parties and non-party states to the Statute, the Pre-Trial Chamber should have given proper and adequate weight to the interests of victims as articulated by them. The failure to listen to the victims while deferring to pressure from the United States – a non-party state – proved detrimental to the Pre-Trial Chamber's assessment of the Prosecutor's request. As the victims themselves argued:

> [T]he broader background to this filing outside the Court and its judicial proceedings cannot be ignored. Blatant attacks on the Court and those contributing to its work have been made at the highest levels, particularly by representatives of the United States government in reaction to the Prosecutor's Request. Such actions cannot but constitute an interference with the independence of the Court and the Prosecution. More troubling still is the apparent suggestion in the Decision (para. 94) that far from resisting such attacks, the Court has allowed itself to be cowed by them.[198]

15. In relation to questions of legitimacy, the Appeals Chamber notes that as a matter of law general concerns regarding the impact of an unsuccessful investigation upon the Court's credibility are immaterial to the Pre-Trial Chamber's determination of whether or not to authorise an investigation under Article 15(4) of the Statute. Ironically, the Impugned Decision had the effect of undermining the Court's legitimacy by deferring to political pressure from the United States.[199] Not only did the focus on the effectiveness of an investigation lead to speculation on the victims' interests, contrary to their express views, but it also denied the victims a right to be heard and to have their views taken into account in determining whether to authorise the investigation.

[196] *Ibid*, § 36.
[197] *Ibid*, § 95.
[198] Victims' Notice of Appeal of the Decision pursuant to Article 15 of the Rome Statute on the Authorisation of an Investigation into the Situation in the Islamic Republic of Afghanistan (ICC-02/17), Appeals Chamber, 10 June 2019, § 43.
[199] 'US threatens to arrest ICC judges', DW, 9 October 2018, available at www.dw.com/en/us-threatens-to-arrest-icc-judges-over-war-crimes-probe/a-45435900.

16. Institutional legitimacy does not take precedence over the actual interests of victims as expressed by the victims themselves in relation to whether or not to authorise an investigation. In the context of victims in Afghanistan, 'international law makes sense only in the context of the lived history of the peoples of the Third World', meaning that it is by evaluating legal rules and procedures and prioritising the lived experience of victims rather than the protection of the Court's legitimacy that this Court may thereby embody and promote global justice effectively.[200]

Gravity of Alleged Crimes in Light of the Interests of Victims

17. The Appeals Chamber notes that the Impugned Decision also fails to consider the interests of victims based on the gravity of the alleged crimes. Since 11 September 2001, Afghanistan has been the subject of military attacks and foreign intervention from the United States in response to terrorism attacks on Washington and New York.[201] Furthermore, the grave and serious allegations of crimes that form the basis of the Prosecutor's request to authorise an investigation form part of the intensification and perpetuation of anti-Muslim violence carried out on a global scale in the wake of the 'war on terror'. Racialised stereotypes of the 'Muslim terrorist' and state policies, practices, and legislation depicting Muslims and their religion through a propensity towards violence have shaped how the war on terror has been carried out by states along intersecting lines of geography, race, ethnicity, religion, and gender.[202] Attacks on civilians, cruel treatment and torture, and humiliating and degrading treatment of detainees in and from Muslim-majority countries are by now are a well-known phenomenon.[203] These harms are not only part of a racialised stereotype of Muslims but also intersect with gender and the effects of prolonged war on women and children.

18. Thus, considering the particular gravity of the alleged crimes, the Appeals Chamber notes that the materials provided by the Prosecutor supported two

[200] A. Anghie and B. S. Chimni, 'Third World Approaches to International Law and Individual Responsibility in Internal Conflicts' 2 *Chinese Journal of International Law* (2003) 77–103, at 78–79.

[201] For an account of the historical context to the armed conflict in Afghanistan, see Public Redacted Version of Request for Authorisation of an Investigation pursuant to Article 15 (ICC-02/17), Pre-Trial Chamber III, 20 November 2017, §§ 13–21.

[202] K. Welch, 'Race, Ethnicity, and the War on Terror', *Oxford Research Encyclopedia of Criminology and Criminal Justice* (online), 29 July 2019, available at https://oxfordre.com/criminology/display/10.1093/acrefore/9780190264079.001.0001/acrefore-9780190264079-e-335;jsessionid=FB9ED687A9B6C3B7CFA557AA4F78E6E1.

[203] Report of the Senate Select Committee on Intelligence: Committee Study of the Central Intelligence Agency's Detention and Interrogation Program (2014) S. Report 113-288, available at www.intelligence.senate.gov/sites/default/files/publications/CRPT-113srpt288.pdf.

outcomes: either the authorisation of an investigation or a request for further additional information from the Prosecutor under Rule 50(4) of the ICC Rules of Procedure and Evidence. Given the Pre-Trial Chamber's particular concern regarding the length of the examination, it could have sought additional information to further clarify the scope and conduct of any potential investigation into cross-border victims of aerial bombardment who are named in the proceedings. For example, cross-border victims made submissions to the Appeals Chamber that they had presented the Prosecutor with information about civilians impacted by drone strikes launched from Afghanistan into Pakistan.[204] They argued that the Prosecutor ignored the submissions in the request, with the result that the position of the cross-border victims as to whether the Prosecutor intended to pursue an investigation into their complaints was unclear.[205]

19. Further, it would have been appropriate to seek additional information regarding the position of women in any future investigation. As was highlighted by the Registry, of 165 individual representations where it was in a position to identify relevant data regarding the gender and age of victims, it found that only 10 representations were introduced by or on behalf of women despite indications that women had clearly suffered harm.[206] In some cases, women were not listed as victims by representatives acting on behalf of women. Several factors may explain this, including the location of women in conflict areas, the predominant role of men in traditional justice resolution practices, and the underreporting of sexual and gender-based violence in Afghanistan.[207] Accordingly, it would have been appropriate to seek clarification on how an investigation would incorporate sexual and gender-based crimes against women given the limited representations by or on behalf of women and the dominant role played by organisations and men in the representation of the victims.

20. Based on the above, the Appeals Chamber finds that the Pre-Trial Chamber plainly abused its discretion when giving priority to factors which it should not have taken into account in the first place while giving insufficient weight to factors that it should have taken into account, such as the interests of victims. Further, it failed to exercise its discretion in an appropriate manner by requesting further information from the Prosecutor in order to determine whether to authorise the investigation.

[204] Submissions on Behalf of the Victims of Cross Border Aerial Bombardment, Appeals Chamber (ICC-02/17), 15 November 2019, § 3.

[205] *Ibid*, § 37.

[206] Public Redacted Version of Annex I-Red to the Final Consolidated Registry Report on Victims' Representations pursuant to the Pre-Trial Chamber's Order of 9 November 2017 (ICC-02/17-29-AnxI-Red), Registry, 20 February 2018, § 35.

[207] *Ibid*, §§ 36–37.

SECOND GROUND OF APPEAL: DID THE PRE-TRIAL CHAMBER ERR IN LAW BY ASSESSING THE PROSECUTOR'S DETERMINATION OF THE INTERESTS OF JUSTICE?

21. Contrary to the Impugned Decision, there are several factors such as the text of Article 53(1) that dictate that an investigation should have been opened in the present situation. Starting with the text of Article 53(1)(C), the Prosecutor is required to consider the following factors when deciding whether to initiate an investigation:

(a) The information available to the Prosecutor provides a reasonable basis to believe that a crime within the jurisdiction of the Court has been or is being committed;

(b) The case is or would be admissible under Article 17; and

(c) Taking into account the gravity of the crime and the interests of the victims, there are nonetheless substantial reasons to believe that an investigation would not serve the interests of justice.

If the Prosecutor determines that there is no reasonable basis to proceed and that determination is based solely on sub-paragraph (c) above, the Prosecutor shall inform the Pre-Trial Chamber.

22. Firstly, in contrast to the first and second criteria, the plain text of the third criterion makes plain that there is no requirement for the Prosecutor to make a positive determination to the effect that an investigation is in the interests of justice when deciding whether to initiate an investigation. The text of Article 53(1)(c) is deliberately formulated in the negative ('would not serve'), meaning that the assessment of the interests of justice generally does not arise unless there are substantial reasons or facts and circumstances to the contrary. Unlike the first and second criteria, which require the application of exacting legal standards, the Prosecutor's evaluation of whether the opening of an investigation would not serve the interests of justice is predicated on the exercise of prosecutorial discretion.[208] As the Pre-Trial Chamber in the Kenya situation correctly identified: Unlike sub-paragraphs (a) and (b), which require an affirmative finding, sub-paragraph (c) does not require the Prosecutor to establish that an investigation is actually in the interests of justice. Indeed, the Prosecutor does not have to present reasons or supporting material in this respect.[209]

[208] *Situation on the Registered Vessels of the Union of the Comoros, the Hellenic Republic, and the Kingdom of Cambodia*, Decision on the Request of the Union of the Comoros to Review the Prosecutor's Decision not to Initiate an Investigation (ICC-01/13-34), Pre-Trial Chamber 1, 16 July 2015, § 14.

[209] *Situation in the Republic of Kenya*, Decision pursuant to Article 15 of the Rome Statute on the Authorization of an Investigation into the Situation in the Republic of Kenya (ICC-01/09), Pre-Trial Chamber II, 31 March 2010, § 6.

23. Secondly, Article 53(1)(c) operates presumptively in favour of a criminal investigation, which is deemed in the interests of justice as a matter of law. This is reflected in the high threshold that the Prosecutor must satisfy to justify a waiver of a criminal investigation. Article 53(1)(c) creates an expectation that the Prosecutor will proceed to an investigation, while limiting the scope of the discretion to waive an investigation.[210] There can be reasons not to proceed with an investigation, but it is only when there are 'substantial reasons to believe' that an investigation would *not* serve the interests of justice that this narrow exception prevails. This is because the function of Article 53(1)(c) is to further the imperative of criminal justice as found in the complementarity principle under Article 17 of the Statute. It must be remembered that the text of Article 53(1)(c) is designed to limit the Prosecutor's ability to waive a criminal investigation and therefore the criminal law nature of the Statute guides the meaning and scope of the interests of justice.

24. Thirdly, the Pre-Trial Chamber is not called on under Article 15(4) of the Statute to review the Prosecutor's assessment under Article 53(1)(a)–(c) of the Statute. Under the text of Article 15(4), the Pre-Trial Chamber's function is confined to an assessment of questions of fact and jurisdiction when it is determining whether to authorise an investigation, that is: (1) is there a 'reasonable basis to proceed with an investigation' in the sense of whether crimes have been committed and (2) does the situation or case appear to fall within the jurisdiction of the Court? If both questions are answered in the affirmative, then the Pre-Trial Chamber must authorise the investigation. Prior to making its decision, it remains open to the Pre-Trial Chamber to request further information to determine whether the factual or jurisdictional requirements of a situation have been satisfied in accordance with Article 15(4) of the Statute. Having found that these requirements were met in the present situation, the Pre-Trial Chamber should have authorised the investigation.

25. Fourthly, to the extent that judicial review is available regarding the Prosecutor's assessment of the interests of justice, then the sole basis for such review lies with Article 53(3)(b) of the Statute. In contrast to Article 53(3)(a), which refers to the referral provisions of the Statute specifically, Article 53(3)(b) is broadly worded and nothing in the wording of this provision suggests it is limited to referrals. Under Article 53(3)(b), and consistent with the imperative of criminal justice under the complementarity principle, the Pre-Trial Chamber's review powers are triggered only when the Prosecutor decides *not* to proceed with an investigation based solely on the interests of justice in Article 53(1)(c).

26. If a Prosecutor determines that there is no reasonable basis to proceed based solely on Article 53(1)(c), then they must notify the Pre-Trial Chamber of their

[210] Judgment on the Appeal against the Decision on the Authorisation of an Investigation into the Situation in the Islamic Republic of Afghanistan (ICC-02/17 OA 4), Appeals Chamber, 5 March 2020, § 29 ('Article 53(1) of the Statute thus reflects an expectation that the Prosecutor will proceed to investigate referred situations, while allowing the Prosecutor not to proceed in the limited circumstances set out in article 53(1)(a) to (c) of the Statute').

decision. In these circumstances, the Pre-Trial Chamber may, on its own motion, conduct a review of the decision by invoking Article 53(3)(b) of the Statute. Its judicial review, however, moves in only one direction, towards confirming the Prosecutor's discretion to waive a criminal investigation. The Pre-Trial Chamber has no power to review a decision by the Prosecutor to proceed with an investigation and cannot compel the Prosecutor to start a criminal investigation. The Prosecutor may, at any time, reconsider the decision not to initiate an investigation pursuant to Article 53(4) based on new facts or information.

27. The Appeals Chamber finds that a plain reading of Article 53, in conjunction with Article 15(4) of the Statute, shows that the Pre-Trial Chamber is only required to assess the information contained in the Prosecutor's request in relation to two matters: whether there is a factual basis to proceed where crimes have been committed and whether the alleged crimes fall within the Court's jurisdiction. In this regard, a decision by the Prosecutor to proceed with an investigation is not reviewable by the Pre-Trial Chamber. Judicial review is available only when the Prosecutor decides that a criminal investigation would *not* serve the interests of justice. In these circumstances, there is only a narrow scope for judicial review and the Pre-Trial Chamber can only confirm the Prosecutor's decision to waive a criminal investigation. Based on the foregoing, the Pre-Trial Chamber plainly erred when assessing the Prosecutor's determination of the interests of justice.

DETERMINATION ON THE MERITS OF THE APPEAL

28. The Appeals Chamber finds that the Pre-Trial Chamber plainly exercised its discretion incorrectly due to taking into account factors it should not have taken into account while ignoring factors it should have taken into account and failing to exercise its discretion by requesting further information. It thereby abused its discretion when determining whether to authorise an investigation.

29. Furthermore, the Appeals Chamber concludes that the Pre-Trial Chamber had no role in assessing the Prosecutor's determination regarding the interests of justice in this situation. In reaching this conclusion, the Appeals Chamber notes that the Pre-Trial Chamber should have limited its assessment to the factual and jurisdictional basis of the request which required it to authorise the investigation. Instead, it sought to block the investigation by choosing to exercise its discretion in a manner that was contrary to the express views of the victims and the plain text of Articles 15(4) and 53(1)(c) of the Statute. As a result, victims were denied the right to be properly heard and to have their interests reflected in the Pre-Trial Chamber's decision regarding the authorisation of an investigation. Had it exercised its discretion correctly, then it is likely the Pre-Trial Chamber would have reached a different outcome.

CONCLUSION ON APPROPRIATE RELIEF

30. In sum, the Appeals Chamber considers it appropriate to amend the Impugned Decision to the effect that the Prosecutor is authorised to commence an investigation into allegations of crimes set out in the Prosecutor's request. The Appeals Chamber also considers it appropriate for the Prosecutor to clarify the scope of any potential investigation in response to the cross-border victims of aerial bombardment. Finally, it considers it appropriate for the Prosecutor to clarify the position of women within the scope of any future investigation and how the Prosecutor intends to incorporate the interests of victims of sexual and gender-based violence where there are insufficient contributions by or on behalf of women in the victims' representation.

Judge Souheir Edelbi

16.6 GENDER-BASED PERSECUTION IN THE AFGHANISTAN INVESTIGATION AUTHORISATION

Susana SáCouto

In 2019, Pre-Trial Chamber II denied[211] the Prosecutor's request to authorise an investigation into crimes allegedly committed on the territory of the Islamic Republic of Afghanistan since 1 March 2003.[212] While the Pre-Trial Chamber agreed that the jurisdiction, complementarity, and gravity tests were met, ultimately the Chamber decided an investigation would not be in the interests of justice.

In this rewritten decision, Susana SáCouto focuses on the allegations concerning gender-based persecution by the Taliban and other armed groups and closely analyses the Rome Statute's definition of 'gender' per Article 7(3) and the definition of 'persecution' per Articles 7(1)(h) and 7(2)(g) of the Rome Statute. Using the Vienna Convention on the Law of Treaties as well as the ICC Office of the Prosecutor's 2014 Policy Paper on Gender-based Crimes, SáCouto concludes that gender-based persecution includes persecutory acts that are motivated by the perpetrators' beliefs, attitudes, and perceptions regarding appropriate social behaviour based on gender. Her decision stresses that without this understanding of gender, the Court would not be able to recognise the full scope of gender-based harms committed against women and girls in Afghanistan, including the attacks by the Taliban and affiliated armed groups aimed at preventing women and girls from studying,

[211] Decision pursuant to Article 15 of the Rome Statute on the Authorisation of an Investigation into the Situation in the Islamic Republic of Afghanistan, *Situation in Afghanistan* (ICC-02/17-33), Pre-Trial Chamber II, 12 April 2019.

[212] Public Redacted Version of Request for Authorisation of an Investigation pursuant to Article 15, 20 November 2017, ICC-02/17-7-Conf-Exp, *Situation in Afghanistan* (ICC-02/17-7-Red), Pre-Trial Chamber III, 20 November 2017.

teaching, working, or participating in public affairs. Moreover, Judge SáCouto addresses whether and how gender-based persecution intersects with other grounds of persecution, and finds that characterising the persecution against Afghan female politicians, public servants, and students as having been based on intersecting gender and political grounds more accurately captures the basis of the discrimination underlying this crime and the aggravated nature of the harms resulting from it.

No.: ICC-02/17
Date: 12 April 2019

Original: English

PRE-TRIAL CHAMBER II(B)

Before: Judge Susana SÁCOUTO[213]
SITUATION IN THE ISLAMIC REPUBLIC OF AFGHANISTAN

Public

Decision pursuant to Article 15 of the Rome Statute on the Authorisation of an Investigation into the Situation in the Islamic Republic of Afghanistan

PRE-TRIAL CHAMBER II (the Chamber) of the International Criminal Court (the Court) issues this Decision pursuant to Article 15 of the Rome Statute (the Statute) on the authorisation of an investigation into the situation in the Islamic Republic of Afghanistan (Afghanistan).

PROCEDURAL HISTORY

1. By a letter of 30 October 2017, the Prosecutor notified the President of the Court, in accordance with Regulation 45 of the Regulations, of her intention to submit a request for authorisation of an investigation into the situation in the Islamic Republic of Afghanistan pursuant to Article 15(3) of the Statute.[214]

2. On 20 November 2017, the Prosecutor submitted the Request for Authorisation of an Investigation pursuant to Article 15 (Prosecutor's Request), together with 14 annexes, in which the Pre-Trial Chamber is requested 'to authorise the commencement of an investigation into the Situation in the Islamic Republic of Afghanistan in relation to alleged crimes committed on the territory of Afghanistan in the period since 1 May 2003, as well as other alleged crimes that have a nexus to the armed

[213] The author wishes to recognise the contributions of Indira Rosenthal to this judgment.

[214] Situation in the Islamic Republic of Afghanistan, The Presidency, Decision Assigning the Situation in the Islamic Republic of Afghanistan (ICC-02/17-1, ICC-02/17-1-AnxI), 3 November 2017.

conflict in Afghanistan and are sufficiently linked to the situation and were committed on the territory of other States Parties in the period since 1 July 2002'.[215]

3. Throughout the period 20 November 2017 to 31 January 2018, the Court received the representations of victims, which were transmitted to Pre-Trial Chamber III on a rolling basis, together with reports containing a preliminary assessment of the representations.[216]

4. On 20 February 2018, the Registry submitted a final consolidated report summarising the process of collecting the victims' representations and the victims' views on whether or not they wish an investigation into the situation in Afghanistan to be authorised.[217]

5. On 16 March 2018, the Presidency recomposed the Chambers of this Court and assigned the situation in Afghanistan to this Chamber.[218]

[215] Situation in the Islamic Republic of Afghanistan, Public Redacted Version of Request for Authorisation of an Investigation pursuant to Article 15 (ICC-02/17-7-Conf-Exp), and Public Redacted Version (ICC-02/17-7-Red), 20 November 2017 (hereafter Prosecutor's Request), § 376.

[216] Situation in the Islamic Republic of Afghanistan, First Transmission and Report on 7 December 2017: ICC-02/17-10 with five confidential *ex parte* annexes; ICC-02/1 7-1 1-Red with two confidential *ex parte* annexes; the Court received one individual and four collective representation forms; Situation in the Islamic Republic of Afghanistan, Second Transmission and Report on 21 December 2017: ICC-02117-15 with seven confidential *ex parte* annexes; ICC-02117-16-Red with one confidential *ex parte* annex; the Court received three individual and four collective representation forms; Situation in the Islamic Republic of Afghanistan, Third Transmission and Report on 11 January 2018: ICC-02/I 7-17 with twenty-eight confidential *ex parte* annexes; ICC-02/17-18 with one confidential *ex parte* annex; the Court received five individual and twenty-three collective representation forms; Situation in the Islamic Republic of Afghanistan, Fourth Transmission and Report on 25 January 2018: ICC-02/17-19 with forty-seven confidential *ex parte* annexes; ICC-02/1 7-20-Red with three confidential *ex parte* annexes; the Court received five individual and forty-two collective representation forms; Situation in the Islamic Republic of Afghanistan, Fifth Transmission and Report on 2 February 2018: ICC-02/17-21 with 138 confidential *ex parte* annexes; ICC-02/1 7-22-Red with three confidential *ex parte* annexes; the Court received fifty-eight individual and eighty collective representation forms; Situation in the Islamic Republic of Afghanistan, Sixth Transmission and Report on 5 February 2018, ICC-02/1 7-24 with 165 confidential *ex parte* annexes; ICC-02/17-25 with 2 confidential *ex parte* annexes; the Court received 29 individual and 136 collective representation forms; Situation in the Islamic Republic of Afghanistan, Seventh Transmission and Report on 9 February 2018: ICC-02/17-27 with 309 confidential *ex parte* annexes; ICC-02/17-28 with 2 confidential *ex parte* annexes; the Court received 72 individual and 237 collective representation forms.

[217] Situation in the Islamic Republic of Afghanistan, Final Consolidated Registry Report on Victims' Representations pursuant to the Pre-Trial Chamber's Order ICC-02/17-6 of 9 November 2017, ICC-02/17-29, with a confidential annex (a public redacted version is also available) and a confidential *ex parte* annex, 20 February 2018 (hereafter Final Consolidated Registry Report).

[218] Situation in the Islamic Republic of Afghanistan, The Presidency, Decision Assigning Judges to Divisions and Recomposing Chambers (ICC-02/17-30), 16 March 2018, at 9.

PROSECUTOR'S SUBMISSIONS

6. The Prosecutor's submission asserts that the people of Afghanistan have suffered acts of serious violence and other violations of their fundamental rights over the past four decades as waves of armed conflict and security crises have plagued the country.[219] The Prosecutor submits that some of these acts constitute crimes within the jurisdiction of the Court, namely crimes against humanity under Article 7 and war crimes under Article 8 of the Statute, and seeks authorisation to open a formal investigation into such crimes.

7. The Request lists the groups allegedly responsible for the crimes for which authorisation to investigate is sought as follows: (1) the Taliban and other armed groups; (2) the Afghan National Security Forces, including the Afghan National Army, the Afghan National Police, the Afghan Local Police, the Afghan National Border Police, and the National Directorate for Security); and (3) US armed forces and the Central Intelligence Agency. The prosecution alleges that each of these groups is responsible for war crimes in the context of an armed conflict not of an international character under Article 8 of the Statute. Further, the prosecution asserts that the first category, the Taliban and other armed groups, are also responsible for crimes against humanity under Article 7, including persecution on the ground of 'gender' under Article 7(1)(h) of the Statute.

VICTIMS' REPRESENTATIONS

8. Overall, the Court has received a total of 794 representations in Dari and Pashto, as well as Arabic, English, and German of which 699 were transmitted to the Pre-Trial Chamber on behalf of the following victims: 668 representations on behalf of 6,220 individuals; 17 representations on behalf of 1,690 families; 13 representations on behalf of several millions of victims, including 26 villages; and 1 representation on behalf of an institution.

9. Notably, the report received from the Registry on Victims' Representations pursuant to the Pre-Trial Chamber's Order ICC-02/17-6 of 9 November 2017 indicates that one of the representations it received 'called on the Prosecutor to investigate all crimes perpetrated against women' and that 'a number of representations requested the persecution against certain specific groups . . . be investigated'.[220]

[219] Prosecutor's Request, *supra* note 215, §§ 115–121. The Chamber recognises that there have been reports of additional violations occurring in Afghanistan since the prosecution's submission, but does not address those violations here as the prosecution's request relates to events occurring between July 2002 and November 2017.

[220] Situation in the Islamic Republic of Afghanistan, ICC-02/17, Final Consolidated Registry Report on Victims' Representations pursuant to the Pre-Trial Chamber's Order, ICC-02/17-6 of 9 November 2017, with Confidential and Public Redacted Versions of Annex I, and Confidential ex parte Annex II, only available to the Registry, 20 February 2018, Annex 1 (hereafter Annex 1 of Final Consolidated Registry Report), at § 45.

10. Further, the Registry found that 'victims overwhelmingly support an investigation into all crimes against humanity and war crimes committed in Afghanistan since 1 May 2003'.[221]

DETERMINATION BY THE CHAMBER ON THE EXISTENCE OF A REASONABLE BASIS TO PROCEED

Jurisdiction Ratione Materiae

11. Although at the Article 15 stage, the Appeals Chamber has stated that '[o]ften no individual suspects will have been identified at this stage, nor will the exact conduct nor its legal classification be clear',[222] the facts presented in the Prosecutor's submissions and victims' representations suggest that there is a reasonable basis to believe that a number of crimes within the jurisdiction of the ICC have been committed.

12. The Chamber will first consider the allegation that the Taliban and other armed groups are responsible for the crime against humanity of gender-based persecution.

Gender-Based Persecution by the Taliban and Other Armed Groups

13. According to the Prosecutor's Request, since mid-2003 civilians have suffered greatly as anti-government forces, aligned with the Taliban and other armed groups, attacked civilians perceived or believed to be associated with or supportive of the Afghan government, related to or working with the international community, and/or perceived to oppose Taliban rule and ideology, including women and girls who worked, took part in public affairs, and attended school past the age of puberty.[223] Attacks were also directed at civilian property and objects related to the targeted civilians, and carried out in public places, including schools, hospitals, and mosques, and in private.[224] The prosecution submits that the nature of the attacks varied, and included killings, severe deprivation of physical liberty, and other fundamental human rights.[225] The prosecution submits that conduct underlying

[221] *Ibid*, at § 47.

[222] Judgment on the appeal of the Republic of Kenya against the decision of Pre-Trial Chamber II of 30 May 2011 entitled 'Decision on the Application by the Government of Kenya Challenging the Admissibility of the Case Pursuant to Article 19(2)(b) of the Statute', *Ruto and others* (ICC-01/09-01/11-307), Appeals Chamber, 30 August 2011, § 39; *Prosecutor v. Muthaura et al.*, Appeals Chamber, Judgment on the appeal of the Republic of Kenya against the decision of Pre-Trial Chamber II of 30 May 2011 entitled 'Decision on the Application by the Government of Kenya Challenging the Admissibility of the Case Pursuant to Article 19(2)(b) of the Statute' (ICC-01/09-02/11-274), 30 August 2011 (hereafter Muthaura Admissibility Appeals Judgment), § 38.

[223] Prosecutor's Request, *supra* note 215 at §§ 74, 75, 87.

[224] *Ibid*, at § 75.

[225] *Ibid*, at §§ 95–121.

some of these attacks qualifies as the crime against humanity of persecution on the ground of gender under Article 7(1)(h) of the Statute,[226] which defines the crime as follows:

> Persecution against any identifiable group or collectivity on political, racial, national, ethnic, cultural, religious, gender as defined in paragraph 3, or other grounds that are universally recognized as impermissible under international law, in connection with any act referred to in this paragraph or any crime within the jurisdiction of the Court.

14. The term 'persecution' is defined in paragraph 7(2)(g) as 'the intentional and severe deprivation of fundamental rights contrary to international law by reason of the identity of the group or collectivity'. In its Request, the prosecution submits that the Taliban and other armed groups targeted civilians and deprived them of their fundamental rights on the basis of their gender and political opinion.

INTERPRETATION OF THE LAW

Definition of Gender under the Rome Statute

15. Paragraph 7(3), which is referenced in Article 7(1)(h), defines gender as follows: 'For the purpose of this Statute, it is understood that the term "gender" refers to the two sexes, male and female, within the context of society. The term "gender" does not indicate any meaning different from the above.'

16. In interpreting the Rome Statute, this Court has routinely applied the Vienna Convention on the Law Treaties (VCLT).[227] Article 31(1) of the VCLT states that: 'A treaty shall be interpreted in good faith in accordance with the ordinary meaning to be given to the terms of the treaty in their context and in the light of its object and purpose.'[228]

17. The phrase 'the two sexes, male and female, *within the context of society*' suggests that the definition includes societal perceptions and experiences of what it means to be 'male' and 'female'. Although this phrase could be read to define gender merely as a biological category, doing so would ignore the second part of the phrase, 'within the context of society', and would, thus, be inconsistent with a good-faith reading of the phrase.

[226] *Ibid*, at § 116.

[227] See e.g. *Prosecutor v. Lubanga*, Judgment on the appeal of Mr Thomas Lubanga Dyilo against his conviction (ICC-01/04-01/06-3121-Red), Appeals Chamber, 1 December 2014, at § 227; Final Submissions of the Prosecution following the Appeal Hearing, Al Bashir (ICC-02/05-01/09-392), Appeals Chamber, 28 September 2018, at § 6.

[228] Vienna Convention on the Law of Treaties (adopted 23 May 1969, entered into force 1 January 1980) 1155 UNTS 331 (VCLT).

18. Moreover, the drafting history of Article 7(3) – which is relevant as a supplementary means of interpretation under Article 32 of the VCLT[229] – affirms that the definition of gender encompasses more than a biological category.[230] The Chamber will briefly detail that history here in order to shed light on the meaning of the Article 7 definition of 'gender', and thereby the crime of gender-based persecution under the Statute.

19. The inclusion of gender-based persecution as a crime against humanity in the Statute was novel. 'Gender' as a ground for persecution had not previously been enumerated or defined either in statute or international criminal jurisprudence. The Court's twentieth-century antecedents, the ad hoc international criminal tribunals for the former Yugoslavia (ICTY) and Rwanda (ICTR), created by the UN Security Council, had jurisdiction over persecution as a crime against humanity, but only on political, racial, and religious grounds.[231] Gender-based persecution therefore required delineation in the Statute. Defining the 'gender' part of the crime proved contentious in the negotiations leading up to the adoption of the Rome Statute.[232]

20. A majority of states favoured a definition that was consistent with the way in which the term had been used in the UN and other international fora: 'gender' refers to a social construction of what it means to be male or female in a given time and place.[233] In this understanding, these social constructs dictate and moderate norms of behaviour and appearance for all individuals, as well as power relations between people of different genders and their respective access to opportunities and resources.[234]

[229] Article 32 of the VCLT states: 'Recourse may be had to supplementary means of interpretation, including the preparatory work of the treaty and the circumstances of its conclusion, in order to confirm the meaning resulting from the application of article 31.'

[230] See e.g. B. Bedont and K. Hall-Martinez, 'Ending Impunity for Gender Crimes under the International Criminal Court' 6 *Brown Journal of World Affairs* (1999) 65–85; Valerie Oosterveld, 'The Definition of "Gender" in the Rome Statute of the International Criminal Court: A Step Forward or Back for International Criminal Justice?' 18 *Harvard Human Rights Journal* (2005) 55–84.

[231] Statute of the International Criminal Tribunal for the former Yugoslavia, adopted on 25 May 1993, Article 5, Statute of the International Tribunal for Rwanda, adopted on 8 November 1994, Article 3.

[232] C. Steains, 'Gender Issues' in R. S. Lee (ed.), *The International Criminal Court: The Making of the Rome Statute* (Alphen aan den Rijn: Kluwer Law International, 1999) 357–390; Oosterveld, *supra* note 230; R. Grey et al., 'Gender-Based Persecution as a Crime against Humanity: The Road Ahead' 17(5) *Journal of International Criminal Justice* (2019) 957–979, at 964–966; I. Rosenthal, V. Oosterveld, and S. SáCouto, 'What Is Gender in International Criminal Law?', in *Gender and International Criminal Law* (Oxford: Oxford University Press, 2022).

[233] Steains, *supra* note 232, at 373; Oosterveld, *supra* note 230, at 64 (according to Valerie Oosterveld, who was a member of the Canadian delegation during the negotiations: 'Countries supporting use of the term were committed to ensuring that any definition adopted would reflect that "gender" refers to socially constructed understandings of what it means to be male or female').

[234] Steains, *supra* note 232, at 373–374.

21. On the opposing side was a small minority of states that insisted on a narrow definition that confined 'gender' to a description of only two biological sexes, namely female and male.[235] In their view, there are only two 'genders' which are not mutable, and which are wholly biologically determined.[236]

22. As is the way in treaty negotiations, compromises were made. A definition of 'gender' was included in Article 7(3) that appears to attempt to balance the two opposing views as to the correct meaning of 'gender'. The definition has been described as 'intentionally opaque'[237] and 'constructively ambiguous'.[238]

23. In the ICC's 'Policy Paper on Sexual and Gender-Based Crimes' (the SGBC Policy Paper) adopted in 2014,[239] the ICC Prosecutor interprets the definition of gender as follows: '"Gender", in accordance with article 7(3) of the Rome Statute . . . refers to males and females, within the context of society. This definition acknowledges the social construction of gender, and the accompanying roles, behaviours, activities, and attributes assigned to women and men, and to girls and boys.'[240]

24. Notably, the SGBC Policy Paper distinguishes 'gender' from 'sex'. Therefore, it defines 'sex' for the purpose of the policy as: '"Sex" refers to the biological and physiological characteristics that define men and women.'[241]

25. The SGBC Policy Paper's approach is not only consistent with a good-faith reading of Article 7(3) and the Statute's drafting history of this article, but also with international human rights law and practice,[242] as required by Article 21(3) of the Rome Statute.[243]

26. Indeed, twenty-four UN experts who provided comments on the definition of gender contemplated by the International Law Commission in its consideration of a new draft treaty on crimes against humanity observed that '[i]nternational human rights law recognizes gender as the social attributes associated with being male and female', and that twenty-five years of practice has demonstrated 'wide recognition of

[235] Oosterveld, *supra* note 230, at 64.

[236] *Ibid*.

[237] Rosenthal et al., *supra* note 232, at 21.

[238] V. Oosteveld, 'Constructive Ambiguity and the Meaning of Gender for the International Criminal Court' 16 *International Feminist Journal of Politics* (2014) 563; Rosenthal et al., *supra* note 232, at 21; T. Rahimian, 'Afghanistan and the International Criminal Court: A Gender Perspective', *Journal of International Affairs*, 20 June 2018, https://jia.sipa.columbia.edu/news/afghanistan-and-international-criminal-court-gender-perspective.

[239] ICC OTP, Policy Paper on Sexual and Gender-Based Crimes (2014) (hereafter SGBC Policy Paper).

[240] *Ibid*, at 3.

[241] *Ibid*, at 3.

[242] Grey et al., *supra* note 232, at 957–979.

[243] See Rome Statute, Art. 21(3) ('The application and interpretation of law pursuant to this article must be consistent with internationally recognized human rights, and be without any adverse distinction founded on grounds such as gender as defined in article 7, paragraph 3, age, race, colour, language, religion or belief, political or other opinion, national, ethnic or social origin, wealth, birth or other status').

gender as a social construct that permeates the context in which human rights abuses take place'.[244]

27. Thus, this Chamber understands 'gender' to mean not only biological differences between males and females, but also societal beliefs, attitudes, perceptions, and experiences of what it means to be 'male' and 'female'.

28. Moreover, in the context of Article 7(1)(h) and in line with the ICC Elements of Crimes,[245] the term 'gender' describes the grounds on which a group is victimised, meaning persecution on the grounds of gender includes persecution that takes place on the grounds of socially constructed ideas about what it means to be male or female, rather than solely because the members of the group are male or female. Thus, gender-based persecution includes persecutory acts that are motivated by the beliefs, attitudes, and perceptions of the perpetrators regarding appropriate social behaviour for males and females.

29. This Chamber considers it important to make clear, as other tribunals have, that as long as the acts constitute a severe deprivation of victims' fundamental rights

[244] Twenty-four Special Rapporteurs, Working Groups, and Independent Experts' submission to the International Law Commission, 'Re: Comments to the Draft Crimes against Humanity Convention', 30 November 2018, available at www.ohchr.org/Documents/Issues/Executions/LetterGender.pdf (hereafter Comments by UN Experts), at 2, 6. Notably, the one treaty besides the Rome Statute that explicitly includes a definition of 'gender', namely the Council of Europe Convention on Preventing and Combating Violence against Women and Domestic Violence, defines 'gender' as 'the socially constructed roles, behaviours, activities and attributes that a given society considers appropriate for women and men'. Council of Europe Convention on preventing and combating violence against women and domestic violence (Istanbul Convention), CETS 210, 11 May 2011 (entered into force 1 August 2014), Art. 3(c). In addition, human rights treaty bodies, UN Human Rights Council special procedures and UN agencies involved in the promotion and protection of human rights all define the term 'gender' as a social construct. See e.g. CEDAW, General Recommendation 28, UN Doc. CEDAW/C/GC/28, 16 December 2010, at § 7 (explaining that whereas 'sex' means 'biological differences between men and women', the term 'gender' refers to 'socially constructed identities, attributes and roles for women and men and society's social and cultural meaning for these biological differences resulting in hierarchical relationships between women and men and in the distribution of power and rights favouring men and disadvantaging women'); Report of the Special Rapporteur on Extrajudicial, Summary or Arbitrary Executions on a Gender-Sensitive Approach to Arbitrary Killings, Agnes Callamard, UN Doc. A/HRC/35/23, 6 June 2017, at §§ 16–17 (defining 'gender' as a social construct); Office of the Special Advisor on Gender Issues and Advancement of Women, Gender Mainstreaming: Strategy for Promoting Gender Equality (2001), available at www.un.org/womenwatch/osagi/pdf/factsheet1.pdf (same); Office of the High Commissioner for Human Rights, Integrating a Gender Perspective into Human Rights Investigations: Guidance and Practice (2018), at 7; UNHCHR Guidelines on International Protection: Gender-Related Persecution within the Context of Article 1A(2) of the 1951 Convention and/or Its 1967 Protocol Relating to the Status of Refugees, UN Doc. HCR/GIP/02/01, 7 May 2002, at § 3 (same); UN Women, Concepts and Definitions, at www.un.org/womenwatch/osagi/conceptsandefinitions.htm (same). This approach is also consistent with that of scholars and experts in the area of gender and international law. See e.g. Grey et al, *supra* note 232, at 966–968.

[245] ICC Elements of Crimes, Art. 7(1)(h), Elements (2) and (3) (separately listing as elements the targeting of the group and the grounds on which that group was targeted).

under international law, it is legally irrelevant whether local laws, religion, or customs permit the behaviour that resulted in those violations.[246] Thus, even in societies where the idea of equality among certain groups is contentious, or where discrimination on the basis of gender is the norm, severe violations of fundamental rights contrary to international law can amount to persecution. Indeed, such violations may constitute persecution regardless of whether they are accepted, tolerated, or formally legalised in a given community.

30. Finally, this Chamber recognises that groups may be targeted, or have different experiences of crimes, because of intersecting and inextricably linked identity factors, which may include gender but also political, racial, national, ethnic, cultural, religious, or other grounds. As such, it will take an intersectional approach to the crime of persecution, meaning the Chamber will assess not only whether harms were inflicted on victims on the grounds of gender but also whether and how gender-based persecution intersected with other grounds of persecution, and the impact of persecution on the basis of these intersecting grounds on the targeted group.[247] The Chamber considers that this approach most accurately captures the lived experiences of those who are targeted for persecution.

Intentional and Severe Deprivation of Fundamental Rights Contrary to International Law

31. The Chamber considers that, as this Court has previously found, for the purpose of identifying those rights the intentional and severe deprivation of which may constitute persecution, it should look to international standards on human rights such as those laid down in the Universal Declaration of Human Rights (UDHR), the two United Nations Covenants on Human Rights, and other international instruments on international human rights.[248] Drawing upon various provisions of these texts, the Chamber considers that it is possible to identify a set of fundamental rights pertaining to any human being, the gross infringement of which

[246] See e.g. *Prosecutor v. Zoran Kupreškić et al.*, IT 95-16, Judgment, 14 January 2000 (hereafter Kupreškić Trial Judgment), § 614 (noting: 'It is well-known that the Nazis passed many discriminatory laws through the available constitutional and legislative channels which were subsequently enforced by their judiciary. This does not detract from the fact that these laws were contrary to international legal standards. The Trial Chamber therefore rejects the Defence submission that persecution should not include acts which are legal under national laws'). See also Grey et al., *supra* note 232, at 973 ('The fact that a violation may be commonplace or even ubiquitous does not make it any less "severe"').

[247] Notably, this approach is consistent with that adopted by the Prosecutor in both the SGBC Policy Paper and the OTP's Policy on Children. See SGBC Policy Paper, *supra* note 239, at 13, 116; ICC OTP, Policy on Children (2016), available at www.icc-cpi.int/sites/default/files/20161115_OTP_ICC_Policy-on-Children_Eng.PDF, at 19.

[248] See *Prosecutor v. Ntaganda* (ICC-01/04-02/06), Judgment, 8 July 2019 (hereafter Ntaganda Trial Judgment), § 991. This, of course, is also consistent with Article 21(3) of the Rome Statute, which requires that the application and interpretation of the Rome Statute 'be consistent with internationally recognized human rights'.

may amount to persecution. For instance, the deprivation of rights infringed by the crimes of genocide, crimes against humanity, or war crimes – such as the right to life, liberty, and the security of person, and the right not to be subjected to torture or cruel, inhuman, or degrading treatment or punishment, or to rape and sexual slavery, or to arbitrary arrest, detention, exile, or imprisonment – certainly amount to persecution.[249]

32. However, as other tribunals have found, 'there is no comprehensive list of what acts can' amount to violations of fundamental rights contrary to international law.[250] Indeed, they may also include discriminatory acts not enumerated in the court's statute, such as those involving 'physical or mental harm or infringements upon individual freedom'.[251] For instance, as the ICTY has noted:

> The Judgment of the [International Military Tribunal at Nuremberg] included in the notion of persecution a variety of acts which, at present, may not fall under the Statute of the International Tribunal, such as *the passing of discriminatory laws, the exclusion of members of an ethnic or religious group from aspects of social, political, and economic life*, the imposition of a collective fine on them, *the restriction of their movement* and their seclusion in ghettos, and the requirement that they mark themselves out by wearing a yellow star. Moreover, and as mentioned above, several individual defendants were convicted of persecution in the form of *discriminatory economic acts*.[252]

33. Moreover, the *Justice* case, prosecuted by the United States after World War II, recognised the use of 'judicial process as a powerful weapon for the persecution and extermination of all opponents of the Nazi regime'.[253] This case recognised that acts of persecution could include the 'passing of a decree by which Jews were excluded from the legal profession; the prohibition of intermarriage between Jews and persons of German blood and the severe punishment of sexual intercourse between these groups; and decrees expelling Jews from public services, educational institutions, and from many business enterprises'.[254]

34. Thus, acts such as: other forms of sexual violence; harassment, humiliation, and psychological abuse; destruction of means of subsistence; restrictions on the types of professions and on family life; and other attacks on political, social, or

[249] *Ibid*, at §§ 991, 993.

[250] See e.g. *Prosecutor v. Vasiljević*, IT-98-32-T, Judgment, 29 November 2002, § 246.

[251] *Ibid*. See also Kupreškić Trial Judgment, *supra* note 246, at §§ 610–614 (14 January 2000); *Prosecutor v. Kvočka*, IT-98-30/1-T, Judgment, 2 November 2001, § 185.

[252] Kupreškić Trial Judgment, *supra* note 246, § 610 (emphasis added) (internal citations omitted).

[253] *Ibid*, § 611 (citing Justice Case, Indictment, Nuremberg Military Tribunal, Vol. III, at 18).

[254] *Ibid*, § 612 (citing Justice Case, Judgment, Nuremberg Military Tribunal, Vol. III, at 1063–1064).

economic rights[255] can also amount to persecution, as long those acts were committed 'in connection with any crime within the jurisdiction of the Court'.[256]

35. As this Court has previously held, the determination as to which acts will result in the *severe* deprivation of one or more individuals' fundamental rights must be made on a case-by-case basis.[257] Further, it is this Chamber's view that all acts must be examined in context and cumulatively because although certain acts may not on their own amount to a violation of fundamental rights (and therefore persecution), they may do so when considered in light of other acts and the context in which they occur.[258] When assessing the severity of deprivations of fundamental rights, this Chamber considers it important to conduct a detailed analysis not only of the harms but also the impact of the discriminatory acts on the targeted group.

LEGAL FINDINGS: GENDER-BASED PERSECUTION BY THE TALIBAN

36. Although this is not this Court's first opportunity to address the crime of gender-based persecution,[259] in the one case where it was considered at the confirmation of charges stage, persecution was not confirmed and gender-based persecution was ultimately not discussed in the confirmation of charges decision.[260] The Chamber considers that – in light of enduring misconceptions about 'gender-based crimes', such as the notion that such crimes are limited to rape and other forms of sexual violence[261] – it is particularly important for this Chamber to address the scope and contours of gender-based persecution in the context of the Afghanistan situation. Indeed, this Chamber finds it critical to examine both individual and cumulative harms, in particular non-sexual gendered harms, experienced by victims of persecution and to explore the breadth of fundamental rights the deprivation of which are implicated by this crime and which rarely have been made visible.

255 See e.g. Kupreškić Trial Judgment, *supra* note 246, at § 615; *Prosecutor v. Tadic*, Judgment, IT-94-1, 7 May 1997, § 704.

256 See Article 7(1)(h) and (7)(2)(g) of the Rome Statute.

257 Ntaganda Trial Judgment, *supra* note 248, § 992.

258 *Ibid*. In addition, as this Court has previously determined, with respect to the element requiring that the deprivation of a fundamental right must be contrary to international law, the Chamber considers this to mean that no justification exists under international law for the impediment of the concerned right, whether the act is committed by a state or non-state actor. *Ibid*, at § 993.

259 See e.g. *Prosecutor v. Mbarushimana*, Prosecution's Application under Article 58 (ICC-01/04-01/ 10-11-Red2), 20 August 2010, Count 11 (including gender-based persecution); *Prosecutor v. Mbarushimana*, Arrest Warrant (ICC-01/04-01/ 10-2-tENG), 28 September 2010, at § 10 (same); *Prosecutor v. Al Hassan Ag Abdoul Aziz Ag Mohamed Ag Mahmoud* (ICC-01/12-01/ 18), Decision on the Prosecutor's Application for the Issuance of a Warrant of Arrest for Al Hassan Ag Abdoul Aziz Ag Mohamed Ag Mahmoud, 28 May 2018, at § 96 (finding reasonable grounds to believe that the crime against humanity of persecution on religious and gender grounds was committed).

260 *Prosecutor v. Mbarushimana* (ICC-01/04-01/10), Decision on the Confirmation of Charges, 15 December 2011.

261 See e.g. Rosenthal et al., *supra* note 232, at 14.

37. In this regard, the Chamber finds it particularly noteworthy that one of the organisations consulted during the Registry's review of victims' views on the opening of this investigation stressed that 'most "traditional justice resolution" practices ("jirgas") are male-only affairs, with crimes against women almost entirely unrepresented in these fora, unless as a matter of family "honour"'. The organisation 'concluded that the obstacles to women using a "formal" justice system are enormous'.[262]

Deprivation of Fundamental Rights

38. The Prosecutor's allegations of gender-based persecution include crimes committed by the Taliban and affiliated armed groups against female politicians, public servants, and students in Afghanistan.[263] The Prosecutor alleges that: 'Pursuant to the ideology and rules of the Taliban, women and girls have been deliberately attacked by the Taliban and affiliated armed groups to prevent them from studying, teaching, working or participating in public affairs, through intimidation, death threats, abductions and killings.'[264]

39. Specifically, the Prosecutor's allegations and supporting documents indicate that the Taliban destroyed girls' schools and directed threats and acts of violence at teachers, administrators, and students 'who refused to abide by the Taliban's rules'.[265] These attacks deprived 'thousands of girls of their right to education'.[266]

40. Moreover, the Taliban threatened and/or killed female politicians, female police officers, and women at or on their way to work.[267] As the prosecution notes, the 'efforts to prevent women from participating in the workforce, education, and governance and politics, have resulted in major disruption to the ability of women to exercise many of their fundamental rights'.[268]

41. In other words, women and girls were deprived of their fundamental rights to education, to work, to participate in public life, to physical and bodily integrity, to liberty and freedom of movement, to expression, to assemble, and to be free from arbitrary deprivations of life, inhuman and degrading treatment or punishment, and discrimination on the basis of sex, all of which they enjoyed pursuant to international law.[269]

262 Annex 1 of Final Consolidated Registry Report, *supra* note 217, at § 37. This Chamber believes that, in light of these challenges, it is vital that it expand on the contours of the crime of gender-based persecution, such that future investigations adequately include the full scope of gender-based harms relevant to this crime.

263 Prosecutor's Request, *supra* note 215, at § 115.

264 *Ibid*, §§ 115–116.

265 *Ibid*, § 119.

266 *Ibid*, § 343.

267 *Ibid*, §§ 117–120.

268 *Ibid*, § 121.

269 These rights are included in human rights instruments, such as the International Covenant for Civil and Political Rights, the International Covenant on Economic, Social and Cultural Rights, the Convention against Torture and Other Cruel Inhuman or Degrading Treatment of

42. Moreover, these deprivations had far-reaching consequences, with long-lasting impacts on the lives of the victims, their families, and their communities. For instance, the attacks against schools, as well as the threats and violence directed at female students who refused to abide by the Taliban's rules by attending school, not only resulted in the violation of the girls' physical and bodily integrity – some of whom were burned, blinded, and disfigured through acid attacks[270] – but also reduced or eliminated their prospects of continuing their education, disrupting and/or limiting their future ability to work or participate in public life. As the Prosecutor's Request indicates, these restrictions 'led to severe economic hardship due to loss of employment and income'.[271]

43. Importantly, these consequences affected not only those who actually opposed or were perceived to oppose Taliban rule and ideology, but also those who complied with the restrictions in order to avoid punishments or reprisals. As the Prosecutor's Request and supporting documentation demonstrate, as a result of the attacks, 'countless *other* women and girls have reportedly stopped going to school or working due to the attendant climate of fear'.[272] Given the high rate of male casualties during the conflicts in Afghanistan, many women were the primary or only breadwinners in the family. The systematic deprivation of the right to education and to work meant increased levels of impoverishment for women, girls, and their families, 'with poverty forcing many women to give their daughters in marriage in exchange for debts or to take their children out of school often to work'.[273]

44. Some of these acts – such as the killings and acid attacks – violate rights infringed by other Rome Statute crimes, such as murder and inhumane acts, and thus clearly amount to persecutory acts if committed on the basis of one of the grounds within Article 7(1)(h). This Chamber finds it important to stress, however, that other acts – such as preventing women and girls from participating in aspects of social, political, and economic life – also deprive victims of fundamental rights and constitute persecutory acts when committed on the basis of one of the protected grounds.[274]

45. Further, this Chamber finds that when viewed in context and cumulatively, these acts constitute a *severe* deprivation of victims' fundamental rights. Having examined not only direct harms to the women and girls targeted by the Taliban, but also the long-lasting adverse impacts of these acts on the ability of victims and their families to subsist and on women's and girl's access to critical services and

Punishment, and the Convention to Eliminate all Forms of Discrimination Against Women, all of which were ratified by Afghanistan. See UN Treaty Body Database, at https://tbinternet.ohchr.org/_layouts/15/TreatyBodyExternal/Treaty.aspx?CountryID=1&Lang=EN.

270 Prosecutor's Request, *supra* note 215, § 120.

271 *Ibid*, § 121.

272 *Ibid*, at § 116 (emphasis added).

273 *Ibid*, at § 343.

274 See *supra* notes 250–256 and accompanying text.

support, this Chamber finds that women and girls in Afghanistan were severely deprived of their fundamental rights.

46. In addition, this Chamber finds that these acts were committed 'in connection with' other ICC crimes, as required per Articles 7(1)(h) and 7(2)(g) of the Rome Statue. As the Prosecutor's Request and supporting documents indicate, the Taliban had a policy 'to attack the civilian population in order to seize power from the Government of Afghanistan by lethal force' and pursued this policy by deliberately targeting civilians perceived or believed to be associated with or supportive of the Afghan government, related to or working with the international community, and/or perceived to oppose Taliban rule and ideology, 'including women and girls who worked, took part in public affairs, and attended school past the age of puberty'.[275] Thus, the persecutory acts against women and girls were committed in connection with the other crimes against humanity in furtherance of this policy, including murder and deprivations of physical liberty.

On the Grounds of Gender

47. As discussed earlier, persecution on the grounds of gender includes persecution that takes place on the grounds of the perpetrators' socially constructed ideas about what it means to be male or female, rather than solely because the members of the group are biologically male or female. Thus, gender-based persecution includes persecutory acts that are motivated by the perpetrators' beliefs, attitudes, and perceptions regarding appropriate social behaviour for males and females. Significantly, without this understanding of gender, this Chamber would not be able to recognise the full scope of gender-based harms committed against women and girls in Afghanistan, including the attacks by the Taliban and affiliated armed groups aimed at preventing them from studying, teaching, working, or participating in public affairs.

48. The sources supporting the Prosecutor's Request indicate that the Taliban's attacks against women and girls were animated by their interpretation of Islam and beliefs about the proper role of women and girls in society. For instance, credible sources cited by the prosecution demonstrate that the Taliban and affiliated armed groups 'believe that girls should stop attending school past puberty'.[276] These and other sources likewise show that the Taliban and affiliated groups believe that women should not teach, work, or participate in public affairs.[277] For example,

[275] Prosecutor's Request, *supra* note 215, at §§ 74, 75, 87.

[276] *Ibid*, § 116, n. 175 (citing HRW, The Ten-Dollar Talib, AFG-OTP-0002-3071 at 3104; A. Giustozzi and C. Franco, 'The Ongoing Battle for the Schools: Uprisings, Negotiations and Taleban Tactics', Afghanistan Analysts Network, June 2013, AFG-OTP-0003-0172 at 0175; UNAMA, 'Silence Is Violence: End the Abuse of Women in Afghanistan', 8 July 2009, AFG-OTP-0001-3204, at 3225). See also Prosecutor's Request, *supra* note 215, § 119.

[277] Prosecutor's Request, *supra* note 215, § 116 (citing UNAMA, *supra* note 276, at 3218–3228; R. Reid, 'The Taliban war on women continues', *Wall Street Journal*, 14 July 2010, AFG-OTP-0003-3744; Amnesty International, 'Their Lives on the Line: Attacks on Women Human Rights Defenders in Afghanistan', 6 April 2015, AFG-OTP-0003-0444 at 0470-0496).

the prosecution cites sources indicating that the Taliban had a practice of distributing 'night letters' to 'induce compliance with social norms favored by the Taliban',[278] and that one of these letters addressed to an Afghan woman stated: 'We Taliban warn you to stop working otherwise we will take your life away. We will kill you in such a harsh way that no woman has so far been killed in that manner. This will be a good lesson for those women like you who are working. The money you receive is *haram* [prohibited under Islam] and coming from the infidels.'[279]

49. Thus, it is clear that the deprivation of fundamental human rights was inflicted on women and girls because of the Taliban's beliefs, attitudes, and perceptions regarding appropriate social behaviour for females.

50. This Chamber recognises that the definition of gender under Article 7(3) of the Rome Statute, in particular the phrase 'within the context of society' – even if interpreted to include societal perceptions and attitudes about what it means to be 'male' and 'female' – could be read as referring to perceptions and attitudes about the proper role and behaviour of males and females *within the context of Afghan society*. Notably, historians and social scientists who have written about Afghanistan have indicated that gender-discriminatory attitudes, beliefs, and perceptions were prevalent within Afghan society during the period under review here.[280]

51. This Chamber notes, however, that even those sources acknowledge that such discriminatory beliefs were 'largely attributed to the patriarchal social structure' in Afghanistan, where '[m]en [we]re still largely in control of the means of production,

[278] *Ibid*, § 94 (citing Report of the UN Special Rapporteur on Extrajudicial, Summary or Arbitrary Executions, Philip Alston, Addendum: Mission to Afghanistan", A/HRC/11/2/Add.4, 6 May 2009, AFG-OTP-0003-3233, at 3248).

[279] *Ibid*, § 118. See also P. R. Blood (ed.), *Afghanistan: A Country Study* (2001), available at http://countrystudies.us/afghanistan/58.htm (explaining that in 1978, '[c]onservative mujahidin leaders waging a jihad (struggle) against foreign encroachment [in Afghanistan], both military and ideological, were imbued with the belief that sexual anarchy would result if women continued to move freely in public; and that society would fall into ruin as a result. These attitudes … intensified under the Taliban. Mostly rural Pushtun from strongly patriarchal backgrounds, the Taliban project ultraconservative interpretations of Islam and apply customary practices as societal ideals').

[280] See e.g. Blood, *supra* note 279 (explaining the 'zealous need to protect women's morality stems from the fact that Afghan society regards women as the perpetuators of the ideals of the society. As such they symbolize honor – of family, community and nation – and must be controlled as well as protected so as to maintain moral purity'); H. Emadi, 'Women in the Post-Taliban Afghanistan: The Socio-economic System and Its Corresponding Culture, Race, Gender & Class' 22(3–4) *Environment, Race, Culture, Gender, Crime, and Other Issues* (2015) 244–259, at 247 (noting that the 'socio-economic system and its corresponding culture and religion regards women as men's private property … Such a belief system suppresses women and restricts their activities to the domestic realm and household tasks such as cooking, cleaning and bearing and rearing children as well as helping men with farming and harvesting. Women are regarded as chattel to be sold and bought by men, treated as second-class citizens and are routinely deprived of their basic civil rights. It is suggested that 87 percent of women in the country are illiterate. … 70–80 percent are forced to marry against their will, often to much older men. … In a male-dominated society it is difficult even for educated women to engage in socio-political and cultural activities that are usually regarded an exclusively male domain').

religious educational institutions and decision-making bodies inside and outside … state [institutions], and other social and cultural institutions'.[281] This suggests that while these beliefs might have been shared by a segment of the population, they likely did not reflect all or even a majority of Afghans' views. In fact, during debates surrounding the drafting of a new Afghan constitution in 2003 and 2004, 'a number of women delegates … spoke against societal injustice and violation of human and women['s] rights by the Islamic warriors'.[282]

52. More importantly, even if these beliefs, attitudes, and perceptions had been prevalent within the context of Afghan society, as discussed above, if they resulted in conduct that constitutes a *severe* violation of victims' fundamental rights under international law, it is legally irrelevant whether local laws, religion, or customs permit the behaviour that resulted in those violations.[283] Thus, the severe deprivation of fundamental rights of individuals who act contrary to prescribed gender roles, even if accepted or tolerated in a particular society, amounts to persecution on the grounds of gender.

On Intersecting Grounds of Gender and Political Opinion

53. As mentioned earlier, this Chamber recognises that groups may be targeted, or have different experiences of crimes, because of intersecting and inextricably linked identity factors. Thus, the Chamber will assess not only whether harms were inflicted on victims on the grounds of gender but also whether and how gender-based persecution intersected with other grounds of persecution, and the impact of persecution on the basis of these intersecting grounds on the targeted group.

54. The Prosecutor's Request notes that 'it appears that female politicians, public servants and students were also killed based on their *political* affiliation or beliefs'.[284] The Prosecutor's allegations and supporting documents note, for instance, that the Taliban killed two female heads of a provincial Department of Women's Affairs (DWA), one of whom was a 'prominent politician who had for years been a leading advocate for the fair treatment of women'.[285] Although the prosecution uses this as an example of gender-based persecution, the Taliban appears to have targeted these women both because they acted contrary to the gender norms espoused by the Taliban *and* because of their political opinions and activities. In fact, as the Prosecutor's Request makes clear, the second victim, who was Acting Head of the DWA, was killed on her way to work.[286] Moreover, other DWA staff members were also subject to threats.[287]

[281] Emadi, *supra* note 280, at 257.
[282] *Ibid*, at 250.
[283] See *supra* note 246 and accompanying text.
[284] Prosecutor's Request, *supra* note 215, at § 116 (emphasis added).
[285] *Ibid*, § 117.
[286] *Ibid*.
[287] *Ibid*. See also ibid, § 120 (noting an 'August 2013 attack on the convoy of a female senator from Nimroz Province on the Kandahar-Kabul highway').

55. Importantly, recognising the intersectional grounds animating the Taliban's conduct makes clear both the enhanced vulnerability of the victims to the Taliban's attacks and the aggravated harms flowing from their conduct. Indeed, the killings not only deprived the victims of their lives and the victims' families of their loved ones, but also resulted in reduced advocacy for and availability of services and support for women and girls in their community. As the Prosecutor's allegations and supporting sources show, 'by targeting ... two prominent female figures ... the Taliban terrorised and effectively prevented women and girls from approaching an important social institution where they could seek protection and file complaints in efforts to improve the living conditions of Afghan women and girls'.[288]

56. Thus, this Chamber finds that characterising the persecution against female politicians, public servants, and students as having been based on intersecting gender and political grounds more accurately captures the basis of the discrimination underlying this crime and the aggravated nature of the harms resulting from it.

Chapeau Elements

57. The Chamber finds that the persecution on intersecting gender and political grounds was committed as part of a widespread or systematic attack directed against a civilian population. It further finds that the perpetrators knew that such persecution was part of or intended the conduct to be part of a widespread or systematic attack directed against the civilian population.

Conclusion

58. Having considered the Prosecutor's Request and the evidence adduced in support of it, the Chamber is satisfied that there is a reasonable basis to believe that the crime against humanity of persecution on intersecting gender and political grounds has been committed.

FOR THESE REASONS, THE CHAMBER HEREBY:

DECIDES to authorise an investigation into the situation in Afghanistan and, accordingly, **APPROVES THE REQUEST**;

ORDERS the Victims' Participation and Reparations Section of the Registry to notify the present Decision to the victims who have made representations to the Chamber in relation to the situation in Afghanistan.

Judge Susana SáCouto

[288] *Ibid*, § 117.

17

The Situations and Cases That Are Yet to Be

Suzanne Varrall, Rosemary Grey, Kcasey McLoughlin, and Louise Chappell

As noted in Chapter 2, the selection of situations and cases that authors have reimagined in this collection was shaped by several constraints. One of the most significant was the constraint of being limited to those situations and cases that have actually commenced in the ICC, thereby providing judicial decisions to rewrite.[1] As editors and contributors, we struggled with this limitation in the feminist judgment method because it meant that the selection of cases and situations in this collection necessarily replicated the gaps and silences in ICC jurisprudence.

Allegations of selectivity have long shrouded the search for international criminal justice, and the ICC has been a lightning rod for criticisms on this front, from concerns about its preliminary examinations and investigations, to concerns about case selection and prioritisation and the selection of charges. Myriad factors – legal and political – determine which situations, cases, and persons ultimately come before the court. In this way, any reimagining of law is limited in its ability to examine the road not taken – 'the situations that never were', so to speak.

At the time of writing in 2023, one of the many gaps in the ICC's quest for accountability and justice concerns the Palestine/Israel conflict. In 2009, the Palestinian National Authority lodged a declaration to the ICC, accepting the Court's jurisdiction for potential crimes committed on Palestinian territory since the Rome Statute's entry into force in 2002. Had that declaration been valid, the ICC Prosecutor could theoretically open an investigation, after obtaining authorisation of the Pre-Trial Chamber. However, in 2012 Prosecutor Luis Moreno Ocampo concluded that no such progress was possible because Palestine was, at that stage, an

[1] This includes investigations that have been opened following an Article 15 authorisation decision by the Pre-Trial Chambers, and cases that have progressed, at least, to an arrest warrant decision. However, it excludes situations that were opened by the Prosecutor *proprio motu*, and which do not yet include any cases, because in such situations the judges are yet to be involved.

'observer entity' rather than a state in the UN, with the result that its ICC declaration was not legally valid.[2]

Subsequently, Palestine became a UN 'observer state', enabling it to become a state party to the Rome Statute in 2015. In 2018, Palestine referred the situation to the (then) ICC Prosecutor, Fatou Bensouda, who in 2021 opened an investigation into potential Rome Statute crimes committed since 2014 in Palestine, including in Gaza and the West Bank, or by Palestinian nationals in Israel.[3] This enabled the investigation of possible crimes by both Hamas and the Israeli Defence Forces (IDF). Bensouda's successor, prosecutor Karim Khan, has committed additional resources to the Palestine investigation, stating that 'the Palestine investigation has always been, and remains, a very important investigation in the ICC. It's one that cannot be forgotten, and it is one that is being conducted as effectively as we can'.[4] When we designed this book project, there were yet to be any cases on the public record from this situation.[5]

To address this concern, we commissioned a poetic intervention to acknowledge the silence rendered in such instances of 'absent jurisprudence'.

Sara Saleh's *The Checkpoint* is a thoughtful and evocative meditation on the daily realities of life in Palestine, drawing links with other colonised, indigenous, and subjugated peoples elsewhere in the world. Saleh's attention to the routine yet extraordinary hardships experienced by women, children, older people, and many others in Palestine are cleverly woven through with references to the international legal architecture designed to protect them and facilitate justice, but which has so manifestly failed to do so. In this context, the narrator of the poem reflects, 'words are the sharpest weapon I wield'.

The editors are acutely aware that the complex context of the Palestine/Israel conflict, as in all conflicts, cannot be fully captured in a single intervention, or by a single voice. Accountability for the crimes committed against people on all sides of this conflict must be pursued with urgency.

Although Saleh's poem responds specifically to the ICC's limited response to war crimes in Palestine, we intend for it to provoke broader reflections about the many situations and cases that, for legal and political reasons, are yet to progress in the ICC. In this way, the poem also speaks to the strictures of the feminist judgment

[2] See F. Bensouda, 'The truth about the ICC and Gaza', *The Guardian*, 30 August 2014, available at www.theguardian.com/commentisfree/2014/aug/29/icc-gaza-hague-court-investigate-war-crimes-palestine.

[3] F. Bensouda, Statement of ICC Prosecutor, Fatou Bensouda, respecting an investigation of the Situation in Palestine, 3 March 2021, available at www.icc-cpi.int/news/statement-icc-prosecutor-fatou-bensouda-respecting-investigation-situation-palestine.

[4] K. Khan, 'Statement of ICC Prosecutor Karim A. A. Khan KC from Cairo on the Situation in the State of Palestine and Israel', 20 October 2023, available at www.icc-cpi.int/news/statement-icc-prosecutor-karim-khan-kc-cairo-situation-state-palestine-and-israel.

[5] Subsequently, in May 2024, Prosecutor Khan applied for arrest warrants against certain Hamas and Israeli leaders. For updates, see www.icc-cpi.int/palestine.

method, and gestures towards an even more radical and inclusive reimagination of the ICC's case load.

[*Editors' Note: In May 2024, the ICC Prosecutor sought arrest warrants against certain leaders of Hamas and Israel. The Pre-Trial Chamber issued warrants for Hamas's highest military commander and Israel's Prime Minister and (then) Defence Minister in November 2024.*]

18

The Checkpoint

Sara Saleh

PRELUDE

Hey. *Psst.*
Ya zalameh? *Psst.*
Did you hear about the pregnant woman?
The one who gave birth to a stillborn right here?
They say it took the ambulance four hours – *four hours* – to drive two kilometres.
Ya zalameh? Psst.
Can you hear me? I'm talking to you.
*

Stillborn or not . . . You don't say a thing.
You don't want to talk to the other Palestinian man in line because hopefully at least one of you will make it out.
Or hopefully, he won't drag you down if he doesn't.
*

YOU! AT THE BACK. WITH THE BIG MOUTH. QUIET!
DID I TELL YOU YOU CAN TALK?
SHUT UP!
STAND OVER THERE. DON'T MOVE.
DON'T EVEN BREATHE.
*

How long have you been waiting?
I just got here.
How long have you been waiting?
A few hours.
How long have you been waiting?
All night.

How long have you been waiting?
Since the day I was born.
*

YOU. STOP. YOU'RE NOT ALLOWED.
EVEN YOUR SHADOW WILL NOT PASS THROUGH.
NO, I'M NOT INTERESTED IN WHAT YOU HAVE TO SAY.
STOP. YOU WANNA GET SMART WITH ME? I WILL SHOOT YOU.
COME BACK TOMORROW. TODAY IS NOT YOUR DAY.
*

You breathe when they tell you to breathe. And you calmly nod and smile.
That right there is resistance. It is survival.

READING DARWISH AT QALANDIA

A woman is standing too close behind me in this
swollen crowd, her breath foggy on my neck.
I thumb the pages of my book
and sigh loudly. She sighs back.
And I can feel all the ghosts through
the towers of barbed wire and cameras:
The baba holding his clothes up like a flag
at the guards behind the tinted glass.
The student eager to make it to the final exam,
her messy bun in place with pencils.
The Teta, ready since the rooster sang sunrise in,
with her long-awaited permit to begin chemotherapy.
The devoted husband on his wedding day, he doesn't know
his body will be a bargaining chip held hostage by authorities.
The young man with autism who was chased
and shot on the spot by police. Investigation pending.
And I think of Cassius Turvey, fifteen-year-old Indigenous boy
who was punched and stabbed simply for being Black.
Palestinians know about going to school
and not making it back.
Palestinians know about bulldozers demolishing villages
and settlers torching trees, homes, and shops.
No resolution, no report, no textbook has
been able to stop the violence or remedy the wrongs.
No amount of objections and condemnations have saved
the twelve-year-old boy from the military court system.
The official explanations will state that this twelve-year-old
boy is undoubtedly the assailant in this story.

And I think about how he will be blindfolded,
thrown in solitary confinement without food or water,
tried as an adult for a traffic offence,
convicted in a language not his own.
~~The evidence~~ – REDACTED
~~His rights~~ – REDACTED
~~His childhood~~ – REDACTED
At Qalandia, the soldier cradles his Uzi unrelentingly,
like an instrument he is performing,
the olive branch insignia on his uniform glimmers
in the haze of lights and multilingual
Ramadan greetings signs behind him.
I think of Article 7 of the Rome Statute:
the crime of apartheid,
and all the other rules, customs, and conventions
that missed the irony.
We find ways to survive this daily exercise
in humiliation, to numb infinite time. Each
moment any of us remains alive is a miracle.
The soldier turns to his comrade just starting a shift
and smiles hello, revealing teeth that match their belts
of ammo. They talk about the settlements that are expanding.
'Thank God for cheap social housing',
but no God gave them this land,
and no God made us the cattle in this allegory.
Just law and policy. The neat and natural geometry,
the architected 'safety', all this freedom is illusory.
The very things keeping us out, keep you in.
I think of peace talks and frameworks and negotiations,
contradictory definitions and competing legal and political interpretations.
Of terms like 'conflict' and 'ethnic cleansing' and 'casualty'
that have sanctioned seventy-five years of this.
Of whole cities/towns/villages/valleys split in bantustans and quarters.
We grow oranges in our backyards and guerrillas on our balconies.
Power constructs borders, the faultlines of global empires.
I think of Jerusalem, al-Quds.
Of the boot soles on necks young and old in Sheikh Jarrah,
of the mobs with bats chanting 'death to Arabs',
of the occupying forces besieging al-Aqsa mosque,
prayers and bullets ricocheting off its ancient walls.
I think of Gaza, the forty-five-kilometre-long strip by the sea.
Of another aerial bombardment disrupting medical supplies and electricity.

Of schools, hospitals, highways, and media organisations flattened to 'collateral damage'.
Where the water is contaminated and the food rots and the people consume it anyway.
I think of Akka and Haifa and An-Nasira.
Of the Palestinian residents called 'second-class citizens'
who must pay taxes but still face an environmental crisis,
piles of used needles, plastic bags, and garbage spilling on their streets.
Where 'democracy' means no accountability for war crimes,
and the same fascist government is voted in for a fifth time
and no one seems to mind the International Criminal Court's jurisdiction.
The people march against 'right wing' and corruption
with little thought for the millions living under occupation.
I think of Ramallah, the so-called capital of a 'future state'.
Of children selling lemonade in sweltering afternoon traffic,
of peeling yellow taxis and the rolling fruit and vegetable carts that feed families.
Of the ugly concrete wall looming twenty years after the International Court of Justice's Advisory Opinion,
Of whole neighbourhoods fractured and farms confiscated and social services isolated and somehow our subjugation is still up for debate.
How do we not dissolve under this unbearable weight?
Then I think of the ruptures. 'The reservoirs of hope.'
The refusals. Those who keep rising from the rubble.
The ratification of the First Additional Protocol
recognised my people and all people fighting against
colonial domination, alien occupation or racist regimes.
We need more than stock photos of refugees from Balata to Jenin.
We need more than another fundraiser,
than another NGO worker,
than another journalist,
we need more than another poem.
Still, I frantically flip through the pages of
my book. *Reading Darwish at Qalandia*
is a provocation and words are
the sharpest weapon I wield.
I confront the bare iron grids,
they are bone waiting for skin,
the toothed bars not wide enough
to squeeze a single orange in.
And I think of the generations of Palestinian women
who march in our name, banners and fists raised.

Who won't accept a piecemeal or a truncation
Who fight on every front for our self-determination. Who birth revolutions.
Who are building with other women from Turtle Island to so-called Australia.
Who are questioning, deconstructing, scratching off old laws,
breaking this apart so they can put it together …
finally, justice for us all.

PART III

Conclusion

19

Envisioning the Future 'Art and Craft' of Judicial Decision-Making at the ICC

Louise Chappell, Suzanne Varrall, Kcasey McLoughlin, and Rosemary Grey

This collection of feminist judgments shines a spotlight on the work of the International Criminal Court (ICC) over the course of its first twenty-five years since the adoption of the Rome Statute. Through a curated selection of cases, its reimagined judgments and reflections expose the limitations of ICC judicial adjudication and, in several instances, the limits of international criminal law (ICL) more generally. Importantly, too, these rewritten decisions point out clear directions for the ICC Chambers to advance gender-sensitive jurisprudence for atrocity crimes, while staying safely within the guard rails of the Rome Statute.[1] In doing so, this volume showcases the possibilities for harnessing the existing gender justice provisions embedded within the Rome Statute,[2] and the scope of the 'art and craft' of judicial decision-making.

The need to maintain legal plausibility by staying within these guard rails has been one of the most revealing aspects of this feminist judgment project (see Marshall, Chapter 16.3). Given the Rome Statute's reputation for providing the

[1] Our contributors were instructed to imagine themselves in the robes and wigs of the judiciary in rendering a judgment that was legally plausible and relied upon evidence available to the judiciary at the time of the original decision. For a select few authors, these restraints proved too great, compromising their vision of gender justice. In particular, Sophie Rigney's piece (Chapter 9.2) invites considerations of issues of morality, responsibility, power, and violence which are not provided for by the Rome Statute, in rejecting the concept of ICL as it exists today.

[2] Examples include Article 21(3), which requires that all sources of applicable law are interpreted without adverse distinction on gender grounds, Article 68(1), which requires the Court to take measures to protect survivors of sexual and gender-based violence, and Articles 7 and 8, which identify a wider range of sexual and gender-based crimes as crimes against humanity and war crimes than any previous instrument of international criminal law. For a full discussion see R. Grey, K. McLoughlin, and L. Chappell, 'Gender and Judging at the International Criminal Court: Lessons from "Feminist Judgment Projects"' 34(1) *Leiden Journal of International Law* (2021) 247–264, at 250.

most advanced ever set of gender justice rules under international criminal law,[3] these reimagined judgments are instructive in demonstrating the potential of the Rome Statute to advance gender justice but also just how most ICC judges have been in using the existing rules to achieve this outcome. Whether through gendered norms of 'impartiality',[4] blindness, timidity, or lack of training in gender analysis, the ICC judiciary has been highly constrained in its approach to reading the law through a gender lens, unlike the judgments and reflections in this collection. At the ICC, it remains rare for judges to employ the modes of contextualised and gender-informed reasoning that are at the heart of the feminist judgment method.[5] *And yet, 'it is possible to be both a judge and a feminist', as Judge Pillay writes in her foreword to this book.*

The feminist judgments included in this collection provide insights for current and future ICC judges as to how the Rome Statute can be used to achieve more gender-just outcomes, as well as to scholars and activists about where limitations and obstacles remain. However, it should be noted that for some of our contributors, these efforts towards change are likely to be futile. For some authors, to paraphrase Audre Lorde,[6] regardless of the tools for reform, the Master will always remain in charge of the ICL house given its gendered, imperialist, patriarchal, racial, and cultural foundations. In particular, the contributions by Sophie Rigney (Chapter 9.2), Souheir Edelbi (Chapter 16.5), Jill Marshall (Chapter 16.3), and Immi Tallgren (Chapter 12.1) posit, to varying extents, that the system of international criminal law itself is incompatible with a feminist approach to justice, and challenge readers to rethink the entire premise of the ICC, to focus on building local ethnically, culturally, and gender-sensitive (non-carceral) processes to achieve conflict-related accountability and justice. These important critiques push us to think harder about the meaning of 'feminism' in the feminist judgments projects, and to consider more expansive ways of engaging with legal institutions.

In making the case for 'yet another' feminist judgment project, Kcasey McLoughlin (Chapter 3) revisits the fairy-tale motif which has been so prominent in accounts of judging (both 'traditional' and 'critical'), and, in so doing, explores the implications of imagination and reimagination. According to Erika Rackley, like

3 L. Chappell, *The Politics of Gender Justice at the International Criminal Court* (Cambridge: Cambridge University Press, 2016), at 36; P. Spees, 'Women's Advocacy in the Creation of the International Criminal Court: Changing the Landscapes of Justice and Power' 28(4) *Journal of Women in Culture and Society* (2003) 1233–1254; C. Steains, 'Gender Issues' in R. S. Lee (ed.), *The International Criminal Court: The Making of the Rome Statute* (The Hague: Kluwer Law International, 1999), at 357.

4 A. Phillips, *The Politics of Presence* (Oxford: Oxford University Press, 1995), at 186. Phillips suggests that, whilst impartiality is often interpreted as a 'view from nowhere' it should actually reflect 'views from everywhere', which makes securing judicial diversity so important.

5 Grey, McLoughlin, and Chappell, *supra* note 2, at 248.

6 A. Lorde, 'The Master's Tools Will Never Dismantle the Master's House' in *Sister Outsider: Essays and Speeches* (New York: Crossing Press, 2007) 110–114.

Hans Christian Andersen's little mermaid, the woman judge must 'shed her difference and fit the fairy tale'[7] – the fairy tale being the liberal legal world. We argue that feminist judgment writing as feminist method is not (merely) the stuff of fairy tales, but rather a practical demonstration of what *is possible* within the bounds (sometimes pushing them) of law. Although we acknowledge the challenges and tensions which arise through feminist engagement with law and its institutions (especially when those very institutions have shown how impervious they are to feminist interventions), we nonetheless think that there are important practical, educative, and political reasons justifying such engagement.

In this concluding chapter, we start by considering some general points for the feminist judgment method which have emerged from the collection, including the importance of context and intersectionality, before drawing out internal and external opportunities and barriers for transforming the ICC into a tool for advancing gender justice.

LESSONS FOR THE FEMINIST JUDGMENT METHOD

As explained in the introductory Chapter 2, the story of feminist engagement with law is the story of pressing and redrawing boundaries. Feminist accounts have demonstrated the consequences which stem from women's exclusion from the development of international law: 'a narrow and inadequate jurisprudence that has legitimated the unequal position of women worldwide'.[8] In ICL, women's exclusion has shaped the development of law and its institutions (notwithstanding the work of feminist scholars in seeking to shape the Rome Statute).[9] In this book, we have continued to press the boundaries of imagination and judgment within the bounds of the Statute, interrogating how *gender* has been framed in international criminal law. Gender is not a synonym for woman/women; nor is it possible to view the world through a gender-free lens – this is the fiction of neutrality which has held sway in traditional accounts of law:

> Many people do not recognize how obvious gender is because they think it means women: if women are not there it is not gendered. In this view, we need to add a gender perspective to explain where women are, notice their hidden activities, and denounce the injustice of their exclusion. On the contrary, I propose that it is

7 E. Rackley, 'Representations of the (Woman) Judge: Hercules, the Little Mermaid, and the Vain and Naked Emperor' 22(4) *Legal Studies* (2002) 602–624, at 602.

8 H. Charlesworth and C. Chinkin, *The Boundaries of International Law: A Feminist Analysis* (Manchester: Manchester University Press, 2000), at 13.

9 See for example, B. Bedont and K. Hall-Martinez, 'Ending Impunity for Gender Crimes under the International Criminal Court' 6 *Brown Journal of World Affairs* (1999) 65–85; R. Copelon, 'Gender Crimes as War Crimes: Integrating Crimes against Women into International Criminal Law' 46(1) *McGill Law Journal* (2000) 217–240; V. Oosterveld, 'The Definition of Gender in the Rome Statute of the International Criminal Court: A Step Forward or Back for International Criminal Justice?' 18 *Harvard Human Rights Journal* (2005) 55–84.

> ontologically impossible not to have a gender perspective: it is implicit in all domains of academic inquiry. The more interesting question then becomes: what research agendas and hypotheses will lead us towards a better understanding of gender?[10]

Rather, adopting a gender lens entails making visible all people who are targeted in conflicts for contravening assigned gender narratives that regulate what is 'acceptable' behaviour, in terms of societal norms and values, and understanding their distinct experiences.[11] It further involves asking the 'why question', understanding what motivates the commission of gender-based crimes, in order to move towards sustainable peace.[12] By setting out what might be possible if feminist and gender-sensitive voices echoed from the judiciary, this book imagines a new jurisprudence, one where marginalised voices are included.

One of the major themes to emerge from this collection is the need for judges to make decisions from the perspective of the *context* and *lived experiences* of those closest to the commission of international crimes, whether as victims/survivors, as perpetrators, or, in some cases, as both. *The photo essay by Omal Khair, Dil Kayas and Azimul Hassan (Chapter 15), which disrupts the text to offer a visual window into lived experiences of Rohingya people, underscores this point.* By placing context at the forefront, our authors have demonstrated the value of the feminist judgment method in advancing justice. In a nutshell, situating people in their historical and political context rather than imagining them as genderless, raceless beings has resulted in greater clarity in understanding how gender relations, and their intersection with other structural power relations, influence the meaning, experience, processes, and outcomes of justice.

Contextualisation and Gender

Feminist judgments in this collection demonstrate that by adopting a contextual view it is possible to disrupt gender stereotypes. Contextualisation leads to an emphasis on the fluid and dynamic nature of the meaning of the term 'gender' in relation to the statute, and the need to understand gender as a social construction (for example, Davis and Kumskova, Chapter 10.5; SáCouto, Chapter 16.6). As Loyce Mrewa (Chapter 11.3) states, a contextual approach enables judges to 'better reflect the full culpability of the accused and the extent of the harm suffered by victims'. Judgments in this book highlight how seemingly gender-neutral crimes are experienced differently based on gender, including genocide (Radhakrishnan and Shubin, Chapter 10.2), pillage (Keith, Chapter 11.4), deportation (Palmer and Oo, Chapter 14.2), the enlistment,

[10] M. Htun, 'What It Means to Study Gender and the State' 1 *Politics and Gender* (2005) 157–166, at 162.

[11] L. Davis, 'Dusting off the Law Books: Recognising Gender Persecution in Conflicts and Atrocities' 20(1) *Northwestern Journal of Human Rights* (2021) 63–126.

[12] *Ibid*, at 66.

conscription, and use of child soldiers (Wilmet, Chapter 8.2), and the destruction of cultural property (Ismail, Chapter 13.2; Graham and Jones, Chapter 13.4). The specific disadvantage of those who are persecuted because they are something other than male or female, such as the Hijra people in Myanmar, is also apparent (Palmer and Oo, Chapter 14.2; O'Hara, Chapter 14.3).

A contextualised gender analysis surfaces the multitude of harms experienced by women and their children who are born because of conflict-related rape (Kirabira, Ringin, and Grey, Chapter 9.3; Naigaga Kyobika, Chapter 9.4), and by male victims of sexual violence (Eichert, Chapter 11.2). Suzanne Varrall and Sarah Williams' reimagined *Bemba* judgment in the Central African Republic (CAR) situation (Chapter 11.5) draws attention to the persistence of sexual and gender-based violence in conflict, and calls for it to be better recognised in the Court's interpretation and application of the doctrine of command responsibility, which they argue is informed by the concept of protection under international humanitarian law (IHL).[13] Moreover, they remind us that while the majority of sexual and gender-based violence in conflict affects women and girls, a gender-sensitive approach to IHL needs to challenge traditional views of gender roles that cast men as combatants and, as a result, potentially under-protect civilian men and boys.

Contextualisation through a gender lens also enables a deeper reflection on victim/survivor agency. Such a view is often missing in legal judgments where those experiencing crime tend to be objectified and seen only through the prism of disempowerment. In this collection, victim/survivor agency is recognised – for example, in Souheir Edelbi's interpretation of the 'interests of justice' test (Chapter 16.5), in Anushka Sehmi's emphasis on the right of victims to choose their own legal representation (Chapter 10.4), and in the reflection by Salima Ahmadi and Sari Kouvo (Chapter 16.1), which reaffirms the need to challenge narratives that Afghani women are all oppressed victims to be saved by the West. Judgments also focus on the complementarity and jurisdictional aspects of the Rome Statute, supporting the view that victims of gender-based crimes should be able to access the ICC when the domestic-level courts are demonstrably not fit for purpose, thus expanding the interpretation of 'unable or unwilling' (Easy, Chapter 12.3; Gooding, Chapter 16.4).

Other judgments and reflections challenge existing legal tropes related to perpetrators, bringing into view the role of women as war criminals, in the case of Simone Gbagbo in Côte d'Ivoire (Hodgson, Chapter 12.2). In the Uganda section, Sophie Rigney's rewritten judgment in the *Ongwen* case explicitly confronts the defendants' position as both the victim and the perpetrator of crimes under international law (Chapter 9.2). In the Afghanistan situation, Mashal Aamir and Adrienne Ringin (Chapter 16.2) identify the need for the ICC to rigorously prosecute crimes

[13] Additional Protocol I to the Geneva Convention, Art. 4; Additional Protocol II to the Geneva Convention, Arts. 24–25.

committed by all forces, not just the Taliban, but also the United States, the former Islamic Republic, and other international forces. In demonstrating this point, Aamir and Ringin rely upon evidence of torture, rape, and outrages upon personal dignity committed by US forces in Central Intelligence Agency (CIA) facilities in Afghanistan, Poland, Romania, and Lithuania.

Viewing ICC *processes* contextually allows judges to see intrinsic connections between: gender and head-of-state immunity in ending impunity for crimes of sexual and gender-based violence (Uma and Kudekallu, Chapter 10.3); the rules of procedure relating to the amendment of charges (Oosterveld, Chapter 11.6), and video evidence (Zarmsky and Irving, Chapter 13.5). Melissa McKay (Chapter 13.3) also reminds readers of one of the oft-forgotten purposes of sentencing, which is the process of rehabilitation. Echoing other chapters that advance a non-carceral approach, she raises the prospect of community service through the ICC's Trust Fund for Victims as a potentially more fruitful avenue of punishment than incarceration.

Gender and Intersectionality

Our authors also point to the importance of bringing an *intersectional* lens to their gender analysis. As the introductory chapters by Priya Gopalan (Chapter 7) and Angela Mudukuti and Louise Chappell (Chapter 5) show, the ICC is a long way from recognising the impact of intersectional power structures which can co-constitute and exacerbate the perpetration and impact of atrocity crimes. The rewritten judgments highlight the importance of intersectionality, demonstrating how the effects of crimes are shaped not only by gender structures alone, but are also intertwined and interact with structural religious, racial, dis/ability, and economic dis/advantages in communities where atrocity crimes are committed.

Judgments grapple with crimes whose commission is enabled by gender and intersecting power structures including political affiliation, ethnicity, and religion (Davis and Kumskova, Chapter 10.5; Radhakrishnan and Shubin, Chapter 10.2; O'Hara, Chapter 14.3), and age (Maravall-Buckwater, Chapter 8.4; Gopalan and Jurasz, Chapter 8.3). Susana SáCouto's reimagined decision in the Afghanistan situation characterises the persecution of Afghan female politicians, public servants, and students through the intersection of gender and political grounds (Chapter 16.6). And in the contribution by Patricia Sellers and Rosemary Grey (Chapter 4), the intersecting gender, racialised, and economic dimensions of slavery crimes are front and centre.

These judgments and the chapters reflecting on them helpfully demonstrate that an intersectional approach is not only both feasible and plausible but can result in the ICC providing a more expansive form of justice.

Temporality

As editors, we've also noted in judgments and other chapters the emergence of temporality as a feature influencing judicial deliberations and outcomes at the ICC. This point is raised most starkly in the 'in conversation' chapter between Sellars and Grey (Chapter 4). Reflecting on 'absent jurisprudence', Sellers challenges us to think of how an alternative past – a past in which the gendered dimensions of criminal conduct were more fully captured in the jurisprudence of the various international courts and tribunals – would arguably have gifted us a different legal present. As Grey notes in Chapter 3, using a 'time travelling imaginative approach', Sellars 'conjures up an alternative legal present and paves the way for an alternative legal future'.

Time also emerges as a relevant factor in other judgments and reflections. Valerie Oosterveld (Chapter 11.6) strikes an appropriate balance between the duty to establish the truth in allowing the Prosecutor to add additional charges of sexual violence and the need to balance the interests of the defence in the *Yekatom* case. She notes that, as there has been a delay in setting a trial date, the interests of the defence are not materially affected by allowing the charges, which more fully reflect the alleged culpability. In the Myanmar reflection (Chapter 14.1), Catherine Renshaw and Afroza Anwary also highlight how using a linear time frame 'preclude[s] more multi-layered, complex, interactive, and cyclical notions of time that encompass longer-term and inter-generational pain'. The Afghanistan reflection by Salima Ahmadi and Sari Kouvo (Chapter 16.1) raises temporality in another sense by positing that drawing time boundaries around cases limits the scope of crimes, perpetrators, and victims. In relation to Afghanistan, the singular focus on the crimes committed by the Taliban has meant that the victims of crimes perpetrated by the Islamic Republic of Afghanistan government and international forces have no current avenue to justice.

Together, the feminist judgment method as used in this volume can unearth the gendered context, intersectional power relations, and time as factors. The judgments show that once recognised, these factors can reshape judges' understanding of the perpetration, experience, and impact of international crimes. As discussed in the next section, the results of this methodology are a prompt to the ICC to rethink court processes and the use and relevance of different types of evidence, as well as verdicts and sentencing decisions.

Inspiring the Future: What Can Be Done to Advance Feminist Judging at the ICC?

The judgments that are reimagined in this book may form part of the legal history of the ICC, yet the value of speculating about 'what could have been' can be framed not only in the critical sense of 'what went wrong' but in the imaginative sense of providing inspiration for the future. Inspired by Immi Tallgren's contribution (Chapter 12.1), all our reflection writers were specifically asked to take on the task of 'thinking outside the box' to determine their vision of gender justice. That is, we asked reflection writers to consider what justice would entail, in their particular situation, if it was not limited by the parameters of the Rome Statute. These insights compel us to view the present day as tomorrow's past, as Patricia Sellers has done (Chapter 4), and give us an opportunity to think creatively about how to shape the future of the ICC in relation to gender justice.

Just as critiques of the Court take many forms in this volume, so too do proposals for reform, which are articulated most clearly in the reflection chapters. These writers take very different positions in terms of envisioning what could be done to enhance opportunities for strengthening gender justice in international criminal law, ranging from abandonment of the ICC, through to reform of the Statute, and more minimalist (yet no doubt radical in the eyes of existing judges) efforts to bring a feminist sensibility to adjudicating atrocity crimes.

For some reflection writers, the guard rails of the Rome Statute will always prove too restrictive for achieving gender justice. For instance, reflecting on Côte d'Ivoire, Immi Tallgren writes: 'A feminist rethinking might even ask to what extent does the ICC and the overwhelming, passionate commitment, activism, and academic investment in international criminal punishment form part of a global political economy that adds to the already manifold challenges faced by post-colonial states?' (Chapter 11.1). Reflecting on Darfur, Sareta Ashraph is encouraged by the reimagined judgments in this volume (Chapter 10.1). However, she calls into question whether the Rome Statute and ICC Rules of Evidence and Procedure are suitable instruments for achieving gender equality, at least until international justice actors engage in a more radical questioning of political and philosophical underpinnings of international criminal law. Salina Ahmadi and Sari Kouvo (Chapter 16.1), who focus on Afghanistan, are equivocal about how far the law can be relied upon to advance gender justice. Their approach might be described as 'ICC+', recognising that the Court will only ever provide a partial solution to accountability, and justice seekers will also need to look for justice through other social, economic, and political institutions.

Some of our other reflection writers think that future progress may be possible by working within the boundaries of the law, but only with reform of the Statute. For instance, Catherine Renshaw and Afroza Anway, discussing Myanmar/Bangladesh, suggest that to adequately address gender persecution it is necessary to reform the rules, to replace the current definition of 'gender' with one that is without the current constraints contained in the reference to the 'two sexes' (Chapter 14.1).[14]

[14] Art. 7(3) of the ICC Statute defines 'gender' as: 'For the purpose of this Statute, it is understood that the term "gender" refers to the two sexes, male and female, within the context of society. The term "gender" does not indicate any meaning different from the above.'

Such a change would inevitably require an amendment to the Rome Statute. However, the process for altering the Court's foundational document requires meeting a high threshold in terms of the agreement of states parties,[15] and, perhaps unsurprisingly, there have to date been few successful attempts to amend it.[16]

For other authors, reform of the Rome Statute is unnecessary to ensure gender justice is better embedded in the practice of the ICC, as the Court arguably already possesses the tools needed to properly acknowledge and account for the gendered and intersectional nature of atrocity crimes.[17] The true challenge, therefore, lies in the implementation of this aspirational treaty to achieve its gender mandate.[18] Some of the reflection writers suggest avenues for surfacing the still (under-)utilised aspects of the Statute. Melanie O'Brien, writing on Uganda, suggests one important intervention would be to better honour the wishes of victims in making reparation orders, as well as expanding the vision of who counts as a victim, such as children born of conflict-related rape (Chapter 9.1). For Kerstin Braun, reflecting on Mali, attitudinal change among the judiciary is necessary to advance gender justice, alongside broadening conventional understandings of specific contexts, such as expanding the definition of cultural property to encompass women's relationship to cultural objects and practices (Chapter 13.1). From the DRC situation, Aparajitha Narayanan and Sandrine de Herdt suggest judges need to be more attuned to the socio-economic effects of sexual violence crimes (Chapter 8.1). Alice Dieci and Cassandra Mudgway use the CAR situation to make this contextual point more broadly, suggesting that judicial reasoning based on context rather than abstract situations is the best way to capture the lived experiences of victims, including the operation of gender norms as they relate to gender-diverse people (Chapter 11.1).

[15] Art. 121 of the ICC Statute provides the mechanics for amendments, which require a two-thirds majority vote in favour by states parties to be adopted as per sub-section (3). Under Art. 121(5), amendments to provisions concerning the substantive crimes within the jurisdiction of the Court shall only enter into force for those states parties which accept the amendment; those which do not accept an amendment to these provisions will not be bound by any changes. Such an 'opt-in' approach presents significant problems for the Court's universality and jurisdiction. Amendments to other provisions shall enter into force for all states parties one year after acceptance or ratification by seven-eighths of all states parties as per Art 121(4) – an extremely high threshold to meet.

[16] As a result of the Review Conference in Kampala in 2010, which was held in accordance with Art. 123 of the ICC Statute, amendments were made which provided the Court jurisdiction over the crime of aggression. An amendment to Art. 8 of the ICC Statute was also adopted to harmonise provisions on war crimes in non-international armed conflict and international armed conflict. At the fourteenth session of the Assembly of States Parties in 2015, the deletion of Art. 124 (concerning declarations of transitional acceptance of jurisdiction) was agreed unanimously.

[17] Chappell, *supra* note 3, at 51–86.

[18] *Ibid.*

OPPORTUNITIES FOR AND BARRIERS TO REFORM

Having identified some key areas for reform, in this final section we want to reflect on what might be some of the main practical opportunities for and barriers to realising gender justice at the ICC. We look first at some of the internal issues before widening the lens to think about the Court in the broader international context.

Internal Opportunities

A key point made by Mudukuti in her conversation with Chappell (Chapter 5), by Dawuni (Chapter 6), and in our introductory chapters (Chapters 2–4), was the critical importance of having a diversity of judges on the bench capable of 'seeing' context to bring about more gender-just judgments. The need for a systematic effort to integrate gender sensitivity and competence into how the ICC Chamber performs its role provides one of the most significant opportunities for positive change within the ICC, in terms of realising gender justice. This starts with processes and policies within the Assembly of States Parties (ASP) to ensure the bench is composed of judges who are both gender diverse and gender competent, but also requires the provision of institutional support to maintain gender expertise among the judges and translate that expertise into judicial decision-making.

While the ASP has established minimum requirements for judicial appointments in relation to criminal law and international law competence and fair representation of sexes and regional groups,[19] it has not mandated any requirements with regard to judicial candidates who possess legal expertise in violence against women or children. As we have argued elsewhere, we believe that such a measure would be a first step in building the gender expertise of the ICC Chambers.[20]

Beyond the selection of diverse and gender-competent judges, it is critical that these judicial officers are provided institutional support if they are to deliver gender-sensitive outcomes, in the form of relevant and ongoing training and materials. For example, in relation to the crime of gender persecution and the recent policy of the Office of the Prosecutor (OTP) in this area,[21] a corresponding training module and practice manual for the judiciary would ensure a systematic institutional approach to this issue. Of course, as our chapters have indicated, gender persecution is only one area of substantive law in which further training and materials could assist the Bench in building and maintaining gender expertise. Judges need stronger skills for

[19] Resolution ICC-ASP/3/Res.6, 10 September 2004, § 20. See also Open Society Justice Initiative, Electing the Next judges of the International Criminal Court: Expertise and Skills, available at www.justiceinitiative.org/publications/electing-the-next-judges-of-the-international-criminal-court-principles-and-essential-skills, at 19.

[20] Grey, McLoughlin, and Chappell, *supra* note 2, at 253.

[21] Office of the Prosecutor, Policy on the Crime of Gender Persecution, December 2022.

understanding how gender relates to socio-economic, cultural, and religious structures in any given setting. Meanwhile, adjudication in areas not usually considered gender related – including the types of evidence available, court processes for witness and victim protection, the impact of delayed trials on specific victims – can all be enriched by a gender analysis.

In sum, the nomination, selection, and training of ICC judges to ensure gender diversity *and* expertise must be an area of increased attention.[22] This cannot occur in isolation, but must take place alongside approaches to prosecution and investigation which work together to better embed gender sensitivity in the organisational culture and the staff of the ICC.

External Pressures and Opportunities

Numerous external factors are currently affecting the ICC's effectiveness and will continue to make it difficult for it fulfil its mandate. Of these, none perhaps is more significant than the febrile geopolitical context in which the Court operates. As one of many international institutions, the ICC operates within the broader international relations context in which states interact, which has consequences for its ability to realise global gender justice outcomes. At a macro level, for example, the prospects for universalisation of the Rome Statute are limited by continuing strategic competition between major powers which makes membership of China, Russia, and/or the United States highly unlikely.[23] It also limits the likelihood of referrals by the UN Security Council of any situations that may touch upon the interests of one of the permanent five Council members, given their veto power.[24] This situation serves to reinforce the selectivity problems which have plagued the Court,[25] as reflected so powerfully in Sara Saleh's poem on Palestine (Chapter 18). The absence of major global powers from the ICC regime thus affects the Court's legitimacy and credibility, a problem that is further undermined by comparatively weak Asian representation,[26] and the continuing risk of withdrawal of African states, including South Africa.[27] As Mudukuti notes in her in conversation with Chappell (Chapter 5), if the

[22] Grey, McLoughlin, and Chappell, *supra* note 2.

[23] A. Bower, *Norms without the Great Powers: International Law and Changing Social Standards in World Politics* (Oxford: Oxford University Press, 2016).

[24] K. Clarke and S. Koulen, 'The Legal Politics of the Article 16 Decision: the International Criminal Court, the UN Security Council and Ontologies of a Contemporary Compromise' 7 (3) *African Journal of Legal Studies* (2014) 297–319.

[25] B. Kotecha, 'The International Criminal Court's Selectivity and Procedural Justice' 18(1) *Journal of International Criminal Justice* (2020) 107–139.

[26] On the reluctance among Asian states, see A. Kapur, 'Asian Values v. The Paper Tiger' 11 *Journal of International Criminal Justice* (2013) 1059–1090.

[27] On 26 April 2023, South Africa's President Cyril Ramaphosa rescinded a statement that the country planned to withdraw from the International Criminal Court ahead of hosting the BRICS (Brazil, Russia, India, China, and South Africa) summit, which Russia's President Vladimir Putin, wanted by the Court for war crimes, would otherwise be expected to attend.

focus of the ICC is not impartial, and seen not to be impartial, it risks failing to effectively engage with and address the gendered dimensions and intersectional nature of atrocity around the globe.

Within the broader geopolitical context, the range and nature of current and emerging conflicts also gives rise to issues which impact the pursuit of gender justice at the ICC. These include the impacts of protracted conflict, inter-state conflicts, the role and use of technology in war, as well as the persistence of sexualised violence and the intersectional nature of atrocity crimes.

Around 110 instances of armed conflict are underway around the world at the time of writing, the majority of which are in Africa and the Middle East.[28] Of the eight countries covered in this volume, most continue to experience armed conflicts on their territory,[29] which is indicative of the prolonged and intractable nature of many of today's (and potentially tomorrow's) wars. It is well established that conflict exacerbates previously existing gender inequalities, while often entrenching gender roles. For example, research demonstrates that during armed conflict women have less access to health services than men, and especially in protracted conflicts.[30] The lack of access is particularly notable in the context of maternal mortality, as more than 50 per cent of maternal deaths worldwide occur in settings affected by armed conflict or natural disasters.[31] The persistence of conflicts over long periods therefore has significant and broad gendered implications, which need to be recognised in the ICC's approach to investigating, characterising, adjudicating, and punishing perpetrators of atrocity crimes in these contexts, as well as awarding reparations to victims who have experienced years of loss.

Although the majority of conflicts are still largely conducted with conventional small arms and light weapons, such as the infamous AK47,[32] the way that technology is used in war is changing, as demonstrated by the growing application of artificial intelligence and machine learning in weapons and weapons systems.[33] What is often lacking from the discourse around technology, weapons, and war, however, is the differential and gendered impacts of technology use in situations of conflict and repression. The International Committee of the Red Cross has recognised that 'sex-specific harms arise from the use of certain weapons', and gender analysis of civilian casualty data indicates that 'women, men, boys and girls are killed at different rates

28 This number includes international and non-international armed conflicts as well as military occupations. Source: RULAC, 'Conflicts', available at www.rulac.org/browse/conflicts.

29 The exceptions at the time of writing were Cote d'Ivoire and Uganda. See *ibid.*

30 K. Meagher, B. Attal, and P. Patel, 'Exploring the Role of Gender and Women in the Political Economy of Health in Armed Conflict: A Narrative Review' 17 *Global Health* (2021) 1–9.

31 V. Pillai, Y. C. Wang, and A. Maleku, 'Women, War, and Reproductive Health in Developing Countries' 56(1) *Social Work in Health Care* (2017) 28–44.

32 ICRC, 'Arms Availability', available at www.icrc.org/en/war-and-law/weapons/arms-availability.

33 S. Longpre, M. Storm, and R. Shah, 'Lethal Autonomous Weapons Systems & Artificial Intelligence: Trends, Challenges, and Policies' 3(1) *MIT Science Policy Review* (2022) 47–56.

depending on the context and weapon used'.[34] These are factors that need to be understood by those involved in investigating and prosecuting international crimes, not only to comprehend the impacts on victims, but also to assess basic legality of the use of weapons and weapons systems under international humanitarian law.[35] This is particularly relevant to those war crimes under Article 8 of the Rome Statute, but has a broader significance as well.

External pressures are also affecting the ICC in terms of jurisdiction, particularly the principles of complementarity and universal jurisdiction. The principle of complementarity was central to the Rome Statute's negotiation and remains central to its interpretation. The principle recognises a hierarchy in which national jurisdictions have the primary authority to prosecute suspected perpetrators, with the jurisdiction of the ICC being of a subsidiary nature.[36] This means that, where affected states are unable or unwilling to genuinely investigate and/or prosecute international crimes, the ICC's mandate (as well as the exercise of universal jurisdiction) can be critical to promoting gender justice. Yet, as noted by Chappell, Grey, and Waller,[37] complementarity has also served to limit the reach of the ICC's gender mandate, and to restrict the expressive power of the Court to influence reforms and address gender-discriminatory practices in national jurisdictions. Questions of complementarity and the interaction of this principle with gender issues are highlighted in the reimagined decisions of Kathryn Gooding in the Afghanistan situation (Chapter 16.3) and Sarah Easy in the Côte d'Ivoire situation (Chapter 12.3). These contributions give pause for reflection upon the barriers faced by women and gender-diverse people in accessing justice globally, and how the ICC's interpretation and application of the principle of complementarity can also limit the reach of the Court's gender mandate.

In other contexts, the hierarchy implicit in the complementarity regime has been less strictly adhered to, creating a different set of challenges for the ICC and international criminal justice goals. For example, despite ongoing investigations and prosecutions of atrocities by Ukrainian officials,[38] the 2022 Russian invasion of Ukraine has been referred to the ICC by forty-three states parties, and several third

[34] H. Durham et al., 'Gendered Impacts of Armed Conflict and Implications for the Application of IHL', ICRC (2022), available at https://blogs.icrc.org/law-and-policy/2022/06/30/gendered-impacts-of-armed-conflict-and-implications-for-the-application-of-ihl/.

[35] Art. 36 of Additional Protocol I to the Geneva Conventions obliges states to review new weapons, means, or methods of warfare, which includes physical and digital systems.

[36] The preamble to the Rome Statute states: 'Emphasizing that the International Criminal Court established under this Statute shall be complementary to national criminal jurisdictions', while Art. 17(1)(a) requires deference to state prosecutions where the state is able and willing.

[37] Grey, McLoughlin, and Chappell, *supra* note 2; R. Grey and E. Waller, 'The Gender Justice Shadow of Complementarity: Lessons from the International Criminal Court's Preliminary Examinations in Guinea and Colombia' 7(3) *International Journal of Transitional Justice* (2013) 455–475.

[38] As at May 2023, more than 88,500 atrocities have been reported in Ukraine since Russia invaded, according to the Prosecutor General's office in Kyiv.

states are conducting their own investigations with a view to prosecution based on universal jurisdiction.[39] There are also plans to create a new tribunal to prosecute the Russian invasion as a crime of aggression.[40] Evidence of alleged sexual crimes such as rape and other abuses has been gathered across the country, including by a Ukrainian special war crimes unit for sexual violence. The broad-based international commitment to accountability in this situation should be welcomed, albeit notwithstanding obvious questions of selectivity.[41] Yet this situation also results in potential inefficiencies and a dilution of responsibility as multiple efforts overlap and even interfere with one another, which does not benefit the realisation of gender-justice goals in this situation. The ICC's ability to exercise jurisdiction in any Russia/ Ukraine cases will depend on the scope and 'genuineness' of those various national proceedings.

The growing exercise of universal jurisdiction by third states in relation to international crimes also has potential to contribute to the realisation of gender justice globally, but adjacent to, rather than inside of, the ICC framework. The situation in Myanmar provides an illustrative example. Internal conflict in this country since at least 2016 has been characterised by significant instances of sexual and gender-based violence, potentially amounting to international crimes. Yet despite authorisation in 2019 of an ICC investigation into the Myanmar/ Bangladesh situation, to date no charges have been laid, leading to criticism of the apparent lack of progress by the OTP in this situation.[42] The reimagined judgments from the Myanmar/Bangladesh situation contained in this volume (Chapters 14.1–14.3) demonstrate that there are significant gender justice dimensions to this situation which will remain unresolved pending further developments in the ICC's investigation, including the issuance of arrest warrants for alleged perpetrators. In such circumstances, third states acting on the basis of universal jurisdiction may be able to progress gender-justice goals. In Argentina, a judicial investigation into crimes against Rohingya people committed by the Myanmar military is

[39] For instance, on 3 July 2023 the International Centre for the Prosecution of the Crime of Aggression against Ukraine (ICPA) started its operations in the Hague, hosted by the European Union Agency for Criminal Justice Cooperation.

[40] In September 2022, the Council of Europe proposed to create a tribunal that would have a mandate to 'investigate and prosecute the crime of aggression' committed by 'the political and military leadership of the Russian Federation'. Additionally, on 19 January 2023, the European Parliament called for the creation of an international tribunal to carry out investigations and prosecutions for Russian and Belarusian responsibility for the crime of aggression, complementary to the ICC. The text was adopted with 472 votes in favour, 19 against, and 33 abstentions.

[41] P. Labuda, 'Beyond Rhetoric: Interrogating the Eurocentric Critique of International Criminal Law's Selectivity in the Wake of the 2022 Ukraine Invasion' *Leiden Journal of International Law* (2023) 1–22.

[42] R. Ahmed, 'International Criminal Court and Its Tryst with Justice: The Case of Myanmar' 4 (10) *International Journal of Arts Humanities and Social Sciences Studies* (2019) 23–33.

occurring on the basis of universal jurisdiction,[43] and through this process the testimony of sexual violence victims in that conflict can be heard – an initial step towards achieving justice for the survivors of these crimes.

Creating a court sensitive to these pressures, their influence on the gendered dynamics of conflict, and the resultant specific targeted crimes against men and women and gender-diverse people is critical to ending impunity and to advancing gender justice. Following Patricia Sellers (Chapter 4), by adopting a contextual and intersectional approach to atrocity crimes we can create a new future for international criminal law in general, and the ICC specifically.

In her poem at the start of this book, Maxine Beneba Clarke wisely writes: 'Some say the law ought not to bend. That it should be a neutral, certain thing. But there are reasons judgement and interpretation are bequeathed to human – humane – hearts, and heads.' There is clearly much work to be done to deliver gender-inclusive international justice as far as the ICC is concerned, and a significant role for the judiciary to play in realising this goal. It is the transformative power of judges that makes international criminal law, and the ICC in particular, fertile ground for the Feminist Judgment Project and its methodology to have effect and inspire change.

43 TRIAL, 'Universal Jurisdiction Database', available at https://trialinternational.org/latest-post/universal-jurisdiction-case-in-argentina-an-important-decision-for-the-rohingyas.

Bibliography

Abebe, AM 'Displacement of Civilians during Armed Conflict in the Light of the Case Law of the Eritrea-Ethiopia Claims Commission' 22 *Leiden Journal of International Law* (2009) 823–851.

Ahmed, R 'International Criminal Court and Its Tryst with Justice: The Case of Myanmar' 4(10) *International Journal of Arts Humanities and Social Sciences Studies* (2019) 23–33.

Akhaven P 'The Radically Routine *Rohungya* Case: Territorial Jurisdiction and the Crime of Deportation under the ICC Statute' 17 *Journal of International Criminal Justice* (2019) 325–345.

Alcici, L and Pipia, S 'Displacement of the Rohingya before the ICJ and the ICC: Same Conduct, Different Crimes in International Law?' 2 *Asia Pacific Journal of International Humanitarian Law* (2021) 116–142.

Alison, M *Women and Political Violence: Female Combatants in Ethno-National Conflict* (London: Routledge, 2009).

Allar, K 'Setting the Picture Straight: The Ordinary Women of Nazi Germany and Rwanda Who Participated in Genocide' in K Auerbach (ed.), *Aftermath – Genocide, Memory and History* (Clayton: Monash University Publishing, 2015).

Amann, DM 'International Child Law and the Settlement of Ukraine–Russia and Other Conflicts' 99 *International Law Studies* (2022) 599–601.

Anghie, A and Chimni, BS 'Third World Approaches to International Law and Individual Responsibility in Internal Conflicts' 2(1) *Chinese Journal of International Law* (2003) 77–103.

Aparna, C, Sen, J, and Chaudhary, R 'Righting Together: An Introduction to the Indian Feminist Judgments Project' 56(1) *VRÜ Verfassung und Recht in Übersee* (2023) 5–16.

Apple, B *School for Rape: The Burmese Military and Sexual Violence* (EarthRights International Report, 1998). https://earthrights.org/wp-content/uploads/publications/school-for-rape.pdf.

Ashworth, A 'Principles and Policies' in A Ashworth (ed.), *Principles of Criminal Law* (New York: Oxford University Press, 5th ed. 2006; 6th ed. 2009).

Askin, KD *War Crimes against Women: Prosecutions in International War Crimes Tribunals* (The Hague: Martinus Nijhoff, 1997).

'Prosecuting Wartime Rape and Other Gender Related Crimes: Extraordinary Advances, Enduring Obstacles' 21 *Berkeley Journal of International Law* (2003) 288–349.

'Gender Crimes Jurisprudence in the ICTR: Positive Developments' 3 *Journal of International Criminal Justice* (2005) 1007–1018.

Ba, O, Bluen, KJ, and Owiso, O 'The Geopolitics of Race, Empire, and Expertise at the ICC' *International Studies* (2023). https://doi.org/10.1093/acrefore/9780190846626.013.717.

Baetens, F (ed.) *Identity and Diversity on the International Bench* (Oxford: Oxford University Press, 2020).

Baines, EK 'Complex Political Perpetrators: Reflections on Dominic Ongwen' 47 (2) *Journal of Modern African Studies* (2009) 163–191.

Balungi, SB and Dossan, GL 'Ethnicity, Religion and Diversity at the International Criminal Court: Is More Too Much?' in F Baetens (ed.), *Identity and Diversity on the International Bench* (Oxford: Oxford University Press, 2020).

Barnett, H *Sourcebook on Feminist Jurisprudence* (London: Cavendish Publishing, 1996).

Barr, A and Herfroy-Mischler, A 'ISIL's Execution Videos: Audience Segmentation and Terrorist Communication in the Digital Age' 41 *Studies in Conflict & Terrorism* (2018) 946–967.

Bartlett, KT 'Feminist Legal Methods' 103 *Harvard Law Review* (1990) 829–888.

Bauer, S *American Prison: A Reporter's Undercover Journey into the Business of Punishment* (New York: Penguin Books, 2019).

Bazyler MJ and Tuerkheimer, FM 'The Hamburg Ravensbrück Trials in British-Occupied Germany: Women as Perpetrators, Women as Victims' in MJ Bazyler and FM Tuerkheimer (eds.), *Forgotten Trials of the Holocaust* (New York: New York University Press, 2014).

Beccaria, C *Dei delitti e delle pene (Crimes and Punishment)*, edited by F Venturi (New York: Cambridge University Press, 1965, originally published 1766).

Bedont, B and Hall-Martinez, K 'Ending Impunity for Gender Crimes under the International Criminal Court' 6 *Brown Journal of World Affairs* (1999) 65–85.

Bennoune, K 'Multi-directionality and Universality: Global Feminisms and International Law in the Twenty-First Century' 116 *AJIL Unbound* (2022) 275–280.

Berger, L, Stanchi, K, and Crawford, B 'Learning from Feminist Judgments: Lessons in Language and Advocacy' 98 *Texas Law Review Online* (2019) 40–70.

Bitti, G 'Part IV: The ICC and Its Applicable Law: Article 21and the Hierarchy or Sources of Law before the ICC' in C Stahn (ed.), *The Law and Practice of the International Criminal Law* (Oxford: Oxford University Press, 2022).

Bjorge, E *The Evolutionary Interpretation of Treaties* (Oxford: Oxford University Press, 2014).

Blood, PR (ed.) *Afghanistan: A Country Study* (2001). http://public-library.uk/ebooks/10/35.pdf.

Blue, AW and Blue, MA 'The Case for Aboriginal Justice and Healing: The Self Perceived Through a Broken Mirror' in ML Hadley (ed.), *The Spiritual Roots of Restorative Justice* (New York: SUNY Press, 2001).

Bock, G 'Equality and Difference in National Socialist Racism' in J Scott (ed.), *Feminism and History* (Oxford: Oxford University Press, 1996).

Bouchenaki, M 'Editorial' 56 *Museum International* (2004) 10.

Bower, A *Norms without the Great Powers: International Law and Changing Social Standards in World Politics* (Oxford: Oxford University Press, 2016).

Bradfield, B 'Preserving Vulnerable Evidence at the International Criminal Court – the Article 56 Milestone in Ongwen' 19(3) *International Criminal Law Review* (2019) 373–411.

Brammertz, S and Jarvis, M (eds.) *Prosecuting Conflict-Related Sexual Violence at the ICTY* (Oxford: Oxford University Press, 2016).

Brandon, E 'Grave Breaches and Justifications: The War Crime of Forcible Transfer or Deportation of Civilians and the Exception for Evacuations for Imperative Military Reasons' 6(2) *Oslo Law Review* (2019) 107–124.

Brown, D *The Beautiful Beast: The Life and Crimes of SS-Aufseherin Irma Grese* (Racine, WI: Golden West Historical Publications, 1996).

Brown, S 'Female Perpetrators of the Rwandan Genocide' 16 *International Feminist Journal of Politics* (2014) 448–469.

'Foreword' in H Douglas et al. (eds.), *Australian Feminist Judgments: Righting and Rewriting Law* (Oxford: Hart, 2014).

Brownmiller, S *Against Our will: Men, Women and Rape* (Harmondsworth: Penguin Books, 1986).

Bruce Jr, DD 'W.E.B. Du Bois and the Idea of Double Consciousness' 64(2) *Journal of Literary History, Criticism, and Bibliography* (1992) 299–309.

Brunger, YM, Irving, E, and Sankey, D 'The Prosecutor v Thomas Lubanga Dyilo' in L Hodson and T Lavers (eds.), *Feminist Judgements in International Law* (Oxford: Hart, 2019).

Buchowska, N 'Violated or Protected. Women's Rights in Armed Conflicts after the Second World War' 2(2) *International Comparative Jurisprudence* (2016) 72–80.

Burgis-Kasthala, M 'Scholarship as Dialogue? TWAIL and the Politics of Methodology' 14(4) *Journal of International Criminal Justice* (2016) 921–937.

Burman, E 'Beyond "Women vs Children" or "Womenandchildren": Engendering Childhood and Reforming Motherhood' 16 *Journal of Children's Rights* (2008) 177–194.

Buss, D 'Seeing Sexual Violence in Conflict and Post-Conflict Societies: The Limits of Visibility' in D Buss et al. (eds.), *Sexual Violence in Conflict and Post-Conflict Societies: International Agendas and African Contexts* (Oxon: Routledge, 2014).

Calleja, C 'Jack Mezirow's Conceptualisation of Adult Transformative Learning: A Review' 20(1) *Journal of Adult and Continuing Education* (2014) 117–136.

Campbell, K 'The Gender of Transitional Justice: Law, Sexual Violence and the International Criminal Tribunal for the Former Yugoslavia' 1 *International Journal of Transitional Justice* (2007) 411–432.

Carastathis, A 'The Invisibility of Privilege: A Critique of Intersectional Models of Identity' 3(2) *Les Ateliers de l'Ethique* (2008) 23–38.

'Intersectionality and Decolonial Feminism' in *Intersectionality: Origins, Contestations, Horizons* (Lincoln: University of Nebraska Press, 2016) 199–232, available at https://doi.org/10.2307/j.ctt1fzhfz8.11.

Cardi, C and Pruvost, G 'Thinking Women's Violence' 5 *History of the Present* (2015) 200–216.

Casey, E (ed.) *Getting Back into Place: Towards a Renewed Understanding of the Place-World* (Bloomington: Indiana University Press, 2009).

Chalmers, J and Leverick, F 'Fair Labelling in Criminal Law' 71(2) *Modern Law Review* (2008) 217–246.

Chan, A 'The Development of a Muslim Enclave in Arakan (Rakhine) State of Burma (Myanmar)' 3 *SOAS Bulletin of Burma Research* (2005) 396–420.

Chappell, L 'Women, Gender and International Institutions: Exploring New Opportunities at the International Criminal Court' 22(1) *Policy and Society* (2003) 3–25.

'Women's Rights and Religious Opposition: The Politics of Gender at the International Criminal Court' in Y Abu-Laban (ed.), *Gendering the Nation-State: Canadian and Comparative Perspectives* (Vancouver: University of British Columbia Press, 2009).

'The Role of the ICC in Transitional Gender Justice: Capacity and Limitations' in S Buckley-Zistal and R Stanley (eds.), *Gender in Transitional Justice* (Basingstoke: Palgrave Macmillan, 2011).

'Conflicting Institutions and the Search for Gender Justice at the International Criminal Court' 67(1) *Political Research Quarterly* (2014) 183–196.

'"Newness", "Oldness", "Nestedness" and Gender Justice Outcomes' 10(4) *Politics & Gender* (2014) 572–594.

The Politics of Gender Justice at the International Criminal Court: Legacies and Legitimacy (Oxford: Oxford University Press, 2016).

'The Gender Injustice Cascade: "Transformative" Reparations for Victims of Sexual and Gender-Based Crimes in the Lubanga Case at the International Criminal Court' 21(9) *International Journal of Human Rights* (2017) 1223–1242.

Chappell, L and Grey, R '"Gender Just Judging" in International Criminal Courts: New Directions for Research' in S Rimmer and K Ogg (eds.), *Research Handbook on Feminist Engagement with International Law* (Cheltenham: Edward Elgar, 2019).

Chappell, L, Grey, R, and Walker, E 'The Gender Justice Shadow of Complementarity: Lessons from the International Criminal Court's Preliminary Examinations in Guinea and Colombia' 7(3) *International Journal of Transitional Justice* (2013) 455–475.

Charlesworth, H 'Are Women Peaceful? Reflections on the Role of Women in Peace-building' 16(3) *Feminist Legal Studies* (2008) 347–361.

'L'IDI dans le monde d'aujourd'hui' in M Kohen and I van der Heijden (eds.), *150 ans de contributions au développement du droit international: livre du sesquicentenaire de l'Institut de droit international (1873–2023) [150 Years of Contributing to the Development of International Law: Sesquicentenary Book of the Institute of International Law (1873–2023)[* (Paris: Éditions A. Pedon, 2023).

Charlesworth, H and Chinkin, C *The Boundaries of International Law: A Feminist Analysis* (Manchester: Manchester University Press, 2000).

Charlesworth, H, Chinkin, C, and Wright, S 'Feminist Approaches to International Law' 85 *American Journal of International Law* (1991) 613–645.

Cheesman, N 'How in Myanmar "National Races" Came to Surpass Citizenship and Exclude Rohingya' 47(3) *Journal of Contemporary Asia* (2017) 461–483.

Chetail, V 'Is There Any Blood on My Hands? Deportation as a Crime of International Law' 29 *Leiden Journal of International Law* (2016) 926–928.

Chinkin, C and Charlesworth, H *The Boundaries of International Law: A Feminist Analysis* (Manchester: Manchester University Press, 2000).

Chinkin, C et al. '*Bozkurt Case*, aka the *Lotus Case (France v Turkey)*: Ships that Go Bump in the Night', in L Hodson and T Lavers (eds.), *Feminist Judgments in International Law* (Oxford: Hart, 2019).

Chua, LJ and Gilbert, D 'State Violence, Human-Rights Violations and the Case of Apwint in Myanmar' in A Barrow and JL Chia (eds.), *Gender, Violence and the State of Asia* (London: Routledge, 2016).

Clark, P *Distant Justice: The Impact of the International Criminal Court on African Politics* (Cambridge: Cambridge University Press, 2018).

Clarke, K and Koulen, S 'The Legal Politics of the Article 16 Decision: The International Criminal Court, the UN Security Council and Ontologies of a Contemporary Compromise' (2014) 7(3) *African Journal of Legal Studies* 297–319.

Collins, PH 'Black Feminist Thought in the Matrix of Domination' in CC Lemert (ed.), *Social Theory: The Multicultural and Classic Readings* (Boulder, CO: Westview Press, 1993).

Black Feminist Thought: Knowledge, Consciousness, and the Politics of Empowerment (London: Routledge, 2000).

Collins, PH and Bilge, S *Intersectionality: Key Concepts* (Cambridge: Polity, 2016).

Colvin, V and Orchard, P 'A Forgotten History: Forcible Transfers and Deportations in International Criminal Law' 32 *Criminal Law Forum* (2021) 51–95.

Copelon, R 'Surfacing Gender: Re-engraving Crimes against Women in Humanitarian Law' 5 *Hastings Women' s Law Journal* (1994) 243–265.

'Gender Crimes as War Crimes: Integrating Crimes against Women into International Criminal Law' 46(1) *McGill Law Journal* (2000) 217–240.

Cornell, D and Thurschwell, A 'Feminism, Negativity, Intersubjectivity' in S Benhabib and D Cornell (eds.), *Feminism as Critique* (Minneapolis: University of Minnesota Press, 1987).

Coutler, C 'Female Fighters in the Sierra Leone War: Challenging the Assumptions?' 88 *Feminist Review* (2008) 54–73.

Cowan, S, Kennedy, C, and Munro, VE (eds.), *Scottish Feminist Judgments: (Re)Creating Law from the Outside In* (Oxford: Hart, 2019).

Crawford BJ et al. 'Teaching with Feminist Judgments: A Global Conversation' 38(1) *Law and Inequality* (2020) 1–67.

Crenshaw, K 'Demarginalizing the Intersection of Race and Sex: A Black Feminist Critique of Antidiscrimination Doctrine, Feminist Theory and Antiracist Politics' 1 *University of Chicago Legal Forum* (1989) 139–167.

'Mapping the Margins: Intersectionality, Identity Politics, and Violence against Women of Color' 43 *Stanford Law Review* (1991) 1241–1299.

Davies M (ed.) *Asking the Law Question* (3rd ed., Sydney: Lawbook Company, 2008).

Davies, M 'The Law Becomes Us: Rediscovering Judgment, review of Feminist Judgments: From Theory to Practice' 20(2) *Feminist Legal Studies* (2012) 167–181.

Davis, AY et al. *Abolition. Feminism. Now* (Chicago: Haymarket, 2022).

Davis, J 'The Anthropology of Suffering' 5 *Journal of Refugee Studies* (1992) 149–161.

Davis, L 'Reimagining Justice for Gender-Based Crimes at the Margins: New Legal Strategies for Prosecuting ISIS Crimes against Women and LGBTIQ Persons' 3 *William & Mary Journal of Race, Gender, and Social Justice* (2018) 513–558.

'Dusting off the Law Books: Recognising Gender Persecution in Conflicts and Atrocities' 20(1) *Northwestern Journal of Human Rights* (2021) 63–126.

Davis, LM et al. *Evaluating the Effectiveness of Correctional Education: A Meta-Analysis of Programs That Provide Education to Incarcerated Adults* (Santa Monica, CA: RAND Corporation, 2013).

Dawuni, J 'Matri-legal Feminism: An African Feminist Response to International Law' in K Ogg and SH Rimmer (eds.), *Feminist Approaches to International Law* (Cheltenham: Edward Elgar, 2019).

(ed.) *Intersectionality and Women's Access to Justice in Africa* (Lanham, MD: Rowman and Littlefield, 2022).

De Souza Dias, T 'Recharacterisation of Crimes and the Principle of Fair Labelling in International Criminal Law' 18(5) *International Criminal Law Review* (2018) 788–821.

De Zayas, A 'The Illegality of Population Transfers and the Application of Emerging International Norms in the Palestinian Context' 6 *Palestine Yearbook of International Law* (1990) 17–55.

DeFalco, RC and Mégret, F 'The Invisibility of Race at the ICC: Lessons from the US Criminal Justice System' 7(1) *London Review of International Law* (2019) 55–87.

Delgado, R and Stefancic, J 'Introduction' in R Delgado and J Stefancic (eds.), *Critical Race Theory: The Cutting Edge* (2nd ed., Philadelphia: Temple University Press, 2000).

Dolgopol, T 'The Tokyo Women's Tribunal' in A Byrnes and G Simm (eds.), *Peoples' Tribunals and International Law* (Cambridge: Cambridge University Press, 2018).

Douglas, H et al. *Australian Feminist Judgments: Righting and Rewriting Law* (1st ed., London: Bloomsbury, 2014).

Drumbl, MA *Atrocity, Punishment, and International Law* (Cambridge: Cambridge University Press, 2007).

Reimagining Child Soldiers in International Law and Policy (Oxford: Oxford University Press, 2012)

'"She Makes Me Ashamed to Be a Woman": The Genocide Conviction of Pauline Nyiramasuhuko, 2011' 34 *Michigan Journal of International Law* (2013) 559–603.

'Victims Who Victimise' 4(2) *London Review of International Law* (2016) 217–246.

Durham, H and O'Byrne, K 'The Dialogue of Difference: Gender Perspectives on International Humanitarian Law' 92(877) *International Review of the Red Cross* (2010) 31–52.

Durlauf, S and Nagin, D 'Imprisonment and Crime: Can Both Be Reduced?' 10(1) *Criminology & Public Policy* (2011) 13–54.

Dworkin, R *Taking Rights Seriously* (London: Duckworth, 1977).

Eckenwiler, L 'Displacement and Solidarity: An Ethic of Place-Making' 32 *Bioethics* (2018) 562–568.

Eichert, D '"Homosexualization" Revisited: An Audience-Focused Theorization of Wartime Male Sexual Violence' 21 *International Feminist Journal of Politics* (2019) 409–433.

'Decolonizing the Corpus: A Queer Decolonial Re-Examination of Gender in International Law's Origins' 43 *Michigan Journal of International Law* (2022) 557–594.

Elshtain, JB *Women and War* (New York: Basic Books, 1987).

Emadi, H 'Women in the Post-Taliban Afghanistan: The Socio-economic System and Its Corresponding Culture, Race, Gender & Class' 22(3–4) *Environment, Race, Culture, Gender, Crime and other Issues* (2015) 244–259.

England, K 'Getting Personal: Reflexivity, Positionality, and Feminist Research' 46 *The Professional Geographer* (1994) 80–89.

Engle, J 'Judging Sex in War' 106 *Michigan Law Review* (2008) 941–961.

Engle, K 'Anti-Impunity and the Turn to Criminal Law in Human Rights Law and Advocacy' 100(5) *Cornell Law Review* (2015) 1069–1127.

The Grip of Sexual Violence in Conflict: Feminist Interventions in International Law (Redwood City, CA: Stanford University Press, 2020).

Enloe, C *The Morning After: Sexual Politics at the End of the Cold War* (Berkeley: University of California Press, 1993).

Enright, M, McCandless J, and O'Donoghue A (eds.) *Northern/Irish Feminist Judgments: Judges' Troubles and the Gendered Politics of Identity* (London: Bloomsbury, 2017).

Eriksson Baaz, M and Stern, M *Sexual Violence as a Weapon of War? Perceptions, Prescriptions, Problems in the Congo and Beyond* (London: Zed Books, 2013).

Esposito J and Evans-Winters, V *Introduction to Intersectional Qualitative Research* (Thousand Oaks, CA: Sage, 2021).

Evans, C *The Right to Reparations in International Law for Victims of Armed Conflict* (Cambridge: Cambridge University Press, 2012).

Facio, A 'All Roads Lead to Rome, but Some Are Bumpier than Others' in S Pickering and C Lambert (eds.), *Global Issues, Women and Justice* (Sydney: Federation Press, 2004).

Fletcher, L 'Refracted Justice: The Imagined Victim and the International Criminal Court' in C De Vos, S Kendall, and C Stahn (eds.), *Contested Justice: The Politics and Practice of International Criminal Court Interventions* (Cambridge: Cambridge University Press, 2015).

Flint, J and de Waal, A *Darfur: A New History of a Long War* (London: Zed Books, 2008).

Fountain, J 'Sexual Violence, the Ad Hoc Tribunals and the International Criminal Court: Reconciling Akayesu and Kunarac' 19(2) *ILSA Journal of International and Comparative Law* (2013) 251–262.

Fraser, N *Scales of Justice: Reimaging Political Space in a Globalizing World* (New York: Colombia University Press, 2009).

Garbett, C 'From Passive Objects to Active Agents: Changing Conceptions of Victim Identities at the ICTY and ICC' 15(1) *Journal of Human Rights* (2016) 40–59.

Gardam, JG 'The Law of Armed Conflict: A Gendered Regime?' in DG Dallmeyer (ed.), *Reconceiving Reality: Women and International Law*, Studies in Transnational Legal Policy No. 25 (Washington, DC: American Society of International Law ASIL, 1993).

'Women and the Law of Armed Conflict – Why the Silence?' 46(1) *International and Comparative Law Quarterly* (1997) 55–80.

'The Neglected Aspect of Women and Armed Conflict: Progressive Development of the Law' 52(2) *Netherlands International Law Review*, (2005) 197–219.

'A New Frontline for Feminism and International Humanitarian Law' in M Davies and V Munro (eds.), *The Ashgate Research Companion to Feminist Legal Theory* (Farnham: Ashgate, 2013).

Gathii, J 'Alternative and Critical: The Contribution of Research and Scholarship on Developing Countries to International Legal Theory' 41 *Harvard International Law Journal* (2000) 263–275.

Gebhardt, M *Crimes Unspoken: The Rape of German Women at the End of the Second World War* (trans. N Somers, Cambridge: Polity, 2016).

Gentry, C and Sjoberg, L *Beyond Mothers, Monsters, Whores: Thinking About Women's Violence in Global Politics* (London: Zed Books, 2015).

Germain, S and Yong A (eds.) *Beyond the Virus: Multidisciplinary and International Perspectives on Inequities raised by Covid-19* (Bristol: Bristol University Press, 2023).

Ghosh, B 'A Diachronic Perspective of Hijra Identity in India' in S Manna, S Patra, and S Roy (eds.), *Sociology of Motherhood and Beyond* (Kolkata: Levant Books, 2018).

Gidding, P *When and Where I Enter: The Impact of Black Women on Race and Sex in America* (New York: W Morrow, 1984).

Gilbert, D *Everyday Transgender Belonging in Transitioning Yangon* (PhD Thesis, ANU, March 2016).

Gilbert D and Thar, NHM 'Moving from the Shadows: Law and SOGIE Rights in Myanmar's Democratic Transition' 20(1) *Australian Journal of Asian Law* (2019) 187–195.

Gilligan, C *In a Different Voice: Psychological Theory and Women's Development* (Cambridge, MA: Harvard University Press, 1982).

Glasius, M *The International Criminal Court: A Global Civil Society Achievement* (London: Routledge, 2006).

Gooding, K 'How Can the Methodology of Feminist Judgment Writing Improve Gender Sensitivity in International Criminal Law' 5 *LSE Law Review* (2020) 115–152.

Gorris, EAP 'Invisible Victims? Where Are Male Victims of Conflict-Related Sexual Violence in international Law and Policy?' 22 *European Journal of Women's Studies* (2015) 412–427.

Gottschall, J 'Explaining Wartime Rape' 41 *Journal of Sex Research* (2004) 129–136.

Graham, M et al. 'Working at Home' 63(11) *Journal of Occupational and Environmental Medicine* (2021) 938–943.

Gravenshort, L and Tatschmurat, L (eds.) *Töchter-Fragen, NS-Frauen-Geschichte* (Freiburg im Breisgau: Kore, 1990).

Gravers, M 'Exploring Ethnic Diversity in Burma' 40 *Nordic Institute of Asian Studies* (2007) 191–283.

Gready P and Robins, S 'From Transitional to Transformative Justice: A New Agenda for Practice' 8 *International Journal of Transitional Justice* (2014) 339–361.

Green, L 'First-Class Crimes, Second-Class Justice: Cumulative Charges for Gender-Based Crimes at the International Criminal Court' 11 *International Criminal Law Review* (2011) 529–541.

Greene, J 'Hostis Humani Generis' 34(4) *Critical Inquiry* (2008) 683–705.

Grey, R 'The Limits and Potential of International Criminal Law' 16(4) *International Feminist Journal of Politics* (2014) 601–621.

'Sexual Violence against Child Soldiers: The Limits and Potential of International Criminal Law' 16(4) *International Feminist Journal of Politics* (2014) 601–621.

'Interpreting International Crimes from a Female Perspective: Opportunities and Challenges for the International Criminal Court' 17(2) *International Criminal Law Review* (2016) 325–350.

'ICC's First "Forced Pregnancy" Case in Historical Perspective' 15(4) *Journal of International Criminal Justice* (2017) 905–930.

Prosecuting Sexual and Gender-Based Crimes at the International Criminal Court (Cambridge: Cambridge University Press, 2019).

Grey, R and Chappell, L 'Prosecuting Sexual and Gender-Based Crimes in the International Criminal Court: Inching Towards Gender Justice' in S Mouthaan and O Jurasz (eds.), *Gender and War: International and Transitional Justice Perspectives* (Cambridge: Intersentia, 2019).

Grey, R and Waller, E 'The Gender Justice Shadow of Complementarity: Lessons from the International Criminal Court's Preliminary Examinations in Guinea and Colombia' 7(3) *International Journal of Transitional Justice* (2013) 455–475.

Grey, R et al. 'Gender-Based Persecution as a Crime against Humanity' 17(5) *Journal of International Criminal Justice* (2019) 957–979.

Grey, R, McLoughlin, K, and Chappell, L 'Gender and Judging at the International Criminal Court: Lessons from "Feminist Judgment Projects"' 34(1) *Leiden Journal of International* (2021) 247–264.

Grossman, N 'Sex on the Bench: Do Women Judges Matter to the Legitimacy of International Courts?' 12(2) *Chicago Journal of International Law* (2012) 647–648.

'Achieving Sex-Representative International Court Benches' 110 *American Journal of International Law* (2016) 82–95.

'Julia Sebutinde: An Unbreakable Cloth' in J Dawuni and A Kuenyehia (eds.), *International Courts and the African Woman Judge: Unveiled Narratives* (London: Routledge, 2018).

'The "Invisible Court": Gender and Nationality in Registries and Secretariats' in N Grossman et al. (eds.), *Women and International Law* (Oxford: Oxford University Press, 2024).

Guilfoyle, D 'The ICC Pre-Trial Chamber Decision on Jurisdiction over the Situation in Myanmar' 73(1) *Australian Journal of International Affairs* (2019) 2–8.

Gunnison, E et al., 'Correctional Practitioners on Reentry: A Missed Perspective' 2(1) *Journal of Prison Education and Reentry* (2015) 32–54.

Hale, B 'Foreword' in R Hunter, C McGlynn, and E Rackley (eds.), *Feminist Judgments: From Theory to Practice* (Oxford: Hart, 2010).

Halley, J 'Rape in Berlin: Reconsidering the Criminalisation of Rape in the International Law of Armed Conflict' 9(1) *Melbourne Journal of International Law* (2008) 78–124.

'Rape in Rome: Feminist Interventions in the Criminalization of Sex-Related Violence in Positive International Criminal Law' 30(1) *Michigan Journal of International Law* (2008) 1–123.

Hallperin, L 'Beyond Clueless Mothers: Israel "Women Wage Peace": Activists' Perception of Why Women Are Key to Peacemaking' 31(2) *Social Politics* (2023) 249–272.

Harris, A 'Race and Essentialism in Feminist Legal Theory' 42 *Stanford Law Review* (1989) 581–616.

Haslam, E 'Unlawful Population Transfer and the Limits of International Criminal Law' 61(1) *Cambridge Law Journal* (2002) 66–75.

Haslam, E and Edmunds, R 'Whose Number Is It Anyway? Common Legal Representation, Consultations, and the "Statistical Victim"' 15(5) *Journal of International Criminal Justice* (2017) 931–952.

Hayes, N 'Sisyphus Wept: Prosecuting Sexual Violence at the International Criminal Court' in W Schabas, N Hayes, and Y Mcdermott (eds.), *Ashgate Research Companion to International Criminal Law: Critical Perspectives* (London: Routledge, 2013).

Henckaerts, JM and Doswald-Beck, L *International Committee of the Red Cross: Customary International Humanitarian Law (Vol. I)* (Cambridge: Cambridge University Press, 2005).

Henn, E *International Human Rights Law and Structural Discrimination: The Example of Violence Against Women* (1st ed., Berlin: Springer, 2019).

Hessler, K 'The Significance of Religious Diversity in International Human Rights Adjudication' in F Baetens (ed.), *Identity and Diversity on the International Bench* (Oxford: Oxford University Press, 2021).

Hodgson, N 'Gender Justice or Gendered Justice? Female Defendants in International Criminal Tribunals' 25 *Feminist Legal Studies* (2017) 337–357.

Hodson, L 'Gender and the International Judge: Towards a Transformative Equality Approach' 35 *Leiden Journal of International Law* (2022) 913–930.

Hodson, L and Lavers, T (eds.) *Feminist Judgements in International Law* (Oxford: Hart, 2019).

Hogg, N 'Women's Participation in the Rwandan Genocide: Mothers or Monsters?' 92(877) *International Review of the Red Cross* (2010) 69–102.

Holslag, A 'Exposed Bodies: A Conceptual Approach to Sexual Violence during the Armenian Genocide' in E Randall (ed.), *Genocide and Gender in the Twentieth Century: A Comparative Survey* (London: Bloomsbury Academic, 2015).

Honwana, A *Child Soldiers in Africa* (Pittsburgh: University of Pennsylvania Press, 2006).

Hospodaryk, V 'Male and Gender-Diverse Victims of Sexual Violence in the Rohingya Genocide: The Selective Narrative of International Courts' 17(2) *International Journal of Transitional Justice* (2023) 252–267.

Hossain, A 'Beyond Emasculation: Being Muslim and Becoming *Hijra* in South Asia' 36(4) *Asian Studies Review* (2012) 495–513.

'The Paradox of Recognition: *Hijra*, Third Gender and Sexual Rights in Bangladesh' 19(12) *Culture, Health & Sexuality* (2017) 1418–1431.

Htun, M 'What It Means to Study Gender and the State' 1 *Politics and Gender* (2005) 157–166.

Hunter, R 'Can Feminist Judges Make a Difference?' 15(1–2) *International Journal of the Legal Profession* (2008) 7–36.

'An Account of Feminist Judging' in R Hunter, C McGlynn, and E Rackley (eds.), *Feminist Judgments: From Theory to Practice* (Oxford: Hart, 2010).

Hunter, R and Rackley, E 'Feminist Judgments on the UK Supreme Court' 32 *Canadian Journal of Women and the Law* (2020) 85–113.

Hunter, R, McGlynn C, and Rackley E (eds.) *Feminist Judgments: From Theory to Practice* (Oxford: Hart, 2010).

Indra, D (ed.) *Engendering Forced Migration: Theory and Practice* (New York; Berghahn Books, 2001).

Islam F et al. 'Situation of Sexual and Gender Based Violence among the Rohingya Migrants Residing in Bangladesh' 22(2) *Injury Prevention* (2016). https://injuryprevention.bmj.com/content/22/Suppl_2/A260.1.

Jarvis, M 'Overview: The Challenge of Accountability for Conflict-Related Sexual Violence Crimes' in S Brammertz and M Jarvis (eds.), *Prosecuting Conflict-Related Sexual Violence at the ICTY* (Oxford: Oxford University Press, 2016).

Jarvis, M and Vigneswaran, K 'Challenges to Successful Outcomes in Sexual Violence Cases' in S Brammertz and M Jarvis (eds.), *Prosecuting Conflict-Related Sexual Violence at the ICTY* (Oxford: Oxford University Press, 2016).

Jessberger, F and Geneuss, J (eds.) *Why Punish Perpetrators of Mass Atrocities? Purposes of Punishment in International Criminal Law* (Cambridge: Cabridge University Press, 2020).

Jjuko, D 'Double Victimization? Using a Human Security Framework to Assess the Effectiveness of the Witness Protection Regime in Kenya' 15(3) *African Security* (2022) 189–212.

Jones, A 'Gender and Genocide in Rwanda' 4 *Journal of Genocide Research* (2002) 65–94.

Kalra, G '*Hijras*: The Unique Transgender Culture of India' 5(2) *International Journal of Culture and Mental Health* (2012) 121–126.

Kapur, A 'Asian Values v. The Paper Tiger' 11 *Journal of International Criminal Justice* (2013) 1059–1090.

Kapur, R '"The First Feminist War in All History": Epistemic Shifts and Relinquishing the Mission to Rescue the "Other Woman"' 116 *AJIL Unbound* (2022) 270–274.

Kasozi, ABK *Social Origins of Violence in Uganda, 1964–1985* (Montreal: McGill-Queen's University Press, 1994).

Kendall, S 'Commodifying Global Justice: Economics of Accountability at the International Criminal Court' 13(1) *Journal of International Criminal Justice* (2015) 113–134.

Kendall, S and Nouwen, S 'Representational Practices at the International Criminal Court: The Gap between Juridified and Abstract Victimhood' 76 *Law and Contemporary Problems* (2013) 235–262.

Kenney, SJ 'New Research on Gendered Political Institutions' 49(2) *Political Research Quarterly* (1996) 445–466.

'Thinking about Gender and Judging' 15(1) *International Journal of the Legal Profession* (2008) 87–110.

Gender and Justice: Why Women in the Judiciary Really Matter (New York: Routledge, 2013).

Kim, M 'Transformative Justice and Restorative Justice: Gender-Based Violence and Alternative Visions of Justice in the United States' 27(2) *International Review of Victimology* (2021) 162–172.

King, KL and Greening, M 'Gender Justice or Just Gender? The Role of Gender in Sexual Assault Decisions at the International Criminal Tribunal for Former Yugoslavia' 88 *Social Science Quarterly* (2007) 1049–1071.

Knibiehler, Y La virginité féminine: Mythes, fantasmes, émancipation (Paris: Odile Jacob, 2012).

Koenig, A and Egan, U 'Power and Privilege: Investigating Sexual Violence with Digital Open Source Information' 19 *Journal of International Criminal Justice* (2021) 55–84.

Kompisch, K *Täterinnen: Frauen im Nationalsozialismus* (Cologne: Böhlau Köln, 2008).

Koonz, C *Mothers in the Fatherland* (New York: St Martin's Press, 1987).

Korman R 'The Tutsi Body in the 1994 Genocide: Ideology, Physical Destruction, and Memory' in E Anstett and J-M Dreyfus (eds.), *Destruction and Human Remains: Disposal and Concealment in Genocide and Mass Violence* (Manchester: Manchester University Press, 2014).

Koskenniemi, M 'Between Impunity and Show Trials' 6(1) *Max Planck Yearbook of United Nations Law* (2002) 1–35.

Kotecha, B 'The International Criminal Court's Selectivity and Procedural Justice' 18(1) *Journal of International Criminal Justice* (2020) 107–139.

Kouvo, S and Levine, C 'Law as a Placeholder for Change? Women's Rights and Realities in Afghanistan' in K Rubenstein and KG Young (eds.), *The Public Law of Gender: From the Local to the Global* (Cambridge: Cambridge University Press, 2016).

Krever, T 'International Criminal Law: An Ideology Critique' 26(3) *Leiden Journal of International Law* (2013) 701–723.

Labenski, SA *The Importance of Women as Villains and Violators: Scenes from the ICTY, the ICTR, and Abu Ghraib* (Master's thesis, American University of Cairo, 2013).

Labuda, P 'Beyond Rhetoric: Interrogating the Eurocentric Critique of International Criminal Law's Selectivity in the Wake of the 2022 Ukraine Invasion' 36(4) *Leiden Journal of International Law* (2023) 1095–1116.

Leddy, N 'Investigative and Charging Considerations for International Crimes Targeting Individuals on the Basis of Sexual Orientation and Gender Identity' 20(4) *Journal of International Criminal Justice* (2022) 911–942.

Leider, JP 'Competing Identities and the Hybridized History of the Rohingyas' in R Egreteau and F Robin (eds.), *Metamorphosis: Studies in Social and Political Change in Myanmar* (Singapore: NUS Press, 2015).

Lewa, C 'North Arakan: An Open Prison for the Rohingya in Burma. Statelessness' 32 *Forced Migration Online* (2009) 11–13.

Lewis, D 'Unrecognized Victims: Sexual Violence against Men in Conflict Settings under International Law' 27 *Wisconsin International Law Journal* (2009) 1–49.

Linton, S 'Women Accused of International Crimes: A Trans-Disciplinary Inquiry and Methodology' 27(2) *Criminal Law Forum* (2016) 159–226.

Longpre, S, Storm, M, and Shah, R 'Lethal Autonomous Weapons Systems & Artificial Intelligence: Trends, Challenges, and Policies' 3(1) *MIT Science Policy Review* (2022) 47–56.

Lord Reid 'The Judge as Law Maker' 12 *Journal of the Society of Public Teachers of Law* (1972) 22–29.

Lorde, A *Sister Outsider* (Harmondsworth: Penguin Modern Classics, 2019, originally 1984).

'The Master's Tools Will Never Dismantle the Master's House' in *Sister Outsider: Essays and Speeches* (Trumansburg, NY: Crossing Press, 2007).

Loucou, JN *Côte d'Ivoire: les résistances à la conquête coloniale* (Abidjan: Éditions CERAP, 2007).

Lubaale, EC and Dyani-Mhango N *National Accountability for International Crimes in Africa* (London: Palgrave Macmillan, 2022).

Luban, D 'Calling Genocide by Its Rightful Name: Lemkin's Word, Darfur, and the UN Report' 7(1) *Chicago Journal of International Law* (2006) 303–320.

Macbeth, D 'On "Reflexivity" in Qualitative Research: Two Readings, and a Third' 7(1) *Qualitative Inquiry* (2001) 35–68.

Mackenzie R et al. *Selecting International Judges: Principle, Process and Politics* (Oxford: Oxford University Press, 2010).

MacKinnon, CA 'Feminism, Marxism, Method, and the State: Toward Feminist Jurisprudence' 8(4) *Signs* (1983) 635–658.

'The ICTR's Legacy on Sexual Violence' 14 *New England Journal of International and Comparative Law* (2008) 211–221.

'Intersectionality as Method: A Note' 38(4) *Signs* (2013) 1019–1030.

Madkour, AS et al. 'Early Adolescent Sexual Initiation as a Problem Behavior: A Comparative Study of Five Nations' 47(4) *Journal of Adolescent Health* (2010) 389–398.

Mal, S 'The Hijras of India: A Marginal Community with Paradox Sexual Identity' 34(1) *Indian Journal of Social Psychiatry* (2018) 79–85.

Maravall-Buckwalter, I 'The Inconsistencies of Age-Related Incapacity Thresholds in International Law: Child Rape Victims at a Disadvantage' 22(2) *Human Rights Law Review* (2022) 1–21.

Margalit, A 'Still a Blind Spot: The Protection of LGBT Persons during Armed Conflict and Other Situations of Violence' 100 *International Review of the Red Cross* (2018) 237–265.

Marshall, J 'Law, Everyday Spaces and Objects, and Being Human' in C Stychin (ed.), *Law, Humanities and the COVID Crisis* (London: University of London Press, 2023).

Mathey, MJ et al. 'The Role Played by Women of the Central African Republic in the Prevention and Resolution of Conflicts' in *Women and Peace in Africa: Case Studies on Traditional Conflict Resolution Practices* (Paris: UNESCO, 2003). https://unesdoc.unesco.org/ark:/48223/pf0000133274.

Matsuda, M 'When the First Quail Calls: Multiple Consciousness as Jurisprudential Method' 7(9) *Women's Rights Law Report* (1989) 297–300.

Matthews, H 'Redeeming Rape: Berlin 1945 and the Making of Modern International Criminal Law' in I Tallgren and T Skouteris (eds.), *The New Histories of International Criminal Law – Retrials* (Oxford: Oxford University Press, 2019).

Maxine Clarke, K *Fictions of Justice: The International Criminal Court and the Challenge of Legal Pluralism in Sub-Saharan Africa* (Cambridge: Cambridge University Press, 2010).

'Refiguring the Perpetrator: Culpability, History and International Criminal Law's Impunity Gap' 19(5) *International Journal of Human Rights* (2015) 592–614.

'We Ask for Justice, You Give Us Law: The Rule of Law, Economic Markets, and the Reconfiguration of Victimhood' in C De Vos, S Kendall, and C Stahn (eds.), *Contested Justice: The Politics and Practice of International Criminal Court Interventions* (Cambridge: Cambridge University Press, 2015).

Maxwel, C and Garner, J 'The Crime Control Effects of Criminal Sanctions for Intimate Partner Violence' 3(4) *Partner Abuse* (2012) 469–500.

McCall, L 'The Complexity of Intersectionality' 30(3) *Signs* (2005) 1771–1800.

McCall-Smith, K, Smith, R, and Yahyaoui Krivenko, E 'Reservations to the Convention on the Prevention and Punishment of the Crime of Genocide' in L Hodson and T Lavers (eds.), *Feminist Judgments in International Law* (Oxford: Hart, 2019).

McDonald, E et al. (eds.) *Feminist Judgments of Aotearoa New Zealand Te Rino, a Two-Stranded Rope* (Oxford: Hart, 2017).

McGlynn, C *The Woman Lawyer: Making the Difference* (London: Butterworths, 1998).

'Rape as "Torture"? Catherine MacKinnon and Questions of Feminist Strategy' 16(1) *Feminist Legal Studies* (2008) 71–85.

'Challenging Anti-Carceral Feminism: Criminalisation, Justice and Continuum Thinking' (2022) 93 *Women's Studies International Forum* 1–8.

McLoughlin, K 'A Particular Disappointment? Judging Women and the High Court of Australia' 23(3) *Feminist Legal Studies* (2015) 273–294.

Law, Women Judges and the Gender Order: Lessons from the High Court of Australia (London: Routledge, 2022).

Meagher, K 'Exploring the Role of Gender and Women in the Political Economy of Health in Armed Conflict: A Narrative Review' 17 *Global Health* (2021) 88–96.

Mégret, F 'What Sort of Global Justice Is "International Criminal Justice"?' 13 *Journal of International Criminal Justice* (2015) 77–96.

'The Strange Case of the Victim Who Did Not Want Justice' 12(3) *International Journal of Transitional Justice* (2018) 444–463.

Meier, AM 'Adolescent First Sex and Subsequent Mental Health' 112(6) *American Journal of Sociology* (2007) 1811–1847.

Menkel-Meadow, C 'Portia in a Different Voice: Speculations on a Women's Lawyering Process' 1 *Berkeley Women's Law Journal* (1985) 39–63.

Mennecke, M 'Punishing Genocidaires: A Deterrent Effect or Not?' in S Totten (ed.), *The Prevention and Intervention of Genocide* (New York: Routledge, 2008).

Merope S, 'Recharacterizing the Lubanga Case: Regulation 55 and the Consequences for Gender Justice at the ICC' 22 *Criminal Law Forum* (2011) 311–346.

Mickelson, K 'Rhetoric and Rage: Third World Voices in International Legal Discourse' 16 *Wisconsin International Law Journal* (1998) 353–419.

Min, PG 'Korean "Comfort Women": The Intersection of Colonial Power, Gender, and Class' 17(6) *Gender and Society* (2003) 938–957.

Mitchell, DS 'The Prohibition of Rape in International Humanitarian Law as a Norm of Jus Cogens: Clarifying the Doctrine' 15 *Duke Journal of Comparative Law & International Law* (2005) 219–257.

Miyoshi, MA 'Borderless World? From Colonialism to Transnationalism and the Decline of the Nation-State' 19(4) *Critical Inquiry* (1993) 726–751.

Moffett, L *Justice for Victims before the International Criminal Court* (London: Routledge, 2014).

Reparations and War: Finding Balance in Repairing the Past (Oxford: Oxford University Press, 2023).

Mohanty, CT *Feminism without Borders: Decolonizing Theory, Practicing Solidarity* (Durham, NC: Duke University Press, 2003).

'Transnational Feminist Crossings: On Neoliberalism and Radical Critique' 38(4) *Signs* (2013) 967–991.

Mohanty, CT, Russo, A, and Torres, L (eds.) *Third World Women and the Politics of Feminism* (Bloomington: Indiana University Press, 1991).

Moser, C and Clark, F (eds.) *Victims, Perpetrators or Actors? Gender, Armed conflict and Political Violence* (London: Zed Books, 2001).

Mossman, MJ 'Feminism and Legal Method: The Difference It Makes' 3 *Wisconsin Women's Law Journal* (1987) 147–168.

Mouthaan, S 'The Prosecution of Gender-Based Crimes at the ICC: Challenges and Opportunities' 11(4) *International Criminal Law Review* (2011) 775–802.

'Sexual Violence against Men and International Law – Criminalising the Unmentionable' 13(3) *International Law Review* (2013) 665–695.

Mudukuti, A 'Gender Imbalance at the ICC: The Continued Hegemonic Entrenchment of Male Privilege in International Criminal Law' in F Jeßberger, L Steinl, and K Mehta (eds.), *International Criminal Law – A Counter-Hegemonic Project* (The Hague: TMC Asser Press, 2022).

Mukasa, N 'War-Child Mothers in Northern Uganda: The Civil War Forgotten Legacy' 27 *Development in Practice* (2017) 354–367.

Munro, V 'Feminist Judgments Projects at the Intersection' 29 *Feminist Legal Studies* (2021) 251–261.

Mutcherson, KM (ed.) *Feminist Judgments: Reproductive Justice Rewritten* (Cambridge: Cambridge University Press, 2020).

Mutua, M 'What Is TWAIL?' 94 *American Society of International Law Proceedings* (2000) 31–38.

Nagakoshi, Y 'The Scope and Implications of the International Criminal Court's Jurisdictional Decision over the Rohingya Crisis' 43(2) *Human Rights Quarterly* (2021) 259–289.

Nash, JC 'Re-thinking Intersectionality' 89 *Feminist Review* (2008) 1–15.

Neikirk, A '. . .Happily Ever After (Or What Fairytales Teach Girls about Being Women)' 8 *Hohonu: A Journal of Academic Writing* (2009) 38–42.

Nesiah, V 'The Ground Beneath Her Feet: "Third World" Feminisms' 4(3) *Journal of International Women's Studies* (2003) 30–38.

'Missionary Zeal for a Secular Mission: Bringing Gender to Transitional Justice and Redemption to Feminism' in S Kouvo and Z Pearson (eds.), *Feminist Perspectives on Contemporary International Law: Between Resistance and Compliance* (Oxford: Bloomsbury, 2014).

Ni Aolain, F 'Exploring a Feminist Theory of Harm in the Context of Conflicted and Post-Conflict Societies' 35 *Queen's Law Journal* (2009) 219–244.

Ní Aoláin, F, Haynes, DF, and Cahn, N *On the Frontlines: Gender, War, and the Post-Conflict Process* (New York: Oxford University Press, 2011).

Nilsson, J 'The Vucković Trial in Kosovo – Deportation and Forcible Transfer under the Definition of Genocide' 71 *Nordic Journal of International Law* (2002) 545–555.

Nolin C (ed.) *Transnational Ruptures: Gender and Forced Migration (Gender in a Global/Local World)* (London: Routledge, 2001).

Nortje, W and Quénivet, N *Child Soldiers and the Defence of Duress under International Criminal Law* (Cham: Palgrave Macmillan, 2019).

Nosworthy, J 'Diversity, Inclusion, and Legitimacy in International Courts and Tribunals: Insights from Within, Perspectives from the Periphery – An Island Girl Speaks' in F Baetens (ed.), *Identity and Diversity on the International Bench* (Oxford: Oxford University Press, 2020).

Nour, NM 'Health Consequences of Child Marriage in Africa' 12(11) *Emerging Infectious Diseases* (2006) 1644–1649.

Nouwen, S 'Justifying Justice' in J Crawford and M Koskenniemi (eds.), *The Cambridge Companion to International Law* (Cambridge: Cambridge University Press, 2012).

Nove, A et al. 'Maternal Mortality in Adolescents Compared with Women of Other Ages: Evidence from 144 Countries' 2(3) *Lancet Global Health* (2014) 155–164.

Nyseth Brehm, HN 'Re-examining Risk Factors of Genocide' 12(1) *Journal of Genocide Research* (2017) 61–87.

O'Brien, M 'Gender Dimensions of Forced Marriage in International Criminal Law' in I Rosenthal, V Oosterveld, and S SáCouto (eds.), *Gender and International Criminal Law* (Oxford: Oxford University Press, 2022).

From Discrimination to Death: Genocide Process through a Human Rights Lens (Abingdon: Routledge, 2023).

O'Brien, M, Rosenthal, I, and Grey, R 'Historic Feminist Intervention at the International Criminal Court – The Appeals Hearing in *Prosecutor v Dominic Ongwen*' 28(1) *Australian Journal of Human Rights* (2022) 176–182.
O'Rourke, C *Gender Politics in Transitional Justice* (London: Routledge, 2013).
O'Smith, K 'Prosecutor v Lubanga: How the ICC failed the Women and Girls of the Congo' 54(2) *Howard Law Journal* (2010–2011) 467–504.
Okafor, OC 'Critical Third World Approaches to International Law (TWAIL): Theory, Methodology, or Both?' 10 *International Community Law Review* (2008) 371–378.
Oosterveld, V 'The Definition of "Gender" in the Rome Statute of the International Criminal Court: A Step Forward or Back for International Criminal Justice?' 18 *Harvard Human Rights Journal* (2005) 55–84.
'Constructive Ambiguity and the Meaning of Gender for the International Criminal Court' 16 *International Feminist Journal of Politics* (2014) 563–580.
'Sexual Violence Directed at Men and Boys in Armed Conflict or Mass Atrocity' 10 *International Law & International Relations* (2014) 107–128.
'The ICC Policy Paper on Sexual and Gender-Based Crimes: A Crucial Step for International Criminal Law' 24(3) *William & Mary Journal of Women and the Law* (2018) 1–15.
Otto, D (ed.) *Queering International Law: Possibilities, Alliances, Complicities, Risks* (London: Routledge, 2018).
'Feminist Judging in Action: Reflecting on the Feminist Judgments in International Law Project' 28(2) *Feminist Legal Studies* (2020) 206–207.
Parry, BR and Gordon, E 'The Shadow Pandemic: Inequitable Gendered Impacts of COVID-19 in South Africa' 28(2) *Gender, Work & Organization* (2021) 795–806.
Pena, M and Carayon, G 'Is the ICC Making the Most of Victim Participation?' 7(3) *International Journal of Transitional Justice* (2013) 518–535.
Petersilia, J *When Prisoners Come Home: Parole and Prisoner Reentry* (New York: Oxford University Press 2003).
Phillip, A *The Politics of Presence* (Oxford: Oxford University Press, 1995).
Picart CJ (Kay) S 'Attempting to Go Beyond Forgetting: The Legacy of the Tokyo IMT and Crimes of Violence against Women' 7 *University of Pennsylvania East Asia Law Review* (2011) 1–49.
Pillai, V 'Women, War, and Reproductive Health in Developing Countries' 56(1) *Social Work in Health Care* (2017) 28–44.
Plavšić, B *Svedocim* (Banjaluka: Trioprint, 2005).
Quénivet, N 'Girl Soldiers and Participation in Hostilities' 16(2) *African Journal of International and Comparative Law* (2008) 219–235.
Quinn, JR 'Getting to Peace? Negotiating with the LRA in Northern Uganda' 10(1) *Human Rights Review* (2009) 55–71.
Rackley, E 'Representations of the (Woman) Judge: Hercules, the Little Mermaid, and the Vain and Naked Emperor' 22(4) *Legal Studies* (2002) 602–624.
'Why Feminist Legal Scholars Should Write Judgments: Reflections on the Feminist Judgments Project in England and Wales' 24(2) *Canadian Journal of Women and Law* (2012) 389–413.
'A Short History of Judicial Diversity' 76 *Current Legal Problems* (2023) 1–32.
Rafter, N and Stanko, EA *Judge, Lawyer, Victim, Thief: Women, Gender Roles, and Criminal Justice* (Boston: Northeastern University Press, 1982).
Rahimian, T 'Afghanistan and the International Criminal Court: A Gender Perspective' *Journal of International Affairs* (2018). https://jia.sipa.columbia.edu/news/afghanistan-and-international-criminal-court-gender-perspective.

Rami-Nogales, J 'Revisiting the Category "Women"' in K Ogg and SH Rimmer (eds.), *Feminist Approaches to International Law* (Cheltenham: Edward Elgar, 2019).
Rauxloh, RE 'Negotiated History: The Historical Record in International Criminal Law and Plea Bargaining' 10 *International Criminal Law Review* (2010) 739–770.
Reddy, G *With Respect to Sex: Negotiating Hijra Identity in South Asia* (Chicago: Chicago University Press, 2005).
Rees, M and Chinkin, C 'Exposing the Gendered Myth of Post Conflict Transition: The Transformative Power of Economic and Social Rights' 48(4) *New York University Journal of International Law and Politics* (2016) 1211–1226.
Renshaw, C 'Myamar's Genocide and the Legacy of Forgetting' 48 *Georgia Journal of International and Comparative Law* (2019) 425–472.
Reynolds, J and Xavier, S '"The Dark Corners of the World": TWAIL and International Criminal Justice' 14(4) *Journal of International Criminal Justice* (2016) 959–983.
Rigney, S 'Postcard from the ICTY: Examining International Criminal Law's Narratives' in D Joyce and J Hohmann (eds.), *International Law's Objects* (Oxford: Oxford University Press, 2018).
'Distant Justice: The Impact of the International Criminal Court on African Politics (Book Review)' 31(3) *European Journal of International Law* (2020) 1157–1161.
Fairness and Rights in International Criminal Procedure (Edinburgh: Edinburgh University Press, 2023).
Roberts, DE 'Abolition Constitutionalism' 133(1) *Harvard Law Review* (2019) 3–122.
Roberts K and Stewart, JG 'Delimiting Deportation, Unlawful Transfer, Forcible Transfer and Forcible Displacement in International Criminal Law: A Jurisprudential History' 5(1) *African Journal of International Criminal Justice* (2019) 56–95.
Robins, S 'Failing Victims? The Limits of Transitional Justice in Addressing the Needs of Victims of Violations' 11(1) *Human Rights and International Legal Discourse* (2017) 41–58.
Robinson, D 'Serving the Interests of Justice: Amnesties, Truth Commissions and the International Criminal Court' 14 *European Journal of International Law* (2003) 481–505.
Ronel, N and Elisha, E 'A Different Perspective: Introducing Positive Criminology' 55(2) *International Journal of Offender Therapy and Comparative Criminology* (2011) 305–325.
Rose, G *Feminism and Geography: The Limits of Geographical Knowledge* (Minneapolis: University of Minnesota Press, 1993).
Rosenthal, I, Oosterveld, V, and SáCouto, S 'What Is "Gender" in I Rosenthal, V Oosterveld, and S SáCouto (eds.), International Criminal Law?' in *Gender and International Criminal Law* (Oxford: Oxford University Press, 2022).
Roth, BB et al. 'The Relationship between Prisoners' Academic Self-Efficacy and Participation in Education, Previous Convictions, Sentence Length, and Portion of Sentence Served' 3(2) *Journal of Prison Education and Reentry* (2016) 106–121.
SáCouto, S and Cleary, K 'The Importance of Effective Investigation of Sexual Violence and Gender-Based Crimes at the International Criminal Court' 17(2) *American University Journal of Gender, Social Policy and Law* (2009) 337–359.
SáCouto, S and Sellers, PV 'The Bemba Appeals Chamber Judgment: Impunity for Sexual and Gender-based Crimes' 27 *William & Mary Bill of Rights Journal* (2019) 599–622.
Samady, SR *Education and Afghan Society in the Twentieth Century* (Paris: UNESCO, 2001). https://unesdoc.unesco.org/ark:/48223/pf0000124627.
Samar, S 'Feminism, Peace and Afghanistan' 72(2) *Journal of International Affairs* (2019) 145–158.
Sanchi, K, Berger, L, and Crawford, B *Feminist Judgments (Feminist Judgment Series: Rewritten Judicial Opinions)* (Cambridge: Cambridge University Press, 2016).

Sandberg, S and Ugelvik, T 'Why Do Offenders Tape Their Crimes? Crime and Punishment in the Age of the Selfie' 57 *British Journal of Criminology* (2017) 1023–1040.

Scales, A 'The Emergence of Feminist Jurisprudence: An Essay' 95(7) *Yale Law Journal* (1986) 1373–1403.

Schabas, W 'Problems of International Codification – Were the Atrocities in Cambodia and Kosovo Genocide?' 35(1) *New England Law Review* (2001) 287–302.

The International Criminal Court: A Commentary on the Rome Statute (2nd ed., Oxford: Oxford University Press, 2016).

Schabas, W, Stahn, C, and El Zeidy, M 'The International Criminal Court and Complementarity: Five Years On' 19 *Criminal Law Forum* (2008) 1–3.

Schiff, B *Building the International Criminal Court* (Cambridge: Cambridge University Press, 2008).

Schmid, E *Taking Economic, Social and Cultural Rights Seriously in International Criminal Law* (Cambridge: Cambridge University Press, 2015).

Schomerus, M *The Lord's Resistance Army: Violence and Peacemaking in Africa* (Cambridge: Cambridge University Press, 2021).

Schwöbel-Patel, C 'The Market and Marketing Culture of International Criminal Law' in C Schwöbel (ed.), *Critical Approaches to International Criminal Law* (London: Routledge, 2014).

'The "Ideal" Victim of International Criminal Law' 29(3) *European Journal of International Law* (2018) 703–724.

'The Core Crimes of International Criminal Law' in K Heller et al. (eds.), *The Oxford Handbook of International Criminal Law* (Oxford: Oxford University Press, 2020).

Marketing Global Justice: The Political Economy of International Criminal Law (Cambridge: Cambridge University Press, 2021).

Sehmi, A 'Now That We Have No Voice, What Will Happen to Us?': Experiences of Victim Participation in the *Kenyatta* Case' 16(3) *Journal of International Criminal Justice* (2018) 571–591.

'Emphasising Socio-economic Narratives of Truth, Justice and Reparations in the Prosecutor v. Dominic Ongwen' 26(6) *International Journal of Human Rights* (2022) 1083–1106.

Sellers, PV 'Gender Strategy Is Not Luxury for International Courts Symposium: Prosecuting Sexual and Gender Based Crimes Before International/ized Criminal Courts' 17(2) *American University Journal of Gender, Social Policy & the Law* (2009) 327–335.

'Wartime Female Slavery: Enslavement?' 44 *Cornell International Law Journal* (2011) 115–142.

Sellers, PV and Kestenbaum, JG 'Missing in Action: The International Crime of the Slave Trade' 18 *Journal of International Criminal Justice* (2020) 517–542.

'The International Crimes of Slavery and the Slave Trade A Feminist Critique' in I Rosenthal, V Oosterveld, and S SáCouto (eds.), *Gender and International Criminal Law* (Oxford: Oxford University Press, 2022).

Sellers PV and Rosenthal, I 'Chapter 17. Rape and Other Sexual Violence' in A Clapham et al. (eds.), *The 1949 Geneva Conventions: A Commentary* (Oxford: Oxford University Press, 2015).

Sharlach, L 'Gender and Genocide in Rwanda: Women as Agents and Objects of Genocide' 1(3) *Journal of Genocide Research* (1999) 387–399.

Sherry, S 'The Gender of Judges' 4 *Law and Inequality* (1986) 159–169.

Sivakumaran, S 'Sexual Violence against Men in Armed Conflict' 18 *European Journal of International Law* (2007) 253–276.

'Lost in Translation: UN Responses to Sexual Violence against Men and Boys in Situations of Armed Conflict' 92 *International Review of the Red Cross* (2010) 259–277.
Sjoberg, L and Gentry, C *Mothers, Monsters, Whores: Women's Violence in Global Politics* (London: Zed Books, 2007).
Smart, C *Feminism and the Power of Law* (New York: Routledge, 1990).
Law, Crime and Sexuality (London: Sage, 1995).
'Reflection' 20 *Feminist Legal Studies* (2012) 161–165.
Smeulers, A 'Female Perpetrators: Ordinary or Extra-ordinary Women?' 15(2) *International Criminal Law Review* (2015) 207–253.
Special Issue: 'Rewriting Equality' 18(1) *Canadian Journal of Women and the Law* (2006).
Spees, P 'Women's Advocacy in the Creation of the International Criminal Court: Changing the Landscapes of Justice and Power' 28(4) *Journal of Women in Culture and Society* (2003) 1233–1254.
Sperling, C 'Mother of Atrocities: Pauline Nyiramasuhuko's Role in the Rwandan Genocide' 33(2) *Fordham Urban Law Journal* (2006) 637–656.
Spivak, GC 'A Borderless World?' in R Braidotti and P Gilroy (eds.), *Conflicting Humanities* (London: Bloomsbury, 2016).
Spriggs, AL and Halpern, CT 'Sexual Debut Timing and Depressive Symptoms in Emerging Adulthood' 37(9) *Journal of Youth and Adolescence* (2008) 1085–1096.
Steains, C 'Gender Issues' in RS Lee (ed.), *The International Criminal Court: The Making of the Rome Statute* (The Hague: Kluwer Law International, 1999).
Steinfeld, M 'When Ethnic Cleansing Is Not Genocide: A Critical Appraisal of the ICJ's Ruling in *Croatia v Serbia* in Relation to Deportation and Population Transfer' 28(4) *Leiden Journal of International Law* (2015) 937–944.
Stephenson, J *Women in Nazi Germany* (London: Routledge, 2001).
Stone-Mediatore, S 'Chandra Mohanty and the Revaluing of "Experience"' 13 *Hypatia* (1998) 116–133.
Sugarman, E et al. *An Introduction to the Criminal Law of Afghanistan* (2nd ed., Stanford, CA: Stanford Law School, 2009).
Suhr, V (ed.) *Rainbow Jurisdiction at the International Criminal Court – Protection of Sexual and Gender Minorities under the Rome Statute* (The Hague: TMC Asser Press, 2021).
Swaine, A 'Beyond Strategic Rape and between the Public and Private: Violence against Women in Armed Conflict' 37(3) *Human Rights Quarterly* (2015) 755–786.
Conflict-related Violence against Women: Transforming Transition (Cambridge: Cambridge University Press, 2018).
Swigart, L 'The Impacts of English-Language Hegemony on the ICC' in F Jeßberger, L Steinl, and K Mehta (eds.), *International Criminal Law—A Counter-Hegemonic Project?* (The Hague: TMC Asser Press, 2022).
Tabak, S 'False Dichotomies of Transitional Justice: Gender, Conflict and Combatants in Colombia' 44 *NYU Journal of International Law and Policy* (2011) 103–161.
Tallgren, I 'Sensibility and Sense of International Criminal Law' 13(3) *European Journal of International Law* (2002) 561–595.
Taylor, C 'Anti-Carceral Feminism and Sexual Assault – A Defense: A Critique of the Critique of the Critique of Carceral Feminism' 34 *Social Philosophy Today* (2018) 29–49.
Terris, D, Romano, CPR, and Swigart, L *The International Judge: An Introduction to the Men and Women Who Decide the World's Cases* (Waltham, MA: Brandeis University Press, 2007).
Tønnessen, L 'Women at Work in Sudan: Marital Privilege or Constitutional Right?' 26 *Social Politics* (2019) 223–244.

Toy Cronin, B 'Feminist Judgments of Aotearoa, New Zealand and Te Rino: A Two-Stranded Rope' 1 *New Zealand Women's Law Journal* (2017) 192–199.

True, J 'The Political Economy of Gender in UN Peacekeeping' in G Heathcote and D Otto (eds.), *Rethinking Peacekeeping, Gender Equality and Collective Security* (London: Palgrave Macmillan, 2014).

Uggen, C 'Work as a Turning Point in the Life Course of Criminals: A Duration Model of Age, Employment, and Recidivism' 65(4) *American Sociological Review* (2000) 529–546.

Umbreit et al. 'The Impact of Restorative Justice Conferencing: A Multinational Perspective' 1(2) *British Journal of Community Justice* (2002) 21–48.

United Nations Office on Drugs and Crime *Handbook on Restorative Justice Programmes* (1st ed., New York: UNODC, 2006).

Vasiliev, S 'Victim Participation Revisited – What the ICC Is Learning about Itself' in C Stahn (ed.), *The Law and Practice of the International Criminal Court: A Critical Account of Challenges and Achievements* (Oxford: Oxford University Press, 2015).

Vauchez, V 'More Women – But Which Women? The Rule and Politics of Gender Balance at the European Court of Human Rights' 26(1) *European Journal of International Law* (2015) 195–221.

Velez, ED 'Decolonial Feminism at the Intersection: A Critical Reflection on the Relationship between Decolonial Feminism and Intersectionality' 33(3) *Journal of Speculative Philosophy* (2019) 390–406.

Vigneswaran, K 'Annex B: Charges and Outcomes in ICTY Cases Involving Sexual Violence' in S Brammertz and M Jarvis (eds.), *Prosecuting Conflict-Related Sexual Violence at the ICTY* (Oxford: Oxford University Press, 2016) 429–481.

Viseur Sellers, P 'Gender Strategy Is Not Luxury for International Courts' 17(2) *American University Journal of Gender, Social Policy & the Law* (2009) 301–326.

'Wartime Female Slavery: Enslavement?' 44 *Cornell International Law Journal* (2011) 115–142.

'Ntaganda: Re-Alignment of a Paradigm' in F Pocar (ed.), *The Additional Protocols 40 Years Later* (Sanremo: International Institute of Humanitarian Law, 2018).

Viseur Sellers, P and Kestenbaum, JG 'The International Crimes of Slavery and the Slave Trade: A Feminist Critique', in I Rosenthal, V Oosterveld, and S SáCouto (eds.), *Gender and International Criminal Law* (Oxford: Oxford University Press, 2022).

Watson, I 'Response to *Kartinyeri v Commonwealth of Australia* (1998) 195 CLR H' in H Douglas et al. (eds.), *Australian Feminist Judgments: Righting and Rewriting Law* (Oxford: Hart, 2014).

Watson, N 'In the Matter of Djaparri (Re Tuckiar)' in H Douglas et al. (eds.), *Australian Feminist Judgments: Righting and Rewriting Law* (Oxford: Hart, 2014).

Watson, N and Broderick, T 'Dempsey v Rigg [1914] St R Qd 245' in N Watson and H Douglas (eds.), *Indigenous Legal Judgments: Bringing Indigenous Voices into Judicial Decision Making* (London: Routledge, 2021).

Watson, N and Douglas, H (eds.) *Indigenous Legal Judgments: Bringing Indigenous Voices into Judicial Decision Making* (London: Routledge, 2021).

Weckel, U and Wolfrum, E *'Bestien' und 'Befehlsempfänger': Frauen und Männer in NS-Prozessen nach 1945* (Göttingen: Vandenhoeck & Ruprecht, 2003).

Welang, N 'Triple Consciousness: The Reimagination of Black Female Identities in Contemporary American Culture' 2 *Open Cultural Studies* (2018) 296–306.

Wheeler, C 'Human Rights Enforcement at the Borders: International Criminal Court Jurisdiction over the Rohingya Situation' 17 *Journal of International Criminal Justice* (2019) 609–631.

White, SC 'Depoliticising Development: The Uses and Abuses of Participation' in J Pearce (ed.), *Development, NGOs, and Civil Society: Selected essays from Development in Practice* (Oxford: Oxfam GB, 2000).

Williams, P *The Alchemy of Race and Rights: Diary of a Law Professor* (Cambridge, MA: Harvard University Press, 1991).

Win, C and Kean, T 'Communal Conflict in Myanmar: The Legislature's Response, 2012–2015' 47(3) *Journal of Contemporary Asia* (2017) 413–439.

Wing, A 'International Human Rights and Black Women: Justice or Just Us?' in J Levitt (ed.), *Black Women and International Law: Deliberate Interactions, Movements and Actions* (Cambridge: Cambridge University Press, 2015).

Worrall, A *Offending Women: Female Lawbreakers and the Criminal Justice System* (London: Routledge, 1990).

Yarwood, L (ed.) *Women and Transitional Justice: The Experience of Women as Participants* (London: Routledge, 2013).

York, J 'The Truth about Women and Peace' in LA Lorentzen and J Turpin (eds.), *The Women and War Reader* (New York: New York University Press, 1998) 19–25.

Zarni, M and Cowley, A 'The Slow-Burning Genocide of Myanmar's Rohingya' 23(3) *Pacific Rim Law & Policy Journal* (2014) 681–752.

Zawati, H 'Fair Labelling as a Common Legal Principle in Criminal Law' in H Zawati (ed.), *Fair Labelling and the Dilemma of Prosecuting Gender-Based Crimes at the International Criminal Tribunals* (New York: Oxford University Press, 2014).

'Introduction: Structure and Scope' in H Zawati (ed.), *Fair Labelling and the Dilemma of Prosecuting Gender-Based Crimes at the International Criminal Tribunals* (New York: Oxford University Press, 2014).

Zulfacar, M 'The Pendulum of Gender Politics in Afghanistan' 25(1–2) *Central Asian Survey* (2006) 27–59.

For EU product safety concerns, contact us at Calle de José Abascal, 56–1°,
28003 Madrid, Spain or eugpsr@cambridge.org.

www.ingramcontent.com/pod-product-compliance
Lightning Source LLC
LaVergne TN
LVHW011510220926
848484LV00024B/826

* 9 7 8 1 0 0 9 2 5 5 2 8 8 *